WORDSWORTH CLASSICS
OF WORLD LITERATURE
General Editor: Tom Griffith

THE LIFE OF SAMUEL JOHNSON, LL.D.

James Boswell

The Life of
Samuel Johnson, LL.D.

❖

With an Introduction by Angus Calder

WORDSWORTH CLASSICS
OF WORLD LITERATURE

For my husband
ANTHONY JOHN RANSON
with love from your wife, the publisher
Eternally grateful for your
unconditional love

Readers who are interested in other titles from
Wordsworth Editions are invited to visit our
website at www.wordsworth-editions.com

For our latest list and a full mail order service contact
Bibliophile Books, Unit 5 Datapoint,
South Crescent, London E16 4TL
Tel: +44 (0) 20 74 74 24 74
Fax: +44 (0) 20 74 74 85 89
orders@bibliophilebooks.com
www.bibliophilebooks.com

This edition published 1999 by Wordsworth Editions Limited
8B East Street, Ware, Hertfordshire SG12 9HJ
Reissued in this smaller format 2008

ISBN 978 1 84022 068 1

Text © Wordsworth Editions Limited 1999
Introduction © Angus Calder 1999

Wordsworth® is a registered trademark of
Wordsworth Editions Limited

Wordsworth Editions is
the company founded in 1987 by
MICHAEL TRAYLER

Typeset in Great Britain by Antony Gray
Printed and bound by Clays Ltd, St Ives plc

CONTENTS

INTRODUCTION

Verbally, at times, the relationship of Johnson and Boswell was pitched almost as high as any romance in history. When Johnson, in company, referred to Boswell as 'the best travelling companion in the world', or when he told Boswell, 'Were I in distress, there is no man to whom I should sooner come than you', that was the least of it. When Boswell described himself as 'trusting always, that in another state, we shall meet never to be separated' this might have been the language of an ardent absent lover. 'I do not believe', he had written earlier, 'that a more perfect attachment ever existed in the history of mankind.' He was referring to his own feeling for Johnson, inspired by 'Genius, Learning, and Piety'. When he found himself 'easy', at one point, in the Doctor's company, he rebounded into regret: he 'missed that awful reverence with which I used to contemplate . . . the complex magnitude of his literary, moral and religious character.' The older man, who could never have felt 'awe' before Boswell, was more measured in his expressions, but extremely encouraging – 'I set a very high value upon your friendship, and count your kindness as one of the chief felicities of my life.' They were more than a team. They were a couple, each inspired by noble versions of male friendship found in the writings of antiquity.

Dr Samuel Johnson, the son of a provincial bookseller, rose to be the most celebrated literary eminence in what was already known in his lifetime as 'the Augustan Age' of English writing. Self-comparison with the Rome of the Emperor Augustus worked in two related ways. Boisterous British soldiers and sailors, pursuing the aims of British merchants and planters, had fought French and Spanish rivals from the Bay of Biscay to the Philippines in wars (1740–48 and 1756–63) which had ensured control over territories as widely different as the ricefields of Bengal and the snowy steppes of Canada. The British Empire was bigger than the Romans' had ever been. The British usually abhorred 'Caesarism' and despotism as such, and venerated a constitution in which the King's power was in effect controlled by an elected, though unrepresentative, House of Commons. But sculptors presented great Britons with togas. Secondly, it might be supposed that the fellow-countrymen of Shakespeare, whose supreme if rather wild greatness was taken for granted, were not incapable of matching the admired writers of ancient Rome, whom they knew by heart, imitated freely and set up as standards of excellence. To hold your own in Johnson's talented circle, you needed to understand disputes over the exact meaning of famous lines in Horace, and to sustain comparisons between Augustan Virgil and barbaric yet exemplary Homer.

Johnson was what a later age would call a 'miscellaneous' writer. He wrote much-admired poetry, philosophical fiction, an ineffectual but respected tragedy for the stage, genteel periodical moralising essays, political pamphlets and biographical introductions to a massive uniform republication of major and minor English poets. He was honoured above all for his pioneering Dictionary of the English Language. He was 'Dictionary Johnson'. He was not the first major full-time writer to subsist without aristocratic patronage (and a pension from the Crown eventually made him less than ideally independent). But Johnson stood forth signally as his own man. His wit, deployed at whatever level of society he happened to find himself placed in, became legendary in his own lifetime.

James Boswell, like many Scottish lawyers of his time, came of landowning stock. His father, a judge, was the Laird of Auchinleck, of ancient lineage. Boswell was on uneasy terms with him. His own rage for drink and loose women was not openly acceptable in a country dominated by a Calvinistic tradition of 'grave living'. He roamed the Continent as a young man, met the impious Voltaire, and claimed to have slept with the mistress of the notorious Rousseau. In Corsica he tracked down General Paoli, leader of a nationalistic revolt first against Genoese rule, then against the French whom he had invited in as allies. Boswell's account of this trip gave him some fame as 'Corsica Boswell'. He mingled on familiar terms with the legal luminaries, scientists and philosophers whose writings marked the 'Scottish Enlightenment' and profoundly affected thought in the European world from that day to this. Otherwise, he practised without vast acclaim as an advocate in Scotland, then as a barrister in London. Despite his influential acquaintance, his hopes of Government office came to nothing. He died, worn-out, sodden with drink, in his mid-fifties.

When the two men met in a bookseller's shop in Covent Garden on May 16th 1763, Johnson (1709–1784) was fifty-two, Boswell (1740–1795) only twenty-two. Johnson, who had been married to a woman, now dead, much older than himself, had never had, nor wanted, children, but the company of young men perhaps gave him a gratifying sense of surrogate paternity. In 1752 he had made a lifelong friend of Bennet Langton, young son of a Lincolnshire gentleman. And he then became friendly with Langton's fellow student at Oxford, Topham Beauclerk. Boswell records how these two once knocked him up at 3 a.m. in London and carried him off for a drinking bout in Covent Garden. Dictionary Johnson seems to have found some relief from his fame and dignity in the company of unformed youth. 'Sir,' he told Boswell early in their relationship, 'I love the acquaintance of young people; because, in the first place, I don't like to think of myself as growing old. In the next place, young acquaintances must last longest, if they do last; and then, Sir, young men have more virtue than old men; they have more generous sentiments in every respect.' And Boswell was a much more talented and complex person than Langton or Beauclerk. They were soon talking about going to the

Hebrides together, a project realised in 1773, which produced an imposing book by Johnson and a miraculously lively one by Boswell.

Without Boswell we would now know Johnson, if at all, as an extraordinary arbiter in English prose whose latinate periods and magisterial wit reverberate through later writers as diverse as Jane Austen and Dickens, as the author of fine poetry never excluded from general anthologies of English verse, and, for readers with rather specialised curiosity, the deviser in his *Rasselas* of a philosophical fable, published in 1759, such as might be read as a Christian antidote to Voltaire's *Candide*, which had appeared in the previous year. Students of the history of criticism would needfully peruse his seminal introduction to his edition of Shakespeare and his *Lives of the Poets*. Literary and cultural historians would discuss his brilliant circle of artists and intellectuals. But he might seem not much more attractive than those composers whom the music critic Tovey described as Interesting Historical Figures.

Without Johnson, Boswell would seem to be merely a minor hanger-on of the Scottish Enlightenment. It is true that his vivid and candid journals now provide an independent basis for his reputation as a major writer, but the rediscovery of his papers, in instalments, first at Malahide Castle in Ireland in 1926, then at Fettercairn in Scotland in 1930, then at Malahide again in 1937, 1944 and 1948, would hardly have triggered acquisition by Yale University, and multi-volume scholarly editions, had he not been the author of *Tour of the Hebrides* and the *Life of Johnson*. The *Life*, appearing in 1791, established both men as major, indeed archetypal, figures, not merely in the canon of Literature, but in the imaginations of general readers, where the rough and loveable Bear and Bozzie, his somewhat ridiculous bear-leader, proceed forever over the sea to Skye and sit together shaking their heads over Goldsmith's *faux pas* in conversation, or swapping erudition and political prejudices with learned men at Oxford University.

It was crucial to the relationship that Boswell, while not as prodigiously well-read as Johnson, was a highly intelligent man. If he exposes his own taste in poetry as, sometimes risibly, defective, at least he made it his business to read poetry. If he could hardly contend on equal terms with the great David Hume, at least he had conversed with him and taken his arguments seriously. Not a great legal brain himself, he knew the best in Scotland of his day. His political views were hardly as deep-brewed as Burke's, but he could stand up sturdily with Burke and against Johnson over the revolt of the American colonists. However, Johnson knew lots of bright people, old and young. His profound affinity with Boswell derived from the fact that both men were guilt-ridden depressives, forming a sombre communion of two on Johnson's penitential Good Fridays, discussing predestination and the afterlife with a seriousness less unusual in their age than ours, but still counter to the overall *mores* of a period in which worldly Anglicanism ruled the ecclesiological roost in England, and the bland, dominant Moderate faction led by the historian Robertson negated the stark Calvinist tradition of the established Church of Scotland. It is significant that Boswell records without dissent Johnson's friendly disposition towards John Wesley, whose mission to re-energise Christianity in worldly days and bring severe but saving truths to the unwashed and disregarded set him at odds with churchmen and magistrates whose authority the fiercely Tory Doctor would normally have upheld. (At what now seems a ridiculous extreme, Johnson expressed approval of the Indian caste system.) In so far as Boswell could be truly pious – his religious principles were always in combat with his own rakish behaviour – he shared Johnson's simple and far from consolatory faith in a God whose existence was proved by instinct not reasoning and who must condemn sinful persons to Hell. As Johnson ages, death and the afterlife become more and more insistent themes in Boswell's biography. There is a painful conclusion to their relationship, exposed by Boswell with his usual candour. Johnson is mortally ill in London (and Boswell did not really serve his idol well by printing letter after letter in which he lamentingly recounts his deadly symptoms to his friends, making him seem grimly self-obsessed near his end). Boswell is horribly depressed. Johnson (to use a Johnsonian phrase memorably devised by that worthy successor in prose, Beatrix Potter) 'implores him to exert himself'. Boswell cannot bring himself to print a passage in Johnson's last letter to him in which 'he still persevered in arraigning me as before, which was strange in him who had so much experience of what I suffered.' He expresses implicitly one dire fact about depression – that it incorporates the sufferings of others, if at all, solipsistically into the paranoid sufferer's own misery – and almost explicitly the important fact that depression is a mental disease beyond the control of its victims. Boswell recurs again and again to the 'indolence' which somehow did not prevent Johnson being mightily productive. Perhaps because he himself when low resorted to the bottle rather than books, he does not seem to have fully appreciated the connection between Johnson's depressive insomnia and his vast up-to-date learning, and because he was activated professionally as a lawyer he did not recognise Johnson's 'indolence' as the form of depression now known as 'writer's block'.

Readers will be drawn to the *Life*, most likely, because it contains scores of wonderful examples of Johnson's wit. The temptation is always there to seek these out and skip the rest of what seems by our present-day standards a defective and shapeless biography. Less than one-fifth deals with Johnson's life before he met Boswell (though light is thrown on it in subsequent conversations and anecdotes). More than half of the book is concerned with the last eight years of the Doctor's existence. Every lengthy opinion which Johnson provided when Boswell applied for his advice about legal cases is given in full. Letters to Boswell himself and to many others are thrown in precipitously in their chronological order. When short of matter about some phase of Johnson's life, Boswell will intrude sayings collected by others. His own general philosophisings take over quite frequently. Though he never wavers in his view of Johnson as a great man whose eccentricities were in the last analysis wholly forgiveable, Boswell is fitful in his evocation of his subject's physical peculiarities and disconcerting mannerisms and habits, and repetitious in his compensatory praise of Johnson's learning and Christian virtues.

Yet the book is best read right through, though items to skip will present themselves frequently. What Boswell achieves – the essence of his immediate and enduring appeal – is an astonishing sense of Johnson's presence, so strong that we can interpret him in different ways than his biographer. In his summing up, Boswell writes, 'The character of Samuel Johnson has, I trust, been so developed in the course of this work, that they, who have honoured it with a perusal, may be considered as well acquainted with him.' Importantly, we know Johnson in his context, not by summary, but through our own apprehension. Boswell succeeds in the aim advertised on his title page, of 'exhibiting a view of literature and literary men in Great Britain, for near half-a-century.'

Johnson's friends are not all fully characterised. Garrick, often present and much discussed, impresses us with his independent stature, not undermined by Johnson's real or feigned contempt for mere actors. Goldsmith impacts on us because his combination of great literary skill and much learning with ineffectual attempts to match Johnson's wit is discussed sadly and fondly for years after his early death. The genial, equable Joshua Reynolds makes his presence felt, but Burke, of whom even Johnson stood in awe, remains a rather vague compound of unquotable intellectual brilliance and occasional benevolence. (Ugly, crotchety Edward Gibbon is briefly more vivid.) If Mr Thrale the brewer is shadowy, a virtuous cipher, his lively wife, presented with a mixture of strained fairness and calculated waspishness (because Boswell is anxious to expose her as deficient both in understanding and powers of memory, so that her own rival memoirs of Johnson will not be trusted) does impinge on our minds with some vividness. Johnson's extraordinary household, which stands as proof that he was indeed a truly great-hearted man, comes down to us powerfully as a wholly eccentric entity. But its most exceptional inmate, Francis Barber, the black slave whom Johnson freed, educated, and made his amanuensis and finally his legatee, is only casually referred to, and Boswell makes less than he might have done of the good and unworldly medical Doctor Levett, for whom Johnson wrote one of the most moving elegies in the tradition of English verse. The disagreeable and impoverished Mrs Williams, to whom Johnson paid such unfailing attention, and whom he sat down with to dinner with quite fine company, is often uncomfortably present in our mind's eyes, that more gracious unfortunate Mrs Desmoulins less so. But we have already in this paragraph spanned from wealthy Thrale, honoured Sir Joshua, and world-famous Burke to a household, visited by titled men, but crammed with folk who without Johnson's kindness might have died in destitution. And what Boswell's assortment of materials gives us is means of putting together a vision of a very complex society in which Johnson was as much himself with the lowest as with some of the very highest. 'He associated', Boswell writes, 'with persons the most widely different in manners, abilities, rank and accomplishments. He was at once the companion of the brilliant Colonel Forrester of the Guards, who wrote *The Polite Philosopher*, and of awkward and uncouth Robert Levett; of Lord Thurlow, and Mr Sastres, the Italian master; and has dined one day with the beautiful, gay and fascinating Lady Craven and the next with good Mrs Gardiner, the tallow-chandler, on Snow-hill.'

Surely that is why Boswell's Johnson has been so much loved by generations of readers. A staunch believer in divine right of kings, hierarchy and authority, Johnson's behaviour marked his silent assent to the Burnsian creed that a man's a man for a' that. John-Bully Johnson would knock men down in his rages. Sailors upon the Thames had the custom of accosting each other as they passed 'in the most abusive language they could invent . . . Johnson [as Langton recalled for Boswell] was once eminently successful in this species of contest; a fellow having attacked him with some coarse raillery, Johnson answered him thus, "Sir, your wife, *under pretence of keeping a bawdy house*, is a receiver of stolen goods." ' In conversation with John Wilkes, that erstwhile master of the London mob, Johnson suddenly introduced Bet Flint – 'a woman of the town, who, with some eccentric talents and much effrontery, forced herself upon his acquaintance. "Bet (said he) wrote her own life in verse, which she brought to me, wishing that I would furnish her with a Preface to it. (Laughing) I used to say of her, that she was generally slut and drunkard; occasionally, whore and thief. She had, however, genteel lodgings, a spinet on which she played, and a boy that walked before her chair. Poor Bet was taken up on a charge of stealing a counterpane, and tried at the Old Bailey. Chief Justice —, who loved a wench, summed up favourably. and she was acquitted. After which Bet said, with a gay and satisfied air, 'Now that the counterpane is *my own*, I shall make a petticoat out of it.' " ' Through Captain Cook's first expedition to the Pacific there came to London Omai, a Tahitian, who was dressed in fine clothes and paraded through high society. Johnson despised Rousseauesque prattle about the nobility of savages, and in principle looked up to the British aristocracy. But he could not resist a levelling joke regarding Omai. 'Sir, he had passed all his time, while in England, only in the best company; so that all that he had acquired of our manners was genteel. As a proof of this, Sir, Lord Musgrave and he one day dined at Streatham [with the Thrales]; they sat with their backs to the light fronting me, so that I could not see distinctly; and there was so little of the savage in Omai, that I was afraid to speak to either, lest I should mistake one for the other.' Johnson seems to have been totally free of racial prejudice, and Boswell, who himself approved of the slave trade, gave armament to the new movement against it when he recalled his hero's toast, in company with grave gentlemen at Oxford University – 'Here's to the next slave rebellion in the West Indies!'

But what about Johnson's famous prejudice against the Scots? There is a rather ugly scene in the *Life*, where Johnson, now fully at peace with John Wilkes, whose anti-Government rabble-rousing and support for the American colonists he had abhorred, sits with him in company, not only with Boswell, but also with the distinguished Scottish philosopher Beattie, who had attempted to refute the atheistical arguments of Hume, engaging 'in extravagant sportive raillery' against the Scots, once the focus of attack in Wilkes's 'seditious' journal the *North Briton*. As usual, Boswell conscientiously sets down remarks by his hero which displease him. But a thorough reader of the *Life* will realise that Scotophobia was a problem in Boswell's own mind, not a factor in Johnson's actual behaviour. His notorious definition in his Dictionary of oats as something fed to the horses in England but eaten by people in Scotland, and his equally pungent, and wholly misleading, observation that there were no trees in Scotland, exaggerated a fact which intelligent Scots willingly conceded – that Scotland was a poorer country than England, with a lower ratio of fertile land and, historically, less involvement in the richer trades. The Union of Parliaments in 1707 was willed by many Scots because it gave them a chance to share in the opulence of England and empire. By the time that Boswell met Johnson, Scots seemed to have done rather more than catch up. The gist of Wilkes's jibes against George III's first Ministry, headed by the 'Scotch' Lord Bute, was that insidious and pushy Scots were commandeering the Roast Beef of Old England. A mania for agricultural improvement – including, as Boswell notes in passing, the planting of trees – had gripped the landed classes north of the border. The rich West Indian sugar islands had been invaded, sometimes to the point of domination, by Scottish planters and professional men. Scots within the East India Company, most notably that cynical plunderer John Johnstone, had gladly assisted Clive in the Rape of Bengal, and much of the ill-gotten cash of the 'nabobs' was returning to Scotland to fund further 'improvement' and industrialisation, along with commercial profits from Glasgow, which by this time had acquired a monopolistic grip on the Europe-wide trade in Virginian tobacco. Scottish lawyers – Mansfield, Wedderburn, not, alas, Boswell – rose to the highest rank in the English legal establishment, and Scottish politicians sat for English parliamentary seats at a time when no Englishman practised Scots law and no southerner penetrated the Scottish electoral system, which was manipulated so successfully by Henry Dundas, a lawyer of minor landed family, that by the time of Boswell's death 'King Harry the Ninth' was arguably even more powerful at Westminster than his protégé, Prime Minister William Pitt.

Boswell exemplified three features common among Scots of his day. He was an intense, though deeply confused, patriot, conscious of his family's share in Scottish history, and absurdly over-sensitive to Johnson's teasing. He shared the zest for 'improvement' among the overlapping landed and legal classes, which made English agriculture, trade and industry models to be imitated. And he was involved in the soul-searching and mind-searching with which Scottish intellectuals met the exciting but disturbing changes in their country which accelerated after the crushing of the last Jacobite rebellion in 1746 had opened up the last 'barbaric' area of Britain to capitalist exploitation. Was not the triumph of commerce destroying the old heroic virtues, as seen in ancient epic and the disinterested support which many had given to the Jacobite cause? On such ground, as their books about their tour of the highlands and islands show, he had great affinity with Johnson. As a vehement supporter of hierarchy in Church and State, Johnson came to accept the Hanoverian dynasty (along with his royal pension). George III was better than no king. But he still preferred the overthrown Stuarts, to such a degree that an absurd speculation has been seen in print that he actually fought in Bonny Prince Charlie's plaided host. Temperamentally, as Boswell inferred acutely, he was aligned with the 'non-jurors' – Anglicans who had passed into semi-legal nonconformity by refusing to swear allegiance to William of Orange after the

'Glorious Revolution' of 1688–89, or to Anne in 1702. English non-jurors had close links with Scottish episcopalians. Both groups maintained their own shadow hierarchies. Furthermore, Johnson was rather passionately attracted by the vestigial feudalism of the Scottish highlands. His complaint on Skye against Sir Alexander Macdonald was that he spent too much time away from his own people, and was undeserving of their loyalty. The notion that Johnson was seriously anti-Scottish is belied by detail after detail in Boswell's own presentation of him. He became a patron of studies in the Gaelic language. He admired Beattie and respected William Robertson. Scottish booksellers and authors in London were part of his own intimate literary community. But he knew how to wind his friend Boswell up by making routine anti-Scottish jokes. The prevalence of these was based on quite genuine English fears that pushy Scots mindful of gain were infiltrating and conquering by stealth the green and pleasant land south of their border – a myth finally crystallised towards the end of the nineteenth century in Hardy's fable of the Wessex *Mayor of Casterbridge* ousted by the personable Scottish incomer Farfrae.

By Hardy's day, a respectable Scottish accent was if anything an asset in British professional, commercial, financial and public life. It had the advantages of clear enunciation and, in relation to England, reassuring 'classlessness'. The Scottish doctor, bank manager or policeman was peculiarly trustworthy. Nowadays companies setting up telephone services for customers recognise these virtues by locating in Scotland. Boswell would have boggled.

Consider the circumstances around his first meeting with Johnson. 'In the summer of 1761, Mr Thomas Sheridan was at Edinburgh, and delivered lectures upon the English Language and Public Speaking to large and respectable audiences.' Historians do not pass over the irony that the genteel classes in Scotland's capital flocked to take instruction upon the proper pronunciation of English from an Irish actor. Even the great Hume would be said to have died confessing not his sins but his 'Scotticisms'. Boswell attached himself to Sheridan and heard him 'frequently expatiate upon Johnson's extraordinary knowledge, talents, and virtues . . . and boast of his being his guest sometimes till two or three in the morning.' In London in 1762, Boswell was mortified to find that his friend Sheridan had fallen out with Johnson, who had reacted scoffingly or peevishly when he heard that the Irishman had received a royal pension, 'Johnson', Boswell comments with perhaps unconscious Scottish patriotism, 'should have recollected that Mr Sheridan had taught pronunciation to Mr Alexander Wedderburn, whose sister was married to Sir Harry Erskine, an intimate friend of Lord Bute, who was the favourite of the King; and surely the most outrageous Whig will not maintain, that . . . a *pension* ought never to be granted from any bias of court connection.' Wedderburn had gone on to become Solicitor General for the United Kingdom and eventually a peer with an English title. Boswell's next comment exposes his painful self-contradiction. 'Mr Macklin [another Irish actor], indeed, shared with Mr Sheridan the honour of instructing Mr Wedderburn; and though it was too late in life for a Caledonian to acquire the genuine English cadence, yet so successful were Mr Wedderburn's instructors, and his own unabating endeavours, that he got rid of the coarse part of his Scotch accent, retaining only so much of the "native wood-notes wild" as to mark his country; *which, if any Scotchman should affect to forget, I should heartily despise him.*' (My italics.)

It was with a mental constitution mingling awe for the great arbiter of English lexicography and prose style with prickly defensiveness about his own cherished Scottish identity that Boswell sought an alternative route to Johnson through another actor, Thomas Davies, turned bookseller. He was not alone in seeing London, the mart of world trade, the site of imperial government and, in Johnson's person, the fountainhead of the best English, as necessary to his self-advancement intellectually, socially and professionally. Though Hume scoffed at 'barbarians who dwell by the banks of the Thames', a great proportion of the most talented persons in the English-speaking countries converged upon the metropolis. Even the cynical revolutionary-to-be Benjamin Franklin was long seduced by its amenities. Here the provincial Englishmen, Johnson, Reynolds (arbiter of taste in painting) and Garrick (model for Shakespearian acting) consorted with the brilliant Irishmen, Goldsmith, Burke, and later Thomas Sheridan's son, the dramatist and orator Richard, while the Scot Robert Adam adorned what we now call English heritage with magnificent houses such as Kedleston. Adam Smith did not shine in their company, but his *Wealth of Nations* (1776) electrified intelligent public men, who would soon be grieved to hear of the death, on his third Pacific voyage, of a Yorkshire-born navigator with a Scottish father, Captain James Cook. As Linda Colley has argued in her justly influential book *Britons*, a sense of *British* identity was evolving strongly at this time. When Boswell, defending his pro-colonist view of the American war to Johnson in the last year of the latter's life, referred to himself as an 'ancient and faithful Briton', he was expressing a sense which Burke would have shared with him that the peoples of the British Isles, Celts and Saxons together, were all now in the business of creating and sustaining a great and prosperous empire under the unwritten but august British Constitution. When Johnson himself memorably stated that 'Patriotism is the last refuge of a scoundrel', he was not, as many have supposed, attacking 'national' feeling as such, but jibing at people in Britain and the Thirteen Colonies, Wilkesites and Virginian slave-owners, who inscribed 'Patriotism' on the banner of mob action and seditious insurrection.

If the American colonies astonished the world with their absence of European hierarchies – almost everybody, apart from slaves and servants, could be re-garded as 'middle class' – the English seemed almost equally strange to Europeans in the extreme fluidity of their hierarchical social system and the porousness of its upper sections. This had something to do with the revolution of the 1640s, which had briefly made England a republic under the control of commoners, but much more with the commercial afflatus since which had put wealth and, accordingly, influence into the hands of men of middling degree. Thrale the great self-made brewer and Mrs Gardiner the little philanthropical tallow-chandler both belonged to a relatively vast, multisectioned 'middle class' together with Johnson and his bookseller friends. Garrick's prowess helped to secure the status of some actors within that class, Reynolds gave portrait-painters a fair chance of an honoured status in society. Handel the composer had soared high as a great man of his own kind, in his own right, at a time when his equally masterly younger contemporary Haydn was merely an upper-servant under of a Hungarian aristocrat. The consequence of such phenomena, and of parliamentary representation, however imperfect, was that authority was debatable. Johnson hated the Whigs who dominated British politics from early in the reign of George I to the accession of George III because they presumed that control of Parliament gave them control of the King, his finances and his powers. Famously, he exclaimed in 1778, when the revolt of the Thirteen Colonies was in full flood, ' "Subordination is sadly broken down in this age. No man, now, has the same authority which his father had – except a gaoler. No master has it over his servants: it is diminished in our colleges; nay, in our grammar schools." BOSWELL. "What is the cause of this, Sir?" JOHNSON. "Why, Sir, the coming in of the Scotch" (laughing sarcastically).' Boswell for once saw that he was teasing and asked him for his 'serious cause', and Johnson very plausibly evinced 'the great increase of money. No man now depends upon the Lord of the Manor, when he can send to another country and fetch provisions . . . I have explained, in my *Journey to the Hebrides*, how gold and silver destroy feudal subordination.' In short, what Adam Smith had recently declared to be a universal propensity to 'truck, barter and exchange' had swept away the actual foundations of hierarchy in England, though we can now see clearly that hierarchical thinking about society remained strong, even dominant, down to the present day (as when Mrs Thatcher defended hereditary peerages).

The 'Scotch', however, retained respect for Lords in Johnson's day. Members of a clan or a Lowland surname retained a sense of being part of the same family as the titled men of their name – and the position of head of the family, *pace* Johnson, remained even in England very powerful. While Wilkesite rioters were terrorising London and a New England mob was throwing tea into Boston harbour in protest against George III's 'Tory' henchmen, and Irish Protestants were drilling to express their desire for a free Parliament of their own, Scotland remained the calmest part of the empire. This can be partly attributed to the fact that the patriotic cause of 'improvement' drew intelligent landowners together with inventive men of artisan origins, while the ideas of Enlightenment rapidly reached the most literate lower orders in Europe. Scots were capable simultaneously of defining more clearly than most others the rationality and value of commerce, and of observing principles of hierarchy. The radical thinking of such men as the philosopher Hume, the sociologist Ferguson and the scientists Black and Cullen stopped dead in professed Toryism. As chief of Scotland the Clan (we might now add, plc), Henry Dundas, used the avenues and side-lanes of aristocratic patronage to make many humble families grateful to his Government. Scottish influence on English affairs was anything but anti-hierarchical. The near-non-juring Johnson and the loosened Calvinist Boswell found common political ground very easily.

Both were thoroughly engaged with worldly matters. Boswell's legal work, as well as his rakish proclivities, brought him into touch with drastically unhoused sections of society, as well as with the most respectable. Johnson made it his business to acquire astonishing knowledge of crafts and trades, and his hobby was chemical experiment. But both struggled constantly with a melancholy apprehension of the transience of the busy world and the imminence of Divine Judgement. If Boswell, usually when out of Johnson's sight, found oblivion in drink, Johnson constantly sought relief in company. And here we come to the presence which dominates Boswell's *Life* – the otherwise kindly and friendly Doctor Johnson 'talking for victory'.

His eloquence and wit even in the most private conversation were, according to Boswell and others, remarkable. But in an age when news travelled slowly and modern aviation and television were almost equally inconceivable (Johnson correctly observed that hot air balloons would add nothing to human experience until they could rise above the clouds), the man of clever words, whose witticisms ran round the town's gossip in accurate or garbled form, could be as much a star as a great opera singer or actor. Johnson, like most effective performers, was clearly nervous before big occasions. To joust with Wilkes, or appear at an aristocratic salon, was a test of his abilities, and if frequent comparisons with the unfortunate Goldsmith served to inflate his sense of superiority, the daunting example of Burke called into question even the validity of his own art – better, it might seem, to be truly profound than merely amusing, like the actor Foote, also in rivalry. 'Once,' Boswell records, 'when Johnson was ill, and unable to exert himself as much as usual without fatigue, Mr Burke having been mentioned, he said, "That fellow calls forth all my powers. Were I to see Burke now, it would kill me." So much was he accustomed to consider conversation as a contest . . .'

Boswell again and again ponders upon Johnson's act as conversational pugilist or solo performer. He expresses remorse over missing verbal gems for want of opportunity to apply his own method of shorthand or time to write things down immediately from memory. He believed as devoutly as any follower of a great pioneer in religion that every utterance of his hero was worth preserving. 'I cannot allow any fragment whatever that floats in my memory concerning the great subject of this work to be lost.' This explains his recording of occasions when Johnson said bad things to his face, even in front of others, about him, and his rather painful candour about the coolness between Johnson and Mrs Boswell. But he was equally candid about Johnson's least appealing traits. Ugly as childhood disease had made him, the great Doctor did not need to compound uneasiness stirred by his physical presence with slovenly dress and with fiercely greedy eating habits which 'could not but be disgusting' to those whose 'sensations were delicate'. His rolling gait and random shouts in the street might be constitutional, he might not be able to control the violence of his outbursts of laughter, but he might never have been forgiven (and indeed, old Sheridan never forgave him) for witticisms directed roughly even against those whom he normally wished well. It was Goldsmith who pilfered an idea from one of Cibber's plays to evoke Johnson's pugnacity when he felt someone might have scored a point over him: 'There is no arguing with Johnson: for if his pistol misses fire, he knocks you down with the butt end of it.' Boswell quotes this in a context where Johnson has been contradicted by someone quoting his own writings against his just-expressed opinion – whom he promptly accuses of being drunk. He would deliberately argue a case which he did not believe in, then take evasive action when he had been worsted, having recourse to some 'sudden mode of robust sophistry'. And though many of his best-known sayings are in pithy plain English, he was aware that he was famous for orotund Latinity provided by his exceptional knowledge of the classics and the efforts which had produced his Dictionary. 'He seemed to take a pleasure in speaking in his own style; for when he had carelessly missed it, he would repeat the thought translated into it. Talking of the comedy of "The Rehearsal", he said, "It has not wit enough to keep it sweet." This was easy – he therefore caught himself, and pronounced a more round sentence; "It has not vitality enough to preserve it from putrefaction." '

Conversation as an art, for Johnson, was, as he once remarked, not *talk* but *discussion*. ' "There must", he said on another occasion, "in the first place, be knowledge, there must be materials; – in the second place, there must be command of words; – in the third place, there must be imagination, to place things in such views as they are not commonly seen in; – and in the fourth place, there must be presence of mind, and a resolution that is not to be overcome by failures." '

He might privately acknowledge afterwards, as the Shakespearean critic Maurice Morgann testified to Boswell, that he had been in the wrong, but in company which expected him to mount a display, he argued, according to the rules of his art, always for victory and conclusive effect.

It is important to know that like his anti-Scotch jokes, some of Johnson's best known sayings exaggerated, for immediate impact, his settled views, and provided no guide to his social practices. He is famous for sneering at the (anti-hierarchical) idea of a woman preaching, but Boswell shows that he especially enjoyed the company of intelligent women – if he looked askance at the ultra-Whig, and famous, historian Catherine Macaulay, a serious rival, he accepted other literary women on cordially equal terms. One was Mrs Knowles, the ingenious Quaker lady who tilted at him on the subject of female subordination to men. She was not a wit, but a genuinely religious woman, and mention of her brings us to a fact about Johnson's milieu which would have staggered many foreigners, but which we are now in danger of taking for granted – its spontaneous and even festive tolerance.

Johnson was unbending in what he thought were correct Anglican and Tory principles. But he respected intelligent nonconformists and Catholics, and would not have dreamt of shunning Burke over differences in politics. He entertained Wesley's sister and asked that the poems of the nonconformist hymn-writer Watts be included in the series for which he wrote his *Lives*. He explained why he was for Charles James Fox, a libertarian Whig, against the King's Prime Minister William Pitt, in a most illuminating fashion. 'The King is my master; but I do not know Pitt; and Fox is my friend.' The British metropolis was self-confident enough to accomodate all manner of debate and dissent, until the Jacobin phase of the French Revolution prompted most of the well-to-do to rally in intolerant and punitive defence of hierarchy. We would have a less genial image of Johnson had he survived to react to Robespierre, at a moment when Boswell's friends on the Scottish bench were scourging a local outbreak of democratical ideas with fierce sentences.

The good Doctor's belief that he himself might have committed such sins that God might punish him was a basis for general tolerance. A virtuous Quaker, or even a guilt-smitten womaniser like Boswell, might be more worthy of Heaven than himself. He did sometimes chide Boswell's drunkenness, and reminded him often of the importance of his family life and of full reconciliation with his father. But Boswell with him was usually on his best behaviour, and Boswell as he wished himself always to be was grateful in Johnson's presence for the countenance of a man whose goodness he wholly respected.

The couple are seen together at their mutual best in Boswell's passages describing their stay together, in 1777, with Johnson's old friend Dr Taylor in Ashbourne. With no famous intellectual to conquer or titled ladies to delight, Johnson is genial and relaxed. 'Basking in the sun' in the garden of the local school, he holds forth on the finances of the Church of England. One evening he talks with respect and affection of 'the late Mr Fitzherbert of Derbyshire', a person with 'no sparkle, no brilliancy . . . but I never knew a man who was so generally acceptable.' Boswell tries to interest him in the works of a minor Scottish poet, Hamilton of Bangour, and Johnson refuses to concede him merit. Boswell, endearingly, quotes two lamentable couplets which he thinks fine, but which for most readers will confirm the justice of Johnson's verdict. He confesses to Johnson how disturbed he had been when Hume had died persisting in his 'infidelity'. Johnson says that Hume should have studied the New Testament thoroughly, and refuses to believe that the philosopher was not afraid of death. 'The horror of death, which I had always observed in Dr. Johnson, appeared strong tonight', remarks Boswell, perhaps tacitly envying Hume. They discuss the art of biography. Johnson knows, and approves, of Boswell's ambition to write his Life, and Boswell is rather put out when the great man, who had told him in the Hebrides that 'a man's intimate friend should mention his faults, if he writes his life', now suggests that perhaps such matters as the drunkenness of certain great authors should be suppressed, lest their mention encourages vice. He attempts to overpower his Whig friend Taylor with vehement contentions that the people of England, given a vote on it, would prefer the exiled Stuarts to their actual Hanoverian monarchs. And so on. Johnson and Boswell inspect the great house at Kedleston, and are delighted to find a copy of Johnson's dictionary in the owner Lord Scarsdale's, dressing room, amidst magnificence awesome for both of them. A physician in Derby shows them the local china factory. Then the doctor's Scottish wife takes Boswell to see Mr Lombe's renowned silk-mill, a famous pioneering venture in what has since been called the' Industrial Revolution'. Boswell, 'not very conversant with mechanics', is nevertheless pleased by 'the simplicity of this machine, and its multiplied operations'. Mechanics, at that time, was still termed an 'art'. Boswell says he had learnt from Johnson 'not to think with a dejected indifference of the works of art and the pleasures of life, because life is uncertain and short; but to consider such indifference as a failure of reason, a morbidness of mind.' Johnson that day had reiterated 'his love of driving fast in a post-chaise. "If (said he), I had no duties and no reference to futurity, I would spend my life in driving briskly in a post-chaise with a pretty woman; but she should be one who could understand me, and would add something to the conversation." ' 'Happiness', Boswell broods on, moving into one of those moralising little essays with which he occasionally studs his biography, 'should be cultivated as much as we can, and the objects which are instrumental in it should be steadily considered as of importance, with reference not only to ourselves, but to multitudes in successive ages.' He goes on to write well about the difficult fact that people will still be young and flowers will still bloom when we are dead, and the last pages of his book will be almost choked with reference to sickness, melancholy and death. But his relative perkiness in Derby provides an apt text for a conclusion here which might launch a reader into Boswell's huge and, in its odd way, great book. However gloomy Boswell's own existence was while he wrote it, the book brought him what he had always craved – great, and, so time has proved, enduring fame – and the happiness which he felt at times in Johnson's company as the master of wit gave pleasure to others, or merely flattered his Scottish friend by uttering his intimate thoughts aloud to him, has translated into the delight of millions of readers introduced in his pages to a most extraordinary person.

ANGUS CALDER
Edinburgh

SUGGESTIONS FOR FURTHER READING

The most obvious place to go next is one of the volumes combining Johnson's *A Journey to the Western Islands of Scotland* (1775) and Boswell's *The Journal of a Tour to the Hebrides* (1785), edited by R.W. Chapman in 1924 and Peter Levi in 1984. Comparison with Boswell's original *Journal of a Tour to the Hebrides, 1773*, published by Yale University Press in 1961 as part of its multi-volume edition of Boswell's diaries, is very interesting and instructive.

The lists of publications by and on Johnson are immense. There is a convenient selection of his poetry and prose in the Oxford Authors series, edited by Donald Greene (1984), and at the other extreme a vast ongoing Yale Edition of his Works. Modern biographies include W.J. Bate, *Samuel Johnson* (1977); James L. Clifford, *Young Sam Johnson* (1955) and *Dictionary Johnson: Samuel Johnson's Middle Years* (1979); and John Wain, *Samuel Johnson* (1974).

David Daiches, *James Boswell and His World* (1976) is a lively short introduction. The standard biographies are by F.A. Pottle, *James Boswell: The Earlier Years, 1740–1769* (1966) and Frank Brady, *James Boswell: The Later Years, 1769–1795* (1984). The most popular volume in the Yale series, Boswell's *London Journal, 1762–1763*, has been available in paperback.

NOTE ON THE TEXT

We have chosen to copy the edition made for Percy Fitzgerald for Bickers and Son, London, in 1874. This reprints Boswell's first edition of 1791 – the book which took the market by storm – with Boswell's amendments for the second edition of 1793 and some of his notes towards a third edition. After his death, his friend and Johnson's, Edmond Malone, a fine Irish scholar, freely added new letters and notes in four subsequent editions down to 1811. George Birkbeck Hill's edition of 1887, revised and augmented by L.F. Powell (1934–64), is the standard scholarly edition, in six volumes.

THE LIFE OF SAMUEL JOHNSON, LL.D

DEDICATION

To Sir Joshua Reynolds

My Dear Sir – Every liberal motive that can actuate an Author in the dedication of his labours, concurs in directing me to you, as the person to whom the following work should be inscribed.

If there be a pleasure in celebrating the distinguished merit of a contemporary, mixed with a certain degree of vanity not altogether inexcusable, in appearing fully sensible of it, where can I find one in complimenting whom I can with more general approbation gratify those feelings? Your excellence, not only in the Art over which you have long presided with unrivalled fame, but also in Philosophy and elegant Literature, is well known to the present, and will continue to be the admiration of future ages. Your equal and placid temper, your variety of conversation, your true politeness, by which you are so amiable in private society, and that enlarged hospitality which has long made your house a common centre of union for the great, the accomplished, the learned, and the ingenious; all these qualities I can, in perfect confidence of not being accused of flattery, ascribe to you.

If a man may indulge an honest pride, in having it known to the world, that he has been thought worthy of particular attention by a person of the first eminence in the age in which he lived, whose company has been universally courted, I am justified in availing myself of the usual privilege of a Dedication, when I mention that there has been a long and uninterrupted friendship between us.

If gratitude should be acknowledged for favours received, I have this opportunity, my dear Sir, most sincerely to thank you for the many happy hours which I owe to your kindness – for the cordiality with which you have at all times been pleased to welcome me – for the number of valuable acquaintances to whom you have introduced me – for the *noctes coenaeque Deum*, which I have enjoyed under your roof.

If a work should be inscribed to one who is master of the subject of it, and whose approbation, therefore, must ensure it credit and success, the Life of Dr Johnson is, with the greatest propriety, dedicated to Sir Joshua Reynolds, who was the intimate and beloved friend of that great man; the friend, whom he declared to be 'the most invulnerable man he knew; with whom, if he should quarrel, he should find the most difficulty how to abuse.' You, my dear Sir, studied him, and knew him well: you venerated and admired him. Yet, luminous as he was upon the whole, you perceived all the shades which mingled in the grand composition, all the little peculiarities and slight blemishes which marked the literary Colossus. Your very warm commendation of the specimen which I gave in my *Journal of a Tour to the Hebrides*, of my being able to preserve his conversation in an authentic and lively manner, which opinion the Public has confirmed, was the best encouragement for me to persevere in my purpose of producing the whole of my stores.

In one respect this work will in some passages be different from the former. In my *Tour* I was almost unboundedly open in my communications; and from my eagerness to display the wonderful fertility and readiness of Johnson's wit, freely showed to the world its dexterity, even when I was myself the object of it. I trusted that I should be liberally understood, as knowing very well what I was about, and by no means as simply unconscious of the pointed effects of the satire. I own, indeed, that I was arrogant enough to suppose that the tenor of the rest of the book would sufficiently guard me against such a strange imputation. But it seems I judged too well of the world; for, though I could scarcely believe it, I have been undoubtedly informed, that many persons, especially in distant quarters, not penetrating enough into Johnson's character so as to understand his mode of treating his friends, have arraigned my judgement, instead of seeing that I was sensible of all that they could observe.

It is related of the great Dr Clarke, that when in one of his leisure hours he was unbending himself with a few friends in the most playful and frolicsome manner, he observed Beau Nash approaching; upon which he suddenly stopped: 'My boys (said he), let us be grave: here comes a fool.' The world, my friend, I have found to be a great fool, as to that particular, on which it has become necessary to speak very plainly. I have, therefore, in this work been more reserved; and though I tell nothing but the truth, I have still kept in my mind that the whole truth is not always to be exposed. This, however, I have managed so as to occasion no diminution of the pleasure which my book should afford; though malignity may sometimes be disappointed of its gratifications.

I am,

My dear Sir,

Your much obliged friend,

And faithful humble servant,

JAMES BOSWELL.

London, April 20, 1791.

ADVERTISEMENT

I at last deliver to the world a Work which I have long promised and of which I am afraid too high expectations have been raised. The delay of its publication must be imputed, in a considerable degree, to the extraordinary zeal which has been shown by distinguished persons in all quarters to supply me with additional information concerning its illustrious Subject; resembling in this the grateful tribes of ancient nations, of which every individual was eager to throw a stone upon the grave of a departed Hero, and thus to share in the pious office of erecting an honourable monument to his memory.

The labour and anxious attention with which I have collected and arranged the materials of which these volumes are composed, will hardly be conceived by those who read them with careless faculty. The stretch of mind and prompt assiduity by which so many conversations were preserved, I myself, at some distance of time, contemplate with wonder; and I must be allowed to suggest, that the nature of the work in other respects, as it consists of innumerable detached particulars, all which, even the most minute, I have spared no pains to ascertain with a scrupulous authenticity, has occasioned a degree of trouble far beyond that of any other species of composition. Were I to detail the books which I have consulted, and the inquiries I have found it necessary to make by various channels, I should probably be thought ridiculously ostentatious. Let me only observe, as a specimen of my trouble, that I have sometimes had to run half over London in order to fix a date correctly; which, when I had accomplished, I well knew would obtain me no praise, though a failure would have been to my discredit. And after all perhaps, hard as it may be, I shall not be surprised if omissions or mistakes be pointed out with invidious severity. I have also been extremely careful as to the exactness of my quotations; holding that there is a respect due to the Public which should oblige every Author to attend to this, and never to presume to introduce them with – 'I think I have read;' – or, – 'If I remember right;' – when the originals may be examined.

I beg leave to express my warmest thanks to those who have been pleased to favour me with communications and advice in the conduct of my Work. But I cannot sufficiently acknowledge my obligations to my friend Mr Malone, who was so good as to allow me to read to him almost the whole of my manuscript, and made such remarks as were greatly for the advantage of the work; though it is but fair to him to mention, that upon many occasions I differed from him and followed my own judgement. I regret exceedingly that I was deprived of the benefit of his revision, when but about one half of the book had passed through the press; but after having completed his very laborious and admirable edition of Shakspeare, for which he generously would accept of no other reward but that fame which he has so deservedly obtained, he fulfilled his promise of a long-wished-for visit to his relations in Ireland; from whence his safe return *finibus Atticis* is desired by his friends here, with all the classical ardour of *Sic te Diva potens Cypri*; for there is no man in whom more elegant and worthy qualities are united; and whose society therefore is more valued by those who know him.

It is painful to me to think, that while I was carrying on this Work, several of those to whom it would have been most interesting have died. Such melancholy disappointments we know to be incident to humanity; but we do not feel them the less. Let me particularly lament the Reverend Thomas Warton, and the Reverend Dr Adams. Mr Warton, amidst his variety of genius and learning, was an excellent Biographer. His contributions to my Collection are highly estimable; and as he had a true relish of my *Tour to the Hebrides*, I trust I should now have been gratified with a larger share of his kind approbation. Dr Adams, eminent as the Head of a College, as a writer, and as a most amiable man, had known Johnson from his early years, and was his friend through life. What reason I had to hope for the countenance of that venerable Gentleman to this Work, will appear from what he wrote to me upon a former occasion from Oxford, November 17, 1785: 'DEAR SIR – I hazard this letter, not knowing where it will find you, to thank you for your very agreeable *Tour*, which I found here on my return from the country, and in which you have depicted our friend so perfectly to my fancy, in every attitude, every scene and situation, that I have thought myself in the company, and of the party almost throughout. It has given very general satisfaction; and those who have found most fault with a passage here and there, have agreed that they could not help going through, and being entertained through the whole. I wish, indeed, some few gross expressions had been softened, and a few of our hero's foibles had been a little more shaded; but it is useful to see the weaknesses incident to great minds; and you have given us Dr Johnson's authority that in history all ought to be told.'

Such a sanction to my faculty of giving a just representation of Dr Johnson I could not conceal. Nor will I suppress my satisfaction in the consciousness, that by recording so considerable a portion of the wisdom and wit of 'the brightest ornament of the eighteenth century',[1] I have largely provided for the instruction and entertainment of mankind.

London, April 20, 1791.

---

1 See Mr Malone's Preface to his edition of Shakspeare.

ADVERTISEMENT TO THE SECOND EDITION

That I was anxious for the success of a Work which had employed much of my time and labour, I do not wish to conceal: but whatever doubts I at any time entertained have been entirely removed by the very favourable reception with which it has been honoured. That reception has excited my best exertions to render my Book more perfect; and in this endeavour I have had the assistance not only of some of my particular friends, but of many other learned and ingenious men, by which I have been enabled to rectify some mistakes, and to enrich the work with many valuable additions. These I have ordered to be printed separately in quarto, for the accommodation of the purchasers of the first edition. May I be permitted to say that the typography of both editions does honour to the press of Mr Henry Baldwin, now Master of the Worshipful Company of Stationers, whom I have long known as a worthy man and an obliging friend.

In the strangely mixed scenes of human existence, our feelings are often at once pleasing and painful. Of this truth the progress of the present Work furnishes a striking instance. It was highly gratifying to me that my friend, Sir Joshua Reynolds, to whom it is inscribed, lived to peruse it, and to give the strongest testimony to its fidelity; but before a second edition, which he contributed to improve, could be finished, the world has been deprived of that most valuable man; a loss of which the regret will be deep, and lasting, and extensive, proportionate to the felicity which he diffused through a wide circle of admirers and friends.

In reflecting that the illustrious subject of this Work, by being more extensively and intimately known, however elevated before, has risen in the veneration and love of mankind, I feel a satisfaction beyond what fame can afford. We cannot, indeed, too much or too often admire his wonderful powers of mind, when we consider that the principal store of wit and wisdom which this Work contains, was not a particular selection from his general conversation, but was merely his occasional talk at such times as I had the good fortune to be in his company; and, without doubt, if his discourse at other periods had been collected with the same attention, the whole tenor of what he uttered would have been found equally excellent.

His strong, clear, and animated enforcement of religion, morality, loyalty, and subordination, while it delights and improves the wise and the good, will, I trust, prove an effectual antidote to that detestable sophistry which has been lately imported from France, under the false name of philosophy, and with a malignant industry has been employed against the peace, good order, and happiness of society, in our free and prosperous country; but thanks be to GOD, without producing the pernicious effects which were hoped for by its propagators.

It seems to me in my moments of self-complacency, that this extensive biographical work, however inferior in its nature, may in one respect be assimilated to the ODYSSEY. Amidst a thousand entertaining and instructive episodes the HERO is never long out of sight; for they are all in some degree connected with him; and HE in the whole course of the History is exhibited by the Author for the best advantage of his readers.

> — Quid virtus et quid sapientia possit,
> Utile proposuit nobis exemplar Ulyssen.

Should there be any cold-blooded and morose mortals who really dislike this Book, I will give them a story to apply. When the great Duke of Marlborough, accompanied by Lord Cadogan, was one day reconnoitering the army in Flanders, a heavy rain came on, and they both called for their cloaks. Lord Cadogan's servant, a good-humoured alert lad, brought his Lordship's in a minute. The Duke's servant, a lazy sulky dog, was so sluggish, that his Grace being wet to the skin, reproved him, and had for answer with a grunt, 'I came as fast as I could', upon which the Duke calmly said, 'Cadogan, I would not for a thousand pounds have that fellow's temper.'

There are some men, I believe, who have, or think they have, a very small share of vanity. Such may speak of their literary fame in a decorous style of diffidence. But I confess, that I am so formed by nature and by habit, that to restrain the effusion of delight, on having obtained such fame, to me would be truly painful. Why then should I suppress it? Why 'out of the abundance of the heart' should I not speak? Let me then mention with a warm, but no insolent exultation, that I have been regaled with spontaneous praise of my work by many and various persons eminent for their rank, learning, talents and accomplishments; much of which praise I have under their hands to be reposited in my archives at Auchinleck. An honourable and reverend friend speaking of the favourable reception of my volumes, even in the circles of fashion and elegance, said to me, 'you have made them all talk Johnson,' - Yes, I may add, I have *Johnsonised* the land; and I trust they will not only *talk* but *think* Johnson.

To enumerate those to whom I have been thus indebted, would be tediously ostentatious. I cannot however but name one whose praise is truly valuable, not only on account of his knowledge and abilities, but on account of the magnificent, yet dangerous embassy, in which he is now employed, which makes everything that relates to him peculiarly interesting. Lord MACARTNEY favoured me with his own copy of my book, with a number of notes, of which I have availed myself. On the first leaf I found in his Lordship's handwriting, an inscription of such high commendation, that even I, vain as I am, cannot prevail on myself to publish it.

We the Circumscribers,
having read with great pleasure, an
intended Epitaph for the Monument of Dr
Goldsmith; which considered abstractedly, appears to
be, for elegant Composition and Masterly Style, in
every respect worthy of the pen of its learned Author;
are yet of opinion, that the Character of the Deceased as
a Writer, particularly as a Poet, is, perhaps, not delineated
with all the exactness which Dr Johnson is Capable of
giving it. — We therefore, with deference to his Superior Judgement, humbly request, that he would at least take the trouble
of revising it; & of making such additions and alterations
as he shall think proper, upon a further perusal: But
if We might venture to express our Wishes, they would
lead us to request, that he would write the Epitaph
in English; rather than in Latin: As We think that the
Memory of so eminent an English Writer ought to be
perpetuated in the language, to which his Works are
likely to be so lasting an Ornament, Which we
also know to have been the opinion of
The late Doctor
himself.

TO WRITE THE LIFE of him who excelled all mankind in writing the lives of others, and who, whether we consider his extraordinary endowments, or his various works, has been equalled by few in any age, is an arduous, and may be reckoned in me a presumptuous task.

Had Dr Johnson written his own life, in conformity with the opinion which he has given,[1] that every man's life may be best written by himself; had he employed in the preservation of his own history, that clearness of narration and elegance of language in which he has embalmed so many eminent persons, the world would probably have had the most perfect example of biography that was ever exhibited. But although he at different times, in a desultory manner, committed to writing many particulars of the progress of his mind and fortunes, he never had persevering diligence enough to form them into a regular composition. Of these memorials a few have been preserved; but the greater part was consigned by him to the flames, a few days before his death.

As I had the honour and happiness of enjoying his friendship for upwards of twenty years; as I had the scheme of writing his life constantly in view; as he was well apprised of this circumstance, and from time to time obligingly satisfied my inquiries, by communicating to me the incidents of his early years; as I acquired a facility in recollecting, and was very assiduous in recording his conversation, of which the extraordinary vigour and vivacity constituted one of the first features of his character; and as I have spared no pains in obtaining materials concerning him, from every quarter where I could discover that they were to be found, and have been favoured with the most liberal communications by his friends; I flatter myself that few biographers have entered upon such a work as this, with more advantages, independent of literary abilities, in which I am not vain enough to compare myself with some great names who have gone before me in this kind of writing.

Since my work was announced, several Lives and Memoirs of Dr Johnson have been published, the most voluminous of which is one compiled for the Booksellers of London, by Sir John Hawkins, Knight,[2] a man, whom, during

1 *Idler*, No. 84.

2 The greatest part of this book was written while Sir John Hawkins was alive, and I avow, that one object of my strictures was to make him feel some compunction for his illiberal treatment of Dr Johnson. Since his decease, I have suppressed several of my remarks upon his work. But though I would not 'war with the dead' *offensively*, I think it necessary to be strenuous in *defence* of my illustrious friend, which I cannot be, without strong animadversion upon a writer who has greatly injured him. Let me add, that though I doubt I should not have been very prompt to gratify Sir John Hawkins with any compliment in his life-time, I do now frankly acknowledge, that, in my

my long intimacy with Dr Johnson, I never saw in his company, I think but once, and I am sure not above twice. Johnson might have esteemed him for his decent, religious demeanour, and his knowledge of books and literary history; but from the rigid formality of his manners, it is evident that they never could have lived together with companionable ease and familiarity; nor had Sir John Hawkins that nice perception which was necessary to mark the finer and less obvious parts of Johnson's character. His being appointed one of his executors, gave him an opportunity of taking possession of such fragments of a diary and other papers as were left, of which, before delivering them up to the residuary legatee, whose property they were, he endeavoured to extract the substance. In this he has not been very successful, as I have found upon a perusal of those papers, which have been since transferred to me. Sir John Hawkins's ponderous labours, I must acknowledge, exhibit a *farrago,* of which a considerable portion is not devoid of entertainment to the lovers of literary gossiping; but besides its being swelled out with long unnecessary extracts from various works (even one of several leaves from Osborne's Harleian Catalogue, and those not compiled by Johnson, but by Oldys), a very small part of it relates to the person who is the subject of the book; and, in that, there is such an inaccuracy in the statement of facts, as in so solemn an author is hardly excusable, and certainly makes his narrative very unsatisfactory. But what is still worse, there is throughout the whole of it a dark uncharitable cast, by which the most unfavourable construction is put upon almost every circumstance in the character and conduct of my illustrious friend; who, I trust, will, by a true and fair delineation, be vindicated both from the injurious misrepresentations of this author, and from the slighter aspersions of a lady who once lived in great intimacy with him.

There is, in the British Museum, a letter from Bishop Warburton to Dr Birch, on the subject of biography; which, though I am aware it may expose me to a charge of artfully raising the value of my own work, by contrasting it with that of which I have spoken, is so well conceived and expressed, that I cannot refrain from here inserting it:

> I shall endeavour (says Dr Warburton) to give you what satisfaction I can in any thing you want to be satisfied in on the subject of Milton, and am extremely glad you intend to write his life. Almost all the life-writers we have had before Toland and Desmaiseaux, are indeed strange insipid creatures; and yet I had rather read the worst of them, than be obliged to go through with this of Milton's, or the other's life of Boileau, where there is such a dull, heavy succession of long quotations of disinteresting passages, that it makes their method quite nauseous. But the verbose, tasteless Frenchman seems to lay it down as a principle, that every life must be a

---

opinion, his volume, however inadequate and improper as a life of Dr Johnson, and however discredited by unpardonable inaccuracies in other respects, contains a collection of curious anecdotes and observations, which few men but its author could have brought together.

book, and what's worse, it proves a book without a life; for what do we know of Boileau, after all his tedious stuff? You are the only one (and I speak it without a compliment) that by the vigour of your style and sentiments, and the real importance of your materials, have the art (which one would imagine no one could have missed) of adding agreements to the most agreeable subject in the world, which is literary history.[1]

Nov. 24, 1737.

Instead of melting down my materials into one mass, and constantly speaking in my own person, by which I might have appeared to have more merit in the execution of the work, I have resolved to adopt and enlarge upon the excellent plan of Mr Mason, in his Memoirs of Gray. Wherever narrative is necessary to explain, connect, and supply, I furnish it to the best of my abilities; but in the chronological series of Johnson's life, which I trace as distinctly as I can, year by year, I produce, whenever it is in my power, his own minutes, letters, or conversation, being convinced that this mode is more lively, and will make my readers better acquainted with him, than even most of those were who actually knew him, but could know him only partially; whereas there is here an accumulation of intelligence from various points, by which his character is more fully understood and illustrated.

Indeed I cannot conceive a more perfect mode of writing any man's life, than not only relating all the most important events of it in their order, but interweaving what he privately wrote, and said, and thought; by which mankind are enabled as it were to see him live, and to 'live o'er each scene' with him, as he actually advanced through the several stages of his life. Had his other friends been as diligent and ardent as I was, he might have been almost entirely preserved. As it is, I will venture to say that he will be seen in this work more completely than any man who has ever yet lived.

And he will be seen as he really was; for I profess to write, not his panegyric, which must be all praise, but his life; which, great and good as he was, must not be supposed to be entirely perfect. To be as he was, is indeed subject of panegyric enough to any man in this state of being; but in every picture there should be shade as well as light, and when I delineate him without reserve, I do what he himself recommended, both by his precept and his example:

If the biographer writes from personal knowledge, and makes haste to gratify the public curiosity, there is danger lest his interest, his fear, his gratitude, or his tenderness overpower his fidelity, and tempt him to conceal, if not to invent. There are many who think it an act of piety to hide the faults or failings of their friends, even when they can no longer suffer by their detection; we therefore see whole ranks of characters adorned with uniform panegyric, and not to be known from one another but by extrinsic and casual circumstances. 'Let me remember (says Hale), when I find myself inclined to pity a criminal, that there is likewise a pity

1 Brit. Mus. 4320, Ascough's Catal. Sloane MSS.

due to the country.' If we owe regard to the memory of the dead, there is yet more respect to be paid to knowledge, to virtue, and to truth.'[1]

What I consider as the peculiar value of the following work, is, the quantity that it contains of Johnson's conversation; which is universally acknowledged to have been eminently instructive and entertaining; and of which the specimens that I have given upon a former occasion, have been received with so much approbation, that I have good grounds for supposing that the world will not be indifferent to more ample communications of a similar nature.

That the conversation of a celebrated man, if his talents have been exerted in conversation, will best display his character, is, I trust, too well established in the judgement of mankind, to be at all shaken by the sneering observation of Mr Mason, in his Memoirs of Mr William Whitehead, in which there is literally no *Life,* but a mere dry narrative of facts. I do not think it was quite necessary to attempt a depreciation of what is universally esteemed, because it was not to be found in the immediate object of the ingenious writer's pen; for in truth, from a man so still and so tame, as to be contented to pass many years as the domestic companion of a superannuated lord and lady, conversation worth recording could no more be expected, than from a Chinese mandarin on a chimney-piece, or the fantastic figures on a gilt leather screen.

If authority be required, let us appeal to Plutarch, the prince of ancient biographers. Οὔτε ταῖς ἐπιφανεστάταις πράξεσι πάντως ἔνεστι δήλωσις ἀρετῆς, ἀλλὰ πρᾶγμα βραχὺ πολλάκις καὶ ῥῆμα, καὶ παιδιά τις ἔμφασιν ἤθους ἐποίησεν μᾶλλον ἢ μάχαι μυριόνεκροι, καὶ παρατάξεις αἱ μέγισται, καὶ πολιορκίαι πόλεων. 'Nor is it always in the most distinguished achievements that men's virtues or vices may be best discerned; but very often an action of small note, a short saying, or a jest, shall distinguish a person's real character more than the greatest sieges, or the most important battles.'[2]

To this may be added the sentiments of the very man whose life I am about to exhibit.

The business of the biographer is often to pass slightly over those perform-ances and incidents which produce vulgar greatness, to lead the thoughts into domestic privacies, and display the minute details of daily life, where exterior appendages are cast aside, and men excel each other only by prudence and by virtue. The account of Thuanus is with great propriety said by its author to have been written, that it might lay open to posterity the private and familiar character of that man, *cujus ingenium et candorem ex ipsius scriptis sunt olim semper miraturi,* whose candour and genius will to the end of time be by his writings preserved in admiration.

---

1 *Rambler,* No. 60.
2 Plutarch's *Life of Alexander,* Langhorne's translation.

There are many invisible circumstances, which whether we read as enquirers after natural or moral knowledge, whether we intend to enlarge our science, or increase our virtue, are more important than public occurrences. Thus Sallust, the great master of nature, has not forgot in his account of Catiline to remark, that his walk was now quick, and again slow, as an indication of a mind revolving with violent commotion. Thus the story of Melancthon affords a striking lecture on the value of time, by informing us, that when he had made an appointment, he expected not only the hour, but the minute to be fixed, that the day might not run out in the idleness of suspense; and all the plans and enterprises of De Wit are now of less importance to the world than that part of his personal character, which represents him as careful of his health and negligent of his life.

But biography has often been allotted to writers, who seem very little acquainted with the nature of their task, or very negligent about the performance. They rarely afford any other account than might be collected from public papers, but imagine themselves writing a life, when they exhibit a chronological series of actions or preferments; and have so little regard to the manners or behaviour of their heroes, that more knowledge may be gained of a man's real character, by a short conversation with one of his servants, than from a formal and studied narrative, begun with his pedigree, and ended with his funeral.

There are, indeed, some natural reasons why these narratives are often written by such as were not likely to give much instruction or delight, and why most accounts of particular persons are barren and useless. If a life be delayed till interest and envy are at an end, we may hope for impartiality, but must expect little intelligence; for the incidents which give excellence to biography are of a volatile and evanescent kind, such as soon escape the memory, and are transmitted by tradition. We know how few can portray a living acquaintance, except by his most prominent and observable particularities, and the grosser features of his mind; and it may be easily imagined how much of this little knowledge may be lost in imparting it, and how soon a succession of copies will lose all resemblance of the original.[1]

I am fully aware of the objections which may be made to the minuteness on some occasions of my detail of Johnson's conversation, and how happily it is adapted for the petty exercise of ridicule by men of superficial understanding, and ludicrous fancy; but I remain firm and confident in my opinion, that minute particulars are frequently characteristic, and always amusing, when they relate to a distinguished man. I am therefore exceedingly unwilling that almost any thing[a] which my illustrious friend thought it worth his while to

---

[1] *Rambler*, No. 60.
[a] For 'almost anything', read 'anything, however slight'.

express, with any degree of point, should perish. For this almost superstitious reverence, I have found very old and venerable authority, quoted by our great modern prelate, Secker, in whose tenth sermon there is the following passage:

> *Rabbi David Kimchi*, a noted Jewish commentator who lived above five hundred years ago, explains that passage in the first Psalm, *His leaf also shall not wither*, from Rabbins yet older than himself, thus: That *even the idle talk*, so he expresses it, *of a good man ought to be regarded*; the most superfluous things he saith are always of some value. And other ancient authors have the same phrase, nearly in the same sense.

Of one thing I am certain, that considering how highly the small portion which we have of the table-talk and other anecdotes of our celebrated writers is valued, and how earnestly it is regretted that we have not more, I am justified in preserving rather too many of Johnson's sayings than too few; especially as from the diversity of dispositions it cannot be known with certainty beforehand, whether what may seem trifling to some, and perhaps to the collector himself, may not be most agreeable to many; and the greater number that an author can please in any degree, the more pleasure does there arise to a benevolent mind.

To those who are weak enough to think this a degrading task, and the time and labour which have been devoted to it misemployed, I shall content myself with opposing the authority of the greatest man of any age, JULIUS CAESAR, of whom Bacon observes, that 'in his book of Apothegms which he collected, we see that he esteemed it more honour to make himself but a pair of tables, to take the wise and pithy words of others, than to have every word of his own to be made an apothegm or an oracle.'[1]

Having said thus much by way of introduction, I commit the following pages to the candour of the public.

SAMUEL JOHNSON was born at Lichfield, in Staffordshire, on the 18th of September, N.S., 1709; and his initiation into the Christian Church was not delayed; for his baptism is recorded, in the register of St Mary's parish in that city, to have been performed on the day of his birth. His father is there styled *Gentleman*, a circumstance of which an ignorant panegyrist has praised him for not being proud; when the truth is, that the appellation of Gentleman, though now lost in the indiscriminate assumption of *Esquire*, was commonly taken by those who could not boast of gentility. His father was Michael Johnson, a native of Derbyshire, of obscure extraction, who settled in Lichfield as a bookseller and stationer. His mother was Sarah Ford, descended of an ancient race of substantial yeomanry in Warwickshire. They were well advanced in years when they married, and never had more than two children, both sons; Samuel, their first born, who lived to be the illustrious character whose various excellence I am to endeavour to record, and Nathanael, who died in his twenty-fifth year.

1 Bacon's *Advancement of Learning*, Book I.

Mr Michael Johnson was a man of a large and robust body, and of a strong and active mind; yet, as in the most solid rocks veins of unsound substance are often discovered, there was in him a mixture of that disease, the nature of which eludes the most minute enquiry, though the effects are well known to be a weariness of life, an unconcern about those things which agitate the greater part of mankind, and a general sensation of gloomy wretchedness. From him, then, his son inherited, with some other qualities, 'a vile melancholy', which, in his too strong expression of any disturbance of the mind, 'made him mad all his life, at least not sober'.[1] Michael was, however, forced by the narrowness of his circumstances to be very diligent in business, not only in his shop, but by occasionally resorting to several towns in the neighbourhood, some of which were at a considerable distance from Lichfield. At that time booksellers' shops in the provincial towns of England were very rare, so that there was not one even in Birmingham, in which town old Mr Johnson used to open a shop every market-day. He was a pretty good Latin scholar, and a citizen so creditable as to be made one of the magistrates of Lichfield; and, being a man of good sense, and skill in his trade, he acquired a reasonable share of wealth, of which however he afterwards lost the greatest part, by engaging unsuccessfully in a manufacture of parchment. He was a zealous high-churchman and royalist, and retained his attachment to the unfortunate house of Stuart, though he reconciled himself, by casuistical arguments of expediency and necessity, to take the oaths imposed by the prevailing power.

There is a circumstance in his life somewhat romantic, but so well authenticated, that I shall not omit it. A young woman of Leek, in Staffordshire, while he served his apprenticeship there, conceived a violent passion for him; and though it met with no favourable return, followed him to Lichfield, where she took lodgings opposite to the house in which he lived, and indulged her hopeless flame. When he was informed that it so preyed upon her mind that her life was in danger, he with a generous humanity went to her and offered to marry her, but it was then too late: her vital power was exhausted; and she actually exhibited one of the very rare instances of dying for love. She was buried in the cathedral of Lichfield; and he, with a tender regard, placed a stone over her grave with this inscription:

Here lies the body of
Mrs ELIZABETH BLANEY, a stranger.
She departed this life
20 of September, 1694.

Johnson's mother was a woman of distinguished understanding. I asked his old school-fellow Mr Hector, surgeon, of Birmingham, if she was not vain of her son. He said, 'she had too much good sense to be vain, but she knew her son's value.' Her piety was not inferior to her understanding; and to her must be ascribed those early impressions of religion upon the mind of her son, from

1 *Journal of a Tour to the Hebrides*, 3rd edit. p. 213.

which the world afterwards derived so much benefit. He told me, that he remembered distinctly having had the first notice of Heaven, 'a place to which good people went', and Hell, 'a place to which bad people went', communicated to him by her, when a little child in bed with her; and that it might be the better fixed in his memory, she sent him to repeat it to Thomas Jackson, their manservant. He not being in the way, this was not done; but there was no occasion for any artificial aid for its preservation.

In following so very eminent a man from his cradle to his grave, every minute particular, which can throw light on the progress of his mind, is interesting. That he was remarkable, even in his earliest years, may easily be supposed; for to use his own words in his Life of Sydenham, 'That the strength of his understanding, the accuracy of his discernment, and ardour of his curiosity, might have been remarked from his infancy, by a diligent observer, there is no reason to doubt. For, there is no instance of any man, whose history has been minutely related, that did not in every part of life discover the same proportion of intellectual vigour.'

In all such investigations it is certainly unwise to pay too much attention to incidents which the credulous relate with eager satisfaction, and the more scrupulous or witty enquirer considers only as topics of ridicule: Yet there is a traditional story of the infant Hercules of toryism, so curiously characteristic, that I shall not withhold it. It was communicated to me in a letter from Miss Mary Adye, of Lichfield.

> When Dr Sacheverel was at Lichfield, Johnson was not quite three years old. My grandfather Hammond observed him at the cathedral perched upon his father's shoulders, listening, and gaping, at the much celebrated preacher. Mr Hammond asked Mr Johnson how he could possibly think of bringing such an infant to church, and in the midst of so great a crowd. He answered, because it was impossible to keep him at home; for, young as he was, he believed he had caught the public spirit and zeal for Sacheverel, and would have staid for ever in the church, satisfied with beholding him.

Nor can I omit a little instance of that jealous independence of spirit, and impetuosity of temper, which never forsook him. The fact was acknowledged to me by himself, upon the authority of his mother. One day, when the servant who used to be sent to school to conduct him home, had not come in time, he set out by himself, though he was then so near-sighted, that he was obliged to stoop down on his hands and knees to take a view of the kennel before he ventured to step over it. His schoolmistress, afraid that he might miss his way, or fall into the kennel, or be run over by a cart, followed him at some distance. He happened to turn about and perceive her. Feeling her careful attention as an insult to his manliness, he ran back to her in a rage, and beat her, as well as his strength would permit.

Of the strength of his memory, for which he was all his life eminent to a degree almost incredible, the following early instance was told me in his presence at Lichfield, in 1776, by his stepdaughter, Mrs Lucy Porter, as related to her by his mother. When he was a child in petticoats, and had learnt to read, Mrs Johnson one morning put the common prayer-book into his hands, pointed to the collect for the day, and said, 'Sam, you must get this by heart.' She went up stairs, leaving him to study it: But by the time she had reached the second floor, she heard him following her. 'What's the matter?' said she. 'I can say it,' he replied; and repeated it distinctly, though he could not have read it over more than twice.

But there has been another story of his infant precocity generally circulated, and generally believed, the truth of which I am to refute upon his own authority. It is told,[1] that, when a child of three years old, he chanced to tread upon a duckling, the eleventh of a brood, and killed it; upon which, it is said, he dictated to his mother the following epitaph:

> 'Here lies good master duck,
>   Whom Samuel Johnson trod on;
> If it had liv'd, it had been *good luck*,
>   For then we'd had an *odd òne*.'

There is surely internal evidence that this little composition combines in it, what no child of three years old could produce, without an extension of its faculties by immediate inspiration; yet Mrs Lucy Porter, Dr Johnson's step-daughter, positively maintained to me, in his presence, that there could be no doubt of the truth of this anecdote, for she had heard it from his mother.[2] So difficult is it to obtain an authentic relation of facts, and such authority may there be for error; for he assured me, that his father made the verses, and wished to pass them for his child's. He added, 'my father was a foolish old man; that is to say, foolish in talking of his children.'

Young Johnson had the misfortune to be much afflicted with the scrofula,

1 *Anecdotes of Dr Johnson*, by Hester Lynch Piozzi, p. 11. *Life of Dr Johnson*, by Sir John Hawkins, p. 6.

2 This anecdote of the duck, though disproved by internal and external evidence, has nevertheless, upon supposition of its truth, been made the foundation of the following ingenious and fanciful reflections by Miss Seward, amongst the communications concerning Dr Johnson with which she has been pleased to favour me: 'These infant numbers contain the seeds of those propensities which through his life so strongly marked his character, of that poetic talent which afterwards bore such rich and plentiful fruits; for, excepting his orthographic works, everything which Dr Johnson wrote was Poetry, whose essence consists not in numbers, or in jingle, but in the strength and glow of a fancy, to which all the stores of nature and of art stand in prompt administration; and in an eloquence which conveys their blended illustrations in a language "more tuneable than needs or rhyme or verse to add more harmony."

'The above little verses also show that superstitious bias which "grew with his **growth, and strengthened with** his strength", and of late years particularly injured his happiness, by presenting to him the gloomy side of religion, rather than that bright and cheering one which gilds the period of closing life, with the light of pious hope.'

This is so beautifully imagined, that I would not suppress it. But, like many other theories, it is deduced from a supposed fact, which is, indeed, a fiction.

or king's evil, which disfigured a countenance naturally well formed, and hurt his visual nerves so much, that he did not see at all with one of his eyes, though its appearance was little different from that of the other. There is amongst his prayers, one inscribed, '*When my* EYE *was restored to its use*,'[1] which ascertains a defect that many of his friends knew he had, though I never perceived it. I supposed him to be only near-sighted; and indeed I must observe, that in no other respect could I discern any defect in his vision; on the contrary, the force of his attention and perceptive quickness made him see and distinguish all manner of objects, whether of nature or of art, with a nicety that is rarely to be found. When he and I were travelling in the Highlands of Scotland, and I pointed out to him a mountain which I observed resembled a cone, he corrected my inaccuracy by showing me, that it was indeed pointed at the top, but that one side of it was larger than the other. And the ladies with whom he was acquainted agree, that no man was more nicely and minutely critical in the elegance of female dress. When I found that he saw the romantic beauties of Islam, in Derbyshire, much better than I did, I told him that he resembled an able performer upon a bad instrument. How false and contemptible then are all the remarks which have been made to the prejudice either of his candour or of his philosophy, founded upon a supposition that he was almost blind. It has been said, that he contracted this grievous malady from his nurse. His mother yielding to the superstitious notion, which, it is wonderful to think, prevailed so long in this country, as to the virtue of the regal touch; a notion, which our kings encouraged, and to which a man of such inquiry and such judgement as Carte could give credit; carried him to London, where he was actually touched by Queen Anne. Mrs Johnson indeed, as Mr Hector informed me, acted by the advice of the celebrated Sir John Floyer, then a physician in Lichfield. Johnson used to talk of this very frankly; and Mrs Piozzi has preserved his very picturesque description of the scene, as it remained upon his fancy. Being asked if he could remember Queen Anne, 'He had (he said) a confused, but somehow a sort of solemn recollection of a lady in diamonds, and a long black hood.'[2] This touch, however, was without any effect. I ventured to say to him, in allusion to the political principles in which he was educated, and of which he ever retained some odour, that 'his mother had not carried him far enough; she should have taken him to ROME.'

He was first taught to read English by Dame Oliver, a widow, who kept a school for young children in Lichfield. He told me she could read the black letter, and asked him to borrow for her, from his father, a bible in that character. When he was going to Oxford, she came to take leave of him, brought him, in the simplicity of her kindness, a present of gingerbread, and said he was the best scholar she had ever had. He delighted in mentioning this early compliment; adding, with a smile, that 'this was as high a proof of his

1 *Prayers and Meditations*, p. 27.
2 *Anecdotes*, p. 10.

merit as he could conceive.' His next instructor in English was a master, whom, when he spoke of him to me, he familiarly called Tom Brown, who, said he, 'published a spelling-book, and dedicated it to the UNIVERSE; but, I fear, no copy of it can now be had.'

He began to learn Latin with Mr Hawkins, usher, or under-master of Lichfield school, 'a man (said he), very skilful in his little way.' With him he continued two years, and then rose to be under the care of Mr Hunter the headmaster, who, according to his account, 'was very severe, and wrong-headedly severe. He used (said he), to beat us unmercifully; and he did not distinguish between ignorance and negligence; for he would beat a boy equally for not knowing a thing, as for neglecting to know it. He would ask a boy a question; and if he did not answer it, he would beat him, without considering whether he had an opportunity of knowing how to answer it. For instance, he would call up a boy and ask him Latin for a candlestick, which the boy could not expect to be asked. Now, Sir, if a boy could answer every question, there would be no need of a master to teach him.'

It is, however, but justice to the memory of Mr Hunter to mention, that though he might err in being too severe, the school of Lichfield was very respectable in his time. The late Dr Taylor, Prebendary of Westminster, who was educated under him, told me, that he was an excellent master, and that his ushers were most of them men of eminence; that Holbrook, one of the most ingenious men, best scholars, and best preachers of his age, was usher during the greatest part of the time that Johnson was at school. Then came Hague, of whom as much might be said, with the addition that he was an elegant poet. Hague was succeeded by Green, afterwards Bishop of Lincoln, whose character in the learned world is well known. In the same form with Johnson was Congreve, who afterwards became chaplain to Archbishop Boulter, and by that connection obtained good preferment in Ireland. He was a younger son of the ancient family of Congreve, in Staffordshire, of which the poet was a branch. His brother sold the estate. There was also Lowe, afterwards Canon of Windsor; who was tutor to the present Marquis Townshend, and his brother Charles.

Indeed Johnson was very sensible how much he owed to Mr Hunter. Mr Langton one day asked him how he had acquired so accurate a knowledge of Latin, in which, I believe, he was exceeded by no man of his time; he said, 'My master whipped me very well. Without that, Sir, I should have done nothing.' He told Mr Langton, that while Hunter was flogging his boys unmercifully, he used to say, 'And this I do to save you from the gallows.' Johnson, upon all occasions, expressed his approbation of enforcing instruction by means of the rod. 'I would rather (said he) have the rod to be the general terror to all, to make them learn, than tell a child, if you do thus, or thus, you will be more esteemed than your brothers or sisters. The rod produces an effect which terminates in itself. A child is afraid of being whipped, and gets his task, and there's an end on't; whereas, by exciting emulation and comparisons of superiority, you lay the foundation of lasting mischief; you make brothers and sisters hate each other.'

Mr Langton told me, that when Johnson saw some young ladies in Lincoln-shire who were remarkably well behaved, owing to their mother's strict discipline, and severe correction, he exclaimed, in one of Shakspeare's lines a little varied, '*Rod*, I will honour thee for this thy duty.'

That superiority over his fellows, which he maintained with so much dignity in his march through life, was not assumed from vanity and ostenta-tion, but was the natural and constant effect of those extraordinary powers of mind, of which he could not but be conscious by comparison; the intellectual difference, which in other cases of comparison of characters is often a matter of undecided contest, being as clear in his case as the superiority of stature in some men above others. Johnson did not strut or stand on tiptoe: He only did not stoop. From his earliest years, his superiority was perceived and acknow-ledged. He was from the beginning ἄναξ ἀνδρῶν, a king of men. His schoolfellow, Mr Hector, has obligingly furnished me with many particulars of his boyish days; and assured me, that he never knew him corrected at school, but for talking and diverting other boys from their business. He seemed to learn by intuition; for though indolence and procrastination were inherent in his constitution, whenever he made an exertion he did more than any one else. In short, he is a memorable instance of what has been often observed, that the boy is the man in miniature; and that the distinguishing characteristics of each individual are the same, through the whole course of life. His favourites used to receive very liberal assistance from him; and such was the submission and deference with which he was treated, such the desire to obtain his regard, that three of the boys, of whom Mr Hector was sometimes one, used to come in the morning as his humble attendants, and carry him to school. One in the middle stooped, while he sat upon his back, and one on each side supported him; and thus he was borne triumphant. Such a proof of the early predominance of intellectual vigour is very remarkable, and does honour to human nature. Talking to me once himself of his being much distinguished at school, he told me, 'they never thought to raise me by comparing me to any one; they never said, Johnson is as good a scholar as such a one; but such a one is as good a scholar as Johnson; and this was said but of one, but of Lowe; and I do not think he was as good a scholar.'

He discovered a great ambition to excel, which roused him to counteract his indolence. He was uncommonly inquisitive; and his memory was so tenacious, that he never forgot anything that he either heard or read. Mr Hector remembers having recited to him eighteen verses, which, after a little pause, he repeated *verbatim*, varying only one epithet, by which he improved the line.

He never joined with the other boys in their ordinary diversions; his only amusement was in winter, when he took a pleasure in being drawn upon the ice by a boy barefooted, who pulled him along by a garter fixed round him; no very easy operation, as his size was remarkably large. His defective sight, indeed, prevented him from enjoying the common sports; and he once pleasantly remarked to me, how wonderfully well he had contrived to be idle without them. Lord Chesterfield, however, has justly observed in one of his letters, when earnestly cautioning a friend against the pernicious effects of idleness, that active sports are not to be reckoned idleness in young people; and that the listless torpor of doing nothing, alone deserves that name. Of this dismal inertness of disposition, Johnson had all his life too great a share. Mr Hector relates, that 'he could not oblige him more than by sauntering away the hours of vacation in the fields, during which he was more engaged in talking to himself than to his companion.'

Dr Percy, the Bishop of Dromore, who was long intimately acquainted with him, and has preserved a few anecdotes concerning him, regretting that he was not a more diligent collector, informs me, that 'when a boy he was immoderately fond of reading romances of chivalry, and he retained his fondness for them through life; so that (adds his Lordship) spending part of a summer at my parsonage-house in the country, he chose for his regular reading the old Spanish romance of *Felixmarte of Hircania*, in folio, which he read quite through. Yet I have heard him attribute to these extravagant fictions, that unsettled turn of mind which prevented his ever fixing in any profession.'

After having resided for some time at the house of his uncle, Cornelius Ford, Johnson was, at the age of fifteen, removed to the school of Stourbridge, in Worcestershire, of which Mr Wentworth was then master. This step was taken by the advice of his cousin, the Reverend Mr Ford, a man in whom both talents and good dispositions were disgraced by licentiousness,[1] but who was a very able judge of what was right. At this school he did not receive so much benefit as was expected. It has been said, that he acted in the capacity of an assistant to Mr Wentworth, in teaching the younger boys. 'Mr Wentworth (he told me) was a very able man, but an idle man, and to me very severe; but I cannot blame him much. I was then a big boy; he saw I did not reverence him; and that he should get no honour by me. I had brought enough with me, to carry me through; and all I should get at his school would be ascribed to my own labour, or to my former master. Yet he taught me a great deal.'

He thus discriminated, to Dr Percy, Bishop of Dromore, his progress at his two grammar-schools. 'At one, I learnt much in the school, but little from the master; in the other, I learnt much from the master, but little in the school.'

The Bishop also informs me, that Dr Johnson's father, before he was received at Stourbridge, applied to have him admitted as a scholar and assistant to the Reverend Samuel Lea, M.A., head master of Newport School, in Shropshire (a very diligent good teacher, at that time in high reputation, under whom Mr Hollis is said, in the Memoirs of his Life, to have been also educated[2]). This application to Mr Lea was not successful; but Johnson had afterwards the gratification to hear that the old gentleman, who lived to a very advanced age, mentioned it as one of the most memorable events of his life, that 'he was *very near* having that great man for his scholar.'

He remained at Stourbridge little more than a year, and then returned home, where he may be said to have loitered, for two years, in a state very

---

1   He is said to be the original of the parson in Hogarth's *Modern Midnight Conversation*.
2   As was likewise the Bishop of Dromore many years afterwards.

unworthy his uncommon abilities. He had already given several proofs of his
poetical genius, both in his school-exercises and in other occasional compositions. Of these I have obtained a considerable collection, by the favour of Mr
Wentworth, son of one of his masters, and of Mr Hector, his school-fellow
and friend; from which I select the following specimens:

Translation of VIRGIL. *Pastoral* I.

MELIBOEUS.

Now, Tityrus, you, supine and careless laid,
Play on your pipe beneath this beechen shade;
While wretched we about the world must roam,
And leave our pleasing fields and native home,
Here at your ease you sing your amorous flame,
And the wood rings with Amarillis' name.

TITYRUS.

Those blessings, friend, a deity bestow'd,
For I shall never think him less than God;
Oft on his altar shall my firstlings lie,
Their blood the consecrated stones shall dye;
He gave my flocks to graze the flowery meads,
And me to tune at ease th' unequal reeds.

MELIBOEUS.

My admiration only I exprest,
(No spark of envy harbours in my breast)
That when confusion o'er the country reigns,
To you alone this happy state remains.
Here I, though faint myself, must drive my goats,
Far from their antient fields and humble cots.
This scarce I lead, who left on yonder rock
Two tender kids, the hopes of all the flock.
Had we not been perverse and careless grown,
This dire event by omens was foreshown;
Our trees were blasted by the thunder stroke,
And left-hand crows, from an old hollow oak,
Foretold the coming evil by their dismal croak.

Translation of HORACE. *Book* I. *Ode* xii.

The man, my friend, whose conscious heart
   With virtue's sacred ardour glows,
Nor taints with death the envenom'd dart,
   Nor needs the guard of Moorish bows:

Though Scythia's icy cliffs he treads,
   Or horrid Africk's faithless sands;
Or where the fam'd Hydaspes spreads
   His liquid wealth o'er barbarous lands.

For while by Chloe's image charm'd,
   Too far in Sabine woods I stray'd;
Me singing, careless and unarm'd,
   A grizly wolf surprised, and fled.

No savage more portentous stain'd
   Apulia's spacious wilds with gore;
None fiercer Juba's thirsty land,
   Dire nurse of raging lions, bore.

Place me where no soft summer gale
   Among the quivering branches sighs;
Where clouds condens'd for ever veil
   With horrid gloom the frowning skies:

Place me beneath the burning line,
   A clime deny'd to human race;
I'll sing of Chloe's charms divine,
   Her heav'nly voice, and beauteous face.

Translation of HORACE. *Book* II. *Ode* ix.

Clouds do not always veil the skies,
   Nor showers immerse the verdant plain;
Nor do the billows always rise,
   Or storms afflict the ruffled main.

Nor, Valgius, on th' Armenian shores
   Do the chain'd waters always freeze;
Not always furious Boreas roars,
   Or bends with violent force the trees.

But you are ever crown'd in tears,
   For Mystes dead you ever mourn;
No setting Sol can ease your care,
   But finds you sad at his return.

The wise experienc'd Grecian sage
   Mourn'd not Antilochus so long;
Nor did King Priam's hoary age
   So much lament his slaughter'd son.

Leave off, at length, these woman's sighs,
   Augustus' numerous trophies sing;
Repeat that prince's victories,
   To whom all nations tribute bring.

Niphates rolls an humbler wave,
   At length the undaunted Scythian yields,
Content to live the Romans' slave,
   And scarce forsakes his native fields.

Translation of part of the Dialogue between HECTOR *and* ANDROMACHE;
from the sixth Book of HOMER'S ILIAD.

She ceas'd; then Godlike Hector answer'd kind, –
(His various plumage sporting in the wind)
That post, and all the rest, shall be my care;
But shall I, then, forsake the unfinish'd war?
How would the Trojans brand great Hector's name!
And one base action sully all my fame,
Acquir'd by wounds, and battles bravely fought!
Oh! how my soul abhors so mean a thought.
Long since I learn'd to slight this fleeting breath,
And view with cheerful eyes approaching death.
The inexorable sisters have decreed
That Priam's house, and Priam's self shall bleed:
The day will come, in which proud Troy shall yield,
And spread its smoking ruins o'er the field.
Yet Hecuba's, nor Priam's hoary age,
Whose blood shall quench some Grecian's thirsty rage,
Nor my brave brothers, that have bit the ground,
Their souls dismiss'd through many a ghastly wound,
Can in my bosom half that grief create,
As the sad thought of your impending fate:
When some proud Grecian dame shall tasks impose,
Mimick your tears, and ridicule your woes;
Beneath Hyperia's waters shall you sweat,
And, fainting, scarce support the liquid weight:
Then shall some Argive loud insulting cry,
Behold the wife of Hector, guard of Troy!
Tears, at my name, shall drown those beauteous eyes,
And that fair bosom heave with rising sighs!
Before that day, by some brave hero's hand,
May I lie slain, and spurn the bloody sand!

To a YOUNG LADY on her BIRTH-DAY.[1]

This tributary verse receive, my fair,
Warm with an ardent lover's fondest pray'r.
May this returning day for ever find
Thy form more lovely, more adorn'd thy mind;
All pains, all cares, may favouring heav'n remove,
All but the sweet solicitudes of love!
May powerful nature join with grateful art,
To point each glance, and force it to the heart!
O then, when conquer'd crouds confess thy sway,
When even proud wealth and prouder wit obey,
My fair, be mindful of the mighty trust,
Alas! 'tis hard for beauty to be just.
Those sovereign charms with strictest care employ;
Nor give the generous pain, the worthless joy:
With his own form acquaint the forward fool,
Shewn in the faithful glass of ridicule;
Teach mimick censure her own faults to find,
No more let coquets to themselves be blind,
So shall Belinda's charms improve mankind.

THE YOUNG AUTHOUR.[2]

When first the peasant, long inclin'd to roam,
Forsakes his rural sports and peaceful home,
Pleased with the scene the smiling ocean yields,
He scorns the verdant meads and flow'ry fields;
Then dances jocund o'er the watery way,
While the breeze whispers, and the streamers play:
Unbounded prospects in his bosom roll,
And future millions lift his rising soul;
In blissful dreams he digs the golden mine,
And raptur'd sees the new-found ruby shine.
Joys insincere! thick clouds invade the skies,
Loud roar the billows, high the waves arise;
Sick'ning with fear, he longs to view the shore,
And vows to trust the faithless deep no more.
So the young Authour, panting after fame,
And the long honours of a lasting name,
Entrusts his happiness to human kind,
More false, more cruel, than the seas or wind.
'Toil on, dull croud,' in extacies he cries,
'For wealth or title, perishable prize;

1 Mr Hector informs me, that this was made almost impromptu, in his presence.
2 This he inserted, with many alterations, in the *Gentleman's Magazine*, 1743.

While I those transitory blessings scorn,
Secure of praise from ages yet unborn.'
This thought once form'd, all counsel comes too late,
He flies to press, and hurries on his fate;
Swiftly he sees the imagin'd laurels spread,
And feels the unfading wreath surround his head.
Warn'd by another's fate, vain youth, be wise,
Those dreams were Settle's once, and Ogilby's:
The pamphlet spreads, incessant hisses rise,
To some retreat the baffled writer flies;
Where no sour criticks snarl, no sneers molest,
Safe from the tart lampoon, and stinging jest;
There begs of heav'n a less distinguish'd lot,
Glad to be hid, and proud to be forgot.

EPILOGUE, *intended to have been spoken by a* LADY
who was to personate the Ghost of HERMIONE.[1]

Ye blooming train, who give despair or joy,
Bless with a smile, or with a frown destroy;
In whose fair cheeks destructive Cupids wait,
And with unerring shafts distribute fate;
Whose snowy breasts, whose animated eyes,
Each youth admires, though each admirer dies;
Whilst you deride their pangs in barb'rous play,
Unpitying see them weep, and hear them pray,
And unrelenting sport ten thousand lives away;
For you, ye fair, I quit the gloomy plains,
Where sable night in all her horrour reigns;
No fragrant bowers, no delightful glades,
Receive th' unhappy ghosts of scornful maids.
For kind, for tender nymphs the myrtle blooms,
And weaves her bending boughs in pleasing glooms;
Perennial roses deck each purple vale,
And scents ambrosial breathe in every gale:
Far hence are banish'd vapours, spleen, and tears,
Tea, scandal, ivory teeth, and languid airs;
No pug, nor favourite Cupid there enjoys
The balmy kiss, for which poor Thyrsis dies;
Form'd to delight, they use no foreign arms,
Nor torturing whalebones pinch them into charms;
No conscious blushes there their cheeks inflame,
For those who feel no guilt can know no shame;

---

1 Some young ladies at Lichfield having proposed to act *The Distressed Mother*,
Johnson wrote this, and gave it to Mr Hector to convey it privately to them.

Unfaded still their former charms they shew,
Around them pleasures wait, and joys for ever new.
But cruel virgins meet severer fates;
Expell'd and exil'd from the blissful seats,
To dismal realms, and regions void of peace,
Where furies ever howl, and serpents hiss.
O'er the sad plains perpetual tempests sigh;
And pois'nous vapours, black'ning all the sky,
With livid hue the fairest face o'ercast,
And every beauty withers at the blast:
Where e'er they fly their lovers' ghosts pursue,
Inflicting all those ills which once they knew;
Vexation, Fury, Jealousy, Despair,
Vex ev'ry eye, and ev'ry bosom tear;
Their foul deformities by all descry'd,
No maid to flatter, and no paint to hide.
Then melt, ye fair, while crouds around you sigh,
Nor let disdain sit low'ring in your eye;
With pity soften every awful grace,
And beauty smile auspicious in each face;
To ease their pains exert your milder power,
So shall you guiltless reign, and all mankind adore.

The two years which he spent at home, after his return from Stourbridge, he passed in what he thought idleness, and was scolded by his father for his want of steady application. He had no settled plan of life, nor looked forward at all, but merely lived from day to day. Yet he read a great deal in a desultory manner, without any scheme of study, as chance threw books in his way, and inclination directed him through them. He used to mention one curious instance of his casual reading, when but a boy. Having imagined that his brother had hid some apples behind a large folio upon an upper shelf in his father's shop, he climbed up to search for them. There were no apples; but the large folio proved to be Petrarch, whom he had seen mentioned, in some preface, as one of the restorers of learning. His curiosity having been thus excited, he sat down with avidity, and read a great part of the book. What he read during these two years, he told me, was not works of mere amusement, 'not voyages and travels, but all literature, Sir, all ancient writers, all manly; though but little Greek, only some of Anacreon and Hesiod; but in this irregular manner (added he) I had looked into a great many books, which were not commonly known at the Universities, where they seldom read any books but what are put into their hands by their tutors; so that when I came to Oxford, Dr Adams,[a] master of Pembroke College, told me, I was the best qualified for the University that he had ever known come there.'

---

[a] After 'Dr Adams,' read 'now'.

In estimating the progress of his mind during these two years, as well as in future periods of his life, we must not regard his own hasty confession of idleness; for we see, when he explains himself, that he was acquiring various stores; and, indeed, he himself concluded the account, with saying, 'I would not have you think I was doing nothing then.' He might, perhaps, have studied more assiduously; but it may be doubted, whether such a mind as his was not more enriched by roaming at large in the fields of literature, than if it had been confined to any single spot. The analogy between body and mind is very general, and the parallel will hold as to their food, as well as any other particular. The flesh of animals who feed excursively, is allowed to have a higher flavour than that of those who are cooped up. May there not be the same difference between men who read as their taste prompts, and men who are confined in cells and colleges to stated tasks?

That a man in Mr Michael Johnson's circumstances should think of sending his son to the expensive University of Oxford, at his own charge, seems very improbable. The subject was too delicate to question Johnson upon. But I have been assured by Dr Taylor, that the scheme never would have taken place, had not a gentleman of Shropshire, one of his schoolfellows, spontaneously undertaken to support him at Oxford, in the character of his companion; though, in fact, he never received any assistance whatever from that gentleman.

He, however, went to Oxford, and was entered a Commoner of Pembroke College, on the 31st of October, 1728, being then in his nineteenth year.

The Reverend Dr Adams, who afterwards presided over Pembroke College with universal esteem, told me he was present, and gave me some account of what passed on the night of Johnson's arrival at Oxford. On that evening, his father, who had anxiously accompanied him, found means to have him introduced to Mr Jorden, who was to be his tutor. His being put under any tutor, reminds us of what Wood says of Robert Burton, author of the *Anatomy of Melancholy*, when elected student of Christ Church; 'for form's sake, though he wanted not a tutor, he was put under the tuition of Dr John Bancroft, afterwards Bishop of Oxon.'[1]

His father seemed very full of the merits of his son, and told the company he was a good scholar, and a poet, and wrote Latin verses. His figure and manner appeared strange to them; but he behaved modestly, and sat silent, till upon something which occurred in the course of conversation, he suddenly struck in and quoted Macrobius; and thus he gave the first impression of that more extensive reading in which he had indulged himself.

His tutor, Mr Jorden, fellow of Pembroke, was not, it seems, a man of such abilities as we should conceive requisite for the instructor of Samuel Johnson, who gave me the following account of him. 'He was a very worthy man, but a heavy man, and I did not profit much by his instructions. Indeed, I did not attend him much. The first day after I came to college, I waited upon him, and then staid away four. On the sixth, Mr Jorden asked me why I had not

---

1 *Athen. Oxon.* edit. 1721, p. 628.

attended. I answered, I had been sliding in Christ Church meadow. And this I said with as much *nonchalance* as I am now[1] talking to you. I had no notion that I was wrong or irreverent to my tutor.' BOSWELL. 'That, Sir, was great fortitude of mind.' JOHNSON. 'No, Sir; stark insensibility.'[2]

The fifth of November was at that time kept with great solemnity at Pembroke College, and exercises upon the subject of the day were required. Johnson neglected to perform his, which is much to be regretted; for his vivacity of imagination, and force of language, would probably have produced something sublime upon the gunpowder plot. To apologise for his neglect, he gave in a short copy of verses, entitled *Somnium*, containing a common thought; 'that the Muse had come to him in his sleep, and whispered that it did not become him to write on such subjects as politics; he should confine himself to humbler themes': but the versification was truly Virgilian.

He had a love and respect for Jorden, not for his literature, but for his worth. 'Whenever (said he) a young man becomes Jorden's pupil, he becomes his son.'

Having given such a specimen of his poetical powers, he was asked by Mr Jorden to translate Pope's Messiah into Latin verse, as a Christmas exercise. He performed it with uncommon rapidity, and in so masterly a manner, that he obtained great applause from it, which ever after kept him high in the estimation of his College, and, indeed, of all the University.

It is said, that Mr Pope expressed himself concerning it in terms of strong approbation. Dr Taylor told me, that it was first printed for old Mr Johnson, without the knowledge of his son, who was very angry when he heard of it. A miscellany of Poems, collected by a person of the name of Husbands, was published at Oxford in 1731. In that miscellany Johnson's Translation of the Messiah appeared, with this modest motto from Scaliger's Poetics, '*Ex alieno ingenio Poeta, ex suo tantum versificator.*'

I am not ignorant that critical objections have been made to this and other specimens of Johnson's Latin Poetry. I acknowledge myself not competent to decide on a question of such extreme nicety. But I am satisfied with the just and discriminative eulogy pronounced upon it by my friend Mr Courtenay.

> And with like ease his vivid lines assume
> The garb and dignity of ancient Rome.
> Let college *verse-men* trite conceits express,
> Trick'd out in splendid shreds of Virgil's dress;
> From playful Ovid cull the tinsel phrase,
> And vapid notions hitch in pilfer'd lays;
> Then with mosaick art the piece combine,
> And boast the glitter of each dulcet line:

---

1 Oxford, 20th March, 1776.

2 It ought to be remembered, that Dr Johnson was apt, in his literary as well as moral exercises, to overcharge his defects. Dr Adams informed me, that he attended his tutor's lectures, and also the lectures in the College Hall, very regularly.

> Johnson adventured boldly to transfuse
> His vigorous sense into the Latin muse;
> Aspir'd to shine by unreflected light,
> And with a Roman's ardour *think* and write.
> He felt the tuneful Nine his breast inspire,
> And, like a master, wak'd the soothing lyre:
> Horatian strains a grateful heart proclaim,
> While Sky's wild rocks resound his Thalia's name.
> Hesperia's plant, in some less skilful hands,
> To bloom a while, factitious heat demands;
> Though glowing Maro a faint warmth supplies,
> The sickly blossom in the hot-house dies:
> By Johnson's genial culture, art, and toil,
> Its roots strike deep, and owns the fost'ring soil;
> Imbibes our sun through all its swelling veins,
> And grows a native of Britannia's plains.[1]

The 'morbid melancholy' which was lurking in his constitution, and to which we may ascribe those particularities, and that aversion to regular life, which, at a very early period, marked his character, gathered such strength in his twentieth year, as to afflict him in a dreadful manner. While he was at Lichfield, in the College vacation of the year 1729, he felt himself overwhelmed with an horrible hypochondria, with perpetual irritation, fretfulness, and impatience; and with a dejection, gloom, and despair, which made existence misery. From this dismal malady he never afterwards was perfectly relieved; and all his labours, and all his enjoyments, were but temporary interruptions of its baleful influence. How wonderful, how unsearchable are the ways of GOD! Johnson, who was blest with all the powers of genius and understanding in a degree far above the ordinary state of human nature, was at the same time visited with a disorder so afflictive, that they who know it by dire experience, will not envy his exalted endowments. That it was, in some degree, occasioned by a defect in his nervous system, that inexplicable part of our frame, appears highly probable. He told Mr Paradise that he was sometimes so languid and inefficient, that he could not distinguish the hour upon the town-clock.

Johnson, upon the first violent attack of this disorder, strove to overcome it by forcible exertions. He frequently walked to Birmingham and back again, and tried many other expedients, but all in vain. His expression concerning it to me was, 'I did not then know how to manage it.' His distress became so intolerable that he applied to Dr Swinfen, physician in Lichfield, his godfather, and put into his hands a state of his case written in Latin. Dr Swinfen was so much struck with the extraordinary acuteness, research, and eloquence

---

1 *Poetical Review of the Literary and Moral Character of Dr Johnson*, by John Courtenay, Esq., M.P.

of this paper, that in his zeal for his godson he showed it to several people. His daughter, Mrs Desmoulins, who was many years humanely supported in Dr Johnson's house in London, told me, that upon his discovering that Dr Swinfen had communicated his case, he was so much offended, that he was never afterwards fully reconciled to him. He indeed had good reason to be offended; for though Dr Swinfen's motive was good, he inconsiderately betrayed a matter deeply interesting and of great delicacy, which had been entrusted to him in confidence; and exposed a complaint of his young friend and patient, which, in the superficial opinion of the generality of mankind, is attended with contempt and disgrace.

But let not little men triumph upon knowing that Johnson was an HYPO-CHONDRIAC, was subject to what the learned, philosophical, and pious Dr Cheyne has so well treated, under the title of 'The English Malady'. Though he suffered severely from it, he was not therefore degraded. The powers of his great mind might be troubled, and their full exercise suspended at times, but the mind itself was ever entire. As a proof of this, it is only necessary to consider, that, when he was at the very worst, he composed that state of his own case, which showed an uncommon vigour, not only of fancy and taste, but of judgement. I am aware that he himself was too ready to call such a complaint by the name of *madness*; in conformity with which notion, he has traced its gradations, with exquisite nicety, in one of the chapters of his *Rasselas*. But there is surely a clear distinction between a disorder which affects only the imagination and spirits, while the judgement is sound, and a disorder by which the judgement itself is impaired. This distinction was made to me by the late Professor Gaubius of Leyden, physician to the Prince of Orange, in a conversation which I had with him several years ago, and he expanded it thus: 'If (said he) a man tells me that he is grievously disturbed, for that he *imagines* he sees a ruffian coming against him with a drawn sword, though at the same time he is *conscious* it is a delusion, I pronounce him to have a disordered imagination; but if a man tells me that he sees this, and in consternation calls to me to look at it, I pronounce him to be *mad*.'

It is a common effect of low spirits or melancholy, to make those who are afflicted with it imagine that they are actually suffering those evils which happen to be most strongly presented to their minds. Some have fancied themselves to be deprived of the use of their limbs, some to labour under acute diseases, others to be in extreme poverty, when, in truth, there was not the least reality in any of the suppositions; so that when the vapours were dispelled, they were convinced of the delusion. To Johnson, whose supreme enjoyment was the exercise of his reason, the disturbance or obscuration of that faculty was the evil most to be dreaded. Insanity, therefore, was the object of his most dismal apprehension; and he fancied himself seized by it, or approaching to it, at the very time when he was giving proofs of a more than ordinary soundness and vigour of judgement. That his own diseased imagination should have so far deceived him, is strange; but it is stranger still that some of his friends should have given credit to his groundless opinion, when they had such undoubted proofs that it was totally fallacious; though it is by no means surprising that those who wish to depreciate him, should, since his death, have laid hold of this circumstance, and insisted upon it with very unfair aggravation.

Amidst the oppression and distraction of a disease which very few have felt in its full extent, but many have experienced in a slighter degree, Johnson, in his writings, and in his conversation, never failed to display all the varieties of intellectual excellence. In his march through this world to a better, his mind still appeared grand and brilliant, and impressed all around him with the truth of Virgil's noble sentiment – '*Igneus est ollis vigor et caelestis origo.*'

The history of his mind as to religion is an important article. I have mentioned the early impressions made upon his tender imagination by his mother, who continued her pious care with assiduity, but, in his opinion, not with judgement. 'Sunday (said he) was a heavy day to me when I was a boy. My mother confined me on that day, and made me read *The Whole Duty of Man*, from a great part of which I could derive no instruction. When, for instance, I had read the chapter on theft, which from my infancy I had been taught was wrong, I was no more convinced that theft was wrong than before; so there was no accession of knowledge. A boy should be introduced to such books, by having his attention directed to the arrangement, to the style, and other excellencies of composition; that the mind being thus engaged by an amusing variety of objects, may not grow weary.'

He communicated to me the following particulars upon the subject of his religious progress. 'I fell into an inattention to religion, or an indifference about it, in my ninth year. The church at Lichfield, in which we had a seat, wanted reparation, so I was to go and find a seat in other churches; and having bad eyes, and being awkward about this, I used to go and read in the fields on Sunday. This habit continued till my fourteenth year; and still I find a great reluctance to go to church. I then became a sort of lax *talker* against religion, for I did not much *think* against it; and this lasted till I went to Oxford, where it would not be suffered. When at Oxford, I took up Law's *Serious Call to the Unconverted*,[a] expecting to find it a dull book (as such books generally are), and perhaps to laugh at it. But I found Law quite an over-match for me; and this was the first occasion of my thinking in earnest of religion, after I became capable of rational inquiry.'[1] From this time forward, religion was the

---

[a] For '*the Unconverted*', read '*a Holy Life.*'

1 Mrs Piozzi has given a strange fantastical account of the origin of Dr Johnson's belief in our most holy religion. 'At the age of *ten* years his mind was disturbed by scruples of infidelity, which preyed upon his spirits, and made him very uneasy, the more so, as he revealed his uneasiness to none, being naturally (as he said) of a sullen temper, and reserved disposition. He searched, however, diligently, but fruitlessly, for evidence of the truth of revelation; and, at length, *recollecting* a book he had *once* seen [*I suppose at five years old*] in his father's shop, intitled *De veritate Religionis, &c.*, he began to think himself *highly culpable* for neglecting such a means of information, and took himself severely to task for his sin, adding many acts of voluntary, and, to others, unknown *penance*. The first opportunity which offered, of course, he seized the book with avidity; but, on examination, *not finding himself scholar enough to peruse its contents*,

predominant object of his thoughts; though, with the just sentiments of a conscientious Christian, he lamented that his practice of its duties fell far short of what it ought to be.

This instance of a mind such as that of Johnson being first disposed, by an unexpected incident, to think with anxiety of the momentous concerns of eternity, and of 'what he should do to be saved', may for ever be produced in opposition to the superficial and sometimes profane contempt that has been thrown upon those occasional impressions which it is certain many Christians have experienced; though it must be acknowledged that weak minds, from an erroneous supposition that no man is in a state of grace who has not felt a particular conversion, have, in some cases, brought a degree of ridicule upon them; a ridicule, of which it is inconsiderate or unfair to make a general application.

How seriously Johnson was impressed with a sense of religion, even in the vigour of his youth, appears from the following passage in his minutes, kept by way of diary: 'Sept. 7, 1736. I have this day entered upon my 28th year. Mayest thou, O GOD, enable me, for JESUS CHRIST's sake, to spend this in such a manner that I may receive comfort from it at the hour of death, and in the day of judgement! Amen.'

The particular course of his reading while at Oxford, and during the time of vacation which he passed at home, cannot be traced. Enough has been said of his irregular mode of study. He told me, that from his earliest years he loved to read poetry, but hardly ever read any poem to an end; that he read Shakspeare at a period so early, that the speech of the Ghost in *Hamlet* terrified him when he was alone; that Horace's Odes were the compositions in which he took most delight, and it was long before he liked his Epistles and Satires. He told me what he read *solidly* at Oxford was Greek; not the Grecian historians, but Homer and Euripides, and now and then a little Epigram; that the study of which he was most fond was Metaphysics, but he had not read much, even in that way. I always thought that he did himself injustice in his account of what he had read, and that he must have been speaking with reference to the vast

---

set his heart at rest; and not thinking to enquire whether there were any English books written on the subject, followed his usual amusements, and *considered his conscience as lightened of a crime.* He redoubled his diligence to learn the language that contained the information he most wished for; but from the pain which *guilt* [*namely, having omitted to read what he did not understand*] had given him, he now began to deduce the soul's immortality, [*a sensation of pain in this world being an unquestionable proof of existence in another*] which was the point that belief first stopped at; *and from that moment resolving to be a Christian,* became one of the most zealous and pious ones our nation ever produced.' – *Anecdotes,* p. 17.

This is one of the numerous misrepresentations of this lively lady, which it is worth while to correct; for if credit should be given to such a childish, irrational, and ridiculous statement of the foundation of Dr Johnson's faith in Christianity, how little credit would be due to it. Mrs Piozzi seems to wish, that the world should think Dr Johnson also under the influence of that easy logic, *Stet pro ratione voluntas.*

portion of study which is possible, and to which a few scholars in the whole history of literature have attained; for when I once asked him whether a person whose name I have now forgotten, studied hard, he answered, 'No, Sir. I do not believe he studied hard. I never knew a man who studied hard. I conclude, indeed, from the effects, that some men have studied hard, as Bentley and Clarke.' Trying him by that criterion upon which he formed his judgement of others, we may be absolutely certain, both from his writings and his conversation, that his reading was very extensive. Dr Adam Smith, than whom few are better judges on this subject, once observed to me that 'Johnson knew more books than any man alive.' He had a peculiar facility in seizing at once what was valuable in any book, without submitting to the labour of perusing it from beginning to end. He had, from the irritability of his constitution, at all times, an impatience and hurry when he either read or wrote. A certain apprehension, arising from novelty, made him write his first exercise at College twice over, but he never took that trouble with any other composition; and we shall see that his most excellent works were struck off at a heat, with rapid exertion.

Yet he appears, from his early notes and memorandums, in my possession, to have at various times attempted, or at least planned, a methodical course of study, according to computation, of which he was all his life fond, as it fixed his attention steadily upon something without, and prevented his mind from preying upon itself. Thus I find in his handwriting the number of lines in each of two of Euripides's Tragedies, of the *Georgics* of Virgil, of the first six books of the *Aeneid*, of Horace's *Art of Poetry*, of three of the books of Ovid's *Metamorphosis*, of some parts of Theocritus, and of the tenth Satire of Juvenal; and a table, showing at the rate of various numbers a day (I suppose verses to be read), what would be, in each case, the total amount in a week, month, and year.

No man had a more ardent love of literature, or a higher respect for it, than Johnson. His apartment in Pembroke College was that upon the second floor, over the gateway. The enthusiasts of learning will ever contemplate it with veneration. One day, while he was sitting in it quite alone, Dr Panting, then master of the College, whom he called 'a fine Jacobite fellow', overheard him uttering this soliloquy in his strong emphatic voice: 'Well, I have a mind to see what is done in other places of learning. I'll go and visit the Universities abroad. I'll go to France and Italy. I'll go to Padua. – And I'll mind my business. For an *Athenian* blockhead is the worst of all blockheads.'[1]

Dr Adams told me, that Johnson, while he was at Pembroke College, 'was caressed and loved by all about him, was a gay and frolicsome fellow, and passed there the happiest part of his life.' But this is a striking proof of the fallacy of appearances, and how little any of us know of the real internal state even of those whom we see most frequently; for the truth is, that he was then depressed by poverty, and irritated by disease. When I mentioned to him this

---

1 I had this anecdote from Dr Adams, and Dr Johnson confirmed it. Bramston, in his 'Man of Taste', has the same thought:

'Sure, of all blockheads, scholars are the worst.'

account as given me by Dr Adams, he said, 'Ah, sir, I was mad and violent. It was bitterness which they mistook for frolic. I was miserably poor, and I thought to fight my way by my literature and my wit; so I disregarded all power and all authority.'

The Bishop of Dromore observes in a letter to me, 'The pleasure he took in vexing the tutors and fellows has been often mentioned. But I have heard him say, what ought to be recorded to the honour of the present venerable master of that College, the Reverend William Adams, D.D., who was then very young, and one of the junior fellows; that the mild but judicious expostulations of this worthy man, whose virtue awed him, and whose learning he revered, made him really ashamed of himself, "though I fear (said he), I was too proud to own it."

'I have heard from some of his contemporaries that he was generally seen lounging at the College gate, with a circle of young students round him, whom he was entertaining with wit, and keeping from their studies, if not spiriting them up to rebellion against the College discipline, which in his maturer years he so much extolled.'

He very early began to attempt keeping notes or memorandums, by way of a diary of his life. I find, in a parcel of loose leaves, the following spirited resolution to contend against his natural indolence: '*Oct.* 1729. *Desidiae valedixi; syrenis istius cantibus surdam posthac aurem obversurus.* – I bid farewell to Sloth, being resolved henceforth not to listen to her siren strains.' I have also in my possession a few leaves of another *Libellus*, or little book, entitled ANNALES, in which some of the early particulars of his history are registered in Latin.

I do not find that he formed any close intimacies with his fellow-collegians. But Dr Adams told me, that he contracted a love and regard for Pembroke College, which he retained to the last. A short time before his death he sent to that College a present of all his works, to be deposited in their library, and he had thoughts of leaving to it his house at Lichfield; but his friends who were about him very properly dissuaded him from it, and he bequeathed it to some poor relations. He took a pleasure in boasting of the many eminent men who had been educated at Pembroke. In this list are found the names of Spenser,[a] Mr Hawkins the Poetry Professor, Mr Shenstone, Sir William Blackstone, and others,[1] not forgetting the celebrated popular preacher, Mr George Whitefield, of whom, though Dr Johnson did not think very highly, it must be acknowledged that his eloquence was powerful, his views pious and charitable, his assiduity almost incredible; and, that since his death, the integrity of his character has been fully vindicated. Being himself a poet, Johnson was peculiarly happy in mentioning how many of the sons of Pembroke were poets; adding, with a smile of sportive triumph, 'Sir, we are a nest of singing birds.'

[a] Delete 'Spenser'. He was of Pembroke Hall, Cambridge.
1 See Nash's *History of Worcestershire*, Vol. I, p. 529.

He was not, however, blind to what he thought the defects of his own College; and I have, from the information of Dr Taylor, a very strong instance of that rigid honesty which he ever inflexibly preserved. Taylor had obtained his father's consent to be entered of Pembroke, that he might be with his schoolfellow Johnson, with whom, though some years older than himself, he was very intimate. This would have been a great comfort to Johnson. But he fairly told Taylor that he could not, in conscience, suffer him to enter where he knew he could not have an able tutor. He then made inquiry all round the University, and having found that Mr Bateman, of Christ Church, was the tutor of highest reputation, Taylor was entered of that College. Mr Bateman's lectures were so excellent, that Johnson used to come and get them at second-hand from Taylor, till his poverty being so extreme, that his shoes were worn out, and his feet appeared through them, he saw that this humiliating circumstance was perceived by the Christ Church men, and he came no more. He was too proud to accept of money, and somebody having set a pair of new shoes at his door, he threw them away with indignation. How must we feel when we read such an anecdote of Samuel Johnson!

His spirited refusal of an eleemosynary supply of shoes arose, no doubt, from a proper pride. But, considering his ascetic disposition at times, as acknowledged by himself in his Meditations and the exaggeration with which some have treated the peculiarities of his character, I should not wonder to hear it ascribed to a principle of superstitious mortification; as we are told by Tursellinus, in his Life of St Ignatius Loyola, that this intrepid founder of the order of Jesuits, when he arrived at Goa, after having made a severe pilgrimage through the eastern deserts, persisted in wearing his miserable shattered shoes, and when new ones were offered him, rejected them as an unsuitable indulgence.

The *res angusta domi* prevented him from having the advantage of a complete academical education. The friend to whom he had trusted for support had deceived him. His debts in College, though not great, were increasing; and his scanty remittances from Lichfield, which had all along been made with great difficulty, could be supplied no longer, his father having fallen into a state of insolvency. Compelled, therefore, by irresistible necessity, he left the College in autumn 1731, without a degree, having been a member of it little more than three years.

Dr Adams, the worthy and respectable master of Pembroke College, has generally had the reputation of being Johnson's tutor. The fact, however, is, that in 1731 Mr Jorden quitted the College, and his pupils were transferred to Dr Adams; so that had Johnson returned, Dr Adams *would have been his tutor*. It is to be wished, that this connection had taken place. His equal temper, mild disposition, and politeness of manners, might have insensibly softened the harshness of Johnson, and infused into him those more delicate charities, that *petite morale*, in which, it must be confessed, our great moralist was more deficient than his best friends could fully justify. Dr Adams paid Johnson this high compliment. He said to me at Oxford, in 1776, 'I was his nominal tutor, but he was above my mark.' When I repeated it to Johnson, his eyes flashed with grateful satisfaction, and he exclaimed, 'That was liberal and noble.'

And now (I had almost said *poor*) Samuel Johnson returned to his native city, destitute, and not knowing how he should gain even a decent livelihood. His father's misfortunes in trade rendered him unable to support his son; and for some time there appeared no means by which he could maintain himself. In the December of this year his father died.

The state of poverty in which he died, appears from a note in one of Johnson's little diaries of the following year, which strongly displays his spirit and virtuous dignity of mind. '1732, *Julii* 15. *Undecim aureos deposui, quo die quicquid ante matris funus (quod serum sit precor) de paternis bonis sperari licet, viginti scilicet libras accepi. Usque adeo mihi fortuna fingenda est. Interea, ne paupertate vires animi languescant, nec in flagitia egestas abigat, cavendum.* – I layed by eleven guineas on this day, when I received twenty pounds, being all that I have reason to hope for out of my father's effects, previous to the death of my mother; an event which I pray GOD may be very remote. I now, therefore, see that I must make my own fortune. Meanwhile, let me take care that the powers of my mind may not be debilitated by poverty, and that indigence do not force me into any criminal act.'

Johnson was so far fortunate, that the respectable character of his parents, and his own merit, had, from his earliest years, secured him a kind reception in the best families at Lichfield. Among these I can mention Mr Howard, Dr Swinfen, Mr Simpson, Mr Levett, Captain Garrick, father of the great ornament of the British stage; but above all, Mr Gilbert Walmsley,[1] Register of the Prerogative Court of Lichfield, whose character, long after his decease, Dr Johnson has, in his life of Edmund Smith, thus drawn in the glowing colours of gratitude:

> Of Gilbert Walmsley, thus presented to my mind, let me indulge myself in the remembrance. I knew him very early; he was one of the first friends that literature procured me, and I hope that, at least, my gratitude made me worthy of his notice.
>
> He was of an advanced age, and I was only not a boy; yet he never received my notions with contempt. He was a whig, with all the virulence and malevolence of his party; yet difference of opinion did not keep us apart. I honoured him, and he endured me.
>
> He had mingled with the gay world without exemption from its vices or its follies; but had never neglected the cultivation of his mind. His belief of revelation was unshaken; his learning preserved his principles; he grew first regular, and then pious.
>
> His studies had been so various, that I am not able to name a man of

---

1 Mr Warton informs me, that this early friend of Johnson was entered a Commoner of Trinity College, Oxford, aged 17, in 1698; and is the author of many Latin verse translations in the *Gentleman's Magazine*. One of them is a translation of

My time, O ye Muses, was happily spent, &c.

equal knowledge. His acquaintance with books was great, and what he did not immediately know, he could, at least, tell where to find. Such was his amplitude of learning, and such his copiousness of communication, that it may be doubted whether a day now passes, in which I have not some advantage from his friendship.

At this man's table I enjoyed many cheerful and instructive hours, with companions, such as are not often found – with one who has lengthened, and one who has gladdened life; with Dr James, whose skill in physic will be long remembered; and with David Garrick, whom I hoped to have gratified with this character of our common friend. But what are the hopes of man! I am disappointed by that stroke of death, which has eclipsed the gaiety of nations, and impoverished the public stock of harmless pleasure.

In these families he passed much time in his early years. In most of them, he was in the company of ladies, particularly at Mr Walmsley's, whose wife and sisters-in-law, of the name of Aston, and daughters of a baronet, were remarkable for good breeding; so that the notion which has been industriously circulated and believed, that he never was in good company till late in life, and, consequently, had been confirmed in coarse and ferocious manners by long habits, is wholly without foundation. Some of the ladies have assured me, they recollected him well when a young man, as distinguished for his complaisance.

And that this politeness was not merely occasional and temporary, or confined to the circles of Lichfield, is ascertained by the testimony of a lady, who, in a paper with which I have been favoured by a daughter of his intimate friend and physician, Dr Lawrence, thus describes Dr Johnson some years afterwards:

As the particulars of the former part of Dr Johnson's life do not seem to be very accurately known, a lady hopes that the following information may not be unacceptable.

She remembers Dr Johnson on a visit to Dr Taylor, at Ashbourn, some time between the end of the year 37, and the middle of the year 40; she rather thinks it to have been after he and his wife were removed to London. During his stay at Ashbourn, he made frequent visits to Mr Meynell, at Brodley, where his company was much desired by the ladies of the family, who were, perhaps, in point of elegance and accomplishments, inferior to few of those with whom he was afterwards acquainted. Mr Meynell's eldest daughter was afterwards married to Mr Fitzherbert, father to Mr Alleyne Fitzherbert, lately minister to the court of Russia. Of her, Dr Johnson said, in Dr Lawrence's study, that she had the best understanding he ever met with in any human being. At Mr Meynell's he also commenced that friendship with Mrs Hill Boothby, sister to the present Sir Brook Boothby, which continued till her death. The *young woman whom he used to call Molly Aston*,[1] was sister to Sir Thomas Aston, and daughter to a Baronet; she was likewise

1 The words of Sir John Hawkins, p. 316.

sister to the wife of his friend Mr Gilbert Walmsley. Besides his intimacy with the above-mentioned persons, who were surely people of rank and education, while he was yet at Lichfield he used to be frequently at the house of Dr Swinfen, a gentleman of a very ancient family in Staffordshire, from which, after the death of his elder brother, he inherited a good estate. He was, besides, a physician of very extensive practice; but for want of due attention to the management of his domestic concerns, left a very large family in indigence. One of his daughters, Mrs Desmoulins, afterwards found an asylum in the house of her old friend, whose doors were always open to the unfortunate, and who well observed the precept of the gospel, for he was kind to the unthankful and to the evil.

In the forlorn state of his circumstances he accepted of an offer to be employed as usher in the school of Market Bosworth, in Leicestershire, to which it appears, from one of his little fragments of a diary, that he went on foot, on the 16th of July, - '*Julii 16. Bosvortiam pedes petii.*' But it is not true, as has been erroneously related, that he was assistant to the famous Anthony Blackwall, whose merit has been honoured by the testimony of Bishop Hurd, who was his scholar; for Mr Blackwall died on the 8th of April, 1730,[1] more than a year before Johnson left the University.

This employment was very irksome to him in every respect, and he complained grievously of it in his letters to his friend Mr Hector, who was now settled as a surgeon at Birmingham. The letters are lost; but Mr Hector recollects his writing 'that the poet had described the dull sameness of his existence in these words, *Vitam continet una dies* (one day contains the whole of my life); that it was unvaried as the note of the cuckoo; and that he did not know whether it was more disagreeable for him to teach, or the boys to learn, the grammar rules.' His general aversion to this painful drudgery was greatly enhanced by a disagreement between him and Sir Woolston Dixey, the patron of the school, in whose house, I have been told, he officiated as a kind of domestic chaplain, so far, at least, as to say grace at table, but was treated with what he represented as intolerable harshness; and, after suffering for a few months such complicated misery, he relinquished a situation which all his life afterwards he recollected with the strongest aversion, and even a degree of horror. But it is probable that at this period, whatever uneasiness he may have endured, he laid the foundation of much future eminence by application to his studies.

Being now again totally unoccupied, he was invited by Mr Hector to pass some time with him at Birmingham, as his guest, at the house of Mr Warren, with whom Mr Hector lodged and boarded. Mr Warren was the first established bookseller in Birmingham, and was very attentive to Johnson, who he soon found could be of much service to him in his trade, by his knowledge of literature; and he even obtained the assistance of his pen in furnishing some numbers of a periodical Essay printed in the newspaper, of which Warren was

1 See *Gent. Mag.*, Dec. 1784, p. 957.

proprietor. After very diligent inquiry, I have not been able to recover those early specimens of that particular mode of writing by which Johnson afterwards so greatly distinguished himself.

He continued to live as Mr Hector's guest for about six months, and then hired lodgings in another part of the town, finding himself as well situated at Birmingham as he supposed he could be any where, while he had no settled plan of life, and very scanty means of subsistence. He made some valuable acquaintances there, amongst whom were Mr Porter, a mercer, whose widow he afterwards married, and Mr Taylor, who by his ingenuity in mechanical inventions, and his success in trade, acquired an immense fortune. But the comfort of being near Mr Hector, his old schoolfellow and intimate friend, was Johnson's chief inducement to continue here.

In what manner he employed his pen at this period, or whether he derived from it any pecuniary advantage, I have not been able to ascertain. He probably got a little money from Mr Warren; and we are certain, that he executed here one piece of literary labour, of which Mr Hector has favoured me with a minute account. Having mentioned that he had read at Pembroke College a Voyage to Abyssinia, by Lobo, a Portuguese Jesuit, and that he thought an abridgement and translation of it from the French into English might be an useful and profitable publication, Mr Warren and Mr Hector joined in urging him to undertake it. He accordingly agreed; and the book not being to be found in Birmingham, he borrowed it of Pembroke College. A part of the work being very soon done, one Osborn, who was Mr Warren's printer, was set to work with what was ready, and Johnson engaged to supply the press with copy as it should be wanted; but his constitutional indolence soon prevailed, and the work was at a stand. Mr Hector, who knew that a motive of humanity would be the most prevailing argument with his friend, went to Johnson, and represented to him, that the printer could have no other employment till this undertaking was finished, and that the poor man and his family were suffering. Johnson upon this exerted the powers of his mind, though his body was relaxed. He lay in bed with the book, which was a quarto, before him, and dictated while Hector wrote. Mr Hector carried the sheets to the press, and corrected almost all the proof sheets, very few of which were even seen by Johnson. In this manner, with the aid of Mr Hector's active friendship, the book was completed, and was published in 1735, with LONDON upon the title-page, though it was in reality printed at Birmingham, a device too common with provincial publishers. For this work he had from Mr Warren only the sum of five guineas.

This being the first prose work of Johnson, it is a curious object of inquiry how much may be traced in it of that style which marks his subsequent writings with such peculiar excellence; with so happy an union of force, vivacity, and perspicuity. I have perused the book with this view, and have found that here, as I believe in every other translation, there is in the work itself no vestige of the translator's own style; for the language of translation being adapted to the thoughts of another person, insensibly follows their cast, and, as it were, runs into a mould that is ready prepared.

Thus, for instance, taking the first sentence that occurs at the opening of the book, p. 4. 'I lived here above a year, and completed my studies in divinity; in which time some letters were received from the fathers in Ethiopia, with an account that Sultan Segned, Emperor of Abyssinia, was converted to the Church of Rome; that many of his subjects had followed his example, and that there was a great want of missionaries to improve these prosperous beginnings. Everybody was very desirous of seconding the zeal of our fathers, and of sending them the assistance they requested; to which we were the more encouraged, because the Emperor's letter informed our Provincial, that we might easily enter his dominions by the way of Dancala; but, unhappily, the secretary wrote Geila for Dancala, which cost two of our fathers their lives.' Every one acquainted with Johnson's manner will be sensible that there is nothing of it here, but that this sentence might have been composed by any other man.

But, in the Preface, the Johnsonian style begins to appear; and though use had not yet taught his wing a permanent and equable flight, there are parts of it which exhibit his best manner in full vigour. I had once the pleasure of examining it with Mr Edmund Burke, who confirmed me in this opinion, by his superior critical sagacity, and was, I remember, much delighted with the following specimen:

> The Portuguese traveller, contrary to the general vein of his countrymen, has amused his reader with no romantic absurdity, or incredible fictions; whatever he relates, whether true or not, is at least probable; and he who tells nothing exceeding the bounds of probability, has a right to demand that they should believe him who cannot contradict him.
>
> He appears, by his modest and unaffected narration, to have described things as he saw them, to have copied nature from the life, and to have consulted his senses, not his imagination. He meets with no basilisks that destroy with their eyes, his crocodiles devour their prey without tears, and his cataracts fall from the rocks without deafening the neighbouring inhabitants.
>
> The reader will here find no regions cursed with irremediable barrenness, or blessed with spontaneous fecundity; no perpetual gloom, or unceasing sunshine; nor are the nations here described either devoid of all sense of humanity, or consummate in all private or social virtues. Here are no Hottentots without religious polity or articulate language; no Chinese perfectly polite, and completely skilled in all sciences; he will discover, what will always be discovered by a diligent and impartial enquirer, that wherever human nature is to be found, there is a mixture of vice and virtue, a contest of passion and reason; and that the Creator doth not appear partial in his distributions, but has balanced, in most countries, their particular inconveniences by particular favours.

Here we have an early example of that brilliant and energetic expression, which, upon innumerable occasions in his subsequent life, justly impressed the world with the highest admiration.

Nor can any one, conversant with the writings of Johnson, fail to discern his hand in this passage of the Dedication to John Warren, Esq., of Pembrokeshire, though it is ascribed to Warren the bookseller. 'A generous and elevated mind is distinguished by nothing more certainly than an eminent degree of curiosity; nor is that curiosity ever more agreeably or usefully employed, than in examining the laws and customs of foreign nations. I hope, therefore, the present I now presume to make, will not be thought improper; which, however, it is not my business as a dedicator to commend, nor as a bookseller to depreciate.'

It is reasonable to suppose, that his having been thus accidentally led to a particular study of the history and manners of Abyssinia, was the remote occasion of his writing, many years afterwards, his admirable philosophical tale, the principal scene of which is laid in that country.

Johnson returned to Lichfield early in 1734, and in August that year he made an attempt to procure some little subsistence by his pen; for he published proposals for printing by subscription the Latin poems of Politian: '*Angeli Politiani Poemata Latina, quibus Notas, cum historia Latinae poeseos, a Petrarchae aevo ad Politiani tempora deducta, et vita Politiani fusius quam antehac enarrata addidit* SAM. JOHNSON.'[1]

It appears that his brother Nathanael had taken up his father's trade; for it is mentioned, that 'subscriptions are taken in by the Editor, or N. Johnson, bookseller, of Lichfield.' Notwithstanding the merit of Johnson, and the cheap price at which this translation, with its accompaniments, was offered, there were not subscribers enough to insure a sufficient sale; so the work never appeared, and, probably, never was executed.

We find him again this year at Birmingham, and there is preserved the following letter from him to Mr Edward Cave,[2] the original compiler and editor of the *Gentleman's Magazine*:

To Mr CAVE.

Nov. 25, 1734.

SIR – As you appear no less sensible than your readers of the defects of your poetical article, you will not be displeased, if, in order to the improvement of it, I communicate to you the sentiments of a person, who will undertake, on reasonable terms, sometimes to fill a column.

His opinion is, that the public would not give you a bad reception, if, beside the current wit of the month, which a critical examination would

---

1 The book was to contain more than thirty sheets, the price to be two shillings and six-pence at the time of subscribing, and two shillings and six-pence at the delivery of a perfect book in quires.

2 Miss Cave, the grand-niece of Mr Edward Cave, has obligingly shown me the originals of this and the other letters of Dr Johnson, to him, which were first published in the *Gentleman's Magazine*, with notes by Mr John Nichols, the worthy and indefatigable editor of that valuable miscellany, signed N; some of which I shall occasionally transcribe in the course of this work.

generally reduce to a narrow compass, you admitted not only poems, inscriptions, &c., never printed before, which he will sometimes supply you with; but likewise short literary dissertations in Latin or English, critical remarks on authors ancient or modern, forgotten poems that deserve revival, or loose pieces, like Floyer's,[a] worth preserving. By this method your literary article, for so it might be called, will, he thinks, be better recommended to the public, than by low jests, awkward buffoonery, or the dull scurrilities of either party.

If such a correspondence will be agreeable to you, be pleased to inform me in two posts, what the conditions are on which you shall expect it. Your late offer[1] gives me no reason to distrust your generosity. If you engage in any literary projects besides this paper, I have other designs to impart, if I could be secure from having others reap the advantage of what I should hint.

Your letter, by being directed to S. Smith, to be left at the Castle in Birmingham, Warwickshire, will reach

Your humble servant.

Mr Cave has put a note on this letter, 'Answered Dec. 2.' But whether anything was done in consequence of it we are not informed.

Johnson had, from his early youth, been sensible to the influence of female charms. When at Stourbridge school, he was much enamoured of Olivia Lloyd, a young quaker, to whom he wrote a copy of verses, which I have not been able to recover, and I am assured[b] by Miss Seward, that he conceived a tender passion for Miss Lucy Porter, daughter of the lady whom he afterwards married. Miss Porter was sent very young on a visit to Lichfield, where Johnson had frequent opportunities of seeing and admiring her; and he addressed to her the following verses, on her presenting him with a nosegay of myrtle:

> What hopes, what terrors does thy gift create,
> Ambiguous emblem of uncertain fate:
> The myrtle, ensign of supreme command,
> Consigned by Venus to Melissa's hand;
> Not less capricious than a reigning fair,
> Now grants, and now rejects a lover's prayer.
> In myrtle shades oft sings the happy swain,
> In myrtle shades despairing ghosts complain;
> The myrtle crowns the happy lovers' heads,

---

[a] Add note: Sir John Floyer's Treatise on 'Cold Baths'. *Gent. Mag.* 1734, p. 147.

1 A prize of fifty pounds for the best poem 'on Life, Death, Judgement, Heaven, and Hell.' See *Gentleman's Magazine*, Vol. IV. p. 60. N.

[b] Instead of 'and I am assured', &c., to the end of the paragraph, read, 'but with what facility and elegance he could warble the amorous lay will appear from the following lines, which he wrote for his friend, Mr Edmund Hector.'

The unhappy lovers' grave the myrtle spreads:
O then the meaning of thy gift impart,
And ease the throbbings of an anxious heart!
Soon must this bough, as you shall fix his doom,
Adorn Philander's head, or grace his tomb.[1a]

His juvenile attachments to the fair sex were, however, very transient; and it is certain, that he formed no criminal connection whatsoever. Mr Hector, who lived with him in his younger days, in the utmost intimacy and social freedom, has assured me, that even at that ardent season his conduct was strictly virtuous in that respect; and that though he loved to exhilarate himself with wine, he never knew him intoxicated but once.

In a man whom religious education has secured from licentious indulgences, the passion of love, when once it has seized him, is exceedingly strong, being

1 Mrs Piozzi, in her *Anecdotes*, asserts that Johnson wrote this effusion of elegant tenderness not in his own person, but for a friend who was in love. But that lively lady is as inaccurate in this instance as in many others, for Miss Seward writes to me – '*I know* those verses were addressed to Lucy Porter when he was enamoured of her in his boyish days, two or three years before he had seen her mother, his future wife. He wrote them at my grandfather's, and gave them to Lucy in the presence of my mother, to whom he showed them on the instant. She used to repeat them to me, when I asked her for *the verses Dr Johnson gave her on a sprig of myrtle, which he had stolen or begged from her bosom*. We all know honest Lucy Porter to have been incapable of the mean vanity of applying to herself a compliment not *intended* for her.'

a On *tomb* put the following note: Mrs Piozzi gives the following account of this little composition from Dr Johnson's own relation to her, on her inquiring whether it was rightly attributed to him: 'I think it is now just forty years ago, that a young fellow had a sprig of myrtle given him by a girl he courted, and asked me to write him some verses that he might present her in return. I promised, but forgot, and when he called for his lines at the time agreed on – sit still a moment (says I), dear Mund, and I'll fetch them thee – So stepped aside for five minutes, and wrote the nonsense you now keep such a stir about.' *Anecdotes*, p. 34.

In my first edition I was induced to doubt the authenticity of this account, by the following circumstantial statement in a letter to me from Miss Seward, of Lichfield: 'I *know* those verses were addressed to Lucy Porter, when he was enamoured of her in his boyish days, two or three years before he had seen her mother, his future wife. He wrote them at my grandfather's, and gave them to Lucy in the presence of my mother, to whom he showed them on the instant. She used to repeat them to me, when I asked her *for the verses Dr Johnson gave her on a sprig of myrtle, which he had stolen or begged from her bosom*. We all know honest Lucy Porter to have been incapable of the mean vanity of applying to herself a compliment not *intended* for her.' Such was this lady's statement, which I make no doubt she supposed to be correct; but it shows how dangerous it is to trust too implicitly to traditional testimony and ingenious inference; for Mr Hector has lately assured me that Mrs Piozzi's account is in this instance accurate, and that he was the person for whom Johnson wrote those verses, which have been erroneously ascribed to Mr Hammond.

I am obliged in so many instances to notice Mrs Piozzi's incorrectness of relation, that I gladly seize this opportunity of acknowledging, that however often, she is not always inaccurate.

unimpaired by dissipation, and totally concentrated in one object. This was experienced by Johnson when he became the fervent admirer of Mrs Porter, after her first husband's death. Miss Porter told me, that when he was first introduced to her mother, his appearance was very forbidding: He was then lean and lank, so that his immense structure of bones was hideously striking to the eye, and the scars of the scrofula were deeply visible. He also wore his hair, which was straight and stiff, and separated behind; and he often had, seemingly, convulsive starts and odd gesticulations, which tended to excite at once surprise and ridicule. Mrs Porter was so much engaged by his conversation that she overlooked all these external disadvantages, and said to her daughter, 'this is the most sensible man that I ever saw in my life.'

Though Mrs Porter was double the age of Johnson, and her person and manners, as described to me by the late Mr Garrick, were by no means pleasing to others, she must have had a superiority of understanding and talents, as she certainly inspired him with a more than ordinary passion; and she having signified her willingness to accept of his hand, he went to Lichfield to ask his mother's consent to the marriage, which he could not but be conscious was a very imprudent scheme, both on account of their disparity of years, and her want of fortune. But Mrs Johnson knew too well the ardour of her son's temper, and was too tender a parent to oppose his inclinations.

I know not for what reason the marriage ceremony was not performed at Birmingham; but a resolution was taken that it should be at Derby, for which place the bride and bridegroom set out on horseback, I suppose in very good humour. But though Mr Topham Beauclerk used archly to mention Johnson's having told him, with much gravity, 'Sir, it was a love-marriage upon both sides', I have had from my illustrious friend the following curious account of their journey to church upon the nuptial morn. 'Sir, she had read the old romances, and had got into her head the fantastical notion that a woman of spirit should use her lover like a dog. So, Sir, at first she told me that I rode too fast, and she could not keep up with me; and, when I rode a little slower, she passed me, and complained that I lagged behind. I was not to be made the slave of caprice; and I resolved to begin as I meant to end. I therefore pushed on briskly, till I was fairly out of her sight. The road lay between two hedges, so I was sure she could not miss it; and I contrived that she should soon come up with me. When she did, I observed her to be in tears.'

This, it must be allowed, was a singular beginning of connubial felicity; but there is no doubt that Johnson, though he thus showed a manly firmness, proved a most affectionate and indulgent husband to the last moment of Mrs Johnson's life; and in his *Prayers and Meditations*, we find very remarkable evidence that his regard and fondness for her never ceased, even after her death.

He now set up a private academy, for which purpose he hired a large house, well situated near his native city. In the *Gentleman's Magazine* for 1736, there is the following advertisement: 'At Edial, near Lichfield, in Staffordshire, young gentlemen are boarded and taught the Latin and Greek languages, by SAMUEL JOHNSON.' But the only pupils that were put under his care were the celebrated David Garrick and his brother George, and a Mr Offely, a young gentleman of good fortune, who died early. As yet, his name had nothing of that celebrity which afterwards commanded the highest attention and respect of mankind. Had such an advertisement appeared after the publication of his *London*, or his *Rambler*, or his *Dictionary*, how would it have burst upon the world! With what eagerness would the great and the wealthy have embraced an opportunity of putting their sons under the learned tuition of SAMUEL JOHNSON. The truth, however, is, that he was not so well qualified for being a teacher of elements, and a conductor in learning by regular gradations, as men of inferior powers of mind. His own acquisitions had been made by fits and starts, by violent irruptions into the regions of knowledge; and it could not be expected that his impatience would be subdued, and his impetuosity restrained, so as to fit him for a quiet guide to novices. The art of communicating instruction, of whatever kind, is much to be valued; and I have ever thought that those who devote themselves to this employment, and do their duty with diligence and success, are entitled to very high respect from the community, as Johnson himself often maintained. Yet I am of opinion, that the greatest abilities are not only not required for this office, but render a man less fit for it.

While we acknowledge the justness of Thomson's beautiful remark,

> 'Delightful task! to rear the tender thought
> And teach the young idea how to shoot!'

we must consider that this delight is perceptible only by 'a mind at ease', a mind at once calm and clear; but that a mind gloomy and impetuous like that of Johnson, cannot be fixed for any length of time in minute attention, and must be so frequently irritated by unavoidable slowness and error in the advances of scholars, as to perform the duty with little pleasure to the teacher, and no great advantage to the pupils. Good temper is a most essential requisite in a preceptor. Horace paints the character as *bland*:

> — *Ut pueris olim dant crustula* blandi
> *Doctores, elementa velint ut discere prima.*

Johnson was not more satisfied with his situation as the master of an academy, than with that of the usher of a school; we need not wonder, therefore, that he did not keep his academy above a year and a half. From Mr Garrick's account he did not appear to have been profoundly reverenced by his pupils. His oddities of manner, and uncouth gesticulations, could not but be the subject of merriment to them; and, in particular, the young rogues used to listen at the door of his bed-chamber, and peep through the keyhole, that they might turn into ridicule his tumultuous and awkward fondness for Mrs Johnson, whom he used to name by the familiar appellation of *Tetty* or *Tetsy*, which, like *Betty* or *Betsy*, is provincially used as a contraction for *Elizabeth*, her Christian name, but which to us seems ludicrous, when applied to a woman of her age and appearance. Mr Garrick described her to me as very fat, with a bosom of more than ordinary protuberance, with swelled cheeks, of a florid red, produced by thick painting, and increased by the liberal use of cordials; flaring and fantastic in her dress, and affected both in her speech and her general behaviour. I have seen Garrick exhibit her, by his exquisite talent for mimicry, so as to excite the heartiest bursts of laughter; but he, probably, as is the case in all such representations, considerably aggravated the picture.

That Johnson well knew the most proper course to be pursued in the instruction of youth, is authentically ascertained by the following paper in his own handwriting, given about this period to a relation, and now in the possession of Mr John Nichols:

Scheme *for the* Classes *of a* Grammar School

When the introduction, or formation of nouns and verbs, is perfectly mastered, let them learn

Corderius by Mr Clarke, beginning at the same time to translate out of the introduction, that by this means they may learn the syntax. Then let them proceed to

Erasmus, with an English translation by the same author.

Class II. Learns Eutropius and Cornelius Nepos, or Justin, with the translation.

N. B. The first class gets for their part every morning the rules which they have learned before, and in the afternoon learns the Latin rules of the nouns and verbs.

They are examined in the rules which they have learned every Thursday and Saturday.

The second class doth the same whilst they are in Eutropius; afterwards their part is in the irregular nouns and verbs, and in the rules for making and scanning verses. They are examined as the first.

Class III. Ovid's Metamorphoses in the morning, and Caesar's Commentaries in the afternoon.

Practise in the Latin rules till they are perfect in them, afterwards in Mr Leed's Greek Grammar. Examined as before.

Afterwards they proceed to Virgil, beginning at the same time to write themes and verses, and to learn Greek; from thence passing on to Horace, &c. as shall seem most proper.

I know not well what books to direct you to, because you have not informed me what study you will apply yourself to. I believe it will be most for your advantage to apply yourself wholly to the languages, till you go to the University. The Greek authors I think it best for you to read are these:

Cebes	
Aelian	
Lucian by Leeds	Attic
Xenophon	
Homer	Ionic
Theocritus	Doric
Euripides	Attic and Doric

Thus you will be tolerably skilled in all the dialects, beginning with the Attic, to which the rest must be referred.

In the study of Latin, it is proper not to read the latter authors, till you are well versed in those of the purest ages; as, Terence, Tully, Caesar, Sallust, Nepos, Velleius Paterculus, Virgil, Horace, Phaedrus.

The greatest and most necessary task still remains, to attain a habit of expression, without which knowledge is of little use. This is necessary in Latin, and more necessary in English; and can only be acquired by a daily imitation of the best and correctest authors.

SAM. JOHNSON.

While Johnson kept his academy, there can be no doubt that he was insensibly furnishing his mind with various knowledge; but I have not discovered that he wrote any thing except a great part of his tragedy of *Irene*. Mr Peter Garrick, the elder brother of David, told me that he remembered Johnson's borrowing the Turkish History of him, in order to form his play from it. When he had finished some part of it, he read what he had done to Mr Walmsley, who objected to his having already brought his heroine into great distress, and asked him 'how can you possibly contrive to plunge her into deeper calamity?' Johnson, in sly allusion to the supposed oppressive proceedings of the court of which Mr Walmsley was register, replied, 'Sir, I can put her into the Spiritual Court!'

Mr Walmsley, however, was well pleased with this proof of Johnson's abilities as a dramatic writer, and advised him to finish the tragedy, and produce it on the stage.

Johnson now thought of trying his fortune in London, the great field of genius and exertion, where talents of every kind have the fullest scope, and the highest encouragement. It is a memorable circumstance that his pupil David Garrick went thither at the same time, with intention to complete his education, and follow the profession of the law, from which he was soon diverted by his decided preference for the stage.[a]

This joint expedition of these two eminent men to the metropolis, was many years afterwards noticed in an allegorical poem on Shakspeare's Mulberry Tree, by Mr Lovibond, the ingenious author of *The Tears of Old May-day*.

---

[a] Add: Both of them used to talk pleasantly of this their first journey to London. Garrick, evidently meaning to embellish a little, said one day in my hearing, 'we rode and tied.' And the Bishop of Killaloe informed me, that at another time, when Johnson and Garrick were dining together in a pretty large company, Johnson humorously ascertaining the chronology of something, expressed himself thus: 'that was the year when I came to London with two-pence half-penny in my pocket.' Garrick overhearing him, exclaimed, 'Eh? What do you say? With two-pence half-penny in your pocket?' JOHNSON, 'Why – yes; when I came with two-pence half-penny in my pocket, and thou, Davy, with three half-pence in thine.'

[In the 'corrections' this passage is directed to be placed as part of the text: in the second edition as a note.]

They were recommended to Mr Colson, an eminent mathematician and master of an academy, by the following letter from Mr Walmsley:

To the Reverend Mr COLSON.

Lichfield, March 2, 1737.

DEAR SIR – I had the favour of yours, and am extremely obliged to you; but I cannot say I had a greater affection for you upon it than I had before, being long since so much endeared to you, as well by an early friendship, as by your many excellent and valuable qualifications; and, had I a son of my own, it would be my ambition, instead of sending him to the University, to dispose of him as this young gentleman is.

He and another neighbour of mine, one Mr Samuel Johnson, set out this morning for London together. Davy Garrick is to be with you early the next week, and Mr Johnson to try his fate with a tragedy, and to see to get himself employed in some translation either from the Latin or the French. Johnson is a very good scholar and poet, and I have great hopes will turn out a fine tragedy-writer. If it should any way lie in your way, doubt not but you would be ready to recommend and assist your countryman.

G. WALMSLEY.

How he employed himself upon his first coming to London is not particularly known.[a] I never heard that he found any protection or encouragement by the means of Mr Colson, to whose academy David Garrick went. Mrs Lucy Porter told me, that Mr Walmsley gave him a letter of introduction to Lintot his bookseller, and that Johnson wrote some things for him; but I imagine this to be a mistake, for I have discovered no trace of it, and I am pretty sure he told me, that Mr Cave was the first publisher by whom his pen was engaged in London.

He had a little money when he came to town, and he knew how he could live in the cheapest manner. His first lodgings were at the house of Mr Norris, a staymaker, in Exeter-street, adjoining Catharine-street, in the Strand. 'I dined (said he) very well for eight-pence, with very good company, at the Pine Apple in New-street, just by. Several of them had travelled. They expected to meet every day; but did not know one another's names. It used to cost the rest a shilling, for they drank wine; but I had a cut of meat for sixpence, and bread for a penny, and gave the waiter a penny; so that I was quite well served, nay, better than the rest, for they gave the waiter nothing.'

He at this time, I believe, abstained entirely from fermented liquors; a practice to which he rigidly conformed for many years together, at different periods of his life.

[a] Add following note: One curious anecdote was communicated by himself to Mr John Nichols. Mr Wilcox, the bookseller, on being informed by him that his intention was to get his livelihood as an author, eyed his robust frame attentively, and with a significant look, said, 'You had better buy a porter's knot.' He however added, 'Wilcox was one of my best friends.'

His OFELLUS in the *Art of Living in London*, I have heard him relate, was an Irish painter, whom he knew at Birmingham, and who had practised his own precepts of economy for several years in the British capital. He assured Johnson, who, I suppose, was then meditating to try his fortune in London, but was apprehensive of the expense, 'that thirty pounds a year was enough to enable a man to live there without being contemptible. He allowed ten pounds for clothes and linen. He said a man might live in a garret at eighteen-pence a week; few people would inquire where he lodged; and if they did, it was easy to say, "Sir, I am to be found at such a place." By spending three-pence in a coffee-house, he might be for some hours every day in very good company; he might dine for six-pence, breakfast on bread and milk for a penny, and do without supper. On *clean-shirt-day* he went abroad, and paid visits.' I have heard him more than once talk of this frugal friend, whom he recollected with esteem and kindness, and did not like to have any one smile at the recital. 'This man (said he, gravely), was a very sensible man, who perfectly understood common affairs: a man of a great deal of knowledge of the world, fresh from life, not strained through books. He borrowed a horse and ten pounds at Birmingham. Finding himself master of so much money, he set off for West Chester, in order to get to Ireland. He returned the horse, and probably the ten pounds too, after he got home.'

Considering Johnson's narrow circumstances in the early part of his life, and particularly at the interesting era of his launching into the ocean of London, it is not to be wondered at, that an actual instance, proved by experience, of the possibility of enjoying the intellectual luxury of social life, upon a very small income, should deeply engage his attention, and be ever recollected by him as a circumstance of much importance. He amused himself, I remember, by computing how much more expense was absolutely necessary to live upon the same scale with that which his friend described, when the value of money was diminished by the progress of commerce. It may be estimated that double the money might now with difficulty be sufficient.

Amidst this cold obscurity, there was one brilliant circumstance to cheer him; he was well acquainted with Mr Henry Hervey,[a] one of the branches of the noble family of that name, who had been quartered at Lichfield as an officer of the army, and had at this time a house in London, where Johnson was frequently entertained, and had an opportunity of meeting genteel company. Not very long before his death, he mentioned this, among other particulars of his life, which he was kindly communicating to me; and he described this early friend 'Harry Hervey', thus: 'He was a vicious man, but very kind to me. If you call a dog HERVEY, I shall love him.'

He told me he had now written only three acts of his *Irene*, and that he retired for some time to lodgings at Greenwich, where he proceeded in it

---

[a] Add following note: The Honourable Henry Hervey, third son of the first Earl of Bristol, quitted the army and took orders. He married a sister of Sir Thomas Aston, by whom he got the Aston Estate, and assumed the name and arms of that family. *Vide* Collins's *Peerage*.

somewhat farther, and used to compose, walking in the Park; but did not stay long enough at that place to finish it.

At this period we find the following letter from him to Mr Edward Cave, which, as a link in the chain of his literary history, it is proper to insert:

To Mr CAVE.

> Greenwich, next door to the Golden Heart,
> Church-street, July 12, 1737.

SIR – Having observed in your papers very uncommon offers of encouragement to men of letters, I have chosen, being a stranger in London, to communicate to you the following design, which, I hope, if you join in it, will be of advantage to both of us.

The History of the Council of Trent having been lately translated into French, and published with large Notes by Dr Le Courayer, the reputation of that book is so much revived in England, that, it is presumed, a new translation of it from the Italian, together with Le Courayer's Notes from the French, could not fail of a favourable reception.

If it be answered, that the History is already in English, it must be remembered, that there was the same objection against Le Courayer's undertaking, with this disadvantage, that the French had a version by one of their best translators, whereas you cannot read three pages of the English History without discovering that the style is capable of great improvements; but whether those improvements are to be expected from this attempt, you must judge from the specimen, which, if you approve the proposal, I shall submit to your examination.

Suppose the merit of the versions equal, we may hope that the addition of the Notes will turn the balance in our favour, considering the reputation of the Annotator.

Be pleased to favour me with a speedy answer, if you are not willing to engage in this scheme; and appoint me a day to wait upon you, if you are. I am, sir,

> Your humble servant,
>
> SAM. JOHNSON.

It should seem from this letter, though subscribed with his own name, that he had not yet been introduced to Mr Cave. We shall presently see what was done in consequence of the proposal which it contains.

In the course of the summer he returned to Lichfield, where he had left Mrs Johnson, and there he at last finished his tragedy, which was not executed with his rapidity of composition upon other occasions, but was slowly and painfully elaborated. A few days before his death, while burning a great mass of papers, he picked out from among them the original unformed sketch of this tragedy, in his own handwriting, and gave it to Mr Langton, by whose favour a copy of it is now in my possession. It contains fragments of the intended plot, and speeches for the different persons of the drama, partly in the raw materials of prose, partly worked up into verse; as also a variety of hints for illustration borrowed from the Greek, Roman, and modern writers. The handwriting is very difficult to be read, even by those who were best acquainted with Johnson's mode of penmanship, which at all times was very particular. The King having graciously accepted of this manuscript as a literary curiosity, Mr Langton made a fair and distinct copy of it, which he ordered to be bound up with the original and the printed tragedy; and the volume is deposited in the King's library. His Majesty was pleased to permit Mr Langton to take a copy of it for himself.

The whole of it is rich in thought and imagery, and happy expressions; and of the *disjecta membra* scattered throughout, and as yet unarranged, a good dramatic poet might avail himself with considerable advantage. I shall give my readers some specimens of different kinds, distinguishing them by the Italic character.

> *Nor think to say, here will I stop,*
> *Here will I fix the limits of transgression,*
> *Nor farther tempt the avenging rage of heaven.*
> *When guilt like this once harbours in the breast,*
> *Those holy beings, whose unseen direction*
> *Guides through the maze of life the steps of man,*
> *Fly the detested mansions of impiety,*
> *And quit their charge to horror and to ruin.*

A small part only of this interesting admonition is preserved in the play, and is varied, I think, not to advantage:

> The soul once tainted with so foul a crime,
> No more shall glow with friendship's hallow'd ardour:
> Those holy beings whose superior care
> Guides erring mortals to the paths of virtue,
> Affrighted at impiety like thine,
> Resign their charge to baseness and to ruin.

> *I feel the soft infection*
> *Flush in my cheek, and wander in my veins.*
> *Teach me the Grecian arts of soft persuasion.*

Sure this is love, which heretofore I conceived the dream of idle maids and wanton poets.

Though no comets or prodigies foretold the ruin of Greece, signs which heaven must by another miracle enable us to understand, yet might it be foreshown, by tokens no less certain, by the vices which always bring it on.

This last passage is worked up in the tragedy itself, as follows:

LEONTIUS.

That power that kindly spreads
The clouds, a signal of impending showers,
To warn the wand'ring linnet to the shade,
Beheld, without concern, expiring Greece,
And not one prodigy foretold our fate.

DEMETRIUS.

A thousand horrid prodigies foretold it;
A feeble government, eluded laws,
A factious populace, luxurious nobles,
And all the maladies of sinking states.
When public villainy, too strong for justice,
Shows his bold front, the harbinger of ruin,
Can brave Leontius call for airy wonders,
Which cheats interpret, and which fools regard?
When some neglected fabric nods beneath
The weight of years, and totters to the tempest,
Must heaven dispatch the messengers of light,
Or wake the dead, to warn us of its fall?

MAHOMET (to IRENE). '*I have tried thee, and joy to find that thou deservest to be loved by Mahomet – with a mind great as his own. Sure, thou art an error of nature, and an exception to the rest of thy sex, and art immortal; for sentiments like thine were never to sink into nothing. I thought all the thoughts of the fair had been to select the graces of the day, dispose the colours of the flaunting (flowing) robe, tune the voice and roll the eye, place the gem, choose the dress, and add new roses to the fading cheek, but – sparkling.*'

Thus in the tragedy:

Illustrious maid, new wonders fix me thine;
Thy soul completes the triumphs of thy face:
I thought, forgive my fair, the noblest aim,
The strongest effort of a female soul,
Was but to choose the graces of the day,
To tune the tongue, to teach the eyes to roll,
Dispose the colours of the flowing robe,
And add new colours to the faded cheek.

I shall select one other passage, on account of the doctrine which it illustrates. IRENE observes, '*that the Supreme Being will accept of virtue, whatever outward circumstances it may be accompanied with, and may be delighted with varieties of worship*' – but is answered, '*that variety cannot affect that Being, who, infinitely happy in his own perfections, wants no external gratifications; nor can infinite truth be delighted with falsehood; that though he may guide or pity those he leaves in darkness, he abandons those who shut their eyes against the beams of day.'*

Johnson's residence at Lichfield, on his return to it at this time, was only for three months; and as he had as yet seen but a small part of the wonders of the metropolis, he had little to tell his townsmen. He related to me the following minute anecdote of this period: 'In the last age, when my mother lived in London, there were two sets of people, those who gave the wall, and those who took it; the peaceable and the quarrelsome. When I returned to Lichfield, after having been in London, my mother asked me whether I was one of those who gave the wall, or those who took it. Now it is fixed that every man keeps to the right; or, if one is taking the wall, another yields it; and it is never a dispute.'[1]

He now removed to London with Mrs Johnson; but her daughter, who had lived with them at Edial, was left with her relations in the country. His lodgings were for some time in Woodstock-street, near Hanover-square, and afterwards in Castle-street, near Cavendish-square. As there is something pleasingly interesting, to many, in tracing so great a man through all his different habitations, I shall, before this work is concluded, present my readers with an exact list of his lodgings and houses, in order of time, which, in placid condescension to my respectful curiosity, he one evening dictated to me, but without specifying how long he lived at each. In the progress of his life I shall have occasion to mention some of them as connected with particular incidents, or with the writing of particular parts of his works. To some, this minute attention may appear trifling; but when we consider the punctilious exactness with which the different houses in which Milton resided have been traced by the writers of his life, a similar enthusiasm may be pardoned in the biographer of Johnson.

His tragedy being by this time, as he thought, completely finished and fit for the stage, he was very desirous that it should be brought forward. Mr Peter Garrick told me, that Johnson and he went together to the Fountain tavern, and read it over, and that he afterwards solicited Mr Fleetwood, the patentee of Drury-lane theatre, to have it acted at his house; but Mr Fleetwood would not accept it, probably because it was not patronised by some man of high rank; and it was not acted till 1749, when his friend David Garrick was manager of that theatre.

The Gentleman's Magazine, begun and carried on by Mr Edward Cave, under the name of SYLVANUS URBAN, had attracted the notice and esteem of Johnson, in an eminent degree, before he came to London as an adventurer in literature. He told me, that when he first saw St John's Gate, the place where that deservedly popular miscellany was originally printed, he 'beheld it with reverence'. I suppose, indeed, that every young author has had the same kind of feeling for the magazine or periodical publication which has first entertained him, and in which he has first had an opportunity to see himself in print, without the risk of exposing his name. I myself recollect such impressions from

1 *Journal of a Tour to the Hebrides*, 3rd edit. p. 232.

The Scots Magazine, which was begun at Edinburgh in the year 1739, and has been ever conducted with judgement, accuracy and propriety. I yet cannot help thinking of it with an affectionate regard. Johnson has dignified the *Gentleman's Magazine*, by the importance with which he invests the life of Cave; but he has given it still greater lustre by the various admirable Essays which he wrote for it.

Though Johnson was often solicited by his friends to make a complete list of his writings, and talked of doing it, I believe with a serious intention that they should all be collected on his own account, he put it off from year to year, and at last died without having done it perfectly. I have one in his own handwriting, which contains a certain number; I indeed doubt if he could have recollected every one of them, as they were so numerous, so various, and scattered in such a multiplicity of unconnected publications; nay, several of them published under the names of other persons, to whom he liberally contributed from the abundance of his mind. We must, therefore, be content to discover them, partly from occasional information given by him to his friends, and partly from internal evidence.[1]

His first performance in the *Gentleman's Magazine*, which for many years was his principal resource for employment and support, was a copy of Latin verses, in March, 1738, addressed to the editor in so happy a style of compliment, that Cave must have been destitute both of taste and sensibility, had he not felt himself highly gratified.

Ad URBANUM.*

> URBANE, *nullis fesse laboribus,*
> URBANE, *nullis victe calumniis,*
>   *Cui fronte sertum in erudita*
>   *Perpetuo viret et virebit;*
>
> *Quid moliatur gens imitantium,*
> *Quid et minetur, solicitus parum,*
>   *Vacare solis perge Musis,*
>   *Juxta animo studiisque felix.*
>
> *Linguae procacis plumbea spicula,*
> *Fidens, superbo frange silentio;*
>   *Victrix per obstantes catervas*
>   *Sedulitas animosa tendet.*

---

1 While in the course of my narrative I enumerate his writings, I shall take care that my readers shall not be left to waver in doubt, between certainty and conjecture, with regard to their authenticity; and, for that purpose, shall mark with an *asterisk* * those which he acknowledged to his friends, and with a *dagger* † those which are ascertained to be his by internal evidence. When any other pieces are ascribed to him, I shall give my reasons.

Intende nervos, fortis, inanibus
Risurus olim nisibus aemuli;
   Intende jam nervos, habebis
     Participes operae Camoenas.

Non ulla Musis pagina gratior,
Quam quae severis ludicra jungere
   Novit, fatigatamque nugis
     Utilibus recreare mentem.

Texente Nymphis serta Lycoride,
Rosae ruborem sic viola adjuvat
   Immista, sic Iris refulget
     Aethereis variata fucis.[1]

                    S. J.

It appears that he was now enlisted by Mr Cave as a regular coadjutor in his magazine, by which he probably obtained a tolerable livelihood. At what time, or by what means, he had acquired a competent knowledge both of French and Italian, I do not know; but he was so well skilled in them, as to be sufficiently qualified for a translator. That part of his labour which consisted in emendation and improvement of the productions of other contributors, like that employed in levelling ground, can be perceived only by those who had an opportunity of comparing the original with the altered copy. What we certainly know to have

---

1 A translation of this Ode, by an unknown correspondent, appeared in the Magazine for the month of May following:

   Hail URBAN! indefatigable man,
Unwearied yet by all thy useful toil!
   Whom num'rous slanderers assault in vain;
Whom no base calumny can put to foil.
   But still the laurel on thy learned brow
   Flourishes fair, and shall for ever grow.

   What mean the servile imitating crew,
What their vain blust'ring, and their empty noise,
   Ne'er seek: but still thy noble ends pursue,
Unconquer'd by the rabble's venal voice.
   Still to the Muse thy studious mind apply,
   Happy in temper as in industry.

   The senseless sneerings of an haughty tongue,
Unworthy thy attention to engage,
   Unheeded pass: and tho' they mean thee wrong,
By manly silence disappoint their rage.
   Assiduous diligence confounds its foes,
   Resistless, tho' malicious crouds oppose.

been done by him in this way, was the Debates in both houses of Parliament, under the name of 'The Senate of Lilliput', sometimes with feigned denominations of the several speakers, sometimes with denominations formed of the letters of their real names, in the manner of what is called anagram, so that they might easily be decyphered. Parliament then kept the press in a kind of mysterious awe, which made it necessary to have recourse to such devices. In our time it has acquired an unrestrained freedom, so that the people in all parts of the kingdom have a fair, open, and exact report of the actual proceedings of their representatives and legislators; which in our constitution is highly to be valued, though, unquestionably, there has of late been too much reason to complain of the petulance with which obscure scribblers have presumed to treat men of the most respectable character and situation.

This important article of the *Gentleman's Magazine* was, for several years, executed by Mr William Guthrie, a man who deserves to be respectably recorded in the literary annals of this country. He was descended of an ancient family in Scotland; but having a small patrimony, and being an adherent of the unfortunate house of Stuart, he could not accept of any office in the state; he therefore came to London, and employed his talents and learning as an 'Author by profession'. His writings in history, criticism, and politics, had considerable merit.[1] He was the first English historian who had recourse to

---

Exert thy powers, nor slacken in the course,
Thy spotless fame shall quash all false reports:
    Exert thy powers, nor fear a rival's force,
But thou shalt smile at all his vain efforts;
    Thy labours shall be crown'd with large success;
    The Muse's aid thy magazine shall bless.

No page more grateful to th' harmonious nine
Than that wherein thy labours we survey:
    Where solemn themes in fuller splendour shine,
(Delightful mixture), blended with the gay.
    Where in improving, various joys we find,
    A welcome respite to the wearied mind.

Thus when the nymphs in some fair verdant mead,
Of various flow'rs a beauteous wreath compose,
    The lovely violet's azure-painted head
Adds lustre to the crimson-blushing rose.
    Thus splendid Iris, with her varied dye,
    Shines in the aether, and adorns the sky.

'BRITON.'

1 How much poetry he wrote, I know not; but he informed me, that he was the author of the beautiful little piece, 'The Eagle and Robin Redbreast', in the collection of poems entitled *The Union*, though it is there said to be written by Archibald Scott, before the year 1600.

that authentic source of information, the Parliamentary Journals; and such was the power of his political pen, that, at an early period, government thought it worth their while to keep it quiet by a pension, which he enjoyed till his death. Johnson esteemed him enough to wish that his life should be written. The debates in Parliament, which were brought home and digested by Guthrie, whose memory, though surpassed by others who have since followed him in the same department, was yet very quick and tenacious, were sent by Cave to Johnson for his revision; and, after some time, when Guthrie had attained to greater variety of employment, and the speeches were more and more enriched by the accession of Johnson's genius, it was resolved that he should do the whole himself, from the scanty notes furnished by persons employed to attend in both houses of Parliament. Sometimes, however, as he himself told me, he had nothing more communicated to him but the names of the several speakers, and the part which they had taken in the debate.

Thus was Johnson employed, during some of the best years of his life, as a mere literary labourer 'for gain, not glory', solely to obtain an honest support. He however indulged himself in occasional little sallies, which the French so happily express by the term *jeux d'esprit*, and which will be noticed in their order, in the progress of this work.

But what first displayed his transcendent powers, and 'gave the world assurance of the MAN', was his 'LONDON, a Poem, in Imitation of the Third Satire of Juvenal', which came out in May this year, and burst forth with a splendour, the rays of which will for ever encircle his name. Boileau had imitated the same satire with great success, applying it to Paris; but an attentive comparison will satisfy every reader, that he is much excelled by the English Juvenal. Oldham had also imitated it, and applied it to London; all which performances concur to prove, that great cities, in every age, and in every country, will furnish similar topics of satire. Whether Johnson had previously read Oldham's imitation, I do not know; but it is not a little remarkable, that there is scarcely any coincidence found between the two performances, though upon the very same subject. The only instances are, in describing London as the *sink* of foreign worthlessness:

> the *common shore*,
> Where France does all her filth and ordure pour.
>
> OLDHAM.

> The *common shore* of Paris and of Rome.
>
> JOHNSON.

and,

> No calling or profession comes amiss,
> A *needy monsieur* can be what he please.
>
> OLDHAM.

> All sciences a *fasting monsieur* knows.
>
> JOHNSON.

The particulars which Oldham has collected, both as exhibiting the horrors of London, and of the times, contrasted with better days, are different from those of Johnson, and in general well chosen, and well expressed.[1]

There are, in Oldham's imitation, many prosaic verses and bad rhymes, and his poem sets out with a strange inadvertent blunder:

> Tho' much concern'd to *leave* my dear old friend,
> I must, however, *his* design commend
> Of fixing in the country . . .

It is plain he was not going to leave his *friend*; his friend was going to leave *him*. A young lady at once corrected this with good critical sagacity to

> Tho' much concern'd to *lose* my dear old friend.

There is one passage in the original, better transfused by Oldham than by Johnson:

> *Nil habet infelix paupertas durius in se,*
> *Quam quod ridiculos homines facit.*

which is an exquisite remark on the galling meanness and contempt annexed to poverty: JOHNSON's imitation is,

> Of all the griefs that harass the distrest,
> Sure the most bitter is a scornful jest.

OLDHAM's, though less elegant, is more just:

> Nothing in poverty so ill is borne,
> As its exposing men to grinning scorn.

Where, or in what manner this poem was composed, I am sorry that I neglected to ascertain with precision from Johnson's own authority. He has marked upon his corrected copy of the first edition of it, 'Written in 1738'; and, as it was published in the month of May in that year, it is evident that

---

1 I own it pleased me to find amongst them one trait of the manners of the age in London, in the last century, to shield from the sneer of English ridicule, what was some time ago too common a practice in my native city of Edinburgh:

> If what I've said can't from the town affright,
> Consider other *dangers of the night*;
> When brickbats are from upper stories thrown,
> And *emptied chamberpots come pouring down*
> *From garret windows.*

much time was not employed in preparing it for the press. The history of its publication I am enabled to give in a very satisfactory manner; and judging from myself, and many of my friends, I trust that it will not be uninteresting to my readers.

We may be certain, though it is not expressly named in the following letters to Mr Cave in 1738, that they all relate to it:

To Mr CAVE.

Castle-street, Wednesday morning.
[No date. 1738.]

SIR – When I took the liberty of writing to you a few days ago, I did not expect a repetition of the same pleasure so soon; for a pleasure I shall always think it, to converse in any manner with an ingenious and candid man; but having the enclosed poem in my hands to dispose of for the benefit of the author (of whose abilities I shall say nothing, since I send you his perform-ance), I believed I could not procure more advantageous terms from any person than from you, who have so much distinguished yourself by your generous encouragement of poetry; and whose judgement of that art nothing but your commendation of my trifle[1] can give me any occasion to call in question. I do not doubt but you will look over this poem with another eye, and reward it in a different manner, from a mercenary bookseller, who counts the lines he is to purchase, and considers nothing but the bulk. I cannot help taking notice, that, besides what the author may hope for on account of his abilities, he has likewise another claim to your regard, as he lies at present under very disadvantageous circumstances of fortune. I beg, therefore, that you will favour me with a letter tomorrow, that I may know what you can afford to allow him, that he may either part with it to you, or find out (which I do not expect) some other way more to his satisfaction.

I have only to add, that as I am sensible I have transcribed it very coarsely, which, after having altered it, I was obliged to do, I will, if you please to transmit the sheets from the press, correct it for you; and take the trouble of altering any stroke of satire which you may dislike.

By exerting on this occasion your usual generosity, you will not only encourage learning, and relieve distress, but (though it be in comparison of the other motives of very small account) oblige in a very sensible manner, Sir,

Your very humble servant,

SAM. JOHNSON.

---

1 [His Ode 'Ad Urbanum' probably. Nichols.]

To Mr CAVE.

Monday, No. 6, Castle-street.

SIR – I am to return you thanks for the present you were so kind as to send by me, and to entreat that you will be pleased to inform me by the penny-post, whether you resolve to print the poem. If you please to send it me by the post, with a note to Dodsley, I will go and read the lines to him, that we may have his consent to put his name in the title-page. As to the printing, if it can be set immediately about, I will be so much the author's friend, as not to content myself with mere solicitations in his favour. I propose, if my calculation be near the truth, to engage for the reimburse-ment of all that you shall lose by an impression of 500, provided, as you very generously propose, that the profit, if any, be set aside for the author's use, excepting the present you made, which, if he be a gainer, it is fit he should repay. I beg that you will let one of your servants write an exact account of the expense of such an impression, and send it with the poem, that I may know what I engage for. I am very sensible, from your generosity on this occasion, of your regard to learning, even in its unhap-piest state, and cannot but think such a temper deserving of the gratitude of those who suffer so often from a contrary disposition. I am, Sir,

Your most humble servant,

SAM. JOHNSON.

To Mr CAVE.

[No date.]

SIR – I waited on you to take the copy to Dodsley's: as I remember the number of lines which it contains, it will be longer than 'Eugenio', with the quotations, which must be subjoined at the bottom of the page, part of the beauty of the performance (if any beauty be allowed it) consisting in adapting Juvenal's sentiments to modern facts and persons. It will, with those additions, very conveniently make five sheets. And since the expense will be no more, I shall contentedly insure it, as I mentioned in my last. If it be not therefore gone to Dodsley's, I beg it may be sent me by the penny-post, that I may have it in the evening. I have composed a Greek Epigram to Eliza,[1] and think she ought to be celebrated in as many different languages as Lewis le Grand. Pray send me word when you will begin upon the poem, for it is a long way to walk. I would leave my Epigram, but have not daylight to transcribe it. I am, sir,

Your's, &c.

SAM. JOHNSON.

1 The learned Mrs Elizabeth Carter.

To Mr Cave.

[No date.]

Sir — I am extremely obliged by your kind letter, and will not fail to attend you tomorrow with *Irene*, who looks upon you as one of her best friends.

I was today with Mr Dodsley, who declares very warmly in favour of the paper you sent him, which he desires to have a share in, it being, as he says, *a creditable thing to be concerned in*. I knew not what answer to make till I had consulted you, nor what to demand on the author's part, but am very willing that, if you please, he should have a part in it, as he will undoubtedly be more diligent to disperse and promote it. If you can send me word tomorrow what I shall say to him, I will settle matters, and bring the poem with me for the press, which as the town empties, we cannot be too quick with. I am, Sir,

Your's, &c.

SAM. JOHNSON.

To us who have long known the manly force, bold spirit, and masterly versification of this poem, it is a matter of curiosity to observe the diffidence with which its author brought it forward into public notice, while he is so cautious as not to avow it to be his own production; and with what humility he offers to allow the printer to 'alter any stroke of satire which he might dislike'. That any such alteration was made, we do not know. If we did, we could not but feel an indignant regret; but how painful is it to see that a writer of such vigorous powers of mind was actually in such distress, that the small profit which so short a poem, however excellent, could yield, was courted as a 'relief'.

It has been generally said, I know not with what truth, that Johnson offered his *London* to several booksellers, none of whom would purchase it. To this circumstance Mr Derrick alludes in the following lines of his 'Fortune, a Rhapsody':

> Will no kind patron JOHNSON own?
> Shall JOHNSON friendless range the town?
> And every publisher refuse
> The offspring of his happy Muse?

But we have seen that the worthy, modest, and ingenious Mr Robert Dodsley had taste enough to perceive its uncommon merit, and thought it creditable to have a share in it. The fact is, that, at a future conference, he bargained for the whole property of it, for which he gave Johnson ten guineas, who told me, 'I might, perhaps, have accepted of less; but that Paul Whitehead had a little before got ten guineas for a poem; and I would not take less than Paul Whitehead.'

I may here observe, that Johnson appeared to me to undervalue Paul Whitehead upon every occasion when he was mentioned, and, in my opinion, did not do him justice; but when it is considered that Paul Whitehead was a member of a riotous and profane club, we may account for Johnson's having a prejudice against him. Paul Whitehead was, indeed, unfortunate in being not only slighted by Johnson, but violently attacked by Churchill, who utters the following imprecation:

> May I (can worse disgrace on manhood fall?)
> Be born a Whitehead, and baptiz'd a Paul!

yet I shall never be persuaded to think meanly of the author of so brilliant and pointed a satire as 'Manners'.

Johnson's *London* was published in May, 1738;[1] and it is remarkable, that it came out on the same morning with Pope's satire, entitled '1738'; so that England had at once its Juvenal and Horace as poetical monitors. The Reverend Dr Douglas, now Bishop of Carlisle, to whom I am indebted for some obliging communications, was then a student at Oxford, and remembers well the effect which *London* produced. Everybody was delighted with it; and there being no name to it, the first buz of the literary circles was 'here is an unknown poet, greater even than Pope.' And it is recorded in the *Gentleman's Magazine* of that year,[2] that it 'got to the second edition in the course of a week.'

One of the warmest patrons of this poem on its first appearance was General OGLETHORPE, whose 'strong benevolence of soul' was unabated during the course of a very long life: though it is painful to think, that he had but too much reason to become cold and callous, and discontented with the world, from the neglect which he experienced of his public and private worth, by those in whose power it was to gratify so gallant a veteran with marks of distinction. This extraordinary person was as remarkable for his learning and taste, as for his other eminent qualities; and no man was more prompt, active, and generous in encouraging merit. I have heard Johnson gratefully acknowledge, in his presence, the kind and effectual support which he gave to his *London*, though unacquainted with its author.

POPE, who then filled the poetical throne without a rival, it may reasonably be presumed, must have been particularly struck by the sudden appearance of such a poet; and, to his credit, let it be remembered, that his feelings and conduct on the occasion were candid and liberal. He requested Mr

---

1 Sir John Hawkins, p. 86, tells us 'The event is *antedated*, in the poem of *London*; but in every particular, except the difference of a year, what is there said of the departure of Thales, must be understood of Savage, and looked upon as *true history*.' This conjecture is, I believe, entirely groundless. I have been assured that Johnson said he was not so much as acquainted with Savage when he wrote his *London*. If the departure mentioned in it was the departure of Savage, the event was not *antedated* but *foreseen*; for *London* was published in May, 1738, and Savage did not set out for Wales till July, 1739. However well Johnson could defend the credibility of *second sight*, he did not pretend that he himself was possessed of that faculty.

2 p. 269.

Richardson, son of the painter, to endeavour to find out who this new author was. Mr Richardson, after some inquiry, having informed him that he had discovered only that his name was Johnson, and that he was some obscure man, Pope said, 'He will soon be *deterré*.'[1] We shall presently see, from a note written by Pope, that he was himself afterwards more successful in his inquiries than his friend.

That in this justly-celebrated poem may be found a few rhymes which the critical precision of English prosody at this day would disallow, cannot be denied; but with this small imperfection, which in the general blaze of its excellence is not perceived, till the mind has subsided into cool attention, it is, undoubtedly, one of the noblest productions in our language, both for sentiment and expression. The nation was then in that ferment against the court and the ministry, which some years after ended in the downfall of Sir Robert Walpole; and as it has been said, that Tories are Whigs when out of place, and Whigs, Tories when in place; so, as a whig administration ruled with what force it could, a tory opposition had all the animation and all the eloquence of resistance to power, aided by the common topics of patriotism, liberty, and independence! Accordingly, we find in Johnson's *London* the most spirited invectives against tyranny and oppression, the warmest predilection for his own country, and the purest love of virtue; interspersed with traits of his own particular character and situation, not omitting his prejudices as a 'true-born Englishman',[2] not only against foreign countries, but against Ireland and Scotland. On some of these topics I shall quote a few passages:

> The cheated nation's happy fav'rites see;
> Mark whom the great caress, who frown on me.

> Has heaven reserv'd, in pity to the poor,
> No pathless waste, or undiscover'd shore?
> No secret island in the boundless main?
> No peaceful desart yet unclaim'd by Spain?
> Quick let us rise, the happy seats explore,
> And bear Oppression's insolence no more.

> How, when competitors like these contend,
> Can *surly Virtue* hope to fix a friend?

> This mournful truth is every where confess'd,
> SLOW RISES WORTH, BY POVERTY DEPRESS'D!

1 Sir Joshua Reynolds, from the information of the younger Richardson.
2 It is, however, remarkable, that he uses the epithet, which, undoubtedly, since the union between England and Scotland, ought to denominate the natives of both parts of our island:

> 'Was early taught a BRITON'S rights to prize.'

We may easily conceive with what feeling a great mind like his, cramped and galled by narrow circumstances, uttered this last line, which he marked by capitals. The whole of the poem is eminently excellent, and there are in it such proofs of a knowledge of the world, and of a mature acquaintance with life, as cannot be contemplated without wonder, when we consider that he was then only in his twenty-ninth year, and had yet been so little in the 'busy haunts of men'.

Yet, while we admire the poetical excellence of this poem, candour obliges us to allow, that the flame of patriotism and zeal for popular resistance with which it is fraught, had no just cause. There was, in truth, *no* 'oppression'; the 'nation' was *not* 'cheated'. Sir Robert Walpole was a wise and a benevolent minister, who thought that the happiness and prosperity of a commercial country like ours, would be best promoted by peace, which he accordingly maintained, with credit, during a very long period. Johnson himself afterwards honestly acknowledged the merit of Walpole, whom he called 'a fixed star'; while he characterised his opponent, Pitt, as 'a meteor'. But Johnson's juvenile poem was naturally impregnated with the fire of opposition, and upon every account was universally admired.

Though thus elevated into fame, and conscious of uncommon powers, he had not that bustling confidence, or, I may rather say, that animated ambition, which one might have supposed would have urged him to endeavour at rising in life. But such was his inflexible dignity of character, that he could not stoop to court the great; without which, hardly any man has made his way to high station. He could not expect to produce many such works as his *London*, and he felt the hardship of writing for bread; he was, therefore, willing to resume the office of a schoolmaster, so as to have a sure, though moderate income for his life; and an offer being made to him of a school in Staffordshire,[1a] provided he could obtain the degree of Master of Arts, Dr Adams was applied to, by a

---

1 In a billet written by Mr Pope in the following year, this school is said to have been in *Shropshire*; but as it appears from a letter from Earl Gower, that the trustees of it were 'some worthy gentlemen in Johnson's neighbourhood', I conclude that Pope must have, by mistake, written Shropshire instead of Staffordshire.

a Delete 'in Staffordshire'. After the note add: Mr Spearing, attorney-at-law, was so good as to furnish me with several circumstances of probable conjecture that it was the school of Newport, in Shropshire. But Mr Henn, one of the masters of the school of Appleby, in Leicestershire, in a letter to the *Gentleman's Magazine* for May, 1793, demonstrated *that* to be the school for which Johnson was a candidate.

Second Edition. In a billet written by Mr Pope in the following year, this school is said to have been in *Shropshire*; but as it appears from a letter from Earl Gower, that the trustees of it were 'some worthy gentlemen in Johnson's neighbourhood', I in my first edition suggested that Pope must have, by mistake, written Shropshire, instead of Staffordshire. But I have since been obliged to Mr Spearing, attorney-at-law, for the following information: 'William Adams, formerly citizen and haberdasher of London, founded a school at Newport, in the county of Salop, by deed dated 27th November, 1656, by which he granted the "yearly sum of *sixty pounds* to such able and learned schoolmaster, from time to time, being of godly life and conversation, who should

common friend, to know whether that could be granted him as a favour from the University of Oxford. But though he had made such a figure in the literary world, it was then thought too great a favour to be asked.

Pope, without any knowledge of him but from his *London*, recommended him to Earl Gower, who endeavoured to procure for him a degree from Dublin, by the following letter to a friend of Dean Swift:

> SIR – Mr Samuel Johnson (author of *London*, a satire, and some other poetical pieces) is a native of this county, and much respected by some worthy gentlemen in his neighbourhood, who are trustees of a charity school now vacant; the certain salary is sixty pounds a year, of which they are desirous to make him master; but, unfortunately, he is not capable of receiving their bounty, which *would make him happy for life*, by not being a *Master of Arts*; which by the statutes of this school, the master of it must be.
>
> Now these gentlemen do me the honour to think that I have interest enough in you, to prevail upon you to write to Dean Swift, to persuade

---

have been educated at one of the Universities of Oxford or Cambridge, and had taken the degree of *Master of Arts*, and was well read in the Greek and Latin tongues, as should be nominated from time to time by the said William Adams, during his life, and after the decease of the said William Adams by the governors (namely, the Master and Wardens of the Haberdashers' Company of the City of London) and their successors." The manor and lands out of which the revenues for the maintenance of the school were to issue are situate at *Knighton and Adbaston, in the county of Stafford.*' From the foregoing account of this foundation, particularly the circumstances of the salary being sixty pounds, and the degree of Master of Arts being a requisite qualification in the teacher, it seemed probable that this was the school in contemplation; and that Lord Gower erroneously supposed that the gentlemen who possessed the lands, out of which the revenues issued, were trustees of the charity.

Such was probable conjecture. But in the *Gentleman's Magazine* for May, 1793, there is a letter from Mr Henn, one of the masters of the school of Appleby, in Leicestershire, in which he writes as follows:

'I compared time and circumstance together, in order to discover whether the school in question might not be this of Appleby. Some of the trustees at that period were "worthy gentlemen of the neighbourhood of Lichfield". Appleby itself was not far from the neighbourhood of Lichfield: the salary, the degree requisite, together with the time of election, all agreeing with the statutes of Appleby. The election, as said in the letter, "could not be delayed longer than the 11th of next month", which was the 11th of September, just three months after the annual audit day of Appleby school, which is always on the 11th of June, and the statutes enjoin *ne ullius praeceptorum electio diutius tribus mensibus moraretur.*

'These I thought to be convincing proofs that my conjecture was not ill-founded, and that in a future edition of that book the circumstances might be recorded as a fact.

'But what banishes every shadow of doubt is the *Minute Book* of the school, which declares the head-mastership to be *at that time* VACANT.'

I cannot omit returning thanks to this learned gentleman for the very handsome manner in which he has, in that letter, been so good as to speak of my work.

the University of Dublin to send a diploma to me, constituting this poor man Master of Arts in their University. They highly extol the man's learning and probity; and will not be persuaded, that the University will make any difficulty of conferring such a favour upon a stranger, if he is recommended by the Dean. They say he is not afraid of the strictest examination, though he is of so long a journey; and will venture it, if the Dean thinks it necessary; choosing rather to die upon the road, *than be starved to death in translating for booksellers*; which has been his only subsistence for some time past.

I fear there is more difficulty in this affair, than those good-natured gentlemen apprehend; especially as their election cannot be delayed longer than the 11th of next month. If you see this matter in the same light that it appears to me, I hope you will burn this and pardon me for giving you so much trouble about an impracticable thing; but, if you think there is a probability of obtaining the favour asked, I am sure your humanity, and propensity to relieve merit in distress, will incline you to serve the poor man, without my adding any more to the trouble I have already given you, than assuring you, that I am, with great truth, Sir,

Your faithful humble servant,

GOWER.

Trentham, Aug. 1, 1739.

It was, perhaps, no small disappointment to Johnson that this respectable application had not the desired effect; yet how much reason has there been, both for himself and his country, to rejoice that it did not succeed, as he might probably have wasted in obscurity those hours in which he afterwards produced his incomparable works.

About this time he made one other effort to emancipate himself from the drudgery of authorship. He applied to Dr Adams, to consult Dr Smalbroke of the Commons, whether a person might be permitted to practice as an advocate there, without a doctor's degree in Civil Law. 'I am (said he) a total stranger to these studies; but whatever is a profession, and maintains numbers, must be within the reach of common abilities, and some degree of industry.' Dr Adams was much pleased with Johnson's design to employ his talents in that manner, being confident he would have attained to great eminence. And, indeed, I cannot conceive a man better qualified to make a distinguished figure as a lawyer; for, he would have brought to his profession a rich store of various knowledge, an uncommon acuteness, and a command of language, in which few could have equalled, and none have surpassed him. He who could display eloquence and wit in defence of the decision of the House of Commons' upon Mr Wilkes's election for Middlesex, and of the unconstitutional taxation of our fellow subjects in America, must have been a powerful advocate in any cause. But here, also, the want of a degree was an insurmountable bar.

He was, therefore, under the necessity of persevering in that course, into which he had been forced; and we find, that his proposal from Greenwich to

Mr Cave, for a translation of Father Paul Sarpi's History, was accepted.[1]

Some sheets of this translation were printed off, but the design was dropped; for it happened, oddly enough, that another person of the name of Samuel Johnson, Librarian of St Martin's in the Fields, and curate of that parish, engaged in the same undertaking, and was patronized by the Clergy, particularly by Dr Pearce, afterwards Bishop of Rochester. Several light skirmishes passed between the rival translators, in the newspapers of the day; and the consequence was, that they destroyed each other, for neither of them went on with the work. It is much to be regretted, that the able performance of that celebrated genius FRA PAOLO lost the advantage of being incorporated into British literature by the masterly hand of Johnson.

I have in my possession, by the favour of Mr John Nichols, a paper in Johnson's handwriting, entitled 'Account between Mr Edward Cave and Sam. Johnson, in relation to a version of Father Paul, &c. begun August the 2d, 1738'; by which it appears, that from that day to the 21st of April, Johnson received for this work £49. 7s. in sums of one, two, three, and sometimes four guineas at a time, most frequently two. And it is curious to observe the minute and scrupulous accuracy with which Johnson has pasted upon it a slip of paper, which he has entitled 'Small Account', and which contains one article, 'Sept. 9th, Mr Cave laid down 2s. 6d.' There is subjoined to this account, a list of some subscribers to the work, partly in Johnson's handwriting, partly in that of another person; and there follows a leaf or two on which are written a number of characters which have the appearance of a short hand, which, perhaps, Johnson was then trying to learn.

1 In the *Weekly Miscellany*, October 21, 1738, there appeared the following advertisement:

Just published, Proposals for Printing the *History of the Council of Trent*, translated from the Italian of Father Paul Sarpi; with the Authour's Life, and Notes theological, historical, and critical, from the French edition of Dr Le Courayer. To which are added, Observations on the History, and Notes and Illustrations from various Authours, both printed and manuscript. By S. Johnson.
1. The work will consist of two hundred sheets, and be two volumes in quarto, printed on good paper and letter.
2. The price will be 18s. each volume, to be paid, half a guinea at the time of subscribing, half a guinea at the delivery of the first volume, and the rest at the delivery of the second volume in sheets.
3. Two-pence to be abated for every sheet less than two hundred. It may be had on a large paper, in three volumes, at the price of three guineas; one to be paid at the time of subscribing, another at the delivery of the first, and the rest at the delivery of the other volumes.
The work is now in the press, and will be diligently prosecuted. Subscriptions are taken in by Mr Dodsley in Pall-Mall, Mr Rivington in St Paul's Church-yard, by E. Cave at St John's Gate, and the Translator, at No. 6 in Castle-street, by Cavendish-square.

To Mr CAVE.

Wednesday.

SIR – I did not care to detain your servant while I wrote an answer to your letter, in which you seem to insinuate that I had promised more than I am ready to perform. If I have raised your expectations by any thing that may have escaped my memory, I am sorry; and if you remind me of it, shall thank you for the favour. If I made fewer alterations than usual in the Debates, it was only because there appeared, and still appears to be, less need of alteration. The verses to Lady Firebrace[1] may be had when you please, for you know that such a subject neither deserves much thought, nor requires it.

The Chinese Stories[2] may be had folded down when you please to send, in which I do not recollect that you desired any alterations to be made.

An answer to another query I am very willing to write, and had consulted with you about it last night if there had been time; for I think it the most proper way of inviting such a correspondence as may be an advantage to the paper, not a load upon it.

As to the Prize Verses, a backwardness to determine their degrees of merit is not peculiar to me. You may, if you please, still have what I can say; but I shall engage with little spirit in an affair, which I shall *hardly* end to my own satisfaction, and *certainly* not to the satisfaction of the parties concerned.[3]

As to Father Paul, I have not yet been just to my proposal, but have met with impediments, which, I hope, are now at an end; and if you find the progress hereafter not such as you have a right to expect, you can easily stimulate a negligent translator.

If any or all of these have contributed to your discontent, I will endeavour to remove it; and desire you to propose the question to which you wish for an answer. I am, Sir,

Your humble servant,

SAM. JOHNSON.

To Mr CAVE.

[No date.]

SIR – I am pretty much of your opinion, that the Commentary cannot be prosecuted with any appearance of success; for as the names of the authors concerned are of more weight in the performance than its own intrinsic

1 They afterwards appeared in the *Gentleman's Magazine* with this title, 'Verses to Lady Firebrace, at Bury Assizes'.

2 [Du Halde's Description of China was then publishing by Mr Cave in weekly numbers, whence Johnson was to select pieces for the embellishment of the magazine. Nichols.]

3 [The premium of forty pounds proposed for the best poem on the Divine Attributes is here alluded to. Nichols.]

merit, the public will be soon satisfied with it. And I think the Examen should be pushed forward with the utmost expedition. Thus, 'This day, &c., An Examen of Mr Pope's Essay, &c., containing a succinct Account of the Philosophy of Mr Leibnitz on the system of the Fatalists, with a Confutation of their Opinions, and an Illustration of the Doctrine of Free-will' [with what else you think proper].

It will, above all, be necessary to take notice, that it is a thing distinct from the Commentary.

I was so far from imagining they stood still,[1] that I conceived them to have a good deal beforehand, and therefore was less anxious in providing them more. But if ever they stand still on my account, it must doubtless be charged to me; and whatever else shall be reasonable, I shall not oppose; but beg a suspense of judgement till morning, when I must entreat you to send me a dozen proposals, and you shall then have copy to spare. I am, Sir,

Your's, *impransus*,

SAM. JOHNSON.

Pray muster up the Proposals if you can, or let the boy recall them from the bookseller.

But although he corresponded with Mr Cave concerning a translation of Crousaz's Examen of Pope's *Essay on Man*, and gave advice as one anxious for its success, I was long ago convinced by a perusal of the Preface, that this translation was erroneously ascribed to him; and I have found this point ascertained, beyond all doubt, by the following article in Dr Birch's Manuscripts in the British Museum:

ELISAE CARTERAE S. P. D. THOMAS BIRCH.

Versionem tuam Examinis Crousaziani jam perlegi. Summam styli et elegantiam, et in re difficillima proprietatem, admiratus.

Dabam Novemb. 27° 1738.[2]

Indeed Mrs Carter has lately acknowledged to Mr Seward, that she was the translator of the Examen.

It is remarkable, that Johnson's last quoted letter to Mr Cave concludes with a fair confession that he had not a dinner, and it is no less remarkable, that, though in this state of want himself, his benevolent heart was not insensible to the necessities of an humble labourer in literature, as appears from the very next letter:

---

1 [The compositors in Mr Cave's printing-office, who appear by this letter to have then waited for copy. Nichols.]
2 Birch MSS. Brit. Mus. 4320.

To Mr CAVE.

[No date.]

DEAR SIR — You may remember I have formerly talked with you about a Military Dictionary. The eldest Mr Macbean, who was with Mr Chambers, has very good materials for such a work, which I have seen, and will do it at a very low rate.[a] I think the terms of War and Navigation might be comprised, with good explanations, in one 8vo. Pica, which he is willing to do for twelve shillings a sheet, to be made up a guinea at the second impression. If you think on it, I will wait on you with him. I am, Sir,

Your humble servant,

SAM. JOHNSON.

Pray lend me Topsel on Animals.

I must not omit to mention, that this Mr Macbean was a native of Scotland.

In the *Gentleman's Magazine* of this year, Johnson gave a Life of Father Paul;* and he wrote the Preface to the Volume,[†] which, though prefixed to it when bound, is always published with the Appendix, and is therefore the last composition belonging to it. The ability and nice adaptation with which he could draw up a prefatory address, was one of his peculiar excellencies.

It appears too, that he paid a friendly attention to Mrs Elizabeth Carter; for, in a letter from Mr Cave to Dr Birch, November 28, this year, I find 'Mr Johnson advises Miss C. to undertake a translation of *Boethius de Cons.* because there is prose and verse, and to put her name to it when published.' This advice was not followed, probably from an apprehension that the work was not sufficiently popular for an extensive sale. How well Johnson himself could have executed a translation of this philosophical poet, we may judge from a specimen which he has given in the *Rambler*:[1]

> *O qui perpetua mundum ratione gubernas,*
> *Terrarum caelique sator! . . .*
> *Disjice terrenae nubulas et pondera molis,*
> *Atque tuo splendore mica! Tu namque serenum,*
> *Tu requies tranquilla piis. Te cernere finis,*
> *Principium, vector, dux, semita, terminus, idem.*

> O THOU whose power o'er moving worlds presides,
> Whose voice created, and whose wisdom guides,
> On darkling man in pure effulgence shine,
> And cheer the clouded mind with light divine.
> 'Tis thine alone to calm the pious breast,
> With silent confidence and holy rest;
> From thee, great GOD! we spring, to thee we tend,
> Path, motive, guide, original, and end!'

[a] This book was published.

[1] Motto No. 7.

In 1739, beside the assistance which he gave to the Parliamentary Debates, his writings in the *Gentleman's Magazine* were, 'The Life of Boerhaave',* in which it is to be observed, that he discovers that love of chemistry which never forsook him; 'An Appeal to the Public in behalf of the Editor'; † 'An address to the Reader';† 'An epigram both in Greek and Latin to Eliza',* and also English verses to her;* and, 'A Greek Epigram to Dr Birch'.* It has been erroneously supposed, that an Essay published in that Magazine this year, entitled 'The Apotheosis of Milton', was written by Johnson; and on that supposition it has been improperly inserted in the edition of his works by the booksellers, after his decease. Were there no positive testimony as to this point, the style of the performance, and the name of Shakspeare not being mentioned in an Essay professedly reviewing the principal English poets, would ascertain it not to be the production of Johnson. But there is here no occasion to resort to internal evidence; for my Lord Bishop of Carlisle has assured me, that it was written by Guthrie. His separate publications were, 'A Complete Vindication of the Licensers of the Stage, from the malicious and scandalous Aspersions of Mr Brooke, Author of Gustavus Vasa',* being an ironical Attack upon them for their Suppression of that Tragedy; and 'Marmor Norfolciense; or an Essay on an ancient prophetical Inscription in monkish Rhyme, lately discovered near Lynne in Norfolk, by PROBUS BRITANNICUS'.* In this performance, he, in a feigned inscription, supposed to have been found in Norfolk, the county of Sir Robert Walpole, then the obnoxious prime minister of this country, inveighs against the Brunswick succession, and the measures of government consequent upon it. To this supposed prophecy he added a Commentary, making each expression apply to the times, with warm Anti-Hanoverian zeal.

This anonymous pamphlet, I believe, did not make so much noise as was expected, and, therefore, had not a very extensive circulation. Sir John Hawkins relates, that 'warrants were issued, and messengers employed to apprehend the author; who, though he had forborne to subscribe his name to the pamphlet, the vigilance of those in pursuit of him had discovered'; and we are informed, that he lay concealed in Lambeth-marsh till the scent after him grew cold. This, however, is altogether without foundation; for Mr Steele, one of the Secretaries of the Treasury, who, amidst a variety of important business, politely obliged me with his attention to my inquiry, informs me, that 'he directed every possible search to be made in the records of the Treasury and Secretary of State's Office, but could find no trace whatever of any warrant having been issued to apprehend the author of this pamphlet.'

'Marmor Norfolciense' became exceedingly scarce, so that I, for many years, endeavoured in vain to procure a copy of it. At last I was indebted to the malice of one of Johnson's numerous petty adversaries, who, in 1775, published a new edition of it, 'with Notes and a Dedication to SAMUEL JOHNSON, LL.D. by TRIBUNUS'; in which some puny scribbler invidiously attempted to found upon it a charge of inconsistency against its author, because he had accepted of a pension from his present Majesty, and had written in support of the measures of government. As a mortification to such impotent malice, of which there are so many instances towards men of eminence, I am happy to relate, that this *telum imbelle* did not reach its exalted object, till about a year after it thus appeared, when I mentioned it to him, supposing that he knew of the re-publication. To my surprise, he had not yet heard of it. He requested me to go directly and get it for him, which I did. He looked at it and laughed, and seemed to be much diverted with the feeble efforts of his unknown adversary, who, I hope, is alive to read this account. 'Now (said he) here is somebody who thinks he has vexed me sadly; yet, if it had not been for you, you rogue, I should probably never have seen it.'

As Mr Pope's note concerning Johnson, alluded to in a former page, refers both to his *London*, and his 'Marmor Norfolciense', I have deferred inserting it till now. I am indebted for it to Dr Percy, the Bishop of Dromore, as presented to his Lordship by Sir Joshua Reynolds, to whom it was given by the son of Mr Richardson the painter, the person to whom it is addressed. I have transcribed it with minute exactness, that the peculiar mode of writing, and imperfect spelling of that celebrated poet, may be exhibited to the curious in literature. It justifies Swift's epithet of 'paper-sparing Pope', for it is written on a slip no larger than a common message-card, and was sent to Mr Richardson, along with the Imitation of Juvenal.

> This is imitated by one Johnson who put in for a Public School in Shropshire,[1] but was Disappointed. He has an Infirmity of the convulsive kind, that attacks him sometimes, so as to make Him a sad Spectacle. Mr P. from the Merit of This Work which was all the knowledge he had of Him endeavour'd to serve Him without his own application; & wrote to my L^d. gore, but he did not succeed. Mr Johnson publish'd afterw^{ds}. another Poem in Latin with Notes the whole very Humerous call'd the Norfolk Prophecy.   P.

Johnson had been told of this note by Pope; and Sir Joshua Reynolds informed him of the compliment which it contained, but, from delicacy, avoided showing him the paper itself. When Sir Joshua observed to Johnson that he seemed very desirous to see Pope's note, he answered, 'Who would not be proud to have such a man as Pope so solicitous in inquiring about him?'

The infirmity to which Mr Pope alludes, appeared to me also, as I have elsewhere[2] observed, to be of the convulsive kind, and of the nature of that distemper called St Vitus's dance; and in this opinion I am confirmed by the description which Sydenham gives of that disease. 'This disorder is a kind of convulsion. It manifests itself by halting or unsteadiness of one of the legs, which the patient draws after him like an idiot. If the hand of the same side be applied to the breast, or any other part of the body, he cannot keep it a moment in the same posture, but it will be drawn into a different one by a

---

1 See note, p. 59.
2 *Journal of a Tour to the Hebrides*, 3d edit. p. 8.

convulsion, notwithstanding all his efforts to the contrary.' Sir Joshua Reynolds, however, is of a different opinion, and has favoured me with the following paper.

> Those motions or tricks of Dr Johnson are improperly called convulsions. He could sit motionless, when he was told so to do, as well as any other man; my opinion is, that it proceeded from a habit he had indulged himself in, of accompanying his thoughts with certain untoward actions, and those actions always appeared to me as if they were meant to reprobate some part of his past conduct. Whenever he was not engaged in conversation, such thoughts were sure to rush into his mind; and, for this reason, any company, any employment whatever, he preferred to being alone. The great business of his life (he said) was to escape from himself; this disposition he considered as the disease of his mind, which nothing cured but company.

> One instance of his absence and particularity, as it is characteristic of the man, may be worth relating. When he and I took a journey together into the West, we visited the late Mr Banks, of Dorsetshire; the conversation turning upon pictures, which Johnson could not well see, he retired to a corner of the room, stretching out his right leg as far as he could reach before him, then bringing up his left leg, and stretching his right still further on. The old gentleman observing him, went up to him, and in a very courteous manner assured him, that though it was not a new house, the flooring was perfectly safe. The Doctor started from his reverie, like a person waked out of his sleep, but spoke not a word.

While we are on this subject, my readers may not be displeased with another anecdote, communicated to me by the same friend, from the relation of Mr Hogarth.

Johnson used to be a pretty frequent visitor at the house of Mr Richardson, author of *Clarissa*, and other novels of extensive reputation. Mr Hogarth came one day to see Richardson, soon after the execution of Dr Cameron, for having taken arms for the house of Stuart in 1745–6; and being a warm partisan of George the Second, he observed to Richardson, that certainly there must have been some very unfavourable circumstances lately discovered in this particular case, which had induced the King to approve of an execution for rebellion so long after the time when it was committed, as this had the appearance of putting a man to death in cold blood,[1] and was very unlike his

---

1 Impartial posterity may, perhaps, be as little inclined as Dr Johnson was to justify the uncommon rigour exercised in the case of Dr Archibald Cameron. He was an amiable and truly honest man and his offence was owing to a generous, though mistaken principle of duty. Being obliged, after 1746, to give up his profession as a physician, and go into foreign parts, he was honoured with the rank of Colonel, both in the French and Spanish service. He was a son of the ancient and respectable family of Cameron, of Lochiel; and his brother, who was the Chief of that brave clan,

Majesty's usual clemency. While he was talking, he perceived a person standing at a window in the room, shaking his head, and rolling himself about in a strange ridiculous manner. He concluded that he was an idiot, whom his relations had put under the care of Mr Richardson, as a very good man. To his great surprise, however, this figure stalked forwards to where he and Mr Richardson were sitting, and all at once took up the argument, and burst out into an invective against George the Second, as one, who, upon all occasions, was unrelenting and barbarous; mentioning many instances, particularly, that when an officer of high rank had been acquitted by a Court Martial, George the Second had, with his own hand, struck his name off the list. In short, he displayed such a power of eloquence, that Hogarth looked at him with astonishment, and actually imagined that this idiot had been at the moment inspired. Neither Hogarth nor Johnson were made known to each other at this interview.

In 1740 he wrote for the *Gentleman's Magazine* the 'Preface',† 'Life of Sir Francis Drake',* and the first parts of those of 'Admiral Blake',* and of 'Philip Baretier',* both which he finished the year after. He also wrote an 'Essay on Epitaphs',† and an 'Epitaph on Philips, a Musician',* which was afterwards published with some other pieces of his, in Mrs Williams's *Miscellanies*. This Epitaph is so exquisitely beautiful, that I remember even Lord Kames, strangely prejudiced as he was against Dr Johnson, was compelled to allow it very high praise. It has been ascribed to Mr Garrick, from its appearing at first with the signature G; but I have heard Mr Garrick declare, that it was written by Dr Johnson, and give the following account of the manner in which it was composed. Johnson and he were sitting together; when, amongst other things, Garrick repeated an Epitaph upon this Philips by a Dr Wilkes, in these words:

> Exalted soul! whose harmony could please
> The love-sick virgin, and the gouty ease;
> Could jarring discord, like Amphion, move
> To beauteous order and harmonious love;
> Rest here in peace, till angels bid thee rise,
> And meet thy blessed Saviour in the skies.

Johnson shook his head at these common-place funereal lines, and said to Garrick, 'I think, Davy, I can make a better.' Then, stirring about his tea for a little while, in a state of meditation, he almost extempore produced the following verses:

---

distinguished himself by moderation and humanity, while the Highland army marched victorious through Scotland. It is remarkable of this Chief, that though he had earnestly remonstrated against the attempt as hopeless, he was of too heroic a spirit not to venture his life and fortune in the cause, when personally asked by him whom he thought his Prince.

> Philips, whose touch harmonious could remove
> The pangs of guilty power or hapless love;
> Rest here, distress'd by poverty no more,
> Here find that calm thou gav'st so oft before:
> Sleep, undisturb'd, within this peaceful shrine,
> Till angels wake thee with a note like thine!

At the same time that Mr Garrick favoured me with this anecdote, he repeated a very pointed Epigram by Johnson, on George the Second and Colley Cibber, which has never yet appeared, and of which I know not the exact date. Dr Johnson afterwards gave it to me himself.

> Augustus still survives in Maro's strain,
> And Spenser's verse prolongs Eliza's reign;
> Great George's acts let tuneful Cibber sing;
> For Nature form'd the Poet for the King.

In 1741 he wrote for the *Gentleman's Magazine* 'the Preface',[†] 'Conclusion of his Lives of Drake and Baretier',* 'A free Translation of the Jests of Hierocles, with an Introduction'; [†] and, I think, the following pieces: 'Debate on the Proposal of Parliament to Cromwell, to assume the Title of King, abridged, methodised, and digested';[†] 'Translation of Abbé Guyon's Dissertation on the Amazons';[†] 'Translation of Fontenelle's Panegyric on Dr Morin'.[†] Two notes upon this appear to me undoubtedly his. He this year, and the two following, wrote the Parliamentary Debates. He told me himself, that he was the sole composer of them for those three years only. He was not, however, precisely exact in his statement, which he mentioned from hasty recollection; for it is sufficiently evident, that his composition of them began November 19, 1740, and ended February 23, 1742–3.

It appears from some of Cave's letters to Dr Birch, that Cave had better assistance for that branch of his Magazine, than has been generally supposed; and that he was indefatigable in getting it made as perfect as he could.

Thus, 21st July, 1735, 'I trouble you with the enclosed, because you said you could easily correct what is herein given for Lord C—ld's speech. I beg you will do so as soon as you can for me, because the month is far advanced.'

And, 15th July, 1737. 'As you remember the Debates so far as to perceive the speeches already printed are not exact, I beg the favour that you will peruse the enclosed, and, in the best manner your memory will serve, correct the mistaken passages, or add anything that is omitted. I should be very glad to have something of the Duke of N—le's speech, which would be particularly of service.

'A gentleman has Lord Bathurst's speech to add something to.'

And, July 3, 1744, 'You will see what stupid, low, abominable stuff is put[1]

---

1 I suppose in another compilation of the same kind.

upon your noble and learned friend's[1] character, such as I should quite reject, and endeavour to do something better towards doing justice to the character. But as I cannot expect to attain my desires in that respect, it would be a great satisfaction to me, as well as an honour to our work, to have the favour of the genuine speech. It is a method that several have been pleased to take, as I could show, but I think myself under a restraint. I shall say so far, that I have had some by a third hand, which I understood well enough to come from the first; others by penny-post, and others by the speakers themselves, who have been pleased to visit St John's Gate, and show particular marks of their being pleased.'[2]

There is no reason, I believe, to doubt the veracity of Cave. It is, however, remarkable, that none of these letters are in the years during which Johnson alone furnished the Debates, and one of them is in the very year after he ceased from that labour. Johnson told me, that as soon as he found that the speeches were thought genuine, he determined that he would write no more of them, for 'he would not be accessary to the propagation of falsehood.' And such was the tenderness of his conscience, that a short time before his death he expressed a regret for his having been the author of fictions, which had passed for realities.

He nevertheless agreed with me in thinking, that the Debates which he had framed were to be valued as Orations upon questions of public importance. They have accordingly been collected in volumes, properly arranged, and recommended to the notice of parliamentary speakers by a Preface, written by no inferior hand.[3] I must, however, observe, that although there is in those Debates a wonderful store of political information, and very powerful elo-quence, I cannot agree that they exhibit the manner of each particular speaker, as Sir John Hawkins seems to think. But indeed, what opinion can we have of his judgement, and taste in public speaking, who presumes to give, as the characteristics of two celebrated orators, 'the deep-mouthed rancour of Pulteney, and the yelping pertinacity of Pitt'.[4]

This year I find that his tragedy of *Irene* had been for some time ready for the stage, and that his necessities made him desirous of getting as much as he could for it, without delay; for there is the following letter from Mr Cave to Dr Birch, in the same volume of manuscripts in the British Museum from whence I copied those above quoted. They were most obligingly pointed out to me by Sir William Musgrave, one of the Curators of that noble repository.

---

1 Doubtless, Lord Hardwick.
2 Birch's MSS. in the British Museum, 4302.
3 I am well assured, that the editor is Mr George Chalmers, whose commercial works are well known and esteemed.
4 Hawkins's Life of Johnson, p. 100.

Sept. 9, 1741.

I have put Mr Johnson's play into Mr Gray's[1] hands, in order to sell it to him, if he is inclined to buy it; but I doubt whether he will or not. He would dispose of the copy, and whatever advantage may be made by acting it. Would your society,[2] or any gentleman or body of men that you know, take such a bargain? He and I are very unfit to deal with theatrical persons. Fleetwood was to have acted it last season, but Johnson's diffidence or [3] prevented it.

I have already mentioned that *Irene* was not brought into public notice till Garrick was manager of Drury-lane theatre.

In 1742 he wrote for the *Gentleman's Magazine* the 'Preface',[†] the 'Parliamentary Debates,'[*] 'Essay on the Account of the Conduct of the Duchess of Marlborough',[*] then the popular topic of conversation. This Essay is a short but masterly performance. We find him in No. 13 of his *Rambler*, censuring a profligate sentiment in that 'Account'; and again insisting upon it strenuously in conversation.[4] 'An Account of the Life of Peter Burman',[*] I believe chiefly taken from a foreign publication; as, indeed, he could not himself know much about Burman; 'Additions to his Life of Baretier';[*] 'The Life of Sydenham',[*] afterwards prefixed to Dr Swan's edition of his works; 'Proposals for printing Bibliotheca Harleiana, or a Catalogue of the Library of the Earl of Oxford'.[*] His account of that celebrated collection of books, in which he displays the importance to literature, of what the French call a *catalogue raisonnée*, when the subjects of it are extensive and various, and it is executed with ability, cannot fail to impress all his readers with admiration of his philological attainments. It was afterwards prefixed to the first volume of the Catalogue, in which the Latin accounts of books were written by him. He was employed in this business by Mr Thomas Osborne the bookseller, who purchased the library for £13,000, a sum, which Mr Oldys says, in one of his manuscripts, was not more than the binding of the books had cost; yet, as Dr Johnson assured me, the slowness of the sale was such, that there was not much gained by it. It has been confidently related, with many embellishments, that Johnson one day knocked Osborne down in his shop, with a folio, and put his foot upon his neck. The simple truth I had from Johnson himself. 'Sir, he was impertinent to me, and I beat him. But it was not in his shop: it was in my own chamber.'

---

1 A bookseller of London.

2 It is strange, that a printer who knew so much as Cave, should conceive so ludicrous a fancy as that the Royal Society would purchase a Play.[a]

3 There is no erasure here, but a mere blank; to fill up which may be an exercise for ingenious conjecture.

4 *Journal of a Tour to the Hebrides*, 3d edit. p. 167.

[a] Delete note 2, and read as follows: Not the Royal Society, but the Society for the encouragement of learning, of which Dr Birch was a leading member. Their object was, to assist authors in printing expensive works. It existed from about 1735 to 1746, when, having incurred a considerable debt, it was dissolved.

A very diligent observer may trace him where we should not easily suppose him to be found. I have no doubt that he wrote the little abridgement entitled 'Foreign History', in the *Magazine* for December. To prove it, I shall quote the introduction. 'As this is that season of the year in which Nature may be said to command a suspension of hostilities, and which seems intended, by putting a short stop to violence and slaughter, to afford time for malice to relent, and animosity to subside; we can scarce expect any other accounts than of plans, negotiations and treaties, of proposals for peace, and preparations for war.' As also this passage: 'Let those who despise the capacity of the Swiss, tell us by what wonderful policy, or by what happy conciliation of interests, it is brought to pass, that in a body made up of different communities and different religions, there should be no civil commotions, though the people are so warlike, that to nominate and raise an army is the same.'

I am obliged to Mr Astle for his ready permission to copy the two following letters, of which the originals are in his possession. Their contents show that they were written about this time, and that Johnson was now engaged in preparing an historical account of the British Parliament.

To Mr CAVE.

[No date.]

SIR – I believe I am going to write a long letter, and have therefore taken a whole sheet of paper. The first thing to be written about is our historical design.

You mentioned the proposal of printing in numbers, as an alteration in the scheme, but I believe you mistook, some way or other, my meaning; I had no other view than that you might rather print too many of five sheets, than of five and thirty.

With regard to what I shall say on the manner of proceeding, I would have it understood as wholly indifferent to me, and my opinion only, not my resolution. *Emptoris sit eligere.*

I think the insertion of the exact dates of the most important events in the margin, or of so many events as may enable the reader to regulate the order of facts with sufficient exactness, the proper medium between a journal which has regard only to time, and a history which ranges facts according to their dependence on each other, and postpones or anticipates according to the convenience of narration. I think the work ought to partake of the spirit of history, which is contrary to minute exactness, and of the regularity of a journal, which is inconsistent with spirit. For this reason, I neither admit numbers or dates, nor reject them.

I am of your opinion with regard to placing most of the resolutions, &c. in the margin, and think we shall give the most complete account of parliamentary proceedings that can be contrived. The naked papers, without an historical treatise interwoven, require some other book to make them understood. I will date the succeeding facts with some exactness, but I think in the margin. You told me on Saturday that I had received money on this work, and found set down £13. 2s. 6d. reckoning the half guinea of last Saturday. As you hinted to me that you had many calls tor money, I would not press you too hard, and therefore shall desire only, as I send it in, two guineas for a sheet of copy, the rest you may pay me when it may be more convenient; and even by this sheet-payment I shall, for some time, be very expensive.

The Life of Savage I am ready to go upon; and in Great Primer, and Pica notes, I reckon on sending in half a sheet a day; but the money for that shall likewise lye by in your hands till it is done. With the debates, shall I not have business enough? if I had but good pens.

Towards Mr Savage's Life what more have you got? I would willingly have his trial, &c. and know whether his defence be at Bristol; and would have his collection of poems, on account of the preface – The Plain Dealer, – all the magazines that have anything of his, or relating to him.

I thought my letter would be long, but it is now ended; and I am, Sir, Your's, &c.

SAM. JOHNSON.

The boy found me writing this almost in the dark, when I could not quite easily read yours.

I have read the Italian – nothing in it is well.

I had no notion of having any thing for the inscription. I hope you don't think I kept it to extort a price. I could think of nothing, till to day. If you could spare me another guinea for the history, I should take it very kindly, to night; but if you do not, I shall not think it an injury. I am almost well again.

To Mr CAVE.

SIR – You did not tell me your determination about the Soldier's Letter,[1] which I am confident was never printed. I think it will not do by itself, or in any other place, so well as the Mag. Extraordinary. If you will have it at all, I believe you do not think I set it high, and I will be glad if what you give, you will give quickly.

You need not be in care about something to print, for I have got the State Trials, and shall extract Layer, Atterbury, and Macclesfield from them, and shall bring them to you in a fortnight; after which I will try to get the South Sea Report.

[No date, nor signature.]

I would also ascribe to him an 'Essay on the Description of China, from the French of Du Halde'.[†]

His writings in the Gentleman's Magazine in 1743, are, the Preface,[†] the Parliamentary Debates,[†] 'Considerations on the Dispute between Crousaz and

1 I have not discovered what this was.

Warburton, on Pope's *Essay on Man*',[†] in which, while he defends Crousaz, he shows an admirable metaphysical acuteness and temperance in controversy; '*Ad Lauram parituram Epigramma*';*[1] and, 'A Latin Translation of Pope's Verses on his Grotto';* and, as he could employ his pen with equal success upon a small matter as a great, I suppose him to be the author of an advertisement for Osborn, concerning the great Harleian Catalogue.

But I should think myself much wanting, both to my illustrious friend and my readers, did I not introduce here, with more than ordinary respect, an exquisitely beautiful Ode, which has not been inserted in any of the collections of Johnson's poetry, written by him at a very early period, as Mr Hector informs me, and inserted in the *Gentleman's Magazine* of this year.

Friendship, an Ode.*

Friendship, peculiar boon of heaven,
    The noble mind's delight and pride,
To men and angels only given,
    To all the lower world deny'd.

While love, unknown among the blest,
    Parent of thousand wild desires,
The savage and the human breast
    Torments alike with raging fires.

With bright, but oft destructive, gleam,
    Alike o'er all his lightnings fly;
Thy lambent glories only beam
    Around the fav'rites of the sky.

Thy gentle flows of guiltless joys
    On fools and villains ne'er descend;
In vain for thee the tyrant sighs,
    And hugs a flatterer for a friend.

Directress of the brave and just,
    O guide us through life's darksome way!
And let the tortures of mistrust
    On selfish bosoms only prey.

1   *Angliacas inter pulcherrima Laura puellas*
                Mox uteri pondus depositura grave,
            Adsit, Laura, tibi facilis Lucina dolenti,
                Neve tibi noceat praenituisse Deae.

Mr Hector was present when this Epigram was made *impromptu*. The first line was proposed by Dr James, and Johnson was called upon by the company to finish it, which he instantly did.

> Nor shall thine ardours cease to glow,
>   When souls to blissful climes remove:
> What rais'd our virtue here below,
>   Shall aid our happiness above.

Johnson had now an opportunity of obliging his schoolfellow Dr James, of whom he once observed, 'no man brings more mind to his profession.' James published this year his *Medicinal Dictionary*, in three volumes folio. Johnson, as I understood from him, had written, or assisted in writing, the proposals for this work; and being very fond of the study of physic, in which James was his master, he furnished some of the articles. He, however, certainly wrote for it the Dedication to Dr Mead,[†] which is conceived with great address, to conciliate the patronage of that very eminent man.[1]

It has been circulated, I know not with what authenticity, that Johnson considered Dr Birch as a dull writer, and said of him, 'Tom Birch is as brisk as a bee in conversation; but no sooner does he take a pen in his hand, than it becomes a torpedo to him, and benumbs all his faculties.' That the literature of this country is much indebted to Birch's activity and diligence, must certainly be acknowledged. We have seen that Johnson honoured him with a Greek Epigram; and his correspondence with him, during many years, proves that he had no mean opinion of him.

To Dr BIRCH.

Thursday, Sep. 29, 1743.

SIR – I hope you will excuse me for troubling you on an occasion on which I know not whom else I can apply to; I am at a loss for the Lives and Characters of Earl Stanhope, the two Craggs, and the Minister Sunderland; and beg that you will inform [me] where I may find them, and send any pamphlets, &c., relating to them to Mr Cave, to be perused for a few days by, Sir,

Your most humble servant,

SAM. JOHNSON.

1   To Dr MEAD.

SIR – That the *Medicinal Dictionary* is dedicated to you, is to be imputed only to your reputation for superior skill in those sciences which I have endeavoured to explain and facilitate: and you are, therefore, to consider this address, if it be agreeable to you, as one of the rewards of merit; and, if otherwise, as one of the inconveniencies of eminence.

   However you shall receive it, my design cannot be disappointed; because this public appeal to your judgement will show that I do not found my hopes of approbation upon the ignorance of my readers, and that I fear his censure least, whose knowledge is most extensive.

   I am, Sir,

   Your most obedient humble servant,

R. JAMES.

His circumstances were at this time much embarrassed; yet his affection for his mother was so warm, and so liberal, that he took upon himself a debt of hers, which, though small in itself, was then considerable to him. This appears from the following letter which he wrote to Mr Levett, of Lichfield, the original of which now lies before me.

To Mr LEVETT, in Lichfield.

December 1, 1743.

SIR – I am extremely sorry that we have encroached so much upon your forbearance with respect to the interest, which a great perplexity of affairs hindered me from thinking of with that attention that I ought, and which I am not immediately able to remit to you, but will pay it (I think twelve pounds), in two months. I look upon this, and on the future interest of that mortgage, as my own debt; and beg that you will be pleased to give me directions how to pay it, and not mention it to my dear mother. If it be necessary to pay this in less time, I believe I can do it; but I take two months for certainty, and beg an answer whether you can allow me so much time. I think myself very much obliged to your forbearance, and shall esteem it a great happiness to be able to serve you. I have great opportunities of dispersing any thing that you may think it proper to make public. I will give a note for the money, payable at the time mentioned, to any one here that you shall appoint. I am, Sir,

Your most obedient,

And most humble servant,

SAM. JOHNSON,

At Mr Osborne's, bookseller, in Gray's Inn.

It does not appear that he wrote any thing in 1744 for the *Gentleman's Magazine*, but the Preface.† His life of Baretier was now republished in a pamphlet by itself. But he produced one work this year, fully sufficient to maintain the high reputation which he had acquired. This was *The Life of Richard Savage*;* a man, of whom it is difficult to speak impartially, without wondering that he was for some time the intimate companion of Johnson; for his character was marked by profligacy, insolence, and ingratitude:[1] yet, as he undoubtedly

---

1 As a specimen of his temper, I insert the following letter from him to a noble Lord, to whom he was under great obligations, but who, on account of his bad conduct, was obliged to discard him. The original is in the hands of one of his Majesty's Counsel learned in the law:

Right Honourable BRUTE, and BOOBY – I find you want (as Mr — is pleased to hint,) to swear away my life, that is, the life of your creditor, because he asks you for a debt. The public shall soon be acquainted with this, to judge whether you are not fitter to be an Irish Evidence, than to be an Irish Peer. I defy and despise you. I am, Your determined adversary,

R. S.

had a warm and vigorous, though unregulated mind, had seen life in all its varieties, and been much in the company of the statesmen and wits of his time, he could communicate to Johnson an abundant supply of such materials as his philosophical curiosity most eagerly desired; and as Savage's misfortunes and misconduct had reduced him to the lowest state of wretchedness as a writer for bread, his visits to St John's Gate naturally brought Johnson and him together.[1]

It is melancholy to reflect, that Johnson and Savage were sometimes in such extreme indigence, that they could not pay for a lodging; so that they have wandered together whole nights in the streets. Yet in these almost incredible scenes of distress, we may suppose that Savage mentioned many of the anecdotes with which Johnson afterwards enriched the life of his unhappy companion, and those of other Poets.

He mentioned to Sir Joshua Reynolds, that one night in particular, when Savage and he walked round St James's-square for want of a lodging, they were not at all depressed by their situation, but in high spirits and brimful of patriotism, traversed the square for several hours, inveighed against the minister, and 'resolved they would *stand by their country*.'

I am afraid, however, that by associating with Savage, who was habituated to the dissipation and licentiousness of the Town, Johnson, though his good principles remained steady, did not entirely preserve that conduct, for which, in days of greater simplicity, he was remarked by his friend Mr Hector; but was imperceptibly led into some indulgences which occasioned much distress to his virtuous mind.

That Johnson was anxious that an authentic and favourable account of his extraordinary friend should first get possession of the public attention, is evident from a letter which he wrote in the *Gentleman's Magazine* for August of the year preceding its publication.

---

1 Sir John Hawkins gives the world to understand, that Johnson, 'being an admirer of genteel manners, was captivated by the address and demeanour of Savage, who as to his exterior, was, to a remarkable degree, accomplished.' Hawkins's *Life*, p. 52. But Sir John's notion of gentility must appear somewhat ludicrous, from his stating the following circumstance as presumptive evidence that Savage was a good swordsman: 'That he understood the exercise of a gentleman's weapon, may be inferred from the use made of it in that rash encounter which is related in his life.' The dexterity here alluded to was, that Savage, in a nocturnal fit of drunkenness, stabbed a man at a coffee-house, and killed him; for which he was tried at the Old-Bailey, and found guilty of murder.

Johnson, indeed, describes him as having 'a grave and manly deportment, a solemn dignity of mien; but which, upon a nearer acquaintance, softened into an engaging easiness of manners.' How highly Johnson admired him for that knowledge which he himself so much cultivated, and what kindness he entertained for him, appears from the following lines in the *Gentleman's Magazine* for April, 1738, which I am assured were written by Johnson:

Ad Ricardum Savage.
Humani studium generis cui pectore fervet,
    O colat humanum te foveatque genus.

Mr URBAN – As your collections show how often you have owed the ornaments of your poetical pages to the correspondence of the unfortunate and ingenious Mr Savage, I doubt not but you have so much regard to his memory as to encourage any design that may have a tendency to the preservation of it from insults or calumnies; and, therefore, with some degree of assurance, entreat you to inform the public, that his life will speedily be published by a person who was favoured with his confidence, and received from himself an account of most of the transactions which he proposes to mention, to the time of his retirement to Swansea in Wales.

From that period, to his death in the prison of Bristol, the account will be continued from materials still less liable to objection; his own letters, and those of his friends, some of which will be inserted in the work, and abstracts of others subjoined in the margin.

It may be reasonably imagined, that others may have the same design; but as it is not credible that they can obtain the same materials, it must be expected they will supply from invention the wants of intelligence; and that under the title of *The Life of Savage*, they will publish only a novel, filled with romantic adventures, and imaginary amours. You may therefore, perhaps, gratify the lovers of truth and wit, by giving me leave to inform them in your magazine, that my account will be published in 8vo. by Mr Roberts, in Warwick-lane.

[No Signature.]

In February, 1744, it accordingly came forth from the shop of Roberts, between whom and Johnson I have not traced any connection, except the casual one of this publication. In this work, although it must be allowed that its moral is the reverse of – *Respicere exemplar vitae morumque jubebo*, a very useful lesson is inculcated, to guard men of warm passions from a too free indulgence of them; and the various incidents are related in so clear and animated a manner, and illuminated throughout with so much philosophy, that it is one of the most interesting narratives in the English language. Sir Joshua Reynolds told me, that upon his return from Italy he met with it in Devonshire, knowing nothing of its author, and began to read it while he was standing with his arm leaning against a chimney-piece. It seized his attention so strongly, that, not being able to lay down the book till he had finished it, when he attempted to move, he found his arm totally benumbed. The rapidity with which this work was composed, is a wonderful circumstance. Johnson has been heard to say, 'I wrote forty-eight of the printed octavo pages of the Life of Savage at a sitting; but then I sat up all night.'[1]

He exhibits the genius of Savage to the best advantage, in the specimens of his poetry which he has selected, some of which are of uncommon merit. We, indeed, occasionally find such vigour and such point, as might make us suppose that the generous aid of Johnson had been imparted to his friend. Mr Thomas Warton made this remark to me; and, in support of it, quoted from

1 *Journal of a Tour to the Hebrides*, 3d edit. p. 35.

the poem entitled 'The Bastard', a line in which the fancied superiority of one 'stamped in Nature's mint with ecstasy', is contrasted with a regular lawful descendant of some great and ancient family:

> No tenth transmitter of a foolish face.

but the fact is, that this poem was published some years before Johnson and Savage were acquainted.

It is remarkable, that in this biographical disquisition there appears a very strong symptom of Johnson's prejudice against players; a prejudice, which may be attributed to the following causes: first, the imperfection of his organs, which were so defective that he was not susceptible of the fine impressions which theatrical excellence produces upon the generality of mankind; secondly, the cold rejection of his tragedy; and, lastly, the brilliant success of Garrick, who had been his pupil, who had come to London at the same time with him, not in a much more prosperous state than himself, and whose talents he undoubtedly rated low, compared with his own. His being outstripped by his pupil in the race of immediate fame, as well as of fortune, probably made him feel some indignation, as thinking that whatever might be Garrick's merits in his art, the reward was too great when compared with what the most successful efforts of literary labour could attain. At all periods of his life Johnson used to talk contemptuously of players; but in this work he speaks of them with peculiar acrimony; for which, perhaps, there was formerly too much reason from the licentious and dissolute manners of those engaged in that profession. It is but justice to add, that in our own time such a change has taken place, that there is no longer room for such an unfavourable distinction.

His schoolfellow and friend, Dr Taylor, told me a pleasant anecdote of Johnson's triumphing over his pupil David Garrick. When that great actor had played some little time at Goodman's-fields, Johnson and Taylor went to see him perform, and afterwards passed the evening at a tavern with him and old Giffard. Johnson, who was ever depreciating stage-players, after censuring some mistakes in emphasis which Garrick had committed in the course of that night's acting, said, 'The players, Sir, have got a kind of rant, with which they run on, without any regard either to accent or emphasis.' Both Garrick and Giffard were offended at this sarcasm, and endeavoured to refute it; upon which Johnson rejoined, 'Well now, I'll give you something to speak, with which you are little acquainted, and then we shall see how just my observation is. That shall be the criterion. Let me hear you repeat the ninth Commandment, 'Thou shalt not bear false witness against thy neighbour.' Both tried at it, said Dr Taylor, and both mistook the emphasis, which should be upon *not* and *false witness*.[a] Johnson put them right, and enjoyed his victory with great glee.

[a] Add the following note: I suspect Dr Taylor was inaccurate in this statement. The emphasis should be equally upon *shalt* and *not*, as both concur to form the negative injunction; and *false witness*, like the other acts prohibited in the Decalogue, should not be marked by any peculiar emphasis, but only be distinctly enunciated.

His *Life of Savage* was no sooner published, than the following liberal praise was given to it, in *The Champion*, a periodical paper: 'This pamphlet is, without flattery to its author, as just and well written a piece as of its kind I ever saw; so that at the same time that it highly deserves, it certainly stands very little in need of this recommendation. As to the history of the unfortunate person, whose memoirs compose this work, it is certainly penned with equal accuracy and spirit, of which I am so much the better judge, as I know many of the facts mentioned to be strictly true, and very fairly related. Besides, it is not only the story of Mr Savage, but innumerable incidents relating to other persons, and other affairs, which renders this a very amusing, and, withal, a very instructive and valuable performance. The author's observations are short, significant, and just, as his narrative is remarkably smooth and well disposed. His reflections open to all the recesses of the human heart; and, in a word, a more just or pleasant, a more engaging or a more improving treatise, on all the excellencies and defects of human nature, is scarce to be found in our own, or, perhaps, any other language.'[a] This paper is well known to have been written by the celebrated Henry Fielding.[b] But, I suppose, Johnson was not informed of his being indebted to him for this civility; for if he had been apprised of that circumstance, as he was very sensible of praise, he probably would not have spoken with so little respect of Fielding, as we shall find he afterwards did.

Johnson's partiality for Savage made him entertain no doubt of his story, however extraordinary and improbable. It never occurred to him to question his being the son of the Countess of Macclesfield, of whose unrelenting barbarity he so loudly complained, and the particulars of which are related in so strong and affecting a manner in Johnson's life of him. Johnson was certainly well warranted in publishing his narrative, however offensive it might be to the Lady and her relations, because her alleged unnatural and cruel conduct to her son, and shameful avowal of guilt, were stated in a life of Savage now lying before me, which came out so early as 1727, and no attempt had been made to confute it, or to punish the author or printer as a libeller: but, for the honour of human nature, we should be glad to find the shocking tale not true; and, from a respectable gentleman[c] connected with the Lady's family, I have received such information and remarks, as joined to my own inquiries, will, I think, render it at least somewhat doubtful, especially when we consider that it must have originated from the person himself who went by the name of Richard Savage.

---

[a] Add the following note: This character of the Life of Savage was not written by Fielding, as was been supposed, but most probably by Ralph, who, as appears from the minutes of the Partners of 'The Champion,' in the possession of Mr Reed of Staple Inn, succeeded Fielding in his share of the paper, before the date of that eulogium.

[b] Delete 'This paper, &c.', to the end of the paragraph.

[c] Add the following note: The late Francis Cockayne Cust, Esq., one of his Majesty's Counsel.

If the maxim *falsum in uno, falsum in omnibus* were to be received without qualification, the credit of Savage's narrative, as conveyed to us, would be annihilated; for it contains some assertions which, beyond a question, are not true.

1. In order to induce a belief that Earl Rivers, on account of a criminal connection with whom, Lady Macclesfield is said to have been divorced from her husband, by Act of Parliament,[1] had a peculiar anxiety about the child which she bore to him, it is alleged, that his Lordship gave him his own name, and had it duly recorded in the register of St Andrews, Holborn. I have carefully inspected that register, but no such entry is to be found.

2. It is stated, that 'Lady Macclesfield having lived for some time upon very uneasy terms with her husband, thought a public confession of adultery the most obvious and expeditious method of obtaining her liberty'; and Johnson, assuming this to be true, stigmatises her with indignation, as 'the wretch who had, without scruple, proclaimed herself an adulteress'. But I have perused the Journals of both houses of Parliament at the period of her divorce, and there find it authentically ascertained, that so far from voluntarily submitting to the ignominious charge of adultery, she made a strenuous defence by her Counsel; the bill having been first moved 15th January, 1697, in the House of Lords, and proceeded on (with various applications for time to bring up witnesses at a distance, &c.) at intervals, till the 3rd of March, when it passed. It was brought to the Commons, by a message from the Lords, the 5th of March, proceeded on the 7th, 10th, 11th, 14th, and 15th, on which day, after a full examination of witnesses on both sides, and hearing of Counsel, it was reported without amendments, passed, and carried to the Lords.

That Lady Macclesfield was convicted of the crime of which she was accused, cannot be denied; but the question now is, whether the person calling himself Richard Savage was her son.

It has been said, that when Earl Rivers was dying, and anxious to provide for all his natural children, he was informed by Lady Macclesfield that her son by him was dead. Whether, then, shall we believe that this was a malignant lie, invented by a mother to prevent her own child from receiving the bounty of his father, which was accordingly the consequence, if the person whose life Johnson wrote, was her son; or shall we not rather believe that the person who then assumed the name of Richard Savage was an impostor, being in reality the son of the shoemaker, under whose wife's care Lady Macclesfield's child was placed; that after the death of the real Richard Savage, he attempted to personate him, and that the fraud being known to Lady Macclesfield, he was therefore repulsed by her with just resentment.

There is a strong circumstance in support of the last supposition, though it has been mentioned as an aggravation of Lady Macclesfield's unnatural conduct, and that is, her having prevented him from obtaining the benefit of a legacy left to him by Mrs Lloyd his godmother. For if there was such a legacy

1 1697.

left, his not being able to obtain payment of it, must be imputed to his consciousness that he was not the real person. The just inference should be, that by the death of Lady Macclesfield's child before its godmother, the legacy became lapsed, and therefore that Johnson's Richard Savage was an impostor. If he had a title to the legacy, he could not have found any difficulty in recovering it; for had the executors resisted his claim, the whole costs, as well as the legacy, must have been paid by them, if he had been the child to whom it was given.

The talents of Savage, and the mingled fire, rudeness, pride, meanness, and ferocity of his character,[1] concur in making it credible that he was fit to plan and carry on an ambitious and daring scheme of imposture, similar instances of which have not been wanting in higher spheres, in the history of different countries, and have had a considerable degree of success.

Yet, on the other hand, to the companion of Johnson (who through whatever medium he was conveyed into this world, be it ever so doubtful 'to whom related, or by whom begot', was unquestionably a man of no common endowments), we must allow the weight of general repute as to his *Status* or parentage, though illicit; and supposing him to be an impostor, it seems strange that Lord Tyrconnel, the nephew of Lady Macclesfield, should patronise him, and even admit him as a guest in his family.[2] Lastly, it must ever appear very suspicious, that three different accounts of the Life of Richard Savage, one published in *The Plain Dealer*, in 1724, another in 1727, and

---

1 Johnson's companion appears to have persuaded that lofty-minded man, that he resembled him in having a noble pride; for Johnson, after painting in strong colours the quarrel between Lord Tyrconnel and Savage, asserts that 'the spirit of Mr Savage, indeed, never suffered him to solicit a reconciliation; he returned reproach for reproach, and insult for insult.' But the respectable gentleman to whom I have alluded, has in his possession a letter from Savage, after Lord Tyrconnel had discarded him, addressed to the Reverend Mr Gilbert, his Lordship's Chaplain, in which he requests him, in the humblest manner, to represent his case to the Earl.[a]

[a] For Earl, read Viscount.

2 Trusting to Savage's information, Johnson represents this unhappy man's being received as a companion by Lord Tyrconnel, and pensioned by his Lordship, as if posterior to Savage's conviction and pardon. But I am assured, that Savage had received the voluntary bounty of Lord Tyrconnel, and had been dismissed by him long before the murder was committed, and that his Lordship was very instrumental in procuring Savage's pardon, by his intercession with the Queen, through Lady Hertford. If, therefore, he had been desirous of preventing any publication by Savage, he would have left him to his fate. Indeed I must observe, that although Johnson mentions that Lord Tyrconnel's patronage of Savage was 'upon his promise to lay aside his design of exposing the cruelty of his mother', the great biographer has forgotten that he himself has mentioned, that Savage's story had been told several years before in *The Plain Dealer*, from which he quotes this strong saying of the generous Sir Richard Steele, that 'the inhumanity of his mother had given him a right to find every good man his father.' At the same time it must be acknowledged, that Lady Macclesfield and her relations might still wish that her story should not be brought into more conspicuous notice by the satirical pen of Savage.

another by the powerful pen of Johnson, in 1744, and all of them while Lady Macclesfield was alive, should, notwithstanding the severe attacks upon her, have been suffered to pass without any public and effectual contradiction.

I have thus endeavoured to sum up the evidence upon the case, as fairly as I can; and the result seems to be, that the world must vibrate in a state of uncertainty as to what was the truth.

This digression, I trust, will not be censured, as it relates to a matter exceedingly curious, and very intimately connected with Johnson, both as a man and an author.[1]

He this year wrote the 'Preface to the *Harleian Miscellany*'.* The selection of the pamphlets of which it was composed was made by Mr Oldys, a man of eager curiosity and indefatigable diligence, who first exerted that spirit of inquiry into the literature of the old English writers, by which the works of our great dramatic poet have of late been so signally illustrated.

In 1745 he published a pamphlet entitled 'Miscellaneous Observations on the Tragedy of *Macbeth*, with Remarks on Sir T. H.'s (Sir Thomas Hanmer's) Edition of Shakspeare'.* To which he affixed, proposals for a new edition of that poet.

As we do not trace any thing else published by him during the course of this year, we may conjecture that he was occupied entirely with that work. But the little encouragement which was given by the public to his anonymous proposals for the execution of a task which Warburton was known to have undertaken, probably damped his ardour. His pamphlet, however, was highly esteemed, and was fortunate enough to obtain the approbation even of the supercilious Warburton himself, who, in the Preface to his Shakspeare published two years afterwards, thus mentioned it: 'As to all those things which have been published under the titles of *Essays, Remarks, Observations,* &c., on Shakspeare, if you except some critical notes on *Macbeth*, given as a specimen of a projected edition, and written, as appears, by a man of parts and genius, the rest are absolutely below a serious notice.'

Of this flattering distinction shown to him by Warburton, a very grateful remembrance was ever entertained by Johnson, who said, 'He praised me at a time when praise was of value to me.'

In 1746 it is probable that he was still employed upon his Shakspeare, which perhaps he laid aside for a time, upon account of the high expectations which

---

1 Miss Mason, after having forfeited the title of Lady Macclesfield by divorce, was married to Colonel Brett, and, it is said, was well known in all the polite circles. Colley Cibber, I am informed, had so high an opinion of her taste and judgement as to genteel life and manners, that he submitted every scene of his *Careless Husband*, to Mrs Brett's revisal and correction. Colonel Brett was reported to be too free in his gallantry with his Lady's maid. Mrs Brett came into a room one day in her own house, and found the Colonel and her maid both fast asleep in two chairs. She tied a white handkerchief round her husband's neck, which was a sufficient proof that she had discovered his intrigue; but she never at any time took notice of it to him. This incident, as I am told, gave occasion to the well-wrought scene of Sir Charles and Lady Easy and Edging.

were formed of Warburton's edition of that great poet. It is somewhat curious, that his literary career appears to have been almost totally suspended in the years 1745 and 1746, those years which were marked by a civil war in Great-Britain, when a rash attempt was made to restore the House of Stuart to the throne. That he had a tenderness for that unfortunate House, is well known; and some may fancifully imagine, that a sympathetic anxiety impeded the exertion of his intellectual powers: but I am inclined to think, that he was, during this time, sketching the outlines of his great philological work.

None of his letters during those years are extant, so far as I can discover. This is much to be regretted. It might afford some entertainment to see how he then expressed himself to his private friends, concerning state affairs. Dr Adams informs me, that 'at this time a favourite object which he had in contemplation was *The Life of Alfred*, in which, from the warmth with which he spoke about it, he would, I believe, had he been master of his own will, have engaged himself, rather than on any other subject.'

In 1747 it is supposed that the *Gentleman's Magazine* for May was enriched by him with five short poetical pieces, distinguished by three asterisks. The first is a translation, or rather a paraphrase, of a Latin Epitaph on Sir Thomas Hanmer. Whether the Latin was his, or not, I have never heard, though I should think it probably was, if it be certain that he wrote the English; as to which my only cause of doubt is, that his slighting character of Hanmer as an editor, in his 'Observations on Macbeth', is very different from that in the Epitaph. It may be said, that there is the same contrariety between the character in the Observations, and that in his own Preface to Shakspeare; but a considerable time elapsed between the one publication and the other, whereas the Observations and the Epitaph came close together. The others are, 'To Miss —, on her giving the Author a gold and silk net-work Purse of her own weaving'; 'Stella in Mourning', 'The Winter's Walk'; 'An Ode'; and, 'To Lyce, an elderly Lady'. I am not positive that all these were his productions; but as 'The Winter's Walk,' has never been controverted to be his, and all of them have the same mark, it is reasonable to conclude that they are all written by the same hand. Yet to the Ode, in which we find a passage very characteristic of him, being a learned description of the gout,

> Unhappy, whom to beds of pain
> Arthritic tyranny consigns;

there is the following note: 'The author being ill of the gout': but Johnson was not attacked with that distemper till at a very late period of his life. May not this, however, be a poetical fiction? Why may not a poet suppose himself to have the gout, as well as suppose himself to be in love, of which we have innumerable instances, and which has been admirably ridiculed by Johnson in his *Life of Cowley*? I have also some difficulty to believe that he could produce such a group of conceits as appear in the verses to Lyce, in which he claims for this ancient personage as good a right to be assimilated to *heaven*, as nymphs whom other poets have flattered; he therefore ironically ascribes to her the attributes of the sky, in such stanzas as this:

> Her teeth the *night* with *darkness* dies,
>   She's *starr'd* with pimples o'er;
> Her tongue like nimble *lightning* plies,
>   And can with *thunder* roar.

But as at a very advanced age he could condescend to trifle in *namby pamby* rhymes to please Mrs Thrale and her daughter, he may have, in his earlier years, composed such a piece as this.

It is remarkable, that in this first edition of 'The Winter's Walk', the concluding line is much more Johnsonian than it was afterwards printed; for in subsequent editions after praying Stella to 'snatch him to her arms' he says,

> And *shield* me from the *ills* of life.

Whereas in the first edition it is

> And *hide* me from the *sight* of life.

A horror at life in general is more consonant with Johnson's habitual gloomy cast of thought.

I have heard him repeat with great energy the following verses, which appeared in the *Gentleman's Magazine* for April this year; but I have no authority to say they were his own. Indeed one of the best critics of our age suggests to me, that the word *indifferently* being used in the sense of *without concern*, renders it improbable that they should have been his composition.

On Lord LOVAT's Execution.

> Pity'd by *gentle minds* KILMARNOCK died;
> The *brave*, BALMERINO, were on thy side;
> RADCLIFFE, unhappy in his crimes of youth,
> Steady in what he still mistook for truth,
> Beheld his death so decently unmoved,
> The *soft* lamented, and the *brave* approved.
> But LOVAT's fate indifferently we view,
> True to no *King*, to no *religion* true:
> No *fair* forgets the *ruin* he has done;
> No *child* laments the *tyrant* of his *son*;
> No *tory* pities, thinking what he was;
> No *whig* compassions, *for he left the cause*;
> The *brave* regret not, for he was not brave;
> The *honest* mourn not, knowing him a knave!'[1]

This year his old pupil and friend, David Garrick, having become joint patentee and manager of Drury-lane theatre, Johnson honoured his opening

---

1 These verses are somewhat too severe on the extraordinary person who is the chief figure in them, for he was undoubtedly brave. His pleasantry during his solemn trial

of it with a Prologue,* which for just and manly dramatic criticism, on the whole range of the English stage, as well as for poetical excellence, is unrivalled. Like the celebrated Epilogue to the *Distressed Mother*, it was, during the season, often called for by the audience. The most striking and brilliant passages of it have been so often repeated, and are so well recollected by all the lovers of the drama and of poetry, that it would be superfluous to point them out. In the *Gentleman's Magazine* for December this year, he inserted an 'Ode on Winter', which is, I think, an admirable specimen of his genius for lyric poetry.

But the year 1747 is distinguished as the epoch, when Johnson's arduous and important work, his DICTIONARY OF THE ENGLISH LANGUAGE, was announced to the world, by the publication of its Plan or *Prospectus*.

How long this immense undertaking had been the object of his contemplation, I do not know. I once asked him by what means he had attained to that astonishing knowledge of our language, by which he was enabled to realize a design of such extent, and accumulated difficulty. He told me, that 'it was not the effect of particular study; but that it had grown up in his mind insensibly.' I have been informed by Mr James Dodsley, that several years before this period, when Johnson was one day sitting in his brother Robert's shop, he heard his brother suggest to him, that a Dictionary of the English Language would be a work that would be well received by the public; that Johnson seemed at first to catch at the proposition, but, after a pause, said, in his abrupt decisive manner, 'I believe I shall not undertake it.' That he, however, had bestowed much thought upon the subject, before he published his 'Plan', is evident from the enlarged, clear, and accurate views which it exhibits; and we find him mentioning in that tract, that many of the writers whose testimonies were to be produced as authorities, were selected by Pope, which proves that he had been furnished, probably by Mr Robert Dodsley, with whatever hints that eminent poet had contributed towards a great literary project, that had been the subject of important consideration in a former reign.

The booksellers who contracted with Johnson, single and unaided, for the execution of a work, which in other countries has not been effected but by the co-operating exertions of many, were Mr Robert Dodsley, Mr Charles Hitch, Mr Andrew Millar, the two Messieurs Longman, and the two Messieurs Knapton. The price stipulated was fifteen hundred and seventy-five pounds.

(in which, by the way, I have heard Mr David Hume observe, that we have one of the very few speeches of Mr Murray, now Earl of Mansfield, authentically given) was very remarkable. When asked if he had any questions to put to Sir Everard Fawkener, who was one of the strongest witnesses against him, he answered, 'I only wish him joy of his young wife.' And after sentence of death in the horrible terms in cases of treason was pronounced upon him, and he was retiring from the bar, he said, 'Fare you well, my Lords, we shall not all meet again in one place.' He behaved with perfect composure at his execution, and called out '*Dulce et decorum est pro patria mori.*'

The 'Plan' was addressed to Philip Dormer, Earl of Chesterfield, then one of his Majesty's Principal Secretaries of State, a nobleman who was very ambitious of literary distinction, and who, upon being informed of the design, had expressed himself in terms very favourable to its success. There is, perhaps, in every thing of any consequence, a secret history which it would be amusing to know, could we have it authentically communicated. Johnson told me,[1] 'Sir, the way in which the Plan of my Dictionary came to be inscribed to Lord Chesterfield, was this: I had neglected to write it by the time appointed. Dodsley suggested a desire to have it addressed to Lord Chesterfield. I laid hold of this as a pretext for delay, that it might be better done, and let Dodsley have his desire. I said to my friend Dr Bathurst, "Now if any good comes of my addressing to Lord Chesterfield, it will be ascribed to deep policy, when, in fact, it was only a casual excuse for laziness." '

It is worthy of observation, that the 'Plan' has not only the substantial merit of comprehension, perspicuity, and precision, but that the language of it is unexceptionably excellent, it being altogether free from that inflation of style, and those uncommon but apt and energetic words, which in some of his writings have been censured with more petulance than justice; and never was there a more dignified strain of compliment, than that in which he courts the attention of one whom he had been persuaded to believe would be a respectable patron.

> With regard to questions of purity or propriety (says he), I was once in doubt whether I should not attribute to myself too much in attempting to decide them, and whether my province was to extend beyond the proposition of the question, and the display of the suffrages on each side; but I have been since determined by your Lordship's opinion, to interpose my own judgement, and shall therefore endeavour to support what appears to me most consonant to grammar and reason. Ausonius thought that modesty forbade him to plead inability for a task to which Caesar had judged him equal:
>
> *Cur me posse negem posse quod ille putat?*
>
> And I may hope, my Lord, that since you, whose authority in our language is so generally acknowledged, have commissioned me to declare my own opinion, I shall be considered as exercising a kind of vicarious jurisdiction, and that the power which might have been denied to my own claim, will be readily allowed me as the delegate of your Lordship.

This passage proves, that Johnson's addressing his 'Plan' to Lord Chesterfield was not merely in consequence of the result of a report by means of Dodsley, that the Earl favoured the design; but that there had been a particular communication with his Lordship concerning it. Dr Taylor told me, that

1 September 22, 1777, going from Ashbourne in Derbyshire, to see Islam.

Johnson sent his 'Plan' to him in manuscript, for his perusal; and that when it was lying upon his table, Mr William Whitehead happened to pay him a visit, and being shown it, was highly pleased with such parts of it as he had time to read, and begged to take it home with him, which he was allowed to do; that from him it got into the hands of a noble Lord, who carried it to Lord Chesterfield. When Taylor observed this might be an advantage, Johnson replied, 'No, Sir; it would have come out with more bloom, if it had not been seen before by any body.'

The opinion conceived of it by another noble author, appears from the following extract of a letter from the Earl of Orrery to Dr Birch:

> Caledon, Dec. 30, 1747.
>
> I have just now seen the specimen of Mr Johnson's Dictionary, addressed to Lord Chesterfield. I am much pleased with the plan, and I think the specimen is one of the best that I have ever read. Most specimens disgust, rather than prejudice us in favour of the work to follow; but the language of Mr Johnson's is good, and the arguments are properly and modestly expressed. However, some expressions may be cavilled at, but they are trifles. I'll mention one. The *barren* Laurel. The laurel is not barren, in any sense whatever; it bears fruits and flowers. *Sed hae sunt nugae,* and I have great expectations from the performance.[1]

That he was fully aware of the arduous nature of the undertaking, he acknowledges, and shows himself perfectly sensible of it in the conclusion of his 'Plan'; but he had a noble consciousness of his own abilities, which enabled him to go on with undaunted spirit.

Dr Adams found him one day busy at his Dictionary, when the following dialogue ensued. 'ADAMS. This is a great work, Sir. How are you to get all the etymologies? JOHNSON. Why, Sir, here is a shelf with Junius, and Skinner, and others; and there is a Welch gentleman who has published a collection of Welch proverbs, who will help me with the Welch. ADAMS. But, Sir, how can you do this in three years? JOHNSON. Sir, I have no doubt that I can do it in three years. ADAMS. But the French Academy, which consists of forty members, took forty years to compile their Dictionary. JOHNSON. Sir, thus it is. This is the proportion. Let me see; forty times forty is sixteen hundred. As three to sixteen hundred, so is the proportion of an Englishman to a Frenchman.' With so much ease and pleasantry could he talk of that prodigious labour which he had undertaken to execute.

The public has had, from another pen,[a] a long detail of what had been done in this country by prior Lexicographers, and no doubt Johnson was wise to avail himself of them so far as they went; but the learned, yet judicious

---

1 Birch. MSS. Brit. Mus. 4303.

a Add the following note: See Sir John Hawkins's *Life of Johnson*.

research of etymology, the various, yet accurate display of definition, and the rich collection of authorities, were reserved for the superior mind of our great philologist. For the mechanical part, he employed, as he told me, six amanuenses; and let it be remembered by the natives of North Britain, to whom he is supposed to have been so hostile, that five of them were of that country. There were two Messieurs Macbean; Mr Shiels, the writer of the Lives of the Poets to which the name of Cibber is affixed; Mr Stewart, son of Mr George Stewart, bookseller at Edinburgh; and, a Mr Maitland. The sixth of these humble assistants was Mr Peyton, who, I believe, taught French, and published some elementary tracts.

To all these painful labourers, Johnson showed a never-ceasing kindness, so far as they stood in need of it. The elder Mr Macbean had afterwards the honour of being Librarian to Archibald, Duke of Argyle, for many years, but was left without a shilling. Johnson wrote for him a Preface to 'A System of ancient Geography'; and, by the favour of Lord Thurlow, got him admitted a poor brother of the Charterhouse. For Shiels, who died of a consumption, he had much tenderness; and it has been thought that some choice sentences in the Lives of the Poets were supplied by him. Peyton, when reduced to penury, had frequent aid from the bounty of Johnson, who at last was at the expense of burying both him and his wife.

While the Dictionary was going forward, Johnson lived part of the time in Holborn, part in Gough-square, Fleet-street; and he had an upper room fitted up like a counting-house for the purpose, in which he gave to the copyists their several tasks. The words, partly taken from other dictionaries, and partly supplied by himself, having been first written down with spaces left between them, he delivered in writing their etymologies, definitions, and various significations. The authorities were copied from the books themselves, in which he had marked the passages with a black-lead pencil, the traces of which could easily be effaced. I have seen several of them, in which that trouble had not been taken, so that they were just as when used by the copyists. It is remarkable, that he was so attentive in the choice of the passages in which words were authorised, that one may read page after page of his Dictionary with improvement and pleasure; and it should not pass unobserved, that he has quoted no author whose writings had a tendency to hurt sound religion and morality.

The necessary expense of preparing a work of such magnitude for the press, must have been a considerable deduction from the price stipulated to be paid for the copy-right. I understand that nothing was allowed by the booksellers on that account; and I remember his telling me, that a large portion of it having, by mistake, been written upon both sides of the paper, so as to be inconvenient for the compositor, it cost him twenty pounds to have it transcribed upon one side only.

He is now to be considered as 'tugging at his oar', as engaged in a steady continued course of occupation, sufficient to employ all his time for some years, and which was the best preventive of that constitutional melancholy which was ever lurking about him, ready to trouble his quiet. But his enlarged and lively mind could not be satisfied without more diversity of employment, and the pleasure of animated relaxation. He therefore not only exerted his talents in occasional composition very different from Lexicography, but formed a club in Ivy-lane, Paternoster-row, with a view to enjoy literary discussion, and amuse his evening hours. The members associated with him in this little society were his beloved friend Dr Richard Bathurst, Mr Hawkesworth, afterwards well known by his writings, Mr John Hawkins, an attorney,[1] and a few others of different professions.

In the *Gentleman's Magazine* for May of this year he wrote a 'Life of Lord Roscommon',* with Notes, which he afterwards much improved, indented the notes into text, and inserted it amongst his Lives of the English Poets.

Mr Dodsley this year brought out his PRECEPTOR, one of the most valuable books for the improvement of young minds that has appeared in any language; and to this meritorious work Johnson furnished 'The Preface',* containing a general sketch of the book, with a short and perspicuous recommendation of each article; as also, 'The Vision of Theodore the Hermit, found in his Cell',* a most beautiful allegory of human life, under the figure of ascending the mountain of Existence. The Bishop of Dromore heard Dr Johnson say, that he thought this was the best thing he ever wrote.

In January, 1749, he published 'THE VANITY OF HUMAN WISHES, being the Tenth Satire of Juvenal imitated'. He, I believe, composed it the preceding year.[2] Mrs Johnson, for the sake of country air, had lodgings at Hampstead, to which he resorted occasionally, and there the greatest part, if not the whole, of this Imitation was written. The fervid rapidity with which it was produced, is scarcely credible. I have heard him say, that he composed seventy lines of it in one day, without putting one of them upon paper till they were finished. I remember when I once regretted to him that he had not given us more of Juvenal's Satires, he said he probably should give more, for he had them all in his head; by which I understood, that he had the originals and correspondent allusions floating in his mind, which he could, when he pleased, embody and render permanent without much labour. Some of them, however, he observed, were too gross for imitation.

The profits of a single poem, however excellent, appear to have been very small in the last reign, compared with what a publication of the same size has since been known to yield. I have mentioned, upon Johnson's own authority, that for his *London* he had only ten guineas; and now, after his fame was

---

1 He was afterwards for several years Chairman of the Middlesex Justices, and upon occasion of presenting some address to the King, accepted the usual offer of Knighthood. He is author of *A History of Musick*, in five volumes in quarto. By assiduous attendance upon Johnson in his last illness, he obtained the office of one of his executors; in consequence of which, the booksellers of London employed him to publish an edition of Dr Johnson's works, and to write his Life.

2 Sir John Hawkins, with solemn inaccuracy, represents this poem as a consequence of the indifferent reception of his tragedy. But the fact is, that the poem was published on the 9th of January, and the tragedy was not acted till the 6th of the February, following.

established, he got for his *Vanity of Human Wishes* but five guineas more, as is proved by an authentic document in my possession.[1]

It will be observed, that he reserves to himself the right of printing one edition of this satire, which was his practice upon occasion of the sale of all his writings; it being his fixed intention to publish at some period, for his own profit, a complete collection of his works.

His *Vanity of Human Wishes* has less of common life, but more of a philo-sophic dignity than his *London*. More readers, therefore, will be delighted with the pointed spirit of *London*, than with the profound reflection of *The Vanity of Human Wishes*. Garrick, for instance, observed, in his sprightly manner, with more vivacity than regard to just discrimination, as is usual with wits, 'When Johnson lived much with the Herveys, and saw a good deal of what was passing in life, he wrote his *London*, which is lively and easy. When he became more retired, he gave us his *Vanity of Human Wishes*, which is as hard as Greek. Had he gone on to imitate another satire, it would have been as hard as Hebrew.'[2]

But *The Vanity of Human Wishes* is, in the opinion of the best judges, as high an effort of ethic poetry as any language can show. The instances of variety of disappointment are chosen so judiciously, and painted so strongly, that, the moment they are read, they bring conviction to every thinking mind. That of the scholar must have depressed the too sanguine expectations of many an ambitious student.[3] That of the warrior, Charles of Sweden, is, I think, as highly finished a picture as can possibly be conceived.

---

1 'Nov. 25, 1748. I received of Mr Dodsley fifteen guineas, for which I assign to him the right of copy of an Imitation of the Tenth Satire of Juvenal, written by me; reserving to myself the right of printing one edition.   SAM. JOHNSON.'

'London, 29 June, 1746. A true copy from the original in Dr Johnson's handwriting –
JAS. DODSLEY.'

2 From Mr Langton.

3 In this poem one of the instances mentioned of unfortunate learned men is *Lydiat*:

Hear Lydiat's life, and Galileo's end.

The history of Lydiat being little known, the following account of him may be acceptable to many of my readers. It appeared as a note in the Supplement to the *Gentleman's Magazine* for 1748, in which some passages extracted from Johnson's poem were inserted, and it should have been added in the subsequent editions. – 'A very learned divine and mathematician, fellow of New College, Oxon, and Rector of Okerton, near Banbury. He wrote, among many others, a Latin treatise '*De natura caeli*, &c.' in which he attacked the sentiments of Scaliger and Aristotle, not bearing to hear it urged, *that some things are true in philosophy and false in divinity*. He made above 600 sermons on the harmony of the Evangelists. Being unsuccessful in publishing his works, he lay in the prison of Bocardo at Oxford, and in the King's Bench, till Bishop Usher, Dr Laud, Sir William Boswel, and Dr Pink, released him by paying his debts. He petitioned King Charles I to be sent into Ethiopia, &c. to procure MSS. Having spoken in favour of monarchy and bishops, he was plundered by the parliament forces, and twice carried away prisoner from his rectory; and afterwards had not a shirt to shift him in three months, without he borrowed it, and died very poor in 1646.'

Were all the excellencies of this poem annihilated, it must ever have our grateful reverence from its noble conclusion; in which we are consoled with the assurance that happiness may be attained, if we 'apply our hearts' to piety:

> Where then shall hope and fear their objects find?
> Shall dull suspense corrupt the stagnant mind?
> Must helpless man, in ignorance sedate,
> Roll darkling down the torrent of his fate?
> Shall no dislike alarm, no wishes rise,
> No cries attempt the mercy of the skies?
> Enthusiast, cease; petitions yet remain,
> Which heav'n may hear, nor deem religion vain.
> Still raise for good the supplicating voice,
> But leave to heav'n the measure and the choice.
> Safe in his hand, whose eye discerns afar
> The secret ambush of a specious pray'r;
> Implore his aid, in his decisions rest,
> Secure whate'er he gives he gives the best.
> Yet when the sense of sacred presence fires,
> And strong devotion to the skies aspires,
> Pour forth thy fervours for a healthful mind,
> Obedient passions, and a will resign'd;
> For love, which scarce collective man can fill,
> For patience sovereign o'er transmuted ill;
> For faith, which panting for a happier seat,
> Counts death kind Nature's signal for retreat.
> These goods for man the laws of heaven ordain,
> These goods he grants, who grants the power to gain:
> With these celestial wisdom calms the mind,
> And makes the happiness she does not find.

Garrick being now vested with theatrical power by being manager of Drury-lane theatre, he kindly and generously made use of it to bring out Johnson's tragedy, which had been long kept back for want of encouragement. But in this benevolent purpose he met with no small difficulty from the temper of Johnson, which could not brook that a drama which he had formed with much study, and had been obliged to keep more than the nine years of Horace, should be revised and altered at the pleasure of an actor. Yet Garrick knew well, that without some alterations it would not be fit for the stage. A violent dispute having ensued between them, Garrick applied to the Reverend Dr Taylor to interpose. Johnson was at first very obstinate. 'Sir (said he), the fellow wants me to make Mahomet run mad, that he may have an opportunity of tossing his hands and kicking his heels.'[1] He was, however, at last, with

---

1 Mahomet was, in fact, played by Mr Barry, and Demetrius by Mr Garrick; but probably at this time the parts were not yet cast.

difficulty, prevailed on to comply with Garrick's wishes, so as to allow of some changes; but still there were not enough.

Dr Adams was present the first night of the representation of *Irene*, and gave me the following account: 'Before the curtain drew up, there were catcalls whistling, which alarmed Johnson's friends. The Prologue, which was written by himself in a manly strain, soothed the audience,[1] and the play went off tolerably till it came to the conclusion, when Mrs Pritchard, the heroine of the piece, was to be strangled upon the stage, and was to speak two lines with the bowstring round her neck. The audience cried out "Murder, murder". She several times attempted to speak, but in vain. At last she was obliged to go off the stage alive.' This passage was afterwards struck out, and she was carried off to be put to death behind the scenes, as the play now has it. The Epilogue was written by Sir William Young.[a] I know not how Johnson's play came to be thus graced by the pen of a person then so eminent in the political world.

Notwithstanding all the support of such performers as Garrick, Barry, Mrs Cibber, Mrs Pritchard, and every advantage of dress and decoration, the tragedy of *Irene* did not please the public. Mr Garrick's zeal carried it through for nine nights, so that the author had his three nights' profits; and from a receipt signed by him, now in the hands of Mr James Dodsley, it appears that his friend Mr Robert Dodsley gave him one hundred pounds for the copy, with his usual reservation of the right of one edition.

Irene, considered as a poem, is entitled to the praise of superior excellence. Analysed into parts, it will furnish a rich store of noble sentiments, fine imagery, and beautiful language; but it is deficient in pathos, in that delicate power of touching the human feelings, which is the principal end of the drama.[b] Indeed Garrick has complained to me, that Johnson not only had not

---

1 The expression used by Dr Adams was 'soothed'. I should rather think the audience was *awed* by the extraordinary spirit and dignity of the following lines:

> Be this at least his praise, be this his pride,
> To force applause no modern arts are tried:
> Should partial catcalls all his hopes confound,
> He bids no trumpet quell the fatal sound;
> Should welcome sleep relieve the weary wit,
> He rolls no thunders o'er the drowsy pit;
> No snares to captivate the judgement spreads,
> Nor bribes your eyes to prejudice your heads.
> Unmov'd, though witlings sneer and rivals rail,
> Studious to please, yet not ashamed to fail,
> He scorns the meek address, the suppliant strain,
> With merit needless, and without it vain:
> In Reason, Nature, Truth, he dares to trust;
> Ye fops be silent, and ye wits be just!

[a] For 'Young,' read 'Yonge.' *Second Edition*: 'as Johnson informed me,' inserted.

[b] Add the following note: Aaron Hill (Vol. II, p. 355), in a letter to Mr Mallet, gives the following account of *Irene* after having seen it: 'I was at the anomalous Mr

the faculty of producing the impressions of tragedy, but that he had not the sensibility to perceive them. His great friend Mr Walmsley's prediction, that he would 'turn out a fine tragedy-writer', was, therefore, ill founded. Johnson was wise enough to be convinced that he had not the talents necessary to write successfully for the stage, and never made another attempt in that species of composition.

When asked how he felt upon the ill success of his tragedy, he replied, 'Like the Monument'; meaning that he continued firm and unmoved as that column. And let it be remembered, as an admonition to the *genus irritabile* of dramatic writers, that this great man, instead of peevishly complaining of the bad taste of the town, submitted to its decision without a murmur. He had, indeed, upon all occasions a great deference for the general opinion: 'A man (said he) who writes a book, thinks himself wiser or wittier than the rest of mankind; he supposes that he can instruct or amuse them, and the public to whom he appeals, must, after all, be the judges of his pretensions.'

On occasion of his play being brought upon the stage, Johnson had a fancy that as a dramatic author his dress should be more gay than what he ordinarily wore; he therefore appeared behind the scenes, and even in one of the side boxes, in a scarlet waistcoat, with rich gold lace.[a] His necessary attendance while his play was in rehearsal, and during its performance, brought him acquainted with many of the performers of both sexes, which produced a more favourable opinion of their profession than he had harshly expressed in his Life of Savage. With some of them he kept up an acquaintance as long as he and they lived, and was ever ready to show them acts of kindness. He for a considerable time used to frequent the *Green Room*, and seemed to take delight in dissipating his gloom, by mixing in the sprightly chit-chat of the motley circle then to be found there. Mr David Hume related to me from Mr Garrick, that Johnson at last denied himself this amusement, from considerations of rigid virtue; saying, 'I'll come no more behind your scenes, David; for the silk stockings and white bosoms of your actresses excite my amorous propensities.'

In 1750 he came forth in the character for which he was eminently qualified, a majestic teacher of moral and religious wisdom. The vehicle which he chose was that of a periodical paper, which he knew had been, upon former occasions, employed with great success. The *Tatler*, *Spectator*, and *Guardian*, were the last of the kind published in England, which had stood the test of a long trial; and such an interval had now elapsed since their publication, as made him justly think that, to many of his readers, this form of instruction would, in some degree, have the advantage of novelty. A few days before the first of his Essays came out, there started another competitor for fame in the same form, under the title of the *Tatler Revived*, which I believe was 'born but

---

Johnson's benefit, and found the play his proper representative; strong sense ungraced by sweetness or decorum.'

[a] Add, 'and a gold laced hat'.

to die'. Johnson was, I think, not very happy in the choice of his title, the *Rambler*, which certainly is not suited to a series of grave and moral discourses; which the Italians have literally, but ludicrously, translated by *Il Vagabondo*; and which has been lately assumed as the denomination of a vehicle of licentious tales, *The Rambler's Magazine*. He gave Sir Joshua Reynolds the following account of its getting this name: 'What *must* be done, Sir, *will* be done. When I was to begin publishing that paper, I was at a loss how to name it. I sat down at night upon my bedside, and resolved that I would not go to sleep till I had fixed its title. The *Rambler* seemed the best that occurred, and I took it.'[1]

With what devout and conscientious sentiments this paper was undertaken, is evidenced by the following prayer, which he composed and offered up on the occasion: 'Almighty GOD, the giver of all good things, without whose help all labour is ineffectual, and without whose grace all wisdom is folly; grant, I beseech Thee, that in this undertaking thy Holy Spirit may not be withheld from me, but that I may promote thy glory, and the salvation of myself and others: grant this, O LORD, for the sake of thy son JESUS CHRIST. Amen.'[2]

The first paper of the *Rambler* was published on Tuesday the 20th of March, 1750; and its author was enabled to continue it, without interruption, every Tuesday and Friday, till Saturday the 17th of March, 1752, on which day it closed. This is a strong confirmation of the truth of a remark of his, which I have had occasion to quote elsewhere,[3] that 'a man may write at any time, if he will set himself doggedly to it'; for, notwithstanding his constitutional indolence, his depression of spirits, and his labour in carrying on his Dictionary, he answered the stated calls of the press twice a week from the stores of his mind, during all that time having received no assistance, except four billets in No. 10 by Miss Mulso, now Mrs Chapone; No. 30, by Mrs Catharine Talbot; No. 97, by Mr Samuel Richardson, whom he describes in an introductory note as 'An author who has enlarged the knowledge of human nature, and taught the passions to move at the command of virtue'; and Numbers 44 and 100, by Mrs Elizabeth Carter.

Posterity will be astonished when they are told, upon the authority of Johnson himself, that many of these discourses, which we should suppose had been laboured with all the slow attention of literary leisure, were written in

---

1 I have heard Dr Warton mention, that he was at Mr Robert Dodsley's with the late Mr Moore, and several others of his friends, considering what should be the name of the periodical paper which Moore had undertaken. Garrick proposed the *Sallad*, which, by a curious coincidence, was afterwards applied to himself by Goldsmith:

> Our Garrick's a sallad, for in him we see
> Oil, vinegar, sugar, and saltness agree!

At last the company having separated, without any thing of which they approved having been offered, Dodsley himself thought of *The World*.

2 *Prayers and Meditations*, p. 9.

3 *Journal of a Tour to the Hebrides*, 3d edit. p. 28.

haste as the moment pressed, without even being read over by him before they were printed. It can be accounted for only in this way; that by reading and meditation, and a very close inspection of life, he had accumulated a great fund of miscellaneous knowledge, which, by a peculiar promptitude of mind, was ever ready at his call, and which he had constantly accustomed himself to clothe in the most apt and energetic expression. Sir Joshua Reynolds once asked him by what means he had attained his extraordinary accuracy and flow of language. He told him, that he had early laid it down as a fixed rule to do his best on every occasion, and in every company; to impart whatever he knew in the most forcible language he could put it in; and that by constant practice, and never suffering any careless expressions to escape him, or attempting to deliver his thoughts without arranging them in the clearest manner, it became habitual to him.

Yet he was not altogether unprepared as a periodical writer; for I have in my possession a small duodecimo volume, in which he has written, in the form of Mr Locke's *Common-Place Book*, a variety of hints for essays on different subjects. He has marked upon the first blank leaf of it, 'To the 128th page, collections for the *Rambler*', and in another place, 'In fifty-two there were seventeen provided; in 97 – 21; in 190 – 25.' At a subsequent period (probably after the work was finished) he added, 'In all, taken of provided materials, 30.'

Sir John Hawkins, who is unlucky upon all occasions, tells us, that 'this method of accumulating intelligence had been practised by Mr Addison, and is humorously described in one of the *Spectators*, wherein he feigns to have dropped his paper of *notanda*, consisting of a diverting medley of broken sentences and loose hints, which he tells us he had collected, and meant to make use of. Much of the same kind is Johnson's *Adversaria*.'[1] But the truth is, that there is no resemblance at all between them. Addison's note was a fiction, in which unconnected fragments of his lucubrations were purposely jumbled together, in as odd a manner as he could, in order to produce a laughable effect. Whereas Johnson's abbreviations are all distinct, and applicable to each subject of which the head is mentioned.

For instance, there is the following specimen:

Youth's Entry, &c.

Baxter's account of things in which he had changed his mind as he grew up. Voluminous. – No wonder. – If every man was to tell, or mark, on how many subjects he has changed, it would make vols. but the changes not always observed by man's self. – From pleasure to bus. [business] to quiet; from thoughtfulness to reflect. to piety; from dissipation to domestic. by impercept. gradat. but the change is certain. Dial *non progredi, progress. esse conspicimus*. Look back, consider what was thought at some dist. period.

1 Hawkins's *Life of Johnson*, p. 268.

Hope predom. in youth. Mind not willingly indulges unpleasing thoughts. The world lies all enamelled before him, as a distant prospect sun-gilt:[1] – inequalities only found by coming to it. *Love is to be all joy – children excellent –* Fame to be constant – caresses of the great – applauses of the learned – smiles of Beauty.

Fear of disgrace – Bashfulness – Finds things of less importance. Miscarriages forgot like excellencies; – if remembered, of no import. Danger of sinking into negligence of reputation. Lest the fear of disgrace destroy activity.

Confidence in himself. Long tract of life before him. – No thought of sickness. – Embarrassment of affairs. – Distraction of family. – Public calamities. – No sense of the prevalence of bad habits. – Negligent of time – ready to undertake – careless to pursue – all changed by time.

Confident of others – unsuspecting as unexperienced – imagining himself secure against neglect, never imagines they will venture to treat him ill. Ready to trust; expecting to be trusted. Convinced by time of the selfishness, the meanness, the cowardice, the treachery of men.

Youth ambitious, as thinking honours easy to be had.

Different kinds of praise pursued at different periods. Of the gay in youth. dang. hurt, &c. despised.

Of the fancy in manhood. Ambit. – stocks – bargains. – Of the wise and sober in old age – seriousness – formality maxims, but general – only of the rich, otherwise age is happy – but at last every thing referred to riches – no having fame, honour, influence, without subjection to caprice.

Horace.

Hard it would be if men entered life with the same views with which they leave it, or left as they enter it. – No hope – no undertaking – no regard to benevolence – no fear of disgrace, &c.

Youth to be taught the piety of age – age to retain the honour of youth.

This, it will be observed, is the sketch of No. 196 of the *Rambler.* I shall gratify my readers with another specimen:

Confederacies difficult; why.

Seldom in war a match for single persons – nor in peace; therefore kings make themselves absolute. Confederacies in learning – every great work the work of one. *Bruy.* Scholars' friendship like ladies. Scribebamus &c. Mart. The apple of discord – the laurel of discord – the poverty of criticism. Swift's opinion of the power of six geniuses united. That union scarce possible. His remarks just – man a social, not steady nature. Drawn to man by words, repelled by passions. Orb drawn by attraction rep. [repelled] by centrifugal.

---

1 This most beautiful image of the enchanting delusion of youthful prospect had not been used in any of Johnson's essays.

Common danger unites by crushing other passions – but they return. Equality hinders compliance. Superiority produces insolence and envy. Too much regard in each to private interest – too little.

The mischiefs of private and exclusive societies – the fitness of social attraction diffused through the whole. The mischiefs of too partial love of our country. Contraction of moral duties ᾧ φίλοι οὐ φίλος.

Every man moves upon his own centre, and therefore repels others from too near a contact, though he may comply with some general laws.

Of confederacy with superiors, every one knows the inconvenience. With equals, no authority; – every man his own opinion – his own interest.

Man and wife hardly united; – scarce ever without children. Computation, if two to one against two, how many against five? If confederacies were easy – useless; – many oppresses many. – If possible only to some, dangerous. *Principum amicitias*.

Here we see the embryo of No. 45 of the *Adventurer*; and it is a confirmation of what I have mentioned, that the papers in that collection marked T. were written by Johnson.

This scanty preparation of materials will not, however, much diminish our wonder at the extraordinary fertility of his mind; for the proportion which they bear to the number of essays which he wrote, is very small; and it is remarkable, that those for which he had made no preparation, are as rich and as highly finished, as those for which the hints were lying by him. It is also to be observed, that the papers formed from his hints are worked up with such strength and elegance, that we almost lose sight of the hints, which become like 'drops in the bucket'. Indeed, in several instances, he has made a very slender use of them, so that many of them remain still unapplied.[1]

As the *Rambler* was entirely the work of one man, there was, of course, such an uniformity in its texture, as very much to exclude the charm of variety; and the grave and often solemn cast of thinking, which distinguished it from other periodical papers, made it, for some time, not generally liked. So slowly did this excellent work, of which twelve editions have now issued from the press,

---

1 Sir John Hawkins has selected from this little collection of materials, what he calls the 'Rudiments of two of the papers of the *Rambler*.' But he has not been able to read the manuscript distinctly. Thus he writes, p. 266, 'Sailors fate any mansion'; whereas the original is, 'Sailor's life my aversion'. He has also transcribed the unappropriated hints on *Writers for bread*, in which he decyphers these notable passages, one in Latin, *fatui non famae*, instead of *fami non famae*; Johnson having in his mind what Thuanus says of the learned German antiquary and linguist, Xylander, who, he tells us, lived in such poverty, that he was supposed *fami non famae scribere*; and another in French, *Degente de fate et affamé d'argent*, instead of *Dégouté de fame* (an old word for *renommée*) *et affamé de argent*. The manuscript being written in an exceedingly small hand is indeed very hard to read; but it would have been better to have left blanks than to write nonsense.

gain upon the world at large, that even in the closing number the author says, 'I have never been much a favourite of the public.'

Yet, very soon after its commencement, there were who felt and acknowledged its uncommon excellence. Verses in its praise appeared in the newspapers; and the editor of the *Gentleman's Magazine* mentions, in October, his having received several letters to the same purpose from the learned. *The Student, or Oxford and Cambridge Miscellany*, in which Mr Bonnell Thornton and Mr Colman were the principal writers, describes it as 'a work that exceeds any thing of the kind ever published in this kingdom, some of the *Spectators* excepted, – if indeed they may be excepted.' And, afterwards, 'May the public favours crown his merits, and may not the English, under the auspicious reign of GEORGE the Second, neglect a man, who, had he lived in the first century, would have been one of the greatest favourites of AUGUSTUS.' This flattery of the monarch had no effect. It is too well known, that the second George never was an Augustus to learning or genius.

Johnson told me, with an amiable fondness, a little pleasing circumstance relative to this work. Mrs Johnson, in whose judgement and taste he had great confidence, said to him, after a few numbers of the *Rambler* had come out, 'I thought very well of you before; but I did not imagine you could have written any thing equal to this.' Distant praise, from whatever quarter, is not so delightful as that of a wife whom a man loves and esteems. Her approbation may be said to 'come home to his *bosom*'; and being so near, its effect is most sensible and permanent.

Mr James Elphinston, who has since published various works, and who was ever esteemed by Johnson as a worthy man, happened to be in Scotland while the *Rambler* was coming out in single papers at London. With a laudable zeal at once for the improvement of his countrymen and the reputation of his friend, he suggested and took the charge of an edition of those Essays at Edinburgh, which followed progressively the London publication.[1]

The following letter written at this time, though not dated, will show how much pleased Johnson was with this publication, and what kindness and regard he had for Mr Elphinston.

To Mr JAMES ELPHINSTON.

[No date.]

DEAR SIR – I cannot but confess the failures of my correspondence, but hope the same regard which you express for me on every other occasion, will incline you to forgive me. I am often, very often ill; and, when I am

---

1 It was executed in the printing-office of Sands, Murray, and Cochran, with uncommon elegance, upon writing-paper, of a duodecimo size, and with the greatest correctness, and Mr Elphinston enriched it with translations of the mottos. When completed, it made eight handsome volumes. It is, unquestionably, the most accurate and beautiful edition of this work; and there being but a small impression, it is now become scarce, and sells at a very high price.

well, am obliged to work: and, indeed, have never much used myself to punctuality. You are, however, not to make unkind inferences, when I forbear to reply to your kindness; for be assured, I never receive a letter from you without great pleasure, and a very warm sense of your generosity and friendship, which I heartily blame myself for not cultivating with more care. In this, as in many other cases, I go wrong, in opposition to conviction; for I think scarce any temporal good equally to be desired with the regard and familiarity of worthy men. I hope we shall be some time nearer to each other, and have a more ready way of pouring out our hearts.

I am glad that you still find encouragement to proceed in your publication, and shall beg the favour of six more volumes to add to my former six, when you can, with any convenience, send them me. Please to present a set, in my name, to Mr Ruddiman,[1] of whom, I hear, that his learning is not his highest excellence. I have transcribed the mottos, and returned them, I hope not too late, of which I think many very happily performed. Mr Cave has put the last in the magazine, in which I think he did well. I beg of you to write soon, and to write often, and to write long letters, which I hope in time to repay you; but you must be a patient creditor. I have, however, this of gratitude, that I think of you with regard, when I do not, perhaps, give the proofs which I ought, of being, Sir,

Your most obliged and humble servant,

SAM. JOHNSON.

Soon after this he wrote to the same gentleman another letter upon a mournful occasion.

To Mr JAMES ELPHINSTON.

September 25, 1750.

DEAR SIR — You have, as I find by every kind of evidence, lost an excellent mother; and I hope you will not think me incapable of partaking of your grief. I have a mother, now eighty-two years of age, whom, therefore, I must soon lose, unless it please GOD that she rather should mourn for me. I read the letters in which you relate your mother's death to Mrs Strahan, and think I do myself honour, when I tell you that I read them with tears; but tears are neither to *you* nor to *me* of any further use, when once the tribute of nature has been paid. The business of life summons us away from useless grief, and calls us to the exercise of those virtues of which we are lamenting our deprivation. The greatest benefit which one friend can confer upon another, is to guard, and excite, and elevate his virtues. This your mother will still perform, if you diligently preserve the memory of her life, and of

1 Mr Thomas Ruddiman, the learned grammarian of Scotland, well known for his various excellent works, and for his accurate editions of several authors. He was also a man of a most worthy private character. His zeal for the Royal House of Stuart did not render him less estimable in Dr Johnson's eye.

her death: a life, so far as I can learn, useful, wise, and innocent; and a death resigned, peaceful, and holy. I cannot forbear to mention, that neither reason nor revelation denies you to hope, that you may increase her happiness by obeying her precepts; and that she may in her present state look with pleasure upon every act of virtue to which her instructions or example have contributed. Whether this be more than a pleasing dream, or a just opinion of separate spirits, is, indeed, of no great importance to us, when we consider ourselves as acting under the eye of GOD: yet, surely, there is something pleasing in the belief, that our separation from those whom we love is merely corporeal; and it may be a great incitement to virtuous friendship, if it can be made probable, that that union that has received the divine approbation shall continue to eternity.

There is one expedient by which you may, in some degree, continue her presence. If you write down minutely what you remember of her from your earliest years, you will read it with great pleasure, and receive from it many hints of soothing recollection, when time shall remove her yet farther from you, and your grief shall be matured to veneration. To this, however painful for the present, I cannot but advise you, as a source of comfort and satisfaction in the time to come; for all comfort and all satisfaction is sincerely wished you by, dear Sir,

Your most obliged, most obedient,

And most humble servant,

SAM. JOHNSON.

The *Rambler* has increased in fame as in age. Soon after its first folio edition was concluded, it was published in four octavo[a] volumes; and its author lived to see ten numerous editions of it in London, beside those of Ireland and Scotland.

I profess myself to have ever entertained a profound veneration for the astonishing force and vivacity of mind, which the *Rambler* exhibits. That Johnson had penetration enough to see, and seeing would not disguise the general misery of man in this state of being, may have given rise to the superficial notion of his being too stern a philosopher. But men of reflection will be sensible that he has given a true representation of human existence, and that he has, at the same time, with a generous benevolence, displayed every consolation which our state affords us; not only those arising from the hopes of futurity, but such as may be attained in the immediate progress through life. He has not depressed the soul to despondency and indifference. He has every where inculcated study, labour, and exertion. Nay, he has shown, in a very odious light, a man whose practice is to go about darkening the views of others, by perpetual complaints of evil, and awakening those considerations of danger

---

[a] For 'four octavo', read 'six duodecimo'. [Boswell was nearly right in both versions. Four volumes were first published when the work was in progress, and two more after its conclusion.]

and distress, which are, for the most part, lulled into a quiet oblivion. This he has done very strongly in his character of Suspirius,[1] from which Goldsmith took that of Croaker, in his comedy of *The Good-Natured Man*, as Johnson told me he acknowledged to him, and which is, indeed, very obvious.

To point out the numerous subjects which the *Rambler* treats with a dignity and perspicuity which are there united in a manner which we shall in vain look for any where else, would take up too large a portion of my book, and would, I trust, be superfluous, considering how universally those volumes are now disseminated. Even the most condensed and brilliant sentences which they contain, and which have very properly been selected under the name of *Beauties*,[2] are of considerable bulk. But I may shortly observe, that the *Rambler* furnishes such an assemblage of discourses on practical religion and moral duty, of critical investigations, and allegorical and oriental tales, that no mind can be thought very deficient that has, by constant study and meditation, assimilated to itself all that may be found there. No. 7, written in Passion-week on abstraction and self-examination, and No. 110, on penitence and the placability of the Divine Nature, cannot be too often read. No. 54, on the effect which the death of a friend should have upon us, though rather too dispiriting, may be occasionally very medicinal to the mind. Every one must suppose the writer to have been deeply impressed by a real scene; but he told me that was not the case, which shows how well his fancy could conduct him to the house of mourning. Some of these more solemn papers, I doubt not, particularly attracted the notice of Dr Young, the author of 'The Night Thoughts', of whom my estimation is such, as to reckon his applause an honour even to Johnson. I have seen some volumes of Dr Young's copy of the *Rambler*, in which he has marked the passages which he thought particularly excellent, by folding down a corner of the page; and such as he rated in a super-eminent degree, are marked by double folds. I am sorry that some of the volumes are lost. Johnson was pleased when told of the minute attention with which Young had signified his approbation of his Essays.

I will venture to say, that in no writings whatever can be found more *bark and steel for the mind*, if I may use the expression; more that can brace and invigorate every manly and noble sentiment. No. 32 on patience, even under extreme misery, is wonderfully lofty, and as much above the rant of stoicism, as the Sun of Revelation is brighter than the twilight of Pagan philosophy. I never read the following sentence without feeling my frame thrill: 'I think there is some reason for questioning whether the body and mind are not so proportioned, that the one can bear all which can be inflicted on the other;

---

1 No. 55.

2 Dr Johnson was gratified by seeing this selection, and wrote to Mr Kearsley, bookseller in Fleet-street, the following note:

> Mr Johnson sends compliments to Mr Kearsley, and begs the favour of seeing him as soon as he can. Mr Kearsley is desired to bring with him the last edition of what he has honoured with the name of *Beauties*.

> May 20, 1782.

whether virtue cannot stand its ground as long as life, and whether a soul well principled will not be sooner separated than subdued.'

Though instruction be the predominant purpose of the *Rambler*, yet it is enlivened with a considerable portion of amusement. Nothing can be more erroneous than the notion which some persons have entertained, that Johnson was then a retired author, ignorant of the world; and, of consequence, that he wrote only from his imagination when he described characters and manners. He said to me, that before he wrote that work, he had been 'running about the world', as he expressed it, more than almost any body; and I have heard him relate, with much satisfaction, that several of the characters in the *Rambler* were drawn so naturally, that when it first circulated in numbers, a club in one of the towns in Essex imagined themselves to be severally exhibited in it, and were much incensed against a person who, they suspected, had thus made them objects of public notice; nor were they quieted till authentic assurance was given them, that the *Rambler* was written by a person who had never heard of any one of them. Some of the characters are believed to have been actually drawn from the life, particularly that of Prospero from Garrick, who never entirely forgave its pointed satire. For instances of fertility of fancy, and accurate description of real life, I appeal to No. 19, a man who wanders from one profession to another, with most plausible reasons for every change. No. 34, female fastidiousness and timorous refinement. No. 82, a Virtuoso who has collected curiosities. No. 88, petty modes of entertaining a company, and conciliating kindness. No. 182, fortune-hunting. No. 194–195, a tutor's account of the follies of his pupil. No. 197–198, legacy-hunting. He has given a specimen of his nice observation of the mere external appearances of life, in this passage in No. 179, against affectation, that frequent and most disgusting quality: 'He that stands to contemplate the crowds that fill the streets of a populous city, will see many passengers whose air and motion it will be difficult to behold without contempt and laughter; but if he examine what are the appearances that thus powerfully excite his risibility, he will find among them neither poverty nor disease, nor any involuntary or painful defect. The disposition to derision and insult, is awakened by the softness of foppery, the swell of insolence, the liveliness of levity, or the solemnity of grandeur; by the sprightly trip, the stately stalk, the formal strut, and the lofty mien; by gestures intended to catch the eye, and by looks elaborately formed as evidences of importance.'

Every page of the *Rambler* shows a mind teeming with classical allusion and poetical imagery: illustrations from other writers are, upon all occasions, so ready, and mingle so easily in his periods, that the whole appears of one uniform vivid texture.

The style of this work has been censured by some shallow critics as involved and turgid, and abounding with antiquated and hard words. So ill founded is the first part of this objection, that I will challenge all who may honour this book with a perusal, to point out any English writer whose language conveys his meaning with equal force and perspicuity. It must, indeed, be allowed, that the structure of his sentences is expanded, and often has somewhat of the inversion of Latin; and that he delighted to express familiar thoughts in philosophical language; being in this the reverse of Socrates, who, it was said, reduced philosophy to the simplicity of common life. But let us attend to what he himself says in his concluding paper: 'When common words were less pleasing to the ear, or less distinct in their signification, I have familiarized the terms of philosophy, by applying them to popular ideas.'[1] And, as to the second part of this objection, upon a late careful revision of the work, I can with confidence say, that it is amazing how few of those words, for which it has been unjustly characterized, are actually to be found in it; I am sure, not the proportion of one to each paper. This idle charge has been echoed from one babbler to another, who have confounded Johnson's Essays with Johnson's Dictionary; and because he thought it right in a Lexicon of our language to collect many words which had fallen into disuse, but were supported by great authorities, it has been imagined that all of these have been interwoven into his own compositions. That some of them have been adopted by him unnecessarily, may, perhaps, be allowed; but, in general they are evidently an advantage, for without them his stately ideas would be confined and cramped. 'He that thinks with more extent than another, will want words of larger meaning.'[2] He once told me, that he had formed his style upon that of Sir William Temple, and upon Chambers's Proposal for his Dictionary. He certainly was mistaken; or if he imagined at first that he was imitating Temple, he was very unsuccessful; for nothing can be more unlike than the simplicity of Temple, and the richness of Johnson. Their styles differ as plain cloth and brocade. Temple, indeed, seems equally erroneous in supposing that he himself had formed his style upon Sandy's History of all Religions.[a]

The style of Johnson was, undoubtedly, much formed upon that of the great writers in the last century, Hooker, Bacon, Sanderson, Hakewell, and others; those 'GIANTS', as they were well characterised by one[b] whose authority, were I to name him, would stamp a reverence on the opinion.

We may, with the utmost propriety, apply to his learned style that passage of Horace, a part of which he has taken as the motto to his Dictionary:

> *Cum tabulis animum censoris sumet honesti:*
> *Audebit quaecumque parum splendoris habebunt*
> *Et sine pondere erunt, et honore indigna ferentur,*
> *Verba movere loco, quamvis invita recedant,*
> *Et versentur adhuc intra penetralia Vestae.*
> *Obscurata diu populo bonus eruet, atque*
> *Proferet in lucem speciosa vocabula rerum,*

---

1 Yet his style did not escape the harmless shafts of pleasant humour, for the ingenious Bonnell Thornton published a mock *Rambler* in the *Drury-lane Journal*.

2 *Idler*, No. 70.

a For 'History of all Religions', read 'View'.

b For 'one', read 'A GREAT PERSONAGE'.

Quae priscis memorata Catonibus atque Cethegis,
Nunc situs informis premit et deserta vetustas:
Adsciscet nova, quae genitor produxerit usus:
Vehemens, et liquidus, puroque simillimus amni,
Fundet opes Latiumque beabit divite lingua. [1]

To so great a master of thinking, to one of such vast and various knowledge as Johnson, might have been allowed a liberal indulgence of that licence which Horace claims in another place:

Si forte necesse est
Indiciis monstrare recentibus abdita rerum,
Fingere cinctutis non exaudita Cethegis
Continget, dabiturque licentia sumpta pudenter:
Et nova fictaque nuper habebunt verba fidem si
Graeco fonte cadant, parce detorta. Quid autem
Caecilio Plautoque dabit Romanus, ademptum
Virgilio Varioque? Ego cur, acquirere pauca
Si possum, invideor; cum lingua Catonis et Enni
Sermonem patrium ditaverit, et nova rerum
Nomina protulerit? Licuit semperque licebit
Signatum praesente nota producere nomen.[2]

Yet Johnson assured me, that he had not taken upon him to add more than four or five words to the English language, of his own formation; and he was very much offended at the general licence by no means 'modestly taken' in his time, not only to coin new words, but to use many words in senses quite different from their established meaning, and those frequently very fantastical.

Sir Thomas Brown, whose life Johnson wrote, was remarkably fond of Anglo-Latian diction; and to his example we are to ascribe Johnson's some-times indulging himself in this kind of phraseology.[3] Johnson's comprehension of mind was the mould for his language. Had his conceptions been narrower, his expression would have been easier. His sentences have a dignified march; and, it is certain, that his example has given a general elevation to the language of his country, for many of our best writers have approached very near to him; and, from the influence which he has had upon our composition, scarcely any thing is written now that is not better expressed than was usual before he appeared to lead the national taste.

---

1 Horat. *Epist.* Lib. II. Epist. ii.
2 Horat. *De Arte Poetica.*
3 The observation of his having imitated Sir Thomas Brown has been made by many people; and lately it has been insisted on and illustrated by a variety of quotations from Brown in one of the popular Essays written by the Rev. Mr Knox, master of Tunbridge school, whom I have set down in my list of those who have sometimes not unsuccessfully imitated Dr Johnson's style.

This circumstance, the truth of which must strike every critical reader, has been so happily enforced by Mr Courtenay, in his 'Moral and Literary Character of Dr Johnson', that I cannot prevail on myself to withhold it, notwithstanding his, perhaps, too great partiality for one of his friends:

> By Nature's gifts ordain'd mankind to rule,
> He, like a Titian, form'd his brilliant school;
> And taught congenial spirits to excel,
> While from his lips impressive wisdom fell.
> Our boasted GOLDSMITH felt the sovereign sway;
> From him deriv'd the sweet, yet nervous lay.
> To Fame's proud cliff he bade our Raphael rise;
> Hence REYNOLDS' pen with REYNOLDS' pencil vies.
> With Johnson's flame melodious BURNEY glows,
> While the grand strain in smoother cadence flows.
> And you, MALONE, to critic learning dear,
> Correct and elegant, refin'd, though clear,
> By studying him, acquir'd that classic taste,
> Which high in Shakspeare's fane thy statue plac'd.
> Near Johnson STEEVENS stands, on scenic ground,
> Acute, laborious, fertile, and profound.
> Ingenious HAWKESWORTH to this school we owe,
> And scarce the pupil from the tutor know.
> Here early parts accomplish'd JONES sublimes,
> And science blends with Asia's lofty rhymes:
> Harmonious JONES! who in his splendid strains
> Sings Camdeo's sports, on Agra's flowery plains;
> In Hindu fiction while we fondly trace
> Love and the Muses deck'd with Attic grace.
> Amid these names can BOSWELL be forgot,
> Scarce by North Britons now esteem'd a Scot?[1]
> Who to the sage devoted from his youth,
> Imbib'd from him the sacred love of truth;
> The keen research, the exercise of mind,
> And that best art, the art to know mankind. –

1 The following observation in Mr Boswell's *Journal of a Tour to the Hebrides* may sufficiently account for that gentleman's being 'now scarcely esteem'd a Scot' by many of his countrymen: 'If he [Dr Johnson] was particularly prejudiced against the Scots, it was because they were more in his way; because he thought their success in England rather exceeded the due proportion of their real merit; and because he could not but see in them that nationality which, I believe, no liberal-minded Scotchman will deny.' Mr Boswell, indeed, is so free from national prejudice, that he might with equal propriety have been described as –

> Scarce by *South* Britons now esteem'd a Scot.

COURTENAY.

Nor was his energy confin'd alone
To friends around his philosophic throne;
Its influence wide improv'd our letter'd isle,
And lucid vigour mark'd the general style:
As Nile's proud waves, swol'n from their oozy bed,
First o'er the neighbouring meads majestic spread;
Till gathering force, they more and more expand,
And with new virtue fertilise the land.

Johnson's language, however, must be allowed to be too masculine for the delicate gentleness of female writing. His ladies, therefore, seem strangely formal, even to ridicule; and seem well denominated by the names which he has given them, as, Misella, Zozima, Properantia, Rhodoclia.

It has of late been the fashion to compare the style of Addison and Johnson, and to depreciate, I think very unjustly, the style of Addison as nerveless and feeble, because it has not the strength and energy of that of Johnson. Their prose may be balanced like the poetry of Dryden and Pope. Both are excellent, though in different ways. Addison writes with the ease of a gentleman. His readers fancy that a wise and accomplished companion is talking to them, so that he insinuates his sentiments and taste into their minds by an imperceptible influence. Johnson writes like a teacher. He dictates to his readers as if from an academical chair. They attend with awe and admiration; and his precepts are impressed upon them by his commanding eloquence. Addison's style, like a light wine, pleases every body from the first. Johnson's, like a liquor of more body, seems too strong at first, but, by degrees, is highly relished; and such is the melody of his periods, so much do they captivate the ear, and seize upon the attention, that there is scarcely any writer, however inconsiderable, who does not aim, in some degree, at the same species of excellence. But let us not ungratefully undervalue that beautiful style, which has pleasingly conveyed to us much instruction and entertainment. Though comparatively weak, when opposed to Johnson's Herculean vigour, let us not call it positively feeble. Let us remember the character of his style, as given by Johnson himself: 'What he attempted, he performed; he is *never feeble*, and he did not wish to be energetic; he is never rapid, and he never stagnates. His sentences have neither studied amplitude, nor affected brevity: his periods, though not diligently rounded, are voluble and easy. Whoever wishes to attain an English style, familiar but not coarse, and elegant but not ostentatious, must give his days and nights to the volumes of Addison.'[1]

Though the *Rambler* was not concluded till the year 1752, I shall, under this year, say all that I have to observe upon it. Some of the translations of the mottos by himself, are admirably done. He acknowledges to have received 'elegant translations' of many of them from Mr James Elphinston; and some are

1 I shall probably, in another work, maintain the merit of Addison's poetry, which has been very unjustly depreciated.

very happily translated by a Mr *F. Lewis*, of whom I never heard more, except that Johnson thus described him to Mr Malone: 'Sir, he lived in London, and hung loose upon society.' The concluding paper of his *Rambler* is at once dignified and pathetic. I cannot, however, but wish, that he had not ended it with an unnecessary Greek verse, translated also into an English couplet. It is too much like the conceit of those dramatic poets, who used to conclude each act with a rhyme; and the expression in the first line of his couplet, '*Celestial powers*', though proper in Pagan poetry, is ill suited to Christianity, with a conformity to which he consoles himself. How much better would it have been, to have ended with the prose sentence, 'I shall never envy the honours which wit and learning obtain in any other cause, if I can be numbered among the writers who have given ardour to virtue, and confidence to truth.'

His friend Dr Birch being now engaged in preparing an edition of Raleigh's smaller pieces, Dr Johnson wrote the following letter to that gentleman:

To Dr BIRCH.

Gough-square, May 12, 1750.

SIR – Knowing that you are now preparing to favour the public with a new edition of Raleigh's miscellaneous pieces, I have taken the liberty to send you a Manuscript, which fell by chance within my notice. I perceive no proofs of forgery in my examination of it; and the owner tells me, that, as *he* has heard, the handwriting is Sir Walter's. If you should find reason to conclude it genuine, it will be a kindness to the owner, a blind person,[1] to recommend it to the booksellers. I am, Sir,

Your most humble servant,

SAM. JOHNSON.

His just abhorrence of Milton's political notions was ever strong. But this did not prevent his warm admiration of Milton's great poetical merit, to which he has done illustrious justice, beyond all who have written upon the subject. And this year he not only wrote a Prologue, which was spoken by Mr Garrick before the acting of *Comus* at Drury-lane theatre, for the benefit of Milton's grand-daughter, but took a very zealous interest in the success of the charity. On the day preceding the performance, he published the following letter in the *General Advertiser*, addressed to the printer of that paper:

SIR – That a certain degree of reputation is acquired merely by approving the works of genius, and testifying a regard to the memory of authors, is a truth too evident to be denied; and therefore to ensure a participation of fame with a celebrated poet, many who would, perhaps, have contributed to starve him when alive, have heaped expensive pageants upon his grave.

It must, indeed, be confessed, that this method of becoming known to posterity with honour is peculiar to the great, or at least to the wealthy; but

---

1 Mrs Williams is probably the person meant.

an opportunity now offers for almost every individual to secure the praise of paying a just regard to the illustrious dead, united with the pleasure of doing good to the living. To assist illustrious[a] indigence, struggling with distress and debilitated by age, is a display of virtue, and an acquisition of happiness and honour.

Whoever, then, would be thought capable of pleasure in reading the works of our incomparable Milton, and not so destitute of gratitude as to refuse to lay out a trifle in rational and elegant entertainment for the benefit of his living remains, for the exercise of their own virtue, the increase of their reputation, and the pleasing consciousness of doing good, should appear at Drury-lane theatre tomorrow, April 5, when Comus will be performed for the benefit of Mrs Elizabeth Foster, grand-daughter to the author, and the only surviving branch of his family.

N.B. There will be a new prologue on the occasion, written by the author of Irene, and spoken by Mr Garrick; and, by particular desire, there will be added to the Masque a dramatic satire, called Lethe, in which Mr Garrick will perform.

In 1751 we are to consider him as carrying on both his Dictionary and *Rambler*. But he also wrote 'The Life of Cheynel',* in the miscellany called *The Student*; and the Reverend Dr Douglas having, with uncommon acuteness, clearly detected a gross forgery and imposition upon the public by William Lauder, a Scotch schoolmaster, who had, with equal impudence and ingenuity, represented Milton as a plagiary from certain modern Latin poets, Johnson, who had been so far imposed upon as to furnish a Preface and Postscript to his work, now dictated a letter for Lauder, addressed to Dr Douglas, acknowledging his fraud in terms of suitable contrition.[1]

This extraordinary attempt of Lauder was no sudden effort. He had brooded over it for many years; and to this hour it is uncertain what his principal motive was, unless it were a vain notion of his superiority, in being able, by whatever means, to deceive mankind. To effect this, he produced certain passages from Grotius, Masenius, and others, which had a faint resemblance to some parts of

---

[a] For 'illustrious,' read 'industrious'.

1 Lest there should be any person, at any future period, absurd enough to suspect that Johnson was a partaker in Lauder's fraud, or had any knowledge of it, when he assisted him with his masterly pen, it is proper here to quote the words of Dr Douglas, now Bishop of Carlisle, at the time when he detected the imposition. 'It is to be hoped, nay it is *expected*, that the elegant and nervous writer, whose judicious sentiments and inimitable style point out the author of Lauder's Preface and Postscript, will no longer allow one to *plume himself with his feathers*, who appeareth so little to deserve his assistance: an assistance which I am persuaded would never have been communicated, had there been the least suspicion of those facts which I have been the instrument of conveying to the world in these sheets.' *Milton no Plagiary*, 2d edit. p. 78. And his Lordship has been pleased now to authorise me to say, in the strongest manner, that there is no ground whatever for any unfavourable reflection against Dr Johnson, who expressed the strongest indignation against Lauder.

the *Paradise Lost*. In these he interpolated some fragments of Hog's Latin translation of that poem, alleging that the mass thus fabricated was the archetype from which Milton copied. These fabrications he published from time to time in the *Gentleman's Magazine*; and, exulting in his fancied success, he in 1750 ventured to collect them into a pamphlet, entitled 'An Essay on Milton's Use and Imitation of the Moderns in his *Paradise Lost*'. To this pamphlet Johnson wrote a Preface, in full persuasion of Lauder's honesty, and a Postscript recommending, in the most persuasive terms, a subscription for the relief of a grand-daughter of Milton, of whom he thus speaks: 'It is yet in the power of a great people to reward the poet whose name they boast, and from their alliance to whose genius, they claim some kind of superiority to every other nation of the earth; that poet, whose works may possibly be read when every other monument of British greatness shall be obliterated; to reward him, not with pictures or with medals, which, if he sees, he sees with contempt, but with tokens of gratitude, which he, perhaps, may even now consider as not unworthy the regard of an immortal spirit.' Surely this is inconsistent with 'enmity towards Milton', which Sir John Hawkins imputes to Johnson upon this occasion, adding, 'I could all along observe that Johnson seemed to approve not only of the design, but of the argument; and seemed to exult in a persuasion, that the reputation of Milton was likely to suffer by this discovery. That he was not privy to the imposture, I am well persuaded; but that he wished well to the argument, may be inferred from the Preface, which indubitably was written by Johnson.' Is it possible for any man of clear judgement to suppose that Johnson, who so nobly praised the poetical excellence of Milton in a Postscript to this very 'discovery', as he then supposed it, could, at the same time, exult in a persuasion that the great poet's reputation was likely to suffer by it? This is an inconsistency of which Johnson was incapable; nor can any thing more be fairly inferred from the Preface, than that Johnson, who was alike distinguished for ardent curiosity and love of truth, was pleased with an investigation by which both were gratified. That he was actuated by these motives, and certainly by no unworthy desire to depreciate our great epic poet, is evident from his own words; for, after mentioning the general zeal of men of genius and literature 'to advance the honour, and distinguish the beauties of *Paradise Lost*,' he says, 'Among the inquiries to which this ardour of criticism has naturally given occasion, none is more sure in itself, or more worthy of rational curiosity than a retrospection of the progress of this mighty genius in the construction of his work; a view of the fabric gradually rising, perhaps, from small beginnings, till its foundation rests in the centre, and its turrets sparkle in the skies; to trace back the structure through all its varieties, to the simplicity of its first plan; to find what was first projected, whence the scheme was taken, how it was improved, by what assistance it was executed, and from what stores the materials were collected; whether its founder dug them from the quarries of Nature, or demolished other buildings to embellish his own.' – Is this the language of one who wished to blast the laurels of Milton?

Though Johnson's circumstances were at this time far from being easy, his humane and charitable disposition was constantly exerting itself. Mrs Anna

Williams, daughter of a very ingenious Welsh physician, and a woman of more than ordinary talents and literature, having come to London in hopes of being cured of a cataract in both her eyes, which afterwards ended in total blindness, was kindly received as a constant visitor at his house while Mrs Johnson lived; and after her death having come under his roof in order to have an operation upon her eyes performed with more comfort to her than in lodgings, she had an apartment from him during the rest of her life, at all times when he had a house.

In 1752 he was almost entirely occupied with his Dictionary. The last paper of his *Rambler* was published March 2, this year; after which, there was a cessation for some time of any exertion of his talents as an essayist. But, in the same year, Dr Hawkesworth, who was his warm admirer, and a studious imitator of his style, and then lived in great intimacy with him, began a periodical paper, entitled *The Adventurer*, in connection with other gentlemen, one of whom was Johnson's much-loved friend, Dr Bathurst; and, without doubt, they received many valuable hints from his conversation, most of his friends having been so assisted in the course of their works.

That there should be a suspension of his literary labours during a part of the year 1752, will not seem strange, when it is considered that soon after closing his *Rambler*, he suffered a loss which, there can be no doubt, affected him with the deepest distress. For on the 17th of March, O. S. his wife died. Why Sir John Hawkins should unwarrantably take upon him even to suppose that Johnson's fondness for her was *dissembled* (meaning simulated or assumed), and to assert, that if it was not the case, 'it was a lesson he had learned by rote', I cannot conceive; unless it proceeded from a want of similar feelings in his own breast. To argue from her being much older than Johnson, or any other circumstances, that he could not really love her, is absurd; for love is not a subject of reasoning, but of feeling, and therefore there are no common principles upon which one can persuade another concerning it. Every man feels for himself, and knows how he is affected by particular qualities in the person he admires, the impressions of which are too minute and delicate to be substantiated in language.

That his love for her was of the most ardent kind, and, during the long period of fifty years, was unimpaired by the lapse of time, is evident from various passages in the series of his *Prayers and Meditations*, published by the Reverend Mr Strahan, as well as from other memorials, one[a] of which I select, as strongly marking the tenderness and sensibility of his mind.

> April 23, 1753. I know not whether I do not too much indulge the vain longings of affection; but I hope they intenerate my heart, and that when I die like my Tetty, this affection will be acknowledged in a happy interview, and that in the mean time I am incited by it to piety. I will, however, not deviate too much from common and received methods of devotion.[b]

---

[a] For 'one', read 'two'.

[b] Add as a separate paragraph: 'March 28, 1753. I kept this day as the anniversary of my Tetty's death, with prayer and tears in the morning. In the evening I prayed for her conditionally, if it were lawful.'

Her wedding-ring, when she became his wife, was, after her death, preserved by him as long as he lived with an affectionate care, in a little round wooden box, in the inside of which he pasted a slip of paper, thus inscribed by him in fair characters, as follows:

Eheu!
Eliz. Johnson,
Nupta Jul. 9⁰ 1736,
Mortua, eheu!
Mart. 17⁰ 1752.

After his death, Mr Francis Barber, his faithful servant and residuary legatee, offered this memorial of tenderness to Mrs Lucy Porter, Mrs Johnson's daughter; but she having declined to accept of it, he had it enamelled as a mourning-ring for his old master, and presented it to his wife, Mrs Barber, who now has it.

The state of mind in which a man must be upon the death of a woman whom he sincerely loves, had been in his contemplation many years before. In his *Irene*, we find the following fervent and tender speech of Demetrius, addressed to his Aspasia:

> From those bright regions of eternal day,
> Where now thou shin'st amongst thy fellow saints,
> Array'd in purer light, look down on me!
> In pleasing visions and assuasive dreams,
> O! sooth my soul, and teach me how to lose thee.

I have, indeed, been told by Mrs Desmoulins, who, before her marriage, lived for some time with Mrs Johnson at Hampstead, that she indulged herself in country air and nice living, at an unsuitable expense, while her husband was drudging in the smoke of London, and that she by no means treated him with that complacency which is the most engaging quality in a wife. But all this is perfectly compatible with his fondness for her, especially when it is remembered that he had a high opinion of her understanding, and that the impression which her beauty, real or imaginary, had originally made upon his fancy, being continued by habit, had not been effaced, though she herself was doubtless much altered for the worse. The dreadful shock of separation took place in the night; and he immediately dispatched a letter to his friend, the Reverend Dr Taylor, which, as Taylor told me, expressed grief in the strongest manner he had ever read; so that it is much to be regretted it has not been preserved. The letter was brought to Dr Taylor, at his house in the Cloisters, Westminster, about three in the morning; and as it signified an earnest desire to see him, he got up, and went to Johnson as soon as he was dressed, and found him in tears and in extreme agitation. After being a little while together, Johnson requested him to join with him in prayer. He then prayed extempore, as did Dr Taylor; and thus, by means of that piety which was ever his primary object, his troubled mind was, in some degree, soothed and composed.

The next day he wrote as follows:

To the Reverend Dr TAYLOR.

DEAR SIR – Let me have your company and instruction. Do not live away from me. My distress is great.

Pray desire Mrs Taylor to inform me what mourning I should buy for my mother and Miss Porter, and bring a note in writing with you.

Remember me in your prayers, for vain is the help of man.

I am, dear Sir, &c.

SAM. JOHNSON.

March 18, 1752.

That his sufferings upon the death of his wife were severe beyond what are commonly endured, I have no doubt, from the information of many who were then about him, to none of whom I give more credit than to Mr Francis Barber, his faithful negro servant,[1] who came into his family about a fortnight after the dismal event. These sufferings were aggravated by the melancholy inherent in his constitution; and although he probably was not oftener in the wrong than she was, in the little disagreements which sometimes troubled his married state, during which, he owned to me, that the gloomy irritability of his existence was more painful to him than ever, he might very naturally, after her death, be tenderly disposed to charge himself with slight omissions and offences, the sense of which would give him much uneasiness. Accordingly we find, about a year after her decease, that he thus addressed the Supreme Being: 'O LORD, who givest the grace of repentance, and hearest the prayers of the penitent, grant that by true contrition I may obtain forgiveness of all the sins committed, and of all duties neglected in my union with the wife whom thou hast taken from me; for the neglect of joint devotion, patient exhortation, and mild instruction.'[2] The kindness of his heart, notwithstanding the impetuosity of his temper, is well known to his friends; and I cannot trace the smallest foundation for the following dark and uncharitable assertion by Sir John Hawkins: 'The apparition of his departed wife was altogether of the terrific kind, and hardly afforded him a hope that

---

1 Francis Barber was born in Jamaica, and was brought to England in 1750 by Colonel Bathurst, father of Johnson's very intimate friend, Dr Bathurst. He was sent, for some time, to the Reverend Mr Jackson's school, at Barton, in Yorkshire. The Colonel by his will left him his freedom, and Dr Bathurst was willing that he should enter into Johnson's service, in which he continued from 1752 till Johnson's death, with the exception of two intervals; in one of which, upon some difference with his master, he went and served an apothecary in Cheapside, but still visited Dr Johnson occasionally; in another, when he took a fancy to go to sea. Part of the time, indeed, he was, by the kindness of his master, at a school in Northamptonshire, that he might have the advantage of some learning. So early and so lasting a connection was there between Dr Johnson and this humble friend.

2 *Prayers and Meditations*, p. 19.

she was in a state of happiness.'[1] That he, in conformity with the opinion of many of the most able, learned, and pious Christians in all ages, supposed that there was a middle state after death, previous to the time at which departed souls are finally received to eternal felicity, appears, I think, unquestionably from his devotions: 'And, O LORD, so far as it may be lawful in me, I commend to thy fatherly goodness *the soul of my departed wife*; beseeching thee to *grant* her whatever is best in her *present state*, and *finally to receive her to eternal happiness*.'[2] But this state has not been looked upon with horror, but only as less gracious.

He deposited the remains of Mrs Johnson in the church of Bromley in Kent, to which he was probably led by the residence of his friend Hawkesworth at that place. The funeral sermon which he composed for her, which was never preached, but having been given to Dr Taylor, has been published since his death, is a performance of uncommon excellence, and full of rational and pious comfort to such as are depressed by that severe affliction which Johnson felt when he wrote it. When it is considered that it was written in such an agitation of mind, and in the short interval between her death and burial, it cannot be read without wonder.[a]

From Mr Francis Barber I have had the following authentic and artless account of the situation in which he found him recently after his wife's death:

He was in great affliction. Mrs Williams was then living in his house, which was in Gough-square. He was busy with the Dictionary. Mr Shiels,

---

1 Hawkins's *Life of Johnson*, p. 316.
2 *Prayers and Meditations*, p. 20.
[a] Add: The following very solemn and affecting prayer was found after Dr Johnson's decease, by his servant, Mr Francis Barber, who delivered it to my worthy friend, the Reverend Dr Strahan, vicar of Islington, who at my earnest request has obligingly favoured me with a copy of it, which he and I compared with the original. I present it to the world as an undoubted proof of a circumstance in the character of my illustrious friend, which, though some whose hard minds I never shall envy, may attack as superstitious, will I am sure endear him more to numbers of good men. I have an additional, and that a personal motive for presenting it, because it sanctions what I myself have always maintained and am fond to indulge:

April 26, 1752, being after 12 at Night of the 25th.
O Lord! Governor of heaven and earth, in whose hands are embodied and departed Spirits, if thou hast ordained the Souls of the Dead to minister to the Living, and appointed my departed wife to have care of me, grant that I may enjoy the good effects of her attention and ministration, whether exercised by appearance, impulses, dreams, or in any other manner agreeable to Thy Government. Forgive my presumption, enlighten my ignorance, and however meaner agents are employed, grant me the blessed influences of Thy holy Spirit, through Jesus Christ, our Lord, Amen.

What actually followed upon this most interesting piece of devotion by Johnson, we are not informed; but I, whom it has pleased God to afflict in a similar manner to that which occasioned it, have certain experience of benignant communication by dreams.

and some others of the gentlemen who had formerly written for him, used to come about him. He had then little for himself, but frequently sent money to Mr Shiels when in distress. The friends who visited him at that time, were chiefly Dr Bathurst,[a] and Mr Diamond, an apothecary in Cork-street, Burlington-gardens, with whom he and Mrs Williams generally dined every Sunday. There was a talk of his going to Iceland with him, which would probably have happened had he lived. There were also Mr Cave, Dr Hawkesworth, Mr Ryland, merchant on Tower-hill, Mrs Masters the poetess, who lived with Mr Cave, Mrs Carter, and sometimes Mrs Macaulay; also, Mrs Gardiner, wife of a tallow-chandler on Snow-hill, not in the learned way, but a worthy good woman; Mr (now Sir Joshua) Reynolds; Mr Millar, Mr Dodsley, Mr Bouquet, Mr Payne, of Paternoster-row, booksellers; Mr Strahan the printer, the Earl of Orrery, Lord Southwell, Mr Garrick.

Many are, no doubt, omitted in this catalogue of his friends, and, in particular, his humble friend Mr Robert Levet, an obscure practiser in physic amongst the lower people, his fees being sometimes very small sums, sometimes whatever provisions his patients could afford him, but of such extensive practice in that way, that Mrs Williams has told me, his walk was from Houndsditch to Marylebone. It appears from Johnson's diary, that their acquaintance commenced about the year 1746; and such was Johnson's predilection for him, and fanciful estimation of his moderate abilities, that I have heard him say he should not be satisfied, though attended by all the College of Physicians, unless he had Mr Levet with him. Ever since I was acquainted with Dr Johnson, and many years before, as I have been assured by those who knew him earlier, Mr Levet had an apartment in his house, or his chambers, and waited upon him every morning, through the whole course of his late and tedious breakfast. He was of a strange grotesque appearance, stiff and formal in his manner, and seldom said a word while any company was present.

The circle of his friends, indeed, at this time was extensive and various, far beyond what has been generally imagined. To trace his acquaintance with each particular person, if it could be done, would be a task, of which the labour would not be repaid by the advantage. But exceptions are to be made; one of which must be a friend so eminent as Sir Joshua Reynolds, who was truly his *dulce decus*, and with whom he maintained an uninterrupted intimacy to the last hour of his life. When Johnson lived in Castle-street, Cavendish-

---

[a] On Dr Bathurst put the following note: Dr Bathurst, though a physician of no inconsiderable merit, had not the good fortune to get much practice in London. He was, therefore, willing to accept of employment abroad, and, to the regret of all who knew him, fell a sacrifice to the destructive climate, in the expedition against the Havannah. Mr Langton recollects the following passage in a letter from Dr Johnson to Mr Beauclerk: 'The Havannah is taken – a conquest too dearly obtained; for Bathurst died before it.

Vix Priamus tanti totaque Troja fuit.'

square, he used frequently to visit two ladies, who lived opposite to him, Miss Cotterells, daughters of Admiral Cotterell. Reynolds used also to visit there, and thus they met. Mr Reynolds, as I have observed above, had, from the first reading of his *Life of Savage*, conceived a very high admiration of Johnson's powers of writing. His conversation no less delighted him; and he cultivated his acquaintance with the laudable zeal of one who was ambitious of general improvement. Sir Joshua, indeed, was lucky enough at their very first meeting to make a remark, which was so much above the commonplace style of conversation, that Johnson at once perceived that Reynolds had the habit of thinking for himself. The ladies were regretting the death of a friend, to whom they owed great obligations; upon which Reynolds observed, 'You have, however, the comfort of being relieved from a burthen of gratitude.' They were shocked a little at this alleviating suggestion, as too selfish; but Johnson defended it in his clear and forcible manner, and was much pleased with the *mind*, the fair view of human nature, which it exhibited, like some of the reflections of Rochefoucault. The consequence was, that he went home with Reynolds, and supped with him.

Sir Joshua has told me a pleasant characteristical anecdote of Johnson about the time of their first acquaintance. When they were one evening together at Miss Cotterells, the then Duchess of Argyle and another lady of high rank came in. Johnson thinking that the Miss Cotterells were too much engrossed by them, and that he and his friend were neglected, as low company of whom they were somewhat ashamed, grew angry; and resolving to shock their supposed pride, by making their great visitors imagine that his friend and he were low indeed, he addressed himself in a loud tone to Mr Reynolds, saying, 'How much do you think you and I could get in a week, if we were to *work as hard* as we could?' as if they had been common mechanics.

His acquaintance with Bennet Langton, Esq. of Langton, in Lincolnshire, another much valued friend, commenced soon after the conclusion of his *Rambler*, which that gentleman, then a youth, had read with so much admiration, that he came to London chiefly with the view of endeavouring to be introduced to its author. By a fortunate chance he happened to take lodgings in a house where Mr Levet frequently visited; and having mentioned his wish to his landlady, she introduced him to Mr Levet, who readily obtained Johnson's permission to bring Mr Langton to him; as, indeed, Johnson, during the whole course of his life, had no shyness, real or affected, but was easy of access to all who were properly recommended, and even wished to see numbers at his *levee*, as his morning circle of company might, with strict propriety, be called. Mr Langton was exceedingly surprised when the sage first appeared. He had not received the smallest intimation of his figure, dress, or manner. From perusing his writings, he fancied he should see a decent, well-dressed, in short, a remarkably decorous philosopher. Instead of which, down from his bed-chamber, about noon, came, as newly risen, a huge uncouth figure, with a little dark wig which scarcely covered his head, and his clothes hanging loose about him. But his conversation was so rich, so animated, and so forcible, and his religious and political notions so congenial with those in which Mr Langton had been educated, that he conceived for him that veneration and attachment which he ever preserved. Johnson was not the less ready to love Mr Langton, for his being of a very ancient family; for I have heard him say, with pleasure, 'Langton, Sir, has a grant of free warren from Henry the Second; and Cardinal Stephen Langton, in King John's reign, was of this family.'

Mr Langton afterwards went to pursue his studies at Trinity College, Oxford, where he formed an acquaintance with his fellow-student, Mr Topham Beauclerk, who, though their opinions and modes of life were so different, that it seemed utterly improbable that they should at all agree, had so ardent a love of literature, so acute an understanding, such elegance of manners, and so well discerned the excellent qualities of Mr Langton,[a] that they became intimate friends.

Johnson, soon after this acquaintance began, passed a considerable time at Oxford. He at first thought it strange that Langton should associate so much with one who had the character of being loose, – both in his principles and practice; but, by degrees, he himself was fascinated. Mr Beauclerk's being of the St Albans' family, and having, in some particulars, a resemblance to Charles the Second, contributed, in Johnson's imagination, to throw a lustre upon his other qualities; and, in a short time, the moral, pious Johnson, and the gay, dissipated Beauclerk, were companions. 'What a coalition! (said Garrick, when he heard of this); I shall have my old friend to bail out of the Round-house.' But I can bear testimony that it was a very agreeable association. Beauclerk was too polite, and valued learning and wit too much, to offend Johnson by sallies of infidelity or licentiousness; and Johnson delighted in the good qualities of Beauclerk, and hoped to correct the evil. Innumerable were the scenes in which Johnson was amused by these young men. Beauclerk could take more liberty with him, than any body with whom I ever saw him; but, on the other hand, Beauclerk was not spared by his respectable companion, when reproof was proper. Beauclerk had such a propensity to satire, that at one time Johnson said to him, 'You never open your mouth but with intention to give pain; and you have often given me pain, not from the power of what you said, but from seeing your intention.' At another time applying to him, with a slight alteration, a line of Pope, he said, 'Thy love of folly, and thy scorn of fools – Every thing thou dost shows the one, and every thing thou say'st the other.' At another time he said to him, 'Thy body is all vice, and thy mind all virtue.' Beauclerk not seeming to relish the compliment, Johnson said, 'Nay, Sir, Alexander the Great, marching in triumph into Babylon, could not have desired to have had more said to him.'

Johnson was some time with Beauclerk at his house at Windsor, where he was entertained with experiments in natural philosophy. One Sunday, when the weather was very fine, Beauclerk enticed him, insensibly, to saunter about

---

[a] Add: 'a gentleman eminent not only for worth and learning, but for an inexhaustible fund of entertaining conversation.'

all the morning. They went into a church-yard, in the time of divine service, and Johnson laid himself down at his ease upon one of the tomb-stones. 'Now, Sir (said Beauclerk) you are like Hogarth's Idle Apprentice.' When Johnson got his pension, Beauclerk said to him, in the humorous phrase of Falstaff, 'I hope you'll now purge, and live cleanly like a gentleman.'

One night when Beauclerk and Langton had supped at a tavern in London, and sat till about three in the morning, it came into their heads to go and knock up Johnson, and see if they could prevail on him to join them in a ramble. They rapped violently at the door of his chambers in the Temple, till at last he appeared in his shirt, with his little black wig on the top of his head, instead of a nightcap, and a poker in his hand, imagining, probably, that some ruffians were coming to attack him. When he discovered who they were, and was told their errand, he smiled, and with great good humour agreed to their proposal: 'What, is it you, you dogs! I'll have a frisk with you.' He was soon dressed, and they sallied forth together into Covent-Garden, where the green-grocers and fruiterers were beginning to arrange their hampers, just come in from the country. Johnson made some attempts to help them; but the honest gardeners stared so at his figure and manner, and odd interference, that he soon saw his services were not relished. They then repaired to one of the neighbouring taverns, and made a bowl of that liquor called *Bishop*, which Johnson had always liked, while in joyous contempt of sleep, from which he had been roused, he repeated the festive lines,

> Short, O short then be thy reign,
> And give us to the world again!

They did not stay long, but walked down to the Thames, took a boat, and rowed to Billingsgate. Beauclerk and Johnson were so well pleased with their amusement, that they resolved to persevere in dissipation for the rest of the day: but Langton deserted them, being engaged to breakfast with some young ladies. Johnson scolded him for 'leaving his social friends, to go and sit with a set of wretched *un-idea'd* girls.' Garrick being told of this ramble, said to him smartly, 'I heard of your frolic t'other night. You'll be in the Chronicle.' Upon which Johnson afterwards observed, '*He* durst not do such a thing. His wife would not let him!'

He entered upon the year 1753 with his usual piety, as appears from the following prayer transcribed from that part of his diary which he burnt a few days before his death:

'Jan. 1, 1753, N. S. which I shall use for the future.

'Almighty GOD, who hast continued my life to this day, grant that, by the assistance of thy Holy Spirit, I may improve the time which thou shalt grant me, to my eternal salvation. Make me to remember, to thy glory, thy judgements and thy mercies. Make me so to consider the loss of my wife, whom thou hast taken from me, that it may dispose me, by thy grace, to lead the residue of my life in thy fear. Grant this, O LORD, for JESUS CHRIST's sake. Amen.'

He now relieved the drudgery of his Dictionary, and the melancholy of his grief, by taking an active part in the composition of *The Adventurer*, in which he began to write April 10, marking his essays with the signature T, by which most of his papers in that collection are distinguished: those, however, which have that signature and also that of *Mysargyrus*, were not written by him, but, as I suppose, by Dr Bathurst. Indeed Johnson's energy of thought and richness of language, are still more decisive marks than any signature. As a proof of this, my readers, I imagine, will not doubt that No. 39, on sleep, is his; for it not only has the general texture and colour of his style, but the authors with whom he was peculiarly conversant are readily introduced in it in cursory allusion. The translation of a passage in Statius quoted in that paper, and marked C. B. is certainly the performance of Dr Charles Bathurst.[a] How much this amiable man actually contributed to *The Adventurer*, cannot be known. Let me add, that Hawkesworth's imitations of Johnson are sometimes so happy that it is extremely difficult to distinguish them, with certainty, from the compositions of his great archetype. Hawkesworth was his closest imitator, a circumstance of which that writer would once have been proud to be told; though, when he had become elated by having risen into some degree of consequence, he, in a conversation with me, had the provoking effrontery to say he was not sensible of it.

Johnson was truly zealous for the success of the *Adventurer*; and very soon after his engaging in it, he wrote the following letter:

To the Reverend Dr JOSEPH WARTON.

DEAR SIR – I ought to have written to you before now, but I ought to do many things which I do not; nor can I, indeed, claim any merit from this letter; for being desired by the authors and proprietor of the Adventurer to look out for another hand, my thoughts necessarily fix'd upon you, whose fund of literature will enable you to assist them, with very little interruption of your studies.

They desire you to engage to furnish one paper a month, at two guineas a paper, which you may very readily perform. We have considered that a paper should consist of pieces of imagination, pictures of life, and disquisitions of literature. The part which depends on the imagination is very well supplied, as you will find when you read the paper; for descriptions of life, there is now a treaty almost made with an author and an authoress; and the province of criticism and literature they are very desirous to assign to the commentator on Virgil.

I hope this proposal will not be rejected, and that the next post will bring us your compliance. I speak as one of the fraternity, though I have no part in the paper, beyond now and then a motto; but two of the writers are my

---

[a] Delete the words after 'C.B.' and read, 'has been erroneously ascribed to Dr Bathurst, whose Christian name was Richard.'

particular friends, and I hope the pleasure of seeing a third united to them, will not be denied to, dear Sir,

Your most obedient

And most humble servant,

SAM. JOHNSON.

March 8, 1753.

The consequence of this letter was, Dr Warton's enriching the collection with several admirable essays.

Johnson's saying 'I have no part in the paper beyond now and then a motto,' may seem inconsistent with his being the author of the papers marked T. But he had, at this time, written only one number; and besides, even at any after period, he might have used the same expression, considering it as a point of honour not to own them; for Mrs Williams told me, that 'as he had *given* those essays to Dr Bathurst, who sold them at two guineas each, he never would own them; nay, he used to say he did not *write* them: but the fact was, that he *dictated* them, while Bathurst wrote.' I read to him Mrs Williams's account; he smiled, and said nothing.

I am not quite satisfied with the casuistry by which the productions of one person are thus passed upon the world for the productions of another. I allow that not only knowledge, but powers and qualities of mind may be communicated; but the actual effect of individual exertion never can be transferred, with truth, to any other than its original cause. One person's child may be made the child of another person by adoption, as among the Romans, or by the ancient Jewish mode of a wife having children borne to her upon her knees, by her handmaid. But these were children in a different sense from that of nature. It was clearly understood that they were not of the blood of their nominal parents. So in literary children, an author may give the profits and fame of his composition to another man, but cannot make that other the real author. A Highland gentleman, a younger branch of a family, once consulted me if he could not validly purchase the Chieftainship of his family, from the Chief who was willing to sell it. I told him it was impossible for him to acquire, by purchase, a right to be a different person from what he really was; for that the right of Chieftainship attached to the blood of primogeniture, and, therefore, was incapable of being transferred. I added, that though Esau sold his birthright, or the advantages belonging to it, he still remained the first-born of his parents; and that whatever agreement a Chief might make with any of the clan, the Herald's Office could not admit of the metamorphosis, or with any decency attest that the younger was the elder; but I did not convince the worthy gentleman.

Johnson's papers in the *Adventurer* are very similar to those of the *Rambler*; but being rather more varied in their subjects, and being mixed with essays by other writers, upon topics more generally attractive than even the most elegant ethical discourses, the sale of the work, at first, was more extensive. Without meaning, however, to depreciate the *Adventurer*, I must observe, that as the value of the *Rambler* came, in the progress of time, to be better known, it grew upon the public estimation, and that its sale has far exceeded that of any other periodical papers since the reign of Queen Anne.

In one of the books of his diary I find the following entry:

'Apr. 3, 1753. I began the second vol. of my Dictionary, room being left in the first for Preface, Grammar, and History, none of them yet begun.

'O GOD, who hast hitherto supported me, enable me to proceed in this labour, and in the whole task of my present state; that when I shall render up, at the last day, an account of the talent committed to me, I may receive pardon, for the sake of JESUS CHRIST. Amen.'

He this year favoured Mrs Lennox with a dedication to the Earl of Orrery, of her *Shakspeare Illustrated*.

In 1754 I can trace nothing published by him, except his numbers of the *Adventurer*, and 'The Life of Edward Cave', in the *Gentleman's Magazine* for February. In biography there can be no question that he excelled, beyond all who have attempted that species of composition; upon which, indeed, he set the highest value. To the minute selection of characteristical circumstances for which the ancients were remarkable, he added a philosophical research, and the most perspicuous and energetic language. Cave was certainly a man of estimable qualities, and was eminently diligent and successful in his own business, which, doubtless, entitled him to respect. But he was peculiarly fortunate in being recorded by Johnson, who, of the narrow life of a printer and publisher, without any digressions or adventitious circumstances, has made an interesting and agreeable narrative.

The Dictionary, we may believe, afforded Johnson full occupation this year. As it approached to its conclusion, he probably worked with redoubled vigour, as seamen increase their exertion and alacrity when they have a near prospect of their haven.

Lord Chesterfield, to whom Johnson had paid the high compliment of addressing to his Lordship the Plan of his Dictionary, had behaved to him in such a manner as to excite his contempt and indignation. The world has been for many years amused with a story confidently told, and as confidently repeated with additional circumstances, that a sudden disgust was taken by Johnson upon occasion of his having been one day kept long in waiting in his Lordship's antechamber, for which the reason assigned was, that he had company with him; and that at last, when the door opened, out walked Colley Cibber; and that Johnson was so violently provoked when he found for whom he had been so long excluded, that he went away in a passion, and never would return. I remember having mentioned this story to George Lord Lyttelton, who told me, he was very intimate with Lord Chesterfield; and holding it as a well-known truth, defended Lord Chesterfield, by saying, that 'Cibber, who had been introduced familiarly by the back-stairs, had probably not been there above ten minutes.' It may seem strange even to entertain a doubt concerning a story so long and so widely current, and thus implicitly adopted, if not sanctified, by the authority which I have mentioned; but Johnson himself assured me, that there was not the least foundation for it. He told me, that there never was any particular incident which produced a quarrel between Lord Chesterfield and him; but that his Lordship's continued neglect was the reason why he resolved to have no connection with him. When the Dictionary was upon the eve of publication, Lord Chesterfield, who, it is said, had flattered himself with expectations that Johnson would dedicate the work to him, attempted, in a courtly manner, to soothe, and insinuate himself with the sage, conscious, as it should seem, of the cold indifference with which he had treated its learned author; and further attempted to conciliate him, by writing two papers in *The World*, in recommendation of the work; and it must be confessed, that they contain some studied compliments, so finely turned, that if there had been no previous offence, it is probable that Johnson would have been highly delighted. Praise, in general, was pleasing to him; but by praise from a man of rank and elegant accomplishments, he was peculiarly gratified.

His Lordship says, 'I think the public in general, and the republic of letters in particular, are greatly obliged to Mr Johnson, for having undertaken, and executed, so great and desirable a work. Perfection is not to be expected from man: but if we are to judge by the various works of Johnson already published, we have good reason to believe, that he will bring this as near to perfection as any one man could do. The Plan of it, which he published some years ago, seems to me to be a proof of it. Nothing can be more rationally imagined, or more accurately and elegantly expressed. I therefore recommend the previous perusal of it to all those who intend to buy the Dictionary, and who, I suppose, are all those who can afford it . . .

'It must be owned, that our language is, at present, in a state of anarchy, and hitherto, perhaps, it may not have been the worse for it. During our free and open trade, many words and expressions have been imported, adopted, and naturalized from other languages, which have greatly enriched our own. Let it still preserve what real strength and beauty it may have borrowed from others; but let it not, like the Tarpeian maid, be overwhelmed and crushed by unnecessary ornaments. The time for discrimination seems to be now come. Toleration, adoption, and naturalization have run their lengths. Good order and authority are now necessary. But where shall we find them, and, at the same time, the obedience due to them? We must have recourse to the old Roman expedient in times of confusion, and choose a dictator. Upon this principle, I give my vote for Mr Johnson to fill that great and arduous post. And I hereby declare, that I make a total surrender of all my rights and privileges in the English language, as a free-born British subject, to the said Mr Johnson, during the term of his dictatorship. Nay more, I will not only obey him, like an old Roman, as my dictator, but, like a modern Roman, I will implicitly believe in him as my Pope, and hold him to be infallible while in the chair, but no longer. More than this he cannot well require; for, I presume, that obedience can never be expected, when there is neither terror to enforce, nor interest to invite it . . .

'But a Grammar, a Dictionary, and a History of our Language through its several stages, were still wanting at home, and importunately called for from abroad. Mr Johnson's labours will now, I dare say, very fully supply that want, and greatly contribute to the farther spreading of our language in other countries. Learners were discouraged, by finding no standard to resort to; and, consequently, thought it incapable of any. They will now be undeceived and encouraged.'

This courtly device failed of its effect. Johnson, who thought that 'all was false and hollow', despised the honeyed words, and was even indignant that Lord Chesterfield should, for a moment, imagine, that he could be the dupe of such an artifice. His expression to me concerning Lord Chesterfield, upon this occasion, was, 'Sir, after making great professions, he had, for many years, taken no notice of me; but when my Dictionary was coming out, he fell a scribbling in the *World* about it. Upon which, I wrote him a letter, expressed in civil terms, but such as might show him that I did not mind what he said or wrote, and that I had done with him.'

This is that celebrated letter, of which so much has been said, and about which curiosity has been so long excited, without being gratified. I for many years solicited Johnson to favour me with a copy of it, that so excellent a composition might not be lost to posterity. He delayed from time to time to give it me; till at last in 1781, when we were on a visit at Mr Dilly's, at Southill in Bedfordshire, he was pleased to dictate it to me from memory.[a]

He afterwards found among his papers a copy of it, with its title and corrections, in his own handwriting. This he gave to Mr Langton; adding, that if it were to come into print, he wished it to be from that copy. By Mr Langton's kindness, I am enabled to enrich my work with a perfect transcript of what the world has so eagerly desired to see.

To the Right Honourable the EARL OF CHESTERFIELD.

February, 1755.
MY LORD – I have been lately informed, by the proprietor of the *World*, that two papers, in which my Dictionary is recommended to the public, were written by your Lordship. To be so distinguished, is an honour, which, being very little accustomed to favours from the great, I know not well how to receive, or in what terms to acknowledge.

When, upon some slight encouragement, I first visited your Lordship, I was overpowered, like the rest of mankind, by the enchantment of your address; and could not forbear to wish that I might boast myself *Le vainqueur du vainqueur de la terre*; – that I might obtain that regard for which I saw the world contending; but I found my attendance so little encouraged, that

---

[a] Add: Dr Johnson appeared to have had a remarkable delicacy with respect to the circulation of this letter; for Dr Douglas, Bishop of Salisbury, informs me, that having many years ago pressed him to be allowed to read it to the second Lord Hardwicke, who was very desirous to hear it (promising at the same time, that no copy of it should be taken), Johnson seemed much pleased that it had attracted the attention of a nobleman of such a respectable character; but after pausing some time, declined to comply with the request, saying with a smile, 'No, Sir; I have hurt the dog too much already'; or words to that purpose.

neither pride nor modesty would suffer me to continue it. When I had once addressed your Lordship in public, I had exhausted all the art of pleasing which a retired and uncourtly scholar can possess. I had done all that I could; and no man is well pleased to have his all neglected, be it ever so little.

Seven years, my Lord, have now past, since I waited in your outward rooms, or was repulsed from your door; during which time I have been pushing on my work through difficulties, of which it is useless to complain, and have brought it, at last, to the verge of publication, without one act of assistance,[1] one word of encouragement, or one smile of favour. Such treatment I did not expect, for I never had a Patron before.

The shepherd in Virgil grew at last acquainted with Love, and found him a native of the rocks.

Is not a Patron, my Lord, one who looks with unconcern on a man struggling for life in the water, and, when he has reached ground, encumbers him with help? The notice which you have been pleased to take of my labours, had it been early, had it been kind; but it has been delayed till I am indifferent, and cannot enjoy it; till I am solitary, and cannot impart it;[2] till I am known, and do not want it. I hope it is no very cynical asperity not to confess obligations where no benefit has been received, or to be unwilling that the public should consider me as owing that to a Patron, which Providence has enabled me to do for myself.

Having carried on my work thus far with so little obligation to any favourer of learning, I shall not be disappointed though I should conclude it, if less be possible, with less; for I have been long wakened from that dream of hope, in which I once boasted myself with so much exultation,
My Lord,
Your Lordship's most humble,
Most obedient servant,

SAM. JOHNSON.[3]

---

1 The following note is subjoined by Mr Langton. 'Dr Johnson, when he gave me this copy of his letter, desired that I would annex to it his information to me, that whereas it is said in the letter that "no assistance has been received", he did once receive from Lord Chesterfield the sum of ten pounds, but as that was so inconsiderable a sum, he thought the mention of it could not properly find place in a letter of the kind that this was.'

2 In this passage Dr Johnson evidently alludes to the loss of his wife. We find the same tender recollection recurring to his mind upon innumerable occasion; and, perhaps, no man ever more forcibly felt the truth of the sentiment so elegantly. expressed by my friend Mr Malone, in his Prologue to Mr Jephson's tragedy of *Julia*:

> Vain – wealth, and fame, and fortune's fostering care,
> If no fond breast the splendid blessings share;
> And, each day's bustling pageantry once past,
> There, only there, our bliss is found at last.

3 Upon comparing this copy with that which Dr Johnson dictated to me from recollection, the variations are found to be so slight, that this must be added to the many other proofs which he gave of the wonderful extent and accuracy of his memory.

'While this was the talk of the town (says Dr Adams, in a letter to me) I happened to visit Dr Warburton, who finding that I was acquainted with Johnson, desired me earnestly to carry his compliments to him, and to tell him, that he honoured him for his manly behaviour in rejecting these condescensions of Lord Chesterfield, and for resenting the treatment he had received from him, with a proper spirit. Johnson was visibly pleased with this compliment, for he had always a high opinion of Warburton.'[a] – Indeed the force of mind which appeared in this letter, was congenial with that which Warburton himself amply possessed.

There is a curious minute circumstance which struck me, in comparing the various editions of Johnson's imitations of Juvenal. In the tenth Satire, one of the couplets upon the vanity of wishes even for literary distinction stood thus:

> Yet think what ills the scholar's life assail,
> Pride, envy, want, the *garret*, and the jail.

But after experiencing the uneasiness which Lord Chesterfield's fallacious patronage made him feel, he dismissed the word *garret* from the sad group, and in all the subsequent editions the line stands

> Pride, envy, want, the *Patron*, and the jail.

That Lord Chesterfield must have been mortified by the lofty contempt, and polite, yet keen satire with which Johnson exhibited him to himself in this letter, it is impossible to doubt. He, however, with that glossy duplicity which was his constant study, affected to be quite unconcerned. Dr Adams mentioned to Mr Robert Dodsley that he was sorry Johnson had written his letter to Lord Chesterfield. Dodsley, with the true feelings of trade, said 'he was very sorry too; for that he had a property in the Dictionary, to which his Lordship's patronage might have been of consequence.' He then told Dr Adams, that Lord Chesterfield had shown him the letter. 'I should have imagined (replied Dr Adams), that Lord Chesterfield would have concealed it.' 'Poh! (said Dodsley), do you think a letter from Johnson could hurt Lord Chesterfield? Not at all, Sir. It lay upon his table, where any body might see it. He read it to me; said, "this man has great powers", pointed out the severest passages, and observed how well they were expressed.' This air of indifference, which imposed upon the worthy Dodsley, was certainly nothing but a specimen of that dissimulation

---

[a] Add the following note: Soon after Edwards's *Canons of Criticism* came out, Johnson was dining at Tonson the bookseller's, with Hayman the painter, and some more company. Hayman related to Sir Joshua Reynolds that the conversation having turned upon Edwards's book, the gentlemen praised it much, and Johnson allowed its merits. But when they went farther, and appeared to put that author upon a level with Warburton, 'Nay, (said Johnson), he has given him some smart hits to be sure; but there is no proportion between the two men; they must not be named together. A fly, Sir, may sting a stately horse, and make him wince; but one is but an insect, and the other is a horse still.'

which Lord Chesterfield inculcated as one of the most essential lessons for the conduct of life. His Lordship endeavoured to justify himself to Dodsley from the charges brought against him by Johnson; but we may judge of the flimsiness of his defence, from his having excused his neglect of Johnson, by saying that 'he had heard he had changed his lodgings, and did not know where he lived'; as if there could have been the smallest difficulty to inform himself of that circumstance, by enquiring in the literary circle with which his Lordship was well acquainted, and was, indeed, himself one of its ornaments.

Dr Adams expostulated with Johnson, and suggested, that his not being admitted when he called on him, was, probably, not to be imputed to Lord Chesterfield; for his Lordship had declared to Dodsley, that 'he would have turned off the best servant he ever had, if he had known that he denied him to a man who would have been always more than welcome'; and, in confirmation of this, he insisted on Lord Chesterfield's general affability and easiness of access, especially to literary men. 'Sir (said Johnson), that is not Lord Chesterfield; he is the proudest man this day existing.' 'No (said Dr Adams), there is one person, at least, as proud; I think, by your own account, you are the prouder man of the two.' 'But mine (replied Johnson, instantly) was *defensive* pride.' This, as Dr Adams well observed, was one of those happy turns for which he was so remarkably ready.

Johnson having now explicitly avowed his opinion of Lord Chesterfield, did not refrain from expressing himself concerning that nobleman with pointed freedom: 'This man (said he) I thought had been a Lord among wits; but, I find, he is only a wit among Lords!' And when his Letters to his natural son were published, he observed, that 'they teach the morals of a whore, and the manners of a dancing-master.'[1]

The character of a 'respectable Hottentot', in Lord Chesterfield's letters, has been generally understood to be meant for Johnson, and I have no doubt that

---

[1] That collection of letters cannot be vindicated from the serious charge of encouraging, in some passages, one of the vices most destructive to the good order and comfort of society, which his Lordship represents as mere fashionable gallantry; and, in others, of inculcating the base practice of dissimulation, and recommending, with disproportionate anxiety, a perpetual attention to external elegance of manner. But it must, at the same time, be allowed, that they contain many good precepts of conduct, and much genuine information upon life and manners, very happily expressed; and that there was considerable merit in paying so much attention to the improvement of one who was dependent upon his Lordship's protection; it has, probably, been exceeded in no instance by the most exemplary parent; and though I can by no means approve of confounding the distinction between lawful and illicit offspring, which is, in effect, insulting the civil establishment of our country, to look no higher; I cannot help thinking it laudable to be kindly attentive to those, of whose existence we have, in any way, been the cause. Mr Stanhope's character has been unjustly represented as diametrically opposite to what Lord Chesterfield wished him to be. He has been called dull, gross, and awkward: but I knew him at Dresden, when he was Envoy to that court; and though he could not boast of the *graces*, he was, in truth, a sensible, civil, well-behaved man.

it was. But I remember when the *Literary Property* of those letters was contested in the Court of Session in Scotland, and Mr Henry Dundas, one of the Counsel for the proprietors, read this character as an exhibition of Johnson, Sir David Dalrymple, Lord Hailes, one of the Judges, maintained, with some warmth, that it was not intended as a portrait of Johnson, but of a late noble Lord, distinguished for abstruse science. I have heard Johnson himself talk of the character, and say that it was meant for George Lord Lyttelton, in which I could by no means agree; for his Lordship had nothing of that violence which is a conspicuous feature in the composition. Finding that my illustrious friend could bear to have it supposed that it might be meant for him, I said, laughingly, that there was one trait which unquestionably did not belong to him; 'he throws his meat any where but down his throat.' 'Sir (said he), Lord Chesterfield never saw me eat in his life.'

On the 6th of March came out Lord Bolingbroke's works, published by Mr David Mallet. The wild and pernicious ravings, under the name of 'Philosophy', which were thus ushered into the world, gave great offence to all well-principled men. Johnson, hearing of their tendency, which nobody disputed, was roused with a just indignation, and pronounced this memorable sentence upon the noble author and his editor. 'Sir, he was a scoundrel, and a coward: a scoundrel, for charging a blunderbuss against religion and morality; a coward, because he had not resolution to fire it off himself, but left half a crown to a beggarly Scotchman, to draw the trigger after his death!' Garrick, who I can attest from my own knowledge, had his mind seasoned with pious reverence, and sincerely disapproved of the infidel writings of several, whom, in the course of his almost universal gay intercourse with men of eminence, he treated with external civility, distinguished himself upon this occasion. Mr Pelham having died on the very day on which Lord Bolingbroke's works came out, he wrote an elegant Ode on his death, beginning:

> Let others hail the rising sun,
> I bow to that whose course is run;

in which is the following stanza:

> The same sad morn to church and state
> (So for our sins 'twas fix'd by fate),
>   A double stroke was given;
> Black as the whirlwinds of the North,
> St John's fell genius issued forth,
>   And Pelham fled to heaven.

Johnson this year found an interval of leisure to make an excursion to Oxford, for the purpose of consulting the libraries there. Of this, and of many interesting circumstances concerning him, during a part of his life when he conversed but little with the world, I am enabled to give a particular account, by the liberal communications of the Reverend Mr Thomas Warton, who has obligingly furnished me with several of our common friend's letters, which he has illustrated with notes. These I shall insert in their proper places.

To the Reverend Mr THOMAS WARTON.

SIR — It is but an ill return for the book with which you were pleased to favour me,[1] to have delayed my thanks for it till now. I am too apt to be negligent; but I can never deliberately show my disrespect to a man of your character: and I now pay you a very honest acknowledgement, for the advancement of the literature of our native country. You have shown to all, who shall hereafter attempt the study of our ancient authors, the way to success; by directing them to the perusal of the books which those authors had read. Of this method, Hughes,[2] and men much greater than Hughes, seemed never to have thought. The reason why the authors, which are yet read, of the sixteenth century, are so little understood, is, that they are read alone; and no help is borrowed from those who lived with them, or before them. Some part of this ignorance I hope to remove by my book,[3] which now draws towards its end; but which I cannot finish to my mind, without visiting the libraries of Oxford, which I, therefore, hope to see in a fortnight.[4] I know not how long I shall stay, or where I shall lodge; but shall be sure to look for you at my arrival, and we shall easily settle the rest. I am, dear Sir,

Your most obedient, &c.

SAM. JOHNSON.

[London,] July 16, 1754.

Of his conversation while at Oxford at this time, Mr Warton has preserved and communicated to me the following memorial, which, though not written with all the care and attention which that learned and elegant writer bestows on those compositions which he intends for the public eye, is so happily expressed in an easy style, that I should injure it by any alteration:

'When Johnson came to Oxford in 1754, the long vacation was beginning, and most people were leaving the place. This was the first time of his being there, after quitting the University. The next morning after his arrival, he wished to see his old College, Pembroke. I went with him. He was highly pleased to find all the College-servants which he had left there still remaining, particularly a very old butler; and expressed great satisfaction at being recognized by them, and conversed with them familiarly. He waited on the master, Dr Radcliffe, who received him very coldly. Johnson at least expected, that the master would order a copy of his Dictionary, now near publication: but

---

1 [Observations on Spenser's *Fairy Queen*, the first edition of which was now just published. T.W.]

2 [Hughes published an edition of Spenser. T.W.]

3 [His Dictionary. T.W.]

4 [He came to Oxford within a fortnight, and stayed about five weeks. He lodged at a house called Kettle-hall, near Trinity College. But during this visit at Oxford he collected nothing in the libraries for his Dictionary. T.W.]

the master did not choose to talk on the subject, never asked Johnson to dine, nor even to visit him, while he stayed at Oxford. After we had left the Lodgings, Johnson said to me, "*There* lives a man, who lives by the revenues of literature, and will not move a finger to support it. If I come to live at Oxford, I shall take up my abode at Trinity." We then called on the Reverend Mr Meeke, one of the fellows, and of Johnson's standing. Here was a most cordial greeting on both sides. On leaving him, Johnson said, "I used to think Meeke had excellent parts, when we were boys together at the College: but, alas!

> Lost in a convent's solitary gloom!

I remember, at the classical lecture in the Hall, I could not bear Meeke's superiority, and I tried to sit as far from him as I could, that I might not hear him construe."

'As we were leaving the College, he said, "Here I translated Pope's *Messiah*. Which do you think is the best line in it? My own favourite is,

> *Vallis aromaticas fundit Saronica nubes."*

I told him, I thought it a very sonorous hexameter. I did not tell him, it was not in the Virgilian style. He much regretted that his first tutor was dead; for whom he seemed to retain the greatest regard. He said, "I once had been a whole morning sliding [skating], in Christ-Church Meadow, and missed his lecture in logic. After dinner, he sent for me to his room. I expected a sharp rebuke for my idleness, and went with a beating heart. When we were seated, he told me he had sent for me to drink a glass of wine with him, and to tell me, he was *not* angry with me for missing his lecture. This was, in fact, a most severe reprimand. Some more of the boys were then sent for, and we spent a very pleasant afternoon." Besides Mr Meeke, there was only one other Fellow of Pembroke now resident: from both of whom Johnson received the greatest civilities during this visit, and they pressed him very much to have a room in the College.

'In the course of this visit (1754), Johnson and I walked, three or four times, to Ellsfield, a village beautifully situated about three miles from Oxford, to see Mr Wise, Radclivian librarian, with whom Johnson was much pleased. At this place, Mr Wise had fitted up a house and gardens, in a singular manner, but with great taste. Here was an excellent library; particularly, a valuable collection of books in Northern literature, with which Johnson was often very busy. One day Mr Wise read to us a dissertation which he was preparing for the press, intitled, 'A History and Chronology of the fabulous Ages'. Some old divinities of Thrace, related to the Titans, and called the CABIRI, made a very important part of the theory of this piece; and in conversation afterwards, Mr Wise talked much of the CABIRI. As we returned to Oxford in the evening, I out-walked Johnson, and he cried out *Sufflamina*, a Latin word which came from his mouth with peculiar grace, and was as much as to say, *Put on your drag-chain*. Before we got home, I again walked too fast for him; and he now cried out, "Why, you walk as if you were pursued by all the CABIRI in a body." In an evening, we frequently took long walks from Oxford into the country, returning to supper. Once, in our way home, we viewed the ruins of the abbies of Oseney and Rewley, near Oxford. After at least half an hour's silence, Johnson said, "I viewed them with indignation!" We had then a long conversation on Gothic buildings, and in talking of the form of old halls, he said, "In these halls, the fireplace was anciently always in the middle of the room, till the Whigs removed it on one side." – About this time there had been an execution of two or three criminals at Oxford on a Monday. Soon afterwards, one day at dinner, I was saying that Mr Swinton the chaplain of the gaol, and also a frequent preacher before the University, a learned man, but often thoughtless and absent, preached the condemnation sermon on repentance, before the convicts, on the preceding day, Sunday: and that in the close he told his audience that he should give them the remainder of what he had to say on the subject, the next Lord's Day. Upon which, one of our company, a Doctor of Divinity, and a plain matter-of-fact man, by way of offering an apology for Mr Swinton, gravely remarked, that he had probably preached the same sermon before the University: "Yes, Sir (said Johnson), but the University were not to be hanged the next morning."

'I forgot to observe before, that when he left Mr Meeke (as I have told above) he added, "About the same time of life, Meeke was left behind at Oxford to feed on a Fellowship, and I went to London to get my living: now, Sir, see the difference of our literary characters!" '

The following letter was written by Dr Johnson to Mr Chambers, of Lincoln College, now Sir Robert Chambers, one of the Judges in India:[1]

To Mr CHAMBERS, of Lincoln College.

DEAR SIR – The commission which I delayed to trouble you with at your departure, I am now obliged to send you; and beg that you will be so kind as to carry it to Mr Warton, of Trinity, to whom I should have written immediately, but that I know not if he be yet come back to Oxford.

In the Catalogue of MSS. of Gr. Brit. see vol. I. pag. 18. MSS. Bodl. MARTYRIUM XV. *martyrum sub Juliano, auctore Theophylacto.*

It is desired that Mr Warton will inquire, and send word, what will be the cost of transcribing this manuscript.

Vol. II. pag. 32. Num. 1022. 58. COLL. NOV. – *Commentaria in Acta Apostol.* – *Comment. in Septem Epistolas Catholicas.*

He is desired to tell what is the age of each of these manuscripts; and what it will cost to have a transcript of the two first pages of each.

If Mr Warton be not in Oxford, you may try if you can get it done by any body else: or stay till he comes, according to your own convenience. It is for an Italian *literato.*

1 Communicated by the Reverend Mr Thomas Warton, who has the original.

The answer is to be directed to his Excellency Mr Zon, Venetian Resident, Soho-square.

I hope, dear Sir, that you do not regret the change of London for Oxford. Mr Baretti is well, and Miss Williams;[1] and we shall all be glad to hear from you, whenever you shall be so kind as to write to, Sir,

Your most humble servant,

SAM. JOHNSON.

Nov 21, 1754.

The degree of Master of Arts, which, it has been observed, could not be obtained for him at an early period of his life, was now considered as an honour of considerable importance, in order to grace the title-page of his Dictionary; and his character in the literary world being by this time deservedly high, his friends thought that if proper exertions were made, the University of Oxford would pay him the compliment.

To the Reverend Mr THOMAS WARTON.

DEAR SIR – I am extremely obliged to you and to Mr Wise, for the uncommon care which you have taken of my interest:[2] if you can accomplish your kind design, I shall certainly take me a little habitation among you.

The books which I promised to Mr Wise,[3] I have not been able to procure: but I shall send him a Finnick Dictionary, the only copy, perhaps, in England, which was presented me by a learned Swede; but I keep it back, that it may make a set of my own books of the new edition, with which I shall accompany it, more welcome. You will assure him of my gratitude.

1 [I presume she was a relation of Mr Zachariah Williams, who died in his eighty-third year, July 12, 1755. When Dr Johnson was with me at Oxford, in 1755, he gave to the Bodleian Library a thin quarto of twenty-one pages, a work in Italian, with an English translation on the opposite page The English title-page is this: 'An Account of an Attempt to ascertain the Longitude at Sea, by an exact Variation of the Magnetical Needle, &c. By Zachariah Williams. London, printed for Dodsley, 1755.' The English translation, from the strongest internal marks, is unquestionably the work of Johnson. In a blank leaf, Johnson has written the age, and time of death, of the author, Z. Williams, as I have said above. On another blank leaf is pasted a paragraph from a newspaper, of the death and character of Williams, which is plainly written by Johnson. He was very anxious about placing this book in the Bodleian: and, for fear of any omission or mistake, he entered, in the great Catalogue, the title-page of it, with his own hand. T.W.]

2 [In procuring him the degree of Master of Arts by diploma at Oxford. T.W.]

3 [Lately Fellow of Trinity College, and at this time Radclivian librarian, at Oxford. He was a man of very considerable learning and eminently skilled in Roman and Anglo-Saxon antiquities. He died in 1767. T.W.]

Poor dear Collins![1] – Would a letter give him any pleasure? I have a mind to write.

I am glad of your hindrance in your Spenserian design,[2] yet I would not have it delayed. Three hours a day stolen from sleep and amusement will produce it. Let a Servitour[3] transcribe the quotations, and interleave them with references, to save time. This will shorten the work, and lessen the fatigue.

Can I do any thing to promoting the diploma? I would not be wanting to co-operate with your kindness; of which, whatever be the effect, I shall be, dear Sir,

Your most obliged, &c.

SAM. JOHNSON.

[London,] Nov. 28, 1754.

To the same.

DEAR SIR, – I am extremely sensible of the favour done me, both by Mr Wise and yourself. The book[4] cannot, I think, be printed in less than six weeks, nor probably so soon; and I will keep back the title-page, for such an insertion as you seem to promise me. Be pleased to let me know what money I shall send you, for bearing the expense of the affair; and I will take care that you may have it ready at your hand.

I had lately the favour of a letter from your brother, with some account of poor Collins, for whom I am much concerned. I have a notion, that by very great temperance, or more properly abstinence, he may yet recover.

There is an old English and Latin book of poems by Barclay, called *The Ship of Fools*; at the end of which are a number of *Eglogues*, so he writes it, from *Egloga*, which are probably the first in our language. If you cannot find the book, I will get Mr Dodsley to send it to you.

I shall be extremely glad to hear from you again, to know if the affair proceeds.[5] I have mentioned it to none of my friends, for fear of being laughed at for my disappointment.

'You know poor Mr Dodsley has lost his wife; I believe he is much affected. I hope he will not suffer so much as I yet suffer for the loss of mine.

Οἴμι. τι δ' οἴμι; θνητὰ γὰρ πεπόνθαμεν.[6]

I have ever since seemed to myself broken off from mankind; a kind of solitary wanderer in the wild of life, without any direction, or fixed point of

---

1 [Collins (the poet) was at this time at Oxford, on a visit to Mr Warton; but labouring under the most deplorable languor of body, and dejection of mind. T.W.]

2 [Of publishing a volume of Observations on the best of Spenser's works. It was hindered by my taking pupils in this College. T.W.]

3 [Young students of the lowest rank at Oxford are so called. T.W.]

4 [His Dictionary. T.W.]

5 [Of the degree at Oxford. T.W.]

6 ['Alas! Yet why alas? What we suffer is our mortal lot.' Euripides, Frag.]

view: a gloomy gazer on a world to which I have little relation. Yet I would endeavour, by the help of you and your brother, to supply the want of closer union, by friendship; and hope to have long the pleasure of being, dear Sir,

Most affectionately your's,

SAM. JOHNSON.

[London,] Dec. 21, 1754.

In 1755 we behold him to great advantage; his degree of Master of Arts conferred upon him, his Dictionary published, his correspondence animated, his benevolence exercised.

To the Revd. Mr THOMAS WARTON.

DEAR SIR – I wrote to you some weeks ago, but believe did not direct accurately, and therefore know not whether you had my letter. I would, likewise, write to your brother, but know not where to find him. I now begin to see land, after having wandered, according to Mr Warburton's phrase, in this vast sea of words. What reception I shall meet with on the shore, I know not; whether the sound of bells, and acclamations of the people, which Ariosto talks of in his last Canto, or a general murmur of dislike, I know not: whether I shall find upon the coast a Calypso that will court, or a Polypheme that will resist. But if Polypheme comes, have at his eyes. I hope, however, the critics will let me be at peace; for though I do not much fear their skill and strength, I am a little afraid of myself, and would not willingly feel so much ill-will in my bosom as literary quarrels are apt to excite.

Mr Barretti is about a work for which he is in great want of Crescimbeni, which you may have again when you please.

There is nothing considerable done or doing among us here. We are not, perhaps, as innocent as villagers, but most of us seem to be as idle. I hope, however, you are busy; and should be glad to know what you are doing. I am, dearest Sir,

Your most humble servant,

SAM. JOHNSON.

[London,] Feb. 1, 1755.

To the same.

DEAR SIR – I received your letter this day, with great sense of the favour that has been done me;[1] for which I return my most sincere thanks: and entreat you to pay to Mr Wise such returns as I ought to make for so much kindness so little deserved.

I sent Mr Wise the Lexicon, and afterwards wrote to him; but know not

---

1 [His degree had now past, according to the usual form, the suffrages of the heads of Colleges; but was not yet finally granted by the University. It was carried without a single dissentient voice. T.W.]

whether he had either the book or letter. Be so good as to contrive to enquire.

But why does my dear Mr Warton tell me nothing of himself? Where hangs the new volume?[1] Can I help? Let not the past labour be lost, for want of a little more: but snatch what time you can from the Hall, and the pupils, and the coffee-house, and the parks, and complete your design.

I am, dear Sir, &c.

SAM. JOHNSON.

[London,] Feb 4, 1755.

To the same.

DEAR SIR – I had a letter last week from Mr Wise, but have yet heard nothing from you, nor know in what state my affair stands;[2] Of which I beg you to inform me, if you can, tomorrow by the return of the post.

Mr Wise sends me word, that he has not had the Finnick Lexicon yet, which I sent some time ago; and if he has it not, you must enquire after it. However, do not let your letter stay for that.

Your brother, who is a better correspondent than you, and not much better, sends me word, that your pupils keep you in College, but do they keep you from writing too? Let them, at least, give you time to write to, dear Sir,

Your most affectionate, &c.

SAM. JOHNSON.

[London,] Feb. 13, 1755.

To the same.

DEAR SIR – Dr King[3] was with me a few minutes before your letter; this, however, is the first instance in which your kind intentions to me have ever been frustrated.[4] I have now the full effect of your care and benevolence; and am far from thinking it a slight honour, or a small advantage; since it will put the enjoyment of your conversation more frequently in the power of, dear Sir,

Your most obliged and affectionate

SAM. JOHNSON.

P.S. I have enclosed a letter to the Vice-Chancellor,[5] which you will read; and, if you like it, seal and give him.

[London,] Feb. 1755.

---

1 [On Spenser. T.W.]

2 [Of the degree. T.W.]

3 [Principal of Saint Mary Hall at Oxford. He brought with him the diploma from Oxford. T.W.]

4 [I suppose Johnson means that my *kind intention* of being the first to give him the good news of the degree being granted was *frustrated*, because Dr King brought it before my intelligence arrived. T.W.]

5 [Dr Huddesford, President of Trinity College. T.W.]

As the public will doubtless be pleased to see the whole progress of this well-earned academical honour, I shall insert the Chancellor of Oxford's letter to the University,[1] the diploma, and Johnson's letter of thanks to the Vice-Chancellor.

To the Reverend Dr HUDDESFORD, Vice-Chancellor of the University of Oxford, to be communicated to the Heads of Houses, and proposed in Convocation.

MR VICE-CHANCELLOR, AND GENTLEMEN – Mr Samuel Johnson, who was formerly of Pembroke College, having very eminently distinguished himself by the publication of a series of essays, excellently calculated to form the manners of the people, and in which the cause of religion and morality is every where maintained by the strongest powers of argument and language, and who shortly intends to publish a Dictionary of the English Tongue, formed on a new plan, and executed with the greatest labour and judgement; I persuade myself that I shall act agreeably to the sentiments of the whole University, in desiring that it may be proposed in convocation to confer on him the degree of Master of Arts by diploma, to which I readily give my consent; and am,

Mr Vice-Chancellor, and Gentlemen,

Your affectionate friend and servant,

ARRAN.

Grosvenor-street, Feb. 4, 1755.

DIPLOMA MAGISTRI JOHNSON.

CANCELLARIUS, Magistri et Scholares Universitatis Oxoniensis omnibus ad quos hoc presens scriptum pervenerit, salutem in Domino sempiternam.

Cum eum in finem gradus academici a majoribus nostris instituti fuerint, ut viri ingenio et doctrina praestantes titulis quoque praeter caeteros insignirentur; cumque vir doctissimus Samuel Johnson e Collegio Pembrochiensi, scriptis suis popularium mores informantibus dudum literato orbi innotuerit; quin et linguae patriae tum ornandae tum stabiliendae (Lexicon scilicet Anglicanum summo studio, summo a se judicio congestum propediem editurus) etiam nunc utilissimam impendat operam; Nos igitur Cancellarius, Magistri, et Scholares antedicti, ne virum de literis humanioribus optime meritum diutius inhonoratum praetereamus, in solenni Convocatione Doctorum, Magistrorum, Regentium, et non Regentium, decimo die Mensis Februarii Anno Domini Millesimo Septengentessimo Quinquagesimo quinto habita, praefatum virum Samuelem Johnson (conspirantibus omnium suffragiis) magistrum in artibus renunciavimus et constituimus; eumque, virtute praesentis diplomatis, singulis juribus privilegiis et honoribus ad istum gradum quaqua pertinentibus frui et gaudere jussimus.

In cujus rei testimonium sigillum Universitatis Oxoniensis praesentibus apponi fecimus.

---

1 Extracted from the Convocation-Register, Oxford.

Datum in Domo Nostrae Convocationis die 20° Mensis Feb. Anno Dom. praedicto.

Diploma supra scriptum per Registrarium lectum erat, et ex decreto venerabilis Domus communi Universitatis sigillo munitum.[1]

Dom. Doctori Huddesford,
Oxoniensis Academiae Vice-Cancellario.

INGRATUS plane et tibi et mihi videar, nisi quanto me gaudio affecerint, quos nuper mihi honores (te credo auctore) decrevit Senatus Academicus, literarum, quo tamen nihil levius, officio, significem: ingratus etiam, nisi comitatem, qua vir eximius,[2] *mihi vestri testimonium amoris in manus tradidit, agnoscam et laudem. Si quid est unde rei tam gratae accedat gratia, hoc ipso magis mihi placet, quod eo tempore in ordines Academicos denuo cooptatus sim, quo tuam imminuere auctoritatem, famamque Oxonii laedere, omnibus modis conantur homines vafri, nec tamen acuti: quibus ego, prout viro umbratico licuit, semper restiti, semper restiturus. Qui enim, inter has rerum procellas, vel Tibi vel Academiae defuerit, illum virtuti et literis, sibique et posteris, defuturum existimo.*

S. Johnson.

To the Reverend Mr Thomas Warton.

Dear Sir — After I received my diploma, I wrote you a letter of thanks, with a letter to the Vice-Chancellor, and sent another to Mr Wise; but have heard from nobody since, and begin to think myself forgotten. It is true, I sent you a double letter, and you may fear an expensive correspondent; but I would have taken it kindly, if you had returned it treble: and what is a double letter to a *petty king*, that having *fellowship and fines*, can sleep without a *Modus in his head*?[3]

Dear Mr Warton, let me hear from you, and tell me something, I care not what, so I hear it but from you. Something I will tell you: I hope to see my Dictionary bound and lettered, next week; — *vasta mole superbus*. And I have a great mind to come to Oxford at Easter; but you will not invite me. Shall I come uninvited, or stay here where nobody perhaps would miss me if I went? A hard choice! But such is the world to, dear Sir,

Your, &c.

Sam. Johnson.

[London,] March 20, 1755.

1 The original is in my possession.

2 We may conceive what a high gratification it must have been to Johnson to receive his diploma from the hands of the great Dr King, whose principles were so congenial with his own.

3 [The words in Italics are allusions to passages in Mr Warton's poem, called 'The Progress of Discontent', now lately published. T.W.]

To the same.

DEAR SIR — Though not to write, when a man can write so well, is an offence sufficiently heinous, yet I shall pass it by. I am very glad that the Vice-Chancellor was pleased with my note. I shall impatiently expect you at London, that we may consider what to do next. I intend in the winter to open a *Bibliothèque*, and remember, that you are to subscribe a sheet a year; let us try, likewise, if we cannot persuade your brother to subscribe another. My book is now coming *in luminis oras*. What will be its fate I know not, nor think much, because thinking is to no purpose. It must stand the censure of the *great vulgar and the small*; of those that understand it, and that understand it not. But in all this, I suffer not alone: every writer has the same difficulties, and, perhaps, every writer talks of them more than he thinks.

You will be pleased to make my compliments to all my friends: and be so kind, at every idle hour, as to remember, dear Sir,

Your, &c.

SAM. JOHNSON.

[London,] March 25, 1755.

Dr Adams told me, that this scheme of a *Bibliothèque* was a serious one; for upon his visiting him one day, he found his parlour floor covered with parcels of foreign and English literary journals, and he told Dr Adams he meant to undertake a Review. 'How, Sir (said Dr Adams), can you think of doing it alone? All branches of knowledge must be considered in it. Do you know Mathematics? Do you know Natural History?' Johnson answered, 'Why, Sir, I must do as well as I can. My chief purpose is to give my countrymen a view of what is doing in literature upon the continent; and I shall have, in a good measure, the choice of my subject, for I shall select such books as I best understand.' Dr Adams suggested, that as Dr Maty had just then finished his *Bibliothèque Britannique*, which was a well executed work, giving foreigners an account of British publications, he might, with great advantage, assume him as an assistant. '*He* (said Johnson), the little black dog! I'd throw him into the Thames.' The scheme, however, was dropped.

In one of his little memorandum-books I find the following hints for his intended Review or Literary Journal: '*The Annals of Literature, foreign as well as domestic*. Imitate Le Clerk — Bayle — Barbeyrac. Infelicity of Journals in England. Works of the learned. We cannot take in all. Sometimes copy from foreign Journalists. Always tell.'

To Dr BIRCH.

March 29, 1755.

SIR — I have sent some parts of my Dictionary, such as were at hand, for your inspection. The favour which I beg is, that if you do not like them you will say nothing. I am, Sir,

Your most affectionate humble servant,

SAM. JOHNSON.

To Mr Samuel Johnson.

Norfolk-street, April 3, 1755.

Sir – The part of your Dictionary which you have favoured me with the sight of has given me such an idea of the whole, that I most sincerely congratulate the public upon the acquisition of a work long wanted, and now executed with an industry, accuracy, and judgement, equal to the importance of the subject. You might, perhaps, have chosen one in which your genius would have appeared to more advantage; but you could not have fixed upon any other in which your labours would have done such substantial service to the present age and to posterity. I am glad that your health has supported the application necessary to the performance of so vast a task; and can undertake to promise you as one (though perhaps the only) reward of it, the approbation and thanks of every well-wisher to the honour of the English language. I am, with the greatest regard, Sir,

    Your most faithful

And most affectionate humble servant,

THO. BIRCH.

Mr Charles Burney, who has since distinguished himself so much in the science of Music, and obtained a Doctor's degree from the University of Oxford, had been driven from the capital by bad health, and was now residing at Lynn Regis, in Norfolk. He had been so much delighted with Johnson's *Rambler*, and the Plan of his Dictionary, that when the great work was announced in the newspapers as nearly finished, he wrote to Dr Johnson, begging to be informed when and in what manner his Dictionary would be published; entreating, if it should be by subscription, or he should have any books at his own disposal, to be favoured with six copies for himself and friends.

In answer to this application, Dr Johnson wrote the following letter, of which (to use Dr Burney's own words) 'if it be remembered that it was written to an obscure young man, who at this time had not much distinguished himself even in his own profession, but whose name could never have reached the author of *The Rambler*, the politeness and urbanity may be opposed to some of the stories which have been lately circulated of Dr Johnson's natural rudeness and ferocity.'

To Mr Burney, in Lynne Regis, Norfolk.

Sir – If you imagine that by delaying my answer I intended to show any neglect of the notice with which you have favoured me, you will neither think justly of yourself nor of me. Your civilities were offered with too much elegance not to engage attention; and I have too much pleasure in pleasing men like you, not to feel very sensibly the distinction which you have bestowed upon me.

    Few consequences of my endeavours to please or to benefit mankind have delighted me more than your friendship thus voluntarily offered, which now I have it I hope to keep, because I hope to continue to deserve it.

I have no Dictionaries to dispose of for myself, but shall be glad to have you direct your friends to Mr Dodsley, because it was by his recommendation that I was employed in the work.

When you have leisure to think again upon me, let me be favoured with another letter; and another yet, when you have looked into my Dictionary. If you find faults, I shall endeavour to mend them; if you find none, I shall think you blinded by kind partiality: but to have made you partial in his favour, will very much gratify the ambition of, Sir,

Your most obliged
And most humble servant,

SAM. JOHNSON.

Gough-square, Fleet-street, April 8, 1755.

Mr Andrew Millar, bookseller in the Strand, took the principal charge of conducting the publication of Johnson's Dictionary; and as the patience of the proprietors was repeatedly tried and almost exhausted, by their expecting that the work would be completed within the time which Johnson had sanguinely supposed, the learned author was often goaded to dispatch, more especially as he had received all the copy-money, by different drafts, a considerable time before he had finished his task. When the messenger who carried the last sheet to Millar returned, Johnson asked him, 'Well, what did he say?' – 'Sir (answered the messenger), he said, thank GOD I have done with him.' 'I am glad (replied Johnson, with a smile), that he thanks GOD for any thing.'[1] It is remarkable, that those with whom Johnson chiefly contracted for his literary labours were Scotchmen, Mr Millar and Mr Strahan. Millar, though himself no great judge of literature, had good sense enough to have for his friends very able men to give him their opinion and advice in the purchase of copy-right; the consequence of which was his acquiring a very large fortune, with great liberality. Johnson said of him, 'I respect Millar, Sir; he has raised the price of literature.' The same praise may be justly given to Pancoek,[a] the eminent bookseller of Paris. Mr Strahan's liberality, judgement, and success, are well known.[b]

---

1 Sir John Hawkins, p. 341, inserts two notes as having passed formally between Andrew Millar and Johnson, to the above effect. I am assured this was not the case. In the way of incidental remark it was a pleasant play of raillery. To have deliberately written notes in such terms would have been morose.

[a] Alter to 'Panckoucke'.

[b] Postscript (to the 3rd vol. of 2nd edition): After the first two volumes of this Work were printed off, my worthy friend, Mr Langton, in searching among his papers, found the following valuable letters of Dr Johnson, beginning with the first which that gentleman received from him. Though it is impossible, in the present edition, to insert them in chronological order, I cannot withhold from my readers so great a satisfaction as the perusal of them must afford.

To BENNET LANGTON, ESQ. at Langton, near Spilsby, Lincolnshire.

SIR – It has been long observed, that men do not suspect faults which they do not commit; your own elegance of manners, and punctuality of complaisance, did not

To the Reverend Mr THOMAS WARTON.

DEAR SIR – I am grieved that you should think me capable of neglecting your letters; and beg you will never admit any such suspicion again. I purpose to come down next week, if you shall be there; or any other week, that shall be more agreeable to you. Therefore let me know. I can stay this visit but a week, but intend to make preparations for a longer stay next time; being resolved not to lose sight of the University. How goes Apollonius?[1] Don't let him be forgotten. Some things of this kind must be done, to keep us up. Pay my compliments to Mr Wise, and all my other friends. I think to come to Kettel-Hall. I am, Sir,

Your most affectionate, &c.

SAM. JOHNSON.

[London,] May 13, 1755.

---

suffer you to impute to me that negligence of which I was guilty, and which I have not since attoned. I received both your letters, and received them with pleasure proportioned to the esteem which so short an acquaintance strongly impressed, and which I hope to confirm by nearer knowledge, though I am afraid that gratification will be for a time withheld.

I have, indeed, published my book [his Dictionary], of which I beg to know your father's judgement, and yours; and I have now stayed long enough to watch its progress in the world. It has, you see, no patrons, and, I think, has yet had no opponents, except the critics of the coffee-house, whose outcries are soon dispersed into the air, and are thought on no more; from this, therefore, I am at liberty, and think of taking the opportunity of this interval to make an excursion, and why not then into Lincolnshire? or, to mention a stronger attraction, why not to dear Mr Langton? I will give the true reason, which I know you will approve: I have a mother more than eighty years old, who has counted the days to the publication of my book, in hopes of seeing me; and to her, if I can disengage myself here, I resolve to go.

As I know, dear Sir, that to delay my visit for a reason like this, will not deprive me of your esteem, I beg it may not lessen your kindness. I have very seldom received an offer of friendship which I so earnestly desire to cultivate and mature. I shall rejoice to hear from you, till I can see you, and will see you as soon as I can; for when the duty that calls me to Lichfield is discharged, my inclination will carry me to Langton. I shall delight to hear the ocean roar, or see the stars twinkle, in the company of men to whom Nature does not spread her volumes or utter her voice in vain.

Do not, dear Sir, make the slowness of this letter a precedent for delay, or imagine that I approve the incivility that I have committed; for I have known you enough to love you, and sincerely to wish a further knowledge; and I assure you once more, that to live in a house that contains such a father and such a son, will be accounted a very uncommon degree of pleasure, by, dear Sir,

Your most obliged,

And most humble servant,

SAM. JOHNSON.

May 6, 1755.

1 [A translation of Apollonius Rhodius was now intended by Mr Warton. T.W.]

To the same.

Dear Sir – It is strange how many things will happen to intercept every
pleasure, though it [be] only that of two friends meeting together. I have
promised myself every day to inform you when you might expect me at
Oxford, and have not been able to fix a time. The time, however, is, I
think, at last come; and I promise myself to repose in Kettel-Hall, one of
the first nights of the next week. I am afraid my stay with you cannot be
long; but what is the inference? We must endeavour to make it cheerful. I
wish your brother could meet us, that we might go and drink tea with Mr
Wise in a body. I hope he will be at Oxford, or at his nest of British and
Saxon antiquities.[1] I shall expect to see Spenser finished, and many other
things begun. Dodsley is gone to visit the Dutch. The Dictionary sells well.
The rest of the world goes on as it did. Dear Sir,

 Your most affectionate, &c.

                Sam. Johnson.

 [London,] June 10, 1755.

To the same.

Dear Sir – To talk of coming to you, and not yet to come, has an air of
trifling which I would not willingly have among you; and which, I believe,
you will not willingly impute to me, when I have told you, that since my
promise, two of our partners[2] are dead, and that I was solicited to suspend
my excursion till we could recover from our confusion.

 I have not laid aside my purpose; for every day makes me more impatient
of staying from you. But death, you know, hears not supplications, nor
pays any regard to the convenience of mortals. I hope now to see you next
week; but next week is but another name for tomorrow, which has been
noted for promising and deceiving.

 I am, &c.

                Sam. Johnson.

 [London,] June 24, 1755.

To the same.

Dear Sir – I told you, that among the manuscripts are some things of Sir
Thomas More. I beg you to pass an hour in looking on them, and procure
a transcript of the ten or twenty first lines of each, to be compared with
what I have; that I may know whether they are yet unpublished. The
manuscripts are these:

 Catalogue of Bodl. MS. pag. 122. F. 3. Sir Thomas More.

 1. Fall of angels. 2. Creation and fall of mankind. 3. Determination of the

---

1 At Ellsfield, a village three miles from Oxford.
2 Booksellers concerned in his Dictionary.

Trinity for the rescue of mankind. 4. Five lectures of our Saviour's passion. 5. Of the institution of the sacrament, three lectures. 6. How to receive the blessed body of our Lord sacramentally. 7. Neomenia, the new moon. 8. *De tristitia, taedio, pavore, et oratione Christi, ante captionem ejus.*

Catalogue, pag. 154. Life of Sir Thomas More. *Qu.* Whether Roper's? Pag. 363. *De resignatione Magni Sigilli in manus Regis per D. Thomam Morum.* Pag. 364. *Mori Defensio Moriae.*

If you procure the young gentleman in the library to write out what you think fit to be written, I will send to Mr Prince the bookseller to pay him what you shall think proper.

Be pleased to make my compliments to Mr Wise, and all my friends. I am, Sir,

Your affectionate, &c.

SAM. JOHNSON.

[London,] Aug. 7, 1755.

The *Dictionary*, with a Grammar and History of the English Language, being now at length published, in two volumes folio, the world contemplated with wonder so stupendous a work achieved by one man, while other countries had thought such undertakings fit only for whole academies. Vast as his powers were, I cannot but think that his imagination deceived him, when he supposed that by constant application he might have performed the task in three years. Let the Preface be attentively perused, in which is given, in a clear, strong, and glowing style, a comprehensive, yet particular view of what he had done; and it will be evident, that the time he employed upon it was comparatively short. I am unwilling to swell my book with long quotations from what is in every body's hands; and I believe there are few prose compositions in the English language that are read with more delight, or are more impressed upon the memory, than that preliminary discourse. One of its excellencies has always struck me with peculiar admiration; I mean the perspicuity with which he has expressed abstract scientific notions. As an instance of this, I shall quote the following sentence: 'When the radical idea branches out into parallel ramifications, how can a consecutive series be formed of senses in their own nature collateral?' We have here an example of what has been often said, and I believe with justice that there is for every thought a certain nice adaptation of words which no other could equal, and which, when a man has been so fortunate as to hit, he has attained, in that particular case, to the perfection of language.

The extensive reading which was absolutely necessary for the accumulation of authorities, and which alone may account for Johnson's retentive mind being enriched with a very large and various store of knowledge and imagery, must have occupied several years. The Preface furnishes an eminent instance of a double talent, of which Johnson was fully conscious. Sir Joshua Reynolds has heard him say, 'There are two things which I am confident I can do very well: one is an introduction to any literary work, stating what it is to contain, and how it should be executed in the most perfect manner; the other is a conclusion, showing from various causes why the execution has not been equal to what the author promised to himself and to the public.'

How should puny scribblers be abashed and disappointed, when they find him displaying a perfect theory of lexicographical excellence, yet at the same time candidly and modestly allowing that he 'had not satisfied his own expectations'. Here was a fair occasion for the exercise of Johnson's modesty, when he was called upon to compare his own arduous performance, not with those of other individuals (in which case his inflexible regard to truth would have been violated, had he affected diffidence), but with speculative perfection; as he, who can outstrip all his competitors in the race, may yet be sensible of his deficiency when he runs against time. Well might he say, that 'the English Dictionary was written with little assistance of the learned'; for he told me, that the only aid which he received was a paper containing twenty etymologies, sent to him by a person then unknown, who he was afterwards informed was Dr Pearce, Bishop of Rochester. The etymologies, though they exhibit learning and judgement, are not, I think, entitled to the first praise amongst the various parts of this immense work. The definitions have always appeared to me such astonishing proofs of acuteness of intellect and precision of language, as indicate a genius of the highest rank. This it is which marks the superior excellence of Johnson's Dictionary over others equally or even more voluminous, and must have made it a work of much greater mental labour than mere Lexicons, or *Word Books*, as the Dutch call them. They, who will make the experiment of trying how they can define a few words of whatever nature, will soon be satisfied of the unquestionable justice of this observation, which I can assure my readers is founded upon much study, and upon communication with more minds than my own.

A few of his definitions must be admitted to be erroneous. Thus, *Windward* and *Leeward*, though directly of opposite meaning, are defined identically the same way; as to which inconsiderable specks it is enough to observe, that his Preface announces that he was aware there might be many such in so immense a work; nor was he at all disconcerted when an instance was pointed out to him. A lady once asked him how he came to define *Pastern* the *knee* of a horse: instead of making an elaborate defence, as she expected, he at once answered, 'Ignorance, Madam, pure ignorance.' His definition of *Network* has been often quoted with sportive malignity, as obscuring a thing in itself very plain. But to these frivolous censures no other answer is necessary than that with which we are furnished by his own Preface. 'To explain, requires the use of terms less abstruse than that which is to be explained, and such terms cannot always be found. For as nothing can be proved but by supposing something intuitively known, and evident without proof, so nothing can be defined but by the use of words too plain to admit of definition. Sometimes easier words are changed into harder; as, *burial*, into *sepulture* or *interment*; *dry*, into *desiccative*; *dryness*, into *siccity* or *aridity*; *fit*, into *paroxysm*, for, the *easiest* word, whatever it be, can never be translated into one more easy.'

His introducing his own opinions, and even prejudices, under general definitions of words, while at the same time the original meaning of the words is not explained, as his *Tory*, *Whig*, *Pension*, *Oats*, *Excise*,[a] and a few more, cannot be fully defended, and must be placed to the account of capricious and humorous indulgence. Talking to me upon this subject when we were at Ashbourne in 1777, he mentioned a still stronger instance of the predominance of his private feelings in the composition of this work, than any now to be found in it. 'You know, Sir, Lord Gower forsook the old Jacobite interest. When I came to the word *Renegado*, after telling that it meant "one who deserts to the enemy, a revolter", I added, *Sometimes we say a* GOWER. Thus it went to the press; but the printer had more wit than I, and struck it out.'

Let it, however, be remembered, that this indulgence does not display itself only in sarcasm towards others, but sometimes in playful allusion to the notions commonly entertained of his own laborious task. Thus: '*Grub-street*, the name of a street in London, much inhabited by writers of small histories, *dictionaries*, and temporary poems; whence any mean production is called *Grub-street*.' – '*Lexicographer*, a writer of dictionaries, a *harmless drudge*.'

At the time when he was concluding his very eloquent Preface, Johnson's mind appears to have been in such a state of depression, that we cannot contemplate without wonder the vigorous and splendid thoughts which so highly distinguish that performance. 'I (says he) may surely be contented without the praise of perfection, which if I could obtain in this gloom of solitude, what would it avail me? I have protracted my work till most of those whom I wished to please, have sunk into the grave; and success and miscarriage are empty sounds. I therefore dismiss it with frigid tranquillity, having little to fear or hope from censure or from praise.' That this indifference was rather a temporary than an habitual feeling, appears, I think, from his letters to Mr Warton; and however he may have been affected for the moment, certain it is that the honours which his great work procured him, both at home and abroad, were very grateful to him. His friend the Earl of Corke and Orrery, being at Florence, presented it to the *Academia della Crusca*. That Academy sent

---

[a] Add the following note: He thus defines Excise – 'A hateful tax levied upon commodities, and adjudged not by the common judges of property, but wretches hired by those to whom the Excise is paid.' The Commissioners of Excise being offended by this severe reflection, consulted Mr Murray, then the Attorney-General, to know whether redress could be legally obtained. I wished to have procured for my readers a copy of the opinion which he gave, and which may now be justly considered history: but the mysterious secrecy of office it seems would not permit it. I am, however, informed, by very good authority, that its import was, that the passage might be considered as actionable; but that it would be more prudent in the board not to prosecute. Johnson never made the smallest alteration in this passage. We find he still retained his early prejudice against Excise; for in the *Idler*, No. 65, there is the following very extraordinary paragraph: 'The authenticity of *Clarendon's* history, though printed with the sanction of one of the first Universities of the world, had not an unexpected manuscript been happily discovered, would, with the help of factious credulity, have been brought into question, by the two lowest of all human beings, a Scribbler for a party, and a Commissioner of Excise.' The persons to whom he alludes were Mr John Oldmixon, and George Ducket, Esq.

Johnson their *Vocabulario*, and the French Academy sent him their *Dictionnaire*, which Mr Langton had the pleasure to convey to him.

It must undoubtedly seem strange, that the conclusion of his Preface should be expressed in terms so desponding, when it is considered that the author was then only in his forty-sixth year. But we must ascribe its gloom to that miserable dejection of spirits to which he was constitutionally subject, and which was aggravated by the death of his wife two years before. I have heard it ingeniously observed by a lady of rank and elegance, that 'his melancholy was then at its meridian.' It pleased GOD to grant him almost thirty years of life after this time; and once, when he was in a placid frame of mind, he was obliged to own to me that he had enjoyed happier days, and had had many more friends, since that gloomy hour than before.

It is a sad saying, that 'most of those whom he wished to please had sunk into the grave'; and his case at forty-five was singularly unhappy, unless the circle of his friends was very narrow. I have often thought, that as longevity is generally desired, and, I believe, generally expected, it would be wise to be continually adding to the number of our friends, that the loss of some may be supplied by others. Friendship, 'the wine of life', should, like a well-stocked cellar, be thus continually renewed; and it is consolatory to think that although we can seldom add what will equal the generous *first-growths* of our youth, yet friendship becomes insensibly old in much less time than is commonly imagined, and not many years are required to make it very mellow and pleasant. Warmth will, no doubt, make a considerable difference. Men of affectionate temper and bright fancy will coalesce a great deal sooner than those who are cold and dull.

The proposition which I have now endeavoured to illustrate was, at an after period of his life, the opinion of Johnson himself. He said to Sir Joshua Reynolds, 'If a man does not make new acquaintance as he advances through life, he will soon find himself left alone. A man, Sir, should keep his friendship in *constant repair*.'

The celebrated Mr Wilkes, whose notions and habits of life were very opposite to his, but who was ever eminent for literature and vivacity, sallied forth with a little *Jeu d'Esprit* upon the following passage in his Grammar of the English Tongue, prefixed to the *Dictionary*: '*H* seldom, perhaps never, begins any but the first syllable.' In an essay printed in the *Public Advertiser*, this lively writer enumerated many instances in opposition to this remark, for example, 'The author of this observation must be a man of a quick appre-hension, and of a most compre-hensive genius.' The position is undoubtedly expressed with too much latitude.

This light sally, we may suppose, made no great impression on our Lexico-grapher, for we find that he never altered the passage.[a]

---

[a] For 'never altered the passage', read, 'did not alter the passage till many years afterwards'; and on 'afterwards' put the following note: In the third edition, published in 1773, he left out the words *perhaps never*, and added the following paragraph: 'It sometimes begins middle or final syllables in words compounded, as *block-head*, or derived from the Latin, as *comprehended*.'

He had the pleasure of being treated in a very different manner by his old pupil Mr Garrick, in the following complimentary Epigram:

On JOHNSON'S DICTIONARY.

Talk of war with a Briton, he'll boldly advance,
That one English soldier will beat ten of France;
Would we alter the boast from the sword to the pen,
Our odds are still greater, still greater our men:
In the deep mines of science though Frenchmen may toil,
Can their strength be compar'd to Locke, Newton, and Boyle?
Let them rally their heroes, send forth all their pow'rs,
Their verse-men and prose-men; then match them with ours!
First Shakspeare and Milton, like gods in the fight,
Have put their whole drama and epic to flight;
In satires, epistles, and odes, would they cope,
Their numbers retreat before Dryden and Pope;
And Johnson, well-arm'd like a hero of yore,
Has beat forty French,[1] and will beat forty more!

Johnson this year gave at once a proof of his benevolence, quickness of apprehension, and admirable art of composition, in the assistance which he gave to Mr Zachariah Williams, father of the blind lady whom he had humanely received under his roof. Mr Williams had followed the profession of physic in Wales; but having a very strong propensity to the study of natural philosophy, had made many ingenious advances towards a discovery of the longitude, and repaired to London in hopes of obtaining the great parliamentary reward. He failed of success; but Johnson having made himself master of his principles and experiments, wrote for him a pamphlet, published in quarto, with the following title: 'An Account of an Attempt to ascertain the Longitude at Sea, by an exact Theory of the Variation of the magnetical Needle; with a Table of the Variations at the most remarkable Cities in Europe, from the year 1660 to 1860.' To diffuse it more extensively, it was accompanied with an Italian translation on the opposite page, which it is supposed was the work of Signor Baretti, an Italian of considerable literature, who having come to England a few years before, had been employed in the capacity both of a language-master and an author, and formed an intimacy with Dr Johnson. This pamphlet Johnson presented to the Bodleian Library.[2] On a blank leaf of it is pasted a paragraph cut out of a newspaper, containing an account of the death and character of Williams, plainly written by Johnson.[3]

1 The number of the French Academy employed in settling their language.
2 See note by Mr Warton, p. 140.
3 'On Saturday the 12th, about twelve at night, died Mr Zachariah Williams, in his eighty-third year, after an illness of eight months, in full possession of his mental faculties. He has been long known to philosophers and seamen for his skill in magnetism, and his proposal to ascertain the longitude by a peculiar system of the

In July this year he had formed some scheme of mental improvement, the particular purpose of which does not appear. But we find in his *Prayers and Meditations*, p. 24, a prayer entitled 'On the Study of Philosophy, as an instrument of living'; and after it follows a note, 'This study was not pursued.'[a]

In 1756 Johnson found that the great fame of his Dictionary had not set him above the necessity of 'making provision for the day that was passing over him'. No royal or noble patron extended a munificent hand to give independence to the man who had conferred stability on the language of his country. We may feel indignant that there should have been such unworthy neglect, but we must at the same time, congratulate ourselves, that to this very neglect operating to rouse the natural indolence of his constitution, we owe many valuable productions, which otherwise, perhaps, might never have appeared.

He had spent, during the progress of the work, the money for which he had contracted to write his Dictionary. We have seen that the reward of his labour was only fifteen hundred and seventy-five pounds; and when the expense of amanuenses and paper, and other articles are deducted, his clear profit was very inconsiderable. I once said to him, 'I am sorry, Sir, you did not get more for your Dictionary.' His answer was, 'I am sorry too. But it was very well. The booksellers are generous liberal-minded men.' He, upon all occasions, did ample justice to their character in this respect. He considered them as the patrons of literature; and, indeed, although they have eventually been considerable gainers by his Dictionary, it is to them that we owe its having been undertaken and carried through at the risk of great expense, for they were not absolutely sure of being indemnified.

On the first day of this year we find from his private devotions, that he had then recovered from sickness;[1] and in February that his eye was restored to its use.[2] The pious gratitude with which he acknowledges mercies upon every occasion is very edifying; as is the humble submission which he breathes when

---

variation of the compass. He was a man of industry indefatigable, of conversation inoffensive, patient of adversity and disease, eminently sober, temperate and pious; and worthy to have ended life with better fortune.'

[a] After 'pursued', read: On the 13th of the same month he wrote in his Journal the following scheme of life, for Sunday: 'Having lived' (as he with tenderness of conscience expresses himself) 'not without an habitual reverence for the Sabbath, yet without that attention to its religious duties which Christianity requires:

1. To rise early, and in order to it, to go to sleep early on Saturday.
2. To use some extraordinary devotion in the morning.
3. To examine the tenour of my life, and particularly the last week; and to mark my advances in religion, or recession from it.
4. To read the Scripture methodically with such helps as are at hand.
5. To go to church twice.
6. To read books of Divinity, either speculative or practical.
7. To instruct my family.
8. To wear off by meditation any worldly soil contracted in the week. '

1 *Prayers and Meditations*, p. 25.
2 Ibid. p. 27.

it is the will of his heavenly Father to try him with afflictions. As such dispositions become the state of man here, and are the true effects of religious discipline, we cannot but venerate in Johnson one of the most exercised minds that our holy religion hath ever formed. If there be any thoughtless enough to suppose such exercise the weakness of a great understanding, let them look up to Johnson, and be convinced that what he so earnestly practised must have a rational foundation.

His works this year were, an abstract or epitome, in octavo, of his folio Dictionary, and a few essays in a monthly publication, entitled, *The Universal Visiter*. Christopher Smart, with whose unhappy vacillation of mind he sincerely sympathised, was one of the stated undertakers of this miscellany; and it was to assist him that Johnson sometimes employed his pen. All the essays marked with two *asterisks* have been ascribed to him; but I am confident, from internal evidence, that of these, neither 'The Life of Chaucer', 'Reflections on the State of Portugal', nor an 'Essay on Architecture', were written by him. I am equally confident, upon the same evidence, that he wrote 'Further Thoughts on Agriculture',† being the sequel of a very inferior essay on the same subject, and which, though carried on as if by the same hand, is both in thinking and expression so far above it, and so strikingly peculiar, as to leave no doubt of its true parent; and that he also wrote 'A Dissertation on the State of Literature and Authors',† and 'A Dissertation on the Epitaphs written by Pope'.† The last of these, indeed, he afterwards added to his *Idler*. Why the essays truly written by him are marked in the same manner with some he did not write, I cannot explain; but with deference to those who have ascribed to him the three essays which I have rejected, they want all the characteristical marks of Johnsonian composition.

He engaged also to superintend and contribute largely to another monthly publication, entitled *The Literary Magazine, or Universal Review*; the first number of which came out in May this year. What were his emoluments from this undertaking, and what other writers were employed in it, I have not discovered. He continued to write in it, with intermissions, till the fifteenth number; and I think that he never gave better proofs of the force, acuteness and vivacity of his mind, than in this miscellany, whether we consider his original essays, or his reviews of the works of others. The 'Preliminary Address' to the public is a proof how this great man could embellish even so trite a thing as the plan of a magazine with the graces of superior composition.

His original essays are, 'An Introduction to the political State of Great Britain';† 'Remarks on the Militia Bill';† 'Observations on his Britannic Majesty's Treaties with the Empress of Russia and the Landgrave of Hesse Cassel';† 'Observations on the present State of Affairs';† and 'Memoirs of Frederick III. King of Prussia'.† In all these he displays extensive political knowledge and sagacity, expressed with uncommon energy and perspicuity without any of those words which he sometimes took a pleasure in adopting, in imitation of Sir Thomas Browne, of whose *Christian Morals* he this year gave an edition, with his 'Life'* prefixed to it, which is one of Johnson's best biographical performances. In one instance only in these essays has he indulged his

Brownism. Dr Robertson, the historian, mentioned it to me, as having at once convinced him that Johnson was the author of the 'Memoirs of the King of Prussia'. Speaking of the pride which the old King, the father of his hero, took in being master of the tallest regiment in Europe, he says, 'To review this *towering* regiment was his daily pleasure, and to perpetuate it was so much his care, that when he met a tall woman he immediately commanded one of his *Titanian* retinue to marry her, that they might *propagate procerity*.' For this Anglo-Latian word *procerity*, Johnson had, however, the authority of Addison.

His reviews are of the following books: Birch's *History of the Royal Society*;[†] Murphy's *Gray's-Inn Journal*;[†] Warton's 'Essay on the Writings and Genius of Pope, Vol. I';[†] 'Hampton's 'Translation of Polybius';[†] Blackwell's *Memoirs of the Court of Augustus*;[†] Russel's *Natural History of Aleppo*;[†] Sir Isaac Newton's *Arguments in Proof of a Deity*;[†] Borlase's *History of the Isles of Scilly*;[†] Home's *Experiments on Bleaching*;[†] Browne's *Christian Morals*;[†] Hales on distilling 'Sea-Water, Ventilators in Ships, and curing an ill Taste in Milk';[†] Lucas's 'Essay on Waters';[†] Keith's *Catalogue of the Scottish Bishops*;[†] Browne's *History of Jamaica*;[†] *Philosophical Transactions*, Vol. XLIX;[†] Mrs Lennox's 'Translation of Sully's Memoirs';[*] *Miscellanies* by Elizabeth Harrison;[†] Evans's *Map and Account of the middle Colonies in America*;[†] 'Letter on the Case of Admiral Byng';[*] 'Appeal to the People concerning Admiral Byng';[*] Hanway's *Eight Days Journey*, and *Essay on Tea*;[*] 'The Cadet, a military Treatise';[†] 'Some further Particulars in Relation to the Case of Admiral Byng, by a Gentleman of Oxford';[*] 'The Conduct of the Ministry relating to the present War impartially examined';[†] 'A Free Inquiry into the Nature and Origin of Evil'.[*] All these, from internal evidence, were written by Johnson; some of them I know he avowed, and have marked them with an *asterisk* accordingly. Mr Thomas Davies, indeed, ascribed to him the Review of Mr Burke's 'Inquiry into the Origin of our Ideas of the Sublime and Beautiful'; and Sir John Hawkins, with equal discernment, has inserted it in his collection of Johnson's works. Whereas it has no resemblance to Johnson's composition, and is well known to have been written by Mr Murphy, who has acknowledged it to me and many others.

It is worthy of remark, in justice to Johnson's political character, which has been misrepresented as abjectly submissive to power, that his 'Observations on the present State of Affairs', glow with as animated a spirit of constitutional liberty as can be found any where. Thus he begins, 'The time is now come, in which every Englishman expects to be informed of the national affairs, and in which he has a right to have that expectation gratified. For whatever may be urged by ministers, or those whom vanity or interest make the followers of ministers, concerning the necessity of confidence in our governors, and the presumption of prying with profane eyes into the recesses of policy, it is evident that this reverence can be claimed only by counsels yet unexecuted, and projects suspended in deliberation. But when a design has ended in miscarriage or success, when every eye and every ear is witness to general discontent, or general satisfaction, it is then a proper time to disentangle confusion and illustrate obscurity, to show by what causes every event was produced, and in what effects it is likely to terminate; to lay down with distinct particularity what rumour always huddles in general exclamation, or perplexes by indigested narratives; to show whence happiness or calamity is derived, and whence it may be expected; and honestly to lay before the people what inquiry can gather of the past, and conjecture can estimate of the future.'

Here we have it assumed as an incontrovertible principle, that in this country the people are the superintendents of the conduct and measures of those by whom government is administered, of the beneficial effect of which the present reign afforded an illustrious example, when addresses from all parts of the kingdom controlled an audacious attempt to introduce a new power subversive of the crown.

A still stronger proof of his patriotic spirit appears in his review of an 'Essay on Waters', by Dr Lucas; of whom, after describing him as a man well known to the world for his daring defiance of power, when he thought it exerted on the side of wrong, he thus speaks: 'The Irish ministers drove him from his native country by a proclamation, in which they charged him with crimes of which they never intended to be called to the proof, and oppressed him by methods equally irresistible by guilt and innocence.

'Let the man thus driven into exile for having been the friend of his country, be received in every other place as a confessor of liberty; and let the tools of power be taught in time, that they may rob, but cannot impoverish.'

Some of his reviews in this magazine are very short accounts of the pieces noticed, and I mention them only that Dr Johnson's opinion of the works may be known; but many of them are examples of elaborate criticism, in the most masterly style. In his review of the *Memoirs of the Court of Augustus*, he has the resolution to think and speak from his own mind, regardless of the cant transmitted from age to age, in praise of the ancient Romans. Thus: 'I know not why any one but a school-boy in his declamation should whine over the Common-wealth of Rome, which grew great only by the misery of the rest of mankind. The Romans, like others, as soon as they grew rich, grew corrupt; and in their corruption sold the lives and freedoms of themselves, and of one another.' Again, 'A people, who while they were poor robbed mankind; and as soon as they became rich, robbed one another.' In his review of the *Miscellanies* in prose and verse published by Elizabeth Harrison, but written by many hands, he gives an eminent proof at once of his orthodoxy and candour. 'The authors of the essays in prose seem generally to have imitated, or tried to imitate, the copiousness and luxuriance of Mrs *Rowe*. This, however, is not all their praise; they have laboured to add to her brightness of imagery, her purity of sentiments. The poets have had Dr *Watts* before their eyes; a writer, who, if he stood not in the first class of genius, compensated that defect by a ready application of his powers to the promotion of piety. The attempt to employ the ornaments of romance in the decoration of religion, was, I think, first made by Mr Boyle's *Martyrdom of Theodora*; but *Boyle's* philosophical studies did not allow him time for the cultivation of style: and the completion of the great design was reserved for Mrs *Rowe*. Dr Watts was one of the first who taught the Dissenters to write and speak like other men, by showing them that elegance might consist with piety. They would have both done honour to a better society, for they had that charity which might well make their failings be forgotten, and with which the whole Christian world might wish for communion. They were pure from all the heresies of an age, to which every opinion is become a favourite that the universal church has hitherto detested!

'This praise, the general interest of mankind requires to be given to writers who please and do not corrupt, who instruct and do not weary. But to them all human eulogies are vain, whom I believe applauded by angels, and numbered with the just.'

His defence of tea against Mr Jonas Hanway's violent attack upon that elegant and popular beverage, shows how very well a man of genius can write upon the slightest subject, when he writes, as the Italians say, *con amore*: I suppose no person ever enjoyed with more relish the infusion of that fragrant leaf than Johnson. The quantities which he drank of it at all hours were so great, that his nerves must have been uncommonly strong, not to have been extremely relaxed by such an intemperate use of it. He assured me, that he never felt the least inconvenience from it; which is a proof that the fault of his constitution was rather a too great tension of fibres, than the contrary. Mr Hanway wrote an angry answer to Johnson's review of his Essay on Tea, and Johnson, after a full and deliberate pause, made a reply to it; the only instance, I believe, in the whole course of his life, when he condescended to oppose any thing that was written against him. I suppose when he thought of any of his little antagonists, he was ever justly aware of the high sentiment of Ajax in Ovid:

> *Iste tulit pretium jam nunc certaminis hujus*
> *Qui, cum victus erit, mecum certasse feretur.*

But, indeed, the good Mr Hanway laid himself so open to ridicule, that Johnson's animadversions upon his attack were chiefly to make sport.

The generosity with which he pleads the cause of Admiral Byng is highly to the honour of his heart and spirit. Though Voltaire affects to be witty upon the fate of that unfortunate officer, observing that he was shot '*pour encourager les autres*', the nation has long been satisfied that his life was sacrificed to the political fervour of the times. In the vault belonging to the Torrington family, in the church of Southill, in Bedfordshire, there is the following Epitaph upon his monument, which I have transcribed:

TO THE PERPETUAL DISGRACE
OF PUBLICK JUSTICE
THE HONOURABLE JOHN BYNG, ESQ.
ADMIRAL OF THE BLUE,
FELL A MARTYR TO POLITICAL
PERSECUTION,
MARCH 14, IN THE YEAR, 1757;
WHEN BRAVERY AND LOYALTY
WERE INSUFFICIENT SECURITIES
FOR THE LIFE AND HONOUR OF
A NAVAL OFFICER.

Johnson's most exquisite critical essay in the *Literary Magazine*, and indeed any where, is his review of Soame Jennings's[a] *Inquiry Into the Origin of Evil*. Jennings was possessed of lively talents and a style eminently pure and easy, and could very happily play with a light subject, either in prose or verse; but when he speculated on that most difficult and excruciating question, the Origin of Evil, he 'ventured far beyond his depth', and, accordingly, was exposed by Johnson, both with acute argument and brilliant wit. I remember when the late Mr Bicknell's humorous performance, entitled *The Musical Travels of Joel Collyer*, in which a slight attempt is made to ridicule Johnson, was ascribed to Soame Jennings, 'Ha! (said Johnson), I thought I had given *him* enough of it.

His triumph over Jennings is thus described by my friend Mr Courtenay in his 'Poetical Review of the literary and moral Character of Dr Johnson', a performance of such merit, that had I not been honoured with a very kind and partial notice in it, I should echo the sentiments of men of the first taste loudly in its praise:

> When specious sophists with presumption scan
> The source of evil hidden still from man;
> Revive Arabian tales, and vainly hope
> To rival St John, and his scholar Pope:
> Though metaphysics spread the gloom of night,
> By reason's star he guides our aching sight;
> The bounds of knowledge marks, and points the way
> To pathless wastes, where wilder'd sages stray;
> Where, like a farthing link-boy, Jennings stands,
> And the dim torch drops from his feeble hands. [1]

---

[a] For 'Jennings', read 'Jennyns'. [These corrections, though they may seem trifling, are worth preserving, as not till his second edition did Mr Boswell arrive at the proper spelling of the name, *viz*. 'Jenyns'.]

[1] Some time after Dr Johnson's death there appeared in the newspapers and magazines an illiberal and petulant attack upon him, in the form of an Epitaph, under the name of Mr Soame Jennings, very unworthy of that gentleman, who had quietly submitted to the critical lash while Johnson lived. It assumed, as characteristics of him, all the vulgar circumstances of abuse which had circulated amongst the ignorant. It was an unbecoming indulgence of puny resentment, at a time when he himself was at a very advanced age, and had a near prospect of descending to the grave. I was truly sorry for it; for he was then become an avowed, and (as my Lord Bishop of London, who had a serious conversation with him on the subject, assures me) a sincere Christian. He could not expect that Johnson's numerous friends would patiently bear to have the memory of their master stigmatised by no mean pen, but that at least one would be found to retort. Accordingly, this unjust and sarcastic Epitaph was met in the same public field by an answer, in terms by no means soft, and such as wanton provocation only could justify:

This year Mr William Payne, brother of the respectable bookseller of that name, published *An Introduction to the Game of Draughts*, to which Johnson contributed a Dedication to the Earl of Rochford,* and a Preface,* both of which are admirably adapted to the treatise to which they are prefixed. Johnson, I believe, did not play at draughts after leaving College, by which he suffered, for it would have afforded him an innocent soothing relief from the melancholy which distressed him so often. I have heard him regret that he had not learnt to play at cards; and the game of draughts we know is peculiarly calculated to fix the attention without straining it. There is a composure and gravity in draughts which insensibly tranquillises the mind; and, accordingly, the Dutch are fond of it, as they are of smoking, of the sedative influence of which, though he himself never smoked, he had a high opinion.[1] Besides, there is in draughts some exercise of the faculties; and, accordingly, Johnson wishing to dignify the subject in his Dedication with what is most estimable in it, observes, 'Triflers may find or make any thing a trifle; but since it is the great characteristic of a wise man to see events in their causes, to obviate consequences, and ascertain contingencies, your Lordship will think nothing a trifle by which the mind is inured to caution, foresight, and circumspection.'

As one of the little occasional advantages which he did not disdain to take by his pen, as a man whose profession was literature, he this year accepted of a guinea from Mr Robert Dodsley, for writing the introduction to the *London Chronicle*, an evening newspaper; and even in so slight a performance exhibited peculiar talents. This *Chronicle* still subsists, and from what I observed, when I was abroad, has a more extensive circulation upon the Continent than any of the English newspapers. It was constantly read by Johnson himself; and it is but just to observe, that it has all along been distinguished for good sense, accuracy, moderation, and delicacy.

Another instance of the same nature has been communicated to me by the Reverend Dr Thomas Campbell, who has done himself considerable credit by his own writings. 'Sitting with Dr Johnson one morning alone, he asked me if I had known Dr Madden, who was author of the premium-scheme in Ireland.

EPITAPH,

Prepared for a creature not quite dead *yet.*

Here lies a little ugly nauseous elf,
Who judging only from its wretched self,
Feebly attempted, petulant and vain,
The 'Origin of Evil', to explain.
A mighty/Genius at this elf displeas'd,
With a strong critick grasp the urchin squeez'd.
For thirty years its coward spleen it kept,
Till in the dust the mighty Genius slept;
Then stunk and fretted in expiring snuff,
And blink'd at Johnson with its last poor puff.

1 *Journal of a Tour to the Hebrides*, 3d edit. p. 48.

On my answering in the affirmative, and also that I had for some years lived in his neighbourhood, &c. he begged of me that when I returned to Ireland, I would endeavour to procure for him a poem of Dr Madden's, called 'Boulter's Monument'. The reason (said he), why I wish for it, is this: when Dr Madden came to London, he submitted that work to my castigation; and I remember I blotted a great many lines, and might have blotted many more, without making the poem the worse. However, the Doctor was very thankful, and very generous, for he gave me ten guineas, which was to me at that time a great sum.'

He this year resumed his scheme of giving an edition of Shakspeare with notes. He issued Proposals of considerable length; in which he showed that he perfectly well knew what a variety of research such an undertaking required; but his indolence prevented him from pursuing it with that diligence which alone can collect those scattered facts that genius, however acute, penetrating, and luminous, cannot discover by its own force. It is remarkable, that at this time his fancied activity was for the moment so vigorous, that he promised his work should be published before Christmas, 1757. Yet nine years elapsed before it saw the light. His throes in bringing it forth had been severe and remittent, and at last we may almost conclude that the Caesarian operation was performed by the knife of Churchill, whose upbraiding satire, I dare say, made Johnson's friends urge him to dispatch.

> He for subscribers bates his hook,
> And takes your cash; but where's the book?
> No matter where; wise fear, you know,
> Forbids the robbing of a foe;
> But what, to serve our private ends,
> Forbids the cheating of our friends?

About this period he was offered a living of considerable value in Lincoln-shire, if he were inclined to enter into holy orders. It was a rectory in the gift of Mr Langton, the father of his much valued friend. But he did not accept of it; partly I believe from a conscientious motive, being persuaded that his temper and habits rendered him unfit for that assiduous and familiar instruction of the vulgar and ignorant, which he held to be an essential duty in a clergyman; and partly because his love of a London life was so strong, that he would have thought himself an exile in any other place, particularly if residing in the country. Whoever would wish to see his thoughts upon that subject displayed in their full force, may peruse the *Adventurer*, No. 126.

In 1757 it does not appear that he published any thing, except some of those articles in the *Literary Magazine*, which have been mentioned. That magazine, after Johnson ceased to write in it, gradually declined, though the popular epithet of *Antigallican* was added to it; and in July 1758 it expired. He probably prepared a part of his Shakspeare this year, and he dictated a speech on the subject of an Address to the Throne, after the expedition to Rochfort, which was delivered by one of his friends, I know not in what public meeting. It is printed in the *Gentleman's Magazine* for October 1785 as his, and bears sufficient marks of authenticity.

By the favour of Mr Walker, of the Treasury, Dublin, I have obtained a copy of the following letter from Johnson to the venerable author of 'Dissertations on the History of Ireland.'

To CHARLES O'CONOR, Esq.

SIR − I have lately, by the favour of Mr Faulkner, seen your account of Ireland, and cannot forbear to solicit a prosecution of your design. Sir William Temple complains that Ireland is less known than any other country, as to its ancient state. The natives have had little leisure, and little encouragement for enquiry; and strangers, not knowing the language, have had no ability.

I have long wished that the Irish literature were cultivated.[a] Ireland is known by tradition to have been once the seat of piety and learning; and surely it would be very acceptable to all those who are curious either in the original of nations, or the affinities of Languages, to be further informed of the revolutions of a people so ancient, and once so illustrious.

What relation there is between the Welch and Irish languages, or between the language of Ireland and that of Biscay, deserves enquiry. Of these provincial and unextended tongues, it seldom happens that more than one are understood by any one man; and, therefore, it seldom happens that a fair comparison can be made. I hope you will continue to cultivate this kind of learning, which has lain too long neglected, and which, if it be suffered to remain in oblivion for another century, may, perhaps, never be retrieved. As I wish well to all useful undertakings, I would not forbear to let you know how much you deserve, in my opinion, from all lovers of study, and how much pleasure your work has given to, Sir,

Your most obliged

And most humble servant,

SAM. JOHNSON.

London, Apr. 9, 1757.

---

[a] Add the following note: The celebrated orator, Mr Flood, has shown himself to be of Dr Johnson's opinion; having by his will bequeathed his estate, after the death of his wife, Lady Frances, to the University of Dublin; desiring that immediately after the said estate shall come into their possession, they shall appoint two professors, one for the study of the native Erse or Irish language, and the other for the study of Irish antiquities and Irish history, and for the study of any other European language illustrative of, or auxiliary to, the study of Irish antiquities or Irish history; and that they shall give yearly two liberal premiums for two compositions, one in verse, and the other in prose, in the Irish language.

To the Reverend Mr Thomas Warton.

Dear Sir – Dr Marseli of Padua, a learned gentleman, and good Latin poet, has a mind to see Oxford. I have given him a letter to Dr Huddesford;[1] and shall be glad if you will introduce him, and show him any thing in Oxford.

I am printing my new edition of Shakspeare.

I long to see you all, but cannot conveniently come yet. You might write to me now and then, if you were good for any thing. But *honores mutant mores*. Professors forget their friends.[2] I shall certainly complain to Miss Jones.[3] I am

Your, &c.

SAM. JOHNSON.

[London,] June 21, 1757.
Please to make my compliments to Mr Wise.

Mr Burney having enclosed to him an extract from the review of his Dictionary in the *Bibliothèque des Savans*,[4] and a list of subscribers to his Shakspeare, which Mr Burney had procured in Norfolk, he wrote the following answer:

To Mr Burney, in Lynne, Norfolk.

Sir – That I may show myself sensible of your favours, and not commit the same fault a second time, I make haste to answer the letter which I received this morning. The truth is, the other likewise was received, and I wrote an answer; but being desirous to transmit you some proposals and receipts, I waited till I could find a convenient conveyance, and day was passed after day, till other things drove it from my thoughts, yet not so, but that I remember with great pleasure your commendation of my Dictionary. Your praise was welcome, not only because I believe it was sincere, but because praise has been very scarce. A man of your candour will be surprised when I tell you, that among all my acquaintance there were only two, who upon the publication of my book did not endeavour to depress

---

1 [Now, or late, Vice-Chancellor. T.W.]

2 [Mr Warton was elected Professor of Poetry at Oxford in the preceding year. T.W.]

3 [Miss Jones lived at Oxford, and was often of our parties. She was a very ingenious poetess, and published a volume of poems; and, on the whole, was a most sensible, agreeable, and amiable woman. She was sister of the Reverend River Jones, Chanter of Christ Church Cathedral at Oxford, and Johnson used to call her the *Chantress*. I have heard him often address her in this passage from *Il Penseroso*:

> Thee, Chantress, oft the woods among
> I woo, &c.

She died unmarried. T.W.]

4 Tom. III, p. 482.

me with threats of censure from the public, or with objections learned from those who had learned them from my own Preface. Yours is the only letter of good-will that I have received, though, indeed I am promised something of that sort from Sweden.

How my new edition[1] will be received I know not; the subscription has not been very successful. I shall publish about March.

If you can direct me how to send proposals, I should wish that they were in such hands.

I remember, Sir, in some of the first letters with which you favoured me, you mentioned your lady. May I enquire after her? In return for the favours which you have shown me, it is not much to tell you, that I wish you and her all that can conduce to your happiness. I am, Sir,

Your most obliged

And most humble servant,

SAM. JOHNSON.

Gough-square, Dec. 24, 1757.

In 1758 we find him, it should seem, in as easy and pleasant a state of existence, as constitutional unhappiness ever permitted him to enjoy.[a]

---

1 Of Shakspeare.

a Add:

To BENNET LANGTON, ESQ. at Langton, Lincolnshire.

DEAREST SIR − I must have indeed slept very fast, not to have been awakened by your letter. None of your suspicions are true; I am not much richer than when you left me; and, what is worse, my omission of an answer to your first letter, will prove that I am not much wiser. But I go on as I formerly did, designing to be some time or other both rich and wise; and yet cultivate neither mind nor fortune. Do you take notice of my example, and learn the danger of delay. When I was as you are now, towering in confidence of twenty-one, little did I suspect that I should be at forty-nine, what I now am.

But you do not seem to need my admonition. You are busy in acquiring and in communicating knowledge, and while you are studying, enjoy the end of study, by making others wiser and happier. I was much pleased with the tale that you told me of being tutor to your sisters. I, who have no sisters nor brothers, look with some degree of innocent envy on those who may be said to be born to friends; and cannot see, without wonder, how rarely that native union is afterwards regarded. It sometimes, indeed, happens, that some supervenient cause of discord may overpower this original amity; but it seems to me more frequently thrown away with levity, or lost by negligence, than destroyed by injury or violence. We tell the ladies that good wives make good husbands; I believe it is a more certain position that good brothers make good sisters.

I am satisfied with your stay at home, as Juvenal with his friend's retirement to Cumae: I know that your absence is best, though it be not best for me.

> Quamvis digressu veteris confusus amici
> Laudo tamen vacuis quod sedem figere Cumis
> Destinet, atque unum civem donare Sibyllae.

To Mr BURNEY, at Lynne, Norfolk.

SIR – Your kindness is so great, and my claim to any particular regard from you so little, that I am at a loss how to express my sense of your favours;[1] but I am, indeed, much pleased to be thus distinguished by you.

I am ashamed to tell you that my Shakspeare will not be out so soon as I promised my subscribers; but I did not promise them more than I promised myself. It will, however, be published before summer.

I have sent you a bundle of proposals, which, I think, do not profess more than I have hitherto performed. I have printed many of the plays, and have hitherto left very few passages unexplained; where I am quite at a loss, I confess my ignorance, which is seldom done by commentators.

I have, likewise, enclosed twelve receipts; not that I mean to impose upon you the trouble of pushing them with more importunity than may seem proper, but that you may rather have more than fewer than you shall want. The proposals you will disseminate as there shall be opportunity. I

Langton is a good *Cumae*, but who must be Sibylla? Mrs Langton is as wise as Sibyl, and as good; and will live, if my wishes can prolong life, till she shall in time be as old. But she differs in this, that she has not scattered her precepts in the wind, at least not those which she bestowed upon you.

The two Wartons just looked into the town, and were taken to see *Cleone*, where David [Mr Garrick] says, they were starved for want of company to keep them warm. David and Doddy [Mr Dodsley, the author of *Cleone*] have had a new quarrel, and, I think, cannot conveniently quarrel any more. *Cleone* was well acted by all the characters, but Bellamy left nothing to be desired. I went the first night, and supported it as well as I might; for Doddy, you know, is my patron, and I would not desert him. The play was very well received. Doddy, after the danger was over, went every night to the stage-side, and cried at the distress of poor Cleone.

I have left off housekeeping, and therefore made presents of the game which you were pleased to send me. The pheasant I gave to Mr Richardson [Mr Samuel Richardson, author of *Clarissa*], the bustard to Dr Lawrence, and the pot I placed with Miss Williams, to be eaten by myself. She desires that her compliments and good wishes may be accepted by the family; and I make the same request for myself.

Mr Reynolds has within these few days raised his price to twenty guineas a head, and Miss is much employed in miniatures. I know not any body [else] whose prosperity has increased since you left them.

Murphy is to have his *Orphan of China* acted next month; and is therefore, I suppose, happy. I wish I could tell you of any great good to which I was approaching, but at present my prospects do not much delight me; however, I am always pleased when I find that you, dear Sir, remember,

Your affectionate, humble servant

SAM. JOHNSON

Jan. 9, 1758.

1 This letter was in answer to one in which was enclosed a draft for the payment of some subscriptions to his Shakspeare.

once printed them at length in the *Chronicle*, and some of my friends (I believe Mr Murphy, who formerly wrote the *Gray's-Inn Journal*) introduced them with a splendid encomium.

Since the Life of Browne, I have been a little engaged, from time to time, in the *Literary Magazine*, but not very lately. I have not the collection by me, and therefore cannot draw out a catalogue of my own parts, but will do it, and send it. Do not buy them, for I will gather all those that have any thing of mine in them, and send them to Mrs Burney, as a small token of gratitude for the regard which she is pleased to bestow upon me. I am, Sir,

> Your most obliged
> And most humble servant,
>
> SAM. JOHNSON.

London, March 8, 1758.

Dr Burney has kindly favoured me with the following memorandum, which I take the liberty to insert in his own genuine easy style. I love to exhibit sketches of my illustrious friend by various eminent hands.

Soon after this, Mr Burney, during a visit to the capital, had an interview with him in Gough-square, where he dined and drank tea with him, and was introduced to the acquaintance of Mrs Williams. After dinner, Mr Johnson proposed to Mr Burney to go up with him into his garret, which being accepted, he there found about five or six Greek folios, a deal writing-desk, and a chair and a half. Johnson giving to his guest the entire seat, tottered himself on one with only three legs and one arm. Here he gave Mr Burney Mrs Williams's history, and showed him some volumes of his Shakspeare already printed, to prove that he was in earnest. Upon Mr Burney's opening the first volume, at *The Merchant of Venice*, he observed to him, that he seemed to be more severe on Warburton than Theobald. 'O poor Tib.! (said Johnson), he was ready knocked down to my hands; Warburton stands between me and him.' 'But, Sir (said Mr Burney), you'll have Warburton upon your bones, won't you?' 'No, Sir; he'll not come out: he'll only growl in his den.' 'But you think, Sir, that Warburton is a superior critic to Theobald?' – 'O, Sir, he'd make two-and-fifty Theobalds cut into slices! The worst of Warburton is, that he has a rage for saying something when there's nothing to be said.' – Mr. Burney then asked him whether he had seen the letter which Warburton had written in answer to a pamphlet addressed 'To the most impudent Man alive'. He answered in the negative. Mr Burney told him it was supposed to be written by Mallet. The controversy now raged between the friends of Pope and Bolingbroke; and Warburton and Mallet were the leaders of the several parties. Mr Burney asked him then if he had seen Warburton's book against Bolingbroke's Philosophy? 'No, Sir; I have never read Bolingbroke's impiety, and therefore am not interested about its confutation.'

On the fifteenth of April he began a new periodical paper, entitled *The Idler*,* which came out every Saturday in a weekly newspaper, called the *Universal Chronicle, or Weekly Gazette*, published by Newberry. These essays were continued till April 5, 1760. Of one hundred and three, their total number, twelve were contributed by his friends; of which, Numbers 33, 93, and 96, were written by Mr Thomas Warton; No. 67 by Mr Langton; and No. 76, 79, and 82 by Sir Joshua Reynolds; the concluding words of No. 82, 'and pollute his canvas with deformity', being added by Johnson, as Sir Joshua informed me.

The Idler is evidently the work of the same mind which produced the *Rambler*, but has less body, and more spirit. It has more variety of real life, and greater facility of language. He describes the miseries of idleness, with the lively sensations of one who had felt them; and in his private memorandums while engaged in it, we find, 'This year I hope to learn diligence.'[1] Many of these excellent essays were written as hastily as an ordinary letter. Mr Langton remembers Johnson, when on a visit at Oxford, asking him one evening how long it was till the post went out; and on being told about half an hour, he exclaimed, 'then we shall do very well.' He upon this instantly sat down and finished an *Idler*, which it was necessary should be in London the next day. Mr Langton having signified a wish to read it, 'Sir (said he), you shall not do more than I have done myself.' He then folded it up, and sent it off.

Yet there are in the *Idler* several papers which show as much profundity of thought, and labour of language, as any of this great man's writings. No. 14, 'Robbery of time;' No. 24, 'Thinking;' No. 41, 'Death of a friend;' No. 43, 'Flight of time'; No. 51, 'Domestic greatness unattainable'; No. 52, 'Self-denial'; No. 58, 'Actual, how short of fancied excellence'; No. 89, 'Physical evil moral good'; and his concluding paper on 'The horror of the last', will prove this assertion. I know not why a motto, the usual trapping of periodical papers, is prefixed to very few of the *Idlers*, as I have heard Johnson commend the custom, and he never could be at a loss for one, his memory being stored with innumerable passages of the classics. In this series of essays he exhibits admirable instances of grave humour, of which he had an uncommon share. Nor on some occasions has he repressed that power of sophistry which he possessed in so eminent a degree. In No. 11, he treats with the utmost contempt the opinion that our mental faculties depend, in some degree, upon the weather; an opinion, which they who have never experienced its truth are not to be envied, and of which he himself could not but be sensible, as the effects of weather upon him were very visible. Yet thus he declaims: 'Surely nothing is more reproachful to a being endowed with reason, than to resign its powers to the influence of the air, and live in dependence on the weather and the wind for the only blessings which Nature has put into our power, tranquillity and benevolence. – This distinction of seasons is produced only by imagination operating on luxury. To temperance, every day is bright; and every hour is propitious to diligence. He that shall resolutely excite his faculties, or exert his virtues, will soon make himself superior to the seasons;

---

1 *Prayers and Meditations*, p. 30.

and may set at defiance the morning mist and the evening damp, the blasts of the east, and the clouds of the south.'

Alas! it is too certain, that where the frame has delicate fibres, and there is a fine sensibility, such influences of the air are irresistible. He might as well have bid defiance to the ague, the palsy, and all other bodily disorders. Such boasting of the force of mind is false elevation.

> 'I think the Romans call it Stoicism.'

But in this number of his *Idler* his spirits seem to run riot; for in the wantonness of his disquisition he forgets, for a moment, even the reverence for that which he held in high respect; and describes 'the attendant on a *Court*', as one 'whose business is to watch the looks of a being, weak and foolish as himself.'

His unqualified ridicule of rhetorical gesture or action is not, surely, a test of truth; yet we cannot help admiring how well it is adapted to produce the effect which he wished. 'Neither the judges of our laws, nor the representatives of our people, would be much affected by laboured gesticulation, or believe any man the more because he rolled his eyes, or puffed his cheeks, or spread abroad his arms, or stamped the ground, or thumped his breast, or turned his eyes sometimes to the ceiling, and sometimes to the floor.'

A casual coincidence with other writers, or an adoption of a sentiment or image which has been found in the writings of another, and afterwards appears in the mind as one's own, is not unfrequent. The richness of Johnson's fancy, which could supply his page abundantly on all occasions, and the strength of his memory, which at once detected the real owner of any thought, made him less liable to the imputation of plagiarism than, perhaps, any of our writers. In the *Idler*, however, there is a paper, in which conversation is assimilated to a bowl of punch, where there is the same train of comparison as in a poem by Blacklock, in his collection published in 1756; in which a parallel is ingeniously drawn between human life and that liquor. It ends,

> Say then, physicians of each kind,
> Who cure the body or the mind,
> What harm in drinking can there be,
> Since punch and life so well agree?

To the *Idler*, when collected in volumes, he added (beside the Essay on Epitaphs, and the Dissertation on those of Pope), an Essay on the Bravery of the English common Soldiers.

To the Reverend Mr THOMAS WARTON.

DEAR SIR – Your notes upon my poet were very acceptable. I beg that you will be so kind as to continue your searches. It will be reputable to my work, and suitable to your professorship, to have something of yours in the notes. As you have given no directions about your name, I shall therefore put it. I wish your brother would take the same trouble. A commentary must arise from the fortuitous discoveries of many men in devious walks of literature. Some of your remarks are on plays already printed; but I purpose to add an Appendix of Notes, so that nothing comes too late.

You give yourself too much uneasiness, dear Sir, about the loss of the papers.[1] The loss is nothing, if nobody has found them; nor even then, perhaps, if the numbers be known. You are not the only friend that has had the same mischance. You may repair your want out of a stock, which is deposited with Mr Allen, of Magdalen-Hall; or out of a parcel which I have just sent to Mr Chambers,[2] for the use of any body that will be so kind as to want them. Mr Langtons are well; and Miss Roberts, whom I have at last brought to speak, upon the information which you gave me, that she had something to say.

I am, &c.

SAM. JOHNSON.

[London,] April 14, 1758.

To the same.

DEAR SIR – You will receive this by Mr Baretti, a gentleman particularly entitled to the notice and kindness of the professor of poesy. He has time but for a short stay, and will be glad to have it filled up with as much as he can hear and see.

In recommending another to your favour, I ought not to omit thanks for the kindness which you have shown to myself. Have you any more notes on Shakspeare? I shall be glad of them.

I see your pupil[3] sometimes; his mind is as exalted as his stature. I am half afraid of him; but he is no less amiable than formidable. He will, if the forwardness of his spring be not blasted, be a credit to you, and to the University. He brings some of my plays[4] with him, which he has my permission to show you, on condition you will hide them from every body else.

I am, dear Sir, &c.

SAM. JOHNSON.

[London,] June 1, 1758.[a]

---

1 [Receipts for Shakspeare. T.W.]
2 [Then of Lincoln College. Now Sir Robert Chambers, one of the Judges in India. T.W.]
3 [Mr Langton. T.W.]
4 [Part of the impression of the Shakspeare, which Dr Johnson conducted alone, and published by subscription. This edition came out in 1765. T.W.]
a Add two letters after that letter:

To BENNET LANGTON, ESQ. of Trinity College, Oxford.

DEAR SIR – Though I might have expected to hear from you, upon your entrance into a new state of life at a new place, yet recollecting (not without some degree of shame), that I owe you a letter upon an old account, I think it my part to write

In 1759, in the month of January, his mother died, at the great age of ninety, an event which deeply affected him, not that 'his mind had acquired no

---

first. This, indeed, I do not only from complaisance but from interest; for living on in the old way, I am very glad of a correspondent so capable as yourself, to diversify the hours. You have, at present, too many novelties about you to need any help from me to drive along your time.

I know not any thing more pleasant, or more instructive, than to compare experience with expectation, or to register from time to time the difference between idea and reality. It is by this kind of observation that we grow daily less liable to be disappointed. You, who are very capable of anticipating futurity, and raising phantoms before your own eyes, must often have imagined to yourself an academical life, and have conceived what would be the manners, the views, and the conversation, of men devoted to letters; how they would choose their companions, how they would direct their studies, and how they would regulate their lives. Let me know what you expected, and what you have found. At least record it to yourself before custom has reconciled you to the scenes before you, and the disparity of your discoveries to your hopes has vanished from your mind. It is a rule never to be forgotten, that whatever strikes strongly, should be described while the first impression remains fresh upon the mind.

I love, dear Sir, to think on you, and therefore, should willingly write more to you, but that the post will not now give me leave to do more than send my compliments to Mr Warton, and tell you that I am, dear Sir, most affectionately

Your very humble servant,

SAM. JOHNSON.

June 28, 1758.

To BENNET LANGTON, ESQ. at Langton, near Spilsby, Lincolnshire.

DEAR SIR – I should be sorry to think that what engrosses the attention of my friend, should have no part of mine. Your mind is now full of the fate of Dury;[1] but his fate is past, and nothing remains but to try what reflection will suggest to mitigate the terrors of a violent death, which is more formidable at the first glance than on a nearer and more steady view. A violent death is never very painful, the only danger is, lest it should be unprovided. But if a man can be supposed to make no provision for death in war, what can be the state that would have awakened him to the care of futurity? When would that man have prepared himself to die, who went to seek death without preparation? What then can be the reason why we lament more him that dies of a wound, than him that dies of fever? A man that languishes with disease, ends his life with more pain, but with less virtue: he leaves no example to his friends, nor bequeaths any honour to his descendants. The only reason why we lament a Soldier's death, is, that we think he might have lived longer; yet this cause of grief is common to many other kinds of death, which are not so passionately bewailed. The truth is, that every death is violent which is the effect of accident; every death, which is not gradually brought on by the miseries of age, or when life is extinguished for any other reason than that it burnt out.

---

1 Major-General Alexander Dury, of the first regiment of footguards, who fell in the gallant discharge of his duty, near St Cas, in the well-known unfortunate expedition against France, in 1758. His lady and Mr Langton's mother were sisters. He left an only son, Lieutenant-Colonel Dury, who has a company in the same regiment.

firmness by the contemplation of mortality',[1] but that his reverential affection for her was not abated by years, as indeed he retained all his tender feelings even to the latest period of his life. I have been told that he regretted much his not having gone to visit his mother for several years previous to her death. But he was constantly engaged in literary labours, which confined him to London; and though he had not the comfort of seeing his aged parent, he contributed liberally to her support.

Soon after this event, he wrote his *Rasselas, Prince of Abyssinia;** concerning the publication of which Sir John Hawkins guesses vaguely and idly, instead of having taken the trouble to inform himself with authentic precision. Not to trouble my readers with a repetition of the Knight's reveries, I have to mention, that the late Mr Strahan the printer told me, that Johnson wrote it, that with the profits he might defray the expense of his mother's funeral, and pay some little debts which she had left. He told Sir Joshua Reynolds that he composed it in the evenings of one week, sent it to the press in portions as it was written, and had never since read it over. Mr Strahan, Mr Johnston, and Mr Dodsley purchased it for a hundred pounds, but afterwards paid him twenty-five pounds more when it came to a second edition.

Considering the large sums which have been received for compilations, and works requiring not much more genius than compilations, we cannot but wonder at the very low price which he was content to receive for this admirable performance, which, though he had written nothing else, would have rendered his name immortal in the world of literature. None of his writings has been so extensively diffused over Europe; for it has been translated into most, if not all, of the modern languages. This Tale, with all the charms of oriental imagery, and all the force and beauty of which the English language is capable, leads us through the most important scenes of human life, and shows us that this stage of our being is full of 'vanity and vexation of spirit'. To those who look no further than the present life, or who maintain that human nature has not fallen from the state in which it was created, the instruction of this sublime story will be of no avail. But they who think justly, and feel with strong sensibility, will listen with eagerness and admiration to its truth and wisdom. Voltaire's *Candide*, written to refute the

---

He that dies before sixty, of a cold or consumption, dies, in reality, by a violent death; yet his death is borne with patience, only because the cause of his untimely end is silent and invisible. Let us endeavour to see things as they are, and then enquire whether we ought to complain. Whether to see life as it is, will give us much consolation, I know not; but the consolation which is drawn from truth, if any there be, is solid and durable: that which may be derived from error, must be, like its original, fallacious and fugitive.

I am, dear, dear Sir,
Your most humble Servant,

SAM. JOHNSON.

Sept. 21, 1758.

1 Hawkins's *Life of Johnson*, p. 365.

system of Optimism, which it has accomplished with brilliant success, is wonderfully similar in its plan and conduct to Johnson's *Rasselas*; insomuch, that I have heard Johnson say, that if they had not been published so closely one after the other that there was not time for imitation, it would have been in vain to deny that the scheme of that which came latest was taken from the other. Though the proposition illustrated by both these works was the same, namely, that in our present state there is more evil than good, the intention of the writers was very different. Voltaire, I am afraid, meant only by wanton profaneness to obtain a sportive victory over religion, and to discredit the belief of a superintending Providence: Johnson meant, by showing the unsatisfactory nature of things temporal, to direct the hopes of man to things etyernal. *Rasselas*, as was observed to me by a very accomplished lady, may be considered as a more enlarged and more deeply philosophical discourse in prose, upon the interesting truth, which in his *Vanity of Human Wishes* he had so successfully enforced in verse.

The fund of thinking which this work contains is such, that almost every sentence of it may furnish a subject of long meditation. I am not satisfied if a year passes without my having read it through; and at every perusal, my admiration of the mind which produced it is so highly raised, that I can scarcely believe that I had the honour of enjoying the intimacy of such a man.

I restrain myself from quoting passages from this excellent work, or even referring to them, because I should not know what to select, or, rather, what to omit. I shall, however, transcribe one, as it shows how well he could state the arguments of those who believe in the appearance of departed spirits, a doctrine which it is a mistake to suppose that he himself ever positively held.

'If all your fear be of apparitions (said the Prince), I will promise you safety: there is no danger from the dead; he that is once buried will be seen no more.

'That the dead are seen no more (said Imlac), I will not undertake to maintain against the concurrent and unvaried testimony of all ages, and of all nations. There is no people, rude or learned, among whom apparitions of the dead are not related and believed. This opinion, which prevails as far as human nature is diffused, could become universal only by its truth; those that never heard of one another, would not have agreed in a tale which nothing but experience can make credible. That it is doubted by single cavillers, can very little weaken the general evidence; and some who deny it with their tongues, confess it by their fears.'

Notwithstanding my high admiration of *Rasselas*, I will not maintain that the 'morbid melancholy' in Johnson's constitution may not, perhaps, have made life appear to him more insipid and unhappy than it generally is; for I am sure that he had less enjoyment from it than I have. Yet, whatever additional shade his own particular sensations may have thrown on his representation of life, attentive observation and close inquiry have convinced me, that there is but too much of reality in the gloomy picture. The truth, however, is, that we judge of the happiness and misery of life differently at different times, according to the state of our changeable frame. I always remember a remark made to me by a Turkish lady, educated in France, '*Ma foi, Monsieur, notre bonheur depend de la façon que notre sang circule.*' This have I learnt from a pretty hard course of experience, and would, from sincere benevolence, impress upon all who honour this book with a perusal, that until a steady conviction is obtained, that the present life is an imperfect state, and only a passage to a better, if we comply with the divine scheme of progressive improvement; and also that it is a part of the mysterious plan of Providence, that intellectual beings must 'be made perfect through suffering'; there will be a continual recurrence of disappointment and uneasiness. But if we walk with hope in 'the mid-day sun' of revelation, our temper and disposition will be such, that the comforts and enjoyments in our way will be relished, while we patiently support the inconveniencies and pains. After much speculation and various reasonings, I acknowledge myself convinced of the truth of Voltaire's conclusion, '*Après tout c'est un monde passable.*' But we must not think too deeply:

> Where ignorance is bliss, 'tis folly to be wise,

is, in many respects, more than poetically just. Let us cultivate, under the command of good principles, '*la théorie des sensations agréables*'; and, as Mr Burke once admirably counselled a grave and anxious gentleman, 'live pleasant.'

The effect of *Rasselas*, and of Johnson's other moral tales, is thus beautifully illustrated by Mr Courtenay:

> Impressive truth, in splendid fiction drest,
> Checks the vain wish, and calms the troubled breast;
> O'er the dark mind a light celestial throws,
> And soothes the angry passions to repose:
> As oil effus'd illumes and smooths the deep,
> When round the bark the swelling surges sweep.[1]

It will be recollected, that during all this year he carried on his *Idler*,[2] and, no doubt, was proceeding, though slowly, in his edition of Shakspeare. He,

---

1 'Literary and moral Character of Dr Johnson'.

2 This paper was in such high estimation before it was collected into volumes, that it was seized on with avidity by various publishers of newspapers and magazines, to enrich their publications. Johnson, to put a stop to this unfair proceeding, wrote for the *Universal Chronicle* the following advertisement, in which there is, perhaps, more pomp of words than the occasion demanded:

'London, January 5, 1759. Advertisement. The proprietors of the paper entitled *The Idler*, having found that those essays are inserted in the newspapers and magazines with so little regard to justice or decency, that the *Universal Chronicle*, in which they first appear, is not always mentioned, think it necessary to declare to the publishers of those collections, that however patiently they have hitherto endured these injuries, made yet more injurious by contempt, they have now determined to endure them no longer. They have already seen essays, for which a very large price is paid, transferred with the most shameless rapacity, into the

however, from that liberality which never failed, when called upon to assist other labourers in literature, found time to translate for Mrs Lennox's English version of Brumoy, *A Dissertation on the Greek Comedy*,[†] and the General Conclusion of the book.[†]

I would ascribe to this year the following letter to a son of one of his early friends at Lichfield, Mr Joseph Simpson, Barrister and author of a tract entitled 'Reflections on the Study of the Law'.

To JOSEPH SIMPSON, Esq.

DEAR SIR – Your father's inexorability not only grieves but amazes me: he is your father: he was always accounted a wise man; nor do I remember any thing to the disadvantage of his good nature; but in his refusal to assist you there is neither good-nature, fatherhood, nor wisdom. It is the practice of good-nature to overlook faults which have already, by the consequences, punished the delinquent. It is natural for a father to think more favourably than others of his children; and it is always wise to give assistance while a little help will prevent the necessity of greater.

If you married imprudently, you miscarried at your own hazard, at an age when you had a right of choice. It would be hard if the man might not choose his own wife, who has a right to plead before the Judges of his country.

If your imprudence has ended in difficulties and inconveniences, you are yourself to support them; and, with the help of a little better health, you would support them and conquer them. Surely, that want which accident and sickness produces, is to be supported in every region of humanity, though there were neither friends nor fathers in the world. You have certainly from your father the highest claim of charity, though none of right; and therefore I would counsel you to omit no decent nor manly

---

weekly or monthly compilations, and their right, at least for the present, alienated from them, before they could themselves be said to enjoy it. But they would not willingly be thought to want tenderness, even for men by whom no tenderness hath been shown. The past is without remedy, and shall be without resentment. But those who have been thus busy with their sickles in the fields of their neighbours, are henceforward to take notice, that the time of impunity is at an end. Whoever shall, without our leave, lay the hand of rapine upon our papers, is to expect that we shall vindicate our due, by the means which justice prescribes, and which are warranted by the immemorial prescriptions of honourable trade. We shall lay hold, in our turn, on their copies, degrade them from the pomp of wide margin and diffuse typography, contract them into a narrow space, and sell them at an humble price; yet not with a view of growing rich by confiscations, for we think not much better of money got by punishment than by crimes. We shall, therefore, when our losses are repaid, give what profit shall remain to the *Magdalens*; for we know not who can be more properly taxed for the support of penitent prostitutes, than prostitutes in whom there yet appears neither penitence nor shame.'

degree of importunity. Your debts in the whole are not large, and of the whole but a small part is troublesome. Small debts are like small shot; they are rattling on every side, and can scarcely be escaped without a wound: great debts are like cannon; of loud noise, but little danger. You must, therefore, be enabled to discharge petty debts, that you may have leisure, with security, to struggle with the rest. Neither the great nor little debts disgrace you. I am sure you have my esteem for the courage with which you contracted them, and the spirit with which you endure them. I wish my esteem could be of more use. I have been invited, or have invited myself, to several parts of the kingdom; and will not incommode my dear Lucy by coming to Lichfield, while her present lodging is of any use to her. I hope in a few days to be at leisure, and to make visits. Whither I shall fly is matter of no importance. A man unconnected is at home every where; unless he may be said to be at home no where. I am sorry, dear Sir, that where you have parents, a man of your merits should not have an home. I wish I could give it you. I am, my dear Sir,

Affectionately your's,

SAM. JOHNSON.

He now refreshed himself by an excursion to Oxford, of which the following short characteristical notice, in his own words, is preserved: ' —— is now making tea for me. I have been in my gown ever since I came here. It was at my first coming quite new and handsome. I have swum thrice, which I had disused for many years. I have proposed to Vansittart[1] climbing over the wall, but he has refused me. And I have clapped my hands till they are sore, at Dr King's speech.'[2]

His negro servant, Francis Barber, having left him, and been some time at sea, not pressed as has been supposed, but with his own consent, it appears from a letter to John Wilkes, Esq. from Dr Smollet, that his master kindly interested himself in procuring his release from a state of life of which Johnson always expressed the utmost abhorrence. He said, 'No man will be a sailor who has contrivance enough to get himself into a jail; for being in a ship is being in a jail, with the chance of being drowned.'[3] And at another time, 'A man in a jail has more room, better food, and commonly better company.'[4]

The letter was as follows:

1 Dr Robert Vansittart, of the ancient and respectable family of that name in Berkshire. He was eminent for learning and worth, and much esteemed by Dr Johnson.
2 *Gentleman's Magazine*, April 1785.
3 *Journal of a Tour to the Hebrides*, 3d edit. p. 126.
4 Ibid. p. 251.

Chelsea, March 16, 1759.

DEAR SIR – I am again your petitioner, in behalf of that great chum[1a] of literature Samuel Johnson. His black servant, whose name is Francis Barber, has been pressed on board the Stag Frigate, Captain Angel, and our lexicographer is in great distress. He says the boy is a sickly lad, of a delicate frame, and particularly subject to a malady in his throat, which renders him very unfit for his Majesty's service. You know what manner of animosity the said Johnson has against you; and I dare say you desire no other opportunity of resenting it than that of laying him under an obligation. He was humble enough to desire my assistance on this occasion, though he and I were never cater-cousins; and I gave him to understand that I would make application to my friend Mr Wilkes, who, perhaps, by his interest with Dr Hay and Mr Elliott, might be able to procure the discharge of his lacquey. It would be superfluous to say more on the subject, which I leave to your own consideration; but I cannot let slip this opportunity of declaring that I am, with the most inviolable esteem and attachment, dear Sir,

Your affectionate obliged humble servant,

T. SMOLLET.

Mr Wilkes, who upon all occasions has acted, as a private gentleman, with most polite liberality, applied to his friend Sir George Hay, then one of the Lords Commissioners of the Admiralty; and Francis Barber was discharged, as he has told me, without any wish of his own. He recollects the precise time to be three days before King George II died.[b] He found his old master in chambers in the Inner Temple, and returned to his service.

What particular new scheme of life Johnson had in view this year, I have not discovered; but that he meditated one of some sort, is clear from his private devotions, in which we find, 'the change of outward things which I am now to

---

1 Had Dr Smollet been bred at an English University, he would have known that a *chum* is a student who lives with another in a chamber common to them both. A *chum of literature* is nonsense.

[a] For 'chum', read 'cham'. Delete the note on the word, and read: In my first edition this word was printed *chum*, as it appears in one of Mr Wilkes's *Miscellanies*, and I animadverted on Dr Smollett's ignorance: for which let me propitiate the *manes* of that ingenious and benevolent gentleman. CHUM was certainly a mistaken reading for CHAM, the title of the *Sovereign of Tartary*, which is well applied to Johnson, the Monarch of Literature: and was an epithet familiar to Smollett. See *Roderick Random*, chap. 56. For this correction I am indebted to Lord Palmerston, whose talents and literary acquirements accord well with his respectable pedigree of TEMPLE.

[After the publication of the second edition of this work, the author was furnished by Mr Abercrombie of Philadelphia, with the copy of a letter written by Dr John Armstrong, the poet, to Dr Smollett, at Leghorn, containing the following paragraph: 'As to the K. Bench patriot, it is hard to say from what motive he published a letter of yours asking some trifling favour of him in behalf of somebody for whom the great CHAM of literature, Mr Johnson, had interested himself.' Malone]

[b] Delete 'He recollects the precise time to be three days before King George II died.'

make'; and, 'Grant me the grace of thy Holy Spirit, that the course which I am now beginning may proceed according to thy laws, and end in the enjoyment of thy favour.'[1] But he did not, in fact, make any external or visible change.

At this time there being a competition among the architects of London to be employed in the building of Blackfriars-bridge, a question was very warmly agitated whether semicircular or elliptical arches were preferable. In the design offered by Mr Mylne the elliptical form was adopted, and therefore it was the great object of his rivals to attack it. Johnson's regard for his friend Mr Gwyn induced him to engage in this controversy against Mr Mylne;[2] and after being at considerable pains to study the subject, he wrote three several letters in the *Gazetteer*, in opposition to his plan.

If it should be remarked that this was a controversy which lay quite out of Johnson's way, let it be remembered that after all, his employing his powers of reasoning and eloquence upon a subject which he had studied on the moment,

---

1 *Prayers and Meditations*, p. 30 and 40.

2 Sir John Hawkins has given a long detail of it, in that manner vulgarly, but significantly, called *rigmarole*; in which, amidst an ostentatious exhibition of arts and artists, he talks of 'proportions of a column being taken from that of the human figure, and *adjusted by Nature* – masculine and feminine – in a man, *sesquioctave* of the head, and in a woman *sesquinonal*'; nor has he failed to introduce a jargon of musical terms, which do not seem much to correspond with the subject, but serve to make up the heterogeneous mass. To follow the Knight through all this, would be an useless fatigue to myself, and not a little disgusting to my readers. I shall, therefore, only make a few remarks upon his statement. He seems to exult in having detected Johnson in procuring 'from a person eminently skilled in mathematics and the principles of architecture, answers to a string of questions drawn up by himself, touching the comparative strength of semicircular and elliptical arches.' Now I cannot conceive how Johnson could have acted more wisely. Sir John complains that the opinion of that excellent mathematician, Mr Thomas Simpson, did not preponderate in favour of the semicircular arch. But he should have known, that however eminent Mr Simpson was in the higher parts of abstract mathematical science, he was little versed in mixed and practical mechanics. Mr Muller, of Woolwich Academy, the scholastic father of all the great engineers which this country has employed for forty years, decided the question by declaring clearly in favour of the elliptical arch.

It is ungraciously suggested, that Johnson's motive for opposing Mr Mylne's scheme may have been his prejudice against him as a native of North-Britain; when, in truth, as has been stated, he gave the aid of his able pen to a friend, who was one of the candidates; and so far was he from having any illiberal antipathy to Mr Mylne, that he afterwards lived with that gentleman upon very agreeable terms of acquaintance, and dined with him at his house. Sir John Hawkins, indeed, gives full vent to his own prejudice in abusing Blackfriars-bridge, calling it 'an edifice, in which beauty and symmetry are in vain sought for; by which the citizens of London have perpetuated their own disgrace, and subjected a whole nation to the reproach of foreigners.' Whoever has contemplated, *placido lumine*, this stately, elegant, and airy structure, which has so fine an effect, especially on approaching the capital on that quarter, must wonder at such unjust and ill-tempered censure; and I appeal to all foreigners of good taste, whether this bridge be not one of the most distinguished ornaments of London. As to the stability of the fabric, it is certain that the City of London took every

is not more strange than what we often observe in lawyers, who, as *Quicquid agunt homines* is the matter of law-suits, are sometimes obliged to pick up a temporary knowledge of an art or science, of which they understood nothing till their brief was delivered, and appear to be much masters of it. In like manner, members of the legislature frequently introduce and expatiate upon subjects of which they have informed themselves for the occasion.

In 1760 he wrote 'An Address of the Painters to George III. on his Accession to the Throne of these Kingdoms',† which no monarch ever ascended with more sincere congratulations from his people. Two generations of foreign princes had prepared their minds to rejoice in having again a King, who gloried in being 'born a Briton'. He also wrote for Mr Baretti the Dedication† of his Italian and English Dictionary, to the Marquis of Abreu, then Ambassador Extraordinary from Spain at the Court of Great-Britain.

Johnson was now either very idle, or very busy with his Shakspeare; for I can find no other public composition by him except an account which he gave in the *Gentleman's Magazine* of Mr Tytler's acute and able vindication of Mary Queen of Scots.* The generosity of Johnson's feelings shines forth in the following sentence: 'It has now been fashionable, for near half a century, to defame and vilify the house of Stuart, and to exalt and magnify the reign of Elizabeth. The Stuarts have found few apologists; for the dead cannot pay for praise, and who will, without reward, oppose the tide of popularity? Yet there remains still among us, not wholly extinguished, a zeal for truth, a desire of establishing right in opposition to fashion.'

In this year I have not discovered a single private letter written by him to any of his friends. It should seem, however, that he had at this period a floating intention of writing a history of the recent and wonderful successes of the British arms in all quarters of the globe; for among his resolutions or memorandums, September 18, there is, 'Send for books for Hist. of War.'[1] How much is it to be regretted that this intention was not fulfilled. His majestic expression would have carried down to the latest posterity the glorious achievements of his country, with the same fervent glow which they produced on the mind at the time. He would have been under no temptation to deviate in any degree from truth, which he held very sacred, or to take a licence which a learned divine told me he once seemed, in a conversation, jocularly to allow to historians. 'There are (said he) inexcusable lies, and consecrated lies. For

---

precaution to have the best Portland stone for it, but as this is to be found in the quarries belonging to the public, under the direction of the Lords of the Treasury, it so happened that parliamentary interest, which is often the bane of fair pursuits, thwarted their endeavours. Notwithstanding this disadvantage, it is well known that not only has Blackfriars-bridge never sunk either in its foundations or in its arches, which were so much the subject of contest, but any injuries which it has suffered from the effects of severe frosts have been already, in some measure, repaired with sounder stone, and every necessary renewal can be completed at a moderate expense.

1 *Prayers and Meditations*, p. 42.

instance, we are told that on the arrival of the news of the unfortunate battle of Fontenoy, every heart beat, and every eye was in tears. Now we know that no man eat his dinner the worse, but there *should* have been all this concern; and to say there *was* (smiling), may be reckoned a consecrated lie.'

This year Mr Murphy having thought himself ill treated by the Reverend Dr Francklin, who was one of the writers of the *Critical Review*, published an indignant vindication in 'A Poetical Epistle to Samuel Johnson, A.M.' in which he compliments Johnson in a just and elegant manner:

> Transcendant Genius, whose prolific vein
> Ne'er knew the frigid poet's toil and pain;
> To whom APOLLO opens all his store,
> And every Muse presents her sacred lore;
> Say, pow'rful JOHNSON, whence thy verse is fraught
> With so much grace, such energy of thought;
> Whether thy JUVENAL instructs the age
> In chaster numbers, and new-points his rage
> Or fair IRENE sees, alas! too late
> Her innocence exchang'd for guilty state;
> Whate'er you write, in every golden line
> Sublimity and elegance combine;
> Thy nervous phrase impresses every soul,
> While harmony gives rapture to the whole.

Again, towards the conclusion:

> Thou then, my friend, who see'st the dang'rous strife
> In which some daemon bids me plunge my life,
> To the Aonian font direct my feet,
> Say where the Nine thy lonely musings meet?
> Where warbles to thy ear the sacred throng,
> Thy moral sense, thy dignity of song?
> Tell, for you can, by what unerring art
> You wake to finer feelings every heart;
> In each bright page some truth important give,
> And bid to future times thy RAMBLER live.

I take this opportunity to relate the manner in which an acquaintance first commenced between Dr Johnson and Mr Murphy. During the publication of the *Gray's-Inn Journal*, a periodical paper which was successfully carried on by Mr Murphy alone, when a very young man, he happened to be in the country with Mr Foote; and having mentioned that he was obliged to go to London in order to get ready for the press one of the numbers of that Journal, Foote said to him, 'You need not go on that account. Here is a French magazine, in which you will find a very pretty oriental tale; translate that, and send it to your printer.' Mr Murphy having read the tale, was highly pleased with it, and followed Foote's advice. When he returned to town, this tale was pointed out to him in the *Rambler*, from whence it had been translated into the French magazine. Mr Murphy then waited upon Johnson to explain this curious incident. His talents, literature and gentleman-like manners, were soon perceived by Johnson, and a friendship was formed which was never broken.

Johnson, who was ever awake to the calls of humanity, wrote this year an Introduction* to the proceedings of the Committee for clothing the French prisoners.[a]

[a] Add:

To BENNET LANGTON, ESQ. at Langton, near Spilsby, Lincolnshire.

DEAR SIR – You that travel about the world, have more materials for letters, than I who stay at home: and should, therefore, write with frequency equal to your opportunities. I should be glad to have all England surveyed by you, if you would impart your observations in narratives as agreeable as your last. Knowledge is always to be wished to those who can communicate it well. While you have been riding and running, and seeing the tombs of the learned, and the camps of the valiant, I have only staid at home, and intended to do great things, which I have not done. Beau went away to Cheshire, and has not yet found his way back. Chambers passed the vacation at Oxford.

I am very sincerely solicitous for the preservation or curing of Mr Langton's sight, and am glad that the chirurgeon at Coventry gives him so much hope. Mr Sharpe is of opinion that the tedious maturation of the cataract is a vulgar error and that it may be removed as soon as it is formed. This notion deserves to be considered; I doubt whether it be universally true; but if it be true in some cases, and those cases can be distinguished, it may save a long and uncomfortable delay.

Of dear Mrs Langton you give me no account; which is the less friendly, as you know how highly I think of her, and how much I interest myself in her health. I suppose you told her of my opinion, and likewise suppose it was not followed; however, I still believe it to be right.

Let me hear from you again, wherever you are, or whatever you are doing; whether you wander or sit still, plant trees or make *Rustics*,[1] play with your sisters or muse alone; and in return I will tell you the success of Sheridan, who at this instant is playing Cato, and has already played Richard twice. He had more company the second than the first night, and will make I believe a good figure in the whole, though his faults seem to be very many; some of natural deficience, and some of laborious affectation. He has, I think, no power of assuming either that dignity or elegance which some men, who have little of either in common life, can exhibit on the stage. His voice when strained is unpleasing, and when low is not always heard. He seems to think too much on the audience, and turns his face too often to the galleries.

However, I wish him well; and among other reasons, because I like his wife.[2]
Make haste to write to, dear sir,
Your most affectionate servant,

SAM. JOHNSON.

Oct. 18, 1760.

1 Essays with that title, written about this time by Mr Langton, but not published.
2 Mrs Sheridan was author of *Memoirs of Miss Sydney Biddulph*, a novel of great merit, and of some other pieces. – See her character, p. 198.

In 1761 Johnson appears to have done little. He was still, no doubt, proceeding in his edition of Shakspeare; but what advances he made in it cannot be ascertained. He certainly was at this time not active; for in his scrupulous examination of himself on Easter eve, he laments, in his too rigorous mode of censuring his own conduct, that his life, since the communion of the preceding Easter, had been 'dissipated and useless'.[1] He, however, contributed this year the Preface* to Rolt's *Dictionary of Trade and Commerce*, in which he displays such a clear and comprehensive knowledge of the subject, as might lead the reader to think that its author had devoted all his life to it. I asked him, whether he knew much of Rolt, and of his work. 'Sir (said he), I never saw the man, and never read the book. The booksellers wanted a Preface to a *Dictionary of Trade and Commerce*. I knew very well what such a Dictionary should be, and I wrote a Preface accordingly.' Rolt, who wrote a great deal for the booksellers,[a] particularly a *History of the War*, on which, as we have seen, Johnson himself once had thoughts of employing his pen, was, as Johnson told me, a singular character. Though not in the least acquainted with him, he used to say, 'I am just come from Sam. Johnson.' This was a sufficient specimen of his vanity and impudence. But he gave a more eminent proof of it in our sister kingdom, as Dr Johnson informed me. When Akenside's *Pleasures of the Imagination* first came out, he did not put his name to the poem. Rolt went over to Dublin, published an edition of it, and put his own name[b] to it. Upon the fame of this he lived for several months, being entertained at the best tables as 'the ingenious Mr Rolt'. His conversation, indeed, did not discover much of the fire of the poet; but it was recollected, that both Addison and Thomson were equally dull till excited by wine. Akenside having been informed of this imposition, vindicated his right by publishing the poem with its real author's name. Several instances of such literary fraud have been detected. The Reverend Dr Campbell, of St Andrew's, wrote a book on the authenticity of the Gospel History,[c] the manuscript of which he sent to Mr Innys,[d] a clergyman in England, who was his countryman and acquaintance. Innys published it with his own name to it; and before the imposition was discovered, obtained considerable promotion, as a reward of his merit.[e] The celebrated Dr Hugh Blair, and his cousin

---

1 *Prayers and Meditations*, p. 44.

[a] Delete the words between 'booksellers' and 'was'.

[b] Add the following note: I have had enquiry made in Ireland as to this story, but do not find it recollected there. I give it on the authority of Dr Johnson, to which may be added, that of the *Biographical Dictionary*, and *Biographia Dramatica*; in both of which it has stood many years.

[c] For 'a book on the authenticity of the Gospel History', read, 'an enquiry into the origin of Moral Virtue'.

[d] For 'Innys', read, 'Innes'.

[e] Add the following note: 'I have both books.' *Second edition* – add, 'Innes was the clergyman who brought Psalmanazar to England, and was an accomplice in his extraordinary fiction.'

Mr George Ballantine, when students in divinity, wrote a poem, entitled 'Redemption',[a] copies of which were handed about in manuscript. They were, at length, very much surprised to see a pompous edition of it in folio, dedicated to the Queen,[b] by a Dr Douglas, as his own. Some years ago a little novel, entitled, *The Man of Feeling*, was assumed by Mr Eccles, a young Irish clergyman, who was afterwards drowned near Bath. He had been at the pains to transcribe the whole book, with blottings, interlineations, and corrections, that it might be shown to several people as an original. It was, in truth, the production of Mr Henry Mackenzie, an attorney in the Exchequer, at Edinburgh, who is the author of several other ingenious pieces; but the belief with regard to Mr Eccles became so general, that it was thought necessary for Messieurs Strahan and Cadell to publish an advertisement in the newspapers, contradicting the report, and mentioning that they purchased the copy right of Mr Mackenzie. I can conceive this kind of fraud to be very easily practised with successful effrontery. The *filiation* of a literary performance is difficult of proof; seldom is there any witness present at its birth. A man, either in confidence or by improper means, obtains possession of a copy of it in manuscript, and boldly publishes it as his own. The true author, in many cases, may not be able to make his title clear. Johnson, indeed, from the peculiar features of his literary offspring, might bid defiance to any attempt to appropriate them to others:

> 'But Shakspeare's magic could not copied be,
> Within that circle none durst walk but he.'

He this year lent his friendly assistance to correct and improve a pamphlet written by Mr Gwyn, the architect, entitled 'Thoughts on the Coronation of George III'.

Johnson had now for some years admitted Mr Baretti to his intimacy; nor did their friendship cease upon their being separated by Baretti's revisiting his native country, as appears from Johnson's letters to him.

To Mr JOSEPH BARETTI, at Milan.[c]

You reproach me very often with parsimony of writing: but you may discover by the extent of my paper, that I design to recompense rarity by length. A short letter to a distant friend is, in my opinion, an insult like that of a slight bow or cursory salutation – a proof of unwillingness to do much, even where there is a necessity of doing something. Yet it must be

---

[a] For 'Redemption', read 'The Resurrection'.

[b] For 'Queen', read, 'Princess Dowager of Wales'.

[c] Add the following note: The originals of Dr Johnson's three letters to Mr Baretti, which are among the very best he ever wrote, were communicated to the proprietors of that instructive and elegant monthly miscellany, *The European Magazine*, in which they first appeared.

remembered, that he who continues the same course of life in the same place, will have little to tell. One week and one year are very like another. The silent changes made by time are not always perceived; and if they are not perceived, cannot be recounted. I have risen and laid down, talked and mused, while you have roved over a considerable part of Europe: yet I have not envied my Baretti any of his pleasures, though, perhaps, I have envied others his company; and I am glad to have other nations made acquainted with the character of the English, by a traveller who has so nicely inspected our manners, and so successfully studied our literature. I received your kind letter from Falmouth, in which you gave me notice of your departure for Lisbon; and another from Lisbon, in which you told me, that you were to leave Portugal in a few days. To either of these how could any answer be returned? I have had a third from Turin, complaining that I have not answered the former. Your English style still continues in its purity and vigour. With vigour your genius will supply it; but its purity must be continued by close attention. To use two languages familiarly, and without contaminating one by the other, is very difficult; and to use more than two, is hardly to be hoped. The praises which some have received for their multiplicity of languages, may be sufficient to excite industry, but can hardly generate confidence.

I know not whether I can heartily rejoice at the kind reception which you have found, or at the popularity to which you are exalted. I am willing that your merit should be distinguished, but cannot wish that your affections may be gained. I would have you happy wherever you are: yet I would have you wish to return to England. If ever you visit us again, you will find the kindness of your friends undiminished. To tell you how many enquiries are made after you, would be tedious, or if not tedious, would be vain; because you may be told in a very few words, that all who knew you wish you well; and all that you embraced at your departure, will caress you at your return: therefore do not let Italian academicians nor Italian ladies drive us from your thoughts. You may find among us what you will leave behind, soft smiles and easy sonnets. Yet I shall not wonder if all our invitations should be rejected: for there is a pleasure in being considerable at home, which is not easily resisted.

By conducting Mr Southwell to Venice, you fulfilled, I know, the original contract: yet I would wish you not wholly to lose him from your notice, but to recommend him to such acquaintance as may best secure him from suffering by his own follies, and to take such general care both of his safety and his interest as may come within your power. His relations will thank you for any such gratuitous attention: at least they will not blame you for any evil that may happen, whether they thank you or not for any good.

You know that we have a new King and a new Parliament. Of the new Parliament Fitzherbert is a member. We were so weary of our old King, that we are much pleased with his successor; of whom we are so much inclined to hope great things, that most of us begin already to believe them.

The young man is hitherto blameless; but it would be unreasonable to expect much from the immaturity of juvenile years, and the ignorance of princely education. He has been long in the hands of the Scots, and has already favoured them more than the English will contentedly endure. But, perhaps, he scarcely knows whom he has distinguished, or whom he has disgusted.

The Artists have instituted a yearly exhibition of pictures and statues, in imitation, as I am told, of foreign Academies. This year was the second exhibition. They please themselves much with the multitude of spectators, and imagine that the English school will rise in reputation. Reynolds is without a rival, and continues to add thousands to thousands, which he deserves, among other excellencies, by retaining his kindness for Baretti. This exhibition has filled the heads of the artists and lovers of art. Surely life, if it be not long, is tedious, since we are forced to call in the assistance of so many trifles to rid us of our time, of that time which never can return.

I know my Baretti will not be satisfied with a letter in which I give him no account of myself: yet what account shall I give him? I have not, since the day of our separation, suffered or done any thing considerable. The only change in my way of life is, that I have frequented the theatre more than in former seasons. But I have gone thither only to escape from myself. We have had many new farces, and the comedy called *The Jealous Wife*, which, though not written with much genius, was yet so well adapted to the stage, and so well exhibited by the actors, that it was crowded for near twenty nights. I am digressing from myself to the playhouse; but a barren plan must be filled with episodes. Of myself I have nothing to say, but that I have hitherto lived without the concurrence of my own judgement; yet I continue to flatter myself, that, when you return, you will find me mended. I do not wonder that, where the monastic life is permitted, every order finds votaries, and every monastery inhabitants. Men will submit to any rule, by which they may be exempted from the tyranny of caprice and of chance. They are glad to supply by external authority their own want of constancy and resolution, and court the government of others, when long experience has convinced them of their own inability to govern them- selves. If I were to visit Italy, my curiosity would be more attracted by convents than by palaces; though I am afraid that I should find expectation in both places equally disappointed, and life in both places supported with impatience and quitted with reluctance. That it must be so soon quitted, is a powerful remedy against impatience; but what shall free us from reluc- tance? Those who have endeavoured to teach us to die well, have taught few to die willingly; yet I cannot but hope that a good life might end at last in a contented death.

You see to what a train of thought I am drawn by the mention of myself. Let me now turn my attention upon you. I hope you take care to keep an exact journal, and to register all occurrences and observations; for your friends here expect such a book of travels as has not been often seen. You have given us good specimens in your letters from Lisbon. I wish you had staid longer in Spain, for no country is less known to the rest of Europe; but the quickness of your discernment must make amends for the celerity of your motions. He that knows which way to direct his view, sees much in a little time.

Write to me very often, and I will not neglect to write to you; and I may, perhaps, in time get something to write: at least, you will know by my letters, whatever else they may have or want, that I continue to be

Your most affectionate friend,

SAM. JOHNSON.

London, June 10, 1761.

An inquiry into the state of foreign countries was an object that seems at all times to have interested Johnson. Hence Mr Newbery found no great difficulty in persuading him to write the Introduction* to a collection of voyages and travels published by him under the title of *The World Displayed*. The first volume appeared in 1759, and the remaining volumes in subsequent years.

In 1762 he wrote for the Reverend Dr Kennedy, Rector of Bradley in Derbyshire, in a strain of very courtly elegance, a Dedication to the King* of that gentleman's work, entitled 'A complete System of astronomical Chronology, unfolding the Scriptures'. He had certainly looked at this work before it was printed; for the concluding paragraph is undoubtedly of his composition, of which let my readers judge:

> Thus have I endeavoured to free Religion and History from the darkness of a disputed and uncertain chronology; from difficulties which have hitherto appeared insuperable, and darkness which no luminary of learning has hitherto been able to dissipate. I have established the truth of the Mosaical account by evidence which no transcription can corrupt, no negligence can lose, and no interest can pervert. I have shown that the universe bears witness to the inspiration of its historian, by the revolution of its orbs and the succession of its seasons; *that the stars in their courses fight against* incredulity, that the works of GOD give hourly confirmation to the *law*, the *prophets*, and the *gospel*, of which *one day telleth another, and one night certifieth another*; and that the validity of the sacred writings never can be denied, while the moon shall increase and wane, and the sun shall know his going down.

The following letter, which, on account of its intrinsic merit, it would have been unjust both to Johnson and the public to have withheld, was obtained for me by the solicitation of my friend Mr Seward:

To Dr STAUNTON (now Sir GEORGE STAUNTON, Bart.)

DEAR SIR — I make haste to answer your kind letter, in hope of hearing again from you before you leave us. I cannot but regret that a man of your qualifications should find it necessary to seek an establishment in Guadaloupe, which if a peace should restore to the French, I shall think it some alleviation of the loss, that it must restore likewise Dr Staunton to the English.

It is a melancholy consideration, that so much of our time is necessarily to be spent upon the care of living, and that we can seldom obtain ease in one respect but by resigning it in another; yet I suppose we are by this dispensation not less happy in the whole than if the spontaneous bounty of Nature poured all that we want into our hands. A few, if they were thus left to themselves, would, perhaps, spend their time in laudable pursuits; but the greater part would prey upon the quiet of each other, or, in the want of other objects, would prey upon themselves.

This, however, is our condition, which we must improve and solace as we can: and though we cannot choose always our place of residence, we may in every place find rational amusements, and possess in every place the comforts of piety and a pure conscience.

In America there is little to be observed except natural curiosities. The new world must have many vegetables and animals with which philosophers are but little acquainted. I hope you will furnish yourself with some books of natural history, and some glasses and other instruments of observation. Trust as little as you can to report: examine all you can by your own senses. I do not doubt but you will be able to add much to knowledge, and, perhaps, to medicine. Wild nations trust to simples; and, perhaps, the Peruvian bark is not the only specific which those extensive regions may afford us.

Wherever you are, and whatever be your fortune, be certain, dear Sir, that you carry with you my kind wishes; and that whether you return hither, or stay in the other hemisphere, to hear that you are happy will give pleasure to, Sir,

Your most affectionate humble servant,

SAM. JOHNSON.

June 1, 1762.

A lady having at this time solicited him to obtain the Archbishop of Canterbury's patronage to have her son sent to the University, one of those solicitations which are too frequent, where people, anxious for a particular object, do not consider propriety, or the opportunity which the persons whom they solicit have to assist them, he wrote to her the following answer; with a copy of which I am favoured by the Reverend Dr Farmer, Master of Emanuel College, Cambridge.

MADAM – I hope you will believe that my delay in answering your letter could proceed only from my unwillingness to destroy any hope that you had formed. Hope is itself a species of happiness, and, perhaps, the chief happiness which this world affords: but, like all other pleasures immoderately enjoyed, the excesses of hope must be expiated by pain; and expectations improperly indulged, must end in disappointment. If it be asked, what is the improper expectation which it is dangerous to indulge, experience will quickly answer, that it is such expectation as is dictated not by reason, but by desire; expectation raised, not by the common occurrences of life, but by the wants of the expectant; an expectation that requires the common course of things to be changed, and the general rules of action to be broken.

When you made your request to me, you should have considered, Madam, what you were asking. You ask me to solicit a great man to whom I never spoke, for a young person whom I had never seen, upon a supposition which I had no means of knowing to be true. There is no reason why, amongst all the great, I should choose to supplicate the Archbishop, nor why, among all the possible objects of his bounty, the Archbishop should choose your son. I know, Madam, how unwillingly conviction is admitted, when interest opposes it; but surely, Madam, you must allow, that there is no reason why that should be done by me, which every man may do with equal reason, and which, indeed, no man can do properly, without some very particular relation both to the Archbishop and to you. If I could help you in this exigence by any proper means, it would give me pleasure; but this proposal is so very remote from all usual methods, that I cannot comply with it but at the risk of such answer and suspicions as I believe you do not wish me to undergo.

I have seen your son this morning; he seems a pretty youth, and will, perhaps, find some better friend than I can procure him; but, though he should at last miss the University, he may still be wise, useful, and happy. I am, Madam,

Your most humble servant,

SAM. JOHNSON.

June 8, 1762.

To Mr JOSEPH BARETTI, at Milan.

London, July 20, 1762.

SIR – However justly you may accuse me for want of punctuality in correspondence, I am not so far lost in negligence as to omit the opportunity of writing to you, which Mr Beauclerk's passage through Milan affords me.

I suppose you received the *Idlers*, and I intend that you shall soon receive Shakspeare, that you may explain his works to the ladies of Italy, and tell them the story of the editor, among the other strange narratives with which your long residence in this unknown region has supplied you.

As you have now been long away, I suppose your curiosity may pant for some news of your old friends. Miss Williams and I live much as we did.

Miss Cotterel still continues to cling to Mrs Porter, and Charlotte is now big of the fourth child. Mr Reynolds gets six thousands a year. Levet is lately married, not without much suspicion that he has been wretchedly cheated in his match. Mr Chambers is gone this day, for the first time, the circuit with the Judges. Mr Richardson is dead of an apoplexy, and his second daughter has married a merchant.

My vanity, or my kindness, makes me flatter myself, that you would rather hear of me than of those whom I have mentioned; but of myself I have very little which I care to tell. Last winter I went down to my native town, where I found the streets much narrower and shorter than I thought I had left them, inhabited by a new race of people, to whom I was very little known. My play-fellows were grown old, and forced me to suspect that I was no longer young. My only remaining friend has changed his principles, and was become the tool of the predominant faction. My daughter-in-law, from whom I expected most, and whom I met with sincere benevolence, has lost the beauty and gaiety of youth, without having gained much of the wisdom of age. I wandered about for five days, and took the first convenient opportunity of returning to a place, where, if there is not much happiness, there is at least such a diversity of good and evil, that slight vexations do not fix upon the heart.[1]

I think in a few weeks to try another excursion; though to what end? Let me know, my Baretti, what has been the result of your return to your own country: whether time has made any alteration for the better, and whether, when the first raptures of salutation were over, you did not find your thoughts confessed their disappointment.

Moral sentences appear ostentatious and tumid, when they have no greater occasions than the journey of a wit to his own town: yet such pleasures and such pains make up the general mass of life; and as nothing is little to him that feels it with great sensibility, a mind able to see common incidents in their real state, is disposed by very common incidents to very serious contemplations. Let us trust that a time will come, when the present moment shall be no longer irksome; when we shall not borrow all our happiness from hope, which at last is to end in disappointment.

I beg that you will show Mr Beauclerk all the civilities which you have in your power; for he has always been kind to me.

I have lately seen Mr Stratico, Professor of Padua, who has told me of your quarrel with an Abbot of the Celestine order; but had not the particulars very ready in his memory. When you write to Mr Marsili, let him know that I remember him with kindness.

May you, my Baretti, be very happy at Milan, or some other place nearer to, Sir,

Your most affectionate humble servant,

SAM. JOHNSON.

---

1 This is a very just account of the relief which London affords to melancholy minds.

To the same.

Dec. 21, 1762.

SIR — You are not to suppose, with all your conviction of my idleness, that I have passed all this time without writing to my Baretti. I gave a letter to Mr Beauclerk, who, in my opinion, and in his own, was hastening to Naples for the recovery of his health; but he has stopped at Paris, and I know not when he will proceed. Langton is with him.

I will not trouble you with speculations about peace and war. The good or ill success of battles and embassies extends itself to a very small part of domestic life: we all have good and evil, which we feel more sensibly than our petty part of public miscarriage or prosperity. I am sorry for your disappointment, with which you seem more touched than I should expect a man of your resolution and experience to have been, did I not know that general truths are seldom applied to particular occasions; and that the fallacy of our self-love extends itself as[a] our interest or affections. Every man believes that mistresses are unfaithful, and patrons capricious; but he excepts his own mistress and his own patron. We have all learned that greatness is negligent and contemptuous, and that in Courts life is often languished away in ungratified expectation; but he that approaches greatness, or glitters in a Court, imagines that destiny has at last exempted him from the common lot.

Do not let such evils overwhelm you as thousands have suffered, and thousands have surmounted; but turn your thoughts with vigour to some other plan of life, and keep always in your mind, that, with due submission to Providence, a man of genius has been seldom ruined but by himself. Your patron's weakness or insensibility will finally do you little hurt, if he is not assisted by your own passions. Of your love I know not the propriety, nor can estimate the power; but in love, as in every other passion, of which hope is the essence, we ought always to remember the uncertainty of events. There is, indeed, nothing that so much seduces reason from vigilance, as the thought of passing life with an amiable woman; and if all would happen that a lover fancies, I know not what other terrestrial happiness would deserve pursuit. But love and marriage are different states. Those who are to suffer the evils together, and to suffer often for the sake of one another, soon lose that tenderness of look, and that benevolence of mind, which arose from the participation of unmingled pleasure and successive amusement. A woman, we are sure, will not be always fair; we are not sure she will always be virtuous: and man cannot retain through life that respect and assiduity by which he pleases for a day or for a month.

I do not, however, pretend to have discovered that life has any thing more to be desired than a prudent and virtuous marriage; therefore know not what counsel to give you.

If you can quit your imagination of love and greatness, and leave your

---

[a] After 'as', read 'wide as'.

hopes of preferment and bridal rapture to try once more the fortune of literature and industry, the way through France is now open. We flatter ourselves that we shall cultivate, with great diligence, the arts of peace; and every man will be welcome among us who can teach us any thing we do not know. For your own part, you will find all your old friends willing to receive you.

Reynolds still continues to increase in reputation and in riches. Miss Williams, who very much loves you, goes on in the old way. Miss Cotterel is still with Mrs Porter. Miss Charlotte is married to Dean Lewis, and has three children. Mr Levet has married a street-walker. But the gazette of my narration must now arrive to tell you, that Bathurst went physician to the army, and died at the Havannah.

I know not whether I have not sent you word that Huggins and Richardson are both dead. When we see our enemies and friends gliding away before us, let us not forget that we are subject to the general law of mortality, and shall soon be where our doom will be fixed for ever.

I pray GOD to bless you, and am, Sir,

Your most affectionate humble servant,

SAM. JOHNSON

Write soon.

The accession of George the Third to the throne of these kingdoms, opened a new and brighter prospect to men of literary merit, who had been honoured with no mark of royal favour in the preceding reign. His present Majesty's education in this country, as well as his taste and beneficence, prompted him to be the patron of science and the arts; and early this year Johnson having been represented to him as a very learned and good man, without any certain provision, his Majesty was pleased to grant him a pension of three hundred pounds a year. The Earl of Bute was then prime minister, and had the honour to announce this instance of his sovereign's bounty, concerning which many and various stories, all equally erroneous, have been propagated, maliciously representing it as a political bribe to Johnson to desert his avowed principles, and become the tool of a government which he held to be founded in usurpation. I have taken care to have it in my power to refute them from the most authentic information. Lord Bute has told me, that Mr Wedderburn, now Lord Loughborough, was the person who first mentioned this subject to him. Lord Loughborough has told me, that the pension was granted to Johnson solely as the reward of his literary merit, without any stipulation whatever, or even tacit understanding that he should write for administration. His Lordship added, that he was confident the political tracts which Johnson afterwards did write, as they were entirely consonant with his own opinions, would have been written by him, though no pension had been granted to him.

Mr Thomas Sheridan and Mr Murphy, who then lived a good deal both with him and Mr Wedderburn, have told me, that they previously talked with Johnson upon this matter, and that it was perfectly understood by all parties that the pension was merely honorary. Sir Joshua Reynolds has told me, that Johnson called on him after his Majesty's intention had been notified to him, and said he wished to consult his friends as to the propriety of his accepting this mark of the royal favour, after the definitions which he had given in his Dictionary of *pension* and *pensioners*. He said he would not have Sir Joshua's answer till next day, when he would call again, and desired he might think of it. Sir Joshua answered, that he was clear to give his opinion then, that there could be no objection to his receiving from the King a reward for literary merit; and that certainly the definitions in his Dictionary were not applicable to him. Johnson, it should seem, was satisfied, for he did not call again till he had accepted the pension, and had waited on Lord Bute to thank him. He then told Sir Joshua that Lord Bute said to him expressly, 'It is not given you for any thing you are to do, but for what you have done.' His Lordship, he said, behaved in the handsomest manner. He repeated the words twice, that he might be sure that Johnson heard them, and thus set his mind perfectly at ease. This nobleman, who has been so virulently abused, acted with great honour in this instance, and displayed a mind truly liberal. A minister of a more narrow and selfish disposition would have availed himself of such an opportunity to fix an implied obligation on a man of Johnson's powerful talents to give him his support.

Mr Murphy and the late Mr Sheridan severally contended for the distinction of having been the first who mentioned to Mr Wedderburn that Johnson ought to have a pension. When I spoke of this to Lord Loughborough, wishing to know if he recollected the prime mover in the business, he said, 'All his friends assisted': and when I told him that Mr Sheridan strenuously asserted his claim to it, his Lordship said, 'He rang the bell.' And it is but just to add, that Mr Sheridan told me, that when he communicated to Dr Johnson that a pension was to be granted him, he replied, in a fervour of gratitude, 'The English language does not afford me terms adequate to my feelings on this occasion. I must have recourse to the French. I am *penetré* with his Majesty's goodness.' When I repeated this to Dr Johnson, he did not contradict it.[a]

His definitions of *pension* and *pensioner*, partly founded on the satirical verses of Pope, which he quotes, may be generally true; and yet every body must

[a] Add: The present Earl of Bute, having been pleased to favour me with a copy of the following letter to his late father, which does great honour both to the writer and to the noble person to whom it is addressed, I here subjoin it:

To the Right Honourable the Earl of Bute.

MY LORD – When the bills were yesterday delivered to me by Mr Wedderburne, I was informed by him of the future favours which his Majesty has, by your Lordship's recommendation, been induced to intend for me.

Bounty always receives part of its value from the manner in which it is bestowed; your Lordship's kindness includes every circumstance that can gratify delicacy, or enforce obligation. You have conferred your favours on a man who has neither alliance nor interest, who has not merited them by services, nor courted them by officiousness; you have spared him the shame of solicitation, and the anxiety of suspense.

allow, that there may be, and have been, instances of pensions given and received upon liberal and honourable terms. Thus, then, it is clear, that there was nothing inconsistent or humiliating in Johnson's accepting of a pension so unconditionally and so honourably offered to him.

This year his friend Sir Joshua Reynolds paid a visit of some weeks to his native county, Devonshire, in which he was accompanied by Johnson, who was much pleased with this jaunt, and declared he had derived from it a great accession of new ideas. He was entertained at the seats of several noblemen and gentlemen in the west of England;[a] but the greatest part of the time was passed at Plymouth, where the magnificence of the navy, the shipbuilding and all its circumstances, afforded him a grand subject of contemplation. The Commissioner of the Dock-yard paid him the compliment of ordering the yacht to convey him and his friend to the Eddystone, to which they accordingly sailed. But the weather was so tempestuous that they could not land.

Reynolds and he were at this time the guests of Dr Mudge, the celebrated surgeon, and now physician of that place, not more distinguished for quickness of parts and variety of knowledge, than loved and esteemed for his amiable manners; and here Johnson formed an acquaintance with Dr Mudge's father, that very eminent divine, the Reverend Zachary Mudge, Prebendary of Exeter, who was idolised in the west, both for his excellence as a preacher and the uniform perfect propriety of his private conduct. He preached a sermon purposely that Johnson might hear him, and we shall see afterwards that Johnson honoured his memory by drawing his character. While Johnson was at Plymouth, he saw a great many of its inhabitants, and was not sparing of his very entertaining conversation. It was here that he made that frank and truly original confession, that 'ignorance, pure ignorance', was the cause of wrong definition in his Dictionary of the word *pastern*,[1] to the no small surprise of the Lady who put the question to him; who having the most profound reverence for his character, so as almost to suppose him endowed with infallibility, expected to

---

What has been thus elegantly given, will, I hope, not be reproachfully enjoyed; I shall endeavour to give your Lordship the only recompense which generosity desires – the gratification of finding that your benefits are not improperly bestowed. I am, my Lord,

Your Lordship's most obliged,

Most obedient, and most humble servant,

SAM. JOHNSON.

July 20, 1762.

[a] Add the following note: At one of these seats Dr Annyat, Physician in London, told me he happened to meet him. In order to amuse him till dinner should be ready he was taken out to walk in the garden. The master of the house thinking it proper to introduce something scientific into the conversation, addressed him thus: 'Are you a botanist, Dr Johnson?' 'No, Sir,' answered Johnson, 'I am not a botanist; and,' alluding no doubt to his near-sightedness, 'should I wish to become a botanist, I must first turn myself into a reptile.'

1 See p. 152.

hear an explanation (of what, to be sure, seemed strange to a common reader), drawn from some deep-learned source with which she was unacquainted.

Sir Joshua Reynolds, to whom I am obliged for my information concerning this excursion, mentions a very characteristical anecdote of Johnson while at Plymouth. Having observed that in consequence of the Dock-yard a new town had arisen about two miles off as a rival to the old; and knowing from his sagacity, and just observation of human nature, that it is certain if a man hates at all, he will hate his next neighbour; he concluded that this new and rising town could not but excite the envy and jealousy of the old, in which conjecture he was very soon confirmed; he therefore set himself resolutely on the side of the old town, the established town, in which his lot was cast, considering it as a kind of duty to *stand by* it. He accordingly entered warmly into its interests, and upon every occasion talked of the *dockers*, as the inhabitants of the new town were called, as upstarts and aliens. Plymouth is very plentifully supplied with water by a river brought into it from a great distance, which is so abundant that it runs to waste in the town. The Dock, or New-town, being totally destitute of water, petitioned Plymouth that a small portion of the conduit might be permitted to go to them, and this was now under consideration. Johnson, affecting to entertain the passions of the place, was violent in opposition, and half-laughing at himself for his pretended zeal, where he had no concern, exclaimed, 'No, no! I am against the *dockers*; I am a Plymouth-man. Rogues! let them die of thirst. They shall not have a drop!'[a]

---

* Add: Lord Macartney obligingly favoured me with a copy of the following letter, in his own hand-writing, from the original, which was found, by the present Earl of Bute, among his father's papers.

To the Right Honourable the Earl of Bute.

MY LORD — That generosity by which I was recommended to the favour of his Majesty, will not be offended at a solicitation necessary to make that favour permanent and effectual.

The pension appointed to be paid me at Michaelmas I have not received, and know not where or from whom I am to ask it. I beg, therefore, that your lordship will be pleased to supply Mr Wedderburne with such directions as may be necessary, which, I believe, his friendship will make him think it no trouble to convey to me.

To interrupt your Lordship, at a time like this, with such petty difficulties, is improper and unseasonable; but your knowledge of the world has long since taught you, that every man's affairs, however little, are important to himself. Every man hopes that he shall escape neglect; and, with reason, may every man, whose vices do not preclude his claim, expect favour from that beneficence which has been extended to, My Lord,

Your Lordship's
Most obliged,
And
Most humble servant,

SAM. JOHNSON.

Temple Lane, Nov. 3, 1762.

In 1763 he furnished to *The Poetical Calendar*, published by Fawkes and Woty, a character of Collins,* which he afterwards ingrafted into his entire life of that admirable poet, in the collection of lives which he wrote for the body of English poetry, formed and published by the booksellers of London. His account of the melancholy depression with which Collins was severely afflicted, and which brought him to his grave, is, I think, one of the most tender and interesting passages in the whole series of his writings. He also favoured Mr Hoole with the Dedication of his translation of Tasso to the Queen,* which is so happily conceived and elegantly expressed, that I cannot but point it out to the peculiar notice of my readers.

This is to me a memorable year, for in it I had the happiness to obtain the acquaintance of that extraordinary man whose memoirs I am now writing; an acquaintance which I shall ever esteem as one of the most fortunate circumstances in my life. Though then but two-and-twenty, I had for several years read his works with delight and instruction, and had the highest reverence for their author, which had grown up in my fancy into a kind of mysterious veneration, by figuring to myself a state of solemn elevated abstraction, in which I supposed him to live in the immense metropolis of London. Mr Gentleman, a native of Ireland, who passed some years in Scotland as a player, and as an instructor in the English language, a man whose talents and worth were depressed by misfortunes, had given me a representation of his[a] figure and manner;[b] and during my first visit to London, which was for three months in 1760, Mr Derrick the poet, who was Gentleman's friend and countryman, flattered me with hopes that he would introduce me to Johnson, an honour of which I was very ambitious. But he never found an opportunity, which made me doubt that he had promised to do what was not in his power, till Johnson some years afterwards told me, 'Derrick, Sir, might very well have introduced you. I had a kindness for Derrick, and am sorry he is dead.'

In the summer of 1761 Mr Thomas Sheridan was at Edinburgh, and delivered lectures upon the English Language and Public Speaking to large and respectable audiences. I was often in his company, and heard him frequently expatiate upon Johnson's extraordinary knowledge, talents, and virtues, repeat his pointed sayings, describe his particularities, and boast of his being his guest sometimes till two or three in the morning. At his house I hoped to have many opportunities of seeing the sage, as Mr Sheridan obligingly assured me I should not be disappointed.

When I returned to London in the end of 1762, to my surprise and regret I found an irreconcilable difference had taken place between Johnson and

---

[a] For 'his', read 'the'.

[b] After 'manner' read 'of DICTIONARY JOHNSON, as he was then called'; and on *called* put the following note: As great men of antiquity such as Scipio *Africanus* had an epithet added to their names, in consequence of some celebrated action, so my illustrious friend was often called DICTIONARY JOHNSON, from that wonderful achievement of genius and labour, his *Dictionary of the English Language*; the merit of which I contemplate with more and more admiration.

Sheridan. A pension of two hundred pounds a year had been given to Sheridan. Johnson, who as has been already mentioned, thought slightingly of Sheridan's art, upon hearing that he was also pensioned, exclaimed, 'What! have they given *him* a pension? Then it is time for me to give up mine.' Whether this proceeded from a momentary indignation, as if it were an affront to his exalted merit that a player should be rewarded in the same manner with him, or was the sudden effect of a fit of peevishness, it was unluckily said, and, indeed, cannot be justified. Mr Sheridan's pension was granted to him not as a player, but as a sufferer in the cause of government, when he was manager of the Theatre Royal in Ireland, when parties ran high in 1753. And it must also be allowed that he was a man of literature, and had considerably improved the arts of reading and speaking with distinctness and propriety.

Besides, Johnson should have recollected that Mr Sheridan taught pronunciation to Mr Alexander Wedderburn, whose sister was married to Sir Harry Erskine, an intimate friend of Lord Bute, who was the favourite of the King; and surely the most outrageous Whig will not maintain, that, whatever ought to be the principle in the disposal of *offices*, a *pension* ought never to be granted from any bias of court connection. Mr Macklin, indeed, shared with Mr Sheridan the honour of instructing Mr Wedderburn; and though it was too late in life for a Caledonian to acquire the genuine English cadence, yet so successful were Mr Wedderburn's instructors, and his own unabating endeavours, that he got rid of the coarse part of his Scotch accent, retaining only as much of the 'native wood-note wild', as to mark his country; which, if any Scotchman should affect to forget, I should heartily despise him. Notwithstanding the difficulties which are to be encountered by those who have not had the advantage of an English education, he by degrees formed a mode of speaking, to which Englishmen do not deny the praise of elegance. Hence his distinguished oratory, which he exerted in his own country as an advocate in the Court of Session, and a ruling elder of the *Kirk*, has had its fame and ample reward, in much higher spheres. When I look back on this noble person at Edinburgh, in situations so unworthy of his brilliant powers, and behold LORD LOUGHBOROUGH at London, the change seems almost like one of the metamorphoses in Ovid; and as his two preceptors, by refining his utterance, gave currency to his talents, we may say in the words of that poet, '*Nam vos mutastis.*'

I have dwelt the longer upon this remarkable instance of successful parts and assiduity, because it affords animating encouragement to other gentlemen of North-Britain to try their fortunes in the southern part of the island, where they may hope to gratify their utmost ambition; and now that we are one people by the Union, it would surely be illiberal to maintain that they have not an equal title with the natives of any other part of his Majesty's dominions.

Johnson complained that a man who disliked him repeated his sarcasm to Mr Sheridan, without telling him what followed, which was, that after a pause he added, 'However, I am glad that Mr Sheridan has a pension, for he is a very good man.' Sheridan could never forgive this hasty contemptuous expression. It rankled in his mind; and though I informed him of all that Johnson said, and that he would be very glad to meet him amicably, he positively declined repeated offers which I made, and once went off abruptly from a house where he and I were engaged to dine, because he was told that Dr Johnson was to be there. I have no sympathetic feeling with such persevering resentment. It is painful when there is a breach between those who have lived together socially and cordially; and I wonder that there is not, in all such cases, a mutual wish that it should be healed. I could perceive that Mr Sheridan was by no means satisfied with Johnson's acknowledging him to be a good man. That could not soothe his injured vanity. I could not but smile, at the same time that I was offended, to observe Sheridan in the *Life of Swift*,[1] which he afterwards published, attempting, in the writings of his resentment, to depreciate Johnson, by characterising him 'A writer of gigantic fame in these days of little men'; that very Johnson whom he once so highly admired and venerated.

This rupture with Sheridan deprived Johnson of one of his most agreeable resources for amusement in his lonely evenings; for Sheridan's well-informed, animated, and bustling mind never suffered conversation to stagnate; and Mrs Sheridan was a most agreeable companion to an intellectual man. She was sensible, ingenious, unassuming, yet communicative. I recollect, with satisfaction, many pleasing hours which I passed with her under the hospitable roof of her husband, who was to me a very kind friend. Her novel, entitled *Memoirs of Miss Sydney Biddulph*, contains an excellent moral, while it inculcates a future state of retribution;[a] and what it teaches is impressed upon the mind by a series

---

1 p. 447.

[a] Add the following note: My position has been very well illustrated by Mr Belsham of Bedford, in his Essay on Dramatic Poetry. 'The fashionable doctrine (says he) both of moralists and critics in these times is, that virtue and happiness are constant concomitants; and it is regarded as a kind of dramatic impiety to maintain that virtue should not be rewarded, nor vice punished in the last scene of the last act of every tragedy. This conduct in our modern poets is, however, in my opinion, extremely injudicious; for it labours in vain to inculcate a doctrine in theory, which every one knows to be false in fact, *viz*. that virtue in real life is always productive of happiness; and vice of misery. Thus Congreve concludes the Tragedy of *The Mourning Bride* with the following foolish couplet:

> For blessings ever wait on virtuous deeds
> And, though a late, a sure reward succeeds.

'When a man eminently virtuous, a Brutus, a Cato, or a Socrates, finally sinks under the pressure of accumulated misfortune, we are not only led to entertain a more indignant hatred of vice, than if he rose from his distress, but we are inevitably induced to cherish the sublime idea that a day of future retribution will arise when he shall receive not merely poetical, but real and substantial justice.' *Essays Philosophical, Historical, and Literary*, London, 1791, Vol. II. 8vo. p. 317.

This is well reasoned and well expressed. I wish, indeed, that the ingenious author had not thought it necessary to introduce any *instance* of 'a man eminently virtuous'; as he would then have avoided mentioning such a ruffian as Brutus under that description. Mr Belsham discovers in his *Essays* so much reading and thinking, and good composition, that I regret his not having been fortunate enough to be educated a member of our excellent national establishment. Had he not been nursed in nonconformity, he probably would not have been tainted with those heresies (as I

of as deep distress as can affect humanity.[a] Johnson paid her this high compliment upon it: 'I know not, Madam, that you have a right, upon moral principles, to make your readers suffer so much.'

Mr Thomas Davies the actor, who then kept a bookseller's shop in Russel-street,[b] Covent Garden, told me that Johnson was very much his friend, and came frequently to his house, where he more than once invited me to meet him; but by some unlucky accident or other he was prevented from coming to us.

Mr Thomas Davies was a man of good understanding and talents, with the advantage of a liberal education. Though somewhat pompous, he was an entertaining companion; and his literary performances have no inconsiderable share of merit. He was a friendly and very hospitable man. Both he and his wife (who had been celebrated for her beauty), though upon the stage for many years, maintained an uniform decency of character; and Johnson esteemed them, and lived in as easy an intimacy with them as with any family which he used to visit. Mr Davies recollected several of Johnson's remarkable sayings, and was one of the best of the many imitators of his voice and manner, while relating them. He increased my impatience more and more to see the extraordinary man whose works I highly valued, and whose conversation was reported to be so peculiarly excellent.

At last, on Monday the 16th of May, when I was sitting in Mr Davies's back parlour, after having drunk tea with him and Mrs Davies, Johnson unexpectedly came into the shop;[c] and Mr Davies having perceived him through the glass door of the room in which we were sitting, advancing towards us, – he announced his awful approach to me, somewhat in the manner of an actor in the part of Horatio, when he addresses Hamlet on the appearance of his

---

sincerely, and on no slight investigation, think them) both in religion and politics, which, while I read, I am sure, with candour, I cannot read without offence.

[a] After 'humanity', read, 'in the amiable and pious heroine, who goes to her grave unrelieved but resigned, and full of hope of "heaven's mercy".'

[b] No. 8, the very place where I was fortunate enough to be introduced to the illustrious subject of this work, deserves to be particularly marked. I never pass by it without feeling reverence and regret.' [This note is not found in Boswell's two editions, nor in his *Cor. et Ad.* It may, however, have been one of the MS. notes for the new edition in which Boswell was engaged when he died.]

[c] Add the following note: Mr Murphy in his 'Essay on the Life and Genius of Dr Johnson', has given an account of this meeting considerably different from mine, I am persuaded without any consciousness of error. His memory, at the end of near thirty years, has undoubtedly deceived him, and he supposes himself to have been present at a scene, which he has probably heard inaccurately described by others. In my note *taken on the very day*, in which I am confident I marked every thing material that passed, no mention is made of this gentleman; and I am sure, that I should not have omitted one so well known in the literary world. It may easily be imagined that this my first interview with Dr Johnson, with all its circumstances, made a strong impression on my mind, and would be registered with peculiar attention.

father's ghost, 'Look, my Lord, it comes.' I found that I had a very perfect idea of Johnson's figure, from the portrait of him painted by Sir Joshua Reynolds soon after he had published his Dictionary, in the attitude of sitting in his easy chair in deep meditation, which was the first picture his friend did for him, which Sir Joshua has very kindly presented to me, and from which an engraving has been made for this work. Mr Davies mentioned my name, and respectfully introduced me to him. I was much agitated; and recollecting his prejudice against the Scotch, of which I had heard much, I said to Davies, 'Don't tell where I come from.' – 'From Scotland,' cried Davies, roguishly. 'Mr Johnson (said I), I do indeed come from Scotland, but I cannot help it.' I am willing to flatter myself that I meant this as light pleasantry to soothe and conciliate him, and not as any humiliating abasement at the expense of my country. But however that might be, this speech was somewhat unlucky; for with that quickness of wit for which he was so remarkable, he seized the expression 'come from Scotland', which I used in the sense of being of that country; and as if I had said that I had come away from it or left it, retorted, 'That, Sir, I find, is what a very great many of your countrymen cannot help.' This stroke stunned me a good deal; and when we had sat down, I felt myself not a little embarrassed, and apprehensive of what might come next. He then addressed himself to Davies: 'What do you think of Garrick? He has refused me an order for the play for Miss Williams, because he knows the house will be full, and that an order would be worth three shillings.' Eager to take any opening to get into conversation with him, I ventured to say, 'O, Sir, I cannot think Mr Garrick would grudge such a trifle to you.' 'Sir (said he, with a stern look), I have known David Garrick longer than you have done; and I know no right you have to talk to me on the subject.' Perhaps I deserved this check; for it was rather presumptuous in me, an entire stranger, to express any doubt of the justice of his animadversion upon his old acquaintance and pupil.[1] I now felt myself much mortified, and began to think that the hope which I had long indulged of obtaining his acquaintance was blasted. And, in truth, had not my ardour been uncommonly strong, and my resolution uncommonly persevering, so rough a reception might have deterred me for ever from making any further attempts. Fortunately, however, I remained upon the field not wholly discomfited; and was soon rewarded by hearing some of his conversation, of which I preserved the following short minute, without marking the questions and observations by which it was produced.

'People (he remarked) may be taken in once, who imagine that an author is greater in private life than other men. Uncommon parts require uncommon opportunities for their exertion.

---

[1] That this was a momentary sally against Garrick there can be no doubt; for at Johnson's desire he had, some years before, given a benefit-night at his theatre to this very person, by which she got two hundred pounds. Johnson, indeed, upon all other occasions, when I was in his company, praised the very liberal charity of Garrick. I once mentioned to him, 'It is observed, Sir, that you attack Garrick yourself, but will suffer nobody else to do it.' JOHNSON (smiling), 'Why, Sir, that is true.'

'In barbarous society, superiority of parts is of real consequence. Great strength or great wisdom is of much value to an individual. But in more polished times there are people to do every thing for money; and then there are a number of other superiorities, such as those of birth and fortune, and rank, that dissipate men's attention, and leave no extraordinary share of respect for personal and intellectual superiority. This is wisely ordered by Providence, to preserve some equality among mankind.'

'Sir, this book (*The Elements of Criticism*, which he had taken up), is a pretty essay, and deserves to be held in some estimation, though much of it is chimerical.'

Speaking of one who with more than ordinary boldness attacked public measures and the royal family, he said, 'I think he is safe from the law, but he is an abusive scoundrel; and instead of applying to my Lord Chief Justice to punish him, I would send half a dozen footmen and have him well ducked.'

'The notion of liberty amuses the people of England, and helps to keep off the *taedium vitae*. When a butcher tells you that his heart bleeds for his country, he has, in fact, no uneasy feeling.'

'Sheridan will not succeed at Bath with his oratory. Ridicule has gone down before him, and, I doubt, Derrick is his enemy.[1]

'Derrick may do very well, as long as he can outrun his character; but the moment his character gets up with him it is all over.'

It is, however, but just to record, that some years afterwards, when I reminded him of this sarcasm, he said, 'Well, but Derrick has now got a character that he need not run away from.'

I was highly pleased with the extraordinary vigour of his conversation, and regretted that I was drawn away from it by an engagement at another place. I had, for a part of the evening, been left alone with him, and had ventured to make an observation now and then, which he received very civilly; so that I was satisfied that though there was a roughness in his manner, there was no ill-nature in his disposition. Davies followed me to the door, and when I complained to him a little of the hard blows which the great man had given me, he kindly took upon him to console me by saying, 'Don't be uneasy. I can see he likes you very well.'

A few days afterwards I called on Davies, and asked him if he thought I might take the liberty of waiting on Mr Johnson at his Chambers in the Temple. He said I certainly might, and that Mr Johnson would take it as a compliment. So upon Tuesday the 24th, after having been enlivened by the witty sallies of Messieurs Thornton, Wilkes, Churchill and Lloyd, with whom I had passed the morning, I boldly repaired to Johnson. His Chambers were on the first floor of No. 1, Inner Temple-lane, and I entered them with an impression given me by the Reverend Dr Blair, of Edinburgh, who had been introduced to him not long before, and described his having 'found the giant in his den'; an expression, which, when I came to be pretty well acquainted

---

1 Mr Sheridan was then reading lectures upon Oratory at Bath, where Derrick was Master of the Ceremonies, or, as the phrase is, KING.

with Johnson, I repeated to him, and he was diverted at this picturesque account of himself. Dr Blair had been presented to him by Dr James Fordyce. At this time the controversy concerning the pieces published by Mr James Macpherson, as translations of Ossian, was at its height. Johnson had all along denied their authenticity and, what was still more provoking to their admirers, maintained that they had no merit. The subject having been introduced by Dr Fordyce, Dr Blair, relying on the internal evidence of their antiquity, asked Dr Johnson whether he thought any man of a modern age could have written such poems? Johnson replied, 'Yes, Sir, many men, many women, and many children.' Johnson, at this time, did not know that Dr Blair had just published a Dissertation, not only defending their authenticity, but seriously ranking them with the poems of Homer and Virgil; and when he was afterwards informed of this circumstance, he expressed some displeasure at Dr Fordyce's having suggested the topic, and said, 'I am not sorry that they got thus much for their pains. Sir, it was like leading one to talk of a book, when the author is concealed behind the door.'

He received me very courteously; but, it must be confessed, that his apartment, and furniture, and morning dress, were sufficiently uncouth. His brown suit of clothes looked very rusty; he had on a little old shrivelled unpowdered wig, which was too small for his head; his shirt-neck and knees of his breeches were loose, his black worsted stockings ill drawn up; and he had a pair of unbuckled shoes by way of slippers. But all these slovenly particularities were forgotten the moment that he began to talk. Some gentlemen, whom I do not recollect, were sitting with him; and when they went away, I also rose; but he said to me, 'Nay, don't go.' – 'Sir (said I), I am afraid that I intrude upon you. It is benevolent to allow me to sit and hear you.' He seemed pleased with this compliment, which I sincerely paid him, and answered, 'Sir, I am obliged to any man who visits me.' I have preserved the following short minute of what passed this day.

'Madness frequently discovers itself merely by unnecessary deviation from the usual modes of the world. My poor friend Smart showed the disturbance of his mind by falling upon his knees and saying his prayers in the street, or in any other unusual place. Now although, rationally speaking, it is greater madness not to pray at all, than to pray as Smart did, I am afraid there are so many who do not pray, that their understanding is not called in question.'

Concerning this unfortunate poet, Christopher Smart, who was confined in a madhouse, he had, at another time, the following conversation with Dr Burney. JOHNSON. 'It seems as if his mind had ceased to struggle with the disease; for he grows fat upon it.' BURNEY. 'Perhaps, Sir, that may be from want of exercise.' JOHNSON. 'No, Sir; he has partly as much exercise as he used to have, for he digs in the garden. Indeed, before his confinement, he used for exercise to walk to the alehouse; but he was *carried* back again. I did not think he ought to be shut up. His infirmities were not noxious to society. He insisted on people praying with him, and I'd as lief pray with Kit. Smart as any one else. Another charge was, that he did not love clean linen; and I have no passion for it.'

'Mankind have a great aversion to intellectual labour; but even supposing knowledge to be easily attainable, more people would be content to be ignorant than would take even a little trouble to acquire it.'

'The morality of an action depends on the motive from which we act. If I fling half a crown to a beggar with intention to break his head, and he picks it up and buys victuals with it, the physical effect is good; but, with respect to me, the action is very wrong. So, religious exercises, if not performed with an intention to please GOD, avail us nothing. As our Saviour says of those who perform them from other motives, "Verily they have their reward."'

'The Christian Religion has very strong evidences. It, indeed, appears in some degree strange to reason; but in History we have undoubted facts, against which, in reasoning *a priori*, we have more arguments than we have for them; but then, testimony has great weight, and casts the balance. I would recommend to every man whose faith is yet unsettled, Grotius – Dr Pearson – and Dr Clark.'

Talking of Garrick, he said, 'He is the first man in the world for sprightly conversation.'

When I rose a second time he again pressed me to stay, which I did.

He told me, that he generally went abroad at four in the afternoon, and seldom came home till two in the morning. I took the liberty to ask if he did not think it wrong to live thus, and not make more use of his great talents. He owned it was a bad habit. On reviewing, at the distance of many years, my journal of this period, I wonder how, at my first visit, I ventured to talk to him so freely, and that he bore it with so much indulgence.

Before we parted he was so good as to promise to favour me with his company one evening at my lodgings; and, as I took my leave, shook me cordially by the hand. It is almost needless to add, that I felt no little elation at having now so happily established an acquaintance of which I had been so long ambitious.

My readers will, I trust, excuse me for being thus minutely circumstantial, when it is considered that the acquaintance of Dr Johnson was to me a most valuable acquisition, and laid the foundation of whatever instruction and entertainment they may receive from my recollections concerning the great subject of the work which they are now perusing.

I did not visit him again till Monday, June 13, at which time I recollect no part of his conversation, except that when I told him I had been to see Johnson ride upon three horses, he said, 'Such a man, Sir, should be encouraged; for his performances show the extent of the human powers in one instance, and thus tend to raise our opinion of the faculties of man. He shows what may be attained by persevering application; so that every man may hope, that by giving as much application, although perhaps he may never ride three horses at a time or dance upon a wire, yet he may be equally expert in whatever profession he has chosen to pursue.'

He again shook me by the hand at parting, and asked me why I did not come oftener to him. Trusting that I was now in his good graces, I answered, that he had not given me much encouragement, and reminded him of the check I had received from him at our first interview. 'Poh, poh! (said he, with a complacent smile), never mind these things. Come to me as often as you can. I shall be glad to see you.'

I had learnt that his place of frequent resort was the Mitre tavern in Fleet-street, where he loved to sit up late, and I begged I might be allowed to pass an evening with him there soon, which he promised I should. A few days afterwards I met him near Temple-bar, about one o'clock in the morning, and asked if he would then go to the Mitre. 'Sir (said he), it is too late; they won't let us in. But I'll go with you another night with all my heart.'

A revolution of some importance in my plan of life had just taken place; for instead of procuring a commission in the foot-guards, which was my own inclination, I had, in compliance with my father's wishes, agreed to study the law, and was soon to set out for Utrecht, to hear the lectures of an excellent Civilian in that University, and then to proceed on my travels. Though very desirous of obtaining Dr Johnson's advice and instructions on the mode of pursuing my studies, I was at this time so occupied, shall I call it? or so dissipated, by the amusements of London, that our next meeting was not till Saturday, June 25, when happening to dine at Clifton's eating-house, in Butcher-row, I was surprised to perceive Johnson come in and take his seat at another table. The mode of dining, or rather being fed, at such houses in London, is well known to many to be particularly unsocial, as there is no Ordinary, or united company, but each person has his own mess, and is under no obligation to hold any intercourse with any one. A liberal and full-minded man, however, who loves to talk, will break through this churlish and unsocial restraint. Johnson and an Irishman got into a dispute concerning the cause of some part of mankind being black. 'Why, Sir (said Johnson), it has been accounted for in three ways: either by supposing that they are the posterity of Ham, who was cursed; or that GOD at first created two kinds of men, one black and another white; or that by the heat of the sun the skin is scorched, and so acquires a sooty hue. This matter has been much canvassed among naturalists, but has never been brought to any certain issue.' What the Irishman said is totally obliterated from my mind; but I remember that he became very warm and intemperate in his expressions; upon which Johnson rose, and quietly walked away. When he had retired, his antagonist took his revenge, as he thought, by saying, 'He has a most ungainly figure, and an affectation of pomposity unworthy of a man of genius.'

Johnson had not observed that I was in the room. I followed him, however, and he agreed to meet me in the evening at the Mitre. I called on him, and we went thither at nine. We had a good supper, and port wine, of which he then sometimes drank a bottle. The orthodox high-church sound of the Mitre, the figure and manner of the celebrated Samuel Johnson, the extraordinary power and precision of his conversation, and the pride arising from finding myself admitted as his companion, produced a variety of sensations, and a pleasing elevation of mind beyond what I had ever before experienced. I find in my journal the following minute of our conversation, which, though it will give but a very faint notion of what passed, is, in some degree, a valuable record;

and it will be curious in this view, as showing how habitual to his mind were some opinions which appear in his works.

'Colley Cibber, Sir, was by no means a blockhead; but by arrogating to himself too much, he was in danger of losing that degree of estimation to which he was entitled. His friends gave out that he *intended* his birthday Odes should be bad: but that was not the case, Sir; for he kept them many months by him, and a few years before he died he showed me one of them, with great solicitude to render it as perfect as might be, and I made some corrections, to which he was not very willing to submit. I remember the following couplet in allusion to the King and himself:

> Perch'd on the eagle's soaring wing
> The lowly linnet loves to sing.

Sir, he had heard something of the fabulous tale of the wren sitting upon the eagle's wing, and he had applied it to a linnet. Cibber's familiar style, however, was better than that which Whitehead has assumed. *Grand* nonsense is insupportable. Whitehead is but a little man to inscribe verses to players.'

I did not presume to controvert this censure, which was tinctured with his prejudice against players; but I could not help thinking that a dramatic poet might with propriety pay a compliment to an eminent performer, as Whitehead has very happily done in his verses to Mr Garrick.

'Sir, I do not think Gray a first-rate poet. He has not a bold imagination, nor much command of words. The obscurity in which he has involved himself will not persuade us that he is sublime. His Elegy in a church-yard has a happy selection of images, but I don't like what are called his great things. His Ode which begins

> Ruin seize thee, ruthless King,
> Confusion on thy banners wait,

has been celebrated for its abruptness, and plunging into the subject all at once. But such arts as these have no merit, unless when they are original. We admire them only once; and this abruptness has nothing new in it. We have had it often before. Nay, we have it in the old song of Johnny Armstrong:

> Is there ever a man in all Scotland
> From the highest estate to the lowest degree, &c.

And then, Sir,

> Yes, there is a man in Westmoreland,
> And Johnny Armstrong they do him call.

There, now, you plunge at once into the subject. You have no previous narration to lead you to it. — The two next lines in that Ode are, I think, very good:

Though fann'd by conquest's crimson wing,
They mock the air with idle state.'[1]

Here let it be observed, that although his opinion of Gray's poetry was widely different from mine, and I believe from that of most men of taste, by whom it is with justice highly admired, there is certainly much absurdity in the clamour which has been raised, as if he had been culpably injurious to the merit of that bard, and had been actuated by envy. Alas! ye little short-sighted critics, could Johnson be envious of the talents of any of his contemporaries? That his opinion on this subject was what in private and in public he uniformly expressed, regardless of what others might think, we may wonder, and perhaps regret; but it is shallow and unjust to charge him with expressing what he did not think.

Finding him in a placid humour, and wishing to avail myself of the opportunity which I fortunately had of consulting a sage, to hear whose wisdom, I conceived in the ardour of youthful imagination, that men filled with a noble enthusiasm for intellectual improvement would gladly have resorted from distant lands; I opened my mind to him ingenuously, and gave him a little sketch of my life, to which he was pleased to listen with great attention.

I acknowledged, that though educated very strictly in the principles of religion, I had for some time been misled into a certain degree of infidelity; but that I was come now to a better way of thinking, and was fully satisfied of the truth of the Christian revelation, though I was not clear as to every point considered to be orthodox. Being at all times a curious examiner of the human mind, and pleased with an undisguised display of what had passed in it, he called to me with warmth, 'Give me your hand; I have taken a liking to you.' He then began to descant upon the force of testimony, and the little we could know of final causes; so that the objections of, why was it so? or why was it not so? ought not to disturb us: adding, that he himself had at one period been guilty of a temporary neglect of religion, but that it was not the result of argument, but mere absence of thought.

After having given credit to reports of his bigotry, I was agreeably surprised when he expressed the following very liberal sentiment, which has the additional value of obviating an objection to our holy religion, founded upon the discordant tenets of Christians themselves: 'For my part, Sir, I think all Christians, whether Papists or Protestants, agree in the essential articles, and that their differences are trivial, and rather political than religious.'

We talked of belief in ghosts. He said, 'Sir, I make a distinction between what a man may experience by the mere strength of his imagination, and what imagination cannot possibly produce. Thus, suppose I should think that I saw a form, and heard a voice cry "Johnson, you are a very wicked fellow, and unless you repent you will certainly be punished"; my own unworthiness is so

1 My friend Mr Malone, in his valuable comments on Shakspeare, has traced in that great poet the *disjecta membra* of these lines.

deeply impressed upon my mind, that I might *imagine* I thus saw and heard, and therefore I should not believe that an external communication had been made to me. But if a form should appear, and a voice should tell me that a particular man had died at a particular place, and a particular hour, a fact which I had no apprehension of, nor any means of knowing, and this fact with all its circumstances should afterwards be unquestionably proved, I should, in that case, be persuaded that I had supernatural intelligence imparted to me.'

Here it is proper, once for all, to give a true and fair statement of Johnson's way of thinking upon the question whether departed spirits are ever permitted to appear in this world, or in any way to operate upon human life. He has been ignorantly misrepresented as weakly credulous upon that subject; and therefore, though I feel an inclination to disdain and treat with silent contempt so absurd a notion concerning my illustrious friend, yet as I find it has gained ground, it is necessary to refute it. The real fact then is, that Johnson had a very philosophical mind, and such a rational respect for testimony, as to make him submit his understanding to what was authentically proved, though he could not comprehend why it was so. Being thus disposed, he was willing to inquire into the truth of any relation of supernatural agency, a general belief of which has prevailed in all nations and ages. But so far was he from being the dupe of implicit faith, that he examined the matter with a jealous attention, and no man was more ready to refute its falsehood when he had discovered it. Churchill, in his poem entitled 'The Ghost', availed himself of the absurd credulity imputed to Johnson, and drew a caricature of him under the name of 'POMPOSO', representing him as one of the believers of the story of a Ghost in Cock-lane, which in the year 1762 had gained very general credit in London. Many of my readers, I am convinced, are to this hour under an impression that Johnson was thus foolishly deceived. It will therefore surprise them a good deal when they are informed upon undoubted authority, that Johnson was one of those by whom the imposture was detected. The story had become so popular, that he thought it should be investigated; and in this research he was assisted by the Reverend Dr Douglas, now Bishop of Carlisle, the great detector of impostures, who informs me, that after the gentlemen who went and examined into the evidence were satisfied of its falsity, Johnson wrote in their presence an account of it, which was published in the newspapers and *Gentleman's Magazine*, and undeceived the world.[1]

---

1 The account was as follows:

On the night of the 1st of February, many gentlemen, eminent for their rank and character, were by the invitation of the Reverend Mr Aldrich, of Clerkenwell, assembled at his house, for the examination of the noises supposed to be made by a departed spirit, for the detection of some enormous crime.

About ten at night the gentlemen met in the chamber in which the girl supposed to be disturbed by a spirit, had, with proper caution, been put to bed by several ladies. They sat rather more than an hour, and hearing nothing, went down stairs, when they interrogated the father of the girl, who denied, in the strongest terms, any knowledge or belief of fraud.

Our conversation proceeded. 'Sir (said he), I am a friend to subordination, as most conducive to the happiness of society. There is a reciprocal pleasure in governing and being governed.'

'Dr Goldsmith is one of the first men we now have as an author, and he is a very worthy man too. He has been loose in his principles, but he is coming right.'

I mentioned Mallet's tragedy of *Elvira*, which had been acted the preceding winter at Drury-lane, and that the Honourable Andrew Erskine, Mr Dempster, and myself, had joined in writing a pamphlet, entitled 'Critical Strictures' against it.[1] That the mildness of Dempster's disposition had, however, relented; and he had candidly said, 'We have hardly a right to abuse this tragedy; for, bad as it is, how vain should either of us be to write one not near so good.' JOHNSON. 'Why no, Sir; this is not just reasoning. You *may* abuse a tragedy, though you cannot write one. You may scold a carpenter who has made you a bad table, though you cannot make a table. It is not your trade to make tables.'

When I talked to him of the paternal estate to which I was heir, he said, 'Sir, let me tell you, that to be a Scotch landlord, where you have a number of families dependent upon you, and attached to you, is, perhaps, as high a

---

The supposed spirit had before publicly promised, by an affirmative knock, that it would attend one of the gentlemen into the vault under the church of St John Clerkenwell, where the body is deposited, and give a token of her presence there, by a knock upon her coffin; it was therefore determined to make this trial of the existence or veracity of the supposed spirit.

While they were enquiring and deliberating, they were summoned into the girl's chamber by some ladies who were near her bed, and who had heard knocks and scratches. When the gentlemen entered, the girl declared that she felt the spirit like a mouse upon her back, and was required to hold her hands out of bed. From that time, though the spirit was very solemnly required to manifest its existence by appearance, by impression on the hand or body of any present, by scratches, knocks or any other agency, no evidence of any preter-natural power was exhibited.

The spirit was then very seriously advertised that the person to whom the promise was made of striking the coffin, was then about to visit the vault, and that the performance of the promise was then claimed. The company at one o'clock went into the church, and the gentleman to whom the promise was made, went with another into the vault. The spirit was solemnly required to perform its promise, but nothing more than silence ensued: the person supposed to be accused by the spirit, then went down with several others, but no effect was perceived. Upon their return they examined the girl, but could draw no confession from her. Between two and three she desired and was permitted to go home with her father.

It is, therefore, the opinion of the whole assembly, that the child has some art of making or counterfeiting a particular noise, and that there is no agency of any higher cause.

1 The *Critical Review*, in which Mallet himself sometimes wrote, characterised this pamphlet as 'the crude efforts of envy, petulance and self-conceit'. There being thus three epithets, we the three authors had a humorous contention how each should be appropriated.

situation as humanity can arrive at. A merchant upon the 'Change of London, with a hundred thousand pounds, is nothing: an English duke, with an immense fortune, is nothing: he has no tenants who consider themselves as under his patriarchal care, and who will follow him to the field upon any emergency.'

His notion of the dignity of a Scotch landlord had been formed upon what he had heard of the Highland Chiefs; for it is long since a lowland landlord has been so curtailed in his feudal authority, that he has little more influence over his tenants than an English landlord; and of late years most of the Highland Chiefs have destroyed, by means too well known, the princely power which they once enjoyed.

He proceeded: 'Your going abroad, Sir, and breaking off idle habits, may be of great importance to you. I would go where there are courts and learned men. There is a good deal of Spain that has not been perambulated. I would have you go thither. A man of inferior talents to yours may furnish us with useful observations upon that country.' His supposing me, at that period of life, capable of writing an account of my travels that would deserve to be read, elated me not a little.

I appeal to every impartial reader whether this faithful detail of his frankness, complacency, and kindness to a young man, a stranger and a Scotchman, does not refute the unjust opinion of the harshness of his general demeanour. His occasional reproofs of folly, impudence, or impiety, and even the sudden sallies of his constitutional irritability of temper, which have been preserved for the poignancy of their wit, have produced that opinion among those who have not considered that such instances, though collected by Mrs Piozzi into a small volume, and read over in a few hours, were, in fact, scattered through a long series of years; years, in which his time was chiefly spent in instructing and delighting mankind by his writings and conversation, in acts of piety to GOD, and good-will to men.

I complained to him that I had not yet acquired much knowledge, and asked his advice as to my studies. He said, 'Don't talk of study now. I will give you a plan; but it will require some time to consider of it.' 'It is very good in you, Mr Johnson[1] (I replied), to allow me to be with you thus. Had it been foretold to me some years ago that I should pass an evening with the author of the *Rambler*, how should I have exulted!' What I then expressed was sincerely from my heart. He was satisfied that it was, and cordially answered, 'Sir, I am glad we have met. I hope we shall pass many evenings and mornings too, together.' We finished a couple of bottles of port, and sat till between one and two in the morning.

He wrote this year in the *Critical Review* the account of 'Telemachus, a Mask', by the Reverend George Graham, of Eton College. The subject of this beautiful poem was particularly interesting to Johnson, who had much experience of 'the conflict of opposite principles', which he describes as, 'The contention between

---

1 *Second Edition* – 'Mr Johnson' omitted.

pleasure and virtue, a struggle which will always be continued while the present system of nature shall subsist: nor can history or poetry exhibit more than pleasure triumphing over virtue, and virtue subjugating pleasure.'

As Dr Oliver Goldsmith will frequently appear in this narrative, I shall endeavour to make my readers in some degree acquainted with his singular character. He was a native of Ireland, and a contemporary with Mr Burke, at Trinity College, Dublin, but did not then give much promise of future celebrity. He, however, observed to Mr Malone, that 'though he made no great figure in mathematics, which was a study in much repute there, he could turn an Ode of Horace better than any of them.' He afterwards studied physic at Edinburgh, and upon the Continent; and I have been informed, was enabled to pursue his travels on foot, partly by demanding at Universities to enter the lists as a disputant, by which, according to the custom of many of them, he was entitled to the premium of a crown, when luckily for him his challenge was not accepted; so that, as I once observed to Dr Johnson, he disputed his passage through Europe. He then came to England, and was employed successively in the capacities of an usher to an academy, a corrector of the press, a reviewer, and a writer for a newspaper. He had sagacity enough to cultivate assiduously the acquaintance of Johnson, and his faculties were gradually enlarged by the contemplation of such a model. To me and many others it appeared that he studiously copied the manner of Johnson, though, indeed, upon a smaller scale.

At this time I think he had published nothing with his name, though it was pretty generally known that *one Dr Goldsmith* was the author of 'An Essay on the present State of polite Literature', and of *The Citizen of the World*, a series of letters supposed to be written from London by a Chinese. No man had the art of displaying with more advantage as a writer, whatever literary acquisitions he made. '*Nihil quod tetigit non ornavit.*'[1] His mind resembled a fertile, but thin soil. There was a quick, but not a strong vegetation, of whatever chanced to be thrown upon it. No deep root could be struck. The oak of the forest did not grow there; but the elegant shrubbery and the fragrant parterre appeared in gay succession. It has been generally circulated and believed that he was a mere fool in conversation;[2] but, in truth, this has been greatly exaggerated. He

1 See his Epitaph in Westminster Abbey, written by Dr Johnson.
2 In allusion to this, Mr Horace Walpole, who admired his writings, said he was 'an inspired ideot'; and Garrick described him as one

> for shortness call'd Noll,
> Who wrote like an angel, and talk'd like poor Poll.

Sir Joshua Reynolds has mentioned to me that he frequently heard Goldsmith talk warmly of the pleasure of being liked, and observe how hard it would be if literary excellence should preclude a man from that satisfaction, which he perceived it often did, from the envy which attended it; and therefore Sir Joshua was convinced that he was intentionally more absurd, in order to lessen himself in social intercourse, trusting that his character would be sufficiently supported by his works. If it indeed was his intention to appear absurd in company, he was often very successful. But with due deference to Sir Joshua's ingenuity, I think the conjecture too refined.

had, no doubt, a more than common share of that hurry of ideas which we often find in his countrymen, and which sometimes produces a laughable confusion in expressing them. He was very much what the French call *un etourdi*, and from vanity and an eager desire of being conspicuous wherever he was, he frequently talked carelessly without knowledge of the subject, or even without thought. His person was short, his countenance coarse and vulgar, his deportment that of a scholar awkwardly affecting the easy gentleman. Those who were in any way distinguished, excited envy in him to so ridiculous an excess, that the instances of it are hardly credible. When accompanying two beautiful young ladies[a] with their mother on a tour in France, he was seriously angry that more attention was paid to them than to him; and once at the exhibition of the *Fantoccini*, in London, when those who sat next him observed with what dexterity a puppet was made to toss a pike, he could not bear that it should have such praise, and exclaimed with some warmth, 'Pshaw! I can do it better myself.'[b]

He, I am afraid, had no settled system of any sort, so that his conduct must not be strictly scrutinised; but his affections were social and generous, and when he had money he gave it away very liberally. His desire of imaginary consequence predominated over his attention to truth. When he began to rise into notice, he said he had a brother who was Dean of Durham,[c] a fiction so easily detected, that it is wonderful how he should have been so inconsiderate as to hazard it. He boasted to me at this time of the power of his pen in commanding money, which I believe was true in a certain degree, though in the instance he gave he was by no means correct. He told me that he had sold a novel for four hundred pounds. This was his *Vicar of Wakefield*. But Johnson informed me, that he had made the bargain for Goldsmith, and the price was sixty pounds. 'And, Sir (said he), a sufficient price too, when it was sold; for then the fame of Goldsmith had not been elevated, as it afterwards was, by his *Traveller*; and the bookseller had such faint hopes of profit by his bargain, that he kept the manuscript by him a long time, and did not publish it till after the *Traveller* had appealed. Then, to be sure, it was accidentally worth more money.'

Mrs Piozzi[1] and Sir John Hawkins[2] have strangely mis-stated the history of Goldsmith's situation and Johnson's friendly interference, when this novel was sold. I shall give it authentically from Johnson's own exact narration:

[a] Add the following note: Miss Hornecks, one of whom is now married to Henry Bunbury, Esq., and the other to Colonel Gwyn.

[b] Add the following note: He went home with Mr Burke to supper; and broke his shin by attempting to exhibit to the company how much better he could jump over a stick than the puppets.

[c] Add the following note: I am willing to hope that there may have been some mistake as to this anecdote, though I had it from a Dignitary of the church. Dr Isaac Goldsmith, his near relation, was Dean of Cloyne, in 1747.

1　*Anecdotes of Johnson*, p. 119.
2　*Life of Johnson*, p. 420.

I received one morning a message from poor Goldsmith that he was in great distress, and, as it was not in his power to come to me, begging that I would come to him as soon as possible. I sent him a guinea, and promised to come to him directly. I accordingly went as soon as I was drest, and found that his landlady had arrested him for his rent, at which he was in a violent passion. I perceived that he had already changed my guinea, and had got a bottle of Madeira and a glass before him. I put the cork into the bottle, desired he would be calm, and began to talk to him of the means by which he might be extricated. He then told me that he had a novel ready for the press, which he produced to me. I looked into it, and saw its merits; told the landlady I should soon return, and having gone to a bookseller, sold it for sixty pounds. I brought Goldsmith the money, and he discharged his rent, not without rating his landlady in a high tone for having used him so ill.[1]

My next meeting with Johnson was on Friday the 1st of July, when he and I and Dr Goldsmith supped together at the Mitre. I was before this time pretty well acquainted with Goldsmith, who was one of the brightest ornaments of the Johnsonian school. Goldsmith's respectful attachment to Johnson was then at its height; for his own literary reputation had not yet distinguished him so much as to excite a vain desire of competition with his great master. He had increased my admiration of the goodness of Johnson's heart, by incidental remarks in the course of conversation, such as, when I mentioned Mr Levet, whom he entertained under his roof, 'He is poor and honest, which is recommendation enough to Johnson'; and when I wondered that he was very kind to a man of whom I had heard a very bad character, 'He is now become miserable, and that insures the protection of Johnson.'

Goldsmith attempted this evening to maintain, I suppose from an affectation of paradox, that knowledge was not desirable on its own account, for it often was a source of unhappiness. JOHNSON. 'Why, Sir, that knowledge may in some cases produce unhappiness, I allow. But, upon the whole, knowledge *per se* is certainly an object which every man would wish to attain, although, perhaps, he may not take the trouble necessary for attaining it.'

---

1 It may not be improper to annex here Mrs Piozzi's account of this transaction, in her own words, as a specimen of the extreme inaccuracy with which all her anecdotes of Dr Johnson are related, or rather discoloured and distorted. 'I have forgotten the year, but it could scarcely I think be later than 1765 or 1766, that he was *called abruptly from our house after dinner*, and returning *in about three hours*, said he had been with an enraged author, whose landlady pressed him for payment within doors, while the bailiffs beset him without; that he was *drinking himself drunk* with Madeira, to drown care, and fretting over a novel, which, when *finished*, was to be his *whole fortune*, but *he could not get it done for distraction*, nor could he step out of doors to offer it for sale. Mr Johnson, therefore, set away the bottle, and went to the bookseller, recommending the performance, and *desiring some immediate relief*; which when he brought back to the writer, *he called the woman of the house directly to partake of punch, and pass their time in merriment.*' Anecdotes of Johnson, p. 119.

Dr John Campbell, the celebrated political and biographical writer, being mentioned, Johnson said, 'Campbell is a man of much knowledge, and has a good share of imagination. His *Hermippus Redivivus* is very entertaining, as an account of the Hermetic philosophy, and as furnishing a curious history of the extravagances of the human mind. If it were merely imaginary it would be nothing at all. Campbell is not always rigidly careful of truth in his conversation; but I do not believe there is any thing of this carelessness in his books. Campbell is a good man, a pious man. I am afraid he has not been in the inside of a church for many years;[1] but he never passes a church without pulling off his hat. This shows that he has good principles. I used to go pretty often to Campbell's on a Sunday evening, till I began to consider that the shoals of Scotchmen who flocked about him might probably say, when any thing of mine was well done, "Ay, ay, he has learnt this of CAWMELL." '

He talked very contemptuously of Churchill's poetry, observing that 'it had a temporary currency, only from its audacity of abuse, and being filled with living names, and that it would sink into oblivion.' I ventured to hint that he was not quite a fair judge, as Churchill had attacked him violently. JOHNSON. 'Nay, sir! I am a very fair judge. He did not attack me violently till he found I did not like his poetry; and his attack on me shall not prevent me from continuing to say what I think of him, from an apprehension that it may be ascribed to resentment. No, Sir, I called the fellow a blockhead at first, and I will call him a blockhead still. However, I will acknowledge that I have a better opinion of him now, than I once had; for he has shown more fertility than I expected. To be sure, he is a tree that cannot produce good fruit: he only bears crabs. But, sir, a tree that produces a great many crabs is better than a tree which produces only a few.'

In this depreciation of Churchill's poetry I could not agree with him. It is very true that the greatest part of it is upon the topics of the day, on which account, as it brought him great fame and profit at the time, it must proportionally slide out of the public attention as other occasional objects succeed. But Churchill had extraordinary vigour both of thought and expression. His portraits of the players will ever be valuable to the true lovers of the drama; and his strong caricatures of several eminent men of his age, will not be

---

1 I am inclined to think that he was misinformed as to this circumstance. I own I am jealous for my worthy friend Dr John Campbell. For though Milton could without remorse absent himself from public worship I cannot. On the contrary, I have the same habitual impressions upon my mind, with those of a truly venerable Judge, who said to Mr Langton, ' Friend Langton, if I have not been at church on Sunday, I do not feel myself easy.' Dr Campbell was a sincerely religious man. Lord Macartney, who is eminent for his variety of knowledge, and attention to men of talents, and knew him well, told me, that when he called on him in a morning, he found him reading a chapter in the Greek New Testament, which he informed his Lordship was his constant practice. The quantity of Dr Campbell's composition is almost incredible, and his labours brought him large profits. Dr Joseph Warton told me that Johnson said of him, 'He is the richest author that ever grazed the common of literature.'

forgotten by the curious. Let me add, that there are in his works many passages which are of a general nature; and his 'Prophecy of Famine' is a poem of no ordinary merit. It is, indeed, falsely injurious to Scotland; but therefore may be allowed a greater share of invention.

Bonnel Thornton had just published a burlesque 'Ode on St Cecilia's day, adapted to the ancient British music, viz. the salt-box, the Jew's-harp, the marrow-bones and cleaver, the hum-strum or hurdy-gurdy, &c.' Johnson praised its humour, and seemed much diverted with it. He repeated the following passage:

> In strains more exalted the salt-box shall join,
> And clattering and battering and clapping combine;
> With a rap and a tap, while the hollow side sounds,
> Up and down leaps the flap, and with rattling rebounds.

I mentioned the periodical paper called *The Connoisseur*. He said it wanted matter. – No doubt it has not the deep thinking of Johnson's writings. But surely it has just views of the surface of life, and a very sprightly manner. His opinion of *The World* was not much higher than of the *Connoisseur*.

Let me here apologize for the imperfect manner in which I am obliged to exhibit Johnson's conversation at this period. In the early part of my acquaintance with him, I was so wrapped in admiration of his extraordinary colloquial talents, and so little accustomed to his peculiar mode of expression, that I found it extremely difficult to recollect and record his conversation with its genuine vigour and vivacity. In progress of time, when my mind was, as it were, strongly impregnated with the Johnsonian aether, I could, with much more facility and exactness, carry in my memory and commit to paper the exuberant variety of his wisdom and wit.

At this time Miss Williams, as she was then called, though she did not reside with him in the Temple under his roof, but had lodgings in Bolt-court, Fleet-street, had so much of his attention, that he every night drank tea with her before he went home, however late it might be, and she always sat up for him. This, it may be fairly conjectured, was not alone a proof of his regard for her, but of his own unwillingness to go into solitude before that unseasonable hour at which he had habituated himself to expect the oblivion of repose. Dr Goldsmith, being a privileged man, went with him this night, strutting away, and calling to me with an air of superiority, like that of an esoteric over an exoteric disciple of a sage antiquity, 'I go to Miss Williams.' I confess, I then envied him this mighty privilege, of which he seemed so proud; but it was not long before I obtained the same mark of distinction.

On Tuesday the 5th of July, I again visited Johnson. He told me he had looked into the poems of a certain pretty voluminous modern writer,[a] which had lately come out, but could find no thinking in them. BOSWELL. 'Is there

---

[a] Delete 'certain'. After 'writer', add, 'Mr (now Dr) John Ogilvie, one of the Presbyterian Ministers of Scotland.'

not imagination in them, Sir?' JOHNSON. 'Why, Sir, there is in them what *was* imagination, but it is no more imagination in *him*, than sound is sound in the echo. And his diction too is not his own. We have long ago seen *white-robed innocence*, and *flower-bespangled meads.*'

Talking of London, he observed, 'Sir, if you wish to have a just notion of the magnitude of this city, you must not be satisfied with seeing its great streets and squares, but must survey the innumerable little lanes and courts. It is not in the showy evolutions of buildings, but in the multiplicity of human habitations which are crowded together, that the wonderful immensity of London consists.' – I have often amused myself with thinking how different a place London is to different people. They, whose narrow minds are contracted to the consideration of some one particular pursuit, view it only through that medium. A politician thinks of it merely as the seat of government in its different departments; a grazier, as a vast market for cattle; a mercantile man, as a place where a prodigious deal of business is done upon 'Change; a dramatic enthusiast, as the grand scene of theatrical entertainments; a man of pleasure, as an assemblage of taverns, and the great emporium for ladies of easy virtue. But the intellectual man is struck with it, as comprehending the whole of human life in all its variety, the contemplation of which is inexhaustible.

On Wednesday, July 6, he was engaged to sup with me at my lodgings in Downing-street, Westminster. But on the preceding night my landlord having behaved very rudely to me and some company who were with me, I had resolved not to remain another night in his house. I was exceedingly uneasy at the awkward appearance I supposed I should make to Johnson and the other gentlemen whom I had invited, not being able to receive them at home, and being obliged to order supper at the Mitre. I went to Johnson in the morning, and talked of it as of a serious distress. He laughed, and said, 'Consider, Sir, how insignificant this will appear a twelvemonth hence.' – Were this consideration to be applied to most of the little vexatious incidents of life, by which our quiet is too often disturbed, it would prevent many painful sensations. I have tried it frequently, with good effect. 'There is nothing (continued he) in this mighty misfortune; nay, we shall be better at the Mitre.' I told him that I had been at Sir John Fielding's office, complaining of my landlord, and had been informed, that though I had taken my lodgings for a year, I might, upon proof of his bad behaviour, quit them when I pleased, without being under an obligation to pay rent for any longer time than while I possessed them. The fertility of Johnson's mind could show itself even upon so small a matter as this. 'Why, Sir (said he), I suppose this must be the law, since you have been told so in Bow-street. But, if your landlord could hold you to your bargain, and the lodgings should be yours for a year, you may certainly use them as you think fit. So, Sir, you may quarter two life-guardmen upon him; or you may send the greatest scoundrel you can find into your apartments; or you may say that you want to make some experiments in natural philosophy, and may burn a large quantity of assafoetida in his house.'

I cannot allow any fragment whatever that floats in my memory concerning the great subject of this work to be lost. Though a small particular may appear trifling to some, it will be relished by others, while every little spark adds something to the general blaze. And to please the true, candid, warm admirers of Johnson, and in any degree increase the splendour of his reputation, I bid defiance to the shafts of ridicule, or even of malignity; thousands of them have been discharged at my *Journal of a Tour to the Hebrides*, yet it still sails unhurt 'along the stream of time', and as an attendant upon Johnson, – 'Pursues the triumph, and partakes the gale.'[a]

I had as my guests this evening at the Mitre tavern, Dr Johnson, Dr Goldsmith, Mr Thomas Davies, Mr Eccles, an Irish gentleman, for whose agreeable company I was obliged to Mr Davies, and the Reverend Mr[b] Ogilvie, a Scotch clergyman,[c] author of several poems,[d] who was very desirous of being in company with my illustrious friend, while I, in my turn, was proud to have the honour of showing one of my countrymen upon what easy terms Johnson permitted me to live with him.

Goldsmith, as usual, endeavoured, with too much eagerness, to shine, and disputed very warmly with Johnson against the well-known maxim of the British constitution, 'the King can do no wrong'; affirming, that 'what was morally false could not be politically true; and as the King might, in the exercise of his regal power, command and cause the doing of what was wrong, it certainly might be said, in sense and in reason, that he could do wrong.' JOHNSON. 'Sir, you are to consider, that in our constitution, according to its true principles, the King is the head; he is supreme; he is above every thing, and there is no power by which he can be tried. Therefore it is, Sir, that we hold the King can do no wrong, that whatever may happen to be wrong in government may not be above our reach, by being ascribed to Majesty. Redress is always to be had against oppression, by punishing the immediate agents. The King, though he should command, cannot force a Judge to condemn a man unjustly; therefore it is the Judge whom we prosecute and punish. Political institutions are formed upon the consideration of what will most frequently tend to the good of the whole, although now and then exceptions may occur. Thus it is better in general that a nation should have a supreme legislative power, although it may at times be abused. And then, Sir, there is this consideration, that *if the abuse be enormous, Nature will rise up, and claiming her original rights, overturn a corrupt political system.*' I mark this animated sentence with peculiar pleasure, as a noble instance of that truly dignified spirit of

[a] Delete this paragraph, as it is repeated verbatim on page 613.

[b] After 'Mr' read 'John'.

[c] Delete 'a Scotch clergyman'. Add the following note: The Northern bard mentioned page 214. When I asked Dr Johnson's permission to introduce him, he obligingly agreed; adding, however, with a sly pleasantry, 'but he must give us none of his poetry.' It is remarkable that Johnson and Churchill, however much they differed in other points, agreed on this subject. See Churchill's *Journey*. It is, however, but justice to Dr Ogilvie to observe, that his *Day of Judgment*, has no inconsiderable share of merit.

[d] *Second Edition*: 'author of several poems', omitted.

freedom which ever glowed in his heart, though he was charged with slavish tenets by superficial observers, because he was at all times indignant against that false patriotism, that pretended love of freedom, that unruly restlessness, which is inconsistent with the stable authority of any good government.

This generous sentiment, which he uttered with great fervour, struck me exceedingly, and stirred my blood to that pitch of fancied resistance, the possibility of which I am glad to keep in mind, but to which I trust I shall never be forced.

'Great abilities (said he) are not requisite for an Historian; for in historical composition, all the greatest powers of the human mind are quiescent. He has facts ready to his hand; so there is no exercise of invention. Imagination is not required in any high degree; only about as much as is used in the lower kinds of poetry. Some penetration, accuracy, and colouring will fit a man for the task, if he can give the application which is necessary.'

'Bayle's *Dictionary* is a very useful work for those to consult who love the biographical part of literature, which is what I love most.'

Talking of the eminent writers in Queen Anne's reign, he observed, 'I think Dr Arbuthnot the first man among them. He was the most universal genius, being an excellent physician, a man of deep learning, and a man of much humour. Mr Addison was, to be sure, a great man; his learning was not profound; but his morality, his humour, and his elegance of writing, set him very high.'

Mr Ogilvie was unlucky enough to choose for the topic of his conversation the praises of his native country. He began with saying, that there was very rich land round Edinburgh. Goldsmith, who had studied physic there, contradicted this, very untruly, with a sneering laugh. Disconcerted a little by this, Mr Ogilvie then took new ground, where, I suppose, he thought himself perfectly safe; for he observed, that Scotland had a great many noble wild prospects. JOHNSON. 'I believe, Sir, you have a great many. Norway, too, has noble wild prospects; and Lapland is remarkable for prodigious noble wild prospects. But, Sir, let me tell you, the noblest prospect which a Scotchman ever sees, is the high road that leads him to England!' This unexpected and pointed sally produced a roar of applause. After all, however, those, who admire the rude grandeur of Nature, cannot deny it to Caledonia.

On Saturday, July 9, I found Johnson surrounded with a numerous levee, but have not preserved any part of his conversation. On the 14th we had another evening by ourselves at the Mitre. It happening to be a very rainy night, I made some common-place observations on the relaxation of nerves and depression of spirits which such weather occasioned; adding, however, that it was good for the vegetable creation. Johnson, who, as we have already seen, denied that the temperature of the air had any influence on the human frame, answered, with a smile of ridicule, 'Why yes, Sir, it is good for vegetables, and for the animals who eat those vegetables, and for the animals who eat those animals.' This observation of his aptly enough introduced a good supper; and I soon forgot, in Johnson's company, the influence of a moist atmosphere.

Feeling myself now quite at ease as his companion, though I had all possible reverence for him, I expressed a regret that I could not be so easy with my father, though he was not much older than him, and[a] certainly had not more learning and greater abilities to depress me. I asked him the reason of this. JOHNSON. 'Why, Sir, I am a man of the world. I live in the world, and I take, in some degree, the colour of the world as it moves along. Your father is a Judge in a remote part of the island, and all his notions are taken from the old world. Besides, Sir, there must always be a struggle between a father and son, while one aims at power and the other at independence.' I said, I was afraid my father would force me to be a lawyer. JOHNSON. 'Sir, you need not be afraid of his forcing you to be a laborious practising lawyer; that is not in his power. For as the proverb says, "One man may lead a horse to the water, but twenty cannot make him drink." He may be displeased that you are not what he wishes you to be; but that displeasure will not go far. If he insists only on your having as much law as is necessary for a man of property, and then endeavours to get you into Parliament, he is quite in the right.'

He enlarged very convincingly upon the excellence of rhyme over blank verse in English poetry. I mentioned to him that Dr Adam Smith, in his lectures upon composition, when I studied under him in the College of Glasgow, had maintained the same opinion strenuously, and I repeated some of his arguments. JOHNSON. 'Sir, I was once in company with Smith, and we did not take to each other; but had I known that he loved rhyme as much as you tell me he does, I should have HUGGED him.'

Talking of those who denied the truth of Christianity, he said, 'It is always easy to be on the negative side. If a man were now to deny that there is salt upon the table, you could not reduce him to an absurdity. Come, let us try this a little further. I deny that Canada is taken, and I can support my denial by pretty good arguments. The French are a much more numerous people than we; and it is not likely that they would allow us to take it. "But the ministry have assured us, in all the formality of the Gazette, that it is taken." – Very true. But the ministry have put us to an enormous expense by the war in America, and it is their interest to persuade us that we have got something for our money. – 'But the fact is confirmed by thousands of men who were at the taking of it.' – Ay, but these men have still more interest in deceiving us. They don't want you should think the French have beat them, but that they have beat the French. Now suppose you should go over and find that it is really taken, that would only satisfy yourself; for when you come home we will not believe you. We will say you have been bribed. – Yet, Sir, notwithstanding all these plausible objections, we have no doubt that Canada is really ours. Such is the weight of common testimony. How much stronger are the evidences of the Christian religion?'

'Idleness is a disease which must be combated; but I would not advise a rigid adherence to a particular plan of study. I myself have never persisted in any plan for two days together. A man ought to read just as inclination leads him;

---

[a] After 'and', read, 'however respectable'.

for what he reads as a task will do him little good. A young man should read five hours in a day, and so may acquire a great deal of knowledge.'

To a man of vigorous intellect and ardent curiosity like his own, reading without a regular plan may be beneficial; though even such a man must submit to it, if he would attain a full understanding of any of the sciences.

To such a degree of unrestrained frankness had he now accustomed me, that in the course of this evening I talked of the numerous reflections which had been thrown out against him on account of his having accepted a pension from his present Majesty. 'Why, Sir (said he, with a hearty laugh), it is a mighty foolish noise that they make.[1] I have accepted of a pension as a reward which has been thought due to my literary merit; and now that I have this pension, I am the same man in every respect that I have ever been; I retain the same principles. It is true, that I cannot now curse (smiling) the house of Hanover; nor would it be decent for me to drink King James's health in the wine that King George gives me money to pay for. But, Sir, I think that the pleasure of cursing the house of Hanover, and drinking King James's health, are amply overbalanced by the three hundred pounds a year.'

There was here, most certainly, an affectation of more Jacobitism than he really had, and indeed an intention of admitting, for the moment, in a much greater extent than it really existed, the charge of disaffection imputed to him by the world, merely for the purpose of showing how dexterously he could repel an attack, even though he were placed in the most disadvantageous position; for I have heard him declare, that if holding up his right hand would have secured victory at Culloden to Prince Charles's army, he was not sure he would have held it up; so little confidence had he in the right claimed by the house of Stuart, and so fearful was he of the consequences of another revolution on the throne of Great-Britain; and Mr Topham Beauclerk assured me, he had heard him say this before he had his pension. At another time he said to Mr Langton, 'Nothing has ever offered that has made it worth my while to consider the question fully.' He, however, also said to the same gentleman, talking of King James the Second, 'It was become impossible for him to reign any longer in this country.' He no doubt had an early attachment to the house of Stuart; but his zeal had cooled as his reason strengthened. Indeed I heard him once say, that 'after the death of a violent Whig, with whom he used to contend with great eagerness, he felt his Toryism much abated.'[2] I suppose he meant Mr Walmsley.[a]

---

1 When I mentioned the same idle clamour to him several years afterwards, he said, with a smile, 'I wish my pension were twice as large, that they might make twice as much noise.'

2 *Journal of a Tour to the Hebrides*, 3d edit. p. 402.

[a] Add as follows: Yet there is no doubt that at earlier periods he was wont often to exercise both his pleasantry and ingenuity in talking Jacobitism. My much respected friend, Mr Douglas, now Bishop of Salisbury, has favoured me with the following admirable instance from his Lordship's own recollection. One day when dining at old Mr Langton's, where Miss Roberts, his niece, was one of the company, Johnson, with

He advised me, when abroad, to be as much as I could with the Professors in the Universities, and with the Clergy; for from their conversation I might expect the best accounts of every thing in whatever country I should be, with the additional advantage of keeping my learning alive.

It will be observed, that when giving me advice as to my travels, Dr Johnson did not dwell upon cities, and palaces, and pictures, and shows, and Arcadian scenes. He was of Lord Essex's opinion, who advises his kinsman Roger Earl of Rutland, 'rather to go an hundred miles to speak with one wise man, than five miles to see a fair town.'[1]

I described to him an impudent fellow from Scotland, who affected to be a savage, and railed at all established systems. JOHNSON. 'There is nothing surprising in this, Sir. He wants to make himself conspicuous. He would tumble in a hog-stye, as long as you looked at him and called to him to come out. But let him alone, never mind him, and he'll soon give it over.'

I added, that the same person maintained that there was no distinction between virtue and vice. JOHNSON. 'Why, Sir, if the fellow does not think as he speaks, he is lying; and I see not what honour he can propose to himself from having the character of a liar. But if he does really think that there is no distinction between virtue and vice, why, Sir, when he leaves our houses, let us count our spoons.'

Sir David Dalrymple, now one of the Judges of Scotland by the title of Lord Hailes, had contributed much to increase my high opinion of Johnson, on account of his writings, long before I attained to a personal acquaintance with him; I, in return, had informed Johnson of Sir David's eminent character for learning and religion; and Johnson was so much pleased, that at one of our evening meetings he gave him for his toast. I at this time kept up a very frequent correspondence with Sir David; and I read to Dr Johnson to-night the following passage from the letter which I had last received from him:

---

his usual complacent attention to the fair sex, took her by the hand and said, 'My dear, I hope you are a Jacobite.' Old Mr Langton, who, though a high and steady Tory, was attached to the present Royal Family, seemed offended, and asked Johnson, with great warmth, what he could mean by putting such a question to his niece? 'Why, Sir (said Johnson), I meant no offence to your niece, I meant her a great compliment. A Jacobite, Sir, believes in the divine right of Kings. He that believes in the divine right of Kings believes in a Divinity. A Jacobite believes in the divine right of Bishops. He that believes in the divine right of Bishops believes in the divine authority of the Christian religion. Therefore, Sir, a Jacobite is neither an Atheist nor a Deist. That cannot be said of a Whig; for *Whiggism is a negation of all principle*.'[2]

1 Letter to Rutland on Travel, 1596.

2 He used to tell, with great humour, from my relation to him, the following little story of my early years, which was literally true: 'Boswell, in the year 1745, was a fine boy, wore a white cockade, and prayed for King James, till one of his uncles (General Cochran) gave him a shilling on condition that he would pray for King George, which he accordingly did. So you see (says Boswell) that *Whigs of all ages are made the same way*.'

It gives me pleasure to think that you have obtained the friendship of Mr Samuel Johnson. He is one of the best moral writers which England has produced. At the same time, I envy you the free and undisguised converse with such a man. May I beg you to present my best respects to him, and to assure him of the veneration which I entertain for the author of the *Rambler* and of *Rasselas*? Let me recommend this last work to you; with the *Rambler* you certainly are acquainted. In *Rasselas* you will see a tender-hearted operator, who probes the wound only to heal it. Swift, on the contrary, mangles human nature. He cuts and slashes, as if he took pleasure in the operation, like the tyrant who said, *Ita feri ut se sentiat emori.*

Johnson seemed to be much gratified by this just and well-turned compliment.

He recommended to me to keep a journal of my life, full and unreserved. He said it would be a very good exercise, and would yield me great satisfaction when the particulars were faded from my remembrance. I was uncommonly fortunate in having had a previous coincidence of opinion with him upon this subject, for I had kept such a journal for some time; and it was no small pleasure to me to have this to tell him, and to receive his approbation. He counselled me to keep it private, and said I might surely have a friend who would burn it in case of my death. From this habit I have been enabled to give the world so many anecdotes, which would otherwise have been lost to posterity. I mentioned that I was afraid I put into my journal too many little incidents. JOHNSON. 'There is nothing, Sir, too little for so little a creature as man. It is by studying little things that we attain the great art of having as little misery and as much happiness as possible.'

Next morning Mr Dempster happened to call on me, and was so much struck even with the imperfect account which I gave him of Dr Johnson's conversation, that to his honour be it recorded, when I complained that drinking port and sitting up late with him, affected my nerves for some time after, he said, 'One had better be palsied at eighteen than not keep company with such a man.'

On Tuesday, July 18, I found tall Sir Thomas Robinson sitting with Johnson. Sir Thomas said, that the King of Prussia valued himself upon three things – upon being a hero, a musician, and an author. JOHNSON. 'Pretty well, Sir, for one man. As to his being an author, I have not looked at his poetry; but his prose is poor stuff. He writes just as you might suppose Voltaire's footboy to do, who has been his amanuensis. He has such parts as the valet might have, and about as much of the colouring of the style as might be got by transcribing his works.' When I was at Ferney, I repeated this to Voltaire, in order to reconcile him somewhat to Johnson, whom he, in affecting the English mode of expression, had previously characterized as a 'superstitious dog'; but after hearing such a criticism on Frederick the Great, with whom he was then on bad terms, he exclaimed, 'An honest fellow!'

But I think the criticism much too severe; for the *Memoirs of the House of Brandenburgh* are written as well as many works of that kind. His poetry, for the style of which he himself makes a frank apology, *'Jargonnant un François barbare'*, though fraught with pernicious ravings of infidelity, has, in many places, great animation, and in some a pathetic tenderness.

Upon this contemptuous animadversion on the King of Prussia, I observed to Johnson, 'It would seem then, Sir, that much less parts are necessary to make a King than to make an Author; for the King of Prussia is confessedly the greatest King now in Europe, yet you think he makes a very poor figure as an Author.'

Mr Levet this day showed me Dr Johnson's library, which was contained in two garrets over his chambers, where Lintot, son of the celebrated bookseller of that name, had formerly his printing-house. I found a number of good books, but very dusty and in great confusion. The floor was strewed with manuscript leaves, in Johnson's own handwriting, which I beheld with a degree of veneration, supposing they perhaps might contain portions of the *Rambler*, or of *Rasselas*. I observed an apparatus for chemical experiments, of which Johnson was all his life very fond. The place seemed to be very favourable for retirement and meditation. Johnson told me, that he went up thither without mentioning it to his servant, when he wanted to study, secure from interruption; for he would not allow his servant to say he was not at home when he really was. 'A servant's strict regard for truth (said he), must be weakened by such a practice. A philosopher may know that it is merely a form of denial; but few servants are such nice distinguishers. If I accustom a servant to tell a lie for *me*, have I not reason to apprehend that he will tell many lies for *himself*?' I am, however, satisfied that every servant, of any degree of intelligence, understands saying his master is not at home, not at all as the affirmation of a fact, but as customary words, intimating that his master wishes not to be seen; so that there can be no bad effect from it.

Mr Temple, now vicar of St Gluvias, Cornwall, who had been my intimate friend for many years, had at this time chambers in Farrar's-buildings, at the bottom of Inner Temple-lane, which he kindly lent me upon my quitting my lodgings, he being to return to Trinity Hall, Cambridge. I found them particularly convenient for me, as they were so near Dr Johnson's.

On Wednesday, July 20, Dr Johnson, Mr Dempster, and my uncle Dr Boswell, who happened to be now in London, supped with me at these Chambers. JOHNSON. 'Pity is not natural to man. Children are always cruel. Savages are always cruel. Pity is acquired and improved by the cultivation of reason. We may have uneasy sensations from seeing a creature in distress, without pity; for we have not pity unless we wish to relieve them. When I am on my way to dine with a friend, and finding it late, have bid the coachman make haste, if I happen to attend when he whips his horses, I may feel unpleasantly that the animals are put to pain, but I do not wish him to desist. No, Sir, I wish him to drive on.'

Mr Alexander Donaldson, bookseller of Edinburgh, had for some time opened a shop in London, and sold his cheap editions of the most popular English books, in defiance of the supposed common-law right of *Literary Property*. Johnson, though he concurred in the opinion which was afterwards sanctioned by a decree from[a] the House of Lords, that there was no such right,

---

[a] For 'decree from', read, 'Judgment of'.

was at this time very angry that the booksellers of London, for whom he uniformly professed much regard, should suffer from an invasion of what they had ever considered to be secure, and he was loud and violent against Mr Donaldson. 'He is a fellow who takes advantage of the law to injure his brethren; for, notwithstanding that the statute secures only fourteen years of exclusive right, it has always been understood by the trade, that he, who buys the copy-right of a book from the author, obtains a perpetual property; and upon that belief, numberless bargains are made to transfer that property after the expiration of the statutory term. Now Donaldson, I say, takes advantage here, of people who have really an equitable title from usage; and if we consider how few of the books, of which they buy the property, succeed so well as to bring profit, we should be of opinion that the term of fourteen years is too short; it should be sixty years.' DEMPSTER. 'Donaldson, Sir, is anxious for the encouragement of literature. He reduces the price of books, so that poor students may buy them.' JOHNSON (laughing), 'Well, Sir, allowing that to be his motive, he is no better than Robin Hood, who robbed the rich in order to give to the poor.'

It is remarkable, that when the great question concerning Literary Property came to be ultimately tried before the supreme tribunal of this country, in consequence of the very spirited exertions of Mr Donaldson, Dr Johnson was zealous against a perpetuity; but he thought that the term of the exclusive right of authors should be considerably enlarged. He was then for granting a hundred years.

The conversation now turned upon Mr David Hume's style. JOHNSON. 'Why, Sir, his style is not English; the structure of his sentences is French. Now the French structure and the English structure may, in the nature of things, be equally good. But if you allow that the English language is established, he is wrong. My name might originally have been Nicholson, as well as Johnson; but were you to call me Nicholson now, you would call me very absurdly.'

Rousseau's treatise on the inequality of mankind was at this time a fashionable topic. It gave rise to an observation by Mr Dempster, that the advantages of fortune and rank were nothing to a wise man, who ought to value only merit. JOHNSON. 'If man were a savage, living in the woods by himself, this might be true; but in civilised society, we all depend upon each other, and our happiness is very much owing to the good opinion of mankind. Now, Sir, in civilised society, external advantages make us more respected. A man with a good coat upon his back meets with a better reception than he who has a bad one. Sir, you may analyse this, and say what is there in it? But that will avail you nothing, for it is a part of a general system. Pound St Paul's church into atoms, and consider any single atom; it is, to be sure, good for nothing: but, put all these atoms together, and you have St Paul's church. So it is with human felicity, which is made up of many ingredients, each of which may be shown to be very insignificant. In civilised society, personal merit will not serve you so much as money will. Sir, you may make the experiment. Go into the street, and give one man a lecture on morality, and another a shilling, and see which will respect you most. If you wish only to support nature, Sir

William Petty fixes your allowance at three pounds a year; but as times are much altered, let us call it six pounds. This sum will fill your belly, shelter you from the weather, and even get you a strong lasting coat, supposing it to be made of good bull's hide. Now, Sir, all beyond this is artificial, and is desired in order to obtain a greater degree of respect from our fellow-creatures. And, Sir, if six hundred pounds a year procure a man more consequence, and, of course, more happiness than six pounds a year, the same proportion will hold as to six thousand, and so on as far as opulence can be carried. Perhaps he who has a large fortune may not be so happy as he who has a small one; but that must proceed from other causes than from his having the large fortune: for, *ceteris paribus*, he who is rich in a civilised society, must be happier than he who is poor; as riches, if properly used (and it is a man's own fault if they are not), must be productive of the highest advantages. Money, to be sure, of itself is of no use; for its only use is to part with it. Rousseau, and all those who deal in paradoxes, are led away by a childish desire of novelty. When I was a boy, I used always to choose the wrong side of a debate, because most ingenious things, that is to say, most new things, could be said upon it. Sir, there is nothing for which you may not muster up more plausible arguments, than those which are urged against wealth and other external advantages. Why now, there is stealing; why should it be thought a crime? When we consider by what unjust methods property has been often acquired, and that what was unjustly got it must be unjust to keep, where is the harm in one man's taking the property of another from him? Besides, Sir, when we consider the bad use that many people make of their property, and how much better use the thief may make of it, it may be defended as a very allowable practice. Yet, Sir, the experience of mankind has discovered stealing to be so very bad a thing that they make no scruple to hang a man for it. When I was running about this town a very poor fellow, I was a great arguer for the advantages of poverty; but I was, at the same time, very sorry to be poor. Sir, all the arguments which are brought to represent poverty as no evil, show it to be evidently a great evil. You never find people labouring to convince you that you may live very happily upon a plentiful fortune. – So you hear people talking how miserable a king must be; and yet they all wish to be in his place.'

It was suggested that kings must be unhappy, because they are deprived of the greatest of all satisfactions, easy and unreserved society. JOHNSON. 'That is an ill-founded notion. Being a king does not exclude a man from such society. Great kings have always been social. The King of Prussia, the only great king at present, is very social. Charles the Second, the last King of England who was a man of parts, was social; and our Henrys and Edwards were all social.'

Mr Dempster having endeavoured to maintain that intrinsic merit *ought* to make the only distinction amongst mankind. JOHNSON. 'Why, Sir, mankind have found that this cannot be. How shall we determine the proportion of intrinsic merit? Were that to be the only distinction amongst mankind, we should soon quarrel about the degrees of it. Were all distinctions abolished, the strongest would not long acquiesce, but would endeavour to obtain a superiority by their bodily strength. But, Sir, as subordination is very necessary for society, and contentions for superiority very dangerous, mankind, that is to say, all civilised nations, have settled it upon a plain invariable principle. A man is born to hereditary rank; or his being appointed to certain offices, gives him a certain rank. Subordination tends greatly to human happiness. Were we all upon an equality, we should have no other enjoyment than mere animal pleasure.'

I said, I considered distinction of rank to be of so much importance in civilised society, that if I were asked on the same day to dine with the first duke in England, and with the first man in Britain for genius, I should hesitate which to prefer. JOHNSON. 'To be sure, Sir, if you were to dine only once, and it were never to be known where you dined, you would choose rather to dine with the first man for genius; but to gain most respect, you should dine with the first duke in England. For nine people in ten that you meet with, would have a higher opinion of you for having dined with a duke; and the great genius himself would receive you better, because you had been with the great duke.'

He took care to guard himself against any possible suspicion that his settled principles of reverence for rank and respect for wealth were at all owing to mean or interested motives; for he asserted his own independence as a literary man. 'No man (said he) who ever lived by literature, has lived more independently than I have done.' He said he had taken longer time than he needed to have done in composing his Dictionary. He received our compliments upon that great work with complacency, and told us that the Academy *della Crusca* could scarcely believe that it was done by one man.

Next morning I found him alone, and have preserved the following fragments of his conversation. Of a gentleman who was mentioned, he said, 'I have not met with any man for a long time who has given me such general displeasure. He is totally unfixed in his principles, and wants to puzzle other people.' I said, his principles had been poisoned by a noted infidel writer, but that he was, nevertheless, a benevolent good man. JOHNSON. 'We can have no dependence upon that instinctive, that constitutional goodness which is not founded upon principle. I grant you that such a man may be a very amiable member of society. I can conceive him placed in such a situation that he is not much tempted to deviate from what is right; and as every man prefers virtue when there is not some strong incitement to transgress its precepts, I can conceive him doing nothing wrong. But if such a man stood in need of money, I should not like to trust him; and I should certainly not trust him with young ladies, for *there* there is always temptation. Hume, and other sceptical innovators, are vain men, and will gratify themselves at any expense. Truth will not afford sufficient food to their vanity; so they have betaken themselves to error. Truth, Sir, is a cow which will yield such people no more milk, and so they are gone to milk the bull. If I could have allowed myself to gratify my vanity at the expense of truth, what fame might I have acquired. Every thing which Hume has advanced against Christianity had passed through my mind long before he wrote. Always remember this, that after a system is well settled upon positive evidence, a few partial objections ought not to shake it. The human mind is so limited, that it cannot take in all the parts of a subject, so that there may be objections raised against any thing. There are objections against a *plenum*, and objections against a *vacuum*; yet one of them must certainly be true.'

I mentioned Hume's argument against the belief of miracles, that it is more probable that the witnesses to the truth of them are mistaken, or speak falsely, than that the miracles should be true. JOHNSON. 'Why, Sir, the great difficulty of proving miracles should make us very cautious in believing them. But let us consider; although GOD has made Nature to operate by certain fixed laws, yet it is not unreasonable to think that he may suspend those laws, in order to establish a system highly advantageous to mankind. Now the Christian religion is a most beneficial system, as it gives us light and certainty where we were before in darkness and doubt. The miracles which prove it are attested by men who had no interest in deceiving us; but who, on the contrary, were told that they should suffer persecution, and did actually lay down their lives in confirmation of the truth of the facts which they asserted. Indeed, for some centuries the heathens did not pretend to deny the miracles; but said they were performed by the aid of evil spirits. This is a circumstance of great weight. Then, Sir, when we take the proofs derived from prophecies which have been so exactly fulfilled, we have most satisfactory evidence. Supposing a miracle possible, as to which, in my opinion, there can be no doubt, we have as strong evidence for the miracles in support of Christianity, as the nature of the thing admits.'

At night, Mr Johnson and I supped in a private room at the Turk's Head coffee-house, in the Strand. 'I encourage this house (said he); for the mistress of it is a good civil woman, and has not much business.'

'Sir, I love the acquaintance of young people; because, in the first place, I don't like to think myself growing old. In the next place, young acquaintances must last longest, if they do last; and then, Sir, young men have more virtue than old men; they have more generous sentiments in every respect. I love the young dogs of this age: they have more wit and humour and knowledge of life than we had; but then the dogs are not so good scholars. Sir, in my early years I read very hard. It is a sad reflection, but a true one, that I knew almost as much at eighteen as I do now. My judgement, to be sure, was not so good; but, I had all the facts. I remember very well, when I was at Oxford, an old gentleman said to me, "Young man, ply your book diligently now, and acquire a stock of knowledge; for when years come upon you, you will find that poring upon books will be but an irksome task." '

This account of his reading, given by himself in plain words, sufficiently confirms what I have already advanced upon the disputed question as to his application. It reconciles any seeming inconsistency in his way of talking upon it at different times; and shows that idleness and reading hard were with him relative terms, the import of which, as used by him, must be gathered from a comparison with what scholars of different degrees of ardour and assiduity have been known to do. And let it be remembered, that he was now talking spontaneously, and expressing his genuine sentiments; whereas at other times he might be induced from his spirit of contradiction, or more properly from his love of argumentative contest, to speak lightly of his own application to study. It is pleasing to consider that the old gentleman's gloomy prophecy as to the irksomeness of books to men of an advanced age, which is too often fulfilled, was so far from being verified in Johnson, that his ardour for literature never failed, and his last writings had more ease and vivacity than any of his earlier productions.

He mentioned to me now, for the first time, that he had been distressed by melancholy, and for that reason had been obliged to fly from study and meditation, to the dissipating variety of life. Against melancholy he recommended constant occupation of mind, a great deal of exercise, moderation in eating and drinking, and especially to shun drinking at night. He said melancholy people were apt to fly to intemperance for relief, but that it sunk them much deeper in misery. He observed, that labouring men who work hard, and live sparingly, are seldom or never troubled with low spirits.

He again insisted on the duty of maintaining subordination of rank. 'Sir, I would no more deprive a nobleman of his respect than of his money. I consider myself as acting a part in the great system of society, and I do to others as I would have them to do to me. I would behave to a nobleman as I should expect he would behave to me, were I a nobleman and he Sam. Johnson. Sir, there is one Mrs Macaulay[1] in this town, a great republican. One day when I was at her house, I put on a very grave countenance, and said to her, "Madam, I am now become a convert to your way of thinking. I am convinced that all mankind are upon an equal footing; and to give you an unquestionable proof, Madam, that I am in earnest, here is a very sensible, civil, well-behaved fellow-citizen, your footman; I desire that he may be allowed to sit down and dine with us." I thus, Sir, showed her the absurdity of the levelling doctrine. She has never liked me since. Sir, your levellers wish to level *down* as far as themselves; but they cannot bear levelling *up* to themselves. They would all have some people under them; why not then have some people above them?' I mentioned a certain author who disgusted me by his forwardness, and by showing no deference to noblemen into whose company he was admitted. JOHNSON. 'Suppose a shoemaker should claim an equality with him as he does with a Lord; how would he stare. "Why, Sir, do you stare? (says the shoemaker), I do great service to society. 'Tis true, I am paid for doing it; but so are you, Sir: and I am sorry to say it, better paid than I am, for doing something not so necessary. For mankind could do better without your books, than without my shoes." Thus, Sir, there would be a perpetual struggle for precedence, were there no fixed invariable rules for the distinction of rank, which creates no jealousy, as it is allowed to be accidental.'

He said, Dr Joseph Warton was a very agreeable man, and his *Essay on the Genius and Writings of Pope*, a very pleasing book. I wondered that he delayed so long to give us the continuation of it. JOHNSON. 'Why, Sir, I suppose he finds himself a little disappointed, in not having been able to persuade the world to be of his opinion as to Pope.'

We have now been favoured with the concluding volume, in which, to use

1 This *one* Mrs Macaulay was the same personage who afterwards made herself so much known as 'the celebrated female historian'.

a parliamentary expression, he has *explained*, so as not to appear quite so adverse to the opinion of the world concerning Pope, as was at first thought; and we must all agree, that his work is a most valuable accession to English literature.

A writer of deserved eminence being mentioned, Johnson said, 'Why, Sir, he is a man of good parts, but being originally poor, he has got a love of mean company and low jocularity; a very bad thing, Sir. To laugh is good, as to talk is good. But you ought no more to think it enough if you laugh, than you are to think it enough if you talk. You may laugh in as many ways as you talk; and surely *every* way of talking that is practised cannot be esteemed.'

I spoke of Sir James Macdonald as a young man of most distinguished merit, who united the highest reputation at Eton and Oxford, with the patriarchal spirit of a great Highland Chieftain. I mentioned that Sir James had said to me, that he had never seen Mr Johnson, but he had a great respect for him, though at the same time it was mixed with some degree of terror. JOHNSON. 'Sir, if he were to be acquainted with me, it might lessen both.'

The mention of this gentleman led us to talk of the Western Islands of Scotland, to visit which he expressed a wish that then appeared to me a very romantic fancy, which I little thought would be afterwards realized. He told me, that his father had put Martin's account of those islands into his hands when he was very young, and that he was highly pleased with it; that he was particularly struck with the St Kilda man's notion that the high church of Glasgow had been hollowed out of a rock; a circumstance to which old Mr Johnson had directed his attention. He said, he would go to the Hebrides with me, when I returned from my travels, unless some very good companion should offer when I was absent, which he did not think probable; adding, 'There are few people to whom I take so much to as you.' And when I talked of my leaving England, he said, with a very affectionate air, 'My dear Boswell, I should be very unhappy at parting, did I think we were not to meet again.' – I cannot too often remind my readers, that although such instances of his kindness are doubtless very flattering to me, yet I hope my recording them will be ascribed to a better motive than to vanity; for they afford unquestionable evidence of his tenderness and complacency, which some, while they were forced to acknowledge his great powers, have been so strenuous to deny.

He maintained, that a boy at school was the happiest of human beings. I supported a different opinion, from which I have never yet varied, that a man is happier; and I enlarged upon the anxiety and sufferings which are endured at school. JOHNSON. 'Ah! Sir, a boy's being flogged is not so severe as a man's having the hiss of the world against him. Men have a solicitude about fame; and the greater share they have of it, the more afraid they are of losing it.' I silently asked myself, 'Is it possible that the great Samuel Johnson really entertains any such apprehension, and is not confident that his exalted fame is established upon a foundation never to be shaken?'

He this evening drank a bumper to Sir David Dalrymple, as a man of worth, a scholar, and a wit. – 'I have (said he) never heard of him except from you; but let him know my opinion of him: for as he does not show himself much in the world, he should have the praise of the few who hear of him.'

On Tuesday, July 26, I found Mr Johnson alone. It was a very wet day, and I again complained of the disagreeable effects of such weather. JOHNSON. 'Sir, this is all imagination, which physicians encourage; for man lives in air, as a fish lives in water; so that if the atmosphere press heavy from above, there is an equal resistance from below. To be sure, bad weather is hard upon people who are obliged to be abroad; and men cannot labour so well in the open air in bad weather, as in good; but, Sir, a smith or a tailor, whose work is within doors, will surely do as much in rainy weather as in fair. Some very delicate frames, indeed, may be affected by wet weather, but not common constitutions.'

We talked of the education of children; and I asked him what he thought was best to teach them first. JOHNSON. 'Sir, it is no matter what you teach them first, any more than what leg you shall put into your breeches first. Sir, you may stand disputing which is best to put in first, but in the mean time your breech is bare. Sir, while you are considering which of two things you should teach your child first, another boy has learnt them both.'

On Thursday, July 28, we again supped in private at the Turk's Head coffee-house. JOHNSON. 'Swift has a higher reputation than he deserves. His excellence is strong sense; for his humour, though very well, is not remarkably good. I doubt whether the *Tale of a Tub* be his; for he never owned it, and it is much above his usual manner.'[1]

'Thomson, I think, had as much of the poet about him as most writers. Every thing appeared to him through the medium of his favourite pursuit. He could not have viewed those two candles burning but with a poetical eye.'

'Has not ―― a great deal of wit, Sir?' JOHNSON. 'I do not think so, Sir. He is, indeed, continually attempting wit, but he fails. And I have no more pleasure in hearing a man attempting wit and failing, than in seeing a man trying to leap over a ditch and tumbling into it.'

He laughed heartily, when I mentioned to him a saying of his concerning Mr Thomas Sheridan, which Foote took a wicked pleasure to circulate. 'Why, Sir, Sherry is dull, naturally dull; but it must have taken him a great deal of pains to become what we now see him. Such an excess of stupidity, Sir, is not in Nature.' – 'So (said he), I allowed him all his own merit.'

He now added, 'Sheridan cannot bear me. I bring his declamation to a point. I ask him a plain question, "What do you mean to teach?" Besides, Sir, what influence can Mr Sheridan have upon the language of this great country by his narrow exertions? Sir, it is burning a farthing candle at Dover, to show light at Calais.'

Talking of a young man who was uneasy from thinking that he was very deficient in learning and knowledge, he said, 'A man has no reason to complain who holds a middle place and has many below him; and perhaps he has not six of his years above him – perhaps not one. Though he may not know any thing perfectly, the general mass of knowledge that he has acquired is considerable. Time will do for him all that is wanting.'

1 This opinion was given by him more at large at a subsequent period. See *Journal of a Tour to the Hebrides*, 3d edit. p. 32.

The conversation then took a philosophical turn. JOHNSON. 'Human experience, which is constantly contradicting theory, is the great test of truth. A system, built upon the discoveries of a great many minds, is always of more strength, than what is produced by the mere workings of any one mind, which, of itself, can do little. There is not so poor a book in the world but what would be a prodigious effort were it wrought out entirely by a single mind, without the aid of prior investigators. The French writers are superficial, because they are not scholars, and so proceed upon the mere power of their own minds; and we see how very little power they have.'

'As to the Christian religion, Sir, besides the strong evidence which we have for it, there is a balance in its favour from the number of great men who have been convinced of its truth, after a serious consideration of the question. Grotius was an acute man, a lawyer, a man accustomed to examine evidence, and he was convinced. Grotius was not a recluse, but a man of the world, who certainly had no bias to the side of religion. Sir Isaac Newton set out an infidel, and came to be a very firm believer.'

He this evening again recommended to me to perambulate Spain.[1] I said it would amuse him to get a letter from me dated at Salamancha. JOHNSON. 'I love the University of Salamancha; for when the Spaniards were in doubt as to the lawfulness of their conquering America, the University of Salamancha gave it as their opinion that it was not lawful.' He spoke this with great emotion, and with that generous warmth which dictated the lines in his *London*, against Spanish encroachment.

I expressed my opinion of my friend Derrick as but a poor writer. JOHNSON. 'To be sure, Sir, he is; but you are to consider that his being a literary man has got for him all that he has. It has made him King of Bath. Sir, he has nothing to say for himself but that he is a writer. Had he not been a writer, he must have been sweeping the crossings in the streets, and asking halfpence from every body that past.'

In justice, however, to the memory of Mr Derrick, who was my first tutor in the ways of London, and showed me the town in its variety of departments, both literary and sportive, the particulars of which Dr Johnson advised me to put in writing, it is proper to mention what Johnson, at a subsequent period, said of him both as a writer and an editor. 'Sir, I have often said, that if Derrick's letters had been written by one of a more established name, they would have been thought very pretty letters.'[2] And, 'I sent Derrick to Dryden's relations to gather materials for his life; and I believe he got all that I myself should have got.'[3]

---

1 I fully intended to have followed advice of such weight; but having staid much longer both in Germany and Italy than I proposed to do, and having also visited Corsica, I found that I had exceeded the time allowed me by my father, and hastened to France in my way homewards.

2 *Journal of a Tour to the Hebrides*, 3d edit. p. 104

3 Ibid. p. 142.

Poor Derrick! I remember him with kindness. Yet I cannot withhold from my readers a pleasant humorous sally which could not have hurt him had he been alive, and now is perfectly harmless. In his collection of poems, there is one upon entering the harbour of Dublin, his native city, after a long absence. It begins thus:

> Eblana! Much lov'd city, hail!
> Where first I saw the light of day.

And after a solemn reflection on his being 'numbered with forgotten dead', there is the following stanza:

> Unless my lines protract my fame,
>   And those, who chance to read them, cry,
> I knew him! Derrick was his name,
>   In yonder tomb his ashes lie.

Which was thus happily parodied by Mr John Home, to whom we owe the beautiful and pathetic tragedy of *Douglas*:

> Unless my *deeds* protract my fame,
>   *And he who passes sadly sings,*
> I knew him! Derrick was his name,
>   *On yonder tree his carcase swings.*

I doubt much whether the amiable and ingenious author of these burlesque lines will recollect them, for they were produced extempore one evening while he and I were walking together in the dining-room at Eglintoune castle, in 1760, and I have never mentioned them to him since.

Johnson said once to me, 'Sir, I honour Derrick for his presence of mind. One night, when Floyd,[1] another poor author, was wandering about the streets in the night, he found Derrick fast asleep upon a bulk; upon being suddenly waked, Derrick started up, "My dear Floyd, I am sorry to see you in this destitute state; will you go home with me to *my lodgings*?" '

I again begged his advice as to my method of study at Utrecht. 'Come (said he), let us make a day of it. Let us go down to Greenwich and dine, and talk of it there.' The following Saturday was fixed for this excursion.

As we walked along the Strand to-night, arm in arm, a woman of the town accosted us, in the usual enticing manner. 'No, no, my girl (said Johnson), it won't do.' He, however, did not treat her with harshness, and we talked of the wretched life of such women; and agreed, that much more misery than happiness, upon the whole, is produced by illicit commerce between the sexes.

On Saturday, July 30, Dr Johnson and I took a sculler at the Temple-stairs, and set out for Greenwich. I asked him if he really thought a knowledge of the

---

1 He published a biographical work, containing an account of eminent writers, in three vols. 8vo.

Greek and Latin languages an essential requisite to a good education. JOHNSON. 'Most certainly, Sir. For those who know them have a very great advantage over those who do not. Nay, Sir, it is wonderful what a difference learning makes upon people even in the common intercourse of life, which does not appear to be much connected with it.' 'And yet (said I), people will go through the world very well, and carry on the business of life to good advantage, without learning.' JOHNSON. 'Why, Sir, that may be true in cases where learning cannot possibly be of any use; for instance, this boy rows us as well without learning, as if he could sing the song of Orpheus to the Argonauts, who were the first sailors.' He then called to the boy, 'What would you give, my lad, to know about the Argonauts?' 'Sir (said the boy), I would give what I have.' Johnson was much pleased with his answer, and we gave him a double fare. Mr Johnson then turning to me, 'Sir (said he), a desire of knowledge is the natural feeling of mankind; and every human being, whose mind is not debauched, will be willing to give all that he has to get knowledge.'

We landed at the Old Swan, and walked to Billingsgate, where we took oars, and moved smoothly along the silver Thames. It was a very fine day. We were entertained with the immense number and variety of ships that were lying at anchor, and with the beautiful country on each side of the river.

I talked of preaching, and of the great success which those called Methodists[1] have. JOHNSON. 'Sir, it is owing to their expressing themselves in a plain and

---

1 All who are acquainted with the history of Religion (the most important, surely, that concerns the human mind), know that the appellation of *Methodists* was first given to a society of students in the University of Oxford, who about the year 1730, were distinguished by an earnest and methodical attention to devout exercises. This disposition of mind is not a novelty or peculiar to any sect, but has been, and still may be found, in many Christians of every denomination. Johnson himself was, in a dignified manner, a Methodist. In his *Rambler*, No. 110, he mentions with respect 'the whole discipline of regulated piety'; and in his *Prayers and Meditations*, many instances occur of his anxious examination into his spiritual state. That this religious earnestness, and in particular an observation of the influence of the Holy Spirit, has sometimes degenerated into folly, and sometimes been counterfeited for base purposes, cannot be denied. But it is not, therefore, fair to decry it when genuine. The principal argument in reason and good sense against methodism is, that it tends to debase human nature, and prevent the generous exertions of goodness, by an unworthy supposition that GOD will pay no regard to them, although it is positively said in the scriptures that he 'will reward every man according to his works.' But I am happy to have it in my power to do justice to those whom it is the fashion to ridicule, without any knowledge of their tenets; and this I can do by quoting a passage from one of their best apologists, Mr Milner, who thus expresses their doctrine upon this subject. 'Justified by faith, renewed in his faculties, and constrained by the love of Christ, their believer moves in the sphere of love and gratitude, and all his *duties* flow more or less from this principle. And though *they are accumulating for him in heaven a treasure of bliss proportioned to his faithfulness and activity, and it is by no means inconsistent with his principles to feel the force of this consideration,* yet love itself sweetens every duty to his mind; and he thinks there is no absurdity in his feeling the love of GOD as the grand commanding principle of his life.' Essays on several religious Subjects, &c. by Joseph Milner, A.M., Master of the Grammar School of Kingston-upon-Hull, 1789, p. 11.

familiar manner, which is the only way to do good to the common people, and which clergymen of genius and learning ought to do from a principle of duty, when it is suited to their congregations; a practice, for which they will be praised by men of sense. To insist against drunkenness as a crime, because it debases reason, the noblest faculty of man, would be of no service to the common people: but to tell them that they may die in a fit of drunkenness, and show them how dreadful that would be, cannot fail to make a deep impression. Sir, when your Scotch clergy give up their homely manner, religion will soon decay in that country.' Let this observation, as Johnson meant it, be ever remembered.

I was much pleased to find myself with Johnson at Greenwich, which he celebrates in his *London* as a favourite scene. I had the poem in my pocket, and read the lines aloud with enthusiasm:

> On Thames's banks in silent thought we stood,
> Where Greenwich smiles upon the silver flood:
> Pleas'd with the seat which gave ELIZA birth,
> We kneel, and kiss the consecrated earth.

He remarked that the structure of Greenwich hospital was too magnificent for a place of charity, and that its parts were too much detached to make one great whole.

Buchanan, he said, was a very fine poet; and observed, that he was the first who complimented a lady, by ascribing to her the different perfections of the heathen goddesses; but that Johnston improved upon this, by making his lady, at the same time, free from their defects.

He dwelt upon Buchanan's elegant verses to Mary Queen of Scots, *Nympha Caledoniae*, &c. and spoke with enthusiasm of the beauty of Latin verse. 'All the modern languages (said he) cannot furnish so melodious a line as

> *Formosam resonare doces Amarillida silvas.*

Afterwards he entered upon the business of the day, which was to give me his advice as to a course of study. And here I am to mention with much regret, that my record of what he said is miserably scanty. I recollect with admiration an animating blaze of eloquence, which roused every intellectual power in me to the highest pitch, but must have dazzled me so much, that my memory could not preserve the substance of his discourse; for the note which I find of it is no more than this – 'He ran over the grand scale of human knowledge; advised me to select some particular branch to excel in, but to acquire a little of every kind.' The defect of my minutes will be fully supplied by a long letter upon the subject which he favoured me with, after I had been some time at Utrecht, and which my readers will have the pleasure to peruse in its proper place.

We walked in the evening in Greenwich Park. He asked me, I suppose by way of trying my disposition, 'Is not this very fine?' Having no exquisite relish of the beauties of Nature, and being more delighted with 'the busy hum of men', I answered, 'Yes, Sir; but not equal to Fleet-street.' JOHNSON. 'You are right, Sir.'

I am aware that many of my readers may censure my want of taste. Let me, however, shelter myself under the authority of a very fashionable Baronet[a] in the brilliant world, who, on his attention being called to the fragrance of a May evening in the country, observed, 'This may be very well; but, for my part, I prefer the smell of a flambeau at the play-house.'

We staid so long at Greenwich, that our sail up the river, in our return to London, was by no means so pleasant as in the morning; for the night air was so cold that it made me shiver. I was the more sensible of it from having sat up all the night before, recollecting and writing in my journal what I thought worthy of preservation; an exertion, which, during the first part of my acquaintance with Johnson, I frequently made. I remember having sat up four nights in one week, without being much incommoded in the day time.

Johnson, whose robust frame was not in the least affected by the cold, scolded me, as if my shivering had been a paltry effeminacy, saying, 'Why do you shiver?' Sir William Scott, of the Commons, told me, that when he complained of a head-ache in the post-chaise, as they were travelling together to Scotland, Johnson treated him in the same manner: 'At your age, Sir, I had no head-ache.' It is not easy to make allowance for sensations in others, which we ourselves have not at the time. We must all have experienced how very differently we are affected by the complaints of our neighbours, when we are well and when we are ill. In full health, we can scarcely believe that they suffer much; so faint is the image of pain upon our imagination: when softened by sickness, we readily sympathize with the sufferings of others.

We concluded the day at the Turk's Head coffee-house, very socially. He was pleased to listen to a particular account which I gave him of my family, and of its hereditary estate, as to the extent and population of which he asked questions, and made calculations; recommending, at the same time, a liberal kindness to the tenantry, as people over whom the proprietor was placed by Providence. He took delight in hearing my description of the romantic seat of my ancestors. 'I must be there, Sir (said he), and we will live in the old castle; and if there is not a room in it remaining, we will build one.' I was highly flattered, but could scarcely indulge a hope that Auchinleck would indeed be honoured by his presence, and celebrated by a description, as it afterwards was, in his *Journey to the Western Islands*.

After we had again talked of my setting out for Holland, he said, 'I must see thee out of England: I will accompany you to Harwich.' I could not find words to express what I felt upon this unexpected and very great mark of his affectionate regard.

Next day, Sunday, July 31, I told him I had been that morning at a meeting of the people called Quakers, where I had heard a woman preach. JOHNSON, 'Sir,

---

[a] Add the following note: My friend Sir Michael Le Fleming. This gentleman, with all his experience of sprightly and elegant life, inherits, with the beautiful family domain, no inconsiderable share of that love of literature, which distinguished his venerable grandfather, the Bishop of Carlisle. He one day observed to me, of Dr Johnson, in a felicity of phrase, 'There is a blunt dignity about him on every occasion.'

a woman's preaching is like a dog's walking on his hinder legs. It is not done well; but you are surprised to find it done at all.'

On Tuesday, August 2 (the day of my departure from London having been fixed for the 5th), Dr Johnson did me the honour to pass a part of the morning with me at my Chambers. He said, that 'he always felt an inclination to do nothing.' I observed, that it was strange to think that the most indolent man in Britain had written the most laborious work, *The English Dictionary*.

I mentioned an imprudent publication, by a certain friend of his, at an early period of life, and asked him if he thought it would hurt him. JOHNSON. 'No, Sir; not much. It may, perhaps, be mentioned at an election.'

I had now made good my title to be a privileged man, and was carried by him in the evening to drink tea with Mrs Williams, whom, though under the misfortune of having lost her sight, I found to be agreeable in conversation; for she had a variety of literature, and expressed herself well; but her peculiar value was the intimacy in which she had long lived with Johnson, by which she was well acquainted with his habits, and knew how to lead him on to talk.

After tea he carried me to what he called his walk, which was a long narrow paved court in the neighbourhood, overshadowed by some trees. There we sauntered a considerable time; and I complained to him that my love of London and of his company was such, that I shrunk almost from the thought of going away even to travel, which is generally so much desired by young men. He roused me by manly and spirited conversation. He advised me, when settled in any place abroad, to study with an eagerness after knowledge, and to apply to Greek an hour every day; and when I was moving about, to read diligently the great book of mankind.

On Wednesday, August 3, we had our last social evening at the Turk's Head coffee-house, before my setting out for foreign parts. I had the misfortune, before we parted, to irritate him unintentionally. I mentioned to him how common it was in the world to tell absurd stories of him, and to ascribe to him very strange sayings. JOHNSON. 'What do they make me say, Sir?' BOSWELL. 'Why, Sir, as an instance very strange indeed (laughing heartily as I spoke), David Hume told me, you said that you would stand before a battery of cannon, to restore the Convocation to its full powers.' – Little did I apprehend that he had actually said this; but I was soon convinced of my error; for, with a determined look, he thundered out, 'And would I not, Sir? Shall the Presbyterian *Kirk* of Scotland have its General Assembly, and the Church of England be denied its Convocation?' He was walking up and down the room while I told him the anecdote; but when he uttered this explosion of high-church zeal, he had come close to my chair, and his eyes flashed with indignation. I bowed to the storm, and diverted the force of it, by leading him to expatiate on the influence which religion derived from maintaining the church with great external respectability.

I must not omit to mention that he this year wrote 'The Life of Ascham',[†] and the Dedication to the Earl of Shaftesbury,[†] prefixed to the edition of that writer's English works, published by Mr Bennet.

On Friday, August 5, we set out early in the morning in the Harwich stage coach. A fat elderly gentlewoman, and a young Dutchman, seemed the most inclined among us to conversation. At the inn where we dined, the gentle-woman said that she had done her best to educate her children; and, particularly, that she had never suffered them to be a moment idle. JOHNSON. 'I wish, Madam, you would educate me too; for I have been an idle fellow all my life.' 'I am sure, Sir (said she), you have not been idle.' JOHNSON. 'Say, Madam, it is very true; and that gentleman there (pointing to me), has been idle. He was idle at Edinburgh. His father sent him to Glasgow, where he continued to be idle. He then came to London, where he has been very idle; and now he is going to Utrecht, where he will be as idle as ever.' I asked him privately how he could expose me so. JOHNSON. 'Poh, poh! (said he), they knew nothing about you, and will think of it no more.' In the afternoon the gentlewoman talked violently against the Roman Catholics, and of the horrors of the Inquisition. To the utter astonishment of all the passengers but myself, who knew that he could talk upon any side of a question, he defended the Inquisition, and maintained, that 'false doctrine should be checked on its first appearance; that the civil power should unite with the church in punishing those who dared to attack the established religion, and that such only were punished by the Inquisition.' He had in his pocket Pomponius Mela *de situ Orbis* in which he read occasionally, and seemed very intent upon ancient geography. Though by no means niggardly, his attention to what was gener-ally right was so minute, that having observed at one of the stages that I ostentatiously gave a shilling to the coachman, when the custom was for each passenger to give only sixpence, he took me aside and scolded me, saying that what I had done would make the coachman dissatisfied with all the rest of the passengers, who gave him no more than his due. This was a just reprimand; for in whatever way a man may indulge his generosity or his vanity in spending his money, for the sake of others he ought not to raise the price of any article for which there is a constant demand.

He talked of Mr Blacklock's poetry, so far as it was descriptive of visible objects; and observed, that 'as its author had the misfortune to be blind, we may be absolutely sure that such passages are combinations of what he has remembered of the works of other writers who could see. That foolish fellow Spence has laboured to explain philosophically how Blacklock may have done, by means of his own faculties, what it is impossible he should do. The solution, as I have given it, is plain. Suppose, I know a man to be so lame that he is absolutely incapable to move himself, and I find him in a different room from that in which I left him; shall I puzzle myself with idle conjectures, that, perhaps, his nerves have by some unknown change all at once become effective? No, Sir; it is clear how he got into a different room. He was *carried*.'

Having stopped a night at Colchester, Johnson talked of that town with veneration, for having stood a siege for Charles the First. The Dutchman alone now remained with us. He spoke English tolerably well; and thinking to recommend himself to us by expatiating on the superiority of the criminal jurisprudence of this country over that of Holland, he inveighed against the barbarity of putting an accused person to the torture, in order to force a confession. But Johnson was as ready for this, as for the Inquisition. 'Why, sir, you do not, I find, understand the law of your own country. The torture in Holland is considered as a favour to an accused person; for no man is put to the torture there, unless there is as much evidence against him as would amount to conviction in England. An accused person among you, therefore, has one chance more to escape punishment, than those who are tried among us.'

At supper this night he talked of good eating with uncommon satisfaction. 'Some people (said he), have a foolish way of not minding, or pretending not to mind, what they eat. For my part, I mind my belly very studiously, and very carefully; for I look upon it, that he who does not mind his belly will hardly mind any thing else.' He now appeared to me *Jean Bull philosophe*, and he was, for the moment, not only serious but vehement. Yet I have heard him, upon other occasions, talk with great contempt of people who were anxious to gratify their palates; and the 206th number of his *Rambler* is a masterly essay against gulosity. His practice, indeed, I must acknowledge, may be considered as casting the balance of his different opinions upon this subject; for I never knew any man who relished good eating more than he did. When at table, he was totally absorbed in the business of the moment; his looks seemed riveted to his plate; nor would he, unless when in very high company, say one word, or even pay the least attention to what was said by others, till he had satisfied his appetite, which was so fierce, and indulged with such intenseness, that while in the act of eating, the veins of his forehead swelled, and generally a strong perspiration was visible. To those whose sensations were delicate, this could not but be disgusting; and it was doubtless not very suitable to the character of a philosopher, who should be distinguished by self-command. But it must be owned, that Johnson, though he could be rigidly *abstemious*, was not a *temperate* man either in eating or drinking. He could refrain, but he could not use moderately. He told me, that he had fasted two days without inconvenience, and that he had never been hungry but once. They who beheld with wonder how much he eat upon all occasions when his dinner was to his taste, could not easily conceive what he must have meant by hunger; and not only was he remarkable for the extraordinary quantity which he eat, but he was, or affected to be, a man of very nice discernment in the science of cookery. He used to descant critically on the dishes which had been at table where he had dined or supped, and to recollect very minutely what he had liked. I remember, when he was in Scotland, his praising 'Gordon's palates', (a dish of palates at the Honourable Alexander Gordon's), with a warmth of expression which might have done honour to more important subjects. 'As for ——'s imitation of a *made dish* it was a wretched attempt.' He about the same time was so much displeased with the performances of a nobleman's French cook, that he exclaimed with vehemence, 'I'd throw such a rascal into the river'; and he then proceeded to alarm a lady at whose house he was to sup, by the following manifesto of his skill: 'I, Madam, who live at a variety of good tables, am a much better judge of cookery, than any person who has a very tolerable cook, but lives much at home; for his palate is gradually adapted to the taste of his cook; whereas, Madam, in trying by a wider range, I can more exquisitely judge.' When invited to dine, even with an intimate friend, he was not pleased if something better than a plain dinner was not prepared for him. I have heard him say on such an occasion, 'This was a good dinner enough, to be sure; but it was not a dinner to *ask* a man to.' On the other hand, he was wont to express, with great glee, his satisfaction when he had been entertained quite to his mind. One day when he had dined with his neighbour and landlord in Bolt-court, Mr Allen, the printer, whose old housekeeper had studied his taste in every thing, he pronounced this eulogy, 'Sir, we could not have had a better dinner had there been a *Synod of Cooks.*'

While we were left by ourselves, after the Dutchman had gone to bed, Dr Johnson talked of that studied behaviour which many have recommended and practised. He disapproved of it; and said, 'I never considered whether I should be a grave man, or a merry man, but just let inclination, for the time, have its course.'

He flattered me with some hopes that he would, in the course of the following summer, come over to Holland, and accompany me in a tour through the Netherlands.

I teased him with fanciful apprehensions of unhappiness. A moth having fluttered round the candle, and burnt itself, he laid hold of this little incident to admonish me; saying, with a sly look, and in a solemn but quiet tone, 'That creature was its own tormentor, and I believe its name was BOSWELL.'

Next day we got to Harwich to dinner; and my passage in the packet-boat to Helvoetsluys being secured, and my baggage put on board, we dined at our inn by ourselves. I happened to say it would be terrible if he should not find a speedy opportunity of returning to London, and be confined to so dull a place. JOHNSON. 'Don't, Sir, accustom yourself to use big words for little matters. It would *not* be *terrible*, though I *were* to be detained some time here.' The practice of using words of disproportionate magnitude, is, no doubt, too frequent every where; but, I think, most remarkable among the French, of which, all who have travelled in France must have been struck with innumerable instances.

We went and looked at the church, and having gone into it and walked up to the altar, Johnson, whose piety was constant and fervent, sent me to my knees, saying, 'Now that you are going to leave your native country, recommend yourself to the protection of your Creator and Redeemer.'

After we came out of the church, we stood talking for some time together of Bishop Berkeley's ingenious sophistry to prove the non-existence of matter, and that every thing in the universe is merely ideal. I observed, that though we are satisfied his doctrine is not true, it is impossible to refute it. I never shall forget the alacrity with which Johnson answered, striking his foot with mighty force against a large stone, till he rebounded from it, 'I refute it *thus*.' This was a stout exemplification of the *first truths* of Père Bouffier, or the *original principles* of Reid and of Beattie; without admitting which, we can no more argue in metaphysics, than we can argue in mathematics without axioms. To me it is not conceivable how Berkeley can be answered by pure reasoning. But I know that the nice and difficult task was to have been undertaken by one of the most luminous minds of the present age; had not politics 'turned him from calm philosophy aside.' What an admirable display of subtlety, united with brilliance, might his contending with Berkeley have afforded us! How must we, when we reflect on the loss of such an intellectual feast, regret that he should be characterised as the man,

> Who born for the universe narrowed his mind,
> And to party gave up what was meant for mankind?

My revered friend walked down with me to the beach, where we embraced and parted with tenderness, and engaged to correspond by letters. I said, 'I hope, Sir, you will not forget me in my absence.' JOHNSON. 'Nay, Sir, it is more likely you should forget me, than that I should forget you.' As the vessel put out to sea, I kept my eyes upon him for a considerable time, while he remained rolling his majestic frame in his usual manner; at last I perceived him walk back into the town, and he disappeared.

Utrecht seeming at first very dull to me, after the animated scenes of London, my spirits were grievously affected; and I wrote to Johnson a plaintive and desponding letter, to which he paid no regard. Afterwards, when I had acquired a firmer tone of mind, I wrote him a second letter, expressing much anxiety to hear from him. At length I received the following epistle, which was of important service to me, and, I trust, will be so also to many others.

A Mr Mr BOSWELL, à la Cour de l'Empereur, Utrecht.

DEAR SIR – You are not to think yourself forgotten, or criminally neglected, that you have had yet no letter from me. I love to see my friends, to hear from them, to talk to them, and to talk of them; but it is not without a considerable effort of resolution that I prevail upon myself to write. I would not, however, gratify my own indolence by the omission of any important duty, or any office of real kindness.

To tell you that I am or am not well, that I have or have not been in the country, that I drank your health in the room in which we sat last together, and that your acquaintance continue to speak of you with their former kindness, topics with which those letters are commonly filled which are written only for the sake of writing, I seldom shall think worth communicating; but if I can have it in my power to calm any harassing disquiet, to excite any virtuous desire, to rectify any important opinion, or fortify any generous resolution, you need not doubt but I shall at least wish to prefer the pleasure of gratifying a friend much less esteemed than yourself, before the gloomy calm of idle vacancy. Whether I shall easily arrive at an exact punctuality of correspondence, I cannot tell. I shall, at present, expect that you will receive this in return for two which I have had from you. The first, indeed, gave me an account so hopeless of the state of your mind, that it hardly admitted or deserved an answer; by the second I was much better pleased: and the pleasure will still be increased by such a narrative of the progress of your studies, as may evince the continuance of an equal and rational application of your mind to some useful enquiry.

You will, perhaps, wish to ask what study I would recommend. I shall not speak of theology, because it ought not to be considered as a question whether you shall endeavour to know the will of GOD.

I shall, therefore, consider only such studies as we are at liberty to pursue or to neglect; and of these I know not how you will make a better choice than by studying the civil law, as your father advises, and the ancient languages, as you had determined for yourself; at least resolve, while you remain in any settled residence, to spend a certain number of hours every day amongst your books. The dissipation of thought, of which you complain, is nothing more than the vacillation of a mind suspended between different motives, and changing its direction as any motive gains or loses strength. If you can but kindle in your mind any strong desire, if you can but keep predominant any wish for some particular excellence or attainment, the gusts of imagination will break away, without any effect upon your conduct, and commonly without any traces left upon the memory.

There lurks, perhaps, in every human heart a desire of distinction, which inclines every man first to hope, and then to believe, that Nature has given him something peculiar to himself. This vanity makes one mind nurse aversions, and another actuate desires, till they rise by art much above their original state of power, and as affectation, in time, improves to habit, they at last tyrannise over him who at first encouraged them only for show. Every desire is a viper in the bosom, who, while he was chill, was harmless; but when warmth gave him strength, exerted it in poison. You know a gentleman, who, when first he set his foot in the gay world, as he prepared himself to whirl in the vortex of pleasure, imagined a total indifference and universal negligence to be the most agreeable concomitants of youth, and the strongest indication of an airy temper and a quick apprehension. Vacant to every object, and sensible of every impulse, he thought that all appearance of diligence would deduct something from the reputation of genius; and hoped that he should appear to attain, amidst all the ease of carelessness and all the tumult of diversion, that knowledge and those accomplishments which mortals of the common fabric obtain only by mute abstraction and solitary drudgery. He tried this scheme of life awhile, was made weary of it by his sense and his virtue, he then wished to return to his studies; and finding long habits of idleness and pleasure harder to be cured than he expected, still willing to retain his claim to some extraordinary prerogatives, resolved the common consequences of irregularity into an unalterable decree of destiny, and concluded that Nature had originally formed him incapable of rational employment.

Let all such fancies, illusive and destructive, be banished henceforward from your thoughts for ever. Resolve, and keep your resolution; choose and pursue your choice. If you spend this day in study, you will find yourself still more able to study to-morrow; not that you are to expect that you shall at once obtain a complete victory. Depravity is not very easily overcome. Resolution will sometimes relax, and diligence will sometimes be interrupted; but let no accidental surprise or deviation, whether short or long, dispose you to despondency. Consider these failings as incident to all mankind. Begin again where you left off, and endeavour to avoid the seducements that prevailed over you before.

This, my dear Boswell, is advice which, perhaps, has been often given you, and given you without effect. But this advice, if you will not take from others, you must take from your own reflections, if you purpose to do the duties of the station to which the bounty of Providence has called you.

Let me have a long letter from you as soon as you can. I hope you continue your journal, and enrich it with many observations upon the country in which you reside. It will be a favour if you can get me any books in the Frisick language, and can enquire how the poor are maintained in the Seven Provinces. I am, dear Sir,

Your most affectionate servant,

SAM. JOHNSON.

London, Dec. 8, 1763.

I am sorry to observe, that neither in my own minutes, nor in my letters to Johnson which have been preserved by him, can I find any information how the poor are maintained in the Seven Provinces. But I shall extract from one of my letters what I learnt concerning the other subject of his curiosity.

I have made all possible enquiry with respect to the Frisick language, and find that it has been less cultivated than any other of the northern dialects; a certain proof of which is their deficiency of books. Of the old Frisick there are no remains, except some ancient laws preserved by *Schotanus* in his *Beschryvinge van die Heerlykheid van Friesland*; and his *Historia Frisica*. I have not yet been able to find these books. Professor Trotz, who formerly was of the University of Vranyken, in Friesland, and is at present preparing an edition of all the Frisick laws, gave me this information. Of the modern Frisick, or what is spoken by the boors at this day, I have procured a specimen. It is *Gisbert Japix's Rymelerie*, which is the only book that they have. It is amazing, that they have no translation of the bible, no treatises of devotion, nor even any of the ballads and story-books which are so agreeable to country people. You shall have *Japix* by the first convenient opportunity. I doubt not to pick up *Schotanus*. Mynheer Trotz has promised me his assistance.

Early in 1764 Johnson paid a visit to the Langton family, at their seat of Langton, in Lincolnshire, where he passed some time, much to his satisfaction. His friend Bennet Langton, it will not be doubted, did every thing in his power to make the place agreeable to so illustrious a guest; and the elder Mr Langton and his lady, being fully capable of understanding his value, were not wanting in attention. He, however, told me, that old Mr Langton, though a man of considerable learning, had so little allowance to make for his occasional 'laxity of talk,' that because in the course of discussion he sometimes mentioned what might be said in favour of the peculiar tenets of the Romish church, he went to his grave believing him to be of that communion.

Johnson, during his stay at Langton, had the advantage of a good library, and saw several gentlemen of the neighbourhood. I have obtained from Mr Langton the following particulars of this period.

He was now fully convinced that he could not have been satisfied with a country living; for, talking of a respectable clergyman in Lincolnshire, he observed, 'This man, Sir, fills up the duties of his life well. I approve of him, but could not imitate him.'

To a lady who endeavoured to vindicate herself from blame for neglecting social attention to worthy neighbours, by saying, 'I would go to them if it would do them any good'; he said, 'What good, Madam, do you expect to have in your power to do them? It is showing them respect, and that is doing them good.'

So socially accommodating was he, that once when Mr Langton and he were driving together in a coach, and Mr Langton complained of being sick, he insisted that they should go out, and sit on the back of it in the open air, which they did. And being sensible how strange the appearance must be, observed, that a countryman whom they saw in a field would probably be thinking, 'If these two madmen should come down, what would become of me?'

Soon after his return to London, which was in February, was founded that club which existed long without a name, but at Mr Garrick's funeral became distinguished by the title of THE LITERARY CLUB. Sir Joshua Reynolds had the merit of being the first proposer of it, to which Johnson acceded, and the original members were, Sir Joshua Reynolds, Dr Johnson, Mr Edmund Burke, Dr Nugent, Mr Beauclerk, Mr Langton, Dr Goldsmith, Mr Chamier, and Sir John Hawkins. They met at the Turk's Head, In Gerard-street, Soho, one evening in every week, at seven, and generally continued their conversation till a pretty late hour. This club has been gradually increased, and instead of assembling in the evening, they now dine together at a tavern in Dover-street once a fortnight, during the meeting of Parliament. Between the time of its formation, and the time at which this work is passing through the press (1790), the following persons, now dead, were members of it: Mr Dunning (afterwards Lord Ashburton), Mr Dyer, Mr Garrick, Dr Shipley, Bishop of St Asaph, Mr Vesey, and Mr Thomas Warton. The present members are, Sir Joshua Reynolds, Mr Burke, Mr Langton, Dr Percy Bishop of Dromore, Dr Barnard Bishop of Killaloe, Dr Marlay Bishop of Clonfert, Mr Fox, Dr George Fordyce, Sir William Scott, Sir Joseph Banks, Sir Charles Bunbury, Mr Windham of Norfolk, Mr Sheridan, Mr Gibbon, Dr Adam Smith, Lord Charlemont, Sir Robert Chambers, Sir William Jones, Mr Colman, Mr Steevens, Dr Burney, Dr Joseph Warton, Mr Malone, Lord Ossory, Lord Spencer, Lord Lucan, Lord Palmerston, Lord Elliot, Lord Macartney, Mr Richard Burke, junior, Sir William Hamilton, Dr Warren, Mr Courtenay, and the writer of this account.

Sir John Hawkins[1] represents himself as a '*seceder*' from this society, and assigns as the reason of his '*withdrawing*' himself from it, that its late hours were

1 *Life of Johnson*, p. 425.

inconsistent with his domestic arrangements. In this he is not accurate; for the fact was, that he one evening attacked Mr Burke in so rude a manner, that all the company testified their displeasure; and at their next meeting his reception was such, that he never came again.[1]

He is equally inaccurate with respect to Mr Garrick, of whom he says, 'he trusted that the least intimation of a desire to come among us, would procure him a ready admission; but in this he was mistaken. Johnson consulted me upon it; and when I could find no objection to receiving him, exclaimed, "He will disturb us by his buffoonery"; – and afterwards so managed matters, that he was never formally proposed, and, by consequence, never admitted.'[2]

In justice both to Mr Garrick and Dr Johnson, I think it necessary to rectify this mis-statement The truth is, that not very long after the institution of our club, Sir Joshua Reynolds was speaking of it to Garrick. 'I like it much (said he), I think I shall be of you.' When Sir Joshua mentioned this to Dr Johnson, he was much displeased with the actor's conceit. '*He'll be of us* (said Johnson), how does he know we will *permit* him? The first duke in England has no right to hold such language.' However, when Garrick was regularly proposed some time afterwards, Johnson, though he had taken a momentary offence at his arrogance, warmly and kindly supported him, and he was accordingly elected, was a most agreeable member, and continued to attend our meetings to the time of his death.

Mrs Piozzi[3] has also given a similar misrepresentation of Johnson's treatment of Garrick in this particular, as if he had used these contemptuous expressions: 'If Garrick *does* apply, I'll blackball him. – Surely, one ought to sit in a society like ours,

> Unelbow'd by a gamester, pimp, or player.'

I am happy to be enabled by such unquestionable authority as that of Sir Joshua Reynolds, as well as from my own knowledge, to vindicate at once the heart of Johnson and the social merit of Garrick.

In this year, except what he may have done in revising Shakspeare, we do not find that he laboured much in literature. He wrote a review of Grainger's 'Sugar Cane, a Poem,' in the *London Chronicle*. He told me, that Dr Percy wrote the greatest part of this review; but, I imagine, he did not recollect it distinctly, for it appears to be mostly, if not altogether, his own. He also wrote in the *Critical Review*, an account[†] of Goldsmith's excellent poem, 'The Traveller'.

The ease and independence to which he had at last attained by royal munificence, increased his natural indolence. In his *Meditations* he thus accuses himself: 'GOOD FRIDAY, April 20, 1764. I have made no reformation; I have lived totally useless, more sensual in thought, and more addicted to wine and

---

1 From Sir Joshua Reynolds.
2 *Life of Johnson*, p. 425.
3 *Letters to and from Dr Johnson*, Vol. II, p. 278.

meat.'[1] And next morning he thus feelingly complains: 'My indolence, since my last reception of the sacrament, has sunk into grosser sluggishness, and my dissipation spread into wilder negligence. My thoughts have been clouded with sensuality; and, except that from the beginning of this year I have, in some measure, forborne excess of strong drink, my appetites have predominated over my reason. A kind of strange oblivion has overspread me, so that I know not what has become of the last year; and perceive that incidents and intelligence pass over me, without leaving any impression. He then solemnly says, 'This is not the life to which heaven is promised';[2] and he earnestly resolves on amendment.

It was his custom to observe certain days with a pious abstraction; viz. New-year's-day, the day of his wife's death, Good Friday, Easter-day, and his own birthday. He this year says, 'I have now spent fifty-five years in resolving; having, from the earliest time almost that I can remember, been forming schemes of a better life. I have done nothing. The need of doing, therefore, is pressing, since the time of doing is short. O GOD, grant me to resolve aright, and to keep my resolutions, for JESUS CHRIST's sake. Amen.'[3] Such a tenderness of conscience, such a fervent desire of improvement, will rarely be found. It is, surely, not decent in those who are hardened in indifference to spiritual improvement, to treat this pious anxiety of Johnson with contempt.

About this time he was afflicted with a very severe return of the hypochondriac disorder, which was ever lurking about him. He was so ill, as, notwithstanding his remarkable love of company, to be entirely averse to society, the most fatal symptom of that malady. Dr Adams told me, that, as an old friend, he was admitted to visit him, and that he found him in a deplorable state, sighing, groaning, talking to himself, and restlessly walking from room to room. He then used this emphatical expression of the misery which he felt: 'I would consent to have a limb amputated to recover my spirits.'

Talking to himself was, indeed, one of his singularities ever since I knew him. I was certain that he was frequently uttering pious ejaculations, for fragments of the Lord's Prayer have been distinctly overheard. His friend Mr Thomas Davies, of whom Churchill says,

'That Davies hath a very pretty wife',

when Dr Johnson muttered 'lead us not into temptation', used with waggish and gallant humour to whisper Mrs Davies, 'You, my dear, are the cause of this.'

He had another particularity, of which none of his friends ever ventured to ask an explanation. It appeared to me some superstitious habit, which he had contracted early, and from which he had never called upon his reason to disentangle him. This was his anxious care to go out or in at a door or passage,

---

1 *Prayers and Meditations*, p. 50.
2 Ibid. p. 51.
3 Ibid. p. 58.

by a certain number of steps from a certain point, or at least so as that either his right or left foot (I am not certain which), should constantly make the first actual movement when he came close to the door or passage. Thus I conjecture: for I have, upon innumerable occasions, observed him suddenly stop, and then seem to count his steps with a deep earnestness; and when he had neglected or gone wrong in this sort of magical movement, I have seen him go back again, put himself in a proper posture to begin the ceremony, and, having gone through it, break from his abstraction, walk briskly on, and join his companion. A strange instance of something of this nature, even when on horseback, happened when he was in the isle of Sky.[1] Sir Joshua Reynolds has observed him to go a good way about, rather than cross a particular alley in Leicester-fields; but this Sir Joshua imputed to his having had some disagreeable recollection associated with it.

That the most minute singularities which belonged to him, and made very observable parts of his appearance and manner, may not be omitted, it is requisite to mention, that while talking or even musing as he sat in his chair, he commonly shook his head in a tremulous manner, moving his body backwards and forwards, and rubbing his left knee in the same direction, with the palm of his hand. In the intervals of articulating he made various sounds with his mouth, sometimes as if ruminating, or what is called chewing the cud, sometimes giving a half whistle, sometimes making his tongue play backwards from the roof of his mouth, as if clucking like a hen, and sometimes protruding it against his upper gums in front, as if pronouncing quickly under his breath, *too, too, too*: all this accompanied sometimes with a thoughtful look but more frequently with a smile.[a]

I am fully aware how very obvious an occasion I here give for the sneering jocularity of such as have no relish of an exact likeness; which, to render complete, he who draws it must not disdain the slightest strokes. But if witlings should be inclined to attack this account, let them have the candour to quote what I have offered in my defence.

He was for some time in the summer at Easton Maudit, Northamptonshire, on a visit to the Reverend Dr Percy, now Bishop of Dromore. Whatever dissatisfaction he felt at what he considered as a slow progress in intellectual improvement, we find that his heart was tender, and his affections warm, as appears from the following very kind letter:

1 *Journal of a Tour to the Hebrides*, 3d edit. p. 316.

a Add: Generally when he had concluded a period, in the course of a dispute, by which time he was a good deal exhausted by violence and vociferation, he used to blow out his breath like a whale. This I suppose was a relief to his lungs; and seemed in him to be a contemptuous mode of expression, as if he had made the arguments of his opponent fly like chaff before the wind.

To JOSHUA REYNOLDS, Esq. in Leicester-Fields, London.

DEAR SIR — I did not hear of your sickness till I heard likewise of your recovery, and therefore escaped that part of your pain, which every man must feel, to whom you are known as you are known to me.

Having had no particular account of your disorder, I know not in what state it has left you. If the amusement of my company can exhilarate the languor of a slow recovery, I will not delay a day to come to you; for I know not how I can so effectually promote my own pleasure as by pleasing you, or my own interest as by preserving you, in whom, if I should lose you, I should lose almost the only man whom I call a friend.

Pray let me hear of you from yourself, or from dear Miss Reynolds.[a] Make my compliments to Mr Mudge. I am, dear Sir,
Your most affectionate
And most humble servant,

SAM. JOHNSON.

At the Revd Mr Percy's, at Easton Maudit,
Northamptonshire (by Castle Ashby),
Aug. 19, 1764.

Early in the year 1765 he paid a short visit to the University of Cambridge, with his friend Mr Beauclerk. There is a lively picturesque account of his behaviour on this visit, in the *Gentleman's Magazine* for March 1785, being an extract of a letter from the late Dr John Sharp. The two following sentences are very characteristical: 'He drank his large potations of tea with me, interrupted by many an indignant contradiction, and many a noble sentiment.' — 'Several persons got into his company the last evening at Trinity, where, about twelve, he began to be very great; stripped poor Mrs Macaulay to the very skin, then gave her for his toast, and drank her in two bumpers.'

The strictness of his self-examination and scrupulous Christian humility, appear in his pious meditation on Easter-day this year. — 'I purpose again to partake of the blessed sacrament; yet when I consider how vainly I have hitherto resolved at this annual commemoration of my Saviour's death, to regulate my life by his laws, I am almost afraid to renew my resolutions.'[1b]

No man was more gratefully sensible of any kindness done to him than Johnson. There is a little circumstance in his diary this year, which shows him in a very amiable light.

---

[a] Add the following note: Sir Joshua's sister, for whom Johnson had a particular affection, and to whom he wrote many letters which I have seen, and which I am sorry her too nice delicacy will not permit to be published.

[1] *Prayers and Meditations*, p. 61.

[b] Add: The concluding words are very remarkable, and show that he laboured under a severe depression of spirits. 'Since the last Easter I have reformed no evil habit; my time has been unprofitably spent, and seems as a dream that has left nothing behind. *My memory grows confused, and I know not how the days pass over me.* Good Lord, deliver me!'

'July 2. I paid Mr Simpson[1] ten guineas, which he had formerly lent me in my necessity, and for which Tetty expressed her gratitude.'

'July 8. I lent Mr Simpson ten guineas more.'

Here he had a pleasing opportunity of doing the same kindness to an old friend, which he had formerly received from him. Indeed his liberality as to money was very remarkable. The next article in his diary is, 'July 16, I received seventy-five pounds. Lent Mr Davies twenty-five.'

He appears this year to have been seized with a temporary fit of ambition, for he had thoughts both of studying law and of engaging in politics. His 'Prayer before the Study of LAW' is truly admirable:

Sept. 26, 1765.

Almighty GOD, the giver of wisdom, without whose help resolutions are vain, without whose blessing study is ineffectual; enable me, if it be thy will, to attain such knowledge as may qualify me to direct the doubtful, and instruct the ignorant; to prevent wrongs and terminate contentions; and grant that I may use that knowledge which I shall attain, to thy glory and my own salvation, for JESUS CHRIST's sake. Amen.[2]

His prayer in the view of becoming a politician is entitled, 'Engaging in POLITICS with H——n,' no doubt his friend, the Right Honourable William Gerard Hamilton, for whom, during a long acquaintance, he had a great esteem, and to whose conversation he once paid this high compliment: 'I am very unwilling to be left alone, Sir, and therefore I go with my company down the first pair of stairs, in some hopes that they may, perhaps, return again. I go with you, Sir, as far as the street-door.' In what particular department he intended to engage does not appear, nor can Mr Hamilton explain. His prayer is in general terms. 'Enlighten my understanding with knowledge of right, and govern my will by thy laws, that no deceit may mislead me, nor temptation corrupt me; that I may always endeavour to do good, and hinder evil.'[3] There is nothing upon the subject in his diary.

This year was distinguished by his being introduced into the family of Mr Thrale, one of the most eminent brewers in England, and Member of Parliament for the borough of Southwark. Foreigners are not a little amazed when they hear of brewers, distillers, and men in similar departments of trade, held forth as persons of considerable consequence. In this great commercial country it is natural that a situation which produces much wealth should be considered as very respectable; and, no doubt, honest industry is entitled to esteem. But, perhaps, the too rapid advance of men of low extraction tends to

1 Joseph Simpson, Esq. mentioned in p. 176. He wrote a tragedy entitled *The Patriot*; in which Dr Johnson having made some corrections, advantage was taken of this circumstance after his death, and the piece falsely published under his name.

2 *Prayers and Meditations*, p. 66.

3 *Prayers and Meditations*, p. 67.

lessen the value of that distinction by birth and gentility, which has ever been found beneficial to the grand scheme of subordination. Johnson used to give this account of the rise of Mr Thrale's father: 'He worked at six shillings a week for twenty years in the great brewery, which afterwards was his own. The proprietor of it had an only daughter, who was married to a nobleman. It was not fit that a peer should continue the business. On the old man's death, therefore, the brewery was to be sold. To find a purchaser for so large a property was a difficult matter; and, after some time, it was suggested, that it would be advisable to treat with Thrale, a sensible, active, honest man, who had been long employed in the house, and to transfer the whole to him for thirty[a] thousand pounds, security being taken upon the property. This was accordingly settled. In eleven years Thrale paid the purchase-money. He acquired a large fortune, and lived to be Member of Parliament for South-wark. But what was most remarkable was the liberality with which he used his riches. He gave his son and daughters the best education. The esteem which his good conduct procured him from the nobleman who had married his master's daughter, made him be treated with much attention; and his son, both at school and at the University of Oxford, associated with young men of the first rank. His allowance from his father, after he left college, was splendid; no less than a thousand a year. This, in a man who had risen as old Thrale did, was a very extraordinary instance of generosity. He used to say, "If this young dog does not find so much after I am gone as he expects, let him remember that he has had a great deal in my own time." '

The son, though in affluent circumstances, had good sense enough to carry on his father's trade, which was of such extent, that I remember he once told me, he would not quit it for an annuity of ten thousand a year; 'Not (said he), that I get ten thousand a year by it, but it is an estate to a family.' Having left daughters only, the property was sold for the immense sum of one hundred and thirty thousand pounds; a magnificent proof of what may be done by fair trade in no long period of time.

There may be some who think that a new system of gentility[b] might be established, upon principles totally different from what have hitherto pre-vailed. Our present heraldry, it may be said, is suited to the barbarous times in which it had its origin. It is chiefly founded upon ferocious merit, upon military excellence. Why, in civilised times, we may be asked, should there

[a] After 'thirty' read 'five'.

[b] Add the following note: Mrs Burney informs me that she heard Dr Johnson say, 'An English Merchant is a new species of Gentleman.' He, perhaps, had in his mind the following ingenious passage in *The Conscious Lovers*,' Act iv, Scene ii, where Mr Sealand thus addresses Sir John Bevil: 'Give me leave to say, that we merchants are a species of gentry that have grown into the world this last century, and are as honourable, and almost as useful as you landed-folks, that have always thought yourselves so much above us; for your trading forsooth is extended no farther than a load of hay, or a fat ox. – You are pleasant people indeed! Because you are generally bred up to be lazy, therefore, I warrant you, industry is dishonourable.'

not be rank and honours, upon principles, which, independent of long custom, are certainly not less worthy, and which, when once allowed to be connected with elevation and precedency, would obtain the same dignity in our imagination? Why should not the knowledge, the skill, the expertness, the assiduity, and the spirited hazards of trade and commerce, when crowned with success, be entitled to give those flattering distinctions by which mankind are so universally captivated?

Such are the specious, but false arguments for a proposition which always will find numerous advocates, in a nation where men are every day starting up from obscurity to wealth. To refute them is needless. The general sense of mankind cries out, with irresistible force, '*Un gentilhomme est toujours gentilhomme.*'

Mr Thrale had married Miss Hesther Lynch Salusbury, of good Welch extraction, a lady of lively talents, improved by education. That Johnson's introduction into Mr Thrale's family, which contributed so much to the happiness of his life, was owing to her desire for his conversation, is the most probable and general supposition. But it is not the truth. Mr Murphy, who was intimate with Mr Thrale, having spoken very highly of Dr Johnson, he was requested to make them acquainted. This being mentioned to Johnson, he accepted of an invitation to dinner at Thrale's, and was so much pleased with his reception, both by Mr and Mrs Thrale, and they so much pleased with him, that his invitations to their house were more and more frequent, till at last he became one of the family, and an apartment was appropriated to him, both in their house in Southwark, and in their villa at Streatham.

Johnson had a very sincere esteem for Mr Thrale as a man of excellent principles, a good scholar, well skilled in trade, of a sound understanding, and of manners such as presented the character of a plain independent English 'Squire. As this family will frequently be mentioned in the course of the following pages, and as a false notion has prevailed that Mr Thrale was inferior, and in some degree insignificant, compared with Mrs Thrale, it may be proper to give a true state of the case from the authority of Johnson himself, in his own words.

'I know no man (said he), who is more master of his wife and family than Thrale. If he but holds up his finger, he is obeyed. It is a great mistake to suppose that she is above him in literary attainments. She is more flippant; but he has ten times her learning: he is a regular scholar; but her learning is that of a school-boy in one of the lower forms.' My readers may naturally wish for some representation of the figures of this couple. Mr Thrale was tall, well proportioned, and stately. As for *Madam*, or *my Mistress*, by which epithets Johnson used to mention Mrs Thrale, she was short, plump, and brisk. She has herself given us a lively view of the idea which Johnson had of her person, on her appearing before him in a dark-coloured gown: 'You little creatures should never wear those sort of clothes, however; they are unsuitable in every way. What! have not all insects gay colours?'[1] Mr Thrale gave his wife a liberal indulgence, both in the choice of their company, and in the mode of entertaining them. He understood and valued Johnson, without remission,

1 Mrs Piozzi's *Anecdotes*, p. 279.

from their first acquaintance to the day of his death. Mrs Thrale was enchanted with Johnson's conversation for its own sake, and had also a very allowable vanity in appearing to be honoured with the attention of so celebrated a man.

Nothing could be more fortunate for Johnson than this connection. He had at Mr Thrale's all the comforts and even luxuries of life; his melancholy was diverted, and his irregular habits lessened by association with an agreeable and well-ordered family. He was treated with the utmost respect, and even affection. The vivacity of Mrs Thrale's literary talk roused him to cheerfulness and exertion, even when they were alone. But this was not often the case; for he found here a constant succession of what gave him the highest enjoyment, the society of the learned, the witty, and the eminent in every way, who were assembled in numerous companies, called forth his wonderful powers, and gratified him with admiration, to which no man could be insensible.

In the October of this year he at length gave to the world his edition of Shakspeare, which, if it had no other merit but that of producing his Preface, in which the excellencies and defects of that immortal bard are displayed with a masterly hand, the nation would have had no reason to complain. A blind indiscriminate admiration of Shakspeare had exposed the British nation to the ridicule of foreigners. Johnson, by candidly admitting the faults of his poet, had the more credit in bestowing on him deserved and indisputable praise, and doubtless none of all his panegyrists have done him half so much honour. Their praise was, like that of a counsel, upon his own side of the cause: Johnson's was like the grave, well considered, and impartial opinion of the judge, which falls from his lips with weight, and is received with reverence. What he did as a commentator has no small share of merit, though his researches were not so ample, and his investigations so acute as they might have been, which we now certainly know from the labours of other able and ingenious critics who have followed him. He has enriched his edition with a concise account of each play, and of its characteristic excellence. Many of his notes have illustrated obscurities in the text, and placed passages eminent for beauty in a more conspicuous light; and he has, in general, exhibited such a mode of annotation, as may be beneficial to all subsequent editors.

His Shakspeare was virulently attacked by Mr William Kenrick, who obtained the degree of LL.D. from a Scotch University, and wrote for the booksellers in a great variety of branches. Though he certainly was not without considerable merit, he wrote with so little regard to principle and decorum, and in so hasty a manner, that his reputation was neither extensive nor lasting. I remember one evening, when some of his works were mentioned, Dr Goldsmith said, he had never heard of them; upon which Dr Johnson observed, 'Sir, he is one of the many who have made themselves *public*, without making themselves *known*.'

A young student of Oxford, of the name of Barclay, wrote an answer to Kenrick's review of Johnson's Shakspeare. Johnson was at first angry that Kenrick's attack should have the credit of an answer. But afterwards, considering the young man's good intention, he kindly noticed him, and probably would have done more, had not the young man died.

In his Preface to Shakspeare, Johnson treated Voltaire very contemptuously, observing, upon some of his remarks, 'These are the petty criticisms of petty wits.' Voltaire, in revenge, made an attack upon Johnson, in one of his numerous literary sallies, which I remember to have read; but there being no general index to his voluminous works, have searched for it in vain, and therefore cannot quote it.

Voltaire was an antagonist with whom I thought Johnson should not disdain to contend. I pressed him to answer. He said, he perhaps might: but he never did.

Mr Burney having occasion to write to Johnson for some receipts for subscriptions to his Shakspeare, which Johnson had omitted to deliver, when the money was paid, he availed himself of that opportunity of thanking Johnson for the great pleasure which he had received from the perusal of his Preface to Shakspeare; which although it excited much clamour against him at first, is now justly ranked among the most excellent of his writings. To this letter Johnson returned the following answer:

To CHARLES BURNEY, Esq. in Poland-street.

SIR — I am sorry that your kindness to me has brought upon you so much trouble, though you have taken care to abate that sorrow, by the pleasure which I receive from your approbation. I defend my criticism in the same manner with you. We must confess the faults of our favourite, to gain credit to our praise of his excellencies. He that claims, either in himself or for another, the honours of perfection, will surely injure the reputation which he designs to assist.

Be pleased to make my compliments to your family. I am, Sir,
Your most obliged
And most humble servant,

SAM. JOHNSON.[a]

Trinity College, Dublin, at this time surprised Johnson with a spontaneous compliment of the highest academical honours, by creating him Doctor of Laws. The diploma, which is in my possession, is as follows:

---

[a] After the letter to Dr Burney read as follows: From one of his Journals I transcribed what follows:
'At church, Oct.—65.
'To avoid all singularity; *Bonaventura*.[1]
'To come in before service, and compose my mind by meditation, or by reading some portions of scripture. *Tetty*.
'If I can hear the sermon, to attend it, unless attention be more troublesome than useful.
'To consider the act of prayer as a reposal of myself upon God, and a resignation of all into his holy hand.'
1 He was probably proposing to himself the model of this excellent person, who for his piety was named *the Seraphic Doctor*.

OMNIBUS *ad quos praesentes literae pervenerint, salutem. Nos Praepositus et Socii seniores Collegii sacrosanctae et individuae Trinitatis Reginae Elizabethae juxta Dublin, testamur, Samueli Johnson, Armigero, ob egregiam scriptorum elegantiam et utilitatem, gratiam concessam fuisse pro gradu Doctoratus in utroque Jure, octavo die Julii, Anno Domini millesimo septingentesimo sexagesimo-quinto. In cujus rei testimonium singularum manus et sigillum quo in hisce utimur apposuimus; vicesimo tertio die Julii, Anno Domini millesimo septingentesimo sexagesimo-quinto.*

GUL. CLEMENT.	FRAN. ANDREWS.	R. MURRAY.
THO. WILSON.	*Praep*[s]	ROB[tus]. LAW.
THO. LELAND.		MICH. KEARNEY

This unsolicited mark of distinction, conferred on so great a literary charac-ter, did much honour to the judgement and liberal spirit of that learned body. Johnson acknowledged the favour in a letter to Dr Leland, one of their number; but I have not been able to obtain a copy of it.

Both in 1764 and 1765 it should seem that he was so busily employed with his edition of Shakspeare, as to have had little leisure for any other literary exertion, or, indeed, even for private correspondence. He did not favour me with a single letter for more than two years, for which it will appear that he afterwards apologised.

He was, however, at all times ready to give assistance to his friends, and others, in revising their works, and in writing for them, or greatly improving their Dedications. In that courtly species of composition no man excelled Dr Johnson. Though the loftiness of his mind prevented him from ever dedicat-ing in his own person, he wrote a very great number of Dedications for others. Some of these, the persons who were favoured with them are unwilling should be mentioned, from a too anxious apprehension, as I think, that they might be suspected of having received larger assistance, and some, after all the diligence I have bestowed, have escaped my inquiries. He told me, a great many years ago, 'he believed he had dedicated to all the Royal Family round'; and it was indifferent to him what was the subject of the work dedicated, provided it were innocent. He once dedicated some Music for the German Flute to Edward Duke of York. In writing Dedications for others, he consid-ered himself as by no means speaking his own sentiments.

Notwithstanding his long silence, I never omitted to write to him when I had any thing worthy of communicating. I generally kept copies of my letters to him, that I might have a full view of our correspondence, and never be at a loss to understand any reference in his letters. He kept the greater part of mine very carefully; and a short time before his death was attentive enough to seal them up in bundles, and order them to be delivered to me, which was accordingly done. Amongst them I found one, of which I had not made a copy, and which I own I read with pleasure at the distance of almost twenty years. It is dated November, 1765, at the palace of Pascal Paoli, in Corte, the capital of Corsica, and is full of generous enthusiasm. After giving a sketch of what I had seen and heard in that island, it proceeded thus: 'I dare to call this a spirited tour. I dare to challenge your approbation.'

This letter produced the following answer, which I found on my arrival at Paris.

A Mr Mr Boswell, *chez* Mr Waters, *Banquier, à Paris.*

Dear Sir, - Apologies are seldom of any use. We will delay till your arrival the reasons, good or bad, which have made me such a sparing and ungrateful correspondent. Be assured, for the present, that nothing has lessened either the esteem or love with which I dismissed you at Harwich. Both have been increased by all that I have been told of you by yourself or others; and when you return, you will return to an unaltered, and, I hope, unalterable friend.

All that you have to fear from me is the vexation of disappointing me. No man loves to frustrate expectations which have been formed in his favour; and the pleasure which I promise myself from your journals and remarks is so great, that perhaps no degree of attention or discernment will be sufficient to afford it.

Come home, however, and take your chance. I long to see you, and to hear you; and hope that we shall not be so long separated again. Come home, and expect such a welcome as is due to him, whom a wise and noble curiosity has led, where perhaps no native of this country ever was before.

I have no news to tell you that can deserve your notice; nor would I willingly lessen the pleasure that any novelty may give you at your return. I am afraid we shall find it difficult to keep among us a mind which has been so long feasted with variety. But let us try what esteem and kindness can effect.

As your father's liberality has indulged you with so long a ramble, I doubt not but you will think his sickness, or even his desire to see you, a sufficient reason for hastening your return. The longer we live, and the more we think, the higher value we learn to put on the friendship and tenderness of parents and of friends. Parents we can have but once; and he promises himself too much, who enters life with the expectation of finding many friends. Upon some motive, I hope, that you will be here soon; and am willing to think that it will be an inducement to your return, that it is sincerely desired by, dear Sir,

Your affectionate humble servant,

SAM. JOHNSON.

Johnson's-court, Fleet-street,
January 14, 1766.

I returned to London in February, and found Dr Johnson in a good house in Johnson's-court, Fleet-street, in which he had accommodated Miss Williams with an apartment on the ground floor, while Mr Levett occupied his post in the garret: his faithful Francis was still attending upon him. He received me with much kindness. The fragments of our first conversation, which I have preserved, are these: I told him that Voltaire, in a conversation with me, had distinguished Pope and Dryden thus:- 'Pope drives a handsome chariot, with a couple of neat trim nags; Dryden a coach, and six stately horses.' JOHNSON. 'Why, Sir, the truth is, they both drive coaches and six; but Dryden's horses are either galloping or stumbling: Pope's go at a steady even trot.'[1] 'He said of Goldsmith's *Traveller*, which had been published in my absence, 'There has not been so fine a poem since Pope's time.'

And here it is proper to settle, with authentic precision, what has long floated in public report, as to Johnson's being himself the author of a considerable part of that poem. Much, no doubt, both of the sentiments and expression, were derived from conversation with him; and it was certainly submitted to his friendly revision: but in the year 1783, he, at my request, marked with a pencil the lines which he had furnished, which are only line 420,

> To stop too fearful, and too faint to go;

and the concluding ten lines, except the last couplet but one, which I distinguish by the Italic character:

> How small of all that human hearts endure,
> That part which kings or laws can cause or cure.
> Still to ourselves in every place consign'd,
> Our own felicity we make or find;
> With secret course, which no loud storms annoy,
> Glides the smooth current of domestic joy.
> *The lifted axe, the agonizing wheel,*
> *Luke's iron crown, and Damien's bed of steel,*
> To men remote from power, but rarely known,
> Leave reason, faith, and conscience, all our own.

He added, 'These are all of which I can be sure.' They bear a small proportion to the whole, which consists of four hundred and thirty-eight verses. Goldsmith, in the couplet which he inserted, mentions *Luke* as a person well known, and superficial readers have passed it over quite smoothly; while those of more attention have been as much perplexed by *Luke*, as by *Lydiat*, in *The Vanity of Human Wishes*. The truth is, that Goldsmith himself was in a mistake. In the *Respublica Hungarica*, there is an account of a desperate rebellion in the year 1514, headed by two brothers, of the name of *Zeck*, George and Luke.

---

1 It is remarkable, that Mr Gray has employed somewhat the same image to characterize Dryden. He, indeed, furnished his car with but two horses; but they are of ethereal race:

> Behold where Dryden's less presumptuous car,
> Wide o'er the fields of glory bear,
> Two coursers of ethereal race,
> With necks in thunder cloath'd, and long-resounding pace.

Ode on the Progress of Poesy.

When it was quelled, *George*, not *Luke*, was punished by his head being encircled with a red hot iron crown: '*corona candescente ferrea coronatur.*' The same severity of torture was exercised on the Earl of Athol, one of the murderers of King James I of Scotland.

Dr Johnson at the same time favoured me by marking the lines which he furnished to Goldsmith's *Deserted Village*, which are only the four last:

> That trade's proud empire hastes to swift decay,
> As ocean sweeps the labour'd mole away:
> While self-dependent power can time defy,
> As rocks resist the billows and the sky.

Talking of education, 'People have now a-days (said he), got a strange opinion that everything should be taught by lectures. Now, I cannot see that lectures can do so much good as reading the books from which the lectures are taken. I know nothing that can be best taught by lectures, except where experiments are to be shown. You may teach chemistry by lectures. – You might teach making of shoes by lectures!'

At night I supped with him at the Mitre tavern, that we might renew our social intimacy at the original place of meeting. But there was now a considerable difference in his way of living. Having had an illness, in which he was advised to leave off wine, he had, from that period, continued to abstain from it, and drank only water, or lemonade.

I told him that a foreign friend of his, whom I had met with abroad, was so wretchedly perverted to infidelity, that he treated the hopes of immortality with brutal levity; and said, 'As man dies like a dog, let him lie like a dog.' JOHNSON. '*If* he dies like a dog, *let* him lie like a dog.' I added, that this man said to me, 'I hate mankind, for I think myself one of the best of them, and I know how bad I am.' JOHNSON. 'Sir, he must be very singular in his opinion, if he thinks himself one of the best of men; for none of his friends think him so.' He said, 'No honest man could be a Deist; for no man could be so after a fair examination of the proofs of Christianity.' I named Hume. JOHNSON. 'No, Sir; Hume owned to a clergyman in the bishopric of Durham, that he had never read the New Testament with attention.' I mentioned Hume's notion, that all who are happy are equally happy; a little miss with a new gown at a dancing-school ball, a general at the head of a victorious army, and an orator, after having made an eloquent speech in a great assembly. JOHNSON. 'Sir, that all who are happy, are equally happy, is not true. A peasant and a philosopher may be equally *satisfied*, but not equally *happy*. Happiness consists in the multiplicity of agreeable consciousness. A peasant has not capacity for having equal happiness with a philosopher.' I remember this very question very happily illustrated in opposition to Hume, by the Reverend Mr Robert Brown, at Utrecht. 'A small drinking glass and a large one (said he), may be equally full; but the large one holds more than the small.'

Dr Johnson was very kind this evening, and said to me, 'You have now lived five-and-twenty years, and you have employed them well.' 'Alas, Sir (said I), I fear not. Do I know history? Do I know mathematics? Do I know law?' JOHNSON. 'Why, Sir, though you may know no science so well as to be able to teach it, and no profession so well as to be able to follow it, your general mass of knowledge of books and men renders you very capable to make yourself master of any science, or fit yourself for any profession.' I mentioned that a gay friend had advised me against being a lawyer, because I should be excelled by plodding blockheads. JOHNSON. 'Why, Sir, in the formulary and statutory part of law, a plodding blockhead may excel; but in the ingenious and rational part of it a plodding blockhead can never excel.'

I talked of the mode adopted by some to rise in the world, by courting great men, and asked him whether he had ever submitted to it. JOHNSON. 'Why, Sir, I never was near enough to great men to court them. You may be prudently attached to great men, and yet independent. You are not to do what you think wrong; and, Sir, you are to calculate and not pay too dear for what you get. You must not give a shilling's worth of court for six-pence worth of good. But if you can get a shilling's worth of good for six-pence worth of court, you are a fool if you do not pay court.'

He said, 'If convents should be allowed at all, they should only be retreats for persons unable to serve the public, or who have served it. It is our first duty to serve society, and, after we have done that, we may attend wholly to the salvation of our own souls. A youthful passion for abstracted devotion should not be encouraged.'

I introduced the subject of second sight, and other mysterious manifest- ations; the fulfilment of which, I suggested might happen by chance. JOHNSON. 'Yes, Sir; but they have happened so often that mankind have agreed to think them not fortuitous.'

I talked to him a great deal of what I had seen in Corsica, and of my intention to publish an account of it. He encouraged me by saying, 'You cannot go to the bottom of the subject; but all that you tell us will be new to us. Give us as many anecdotes as you can.'

Our next meeting at the Mitre was on Saturday the 15th of February, when I presented to him my old and most intimate friend, the Reverend Mr Temple, then of Cambridge. I having mentioned that I had passed some time with Rousseau in his wild retreat, and having quoted some remark made by Mr Wilkes, with whom I had spent many pleasant hours in Italy, Johnson said (sarcastically), 'It seems, Sir, you have kept very good company abroad, Rousseau and Wilkes!' Thinking it enough to defend one at a time, I said nothing as to my gay friend, but answered with a smile, 'My dear Sir, you don't call Rousseau bad company. Do you really think *him* a bad man?' JOHNSON. 'Sir, if you are talking jestingly of this, I don't talk with you. If you mean to be serious, I think him one of the worst of men; a rascal, who ought to be hunted out of society, as he has been. Three or four nations have expelled him; and it is a shame that he is protected in this country.' BOSWELL. 'I don't deny, Sir, but that his novel may, perhaps, do harm; but I cannot think his intention was bad.' JOHNSON. 'Sir, that will not do. We cannot prove any man's intention to be bad. You may shoot a man through the head, and say you intended to miss him; but the Judge will order you to be hanged. An alleged want of intention, when evil is committed, will not be allowed in a court of justice. Rousseau, Sir, is a very bad man. I would sooner sign a sentence for his transportation, than that of any felon who has gone from the Old Bailey these many years. Yes, I should like to have him work in the plantations.' BOSWELL. 'Sir, do you think him as bad a man as Voltaire?' JOHNSON. 'Why, Sir, it is difficult to settle the proportion of iniquity between them.'

This violence seemed very strange to me, who had read many of Rousseau's animated writings with great pleasure, and even edification, had been much pleased with his society, and was just come from the Continent, where he was very generally admired. Nor can I yet allow that he deserves the very severe censure which Johnson pronounced upon him. His absurd preference of savage to civilised life, and other singularities, are proofs rather of a defect in his understanding, than of any depravity in his heart. And notwithstanding the unfavourable opinion which many worthy men have expressed of his *Profession de Foi du Vicaire Savoyard*, I cannot help admiring it as the performance of a man full of sincere reverential submission to Divine Mystery, though beset with perplexing doubts; a state of mind to be viewed with pity rather than with anger.

On his favourite subject of subordination, Johnson said, 'So far is it from being true that men are naturally equal, that no two people can be half an hour together, but one shall acquire an evident superiority over the other.'

I mentioned the advice given us by philosophers, to console ourselves when distressed or embarrassed, by thinking of those who are in a worse situation than ourselves. This, I observed, could not apply to all, for there must be some who have nobody worse than they are. JOHNSON. 'Why, to be sure, Sir, there are: but they don't know it. There is no being so poor and so contemptible, who does not think there is somebody still poorer, and still more contemptible.'

As my stay in London at this time was very short, I had not many opportunities of being with Dr Johnson; but I felt my veneration for him in no degree lessened, by my having seen *multorum hominum mores et urbes*. On the contrary, by having it in my power to compare him with many of the most celebrated persons of other countries, my admiration of his extraordinary mind was increased and confirmed.

The roughness, indeed, which sometimes appeared in his manners, was more striking to me now, from my having been accustomed to the studied smooth complying habits of the Continent; and I clearly recognised in him, not without respect for his honest conscientious zeal, the same indignant and sarcastical mode of treating every attempt to unhinge or weaken good principles.

One evening, when a young gentleman teased him with an account of the infidelity of his servant, who, he said, would not believe the Scriptures, because he could not read them in the original tongues, and be sure that they were not invented, 'Why, foolish fellow (said Johnson), has he any better authority for almost everything that he believes?' – 'Then the vulgar, Sir, never can know they are right, but must submit themselves to the learned.' JOHNSON. 'To be sure, Sir. The vulgar are the children of the state, and must be taught like children.' - 'Then, Sir, a poor Turk must be a Mahometan, just as a poor Englishman must be a Christian?' - JOHNSON. 'Why yes, Sir; and what then? This now is such stuff as I used to talk to my mother, when I first began to think myself a clever fellow; and she ought to have whipped me for it.'

Another evening Dr Goldsmith and I called on him, with the hope of prevailing on him to sup with us at the Mitre. We found him indisposed, and resolved not to go abroad. 'Come then (said Goldsmith), we will not go to the Mitre tonight, since we cannot have the big man with us.' Johnson then called for a bottle of port, of which Goldsmith and I partook, while our friend, now a water drinker, sat by us. GOLDSMITH. 'I think, Mr Johnson, you don't go near the theatres now. You give yourself no more concern about a new play, than if you had never had any thing to do with the stage.' JOHNSON. 'Why, Sir, our tastes greatly alter. The lad does not care for the child's rattle, and the old man does not care for the young man's whore.' GOLDSMITH. 'Nay, Sir; but your Muse was not a whore.' JOHNSON. 'Sir, I do not think she was. But as we advance in the journey of life, we drop some of the things which have pleased us; whether it be that we are fatigued and don't choose to carry so many things any farther, or that we find other things which we like better.' BOSWELL. 'But, Sir, why don't you give us something in some other way?' GOLDSMITH. 'Ay, Sir, we have a claim upon you.' JOHNSON. 'No, Sir, I am not obliged to do any more. No man is obliged to do as much as he can do. A man is to have part of his life to himself. If a soldier has fought a good many campaigns, he is not to be blamed if he retires to ease and tranquillity. A physician, who has practised long in a great city, may be excused if he retires to a small town, and takes less practice. Now, Sir, the good I can do by my conversation bears the same proportion to the good I can do by my writings, that the practice of a physician, retired to a small town, does to his practice in a great city.' BOSWELL. 'But I wonder, Sir, you have not more pleasure in writing than in not writing.' JOHNSON. 'Sir, you *may* wonder.'

He talked of making verses, and observed, 'The great difficulty is to know when you have made good ones. When composing, I have generally had them in my mind, perhaps fifty at a time, walking up and down in my room; and then I have wrote them down, and often, from laziness, have written only half lines. I have written a hundred lines in a day. I remember I wrote a hundred lines of the *Vanity of Human Wishes* in a day. Doctor (turning to Goldsmith), I am not quite idle; I made one line t'other day; but I made no more.' GOLDSMITH. 'Let us hear it; we'll put a bad one to it.' JOHNSON. 'No, Sir; I have forgot it.'

Such specimens of the easy and playful conversation of the great Dr Samuel Johnson are, I think, to be prized; as exhibiting the little varieties of a mind so enlarged and so powerful when objects of consequence required its exertions, and as giving us a minute knowledge of his character and modes of thinking.[a]

[a] After this passage, read:

To BENNET LANGTON, Esq. at Langton, near Spilsby, Lincolnshire.

DEAR SIR - What your friends have done, that from your departure till now nothing has been heard of you, none of us are able to inform the rest; but as we are all neglected alike, no one thinks himself entitled to the privilege of complaint.

I should have known nothing of you or of Langton, from the time that dear Miss Langton left us, had not I met Mr Simpson, of Lincoln, one day in the street, by whom I was informed that Mr Langton, your Mamma, and yourself, had been all ill, but that you were all recovered.

That sickness should suspend your correspondence, I did not wonder; but hoped that it would be renewed at your recovery.

Since you will not inform us where you are, or how you live, I know not whether you desire to know any thing of us. However, I will tell you that THE CLUB subsists; but we have the loss of Burke's company since he has been engaged in public business, in which he has gained more reputation than perhaps any man at his [first] appearance ever gained before. He made two speeches in the House for repealing the Stamp-act, which were publicly commended by Mr Pitt, and have filled the town with wonder.

Burke is a great man by nature, and is expected soon to attain civil greatness. I am grown greater too, for I have maintained the newspapers these many weeks; and what is greater still, I have risen every morning since New-year's day, at about eight: when I was up, I have indeed done but little; yet it is no slight advancement to obtain for so many hours more the consciousness of being.

I wish you were in my new study; I am now writing the first letter in it. I think it looks very pretty about me.

Dyer is constant at THE CLUB; Hawkins is remiss; I am not over diligent. Dr Nugent, Dr Goldsmith, and Mr Reynolds, are very constant. Mr Lye is printing his Saxon and Gothic Dictionary: all THE CLUB subscribes.

You will pay my respects to all my Lincolnshire friends. I am, dear Sir,

Most affectionately your's,

SAM. JOHNSON.

March 9, 1766.

Johnson's-court, Fleet-street.

To BENNET LANGTON, Esq. at Langton, near Spilsby, Lincolnshire.

DEAR SIR – In supposing that I should be more than commonly affected by the death of Peregrine Langton,[1] you were not mistaken; he was one of those whom I loved at once by instinct and by reason. I have seldom indulged more hope of any thing than of being able to improve our acquaintance to friendship. Many a time have I placed myself again at Langton, and imagined the pleasure with which I should walk to Partney[2] in a summer morning; but this is no longer possible. We must now endeavour to preserve what is left us – his example of piety and economy. I hope you make what enquiries you can, and write down what is told you. The little things which distinguish domestic characters are soon forgotten: if you delay to enquire, you will have no information; if you neglect to write, information will be vain.

His art of life certainly deserves to be known and studied. He lived in plenty and elegance upon an income which to many would appear indigent, and to most, scanty. How he lived, therefore, every man has an interest in knowing. His death, I hope, was peaceful; it was surely happy.

I wish I had written sooner, lest, writing now, I should renew your grief; but I would not forbear saying what I have now said.

1 Mr Langton's uncle.

2 The place of residence of Mr Peregrine Langton.

This loss is, I hope, the only misfortune of a family to whom no misfortune at all should happen, if my wishes could avert it. Let me know how you all go on. Has Mr Langton got him the little horse that I recommended? It would do him good to ride about his estate in fine weather.

Be pleased to make my compliments to Mrs Langton, and to dear Miss Langton, and Miss Di, and Miss Juliet, and to every body else.

THE CLUB holds very well together. Monday is my night.[1] I continue to rise tolerably well, and read more than I did. I hope something will yet come on it. I am, Sir,

Your most affectionate servant,

SAM. JOHNSON.

May 10, 1766.
Johnson's-court, Fleet-street.

Mr Langton did not disregard this counsel, but wrote the following account, which he has been pleased to communicate to me:

The circumstances of Mr Peregrine Langton were these. He had an annuity for life of two hundred pounds per annum. He resided in a village in Lincolnshire: the rent of his house, with two or three small fields, was twenty-eight pounds; the county he lived in was not more than moderately cheap; his family consisted of a sister, who paid him eighteen pounds annually for her board, and a niece. The servants were two maids, and two men in livery. His common way of living, at his table, was three or four dishes; the appurtenances to his table were neat and handsome; he frequently entertained company at dinner, and then his table was well served with as many dishes as were usual at the tables of the other gentlemen in the neighbourhood. His own appearance, as to clothes, was genteelly neat and plain. He had always a post-chaise, and kept three horses.

Such, with the resources I have mentioned, was his way of living, which he did not suffer to employ his whole income: for he had always a sum of money lying by him for any extraordinary expenses that might arise. Some money he put into the stocks; at his death the sum he had there amounted to one hundred and fifty pounds. He purchased out of his income his household furniture and linen, of which latter he had a very ample store; and, as I am assured by those that had very good means of knowing, not less than the tenth part of his income was set apart for charity: at the time of his death, the sum of twenty-five pounds was found, with a direction to be employed in such uses.

He had laid down a plan of living proportioned to his income, and did not practise any extraordinary degree of parsimony, but endeavoured that in his family there should be plenty without waste. As an instance that this was his endeavour, it may be worth while to mention a method he took in regulating a proper allowance of malt liquor to be drunk in his family, that there might not be a deficiency, or any intemperate profusion. On a complaint made that his allowance of a hogshead in a month, was not enough for his own family, he ordered the quantity of a hogshead to be put into bottles, had it locked up from the servants, and distributed out every day, eight quarts, which is the quantity each day at one hogshead in a month; and told his servants that if that did not suffice, he would allow them more; but, by this method, it appeared at once that the allowance was much more than sufficient for his small family; and this proved a clear conviction,

1 Of his being in the chair of THE LITERARY CLUB, which at this time met once a week in the evening.

After I had been some time in Scotland, I mentioned to him in a letter that, 'On my first return to my native country, after some years of absence, I was told of a vast number of my acquaintance who were all gone to the land of forgetfulness, and I found myself like a man stalking over a field of battle, who every moment perceives some one lying dead.' I complained of irresolution, and mentioned my having made a vow as a security for good conduct. I wrote to him again, without being able to move his indolence; nor did I hear from him till he had received a copy of my inaugural Exercise, or Thesis in Civil

---

that could not be answered, and saved all future dispute. He was, in general, very diligently and punctually attended and obeyed by his servants; he was very considerate as to the injunctions he gave, and explained them distinctly; and at their first coming to his service, steadily exacted a close compliance with them, without any remission: and the servants finding this to be the case, soon grew habitually accustomed to the practice of their business, and then very little further attention was necessary. On extraordinary instances of good behaviour, or diligent service, he was not wanting in particular encouragements and presents above their wages: it is remarkable that he would permit their relations to visit them, and stay at his house two or three days at a time.

The wonder, with most that hear an account of his economy, will be, how he was able, with such an income, to do so much, especially when it is considered that he paid for every thing he had. He had no land, except the two or three small fields which I have said he rented; and, instead of gaining any thing by their produce, I have reason to think he lost by them; however, they furnished him with no further assistance towards his housekeeping, than grass for his horses (not hay, for that I know he bought), and for two cows. Every Monday morning he settled his family accounts, and so kept up a constant attention to the confining his expenses within his income; and to do it more exactly, compared those expenses with a computation he had made, how much that income would afford him every week and day of the year. One of his economical practices was, as soon as any repair was wanting in or about his house, to have it immediately performed. When he had money to spare, he chose to lay in a provision of linen or clothes, or any other necessaries; as then, he said, he could afford it, which he might not be so well able to do when the actual want came; in consequence of which method, he had a considerable supply of necessary articles lying by him, besides what was in use.

But the main particular that seems to have enabled him to do so much with his income, was, that he paid for every thing as soon as he had it, except, alone, what were current accounts, such as rent for his house, and servants' wages; and these he paid at the stated times with the utmost exactness. He gave notice to the tradesmen of the neighbouring market-towns that they should no longer have his custom, if they let any of his servants have any thing without their paying for it. Thus he put it out of his power to commit those imprudences to which those are liable that defer their payments by using their money some other way than where it ought to go. And whatever money he had by him, he knew that it was not demanded elsewhere, but that he might safely employ it as he pleased.

His example was confined, by the sequestered place of his abode, to the observation of few, though his prudence and virtue would have made it valuable to all who could have known it. – These few particulars, which I knew myself, or have obtained from those who lived with him, may afford instruction, and be an incentive to that wise art of living, which he so successfully practised.

Law, which I published at my admission as an advocate, as is the custom in Scotland. He then wrote to me as follows:

To JAMES BOSWELL, Esq.

DEAR SIR – The reception of your Thesis put me in mind of my debt to you. Why did you . . . [1] I will punish you for it, by telling you that your Latin wants correction.[2] In the beginning, *Spei alterae*, not to urge that it should be *primae*, is not grammatical: *alterae* should be *alteri*. In the next time you seem to use *genus* absolutely, for what we call *family*, that is, for *illustrious extraction*, I doubt without authority. *Homines nullius originis*, for *Nullis orti majoribus*, or, *Nullo loco nati*, is, I am afraid, barbarous. – Ruddiman is dead.

I have now vexed you enough, and will try to please you. Your resolution to obey your father I sincerely approve; but do not accustom yourself to enchain your volatility by vows: they will sometime leave a

---

1 The passage omitted alluded to a private transaction.
2 This censure of my Latin relates to the Dedication. which was as follows:

VIRO NOBILISSIMO, ORNATISSIMO,

JOANNI,

VICECOMITI MOUNTSTUART,

ATAVIS EDITO REGIBUS,

EXCELSAE FAMILIAE DE BUTE SPEI ALTERAE;

LABENTE SECULO,

QUUM HOMINES NULLIUS ORIGINIS

GENUS AEQUARE OPIBUS AGGREDIUNTUR,

SANGUINIS ANTIQUI ET ILLUSTRIS

SEMPER MEMORI,

NATALIUM SPLENDOREM VIRTUTIBUS AUGENTI:

AD PUBLICA POPULI COMITIA

JAM LEGATO;

IN OPTIMATIUM VERO MAGNAE BRITANNIAE SENATU,

JURE HAEREDITARIO,

OLIM CONSESSURO:

VIM INSITAM VARIA DOCTRINA PROMOVENTE,

NEC TAMEN SE VENDITANTE,

PRAEDITO:

PRISCA FIDE, ANIMO LIBERRIMO,

ET MORUM ELEGANTIA

INSIGNI:

IN ITALIAE VISITANDAE ITINERE,

SOCIO SUO HONORATISSIMO,

HASCE JURISPRUDENTIAE PRIMITIAS

DEVINCTISSIMAE AMICITIAE ET OBSERVANTIAE

MONUMENTUM,

D.D.C.Q.

JACOBUS BOSWELL.

thorn in your mind, which you will, perhaps, never be able to extract or eject. Take this warning, it is of great importance.

The study of the law is what you very justly term it, copious and generous;[1] and in adding your name to its professors, you have done exactly what I always wished, when I wished you best. I hope that you will continue to pursue it vigorously and constantly. You gain, at least, what is no small advantage, security from those troublesome and wearisome discontents, which are always obtruding themselves upon a mind vacant, unemployed, and undetermined.

You ought to think it no small inducement to diligence and perseverance, that they will please your father. We all live upon the hope of pleasing somebody; and the pleasure of pleasing ought to be greatest, and at last always will be greatest, when our endeavours are exerted in consequence of our duty.

Life is not long, and too much of it must not pass in idle deliberation how it shall be spent; deliberation, which those who begin it by prudence, and continue it with subtlety, must, after long expense of thought, conclude by chance. To prefer one future mode of life to another, upon just reasons, requires faculties which it has not pleased our Creator to give us.

If, therefore, the profession you have chosen has some unexpected inconveniencies, console yourself by reflecting that no profession is without them; and that all the importunities and perplexities of business are softness and luxury, compared with the incessant cravings of vacancy, and the unsatisfactory expedients of idleness.

> *Haec sunt quae nostra potui te voce monere;*
> *Vade, age.*

As to your History of Corsica, you have no materials which others have not, or may not have. You have, somehow or other, warmed your imagination. I wish there were some cure, like the lover's leap, for all heads of which some single idea has obtained an unreasonable and irregular possession. Mind your own affairs, and leave the Corsicans to theirs. I am, dear Sir,

Your most humble servant,

SAM. JOHNSON.

London, Aug. 21, 1766.

---

1 This alludes to the first sentence of the Proemium of my Thesis. 'JURISPRUDENTIAE *studio nullum uberius, nullum generosius: in legibus enim agitandis, populorum mores, variasque fortunae vices ex quibus leges oriuntur, contemplari simul solemus.*'

To Dr SAMUEL JOHNSON.

Auchinleck, Nov. 6, 1766.

MUCH ESTEEMED AND DEAR SIR – I plead not guilty to . . . [1]

Having thus, I hope, cleared myself of the charge brought against me, I presume you will not be displeased if I escape the punishment which you have decreed for me unheard. If you have discharged the arrows of criticism against an innocent man, you must rejoice to find they have missed him, or have not been pointed so as to wound him.

To talk no longer in allegory, I am, with all deference, going to offer a few observations in defence of my Latin, which you have found fault with.

You think I should have used *spei primae* instead of *spei alterae*. *Spes* is, indeed, often used to express something on which we have a future dependence, as in Virg. Eclog. i. l.14,

modo namque gemellos
Spem *gregis ah silice in nuda connixa reliquit.*

and in Georg. iii. l.473,

Spemque *gregemque simul,*

for the lambs and the sheep. Yet it is also used to express any thing on which we have a present dependence, and is well applied to a man of distinguished influence, our support, our refuge, our *praesidium*, as Horace calls Maecenas. So, Aeneid xii. l.57, Queen Amata addresses her son-in-law Turnus: 'Spes *tu nunc una*'; and he was then no future hope, for she adds,

decus imperiumque Latini
Te penes.

which might have been said of my Lord Bute some years ago. Now I consider the present Earl of Bute to be '*Excelsae familiae de Bute* spes prima'; and my Lord Mountstuart, as his eldest son, to be '*spes altera*'. So in *Aeneid* xii. l.168, after having mentioned Pater Aeneas, who was the *present* spes, the *reigning* spes, as my German friends would say, the *spes prima*, the poet adds,

Et juxta Ascanius, magnae spes altera *Romae.*

You think *alterae* ungrammatical, and you tell me it should have been *alteri*. You must recollect that in old times *alter* was declined regularly; and when the ancient fragments preserved in the *Juris Civilis Fontes* were written, it was certainly declined in the way that I use it. This, I should think, may protect a lawyer who writes *alterae* in a dissertation upon part of his own science. But as I could hardly venture to quote fragments of old law to so

---

1 The passage omitted explained the transaction to which the preceding letter had alluded.

classical a man as Mr Johnson, I have not made an accurate search into these remains, to find examples of what I am able to produce in poetical composition. We find in Plaut. *Rudens*, act iii. scene 4,

> *Nam huic* alterae *patria quae sit profecto nescio.*

Plautus is, to be sure, an old comic writer: but in the days of Scipio and Lelius, we find, Terent *Heautontim.* act ii. scene 3,

> *hoc ipsa in itinere* alterae
> *Dum narrat, forte audivi.*

You doubt my having authority for using *genus* absolutely, for what we call *family*, that is, for *illustrious extraction.* Now I take *genus* in Latin, to have much the same signification with *birth* in English; both in their primary meaning expressing simply descent, but both made to stand κατ' ἐξοχήν, for noble descent. *Genus* is thus used in Hor. lib. ii. Sat. v. l.8,

> *Et* genus *et virtus, nisi cum re, vilior alga est.*

And in lib. i. Epist. vi. l.37,

> *Et* genus *et formam Regina pecunia donat.*

And in the celebrated contest between Ajax and Ulysses, Ovid's Metamorph. lib. xiii. l.140,

> *Nam* genus *et proavos, et quae non fecimus ipsi,*
> *Vix ea nostra voco.*

Homines nullius originis, for *nullis orti majoribus,* or *nullo loco nati,* is, you are afraid, barbarous.

Origo is used to signify extraction, as in Virg. Aeneid i. l.286,

> *Nascetur pulchra Trojanus* origine *Caesar.*

and in Aeneid x. l.618,

> *Ille tamen nostra decudit* origine *nomen.*

and as *nullus* is used for obscure, is it not in the genius of the Latin language to write *nullius originis,* for obscure extraction?

I have defended myself as well as I could.

Might I venture to differ from you with regard to the utility of vows? I am sensible that it would be very dangerous to make vows rashly, and without a due consideration. But I cannot help thinking that they may often be of great advantage to one of a variable judgement and irregular inclinations. I always remember a passage in one of your letters to our Italian friend Baretti, where talking of the monastic life, you say you do not wonder that serious men should put themselves under the protection of a religious order, when they have found how unable they are to take care of themselves. For my own part, without affecting to be a Socrates, I am sure I have a more than ordinary struggle to maintain with *the Evil Principle*; and all the methods I can devise are little enough to keep me tolerably steady in the paths of rectitude.

. . .

I am ever, with the highest veneration,
Your affectionate humble servant,

JAMES BOSWELL.

It appears from his diary, that he was this year at Mr Thrale's, from before Midsummer till after Michaelmas,* and that he afterwards passed a month at Oxford. He had then contracted a great intimacy with Mr Chambers of that University, now Sir Robert Chambers, one of the Judges in India.

He published nothing this year in his own name; but the noble Dedication* to the King, of Gwyn's 'London and Westminster Improved', was written by him; and he furnished the Preface,[†] and several of the pieces, which compose a volume of *Miscellanies* by Mrs Anna Williams, the blind lady who had an asylum in his house. Of these, there are his 'Epitaph on Philips';* 'Translation of a Latin Epitaph on Sir Thomas Hanmer';[†] 'Friendship, an Ode';* and 'The Ant',* a paraphrase from the Proverbs, of which I have a copy in his own hand-writing; and, from internal evidence, I ascribe to him, 'To Miss —— on her giving the Author a gold and silk net-work Purse of her own weaving';[†] and, 'The happy Life'.[†] – Most of them have evidently received considerable additions from his superior pen, particularly 'Verses to Mr Richardson, on his Sir Charles Grandison'; 'The Excursion'; 'Reflections on a Grave digging in Westminster-Abbey'. There is in this collection a poem 'On the Death of Stephen Grey, the Electrician';* which, on reading it, appeared to me to be undoubtedly Johnson's. I asked Mrs Williams whether it was not his. 'Sir (said she, with some warmth), I wrote that poem before I had the honour of Dr Johnson's acquaintance.' I, however, was so much impressed with my first notion, that I mentioned it to Johnson, repeating, at the same time, what Mrs Williams had said. His answer was, 'It is true, Sir, that she wrote it before she was acquainted with me; but she has not told you that I wrote it all over again, except two lines.' 'The Fountains',[†] a beautiful little Fairy tale in prose, written with exquisite simplicity, is one of Johnson's productions; and I cannot withhold from Mrs Thrale the praise of being the author of that admirable poem, 'The Three Warnings'.

He wrote this year a letter not intended for publication, which has, perhaps, as strong marks of his sentiment and style, as any of his compositions. The original is in my possession. It is addressed to the late Mr William Drummond, bookseller in Edinburgh, a gentleman of good family, but small estate, who took arms for the house of Stuart in 1745; and during his concealment in London till the act of general pardon came out, obtained the acquaintance of Dr Johnson, who justly esteemed him as a very worthy man. It seems, some of the members of the society in Scotland for propagating Christian knowledge had opposed the scheme of translating the holy scriptures into the Erse or Gaelic language, from political considerations of the disadvantage of keeping up the distinction between the Highlanders and the other inhabitants of

North-Britain. Dr Johnson being informed of this, I suppose by Mr Drummond, wrote with a generous indignation as follows:

To Mr WILLIAM DRUMMOND.

SIR – I did not expect to hear that it could be, in an assembly convened for the propagation of Christian knowledge, a question whether any nation uninstructed in religion should receive instruction; or whether that instruction should be imparted to them by a translation of the holy books into their own language. If obedience to the will of GOD be necessary to happiness, and knowledge of his will be necessary to obedience, I know not how he that withholds this knowledge, or delays it, can be said to love his neighbour as himself. He, that voluntarily continues ignorance, is guilty of all the crimes which ignorance produces; as to him, that should extinguish the tapers of a light-house, might justly be imputed the calamities of shipwrecks. Christianity is the highest perfection of humanity; and as no man is good but as he wishes the good of others, no man can be good in the highest degree, who wishes not to others the largest measures of the greatest good. To omit for a year, or for a day, the most efficacious method of advancing Christianity, in compliance with any purposes that terminate on this side of the grave, is a crime of which I know not that the world has yet had an example, except in the practice of the planters of America, a race of mortals whom, I suppose, no other man wishes to resemble.

The Papists have, indeed, denied to the laity the use of the bible; but this prohibition, in few places now very rigorously enforced, is defended by arguments, which have for their foundation the care of souls. To obscure, upon motives merely political, the light of revelation, is a practice reserved for the reformed; and, surely, the blackest midnight of popery is meridian sunshine to such a reformation. I am not very willing that any language should be totally extinguished. The similitude and derivation of languages afford the most indubitable proof of the traduction of nations, and the genealogy of mankind. They add often physical certainty to historical evidence; and often supply the only evidence of ancient migrations, and of the revolutions of ages which left no written monuments behind them.

Every man's opinions, at least his desires, are a little influenced by his favourite studies. My zeal for languages may seem, perhaps, rather overheated, even to those by whom I desire to be well esteemed. To those who have nothing in their thoughts but trade or policy, present power, or present money, I should not think it necessary to defend my opinions; but with men of letters I would not unwillingly compound, by wishing the continuance of every language, however narrow in its extent, or however incommodious for common purposes, till it is reposited in some version of a known book, that it may be always hereafter examined and compared with other languages, and then permitting its disuse. For this purpose, the translation of the bible is most to be desired. It is not certain that the same method will not preserve the Highland language, for the purposes of learning, and abolish it from daily use. When the Highlanders read the Bible, they will naturally wish to have its obscurities cleared, and to know the history, collateral or appendant. Knowledge always desires increase: it is like fire, which must first be kindled by some external agent, but which will afterwards propagate itself. When they once desire to learn, they will naturally have recourse to the nearest language by which that desire can be gratified; and one will tell another that if he would attain knowledge, he must learn English.

This speculation may, perhaps, be thought more subtle than the grossness of real life will easily admit. Let it, however, be remembered, that the efficacy of ignorance has been long tried, and has not produced the consequence expected. Let knowledge, therefore, take its turn; and let the patrons of privation stand awhile aside, and admit the operation of positive principles.

You will be pleased, Sir, to assure the worthy man[a] who is employed in the new translation, that he has my wishes for his success; and if here or at Oxford I can be of any use, that I shall think it more than honour to promote his undertaking.

I am sorry that I delayed so long to write. I am, Sir,

Your most humble servant,

SAM. JOHNSON.

Johnson's-court, Fleet-street,
Aug. 13, 1766.

The opponents of this pious scheme being made ashamed of their conduct, the benevolent undertaking was allowed to go on.

The following letters, though not written till the year after, being chiefly upon the same subject, are here inserted.

To Mr WILLIAM DRUMMOND.

DEAR SIR – That my letter should have had such effects as you mention, gives me great pleasure. I hope you do not flatter me by imputing to me more good than I have really done. Those whom my arguments have persuaded to change their opinion, show such modesty and candour as deserve great praise.

---

[a] Add: The Rev. Mr John Campbell, Minister of the parish of Kippen, near Stirling, who has lately favoured me with a long, intelligent, and very obliging letter upon this work, makes the following remark: 'Dr Johnson has alluded to the worthy man employed in the translation of the New Testament. Might not this have afforded you an opportunity of paying a proper tribute of respect to the memory of the Rev. Mr James Stuart, late Minister of Killin, distinguished by his eminent piety, learning, and taste. The amiable simplicity of his life, his warm benevolence, his indefatigable and successful exertions for civilizing and improving the parish of which he was minister for upwards of fifty years, entitle him to the gratitude of his country, and the veneration of all good men. It certainly would be a pity, if such a character should be permitted to sink into oblivion.'

I hope the worthy translator goes diligently forward. He has a higher reward in prospect, than any honours which this world can bestow. I wish I could be useful to him.

The publication of my letter, if it could be of use in a cause to which all other causes are nothing, I should not prohibit. But first, I would have you consider whether the publication will really do any good; next, whether by printing and distributing a very small number, you may not attain all that you propose; and, what perhaps I should have said first, whether the letter, which I do not now perfectly remember, be fit to be printed.

If you can consult Dr Robertson, to whom I am a little known, I shall be satisfied about the propriety of whatever he shall direct. If he thinks that it should be printed, I entreat him to revise it; there may, perhaps, be some negligent lines written, and whatever is amiss, he knows very well how to rectify.[1]

Be pleased to let me know, from time to time, how this excellent design goes forward.

Make my compliments to young Mr Drummond, whom I hope you will live to see such as you desire him.

I have not lately seen Mr Elphinston, but believe him to be prosperous. I shall be glad to hear the same of you, for I am, Sir,

Your affectionate humble servant,

SAM. JOHNSON.

Johnson's-court, Fleet-street,
April 21, 1767.

To the same.

SIR – I returned this week from the country, after an absence of near six months, and found your letter, with many others, which I should have answered sooner, if I had sooner seen them.

Dr Robertson's opinion was surely right. Men should not be told of the faults which they have mended. I am glad the old language is taught, and honour the translator as a man whom GOD has distinguished by the high office of propagating his word.

I must take the liberty of engaging you in an office of charity. Mrs Heely, the wife of Mr Heely, who had lately some office in your theatre, is my near relation, and now in great distress. They wrote me word of their situation some time ago, to which I returned them an answer which raised hopes of more than it is proper for me to give them. Their representation of their affairs I have discovered to be such as cannot be trusted; and at this distance, though their case requires haste, I know not how to act. She, or her daughters, may be heard of at Canongate Head. I

---

1 This paragraph shows Johnson's real estimation of the character and abilities of the celebrated Scottish Historian, however lightly, in a moment of caprice, he may have spoken of his works.

must beg, Sir, that you will enquire after them, and let me know what is to be done. I am willing to go to ten pounds, and will transmit you such a sum, if upon examination you find it likely to be of use. If they are in immediate want, advance them what you think proper. What I could do, I would do for the women, having no great reason to pay much regard to Heely himself.[1]

I believe you may receive some intelligence from Mrs Baker, of the theatre, whose letter I received at the same time with yours, and to whom, if you see her, you will make my excuse for the seeming neglect of answering her.

Whatever you advance within ten pounds shall be immediately returned to you, or paid as you shall order. I trust wholly to your judgement.

I am, Sir, &c.

SAM. JOHNSON.

London, Johnson's-court, Fleet-street,
Oct. 24, 1767.

Mr Cuthbert Shaw,[2] alike distinguished by his genius, misfortunes, and misconduct, published this year a poem, called 'The Race, by Mercurius Spur, Esq.', in which he whimsically made the living poets of England contend for pre-eminence of fame by running:

> Prove by their heels the prowess of the head.

In this poem there was the following portrait of Johnson:

> Here Johnson comes – unblest with outward grace,
> His rigid morals stamp'd upon his face.
> While strong conceptions struggle in his brain;
> (For even Wit is brought to bed with pain):
> To view him, porters with their loads would rest,
> And babes cling frighted to the nurse's breast.
> With looks convuls'd, he roars in pompous strain,
> And, like an angry lion, shakes his mane.
> The Nine, with terror struck, who ne'er had seen,
> Aught human with so horrible a mien,
> Debating whether they should stay or run,
> Virtue steps forth, and claims him for her son.
> With gentle speech she warns him now to yield,
> Nor stain his glories in the doubtful field;
> But wrapt in conscious worth, content sit down,
> Since Fame, resolv'd his various pleas to crown,

---

1 This is the person concerning whom Sir John Hawkins has thrown out very unwarrantable reflections both against Dr Johnson and Mr Francis Barber.

2 See an account of him in the *European Magazine*, January, 1786.

> Though forc'd his present claim to disavow,
> Had long reserv'd a chaplet for his brow.
> He bows, obeys; for Time shall first expire,
> Ere Johnson stay, when Virtue bids retire.

The Honourable Thomas Hervey and his lady having unhappily disagreed, and being about to separate, Johnson interfered as their friend, and wrote him a letter of expostulation, which I have not been able to find; but the substance of it is ascertained by a letter to Johnson, in answer to it, which Mr Hervey printed. The occasion of this correspondence between Dr Johnson and Mr Hervey, was thus related to me by Mr Beauclerk. 'Tom Hervey had a great liking for Johnson, and in his will had left him a legacy of fifty pounds. One day he said to me, "Johnson may want this money now, more than afterwards. I have a mind to give it him directly. Will you be so good as to carry a fifty pound note from me to him?" This I positively refused to do, as he might, perhaps, have knocked me down for insulting him, and have afterwards put the note in his pocket. But I said, if Hervey would write him a letter, and enclose a fifty pound note, I should take care to deliver it. He accordingly did write him a letter, mentioning that he was only paying a legacy a little sooner. To his letter he added, "*P.S. I am going to part with my wife.*" Johnson then wrote to him, saying nothing of the note, but remonstrating with him against parting with his wife.'

When I mentioned to Johnson this story, in as delicate terms as I could, he told me that the fifty pound note was given to him by Mr Hervey in consideration of his having written for him a pamphlet against Sir Charles Hanbury Williams, who, Mr Hervey imagined, was the author of an attack upon him; but that it was afterwards discovered to be the work of a garretteer, who wrote *The Fool*: so the pamphlet against Sir Charles was not printed.

In February, 1767, there happened one of the most remarkable incidents of Johnson's life, which gratified his monarchical enthusiasm, and which he loved to relate with all its circumstances, when requested by his friends. This was his being honoured by a private conversation with his Majesty, in a library at the Queen's house. He had frequently visited those splendid rooms and noble collection of books,[1] which he used to say was more numerous and curious than he supposed any person could have made in the time which the King had employed. Mr Barnard, the librarian, took care that he should have every accommodation that could contribute to his ease and convenience, while indulging his literary taste in that place; so that he had here a very agreeable resource at leisure hours.

---

1 Dr Johnson had the honour of contributing his assistance towards the formation of this library; for I have read a long letter from him to Mr Barnard, giving the most masterly instructions on the subject. I wished much to have gratified my readers with the perusal of this letter, and have reason to think that his Majesty would have been graciously pleased to permit its publication; but Mr Barnard, to whom I applied, declined it 'on his own account'.

His Majesty having been informed of his occasional visits, was pleased to signify a desire that he should be told when Dr Johnson came next to the library. Accordingly, the next time that Johnson did come, as soon as he was fairly engaged with a book, on which, while he sat by the fire, he seemed quite intent, Mr Barnard stole round to the apartment where the King was, and, in obedience to his Majesty's commands, mentioned that Dr Johnson was then in the library. His Majesty said he was at leisure, and would go to him; upon which Mr Barnard took one of the candles that stood on the King's table, and lighted his Majesty through a suite of rooms, till they came to a private door into the library, of which his Majesty had the key. Being entered, Mr Barnard stepped forward hastily to Dr Johnson, who was still in a profound study, and whispered him, 'Sir, here is the King.' Johnson started up, and stood still. His Majesty approached him, and at once was courteously easy.[1]

His Majesty began by observing, that he understood he came sometimes to the library; and then mentioning his having heard that the Doctor had been lately at Oxford, asked him if he was not fond of going thither. To which Johnson answered, that he was indeed fond of going to Oxford sometimes, but was likewise glad to come back again. The King then asked him what they were doing at Oxford. Johnson answered, he could not much commend their diligence, but that in some respects they were mended, for they had put their press under better regulations, and were at that time printing Polybius. He was then asked whether there were better libraries at Oxford or Cambridge. He answered, he believed the Bodleian was larger than any they had at Cambridge; at the same time adding, 'I hope, whether we have more books or not than they have at Cambridge, we shall make as good use of them as they do.' Being asked whether All-Souls or Christ-Church library was the largest, he answered, 'All-Souls library is the largest we have except the Bodleian.' 'Aye (said the King), that is the public library.'

His Majesty enquired if he was then writing anything. He answered, he was

[1] The particulars of this conversation I have been at great pains to collect with the utmost authenticity, from Dr Johnson's own detail to myself; from Mr Langton, who was present when he gave an account of it to Dr Joseph Warton, and several other friends, at Sir Joshua Reynolds's; from Mr Barnard; from the copy of a letter written by the late Mr Strahan the printer, to Bishop Warburton; and from a minute, the original of which is among the papers of the late Sir James Caldwell, and a copy of which was most obligingly obtained for me from his son Sir John Caldwell, by Sir Francis Lumm. To all these gentlemen I beg leave to make my grateful acknowledgements, and particularly to Sir Francis Lumm, who was pleased to take a great deal of trouble, and even had the minute laid before the King by Lord Caermarthen, now Duke of Leeds, one of his Majesty's Principal Secretaries of State, who announced to Sir Francis the Royal pleasure concerning it by a letter, in these words: 'I have the King's commands to assure you, Sir, how sensible his Majesty is of your attention in communicating the minute of the conversation previous to its publication. As there appears no objection to your complying with Mr Boswell's wishes on the subject, you are at full liberty to deliver it to that gentleman, to make such use of in his Life of Dr Johnson, as he may think proper.'

not, for he had pretty well told the world what he knew, and must now read to acquire more knowledge. The King, as it should seem with a view to urge him to rely on his own stores as an original writer, and to continue his labours, then said, 'I do not think you borrow much from any body.' Johnson said, he thought he had already done his part as a writer. 'I should have thought so too (said the King), if you had not written so well.' – Johnson observed to me, upon this, that 'No man could have paid a handsomer compliment; and it was fit for a King to pay. It was decisive.' When asked by another friend, at Sir Joshua Reynolds's, whether he made any reply to this high compliment, he answered, 'No, Sir. When the King had said it, it was to be so. It was not for me to bandy civilities with my sovereign.' Perhaps no man who had spent his whole life in courts could have shown a more nice and dignified sense of true politeness, than Johnson did in this instance.

His Majesty having observed to him that he supposed he must have read a great deal; Johnson answered that he thought more than he read; that he had read a great deal in the early part of his life, but having fallen into ill health, he had not been able to read much, compared with others: for instance, he said he had not read much compared with Dr Warburton. Upon which the King said, that he heard Dr Warburton was a man of such general knowledge, that you could scarce talk with him on any subject on which he was not qualified to speak; and that his learning resembled Garrick's acting, in its universality.[a] His Majesty then talked of the controversy between Warburton and Lowth, which he seemed to have read, and asked Johnson what he thought of it. Johnson answered, 'Warburton has most general, most scholastic learning; Lowth is the more correct scholar. I do not know which of them calls names best.' The King was pleased to say he was of the same opinion; adding, 'You do not think then, Dr Johnson, that there was much argument in the case.' Johnson said, he did not think there was. 'Why truly (said the King), when once it comes to calling names, argument is pretty well at an end.'

His Majesty then asked him what he thought of Lord Lyttelton's history, which was then just published. Johnson said, he thought his style pretty good, but that he had blamed Henry the Second rather too much. 'Why (said the King), they seldom do these things by halves.' 'No, Sir (answered Johnson), not to Kings.' But fearing to be misunderstood, he proceeded to explain himself; and immediately subjoined, 'That for those who spoke worse of Kings than they deserved, he could find no excuse, but that he could more easily conceive how some might speak better of them than they deserved, without any ill intention; for, as Kings had much in their power to give, those who were favoured by them would frequently, from gratitude, exaggerate their praises; and as this proceeded from a good motive, it was certainly excusable, as far as error could be excusable.'

---

[a] Add a note: The Reverend Mr Strahan clearly recollects having been told by Johnson, that the King observed that Pope made Warburton a Bishop. 'True, Sir, (said Johnson), but Warburton did more for Pope; he made him a Christian': alluding, no doubt, to his ingenious comments on the *Essay on Man*.

The King then asked him what he thought of Dr Hill. Johnson answered, that he was an ingenious man, but had no veracity; and immediately mentioned, as an instance of it, an assertion of that writer, that he had seen objects magnified to a much greater degree by using three or four microscopes at a time, than by using one. 'Now (added Johnson), every one acquainted with microscopes knows, that the more of them he looks through, the less the object will appear.' 'Why (replied the King), this is not only telling an untruth, but telling it clumsily; for, if that be the case, every one who can look through a microscope will be able to detect him.'

'I now (said Johnson to his friends, when relating what had passed), began to consider that I was depreciating this man in the estimation of his sovereign, and thought it was time for me to say something that might be more favourable.' He added, therefore, that Dr Hill was, notwithstanding, a very curious observer; and if he would have been contented to tell the world no more than he knew, he might have been a very considerable man, and needed not to have recourse to such mean expedients to raise his reputation.

The King then talked of literary journals, mentioned particularly the *Journal des Savans*, and asked Johnson if it was well done. Johnson said, it was formerly very well done, and gave some account of the persons who began it, and carried it on for some years: enlarging at the same time, on the nature and use of such works. The King asked him if it was well done now. Johnson answered, he had no reason to think that it was. The King then asked him if there were any other literary journals published in this kingdom, except the *Monthly* and *Critical* Reviews; and on being answered there were no other, his Majesty asked which of them was the best; Johnson answered, that the *Monthly Review* was done with most care, the *Critical* upon the best principles; adding, that the authors of the *Monthly Review* were enemies to the Church. This the King said he was sorry to hear.

The conversation next turned on the *Philosophical Transactions*, when Johnson observed, that they had now a better method of arranging their materials than formerly. 'Aye (said the King), they are obliged to Dr Johnson for that'; for his Majesty had heard and remembered the circumstance, which Johnson himself had forgot.

His Majesty expressed a desire to have the literary biography of this country ably executed, and proposed to Dr Johnson to undertake it. Johnson signified his readiness to comply with his Majesty's wishes.

During the whole of this interview, Johnson talked to his Majesty with profound respect, but still in his firm manly manner, with a sonorous voice, and never in that subdued tone which is commonly used at the levee and in the drawing-room. After the King withdrew, Johnson showed himself highly pleased with his Majesty's conversation and gracious behaviour. He said to Mr Barnard, 'Sir, they may talk of the King as they will; but he is the finest gentleman I have ever seen.' And he afterwards observed to Mr Langton, 'Sir, his manners are those of as fine a gentleman as we may suppose Lewis the Fourteenth or Charles the Second.'

At Sir Joshua Reynolds's, where a circle of Johnson's friends was collected round him to hear his account of this memorable conversation, Dr Joseph Warton, in his frank and lively manner, was very active in pressing him to mention the particulars. 'Come now, Sir, this is an interesting matter; do favour us with it.' Johnson, with great good humour, complied.

He told them, 'I found his Majesty wished I should talk, and I made it my business to talk. I find it does a man good to be talked to by his sovereign. In the first place, a man cannot be in a passion — ' Here some question interrupted him, which is to be regretted, as he certainly would have pointed out, and illustrated many circumstances of advantage, from being in a situation, where the powers of the mind are at once excited to vigorous exertion, and tempered by reverential awe.

During all the time in which Dr Johnson was employed in relating to the circle at Sir Joshua Reynolds's the particulars of what passed between the King and him, Dr Goldsmith remained unmoved upon a sofa at some distance, affecting not to join in the least in the eager curiosity of the company. He assigned as a reason for his gloom and seeming inattention, that he apprehended Johnson had relinquished his purpose of furnishing him with a Prologue to his play, with the hopes of which he had been flattered; but it was strongly suspected that he was fretting with chagrin and envy at the singular honour Dr Johnson had lately enjoyed. At length, the frankness and simplicity of his natural character prevailed. He sprung from the sofa, advanced to Johnson, and in a kind of flutter, from imagining himself in the situation which he had just been hearing described, exclaimed, 'Well, you acquitted yourself in this conversation better than I should have done; for I should have bowed and stammered through the whole of it.'[a]

I received no letter from Johnson this year; nor have I discovered any of the correspondence[1] he had, except the two letters to Mr Drummond, which have been inserted, for the sake of connection with that to the same gentleman

---

[a] After this passage, read:

To BENNET LANGTON, Esq.

At Mr Rothwell's, Perfumer, in New Bond-street.

Lichfield, Oct. 10, 1767.

DEAR SIR — That you have been all summer in London is one more reason for which I regret my long stay in the country. I hope that you will not leave the town before my return. We have here only the chance of vacancies in the passing carriages, and I have bespoken one that may, if it happens, bring me to town on the fourteenth of this month; but this is not certain.

It will be a favour if you communicate this to Mrs Williams: I long to see all my friends. I am, dear Sir, your most humble servant,

SAM. JOHNSON.

[1] It is proper here to mention, that when I speak of his correspondence, I consider it independent of the voluminous collection of letters which, in the course of many years, he wrote to Mrs Thrale, which forms a separate part of his works; and as a proof of the high estimation set on any thing which came from his pen, was sold by that lady for the sum of five hundred pounds.

in 1766. His diary affords no light as to his employment at this time. He passed three months at Lichfield; and I cannot omit an affecting and solemn scene there, as related by himself:

'Sunday, Oct. 18, 1767. Yesterday, Oct. 17, at about ten in the morning, I took my leave for ever of my dear old friend, Catherine Chambers, who came to live with my mother about 1724, and has been but little parted from us since. She buried my father, my brother, and my mother. She is now fifty-eight years old.

'I desired all to withdraw, then told her that we were to part for ever; that as Christians, we should part with prayer, and that I would, if she was willing, say a short prayer beside her. She expressed great desire to hear me; and held up her poor hands, as she lay in bed, with great fervour, while I prayed, kneeling by her, nearly in the following words:

'Almighty and most merciful Father, whose loving-kindness is over all thy works, behold, visit, and relieve this thy servant, who is grieved with sickness. Grant that the sense of her weakness may add strength to her faith, and seriousness to her repentance. And grant that by the help of thy Holy Spirit, after the pains and labours of this short life, we may all obtain everlasting happiness, through JESUS CHRIST our Lord; for whose sake hear our prayers. Amen. Our Father, &c.

'I then kissed her. She told me that to part was the greatest pain that she had ever felt, and that she hoped we should meet again in a better place. I expressed with swelled eyes, and great emotion of tenderness, the same hopes. We kissed and parted. I humbly hope to meet again, and to part no more.'[1]

By those who have been taught to look upon Johnson as a man of a harsh and stern character, let this tender and affectionate scene be candidly read; and let them then judge whether more warmth of heart, and grateful kindness, is often found in human nature.

We have the following notice in his devotional record:

'August 2, 1767. I have been disturbed and unsettled for a long time, and have been without resolution to apply to study or to business, being hindered by sudden snatches.'[1]

He, however, furnished Mr Adams with a Dedication* to the King of that ingenious gentleman's *Treatise on the Globes*, conceived and expressed in such a manner as could not fail to be very grateful to a monarch, distinguished for his love of the sciences.

This year was published a ridicule of his style, under the title of 'Lexiphanes'. Sir John Hawkins ascribes it to Dr Kenrick; but its author was one Campbell, a Scotch purser in the navy. The ridicule consisted in applying Johnson's 'words of large meaning', to insignificant matters, as if one should put the armour of Goliath upon a dwarf. The contrast might be laughable; but the dignity of the armour must remain the same in all considerate minds. This

1 *Prayers and Meditations*, p. 77 and 78.
2 Ibid. p. 73.

malicious drollery, therefore, it may easily be supposed, could do no harm to its illustrious object.

It appears from his notes of the state of his mind,[1] that he suffered great perturbation and distraction in 1768. Nothing of his writing was given to the public this year, except the Prologue* to his friend Goldsmith's comedy of *The Good-natured Man*. The first lines of this Prologue are strongly characteristical of the dismal gloom of his mind; which, in his case, as in the case of all who are distressed with the same malady of imagination, transfers to others its own feelings. Who could suppose that it was to introduce a comedy, when Mr Bensley solemnly began,

> 'Press'd with the load of life, the weary mind
> Surveys the general toil of human kind.'

but this dark ground might make Goldsmith's humour shine the more.

In the spring of this year, having published my 'Account of Corsica, with the Journal of a Tour to that Island', I returned to London, very desirous to see Dr Johnson, and hear him upon the subject. I found he was at Oxford, with his friend Mr Chambers, who was now Vinerian Professor, and lived in New Inn Hall. Having had no letter from him since that in which he criticised the Latinity of my Thesis, and having been told by somebody that he was offended at my having put into my book an extract of his letter to me at Paris, I was impatient to be with him, and therefore followed him to Oxford, where I was entertained by Mr Chambers with a civility which I shall ever gratefully remember. I found that Dr Johnson had sent a letter to me to Scotland, and that I had nothing to complain of but his being more indifferent to my anxiety than I wished him to be. Instead of giving, with the circumstances of time and place, such fragments of his conversation as I preserved during this visit to Oxford, I shall throw them together in continuation.

I asked him whether, as a moralist, he did not think that the practice of the law, in some degree, hurt the nice feeling of honesty. JOHNSON. 'Why no, Sir, if you act properly. You are not to deceive your clients with false represent-ations of your opinion: you are not to tell lies to a judge.' BOSWELL. 'But what do you think of supporting a cause which you know to be bad?' JOHNSON. 'Sir, you do not know it to be good or bad till the Judge determines it. I have said that you are to state facts fairly; so that your thinking, or what you call knowing a cause to be bad, must be from reasoning, must be from your supposing your arguments to be weak and inconclusive. But, Sir, that is not enough. An argument which does not convince yourself, may convince the Judge to whom you urge it: and if it does convince him, why then, Sir, you are wrong, and he is right. It is his business to judge; and you are not to be confident in your own opinion that a cause is bad, but to say all you can for your client, and then hear the Judge's opinion.' BOSWELL. 'But, Sir, does not affecting a warmth when you have no warmth, and appearing to be clearly of

1 *Prayers and Meditations*, p. 81.

one opinion when you are in reality of another opinion, does not such dissimulation impair one's honesty? Is there not some danger that a lawyer may put on the same mask in common life, in the intercourse with his friends?' JOHNSON. 'Why no, Sir. Every body knows you are paid for affecting warmth for your client; and it is, therefore, properly no dissimulation: the moment you come from the bar you resume your usual behaviour. Sir, a man will no more carry the artifice of the bar into the common intercourse of society, than a man who is paid for tumbling upon his hands will continue to tumble upon his hands when he should walk on his feet.'

Talking of some of the modern plays, he said *False Delicacy* was totally void of character. He praised Goldsmith's *Good-natured Man*; said, it was the best comedy that had appeared since *The Provoked Husband*, and that there had not been of late any such character exhibited on the stage as that of Croaker. I observed it was the Suspirius of his *Rambler*. He said, Goldsmith had owned he had borrowed it from thence. 'Sir (continued he), there is all the difference in the world between characters of nature and characters of manners; and *there* is the difference between the characters of Fielding and those of Richardson. Characters of manners are very entertaining; but they are to be understood by a more superficial observer, than characters of nature, where a man must dive into the recesses of the human heart.'

It always appeared to me that he estimated the compositions of Richardson too highly, and that he had an unreasonable prejudice against Fielding. In comparing those two writers, he used this expression; 'that there was as great a difference between them as between a man who knew how a watch was made, and a man who could tell the hour by looking on the dial-plate.' This was a short and figurative state of his distinction between drawing characters of nature and characters only of manners. But I cannot help being of opinion, that the neat watches of Fielding are as well constructed as the large clocks of Richardson, and that his dial-plates are brighter. Fielding's characters, though they do not expand themselves so widely in dissertation, are as just pictures of human nature, and I will venture to say, have more striking features, and nicer touches of the pencil; and though Johnson used to quote with approbation a saying of Richardson's, 'that the virtues of Fielding's heroes were the vices of a truly good man', I will venture to add, that the moral tendency of Fielding's writings, though it does not encourage a strained and rarely possible virtue, is ever favourable to honour and honesty, and cherishes the benevolent and generous affections. He who is as good as Fielding would make him, is an amiable member of society, and may be led on by more regulated instructors, to a higher state of ethical perfection.

Johnson proceeded: 'Even Sir Francis Wronghead is a character of manners, though drawn with great humour.' He then repeated, very happily, all Sir Francis's credulous account to Manly of his being with 'the great man', and securing a place. I asked him if *The Suspicious Husband* did not furnish a well-drawn character, that of Ranger. JOHNSON. 'No, Sir; Ranger is just a rake, a mere rake, and a lively young fellow, but no *character*.

The great Douglas cause was at this time a very general subject of discussion.

I found he had not studied it with much attention, but had only heard parts of it occasionally. He, however, talked of it, and said, 'I am of opinion that positive proof of fraud should not be required of the plaintiff, but that the Judges should decide according as probability shall appear to preponderate, granting to the defendant the presumption of filiation to be strong in his favour. And I think too, that a good deal of weight should be allowed to the dying declarations, because they were spontaneous. There is a great difference between what is said without our being urged to it, and what is said from a kind of compulsion. If I praise a man's book without being asked my opinion of it, that is honest praise, to which one may trust. But if an author asks me if I like his book, and I give him something like praise, it must not be taken as my real opinion.

'I have not been troubled for a long time with authors desiring my opinion of their works. I used once to be sadly plagued with a man who wrote verses, but who literally had no other notion of a verse, but that it consisted of ten syllables. *Lay your knife and your fork across your plate*, was to him a verse:

Lay yōur knife ānd your fōrk, acrōss your plāte.

As he wrote a great number of verses he sometimes by chance made good ones, though he did not know it.'

He renewed his promise of coming to Scotland, and going with me to the Hebrides, but said he would now content himself with seeing one or two of the most curious of them. He said, 'Macaulay who writes the account of St Kilda, set out with a prejudice against prejudices, and wanted to be a smart modern thinker; and yet he affirms for a truth, that when a ship arrives there all the inhabitants are seized with a cold.'[a]

He expatiated on the advantages of Oxford for learning. 'There is here, Sir (said he), such a progressive emulation. The students are anxious to appear well to their tutors; the tutors are anxious to have their pupils appear well in the college; the colleges are anxious to have their students appear well in the University; and there are excellent rules of discipline in every college. That the rules are sometimes ill observed, may be true; but is nothing against the

---

[a] Add: Dr John Campbell, the celebrated writer, took a great deal of pains to ascertain this fact, and attempted to account for it on physical principles, from the effect of effluvia from human bodies. Johnson at another time praised Macaulay for his '*magnanimity*', in asserting this wonderful story, because it was well attested. A lady of Norfolk, by a letter to my friend Dr Burney, has favoured me with the following solution: 'Now for the explication of this seeming mystery, which is so very obvious as, for that reason, to have escaped the penetration of Dr Johnson and his friend, as well as that of the author. Reading the book with my ingenious friend, the late Reverend Mr Christian of Docking – after ruminating a little, "The cause (says he) is a natural one. The situation of St Kilda renders a North-East Wind indispensably necessary before a stranger can land. The wind, not the stranger, occasions an epidemic cold." If I am not mistaken, Mr Macaulay is dead; if living, this solution might please him, as I hope it will Mr Boswell, in return for the many agreeable hours his works have afforded us.'

system. The members of an University may, for a season, be unmindful of their duty. I am arguing for the excellency of the institution.'

Of Guthrie he said, 'Sir, he is a man of parts. He has no great regular fund of knowledge; but by reading so long, and writing so long, he no doubt has picked up a good deal.'

He said he had lately been a long while at Lichfield, but had grown very weary before he left it. BOSWELL. 'I wonder at that, Sir; it is your native place.' JOHNSON. 'Why, so is Scotland *your* native place.'

His prejudice against Scotland appeared remarkably strong at this time. When I talked of our advancement in literature, 'Sir (said he), you have learnt a little from us, and you think yourselves very great men. Hume would never have written History, had not Voltaire written it before him. He is an echo of Voltaire.' BOSWELL. 'But, Sir, we have Lord Kames.' JOHNSON. 'You *have* Lord Kames. Keep him; ha, ha, ha! We don't envy you him. Do you ever see Dr Robertson?' BOSWELL. 'Yes, Sir.' JOHNSON. 'Does the dog talk of me?' BOSWELL. 'Indeed, Sir, he does, and loves you.' Thinking that I now had him in a corner, and being solicitous for the literary fame of my country, I pressed him for his opinion on the merit of Dr Robertson's *History of Scotland*. But, to my surprise, he escaped. – 'Sir, I love Robertson, and I won't talk of his book.'

It is but justice both to him and Dr Robertson to add, that though he indulged himself in this sally of wit, he had too good taste not to be fully sensible of the merits of that admirable work.

An essay, written by Mr Deane, a divine of the Church of England, maintaining the future life of brutes, by an explication of certain parts of the Scriptures, was mentioned, and the doctrine insisted on by a gentleman who seemed fond of curious speculation. Johnson, who did not like to hear of any thing concerning a future state which was not authorised by the regular canons of orthodoxy, discouraged this talk; and being offended at its continuation, he watched an opportunity to give the gentleman a blow of reprehension. So, when the poor speculatist, with a serious metaphysical pensive face, addressed him, 'But really, Sir, when we see a very sensible dog, we don't know what to think of him.' Johnson, rolling with joy at the thought, which beamed in his eye, turned quickly round and replied, 'True, Sir: and when we see a very foolish *fellow*, we don't know what to think of *him*.' He then rose up, strode to the fire, and stood for some time laughing and exulting.

I told him that I had several times, when in Italy, seen the experiment of placing a scorpion within a circle of burning coals; that it ran round and round in extreme pain; and finding no way to escape, retired to the centre, and, like a true Stoic philosopher, darted its sting into its head, and thus at once freed itself from its woes. '*This must end 'em.*' I said, this was a curious fact, as it showed deliberate suicide in a reptile. Johnson would not admit the fact. He said, Maupertuis[a] was of opinion that it does not kill itself, but dies of the heat;

* Add the following footnote: I should think it impossible not to wonder at the variety of Johnson's reading, however desultory it might have been. Who could have

that it gets to the centre of the circle as the coolest place; that its turning its tail in upon its head is merely a convulsion, and that it does not sting itself. He said he would be satisfied if the great anatomist Morgagni, after dissecting a scorpion upon whom[a] the experiment had been tried, should certify that its sting had penetrated into its head.

He seemed pleased to talk of natural philosophy. 'That woodcocks (said he), fly over to the northern countries, is proved, because they have been observed at sea. Swallows certainly sleep all the winter. A number of them conglobulate together, by flying round and round, and then all in a heap throw themselves under water, and lie in the bed of a river.' He told us one of his first essays was a Latin poem upon the glow-worm. I am sorry I did not ask where it was to be found.

Talking of the Russians and the Chinese, he advised me to read Bell's travels. I asked him whether I should read Du Halde's account of China. 'Why yes (said he), as one reads such a book; that is to say, consult it.'

He talked of the heinousness of the crime of adultery, by which the peace of families was destroyed. He said, 'Confusion of progeny constitutes the offence of the crime; and therefore a woman who breaks her marriage vows is much more criminal than a man who does it. A man, to be sure, is criminal in the sight of GOD: but he does not do his wife a very material injury, if he does not insult her; if, for instance, from mere wantonness of appetite, he steals privately to her chambermaid. Sir, a wife ought not greatly to resent this. I would not receive home a daughter who had run away from her husband on that account. A wife should study to reclaim her husband by more attention to please him. Sir, a man will not, once in a hundred instances, leave his wife and go to a harlot, if his wife has not been negligent of pleasing.'[b]

I asked him if it was not hard that one deviation from chastity should so

---

imagined that the High Church of England-man would be so prompt in quoting *Maupertuis*, who, I am sorry to think, stands in the list of those unfortunate mistaken men, who call themselves *esprits forts*. I have, however, a high respect for that Philosopher whom the Great Frederick of Prussia loved and honoured, and addressed pathetically in one of his Poems,

> *Maupertuis, cher Maupertuis,*
> *Que notre vie est peu de chose.*

There was in Maupertuis a vigour and yet a tenderness of sentiment, united with strong intellectual powers, and uncommon ardour of soul. Would he had been a Christian! I cannot help earnestly venturing to hope that he is one now.

[a] For 'upon whom' read 'upon which'.

[b] Add: Here he discovered that acute discrimination, that solid judgement, and that knowledge of human nature, for which he was upon all occasions remarkable. Taking care to keep in view the moral and religious duty, as understood in our nation, he showed clearly from reason and good sense, the greater degree of culpability in the one sex deviating from it than the other; and, at the same time, inculcated a very useful lesson as to *the way to keep him*.

absolutely ruin a young woman. JOHNSON. 'Why no, Sir; it is the great principle which she is taught. When she has given up that principle, she has given up every notion of female honour and virtue, which are all included in chastity.'

A gentleman talked to him of a lady whom he greatly admired and wished to marry, but was afraid of her superiority of talents. 'Sir (said he), you need not be afraid; marry her. Before a year goes about, you'll find that reason much weaker, and that wit not so bright.' Yet the gentleman may be justified in his apprehension by one of Dr Johnson's admirable sentences in his life of Waller: 'He doubtless praised many whom he would have been afraid to marry; and, perhaps, married one whom he would have been ashamed to praise. Many qualities contribute to domestic happiness, upon which poetry has no colours to bestow; and many airs and sallies may delight imagination, which he who flatters them never can approve.'

He praised Signor Baretti. 'His account of Italy is a very entertaining book; and, Sir, I know no man who carries his head higher in conversation than Baretti. There are strong powers in his mind. He has not, indeed, many hooks; but with what hooks he has he grapples very forcibly.'

At this time I observed upon the dial-plate of his watch a short Greek inscription, taken from the New Testament, Νὺξ γαρ ερχεται, being the first words of our Saviour's solemn admonition to the improvement of that time which is allowed us to prepare for eternity; 'the night cometh when no man can work.' He some time afterwards laid aside this dial-plate; and when I asked him the reason, he said, 'It might do very well upon a clock which a man keeps in his closet; but to have it upon his watch which he carries about with him, and which is often looked at by others, might be censured as ostentatious.' Mr Steevens is now possessed of the dial-plate inscribed as above.

He remained at Oxford a considerable time; I was obliged to go to London, where I received his letter, which had been returned from Scotland.

To JAMES BOSWELL, Esq.

MY DEAR BOSWELL – I have omitted a long time to write to you, without knowing very well why. I could now tell why I should not write, for who would write to men who publish the letters of their friends without their leave? Yet I write to you in spite of my caution, to tell you that I shall be glad to see you, and that I wish you would empty your head of Corsica, which I think has filled it rather too long. But, at all events, I shall be glad, very glad to see you. I am, Sir,

Yours affectionately,

SAM. JOHNSON.

Oxford, March 23, 1768.

I answered thus:

To Mr SAMUEL JOHNSON.

London, 26th April, 1768.

MY DEAR SIR – I have received your last letter, which, though very short, and by no means complimentary, yet gave me real pleasure, because it contains these words, 'I shall be glad, very glad to see you.' – Surely, you have no reason to complain of my publishing a single paragraph of one of your letters; the temptation to it was so strong. An irrevocable grant of your friendship, and your dignifying my desire of visiting Corsica with the epithet of 'a wise and noble curiosity', are to me more valuable than many of the grants of kings.

But how can you bid me 'empty my head of Corsica'? My noble-minded friend, do you not feel for an oppressed nation bravely struggling to be free? Consider fairly what is the case. The Corsicans never received any kindness from the Genoese. They never agreed to be subject to them. They owe them nothing; and when reduced to an abject state of slavery, by force, shall they not rise in the great cause of liberty, and break the galling yoke? And shall not every liberal soul be warm for them? Empty my head of Corsica! Empty it of honour, empty it of humanity, empty it of friendship, empty it of piety. No! while I live, Corsica, and the cause of the brave islanders shall ever employ much of my attention, shall ever interest me in the sincerest manner.

. . .

I am, &c.

JAMES BOSWELL.

Upon his arrival in London in May, he surprised me one morning with a visit at my lodgings in Half-Moon-street, was quite satisfied with my explanation, and was in the kindest and most agreeable frame of mind. As he had objected to a part of one of his letters being published, I thought it right to take this opportunity of asking him explicitly whether it would be improper to publish his letters after his death. His answer was, 'Nay, Sir, when I am dead, you may do as you will.'

He talked in his usual style with a rough contempt of popular liberty. 'They make a rout about *universal* liberty, without considering that all that is to be valued, or indeed can be enjoyed by individuals, is private liberty. Political liberty is good only so far as it produces private liberty. Now, Sir, there is the liberty of the press, which you know is a constant topic. Suppose you and I and two hundred more were restrained from printing our thoughts: what then? What proportion would that restraint upon us bear to the private happiness of the nation?'

This mode of representing the inconveniencies of restraint as light and insignificant, was a kind of sophistry in which he delighted to indulge himself, in opposition to the extreme laxity for which it has been fashionable for too many to argue, when it is evident, upon reflection, that the very essence of government is restraint; and certain it is, that as government produces rational happiness, too much restraint is better than too little. But when restraint is unnecessary, and so close as to gall those who are subject to it, the people may and ought to remonstrate; and if relief is not granted, to resist. Of this manly and spirited principle, no man was more convinced than Johnson himself.

About this time Dr Kenrick attacked him, through my sides, in a pamphlet, entitled, 'An Epistle to James Boswell, Esq., occasioned by his having transmitted the moral Writings of Dr Samuel Johnson to Pascal Paoli, General of the Corsicans'. I was at first inclined to answer this pamphlet; but Johnson, who knew that my doing so would only gratify Kenrick, by keeping alive what would soon die away of itself, would not suffer me to take any notice of it.

His sincere regard for Francis Barber, his faithful negro servant, made him so desirous of his further improvement, that he now placed him at a school at Bishop Stortford, in Hertfordshire. This humane attention does Johnson's heart much honour. Out of many letters which Mr Barber received from his master, he has preserved three, which he kindly gave me, and which I shall insert according to their dates.

To Mr FRANCIS BARBER.

DEAR FRANCIS – I have been very much out of order. I am glad to hear that you are well, and design to come soon to see you. I would have you stay at Mrs Clapp's for the present, till I can determine what we shall do. Be a good boy.

My compliments to Mrs Clapp and to Mr Fowler. I am
Yours affectionately,

SAM. JOHNSON.

May 28, 1768.

Soon afterwards, he supped at the Crown and Anchor Tavern, in the Strand, with a company whom I collected to meet him. They were Dr Percy, now Bishop of Dromore, Dr Douglas, now Bishop of Carlisle, Mr Langton, Dr Robertson the Historian, Dr Hugh Blair, and Mr Thomas Davies, who wished much to be introduced to these eminent Scotch literati; but on the present occasion he had very little opportunity of hearing them talk, for with an excess of prudence for which Johnson afterwards found fault with them, they hardly opened their lips, and that only to say something which they were certain would not expose them to the sword of Goliath; such was their anxiety for their fame when in the presence of Johnson. He was this evening in remarkable vigour of mind, and eager to exert himself in conversation, which he did with great readiness and fluency; but I am sorry to find that I have preserved but a small part of what passed.

He allowed high praise to Thomson as a poet; but when one of the company said he was also a very good man, our moralist contested this with great warmth, accusing him of gross sensuality and licentiousness of manners. I was very much afraid that in writing Thomson's life, Dr Johnson would have treated his private character with a stern severity, but I was agreeably disappointed; and I may claim a little merit in it, from my having been at pains to send him authentic accounts of the affectionate and generous conduct of that poet to his sisters, one of whom, the wife of Mr Thomson, schoolmaster at Lanark, I knew, and was presented by her with three of his letters, one of which Dr Johnson has inserted in his life.

He was vehement against old Dr Mounsey, of Chelsea College, as 'a fellow who swore and talked bawdy.' 'I have been often in his company (said Dr Percy), and never heard him swear or talk bawdy.' Mr Davies, who sat next to Dr Percy, having after this had some conversation aside with him, made a discovery which, in his zeal to pay court to Dr Johnson, he eagerly proclaimed aloud from the foot of the table: 'O, Sir, I have found out a very good reason why Dr Percy never heard Mounsey swear or talk bawdy; for he tells me, he never saw him but at the Duke of Northumberland's table.' 'And so, Sir (said Johnson loudly, to Dr Percy), you would shield this man from the charge of swearing and talking bawdy, because he did not do so at the Duke of Northumberland's table. Sir, you might as well tell us that you had seen him hold up his hand at the Old Bailey, and he neither swore nor talked bawdy; or that you had seen him in the cart at Tyburn, and he neither swore nor talked bawdy. And is it thus, Sir, that you presume to controvert what I have related?' Dr Johnson's animadversion was uttered in such a manner that Dr Percy seemed to be displeased, and soon afterwards left the company, of which Johnson did not at that time take any notice.

Swift having been mentioned, Johnson, as usual, treated him with little respect as an author. Some of us endeavoured to support the Dean of St Patrick's, by various arguments. One in particular praised his *Conduct of the Allies*. JOHNSON. 'Sir, his *Conduct of the Allies* is a performance of very little ability.' 'Surely, Sir (said Dr Douglas), you must allow it has strong facts.'[a] JOHNSON. 'Why, yes, Sir; but what is that to the merit of the composition? In the Sessions-paper of the Old Bailey there are strong facts. Housebreaking is a strong fact; robbery is a strong fact; and murder is a *mighty* strong fact: but is great praise due to the historian of those strong facts? No, Sir. Swift has told what he had to tell distinctly enough, but that is all. He had to count ten, and he has counted it right.' – Then recollecting that Mr Davies, by acting as an *informer*, had been the occasion of his talking somewhat too harshly to his friend Dr Percy, for which, probably, when the first ebullition was over, he felt some compunction, he took an opportunity to give him a hit; so added, with a preparatory laugh, 'Why, Sir, Tom Davies might have written the *Conduct of*

[a] Add the following note: My respectable friend, upon reading this passage, observed that he probably must have said not simply 'strong facts', but 'strong facts well arranged'. His lordship, however, knows too well the value of written documents to insist on setting his recollection against my notes taken at the time. He does not attempt to *traverse the record*. The fact, perhaps, may have been, either that the additional words escaped me in the noise of a numerous company, or that Dr Johnson, from his impetuosity, and eagerness to seize an opportunity to make a lively retort, did not allow Dr Douglas to finish his sentence.

the Allies. Poor Tom being thus suddenly dragged into ludicrous notice in presence of the Scottish Doctors, to whom he was ambitious of appearing to advantage, was grievously mortified. Nor did his punishment rest here; for upon subsequent occasions, whenever he, 'statesman all o'er', assumed a strutting importance, I used to hail him – '*the Author of the Conduct of the Allies.*'

When I called upon Dr Johnson next morning, I found him highly satisfied with his colloquial prowess the preceding evening. 'Well (said he), we had good talk.' BOSWELL. 'Yes, Sir; you tossed and gored several persons.'

The late Alexander Earl of Eglintoune, who loved wit more than wine, and men of genius more than sycophants, had a great admiration of Johnson; but from the remarkable elegance of his own manners, was, perhaps, too delicately sensible of the roughness which sometimes appeared in Johnson's behaviour. One evening about this time, when his Lordship did me the honour to sup at my lodgings with Dr Robertson and several other men of literary distinction, he regretted that Johnson had not been educated with more refinement, and lived more in polished society. 'No, no, my Lord (said Signor Baretti), do with him what you would, he would always have been a bear.' 'True (answered the Earl, with a smile), but he would have been a *dancing* bear.'

To obviate all the reflections which have gone round the world to Johnson's prejudice, by applying to him the epithet of a *bear*, let me impress upon my readers a just and happy saying of my friend Goldsmith, who knew him well: 'Johnson, to be sure, has a roughness in his manner; but no man alive has a more tender heart. *He has nothing of the bear but his skin.*'

In 1769, so far as I can discover, the public was favoured with nothing of his composition, either for himself or any of his friends. His *Meditations* too strongly prove that he suffered much both in body and mind; yet was he perpetually striving against *evil*, and nobly endeavouring to advance his intellectual and devotional improvement. Every generous and grateful heart must feel for the distresses of so eminent a benefactor to mankind; and now that his unhappiness is certainly known, must respect that dignity of character which prevented him from complaining.

His Majesty having this[a] year instituted the Royal Academy, Johnson had[b] the honour of being appointed Professor of Ancient Literature. In the course of the year he wrote some letters to Mrs Thrale, passed some part of the summer at Oxford and at Lichfield, and when at Oxford wrote the following letter:

---

[a] For 'this', read 'the preceding'; after 'Academy', read 'of Arts in London'.

[b] Add 'now'; and on 'Literature' put the following note: In which place he has been succeeded by Bennet Langton, Esq. When that truly religious gentleman was elected to this honorary Professorship, at the same time that Edward Gibbon, Esq., noted for introducing a kind of sneering infidelity into his Historical Writings, was elected Professor in Ancient History, in the room of Dr Goldsmith, I observed that it brought to my mind, 'Wicked Will Whiston and good Mr Ditton.' – I am now also of that admirable institution as Secretary for Foreign Correspondence, by the favour of the Academicians, and the approbation of the Sovereign.

To the Reverend Mr THOMAS WARTON.

DEAR SIR – Many years ago, when I used to read in the library of your College, I promised to recompense the College for that permission, by adding to their books a Baskerville's Virgil. I have now sent it, and desire you to reposit it on the shelves in my name.[1]

If you will be pleased to let me know when you have an hour of leisure, I will drink tea with you. I am engaged for the afternoon, tomorrow and on Friday: all my mornings are my own.[2]

I am, &c.,

SAM. JOHNSON.

May 31, 1769.

I came to London in the autumn, and having informed him that I was going to be married in a few months, I wished to have as much of his conversation as I could before engaging in a state of life which would probably keep me more in Scotland, and prevent my seeing him so often as when I was a single man; but I found he was at Brighthelmston with Mr and Mrs Thrale. I was very sorry that I had not his company with me at the Jubilee, in honour of Shakspeare, at Stratford-upon-Avon, the great poet's native town. Johnson's connection both with Shakspeare and Garrick founded a double claim to his presence; and it would have been highly gratifying to Mr Garrick. Upon this occasion I particularly lamented that he had not that warmth of friendship for his brilliant pupil, which we may suppose would have had a benignant effect on both. When almost every man of eminence in the literary world was happy to partake in this festival of genius, the absence of Johnson could not but be wondered at and regretted. The only trace of him there, was in the whimsical advertisement of a haberdasher, who sold *Shakspearian ribbands* of various dyes; and, by way of illustrating their appropriation to the bard, introduced a line from the celebrated Prologue at the opening of Drury-lane theatre:

Each change of *many-colour'd* life he drew.

From Brighthelmston Dr Johnson wrote me the following letter, which they who may think that I ought to have suppressed, must have less ardent feelings than I have always avowed.[a]

1 [It has this inscription in a blank-leaf: '*Hunc librum D.D. Samuel Johnson, eo quod hic loci studiis interdum vacaret.*' Of this library, which is an old Gothic room, he was very fond. On my observing to him that some of the modern libraries of the University were more commodious and pleasant for study, as being more spacious and airy, he replied, 'Sir, if a man has a mind to *prance*, he must study at Christ-Church and All-Souls.' T.W.]

2 [During this visit he seldom or never dined out. He appeared to be deeply engaged in some literary work. Miss Williams was now with him at Oxford. T.W.]

a Add the following note: In the Preface to my Account of Corsica, published in 1768, I thus express myself: 'He who publishes a book affecting not to be an author, and professing an indifference for literary fame, may possibly impose upon many

To James Boswell, Esq.

Dear Sir — Why do you charge me with unkindness? I have omitted nothing that could do you good, or give you pleasure, unless it be that I have forborne to tell you my opinion of your account of Corsica. I believe my opinion, if you think well of my judgement, might have given you pleasure; but when it is considered how much vanity is excited by praise, I am not sure that it would have done you good. Your History is like other histories, but your Journal is in a very high degree curious and delightful. There is between the history and the journal that difference which there will always be found between notions borrowed from without, and notions generated within. Your history was copied from books; your journal rose out of your own experience and observation. You express images which operated strongly upon yourself, and you have impressed them with great force upon your readers. I know not whether I could name any narrative by which curiosity is better excited, or better gratified.

I am glad that you are going to be married; and as I wish you well in things of less importance, wish you well with proportionate ardour in this crisis of your life. What I can contribute to your happiness, I should be very unwilling to with-hold; for I have always loved and valued you, and shall love you and value you still more, as you become more regular and useful: effects which a happy marriage will hardly fail to produce.

I do not find that I am likely to come back very soon from this place. I shall, perhaps, stay a fortnight longer; and a fortnight is a long time to a lover absent from his mistress. Would a fortnight ever have an end?

I am, dear sir,

Your most affectionate humble servant,

SAM. JOHNSON.

Brighthelmston,
Sept. 9, 1769.

---

people such an idea of his consequence as he wishes may be received. For my part I should be proud to be known as an author, and I have an ardent ambition for literary fame; for, of all possessions I should imagine literary fame to be the most valuable. A man who has been able to furnish a book, which has been approved by the world, has established himself as a respectable character in distant society, without any danger of having that character lessened by the observation of his weaknesses. To preserve an uniform dignity among those who see us every day, is hardly possible; and to aim at it, must put us under the fetters of perpetual restraint. The author of an approved book may allow his natural disposition an easy play, and yet indulge the pride of superior genius, when he considers that by those who know him only as an author, he never ceases to be respected. Such an author, when in his hours of gloom and discontent, may have the consolation to think, that his writings are, at that very time, giving pleasure to numbers; and such an author may cherish the hope of being remembered after death, which has been a great object to the noblest minds in all ages.'

After his return to town, we met frequently, and I continued the practice of making notes of his conversation, though not with so much assiduity as I wish I had done. At this time, indeed, I had a sufficient excuse for not being able to appropriate so much time to my journal; for General Paoli, after Corsica had been overpowered by the monarchy of France, was now no longer at the head of his brave countrymen, but having with difficulty escaped from his native island, had sought an asylum in Great-Britain; and it was my duty, as well as my pleasure, to attend much upon him. Such particulars of Johnson's conversation at this period as I have committed to writing, I shall here introduce, without any strict attention to methodical arrangement. Sometimes short notes of different days shall be blended together, and sometimes a day may seem important enough to be separately distinguished.

He said, he would not have Sunday kept with rigid severity and gloom, but with a gravity and simplicity of behaviour.

I told him that David Hume had made a short collection of Scotticisms. 'I wonder (said Johnson), that he should find them.'

He would not admit the importance of the question concerning the legality of general warrants. 'Such a power (he observed), must be vested in every government, to answer particular cases of necessity; and there can be no just complaint but when it is abused, for which those who administer government must be answerable. It is a matter of such indifference, a matter about which the people care so very little, that were a man to be sent over Britain to offer them an exemption from it at a halfpenny a piece, very few would purchase it.' This was a specimen of that laxity of talking, which I have heard him fairly acknowledge; for, surely, while the power of granting general warrants was supposed to be legal, and the apprehension of them hung over our heads, we did not possess that security of freedom, congenial to our happy constitution, and which, by the intrepid exertions of Mr Wilkes, has been happily established.

He said, 'The duration of Parliament, whether for seven years or for the life of the King, appears to me so immaterial, that I would not give half a crown to turn the scale the one way or the other. The *habeas corpus* is the single advantage which our government has over that of other countries.'

On the 30th of September we dined together at the Mitre. I attempted to argue for the superior happiness of the savage life, upon the usual fanciful topics. JOHNSON. 'Sir, there can be nothing more false. The savages have no bodily advantages beyond those of civilised men. They have not better health; and as to care or mental uneasiness, they are not above it, but below it, like bears. No, Sir; you are not to talk such paradox: let me have no more of 't. It cannot entertain, far less can it instruct. Lord Monboddo, one of your Scotch Judges, talked a great deal of such nonsense. I suffered *him*; but I will not suffer *you*.' – BOSWELL. 'But, Sir, does not Rousseau talk such nonsense?' JOHNSON. 'True, Sir; but Rousseau *knows* he is talking nonsense, and laughs at the world for staring at him.' BOSWELL. 'How so, Sir?' JOHNSON. 'Why, Sir, a man who talks nonsense so well, must know that he is talking nonsense. But I am *afraid* (chuckling and laughing), Monboddo does *not* know that he is talking nonsense.'[1] BOSWELL 'Is it wrong then, Sir, to affect singularity, in order to make people stare?' JOHNSON. 'Yes, if you do it by propagating error: and, indeed, it is wrong in any way. There is in human nature a general inclination to make people stare; and, every wise man has himself to cure of it, and does cure himself. If you wish to make people stare by doing better than others, why, make them stare till they stare their eyes out. But consider how easy it is to make people stare, by being absurd. I may do it by going into a drawing-room without my shoes. You remember the gentleman in *The Spectator*, who had a commission of lunacy taken out against him for his extreme singularity, such as never wearing a wig, but a nightcap. Now, Sir, abstractedly, the nightcap was best; but, relatively, the advantage was overbalanced by his making the boys run after him.'

Talking of a London life, he said, 'The happiness of London is not to be conceived but by those who have been in it. I will venture to say, there is more learning and science within the circumference of ten miles from where we now sit, than in all the rest of the kingdom.' BOSWELL. 'The only disadvantage is the great distance at which people live from one another.' JOHNSON. 'Yes, Sir; but that is occasioned by the largeness of it, which is the cause of all the other advantages.' BOSWELL. 'Sometimes I have been in the humour of wishing to retire to a desert.' JOHNSON. 'Sir, you have desert enough in Scotland.'

Although I had promised myself a great deal of instructive conversation with him on the conduct of the married state, of which I had then a near prospect, he did not say much upon that topic. Mr Seward heard him once say, that 'a man has a very bad chance for happiness in that state, unless he marries a woman of very strong and fixed principles of religion.' He maintained to me, contrary to the common notion, that a woman would not be the worse wife for being learned; in which, from all that I have observed of *Artemisias*, I humbly differed from him. That a woman should be sensible and well informed, I allow to be a great advantage; and think that Sir Thomas Overbury,[2] in his rude versification, has very judiciously pointed out that degree of intelligence which is to be desired in a female companion:

> Give me, next *good*, an *understanding wife*,
>   By Nature *wise*, not *learned* by much art;
> Some *knowledge* on her side will all my life
>   More scope of conversation impart;
> Besides, her inborne virtue fortifie;
> They are most firmly good, who best know why.

1 His Lordship having frequently spoken in an abusive manner of Dr Johnson, in my company, I on one occasion during the life-time of my illustrious friend could not refrain from retaliation, and repeated to him this saying.[a]

a Add to the note: He has since published I don't know how many pages in one of his curious books, attempting, in much anger, but with pitiful effect, to persuade mankind that my illustrious friend was not the great and good man which they esteemed and ever will esteem him to be.

2 'A Wife', a poem, 1614.

When I censured a gentleman of my acquaintance for marrying a second time, as it showed a disregard of his first wife, he said, 'Not at all, Sir. On the contrary, were he not to marry again, it might be concluded that his first wife had given him a disgust to marriage; but by taking a second wife he pays the highest compliment to the first, by showing that she made him so happy as a married man, that he wishes to be so a second time.' So ingenious a turn did he give to this delicate question. And yet, on another occasion, he owned that he once had almost asked a promise of Mrs Johnson that she would not marry again, but had checked himself. Indeed I cannot help thinking, that in his case the request would have been unreasonable; for if Mrs Johnson forgot, or thought it no injury to the memory of her first love – the husband of her youth and the father of her children – to make a second marriage, why should she be precluded from a third, should she be so inclined? In Johnson's persevering fond appropriation of his *Tetty*, even after her decease, he seems totally to have overlooked the prior claim of the honest Birmingham trader. I presume that her having been married before had, at times, given him some uneasiness; for I remember his observing upon the marriage of one of our common friends, 'He has done a very foolish thing, Sir; he has married a widow, when he might have married a maid.'

We drank tea with Mrs Williams. I had last year the pleasure of seeing Mrs Thrale at Dr Johnson's one morning, and had conversation enough with her to admire her talents, and to show her that I was as Johnsonian as herself. Dr Johnson had probably been kind enough to speak well of me, for this evening he delivered me a very polite card from Mr Thrale and her, inviting me to Streatham.

On the 6th of October I complied with this obliging invitation, and found, at an elegant villa, six miles from town, every circumstance that can make society pleasing. Johnson, though quite at home, was yet looked up to with an awe, tempered by affection, and seemed to be equally the care of his host and hostess. I rejoiced at seeing him so happy.

He played off his wit against Scotland with a good humoured pleasantry, which gave me, though no bigot to national prejudices, an opportunity for a little contest with him. I having said that England was obliged to us for gardeners, almost all their good gardeners being Scotchmen, – JOHNSON. 'Why, Sir, that is because gardening is much more necessary amongst you than with us, which makes so many of your people learn it. It is all gardening with you. Things which grow wild here, must be cultivated with great care in Scotland. Pray now (throwing himself back in his chair, and laughing), are you ever able to bring the *sloe* to perfection?'

I boasted that we had the honour of being the first to abolish the unhospitable, troublesome, and ungracious custom of giving vails to servants. JOHNSON. 'Sir, you abolished vails, because you were too poor to be able to give them.'

Mrs Thrale disputed with him on the merit of Prior. He attacked him powerfully; said, he wrote of love like a man who had never felt it: his love verses were college verses: and he repeated the song, 'Alexis shunn'd his fellow swains,' &c. in so ludicrous a manner, as to make us all wonder how any one could have been pleased with such fantastical stuff. Mrs Thrale stood to her gun with great courage, in defence of amorous ditties which Johnson despised, till he at last silenced her by saying, 'My dear Lady, talk no more of this. Nonsense can be defended but by nonsense.'

Mrs Thrale then praised Garrick's talent for light gay poetry; and, as a specimen, repeated his song in 'Florizel and Perdita', and dwelt with peculiar pleasure on this line:

> I'd smile with the simple, and feed with the poor.

JOHNSON. 'Nay, my dear Lady, this will never do. Poor David! Smile with the simple! What folly is that! And who would feed with the poor that can help it? No, no; let me smile with the wise, and feed with the rich.' I repeated this sally to Garrick, and wondered to find his sensibility as a writer not a little irritated by it. To sooth him, I observed, that Johnson spared none of us; and I quoted the passage in Horace, in which he compares one who attacks his friends for the sake of a laugh, to a pushing ox that is marked by a bunch of hay put upon his horns: '*faenum habet in cornu.*' 'Aye (said Garrick, vehemently), he has a whole *mow* of it.'

Talking of history, Johnson said, 'We may know historical facts to be true, as we may know facts in common life to be true. Motives are generally unknown. We cannot trust to the characters we find in history, unless when they are drawn by those who knew the persons; as those, for instance, by Sallust and by Lord Clarendon.'

He would not allow much merit to Whitfield's oratory. 'His popularity, Sir (said he), is chiefly owing to the peculiarity of his manner. He would be followed by crowds were he to wear a nightcap in the pulpit, or were he to preach from a tree.'

I know not from what spirit of contradiction he burst out into a violent declamation against the Corsicans, of whose heroism I talked in high terms. 'Sir (said he), what is all this rout about the Corsicans? They have been at war with the Genoese for upwards of twenty years, and have never yet taken their fortified towns. They might have battered down their walls and reduced them to powder in twenty years. They might have pulled the walls in pieces, and cracked the stones with their teeth in twenty years.' It was in vain to argue with him upon the want of artillery: he was not to be resisted for the moment.

On the evening of October 10, I presented Dr Johnson to General Paoli. I had greatly wished that two men, for whom I had the highest esteem, should meet. They met with a manly ease, mutually conscious of their own abilities, and of the abilities of each other. The General spoke Italian, and Dr Johnson English, and understood one another very well, with a little aid of interpretation from me, in which I compared myself to an isthmus which joins two great continents. Upon Johnson's approach, the General said, 'From what I have read of your works, Sir, and from what Mr Boswell has told me of you, I have long held you in great veneration.' The General talked of languages being formed on the particular notions and manners of a people, without knowing which, we cannot know the language. We may know the direct signification of single words; but by these no beauty of expression, no sally of genius, no wit is conveyed to the mind. All this must be by allusion to other ideas. 'Sir (said Johnson), you talk of language as if you had never done anything else but study it, instead of governing a nation.' The General said, 'Questo e un troppo gran complimento,' this is too great a compliment. Johnson answered, 'I should have thought so, Sir, if I had not heard you talk.' The General asked him, what he thought of the spirit of infidelity which was so prevalent. JOHNSON. 'Sir, this gloom of infidelity, I hope, is only a transient cloud passing through the hemisphere, which will soon be dissipated, and the sun break forth with his usual splendour.' 'You think then (said the General), that they will change their principles like their clothes.' JOHNSON. 'Why, Sir, if they bestow no more thought of principles than on dress, it must be so.' The General said, that 'a great part of the fashionable infidelity was owing to a desire of showing courage. Men who have no opportunities of showing it as to things in this life, take death and futurity as objects on which to display it.' JOHNSON. 'That is mighty foolish affectation. Fear is one of the passions of human nature, of which it is impossible to divest it. You remember that the Emperor Charles V, when he read upon the tomb-stone of a Spanish noble-man, "Here lies one who never knew fear," wittily said, "then he never snuffed a candle with his fingers." '

He talked a few words of French to the General; but finding he did not do it with facility, he asked for pen, ink, and paper, and wrote the following note:

'J'ai lu dans la géographie de Lucas de Linda un Pater-noster écrit dans une langue toutafait différente de l'Italienne et de toutes autres lesquelles se derivent du Latin. L'auteur l'appelle linguam Corsicae rusticam; elle a peutetre passé, peu à peu; mais elle a certainement prevalue autrefois dans les montagnes et dans la campagne. Le même auteur dit la même chose en parlant de Sardaigne; qu'il y a deux langues dans l'Isle, une des villes, l'autre de la campagne.'

The General immediately informed him that the lingua rustica was only in Sardinia.

Dr Johnson went home with me, and drank tea till late in the night. He said, General Paoli had the loftiest port of any man he had ever seen. He denied that military men were always the best bred men. Perfect good breeding, he observed, consists in having no particular mark of any profession, but a general elegance of manners: whereas in a military man you can commonly distinguish the brand of a soldier, l'homme d'épée.

Dr Johnson shunned to-night any discussion of the perplexed question of fate and free will, which I attempted to agitate: 'Sir (said he), we know our will is free, and there's an end of 't.'

He honoured me with his company at dinner on the 16th of October, at my lodgings in Old Bond-street, with Sir Joshua Reynolds, Mr Garrick, Dr Goldsmith, Mr Murphy, Mr Bickerstaff, and Mr Thomas Davies. Garrick played round him with a fond vivacity, taking hold of the breasts of his coat, and, looking up in his face with a lively archness, complimented him on the good health which he seemed then to enjoy; while the sage, shaking his head, beheld him with a gentle complacency. One of the company not being come at the appointed hour, I proposed, as usual upon such occasions, to order dinner to be served; adding, 'Ought six people to be kept waiting for one?' 'Why, yes (answered Johnson, with a delicate humanity), if the one will suffer more by your sitting down, than the six will do by waiting.' Goldsmith, to divert the tedious minutes, strutted about, bragging of his dress, and I believe was seriously vain of it, for his mind was wonderfully prone to such impressions. 'Come, come (said Garrick), talk no more of that. You are, perhaps, the worst – eheh!' – Goldsmith was eagerly attempting to interrupt him, when Garrick went on, laughing ironically, 'Nay, you will always *look* like a *gentleman*; but I am talking of being well or ill *dressed*. 'Well, let me tell you (said Goldsmith), when my tailor brought home my bloom-coloured coat, he said "Sir, I have a favour to beg of you. When any body asks you who made your clothes, be pleased to mention John Phielby, at the Harrow, in Water-lane." ' JOHNSON. 'Why, Sir, that was because he knew the strange colour would attract crowds to gaze at it, and thus they might hear of him, and see how well he could make a coat, even of so absurd a colour.'

After dinner, our conversation first turned upon Pope. Johnson said, his characters of men were admirably drawn, those of women not so well. He repeated to us, in his forcible melodious manner, the concluding lines of the *Dunciad*. While he was talking loudly in praise of those lines, one of the company ventured to say, 'Too fine for such a poem – a poem on what?' JOHNSON. (with a disdainful look) 'Why, on *dunces*. It was worth while being a dunce then. Ah, Sir, hadst *thou* lived in those days! It is not worth while being a dunce now, when there are no wits.' Bickerstaff observed, as a peculiar circumstance, that Pope's fame was higher when he was alive than it was then. Johnson said, his Pastorals were poor things, though the versification was fine. He told us, with high satisfaction, the anecdote of Pope's inquiring who was the author of his *London*, and saying he will be soon *deterré*. He observed, that in Dryden's poetry there were passages drawn from a profundity which Pope could never reach. He repeated some fine lines on love, by the former (which I have now forgotten), and gave great applause to the character of Zimri. Goldsmith said, that Pope's character of Addison showed a deep knowledge of the human heart. Johnson said, that the description of the temple, in the *Mourning Bride*, was the finest poetical passage he had ever read; he recollected none in Shakspeare equal to it. – 'But (said Garrick, all alarmed for 'the god of his idolatry'), we know not the extent and variety of his powers. We are to suppose there are such passages in his works. Shakspeare must not suffer from the badness of our memories.' Johnson, diverted by this enthusiastic jealousy, went on with greater ardour: 'No, Sir; Congreve has *nature* (smiling on the tragic eagerness of Garrick); but composing himself, he added, 'Sir, this is not comparing Congreve on the whole with Shakspeare on the whole; but only maintaining that

Congreve has one finer passage than any that can be found in Shakspeare. Sir, a man may have no more than ten guineas in the world, but he may have those ten guineas in one piece; and so may have a finer piece than a man who has ten thousand pounds: but then he has only one ten-guinea piece. – What I mean is, that you can show me no passage where there is simply a description of material objects, without any intermixture of moral notions, which produces such an effect.' Mr Murphy mentioned Shakspeare's description of the night before the battle of Agincourt; but it was observed, it had *men* in it. Mr Davies suggested the speech of Juliet, in which she figures herself awaking in the tomb of her ancestors. Some one mentioned the description of Dover Cliff. JOHNSON. 'No, Sir; it should be all precipice – all vacuum. The crows impede your fall. The diminished appearance of the boats, and other circumstances, are all very good description; but do not impress the mind at once with the horrible idea of immense height. The impression is divided; you pass on by computation from one stage of the tremendous space to another. Had the girl in *The Mourning Bride* said, she could not cast her shoe to the top of one of the pillars in the temple, it would not have aided the idea, but weakened it.'

Talking of a Barrister who had a bad utterance, some one (to rouse Johnson), wickedly said, that he was unfortunate in not having been taught oratory by Sheridan. JOHNSON. 'Nay, sir, if he had been taught by Sheridan, he would have cleared the room.' GARRICK. 'Sheridan has too much vanity to be a good man.' We shall now see Johnson's mode of *defending* a man; taking him into his own hands, and discriminating. JOHNSON. 'No, Sir. There is, to be sure, in Sheridan something to reprehend, and everything to laugh at; but, Sir, he is not a bad man. No, Sir; were mankind to be divided into good and bad, he would stand considerably within the ranks of good. And, Sir, it must be allowed that Sheridan excels in plain declamation, though he can exhibit no character.'

I should, perhaps, have suppressed this disquisition concerning a person of whose merit and worth I think with respect, had he not attacked Johnson so outrageously in his Life of Swift, and, at the same time, treated us his admirers as a set of pigmies. He who has provoked the lash of wit, cannot complain that he smarts from it.

Mrs Montague, a lady distinguished for having written an Essay on Shakspeare, being mentioned; REYNOLDS. 'I think that essay does her honour.' JOHNSON. 'Yes, Sir; it does *her* honour, but it would do nobody else honour. I have, indeed, not read it all. But when I take up the end of a web, and find it packthread, I do not expect, by looking further, to find embroidery. Sir, I will venture to say there is not one sentence of true criticism in her book.' GARRICK. 'But, Sir, surely it shows how much Voltaire has mistaken Shakspeare, which nobody else has done.' JOHNSON. 'Sir, nobody else has thought it worth while. And what merit is there in that? You may as well praise a schoolmaster for whipping a boy who has construed ill. No, Sir, there is no real criticism in it; none showing the beauty of thought, as formed on the workings of the human heart.'

The admirers of this Essay[1] may be offended at the slighting manner in which Johnson spoke of it; but let it be remembered, that he gave his honest opinion, unbiassed by any prejudice, or any proud jealousy of a woman intruding herself into the chair of criticism; for Sir Joshua Reynolds has told me that when the Essay first came out, and it was not known who had written it, Johnson wondered how Sir Joshua could like it. At this time Sir Joshua himself had received no information concerning the author, except being assured by one of our most eminent literati, that it was clear its author did not know the Greek tragedies in the original. One day at Sir Joshua's table, when it was related that Mrs Montague, in an excess of compliment to the author of a modern tragedy, had exclaimed, 'I tremble for Shakspeare'; Johnson said, 'When Shakspeare has got —— for his rival, and Mrs Montague for his defender, he is in a poor state indeed.'

Johnson proceeded: 'The Scotchman has taken the right method in his *Elements of Criticism*. I do not mean that he had taught us anything: but he has told us old things in a new way.' MURPHY. 'He seems to have read a great deal of French criticism, and wants to make it his own; as if he had been for years anatomising the heart of man, and peeping into every cranny of it.' GOLDSMITH. 'It is easier to write that book, than to read it.' JOHNSON. 'We have an example of true criticism in Burke's *Essay on the Sublime and Beautiful*; and, if I recollect, there is also Du Bos; and Bouhours, who shows all beauty to depend on truth. There is no great merit in telling how many plays have ghosts in them, and how this ghost is better than that. You must show how terror is impressed on the human heart. – In the description of night in Macbeth, the beetle and the bat detract from the general idea of darkness – inspissated gloom.'

Politics being mentioned, he said, 'This petitioning is a new mode of distressing government, and a mighty easy one. I will undertake to get petitions either against quarter guineas or half guineas, with the help of a little hot wine. There must be no yielding to encourage this. The object is not important enough. We are not to blow up half a dozen palaces, because one cottage is burning.'

The conversation then took another turn. JOHNSON. 'It is amazing what ignorance of certain points one sometimes finds in men of eminence. A wit about town, who wrote Latin bawdy verses, asked me, how it happened that England and Scotland, which were once two kingdoms, were now one: and Sir Fletcher Norton did not seem to know that there were such publications as the Reviews.'

1 Of whom I acknowledge myself to be one, considering it as a piece of the secondary or comparative species of criticism, and not of that profound species which alone Dr Johnson would allow to be 'real criticism'. It is, besides, clearly and elegantly expressed, and has done effectually what it professed to do, namely, vindicated Shakspeare from the misrepresentations of Voltaire; and considering how many young people were misled by his witty, though false observations, Mrs Montague's Essay was of service to Shakspeare with a certain class of readers, and is, therefore, entitled to praise. Johnson, I am assured, allowed the merit which I have stated, saying (with reference to Voltaire), 'it is conclusive *ad hominem*.'

'The ballad of Hardyknute has no great merit, if it be really ancient. People talk of nature, but mere obvious nature may be exhibited with very little power of mind.'

On Thursday, October 19, I passed the evening with him at his house. He advised me to complete a Dictionary of words peculiar to Scotland, of which I showed him a specimen. 'Sir (said he), Ray has made a collection of north-country words. By collecting those of your country, you will do a useful thing towards the history of the language.' He bade me also go on with collections which I was making upon the antiquities of Scotland. 'Make a large book; a folio.' BOSWELL. 'But of what use will it be, Sir?' JOHNSON. 'Never mind the use; do it.'

I complained that he had not mentioned Garrick in his preface to Shakspeare; and asked him if he did not admire him. JOHNSON. 'Yes, as a poor player, who frets and struts his hour upon the stage; as a shadow.' BOSWELL. 'But has he not brought Shakspeare into notice?' JOHNSON. 'Sir, to allow that would be to lampoon the age. Many of Shakspeare's plays are the worse for being acted: Macbeth, for instance.' BOSWELL. 'What, Sir, is nothing gained by decoration and action? Indeed, I do wish that you had mentioned Garrick.' JOHNSON. 'My dear Sir, had I mentioned him, I must have mentioned many more: Mrs Pritchard, Mrs Cibber – nay, and Mr Cibber too; he too altered Shakspeare.' BOSWELL. 'You have read his apology, Sir? JOHNSON. 'Yes, it is very entertaining. But as for Cibber himself, taking from his conversation all that he ought not to have said, he was a poor creature. I remember when he brought me one of his Odes to have my opinion of it, I could not bear such nonsense, and would not let him read it to the end; so little respect had I for *that great man* (laughing). Yet I remember Richardson wondering that I could treat him with familiarity.'

I mentioned to him that I had seen the execution of several convicts at Tyburn, two days before, and that none of them seemed to be under any concern. JOHNSON. 'Most of them, Sir, have never thought at all.' BOSWELL. 'But is not the fear of death natural to man?' JOHNSON. 'So much so, Sir, that the whole of life is but keeping away the thoughts of it.' He then, in a low and earnest tone, talked of his meditating upon the awful hour of his own dissolution, and in what manner he should conduct himself upon that occasion: 'I know not (said he), whether I should wish to have a friend by me, or have it all between GOD and myself.'

Talking of our feeling for the distresses of others; – JOHNSON. 'Why, Sir, there is much noise made about it, but it is greatly exaggerated. No, Sir, we have a certain degree of feeling to prompt us to do good: more than that, Providence does not intend. It would be misery to no purpose.' BOSWELL. 'But suppose now, Sir, that one of your intimate friends were apprehended for an offence for which he might be hanged.' JOHNSON. 'I should do what I could to bail him, and give him any other assistance; but if he were once fairly hanged, I should not suffer.' BOSWELL. 'Would you eat your dinner that day, Sir?' JOHNSON. 'Yes, Sir; and eat it as if he were eating it with me. Why, there's Baretti, who is to be tried for his life to-morrow, friends have risen up for him on every side; yet if he should be hanged, none of them will eat a slice of plum-pudding the less. Sir, that sympathetic feeling goes a very little way in depressing the mind.'

I told him that I had dined lately at Foote's, who showed me a letter to him from Tom Davies, telling him that he had not been able to sleep from the concern which he felt on account of *this sad affair of Baretti*, begging of him to try if he could suggest anything that might be of service to him; and at the same time recommending to him an industrious young man who kept a pickle-shop. JOHNSON. 'Aye, Sir, here you have a specimen of human sympathy; a friend hanged, and a cucumber pickled. We know not whether Baretti or the pickle-man has kept Davies from sleep, nor does he know himself. And as to his not sleeping, Sir; Tom Davies is a very great man; Tom has been upon the stage, and knows how to do those things: I have not been upon the stage, and cannot do those things.' BOSWELL. 'I have often blamed myself, Sir, for not feeling for others as sensibly as many say they do.' JOHNSON. 'Sir, don't be duped by them any more. You will find these very feeling people are not very ready to do you good. They pay you by feeling.'

BOSWELL. 'Foote has a great deal of humour? JOHNSON. 'Yes, Sir.' BOSWELL. 'He has a singular talent of exhibiting character.' JOHNSON. 'Sir, it is not a talent, it is a vice; it is what others abstain from. It is not comedy, which exhibits the character of a species, as that of a miser gathered from many misers; it is farce, which exhibits individuals.' BOSWELL. 'Did not he think of exhibiting you, Sir?' JOHNSON. 'Sir, fear restrained him; he knew I would have broken his bones. I would have saved him the trouble of cutting off a leg; I would not have left him a leg to cut off.' BOSWELL. 'Pray, Sir, is not Foote an infidel?' JOHNSON. 'I do not know, Sir, that the fellow is an infidel; but if he be an infidel, he is an infidel as a dog is an infidel; that is to say, he has never thought upon the subject.'[1] BOSWELL. 'I suppose, Sir, he has thought superficially, and seized the first notions which occurred to his mind.' JOHNSON. 'Why then, Sir, still he is like a dog, that snatches the piece next him. Did you never observe that dogs have not the power of comparing? A dog will take a small bit of meat as readily as a large, when both are before him.'

'Buchanan (he observed) has fewer *centos* than any modern Latin poet. He not only had great knowledge of the Latin language, but was a great poetical genius. Both the Scaligers praise him.'

---

[1] When Mr Foote was at Edinburgh, he thought fit to entertain a numerous Scotch company with a great deal of coarse jocularity, at the expense of Dr Johnson, imagining it would be acceptable. I felt this as not civil to me, but sat very patiently till he had exhausted his merriment on that subject; and then observed, that surely Johnson must be allowed to have some sterling wit, and that I had heard him say a very good thing of Mr Foote himself. 'Ah, my old friend Sam (cried Foote), no man says better things: do let us have it.' Upon which I told the above story, which produced a very loud laugh from the company. But I never saw Foote so disconcerted. He looked grave and angry, and entered into a serious refutation of the justice of the remark. 'What, Sir (said he), talk thus of a man of liberal education – a man who for years was at the University of Oxford – a man who has added sixteen new characters to the English drama of his country!'

He again talked of the passage in Congreve with high commendation, and said, 'Shakspeare never has six lines together without a fault. Perhaps you may find seven: but this does not refute my general assertion. If I come to an orchard, and say there's no fruit here, and then comes a poring man, who finds two apples and three pears, and tells me, "Sir, you are mistaken, I have found both apples and pears," I should laugh at him: what would that be to the purpose?'

BOSWELL. 'What do you think of Dr Young's *Night Thoughts*, Sir?' JOHNSON. 'Why, Sir, there are very fine things in them.' BOSWELL. 'Is there not less religion in the nation now, Sir, than there was formerly?' JOHNSON. 'I don't know, Sir, that there is.' BOSWELL. 'For instance, there used to be a chaplain in every great family, which we do not find now.' JOHNSON. 'Neither do you find many of the state servants which great families used formerly to have. There is a change of modes in the whole department of life.'

Next day, October 20, he appeared, for the only time I suppose in his life, as a witness in a Court of Justice, being called to give evidence to the character of Mr Baretti, who having stabbed a man in the street, was arraigned at the Old Bailey for murder. Never did such a constellation of genius enlighten the awful Sessions House; Mr Burke, Mr Garrick, Mr Beauclerk, and Dr Johnson: and undoubtedly their favourable testimony had due weight with the Court and Jury. Johnson gave his evidence in a slow, deliberate, and distinct manner, which was uncommonly impressive. It is well known that Mr Baretti was acquitted.

On the 26th of October, we dined together at the Mitre tavern. I found fault with Foote for indulging his talent of ridicule at the expense of his visitors, which I colloquially termed making fools of his company. JOHNSON. 'Why, Sir, when you go to see Foote, you do not go to see a saint: you go to see a man who will be entertained at your house, and then bring you on a public stage; who will entertain you at his house, for the very purpose of bringing you on a public stage. Sir, he does not make fools of his company; they whom he exposes are fools already: he only brings them into action.'

Talking of trade, he observed, 'It is a mistaken notion that a vast deal of money is brought into a nation by trade. It is not so. Commodities come from commodities; but trade produces no capital accession of wealth. However, though there should be little profit in money, there is a considerable profit in pleasure, as it gives to one nation the production of another; as we have wines and fruits, and many other foreign articles, brought to us.' BOSWELL. 'Yes, Sir, and there is a profit in pleasure, by its furnishing occupation to such numbers of mankind.' JOHNSON. 'Why, Sir, you cannot call that pleasure to which all are averse, and which none begin but with the hope of leaving off; a thing which men dislike before they have tried it, and when they have tried it.' BOSWELL. 'But, Sir, the mind must be employed, and we grow weary when idle.' JOHNSON. 'That is, Sir, because, others being busy, we want company; but if we were all idle, there would be no growing weary; we should all entertain one another. There is, indeed, this in trade: it gives men an opportunity of improving their situation. If there were no trade, many who are poor would always remain poor. But no man loves labour for itself.' BOSWELL. 'Yes, Sir, I know a person who does. He is a very laborious Judge, and he loves the labour.' JOHNSON. 'Sir, that is because he loves respect and distinction. Could he have them without labour, he would like it less.' 'He tells me he likes it for itself.' – 'Why, Sir, he fancies so, because he is not accustomed to abstract.'

We went home to his house to tea. Mrs Williams made it with sufficient dexterity, notwithstanding her blindness, though her manner of satisfying herself that the cups were full enough, was a little awkward:[a] she put her finger down a certain way, till she felt the tea touch it.[b] In my first elation at being allowed the privilege of attending Dr Johnson at his late visits to this lady, which was like being *e secretioribus consiliis*, I willingly drank cup after cup, as if it had been the Heliconian spring. But as the charm of novelty went off, I grew more fastidious; and besides, I discovered that she was of a peevish temper.

There was a pretty large circle this evening. Dr Johnson was in very good humour, lively, and ready to talk upon all subjects. Mr Fergusson, the self-taught philosopher, told him of a new-invented machine which went without horses: a man who sat in it turned a handle, which worked a spring that drove it forward. 'Then, Sir (said Johnson), what is gained is, the man has his choice whether he will move himself alone, or himself and the machine too.' Dominicetti being mentioned, he would not allow him any merit. 'There is nothing in all this boasted system. No, Sir; medicated baths can be no better than warm water: their only effect can be that of tepid moisture.' One of the company took the other side, maintaining that medicines of various sorts, and some too of most powerful effect, are introduced into the human frame by the medium of the pores; and, therefore, when warm water is impregnated with salutiferous substances, it may produce great effects as a bath. This appeared to me very satisfactory. Johnson did not answer it; but talking for victory, and determined to be master of the field, he had recourse to the device which Goldsmith imputed to him in the witty words of one of Cibber's comedies: 'There is no arguing with Johnson; for when his pistol misses fire, he knocks you down with the butt end of it.' He turned to the gentleman, 'Well, Sir, go to Dominicetti, and get thyself fumigated, but be sure that the steam be directed to thy head, for *that* is the *peccant part*.' This produced a triumphant roar of laughter from the motley assembly of philosophers, printers, and dependents, male and female,

I know not how so whimsical a thought came into my mind, but I asked, 'If, Sir, you were shut up in a castle, and a newborn child with you, what would you do?' JOHNSON. 'Why, Sir, I should not much like my company.'

---

[a] For 'was', read 'appeared to me'; after 'awkward', read 'for I fancied that'.

[b] Add a note: I have since had reason to think that I was mistaken; for I have been informed by a lady, who was long intimate with her, and likely to be a more accurate observer of such matters, that she had acquired such a niceness of touch, as to know, by the feeling of the outside of the cup, how near it was to being full.

BOSWELL. 'But would you take the trouble of rearing it?' He seemed, as may well be supposed, unwilling to pursue the subject, but upon my persevering in my question, replied, 'Why yes, Sir, I would; but I must have all conveniences. If I had no garden, I would make a shed on the roof, and take it there for fresh air. I should feed it, and wash it much, and with warm water to please it, not with cold water to give it pain. BOSWELL. 'But, Sir, does not heat relax?' JOHNSON. 'Sir, you are not to imagine the water is to be very hot. I would not *coddle* the child. No, Sir, the hardy method of treating children does no good. I'll take you five children from London, who shall cuff five Highland children. Sir, a man bred in London will carry a burthen, or run, or wrestle, as well as a man brought up in the hardiest manner in the country.' BOSWELL. 'Good living, I suppose, makes the Londoners strong.' JOHNSON. 'Why, Sir, I don't know that it does. Our chairmen from Ireland, who are as strong men as any, have been brought up upon potatoes. Quantity makes up for quality.' BOSWELL. 'Would you teach this child that I have furnished you with, any thing?' JOHNSON. 'No, I should not be apt to teach it.' BOSWELL. 'Would not you have a pleasure in teaching it?' JOHNSON. 'No, Sir, I should *not* have a pleasure in teaching it.' BOSWELL. 'Have you not a pleasure in teaching men? – *There* I have you. You have the same pleasure in teaching men, that I should have in teaching children.' JOHNSON, 'Why, something about that.'

BOSWELL. 'Do you think, Sir, that what is called natural affection is born with us? It seems to me to be the effect of habit, or of gratitude for kindness. No child has it for a parent whom it has not seen.' JOHNSON. 'Why, Sir, I think there is an instinctive natural affection in parents towards their children.'

Russia being mentioned as likely to become a great empire, by the rapid increase of population; – JOHNSON. 'Why, Sir, I see no prospect of their propagating more. They can have no more children than they can get. I know of no way to make them breed more than they do. It is not from reason and prudence that people marry, but from inclination. A man is poor; he thinks, "I cannot be worse, and so I'll e'en take Peggy." ' BOSWELL. 'But have not nations been more populous at one period than another?' JOHNSON. 'Yes, Sir; but that has been owing to the people being less thinned at one period than another, whether by emigrations, war, or pestilence, not by their being more or less prolific. Births at all times bear the same proportion to the same number of people.' BOSWELL. 'But, to consider the state of our own country; – does not throwing a number of farms into one hand hurt population?' JOHNSON. 'Why no, Sir; the same quantity of food being produced, will be consumed by the same number of mouths, though the people may be disposed of in different ways. We see, if corn be dear, and butchers' meat cheap, the farmers all apply themselves to the raising of corn, till it becomes plentiful and cheap, and then butchers' meat becomes dear; so that an equality is always preserved. No, Sir, let fanciful men do as they will, depend upon it, it is difficult to disturb the system of life.' BOSWELL. 'But, Sir, is it not a very bad thing for landlords to oppress their tenants by raising their rents?' JOHNSON. 'Very bad. But, Sir, it never can have any general influence; it may distress some individuals. For consider this: landlords cannot do without tenants. Now tenants will not give more for land than land is worth. If they can make more of their money by keeping a shop, or any other way, they'll do it, and so oblige landlords to let land come back to a reasonable rent, in order that they may get tenants. Land, in England, is an article of commerce. A tenant who pays his landlord his rent, thinks himself no more obliged to him than you think yourself obliged to a man in whose shop you buy a piece of goods. He knows the landlord does not let him have his land for less than he can get from others, in the same manner as the shopkeeper sells his goods. No shopkeeper sells a yard of ribband for six-pence, when seven-pence is the current price.' BOSWELL. 'But, Sir, is it not better that tenants should be dependent on landlords?' JOHNSON. 'Why, Sir, as there are many more tenants than land-lords, perhaps, strictly speaking, we should wish not. But if you please you may let your lands cheap, and so get the value, part in money and part in homage. I should agree with you in that.' BOSWELL. 'So, Sir, you laugh at schemes of political improvement.' JOHNSON. 'Why, Sir, most schemes of political improvement are very laughable things.'

He observed, 'Providence has wisely ordered that the more numerous men are, the more difficult it is for them to agree in any thing, and so they are governed. There is no doubt, that if the poor should reason, "We'll be the poor no longer, we'll make the rich take their turn", they could easily do it, were it not that they can't agree. So the common soldiers, though so much more numerous than their officers, are governed by them for the same reason.'

He said, 'Mankind have a strong attachment to the habitations to which they have been accustomed. You see the inhabitants of Norway do not with one consent quit it, and go to some part of America, where there is a mild climate, and where they may have the same produce from land, with the tenth part of the labour. No, Sir; their affection for their old dwellings, and the terror of a general change, keep them at home. Thus, we see many of the finest spots in the world thinly inhabited, and many rugged spots well inhabited.'

The *London Chronicle*, which was the only newspaper he constantly took in, being brought, the office of reading it aloud was assigned to me. I was diverted by his impatience. He made me pass over so many parts of it, that my task was very easy. He would not suffer one of the petitions to the King about the Middlesex election to be read.

I had hired a Bohemian as my servant while I remained in London, and being much pleased with him, I asked Dr Johnson whether his being a Roman Catholic should prevent my taking him with me to Scotland. JOHNSON. 'Why no, Sir. If *he* has no objection, you can have none.' BOSWELL. 'So, Sir, you are no great enemy to the Roman Catholic religion.' JOHNSON. 'No more, Sir, than to the Presbyterian religion.' BOSWELL. 'You are joking.' JOHNSON. 'No, Sir, I really think so. Nay, Sir, of the two, I prefer the Popish.' BOSWELL. 'How so, Sir?' JOHNSON. 'Why, Sir, the Presbyterians have no church, no apostolical ordination.' BOSWELL. 'And do you think that absolutely essential, Sir?' JOHNSON. 'Why, Sir, as it was an apostolical institution, I think it is dangerous to be without it. And, Sir, the Presbyterians have no public worship: they have no form of prayer in which they know they are to join.

They go to hear a man pray, and are to judge whether they will join with him.' BOSWELL. 'But, Sir, their doctrine is the same with that of the Church of England. Their confession of faith, and the thirty-nine articles, contain the same points, even the doctrine of predestination.' JOHNSON. 'Why yes, Sir; predestination was a part of the clamour of the times, so it is mentioned in our articles, but with as little positiveness as could be.' BOSWELL. 'Is it necessary, Sir, to believe all the thirty-nine articles?' JOHNSON. 'Why, Sir, that is a question which has been much agitated. Some have thought it necessary that they should all be believed; others have considered them to be only articles of peace, that is to say, you are not to preach against them.' BOSWELL. 'It appears to me, Sir, that predestination, or what is equivalent to it, cannot be avoided, if we hold an universal presence in the Deity.' JOHNSON. 'Why, Sir, does not GOD every day see things going on without preventing them?' BOSWELL. 'True, Sir; but if a thing be certainly foreseen, it must be fixed, and cannot happen otherwise; and if we apply this consideration to the human mind, there is no free will, nor do I see how prayer can be of any avail.' He mentioned Dr Clarke, and Bishop Bramhall on Liberty and Necessity, and bid me read South's sermons on Prayer; but avoided the question which has excruciated philosophers and divines, beyond any other. I did not press it further, when I perceived that he was displeased, and shrunk from any abridgement of an attribute usually ascribed to the Divinity, however irreconcilable in its full extent with the grand system of moral government. His supposed orthodoxy here cramped the vigorous powers of his understanding. He was confined by a chain which early imagination and long habit made him think massy and strong, but which, had he ventured to try, he could at once have snapped asunder.

I proceeded: 'What do you think, Sir, of Purgatory, as believed by the Roman Catholics?' JOHNSON. 'Why, Sir, it is a very harmless doctrine. They are of opinion that the generality of mankind are neither so obstinately wicked as to deserve everlasting punishment, nor so good as to merit being admitted into the society of blessed spirits; and therefore that GOD is graciously pleased to allow of a middle state, where they may be purified by certain degrees of suffering. You see, Sir, there is nothing unreasonable in this.' BOSWELL. 'But then, Sir, their masses for the dead?' JOHNSON. 'Why, Sir, if it be once established that there are souls in purgatory, it is as proper to pray for them, as for our brethren of mankind who are yet in this life.' BOSWELL. 'The idolatry of the Mass?' – JOHNSON. 'Sir, there is no idolatry in the Mass. They believe GOD to be there, and they adore him.' BOSWELL. 'The worship of Saints?' – JOHNSON. 'Sir, they do not worship saints; they invoke them; they only ask their prayers. I am talking all this time of the *doctrines* of the church of Rome. I grant you that in *practice*, Purgatory is made a lucrative imposition, and that the people do become idolatrous as they recommend themselves to the tutelary protection of particular saints. I think their giving the sacrament only in one kind is criminal, because it is contrary to the express institution of CHRIST, and I wonder how the Council of Trent admitted it. BOSWELL. 'Confession?' – JOHNSON. 'Why, I don't know but that is a good thing. The scripture says, "Confess your faults one to another"; and the priests confess as well as the laity. Then it must be considered that their absolution is only upon repentance, and often upon penance also. You think your sins may be forgiven without penance, upon repentance alone.'

I thus ventured to mention all the common objections against the Roman Catholic Church, that I might hear so great a man upon them. What he said is here accurately recorded. But it is not improbable that if one had taken the other side, he might have reasoned differently.

I must however mention, that he had a respect for '*the old religion*', as the mild Melancthon called that of the Roman Catholic Church, even while he was exerting himself for its reformation in some particulars. Sir William Scott informs me, that he heard Johnson say, 'A man who is converted from Protestantism to Popery, may be sincere: he parts with nothing: he is only superadding to what he already had. But a convert from Popery to Protestantism, gives up so much of what he has held as sacred as any thing that he retains; there is so much *laceration of mind* in such a conversion, that it can hardly be sincere and lasting.' The truth of this reflection may be confirmed by many and eminent instances, some of which will occur to most of my readers.

When we were alone, I introduced the subject of death, and endeavoured to maintain that the fear of it might be got over. I told him that David Hume said, he was no more uneasy to think he should *not be* after this life, than that he *had not been* before he began to exist. JOHNSON. 'Sir, if he really thinks so, his perceptions are disturbed; he is mad: if he does not think so, he lies. He may tell you, he holds his finger in the flame of a candle without feeling pain; would you believe him? When he dies, he at least gives up all he has.' BOSWELL. 'Foote, Sir, told me, that when he was very ill he was not afraid to die.' JOHNSON. 'It is not true, Sir. Hold a pistol to Foote's breast, or to Hume's breast, and threaten to kill them, and you'll see how they behave.' BOSWELL. 'But may we not fortify our minds for the approach of death?' Here I am sensible I was in the wrong, to bring before his view what he ever looked upon with horror; for although when in a celestial frame, in his *Vanity of Human Wishes*, he has supposed death to be 'kind Nature's signal for retreat', from this state of being to 'a happier seat', his thoughts upon this awful change were in general full of dismal apprehensions. His mind resembled the vast amphitheatre, the Coliseum at Rome. In the centre stood his judgement, which, like a mighty gladiator, combated those apprehensions that, like the wild beasts of the *Arena*, were all around in cells, ready to be let out upon him. After a conflict, he drives them back into their dens; but not killing them, they were still assailing him. To my question, whether we might not fortify our minds for the approach of death, he answered, in a passion, 'No, Sir, let it alone. It matters not how a man dies, but how he lives. The act of dying is not of importance, it lasts so short a time.' He added (with an earnest look), 'A man knows it must be so, and submits. It will do him no good to whine.'

I attempted to continue the conversation. He was so provoked, that he said 'Give us no more of this'; and was thrown into such a state of agitation, that he expressed himself in a way that alarmed and distressed me; showed an impatience that I should leave him, and when I was going away, called to me sternly, 'Don't let us meet tomorrow.'

I went home exceedingly uneasy. All the harsh observations which I had ever heard made upon his character, crowded into my mind; and I seemed to myself like the man who had put his head into the lion's mouth a great many times with perfect safety, but at last had it bit off.

Next morning I sent him a note, stating, that I might have been in the wrong, but it was not intentionally; he was therefore, I could not help thinking, too severe upon me. That notwithstanding our agreement not to meet that day, I would call on him in my way to the city, and stay five minutes by my watch. 'You are (said I), in my mind, since last night, surrounded with cloud and storm. Let me have a glimpse of sunshine, and go about my affairs in serenity and cheerfulness.'

Upon entering his study, I was glad that he was not alone, which would have made our meeting more awkward. There were with him, Mr Steevens and Mr Tyers, both of whom I now saw for the first time. My note had, on his own reflection, softened him, for he received me very complacently; so that I unexpectedly found myself at ease, and joined in the conversation.

He said, the critics had done too much honour to Sir Richard Blackmore, by writing so much against him. That in his 'Creation' he had been helped by various wits, a line by Philips and a line by Tickell; so that by their aid, and that of others, the poem had been made out. I defended Blackmore's[a] lines, which have been ridiculed as absolute nonsense:

> A painted vest Prince Voltiger had on,
> Which from a naked Pict his grandsire won.[b]

I maintained it to be a poetical conceit. A Pict being painted, if he is slain in

---

[a] After 'Blackmore's', read 'supposed'.

[b] Add this note: An acute correspondent of the *European Magazine*, April 1792, has completely exposed a mistake which has been unaccountably frequent in ascribing these lines to Blackmore, notwithstanding that Sir Richard Steel, in that very popular work *The Spectator*, mentions them as written by the Author of the *British Princes*, the Honourable Edward Howard. The correspondent above mentioned, shows this mistake to be so inveterate, that not only *I* defended the lines as Blackmore's, in the presence of Dr Johnson, without any contradiction or doubt of their authenticity, but that the Reverend Mr Whitaker has asserted in print, that he understands they were *suppressed* in the late edition or editions of Blackmore. 'After all (says this intelligent writer), it is not unworthy of particular observation, that these lines so often quoted do not exist either in Blackmore or Howard.' In the *British Princes*, 8vo. 1669, now before me, p. 96, they stand thus:

> A vest as admir'd Voltiger had on,
> Which, from this Island's foes, his grandsire won,
> Whose artful colour pass'd the Tyrian dye,
> Oblig'd to triumph in this legacy.

It is probable, I think, that some wag, in order to make Howard still more ridiculous than he really was, has formed the couplet as it now circulates.

battle, and a vest is made of his skin, it is a painted vest won from him, though he was naked.

Johnson spoke unfavourably of a certain pretty voluminous author, saying, 'He used to write anonymous books, and then other books commending those books, in which there was something of rascality.'

I whispered him, 'Well, Sir, you are now in good humour.' JOHNSON. 'Yes, Sir.' I was going to leave him, and had got as far as the stair-case. He stopped me, and smiling, said, 'Get you gone', in a curious mode of inviting me to stay, which I accordingly did for some time longer.

This little incidental quarrel and reconciliation, which, perhaps, I may be thought to have detailed too minutely, must be esteemed as one of many proofs which his friends had, that though he might be charged with bad humour at times, he was always a good-natured man, and I have heard Sir Joshua Reynolds, a nice and delicate observer of manners, particularly remark, that when upon any occasion Johnson had been rough to any person in company, he took the first opportunity of reconciliation, by drinking to him or addressing his discourse to him; but if he found his dignified indirect overtures sullenly neglected, he was quite indifferent, and considered himself as having done all that he ought to do, and the other as now in the wrong.

Being to set out for Scotland on the 10th of November, I wrote to him at Streatham, begging that he would meet me in town on the 9th; but if this should be very inconvenient to him, I would go thither. His answer was as follows:

To JAMES BOSWELL, Esq.

DEAR SIR – Upon balancing the inconveniencies of both parties, I find it will less incommode you to spend your night here, than me to come to town. I wish to see you, and am ordered by the lady of this house to invite you hither. Whether you can come or not, I shall not have any occasion of writing to you again before your marriage, and therefore tell you now, that with great sincerity I wish you happiness. I am, dear Sir,

Your most affectionate humble servant,

SAM. JOHNSON.

Nov. 9, 1769.

I was detained in town till it was too late on the 9th, so went to him early in the morning of the tenth of November. 'Now (said he) that you are going to marry, do not expect more from life, than life will afford. You may often find yourself out of humour, and you may often think your wife not studious enough to please you; and yet you may have reason to consider yourself as upon the whole very happily married.'

Talking of marriage in general, he observed, 'Our marriage service is too refined. It is calculated only for the best kind of marriages; whereas, we should have a form for matches of convenience, of which there are many. He agreed with me that there was no absolute necessity for having the marriage ceremony performed by a regular clergyman, for this was not commanded in scripture.

I was volatile enough to repeat to him a little epigrammatic song of mine, on matrimony, which Mr Garrick had a few days before procured to be set to music.[a]

A Matrimonial Thought.

In the blithe days of honey-moon,
    With Kate's allurements smitten,
I lov'd her late, I lov'd her soon,
    And call'd her dearest kitten.

But now my kitten's grown a cat,
    And cross like other wives,
O! by my soul, my honest Mat,
    I fear she has nine lives.

My illustrious friend said, 'It is very well, Sir; but you should not swear.' Upon which I altered 'O! by my soul,' to 'alas, alas!'

He was so good as to accompany me to London, and see me into the post-chaise which was to carry me on my road to Scotland. And sure I am, that however inconsiderable many of the particulars recorded at this time may appear to some, they will be esteemed by the best part of my readers as genuine traits of his character, contributing together to give a full, fair, and distinct view of it.

In 1770 he published a political pamphlet, entitled 'The False Alarm', intended to justify the conduct of ministry and their majority in the House of Commons, for having virtually assumed it as an axiom, that the expulsion of a Member of Parliament was equivalent to exclusion, and thus having declared Colonel Lutterel to be duly elected for the county of Middlesex, notwithstanding Mr Wilkes had a great majority of votes. This being justly considered as a gross violation of the right of election, an alarm for the constitution extended itself all over the kingdom. To prove this alarm to be false, was the purpose of Johnson's pamphlet; but even his vast powers were inadequate to cope with constitutional truth and reason, and his argument failed of effect; and the House of Commons have since expunged the offensive resolution from their Journals. That the House of Commons might have expelled Mr Wilkes repeatedly, and as often as he should be re-chosen, was not denied; but incapacitation cannot be but by an act of the whole legislature. It was wonderful to see how a prejudice in favour of government in general, and an aversion to popular clamour, could blind and contract such an understanding as Johnson's, in this particular case; yet the wit, the sarcasm, the eloquent vivacity which this pamphlet displayed, made it be read with great avidity at the time, and it will ever be read with pleasure, for the sake of its composition.

[a] After 'music', read 'by Mr Dibdin'.

That it endeavoured to infuse a narcotic indifference, as to public concerns, into the minds of the people, and that it broke out sometimes into an extreme coarseness of contemptuous abuse, is but too evident.

It must not, however, be omitted, that when the storm of his violence subsides, he takes a fair opportunity to pay a grateful compliment to the King, who had rewarded his merit: 'These low-born rulers have endeavoured, surely without effect, to alienate the affections of the people from the only King who for almost a century has much appeared to desire, or much endeavoured to deserve them.' And, 'Every honest man must lament, that the faction has been regarded with frigid neutrality by the Tories, who being long accustomed to signalise their principles by opposition to the Court, do not yet consider, that they have at last a King who knows not the name of party, and who wishes to be the common father of all his people.'

To this pamphlet, which was at once discovered to be Johnson's, several answers came out, in which, care was taken to remind the public of his former attacks upon government, and of his now being a pensioner, without allowing for the honourable terms upon which Johnson's pension was granted and accepted, or the change of system which the British court had undergone upon the accession of his present Majesty. He was, however, soothed in the highest strain of panegyric, in a poem called 'The Remonstrance', by the Reverend Mr Stockdale, to whom he was, upon many occasions, a kind protector.

The following admirable minute made by him, describes so well his own state, and that of numbers to whom self-examination is habitual, that I cannot omit it:

'June 1, 1770. Every man naturally persuades himself that he can keep his resolutions, nor is he convinced of his imbecility but by length of time and frequency of experiment. This opinion of our own constancy is so prevalent, that we always despise him who suffers his general and settled purpose to be overpowered by an occasional desire. They, therefore, whom frequent failures have made desperate, cease to form resolutions; and they who are become cunning, do not tell them. Those who do not make them are very few, but of their effect little is perceived; for scarcely any man persists in a course of life planned by choice, but as he is restrained from deviation by some external power. He who may live as he will, seldom lives long in the observation of his own rules.'[1]

Of this year I have obtained the following letters:

To the Reverend Dr FARMER, Cambridge.

SIR – As no man ought to keep wholly to himself any possession that may be useful to the public, I hope you will not think me unreasonably intrusive, if I have recourse to you for such information as you are more able to give me than any other man.

---

1 *Prayers and Meditations*, p. 95.

In support of an opinion which you have already placed above the need of any more support, Mr Steevens, a very ingenious gentleman, lately of King's College, has collected an account of all the translations which Shakspeare might have seen and used. He wishes his catalogue to be perfect, and therefore entreats that you will favour him by the insertion of such additions as the accuracy of your inquiries has enabled you to make. To this request, I take the liberty of adding my own solicitation.

We have no immediate use for this catalogue, and therefore do not desire that it should interrupt or hinder your more important employments. But it will be kind to let us know that you receive it.

I am, Sir, &c.

SAM. JOHNSON.

Johnson's-court, Fleet-street,
March 21, 1770.

To the Reverend Mr THOMAS WARTON.

Dear Sir – The readiness with which you were pleased to promise me some notes on Shakspeare, was a new instance of your friendship. I shall not hurry you; but am desired by Mr Steevens, who helps me in this edition, to let you know, that we shall print the tragedies first, and shall therefore want first the notes which belong to them. We think not to incommode the readers with a supplement; and therefore, what we cannot put into its proper place, will do us no good. We shall not begin to print before the end of six weeks, perhaps not so soon.

I am, &c.

SAM. JOHNSON.

London, June 23, 1770.

To the Reverend Dr JOSEPH WARTON.

Dear Sir – I am revising my edition of Shakspeare, and remember that I formerly misrepresented your opinion of Lear. Be pleased to write the paragraph as you would have it, and send it. If you have any remarks of your own upon that or any other play, I shall gladly receive them.

Make my compliments to Mrs Warton. I sometimes think of wandering for a few days to Winchester, but am apt to delay. I am, Sir,

Your most humble servant,

SAM. JOHNSON.

Sept. 27, 1770.

To Mr FRANCIS BARBER, at Mrs Clapp's, Bishop-Stortford, Hertfordshire.

DEAR FRANCIS – I am at last sat down to write to you, and should very much blame myself for having neglected you so long, if I did not impute that and many other failings to want of health. I hope not to be so long silent again. I am very well satisfied with your progress, if you can really perform the exercises which you are set; and I hope Mr Ellis does not suffer you to impose on him, or on yourself.

Make my compliments to Mr Ellis, and to Mrs Clapp, and Mr Smith.

Let me know what English books you read for your entertainment. You can never be wise unless you love reading.

Do not imagine that I shall forget or forsake you; for if, when I examine you, I find that you have not lost your time, you shall want no encouragement from

Yours affectionately,

SAM. JOHNSON.

London, Sept. 25, 1770.

To the same.

DEAR FRANCIS – I hope you mind your business. I design you shall stay with Mrs Clapp these holidays. If you are invited out you may go, if Mr Ellis gives leave. I have ordered you some clothes, which you will receive, I believe, next week. My compliments to Mrs Clapp and to Mr Ellis, and Mr Smith, &c. I am

Your affectionate

SAM. JOHNSON.

December 7, 1770.

During this year there was a total cessation of all correspondence between Dr Johnson and me, without any coldness on either side, but merely from procrastination, continued from day to day; and as I was not in London, I had no opportunity of enjoying his company and recording his conversation. To supply this blank, I shall present my readers with some *Collectanea*, obligingly furnished to me by the Rev. Dr Maxwell, of Falkland, in Ireland, some time assistant preacher at the Temple, and for many years the social friend of Johnson, who spoke of him with a very kind regard.

*   *   *

'My acquaintance with that great and venerable character commenced in the year 1754. I was introduced to him by Mr Grierson,[1] his Majesty's printer at Dublin, a gentleman of uncommon learning, and great wit and vivacity. Mr Grierson died in Germany, at the age of twenty-seven. Dr Johnson highly respected his abilities, and often observed, that he possessed more extensive knowledge than any man of his years he had ever known. His industry was equal to his talents; and he particularly excelled in every species of philological learning, and was, perhaps, the best critic of the age he lived in.

'I must always remember with gratitude my obligation to Mr Grierson, for the honour and happiness of Dr Johnson's acquaintance and friendship, which

1 Son of the learned Mrs Grierson, who was patronised by the late Lord Granville, and was the editor of several of the classics.

continued uninterrupted and undiminished to his death: a connection, that was at once the pride and happiness of my life.

'What pity it is, that so much wit and good sense as he continually exhibited in conversation, should perish unrecorded! Few persons quitted his company without perceiving themselves wiser and better than they were before. On serious subjects he flashed the most interesting conviction upon his auditors; and upon lighter topics, you might have supposed – *Albano musas de monte locutas.*

'Though I can hope to add but little to the celebrity of so exalted a character, by any communications I can furnish, yet out of pure respect to his memory, I will venture to transmit to you some anecdotes concerning him, which fell under my own observation. The very *minutiae* of such a character must be interesting, and may be compared to the filings of diamonds.

'In politics he was deemed a Tory, but certainly was not so in the obnoxious or party sense of the term; for while he asserted the legal and salutary prerogatives of the crown, he no less respected the constitutional liberties of the people. Whiggism, at the time of the Revolution, he said, was accompanied with certain principles; but latterly, as a mere party distinction under Walpole and the Pelhams, was no better than the politics of stock-jobbers, and the religion of infidels.

'He detested the idea of governing by parliamentary corruption, and asserted most strenuously, that a prince steadily and conspicuously pursuing the interests of his people, could not fail of parliamentary concurrence. A prince of ability, he contended, might and should be the directing soul and spirit of his own administration; in short, his own minister, and not the mere head of a party: and then, and not till then, would the royal dignity be sincerely respected.

'Johnson seemed to think, that a certain degree of crown influence over the Houses of Parliament (not meaning a corrupt and shameful dependence), was very salutary, nay even necessary, in our mixed government. "For (said he), if the members were under no crown influence, and disqualified from receiving any gratification from Court, and resembled, as they possibly might, Pym and Haslerig, and other stubborn and sturdy members of the long Parliament, the wheels of government would be totally obstructed. Such men would oppose, merely to show their power, from envy, jealousy, and perversity of disposition; and not gaining themselves, would hate and oppose all who did: not loving the person of the prince, and conceiving they owed him little gratitude, from the mere spirit of insolence and contradiction, they would oppose and thwart him upon all occasions."

'The inseparable imperfection annexed to all human governments, consisted, he said, in not being able to create a sufficient fund of virtue and principle to carry the laws into due and effectual execution. Wisdom might plan, but virtue alone could execute. And where could sufficient virtue be found? A variety of delegated, and often discretionary powers must be entrusted somewhere; which, if not governed by integrity and conscience, would necessarily be abused, till at last the constable would sell his for a shilling.

'This excellent person was sometimes charged with abetting slavish and arbitrary principles of government. Nothing in my opinion could be a grosser calumny and misrepresentation, for how can it be rationally supposed, that he should adopt such pernicious and absurd opinions, who supported his philosophical character with so much dignity, was extremely jealous of his personal liberty and independence, and could not brook the smallest appearance of neglect or insult, even from the highest personages?

'But let us view him in some instances of more familiar life.

'His general mode of life, during my acquaintance, seemed to be pretty uniform. About twelve o'clock I commonly visited him, and frequently found him in bed, or declaiming over his tea, which he drank very plentifully. He generally had a levee of morning visitors, chiefly men of letters; Hawksworth, Goldsmith, Murphy, Langton, Steevens, Beauclerk, &c. &c. and sometimes learned ladies, particularly I remember a French lady of wit and fashion doing him the honour of a visit. He seemed to me to be considered as a kind of public oracle, whom every body thought they had a right to visit and consult; and doubtless they were well rewarded. I never could discover how he found time for his compositions. He declaimed all the morning, then went to dinner at a tavern, where he commonly staid late, and then drank his tea at some friend's house, over which he loitered a great while, but seldom took supper. I fancy he must have read and wrote chiefly in the night, for I can scarcely recollect that he ever refused going with me to a tavern, and he often went to Ranelagh, which he deemed a place of innocent recreation.

'He frequently gave all the silver in his pocket to the poor, who watched him, between his house and the tavern where he dined. He walked the streets at all hours, and said he was never robbed, for the rogues knew he had little money, nor had the appearance of having much.

'Though the most accessible and communicative man alive, yet when he suspected he was invited to be exhibited, he constantly spurned the invitation.

'Two young women from Staffordshire visited him when I was present, to consult him on the subject of Methodism, to which they were inclined. "Come (said he), you pretty fools, dine with Maxwell and me at the Mitre, and we will talk over that subject"; which they did, and after dinner he took one of them upon his knee, and fondled her for half an hour together.

'Upon a visit to me at a country lodging near Twickenham, he asked what sort of society I had there. I told him, but indifferent; as they chiefly consisted of opulent traders, retired from business. He said, he never much liked that class of people; "For, Sir (said he), they have lost the civility of tradesmen, without acquiring the manners of gentlemen."

'Johnson was much attached to London: he observed, that a man stored his mind better there, than any where else; and that in remote situations a man's body might be feasted, but his mind was starved, and his faculties apt to degenerate, from want of exercise and competition. No place, he said, cured a man's vanity or arrogance, so well as London; for as no man was either great or good *per se*, but as compared with others not so good or great, he was sure to find in the metropolis many his equals, and some his superiors. He observed, that a man in London was in less danger of falling in love indiscreetly, than any where else; for there the difficulty of deciding between the conflicting pretensions of a vast variety of objects, kept him safe. He told me, that he had frequently been offered country preferment, if he would consent to take orders; but he could not leave the improved society of the capital, or consent to exchange the exhilarating joys and splendid decorations of public life, for the obscurity, insipidity, and uniformity of remote situations.

'Speaking of Mr Harte, Canon of Windsor, and writer of *The History of Gustavus Adolphus*, he much commended him as a scholar, and a man of the most companionable talents he had ever known. He said, the defects in his history proceeded not from imbecility, but from foppery.

'He loved, he said, the old black letter books; they were rich in matter, though their style was inelegant; wonderfully so, considering how conversant the writers were with the best models of antiquity.

'Burton's *Anatomy of Melancholy*, he said, was the only book that ever took him out of bed two hours sooner than he wished to rise.

'He frequently exhorted me to set about writing a History of Ireland, and archly remarked, there had been some good Irish writers, and that one Irishman might at least aspire to be equal to another. He had great compassion for the miseries and distresses of the Irish nation, particularly the Papists; and severely reprobated the barbarous debilitating policy of the British government, which he said was the most detestable mode of persecution. To a gentleman, who hinted such policy might be necessary to support the authority of the English government, he replied by saying, "Let the authority of the English government perish, rather than be maintained by iniquity. Better would it be to restrain the turbulence of the natives by the authority of the sword, and to make them amenable to law and justice by an effectual and vigorous police, than to grind them to powder by all manner of disabilities and incapacities. Better (said he) to hang or drown people at once, than by an unrelenting persecution to beggar and starve them." The moderation and humanity of the present times have, in some measure, justified the wisdom of his observations.

'Dr Johnson was often accused of prejudices, nay, antipathy, with regard to the natives of Scotland. Surely, so illiberal a prejudice never entered his mind: and it is well known, many natives of that respectable country possessed a large share in his esteem; nor were any of them ever excluded from his good offices, as far as opportunity permitted. True it is, he considered the Scotch, nationally, as a crafty, designing people, eagerly attentive to their own interest, and too apt to overlook the claims and pretensions of other people. "While they confine their benevolence, in a manner, exclusively to those of their own country, they expect to share in the good offices of other people. Now (said Johnson), this principle is either right or wrong; if right, we should do well to imitate such conduct; if wrong, we cannot too much detest it."

'Being solicited to compose a funeral sermon for the daughter of a tradesman, he naturally enquired into the character of the deceased; and being told she was remarkable for her humility and condescension to inferiors, he observed, that those were very laudable qualities, but it might not be so easy to discover who the lady's inferiors were.

'Of a certain player he remarked, that his conversation usually threatened and announced more than it performed; that he fed you with a continual renovation of hope, to end in a constant succession of disappointment.

'When exasperated by contradiction, he was apt to treat his opponents with too much acrimony; as "Sir, you don't see your way through that question;" – "Sir, you talk the language of ignorance." On my observing to him that a certain gentleman had remained silent the whole evening, in the midst of a very brilliant and learned society, "Sir (said he), the conversation overflowed and drowned him."

'His philosophy, though austere and solemn, was by no means morose and cynical, and never blunted the laudable sensibilities of his character, or exempted him from the influence of the tender passions. Want of tenderness, he always alleged, was want of parts, and was no less a proof of stupidity than depravity.

'Speaking of Mr Hanway, who published *A Six Weeks Tour through the South of England*, "Jonas (said he), acquired some reputation by travelling abroad, but lost it all by travelling at home."

'Of the passion of love he remarked, that its violence and ill effects were much exaggerated; for who has known any real sufferings on that head, more than from the exorbitancy of any other passion?

'He much commended Law's *Serious Call*, which he said was the finest piece of hortatory theology in any language. "Law (said he) fell latterly into the reveries of Jacob Behmen, whom Law alleged to have been somewhat in the same state with St Paul, and to have seen *unutterable things*. Were it even so (said Johnson), Jacob would have resembled St Paul still more, by not attempting to utter them."

'He observed, that the established clergy in general did not preach plain enough; and that polished periods and glittering sentences flew over the heads of the common people, without any impression upon their hearts. Something might be necessary, he observed, to excite the affections of the common people, who were sunk in languor and lethargy, and therefore he supposed that the new concomitants of methodism might probably produce so desirable an effect. The mind, like the body, he observed, delighted in change and novelty, and even in religion itself, courted new appearances and modifications. Whatever might be thought of some methodist teachers, he said he could scarcely doubt the sincerity of that man, who travelled nine hundred miles in a month, and preached twelve times a week; for no adequate reward, merely temporal, could be given for such indefatigable labour.

'Of Dr Priestly's theological works, he remarked, that they tended to unsettle every thing, and yet settled nothing.

'He was much affected by the death of his mother, and wrote to me to come and assist him to compose his mind, which indeed I found extremely agitated. He lamented that all serious and religious conversation was banished from the society of men, and yet great advantages might be derived from it. All acknowledged, he said, what hardly any body practised, the obligation we were under of making the concerns of eternity the governing principles of our lives. Every man, he observed, at last wishes for retreat: he sees his expectations frustrated in the world, and begins to wean himself from it, and to prepare for everlasting separation.

'He observed, that the influence of London now extended every where, and that from all manner of communication being opened, there shortly would be no remains of the ancient simplicity, nor places of cheap retreat to be found.

'He was no admirer of blank-verse, and said it always failed, unless sustained by the dignity of the subject. In blank-verse, he said, the language suffered more distortion, to keep it out of prose, than any inconvenience or limitation to be apprehended from the shackles and circumscription of rhyme.

'He reproved me once for saying grace without mention of the name of our Lord JESUS CHRIST, and hoped in future I would be more mindful of the apostolical injunction.

'He refused to go out of a room before me at Mr Langton's house, saying, he hoped he knew his rank better than to presume to take place of a Doctor in Divinity. I mention such little anecdotes, merely to shew the peculiar turn and habit of his mind.

'He used frequently to observe, that there was more to be endured than enjoyed, in the general condition of human life; and frequently quoted those lines of Dryden:

> Strange cozenage! None would live past years again,
> Yet all hope pleasure from what still remain.

For his part, he said, he never passed that week in his life which he would wish to repeat, were an angel to make the proposal to him.

'He was of opinion, that the English nation cultivated both their soil and their reason better than any other people; but admitted that the French, though not the highest, perhaps, in any department of literature, yet in every department were very high. Intellectual pre-eminence, he observed, was the highest superiority; and that every nation derived their highest reputation from the splendour and dignity of their writers. Voltaire, he said, was a good narrator, and that his principal merit consisted in a happy selection and arrangement of circumstances.

'Speaking of the French novels, compared with Richardson's, he said they might be pretty baubles, but a wren was not an eagle.

'In a Latin conversation with the Père Boscovitz, at the house of Mrs Cholmondeley, I heard him maintain the superiority of Sir Isaac Newton over all foreign philosophers, with a dignity and eloquence that surprised that learned foreigner. It being observed to him, that a rage for every thing English prevailed much in France after Lord Chatham's glorious war, he said, he did not wonder at it, for that we had drubbed those fellows into a proper reverence for us, and that their national petulance required periodical chastisement.

'Lord Lyttelton's Dialogues, he deemed a nugatory performance. "That man (said he) sat down to write a book, to tell the world what the world had all his life been telling him."

'Somebody observing that the Scotch Highlanders in the year 1745, had made surprising efforts, considering their numerous wants and disadvantages: "Yes, Sir (said he) their wants were numerous, but you have not mentioned the greatest of them all – the want of law."

'Speaking of the *inward light*, to which some methodists pretended, he said, it was a principle utterly incompatible with social or civil security. "If a man (said he) pretends to a principle of action of which I can know nothing, nay, not so much as that he has it, but only that he pretends to it; how can I tell what that person may be prompted to do? When a person professes to be governed by a written ascertained law, I can then know where to find him."

'The poem of Fingal, he said, was a mere unconnected rhapsody, a tiresome repetition of the same images. "In vain shall we look for the *lucidus ordo*, where there is neither end or object, design or moral, *nec certa recurrit imago*."

'Being asked by a young nobleman what was become of the gallantry and military spirit of the old English nobility, he replied, "Why, my Lord, I'll tell you what is become of it; it is gone into the city to look for a fortune."

'Speaking of a dull, tiresome fellow, whom he chanced to meet, he said, "That fellow seems to me to possess but one idea, and that is a wrong one."

'Much inquiry having been made concerning a gentleman who had quitted a company where Johnson was, and no information being obtained; at last Johnson observed, that "he did not care to speak ill of any man behind his back, but he believed the gentleman was an *attorney*."

'He spoke with much contempt of the notice taken of Woodhouse, the poetical shoemaker. He said, it was all vanity and childishness; and that such objects were, to those who patronized them, mere mirrors of their own superiority. "They had better (said he) furnish the man with good implements for his trade, than raise subscriptions for his poems. He may make an excellent shoemaker, but can never make a good poet. A school-boy's exercise may be a pretty thing for a school-boy, but is no treat for a man."

'Speaking of Boetius, who was the favourite writer of the middle ages, he said it was very surprising, that upon such a subject, and in such a situation, he should be *magis philosophus quam Christianus*.

'Speaking of Arthur Murphy, whom he very much loved, "I don't know (said he), that Arthur can be classed with the very first dramatic writers; yet at present I doubt much whether we have any thing superior to Arthur."

'Speaking of the national debt, he said, it was an idle dream to suppose that the country could sink under it. Let the public creditors be ever so clamorous, the interest of millions must ever prevail over that of thousands.

'Of Dr Kennicott's Collations, he observed, that though the text should not be much mended thereby, yet it was no small advantage to know, that we had as good a text as the most consummate industry and diligence could procure.

'Johnson observed, that so many objections might be made to everything, that nothing could overcome them but the necessity of doing something. No man would be of any profession, as simply opposed to not being of it: but every one must do something.

'He remarked that a London parish was a very comfortless thing, for the clergyman seldom knew the face of one out of ten of his parishioners.

'Of the late Mr Mallet he spoke with no great respect: said, he was ready for any dirty job: that he had wrote against Byng at the instigation of the ministry, and was equally ready to write for him, provided he found his account in it.

'A gentleman who had been very unhappy in marriage, married immediately after his wife died: Johnson said, it was the triumph of hope over experience.

'He observed, that a man of sense and education should meet a suitable companion in a wife. It was a miserable thing when the conversation could only be such as, whether the mutton should be boiled or roasted, and probably a dispute about that.

'He did not approve of late marriages, observing, that more was lost in point of time, than compensated for by any possible advantages. Even ill assorted marriages were preferable to cheerless celibacy.

'Of old Sheridan he remarked, that he neither wanted parts or literature, but that his vanity and Quixotism obscured his merits.

'He said, foppery was never cured; it was the bad stamina of the mind, which, like those of the body, were never rectified: once a coxcomb, and always a coxcomb.

'Being told that Gilbert Cowper called him the Caliban of literature; "Well (said he), I must dub him the Punchinello."

'Speaking of the old Earl of Corke and Orrery, he said, "that man spent his life in catching at an object [literary eminence], which he had not power to grasp."

'He often used to quote, with great pathos, those fine lines of Virgil:

> *Optima quaeque dies miseris mortalibus aevi*
> *Prima fugit; subeunt morbi, tristisque senectus,*
> *Et labor, et durae rapit inclementia mortis.*

'To find a substitution for violated morality, he said, was the leading feature in all perversions of religion.'[a]

*   *   *

[a] *Second Edition* – 'The Rev. Dr Maxwell's Additional Communications.'
'Speaking of Homer, whom he venerated as the prince of poets, Johnson remarked that the advice given to Diomed by his father, when he sent him to the Trojan war, was the noblest exhortation that could be instanced in any heathen writer, and comprised in a single line:

αἰὲν ἀριστεύειν, καὶ ὑπείροχον ἔμμεναι ἄλλων·

which, if I recollect well, is translated by Dr Clarke thus: *semper appetere praestantissima, et omnibus aliis antecellere.*

'He observed, "it was a most mortifying reflection for any man to consider, what he had done, compared with what *he might have done.*"

'He said few people had intellectual resources sufficient to forego the pleasures of wine. They could not otherwise contrive how to fill the interval between dinner and supper.

'He went with me, one Sunday, to hear my old master, Gregory Sharpe, preach at the Temple. – In the prefatory prayer, Sharpe ranted about Liberty, as a blessing most fervently to be implored, and its continuance prayed for. Johnson observed that our *liberty* was in no sort of danger – he would have done much better, to pray against our *licentiousness*.

'One evening at Mrs Montagu's, where a splendid company was assembled, consisting of the most eminent literary characters, I thought he seemed highly pleased with the respect and attention that were shown to him, and asked him, on our return home, if he was not highly gratified by his visit: "No, Sir, (said he) not highly gratified; yet I do not recollect to have passed many evenings *with fewer objections*."

'Though of no high extraction himself, he had much respect for birth and family, especially among ladies. He said, "adventitious accomplishments may be possessed by all ranks; but one may easily distinguish the *born gentlewoman*."

'He said, "the poor in England were better provided for, than in any other country of the same extent; he did not mean little Cantons, or petty Republics. Where a great proportion of the people (said he) are suffered to languish in helpless misery, that country must be ill policed and wretchedly governed: a decent provision for the poor is the true test of civilization. – Gentlemen of education, he observed, were pretty much the same in all countries; the condition of the lower orders, the poor especially, was the true mark of national discrimination."

'When the corn-laws were in agitation in Ireland, by which that country has been enabled not only to feed itself, but to export corn to a large amount; Sir Thomas Robinson observed that those laws might be prejudicial to the corn-trade of England. "Sir Thomas, (said he), you talk the language of a savage: what, Sir? would you prevent any people from feeding themselves, if by any honest means they can do it?"

'It being mentioned that Garrick assisted Dr Brown, the author of the *Estimate*, in some dramatic composition, "No, Sir (said Johnson); he would no more suffer Garrick to write a line in his play, than he would suffer him to mount his pulpit."

'Speaking of Burke, he said, "It was commonly observed he spoke too often in parliament; but nobody could say he did not speak well, though too frequently and too familiarly."

'Speaking of economy, he remarked, it was hardly worth while to save anxiously twenty pounds a year. If a man could save to that degree, so as to enable him to assume a different rank in society, then, indeed, it might answer some purpose.

'He observed, a principal source of erroneous judgement was, viewing things partially and only on *one side*; as for instance, *fortune hunters*, when they contemplated the fortunes *singly* and *separately*, it was a dazzling and tempting object; but when they came to possess the wives and their fortunes *together*, they began to suspect they had not made quite so good a bargain.

'Speaking of the late Duke of Northumberland living very magnificently when Lord Lieutenant of Ireland, somebody remarked, it would be difficult to find a suitable successor to him: then, exclaimed Johnson, *he is only fit to succeed himself.*

'He advised me, if possible, to have a good orchard. He knew, he said, a clergyman of small income, who brought up a family very reputably, which he chiefly fed with apple dumplins.

'He said, he had known several good scholars among the Irish gentlemen; but scarcely any of them correct in *quantity*. He extended the same observation to Scotland.

'Speaking of a certain Prelate, who exerted himself very laudably in building churches and parsonage-houses; "however, said he, I do not find that he is esteemed a

In 1771 he published another political pamphlet, entitled 'Thoughts on the late Transactions respecting Falkland's Islands', in which, upon materials furnished to him by ministry, and upon general topics expanded in his richest style, he successfully endeavoured to persuade the nation that it was wise and laudable to suffer the question of right to remain undecided, rather than involve our country in another war. It has been suggested by some, with what truth I shall not take upon me to decide, that he rated the consequence of those Islands to Great Britain too low. But however this may be, every humane mind must surely applaud the earnestness with which he averted the calamity of war; a calamity so dreadful that it is astonishing how civilised, nay, Christian nations, can deliberately continue to renew it. His description of its miseries in this pamphlet, is one of the finest pieces of eloquence in the English language. Upon this occasion, too, we find Johnson lashing the party in opposition with unbounded severity, and making the fullest use of what he ever reckoned a most effectual argumentative instrument, contempt. His character of their very able mysterious champion, JUNIUS, is executed with all the force of his genius, and finished with the highest care. He seems to have exulted in sallying forth to single combat against the boasted and formidable hero who bade defiance to 'principalities and powers, and the rulers of this world'.

---

man of much professional learning, or a liberal patron of it; – yet, it is well, where a man possesses any strong positive excellence. – Few have all kinds of merit belonging to their character. We must not examine matters too deeply. – No, Sir, a *fallible being will fail somewhere.*"

'Talking of the Irish clergy, he said, Swift was a man of great parts, and the instrument of much good to his country. – Berkeley was a profound scholar, as well as a man of fine imagination; but Usher, he said, was the great luminary of the Irish church; and a greater, he added, no church could boast of; at least in modem times.

'We dined *tête-à-tête* at the Mitre, as I was preparing to return to Ireland, after an absence of many years. I regretted much leaving London, where I had formed many agreeable connexions: "Sir (said he), I don't wonder at it; no man, fond of letters, leaves London without regret. But remember, Sir, you have seen and enjoyed a great deal; – you have seen life in its highest decorations, and the world has nothing new to exhibit. – No man is so well qualified to leave public life as he who has long tried it and known it well. We are always hankering after untried situations, and imagining greater felicity from them than they can afford. No, Sir, knowledge and virtue may be acquired in all countries, and your local consequence will make you some amends for the intellectual gratifications you relinquish." Then he quoted the following lines with great pathos:

> He who has early known the pomps of state,
> (For things unknown, 'tis ignorance to condemn);
> And after having viewed the gaudy bait,
> Can boldly say, the trifle I contemn;
> With such a one contented could I live,
> Contented could I die.

'He then took a most affecting leave of me; said, he knew it was a point of *duty* that called me away. – "We shall all be sorry to lose you, said he: *laudo tamen.*" '

This pamphlet, it is observable, was softened in one particular, after the first edition; for the conclusion of Mr George Grenville's character stood thus: 'Let him not, however, be depreciated in his grave. He had powers not universally possessed: could he have enforced payment of the Manilla ransom, *he could have counted it.*' which, instead of retaining its sly, sharp point, was reduced to a mere flat unmeaning expression, or, if I may use the word, – *truism*: 'He had powers not universally possessed: and if he sometimes erred, he was likewise sometimes right.'[a]

Mr Strahan, the printer, who had been long in intimacy with Johnson, in the course of his literary labours, who was at once his friendly agent in receiving his pension for him, and his banker in supplying him with money when he wanted it; who was himself now a Member of Parliament, and who loved much to be employed in political negotiation; thought he should do eminent service, both to government and Johnson, if he could be the means of his getting a seat in the House of Commons. With this view, he wrote a letter to one of the Secretaries of the Treasury, of which he gave me a copy in his own handwriting, which is as follows:

Sɪʀ – You will easily recollect, when I had the honour of waiting upon you some time ago, I took the liberty to observe to you that Dr Johnson would make an excellent figure in the House of Commons, and heartily wished he had a seat there. My reasons are briefly these:

I know his perfect good affection to his Majesty, and his government, which I am certain he wishes to support by every means in his power.

[a] After this passage, read:

To Bᴇɴɴᴇᴛ Lᴀɴɢᴛᴏɴ, Esq.

Dᴇᴀʀ Sɪʀ – After much lingering of my own, and much of the ministry, I have, at length got out my paper.[1] But delay is not yet at an end: Not many had been dispersed, before Lord North ordered the sale to stop. His reasons I do not distinctly know. You may try to find them in the perusal.[2] Before his order, a sufficient number were dispersed to do all the mischief, though, perhaps, not to make all the sport that might be expected from it.

Soon after your departure, I had the pleasure of finding all the danger past with which your navigation was threatened. I hope nothing happens at home to abate your satisfaction; but that Lady Rothes, and Mrs Langton, and the young ladies are all well.

I was last night at ᴛʜᴇ ᴄʟᴜʙ. Dr Percy has written a long ballad in many *fits*; it is pretty enough. He has printed, and will soon publish it. Goldsmith is at Bath, with Lord Clare. At Mr Thrale's, where I am now writing, all are well.

I am, dear Sir,

Your most humble servant,

Sᴀᴍ. Jᴏʜɴsᴏɴ.

March 20, 1771.

1 'Thoughts on the late Transactions respecting Falkland's Islands'.

2 By comparing the first with the subsequent editions, this curious circumstance of ministerial authorship may be discovered.

He possesses a great share of manly, nervous, and ready eloquence; is quick in discerning the strength and weakness of any argument; can express himself with clearness and precision, and fears the face of no man alive.

His known character, as a man of extraordinary sense and unimpeached virtue, would secure him the attention of the House, and could not fail to give him a proper weight there.

He is capable of the greatest application, and can undergo any degree of labour, where he sees it necessary, and where his heart and affections are strongly engaged. His Majesty's ministers might therefore securely depend on his doing, upon every proper occasion, the utmost that could be expected from him. They would find him ready to vindicate such measures as tended to promote the stability of government, and resolute and steady in carrying them into execution. Nor is any thing to be apprehended from the supposed impetuosity of his temper. To the friends of the King you will find him a lamb, to his enemies a lion.

For these reasons, I humbly apprehend that he would be a very able and useful member. And I will venture to say, the employment would not be disagreeable to him; and knowing, as I do, his strong affection to the King, his ability to serve him in that capacity, and the extreme ardour with which I am convinced he would engage in that service, I must repeat that I wish most heartily to see him in the House.

If you think this worthy of attention, you will be pleased to take a convenient opportunity of mentioning it to Lord North. If his Lordship should happily approve of it, I shall have the satisfaction of having been, in some degree, the humble instrument of doing my country, in my opinion, a very essential service. I know your good-nature, and your zeal for the public welfare, will plead my excuse for giving you this trouble. I am, with the greatest respect, Sir,

Your most obedient and humble servant,

WILLIAM STRAHAN.

New-street, March 30, 1771.

This recommendation we know was not effectual; but how, or for what reason, can only be conjectured. It is not to be believed that Mr Strahan would have applied, unless Johnson had approved of it. I never heard him mention the subject; but at a later period of his life, when Sir Joshua Reynolds told him that Mr Edmund Burke had said, that if he had come early into parliament, he certainly would have been the greatest speaker that ever was there, Johnson exclaimed, 'I should like to try my hand now.'

It has been much agitated among his friends and others, whether he would have been a powerful speaker in Parliament, had he been brought in when advanced in life. I am inclined to think, that his extensive knowledge, his quickness and force of mind, his vivacity and richness of expression, his wit and humour, and above all his poignancy of sarcasm, would have had great effect in a popular assembly; and that the magnitude of his figure, and striking peculiarity of his manner, would have aided the effect. But I remember it was observed by Mr Flood, that Johnson having been long used to sententious brevity and the short flights of conversation, might have failed in that continued and expanded kind of argument, which is requisite in stating complicated matters in public speaking; and as a proof of this he mentioned the supposed speeches in Parliament written by him for the magazine, none of which, in his opinion, were at all like real debates. The opinion of one who is himself so eminent an orator, must be allowed to have great weight. It was confirmed by Sir William Scott, who mentioned, that Johnson had told him, that he had several times tried to speak in the Society of Arts and Sciences, but 'had found he could not get on.' From Mr William Gerard Hamilton I have heard, that Johnson, when observing to him that it was prudent for a man who had not been accustomed to speak in public to begin his speech in as simple a manner as possible, acknowledged that he rose in that society to deliver a speech which he had prepared; 'but (said he) all my flowers of oratory forsook me.' I however cannot help wishing, that he *had* 'tried his hand' in parliament; and I wonder that ministry did not make the experiment.

I at length renewed a correspondence which had been too long discontinued:

To Dr JOHNSON.

Edinburgh, April 18, 1771.

MY DEAR SIR – I can now fully understand those intervals of silence in your correspondence with me, which have often given me anxiety and uneasiness; for although I am conscious that my veneration and love for Mr Johnson have never in the least abated, yet I have deferred for almost a year and a half to write to him.

In the subsequent part of this letter, I gave him an account of my comfortable life as a married man, and a lawyer in practice at the Scotch bar; invited him to Scotland, and promised to attend him to the Highlands, and Hebrides.

To JAMES BOSWELL, Esq.

DEAR SIR – If you are now able to comprehend that I might neglect to write without diminution of affection, you have taught me, likewise, how that neglect may be uneasily felt without resentment. I wished for your letter a long time, and when it came, it amply recompensed the delay. I never was so much pleased as now with your account of yourself; and sincerely hope, that between public business, improving studies, and domestic pleasures, neither melancholy nor caprice will find any place for entrance. Whatever philosophy may determine of material nature, it is certainly true of intellectual nature, that it *abhors a vacuum*: our minds cannot be empty; and evil will break in upon them, if they are not preoccupied by good. My dear Sir, mind your studies, mind your business, make your lady happy, and be a good Christian. After this,

—— *tristitiam et metus*
Trades protervis in mare Creticum
Portare ventis.

If we perform our duty, we shall be safe and steady, '*Sive per*', &c. whether we climb the Highlands, or are tossed among the Hebrides, and I hope the time will come when we may try our powers both with cliffs and water. I see but little of Lord Elibank, I know not why; perhaps by my own fault. I am this day going into Staffordshire and Derbyshire for six weeks. I am, dear Sir,

Your most affectionate
And most humble servant,

SAM. JOHNSON.

London, June 20, 1771.

To Sir JOSHUA REYNOLDS, in Leicester-fields.

DEAR SIR – When I came to Lichfield, I found that my portrait had been much visited, and much admired. Every man has a lurking wish to appear considerable in his native place; and I was pleased with the dignity conferred by such a testimony of your regard.

Be pleased, therefore, to accept the thanks of, Sir,
Your most obliged
And most humble servant,

SAM. JOHNSON.

Ashbourn in Derbyshire,
July 17, 1771.

Compliments to Miss Reynolds.

To Dr JOHNSON.

Edinburgh, July 27, 1771.

MY DEAR SIR – The bearer of this, Mr Beattie, Professor of Moral Philosophy at Aberdeen, is desirous of being introduced to your acquaintance. His genius and learning, and labours in the service of virtue and religion, render him very worthy of it; and as he has a high esteem of your character, I hope you will give him a favourable reception. I ever am, &c.

JAMES BOSWELL.[a]

[a] After this letter, read:

To BENNET LANGTON, Esq. at Langton, near Spilsby, Lincolnshire.

DEAR SIR – I am lately returned from Staffordshire and Derbyshire. The last letter mentions two others which you have written to me since you received my pamphlet. Of these two I never had but one, in which you mentioned a design of visiting Scotland, and, by consequence, put my journey to Langton out of my thoughts. My summer wanderings are now over, and I am engaging in a very great

In October I again wrote to him, thanking him for his last letter and his obliging reception of Mr Beattie; informing him that I had been at Alnwick lately, and had good accounts of him from Dr Percy.

In his religious record of this year, we observe that he was better than usual, both in body and mind, and better satisfied with the regularity of his conduct. But he is still 'trying his ways' too rigorously. He charges himself with not rising early enough; yet he mentions what was surely a sufficient excuse for this, supposing it to be a duty seriously required, as he all his life appears to have thought it. 'One great hindrance is want of rest; my nocturnal complaints grow less troublesome towards morning; and I am tempted to repair the deficiencies of the night.'[1] Alas! how hard would it be if this indulgence were to be imputed to a sick man as a crime. In his retrospect on the following Easter Eve, he says, 'When I review the last year, I am able to recollect so little done, that shame and sorrow, though perhaps too weakly, come upon me.' Had he been judging of any one else in the same circumstances, how clear would he have been on the favourable side. How very difficult, and in my opinion almost constitutionally impossible it was for him to be raised early, even by the strongest resolutions, appears from a note in one of his little paper books (containing words arranged for his Dictionary), written, I suppose, about 1753: 'I do not remember that since I left Oxford, I ever rose early by mere choice, but once or twice at Edial, and two or three times for the *Rambler*.' I think he had fair ground enough to have quieted his mind on the subject, by concluding that he was physically incapable of what is at best but a commodious regulation.

In 1772 he was altogether quiescent as an author; but it will be found, from the various evidences which I shall bring together, that his mind was acute, lively, and vigorous.

---

work, the revision of my Dictionary; from which I know not, at present, how to get loose.

If you have observed, or been told, any errors or omissions, you will do me a great favour by letting me know them.

Lady Rothes, I find, has disappointed you and herself. Ladies will have these tricks. The Queen and Mrs Thrale, both ladies of experience, yet both missed their reckoning this summer. I hope, a few months will recompense your uneasiness.

Please to tell Lady Rothes how highly I value the honour of her invitation, which it is my purpose to obey as soon as I have disengaged myself. In the mean time I shall hope to hear often of her ladyship, and every day better news and better, till I hear that you have both the happiness, which to both is very sincerely wished, by, Sir,

Your most affectionate, and

Most humble servant,

SAM. JOHNSON.

August 29, 1771.

1 *Prayers and Meditations*, p. 101.

To Sir JOSHUA REYNOLDS.

DEAR SIR – Be pleased to send to Mr Banks, whose place of residence I do not know, this note, which I have sent open, that, if you please, you may read it.

When you send it, do not use your own seal.

I am, Sir,

Your most humble servant,

SAM. JOHNSON.

Feb. 27, 1772.

To JOSEPH BANKS, Esq.

Perpetua ambita bis terra praemia lactis
Haec habet altrici Capra secunda Jovis.[1]

SIR – I return thanks to you and to Dr Solander for the pleasure which I received in yesterday's conversation. I could not recollect a motto for your Goat, but have given her one. You, Sir, may perhaps have an epic poem from some happier pen than, Sir,

Your most humble servant,

SAM. JOHNSON.

Johnson's court, Fleet-street,
Feb. 27, 1772.

To Dr JOHNSON.

Edinburgh, March 3, 1772.

MY DEAR SIR – It is hard that I cannot prevail on you to write to me oftener. But I am convinced that it is in vain to expect from you a private correspondence with any regularity. I must, therefore, look upon you as a fountain of wisdom, from whence few rills are communicated to a distance, and which must be approached at its source, to partake fully of its virtues.

. . .

I am coming to London soon, and am to appear in an appeal from the Court of Session in the House of Lords. A schoolmaster in Scotland was, by a court of inferior jurisdiction, deprived of his office for being somewhat severe in the chastisement of his scholars. The Court of Session considering it to be dangerous to the interest of learning and education to lessen the dignity of teachers, and make them afraid of too indulgent parents, instigated by the complaints of their children, restored him. His enemies have

1 Thus translated by a friend:

> In fame scarce second to the nurse of Jove,
>   This Goat, who twice the world had travers'd round,
> Deserving both her master's care and love,
>   Ease and perpetual pasture now has found.

appealed to the House of Lords, though the salary is only twenty pounds a year. I was Counsel for him here. I hope there will be little fear of a reversal; but I must beg to have your aid in my plan of supporting the decree. It is a general question, and not a point of particular law.

. . .

I am, &c.

JAMES BOSWELL.

To JAMES BOSWELL, Esq.

DEAR SIR – That you are coming so soon to town I am very glad; and still more glad that you are coming as an advocate. I think nothing more likely to make your life pass happily away, than that consciousness of your own value which eminence in your profession will certainly confer. If I can give you any collateral help, I hope you do not suspect that it will be wanting. My kindness for you has neither the merit of singular virtue, nor the reproach of singular prejudice. Whether to love you be right or wrong, I have many on my side: Mrs Thrale loves you, and Mrs Williams loves you, and what would have inclined me to love you, if I had been neutral before, you are a great favourite of Dr Beattie.

Of Dr Beattie I should have thought much, but that his lady puts him out of my head; she is a very lovely woman.

The ejection which you come hither to oppose, appears very cruel, unreasonable, and oppressive. I should think there could not be much doubt of your success.

My health grows better, yet I am not fully recovered. I believe it is held, that men do not recover very fast after threescore. I hope yet to see Beattie's College: and have not given up the western voyage. But however all this may be or not, let us try to make each other happy when we meet, and not refer our pleasure to distant times or distant places.

How comes it that you tell me nothing of your lady? I hope to see her some time, and till then shall be glad to hear of her.

I am, dear sir, &c.

SAM. JOHNSON.

March 15, 1772.

To BENNET LANGTON, Esq. near Spilsby, Lincolnshire.

DEAR SIR – I congratulate you and Lady Rothes[1] on your little man, and hope you will all be many years happy together.

Poor Miss Langton can have little part in the joy of her family. She this day called her aunt Langton to receive the sacrament with her, and made me talk yesterday on such subjects as suit her condition. It will probably be

---

1 Mr Langton married the Countess Dowager of Rothes.

her *viaticum*. I surely need not mention again that she wishes to see her mother. I am, Sir,

    Your most humble servant,

SAM. JOHNSON.

March 14, 1772.

On the 21st of March, I was happy to find myself again in my friend's study, and was glad to see my old acquaintance Mr Francis Barber, who was now returned home. Dr Johnson received me with a hearty welcome, saying, 'I am glad you are come, and glad you are come upon such an errand' (alluding to the cause of the schoolmaster). BOSWELL. 'I hope, Sir, he will be in no danger. It is a very delicate matter to interfere between a master and his scholars, nor do I see how you can fix the degree of severity that a master may use.' JOHNSON. 'Why, Sir, till you fix the degree of obstinacy and negligence of the scholars, you cannot fix the degree of severity of the master. Severity must be continued until obstinacy be subdued, and negligence be cured.' He mentioned the severity of Hunter, his own master. 'Sir (said I), Hunter is a Scotch name: so it should seem this schoolmaster who beat you so severely was a Scotchman. I can now account for your prejudice against the Scotch.' JOHNSON. 'Sir, he was not Scotch, and abating his brutality, he was a very good master.'

We talked of his two political pamphlets, 'The False Alarm', and 'Thoughts concerning Falkland's Islands'. JOHNSON. 'Well, Sir, which of them did you think the best?' BOSWELL. 'I liked the second best.' JOHNSON. 'Why, Sir, I liked the first best; and Beattie liked the first best. Sir, there is a subtlety of disquisition in the first, that is worth all the fire of the second.' BOSWELL. 'Pray, Sir, is it true that Lord North paid you a visit, and that you got two hundred a year in addition to your pension?' JOHNSON. 'No, Sir. Except what I had from the bookseller, I did not get a farthing by them. And, between you and me, I believe Lord North is no friend to me.' BOSWELL. 'How so, Sir?' JOHNSON. 'Why, Sir, you cannot account for the fancies of men. – Well, how does Lord Elibank? And how does Lord Monboddo?' BOSWELL. 'Very well, Sir. Lord Monboddo still maintains the superiority of the savage life.' JOHNSON. 'What strange narrowness of mind now is that, to think the things we have not known are better than the things which we have known.' BOSWELL. 'Why, Sir, that is a common prejudice.' JOHNSON. 'Yes, Sir; but a common prejudice should not be found in one whose trade it is to rectify error.'

A gentleman having come in who was to go as a Mate in the ship along with Mr Banks and Dr Solander, Dr Johnson asked what were the names of the ships destined for the expedition. The gentleman answered, they were once to be called the *Drake* and the *Raleigh*, but now they were to be called the *Resolution* and the *Adventure*. JOHNSON. 'Much better; for had the *Raleigh* returned without going round the world, it would have been ridiculous. To give them the names of the *Drake* and the *Raleigh* was laying a trap for satire.' BOSWELL. 'Had not you some desire to go upon this expedition, Sir?' JOHNSON. 'Why yes; but I soon laid it aside. Sir, there is very little of intellectual in the course. Besides, I see but at a small distance. So it was not worth my while to go to see birds fly, which I should not have seen fly; and fishes swim, which I should not have seen swim.'

The gentleman being gone, and Dr Johnson having left the room for some time, a debate arose between the Reverend Mr Stockdale and Mrs Desmoulins, whether Mr Banks and Dr Solander were entitled to any share of glory from their expedition. When Dr Johnson returned to us, I told him the subject of their dispute. JOHNSON. 'Why, Sir, it was properly for botany that they went out: I believe they thought only of culling of simples.'

I thanked him for showing civilities to Beattie. 'Sir (said he), I should thank *you*. We all love Beattie. Mrs Thrale says, if ever she has another husband, she'll have Beattie. He sunk[a] upon us that he was married; else we should have shown his lady more civilities. She is a very fine woman. But how can you show civilities to a non-entity? I did not think he had been married. Nay, I did not think about it one way or other; but he did not tell us of his lady till late.'

He then spoke of St Kilda, the most remote of the Hebrides. I told him, I thought of buying it. JOHNSON. 'Pray do, Sir. We shall go and pass a winter amid the blasts there. We shall have fine fish, and we shall take some dried tongues with us, and some books. We shall have a strong built vessel, and some Orkney men to navigate her. We must build a tolerable house: but we may carry with us

---

[a] Add the following note:

To JAMES BOSWELL, ESQ.

Edinburgh, May 3, 1792.

MY DEAR SIR – As I suppose your great work will soon be reprinted, I beg leave to trouble you with a remark on a passage of it, in which I am a little misrepresented. Be not alarmed; the misrepresentation is not imputable to you. Not having the book at hand, I cannot specify the page, but I suppose you will easily find it. Dr Johnson says, speaking of Mrs Thrale's family, 'Dr Beattie *sunk upon us* that he was married, or words to that purpose.' I am not sure that I understand *sunk upon us*, which is a very uncommon phrase: but it seems to me to imply, (and others, I find, have understood it in the same sense), studiously concealed from us his being married. Now, Sir, this was by no means the case. I could have no motive to conceal a circumstance, of which I never was nor can be ashamed; and of which Dr Johnson seemed to think, when he afterwards became acquainted with Mrs Beattie, that I had, as was true, reason to be proud. So far was I from concealing her, that my wife had at that time almost as numerous an acquaintance in London as I had myself; and was, not very long after, kindly invited and elegantly entertained at Streatham by Mr and Mrs Thrale.

My request, therefore is, that you would rectify this matter in your new edition. You are at liberty to make what use you please of this letter.

My best wishes ever attend you and your family. Believe me to be, with the utmost regard and esteem, dear Sir,

Your obliged and affectionate humble servant,

J. BEATTIE.

I have, from my respect for my friend Dr Beattie, and regard to his extreme sensibility, inserted the foregoing letter, though I cannot but wonder at his considering as an imputation a phrase commonly used among the best friends.

a wooden house ready made, and requiring nothing but to be put up. Consider, Sir, by buying St Kilda, you may keep the people from falling into worse hands. We must give them a clergyman, and he shall be one of Beattie's choosing. He shall be educated at Marischal College. I'll be your Lord Chancellor, or what you please.' BOSWELL. 'Are you serious, Sir, in advising me to buy St Kilda? For if you should advise me to go to Japan, I believe I should do it.' JOHNSON. 'Why yes, Sir, I am serious.' BOSWELL. 'Why then, I'll see, what can be done.'

I gave him an account of the two parties in the church of Scotland, those for supporting the rights of patrons, independent of the people, and those against it. JOHNSON. 'It should be settled one way or other. I cannot wish well to a popular election of the clergy, when I consider that it occasions such animosities, such unworthy courting of the people, such slanders between the contending parties, and other disadvantages. It is enough to allow the people to remonstrate against the nomination of a minister for solid reasons' (I suppose he meant heresy or immorality). He was engaged to dine abroad, and asked me to return to him in the evening at nine, which I accordingly did.

We drank tea with Mrs Williams, who told us a story of second sight, which happened in Wales where she was born. – He listened to it very attentively, and said he should be glad to have some instances of that faculty well authenticated. His elevated wish for more and more evidence for spirit, in opposition to the grovelling belief of materialism, led him to a love of such mysterious disquisitions. He again justly observed, that we could have no certainty of the truth of supernatural appearances, unless something was told us which we could not know by ordinary means, or something done which could not be done but by supernatural power; that Pharaoh in reason and justice required such evidence from Moses, nay, that our Saviour said, 'If I had not done among them the works which none other man did, they had not had sin.' He had said in the morning, that Macaulay's *History of St Kilda* was very well written, except some foppery about liberty and slavery. I mentioned to him that Macaulay told me, he was advised to leave out of his book the wonderful story that upon the approach of a stranger all the inhabitants catch cold; but that it had been so well authenticated, he determined to retain it. JOHNSON. 'Sir, to leave things out of a book, merely because people tell you they will not be believed, is meanness. Macaulay acted with more magnanimity.'

We talked of the Roman Catholic religion, and how little difference there was in essential matters between ours and it. JOHNSON. 'True, Sir: all denominations of Christians have really little difference in point of doctrine, though they may differ widely in external forms. There is a prodigious difference between the external form of one of your Presbyterian churches in Scotland, and a church in Italy; yet the doctrine taught is essentially the same.'

I mentioned the petition to Parliament for removing the subscription to the Thirty-nine Articles. JOHNSON. 'It was soon thrown out. Sir, they talk of not making boys at the University subscribe to what they do not understand; but they ought to consider, that our Universities were founded to bring up members for the Church of England, and we must not supply our enemies with arms from our arsenal. No, Sir, the meaning of subscribing is, not that they fully understand all the articles, but that they will adhere to the Church of England. Now take it in this way, and suppose that they should only subscribe their adherence to the Church of England, there would be still the same difficulty; for still the young men would be subscribing to what they do not understand. For if you should ask them, what do you mean by the Church of England? Do you know in what it differs from the Presbyterian Church? from the Romish Church? from the Greek Church? from the Coptic Church? they could not tell you. So, Sir, it comes to the same thing.' BOSWELL. 'But, Sir, would it not be sufficient to subscribe the Bible?' JOHNSON. 'Why no, Sir; for all sects will subscribe the Bible; nay, the Mahometans will subscribe the Bible, for the Mahometans acknowledge JESUS CHRIST, as well as Moses, but maintain that GOD sent Mahomet as a still greater prophet than either.'

I mentioned the motion to abolish the fast of the 30th of January. JOHNSON. 'Why, Sir, I could have wished that it had been a temporary act, perhaps, to have expired with the century. I am against abolishing it; because that would be declaring it was wrong to establish it; but I should have no objection to make an act, continuing it for another century, and then letting it expire.'

He disapproved of the Royal Marriage Bill; 'Because (said he) I would not have the people think that the validity of marriage depends on the will of man, or that the right of a King depends on the will of man. I should not have been against making the marriage of any of the royal family, without the approbation of King and Parliament, highly criminal.'

In the morning we had talked of old families, and the respect due to them. JOHNSON. 'Sir, you have a right to that kind of respect, and are arguing for yourself. I am for supporting the principle, and am disinterested in doing it, as I have no such right.' BOSWELL. 'Why, Sir, it is one more incitement to a man to do well.' JOHNSON. 'Yes, Sir, and it is a matter of opinion, very necessary to keep society together. What is it but opinion, by which we have a respect for authority, that prevents us, who are the rabble, from rising up and pulling down you who are gentlemen from your places, and saying, "We will be gentlemen in our turn?" Now, Sir, that respect for authority is much more easily granted to a man whose father has had it, than to an upstart, and so Society is more easily supported.' BOSWELL. 'Perhaps, Sir, it might be done by the respect belonging to office, as among the Romans, where the dress, the *toga*, inspired reverence.' JOHNSON. 'Why, Sir, we know very little about the Romans. But, surely, it is much easier to respect a man who has always had respect, than to respect a man who we know was last year no better than ourselves, and will be no better next year. In republics there is not a respect for authority, but a fear of power.' BOSWELL. 'At present, Sir, I think riches seem to gain most respect.' JOHNSON. 'No, Sir, riches do not gain hearty respect; they only procure external attention. A very rich man, from low beginnings, may buy his election in a borough; but, *ceteris paribus*, a man of family will be preferred. People will prefer a man for whose father their fathers have voted, though they should get no more money, or even less. That shows that the respect for family is not merely fanciful, but has an actual operation. If gentlemen of family would allow the rich upstarts to spend their money profusely, which they are ready enough to do, and not vie with them in expense, the upstarts would soon be at an end, and the gentlemen would remain: but if the gentlemen will vie in expense with the upstarts, which is very foolish, they must be ruined.'

I gave him an account of the excellent mimicry of a friend of mine in Scotland; observing at the same time, that some people thought it a very mean thing. JOHNSON. 'Why, Sir, it is making a very mean use of a man's powers. But to be a good mimic, requires great powers, great acuteness of observation, great retention of what is observed, and great pliancy of organs, to represent what is observed. I remember a lady of quality in this town, Lady —— ——, who was a wonderful mimic, and used to make me laugh immoderately. I have heard she is now gone mad.' BOSWELL. 'It is amazing how a mimic can not only give you the gestures and voice of a person whom he represents; but even what a person would say on any particular subject.' JOHNSON. 'Why, Sir, you are to consider that the manner and some particular phrases of a person do much to impress you with an idea of him, and you are not sure that he would say what the mimic says in his character.' BOSWELL. 'I don't think Foote a good mimic, Sir.' JOHNSON. 'No, Sir; his imitations are not like. He gives you something different from himself, but not the character which he means to assume. He goes out of himself without going into other people. He cannot take off any person unless he is very strongly marked, such as George Faulkner. He is like a painter, who can draw the portrait of a man who has a wen upon his face, and who, therefore, is easily known. If a man hops upon one leg, Foote can hop upon one leg. But he has not that nice discrimination which your friend seems to possess. Foote is, however, very entertaining, with a kind of conversation between wit and buffoonery.'

On Monday, March 23, I found him busy, preparing a fourth edition of his folio Dictionary. Mr Peyton, one of his original amanuenses, was writing for him. I put him in mind of a meaning of the word *side*, which he had omitted, viz. relationship; as, father's side, mother's side. He inserted it. I asked him if *humiliating* was a good word. He said, he had seen it frequently used, but he did not know it to be legitimate English. He would not admit *civilization*, but only *civility*. With great deference to him, I thought *civilization*, from to *civilize*, better in the sense opposed to *barbarity*, than *civility*, as it is better to have a distinct word for each sense, than one word with two senses, which *civility* is, in his way of using it.

He seemed busy about some sort of chemical operation. I was entertained by observing how he contrived to send Mr Peyton on an errand, without seeming to degrade him. 'Mr Peyton, – Mr Peyton, – will you be so good as to take a walk to Temple-bar? You will there see a chemist's shop; at which you will be pleased to buy for me an ounce of oil of vitriol; not spirit of vitriol, but oil of vitriol. It will cost three half-pence.' Peyton immediately went, and returned with it, and told him it cost but a penny.

I then reminded him of the schoolmaster's cause, and proposed to read to him the printed papers concerning it. 'No, Sir (said he), I can read quicker than I can hear.' So he read them to himself.

After he had read for some time, we were interrupted by the entrance of Mr

Kristrom, a Swede, who was tutor to some young gentlemen in the city. He told me, that there was a very good History of Sweden, by Daline. Having at that time an intention of writing the history of that country, I asked Dr Johnson whether one might write a history of Sweden without going thither. 'Yes, Sir (said he), one for common use.'

We talked of languages. Johnson observed, that Leibnitz had made some progress in a work, tracing all languages up to the Hebrew. 'Why, Sir (said he), you would not imagine that the French *jour*, day, is derived from the Latin *dies*, and yet nothing is more certain; and the intermediate steps are very clear. From *dies*, comes *diurnus*. *Diu* is, by inaccurate ears or inaccurate pronunciation, easily confounded with *giu*; then the Italians form a substantive of the ablative of an adjective, and thence *giurno*, or, as they make it, *giorno*; which is readily contracted into *giour*, or *jour*.' He observed, that the Bohemian language was true Sclavonic. The Swede said, it had some similarity with the German. JOHNSON. 'Why, Sir, to be sure, such parts of Sclavonia as confine with Germany, will borrow German words; and such parts as confine with Tartary, will borrow Tartar words.'

He said, he never had it properly ascertained that the Scotch Highlanders and the Irish understood each other. I told him that my cousin Colonel Graham, of the Royal Highlanders, whom I met at Drogheda, told me they did. JOHNSON. 'Sir, if the Highlanders understood Irish, why translate the New Testament into Erse, as was done lately at Edinburgh, when there is an Irish translation?' BOSWELL. 'Although the Erse and Irish are both dialects of the same language, there may be a good deal of diversity between them, as between the different dialects in Italy.' – The Swede went away, and Mr Johnson continued his reading of the papers. I said, 'I am afraid, Sir, it is troublesome to you.' 'Why, Sir (said he), I do not take much delight in it; but I'll go through it.'

We went to the Mitre, and dined in the room where he and I first supped together. He gave me great hopes of my cause. 'Sir (said he), the government of a schoolmaster is somewhat of the nature of military government; that is to say, it must be arbitrary, it must be exercised by the will of one man, according to particular circumstances. You must show some learning upon this occasion. You must show, that a schoolmaster has a prescriptive right to beat; and that an action of assault and battery cannot be admitted against him, unless there is some great excess, some barbarity. This man has maimed none of his boys. They are all left with the full exercise of their corporeal faculties. In our schools in England many boys have been maimed; yet I never heard of an action against a schoolmaster on that account. Puffendorf, I think, maintains the right of a schoolmaster to beat his scholars.'

On Saturday, March 27, I introduced to him Sir Alexander Macdonald, with whom he had expressed a wish to be acquainted. He received him very courteously.

Sir Alexander observed that the Chancellors in England are chosen from views much inferior to the office, being chosen from temporary political views. JOHNSON. 'Why, Sir, in such a government as ours, no man is appointed to an office because he is the fittest for it, nor hardly in any other government; because there are so many connections and dependencies to be studied. A despotic prince may choose a man to an office, merely because he is the fittest for it. The King of Prussia may do it.' SIR A. 'I think, Sir, almost all great lawyers, such at least as have written upon law, have known only law, and nothing else.' JOHNSON. 'Why no, Sir; Judge Hale was a great lawyer, and wrote upon law; and yet he knew a great many other things, and has written upon other things. Selden too.' SIR A. 'Very true, Sir; and Lord Bacon. But was not Lord Coke a mere lawyer?' JOHNSON. 'Why, I am afraid he was; but he would have taken it very ill if you had told him so. He would have prosecuted you for scandal.' BOSWELL. 'Lord Mansfield is not a mere lawyer.' JOHNSON. 'No, Sir. I never was in Lord Mansfield's company; but, Lord Mansfield was distinguished at the University. Lord Mansfield, when he came first to town, "drank champagne with the wits", as Prior says. He was the friend of Pope.' SIR A. 'Barristers, I believe, are not so abusive now as they were formerly. I fancy they had less law long ago, and so were obliged to take to abuse, to fill up the time. Now they have such a number of precedents, they have no occasion for abuse.' JOHNSON. 'Nay, Sir, they had more law long ago than they have now. As to precedents, to be sure they will increase in course of time; but the more precedents there are, the less occasion is there for law; that is to say, the less occasion is there for investigating principles.' SIR A. 'I have been correcting several Scotch accents in my friend Boswell. I doubt, Sir, if any Scotchman ever attains to a perfect English pronunciation.' JOHNSON. 'Why, Sir, few of them do, because they do not persevere after acquiring a certain degree of it. But, Sir, there can be no doubt that they may attain to a perfect English pronunciation, if they will. We find how near they come to it; and certainly, a man who conquers nineteen parts of the Scottish accent may conquer the twentieth. But, Sir, when a man has got the better of nine tenths, he grows weary, he relaxes his diligence, he finds he has corrected his accent so far as not to be disagreeable, and he no longer desires his friends to tell him when he is wrong; nor does he choose to be told. Sir, when people watch me narrowly, and I do not watch myself, they will find me out to be of a particular county. In the same manner, Dunning may be found out to be a Devonshire man. So most Scotchmen may be found out. But, Sir, little aberrations are of no disadvantage. I never caught Mallet in a Scotch accent; and yet Mallet, I suppose, was past five-and-twenty before he came to London.'

Upon another occasion I talked to him on this subject, having myself taken some pains to improve my pronunciation, by the aid of the late Mr Love, of Drury-lane theatre, when he was a player at Edinburgh, and also of old Mr Sheridan. Johnson said to me, 'Sir, your pronunciation is not offensive.' With this concession I was pretty well satisfied; and let me give my countrymen of North-Britain an advice not to aim at absolute perfection in this respect; not to speak *High English*, as we are apt to call what is far removed from the Scotch, but which is by no means good English, and makes 'the fools who use it', truly ridiculous. Good English is plain, easy, and smooth in the mouth of an unaffected English gentleman. A studied and factitious pronunciation, which requires perpetual attention, and imposes perpetual constraint, is exceedingly disgusting. A small intermixture of provincial peculiarities may, perhaps, have an agreeable effect, as the notes of different birds concur in the harmony of the grove, and please more than if they were all exactly alike. I could name some gentlemen of Ireland, to whom a slight proportion of the accent and recitative of that country is an advantage. The same observation will apply to the gentlemen of Scotland. I do not mean that we should speak as broad as a certain prosperous member of parliament from that country, though it has been well observed, that 'it has been of no small use to him; as it rouses the attention of the House by its uncommonness, and is equal to tropes and figures in a good English speaker.' I would give as an instance of what I mean to recommend to my countrymen, the pronunciation of the late Sir Gilbert Elliot; and may I presume to add that of the present Earl of Marchmont, who told me, with great good humour, that the master of a shop in London, where he was not known, said to him, 'I suppose, Sir, you are an American.' 'Why so, Sir?' (said his Lordship). 'Because, Sir (replied the shopkeeper), you speak neither English nor Scotch, but something different from both, which I conclude is the language of America.'

BOSWELL. 'It may be of use, Sir, to have a Dictionary to ascertain the pronunciation.' JOHNSON. 'Why, Sir, my Dictionary shows you the accent of words, if you can but remember them.' BOSWELL. 'But, Sir, we want marks to ascertain the pronunciation of the vowels. Sheridan, I believe, has finished such a work.' JOHNSON. 'Why, Sir, consider how much easier it is to learn a language by the ear than by any marks. Sheridan's Dictionary may do very well; but you cannot always carry it about with you: and, when you want the word, you have not the Dictionary. It is like a man who has a sword that will not draw. It is an admirable sword, to be sure: but while your enemy is cutting your throat, you are unable to use it. Besides, Sir, what entitles Sheridan to fix the pronunciation of English? He has, in the first place, the disadvantage of being an Irishman: and if he says he will fix it after the example of the best company, why they differ among themselves. I remember an instance: when I published the Plan for my Dictionary, Lord Chesterfield told me that the word *great* should be pronounced so as to rhyme to *state*; and Sir William Young[a] sent me word that it should be pronounced so as to rhyme to *seat*, and that none but an Irishman would pronounce it *grait*. Now here were two men of the highest rank, the one the best speaker in the House of Lords, the other the best speaker in the House of Commons, differing entirely.'

I again visited him at night. Finding him in a very good humour, I ventured to lead him to the subject of our situation in a future state, having much curiosity to know his notions on that point. JOHNSON. 'Why, Sir, the happiness of an unembodied spirit will consist in a consciousness of the favour of GOD, in the contemplation of truth, and in the possession of felicitating ideas.' BOSWELL. 'But, Sir, is there any harm in our forming to ourselves conjectures as to the particulars of our happiness, though the scripture has said but very little on the subject? "We know not what we shall be." ' JOHNSON. 'Sir, there is no harm. What philosophy suggests to us on this topic is probable: what

---

[a] For 'Young' read 'Yonge'.

scripture tells us is certain. Dr Henry More has carried it as far as philosophy can. You may buy both his theological and philosophical works in two volumes folio, for about eight shillings.' BOSWELL. 'One of the most pleasing thoughts is, that we shall see our friends again.' JOHNSON. 'Yes, Sir; but you must consider that when we are become purely rational, many of our friendships will be cut off. Many friendships are formed by a community of sensual pleasures: all these will be cut off. We form many friendships with bad men, because they have agreeable qualities, and they can be useful to us; but, after death, they can no longer be of use to us. We form many friendships by mistake, imagining people to be different from what they really are. After death, we shall see every one in a true light. Then, Sir, they talk of our meeting our relations: but then all relationship is dissolved; and we shall have no regard for one person more than another, but for their real value. However, we shall either have the satisfaction of meeting our friends, or be satisfied without meeting them.' BOSWELL. 'Yet, Sir, we see in scripture that Dives still retained an anxious concern about his brethren.' JOHNSON. 'Why, Sir, we must either suppose that passage to be metaphorical, or hold with many divines, and all the Purgatorians, that departed souls do not all at once arrive at the utmost perfection of which they are capable.' BOSWELL. 'I think, Sir, that is a very rational supposition.' JOHNSON. 'Why, yes, Sir; but we do not know it is a true one. There is no harm in believing it: but you must not compel others to make it an article of faith, for it is not revealed.' BOSWELL. 'Do you think, Sir, it is wrong in a man who holds the doctrine of purgatory, to pray for the souls of his deceased friends?' JOHNSON. 'Why no, Sir.' BOSWELL. 'I have been told, that in the liturgy of the Episcopal Church of Scotland, there was a form of prayer for the dead.' JOHNSON. 'Sir, it is not in the liturgy which Laud framed for the Episcopal Church of Scotland: if there is a liturgy older than that, I should be glad to see it.' BOSWELL. 'As to our employment in a future state, the sacred writings say little. The Revelation, however, of St John gives us many ideas, and particularly mentions music.' JOHNSON. 'Why, Sir, ideas must be given you by means of something which you know: and as to music, there are some philosophers and divines who have maintained that we shall not be spiritualised to such a degree, but that something of matter, very much refined, will remain. In that case, music may make a part of our future felicity.'

BOSWELL. 'I do not know whether there are any well-attested stories of the appearance of ghosts. You know there is a famous story of the appearance of Mrs Veal, prefixed to Drelincourt 'On Death'. JOHNSON. 'I believe, Sir, that is given up. I believe the woman declared upon her death-bed that it was a lie.' BOSWELL. 'This objection is made against the truth of ghosts appearing: that if they are in a state of happiness, it would be a punishment to them to return to this world; and if they are in a state of misery, it would be giving them a respite.' JOHNSON. 'Why, Sir, as the happiness or misery of unembodied spirits does not depend upon place, but is intellectual, we cannot say that they are less happy or less miserable by appearing upon earth.'

We went down between twelve and one to Mrs Williams's room, and drank tea. I mentioned that we were to have the remains of Mr Gray, in prose and verse, published by Mr Mason. JOHNSON. 'I think we have had enough of Gray. I see they have published a splendid edition of Akenside's works. One bad Ode may be suffered, but a number of them together makes one sick.' BOSWELL. 'Akenside's distinguished poem is his 'Pleasures of the Imagination': but, for my part, I never could admire it so much as most people do.' JOHNSON. 'Sir, I could not read it through.' BOSWELL. 'I have read it through; but I did not find any great power in it.'

I mentioned Elwal, the heretic, whose trial Sir John Pringle had given me to read. JOHNSON. 'Sir, Mr Elwal was, I think, an ironmonger at Wolverhampton; and he had a mind to make himself famous, by being the founder of a new sect, which he wished much should be called *Elwallians*. He held, that every thing in the Old Testament that was not typical, was to be of perpetual observance; and so he wore a ribband in the plaits of his coat, and he also wore a beard. I remember I had the honour of dining in company with Mr Elwal. There was one Barter, a miller, who wrote against him; and so you had 'The Controversy between Mr ELWAL and Mr BARTER'. To try to make himself distinguished, he wrote a letter to King George the Second, challenging him to dispute with him, in which he said, "George, if you be afraid to come by yourself, to dispute with a poor old man, you may bring a thousand of your *black*-guards with you; and if you should still be afraid, you may bring a thousand of your *red*-guards." The letter had something of the impudence of Junius to our present King. But the men of Wolverhampton were not so inflammable as the Common Council of London; so Mr Elwal failed in his scheme of making himself a man of great consequence.'

On Tuesday, March 31, he and I dined at General Paoli's. A question was started, whether the state of marriage was natural to man. JOHNSON. 'Sir, it is so far from being natural for a man and woman to live in a state of marriage, that we find all the motives which they have for remaining in that connection, and the restraints which civilized society imposes to prevent separation, are hardly sufficient to keep them together.' The General said, that in a state of nature a man and woman uniting together would form a strong and constant affection, by the mutual pleasure each would receive, and that the same causes of dissension would not arise between them, as occur between husband and wife in a civilized state. JOHNSON. 'Sir, they would have dissensions enough, though of another kind. One would choose to go a hunting in this wood, the other in that; one would choose to go a fishing in this lake, the other in that; or, perhaps, one would choose to go a hunting, when the other would choose to go a fishing; and so they would part. Besides, Sir, a savage man and a savage woman meet by chance; and when the man sees another woman that pleases him better, he will leave the first.'

We then fell into a disquisition whether there is any beauty independent of utility. The General maintained there was not. Dr Johnson maintained that there was; and he instanced a coffee-cup which he held in his hand, the painting of which was of no real use, as the cup would hold the coffee equally well if plain; yet the painting was beautiful.

We talked of the strange custom of swearing in conversation. The General said, that all barbarous nations swore from a certain violence of temper, that could not be confined to earth, but was always reaching at the powers above. He said, too, that there was greater variety of swearing, in proportion as there wag a greater variety of religious ceremonies.

Dr Johnson went home with me to my lodgings in Conduit-street and drank tea, previous to our going to the Pantheon, which neither of us had seen before.

He said, 'Goldsmith's Life of Parnell is poor; not that it is poorly written, but that he had poor materials: for nobody can write the life of a man, but those who have eat and drunk and lived in social intercourse with him.'

I said, that if it was not troublesome and presuming too much, I would request him to tell me all the little circumstances of his life; what schools he attended, when he came to Oxford, when he came to London, &c. &c. He did not disapprove of my curiosity as to these particulars; but said, 'They'll come out by degrees as we talk together.'

He censured Ruffhead's Life of Pope; and said, 'he knew nothing of Pope, and nothing of poetry.' He praised Dr Joseph Warton's Essay on Pope; but said, he supposed we should have no more of it, as the author had not been able to persuade the world to think of Pope as he did. BOSWELL. 'Why, Sir, should that prevent him from continuing his work? He is an ingenious Counsel, who has made the most of his cause: he is not obliged to gain it.' JOHNSON. 'But, Sir, there is a difference when the cause is of a man's own making.'

We talked of the proper use of riches. JOHNSON. 'If I were a man of a great estate, I would drive all the rascals whom I did not like out of the county at an election.'

I asked him how far he thought wealth should be employed in hospitality. JOHNSON. 'You are to consider that ancient hospitality, of which we hear so much, was in an uncommercial country, when men being idle, were glad to be entertained at rich men's tables. But in a commercial country, a busy country, time becomes precious, and therefore hospitality is not so much valued. No doubt there is still room for a certain degree of it; and a man has a satisfaction in seeing his friends eating and drinking around him. But promiscuous hospitality is not the way to gain real influence. You must help some people at table before others; you must ask some people how they like their wine oftener than others. You therefore offend more people than you please. You are like the French statesman, who said, when he granted a favour, '*J'ai fait dix mécontents et un ingrat.*' Besides, Sir, being entertained ever so well at a man's table, impresses no lasting regard or esteem. No, Sir, the way to make sure of power and influence is, by lending money confidentially to your neighbours at a small interest, or, perhaps, at no interest at all, and having their bonds in your possession.' BOSWELL. 'May not a man, Sir, employ his riches to advantage in educating young men of merit?' JOHNSON. 'Yes, Sir, if they fall in your way; but if it is understood that you patronize young men of merit, you will be harassed with solicitations. You will have numbers forced upon you who have no merit; some will force them upon you from mistaken partiality;

and some from downright interested motives, without scruple; and you will be disgraced.'

'Were I a rich man, I would propagate all kinds of trees that will grow in the open air. A greenhouse is childish. I would introduce foreign animals into the country; for instance, the reindeer.'[1]

The conversation now turned on critical subjects. JOHNSON. 'Bayes, in *The Rehearsal*, is a mighty silly character. If it was intended to be like a particular man, it could only be diverting while that man was remembered. But I question whether it was meant for Dryden, as has been reported; for we know some of the passages said to be ridiculed, were written since *The Rehearsal*; at least a passage mentioned in the Preface is of a later date.' I maintained that it had merit as a general satire on the self-importance of dramatic authors. But even in this light he held it very cheap.

We then walked to the Pantheon. The first view of it did not strike us so much as Ranelagh, of which he said, the *coup d'oeil* was the finest thing he had ever seen. The truth is, Ranelagh is of a more beautiful form; more of it, or rather indeed the whole *rotunda*, appears at once, and it is better lighted. However, as Johnson observed, we saw the Pantheon in time of mourning, when there was a dull uniformity; whereas we had seen Ranelagh when the view was enlivened with a gay profusion of colours. Mrs Bosville, of Gunthwait, in Yorkshire, joined us, and entered into conversation with us. Johnson said to me afterwards, 'Sir, this is a mighty intelligent lady.'

I said there was not half a guinea's worth of pleasure in seeing this place. JOHNSON. 'But, Sir, there is half a guinea's worth of inferiority to other people in not having seen it.' BOSWELL. 'I doubt, Sir, whether there are many happy people here.' JOHNSON. 'Yes, Sir, there are many happy people here. There are many people here who are watching hundreds, and who think hundreds are watching them.'

Happening to meet Sir Adam Fergusson, I presented him to Dr Johnson. Sir Adam expressed some apprehension that the Pantheon would encourage luxury. 'Sir (said Johnson), I am a great friend to public amusements; for they keep people from vice. You now (addressing himself to me), would have been with a wench, had you not been here. O! I forgot you were married.'

Sir Adam suggested, that luxury corrupts a people, and destroys the spirit of liberty. JOHNSON. 'Sir, that is all visionary. I would not give half a guinea to live under one form of government rather than another. It is of no moment to the happiness of an individual. Sir, the danger of the abuse of power is nothing to a private man. What Frenchman is prevented from passing his life as he pleases?' SIR ADAM. 'But, Sir, in the British constitution it is surely of importance to keep up a spirit in the people, so as to preserve a balance against the crown.' JOHNSON. 'Sir, I perceive you are a vile Whig. – Why all this childish jealousy of the power of the crown? The crown has not power

---

1 This project has since been realised. Sir Henry Liddel, who made a spirited tour into Lapland, brought two rein-deer to his estate in Northumberland, where they bred; but the race has unfortunately perished.

enough. When I say that all governments are alike, I consider that in no government power can be abused long. Mankind will not bear it. If a sovereign oppresses his people to a great degree, they will rise and cut off his head. There is a remedy in human nature against tyranny, that will keep us safe under every form of government. Had not the people of France thought themselves honoured as sharing in the brilliant actions of the reign of Lewis XIV, they would not have endured him; and we may say the same of the King of Prussia's people.' Sir Adam introduced the ancient Greeks and Romans. JOHNSON. 'Sir, the mass of both of them were barbarians. The mass of every people must be barbarous where there is no printing, and consequently knowledge is not generally diffused. Knowledge is diffused among our people by the newspapers.' Sir Adam mentioned the orators, poets, and artists of Greece. JOHNSON. 'Sir, I am talking of the mass of the people We see even what the boasted Athenians were. The little effect which Demosthenes's orations had upon them, shows that they were barbarians.'

Sir Adam was unlucky in his topics; for he suggested a doubt of the propriety of Bishops having seats in the House of Lords. JOHNSON. 'How so, Sir? Who is more proper for having the dignity of a peer, than a Bishop, provided a Bishop be what he ought to be; and if improper Bishops be made, that is not the fault of the Bishops, but of those who make them.'

On Sunday, April 5, after attending divine service at St Paul's church, I found him alone. Of a schoolmaster of his acquaintance, a native of Scotland, he said, 'He has a great deal of good about him; but he is also very defective in some respects. His inner part is good, but his outer part is mighty awkward. You in Scotland do not attain that nice critical skill in languages, which we get in our schools in England. I would not put a boy to him, whom I intended for a man of learning. But for the sons of citizens, who are to learn a little, get good morals, and then go to trade, he may do very well.'

I mentioned a cause in which I had appeared as counsel at the bar of the General Assembly of the Church of Scotland, where a *Probationer* (as one licensed to preach, but not yet ordained, is called), was opposed in his application to be inducted, because it was alleged that he had been guilty of fornication five years before. JOHNSON. 'Why, Sir, if he has repented, it is not a sufficient objection. A man who is good enough to go to heaven, is good enough to be a clergyman.' This was a humane and liberal sentiment. But the character of a clergyman is more sacred than that of an ordinary Christian. As he is to instruct with authority, he should be regarded with reverence, as one upon whom divine truth has had the effect to set him above such transgressions, as men less exalted by spiritual habits, and yet upon the whole not to be excluded from heaven, have been betrayed into by the predominance of passion. That clergymen may be considered as sinners in general, as all men are, cannot be denied; but this reflection will not counteract their good precepts so much, as the absolute knowledge of their having been guilty of certain specific immoral acts. I told him, that by the rules of the Church of Scotland, in their 'Book of Discipline', if a *scandal*, as it is called, is not prosecuted for five years, it cannot afterwards be proceeded upon, 'unless it be *of a heinous nature*, or again become flagrant'; and that hence a question arose, whether fornication was a sin of a heinous nature; and that I had maintained, that it did not deserve that epithet, in as much as it was not one of those sins which argue very great depravity of heart: in short, was not, in the general acceptation of mankind, a heinous sin. JOHNSON. 'No, Sir, it is not a heinous sin. A heinous sin is that for which a man is punished with death or banishment.' BOSWELL. 'But, Sir, after I had argued that it was not a heinous sin, an old clergyman rose up, and repeating the text of scripture denouncing judgement against whoremongers, asked whether, considering this, there could be any doubt of fornication being a heinous sin.' JOHNSON. 'Why, Sir, observe the word *whoremonger*. Every sin, if persisted in, will become heinous. Whoremonger is a dealer in whores, as ironmonger is a dealer in iron. But as you don't call a man an ironmonger for buying and selling a pen-knife; so you don't call a man a whoremonger for getting one wench with child.'[a]

I spoke of the inequality of the livings of the clergy in England and the scanty provisions of some of the Curates. JOHNSON. 'Why, yes, Sir; but it cannot be helped. You must consider, that the revenues of the clergy are not at the disposal of the state, like the pay of the army. Different men have founded different churches; and some are better endowed, some worse. The State cannot interfere and make an equal division of what has been particularly appropriated. Now when a clergyman has but a small living, or even two small livings, he can afford very little to a Curate.'

He said, he went more frequently to church when there were prayers only, than when there was also a sermon, as the people required more an example for the one than the other; it being much easier for them to hear a sermon, than to fix their minds on prayer.

On Monday, April 6, I dined with him at Sir Alexander Macdonald's, where was a young officer in the regimentals of the Scots Royal, who talked with a vivacity, fluency, and precision so uncommon, that he attracted particular attention. He proved to be the Honourable Thomas Erskine, youngest brother to the Earl of Buchan, who has since risen into such brilliant reputation at the bar in Westminster-hall.

Fielding being mentioned, Johnson exclaimed, 'he was a blockhead'; and upon my expressing my astonishment at so strange an assertion, he said, 'What I mean by his being a blockhead is, that he was a barren rascal.' BOSWELL. 'Will you not allow, Sir, that he draws very natural pictures of human life?' JOHNSON. 'Why, Sir, it is of very low life. Richardson used to say, that had he not known who Fielding was, he should have believed he was an ostler. Sir, there is more knowledge of the heart in one letter of Richardson's, than in all *Tom Jones*. I, indeed, never read *Joseph Andrews*.' ERSKINE. 'Surely, Sir, Richardson is very tedious.' JOHNSON. 'Why, Sir, if you were to read Richardson for the story, your impatience would be so much fretted, that you

---

[a] *Second Edition*: It must not be presumed that Dr Johnson meant to give any countenance to licentiousness, though in the character of an Advocate he made a just and subtle distinction between occasional and habitual transgression.

would hang yourself. But you must read him for the sentiment, and consider the story as only giving occasion to the sentiment.' – I have already given my opinion of Fielding; but I cannot refrain from repeating here my wonder at Johnson's excessive and unaccountable depreciation of one of the best writers that England has produced. *Tom Jones* has stood the test of public opinion with such success, as to have established its great merit, both for the story, the sentiments, and the manners, and also the varieties of diction, so as to leave no doubt of its having an animated truth of execution throughout.

A book of travels, lately published under the title of *Coriat Junior*, and written by Mr Paterson, the auctioneer, was mentioned. Johnson said, this book was an imitation of Sterne,[a] and not of Coriat, whose name Paterson had chosen as a whimsical one. 'Tom Coriat (said he), was a humorist about the court of James the First. He had a mixture of learning, of wit, and of buffoonery. He first travelled through Europe, and published his travels. He afterwards travelled on foot through Asia, and had made many remarks; but he died at Mandoa, and his remarks were lost.'

We talked of gaming, and animadverted on it with severity. JOHNSON. 'Nay, gentlemen, let us not aggravate the matter. It is not roguery to play with a man who is ignorant of the game, while you are master of it, and so win his money; for he thinks he can play better than you, as you think you can play better than he; and the superior skill carries it.' ERSKINE. 'He is a fool, but you are not a rogue.' JOHNSON. 'That's much about the truth, Sir. It must be considered, that a man who only does what every one of the society to which he belongs would do, is not a dishonest man. In the republic of Sparta it was agreed, that stealing was not dishonourable, if not discovered. I do not commend a society where there is an agreement that what would not otherwise be fair, shall be fair; but I maintain, that an individual of any society, who practises what is allowed, is not a dishonest man.' BOSWELL. 'So then, Sir, you do not think ill of a man who wins perhaps forty thousand pounds in a winter?' JOHNSON. 'Sir, I do not call a gamester a dishonest man; but I call him an unsocial man, an unprofitable man. Gaming is a mode of transferring property without producing any intermediate good. Trade gives employment to numbers, and so produces intermediate good.'

Mr Erskine told us, that when he was in the island of Minorca, he not only read prayers, but preached two sermons to the regiment. He seemed to object to the passage in scripture where we are told that the angel of the Lord smote in one night forty thousand Assyrians. 'Sir (said Johnson), you should recollect that there was a supernatural interposition; they were destroyed by pestilence. You are not to suppose that the angel of the Lord went about and stabbed each of them with a dagger, or knocked them on the head, man by man.'

After Mr Erskine was gone, a discussion took place, whether the present Earl of Buchan, when Lord Cardross, did right to refuse to go Secretary of the

---

[a] *Second Edition*: Mr Paterson, in a pamphlet, produced some evidence to show that his work was written before Sterne's *Sentimental Journey* appeared.

Embassy to Spain, when Sir James Gray, a man of inferior rank, went Ambassador. Dr Johnson said, that perhaps in point of interest he did wrong; but in point of dignity he did well. Sir Alexander insisted that he was wrong, and said that Mr Pitt intended it as an advantageous thing for him. 'Why, Sir (said Johnson), Mr Pitt might think it an advantageous thing for him to make him a vintner, and get him all the Portugal trade; but he would have demeaned himself strangely had he accepted of such a situation. Sir, had he gone Secretary while his inferior was Ambassador, he would have been a traitor to his rank and family.'

I talked of the little attachment which subsisted between near relations in London. 'Sir (said Johnson), in a country so commercial as ours, where every man can do for himself, there is not so much occasion for that attachment. No man is thought the worse of here, whose brother was hanged. In uncommercial countries, many of the branches of a family must depend on the stock; so, in order to make the head of the family take care of them, they are represented as connected with his reputation, that, self-love being interested, he may exert himself to promote their interest. You have first large circles, or clans; as commerce increases, the connection is confined to families. By degrees, that too goes off, as having become unnecessary, and there being few opportunities of intercourse. One brother is a merchant in the city, and another is an officer in the guards. How little intercourse can these two have!'

I argued warmly for the old feudal system. Sir Alexander opposed it, and talked of the pleasure of seeing all men free and independent. JOHNSON. 'I agree with Mr Boswell that there must be a high satisfaction in being a feudal Lord; but we are to consider, that we ought not to wish to have a number of men unhappy for the satisfaction of one.' – I maintained that numbers, namely, the vassals or followers, were not unhappy, for that there was a reciprocal satisfaction between the Lord and them: he being kind in his authority over them; they being respectful and faithful to him.

On Thursday, April 9, I called on him to beg he would go and dine with me at the Mitre tavern. He had resolved not to dine at all this day, I know not for what reason; and I was so unwilling to be deprived of his company, that I was content to submit to suffer a want, which was at first somewhat painful, but he soon made me forget it; and a man is always pleased with himself when he finds his intellectual inclinations predominate.

He observed, that to reason too philosophically on the nature of prayer, was very unprofitable.

Talking of ghosts, he said, he knew one friend, who was an honest man and a sensible man, who told him he had seen a ghost, old Mr Edward Cave, the printer at St John's Gate. He said Mr Cave did not like to talk of it, but seemed to be in great horror whenever it was mentioned. BOSWELL. 'Pray, Sir, what did he say was the appearance?' JOHNSON. 'Why, Sir, something of a shadowy being.'

I mentioned witches, and asked him what they properly meant. JOHNSON. 'Why, Sir, they properly mean those who make use of the aid of evil spirits.' BOSWELL. 'There is no doubt, Sir, a general report and belief of their having existed.' JOHNSON. 'Sir, you have not only the general report and belief, but you have many voluntary solemn confessions.' He did not affirm any thing positively upon a subject which it is the fashion of the times to laugh at as a matter of absurd credulity. He only seemed willing, as a candid enquirer after truth, however strange and inexplicable, to show that he understood what might be urged for it.'[1]

On Friday, April 10, I dined with him at General Oglethorpe's, where we found Dr Goldsmith.

Armorial bearings having been mentioned, Johnson said, they were as ancient as the siege of Thebes, which he proved by a passage in one of the tragedies of Euripides.

I started the question whether duelling was consistent with moral duty. The brave old General fired at this, and said, with a lofty air, 'Undoubtedly a man has a right to defend his honour.' GOLDSMITH (turning to me). 'I ask you first, Sir, what you would do if you were affronted?' I answered I should think it necessary to fight. 'Why then (replied Goldsmith), that solves the question.' JOHNSON. 'No, Sir, it does not solve the question. It does not follow that what a man would do is therefore right.' I said, I wished to have it settled, whether duelling was contrary to the laws of Christianity. Johnson immediately entered on the subject, and treated it in a masterly manner; and so far as I have been able to recollect, his thoughts were these: 'Sir, as men become in a high degree refined, various causes of offence arise; which are considered to be of such importance, that life must be staked to atone for them, though in reality they are not so. A body that has received a very fine polish may be easily hurt. Before men arrive at this artificial refinement, if one tells his neighbour he lies, his neighbour tells him he lies; if one gives his neighbour a blow, his neighbour gives him a blow; but in a state of highly polished society, an affront is held to be a serious injury. It must, therefore, be resented, or rather a duel must be fought upon it; as men have agreed to banish from their society one who puts up with an affront without fighting a duel. Now, Sir, it is never unlawful to fight in self-defence. He, then, who fights a duel, does not fight from passion against his antagonist, but out of self-defence; to avert the stigma of the world, and to prevent himself from being driven out of society. I could wish that there was not that superfluity of refinement; but while such notions prevail, no doubt a man may lawfully fight a duel.'

Let it be remembered, that this justification is applicable only to the person who *receives* an affront. All mankind must condemn the aggressor.

The General told us, that when he was a very young man, I think only fifteen, serving under Prince Eugene of Savoy, he was sitting in a company at table with a Prince at Wirtemberg. The Prince took up a glass of wine, and, by a fillip, made some of it fly in Oglethorpe's face. Here was a nice dilemma. To have challenged him instantly, might have fixed a quarrelsome character

---

1 See this curious question treated by him with most acute ability, *Journal of a Tour to the Hebrides*, 3d edit. p. 33

upon the young soldier: to have taken no notice of it might have been considered as cowardice. Oglethorpe, therefore, keeping his eye upon the Prince, and smiling all the time, as if he took what his Highness had done in jest, said, 'Mon Prince, —' (I forget the French words he used, the purport, however, was), 'That's a good joke; but we do it much better in England'; and threw a whole glass of wine in the Prince's face. An old General who sat by, said, 'Il a bien fait, mon Prince, vous l'avez commencé'; and thus all ended in good humour.

Dr Johnson said, 'Pray, General, give us an account of the siege of Bender.'[a] Upon which the General, pouring a little wine upon the table, described everything with a wet finger: 'Here were we, here were the Turks,' &c. &c. Johnson listened with the closest attention.

A question was started, how far people who disagree in any capital point can live in friendship together. Johnson said they might. Goldsmith said they could not, as they had not the *idem velle atque idem nolle* – the same likings and the same aversions. JOHNSON. 'Why, Sir, you must shun the subject as to which you disagree. For instance, I can live very well with Burke; I love his knowledge, his genius, his diffusion, and affluence of conversation; but I would not talk to him of the Rockingham party.' GOLDSMITH. 'But, Sir, when people live together who have something as to which they disagree, and which they want to shun, they will be in the situation mentioned in the story of Bluebeard. "You may look into all the chambers but one." But we should have the greatest inclination to look into that chamber, to talk of that subject." JOHNSON (with a loud voice). 'Sir, I am not saying that *you* could live in friendship with a man from whom you differ as to some point: I am only saying that *I* could do it. You put me in mind of Sappho in Ovid.'

Goldsmith told us, that he was now busy in writing a natural history, and, that he might have full leisure for it, he had taken lodgings at a farmer's house, near to the six mile-stone, on the Edgeware-road, and had carried down his books in two returned post-chaises. He said, he believed the farmer's family thought him an odd character, similar to that in which the *Spectator* appeared to his landlady and children: he was *The Gentleman*. Mr Mickle, the translator of *The Lusiad*, and I, went to visit him at this place a few days afterwards. He was not at home; but having a curiosity to see his apartment, we went in and found curious scraps of descriptions of animals, scrawled upon the walls with a black lead pencil.

The subject of ghosts having been introduced, Johnson repeated what he had told me of a friend of his, an honest man and a man of sense, having asserted to him that he had seen an apparition. Goldsmith told us, he was assured by his brother, the Reverend Mr Goldsmith, that he also had seen one. General Oglethorpe told us, that Pendergrast, an officer in the Duke of Marlborough's army, had mentioned to many of his friends that he should die on a particular day. That upon that day a battle took place with the French;

[a] For 'Bender' read 'Belgrade'.

that after it was over, and Pendergrast was still alive, his brother officers, while they were yet in the field, jestingly asked him where was his prophecy now. Pendergrast gravely answered, 'I shall die, notwithstanding what you see.' Soon afterwards there came a shot from a French battery, to which the orders for a cessation of arms had not yet reached, and he was killed upon the spot. Colonel Cecil, who took possession of his effects, found in his pocketbook the following solemn entry:

[Here the date.] 'Dreamt – or ———[1] Sir John Friend meets me': (here the very day on which he was killed was mentioned.) Pendergrast had been a witness against Sir John Friend, who was executed for high treason. General Oglethorpe said, he was in company with Colonel Cecil when Pope came and enquired into the truth of this story, which made a great noise at the time, and was then confirmed by the Colonel.

On Saturday, April 11, he appointed me to come to him in the evening, when he said he should be at leisure to give me some assistance for the defence of Hastie, the schoolmaster of Campbell-town, for whom I was to appear in the House of Lords. When I came, I found him unwilling to exert himself. I pressed him to write down his thoughts upon the subject. He said, 'There's no occasion for my writing. I'll talk to you.' He was, however, at last prevailed on to dictate to me, while I wrote as follows:

'The charge is, that he has used immoderate and cruel correction. Correction, in itself, is not cruel; children, being not reasonable, can be governed only by fear. To impress this fear, is therefore one of the first duties of those who have the care of children. It is the duty of a parent; and has never been thought inconsistent with parental tenderness. It is the duty of a master, who is in his highest exaltation when he is *loco parentis*. Yet, as good things become evil by excess, correction, by being immoderate, may become cruel. But when is correction immoderate? When it is more frequent or more severe than is required *ad monendum et docendum*, for reformation and instruction. No severity is cruel which obstinacy makes necessary; for the greatest cruelty would be to desist, and leave the scholar too careless for instruction, and too much hardened for reproof. Locke, in his treatise of Education, mentions a mother, with applause, who whipped an infant eight times before she had subdued it; for had she stopped at the seventh act of correction, her daughter, says he, would have been ruined. The degrees of obstinacy in young minds are very different; as different must be the degrees of persevering severity. A stubborn scholar must be corrected till he is subdued. The discipline of a school is military. There must be either unbounded licence or absolute authority. The master who punishes, not only consults the future happiness of him who is the immediate subject of correction; but he propagates obedience through the whole school, and establishes regularity by exemplary

---

1 Here was a blank, which may be filled up thus: '*was told by an apparition*'; the writer being probably uncertain whether he was asleep or awake when his mind was impressed with the solemn presentiment with which the fact afterwards happened so wonderfully to correspond.

justice. The victorious obstinacy of a single boy would make his future endeavours of reformation or instruction totally ineffectual. Obstinacy, therefore, must never be victorious. Yet, it is well known, that there sometimes occurs a sullen and hardy resolution, that laughs at all common punishment, and bids defiance to all common degrees of pain. Correction must be proportioned to occasions. The flexible will be reformed by gentle discipline, and the refractory must be subdued by harsher methods. The degrees of scholastic, as of military punishment, no stated rules can ascertain. It must be enforced till it overpowers temptation; till stubbornness becomes flexible, and perverseness regular. Custom and reason have, indeed, set some bounds to scholastic penalties. The schoolmaster inflicts no capital punishments; nor enforces his edicts by either death or mutilation. The civil law has wisely determined that a master who strikes at a scholar's eye shall be considered as criminal. But punishments, however severe, that produce no lasting evil, may be just and reasonable, because they may be necessary. Such have been the punishments used by the respondent. No scholar has gone from him either blind or lame, or with any of his limbs or powers injured or impaired. They were irregular, and he punished them: they were obstinate, and he enforced his punishment. But, however provoked, he never exceeded the limits of moderation, for he inflicted nothing beyond present pain; and how much of that was required, no man is so little able to determine as those who have determined against him – the parents of the offender. – It has been said, that he used unprecedented and improper instruments of correction. Of this accusation the meaning is not very easy to be found. No instrument of correction is more proper than another, but as it is better adapted to produce present pain without lasting mischief. Whatever were his instruments, no lasting mischief has ensued; and therefore, however unusual, in hands so cautious they were proper. – It has been objected, that the respondent admits the charge of cruelty, by producing no evidence to confute it. Let it be considered, that his scholars are either dispersed at large in the world, or continue to inhabit the place in which they were bred. Those who are dispersed cannot be found: those who remain are the sons of his persecutors, and are not likely to support a man to whom their fathers are enemies. If it be supposed that the enmity of their fathers proves the justice of the charge, it must be considered how often experience shows us, that men who are angry on one ground will accuse on another; with how little kindness, in a town of low trade, a man who lives by learning is regarded; and how implicitly, where the inhabitants are not very rich, a rich man is hearkened to and followed. In a place like Campbelltown it is easy for one of the principal inhabitants to make a party. It is easy for that party to heat themselves with imaginary grievances. It is easy for them to oppress a man poorer than themselves; and natural to assert the dignity of riches, by persisting in oppression. The argument which attempts to prove the impropriety of restoring him to his school, by alleging that he has lost the confidence of the people, is not the subject of juridical consideration; for he is to suffer, if he must suffer, not for their judgement, but for his own actions.

It may be convenient for them to have another master; but it is a convenience of their own making. It would be likewise convenient for him to find
another school; but this convenience he cannot obtain. – The question is not
what is now convenient, but what is generally right. If the people of
Campbelltown be distressed by the restoration of the respondent, they are
distressed only by their own fault; by turbulent passions and unreasonable
desires; by tyranny, which law has defeated, and by malice, which virtue has
surmounted.'

'This, Sir (said he), you are to turn in your mind, and make the best use of it
you can in your speech.'

Of our friend Goldsmith he said, 'Sir, he is so much afraid of being
unnoticed, that he often talks merely lest you should forget that he is in the
company.' BOSWELL. 'Yes, he stands forward.' JOHNSON. 'True, Sir; but if a
man is to stand forward, he should wish to do it not in an awkward posture,
not in rags, not so as that he shall only be exposed to ridicule.' BOSWELL. 'For
my part, I like very well to hear honest Goldsmith talk away carelessly.'
JOHNSON. 'Why yes, Sir; but he should not like to hear himself.'

On Tuesday, April 14, the decree of the Court of Session in the schoolmaster's cause was reversed in the House of Lords, after a very eloquent speech
by Lord Mansfield, who showed himself an adept in school discipline, but I
thought was too rigorous towards my client. On the evening of the next day I
supped with Dr Johnson, at the Crown and Anchor tavern, in the Strand, in
company with Mr Langton and his brother-in-law, Lord Binning. I repeated a
sentence of Lord Mansfield's speech, of which, by the aid of Mr Longlands,
the solicitor on the other side, who obligingly allowed me to compare his note
with my own, I have a full copy: 'My Lords, severity is not the way to govern
either boys or men.'

'Nay (said Johnson), it is the way to *govern* them. I know not whether it be
the way to *mend* them.'

I talked of the recent expulsion of six students from the University of
Oxford, who were methodists, and would not desist from publicly praying
and exhorting. JOHNSON. 'Sir, that expulsion was extremely just and proper.
What have they to do at an University who are not willing to be taught, but
will presume to teach? Where is religion to be learnt but at an University? Sir,
they were examined, and found to be mighty ignorant fellows.' BOSWELL.
'But, was it not hard, Sir, to expel them, for I am told they were good beings?'
JOHNSON. 'Sir, I believe they might be good beings; but they were not fit to be
in the University of Oxford. A cow is a very good animal in the field; but we
turn her out of a garden.' Lord Elibank used to repeat this as an illustration
uncommonly happy.

Desirous of calling Johnson forth to talk, and exercise his wit, though I
should myself be the object of it, I resolutely ventured to undertake the
defence of convivial indulgence in wine, though he was not to-night in the
most genial humour. After urging the common plausible topics, I at last had
recourse to the maxim, *in vino veritas*; a man who is well warmed with wine
will speak truth. JOHNSON. 'Why, Sir, that may be an argument for drinking, if

you suppose men in general to be liars. But, Sir, I would not keep company with a fellow who lies as long as he is sober, and whom you must make drunk before you can get a word of truth out of him.'[1]

Mr Langton told us he was about to establish a school upon his estate, but it had been suggested to him, that it might have a tendency to make the people less industrious. JOHNSON. 'No, Sir. While learning to read and write is a distinction, the few who have that distinction may be the less inclined to work: but when every body learns to read and write, it is no longer a distinction. A man who has a laced waistcoat is too fine a man to work; but if every body had laced waistcoats, we should have people working in laced waistcoats. There are no people whatever more industrious, none who work more, than our manufacturers; yet they have all learnt to read and write. Sir, you must not neglect doing a thing immediately good, from fear of remote evil – from fear of its being abused. A man who has candles may sit up too late, which he would not do if he had not candles; but nobody will deny that the art of making candles, by which light is continued to us beyond the time that the sun gives us light, is a valuable art, and ought to be preserved.' BOSWELL. 'But, Sir, would it not be better to follow Nature; and go to bed and rise just as Nature gives us light or withholds it?' JOHNSON. 'No, Sir; for then we should have no kind of equality in the partition of our time between sleeping and waking. It would be very different in different seasons and in different places. In some of the northern parts of Scotland how little light is there in the depth of winter!'

We talked of Tacitus, and I hazarded an opinion, that with all his merit for penetration, shrewdness of judgement, and terseness of expression, he was too compact, too much broken into hints, as it were, and therefore too difficult to be understood. To my great satisfaction Dr Johnson sanctioned this opinion. 'Tacitus, Sir, seems to me rather to have made notes for an historical work, than to have written a history.'[2]

At this time it appears from his *Prayers and Meditations*, that he had been more than commonly diligent in religious duties, particularly in reading the holy scriptures. It was Passion Week, that solemn season which the Christian world has appropriated to the commemoration of the mysteries of our redemption, and during which, whatever embers of religion are in our breasts, will be kindled into pious warmth.

I paid him short visits both on Friday and Saturday, and seeing his large folio Greek Testament before him, beheld him with a reverential awe, and would

---

1 Mrs Piozzi, in her *Anecdotes*, p. 261, has given an erroneous account of this incident, as of many others. She pretends to relate it from recollection, as if she herself had been present; when the fact is, that it was communicated to her by me. She has represented it as a personality, and the true point has escaped her.

2 It is remarkable, that Lord Monboddo, whom on account of his resembling Dr Johnson in some particulars, Foote called an Elzevir edition of him, has, by coincidence, made the very same remark. *Origin and Progress of Language*, vol. iii. 2d edit. p. 219.

not intrude upon his time. While he was thus employed to such good purpose, and while his friends in their intercourse with him constantly found a vigorous intellect and a lively imagination, it is melancholy to read in his private register, 'My mind is unsettled and my memory confused. I have of late turned my thoughts with a very useless earnestness upon past incidents. I have yet got no command over my thoughts; an unpleasing incident is almost certain to hinder my rest.'[1] What philosophic heroism was it in him to appear with such manly fortitude to the world, while he was inwardly so distressed! We may surely believe that the mysterious principle of being 'made perfect through suffering', was to be strongly exemplified in him.

On Sunday, April 19, being Easter-day, General Paoli and I paid him a visit before dinner. We talked of the notion that blind persons can distinguish colours by the touch. Johnson said, that Professor Sanderson mentions his having attempted to do it, but that he found he was aiming at an impossibility; that to be sure a difference in the surface makes the difference of colours; but that difference is so fine, that it is not sensible to the touch. The General mentioned jugglers and fraudulent gamesters, who could know cards by the touch. Dr Johnson said, 'the cards used by such persons must be less polished than ours commonly are.'

We talked of sounds. The General said, there was no beauty in a simple sound but only in an harmonious composition of sounds. I presumed to differ from this opinion, and mentioned the soft and sweet sound of a fine woman's voice. JOHNSON. 'No, Sir, if a serpent or a toad uttered it, you would think it ugly.' BOSWELL. 'So you would think, Sir, were a beautiful tune to be uttered by one of those animals.' JOHNSON. 'No, Sir, it would be admired. We have seen fine fiddlers whom we liked as little as toads' (laughing).

Talking on the subject of taste in the arts, he said, that difference of taste was, in truth, difference of skill. BOSWELL. 'But, Sir, is there not a quality called taste, which consists merely in perception or in liking? For instance, we find people differ much as to what is the best style of English composition. Some think Swift's the best; others prefer a fuller and grander way of writing.' JOHNSON. 'Sir, you must first define what you mean by style, before you can judge who has a good taste in style, and who has a bad. The two classes of persons whom you have mentioned don't differ as to good and bad. They both agree that Swift has a good neat style; but one loves a neat style, another loves a style of more splendour. In like manner, one loves a plain coat, another loves a laced coat; but neither will deny that each is good in its kind.'

While I remained in London this spring, I was with him at several other times, both by himself and in company. I dined with him one day at the Crown and Anchor tavern, in the Strand, with Lord Elibank, Mr Langton, and Dr Vansittart of Oxford. Without specifying each particular day, I have preserved the following memorable things.

I regretted the reflection in his Preface to Shakspeare against Garrick, to

[1] *Prayers and Meditations*, p. 111.

whom we cannot but apply the following passage: 'I collated such copies as I could procure, and wished for more, but have not found the collectors of these rarities very communicative.' I told him, that Garrick had complained to me of it, and had vindicated himself by assuring me, that Johnson was made welcome to the full use of his collection, and that he left the key of it with a servant, with orders to have a fire and every convenience for him. I found Johnson's notion was, that Garrick wanted to be courted for them, and that, on the contrary, Garrick should have courted him, and sent him the plays of his own accord. But, indeed, considering the slovenly and careless manner in which books were treated by Johnson, it could not be expected that scarce and valuable editions should have been lent to him.

A gentleman having to some of the usual arguments for drinking added this: 'You know, Sir, drinking drives away care, and makes us forget whatever is disagreeable. Would not you allow a man to drink for that reason?' JOHNSON. 'Yes, Sir, if he sat next *you*.'

I expressed a liking for Mr Francis Osborn's works, and asked him what he thought of that writer. He answered, 'A conceited fellow. Were a man to write so now, the boys would throw stones at him.' He however did not alter my opinion of a favourite author, to whom I was first directed by his being quoted in *The Spectator*, and in whom I have found much shrewd and lively sense, expressed indeed in a style somewhat quaint, which, however, I do not dislike. His book has an air of originality. We figure to ourselves an ancient gentleman talking to us.

When one of his friends endeavoured to maintain that a country gentleman might contrive to pass his life very agreeably, 'Sir (said he), you cannot give me an instance of any man who is permitted to lay out his own time, contriving not to have tedious hours.' This observation, however, is equally applicable to gentlemen who live in cities, and are of no profession.

He said, 'there is no permanent national character; it varies according to circumstances. Alexander the Great swept India: now the Turks sweep Greece.'

A learned gentleman who in the course of conversation wished to inform us of this simple fact, that the Counsel upon the circuit at Shrewsbury were much bitten by fleas, took, I suppose, seven or eight minutes in relating it circumstantially. He in a plenitude of phrase told us, that large bales of woollen cloth were lodged in the town-hall; – that by reason of this, fleas nestled there in prodigious numbers; – that the lodgings of the Counsel were near to the town-hall; – and that those little animals moved from place to place with wonderful agility. Johnson sat in great impatience till the gentleman had finished his tedious narrative, and then burst out, 'It is a pity, Sir, that you have not seen a lion, for a flea has taken you such a time, that a lion must have served you a twelvemonth.'[1]

He would not allow Scotland to derive any credit from Lord Mansfield; for

1 Mrs Piozzi, to whom I told this anecdote, has related it, as if the gentleman had given 'the *natural history of the mouse*'. *Anecdotes*, p. 191.

he was educated in England. 'Much (said he) may be made of a Scotchman, if he be *caught* young.'

Talking of a modern historian and a modern moralist, he said, 'There is more thought in the moralist than in the historian. There is but a shallow stream of thought in history.' BOSWELL. 'But surely, Sir, an historian has reflection.' JOHNSON. 'Why yes, Sir; and so has a cat when she catches a mouse for her kitten. But she cannot write like the moralist; neither can the historian.'[a]

He said, 'I am very unwilling to read the manuscripts of authors, and give them my opinion. If the authors who apply to me have money, I bid them boldly print without a name; if they have written in order to get money, I tell them to go to the booksellers, and make the best bargain they can.' BOSWELL. 'But, Sir, if a bookseller should bring you a manuscript to look at.' – JOHNSON. 'Why, Sir, I would desire the bookseller to take it away.'

I mentioned a friend of mine who had resided long in Spain, and was unwilling to return to Britain. JOHNSON. 'Sir, he is attached to some woman.' BOSWELL. 'I rather believe, Sir, it is the fine climate which keeps him there.' JOHNSON. 'Nay, Sir, how can you talk so? What is *climate* to happiness? Place me in the heart of Asia, should I not be exiled? What proportion does climate bear to the complex system of human life? You may advise me to go and live at Bologna to eat sausages. The sausages there, are the best in the world; they lose much by being carried.'

On Saturday, May 9, Mr Dempster and I had agreed to dine by ourselves at the British coffee-house. Johnson, on whom I happened to call in the morning, said, he would join us, which he did, and we spent a very pleasant day, though I recollect but little of what passed.

He said, 'Walpole was a minister given by the King to the people: Pitt was a minister given by the people to the King – as an adjunct.'

'The misfortune of Goldsmith in conversation is this: he goes on without knowing how he is to get off. His genius is great, but his knowledge is small. As they say of a generous man, it is a pity he is not rich; we may say of Goldsmith, it is a pity he is not knowing. He would not keep his knowledge to himself.'

Before leaving London this year, I consulted him upon a question purely of Scotch law. It was held of old, and continued for a long period, to be an established principle in that law, that whoever intermeddled with the effects of a person deceased, without the interposition of legal authority to guard against embezzlement, should be subjected to pay all the debts of the deceased, as having been guilty of what was technically called *vitious intromission*. The Court of Session had gradually relaxed the strictness of this principle, where the interference proved had been inconsiderable. In a case[1] which came before that Court the preceding winter, I had laboured to persuade the Judges to return to the ancient law. It was my own sincere opinion, that they ought to

---

[a] In *Second Edition* altered to: 'She cannot write like —; neither can —.'
1 Wilson against Smith and Armour.

adhere to it; but I had exhausted all my powers of reasoning in vain. Johnson thought as I did; and in order to assist me in my application to a the Court for a revision and alteration of the judgement, he dictated to me the following argument:

'This, we are told, is a law which has its force only from the long practice of the Court; and may, therefore, be suspended or modified as the Court shall think proper.

'Concerning the power of the Court to make or to suspend a law, we have no intention to inquire. It is sufficient for our purpose that every just law is dictated by reason; and that the practice of every legal Court is regulated by equity. It is the quality of reason to be invariable and constant; and of equity, to give to one man what, in the same case, is given to another. The advantage which humanity derives from law is this: that the law gives every man a rule of action, and prescribes a mode of conduct which shall entitle him to the support and protection of society. That the law may be a rule of action, it is necessary that it be known; – it is necessary that it be permanent and stable. The law is the measure of civil right; but if the measure be changeable, the extent of the thing measured never can be settled.

'To permit a law to be modified at discretion, is to leave the community without law. It is to withdraw the direction of that public wisdom, by which the deficiencies of private understanding are to be supplied. It is to suffer the rash and ignorant to act at discretion, and then to depend for the legality of that action on the sentence of the Judge. He that is thus governed, lives not by law, but by opinion: not by a certain rule to which he can apply his intention before he acts, but by an uncertain and variable opinion, which he can never know but after he has committed the act on which that opinion shall be passed. He lives by a law (if a law it be), which he can never know before he has offended it. To this case may be justly applied that important principle, *misera est servitus ubi jus est aut incognitum aut vagum*. If Intromission be not criminal till it exceeds a certain point, and that point be unsettled, and consequently different in different minds, the right of Intromission, and the right of the Creditor arising from it, are all *jura vaga*, and, by consequence, are *jura incognita*; and the result can be no other than a *misera servitus*, an uncertainty concerning the event of action, a servile dependence on private opinion.

'It may be urged, and with great plausibility, that there may be Intromission without fraud; which, however true, will by no means justify an occasional and arbitrary relaxation of the law. The end of law is protection as well as vengeance. Indeed, vengeance is never used but to strengthen protection. That society only is well governed, where life is freed from danger and from suspicion; where possession is so sheltered by salutary prohibitions, that violation is prevented more frequently than punished. Such a prohibition was this, while it operated with its original force. The creditor of the deceased was not only without loss, but without fear. He was not to seek a remedy for an injury suffered; for injury was warded off.

'As the law has been sometimes administered, it lays us open to wounds, because it is imagined to have the power of healing. To punish fraud when it is detected, is the proper act of vindictive justice; but to prevent frauds, and make punishment unnecessary, is the great employment of legislative wisdom. To permit Intromission, and to punish fraud, is to make law no better than a pitfall. To tread upon the brink is safe; but to come a step further is destruction. But, surely, it is better to enclose the gulf, and hinder all access, than by encouraging us to advance a little, to entice us afterwards a little further, and let us perceive our folly only by our destruction.

'As law supplies the weak with adventitious strength, it likewise enlightens the ignorant with extrinsic understanding. Law teaches us to know when we commit injury, and when we suffer it. It fixes certain marks upon actions, by which we are admonished to do or to forbear them. *Qui sibi bene temperat in licitis*, says one of the fathers, *numquam cadet in illicita*. He who never intromits at all, will never intromit with fraudulent intentions.

'The relaxation of the law against vicious intromission has been very favourably represented by a great master of jurisprudence,[1] whose words have been exhibited with unnecessary pomp, and seem to be considered as irresistibly decisive. The great moment of his authority makes it necessary to examine his position. "Some ages ago (says he), before the ferocity of the inhabitants of this part of the island was subdued, the utmost severity of the civil law was necessary, to restrain individuals from plundering each other. Thus, the man who intermeddled irregularly with the moveables of a person deceased, was subjected to all the debts of the deceased without limitation. This makes a branch of the law of Scotland, known by the name of *vicious intromission*; and so rigidly was this regulation applied in our Courts of Law, that the most trifling moveable abstracted *mala fide*, subjected the intermeddler to the foregoing consequences, which proved in many instances a most rigorous punishment. But this severity was necessary, in order to subdue the undisciplined nature of our people. It is extremely remarkable, that in proportion to our improvement in manners, this regulation has been gradually softened, and applied by our sovereign Court with a sparing hand."

'I find myself under a necessity of observing, that this learned and judicious writer has not accurately distinguished the deficiencies and demands of the different conditions of human life, which, from a degree of savageness and independence, in which all laws are vain, passes or may pass, by innumerable gradations, to a state of reciprocal benignity, in which laws shall be no longer necessary. Men are first wild and unsocial, living each man to himself, taking from the weak, and losing to the strong. In their first coalitions of society, much of this original savageness is retained. Of general happiness, the product of general confidence, there is yet no thought. Men continue to prosecute their own advantages by the nearest way; and the utmost severity of the civil law is necessary to restrain individuals from plundering each other. The restraints then necessary, are restraints from plunder, from acts of public violence, and undisguised oppression. The ferocity of our ancestors, as of all

1 Lord Kames, in his *Historical Law Tracts*.

other nations, produced not fraud but rapine. They had not yet learned to cheat, and attempted only to rob. As manners grow more polished, with the knowledge of good, men attain likewise dexterity in evil. Open rapine becomes less frequent, and violence gives way to cunning. Those who before invaded pastures and stormed houses, now begin to enrich themselves by unequal contracts and fraudulent intromissions. It is not against the violence of ferocity, but the circumventions of deceit, that this law was framed; and I am afraid the increase of commerce, and the incessant struggle for riches which commerce excites, give us no prospect of an end speedily to be expected of artifice and fraud. It therefore seems to be no very conclusive reasoning, which connects those two propositions – 'the nation is become less ferocious, and therefore the laws against fraud and *coven* shall be relaxed.'

'Whatever reason may have influenced the Judges to a relaxation of the law, it was not that the nation was grown less fierce; and, I am afraid, it cannot be affirmed that it is grown less fraudulent.

'Since this law has been represented as rigorously and unreasonably penal, it seems not improper to consider what are the conditions and qualities that make the justice or propriety of a penal law.

'To make a penal law reasonable and just, two conditions are necessary, and two proper. It is necessary that the law should be adequate to its end; that, if it be observed, it shall prevent the evil against which it is directed. It is, secondly, necessary that the end of the law be of such importance, as to deserve the security of a penal sanction. The other conditions of a penal law, which though not absolutely necessary, are to a very high degree fit, are, that to the moral violation of the law there are many temptations, and that of the physical observance there is great facility.

'All these conditions apparently concur to justify the law which we are now considering. Its end is the security of property; and property very often of great value. The method by which it effects the security is efficacious, because it admits, in its original rigour, no gradations of injury; but keeps guilt and innocence apart, by a distinct and definite limitation. He that intromits, is criminal; he that intromits not, is innocent. Of the two secondary consider-ations, it cannot be denied that both are in our favour. The temptation to intromit is frequent and strong; so strong and so frequent, as to require the utmost activity of justice, and vigilance of caution, to withstand its prevalence; and the method by which a man may entitle himself to legal intromission is so open and so facile, that to neglect it is a proof of fraudulent intention: for why should a man omit to do (but for reasons which he will not confess), that which he can do so easily, and that which he knows to be required by the law? If temptation were rare, a penal law might be deemed unnecessary. If the duty enjoined by the law were of difficult performance, omission, though it could not be justified, might be pitied. But in the present case, neither equity nor compassion operate against it. A useful, a necessary law is broken, not only without a reasonable motive, but with all the inducements to obedience that can be derived from safety and facility.

'I therefore return to my original position, that a law, to have its effect, must be permanent and stable. It may be said, in the language of the schools, *Lex non recipit majus et minus* – we may have a law, or we may have no law, but we cannot have half a law. We must either have a rule of action, or be permitted to act by discretion and by chance. Deviations from the law must be uniformly punished, or no man can be certain when he shall be safe.

'That from the rigour of the original institution this Court has sometimes departed, cannot be denied. But, as it is evident that such deviations, as they make law uncertain, make life unsafe, I hope, that of departing from it there will now be an end; that the wisdom of our ancestors will be treated with due reverence; and that consistent and steady decisions will furnish the people with a rule of action, and leave fraud and fraudulent intromission no future hope of impunity or escape.'

With such comprehension of mind, and such clearness of penetration, did he thus treat a subject altogether new to him, without any other preparation than my having stated to him the arguments which had been used on each side of the question. His intellectual powers appeared with peculiar lustre, when tried against those of a writer of so much fame as Lord Kames, and that too in his Lordship's own department.

This masterly argument, after being prefaced and concluded with some sentences of my own, and garnished with the usual formularies, was actually printed and laid before the Lords of Session, but without success. My respected friend, Lord Hailes, however, one of that honourable body, had critical sagacity enough to discover a more than ordinary hand in the *Petition*. I told him that Dr Johnson had favoured me with his pen. His Lordship, with wonderful acumen, pointed out exactly where his composition began, and where it ended. But that I may do impartial justice, and conform to the great rule of Courts, *Suum cuique tribuito*, I must add, that their Lordships in general, though they were pleased to call this 'a well-drawn paper', preferred the former very inferior petition which I had written; thus confirming the truth of an observation made to me by one of their number, in a merry mood: 'My dear Sir, give yourself no trouble in the composition of the papers you present to us; for, indeed, it is casting pearls before swine.'

I renewed my solicitations that he would this year accomplish his long-intended visit to Scotland.

To JAMES BOSWELL, Esq.

DEAR SIR – The regret has not been little with which I have missed a journey so pregnant with pleasing expectations, as that in which I could promise myself not only the gratification of curiosity, both rational and fanciful, but the delight of seeing those whom I love and esteem . . . But such has been the course of things, that I could not come; and such has been, I am afraid, the state of my body, that it would not well have seconded my inclination. My body, I think, grows better, and I refer my hopes to another year; for I am very sincere in my design to pay the visit, and take the ramble. In the mean time, do not omit any opportunity of keeping up a favourable opinion of me in the minds of any of my friends. Beattie's book is, I believe, every day more liked; at least I like it more, as I look more upon it.

I am glad if you got credit by your cause, and am yet of opinion that our cause was good, and that the determination ought to have been in your favour. Poor Hastie, I think, had but his deserts.

You promised to get me a little Pindar, and may add to it a little Anacreon.

The leisure which I cannot enjoy, it will be a pleasure to hear that you employ upon the antiquities of the feudal establishment. The whole system of ancient tenures is gradually passing away; and I wish to have the knowledge of it preserved adequate and complete. For such an institution makes a very important part of the history of mankind. Do not forget a design so worthy of a scholar who studies the laws of his country, and of a gentleman who may naturally be curious to know the condition of his own ancestors. I am, dear Sir,

Yours with great affection,

SAM. JOHNSON.

August 31, 1772.

To Dr JOHNSON.

Edinburgh, Dec. 25, 1772.

MY DEAR SIR – . . .

I was much disappointed that you did not come to Scotland last autumn. However, I must own that your letter prevents me from complaining; not only because I am sensible that the state of your health was but too good an excuse, but because you write in a strain which shows that you have agreeable views of the scheme which we have so long proposed.

. . .

I communicated to Beattie what you said of his book in your last letter to me. He writes to me thus: 'You judge very rightly in supposing that Dr Johnson's favourable opinion of my book must give me great delight. Indeed it is impossible for me to say how much I am gratified by it; for there is not a man upon earth whose good opinion I would be more ambitious to cultivate. His talents and his virtues I reverence more than any words can express. The extraordinary civilities (the paternal attentions I should rather say), and the many instructions I have had the honour to receive from him, will to me be a perpetual source of pleasure in the recollection.

Dum memor ipse mei, dum spiritus hos reget artus.

'I had still some thoughts, while the summer lasted, of being obliged to go to London on some little business; otherwise I should certainly have troubled him with a letter several months ago, and given some vent to my gratitude and admiration. This I intend to do as soon as I am left a little at leisure. Mean time, if you have occasion to write to him, I beg you will offer him my most respectful compliments, and assure him of the sincerity of my attachment and the warmth of my gratitude.'

. . .

I am, &c.,   JAMES BOSWELL.

In 1773 his only publication was an edition of his folio Dictionary, with additions and corrections; nor did he, so far as is known, furnish any productions of his fertile pen to any of his numerous friends or dependants, except the Preface* to his old amanuensis Macbean's *Dictionary of ancient Geography*. His Shakspeare, indeed, which had been received with high approbation by the public, and gone through several editions, was this year republished by George Steevens, Esq., a gentleman not only deeply skilled in ancient learning, and of very extensive reading in English literature, especially the early writers, but at the same time of acute discernment and elegant taste. It is almost unnecessary to say, that by his great and valuable additions to Dr Johnson's work, he justly obtained considerable reputation:

> *Divisum imperium cum Jove Caesar habet.*

To JAMES BOSWELL, Esq.

DEAR SIR – I have read your kind letter much more than the elegant Pindar which it accompanied. I am always glad to find myself not forgotten, and to be forgotten by you would give me great uneasiness. My northern friends have never been unkind to me: I have from you, dear Sir, testimonies of affection, which I have not often been able to excite; and Dr Beattie rates the testimony which I was desirous of paying to his merit, much higher than I should have thought it reasonable to expect.

I have heard of your masquerade.[a] What says your Synod to such innovations? I am not studiously scrupulous, nor do I think a masquerade either evil in itself, or very likely to be the occasion of evil; yet as the world thinks it a very licentious relaxation of manners, I would not have been one of the *first* masquers in a country where no masquerade had ever been before.[1]

A new edition of my great Dictionary is printed, from a copy which I was persuaded to revise; but having made no preparation, I was able to do very little. Some superfluities I have expunged, and some faults I have corrected, and here and there have scattered a remark; but the main fabric of the work remains as it was. I had looked very little into it since I wrote it, and, I think, I found it full as often better, as worse, than I expected.

Baretti and Davies have had a furious quarrel; a quarrel, I think, irreconcilable. Dr Goldsmith has a new comedy, which is expected in the spring. No name is yet given it. The chief diversion arises from a stratagem by which a lover is made to mistake his future father-in-law's house for an inn. This, you see, borders upon farce. The dialogue is quick and gay, and

---

[a] *Second Edition*, add note: Given by a lady at Edinburgh.

1 There had been masquerades in Scotland before; but not for a very long time.

the incidents are so prepared as not to seem improbable.

I am sorry that you lost your cause of Intromission, because I yet think the arguments on your side unanswerable. But you seem, I think, to say that you gained reputation even by your defeat; and reputation you will daily gain, if you keep Lord Auchinleck's precept in your mind, and endeavour to consolidate in your mind a firm and regular system of law, instead of picking up occasional fragments.

My health seems in general to improve; but I have been troubled for many weeks with a vexatious catarrh, which is sometimes sufficiently distressful. I have not found any great effects from bleeding and physic; and am afraid, that I must expect help from brighter days and softer air.

Write to me now and then; and whenever any good befalls you, make haste to let me know it, for no one will rejoice at it more than, dear Sir,

Your most humble servant,

SAM. JOHNSON.

London, Feb. 24, 1773.

You continue to stand very high in the favour of Mrs Thrale.[a]

[a] After this passage, insert: While this edition of my work was passing through the press, I was unexpectedly favoured with a packet from Philadelphia, from Mr James Abercrombie, a gentleman of that country, who is pleased to honour me with very high praise of my *Life of Dr Johnson*. To have the fame of my illustrious friend, and his faithful biographer, echoed from the New World is extremely flattering; and my grateful acknowledgements shall be wafted across the Atlantic. Mr Abercrombie has politely conferred on me a considerable additional obligation, by transmitting to me copies of two letters from Dr Johnson to American gentlemen. 'Gladly, Sir (says he), would I have sent you the originals; but being the only relics of the kind in America, they are considered by the possessors of such inestimable value, that no possible consideration would induce them to part with them. In some future publication of your's relative to that great and good man, they may perhaps be thought worthy of insertion.'

Second Edition, add: Though the first part of my narrative of this year was printed off before I received them, they will now come in with very little deviation from chronological order.

To Mr B—D.[1]

SIR – That in the hurry of a sudden departure you should yet find leisure to consult my convenience, is a degree of kindness, and an instance of regard, not only beyond my claims, but above my expectation. You are not mistaken in supposing that I set a high value on my American friends, and that you should confer a very valuable favour upon me by giving me an opportunity of keeping myself in their memory.

I have taken the liberty of troubling you with a packet, to which I wish a safe and speedy conveyance, because I wish a safe and speedy voyage to him that conveys it. I am, Sir,

Your most humble servant,

SAM. JOHNSON.

London, Johnson's-Court,
Fleet-street, March 4, 1773.

1 This gentleman, who now resides in America in a public character of considerable dignity, desired that his name might not be transcribed at full length.

On Saturday, April 3, the day after my arrival in London this year, I went to his house late in the evening, and sat with Mrs Williams till he came home. I found in the *London Chronicle*, Dr Goldsmith's apology to the public for beating Evans, a bookseller, on account of a paragraph in a newspaper published by him, which Goldsmith thought impertinent to him and to a lady of his acquaintance. The apology was written so much in Dr Johnson's manner, that both Mrs Williams and I supposed it to be his; but when he came home he soon undeceived us. When he said to Mrs Williams, 'Well, Dr Goldsmith's *manifesto* has got into your paper,' I asked him if Dr Goldsmith had written it, with an air that made him see I suspected it was his, though

---

To the Reverend Mr WHITE.[1]

DEAR SIR – Your kindness for your friends accompanies you across the Atlantic. It was long since observed by Horace, that no ship could leave care behind: you have been attended in your voyage by other powers – by benevolence and constancy: and I hope care did not often show her face in their company.

I received the copy of *Rasselas*. The impression is not magnificent, but it flatters an author, because the printer seems to have expected that it would be scattered among the people. The little book has been well received, and is translated into Italian, French, German, and Dutch. It has now one honour more by an American edition.

I know not that much has happened since your departure that can engage your curiosity. Of all public transactions the whole world is now informed by the newspapers. Opposition seems to despond; and the dissenters, though they have taken advantage of unsettled times, and a government much enfeebled, seem not likely to gain any immunities.

Dr Goldsmith has a new comedy in rehearsal at Covent-Garden, to which the manager predicts ill success. I hope he will be mistaken. I think it deserves a very kind reception.

I shall soon publish a new edition of my large Dictionary; I have been persuaded to revise it, and have mended some faults, but added little to its usefulness.

No book has been published since your departure, of which much notice is taken. Faction only fills the town with pamphlets, and greater subjects are forgotten in the noise of discord.

Thus have I written, only to tell you how little I have to tell. Of myself I can only add, that having been afflicted many weeks with a very troublesome cough, I am now recovered.

I take the liberty which you give me of troubling you with a letter, of which you will please to fill up the direction. I am, Sir,

    Your most humble servant,

                          SAM. JOHNSON.

Johnson's-Court, Fleet-street,
London, March 4, 1773.

1 Now Doctor White, and Bishop of the Episcopal Church in Pennsylvania During his first visit to England in 1771, as a candidate for holy orders, he was several times in company with Dr Johnson, who expressed a wish to see the edition of Rasselas, which Dr White told him had been printed in America. Dr White, on his return, immediately sent him a copy.

subscribed by Goldsmith. JOHNSON. 'Sir, Dr Goldsmith would no more have asked me to write such a thing as that for him, than he would have asked me to feed him with a spoon, or to do anything else that denoted his imbecility. I as much believe that he wrote it, as if I had seen him do it. Sir, had he shown it to any one friend, he would not have been allowed to publish it. He has, indeed, done it very well; but it is a foolish thing well done. I suppose he has been so much elated with the success of his new comedy, that he has thought every thing that concerned him must be of importance to the public.' BOSWELL. 'I fancy, Sir, this is the first time that he has been engaged in such an adventure.' JOHNSON. 'Why Sir, I believe it is the first time he has *beat*; he may have *been beaten* before. This, Sir, is a new plume to him.'

I mentioned Sir John Dalrymple's *Memoirs of Great-Britain and Ireland*, and his discoveries to the prejudice of Lord Russel and Algernon Sydney. JOHNSON. 'Why, Sir, every body who had just notions of government thought them rascals before. It is well that all mankind now see them to be rascals.' BOSWELL. 'But, Sir, may not those discoveries be true without their being rascals?' JOHNSON. 'Consider, Sir; would any of them have been willing to have had it known that they intrigued with France? Depend upon it, Sir, he who does what he is afraid should be known, has something rotten about him. This Dalrymple seems to be an honest fellow; for he tells equally what makes against both sides. But nothing can be poorer than his mode of writing: it is the mere bouncing of a schoolboy. Great He! but greater She! and such stuff.'

I could not agree with him in this criticism; for though Sir John Dalrymple's style is not regularly formed in any respect, and one cannot help smiling sometimes at his affected *grandiloquence*, there is in his writing a pointed vivacity, and much of a gentlemanly spirit.

At Mr Thrale's, in the evening, he repeated his usual paradoxical declamation against action in public speaking. 'Action can have no effect upon reasonable minds. It may augment noise, but it never can enforce argument. If you speak to a dog, you use action; you hold up your hand thus, because he is a brute; and in proportion as men are removed from brutes, action will have the less influence upon them.' MRS THRALE. 'What then, Sir, becomes of Demosthenes's saying? "Action, action, action!" ' JOHNSON. 'Demosthenes, Madam, spoke to an assembly of brutes; to a barbarous people.'

I thought it extraordinary, that he should deny the power of rhetorical action upon human nature, when it is proved by innumerable facts in all stages of society. Reasonable beings are not solely reasonable. They have fancies which may be pleased, passions which may be roused.

Lord Chesterfield being mentioned, Johnson remarked, that almost all of that celebrated nobleman's witty sayings were puns. He, however, allowed the merit of good wit to his Lordship's saying of Lord Tyrawley and himself, when both very old and infirm: 'Tyrawley and I have been dead these two years; but we don't choose to have it known.'

He talked with approbation of an intended edition of *The Spectator*, with notes; two volumes of which had been prepared by a gentleman eminent in the literary world, and the materials which he had collected for the remainder had been transferred to another hand. He observed, that all works which describe manners, require notes in sixty or seventy years, or less; and told us, he had communicated all he knew that could throw light upon *The Spectator*. He said, 'Addison had made his Sir Andrew Freeport a true Whig, arguing against giving charity to beggars, and throwing out other such ungracious sentiments; but that he had thought better, and made amends by making him found an hospital for decayed farmers.' He called for the volume of *The Spectator* in which that account is contained, and read it aloud to us. He read so well, that every thing acquired additional weight and grace from his utterance.

The conversation having turned on modern imitations of ancient ballads, and some one having praised their simplicity, he treated them with that ridicule which he always displayed when this subject was mentioned.

He disapproved of introducing scripture phrases into secular discourse. This seemed to me a question of some difficulty. A scripture expression may be used, like a highly classical phrase, to produce an instantaneous strong impression; and it may be done without being at all improper. Yet I own there is danger, that applying the language of our sacred book to ordinary subjects may tend to lessen our reverence for it. If therefore it be introduced at all, it should be with very great caution.

On Thursday, April 8, I sat a good part of the evening with him, but he was very silent. He said, Burnet's 'History of his own Times', is very entertaining. The style, indeed, is mere chit-chat. I do not believe that Burnet intentionally lied; but he was so much prejudiced, that he took no pains to find out the truth. He was like a man who resolves to regulate his time by a certain watch; but will not inquire whether the watch is right or not.'

Though he was not disposed to talk, he was unwilling that I should leave him; and when I looked at my watch, and told him it was twelve o'clock, he cried, 'What's that to you and me?' and ordered Frank to tell Mrs Williams that we were coming to drink tea with her, which we did. It was settled that we should go to church together next day.

On the 9th of April, being Good Friday, I breakfasted with him on tea and cross-buns; *Doctor* Levet, as Frank called him, making the tea. He carried me with him to the church of St Clement Danes, where he had his seat; and his behaviour was, as I had imaged to myself, solemnly devout. I never shall forget the tremulous earnestness with which he pronounced the awful petition in the Litany: 'In the hour of death, and at the day of judgement, good LORD deliver us.'

We went to church both in the morning and evening. In the interval between the two services we did not dine, but he read in the Greek New Testament, and I turned over several of his books.

In Archbishop Laud's Diary, I found the following passage, which I read to Dr Johnson:

'1623. February 1, Sunday. I stood by the most illustrious Prince Charles,[1] at dinner. He was then very merry, and talked occasionally of many things with his attendants. Among other things, he said, that if he were necessitated to take

1 Afterwards Charles I.

any particular profession of life, he could not be a lawyer, adding his reasons: "I cannot (saith he), defend a bad, nor yield in a good cause." ' JOHNSON. 'Sir, this is false reasoning; because every cause has a bad side: and a lawyer is not overcome, though the cause which he has endeavoured to support be determined against him.'

I told him that Goldsmith had said to me a few days before, 'As I take my shoes from the shoemaker, and my coat from the tailor, so I take my religion from the priest.' I regretted this loose way of talking. JOHNSON. 'Sir, he knows nothing; he has made up his mind about nothing.'

To my great surprise, he asked me to dine with him on Easter-day. I never supposed that he had a dinner at his house; for I had not then heard of any one of his friends having been entertained at his table. He told me, 'I generally have a meat pie on Sunday: it is baked at a public oven, which is very properly allowed, because one man can attend it; and thus the advantage is obtained of not keeping servants from church to dress dinners.'

April 11, being Easter-Sunday, after having attended divine service at St Paul's, I repaired to Dr Johnson's. I had gratified my curiosity much in dining with JEAN JACQUES ROUSSEAU, while he lived in the wilds of Neufchatel: I had as great a curiosity to dine with Dr SAMUEL JOHNSON, in the dusky recess of a court in Fleet-street. I supposed we should scarcely have knives and forks, and only some strange uncouth ill-dressed dish: but I found every thing in very good order. We had no other company but Mrs Williams and a young woman whom I did not know. As a dinner here was considered as a singular phenomenon, and as I was frequently interrogated on the subject, my readers may perhaps be desirous to know our bill of fare. Foote, I remember, in allusion to Francis, the negro, was willing to suppose that our repast was *black broth*. But the fact was, that we had a very good soup, a boiled leg of lamb and spinach, a veal pie, and a rice pudding.

Of Dr John Campbell, the author, he said, 'He is a very inquisitive and a very able man, and a man of good religious principles, though I am afraid he has been deficient in practice. Campbell is radically right; and we may hope that in time, there will be good practice.'

He owned that he thought Hawkesworth was one of his imitators, but he did not think Goldsmith was. Goldsmith, he said, had great merit. BOSWELL. 'But, Sir, he is much indebted to you for his getting so high in the public estimation.' JOHNSON. 'Why, Sir, he has, perhaps, got *sooner* to it by his intimacy with me.'

Goldsmith, though his vanity often excited him to occasional competition, had a very high regard for Johnson, which he at this time expressed in the strongest manner in the Dedication of his comedy, entitled, *She stoops to conquer.*[1]

---

1 'By inscribing this slight performance to you, I do not mean so much to compliment you, as myself. It may do me some honour to inform the public, that I have lived many years in intimacy with you. It may serve the interests of mankind also to inform them, that the greatest wit may be found in a character, without impairing the most unaffected piety.'

Johnson observed, that there were very few books printed in Scotland before the Union. He had seen a complete collection of them in the possession of the Honourable Archibald Campbell, a non-juring Bishop.[1] I wish this collection had been kept entire. Many of them are in the library of the Faculty of Advocates at Edinburgh. I told Dr Johnson that I had some intention to write the life of the learned and worthy Thomas Ruddiman. He said, 'I should take pleasure in helping you to do honour to him. But his farewell letter to the Faculty of Advocates, when he resigned the office of their Librarian, should have been in Latin.'

I put a question to him upon a fact in common life, which he could not answer, nor have I found any one else who could. What is the reason that women servants, though obliged to be at the expense of purchasing their own clothes, have much lower wages than men servants, to whom a great proportion of that article is furnished, and when in fact our female house servants work much harder than the male?

He told me, that he had twelve or fourteen times attempted to keep a journal of his life, but never could persevere. He advised me to do it. 'The great thing to be recorded (said he), is the state of your own mind; and you should write down every thing that you remember, for you cannot judge at first what is good or bad; and write immediately while the impression is fresh, for it will not be the same a week afterwards.'

I again solicited him to communicate to me the particulars of his early years. He said, 'You shall have them all for two-pence. I hope you shall know a great deal more of me before you write my Life.' He mentioned to me this day many circumstances, which I wrote down when I went home, and have interwoven in the former part of this narrative.

On Tuesday, April 13, he and Dr Goldsmith and I dined at General Oglethorpe's. Goldsmith expatiated on the common topic that the race of our people was degenerated, and that this was owing to luxury. JOHNSON. 'Sir, in the first place, I doubt the fact. I believe there are as many tall men in England now, as ever there were. But, secondly, supposing the stature of our people to be diminished, that is not owing to luxury; for, Sir, consider to how very small a proportion of our people luxury can reach. Our soldiery, surely, are not luxurious, who live on six-pence a day; and the same remark will apply to almost all the other classes. Luxury, so far as it reaches the poor, will do good to the race of people: it will strengthen and multiply them. Sir, no nation was ever hurt by luxury; for, as I said before, it can reach but to a very few. I admit that the great increase of commerce and manufactures hurts the military spirit of a people; because it produces a competition for something else than martial honours – a competition for riches. It also hurts the bodies of the people; for you will observe, there is no man who works at any particular trade, but you may know him from his appearance to do so. One part or other of his body

1 See an account of this learned and respectable gentleman, and of his curious work on the Middle State, *Journal of a Tour to the Hebrides*, 3d edit. p. 371.

being more used than the rest, he is in some degree deformed: but, Sir, that is not luxury. A tailor sits cross-legged; but that is not luxury.' GOLDSMITH. 'Come, you're just going to the same place by another road.' JOHNSON. 'Nay, Sir, I say that is not *luxury*. Let us take a walk from Charing-cross to Whitechapel, through, I suppose, the greatest series of shops in the world, what is there in any of these shops (if you except gin-shops), that can do any human being any harm?' GOLDSMITH. 'Well, Sir, I'll accept your challenge. The very next shop to Northumberland-house is a pickle-shop.' JOHNSON. 'Well, Sir: do we not know that a maid can in one afternoon make pickles sufficient to serve a whole family for a year? Nay, that five pickle-shops can serve all the kingdom? Besides, Sir, there is no harm done to any body by the making of pickles, or the eating of pickles.'

We drank tea with the ladies; and Goldsmith sung Tony Lumpkin's song in his comedy, *She stoops to conquer*,[a] and a very pretty one, to an Irish tune,* which he had designed for Miss Hardcastle; but as Mrs Bulkeley, who played the part, could not sing, it was left out. He afterwards wrote it down for me, by which means it was preserved, and now appears amongst his poems. Dr Johnson, in his way home, stopped at my lodgings in Piccadilly, and sat with me, drinking tea a second time, till a late hour.

I told him that Mrs Macaulay said, she wondered how he could reconcile his political principles with his moral; his notions of inequality and subordination with wishing well to the happiness of all mankind, who might live so agreeably, had they all their portions of land, and none to domineer over another. JOHNSON. 'Why, Sir, I reconcile my principles very well, because mankind are happier in a state of inequality and subordination. Were they to be in this pretty state of equality, they would soon degenerate into brutes; – they would become Monboddo's nation; – their tails would grow. Sir, all would be losers, were all to work to all: they would have no intellectual improvement. All intellectual improvement arises from leisure: all leisure arises from one working for another.'

Talking of the family of Stuart, he said, 'It should seem that the family at present on the throne has now established as good a right as the former family, by the long consent of the people; and that to disturb this right might be considered as culpable. At the same time I own, that it is a very difficult question, when considered with respect to the house of Stuart. To oblige people to take oaths as to the disputed right, is wrong. I know not whether I could take them: but I do not blame those who do.' So conscientious and so delicate was he upon this subject, which has occasioned so much clamour against him.

Talking of law cases, he said, 'The English reports in general, are very poor: only the half of what has been said is taken down; and of that half, much is mistaken. Whereas, in Scotland, the arguments on each side are deliberately put in writing, to be considered by the Court. I think a collection of your cases

[a] Add note: 'The Humours of Ballamagairy'.

upon subjects of importance, with the opinions of the Judges upon them, would be valuable.'

On Thursday, April 15, I dined with him and Dr Goldsmith at General Paoli's. We found here, Signor Martinelli, of Florence, author of a History of England in Italian, printed at London.

I spoke of Allan Ramsay's *Gentle Shepherd*, in the Scottish dialect, as the best pastoral that had ever been written; not only abounding with beautiful rural imagery, and just and pleasing sentiments, but being a real picture of manners; and I offered to teach Dr Johnson to understand it. 'No, Sir (said he), I won't learn it. You shall retain your superiority by my not knowing it.'

This brought on a question whether one man is lessened by another's acquiring an equal degree of knowledge with him. Johnson asserted the affirmative. I maintained that the position might be true in those kinds of knowledge which produce wisdom, power, and force, so as to enable one man to have the government of others; but that a man is not in any degree lessened by others knowing as well as he what ends in mere pleasure: eating fine fruits, drinking delicious wines, reading exquisite poetry.

The General observed, that Martinelli was a Whig. JOHNSON. 'I am sorry for it. It shows the spirit of the times: he is obliged to temporise.' BOSWELL. 'I rather think, Sir, that Toryism prevails in this reign.' JOHNSON. 'I know not why you should think so, Sir. You see your friend Lord Lyttelton, a noble-man, is obliged in his History to write the most vulgar Whiggism.'

An animated debate took place whether Martinelli should continue his History of England to the present day. GOLDSMITH. 'To be sure he should.' JOHNSON. 'No, Sir; he would give great offence. He would have to tell of almost all the living great what they do not wish told.' GOLDSMITH. 'It may, perhaps, be necessary for a native to be more cautious; but a foreigner who comes among us without prejudice, may be considered as holding the place of a judge, and may speak his mind freely.' JOHNSON. 'Sir, a foreigner, when he sends a work from the press, ought to be on his guard against catching the error and mistaken enthusiasm of the people among whom he happens to be.' GOLDSMITH. 'Sir, he wants only to sell his history, and tell truth; one an honest, the other a laudable motive.' JOHNSON. 'Sir, they are both laudable motives. It is laudable in a man to wish to live by his labours; but he should write so as he may live by them, not so as he may be knocked on the head. I would advise him to be at Calais before he publishes his history of the present age. A foreigner who attaches himself to a political party in this country, is in the worst state that can be imagined: he is looked upon as a mere intermeddler. A native may do it from interest.' BOSWELL. 'Or principle.' GOLDSMITH. 'There are people, who tell a hundred political lies every day, and are not hurt by it. Surely, then, one may tell truth with safety.' JOHNSON. 'Why, Sir, in the first place, he who tells a hundred lies has disarmed the force of his lies. But besides; a man had rather have a hundred lies told of him, than one truth which he does not wish should be told.' GOLDSMITH. 'For my part, I'd tell truth, and shame the devil.' JOHNSON. 'Yes, Sir; but the devil will be angry. I wish to shame the devil as much as you do; but I should choose to be out of the reach of his claws.' GOLDSMITH. 'His claws can do you no harm, when you have the shield of truth.'

It having been observed that there was little hospitality in London; JOHNSON. 'Nay, Sir, any man who has a name, or who has the power of pleasing, will be very generally invited in London. The man, Sterne, I have been told, has had engagements for three months.' GOLDSMITH. 'And a very dull fellow.' JOHNSON. 'Why no, Sir.'

Martinelli told us, that for several years he lived much with Charles Townshend, and that he ventured to tell him he was a bad joker. JOHNSON. 'Why, Sir, thus much I can say upon the subject. One day he and a few more agreed to go and dine in the country, and each of them was to bring a friend in his carriage with him. Charles Townshend asked Fitzherbert to go with him, but told him, "You must find somebody to bring you back: I can only carry you there." Fitzherbert did not much like this arrangement. He however consented, observing sarcastically, "It will do very well; for then the same jokes will serve you in returning as in going." '

An eminent public character being mentioned; – JOHNSON. 'I remember being present when he showed himself to be so corrupted, or at least something so different from what I think right, as to maintain, that a member of parliament should go along with his party right or wrong. Now, Sir, this is so remote from native virtue, from scholastic virtue, that a good man must have undergone a great change before he can reconcile himself to such a doctrine. It is maintaining, that you may lie to the public; for you lie when you call that right which you think wrong, or the reverse. A friend of ours, who is too much an echo of that gentleman, observed, that a man who does not stick uniformly to a party, is only waiting to be bought. Why then, said I, he is only waiting to be what that gentleman is already.'

We talked of the King's coming to see Goldsmith's new play. – 'I wish he would,' said Goldsmith; adding, however, with an affected indifference, 'Not that it would do me the least good.' JOHNSON. 'Well then, Sir, let us say it would do *him* good (laughing). No, Sir, this affectation will not pass – it is mighty idle. In such a state as ours, who would not wish to please the chief magistrate?' GOLDSMITH. 'I do wish to please him. I remember a line in Dryden,

And ev'ry poet is the Monarch's friend.

It ought to be reversed.' JOHNSON. 'Nay, there are finer lines in Dryden on this subject:

For colleges on bounteous Kings depend,
And never rebel was to arts a friend.'

General Paoli observed, that successful rebels might. MARTINELLI. 'Happy rebellions.' GOLDSMITH. 'We have no such phrase.' GENERAL PAOLI. 'But have you not the *thing*?' GOLDSMITH. 'Yes; all our *happy* revolutions. They have hurt our constitution, and will hurt it, till we mend it by another HAPPY REVOLUTION.' – I never before discovered that my friend Goldsmith had so much of the old prejudice in him.

General Paoli, talking of Goldsmith's new play, said, '*Il a fait un compliment très gracieux à une certaine grande dame*'; meaning a Duchess of the first rank.

I expressed a doubt whether Goldsmith intended it, in order that I might hear the truth from himself. It, perhaps, was not quite fair to endeavour to bring him to a confession, as he might not wish to avow positively his taking part against the Court. He smiled and hesitated. The General at once relieved him, by this beautiful image: '*Monsieur Goldsmith est comme la mer, qui jette des perles et beaucoup d'autres belles choses, sans s'en appercevoir.*' GOLDSMITH. '*Très bien dit, et très élégamment.*'

A person was mentioned, who it was said could take down in short hand the speeches in parliament with perfect exactness. JOHNSON. 'Sir, it is impossible. I remember one Angel, who came to me to write for him a Preface or Dedication to a book upon short hand, and he professed to write as fast as a man could speak. In order to try him, I took down a book, and read while he wrote; and I favoured him, for I read more deliberately than usual. I had proceeded but a very little way, when he begged I would desist, for 'he could not follow me.' Hearing now for the first time of this Preface or Dedication, I said, 'What an expense, Sir, do you put us to in buying books, to which you have written Prefaces or Dedications.' JOHNSON. 'Why, I have dedicated to the Royal Family all round; that is to say, to the last generation of the Royal Family.' GOLDSMITH. 'And perhaps, Sir, not one sentence of wit in a whole Dedication.' JOHNSON. 'Perhaps not, Sir.' BOSWELL. 'What then is the reason for applying to a particular person to do that which any one may do as well?' JOHNSON. 'Why, Sir, one man has greater readiness at doing it than another.'

I spoke of Mr Harris, of Salisbury, as being a very learned man, and in particular an eminent Grecian. JOHNSON. 'I am not sure of that. His friends give him out as such, but I know not who of his friends are able to judge of it.' GOLDSMITH. 'He is what is much better: he is a worthy humane man.' JOHNSON. 'Nay, Sir, that is not to the purpose of our argument: that will as much prove that he can play upon the fiddle as well as Giardini, as that he is an eminent Grecian.' GOLDSMITH. 'The greatest musical performers have but small emoluments. Giardini, I am told, does not get above seven hundred a year.' JOHNSON. 'That is, indeed, but little for a man to get, who does best that which so many endeavour to do. There is nothing, I think, in which the power of art is shown so much as in playing on the fiddle. In all other things we can do something at first. Any man will forge a bar of iron, if you give him a hammer; not so well as a smith, but tolerably. A man will saw a piece of wood, and make a box, though a clumsy one; but give him a fiddle and a fiddle-stick, and he can do nothing.'

On Monday, April 19, he called on me with Mrs Williams, in Mr Strahan's coach, and carried me out to dine with Mr Elphinston, at his academy at Kensington. A printer having acquired a fortune sufficient to keep his coach, was a good topic for the credit of literature. Mrs Williams said, that another printer, Mr Hamilton, had not waited so long as Mr Strahan, but had kept his coach several years sooner. JOHNSON. 'He was in the right. Life is short. The sooner that a man begins to enjoy his wealth the better.'

Mr Elphinston talked of a new book that was much admired, and asked Dr Johnson if he had read it. JOHNSON. 'I have looked into it.' 'What (said Elphinston), have you not read it through?' Johnson, offended at being thus pressed, and so obliged to own his cursory mode of reading, answered tartly, 'No, Sir; do *you* read books *through*?'

He this day again defended duelling, and put his argument upon what I have ever thought the most solid basis; that if public war be allowed to be consistent with morality, private war must be equally so. Indeed we may observe what strained arguments are used, to reconcile war with the Christian religion. But, in my opinion, it is exceedingly clear that duelling having better reasons for its barbarous violence, is more justifiable than war, in which thousands go forth without any cause of personal quarrel, and massacre each other.

On Wednesday, April 21, I dined with him at Mr Thrale's. A gentleman attacked Garrick for being vain. JOHNSON. 'No wonder Sir, that he is vain; a man who is perpetually flattered in every mode that can be conceived. So many bellows have blown the fire, that one wonders he is not by this time become a cinder.' BOSWELL. 'And such fellows too. Lord Mansfield with his cheeks like to burst: Lord Chatham like an Aeolus.' I have read such notes from them to him as were enough to turn his head.' JOHNSON. 'True. When he whom every body else flatters, flatters me, I then am truly happy.' MRS THRALE. 'The sentiment is in Congreve, I think.' JOHNSON. 'Yes, Madam, in *The Way of the World*:

> If there's delight in love, 'tis when I see
> That heart which others bleed for, bleed for me.

No, Sir, I should not be surprised though Garrick chained the ocean and lashed the winds.' BOSWELL. 'Should it not be, Sir, lashed the ocean and chained the winds?' JOHNSON. 'No, Sir; recollect the original:

> *In Corum atque Eurum solitus saevire flagellis*
> *Barbarus, Aeolio numquam hoc in carcere passos,*
> *Ipsum compedibus qui vinxerat Ennosigaeum.*'

This does very well when both the winds and the sea are personified, and mentioned by their mythological names, as in Juvenal; but when they are mentioned in plain language, the application of the epithets suggested by me, is the most obvious; and accordingly my friend himself, in his imitation of the passage which describes Xerxes, has

> The waves he lashes, and enchains the wind.

The modes of living in different countries, and the various views with which men travel in quest of new scenes, having been talked of, a learned gentleman who holds a considerable office in the law, expatiated on the happiness of a savage life; and mentioned an instance of an officer who had actually lived for some time in the wilds of America, of whom, when in that state, he quoted this reflection with an air of admiration, as if it had been deeply philosophical: 'Here am I, free and unrestrained, amidst the rude magnificence of Nature, with this Indian woman by my side, and this gun, with which I can procure food when I want it: what more can be desired for human happiness?' It did not require much sagacity to foresee that such a sentiment would not be permitted to pass without due animadversion. JOHNSON. 'Do not allow yourself, Sir, to be imposed upon by such gross absurdity. It is sad stuff; it is brutish. If a bull could speak, he might as well exclaim – Here am I with this cow and this grass; what being can enjoy greater felicity?'

We talked of the melancholy end of a gentleman who had destroyed himself. JOHNSON. 'It was owing to imaginary difficulties in his affairs, which, had he talked with any friend, would soon have vanished.' BOSWELL. 'Do you think, Sir, that all who commit suicide are mad?' JOHNSON. 'Sir, they are often not universally disordered in their intellects, but one passion presses so upon them that they yield to it, and commit suicide, as a passionate man will stab another.' He added, 'I have often thought, that after a man has taken the resolution to kill himself, it is not courage in him to do anything, however desperate, because he has nothing to fear.' GOLDSMITH. 'I don't see that.' JOHNSON. 'Nay but, my dear Sir, why should not you see what every one else sees?' GOLDSMITH. 'It is for fear of something that he has resolved to kill himself; and will not that timid disposition restrain him?' JOHNSON. 'It does not signify that the fear of some- thing made him resolve; it is upon the state of his mind after the resolution is taken, that I argue. Suppose a man, either from fear, or pride, or conscience, or whatever motive, has resolved to kill himself; when once the resolution is taken he has nothing to fear. He may then go and take the King of Prussia by the nose at the head of his army. He cannot fear the rack, who is resolved to kill himself. When Eustace Budgel was walking down to the Thames, determined to drown himself, he might, if he pleased, without any apprehension of danger, have turned aside, and first set fire to St James's palace.'

On Tuesday, April 27, Mr Beauclerk and I called on him in the morning. As we walked up Johnson's-court, I said, 'I have a veneration for this court'; and was glad to find that Beauclerk had the same reverential enthusiasm. We found him alone. We talked of Mr Andrew Stuart's elegant and plausible Letters to Lord Mansfield; a copy of which had been sent by the author to Dr Johnson. JOHNSON. 'They have not answered the end. They have not been talked of. I have never heard of them. This is owing to their not being sold. People seldom read a book which is given to them, and few are given. The way to spread a work is to sell it at a low price. No man will send to buy a thing that costs even sixpence, without an intention to read it.' BOSWELL. 'May it not be doubted, Sir, whether it be proper to publish letters, arraigning the ultimate decision of an important cause by the supreme judicature of the nation?' JOHNSON. 'No, Sir, I do not think it was wrong to publish these letters. If they are thought to do harm, why not answer them? But they will do no harm. If Mr Douglas be indeed the son of Lady Jane, he cannot be hurt: if he be not her son, and yet has the great estate of the family of Douglas, he may well submit to have a pamphlet against him by Andrew Stuart. Sir, I think such a publication does good, as it does good to show us the possibilities of human life. And, Sir, you will not say that the Douglas cause was a cause of easy decision, when it divided your Court as much as it could do, to be determined at all. When your Judges were seven and seven, the casting vote of the President must be given on one side or other; no matter, for my argument, on which; one or the other *must* be taken; as when I am to move, there is no matter which leg I move first. And then, Sir, it was otherwise determined here. No, Sir, a more dubious determination of any question cannot be imagined.'[1]

He said, 'Goldsmith should not be for ever attempting to shine in conversation: he has not temper for it, he is so much mortified when he fails. Sir, a game of jokes is composed partly of skill, partly of chance. A man may be beat at times by one who has not the tenth part of his wit. Now Goldsmith's putting himself against another, is like a man laying a hundred to one who cannot spare the hundred. It is not worth a man's while. A man should not lay a hundred to one, unless he can easily spare it, though he has a hundred chances for him: he can get but a guinea, and he may lose a hundred. Goldsmith is in this state. When he contends, if he gets the better, it is a very little addition to a man of his literary reputation: if he does not get the better, he is miserably vexed.'

Johnson's own superlative power of wit set him above any risk of such uneasiness. Garrick had remarked to me of him, a few days before, 'Rabelais and all other wits are nothing compared with him. You may be diverted by them; but Johnson gives you a forcible hug, and shakes laughter out of you, whether you will or no.'

Goldsmith, however, was often very fortunate in his witty contests even when he entered the lists with Johnson himself. Sir Joshua Reynolds was in company with them one day, when Goldsmith said, that he thought he could write a good fable, mentioned the simplicity which that kind of composition requires, and observed, that in most fables the animals introduced seldom talk in character. 'For instance (said he), the fable of the little fishes, who saw birds fly over their heads, and envying them, petitioned Jupiter to changed into birds. The skill (continued he), consists in making them talk like little fishes.' While he indulged himself in fanciful reverie, he observed Johnson shaking his sides, and laughing. Upon which he smartly proceeded, 'Why, Dr Johnson,

---

1 I regretted that Dr Johnson never took the trouble to study a question which interested nations. He would not even read a pamphlet which I wrote upon it, entitled 'The Essence of the Douglas Cause', which, I have reason to flatter myself, had considerable effect in favour of Mr Douglas; of whose legitimate filiation I was then, and am still, firmly convinced. Let me add, that no fact can be more respectably ascertained, than by a judgement of the most august tribunal in the world; a judgement, in which Lord Mansfield and Lord Camden united in 1769, and from which only five of a numerous body entered a protest.

this is not so easy as you seem to think: for if you were to make little fishes talk, they would talk like WHALES.'

Johnson, though remarkable for his great variety of composition, never exercised his talents in fable, except we allow his beautiful tale published in Mrs Williams's *Miscellanies* to be of that species. I have, however, found among his manuscript collections the following sketch of one:

'Glow-worm lying in the garden saw a candle in a neighbouring palace, – and complained of the littleness of his own light – another observed – wait a little; – soon dark; – have outlasted πολλ [many] of these glaring lights which only are brighter as they haste to nothing.'

On Thursday, April 29, I dined with him at General Oglethorpe's, where were Sir Joshua Reynolds, Mr Langton, Dr Goldsmith, and Mr Thrale. I was very desirous to get Dr Johnson absolutely fixed in his resolution to go with me to the Hebrides this year; and I told him that I had received a letter from Dr Robertson the historian upon the subject, with which he was much pleased, and now talked in such a manner of his long-intended tour, that I was satisfied he meant to fulfil his engagement.

The custom of eating dogs at Otaheite being mentioned, Goldsmith observed, that this was also a custom in China; that a dog-butcher is as common there as any other butcher, and that when he walks abroad all the dogs fall on him. JOHNSON. 'That is not owing to his killing dogs, Sir. I remember a butcher at Lichfield, whom a dog that was in the house where I lived, always attacked. It is the smell of carnage which provokes this, let the animals he has killed be what they may.' GOLDSMITH. 'Yes, there is a general abhorrence in animals at the signs of massacre. If you put a tub full of blood into a stable, the horses are like to go mad.' JOHNSON. 'I doubt that.' GOLDSMITH. 'Nay, Sir, it is a fact well authenticated.' THRALE. 'You had better prove it before you put it into your book on natural history. You may do it in my stable if you will.' JOHNSON. 'Nay, Sir, I would not have him prove it. If he is content to take his information from others, he may get through his book with little trouble, and without much endangering his reputation. But if he makes experiments for so comprehensive a book as his, there would be no end to them; his erroneous assertions would then fall upon himself; and he might be blamed for not having made experiments as to every particular.'

The character of Mallet having been introduced, and spoken of slightingly by Goldsmith; JOHNSON. 'Why, Sir, Mallet had talents enough to keep his literary reputation alive as long as he himself lived; and that, let me tell you, is a good deal.' GOLDSMITH. 'But I cannot agree that it was so. His literary reputation was dead long before his natural death. I consider an author's literary reputation to be alive only while his name will ensure a good price for his copy from the bookseller. I will get you (to Johnson), a hundred guineas for anything whatever that you shall write, if you put your name to it.'

Dr Goldsmith's new play, *She stoops to conquer*, being mentioned; JOHNSON. 'I know of no comedy for many years that has so much exhilarated an audience, that has answered so much the great end of comedy, – making an audience merry.'

Goldsmith having said, that Garrick's compliment to the Queen, which he introduced into the play of *The Chances*, which he had altered and revised this year, was mean and gross flattery; JOHNSON. 'Why, Sir, I would not *write*, I would not give solemnly under my hand a character beyond what I thought really true; but a speech on the stage, let it flatter ever so extravagantly, is formular. It has always been formular to flatter Kings and Queens; so much so, that even in our church-service we have "our most religious King", used indiscriminately, whoever is King. Nay, they even flatter themselves; – "we have been graciously pleased to grant". – No modern flattery, however, is so gross as that of the Augustan age, where the Emperor was deified. *"Praesens Divus habebitur Augustus."* And as to meanness (rising into warmth), how is it mean in a player – a showman – a fellow who exhibits himself for a shilling, to flatter his Queen? The attempt, indeed, was dangerous; for if it had missed, what became of Garrick, and what became of the Queen? As Sir William Temple says of a great General, it is necessary not only that his designs should be formed in a masterly manner, but that they should be attended with success. Sir, it is right, at a time when the Royal Family is not generally liked, to let it be seen that the people like at least one of them. SIR JOSHUA REYNOLDS. 'I do not perceive why the profession of a player should be despised; for the great and ultimate end of all the employments of mankind is to produce amusement. Garrick produces more amusement than any body.' BOSWELL. 'You say, Dr Johnson, that Garrick exhibits himself for a shilling. In this respect he is only on a footing with a lawyer who exhibits himself for his fee, and even will maintain any nonsense or absurdity if the case requires it. Garrick refuses a play or a part which he does not like; a lawyer never refuses.' JOHNSON. 'Why, Sir, what does this prove? Only that a lawyer is worse. Boswell is now like Jack in *The Tale of a Tub*, who, when he is puzzled by an argument, hangs himself. He thinks I shall cut him down, but I'll let him hang (laughing vociferously). SIR JOSHUA REYNOLDS. 'Mr Boswell thinks that the profession of a lawyer being unquestionably honourable, if he can show the profession of a player to be more honourable, he proves his argument.'

On Friday, April 30, I dined with him at Mr Beauclerk's, where were Lord Charlemont, Sir Joshua Reynolds, and some more members of the Literary Club, whom he had obligingly invited to meet me, as I was this evening to be balloted for as candidate for admission into that distinguished society. Johnson had done me the honour to propose me, and Beauclerk was very zealous for me.

Goldsmith being mentioned; – JOHNSON. 'It is amazing how little Goldsmith knows. He seldom comes where he is not more ignorant than any one else.' SIR JOSHUA REYNOLDS. 'Yet there is no man whose company is more liked.' JOHNSON. 'To be sure, Sir. When people find a man of the most distinguished abilities as a writer, their inferior while he is with them, it must be highly gratifying to them. What Goldsmith comically says of himself is very true, – he always gets the better when he argues alone; – meaning that he is master of a subject in his study, and can write well upon it; but when he comes into company, grows confused, and unable to talk. Take him as a poet, his *Traveller* is a very fine performance; aye, and so is his *Deserted Village*, were it not sometimes too much the echo of his *Traveller*. Whether, indeed, we take him as a poet, – as a comic writer, – or as an historian, he stands in the first class.' BOSWELL. 'An historian! My dear Sir, you surely will not rank his compilation of the Roman History with the works of other historians of this age?' JOHNSON. 'Why, who are before him?' BOSWELL. 'Hume – Robertson – Lord Lyttelton.' JOHNSON. (His antipathy to the Scotch beginning to rise) I have not read Hume; but, doubtless, Goldsmith's History is better than the verbiage of Robertson, or the foppery of Dalrymple.' BOSWELL. 'Will you not admit the superiority of Robertson, in whose History we find such penetration – such painting?' JOHNSON. 'Sir, you must consider how that penetration and that painting are employed. It is not history, it is imagination. He who describes what he never saw, draws from fancy. Robertson paints minds as Sir Joshua paints faces in a history-piece: he imagines an heroic countenance. You must look upon Robertson's work as romance, and try it by that standard. History it is not. Besides, Sir, it is the great excellence of a writer to put into his book as much as his book will hold. Goldsmith has done this in his History. Now Robertson might have put twice as much into his book. Robertson is like a man who has packed gold in wool: the wool takes up more room than the gold. No, Sir; I always thought Robertson would be crushed by his own weight – would be buried under his own ornaments. Goldsmith tells you shortly all you want to know: Robertson detains you a great deal too long. No man will read Robertson's cumbrous detail a second time; but Goldsmith's plain narrative will please again and again. I would say to Robertson what an old tutor of a College said to one of his pupils: "Read over your composition, and wherever you meet with a passage which you think is particularly fine, strike it out." Goldsmith's abridgement is better than that of Lucius Florus or Eutropius; and I will venture to say, that if you compare him with Vertot, in the same places of the Roman History, you will find that he excels Vertot. Sir, he has the art of compiling, and of saying every thing he has to say in a pleasing manner. He is now writing a Natural History, and will make it as entertaining as a Persian Tale.'

I cannot dismiss the present topic without observing, that it is probable that Dr Johnson, who owned that he often 'talked for victory', rather urged plausible objections to Dr Robertson's excellent historical works, in the ardour of contest, than expressed his real and decided opinion; for it is not easy to suppose, that he should so widely differ from the rest of the literary world.

JOHNSON. 'I remember once being with Goldsmith in Westminster-abbey. While we surveyed the Poets' Corner, I said to him,

> *Forsitan et nostrum nomen miscebitur istis.*[1]

When we got to Temple-bar he stopped me, pointed to the heads upon it, and slily whispered me,

> *Forsitan et nostrum nomen miscebitur* ISTIS.'[2]

---

1 Ovid *de Art. Amand.* l.iii. v.53.
2 In allusion to Dr Johnson's supposed political principles, and perhaps his own.

Johnson praised John Bunyan highly. 'His *Pilgrim's Progress* has great merit, both for invention, imagination, and the conduct of the story; and it has had the best evidence of its merit, the general and continued approbation of mankind. Few books, I believe, have had a more extensive sale. It is remarkable, that it begins very much like the poem of Dante; yet there was no translation of Dante when Bunyan wrote. There is reason to think that he had read Spenser.'

A proposition which had been agitated, that monuments to eminent persons should, for the time to come, be erected in St Paul's church as well as in Westminster-abbey, was mentioned; and it was asked, who should be honoured by having his monument first erected there. Somebody suggested Pope. JOHNSON. 'Why, Sir, as Pope was a Roman Catholic, I would not have his to be first. I think Milton's rather should have the precedence.[a] I think more highly of him now than I did at twenty. There is more thinking in him and in Butler, than in any of our poets.'

Some of the company expressed a wonder why the author of so excellent a book as *The whole Duty of Man* should conceal himself. JOHNSON. 'There may be different reasons assigned for this, any one of which would be very sufficient. He may have been a clergyman, and may have thought that his religious counsels would have less weight when known to come from a man whose profession was Theology. He may have been a man whose practice was not suitable to his principles; so that his character might injure the effect of his book, which he had written in a season of penitence. Or he may have been a man of rigid self-denial, so that he would have no reward for his pious labours while in this world, but refer it all to a future state.'

The gentlemen went away to their club, and I was left at Beauclerk's till the fate of my election should be announced to me.[b] In a short time I received the agreeable intelligence that I was chosen. I hastened to the place of meeting, and was introduced to such a society as can seldom be found. Mr Edmund Burke, whom I then saw for the first time, and whose splendid talents had long made me ardently wish for his acquaintance; Dr Nugent, Mr Garrick, Dr Goldsmith, Mr (now Sir William) Jones, and the company with whom I had dined. Upon my entrance, Johnson placed himself behind a chair, on which he leaned as on a desk or pulpit, and with humorous formality gave me a *Charge*, pointing out the conduct expected from me as a good member of this club.

Goldsmith produced some very absurd verses which had been publicly recited to an audience for money. JOHNSON. 'I can match this nonsense. There was a poem called 'Eugenio', which came out some years ago, and concluded thus:

---

[a] Add this note: Here is another instance of his high admiration of Milton as a Poet, notwithstanding his just abhorrence of that sour Republican's political principles. His candour and discrimination are equally conspicuous. Let us hear no more of his 'injustice to Milton'.

[b] Add: I sat in a state of anxiety which even the charming society of Lady Di Beauclerk could not entirely dissipate.

> And now, ye trifling self-assuming elves,
> Brimful of pride, of nothing, of yourselves,
> Survey Eugenio, view him o'er and o'er,
> Then sink into yourselves, and be no more.[a]

Nay, Dryden in his poem on the Royal Society, has these lines:

> Then we upon our globe's last verge shall go,
>   And see the ocean leaning on the sky;
> From thence our rolling neighbours we shall know,
>   And on the lunar world securely pry.'

Talking of puns, Johnson, who had a great contempt for that species of wit, deigned to allow that there was one good pun in *Menagiana*, I think on the word *corps*.[b]

---

[a] Add this note: Dr Johnson's memory here was not perfectly accurate: 'Eugenia' does not conclude thus. There are eight more lines after the last of those quoted by him; and the passage which he meant to recite is as follows:

> Say now ye fluttering, poor assuming elves,
> Stark full of pride, of folly, of – yourselves;
> Say where's the wretch of all your impious crew
> Who dares confront his character to view?
> Behold Eugenio, view him o'er and o'er,
> Then sink into yourselves, and be no more.

Mr Reed informs me that the author of 'Eugenio', Thomas Beech, a wine merchant at Wrexham in Denbighshire, soon after its publication, viz. 17th May 1737, cut his own throat; and that it appears by Swift's Works, that the poem had been shown to him, and received some of his corrections. Johnson had read 'Eugenio' on his first coming to town, for we see it mentioned in one of his letters to Mr Cave, which has been inserted in this work.

[b] Add the following note: I formerly thought that I had perhaps mistaken the word and imagined it to be *Corps*, from its similarity of sound to the real one. For an accurate and shrewd unknown gentleman, to whom I am indebted for some remarks on my work, observes on this passage – 'Q. if not on the word, *Fort*? A vociferous French preacher said of Bourdaloue, "Il preche *fort bien*, et moi *bien fort.*" – *Menagiana*. See also *Anecdotes Littéraires*, Article Bourdaloue.' But my ingenious and obliging correspondent, Mr Abercrombie of Philadelphia, has pointed out to me the following passage in 'Menagiana'; which renders the preceding conjecture unnecessary, and confirms my original statement:

> Madame de Bourdonne, Chanoinesse de Remiremont, venoit d'entendre un discours plein de feu et d'esprit, mais fort peu solide, et très irrégulier. Une de ses amies, qui y prenoit intérêt pour l'orateur, lui dit en sortant, 'Eh bien, Madame, que vous semble-t-il de ce que vous venez d'entendre? Qu'il y a d'esprit?' – 'Il y a tant,' répondit Madame de Bourdonne, 'que je n'y ai pas vu de *corps*.' *Menagiana*, tome ii. p. 64. Amsterd. 1713.

In *Second Edition* the note ends at 'Bourdaloue.'

Much pleasant conversation passed, which Johnson relished with great good humour. But his conversation alone, or what led to it, or was interwoven with it, is the business of this work.

On Saturday, May 1, we dined by ourselves at our old rendezvous, the Mitre tavern. He was placid, but not much disposed to talk. He observed, that 'The Irish mix better with the English than the Scotch do; their language is nearer to English, as a proof of which, they succeed very well as players, which Scotchmen do not. Then, Sir, they have not that extreme nationality which we find in the Scotch. I will do you, Boswell, the justice to say, that you are the most *unscottified* of your countrymen. You are almost the only instance of a Scotchman that I have known, who did not at every other sentence bring in some other Scotchman.'

We drank tea with Mrs Williams. I introduced a question which has been much agitated in the Church of Scotland, whether the claim of lay-patrons to present ministers to parishes be well founded; and supposing it to be well founded, whether it ought to be exercised without the concurrence of the people? That Church is composed of a series of judicatures: a Presbytery, – a Synod, – and, finally, a General Assembly; before all of which, this matter may be contended: and in some cases the Presbytery having refused to induct or *settle*, as they call it, the person presented by the patron, it has been found necessary to appeal to the General Assembly. He said, I might see the subject well treated in the *Defence of Pluralities*; and although he thought that a patron should exercise his right with tenderness to the inclinations of the people of a parish, he was very clear as to his right. Then supposing the question to be pleaded before the General Assembly, he dictated to me what follows:

'AGAINST the right of patrons is commonly opposed, by the inferior judicatures, the plea of conscience. Their conscience tells them, that the people ought to choose their pastor; their conscience tells them that they ought not to impose upon a congregation a minister ungrateful and unacceptable to his auditors. Conscience is nothing more than a conviction felt by ourselves of something to be done, or something to be avoided, and, in questions of simple unperplexed morality, conscience is very often a guide that may be trusted. But before conscience can determine, the state of the question is supposed to be completely known. In questions of law, or of fact, conscience is very often confounded with opinion. No man's conscience can tell him the rights of another man: they must be known by rational investigation or historical enquiry. Opinion, which he that holds it may call his conscience, may teach some men that religion would be promoted, and quiet preserved, by granting to the people universally the choice of their ministers. But it is a conscience very ill informed that violates the rights of one man, for the convenience of another. Religion cannot be promoted by injustice: and it was never yet found that a popular election was very quietly transacted.

'That justice would be violated by transferring to the people the right of patronage, is apparent to all who know whence that right had its original. The right of patronage was not at first a privilege torn by power from unresisting poverty. It is not an authority at first usurped in times of ignorance, and established only by succession and by precedents. It is not a grant capriciously made from a higher tyrant to a lower. It is a right dearly purchased by the first possessors, and justly inherited by those that succeeded them. When Christianity was established in this island, a regular mode of public worship was prescribed. Public worship requires a public place; and the proprietors of lands, as they were converted, built churches for their families and their vassals. For the maintenance of ministers, they settled a certain portion of their lands; and a district, through which each minister was required to extend his care, was, by that circumscription, constituted a parish. This is a position so generally received in England, that the extent of a manor and of a parish are regularly received for each other. The churches which the proprietors of lands had thus built and thus endowed, they justly thought themselves entitled to provide with minsters; and where the episcopal government prevails, the Bishop has no power to reject a man nominated by the patron, but for some crime that might exclude him from the priesthood. For the endowment of the church being the gift of the landlord, he was consequently at liberty to give it according to his choice, to any man capable of performing the holy offices. The people did not choose him, because the people did not pay him.

'We hear it sometimes urged that this original right is passed out of memory, and is obliterated and obscured by many translations of property and changes of government; that scarce any church is now in the hands of the heirs of the builders; and that the present persons have entered subsequently upon the pretended rights by a thousand accidental and unknown causes. Much of this, perhaps, is true. But how is the right of patronage extinguished? If the right followed the lands, it is possessed by the same equity by which the lands are possessed. It is, in effect, part of the manor, and protected by the same laws with every other privilege. Let us suppose an estate forfeited by treason, and granted by the Crown to a new family. With the lands were forfeited all the rights appendant to those lands: by the same power that grants the lands, the rights also are granted. The right lost to the patron falls not to the people, but is either retained by the Crown, or, what to the people is the same thing, is by the Crown given away. Let it change hands ever so often, it is possessed by him that receives it with the same right as it was conveyed. It may, indeed, like all our possessions, be forcibly seized or fraudulently obtained. But no injury is still done to the people; for what they never had, they have never lost. Caius may usurp the right of Titius; but neither Caius nor Titius injure the people: and no man's conscience, however tender or however active, can prompt him to restore what may be proved to have been never taken away. Supposing what I think cannot be proved, that a popular election of ministers were to be desired, our desires are not the measure of equity. It were to be desired that power should be only in the hands of the merciful, and riches in the possession of the generous; but the law must leave both riches and power where it finds them; and must often leave riches with the covetous, and power with the cruel. Convenience may be a rule in little things, where no other rule has been established. But as the great end of government is to give every man his own, no inconvenience is greater than that of making right uncertain. Nor is any man more an enemy to public peace, than he who fills weak heads with imaginary claims, and breaks the series of civil subordination, by inciting the lower classes of mankind to encroach upon the higher.

'Having thus shown that the right of patronage, being originally purchased, may be legally transferred, and that it is now in the hands of lawful possessors, at least as certainly as any other right, we have left to the advocates of the people no other plea than that of convenience. Let us, therefore, now consider what the people would really gain by a general abolition of the right of patronage. What is most to be desired by such a change is, that the country should be supplied with better ministers. But why should we suppose that the parish will make a wiser choice than the patron? If we suppose mankind actuated by interest, the patron is more likely to choose with caution, because he will suffer more by choosing wrong. By the deficiencies of his minister, or by his vices, he is equally offended with the rest of the congregation; but he will have this reason more to lament them, that they will be imputed to his absurdity or corruption. The qualifications of a minister are well known to be learning and piety. Of his learning the patron is probably the only judge in the parish; and of his piety not less a judge than others; and is more likely to inquire minutely and diligently before he gives a presentation, than one of the parochial rabble, who can give nothing but a vote. It may be urged, that though the parish might not choose better ministers, they would at least choose ministers whom they like better, and who would therefore officiate with greater efficacy. That ignorance and perverseness should always obtain what they like, was never considered as the end of government; of which it is the great and standing benefit, that the wise see for the simple, and the regular act for the capricious. But that this argument supposes the people capable of judging, and resolute to act according to their best judgements, though this be sufficiently absurd, is not all its absurdity. It supposes not only wisdom, but unanimity in those, who upon no other occasions are unanimous or wise. If by some strange concurrence all the voices of a parish should unite in the choice of any single man, though I could not charge the patron with injustice for presenting a minister, I should censure him as unkind and injudicious. But, it is evident, that as in all other popular elections there will be contrariety of judgement and acrimony of passion, a parish upon every vacancy would break into factions, and the contest for the choice of a minister would set neighbours at variance and bring discord into families. The minister would be taught all the arts of a candidate, would flatter some and bribe others; and the electors, as in all other cases, would call for holidays and ale, and break the heads of each other during the jollity of the canvas. The time must, however, come at last, when one of the factions must prevail, and one of the ministers get possession of the church. On what terms does he enter upon his ministry but those of enmity with half his parish? By what prudence or what diligence can he hope to conciliate the affections of that party by whose defeat he has obtained his living? Every man who voted against him will enter the church with hanging head and downcast eyes, afraid to encounter that neighbour by whose vote and influence he has been overpowered. He will hate his neighbour for opposing him, and his minister for having prospered by the opposition; and, as he will never see him but with pain, he will never see him but with hatred. Of a minister presented by the patron, the parish has seldom anything worse to say than that they do not know him. Of a minister chosen by a popular contest, all those who do not favour him have nursed up in their bosoms principles of hatred and reasons of rejection. Anger is excited principally by pride. The pride of a common man is very little exasperated by the supposed usurpation of an acknowledged superior. He bears only his little share of a general evil, and suffers in common with the whole parish: but when the contest is between equals, the defeat has many aggravations; and he that is defeated by his next neighbour is seldom satisfied without some revenge: and it is hard to say what bitterness of malignity would prevail in a parish where these elections should happen to be frequent, and the enmity of opposition should be rekindled before it had cooled.'

Though I present to my readers Dr Johnson's masterly thoughts on this subject, I think it proper to declare, that notwithstanding I am myself a lay-patron, I do not entirely subscribe to his opinion.

On Friday, May 7, I breakfasted with him at Mr Thrale's in the Borough. While we were alone, I endeavoured as well as I could to apologise for a lady who had been divorced from her husband by act of parliament. I said, that he had used her very ill, had behaved brutally to her, and that she could not continue to live with him without having her delicacy contaminated; that all affection for him was thus destroyed; that the essence of conjugal union being gone, there remained only a cold form, a mere civil obligation; that she was in the prime of life, with qualities to produce happiness; that these ought not to be lost; and, that the gentleman on whose account she was divorced had gained her heart while thus unhappily situated. Seduced, perhaps, by the charms of the lady in question, I thus attempted to palliate what I was sensible could not be justified; for, when I had finished my harangue, my venerable friend gave me a proper check: 'My dear Sir, never accustom your mind to mingle virtue and vice. The woman's a whore, and there's an end on't.'

He described the father of one of his friends thus: 'Sir, he was so exuberant a talker at public meetings, that the gentlemen of his county were afraid of him. No business could be done for his declamation.'

He did not give me full credit when I mentioned that I had carried on a short conversation by signs with some Esquimaux, who were then in London, particularly with one of them who was a priest. He thought I could not make them understand me. No man was more incredulous as to particular facts, which were at all extraordinary; and therefore no man was more scrupulously inquisitive, in order to discover the truth.

I dined with him this day at the house of my friends, Messieurs Edward and Charles Dilly, booksellers in the Poultry: there were present, their elder brother Mr Dilly of Bedfordshire, Dr Goldsmith, Mr Langton, Mr Claxton, Reverend Dr Mayo a dissenting minister, the Reverend Mr Toplady, and my friend the Reverend Mr Temple.

Hawkesworth's compilation of the voyages to the South Sea being mentioned; – JOHNSON. 'Sir, if you talk of it as a subject of commerce, it will be gainful; if as a book that is to increase human knowledge, I believe there will not be much of that. Hawkesworth can tell only what the voyagers have told him, and they have found very little, only one new animal, I think.' BOSWELL. 'But many insects, Sir.' JOHNSON. 'Why, Sir, as to insects, Ray reckons of British insects twenty thousand species. They might have staid at home and discovered enough in that way.'

Talking of birds, I mentioned Mr Daines Barrington's ingenious Essay against the received notion of their migration. JOHNSON. 'I think we have as good evidence for the migration of woodcocks as can be desired. We find they disappear at a certain time of the year, and appear again at a certain time of the year; and some of them, when weary in their flight, have been known to alight on the rigging of ships far out at sea.' One of the company observed, that there had been instances of some of them found in summer in Essex. JOHNSON. 'Sir, that strengthens our argument. *Exceptio probat regulam.* Some being found shows, that, if all remained, many would be found. A few sick or lame ones may be found.' GOLDSMITH. 'There is a partial migration of the swallows; the stronger ones migrate, the others do not.'

BOSWELL. 'I am well assured that the people of Otaheite who have the bread-tree, the fruit of which serves them for bread, laughed heartily when they were informed of the tedious process necessary with us to have bread; – plowing, sowing, harrowing, reaping, threshing, grinding, baking.' JOHNSON. 'Why, Sir, all ignorant savages will laugh when they are told of the advantages of civilised life. Were you to tell men who live without houses, how we pile brick upon brick and rafter upon rafter, and that after a house is raised to a certain height, a man tumbles off a scaffold and breaks his neck, he would laugh heartily at our folly in building; but it does not follow that men are better without houses. No, Sir (holding up a slice of a good loaf), this is better than the bread-tree.'

He repeated an argument, which is to be found in his *Rambler*, against the notion that the brute creation is endowed with the faculty of reason: 'birds build by instinct; they never improve: they build their first nest as well as any one that they ever build.' GOLDSMITH. 'Yet we see if you take away a bird's nest with the eggs in it, she will make a slighter nest and lay again.' JOHNSON. 'Sir, that is because at first she has full time, and makes her nest deliberately. In the case you mention she is pressed to lay, and must therefore make her nest quickly, and consequently it will be slight.' GOLDSMITH. 'The nidification of birds is what is least known in natural history, though one of the most curious things in it.'

I introduced the subject of toleration. JOHNSON. 'Every society has a right to preserve public peace and order, and therefore has a good right to prohibit the propagation of opinions which have a dangerous tendency. To say the *magistrate* has this right, is using an inadequate word: it is the *society* for which the magistrate is agent. He may be morally or theologically wrong in restraining the propagation of opinions which he thinks dangerous, but he is politically right.' MAYO. 'I am of opinion, Sir, that every man is entitled to liberty of conscience in religion; and that the magistrate cannot restrain that right.' JOHNSON. 'Sir, I agree with you. Every man has a right to liberty of conscience, and with that the magistrate cannot interfere. People confound liberty of thinking with liberty of talking; nay, with liberty of preaching. Every man has a physical right to think as he pleases; for it cannot be discovered how he thinks. He has not a moral right; for he ought to inform himself and think justly. But, Sir, no member of a society has a right to *teach* any doctrine contrary to what that society holds to be true. The magistrate, I say, may be wrong in what he thinks; but, while he thinks himself right, he may, and ought to enforce what he thinks.' MAYO. 'Then, Sir, we are to remain always in error, and truth never can prevail; and the magistrate was right in persecuting the first Christians.' JOHNSON. 'Sir, the only method by which religious truth can be established is by martyrdom. The magistrate has a right to enforce what he thinks; and he who is conscious of the truth has a right to suffer. I am afraid there is no other way of ascertaining the truth, but by persecution on the one hand and enduring it on the other.' GOLDSMITH. 'But how is a man to act, Sir? Though firmly convinced of the truth of his doctrine, may he not think it wrong to expose himself to persecution? Has he a right to do so? Is it not, as it were, committing voluntary suicide?' JOHNSON. 'Sir, as to voluntary suicide, as you call it, there are twenty thousand men in an army who will go without scruple to be shot at, and mount a breach for five-pence a day.' GOLDSMITH. 'But have they a moral right to do this?' JOHNSON. 'Nay, Sir, if you will not take the universal opinion of mankind, I have nothing to say. If mankind cannot defend their own way of thinking, I cannot defend it. Sir, if a man is in doubt whether it would be better for him to expose himself to martyrdom or not, he should not do it. He must be convinced that he has a delegation from heaven.' GOLDSMITH. 'I would consider whether there is the greater chance of good or evil upon the whole. If I see a man who has fallen into a well, I would wish to help him out; but if there is a greater probability that he shall pull me in than that I shall pull him out, I would not attempt it. So were I to go to Turkey, I might wish to convert the Grand Signor to the Christian faith; but when I considered that I should probably be put to death without effectuating my purpose in any degree, I should keep myself quiet.' JOHNSON. 'Sir, you must consider that we have perfect and imperfect obligations. Perfect obligations, which are generally not to do something, are clear and positive; as, "thou shalt not kill". But charity, for instance, is not definable by limits. It is a duty to give to the poor; but no man can say how much another should give to the poor, or when a man has given too little to save his soul. In the same manner, it is a duty to instruct the ignorant, and of consequence to convert infidels to Christianity; but no man in the common course of things is obliged to carry this to such a degree as to incur the danger of martyrdom, as no man is obliged to strip himself to the shirt in order to give charity. I have said, that a man must be persuaded that he has a particular delegation from heaven.' GOLDSMITH. 'How is this to be known? Our first reformers, who were burnt for not believing bread and wine to be CHRIST' – JOHNSON (interrupting him). 'Sir, they were not burnt for not believing bread and wine to be CHRIST, but for insulting those who did believe it. And, Sir, when the first reformers began, they did not intend to be martyred: as many of them ran away as could.' BOSWELL. 'But, Sir, there was your countryman, Elwal, who you told me challenged King George with his black-guards and his red-guards.' JOHNSON. 'My countryman, Elwal, Sir, should have been put in the stocks; a proper pulpit for him, and he'd have had a numerous audience. A man who preaches in the stocks will always have hearers enough.' BOSWELL. 'But Elwal thought himself in the right.' JOHNSON. 'We are not providing for mad people; there are places for them in the neighbourhood' (meaning Moorfields). MAYO. 'But, Sir, is it not very hard that I should not be allowed to teach my children what I really believe to be the truth?' JOHNSON. 'Why, Sir, you might contrive to teach your children *extra scandalum*; but, Sir, the magistrate, if he knows it, has a right to restrain you. Suppose you teach your children to be thieves?' MAYO. 'This is making a joke of the subject.' JOHNSON. 'Nay, Sir, take it thus – that you teach them the community of goods, for which there are as many plausible arguments as for most erroneous doctrines. You teach them that all things at first were in common, and that no man had a right to any thing but as he laid his hands upon it; and that this still is, or ought to be, the rule amongst mankind. Here, Sir, you sap a great principle in society – property. And don't you think the magistrate would have a right to prevent you? Or, suppose you should teach your children the notions of the Adamites, and they should run naked into the streets, would not the magistrate have a right to flog 'em into their doublets?' MAYO. 'I think the magistrate has no right to interfere till there is some overt act.' BOSWELL. 'So, Sir, though he sees an enemy to the state charging a blunderbuss, he is not to interfere till it is fired off.' MAYO. 'He must be sure of its direction against the state.' JOHNSON. 'The magistrate is to judge of that. – He has no right to restrain your thinking, because the evil centres in yourself. If a man were sitting at this table, and chopping off his fingers, the magistrate, as guardian of the community, has no authority to restrain him, however he might do it from kindness as a parent. – Though, indeed, upon more consideration, I think he may; as it is probable that he who is chopping off his own fingers, may soon proceed to chop off those of other people. If I think it right to steal Mr Dilly's plate, I am a bad man; but he can say nothing to me. If I make an open declaration that I think so, he will keep me out of his house. If I put forth my hand, I shall be sent to Newgate. This is the gradation of thinking, preaching, and acting: if a man thinks erroneously, he may keep his thoughts to himself, and nobody will trouble him; if he preaches erroneous doctrine, society may expel him; if he acts in consequence of it, the law takes place, and he is hanged.' MAYO. 'But, Sir, ought not Christians to have liberty of conscience?' JOHNSON. 'I have already told you so, Sir. You are coming back to where you were.' BOSWELL. 'Dr Mayo is always taking a return post-chaise, and going the stage over again. He has it at half price.' JOHNSON. 'Dr Mayo, like other champions for unlimited toleration, has got a set of words.[1] Sir, it is no matter

---

1 Dr Mayo's calm temper and steady perseverance, rendered him an admirable subject for the exercise of Dr Johnson's powerful abilities. He never flinched; but, after reiterated blows, remained seemingly unmoved as at the first. The scintillations of Johnson's genius flashed every time he was struck, without his receiving any injury. Hence he obtained the epithet of THE LITERARY ANVIL.

politically, whether the magistrate be right or wrong. Suppose a club were to be formed to drink confusion to King George the Third, and a happy restoration to Charles the Third; this would be very bad with respect to the state; but every member of that club must either conform to its rules, or be turned out of it. Old Baxter, I remember, maintains, that the magistrate should "tolerate all things that are tolerable". This is no good definition of toleration upon any principle; but it shows that he thought some things were not tolerable.' TOPLADY. 'Sir, you have untwisted this difficult subject with great dexterity.'

During this argument, Goldsmith sat in restless agitation, from a wish to get in, and shine. Finding himself excluded, he had taken his hat to go away, but remained for some time with it in his hand, like a gamester, who at the close of a long night, lingers for a little while, to see if he can have a favourable opening to finish with success. Once when he was beginning to speak, he found himself overpowered by the loud voice of Johnson, who was at the opposite end of the table, and did not perceive Goldsmith's attempt. Thus disappointed of his wish to obtain the attention of the company, Goldsmith in a passion threw down his hat, looking angrily at Johnson, and exclaiming in a bitter tone, '*Take it.*' When Toplady was going to speak, Johnson uttered some sound, which led Goldsmith to think that he was beginning again, and taking the words from Toplady. Upon which, he seized this opportunity of venting his own envy and spleen, under the pretext of supporting another person: 'Sir (said he to Johnson), the gentleman has heard you patiently for an hour; pray allow us now to hear him.' JOHNSON (sternly). 'Sir, I was not interrupting the gentleman. I was only giving him a signal of my attention. Sir, you are impertinent.' Goldsmith made no reply, but continued in the company for some time.

A gentleman present ventured to ask Dr Johnson if there was not a material difference as to toleration of opinions which lead to action, and opinions merely speculative; for instance, would it be wrong in the magistrate to tolerate those who preach against the doctrine of the TRINITY. Johnson was highly offended, and said, 'I wonder, Sir, how a gentleman of your piety can introduce this subject in a mixed company.' He told me afterwards, that the impropriety was, that perhaps some of the company might have talked on the subject in such terms as would have shocked him; or he might have been forced to appear in their eyes a narrow-minded man. The gentleman, with submissive deference, said, he had only hinted at the question from a desire to hear Dr Johnson's opinion upon it. JOHNSON. 'Why then, Sir, I think that permitting men to preach any opinion contrary to the doctrine of the established church, tends, in a certain degree, to lessen the authority of the church, and, consequently, to lessen the influence of religion.' 'It may be considered (said the gentleman), whether it would not be politic to tolerate in such a case.' JOHNSON. 'Sir, we have been talking of right: this is another question. I think it is not politic to tolerate in such a case.'

Though he did not think it fit that so awful a subject should be introduced in a mixed company, and therefore at this time waived the theological question; yet his own orthodox belief in the sacred mystery of the TRINITY is evinced beyond doubt, by the following passage in his private devotions: 'O LORD, hear my prayers, for JESUS CHRIST'S sake; to whom with thee and the HOLY GHOST, *three persons and one* GOD, be all honour and glory, world without end. Amen.'[1]

BOSWELL. 'Pray, Mr Dilly, how does Dr Leland's *History of Ireland* sell?' JOHNSON. (Bursting forth with a generous indignation), 'The Irish are in a most unnatural state; for we see there the minority prevailing over the majority. There is no instance, even in the ten persecutions, of such severity as that which the Protestants of Ireland have exercised against the Catholics. Did we tell them we have conquered them, it would be above board: to punish them by confiscation and other penalties, as rebels, was monstrous injustice. King William was not their lawful sovereign, he had not been acknowledged by the parliament of Ireland, when they appeared in arms against him.'

I here suggested something favourable of the Roman Catholics. TOPLADY. 'Does not their invocation of saints suppose omnipresence in the saints?' JOHNSON. 'No, Sir, it supposes only pluri-presence; and when spirits are divested of matter, it seems probable that they should see with more extent than when in an embodied state. There is, therefore, no approach to an invasion of any of the divine attributes, in the invocation of saints. But I think it is will-worship, and presumption. I see no command for it, and therefore think it is safer not to practise it.'

He and Mr Langton and I went together to the Club, where we found Mr Burke, Mr Garrick, and some other members, and amongst them our friend Goldsmith, who sat silently brooding over Johnson's reprimand to him after dinner. Johnson perceived this and said aside to some of us, 'I'll make Goldsmith forgive me,' and then called to him in a loud voice, 'Dr Goldsmith, – something passed to-day where you and I dined; I ask your pardon.' Goldsmith answered placidly, 'It must be much from you, Sir, that I take ill.' And so at once the difference was over, and they were on as easy terms as ever, and Goldsmith rattled away as usual.

In our way to the Club to-night, when I regretted that Goldsmith would, upon every occasion, endeavour to shine, by which he often exposed himself, Mr Langton observed, that he was not like Addison, who was content with the fame of his writings, and did not aim also at excellency in conversation, for which he found himself unfit; and that he said to a lady, who complained of his having talked little in company, 'Madam, I have but nine-pence in ready money, but I can draw for a thousand pounds.' I observed that Goldsmith had a great deal of gold in his cabinet, but, not content with that, was always taking out his purse. JOHNSON. 'Yes, Sir, and that so often an empty purse!'

Goldsmith's incessant desire of being conspicuous in company, was the occasion of his sometimes appearing to such disadvantage as one should hardly have supposed possible in a man of his genius. When his literary reputation had risen deservedly high, and his society was much courted, he became very

1 *Prayers and Meditations,* p. 40.

jealous of the extraordinary attention which was everywhere paid to Johnson. One evening, in a circle of wits, he found fault with me for talking of Johnson as entitled to the honour of unquestionable superiority. 'Sir (said he), you are for making a monarchy of what should be a republic.'

He was still more mortified, when talking in a company with fluent vivacity, and, as he flattered himself, to the admiration of all who were present; a German who sat next him, and perceived Johnson rolling himself, as if about to speak, suddenly stopped him, saying, 'Stay, stay — Toctor Shonson is going to say something.' This was, no doubt, very provoking, especially to one so irritable as Goldsmith, who frequently mentioned it with strong expressions of indignation.

It may also be observed, that Goldsmith was sometimes content to be treated with an easy familiarity, but, upon occasions, would be consequential and important. An instance of this occurred in a small particular. Johnson had a way of contracting the names of his friends; as, Beauclerk, Beau; Boswell, Bozzy; Langton, Lanky; Murphy, Mur; Sheridan, Sherry. I remember one day, when Tom Davies was telling that Dr Johnson said, 'We are all in labour for a name to *Goldy's* play', Goldsmith seemed displeased that such a liberty should be taken with his name, and said, 'I have often desired him not to call me *Goldy*.' Tom was remarkably attentive to the most minute circumstance about Johnson. I recollect his telling me once, on my arrival in London, 'Sir, our great friend has made an improvement on his appellation of old Mr Sheridan. He calls him now *Sherry derry*.'

To the Reverend Mr BAGSHAW, at Bromley.[1]

SIR – I return you my sincere thanks for your additions to my Dictionary; but the new edition has been published some time, and therefore I cannot now make use of them. Whether I shall ever revise it more, I know not. If many readers had been as judicious, as diligent, and as communicative as yourself, my work had been better. The world must at present take it as it is. I am, Sir,
　　Your most obliged
　　And most humble servant,

SAM. JOHNSON.

May 8, 1773.

On Sunday, May 8, I dined with Johnson at Mr Langton's, with Dr Beattie and some other company. He descanted on the subject of Literary Property.

---

1 The Reverend Thomas Bagshaw, M.A., who died on November 20, 1787, in the seventy-seventh year of his age, Chaplain of Bromley College, in Kent, and Rector of Southfleet. He had resigned the cure of Bromley parish some time before his death. For this, and another letter from Dr Johnson in 1784, to the same truly respectable man, I am indebted to Dr John Loveday, of the Commons, who has obligingly transcribed them for me from the originals in his possession.

'There seems (said he) to be in authors a stronger right of property than that by occupancy; a metaphysical right, a right, as it were, of creation, which should from its nature be perpetual; but the consent of nations is against it, and indeed reason and the interests of learning are against it; for were it to be perpetual, no book, however useful, could be universally diffused amongst mankind, should the proprietor take it into his head to restrain its circulation. No book could have the advantage of being edited with notes, however necessary to its elucidation, should the proprietor perversely oppose it. For the general good of the world, therefore, whatever valuable work has once been created by an author, and issued out by him, should be understood as no longer in his power, but as belonging to the public; at the same time the author is entitled to an adequate reward. This he should have by an exclusive right to his work for a considerable number of years.'

He attacked Lord Monboddo's strange speculation on the primitive state of human nature; observing, 'Sir, it is all conjecture about a thing useless, even were it known to be true. Knowledge of all kinds is good. Conjecture, as to things useful, is good; but conjecture as to what it would be useless to know, such as whether men went upon all four, is very idle.'

On Monday, May 9, as I was to set out on my return to Scotland next morning, I was desirous to see as much of Dr Johnson as I could. But I first called on Goldsmith to take leave of him. The jealousy and envy which, though possessed of many most amiable qualities, he frankly avowed, broke out violently at this interview. Upon another occasion, when Goldsmith confessed himself to be of an envious disposition, I contended with Johnson that we ought not to be angry with him, he was so candid in owning it. 'Nay, Sir (said Johnson), we must be angry that a man has such a superabundance of an odious quality that he cannot keep it within his own breast, but it boils over.' In my opinion, however, Goldsmith had not more of it than other people have, but only talked of it freely.

He now seemed very angry that Johnson was going to be a traveller; said, 'he would be a dead weight for me to carry, and that I should never be able to lug him along through the Highlands and Hebrides.' Nor would he patiently allow me to enlarge upon Johnson's wonderful abilities; but exclaimed, 'Is he like Burke, who winds into a subject like a serpent?' 'But (said I), Johnson is the Hercules who strangled serpents in his cradle.'

I dined with Dr Johnson at General Paoli's. He was obliged, by indisposition, to leave the company early; he appointed me, however, to meet him in the evening at Mr (now Sir Robert) Chambers's in the Temple, where he accordingly came, though he continued to be very ill. Chambers, as is common on such occasions, prescribed various remedies to him. JOHNSON. (fretted by pain), 'Pr'ythee don't tease me. Stay till I am well, and then you shall tell me how to cure myself.' He grew better, and talked with a noble enthusiasm of keeping up the representation of respectable families. His zeal on this subject was a circumstance in his character exceedingly remarkable, when it is considered that he himself had no pretensions to blood. I heard him once say, 'I have great merit in being zealous for subordination and the honours of birth; for I can hardly tell who was my grandfather.' He maintained the dignity and propriety of male succession, in opposition to the opinion of one of our friends, who had that day employed Mr Chambers to draw his will, devising his estate to his three sisters, in preference to a remote heir male. Johnson called them three *dowdies*, and said, with as high a spirit as the boldest Baron in the most perfect days of the feudal system, 'An ancient estate should always go to males. It is mighty foolish to let a stranger have it, because he marries your daughter, and takes your name. As for an estate newly acquired by trade, you may give it, if you will, to the dog *Towzer*, and let him keep his *own* name.'

I have known him at times exceedingly diverted at what seemed to others a very small sport. He now laughed immoderately, without any reason that we could perceive, at our friend's making his will; called him the *testator*, and added, 'I dare say, he thinks he has done a mighty thing. He won't stay till he gets home to his seat in the country, to produce this wonderful deed: he'll call up the landlord of the first inn on the road; and, after a suitable preface upon mortality and the uncertainty of life, will tell him that he should not delay making his will; and here, Sir, will he say, is my will, which I have just made, with the assistance of one of the ablest lawyers in the kingdom; and he will read it to him (laughing all the time). He believes he has made this will; but he did not make it: you, Chambers, made it for him. I trust you have had more conscience than to make him say, "being of sound understanding"; ha, ha, ha! I hope he has left me a legacy. I'd have his will turned into verse, like a ballad.'

In this playful manner did he run on, exulting in his own pleasantry, which certainly was not such as might be expected from the author of the *Rambler*, but which is here preserved, that my readers may be acquainted even with the slightest occasional characteristics of so eminent a man.

Mr Chambers did not by any means relish this jocularity upon a matter of which *pars magna fait*, and seemed impatient till he got rid of us. Johnson could not stop his merriment, but continued it all the way till we got without the Temple-gate. He then burst into such a fit of laughter, that he appeared to be almost in a convulsion; and, in order to support himself, laid hold of one of the posts at the side of the foot-pavement, and sent forth peals so loud, that in the silence of the night his voice seemed to resound from Temple-bar to Fleet-ditch.

This most ludicrous exhibition of the awful, melancholy, and venerable Johnson, happened well to counteract the feelings of sadness which I used to experience when parting with him for a considerable time. I accompanied him to his door, where he gave me his blessing.

He records of himself this year, 'Between Easter and Whitsun-tide, having always considered that time as propitious to study, I attempted to learn the Low Dutch language.'[1] It is to be observed, that he here admits an opinion of the human mind being influenced by seasons, which he ridicules in his writings. His progress, he says, 'was interrupted by a fever, which, by the imprudent use

1 *Prayers and Meditations*, p. 129.

of a small print, left an inflammation in his useful eye.' We cannot but admire his spirit when we know, that amidst a complication of bodily and mental distress, he was still animated with the desire of intellectual improvement. Various notes of his studies appear on different days, in his manuscript diary of this year; such as, '*Inchoavi lectionem Pentateuchi* – *Finivi lectionem Conf. Fab. Burdonum* – *Legi primum actum Troadum* – *Legi Dissertationem Clerici postremam de Pent* – *2 of Clark's Sermons* – *L. Appolonii pugnam Betriciam* – *L. centum versus Homeri.*' Let this serve as a specimen of what accessions of literature he was perpetually infusing into his mind, while he charged himself with idleness.

This year died Mrs Salusbury (mother of Mrs Thrale), a lady whom he appears to have esteemed much, and whose memory he honoured with an Epitaph.[1]

In a letter from Edinburgh, dated the 29th of May, I pressed him to persevere in his resolution to make this year the projected visit to the Hebrides, of which he and I had talked for many years, and which I was confident would afford us much entertainment.

To JAMES BOSWELL, Esq.

DEAR SIR – When your letter came to me, I was so darkened by an inflammation in my eye, that I could not for some time read it. I can now write without trouble, and can read large prints. My eye is gradually growing stronger; and I hope will be able to take some delight in the survey of a Caledonian loch.

Chambers is going a Judge, with six thousand a year, to Bengal. He and I shall come down together as far as Newcastle, and thence I shall easily get to Edinburgh. Let me know the exact time when your Courts intermit. I must conform a little to Chambers's occasions, and he must conform a little to mine. The time which you shall fix, must be the common point to which we will come as near as we can. Except this eye, I am very well.

Beattie is so caressed, and invited, and treated, and liked, and flattered, by the great, that I can see nothing of him. I am in great hope that he will be well provided for, and then we will live upon him at the Marischal College, without pity or modesty.

—— left the town without taking leave of me, and is gone in deep dudgeon to ——. Is not this very childish? Where is now my legacy?

I hope your dear lady and her dear baby are both well. I shall see them too when I come; and I have that opinion of your choice as to suspect that when I have seen Mrs Boswell, I shall be less willing to go away. I am, dear Sir,

Your affectionate humble servant,

SAM. JOHNSON.

Johnson's-court, Fleet-street,
July 5, 1773.

Write to me as soon as you can. Chambers is now at Oxford.

1 Mrs Piozzi's *Anecdotes of Johnson*, p. 131.

I again wrote to him, informing him that the Court of Session rose on the twelfth of August, hoping to see him before that time, and expressing, perhaps in too extravagant terms, my admiration of him, and my expectation of pleasure from our intended tour.

To JAMES BOSWELL, Esq.

DEAR SIR — I shall set out from London on Friday the sixth of this month, and purpose not to loiter much by the way. Which day I shall be at Edinburgh, I cannot exactly tell. I suppose I must drive to an inn, and send a porter to find you.

I am afraid Beattie will not be at his College soon enough for us, and I shall be sorry to miss him; but there is no staying for the concurrence of all conveniences. We will do as well as we can. I am, Sir,

Your most humble servant,

SAM. JOHNSON.

August 3, 1773.

To the same.

DEAR SIR — Not being at Mr Thrale's when your letter came, I had written the enclosed paper and sealed it; bringing it hither for a frank, I found yours. If any thing could repress my ardour, it would be such a letter as yours. To disappoint a friend is unpleasing: and he that forms expectations like yours, must be disappointed. Think only when you see me, that you see a man who loves you, and is proud and glad that you love him. I am, Sir,

Your most affectionate

SAM. JOHNSON.

August 3, 1773.

To the same.

Newcastle, Aug. 11, 1771.

DEAR SIR — I came hither last night, and hope, but do not absolutely promise, to be in Edinburgh on Saturday. Beattie will not come so soon. I am, Sir,

Your most humble servant,

SAM. JOHNSON.

My compliments to your lady.

To the same.

Mr JOHNSON sends his compliments to Mr Boswell, being just arrived at Boyd's.

Saturday night.

His stay in Scotland was from the 18th of August, on which day he arrived, till the 22nd of November, when he set out on his return to London, and I believe ninety-four days were never passed by any man in a more vigorous exertion.

He came by the way of Berwick upon Tweed to Edinburgh, where he remained a few days, and then went by St Andrew's, Aberdeen, Inverness, and Fort Augustus, to the Hebrides, to visit which was the principal object he had in view. He visited the isles of Sky, Rasay, Col, Mull, Inchkenneth, and Icolmkill. He travelled through Argyleshire by Inveraray, and from thence by Lochlomond and Dunbarton to Glasgow, then by Loudon to Auchinleck in Ayrshire, the seat of my family, and then by Hamilton, back to Edinburgh, where he again spent some time. He thus saw the four Universities of Scotland, its three principal cities, and as much of the Highland and insular life as was sufficient for his philosophical contemplation. I had the pleasure of accompanying him during the whole of this journey. He was respectfully entertained by the great, the learned, and the elegant, wherever he went; nor was he less delighted with the hospitality which he experienced in humbler life.

His various adventures, and the force and vivacity of his mind, as exercised during this peregrination, upon innumerable topics, have been faithfully and to the best of my abilities displayed in my *Journal of a Tour to the Hebrides*, to which, as the public has been pleased to honour it by a very extensive circulation, I beg to refer, as to a separate and remarkable portion of his life, which may be there seen in detail, and which exhibits as striking a view of his powers in conversation, as his works do of his excellence in writing. Nor can I deny to myself the very flattering gratification of inserting here the character which my friend Mr Courtenay has been pleased to give of that work:

> With Reynolds' pencil, vivid, bold, and true,
> So fervent Boswell gives him to our view:
> In every trait we see his mind expand;
> The master rises by the pupil's hand;
> We love the writer, praise his happy vein,
> Grac'd with the naiveté of the sage Montaigne.
> Hence not alone are brighter parts display'd,
> But ev'n the specks of character pourtray'd:
> We *see* the Rambler with fastidious smile
> Mark the lone tree, and note the heath-clad isle;
> But when the heroic tale of Flora[1] charms,
> Deck'd in a kilt, he wields a chieftain's arms:
> The tuneful piper sounds a martial strain,
> And Samuel sings, 'the King shall have his *ain*.'

1 [The celebrated Flora Macdonald. See Boswell's *Tour*.]

During his stay at Edinburgh, after his return from the Hebrides, he was at great pains to obtain information concerning Scotland; and it will appear from his subsequent letters, that he was not less solicitous for intelligence on this subject after his return to London.

To James Boswell, Esq.

Dear Sir – I came home last night, without any incommodity, danger, or weariness, and am ready to begin a new journey. I shall go to Oxford on Monday. I know Mrs Boswell wished me well to go;[1] her wishes have not been disappointed. Mrs Williams has received Sir A's[2] letter.

Make my compliments to all those to whom my compliments may be welcome.

Let the box [3] be sent as soon as it can, and let me know when to expect it.

Enquire, if you can, the order of the Clans: Macdonald is first, Maclean second; further I cannot go. Quicken Dr Webster.[4] I am, Sir,

Yours affectionately,

SAM. JOHNSON.

Nov. 27, 1773.

Mr Boswell to Dr Johnson.

Edinburgh, Dec. 2, 1773.

. . .

You shall have what information I can procure as to the order of the Clans. A gentleman of the name of Grant tells me, that there is no settled order among them; and he says, that the Macdonalds were not placed upon the right of the army at Culloden; the Stuarts were. I shall, however, examine witnesses of every name that I can find here. Dr Webster shall be quickened too. I like your little memorandums; they are symptoms of your being in earnest with your book of northern travels.

---

1 In this he showed a very acute penetration. My wife paid him the most assiduous and respectful attention, while he was our guest; so that I wonder how he discovered her wishing for his departure. The truth is, that his irregular hours and uncouth habits, such as turning the candles with their heads downwards, when they did not burn bright enough, and letting the wax drop upon the carpet, could not but be disagreeable to a lady. Besides, she had not that high admiration of him which was felt by most of those who knew him; and what was very natural to a female mind, she thought he had too much influence over her husband. She once in a little warmth, made, with more point than justice, this remark upon that subject: 'I have seen many a bear led by a man; but I never before saw a man led by a bear.'

2 Sir Alexander Gordon, one of the Professors at Aberdeen.

3 This was a box containing a number of curious things which he had picked up in Scotland, particularly some horn spoons.

4 The Reverend Dr Alexander Webster, one of the ministers of Edinburgh, a man of distinguished abilities, who had promised him information concerning the Highlands and Islands of Scotland.

Your box shall be sent next week by sea. You will find in it some pieces of the broom bush, which you saw growing on the old castle of Auchinleck. The wood has a curious appearance when sawn across. You may either have a little writing-standish made of it, or get it formed into boards for a treatise on witchcraft, by way of a suitable binding.

. . .

Mr BOSWELL to Dr JOHNSON.

Edinburgh, Dec. 18, 1773.

. . .

You promised me an inscription for a print to be taken from an historical picture of Mary Queen of Scots being forced to resign her crown, which Mr Hamilton at Rome has painted for me. The two following have been sent to me:

Maria Scotorum Regina meliori seculo digna, jus regium civibus seditiosis invita resignat.

Cives seditiosi Mariam Scotorum Reginam sese muneri abdicare invitam cogunt.

Be so good as to read the passage in Robertson, and see if you cannot give me a better inscription. I must have it both in Latin and English; so if you should not give me another Latin one, you will at least choose the best of these two, and send a translation of it.

. . .

His humane forgiving disposition was put to a pretty strong test on his return to London, by a liberty which Mr Thomas Davies had taken with him in his absence, which was, to publish two volumes, entitled 'Miscellaneous and fugitive Pieces', which he advertised in the newspapers, 'By the Author of the *Rambler.*' In this collection, several of Dr Johnson's acknowledged writings, and several of his anonymous performances, and some which he had written for others, were inserted; but there were also some in which he had no concern whatever. He was at first very angry, as he had good reason to be. But, upon consideration of his poor friend's narrow circumstances, and that he had only a little profit in view and meant no harm, he soon relented, and continued his kindness to him as formerly.

In the course of his self-examination with retrospect to this year, he seems to have been much dejected; for he says, January 1, 1774, 'This year has past with so little improvement, that I doubt whether I have not rather impaired than increased my learning':[1] and yet we have seen how he *read*, and we know how he *talked* during that period.

He was now seriously engaged in writing an account of our travels in the Hebrides, in consequence of which I had the pleasure of a more frequent correspondence with him.

1 *Prayers and Meditations*, p. 129.

To JAMES BOSWELL, Esq.

DEAR SIR – My operations have been hindered by a cough; at least I flatter myself, that if the cough had not come, I should have been further advanced. But I have had no intelligence from Dr W—— [Webster], nor from the excise-office, nor from you. No account of the little borough.[1] Nothing of the Erse language. I have yet heard nothing of my box.

You must make haste and gather me all you can, and do it quickly, or I will and shall do without it.

Make my compliments to Mrs Boswell, and tell her that I do not love her the less for wishing me away. I gave her trouble enough, and shall be glad, in recompense, to give her any pleasure.

I would send some porter into the Hebrides, if I knew which way it could be got to my kind friends there. Enquire, and let me know.

Make my compliments to all the Doctors of Edinburgh, and to all my friends from one end of Scotland to the other.

Write to me, and send me what intelligence you can: and if any thing is too bulky for the post, let me have it by the carrier. I do not like trusting winds and waves. I am, dear Sir,

Your most, &c.

SAM. JOHNSON.

Jan. 29, 1774.

To the same.

DEAR SIR – In a day or two after I had written the last discontented letter, I received my box, which was very welcome. But still I must entreat you to hasten Dr Webster, and continue to pick up what you can that may be useful.

Mr Oglethorpe was with me this morning. You know his errand. He was not unwelcome.

Tell Mrs Boswell that my good intentions towards her still continue. I should be glad to do any thing that would either benefit or please her.

Chambers is not yet gone, but so hurried, or so negligent, or so proud, that I rarely see him. I have, indeed, for some weeks past, been very ill of a cold and cough, and have been at Mrs Thrale's, that I might be taken care of. I am much better, *novae redeunt in proelia vires*; but I am yet tender, and easily disordered. How happy it was that neither of us were ill in the Hebrides.

The question of Literary Property is this day before the Lords. Murphy drew up the appellants' case, that is, the plea against the perpetual right. I have not seen it, nor heard the decision. I would not have the right perpetual.

I will write to you as any thing occurs, and do you send me something about my Scottish friends. I have very great kindness for them. Let me

1   The ancient Burgh of Prestwick, in Ayrshire.

know likewise how fees come in, and when we are to see you. I am, Sir,
Yours affectionately,

SAM. JOHNSON.

London, Feb. 7, 1774.

He wrote the following letters to Mr Steevens, his able associate in editing
Shakspeare:

To GEORGE STEEVENS, Esq. in Hampstead.

SIR – If I am asked when I have seen Mr Steevens, you know what answer
I must give; if I am asked when I shall see him, I wish you would tell me
what to say.

If you have Lesley's *History of Scotland*, or any other book about Scotland,
except Boetius and Buchanan, it will be a kindness if you send them to, Sir,
Your humble servant,

SAM. JOHNSON.

Feb. 7, 1774.

To the same.

SIR – We are thinking to augment our club, and I am desirous of
nominating you, if you care to stand the ballot, and can attend on Friday
nights at least twice in five weeks; less than that is too little, and rather
more will be expected. Be pleased to let me know before Friday. I am, Sir,
Your most, &c.

SAM. JOHNSON.

Feb. 21, 1774.

To the same.

SIR – Last night you became a member of the club; if you call on me on
Friday, I will introduce you. A gentleman, proposed after you, was rejected.

I thank you for Neander, but wish he were not so fine. I will take care of
him. I am, Sir,
Your humble servant,

SAM. JOHNSON.

March 5, 1774.

To JAMES BOSWELL, Esq.

DEAR SIR – Dr Webster's informations were much less exact and much less
determinate than I expected: they are, indeed, much less positive than, if
he can trust his own book[1] which he laid before me, he is able to give. But

---

1 A manuscript account drawn up by Dr Webster of all the parishes in Scotland,
ascertaining their length, breadth, number of inhabitants, and distinguishing Protestants
and Roman Catholics. This book had been transmitted to Government, and Dr
Johnson saw a copy of it in Dr Webster's possession.

I believe it will always be found, that he who calls much for information will advance his work but slowly.

I am, however, obliged to you, dear Sir, for your endeavours to help me, and hope, that between us something will some time be done, if not on this, on some occasion.

Chambers is either married, or almost married, to Miss Wilton, a girl of sixteen, exquisitely beautiful, whom he has with his lawyer's tongue, persuaded to take her chance with him in the East.

We have added to the club, Charles Fox, Sir Charles Bunbury, Dr Fordyce, and Mr Steevens.

Return my thanks to Dr Webster. Tell Dr Robertson that I have not much to reply to his censure of my negligence; and tell Dr Blair that since he has written hither what I said to him, we must now consider ourselves as even, forgive one another, and begin again. I care not how soon, for he is a very pleasing man. Pay my compliments to all my friends, and remind Lord Elibank of his promise to give me all his works.

I hope Mrs Boswell and little Miss are well. – When shall I see them again? She is a sweet lady, only she was so glad to see me go, that I have almost a mind to come again, that she may again have the same pleasure.

Enquire if it be practicable to send a small present of a cask of porter to Dunvegan, Rasay, and Col. I would not wish to be thought forgetful of civilities. I am, Sir,

Your humble servant,

SAM. JOHNSON.

March 5, 1774.

On the 5th of March I wrote to him, requesting his counsel whether I should this spring come to London. I stated to him on the one hand some pecuniary embarrassments, which, together with my wife's situation at that time, made me hesitate; and, on the other, the pleasure and improvement which my annual visit to the metropolis always afforded me; and particularly mentioned a peculiar satisfaction which I experienced in celebrating the festival of Easter in St Paul's cathedral; that to my fancy it appeared like going up to Jerusalem at the feast of the Passover; and that the strong devotion which I felt on that occasion diffused its influence on my mind through the rest of the year.

To JAMES BOSWELL, Esq.

                                    [Not dated, but written about the 15th of March.]
DEAR SIR – I am ashamed to think that since I received your letter I have passed so many days without answering it.

I think there is no great difficulty in resolving your doubts. The reasons for which you are inclined to visit London, are, I think, not of sufficient strength to answer the objections. That you should delight to come once a year to the fountain of intelligence and pleasure, is very natural; but both information and pleasure must be regulated by propriety. Pleasure, which cannot be obtained but by unseasonable or unsuitable expense, must always end in pain; and pleasure, which must be enjoyed at the expense of another's pain, can never be such as a worthy mind can fully delight in.

What improvement you might gain by coming to London, you may easily supply, or easily compensate, by enjoining yourself some particular study at home, or opening some new avenue to information. Edinburgh is not yet exhausted; and I am sure you will find no pleasure here which can deserve either that you should anticipate any part of your future fortune, or that you should condemn yourself and your lady to penurious frugality for the rest of the year.

I need not tell you what regard you owe to Mrs Boswell's entreaties; or how much you ought to study the happiness of her who studies yours with so much diligence, and of whose kindness you enjoy such good effects. Life cannot subsist in society but by reciprocal concessions. She permitted you to ramble last year, you must permit her now to keep you at home.

Your last reason is so serious, that I am unwilling to oppose it. Yet you must remember, that your image of worshiping once a year in a certain place, in imitation of the Jews, is but a comparison, and *simile non est idem*; if the annual resort to Jerusalem was a duty to the Jews, it was a duty because it was commanded; and you have no such command, therefore no such duty. It may be dangerous to receive too readily, and indulge too fondly, opinions, from which, perhaps, no pious mind is wholly disengaged, of local sanctity and local devotion. You know what strange effects they have produced over a great part of the Christian world. I am now writing, and you, when you read this, are reading under the Eye of Omnipresence.

To what degree fancy is to be admitted into religious offices, it would require much deliberation to determine. I am far from intending totally to exclude it. Fancy is a faculty bestowed by our Creator, and it is reasonable that all his gifts should be used to his glory, that all our faculties should co-operate in his worship; but they are to co-operate according to the will of him that gave them, according to the order which his wisdom has established. As ceremonies prudential or convenient are less obligatory than positive ordinances, as bodily worship is only the token to others or ourselves of mental adoration, so Fancy is always to act in subordination to Reason. We may take Fancy for a companion, but must follow Reason as our guide. We may allow Fancy to suggest certain ideas in certain places, but Reason must always be heard, when she tells us, that those ideas and those places have no natural or necessary relation. When we enter a church we habitually recall to mind the duty of adoration, but we must not omit adoration for want of a temple; because we know, and ought to remember, that the Universal Lord is every where present; and that, therefore, to come to Jona, or to Jerusalem, though it may be useful, cannot be necessary.

Thus I have answered your letter, and have not answered it negligently. I love you too well to be careless when you are serious.

I think I shall be very diligent next week about our travels, which I have too long neglected. I am, dear Sir,

Your most, &c.

SAM. JOHNSON.

Compliments to Madam and Miss.

To the same.

DEAR SIR – The lady who delivers this has a law-suit, in which she desires to make use of your skill and eloquence, and she seems to think that she shall have something more of both for a recommendation from me; which, though I know how little you want any external incitement to your duty, I could not refuse her, because I know that at least it will not hurt her, to tell you that I wish her well. I am, Sir,

Your most humble servant,

SAM. JOHNSON.

May 10, 1774

Mr BOSWELL to Dr JOHNSON.

Edinburgh, May 12, 1774.

LORD HAILES has begged of me to offer you his best respects, and to transmit to you specimens of *Annals of Scotland, from the Accession of Malcolm Kenmore to the Death of James V*, in drawing up which, his Lordship has been engaged for some time. His Lordship writes to me thus: 'If I could procure Dr Johnson's criticisms, they would be of great use to me in the prosecution of my work, as they would be judicious and true. I have no right to ask that favour of him. If you could, it would highly oblige me.'

Dr Blair requests you may be assured that he did not write to London what you said to him, and that neither by word nor letter has he made the least complaint of you; but, on the contrary, has a high respect for you, and loves you much more since he saw you in Scotland. It would both divert and please you to see his eagerness about this matter.

To JAMES BOSWELL, Esq.

Streatham, June 21, 1774.

DEAR SIR – Yesterday I put the first sheets of the *Journey to the Hebrides* to the press. I have endeavoured to do you some justice in the first paragraph. It will be one volume in octavo, not thick.

It will be proper to make some presents in Scotland. You shall tell me to whom I shall give; and I have stipulated twenty-five for you to give in your own name. Some will take the present better from me, others better from you. In this, you who are to live in the place ought to direct. Consider it. Whatever you can get for my purpose, send me; and make my compliments to your lady and both the young ones.

I am, Sir, your, &c.

SAM. JOHNSON.

Mr BOSWELL to Dr JOHNSON.

Edinburgh, June 25, 1774.

YOU do not acknowledge the receipt of the various packets which I have
sent to you. Neither can I prevail with you to *answer* my letters, though
you honour me with *returns*. You have said nothing to me about poor
Goldsmith,[1] nothing about Langton.

I have received for you, from the Society for propagating Christian
Knowledge in Scotland, the following Erse books: *The New Testament* –
Baxter's Call – *The Confession of Faith of the Assembly of Divines at Westminster*
– *The Mother's Catechism* – *A Gaelick and English Vocabulary.*[2]

To JAMES BOSWELL, Esq.

DEAR SIR – I wish you could have looked over my book before the printer,
but it could not easily be. I suspect some mistakes; but as I deal, perhaps,
more in notions than facts, the matter is not great, and the second edition
will be mended, if any such there be. The press will go on slowly for a
time, because I am going into Wales tomorrow.

I should be very sorry if I appeared to treat such a character as that of
Lord Hailes otherwise than with high respect. I return the sheets,[3] to
which I have done what mischief I could; and finding it so little, thought
not much of sending them. The narrative is clear, lively, and short.

I have done worse to Lord Hailes than by neglecting his sheets: I have
run him in debt. Dr Horne, the President of Magdalen College in Oxford,
wrote to me about three months ago, that he purposed to reprint Walton's
Lives, and desired me to contribute to the work: my answer was, that Lord
Hailes intended the same publication; and Dr Horne has resigned it to him.
His Lordship now must think seriously about it.

Of poor dear Dr Goldsmith there is little to be told, more than the papers
have made public. He died of a fever, made, I am afraid, more violent by
uneasiness of mind. His debts began to be heavy, and all his resources were
exhausted. Sir Joshua is of opinion that he owed not less than two thousand
pounds. Was ever poet so trusted before?

You may, if you please, put the inscription thus:

'*Maria Scotorum Regina nata* 15—, *a suis in exilium acta* 15—, *ab hospita neci
data* 15—.' You must find the years.

Of your second daughter you certainly gave the account yourself,
though you have forgotten it. While Mrs Boswell is well, never doubt of a
boy. Mrs Thrale brought, I think, five girls running, but while I was with
you she had a boy.

1 Dr Goldsmith died April 4, this year.
2 These books Dr Johnson presented to the Bodleian Library.
3 On the cover enclosing them, Dr Johnson wrote, 'If my delay has given any reason
for supposing that I have not a very deep sense of the honour done me by asking my
judgement, I am very sorry.'

I am obliged to you for all your pamphlets, and of the last I hope to make some use. I made some of the former. I am, dear Sir,

Your most affectionate servant,

SAM. JOHNSON.

July 4, 1774.

My compliments to all the three ladies.[a]

_____

[a] After this letter read the following:

To BENNET LANGTON, Esq. at Langton, near Spilsby, Lincolnshire.

DEAR SIR — You have reason to reproach me that I have left your last letter so long unanswered, but I had nothing particular to say. Chambers, you find, is gone far, and poor Goldsmith is gone much further. He died of a fever, exasperated, as I believe, by the fear of distress. He had raised money and squandered it, by every artifice of acquisition and folly of expense. But let not his frailties be remembered; he was a very great man.

I have just begun to print my *Journey to the Hebrides*, and am leaving the press to take another journey into Wales, whither Mr Thrale is going, to take possession of, at least, five hundred a year, fallen to his lady. All at Streatham, that are alive, are well.

I have never recovered from the last dreadful illness, but flatter myself that I grow gradually better; much, however, yet remains to mend. Κύριε ἐλέησον.

If you have the Latin version of *Busy, curious, thirsty fly*, be so kind as to transcribe and send it; but you need not be in haste, for I shall be I know not where, for at least five weeks. I wrote the following tetrastick on poor Goldsmith:

> Τὸν τάφον εἰσοράας τὸν Ὀλιβάροιο. κονίην
> Ἄφροσι μὴ σέμνην, Ξεῖνε, πόδεσσι πάτει·
> Οἷσι μέμηλε φύσις, μέτρων χάρις, ἔργα παλαιῶν,
> Κλαίετε ποιητὴν, ἱστορικὸν, φυσικόν.

Please to make my most respectful compliments to all the ladies, and remember me to young George and his sisters. I reckon George begins to show a pair of heels.

Do not be sullen now, but let me find a letter when I come back. I am, dear Sir,

Your affectionate, humble servant,

SAM. JOHNSON.

July 5, 1774.

To Mr ROBERT LEVET.

Llewenny, in Denbighshire, August 16, 1774.

DEAR SIR — Mr Thrale's affairs have kept him here a great while, nor do I know exactly when we shall come hence. I have sent you a bill upon Mr Strahan.

I have made nothing of the Ipecacuanha, but have taken abundance of pills, and hope that they have done me good.

Wales, so far as I have yet seen of it, is a very beautiful and rich country, all enclosed, and planted. Denbigh is not a mean town. Make my compliments to all my friends, and tell Frank I hope he remembers my advice. When his money is out, let him have more. I am, Sir,

Your humble servant,

SAM. JOHNSON.

Mr Boswell to Dr Johnson.

Edinburgh, Aug. 30, 1774.

You have given me an inscription for a portrait of Mary Queen of Scots, in which you, in a short and striking manner, point out her hard fate. But you will be pleased to keep in mind, that my picture is a representation of a particular scene in her history – her being forced to resign her crown, while she was imprisoned in the castle of Lochlevin. I must, therefore, beg that you will be kind enough to give me an inscription suited to that particular scene, or determine which of the two formerly transmitted to you is the best; and, at any rate, favour me with an English translation. It will be doubly kind if you comply with my request speedily.

Your critical notes on the specimen of Lord Hailes's *Annals of Scotland*, are excellent. I agreed with you in every one of them. He himself objected only to the alteration of *free* to *brave*, in the passage where he says that Edward 'departed with the glory due to the conqueror of a free people.' He says, 'to call the Scots brave would only add to the glory of their conqueror.' You will make allowance for the national zeal of our annalist. I now send a few more leaves of the *Annals*, which I hope you will peruse, and return with observations, as you did upon the former occasion. Lord Hailes writes to me thus: 'Mr Boswell will be pleased to express the grateful sense which Sir David Dalrymple has of Dr Johnson's attention to his little specimen. The further specimen will show, that

Even in an *Edward* he can see desert.

It gives me much pleasure to hear that a republication of Isaac Walton's Lives is intended. You have been in a mistake in thinking that Lord Hailes had it in view. I remember one forenoon, while he sat with you in my house, he said, that there should be a new edition of Walton's Lives; and you said, that they should be benoted a little. This was all that passed on that subject. You must, therefore, inform Dr Horne, that he may resume his plan. I enclose a note concerning it; and if Dr Horne will write to me, all the attention that I can give shall be cheerfully bestowed, upon what I think a pious work, the preservation and elucidation of Walton, by whose writings I have been most pleasingly edified.

. . .

Mr Boswell to Dr Johnson.

Edinburgh, Sept. 16, 1774.

Wales has probably detained you longer than I supposed. You will have become quite a mountaineer, by visiting Scotland one year and Wales another. You must next go to Switzerland. Cambria will complain, if you do not honour her also with some remarks. And I find *concessere columnae*, the booksellers expect another book. I am impatient to see your tour to Scotland and the Hebrides. Might you not send me a copy by the post as soon as it is printed off?

. . .

To James Boswell, Esq.

Dear Sir – Yesterday I returned from my Welch journey. I was sorry to leave my book suspended so long; but having an opportunity of seeing, with so much convenience, a new part of the island, I could not reject it. I have been in five of the six counties of North Wales; and have seen St Asaph and Bangor, the two seats of their bishops; have been upon Penmanmaur and Snowden, and passed over into Anglesea. But Wales is so little different from England, that it offers nothing to the speculation of the traveller.

When I came home, I found several of your papers, with some pages of Lord Hailes's *Annals*, which l will consider. I am in haste to give you some account of myself, lest you should suspect me of negligence in the pressing business which I find recommended to my care,[1] and which I knew nothing of till now, when all care is vain.

In the distribution of my books I purpose to follow your advice, adding such as shall occur to me. I am not pleased with your notes of remembrance added to your names, for I hope I shall not easily forget them.

I have received four Erse books, without any direction, and suspect that they are intended for the Oxford library. If that is the intention, I think it will be proper to add the metrical psalms, and whatever else is printed in Erse, that the present may be complete. The donor's name should be told.

I wish you could have read the book before it was printed, but our distance does not easily permit it.

I am sorry Lord Hailes does not intend to publish Walton; I am afraid it will not be done so well, if it be done at all.

I purpose now to drive the book forward. Make my compliments to Mrs Boswell, and let me hear often from you. I am, dear Sir,

Your affectionate humble servant,

SAM. JOHNSON.

London, Octob. 1, 1774.

This tour to Wales, which was made in company with Mr and Mrs Thrale, though it no doubt contributed to his health and amusement, did not give occasion to such a discursive exercise of his mind as our tour to the Hebrides. I do not find that he kept any journal or notes of what he saw there. All that I heard him say of it was, that instead of bleak and barren mountains, there were green and fertile ones; and that one of the castles in Wales would contain all the castles that he had seen in Scotland.

Parliament having been dissolved, and his friend Mr Thrale, who was a steady supporter of government, having again to encounter the storm of a contested election, he wrote a short political pamphlet, entitled 'The Patriot',* addressed to the electors of Great-Britain; a title which, to factious men, who

---

1 I had written to him, to request his interposition in behalf of a convict, who I thought was very unjustly condemned.

consider a patriot only as an opposer of the measures of government, will appear strangely misapplied. It was, however, written with energetic vivacity; and, except those passages in which it endeavours to vindicate the glaring outrage of the House of Commons in the case of the Middlesex election, and to justify the attempt to reduce our fellow-subjects in America to unconditional submission, it contained an admirable display of the properties of a real patriot, in the original and genuine sense, – a sincere, steady, rational, and unbiassed friend to the interests and prosperity of his King and country. It must be acknowledged, however, that both in this and his two former pamphlets, there was, amidst many powerful arguments, not only a considerable portion of sophistry, but a contemptuous ridicule of his opponents, which was very provoking.[a]

To James Boswell, Esq.

Dear Sir – There has appeared lately in the papers an account of a boat overset between Mull and Ulva, in which many passengers were lost, and

[a] After this letter, read:

To Mr Perkins.[1]

Sir – You may do me a great favour. Mrs Williams, a gentlewoman whom you may have seen at Mr Thrale's, is a petitioner for Mr Hetherington's charity: petitions are this day issued at Christ's Hospital.

I am a bad manager of business in a crowd; and if I should send a mean man, he may be put away without his errand. I must therefore entreat that you will go, and ask for a petition for Anna Williams, whose paper of enquiries was delivered with answers at the counting-house of the hospital on Thursday the 20th. My servant will attend you thither, and bring the petition home when you have it.

The petition, which they are to give us, is a form which they deliver to every petitioner, and which the petitioner is afterwards to fill up, and return to them again. This we must have, or we cannot proceed according to their directions. You need, I believe, only ask for a petition; if they enquire for whom you ask, you can tell them.

I beg pardon for giving you this trouble; but it is a matter of great importance. I am, Sir,

Your most humble servant,

Sam. Johnson.

October 25, 1774.

1 Mr Perkins was for a number of years the worthy superintendent of Mr Thrale's great brewery, and after his death became one of the Proprietors of it; and now resides in Mr Thrale's house in Southwark, which was the scene of so many literary meetings, and in which he continues the liberal hospitality for which it was eminent. Dr Johnson esteemed him much. He hung up in the counting-house a fine proof of the admirable mezzotinto of Dr Johnson, by Doughty; and when Mrs Thrale asked him somewhat flippantly, 'Why do you put him up in the counting-house?' he answered, 'Because, Madam, I wish to have one wise man there.' 'Sir (said Johnson), I thank you. It is a very handsome compliment, and I believe you speak sincerely.'

among them Maclean of Col. We, you know, were once drowned;[1] I hope, therefore, that the story is either wantonly or erroneously told. Pray satisfy me by the next post.

I have printed two hundred and forty pages. – I am able to do nothing much worth doing to dear Lord Hailes's book. I will, however, send back the sheets; and hope, by degrees, to answer all your reasonable expectations.

Mr Thrale has happily surmounted a very violent and acrimonious opposition; but all joys have their abatements: Mrs Thrale has fallen from her horse, and hurt herself very much. The rest of our friends, I believe, are well. My compliments to Mrs Boswell. I am, Sir,

Your most affectionate servant,

SAM. JOHNSON.

London, Octob. 27, 1774.

This letter, which shows his tender concern for an amiable young gentleman to whom we had been very much obliged in the Hebrides, I have inserted according to its date, though before receiving it I had informed him of the melancholy event that the young Laird of Col was unfortunately drowned.

To JAMES BOSWELL, Esq.

DEAR SIR – Last night I corrected the last page of our *Journey to the Hebrides*. The printer has detained it all this time, for I had, before I went into Wales, written all except two sheets. 'The Patriot' was called for by my political friends on Friday, was written on Saturday, and I have heard little of it. So vague are conjectures at a distance.[2] As soon as I can, I will take care that copies be sent to you, for I would wish that they might be given before they are bought; but I am afraid that Mr Strahan will send to you and to the booksellers at the same time. Trade is as diligent as courtesy. I have mentioned all that you recommended. Pray make my compliments to Mrs Boswell and the younglings. The club has, I think, not yet met.

Tell me, and tell me honestly, what you think and others say of our travels. Shall we touch the continent?[3] I am, dear Sir,

Your most humble servant,

SAM. JOHNSON.

Nov. 26, 1774.

---

1 In the newspapers.

2 Alluding to a passage in a letter of mine, where speaking of his *Journey to the Hebrides*, I say, 'But has not 'The Patriot' been an interruption, by the time taken to write it, and the time luxuriously spent in listening to its applauses?'

3 We had projected a voyage together up the Baltic, and talked of visiting some of the more northern regions.

In his manuscript diary of this year, there is the following entry:

'Nov. 27. Advent Sunday. I considered that this day, being the beginning of the ecclesiastical year, was a proper time for a new course of life. I began to read the Greek Testament regularly at 160 verses every Sunday. This day I began the Acts.

'In this week I read Virgil's Pastorals. I learned to repeat the Pollio and Gallus. I read carelessly the first Georgic.'

Such evidences of his unceasing ardour, both for 'divine and human lore', when advanced into his sixty-fourth year, and notwithstanding his many disturbances from disease, must make us at once honour his spirit, and lament that it should be so grievously clogged by its material tegument. It is remarkable, that he was very fond of the precision which calculation produces. Thus we find in one of his manuscript diaries, '12 pages in 4to Gr. Test. and 30 pages in Beza's folio, comprise the whole in 40 days.'

Dr JOHNSON to JOHN HOOLE, Esq.

DEAR SIR – I have returned your play,[1] which you will find underscored with red, where there was a word which I did not like. The red will be washed off with a little water.

The plot is so well framed, the intricacy so artful, and the disentanglement so easy, the suspense so affecting, and the passionate parts so properly interposed, that I have no doubt of its success. I am, Sir,

Your most humble servant,

SAM. JOHNSON.

December 19, 1774.

The first effort of his pen in 1775, was, 'Proposals for publishing the works of Mrs Charlotte Lennox',[†] in three volumes quarto. In his diary, January 2, I find this entry: 'Wrote Charlotte's Proposals.' But, indeed, the internal evidence would have been quite sufficient. Her claim to the favour of the public was thus enforced:

'Most of the pieces, as they appeared singly, have been read with approbation, perhaps above their merit, but of no great advantage to the writer. She hopes, therefore, that she shall not be considered as too indulgent to vanity, or too studious of interest, if, from that labour which has hitherto been chiefly gainful to others, she endeavours to obtain at last some profit for herself and her children. She cannot decently enforce her claim by the praise of her own performances; nor can she suppose, that, by the most artful and laboured address, any additional notice could be procured to a publication, of which Her MAJESTY has condescended to be the PATRONESS.'[a]

---

1   *Cleonice.*

[a]   *Second Edition*: He this year also wrote the Preface to Baretti's *Easy Lessons in Italian and English.*

To James Boswell, Esq.

Dear Sir – You never did ask for a book by the post till now, and I did not think on it. You see now it is done. I sent one to the King, and I hear he likes it.

I shall send a parcel into Scotland for presents, and intend to give to many of my friends. In your catalogue you left out Lord Auchinleck.

Let me know, as fast as you read it, how you like it; and let me know if any mistake is committed, or any thing important left out. I wish you could have seen the sheets. My compliments to Mrs Boswell, and to Veronica, and to all my friends. I am, Sir,

Your most humble servant,

Sam. Johnson.

January 14, 1775.

Mr Boswell to Dr Johnson.

Edinburgh, Jan. 19, 1775.

Be pleased to accept of my best thanks for your *Journey to the Hebrides*, which came to me by last night's post. I did really ask the favour twice; but you have been even with me, by granting it so speedily. *Bis dat qui cito dat.* Though ill of a bad cold, you kept me up the greatest part of the last night; for I did not stop till I had read every word of your book. I looked back to our first talking of a visit to the Hebrides, which was many years ago, when sitting by ourselves in the Mitre tavern, in London, I think about *witching time o'night*; and then exulted in contemplating our scheme fulfilled, and a *monumentum perenne* of it erected by your superior abilities. I shall only say, that your book has afforded me a high gratification. I shall afterwards give you my thoughts on particular passages. In the mean time, I hasten to tell you of your having mistaken two names, which you will correct in London, as I shall do here, that the gentlemen who deserve the valuable compliments which you have paid them, may enjoy their honours. In page 106, for *Gordon* read *Murchison*; and in page 357, for *Maclean* read *Macleod*.

. . .

But I am now to apply to you for immediate aid in my profession, which you have never refused to grant when I requested it. I enclose you a petition for Dr Memis, a physician at Aberdeen, in which Sir John Dalrymple has exerted his talents, and which I am to answer as Counsel for the managers of the Royal Infirmary in that city. Mr Jopp, the Provost, who delivered to you your freedom, is one of my clients, and, *as a citizen of Aberdeen*, you will support him.

The fact is shortly this. In a translation of the charter of the Infirmary from Latin into English, made under the authority of the managers, the same phrase in the original is in one place rendered *Physician*, but when applied to Dr Memis is rendered *Doctor of Medicine*. Dr Memis complained of this before the translation was printed, but was not indulged with having it altered, and he has brought an action for damages, on account of a supposed injury, as if the designation given to him were an inferior one, tending to make it be supposed he is *not* a *Physician*, and, consequently, to hurt his practice. My father has dismissed the action as groundless, and now he has appealed to the whole Court.'[1]

To James Boswell, Esq.

Dear Sir – I long to hear how you like the book; it is, I think, much liked here. But Macpherson is very furious; can you give me any more intelligence about him, or his Fingal? Do what you can, and do it quickly. Is Lord Hailes on our side?

Pray let me know what I owed you when I left you, that I may send it to you.

I am going to write about the Americans. If you have picked up any hints among your lawyers, who are great masters of the law of nations, or if your own mind suggests any thing, let me know. But mum, – it is a secret.

I will send your parcel of books as soon as I can; but I cannot do as I wish. However, you find every thing mentioned in the book which you recommended.

Langton is here; we are all that ever we were. He is a worthy fellow, without malice, though not without resentment.

Poor Beauclerk is so ill, that his life is thought to be in danger. Lady Di. nurses him with very great assiduity.

Reynolds has taken too much to strong liquor,[2] and seems to delight in his new character.

This is all the news that I have; but as you love verses, I will send you a few which I made upon Inchkenneth;[3] but remember the condition, that you shall not show them, except to Lord Hailes, whom I love better than any man whom I know so little. If he asks you to transcribe them for him, you may do it, but I think he must promise not to let them be copied again, nor to show them as mine.

I have at last sent back Lord Hailes's sheets. I never think about returning them, because I alter nothing. You will see that I might as well have kept them. However, I am ashamed of my delay; and if I have the honour of receiving any more, promise punctually to return them by the next post.

---

1 In the Court of Session of Scotland an action is first tried by one of the Judges, who is called the Lord Ordinary; and if either party is dissatisfied, he may appeal to the whole Court, consisting of fifteen, the Lord President and fourteen other Judges, who have both in and out of Court the title of Lords, from the name of their estates; as, Lord Auchinleck, Lord Monboddo, &c.

2 It should be recollected, that this fanciful description of his friend was given by Johnson after he had become a water-drinker.

3 See them in *Journal of a Tour to the Hebrides*, 3d edit. p. 337.

Make my compliments to dear Mrs Boswell, and to Miss Veronica. I am, dear Sir,

Yours most faithfully,

SAM. JOHNSON.[1]

January 21, 1775.

Mr BOSWELL to Dr JOHNSON.

Edinburgh, Jan. 27, 1775.

. . .

You rate our lawyers here too high, when you call them great masters of the law of nations.

. . .

As for myself, I am ashamed to say that I have read little and thought little on the subject of America. I will be much obliged to you, if you will direct me where I shall find the best information of what is to be said on both sides. It is a subject vast in its present extent and future consequences. The imperfect hints which now float in my mind, tend rather to the formation of an opinion that our government has been precipitant and severe in the resolutions taken against the Bostonians. Well do you know that I have no kindness for that race. But nations, or bodies of men, should, as well as individuals, have a fair trial, and not be condemned on character alone. Have we not express contracts with our colonies, which afford a more certain foundation of judgement, than general political speculations on the mutual rights of states and their provinces or colonies? Pray let me know immediately what to read, and I shall diligently endeavour to gather for you any thing that I can find. Is Burke's speech on American Taxation published by himself? Is it authentic? I remember to have heard you say, that you had never considered East Indian affairs; though, surely, they are of much importance to Great-Britain. Under the recollection of this, I shelter myself from the reproach of ignorance about the Americans. If you write upon the subject, I shall certainly understand it. But, since you seem to expect that I should know something of it, without your instruction, and that my own mind should suggest something, I trust you will put me in the way.

. . .

1 He now sent me a Latin inscription for my historical picture of Mary Queen of Scots, and afterwards favoured me with an English translation. Mr Alderman Boydell[a] has subjoined them to the engraving from my picture.

Maria Scotorum Regina,	Mary Queen of Scots,
Hominum seditiosorum	Harrassed, terrified, and overpowered
Contumeliis lassata,	By the insults, menaces,
Minis territa, clamoribus victa,	And clamours
Libello, per quem	Of her rebellious subjects,
Regno cedit,	Sets her hand
Lacrimans trepidansque	With tears and confusion,
Nomen apponit.	To a resignation of the kingdom.

a Add: 'that eminent patron of the arts'.

What does Becket mean by the *Originals* of Fingal and other poems of Ossian, which he advertises to have lain in his shop?

. . .

To JAMES BOSWELL, Esq.

DEAR SIR — You sent me a case to consider, in which I have no facts but what are against us, nor any principles on which to reason. It is vain to try to write thus without materials. The fact seems to be against you, at least I cannot know nor say any thing to the contrary. I am glad that you like the book so well. I hear no more of Macpherson. I shall long to know what Lord Hailes says of it. Lend it him privately. I shall send the parcel as soon as I can. Make my compliments to Mrs Boswell. I am, Sir, &c.

SAM. JOHNSON.

January 28, 1775.

Mr BOSWELL to Dr JOHNSON.

Edinburgh, Feb. 2, 1775.

. . .

As to Macpherson, I am anxious to have from yourself a full and pointed account of what has passed between you and him. It is confidently told here, that before your book came out he sent to you, to let you know that he understood you meant to deny the authenticity of Ossian's poems; that the originals were in his possession; that you might have inspection of them, and might take the evidence of people skilled in the Erse language; and that he hoped, after this fair offer, you would not be so uncandid as to assert that he had refused reasonable proof. That you paid no regard to his message, but published your strong attack upon him; that then he wrote a letter to you, in such terms as he thought suited to one who had not acted as a man of veracity. You may believe it gives me pain to hear your conduct represented as unfavourable, while I can only deny what is said, on the ground that your character refutes it, without having any information to oppose. Let me, I beg it of you, be furnished with a sufficient answer to any calumny upon this occasion.

Lord Hailes writes to me (for we correspond more than we talk together), 'As to Fingal, I see a controversy arising, and purpose to keep out of its way. There is no doubt that I might mention some circumstances; but I do not choose to commit them to paper.' What his opinion is, I do not know. He says, 'I am singularly obliged to Dr Johnson for his accurate and useful criticisms. Had he given some strictures on the general plan of the work, it would have added much to his favours.' He is charmed with your verses on Inchkenneth, says they are very elegant, but bids me tell you he doubts whether '*Legitimas faciunt pectora pura preces*', be according to the rubric: but that is your concern; for, you know, he is a Presbyterian.

. . .

To Dr LAWRENCE.[1]

February 7, 1775.

SIR – One of the Scotch physicians is now prosecuting a corporation that in some public instrument have styled him *Doctor of Medicine* instead of *Physician*. Boswell desires, being advocate for the corporation, to know whether *Doctor of Medicine* is not a legitimate title, and whether it may be considered as a disadvantageous distinction. I am to write to-night, be pleased to tell me. I am, Sir, your most, &c.

SAM. JOHNSON.

To JAMES BOSWELL, Esq.

MY DEAR BOSWELL – I am surprised that, knowing as you do the disposition of your countrymen to tell lies in favour of each other,[2] you can be at all affected by any reports that circulate among them. Macpherson never in his life offered me the sight of any original or of any evidence of any kind, but thought only of intimidating me by noise and threats, till my last answer – that I would not be deterred from detecting what I thought a cheat, by the menaces of a ruffian – put an end to our correspondence.

The state of the question is this. He, and Dr Blair, whom I consider as deceived, say, that he copied the poem from old manuscripts. His copies, if he had them, and I believe him to have none, are nothing. Where are the manuscripts? They can be shown if they exist, but they were never shown. *De non existentibus et non apparentibus*, says our law, *eadem est ratio*. No man has a claim to credit upon his own word, when better evidence, if he had it, may be easily produced. But, so far as we can find, the Erse language was never written till very lately for the purposes of religion. A nation that cannot write, or a language that was never written, has no manuscripts.

But whatever he has, he never offered to show. If old manuscripts should now be mentioned, I should, unless there were more evidence than can be easily had, suppose them another proof of Scotch conspiracy in national falsehood.

Do not censure the expression; you know it to be true.

Dr Memis's question is so narrow as to allow no speculation; and I have no facts before me but those which his advocate has produced against you.

I consulted this morning the President of the London College of Physicians, who says, that with us, *Doctor of Physic* (we do not say *Doctor of Medicine*) is the highest title that a practicer of physic can have; that *Doctor* implies not only *Physician*, but teacher of physic; that every *Doctor* is legally a *Physician*, but no man, not a *Doctor*, can *practice physic* but by licence

1 The learned and worthy Dr Lawrence, whom Dr Johnson respected and loved as his physician and friend.
2 My friend has, in this letter, relied upon my testimony with a confidence, of which the ground has escaped my recollection.

particularly granted. The Doctorate is a licence of itself. It seems to us a very slender cause of prosecution.

. . .

I am now engaged, but in a little time I hope to do all you would have. My compliments to Madam and Veronica. I am, Sir,

Your most humble servant,

SAM. JOHNSON.

February 7, 1775.

What words were used by Mr Macpherson in his letter to the venerable Sage, I have never heard; but they are generally said to have been of a nature very different from the language of literary contest. Dr Johnson's answer appeared in the newspapers of the day, and has since been frequently republished; but not with perfect accuracy. I give it as dictated to me by himself, written down in his presence, and authenticated by a note in his own handwriting, 'This, I think, is a true copy.'[a]

Mr JAMES MACPHERSON – I received your foolish and impudent letter. Any violence offered me I shall do my best to repel; and what I cannot do for myself, the law shall do for me. I hope I shall never be deterred from detecting what I think a cheat, by the menaces of a ruffian.

What would you have me retract? I thought your book an imposture; I think it an imposture still. For this opinion I have given my reasons to the public, which I here dare you to refute. Your rage I defy. Your abilities, since your Homer, are not so formidable; and what I hear of your morals inclines me to pay regard not to what you shall say, but to what you shall prove. You may print this if you will.

SAM. JOHNSON.

Mr Macpherson little knew the character of Dr Johnson, if he supposed that he could be easily intimidated; for no man was ever more remarkable for personal courage. He had, indeed, an awful dread of death, or rather 'of something after death'; and what rational man, who seriously thinks of quitting all that he has ever known, and going into a new and unknown state of being, can be without that dread? But his fear was from reflection, his courage natural. His fear, in that one instance, was the result of philosophical and religious consideration. He feared death, but he feared nothing else, not even what might occasion death. Many instances of his resolution may be mentioned. One day, at Mr Beauclerk's house in the country, when two large dogs were fighting, he went up to them, and beat them till they separated; and at another time, when told of the danger there was that a gun might burst if charged with many balls, he put in six or seven, and fired it off against a wall. Mr Langton told me, that when they were swimming together near Oxford,

---

[a] Add this note: I have deposited it in the British Museum.

he cautioned Dr Johnson against a pool, which was reckoned particularly dangerous; upon which Johnson directly swam into it. He told me himself that one night he was attacked in the street by four men, to whom he would not yield, but kept them all at bay, till the watch came up, and carried both him and them to the round-house. In the play-house at Lichfield, as Mr Garrick informed me, Johnson having for a moment quitted a chair which was placed for him between the side-scenes, a gentleman took possession of it, and when Johnson on his return civilly demanded his seat, rudely refused to give it up; upon which Johnson laid hold of him, and tossed him and the chair into the pit. Foote, who so successfully revived the old comedy, by exhibiting living characters, had resolved to imitate Johnson on the stage, expecting great profits from his ridicule of so celebrated a man. Johnson being informed of his intention, and being at dinner at Mr Thomas Davies's the bookseller, from whom I had the story, he asked Mr Davies 'what was the common price of an oak stick'; and being answered six-pence, 'Why then, Sir (said he), give me leave to send our servant to purchase me a shilling one. I'll have a double quantity; for I am told Foote means to *take me off*, as he calls it, and I am determined the fellow shall not do it with impunity.' Davies took care to acquaint Foote of this, which effectually checked the wantonness of the mimic. Mr Macpherson's menaces made Johnson provide himself with the same implement of defence; and had he been attacked, I have no doubt that, old as he was, he would have made his corporal prowess be felt as much as his intellectual.

His *Journey to the Western Islands of Scotland*,* is a most valuable performance. It abounds in extensive philosophical views of society, and in ingenious sentiments and lively description. A considerable part of it, indeed, consists of speculations, which many years before he saw the wild regions which we visited together, probably had employed his attention, though the actual sight of those scenes undoubtedly quickened and augmented them. Mr Orme, the very able historian, agreed with me in this opinion, which he thus strongly expressed: 'There are in that book thoughts, which, by long revolution in the great mind of Johnson, have been formed and polished like pebbles rolled in the ocean!'

That he was to some degree of excess a *true-born Englishman*, so as to have ever entertained an undue prejudice against both the country and the people of Scotland, must be allowed. But it was a prejudice of the head, and not of the heart. He had no ill will to the Scotch; for, if he had been conscious of that, he would never have thrown himself into the bosom of their country, and trusted to the protection of its remote inhabitants with a fearless confidence. His remark upon the nakedness of the country, from its being denuded of trees, was made after having travelled two hundred miles along the eastern coast, where certainly trees are not to be found near the road, and he said it was 'a map of the road' which he gave. His disbelief of the authenticity of the poems ascribed to Ossian, a Highland bard, was confirmed in the course of his journey, by a very strict examination of the evidence offered for it; and although their authenticity was made too much a national point by the Scotch, there were many respectable persons in that country who did not concur in this; so that his judgement upon the question ought not to be decried, even by those who differ from him. As to myself, I can only say, upon a subject now become very uninteresting, that when the fragments of Highland poetry first came out, I was much pleased with their wild peculiarity, and was one of those who subscribed to enable their editor, Mr Macpherson, then a young man, to make a search in the Highlands and Hebrides for a long poem in the Erse language, which was reported to be preserved somewhere in those regions. But when there came forth an Epic Poem in six books, with all the common circumstances of former compositions of that nature; and when, upon an attentive examination of it, there was found a perpetual recurrence of the same images which appear in the fragments; and when no ancient manuscript, to authenticate the work, was deposited in any public library, though that was insisted on as a reasonable proof, *who* could forbear to doubt?

Johnson's grateful acknowledgements of kindnesses received in the course of this tour, completely refute the brutal reflections which have been thrown out against him, as if he had made an ungrateful return; and his delicacy in sparing in his book those who we find from his letters to Mrs Thrale, were just objects of censure, is much to be admired. His candour and amiable disposition is conspicuous from his conduct, when informed by Mr Macleod, of Rasay, that he had committed a mistake, which gave that gentleman some uneasiness. He wrote him a courteous and kind letter, and inserted in the newspapers an advertisement, correcting the mistake.[1]

The observations of my friend Mr Dempster in a letter written to me, soon after he had read Dr Johnson's book, are so just and liberal, that they cannot be too often repeated:

. . . There is nothing in the book, from beginning to end, that a Scotchman need to take amiss. What he says of the country is true; and his observations on the people are what must naturally occur to a sensible, observing, and reflecting inhabitant of a convenient metropolis, where a man on thirty pounds a year may be better accommodated with all the little wants of life, than Col or Sir Allan.

I am charmed with his researches concerning the Erse language, and the antiquity of their manuscripts. I am quite convinced; and I shall rank Ossian, and his Fingals and Oscars, amongst the nursery tales, not the true history of our country, in all time to come.

Upon the whole, the book cannot displease, for it has no pretensions. The author neither says he is a geographer, nor an antiquarian, nor very learned in the history of Scotland, nor a naturalist, nor a fossilist. The manners of the people, and the face of the country, are all he attempts to describe, or seems to have thought of. Much were it to be wished, that they who have travelled into more remote, and of course more curious

---

1 See *Journal of a Tour to the Hebrides*, 3d edit. p. 520.

regions, had all possessed his good sense. Of the state of learning, his observations on Glasgow University show he has formed a very sound judgement. He understands our climate too; and he has accurately observed the changes, however slow and imperceptible to us, which Scotland has undergone, in consequence of the blessings of liberty and internal peace. . . .

Mr Knox, another native of Scotland, who has since made the same tour, and published an account of it, is equally liberal. 'I have read (says he) his book again and again, travelled with him from Berwick to Glenelg, through countries with which I am well acquainted; sailed with him from Glenelg to Rasay, Sky, Rum, Col, Mull, and Icolmkill, but have not been able to correct him in any matter of consequence. I have often admired the accuracy, the precision, and the justness of what he advances, respecting both the country and the people.

'The Doctor has every where delivered his sentiments with freedom, and in many instances with a seeming regard for the benefit of the inhabitants, and the ornament of the country. His remarks on the want of trees and hedges for shade, as well as for shelter to the cattle, are well founded, and merit the thanks, not the illiberal censure of the natives. He also felt for the distresses of the Highlanders, and explodes, with great propriety, the bad management of the grounds, and the neglect of timber in the Hebrides.'

Having quoted Johnson's just compliments on the Rasay family, he says, 'On the other hand, I found this family equally lavish in their encomiums upon the Doctor's conversation, and his subsequent civilities to a young gentleman of that country, who, upon waiting upon him at London, was well received, and experienced all the attention and regard that a warm friend could bestow. Mr Macleod having also been in London, waited upon the Doctor, who provided a magnificent and expensive entertainment, in honour of his old Hebridean acquaintance.'

And talking of the military road by Fort Augustus, he says, 'By this road, though one of the most rugged in Great-Britain, the celebrated Dr Johnson passed from Inverness to the Hebride Isles. His observations on the country and people are extremely correct, judicious, and instructive.'[1][a]

His private letters to Mrs Thrale, written during the course of his journey, which therefore may be supposed to convey his genuine feelings at the time,

---

1 Page 103.

[a] Add: Mr Tytler, the acute and able vindicator of Mary Queen of Scots, in one of his letters to Mr James Elphinstone, published in that gentleman's *Forty Years' Correspondence*, says, 'I read Dr Johnson's Tour with very great pleasure. Some few errors he has fallen into, but of no great importance, and those are lost in the numberless beauties of his work.

'If I had leisure, I could perhaps point out the most exceptionable places; but at present I am in the country, and have not his book at hand. It is plain he meant to speak well of Scotland: and he has in my apprehension done us great honour in the most capital article, the character of the inhabitants.'

abound in such benignant sentiments towards the people who showed him civilities, that no man whose temper is not very harsh and sour, can retain a doubt of the goodness of his heart.

It is painful to recollect with what rancour he was assailed by numbers of shallow irritable North-Britons, on account of his supposed injurious treatment of their country and countrymen, in his *Journey*. Had there been any just ground for such a charge, would the virtuous and candid Dempster have given his opinion of the book, in the terms which I have quoted? Would the patriotic Knox[1] have spoken of it as he has done?[a] And let me add, that, citizen of the world as I hold myself to be, I have that degree of predilection for my *natale solum*, nay, I have that just sense of the merit of an ancient nation, which has been ever renowned for its valour, which in former times maintained its independence against a powerful neighbour, and in modern times has been equally distinguished for its ingenuity and industry in civilised life, that I should have felt a generous indignation at any injustice done to it. Johnson treated Scotland no worse than he did even his best friends, whose characters he used to give as they appeared to him, both in light and shade. Some people, who had not exercised their minds sufficiently, condemned him for censuring his friends. But Sir Joshua Reynolds, whose philosophical penetration and justness of thinking are not less known to those who live with him, than his genius in his art is admired by the world, explained his conduct thus: 'He was fond of discrimination, which he could not show without pointing out the bad as well as the good in every character; and as his friends were those whose characters he knew best, they afforded him the best opportunity for showing the acuteness of his judgement.'

He expressed to his friend Mr Windham of Norfolk, his wonder at the extreme jealousy of the Scotch, and their resentment at having their country described by him as it really was; when, to say that it was a country as good as England, would have been a gross falsehood. 'None of us (said he) would be offended if a foreigner who has travelled here should say, that vines and olives don't grow in England.' And as to his prejudice against the Scotch, which I always ascribed to that nationality which he observed in *them*, he said to the same gentleman, 'When I find a Scotchman to whom an Englishman is as a Scotchman, that Scotchman shall be as an Englishman to me.' His intimacy with many gentlemen of Scotland, and his employing so many natives of that country as his amanuenses, prove that his prejudice was not virulent; and I have deposited in the British Museum, amongst other pieces of his writing, the following note, in answer to one from me, asking if he would meet me at dinner at the Mitre, though a friend of mine, a Scotchman, was to be there: 'Mr Johnson does not see why Mr Boswell should suppose a Scotchman less acceptable than any other man. He will be at the Mitre.'

---

1 I observe with much regret, while this work is passing through the press (August, 1790), that this ingenious gentleman is dead.

a Add: Would Mr Tytler, surely ' . . . a *Scot*, if ever *Scot* there were', have expressed himself thus?

My much valued friend Dr Barnard, now Bishop of Killaloe, having once expressed to him an apprehension, that if he should visit Ireland he might treat the people of that country more unfavourably than he had done the Scotch, he answered with strong pointed double-edged wit, 'Sir, you have no reason to be afraid of me. The Irish are not in a conspiracy to cheat the world by false representations of the merits of their countrymen. No, Sir; the Irish are a FAIR PEOPLE: they never speak well of one another.'

Johnson told me an instance of Scottish nationality, which made a very unfavourable impression upon his mind. A Scotchman, of some consideration in London, solicited him to recommend, by the weight of his learned authority, to be master of an English school, a person of whom he who recommended him confessed he knew no more but that he was his country-man. Johnson was shocked at this unconscientious conduct.

All the miserable cavillings against his *Journey*, in newspapers, magazines, and other fugitive publications, I can speak from certain knowledge, only fur-nished him with sport. At last there came out a scurrilous volume, larger than Johnson's own, filled with malignant abuse, under a name, real or fictitious, of some low man in an obscure corner of Scotland, though supposed to be the work of another Scotchman, who has found means to make himself well known both in Scotland and England. The effect which it had upon Johnson was, to produce this pleasant observation to Mr Seward, to whom he lent the book: 'This fellow must be a blockhead. They don't know how to go about their abuse. Who will read a five shilling book against me? No, Sir, if they had wit, they should have kept pelting me with pamphlets.'

Mr BOSWELL to Dr JOHNSON.

Edinburgh, Feb. 18, 1775.

You would have been very well pleased if you had dined with me to-day. I had for my guests, Macquharrie, young Maclean of Col, the successor of our friend, a very amiable man, though not marked with such active qualities as his brother, Mr Maclean of Torloisk in Mull a gentleman of Sir Allan's family, and two of the clan Grant, so that the Highland and Hebridean genius reigned. We had a great deal of conversation about you, and drank your health in a bumper. The toast was not proposed by me, which is a circumstance to be remarked, for I am now so connected with you, that any thing that I can say or do to your honour has not the value of an additional compliment. It is only giving you a guinea out of that treasure of admiration which already belongs to you, and which is no hidden treasure; for I suppose my admiration of you is co-existent with the knowledge of my character.

I find that the Highlanders and Hebrideans in general are much fonder of your *Journey*, than the low-country or *hither* Scots. One of the Grants said today, that he was sure you were a man of a good heart, and a candid man, and seemed to hope he should be able to convince you of the antiquity of a good proportion of the poems of Ossian. After all that has passed, I think the matter is capable of being proved to a certain degree. I am told that Macpherson got one old Erse MS. from Clanranald, for the restitution of which he executed a formal obligation; and it is affirmed, that the Gaelic (call it Erse or call it Irish) has been written in the Highlands and Hebrides for many centuries. It is reasonable to suppose, that such of the inhabitants as acquired any learning, possessed the art of writing as well as their Irish neighbours and Celtic cousins; and the question is, can sufficient evidence be shown of this?

Those who are skilled in ancient writings can determine the age of MSS. or at least can ascertain the century in which they were written; and if men of veracity, who are so skilled, shall tell us that MSS. in the possession of families in the Highlands and isles, are the works of a remote age, I think we should be convinced by their testimony.

There is now come to this city, Ranald Macdonald, from the Isle of Egg, who has several MSS. of Erse poetry, which he wishes to publish by subscription. I have engaged to take three copies of the book, the price of which is to be six shillings, as I would subscribe for all the Erse that can be printed, be it old or new, that the language may be preserved. This man says, that some of his manuscripts are ancient; and, to be sure, one of them which was shown to me does appear to have the duskiness of antiquity. . . .

The inquiry is not yet quite hopeless, and I should think that the exact truth may be discovered, if proper means be used. I am, &c.

JAMES BOSWELL.

To JAMES BOSWELL, Esq.

DEAR SIR – I am sorry that I could get no books for my friends in Scotland. Mr Strahan has at last promised to send two dozen to you. If they come, put the names of my friends into them; you may cut them out,[1] and paste them with a little starch in the book.

You then are going wild about Ossian. Why do you think any part can be proved? The dusky manuscript of Egg is probably not fifty years old; if it be an hundred, it proves nothing. The tale of Clanranald has no proof. Has Clanranald told it? Can he prove it? There are, I believe, no Erse manuscripts. None of the old families had a single letter in Erse that we heard of. You say it is likely that they could write. The learned, if any learned there were, could; but knowing by that learning some written language, in that language they wrote, as letters had never been applied to their own. If there are manuscripts, let them be shown, with some proof that they are not forged for the occasion. You say many can remember parts of Ossian. I believe all those parts are versions of the English, at least there is no proof of their antiquity.

Macpherson is said to have made some translations himself; and having

1 From a list in his hand-writing.

taught a boy to write it, ordered him to say that he had learned it of his grandmother. The boy, when he grew up, told the story. This Mrs Williams heard at Mr Strahan's table. Do not be credulous; you know how little a Highlander can be trusted. Macpherson is, so far as I know, very quiet. Is not that proof enough? Everything is against him. No visible manuscript; no inscription in the language: no correspondence among friends: no transaction of business, of which a single scrap remains in the ancient families. Macpherson's pretence is, that the character was Saxon. If he had not talked unskilfully of *manuscripts*, he might have fought with oral tradition much longer. As to Mr Grant's information, I suppose he knows much less of the matter than ourselves.

In the mean time, the bookseller says that the sale[1] is sufficiently quick. They printed four thousand. Correct your copy wherever it is wrong, and bring it up. Your friends will all be glad to see you. I think of going myself into the country about May.

I am sorry that I have not managed to send the books sooner. I have left four for you, and do not restrict you absolutely to follow my directions in the distribution. You must use your own discretion.

Make my compliments to Mrs Boswell; I suppose she is now just beginning to forgive me. I am, dear Sir,

Your humble servant,

SAM. JOHNSON.

Feb. 25, 1775.

On Tuesday, March 21, I arrived in London; and on repairing to Dr Johnson's before dinner, found him in his study, sitting with Mr Peter Garrick, the elder brother of David, strongly resembling him in his countenance and voice, but of more sedate and placid manners. Johnson informed me, that 'though Mr Beauclerk was in great pain, it was hoped he was not in danger, and that he now wished to consult Dr Heberden to try the effect of a *new understanding*.' Both at this interview, and in the evening at Mr Thrale's, where he and Mr Peter Garrick and I met again, he was vehement on the subject of the Ossian controversy; observing, 'We do not know that there are any ancient Erse manuscripts; and we have no other reason to disbelieve that there are men with three heads, but that we do not know that there are any such men.' He also was outrageous, upon his supposition that my countrymen 'loved Scotland better than truth', saying, 'All of them, – nay not all, – but *droves* of them, would come up, and attest any thing for the honour of Scotland.' He also persevered in his wild allegation, that he questioned if there was a tree between Edinburgh and the English borders older than himself. I assured him he was mistaken, and suggested that the proper punishment would be that he should receive a stripe at every tree above a hundred years old, that was found within that space. He laughed and said, 'I believe I might submit to it for a *bawbie!*'

1 Of his *Journey to the Western Islands of Scotland.*

The doubts which, in my correspondence with him, I had ventured to state as to the justice and wisdom of the conduct of Great-Britain towards the American colonies, while I at the same time requested that he would enable me to inform myself upon that momentous subject, he had altogether disregarded; and had recently published a pamphlet, entitled, 'Taxation no Tyranny; an Answer to the Resolutions and Address of the American Congress'.*

He had long before indulged most unfavourable sentiments of our fellow subjects in America. For, as early as 1769, I was told by Dr John Campbell, that he had said of them, 'Sir, they are a race of convicts, and ought to be thankful for anything we allow them short of hanging.'

Of this performance I avoided to talk with him; for I had now formed a clear and settled opinion, that the people of America were well warranted to resist a claim that their fellow-subjects in the mother-country should have the entire command of their fortunes, by taxing them without their own consent; and the extreme violence which it breathed, appeared to me so unsuitable to the mildness of a Christian philosopher, and so directly opposite to the principles of peace which he had so beautifully recommended in his pamphlet respecting Falkland's Islands, that I was sorry to see him appear in so unfavourable a light. Besides, I could not perceive in it that ability of argument, or that felicity of expression, for which he was, upon other occasions, so eminent. Positive assertion, sarcastical severity, and extravagant ridicule, which he himself reprobated as a test of truth, were united in this rhapsody.

That this pamphlet was written at the desire of those who were then in power, I have no doubt; and, indeed, he owned to me, that it had been revised and curtailed by some of them. He told me, that they had struck out one passage, which was to this effect: 'that the Colonists could with no solidity argue from their not having been taxed while in their infancy, that they should not now be taxed. We do not put a calf into the plough; we wait till he is an ox.' He said, 'They struck it out either critically, as too ludicrous, or politically, as too exasperating. I care not which. It was their business. If an architect says, I will build five stories, and the man who employs him says, I will have only three, the employer is to decide.' 'Yes, Sir (said I), in ordinary cases. But should it be so when the architect gives his skill and labour *gratis*?'

Unfavourable as I am constrained to say my opinion of this pamphlet was, yet, since it was congenial with the sentiments of numbers at that time, and as every thing relating to the writings of Dr Johnson is of importance in literary history, I shall therefore insert some passages which were struck out, it does not appear why, either by himself or those who revised it. They appear printed in a few proof leaves of it in my possession, marked with corrections in his own handwriting. I shall distinguish them by *Italics*.

In the paragraph where he says, the Americans were incited to resistance by European intelligence from 'men whom they thought their friends, but who were friends only to themselves', there followed – '*and made, by their selfishness, the enemies of their country*.'

And the next paragraph ran thus: 'On the original contriver of mischief, *rather than on those whom they have deluded*, let an insulted nation pour out its vengeance.'

The paragraph which came next was in these words: '*Unhappy is that country, in which men can hope for advancement by favouring its enemies. The tranquillity of stable government is not always easily preserved against the machinations of single innovators; but what can be the hope of quiet, when factions hostile to the legislature can be openly formed and openly avowed?*'

After the paragraph which now concludes the pamphlet, there followed this, in which he certainly means the great Earl of Chatham, and glances at a certain popular Lord Chancellor:

'*If, by the fortune of war, they drive us utterly away, what they will do next can only be conjectured. If a new monarchy is erected, they will want a* KING. *He who first takes into his hand the sceptre of America, should have a name of good omen.* WILLIAM *has been known as both conqueror and deliverer; and perhaps England, however contemned, might yet supply them with* ANOTHER WILLIAM. *Whigs, indeed, are not willing to be governed; and it is possible that* KING WILLIAM *may be strongly inclined to guide their measures; but Whigs have been cheated like other mortals, and suffered their leader to become their tyrant, under the name of their* PROTECTOR. *What more they will receive from England, no man can tell. In their rudiments of empire they may want a* CHANCELLOR.'

Then came this paragraph:

'*Their numbers are, at present, not quite sufficient for the greatness which, in some form of government or other, is to rival the ancient monarchies; but, by Dr Franklin's rule of progression, they will, in a century and a quarter, be more than equal to the inhabitants of Europe. When the Whigs of America are thus multiplied, let the Princes of the earth tremble in their palaces. If they should continue to double and to double, their own hemisphere will not contain them. But let not our boldest oppugners of authority look forward with delight to this futurity of Whiggism.*'

How it ended I know not, as it is cut off abruptly at the foot of the last of these proof pages.

His pamphlets in support of the measures of administration were published on his own account, and he afterwards collected them into a volume, with the title of 'Political Tracts, by the Author of the *Rambler*', with this motto,

> *Fallitur egregio quisquis sub Principe credit*
> *Servitium, numquam libertas gratior extat*
> *Quam sub Rege pio.*
>
>   CLAUDIANUS.

These pamphlets drew upon him numerous attacks. Against the common weapons of literary warfare he was hardened; but there were two instances of animadversion which I communicated to him, and from what I could judge, both from his silence and his looks, appeared to me to impress him much.

One was, 'A Letter to Dr Samuel Johnson, occasioned by his late political Publications'. It appeared previous to his 'Taxation no tyranny', and was written by Dr Joseph Towers. In that performance, Dr Johnson was treated with the respect due to so eminent a man, while his conduct as a political writer was boldly and pointedly arraigned, as inconsistent with the character of one, who, if he did employ his pen upon politics, 'it might reasonably be expected should distinguish himself, not by party violence and rancour, but by moderation and by wisdom.'

It concluded thus: 'I would, however, wish you to remember, should you again address the public under the character of a political writer, that luxuriance of imagination or energy of language will ill compensate for the want of candour, of justice, and of truth. And I shall only add, that should I hereafter be disposed to read, as I heretofore have done, the most excellent of all your performances, the *Rambler*, the pleasure which I have been accustomed to find in it will be much diminished by the reflection that the writer of so moral, so elegant, and so valuable a work, was capable of prostituting his talents in such productions as 'The False Alarm', the 'Thoughts on the Transactions respecting Falkland's Islands', and 'The Patriot'.'

I am willing to do justice to the merit of Dr Towers, of whom I will say, that although I abhor his Whiggish democratical notions and propensities (for I will not call them principles), I esteem him as an ingenious, knowing, and very convivial man.

The other instance was a paragraph of a letter to me, from my old and most intimate friend the Reverend Mr Temple, who wrote the character of Gray, which has had the honour to be adopted both by Mr Mason and Dr Johnson in their accounts of that poet. The words were, 'How can your great, I will not say your *pious*, but your *moral* friend, support the barbarous measures of administration, which they have not the face to ask even their infidel pensioner Hume to defend.'

However confident of the rectitude of his own mind, Johnson may have felt sincere uneasiness that his conduct should be erroneously imputed to unworthy motives, by good men, and that the influence of his valuable writings should on that account be in any degree obstructed or lessened.

He complained to a Right Honourable friend, of distinguished talents and very elegant manners, with whom he maintained a long intimacy, and whose generosity towards him will afterwards appear, that his pension having been given to him as a literary character, he had been applied to by administration to write political pamphlets; and he was even so much irritated, that he declared his resolution to resign his pension. His friend showed him the impropriety of such a measure, and he afterwards expressed his gratitude, and said he had received good advice. To that friend he once signified a wish to have his pension secured to him for his life; but he neither asked nor received from government any reward whatsoever for his political labours.

On Friday, March 24, I met him at the LITERARY CLUB, where were Mr Beauclerk, Mr Langton, Mr Colman, Dr Percy, Mr Vesey, Sir Charles Bunbury, Dr George Fordyce, Mr Steevens, and Mr Charles Fox. Before he came in, we talked of his *Journey to the Western Islands*, and of his coming away, 'willing to believe the second sight',[1] which seemed to excite some ridicule. I was then so impressed with the truth of many of the stories of it which I had

1 Johnson's *Journey to the Western Islands of Scotland*, edit. 1785, p. 256.

been told, that I avowed my conviction, saying, 'He is only *willing* to believe, I *do* believe. The evidence is enough for me, though not for his great mind. What will not fill a quart bottle will fill a pint bottle. I am filled with belief.' 'Are you? (said Colman), then cork it up.'

I found his *Journey* the common topic of conversation in London at this time, wherever I happened to be. At one of Lord Mansfield's formal Sunday evening conversations, strangely called *Levées*, his Lordship addressed me, 'We have all been reading your travels, Mr Boswell.' I answered, 'I was but the humble attendant of Dr Johnson.' The Chief Justice replied, with that air and manner which none, who ever saw and heard him, can forget, 'He speaks ill of nobody but Ossian.'

Johnson was in high spirits this evening at the club, and talked with great animation and success. He attacked Swift, as he used to do upon all occasions. '*The Tale of a Tub* is so much superior to his other writings, that one can hardly believe he was the author of it. There is in it such a vigour of mind, such a swarm of thoughts, so much of nature, and art, and life.' I wondered to hear him say of *Gulliver's Travels*, 'When once you have thought of big men and little men, it is very easy to do all the rest.' I endeavoured to make a stand for Swift, and tried to rouse those who were much more able to defend him; but in vain. Johnson at last of his own accord allowed very great merit to the inventory of articles found in the pockets of the Man Mountain, particularly the description of his watch, which it was conjectured was his GOD, as he consulted it upon all occasions. He observed, that 'Swift put his name to but two things (after he had a name to put), the 'Plan for the Improvement of the English Language', and the last 'Drapier's Letter'.'

From Swift, there was an easy transition to Mr Thomas Sheridan. – JOHNSON. 'Sheridan is a wonderful admirer of the tragedy of *Douglas*, and presented its author with a gold medal. Some years ago, at a coffee-house in Oxford, I called to him, "Mr Sheridan, Mr Sheridan, how came you to give a gold medal to Home, for writing that foolish play?" This, you see, was wanton and insolent; but I meant to be wanton and insolent. A medal has no value but as a stamp of merit. And was Sheridan to assume to himself the right of giving that stamp? If Sheridan was magnificent enough to bestow a gold medal as an honorary reward of dramatic excellence, he should have requested one of the Universities to choose the person on whom it should be conferred. Sheridan had no right to give a stamp of merit: it was counterfeiting Apollo's coin.'

On Monday, March 27, I breakfasted with him at Mr Strahan's. He told us, that he was engaged to go that evening to Mrs Abington's benefit. 'She was visiting some ladies whom I was visiting, and begged that I would come to her benefit. I told her I could not hear: but she insisted so much on my coming, that it would have been brutal to have refused her.' This was a speech quite characteristical. He loved to bring forward his having been in the gay circles of life; and he was, perhaps, a little vain of the solicitations of this elegant and fashionable actress. He told us, the play was to be *The Hypocrite*, altered from Cibber's *Nonjuror*, so as to satirize the Methodists. 'I do not think (said he) the character of the Hypocrite justly applicable to the Methodists; but it was very applicable to the Nonjurors. I once said to Dr Madan, a clergyman of Ireland, who was a great Whig, that perhaps a Nonjuror would have been less criminal in taking the oaths imposed by the ruling power, than refusing them; because refusing them, necessarily laid him under almost an irresistible temptation to be more criminal; for, a man *must* live, and if he precludes himself from the support furnished by the establishment, will probably be reduced to very wicked shifts to maintain himself.'[1] BOSWELL. 'I should think, Sir, that a man who took the oaths contrary to his principles was a determined wicked man, because he was sure he was committing perjury; whereas a Nonjuror might be insensibly led to do what was wrong, without being so directly conscious of it.' JOHNSON. 'Why, Sir, a man who goes to bed to his patron's wife is pretty sure that he is committing wickedness.' BOSWELL. 'Did the nonjuring clergymen do so, Sir?' JOHNSON. 'I am afraid many of them did.'

I was startled at his argument, and could by no means think it convincing. Had not his own father complied with the requisition of government (as to which he once observed to me, when I pressed him upon it, '*That*, Sir, he was to settle with himself'), he would probably have thought more unfavourably of a Jacobite who took the oaths:

> had he not resembled
> My father as he *swore* . . .

Mr Strahan talked of launching into the great ocean of London, in order to have a chance for rising to eminence, and observing that many men were kept back from trying their fortune there, because they were born to a competency, said, 'Small certainties are the bane of men of talents': which

---

1 This was not merely a cursory remark; for in his Life of Fenton he observes, 'With many other wise and virtuous men, who at that time of discord and debate [about the beginning of this century] consulted conscience, well or ill informed, more than interest, he doubted the legality of the government; and refusing to qualify himself for public employment, by taking the oaths required, left the University without a degree.' This conduct, Johnson calls 'perverseness of integrity'.

The question concerning the morality of taking oaths, of whatever kind, imposed by the prevailing power at the time, rather than to be excluded from all consequence, or even any considerable usefulness in society, has been agitated with all the acuteness of casuistry. It is related, that he who devised the oath of abjuration, profligately boasted, that he had framed a test which should damn one half of the nation, and starve the other. Upon minds not exalted to inflexible rectitude, or minds in which zeal for a party is predominant to excess, taking that oath against conviction, may have been palliated under the plea of necessity, or ventured upon in heat, as upon the whole producing more good than evil.

At a county election in Scotland, many years ago, when there was a warm contest between the friends of the Hanoverian succession and those against it, the oath of abjuration having been demanded, the freeholders upon one side rose to go away. Upon which a very sanguine gentleman, one of their number, ran to the door to stop them, calling out with much earnestness, 'Stay, stay, my friends, and let us swear the rogues out of it!'

Johnson confirmed. Mr Strahan put Johnson in mind of a remark which he had made to him; 'There are few ways in which a man can be more innocently employed than in getting money.' 'The more one thinks of this (said Strahan), the juster it will appear.'

Mr Strahan had taken a poor boy from the country as an apprentice, upon Johnson's recommendation. Johnson having inquired after him, said, 'Mr Strahan, let me have five guineas on account, and I'll give this boy one. Nay, if a man recommends a boy, and does nothing for him, it is sad work. Call him down.'

I followed him into the courtyard, behind Mr Strahan's house, and there I had a proof of what I had heard him profess, that he talked alike to all. 'Some people (said he) tell you that they let themselves down to the capacity of their hearers. I never do that. I speak uniformly, in as intelligible a manner as I can.'

'Well, my boy, how do you go on?' – 'Pretty well, Sir; but they are afraid I ain't strong enough for some parts of the business.' JOHNSON. 'Why, I shall be sorry for it; for when you consider with how little mental power and corporeal labour a printer can get a guinea a week, it is a very desirable occupation for you. Do you hear – take all the pains you can; and if this does not do, we must think of some other way of life for you. There's a guinea.'

Here was one of the many, many instances of his active benevolence. At the same time, the slow and sonorous solemnity with which, while he bent himself down, he addressed a little thick short-legged boy, contrasted with the boy's awkwardness and awe, could not but excite some ludicrous emotions.

I met him at Drury-lane play-house in the evening. Sir Joshua Reynolds, at Mrs Abington's request, had promised to bring a body of wits to her benefit; and having secured forty places in the front boxes, had done me the honour to put me in the group. Johnson sat on the seat directly behind me; and as he could neither see nor hear at such a distance from the stage, he was wrapped up in grave abstraction, and seemed quite a cloud, amidst all the sunshine of glitter and gaiety. I wondered at his patience in sitting out a play of five acts, and a farce of two. He said very little; but after the prologue to Bon Ton had been spoken, which he could hear pretty well from the more slow and distinct utterance, he observed, 'Dryden has written prologues superior to any that David Garrick has written; but David Garrick has written more good prologues than Dryden has done. It is wonderful that he has been able to write such a variety of them.'

At Mr Beauclerk's, where I supped, was Mr Garrick, who I made happy with Johnson's praise of his prologues; and I suppose, in gratitude to him, he took up one of his favourite topics, the nationality of the Scotch, which he maintained in his pleasant manner, with the aid of a little poetical fiction. 'Come, come, don't deny it: they are really national. Why, now, the Adams are as liberal-minded men as any in the world: but, I don't know how it is, all their workmen are Scotch. You are, to be sure, wonderfully free from that nationality; but so it happens, that you employ the only Scotch shoe-black in London.' He imitated the manner of his old master with ludicrous exaggeration; repeating, with pauses and half whistlings interjected,

Os homini sublime dedit, – caelumque tueri –
Jussit, – et erectos ad sidera – tollere vultus.

looking downwards all the time, and, while pronouncing the four last words, absolutely touching the ground with a kind of contorted gesticulation.

Garrick, however, when he pleased, could imitate Johnson very exactly; for that great actor, with his distinguished powers of expression which were so universally admired, possessed also an admirable talent of mimicry. He was always jealous that Johnson spoke lightly of him. I recollect his exhibiting him to me one day, as if saying, 'Davy is futile', which he uttered perfectly with the tone and air of Johnson.

I cannot too frequently request of my readers while they peruse my account of Johnson's conversation, to endeavour to keep in mind his deliberate and strong utterance. His mode of speaking was indeed very impressive;[1] and I wish it could be preserved as music is written, according to the very ingenious method of Mr Steele,[2] who has shown how the recitation of Mr Garrick, and other eminent speakers, might be transmitted to posterity *in score*.[a]

Next day I dined with Johnson at Mr Thrale's. He attacked Gray, calling him 'a dull fellow'. BOSWELL. 'I understand he was reserved, and might appear dull in company; but surely he was not dull in poetry.' JOHNSON. 'Sir, he was dull in company, dull in his closet, dull every where. He was dull in a new way, and that made many people think him GREAT. He was a mechanical poet.' He then repeated some ludicrous lines, which have escaped my memory, and said, 'Is not that GREAT, like his Odes?' Mrs Thrale maintained that his Odes were melodious; upon which he exclaimed,

> Weave the warp, and weave the woof;

I added, in a solemn tone,

> 'The winding-sheet of Edward's race.

---

1 My noble friend Lord Pembroke said once to me at Wilton, with a happy pleasantry and some truth, that 'Dr Johnson's sayings would not appear so extraordinary, were it not for his *bow-wow way*.' The sayings themselves are generally of sterling merit; but, doubtless, his *manner* was an addition to their effect. and therefore should be attended to as much as may be. It is necessary, however, to guard those who were not acquainted with him, against overcharged imitations or caricatures of his manner, which are frequently attempted, and many of which are second-hand copies from the late Mr Henderson the actor, who, though a good mimic of some persons, did not represent Johnson correctly.

2 See '*Prosodia Rationalis*; or, an Essay towards establishing the Melody and Measure of Speech, to be expressed and perpetuated by peculiar Symbols'. London, 1779.

a Add the following note: I use the phrase *in score*, as Dr Johnson has explained it in his Dictionary. '*A song in* SCORE, the words with the musical notes of a song annexed.' But I understand that in scientific propriety it means all the parts of a musical composition noted down in the characters by which it is exhibited to the eye of the skilful.

There is a good line.' – 'Aye (said he), and the next line is a good one' (pronouncing it contemptuously):

> 'Give ample verge and room enough –

No, Sir, there are but two good stanzas in Gray's poetry, which are in his *Elegy in a Country Churchyard.*' He then repeated the stanza,

> For who to dumb forgetfulness a prey, &c.

mistaking one word; for instead of *precincts* he said *confines*. He added, 'The other stanza I forget.'

A young lady who had married a man much her inferior in rank being mentioned, a question arose how a woman's relations should behave to her in such a situation; and, while I recapitulate the debate, and recollect what has since happened, I cannot but be struck in a manner that delicacy forbids me to express. While I contended that she ought to be treated with an inflexible steadiness of displeasure, Mrs Thrale was all for mildness and forgiveness, and according to the vulgar phrase, making the best of a bad bargain. JOHNSON. 'Madam, we must distinguish. Were I a man of rank, I would not let a daughter starve who had made a mean marriage; but having voluntarily degraded herself from the station which she was originally entitled to hold, I would support her only in that which she herself has chosen; and would not put her on a level with my other daughters. You are to consider, Madam, that it is our duty to maintain the subordination of civilised society; and when there is a gross and shameful deviation from rank, it should be punished so as to deter others from the same perversion.'

After frequently considering this subject, I am more and more confirmed in what I then meant to express, and which was sanctioned by the authority, and illustrated by the wisdom, of Johnson; and I think it of the utmost consequence to the happiness of Society, to which subordination is absolutely necessary. It is weak, and contemptible, and unworthy, in a parent to relax in such a case. It is sacrificing general advantage to private feelings. And let it be considered, that the claim of a daughter who has acted thus, to be restored to her former situation, is either fanatical or unjust. If there be no value in the distinction of rank, what does she suffer by being kept in the situation to which she has descended? If there be a value in that distinction, it ought to be steadily maintained. If indulgence be shown to such conduct, and the offenders know that in a longer or shorter time they shall be received as well as if they had not contaminated their blood by a base alliance, the great check upon that inordinate caprice which generally occasions low marriages, will be removed, and the fair and comfortable order of improved life will be miserably disturbed.

Lord Chesterfield's letters being mentioned, Johnson said, 'It was not to be wondered at that they had so great a sale, considering that they were the letters of a statesman, a wit, one who had been so much in the mouths of mankind, one long accustomed *virum volitare per ora.*'

On Friday, March 31, I supped with him and some friends at a tavern. One of the company attempted, with too much forwardness, to rally him on his late appearance at the theatre; but had reason to repent of his temerity. 'Why, Sir, did you go to Mrs Abington's benefit? Did you see?' JOHNSON. 'No, Sir.' 'Did you hear?' JOHNSON. 'No, Sir.' 'Why then, Sir, did you go?' JOHNSON. 'Because, Sir, she is a favourite of the public: and when the public cares the thousandth part for you that it does for her, I will go to your benefit too.'

Next morning I won a small bet from Lady Diana Beauclerk, by asking him as to one of his particularities, which her Ladyship laid I durst not do. It seems he had been frequently observed at the club to put into his pocket the Seville oranges, after he had squeezed the juice of them into the drink which he made for himself. Beauclerk and Garrick talked of it to me, and seemed to think that he had a strange unwillingness to be discovered. We could not divine what he did with them; and this was the bold question to be put. I saw on his table the spoils of the preceding night, some fresh peels nicely scraped and cut into pieces. 'O, Sir (said I), I now partly see what you do with the squeezed oranges which you put into your pocket at the club.' JOHNSON. 'I have a great love for them.' BOSWELL. 'And pray, Sir, what do you do with them? You scrape them, it seems, very neatly, and what next?' JOHNSON. 'I let them dry, Sir.' BOSWELL. 'And what next?' JOHNSON. 'Nay, Sir, you shall know their fate no further.' BOSWELL. 'Then the world must be left in the dark. It must be said (assuming a mock solemnity), he scraped them, and let them dry, but what he did with them next, he never could be prevailed upon to tell.' JOHNSON. 'Nay, Sir, you should say it more emphatically – he could not be prevailed upon, even by his dearest friends, to tell.'

He had this morning received his Diploma as Doctor of Laws from the University of Oxford. He did not vaunt of his new dignity, but I understood he was highly pleased with it. I shall here insert the progress and completion of that high academical honour, in the same manner as I have traced his obtaining that of Master of Arts.

To the Reverend Dr FOTHERGILL, Vice-Chancellor of the University of OXFORD, to be communicated to Heads of Houses, and proposed in Convocation.

MR VICE-CHANCELLOR AND GENTLEMEN – The honour of the degree of M.A. by diploma, formerly conferred upon Mr SAMUEL JOHNSON, in consequence of his having eminently distinguished himself by the publication of a series of essays, excellently calculated to form the manners of the people, and in which the cause of religion and morality has been maintained and recommended by the strongest powers of argument and elegance of language, reflected an equal degree of lustre upon the University itself.

The many learned labours which have since that time employed the attention and displayed the abilities of that great man, so much to the advancement of literature and the benefit of the community, render him worthy of more distinguished honours in the republic of letters: and I persuade myself, that I shall act agreeably to the sentiments of the whole University, in desiring that it may be proposed in Convocation to confer on him the degree of Doctor in Civil Law by diploma, to which I readily give my consent; and am,

Mr Vice-Chancellor and Gentlemen,
Your affectionate friend and servant,

NORTH.[1]

Downing-street.
March 23, 1775.

DIPLOMA

CANCELLARIUS, *Magistri, et Scholares Universitatis Oxoniensis, omnibus ad quos praesentes Literae pervenerint, Salutem in Domino Sempiternam.*

SCIATIS, *virum illustrem,* SAMUELEM JOHNSON, *in omni humaniorum literarum genere eruditum, omniumque scientiarum comprehensione felicissimum, scriptis suis, ad popularium mores formandos summa verborum elegantia ac sententiarum gravitate compositis, ita olim inclaruisse, ut dignus videretur cui ab Academia sua eximia quaedam laudis praemia defer[r]entur, quique in venerabilem Magistrorum Ordinem summa cum dignitate cooptaretur:*

Cum vero eundem clarissimum virum tot postea tantique labores, in patria praesertim lingua ornanda et stabilienda feliciter impensi, ita insigniverint, ut in Literarum Republica PRINCEPS *jam et* PRIMARIUS *jure habeatur; Nos* CANCELLARIUS, *Magistri et Scholares Universitatis Oxoniensis, quo talis viri merita pari honoris remuneratione exaequentur, et perpetuum suae simul laudis, nostraeque erga literas propensissimae voluntatis extet monumentum, in solenni Convocatione Doctorum et Magistrorum regentium et non regentium, praedictum* SAMUELEM JOHNSON *Doctorem in Jure Civili renunciavimus et constituimus, eumque virtute praesentis Diplomatis singulis juribus, privilegiis et honoribus, ad istum gradum quaqua pertinentibus, frui et gaudere jussimus. In cujus rei testimonium commune Universitatis Oxoniensis sigillum praesentibus apponi fecimus.*

Datum in Domo nostrae Convocationis die tricesimo mensis Martii, Anno Domini Millesimo septingentesimo, septuagesimo quinto.[2]

---

1 Extracted from the Convocation Register, Oxford.

2 The original is in my possession.[a]

ᵃ *Added for Third Edition*: He showed me the diploma, and allowed me to read it, but would not consent to my taking a copy of it, fearing perhaps that I should blaze it abroad in his life-time. His objection to this appears from his 99th letter to Mrs Thrale, whom in that letter he thus scolds for the grossness of her flattery of him. – 'The other Oxford news is, that they have sent me a degree of Doctor of Laws, with such praises in the Diploma as perhaps ought to make me ashamed; they are very like your praises. I wonder whether I shall ever show it to you.'

It is remarkable that he never, so far as I know, assumed his title of *Doctor*, but called himself *Mr* Johnson, as appears from many of his cards or notes to myself; and I have

Viro reverendo THOMAE FOTHERGILL, S.T.P. *Universitatis Oxoniensis Vice-Cancellario.*

S. P. D.

SAM. JOHNSON.

MULTIS *non est opus, ut testimonium quo, te praeside, Oxonienses nomen meum posteris commendarunt, quali animo acceperim compertum faciam. Nemo sibi placens non laetatur; nemo sibi non placet, qui vobis, literarum arbitris, placere potuit. Hoc tamen habet incommodi tantum beneficium, quod mihi nunquam posthac sine vestrae famae detrimento vel labi liceat vel cessare; semperque sit timendum, ne quod mihi tam eximiae laudi est, vobis aliquando fiat opprobrio. Vale.*[1]

7 Id. Apr. 1775

Dr Johnson revised some sheets of Lord Hailes's *Annals of Scotland*, and wrote a few notes on the margin with red ink, which he bade me tell his Lordship did not sink into the paper, and might be wiped off with a wet sponge, so that he did not spoil his manuscript. I told him there were very few of his friends so accurate as that I could venture to put down in writing what they told me as his sayings. JOHNSON. 'Why should you write down *my* sayings?' BOSWELL. 'I write them when they are good.' JOHNSON. 'Nay, you may as well write down the sayings of any one else that are good.' But *where*, I might with great propriety have added, can I find such?

I visited him by appointment in the evening, and we drank tea with Mrs Williams. He told me that he had been in the company of a gentleman whose extraordinary travels had been much the subject of conversation. But I found that he had not listened to him with that full confidence, without which there is little satisfaction in the society of travellers. I was curious to hear what opinion so able a judge as Johnson had formed of his abilities, and I asked if he was not a man of sense. JOHNSON. 'Why, Sir, he is not a distinct relater; and I should say, he is neither abounding nor deficient in sense. I did not perceive any superiority of understanding.' BOSWELL. 'But will you not allow him a nobleness of resolution, in penetrating into distant regions?' JOHNSON. 'That, Sir, is not to the present purpose: we are talking of his sense. A fighting cock has a nobleness of resolution.'

Next day, Sunday, April 2, I dined with him at Mr Hoole's. We talked of Pope. JOHNSON. 'He wrote his *Dunciad* for fame. That was his primary motive. Had it not been for that, the dunces might have railed against him till they were

---

seen many from him to other persons, in which he uniformly takes that designation. – I once observed on his table a letter directed to him with the addition of *Esquire*, and objected to it as being a designation inferior to that of Doctor; but he checked me, and seemed pleased with it, because, as I conjectured, he liked to be sometimes taken out of the class of literary men, and to be merely *genteel*, – *un gentilhomme comme un autre.*

1 [The original is in the hands of Dr Fothergill, then Vice-Chancellor, who made this transcript. T.W.]

weary, without his troubling himself about them. He delighted to vex them, no doubt; but he had more delight in seeing how well he could vex them.'

The 'Odes to Obscurity and Oblivion', in ridicule of 'cool Mason and warm Gray', being mentioned, Johnson said, 'They are Colman's best things.' Upon it being observed that it was believed these Odes were made by Colman and Lloyd jointly; – JOHNSON. 'Nay, Sir, how can two people make an Ode? Perhaps one made one of them, and onê the other.' I observed that two people had made a play, and quoted the anecdote of Beaumont and Fletcher, who were brought under suspicion of treason, because while concerting the plan of a tragedy when sitting together at a tavern, one of them was overheard saying to the other, 'I'll kill the King.' JOHNSON. 'The first of these Odes is the best: but they are both good. They exposed a very bad kind of writing.' BOSWELL. 'Surely, Sir, Mr Mason's *Elfrida* is a fine poem: at least you will allow there are some good passages in it.' JOHNSON. 'There are now and then some good imitations of Milton's bad manner.'

I often wondered at his low estimation of the writings of Gray and Mason. Of Gray's poetry I have, in a former part of this work, expressed my high opinion; and for that of Mr Mason I have ever entertained a warm admiration. His *Elfrida* is exquisite, both in poetical description and moral sentiment; and his *Caractacus* is a noble drama. Nor can I omit paying my tribute of praise to some of his smaller poems which I have read with pleasure, and which no criticism shall persuade me not to like. If I wondered at Johnson's not tasting the works of Mason and Gray, still more have I wondered at their not tasting his works; that they should be insensible to his energy of diction, to his splendour of images, and comprehension of thought. Tastes may differ as to the violin, the flute, the hautboy, in short, all the lesser instruments: but who can be insensible to the powerful impressions of the majestic organ?

His 'Taxation no Tyranny' being mentioned, he said, 'I think I have not been attacked enough for it. Attack is the reaction. I never think I have hit hard, unless it rebounds.' BOSWELL. 'I don't know, Sir, what you would be at. Five or six shots of small arms in every newspaper, and repeated cannonading in pamphlets, might, I think, satisfy you. But, Sir, you'll never make out this match, of which we have talked, with a certain political lady, since you are so severe against her principles.' JOHNSON. 'Nay, Sir, I have the better chance for that. She is like the Amazons of old; she must be courted by the sword. But I have not been severe upon her.' BOSWELL. 'Yes, Sir, you have made her ridiculous.' JOHNSON. 'That was already done, Sir. To endeavour to make *her* ridiculous, is like blacking the chimney.'

I put him in mind that the landlord at Ellon in Scotland said, that he heard he was the greatest man in England – next to Lord Mansfield. 'Aye, Sir (said he), the exception defined the idea. A Scotchman could go no farther:

The force of Nature could no farther go.'

Lady Miller's collection of verses by fashionable people, which were put into her Vase at Batheaston villa, near Bath, in competition for honorary prizes, being mentioned, he held them very cheap: '*Bouts rimés* (said he), is a mere conceit, and an *old* conceit *now*; I wonder how people were persuaded to write in that manner for this lady.' I named a gentleman of his acquaintance, who wrote for the Vase. JOHNSON. 'He was a blockhead for his pains.' BOSWELL. 'The Duchess of Northumberland wrote.' JOHNSON. 'Sir, the Duchess of Northumberland may do what she pleases: nobody will say any thing to a lady of her high rank. But I should be apt to throw ——'s verses in his face.'

I talked of the cheerfulness of Fleet-street, owing to the constant quick succession of people which we perceive passing through it. JOHNSON. 'Why, Sir, Fleet-street has a very animated appearance; but I think the full tide of human existence is at Charing-cross.'

He made the common remark on the unhappiness which men who have led a busy life experience, when they retire in expectation of enjoying themselves at ease, and that they generally languish for want of their habitual occupation, and wish to return to it. He mentioned as strong an instance of this as can well be imagined. 'An eminent tallow-chandler in London, who had acquired a considerable fortune, gave up the trade in favour of his foreman, and went to live at a country-house near town. He soon grew weary and paid frequent visits to his old shop, where he desired they might let him know their *melting-days*, and he would come and assist them: which he accordingly did. Here, Sir, was a man, to whom the most disgusting circumstance in the business to which he had been used, was a relief from idleness.'

On Wednesday, April 5, I dined with him at Messieurs Dillys, with Mr John Scott of Amwell, the Quaker, Mr Langton, Mr Miller (now Sir John), and Dr Thomas Campbell, an Irish clergyman, whom I took the liberty of inviting to Messieurs Dillys' table, having seen him at Mr Thrale's, and been told that he had come to England chiefly with a view to see Dr Johnson, for whom he entertained the highest veneration. He has since published 'A philosophical Survey of the South of Ireland', a very entertaining book, which has, how-ever, one fault; – that it assumes the fictitious character of an Englishman.

We talked of public speaking. – JOHNSON. 'We must not estimate a man's powers by his being able or not able to deliver his sentiments in public. Isaac Hawkins Browne, one of the first wits of this country, got into parliament, and never opened his mouth. For my own part, I think it is more disgraceful never to try to speak, than to try it and fail; as it is more disgraceful not to fight, than to fight and be beaten.' This argument appeared to me fallacious; for if a man has not spoken, it may be said that he would have done very well if he had tried; whereas, if he has tried and failed, there is nothing to be said for him. 'Why then, (I asked), is it thought disgraceful for a man not to fight, and not disgraceful not to speak in public?' JOHNSON. 'Because there may be other reasons for a man's not speaking in public than want of resolution: he may have nothing to say (laughing). Whereas, Sir, you know courage is reckoned the greatest of all virtues; because unless a man has that virtue, he has no security for preserving any other.'

He observed, that 'the statutes against bribery were intended to prevent upstarts with money from getting into parliament'; adding, that 'if he were a gentleman of landed property, he would turn out all his tenants who did not vote for the candidate whom he supported.' LANGTON. 'Would not that, Sir, be checking the freedom of election?' JOHNSON. 'Sir, the law does not mean that the privilege of voting should be independent of old family interest; of the permanent property of the country.'

On Thursday, April 6, I dined with him at Mr Thomas Davies's, with Mr Hicky the painter, and my old acquaintance Mr Moody the player.

Dr Johnson, as usual, spoke contemptuously of Colley Cibber. 'It is wonderful that a man, who for forty years had lived with the great and the witty, should have acquired so ill the talents of conversation: and he had but half to furnish; for one half of what he said was oaths.' He, however, allowed considerable merit to some of his comedies, and said there was no reason to believe that *The Careless Husband* was not written by himself. Davies said, he was the first dramatic writer who introduced genteel ladies upon the stage. Johnson refuted this observation by instancing several such characters in comedies before his time. DAVIES. (trying to defend himself from a charge of ignorance), 'I mean genteel moral characters.' 'I think (said Hicky), gentility and morality are inseparable.' BOSWELL. 'By no means, Sir. The genteelest characters are often the most immoral. Does not Lord Chesterfield give precepts for uniting wickedness and the graces? A man indeed, is not genteel when he gets drunk; but most vices may be committed very genteely: a man may debauch his friend's wife genteely: he may cheat at cards genteely.' HICKY. 'I do not think *that* is genteel.' BOSWELL. 'Sir, it may not be like a gentleman, but it may be genteel.' JOHNSON. 'You are meaning two different things. One means exterior grace; the other honour. It is certain, that a man may be very immoral with exterior grace. Lovelace, in *Clarissa*, is a very genteel and a very wicked character. Tom Hervey, who died t'other day, though a vicious man, was one of the genteelest men that ever lived.' Tom Davies instanced Charles the Second. JOHNSON. (taking fire at any attack upon this Prince, for whom he had an extraordinary partiality), 'Charles the Second was licentious in his practice; but he always had a reverence for what was good. Charles the Second knew his people, and rewarded merit. The Church was at no time better filled than in his reign. He was the best King we have had from his time till the reign of his present Majesty, except James the Second, who was a very good King, but unhappily believed that it was necessary for the salvation of his subjects that they should be Roman Catholics. *He* had the merit of endeavouring to do what he thought was for the salvation of the souls of his subjects, till he lost a great empire. We, who thought that we should not be saved if we were Roman Catholics, had the merit of maintaining our religion, at the expense of submitting ourselves to the government of King William (for it could not be done otherwise), – to the government of one of the most worthless scoundrels that ever existed. No; Charles the Second was not such a man as —— (naming another King). He did not destroy his father's will. He took money, indeed, from France: but he did not betray those over whom he ruled: he did not let the French fleet pass ours. George the First knew nothing, and desired to know nothing; did nothing, and desired to do nothing: and the only good thing that is told of him is, that he wished to restore the crown to its hereditary successor.' He roared with prodigious violence against George the Second. When he ceased, Moody interjected in an Irish tone, and with a comic look, 'Ah! poor George the Second.'

I mentioned that Dr Thomas Campbell had come from Ireland to London, principally to see Dr Johnson. He seemed angry at this observation. Davies. 'Why, you know, Sir, there came a man from Spain to see Livy;[1] and Corelli came to England to see Purcell, and, when he heard he was dead, went directly back again to Italy.' Johnson. 'I should not have wished to be dead to disappoint Campbell, had he been so foolish as you represent him; but I should have wished to have been a hundred miles off.' This was apparently perverse; and I do believe it was not his real way of thinking: he could not but like a man who came so far to see him. He laughed with some complacency, when I told him Campbell's odd expression to me concerning him: 'That having seen such a man, was a thing to talk of a century hence'; as if he could live so long.

We got into an argument whether the Judges who went to India might with propriety engage in trade. Johnson warmly maintained that they might. 'For why (he urged) should not Judges get riches, as well as those who deserve them less?' I said, they should have sufficient salaries, and have nothing to take off their attention from the affairs of the public. Johnson. 'No Judge, Sir, can give his whole attention to his office; and it is very proper that he should employ what time he has to himself, for his own advantage, in the most profitable manner.' 'Then, Sir (said Davies, who enlivened the dispute by making it somewhat dramatic), he may become an insurer; and when he is going to the bench, he may be stopped – "Your Lordship cannot go yet: here is a bunch of invoices: several ships are about to sail." ' Johnson. 'Sir, you may as well say a Judge should not have a house; for they may come and tell him, "Your Lordship's house is on fire"; and so, instead of minding the business of his Court, he is to be occupied in getting the engine with the greatest speed. There is no end of this. Every Judge who has land, trades to a certain extent in corn or in cattle; and in the land itself, undoubtedly. His steward acts for him, and so do clerks for a great merchant. A Judge may be a farmer; but he is not to geld his own pigs. A Judge may play a little at cards for his amusement; but he is not to play at marbles, or at chuck-farthing in the Piazza. No, Sir; there is no profession to which a man gives a very great proportion of his time. It is wonderful when a calculation is made, how little the mind is actually employed in the discharge of any profession. No man would be a Judge, upon the condition of being obliged to be totally a Judge. The best employed lawyer has his mind at work but for a small proportion of his time: a great deal of his occupation is merely mechanical. – I once wrote for a magazine: I made a calculation, that if I should write but a page a day, at the same rate, I should, in ten years, write nine volumes in folio, of an ordinary size and print.' Boswell. 'Such as Carte's History?' Johnson. 'Yes, Sir. When a man writes from his own

1 Plin. Epist. Lib. ii. Ep. 3.

2 Johnson certainly did, who had a mind stored with knowledge, and teeming with imagery; but the observation is not applicable to writers in general.

mind, he writes very rapidly.[2] The greatest part of a writer's time is spent in reading, in order to write: a man will turn over half a library to make one book.'

I argued warmly against the Judges trading, and mentioned Hale as an instance of a perfect Judge, who devoted himself entirely to his office. JOHNSON. 'Hale, Sir, attended to other things beside law: he left a great estate.' BOSWELL. 'That was, because what he got, accumulated without any exertion and anxiety on his part.'

While the dispute went on, Moody once tried to say something upon our side. Tom Davies clapped him on the back, to encourage him. Beauclerk, to whom I mentioned this circumstance, said, that 'he could not conceive a more humiliating situation than to be clapped on the back by Tom Davies.'

We spoke of Rolt, to whose Dictionary of Commerce, Dr Johnson wrote the Preface. JOHNSON. 'Old Gardner the bookseller employed Rolt and Smart to write a monthly miscellany, called *The Visitor*. There was a formal written contract, which Allen the printer saw. Gardner thought as you do of the Judge. They were bound to write nothing else. They were to have, I think, a third of the profits of this sixpenny pamphlet; and the contract was for ninety-nine years.[a] I wish I had thought of giving this to Thurlow, in the cause about Literary Property. What an excellent instance would it have been of the oppression of booksellers towards poor authors!' (smiling). Davies, zealous for the honour of *the Trade*, said, Gardner was not properly a bookseller. JOHNSON. 'Nay, Sir; he certainly was a bookseller. He had served his time regularly, was a member of the Stationers' company, kept a shop in the face of mankind, purchased copyright, and was a *bibliopole*, Sir, in every sense. I wrote for some months in *The Visitor*, for poor Smart, while he was mad, not then knowing the terms on which he was engaged to write, and thinking I was doing him good. I hoped his wits would soon return to him. Mine returned to me, and I wrote in *The Visitor* no longer.'

Friday, April 7, I dined with him at a tavern, with a numerous company. JOHNSON. 'I have been reading Twiss's *Travels in Spain*, which are just come out. They are as good as the first book of travels that you will take up. They are as good as those of Keysler or Blainville; nay, as Addison's, if you except the learning. They are not so good as Brydone's, but they are better than Pococke's. I have not, indeed, cut the leaves yet; but I have read in them where the pages are open, and I do not suppose that what is in the pages which are closed is worse than what is in the open pages. – It would seem (he added), that Addison had not acquired much Italian learning, for we do not find it introduced into his writings. The only instance that I recollect, is his quoting "*Stavo bene. Per star meglio, sto qui.*" '

I mentioned Addison's having borrowed many of his classical remarks from Leandro Alberti. Mr Beauclerk said, 'It was alleged that he had borrowed also

---

[a] *Second Edition*: There has probably been some mistake as to the terms of this supposed extraordinary contract, the recital of which from hearsay afforded Johnson so much play for his sportive acuteness. Or if it was worded as he supposed, it is so strange that I should conclude it was a joke. Mr Gardner, I am assured, was a worthy and liberal man.

from another Italian author.' JOHNSON. 'Why, Sir, all who go to look for what the Classics have said of Italy must find the same passages; and I should think it would be one of the first things the Italians would do on the revival of learning, to collect all that the Roman authors had said of their country.'

Ossian being mentioned; – JOHNSON. 'Supposing the Irish and Erse languages to be the same, which I do not believe, yet as there is no reason to suppose that the inhabitants of the Highlands and Hebrides ever wrote their native language, it is not to be credited that a long poem was preserved among them. If we had no evidence of the art of writing being practised in one of the counties of England, we should not believe that a long poem was preserved *there*, though in the neighbouring counties, where the same language was spoken, the inhabitants could write.' BEAUCLERK. 'The ballad of Lullabalero was once in the mouths of all the people of this country, and is said to have had a great effect in bringing about the Revolution. Yet I question whether any body can repeat it now; which shows how improbable it is that much poetry should be preserved by tradition.'

One of the company suggested an internal objection to the antiquity of the poetry said to be Ossian's, that we do not find the wolf in it, which must have been the case had it been of that age.

The mention of the wolf had led Johnson to think of other wild beasts; and while Sir Joshua Reynolds and Mr Langton were carrying on a dialogue about something which engaged them earnestly, he, in the midst of it, broke out, 'Pennant tells of Bears — ' [what he added, I have forgotten]. They went on, which he being dull of hearing, did not perceive, or, if he did, was not willing to break off his talk; so he continued to vociferate his remarks, and *Bear* ('like a word in a catch', as Beauclerk said), was repeatedly heard at intervals, which coming from him who, by those who did not know him, had been so often assimilated to that ferocious animal, while we who were sitting around could hardly stifle laughter, produced a very ludicrous effect. Silence having ensued, he proceeded: 'We are told, that the black bear is innocent; but I should not like to trust myself with him.' Mr Gibbon muttered, in a low tone of voice, 'I should not like to trust myself with *you*.' This piece of sarcastic pleasantry was a prudent resolution, if applied to a competition of abilities.

Patriotism having become one of our topics, Johnson suddenly uttered, in a strong determined tone, an apophthegm, at which many will start: 'Patriotism is the last refuge of a scoundrel.' But let it be considered, that he did not mean a real and generous love of our country, but that pretended patriotism which so many, in all ages and countries, have made a cloak for self-interest. I maintained, that certainly all patriots were not scoundrels. Being urged (not by Johnson), to name one exception, I mentioned an eminent person, whom we all greatly admired. JOHNSON. 'Sir, I do not say that he is not honest; but we have no reason to conclude from his political conduct that he is honest. Were he to accept of a place from this ministry, he would lose that character of firmness which he has, and might be turned out of his place in a year. This ministry is neither stable, nor grateful to their friends, as Sir Robert Walpole was: so that he may think it more for his interest to take his chance of his party coming in.'

Mrs Pritchard being mentioned, he said, 'Her playing was quite mechanical. It is wonderful how little mind she had. Sir, she had never read the tragedy of *Macbeth* all through. She no more thought of the play out of which her part was taken, than a shoemaker thinks of the skin, out of which the piece of leather, of which he is making a pair of shoes, is cut.'

On Saturday, May 8,[a] I dined with him at Mr Thrale's, where we met the Irish Dr Campbell. Johnson had supped the night before at Mrs Abington's, with some fashionable people whom he named; and he seemed much pleased with having made one in so elegant a circle.[b]

Mrs Thrale, who frequently practised a coarse mode of flattery, by repeating his *bon mots* in his hearing, told us that he had said, a certain celebrated actor was just fit to stand at the door of an auction-room, with a long pole, and cry, 'Pray, gentlemen, walk in'; and that a certain author, upon hearing this, had said, that another still more celebrated actor was fit for nothing better than that, and would pick your pocket after you came out. JOHNSON. 'Nay, my dear lady, there is no wit in what our friend added; there is only abuse. You may as well say of any man that he will pick a pocket. Besides, the man who is stationed at the door does not pick people's pockets: that is done within, by the auctioneer.'

Mrs Thrale told us, that Tom Davies repeated, in a very bald manner, the story of Dr Johnson's first repartee to me, which I have related exactly.[1] He made me say, 'I *was born* in Scotland,' instead of 'I *come from* Scotland'; so that Johnson's saying, 'That, Sir, is what a great many of your countrymen cannot help,' had no point, or even meaning: and that upon this being mentioned to Mr Fitzherbert, he observed, 'It is not every man that can *carry* a *bon mot*.'

On Monday, April 10, I dined with him at General Oglethorpe's, with Mr Langton and the Irish Dr Campbell, whom the General had obligingly given me leave to bring with me. This learned gentleman was thus gratified with a very high intellectual feast, by not only being in company with Dr Johnson, but with General Oglethorpe, who had been so long a celebrated name both at home and abroad.[2]

---

[a] For 'May' read 'April'.

[b] After 'circle' read: 'Nor did he omit to pique his mistress a little with jealousy of her housewifery; for he said (with a smile), 'Mrs Abington's jelly, my dear lady, was better than yours.'

1 p. 200.

2 Let me here be allowed to pay my tribute of most sincere gratitude to the memory of that excellent person, my intimacy with whom was the more valuable to me, because my first acquaintance with him was unexpected and unsolicited. Soon after the publication of my *Account of Corsica*, he did me the honour to call on me, and approaching me with a frank courteous air, said, 'My name, Sir, is Oglethorpe, and I wish to be acquainted with you.' I was not a little flattered to be thus addressed by an eminent man, of whom I had read in Pope, from my early years,

Or, driven by strong benevolence of soul,
Will fly, like OGLETHORPE, from pole to pole.

I must, again and again, intreat of my readers not to suppose that my imperfect record of conversation contains the whole of what was said by Johnson, or other eminent persons who lived with him. What I have preserved, however, has the value of the most perfect authenticity.

He this day enlarged upon Pope's melancholy remark,

'Man never *is*, but always *to be* blest.'

He asserted, that *the present* was never a happy state to any human being; but that, as every part of life, of which we are conscious, was at some point of time a period yet to come, in which felicity was expected, there was some happiness produced by hope. Being pressed upon this subject, and asked if he really was of opinion that though, in general, happiness was very rare in human life, a man was not sometimes happy in the moment that was present, he answered, 'Never, but when he is drunk.'

He urged General Oglethorpe to give the world his Life. He said, 'I know no man whose Life would be more interesting. If I were furnished with materials, I should be very glad to write it.'[1]

Mr Scott of Amwell's Elegies were lying in the room. Dr Johnson observed, 'They are very well; but such as twenty people might write.' Upon this I took occasion to controvert Horace's maxim,

mediocribus esse poetis
Non Di, non homines, non concessere columnae.

for here (I observed), was a very middle-rate poet, who pleased many readers, and therefore poetry of a middle sort was entitled to some esteem; nor could I see why poetry should not, like every thing else, have different gradations of excellence, and consequently of value. Johnson repeated the common remark, that 'as there is no necessity for our having poetry at all, it being merely a luxury, an instrument of pleasure, it can have no value, unless when exquisite in its kind.' I declared myself not satisfied. 'Why then, Sir, (said he), Horace and you must settle it.' He was not much in the humour of talking.

No more of his conversation for some days appears in my journal, except that when a gentleman told him he had bought a suit of laces for his lady, he said, 'Well, Sir, you have done a good thing, and a wise thing.' 'I have done a

---

I was fortunate enough to be found worthy of his good opinion, insomuch, that I not only was invited to make one in the many respectable companies whom he entertained at his table, but had a cover at his hospitable board every day when I happened to be disengaged; and in his society I never failed to enjoy learned and animated conversation, seasoned with genuine sentiments of virtue and religion.

1 The General seemed unwilling to enter upon it at this time; but upon a subsequent occasion he communicated to me a number of particulars, which I have committed to writing; but I was not sufficiently diligent in obtaining more from him, not apprehending that his friends were so soon to lose him; for notwithstanding his great age, he was very healthy and vigorous, and was at last carried off by a violent fever, which is often fatal at any period of life.

good thing (said the gentleman), but I do not know that I have done a wise thing.' JOHNSON. 'Yes, Sir; no money is better spent than what is laid out for domestic satisfaction. A man is pleased that his wife is drest as well as other people; and a wife is pleased that she is drest.'

On Friday, April 14, being Good-Friday, I repaired to him in the morning, according to my usual custom on this day, and breakfasted with him. I observed that he fasted so very strictly, that he did not even taste bread, and took no milk with his tea, I suppose because it is a kind of animal food.

He entered upon the state of the nation, and thus discoursed: 'Sir, the great misfortune now is, that government has too little power. All that it has to bestow, must of necessity be given to support itself; so that it cannot reward merit. No man, for instance, can now be made a Bishop for his learning and piety;[1] his only chance for promotion is his being connected with somebody who has parliamentary interest. Our several ministries in this reign have outbid each other in concessions to the people. Lord Bute, though a very honourable man, – a man who meant well, – a man who had his blood full of prerogative, – was a theoretical statesman, – a book-minister, – and thought this country could be governed by the influence of the Crown alone. Then, Sir, he gave up a great deal. He advised the King to agree that the Judges should hold their places for life, instead of losing them at the accession of a new King. Lord Bute, I suppose, thought to make the King popular by this concession; but the people never minded it; and it was a most impolitic measure. There is no reason why a Judge should hold his office for life, more than any other person in public trust. A Judge may be partial otherwise than to the Crown: we have seen Judges partial to the populace. A Judge may become corrupt, and yet there may not be legal evidence against him. A Judge may become froward from age. A Judge may grow unfit for his office in many ways. It was desirable that there should be a possibility of being delivered from him by a new King. That is now gone by an act of parliament *ex gratia* of the Crown. Lord Bute advised the King to give up a very large sum of money,[2] for which nobody thanked him. It was of consequence to the King, but nothing to the public, among whom it was divided. When I say Lord Bute advised, I mean, that such acts were done when he was minister, and we are to suppose that he advised

---

1 From this too just observation there are some eminent exceptions.

2 The money arising from the property of the prizes taken before the declaration of war, which were given to his Majesty by the peace of Paris, and amounted to upwards of £700,000, and from the lands in the ceded islands, which were estimated at £200,000 more. Surely, there was a noble munificence in this gift from a Monarch to his people. And let it be remembered, that during the Earl of Bute's administration, the King was graciously pleased to give up the hereditary revenues of the Crown, and to accept, instead of them, of the limited sum of £800,000 a year; upon which Blackstone observes, that 'The hereditary revenues, being put under the same management as the other branches of the public patrimony, will produce more, and be better collected than heretofore; and the public is a gainer of upwards of £100,000 *per annum*, by this disinterested bounty of his Majesty.' Book I. Ch. 8. p. 330.

them. – Lord Bute showed an undue partiality to Scotchmen. He turned out Dr Nichols, a very eminent man, from being physician to the King, to make room for one of his countrymen, a man very low in his profession. He had —— and —— to go on errands for him. He had occasion for people to go on errands for him; but he should not have had Scotchmen; and, certainly, he should not have suffered them to have access to him before the first people in England.'

I told him, that the admission of one of them before the first people in England, which had given the greatest offence, was no more than what happens at every minister's levee, where those who attend are admitted in the order that they have come, which is better than admitting them according to their rank; for if that were to be the rule, a man who has waited all the morning might have the mortification to see a peer, newly come, go in before him, and keep him waiting still. JOHNSON. 'True, Sir; but —— should not have come to the levee, to be in the way of people of consequence. He saw Lord Bute at all times; and could have said what he had to say at any time, as well as at the levee. There is now no Prime Minister: there is only an agent for government in the House of Commons. We are governed by the Cabinet; but there is no one head there, as in Sir Robert Walpole's time.' BOSWELL. 'What then, Sir, is the use of Parliament?' JOHNSON. 'Why, Sir, Parliament is a larger council to the King; and the advantage of such a council is, having a great number of men of property concerned in the legislature, who, for their own interests, will not consent to bad laws. And you must have observed, Sir, that administration is feeble and timid, and cannot act with that authority and resolution which is necessary. Were I in power, I would turn out every man who dared to oppose me. Government has the distribution of offices, that it may be enabled to maintain its authority.'

'Lord Bute (he added) took down too fast, without building up something new.' BOSWELL. 'Because, Sir, he found a rotten building. The political coach was drawn by a set of bad horses: it was necessary to change them.' JOHNSON. 'But he should have changed them one by one.'

I told him that I had been informed by Mr Orme, that many parts of the East Indies were better mapped than the Highlands of Scotland. JOHNSON. 'That a country may be mapped, it must be travelled over.' 'Nay (said I, meaning to laugh with him at one of his prejudices), can't you say, it is not *worth* mapping?'

As we walked to St Clement's church, and saw several shops open upon this most solemn fast-day of the Christian world, I remarked, that one disadvantage arising from the immensity of London, was, that nobody was heeded by his neighbour; there was no fear of censure for not observing Good-Friday, as it ought to be kept, and as it is kept in country towns. He said, it was, upon the whole, very well observed even in London. He, however, owned that London was too large; but added, 'It is nonsense to say the head is too big for the body. It would be as much too big, though the body were ever so large: that is to say, though the country were ever so extensive. It has no similarity to a head connected with a body.'

Dr Wetherell, Master of University College, Oxford, accompanied us home from church; and after he was gone, there came two other gentlemen, one of whom uttered the commonplace complaints, that by the increase of taxes, labour would be dear, other nations would undersell us, and our commerce would be ruined. JOHNSON (smiling). 'Never fear, Sir. Our commerce is in a very good state; and suppose we had no commerce at all, we could live very well on the produce of our own country.' I cannot omit to mention, that I never knew any man who was less disposed to be querulous than Johnson. Whether the subject was his own situation, or the state of the public, or the state of human nature in general, though he saw the evils, his mind was turned to resolution, and never to whining or complaint.

We went again to St Clement's in the afternoon. He had found fault with the preacher in the morning for not choosing a text adapted to the day. The preacher in the afternoon had chosen one extremely proper: 'It is finished.'

After the evening service, he said, 'Come, you shall go home with me, and sit just an hour.' But he was better than his word; for after we had drunk tea with Mrs Williams, he asked me to go up to his study with him, where we sat a long while together in a serene undisturbed frame of mind, sometimes in silence, and sometimes conversing, as we felt ourselves inclined, or more properly speaking, as he was inclined; for during all the course of my long intimacy with him, my respectful attention never abated, and my wish to hear him was such, that I constantly watched every dawning of communication from that great and illuminated mind.

He observed, 'All knowledge is of itself of some value. There is nothing so minute or inconsiderable, that I would not rather know it than not. In the same manner, all power, of whatever sort, is of itself desirable. A man would not submit to learn to hem a ruffle, of his wife, or his wife's maid; but if a mere wish could attain it, he would rather wish to be able to hem a ruffle.'

He again advised me to keep a journal fully and minutely, but not to mention such trifles as, that meat was too much or too little done, or that the weather was fair or rainy. He had, till very near his death, a contempt for the notion that the weather affects the human frame.

I told him that our friend Goldsmith had said to me, that he had come too late into the world, for that Pope and other poets had taken up the places in the Temple of Fame; so that as but a few at any period can possess poetical reputation, a man of genius can now hardly acquire it. JOHNSON. 'That is one of the most sensible things I have ever heard of Goldsmith. It is difficult to get literary fame, and it is every day growing more difficult. Ah, Sir, that should make a man think of securing happiness in another world, which all who try sincerely for it may attain. In comparison of that, how little are all other things! The belief of immortality is impressed upon all men, and all men act under an impression of it, however they may talk, and though, perhaps, they may be scarcely sensible of it.' I said it appeared to me that some people had not the least notion of immortality; and I mentioned a distinguished gentleman of our acquaintance. JOHNSON. 'Sir, if it were not for the notion of immortality, he would cut a throat to fill his pockets.' When I quoted this to Beauclerk, who knew much more of the gentleman than we did, he said, in his acid manner, 'He would cut a throat to fill his pockets, if it were not for fear of being hanged.'

Dr Johnson proceeded: 'Sir, there is a great cry about infidelity; but there are, in reality, very few infidels. I have heard a person, originally a Quaker, but now, I am afraid, a Deist, say, that he did not believe there were, in all England, above two hundred infidels.'

He was pleased to say, 'If you come to settle here, we will have one day in the week on which we will meet by ourselves. That is the happiest conversation where there is no competition, no vanity, but a calm quiet interchange of sentiments.' In his private register this evening is thus marked, 'Boswell sat with me till night; we had some serious talk.'[1] It also appears from the same record, that after I left him he was occupied in religious duties, in 'giving Francis, his servant, some directions for preparation to communicate; in reviewing his life, and resolving on better conduct.' The humility and piety which he discovers on such occasions, is truly edifying. No saint, however, in the course of his religious warfare, was more sensible of the unhappy failure of pious resolves, than Johnson. He said one day, talking to an acquaintance on the subject, 'Sir, Hell is paved with good intentions.'

On Sunday, April 16, being Easter-day, after having attended the solemn service at St Paul's, I dined with Dr Johnson and Mrs Williams. I maintained that Horace was wrong in placing happiness in *Nil admirari*; for that I thought admiration one of the most agreeable of all our feelings; and I regretted that I had lost much of my disposition to admire, which people generally do as they advance in life. JOHNSON. 'Sir, as a man advances in life, he gets what is better than admiration, – judgement, to estimate things at their true value.' I still insisted that admiration was more pleasing than judgement, as love is more pleasing than friendship. The feeling of friendship is like that of being comfortably filled with roast-beef; love, like being enlivened with champagne. JOHNSON. 'No, Sir, admiration and love are like being intoxicated with champagne; judgement and friendship like being enlivened. Waller has hit upon the same thought with you:[2] but I don't believe you have borrowed from Waller. I wish you would enable yourself to borrow more.'[a]

---

1 *Prayers and Meditations*, p. 138.

2   Amoret's as sweet and good
        As the most delicious food;
        Which but tasted does impart
        Life and gladness to the heart.

        Sacharissa's beauty's wine,
        Which to madness does incline;
        Such a liquor as no brain
        That is mortal can sustain.

[a] After this passage, read:

To BENNET LANGTON, ESQ.

DEAR SIR – I have enquired more minutely about the medicine for the rheumatism, which I am sorry to hear that you still want. The receipt is this:

Take equal quantities of flour of sulphur, and *flour* of mustard-seed, make them an electuary with honey or treacle; and take a bolus as big as a nutmeg several times

He then took occasion to enlarge on the advantages of reading, and combated the idle superficial notion, that knowledge enough may be acquired in conversation. 'The foundation (said he) must be laid by reading. General principles must be had from books, which, however, must be brought to the test of real life. In conversation you never get a system. What is said upon a subject is to be gathered from a hundred people. The parts of a truth, which a man gets thus, are at such a distance from each other, that he never attains to a full view.'

On Tuesday, April 18, he and I were engaged to go with Sir Joshua Reynolds to dine with Mr Cambridge, at his beautiful villa on the banks of the Thames, near Twickenham. Dr Johnson's tardiness was such, that Sir Joshua, who had an appointment at Richmond early in the day, was obliged to go by himself on horseback, leaving his coach to Johnson and me. Johnson was in such good spirits, that every thing seemed to please him as we drove along.

Our conversation turned on a variety of subjects. He thought portrait-painting an improper employment for a woman. 'Public practice of any art (he observed), and staring in men's faces, is very indelicate in a female.' I happened to start a question of propriety, whether when a man knows that some of his intimate friends are invited to the house of another friend, with whom they are all equally intimate, he may join them without an invitation. JOHNSON. 'No, Sir; he is not to go when he is not invited. They may be invited on purpose to abuse him' (smiling).

As a curious instance how little a man knows, or wishes to know, his own character in the world, or, rather, as a convincing proof that Johnson's roughness was only external, and did not proceed from his heart, I insert the following dialogue. JOHNSON. 'It is wonderful, Sir, how rare a quality good humour is in life. We meet with very few good humoured men.' I mentioned four of our friends, none of whom he would allow to be good humoured. One was *acid*, another was *muddy*, and to the others he had objections which have escaped me. Then, shaking his head and stretching himself at his ease in the coach, and smiling with much complacency, he turned to me and said, 'I look upon *myself* as a good humoured fellow.' The epithet *fellow*, applied to the great Lexicographer, the stately Moralist, the masterly Critic, as if he had

---

a day, as you can bear it: drinking after it a quarter of a pint of the infusion of the root of Lovage.

Lovage, in Ray's *Nomenclature*, is Levisticum: perhaps the Botanists may know the Latin name.

Of this medicine I pretend not to judge. There is all the appearance of its efficacy, which a single instance can afford: the patient was very old, the pain very violent, and the relief, I think, speedy and lasting.

My opinion of alterative medicine is not high, but *quid tentasse nocebit*? If it does harm, or does no good, it may be omitted; but that it may do good, you have, I hope, reason to think is desired by, Sir, your most affectionate,

Humble servant,

SAM. JOHNSON.

April 17, 1775.

been *Sam* Johnson, a mere pleasant companion, was highly diverting; and this light notion of himself struck me with wonder. I answered, also smiling, 'No, no, Sir; that will not do. You are good natured, but not good humoured: you are irascible. You have not patience with folly and absurdity. I believe you would pardon them, if there were time to deprecate your vengeance; but punishment follows so quick after sentence, that they cannot escape.'

I had brought with me a great bundle of Scotch magazines and newspapers, in which his *Journey to the Western Islands* was attacked in every mode; and I read a great part of them to him, knowing they would afford him entertainment. I wish the writers of them had been present: they would have been sufficiently vexed. One ludicrous imitation of his style, by Mr Maclaurin, now one of the Scotch Judges, with the title of Lord Dreghorn, was distinguished by him from the rude mass. 'This (said he) is the best. But I could caricature my own style much better myself.' He defended his remark upon the general insufficiency of education in Scotland; and confirmed to me the authenticity of his witty saying on the learning of the Scotch; – 'Their learning is like bread in a besieged town: every man gets a little, but no man gets a full meal.' 'There is (said he) in Scotland a diffusion of learning, a certain portion of it widely and thinly spread. A merchant there has as much learning as one of their clergy.'

He talked of Isaac Walton's Lives, which was one of his most favourite books. Dr Donne's Life, he said, was the most perfect of them. He observed, that 'it was wonderful that Walton, who was in a very low situation in life, should have been familiarly received by so many great men, and that at a time when the ranks of society were kept more separate than they are now.' He supposed that Walton had then given up his business as a linen-draper and sempster, and was only an author; and added, 'that he was a great panegyrist.' BOSWELL. 'No quality will get a man more friends than a disposition to admire the qualities of others. I do not mean flattery, but a sincere admiration.' JOHNSON. 'Nay, Sir, flattery pleases very generally. In the first place, the flatterer may think what he says to be true; but, in the second place, whether he thinks so or not, he certainly thinks those whom he flatters of consequence enough to be flattered.'

No sooner had we made our bow to Mr Cambridge, in his library, than Johnson ran eagerly to one side of the room, intent on poring over the backs of the books. Sir Joshua observed (aside), 'He runs to the books, as I do to the pictures: but I have the advantage. I can see much more of the pictures than he can of the books.' Mr Cambridge, upon this, politely said, 'Dr Johnson, I am going, with your pardon, to accuse myself, for I have the same custom which I perceive you have. But it seems odd that one should have such a desire to look at the backs of books.' Johnson, ever ready for contest, instantly started from his reverie, wheeled about, and answered, 'Sir, the reason is very plain. Knowledge is of two kinds. We know a subject ourselves, or we know where we can find information upon it. When we inquire into any subject, the first thing we have to do is to know what books have treated of it. This leads us to look at catalogues, and at the backs of books in libraries.' Sir Joshua observed to me, the extraordinary promptitude with which Johnson flew upon an argument. 'Yes (said I), he has no formal preparation, no flourishing with his sword; he is through your body in an instant.'

Johnson was here solaced with an elegant entertainment, a very accomplished family, and much good company; among whom was Mr Harris of Salisbury, who paid him many compliments on his *Journey to the Western Islands.*

The common remark as to the utility of reading history being made; – JOHNSON. 'We must consider how very little history there is; I mean real authentic history. That certain Kings reigned, and certain battles were fought, we can depend upon as true; but all the colouring, all the philosophy, of history is conjecture.' BOSWELL. 'Then, Sir, you would reduce all history to no better than an almanack, a mere chronological series of remarkable events.' Mr. Gibbon, who must at that time have been employed upon his history, of which he published the first volume in the following year, was present, but did not step forth in defence of that species of writing. He probably did not like to *trust* himself with Johnson.[1]

Johnson observed, that the force of our early habits was so great, that though reason approved, nay, though our senses relished a different course, almost every man returned to them. I do not believe there is any observation upon human nature better founded than this; and, in many cases, it is a very painful truth; for where early habits have been mean and wretched, the joy and elevation resulting from better modes of life, must be damped by the gloomy consciousness of being under an almost inevitable doom to sink back into a situation which we recollect with disgust. It surely may be prevented, by constant attention and unremitting exertion to establish contrary habits of superior efficacy.

The Beggar's Opera, and the common question, whether it was pernicious in its effects, having been introduced; – JOHNSON. 'As to this matter, which has been very much contested, I myself am of opinion, that more influence has been ascribed to *The Beggar's Opera,* than it in reality ever had; for I do not believe that any man was ever made a rogue by being present at its representation. At the same time I do not deny that it may have some influence, by making the character of a rogue familiar, and in some degree pleasing.[2] Then collecting himself, as it were, to give a heavy stroke: 'There is in it such a *labefactation* of all principles, as may be injurious to morality.'

1 See p. 434.

2 A very eminent physician, whose discernment is as acute and penetrating in judging of the human character as it is in his own profession, remarked once at a club where I was, that a lively young man, fond of pleasure and without money, would hardly resist a solicitation from his mistress to go upon the highway, immediately after being present at the representation of *The Beggar's Opera.* I have been told of an ingenious observation by Mr Gibbon, that '*The Beggar's Opera* may, perhaps, have sometimes increased the number of highwaymen; but that it has had a beneficial effect in refining that class of men, making them less ferocious, more polite, in short, more like gentlemen.' Upon this Mr Courtenay said, that 'Gay was the Orpheus of highwaymen.'

While he pronounced this response, we sat in a comical sort of restraint, smothering a laugh, which we were afraid might burst out. In his Life of Gay, he has been still more decisive as to the inefficiency of *The Beggar's Opera*, in corrupting society. But I have ever thought somewhat differently; for, indeed, not only are the gaiety and heroism of a highwayman very captivating to a youthful imagination, but the arguments for adventurous depredation are so plausible, the allusions so lively, and the contrasts with the ordinary and more painful modes of acquiring property are so artfully displayed, that it requires a cool and strong judgement to resist so imposing an aggregate: yet, I own, I should be very sorry to have *The Beggar's Opera* suppressed; for there is in it so much of real London life, so much of brilliant wit, and such a variety of airs, which, from early association of ideas, engage, soothe, and enliven the mind, that no performance which the theatre exhibits, delights me more.

The late '*worthy*' Duke of Queensberry, as Thomson, in his *Seasons*, justly characterises him, told me, that when Gay first showed him *The Beggar's Opera*, his Grace's observation was, 'This is a very odd thing, Gay; I am satisfied that it is either a very good thing, or a very bad thing.' It proved the former, beyond the warmest expectations of the author or his friends. Mr Cambridge, however, showed us to-day, that there was good reason enough to doubt concerning its success. He was told by Quin, that during the first night of its appearance it was long in a very dubious state; that there was a disposition to damn it, and that it was saved by the song, 'Oh ponder well, be not severe'.[a] Quin himself had so bad an opinion of it, that he refused the part of Captain Macheath, and gave it to Walker, who acquired great celebrity by his grave yet animated performance of it.

We talked of a young gentleman's marriage with an eminent singer, and his determination that she should no longer sing in public, though his father was very earnest she should, because her talents would be liberally rewarded so as to make her a good fortune. It was questioned whether the young gentleman, who had not a shilling in the world, but was blest with very uncommon talents, was not foolishly delicate, or foolishly proud, and his father truly rational without being mean. Johnson, with all the high spirit of a Roman senator, exclaimed, 'He resolved wisely and nobly to be sure. He is a brave man. Would not a gentleman be disgraced by having his wife singing publicly for hire? No, Sir, there can be no doubt here. I know not if I should not *prepare* myself for a public singer, as readily as let my wife be one.'

Johnson arraigned the modern politics of this country, as entirely devoid of all principle of whatever kind. 'Politics (said he) are now nothing more than means of rising in the world. With this sole view do men engage in politics, and their whole conduct proceeds upon it. How different in that respect is the

---

[a] Add: The audience being much affected by the innocent looks of Polly, when she came to those two lines, which exhibit at once a painful and ridiculous image,

> For on the rope that hangs my Dear,
> Depends poor Polly's life.

state of the nation now from what it was in the time of Charles the First, during the Usurpation, and after the Restoration, in the time of Charles the Second. *Hudibras* affords a strong proof how much hold political principles had then upon the minds of men. There is in *Hudibras* a great deal of bullion, which will always last. But to be sure the brightest strokes of his wit owed their force to the impression of the characters, which was upon men's minds at the time; to their knowing them, at table and in the street; in short, being familiar with them; and above all, to his satire being directed against those whom a little while before they had hated and feared. The nation in general has ever been loyal, has been at all times attached to the monarch, though a few daring rebels have been wonderfully powerful for a time. The murder of Charles the First was undoubtedly not committed with the approbation or consent of the people. Had that been the case, parliament would not have ventured to consign the regicides to their deserved punishment. And we know what exuberance of joy there was when Charles the Second was restored. If Charles the Second had bent all his mind to it, had made it his sole object, he might have been as absolute as Louis the Fourteenth.' A gentleman observed he would have done no harm if he had. JOHNSON. 'Why, Sir, absolute princes seldom do any harm. But they who are governed by them are governed by chance. There is no security for good government.' CAMBRIDGE. 'There have been many sad victims to absolute power.' JOHNSON. 'So, Sir, have there been to popular factions.' BOSWELL. 'The question is, which is worst, one wild beast or many?'

Johnson praised *The Spectator*, particularly the character of Sir Roger de Coverley. He said, 'Sir Roger did not die a violent death, as had been generally fancied. He was not killed; he died only because others were to die, and because his death afforded an opportunity to Addison for some very fine writing. We have the example of Cervantes making Don Quixote die. – I never could see why Sir Roger is represented as a little cracked. It appears to me that the story of the widow was intended to have something super-induced upon it: but the superstructure did not come.'

Somebody found fault with writing verses in a dead language, maintaining that they were merely arrangements of so many words, and laughed at the Universities of Oxford and Cambridge, for sending forth collections of them not only in Greek and Latin, but even in Syriac, Arabic, and other more unknown tongues. JOHNSON. 'I would have as many of these as possible; I would have verses in every language that there are the means of acquiring. Nobody imagines that an University is to have at once two hundred poets; but it should be able to show two hundred scholars. Peiresc's death was lamented, I think, in forty languages. And I would have at every coronation, and every death of a King, every *Gaudium*, and every *Luctus*, University verses in as many languages as can be acquired. I would have the world to be thus told, 'Here is a school where every thing may be learnt.'

Having set out next day on a visit to the Earl of Pembroke, at Wilton, and to my friend, Mr Temple, at Mamhead, in Devonshire, and not having returned to town till the second of May, I did not see Dr Johnson for a considerable time, and during the remaining part of my stay in London, kept very imperfect notes of his conversation, which had I according to my usual custom written out at large soon after the time, much might have been preserved, which is now irretrievably lost. I can now only record some particular scenes, and a few fragments of his *memorabilia*. But to make some amends for my relaxation of diligence in one respect, I have to present my readers with arguments upon two law cases, with which he favoured me.

On Saturday, the sixth of May, we dined by ourselves at the Mitre, and he dictated to me what follows, to obviate the complaint already mentioned,[1] which had been made in the form of an action in the Court of Session, by Dr Memis, of Aberdeen, that in the same translation of a charter in which *physicians* were mentioned, he was called *Doctor of Medicine*.

'There are but two reasons for which a physician can decline the title of *Doctor of Medicine*, because he supposes himself disgraced by the doctorship, or supposes the doctorship disgraced by himself. To be disgraced by a title which he shares in common with every illustrious name of his profession, with Boerhaave, with Arbuthnot, and with Cullen, can surely diminish no man's reputation. It is, I suppose, to the doctorate, from which he shrinks, that he owes his right of practising physic. A Doctor of Medicine is a physician under the protection of the laws, and by the stamp of authority. The physician who is not a doctor, usurps a profession, and is authorised only by himself to decide upon health and sickness, and life and death. That this gentleman is a Doctor, his diploma makes evident; a diploma not obtruded upon him, but obtained by solicitation, and for which fees were paid. With what countenance any man can refuse the title which he has either begged or bought, is not easily discovered.

'All verbal injury must comprise in it either some false position, or some unnecessary declaration of defamatory truth. That in calling him Doctor, a false appellation was given him, he himself will not pretend, who at the same time that he complains of the title, would be offended if we supposed him to be not a Doctor. If the title of doctor be a defamatory truth, it is time to dissolve our colleges, for why should the public give salaries to men whose approbation is reproach? It may likewise deserve the notice of the public to consider what help can be given to the professors of physic, who all share with this unhappy gentleman the ignominious appellation, and of whom the very boys in the street are not afraid to say, *There goes the Doctor*.

'What is implied by the term Doctor is well known. It distinguishes him to whom it is granted, as a man who has attained such knowledge of his profession as qualifies him to instruct others. A Doctor of Laws is a man who can form lawyers by his precepts. A Doctor of Medicine is a man who can teach the art of curing diseases. There is an old axiom which no man has yet thought fit to deny, *Nil dat quod non habet*. Upon this principle to be a Doctor implies skill, for *nemo docet quod non didicit*. In England, whoever practises physic, not being a Doctor, must practise by a licence: but the doctorate conveys a licence in itself.

'By what accident it happened that he and the other physicians were mentioned in different terms, where the terms themselves were equivalent, or where in effect that which was applied to him was the more honourable, perhaps they who wrote the paper cannot now remember. Had they expected a lawsuit to have been the consequence of such petty variation, I hope they would have avoided it.[1] But, probably, as they meant no ill, they suspected no danger, and, therefore, consulted only what appeared to them propriety or convenience.'

A few days afterwards I consulted him upon a cause, *Paterson and others* against *Alexander and others*, which had been decided by a casting vote in the Court of Session, determining that the Corporation of Stirling was corrupt, and setting aside the election of some of their officers, because it was proved that three of the leading men who influenced the majority, had entered into an unjustifiable compact, of which, however, the majority were ignorant. He dictated to me, after a little consideration, the following sentences upon the subject:

'There is a difference between majority and superiority; majority is applied to number, and superiority to power; and power, like many other things, is to be estimated *non numero sed pondere*. Now though the greater *number* is not corrupt, the greater *weight* is corrupt, so that corruption predominates in the borough, taken *collectively*, though, perhaps, taken *numerically*, the greater part may be uncorrupt. That borough which is so constituted as to act corruptly, is in the eye of reason corrupt, whether it be by the uncontrollable power of a few, or by an accidental pravity of the multititude. The objection, in which is urged the injustice of making the innocent suffer with the guilty, is an objection not only against society, but against the possibility of society. All societies, great and small, subsist upon this condition; that as the individuals derive advantages from union, they may likewise suffer inconveniences; that as those who do nothing and sometimes those who do ill, will have the honours and emoluments of general virtue and general prosperity, so those likewise who do nothing or perhaps do well, must be involved in the consequences of predominant corruption.'

This in my opinion was a very nice case; but the decision was affirmed in the House of Lords.

On Monday, May 8, we went together and visited the mansions of Bedlam. I had been informed that he had once been there before with Mr Wedderburne (now Lord Loughborough), Mr Murphy, and Mr Foote; and I had heard Foote give a very entertaining account of Johnson's happening to have his attention arrested by a man who was very furious, and who, while beating his straw, supposed it to be William Duke of Cumberland, whom he

---

1 In justice to Dr Memis, though I was against him as an Advocate, I must mention, that he objected to the variation very earnestly, before the translation was printed off.

was punishing for his cruelties in Scotland in 1746.[a] There was nothing peculiarly remarkable this day; but the general contemplation of insanity was very affecting. I accompanied him home, and dined and drank tea with him.

Talking of an acquaintance of ours, distinguished for knowing an uncommon variety of miscellaneous articles both in antiquities and polite literature, he observed, 'You know, Sir, he runs about with little weight upon his mind.' And talking of another very ingenious gentleman, who from the warmth of his temper was at variance with many of his acquaintance, and wished to avoid them, he said, 'Sir, he leads the life of an outlaw.'

On Friday, May 12, as he had been so good as to assign me a room in his house, where I might sleep occasionally, when I happened to sit with him to a late hour, I took possession of it this night, found every thing in excellent order, and was attended by honest Francis with a most civil assiduity. I asked him whether I might go to a consultation with another lawyer upon Sunday, as that appeared to me to be doing work as much in my way, as if an artisan should work on the day appropriated for religious rest. JOHNSON. 'Why, Sir, when you are of consequence enough to oppose the practice of consulting upon Sunday, you should do it: but you may go now. It is not criminal, though it is not what one should do, who is anxious for the preservation and increase of piety, to which a peculiar observance of Sunday is a great help. The distinction is clear between what is of moral and what is of ritual obligation.'

On Saturday, May 13, I breakfasted with him by invitation, accompanied by Mr Andrew Crosbie, a Scotch Advocate, whom he had seen at Edinburgh, and the Hon. Colonel (now General) Edward Stopford, brother to Lord Courtown, who was desirous of being introduced to him. His tea and rolls and butter, and whole breakfast apparatus were all in such decorum, and his behaviour was so courteous, that Colonel Stopford was quite surprised, and wondered at his having heard so much said of Johnson's slovenliness and roughness. I have preserved nothing of what passed, except that Crosbie pleased him much by talking learnedly of alchymy, as to which Johnson was not a positive unbeliever, but rather delighted in considering what progress had actually been made in the transmutation of metals, what near approaches there had been to the making of gold; and told us that it was affirmed, that a person in the Russian dominions had discovered the secret, but died without revealing it, as imagining it would be prejudicial to society. He added, that it was not impossible but it might in time be generally known.

It being asked whether it was reasonable for a man to be angry at another whom a woman had preferred to him; — JOHNSON. 'I do not see, Sir, that it is reasonable for a man to be angry at another, whom a woman has preferred to him: but angry he is, no doubt; and he is loath to be angry at himself.'

Before setting out for Scotland on the 23rd, I was frequently in his company

[a] Add this note: My very honourable friend General Sir George Howard, who served in the Duke of Cumberland's army, has assured me that the cruelties were not imputable to his Royal Highness.

at different places, but during this period have recorded only two remarks: one concerning Garrick: 'He has not Latin enough. He finds out the Latin by the meaning, rather than the meaning by the Latin.' And another concerning writers of travels, who, he observed, 'were more defective than any other writers.'

I passed many hours with him on the 17th, of which I find all my memorial is, 'much laughing'. It would seem he had that day been in a humour for jocularity and merriment, and upon such occasions I never knew a man laugh more heartily. We may suppose, that the high relish of a state so different from his habitual gloom, produced more than ordinary exertions of that distinguishing faculty of man, which has puzzled philosophers so much to explain. Johnson's laugh was as remarkable as any circumstance in his manner. It was a kind of good humoured growl. Tom Davies described it drolly enough: 'He laughs like a rhinoceros.'[a]

To JAMES BOSWELL, Esq.

DEAR SIR – I make no doubt but you are now safely lodged in your own habitation, and have told all your adventures to Mrs Boswell and Miss Veronica. Pray teach Veronica to love me. Bid her not mind mamma.

Mrs Thrale has taken cold, and been very much disordered, but I hope is grown well. Mr Langton went yesterday to Lincolnshire, and has invited Nicolaida[1] to follow him. Beauclerk talks of going to Bath. I am to set out on Monday; so there is nothing but dispersion.

I have returned Lord Hailes's entertaining sheets, but must stay till I come back for more, because it will be inconvenient to send them after me in my vagrant state.

I promised Mrs Macaulay[2] that I would try to serve her son at Oxford. I have not forgotten it, nor am unwilling to perform it. If they desire to give him an English education, it should be considered whether they cannot send him for a year or two to an English school. If he comes immediately from Scotland, he can make no figure in our Universities. The schools in the north, I believe, are cheap; and, when I was a young man, were eminently good.

a After this passage, read:

To BENNET LANGTON, Esq.

DEAR SIR – I have an old amanuensis in great distress. I have given what I think I can give, and begged till I cannot tell where to beg again. I put into his hands this morning four guineas. If you could collect three guineas more, it would clear him from his present difficulty. I am, Sir,

Your most humble servant,

SAM. JOHNSON.

May 21, 1775.

1 A learned Greek.

2 Wife of the Reverend Mr Kenneth Macaulay, author of *The History of St Kilda*.

There are two little books published by the Foulis, *Telemachus* and Collins's Poems, each a shilling; I would be glad to have them.

Make my compliments to Mrs Boswell, though she does not love me. You see what perverse things ladies are, and how little fit to be trusted with feudal estates. When she mends and loves me, there may be more hope of her daughters.

I will not send compliments to my friends by name, because I would be loath to leave any out in the enumeration. Tell them, as you see them, how well I speak of Scotch politeness, and Scotch hospitality, and Scotch beauty, and of every thing Scotch, but Scotch oat-cakes and Scotch prejudices.

Let me know the answer of Rasay, and the decision relating to Sir Allan.[1] I am, my dearest Sir, with great affection,

Your most obliged and most humble servant,

SAM. JOHNSON.

May 27, 1775.

After my return to Scotland, I wrote three letters to him, from which I extract the following passages:

'I have seen Lord Hailes since I came down. He thinks it wonderful that you are pleased to take so much pains in revising his *Annals*. I told him that you said you were well rewarded by the entertainment which you had in reading them.'

'There has been a numerous flight of Hebrideans in Edinburgh this summer, whom I have been happy to entertain at my house. Mr Donald Macqueen[2] and Lord Monboddo supped with me one evening. They joined in controverting your proposition, that the Gaelic of the Highlands and Isles of Scotland was not written till of late.'

'My mind has been somewhat dark this summer. I have need of your warming and vivifying rays; and I hope I shall have them frequently. I am going to pass some time with my father at Auchinleck.'

To JAMES BOSWELL, Esq.

DEAR SIR – I am now returned from the annual ramble into the middle counties. Having seen nothing that I had not seen before, I have nothing to relate. Time has left that part of the island few antiquities; and commerce has left the people no singularities. I was glad to go abroad, and, perhaps, glad to come home; which is, in other words, I was, I am afraid, weary of being at home, and weary of being abroad. Is not this the state of life? But, if we confess this weariness, let us not lament it; for all the wise and all the good say, that we may cure it.

1 A law-suit carried on by Sir Allan Maclean, Chief of his Clan, to recover certain parts of his family estate from the Duke of Argyle.
2 A very learned minister in the Isle of Sky, whom both Dr Johnson and I have mentioned with regard.

For the black fumes which rise in your mind, I can prescribe nothing but that you disperse them by honest business or innocent pleasure, and by reading sometimes easy and sometimes serious. Change of place is useful; and I hope that your residence at Auchinleck will have many good effects.
. . .

That I should have given pain to Rasay, I am sincerely sorry; and am therefore very much pleased that he is no longer uneasy. He still thinks that I have represented him as personally giving up the Chieftainship. I meant only that it was no longer contested between the two houses, and supposed it settled, perhaps, by the cession of some remote generation, in the house of Dunvegan. I am sorry the advertisement was not continued for three or four times in the papers.

That Lord Monboddo and Mr Macqueen should controvert a position contrary to the imaginary interest of literary or national prejudice, might be easily imagined; but of a standing fact there ought to be no controversy: If there are men with tails, catch an *homo caudatus*; if there was writing of old in the Highlands or Hebrides, in the Erse language, produce the manuscripts. Where men write, they will write to one another, and some of their letters, in families studious of their ancestry, will be kept. In Wales there are many manuscripts.

I have now three parcels of Lord Hailes's history, which I purpose to return all the next week: that his respect for my little observations should keep his work in suspense, makes one of the evils of my journey. It is in our language, I think, a new mode of history, which tells all that is wanted, and, I suppose, all that is known, without laboured splendour of language, or affected subtilty of conjecture. The exactness of his dates raises my wonder. He seems to have the closeness of Henault without his constraint.

Mrs Thrale was so entertained with your *Journal*,[1] that she almost read herself blind. She has a great regard for you.

Of Mrs Boswell, though she knows in her heart that she does not love me, I am always glad to hear any good, and hope that she and the little dear ladies will have neither sickness nor any other affliction. But she knows that she does not care what becomes of me, and for that she may be sure that I think her very much to blame.

Never, my dear Sir, do you take it into your head to think that I do not love you; you may settle yourself in full confidence both of my love and my esteem; I love you as a kind man, I value you as a worthy man, and hope in time to reverence you as a man of exemplary piety. I hold you as Hamlet has it, 'in my heart of heart', and, therefore, it is little to say, that I am, Sir,

Your affectionate humble servant,

SAM. JOHNSON.

London, August 27, 1775.

1 My *Journal of a Tour to the Hebrides*, which that lady read in the original manuscript.

To the same.

SIR – If in these papers,[1] there is little alteration attempted, do not suppose me negligent. I have read them perhaps more closely than the rest; but I find nothing worthy of an objection.

Write to me soon, and write often, and tell me all your honest heart.

I am, Sir,

Yours affectionately,

SAM. JOHNSON.

August 30, 1775.

To the same.

MY DEAR SIR – I now write to you, lest in some of your freaks and humours you should fancy yourself neglected. Such fancies I must entreat you never to admit, at least never to indulge, for my regard for you is so radicated and fixed, that it is become part of my mind, and cannot be effaced but by some cause uncommonly violent; therefore, whether I write or not, set your thoughts at rest. I now write to tell you that I shall not very soon write again, for I am to set out tomorrow on another journey.

. . .

Your friends are all well at Streatham, and in Leicester-fields.[a] Make my compliments to Mrs Boswell, if she is in good humour with me.

I am, Sir, &c.

SAM. JOHNSON.

September 14, 1775.

What he mentions in such light terms as, 'I am to set out to-morrow on another journey', I soon afterwards discovered was no less than a tour to France with Mr and Mrs Thrale. This was the only time in his life that he went upon the continent.[b]

1 Another parcel of Lord Hailes's *Annals of Scotland*.
a Add note: Where Sir Joshua Reynolds lived.
b After this passage, read:

To SIR ROBERT LEVET.

Sept. 18, 1775, Calais.

DEAR SIR – We are here in France, after a very pleasing passage of no more than six hours. I know not when I shall write again, and therefore I write now, though you cannot suppose that I have much to say. You have seen France yourself. From this place we are going to Rouen, and from Rouen to Paris, where Mr Thrale designs to stay about five or six weeks. We have a regular recommendation to the English resident, so we shall not be taken for vagabonds. We think to go one way and return another, and for as much as we can, I will try to speak a little French; I tried hitherto but little, but I spoke sometimes. If I heard better, I suppose I should learn faster. I am, Sir,

Your humble servant,   SAM. JOHNSON.

To Dr SAMUEL JOHNSON.

Edinburgh, Oct. 24, 1775.

MY DEAR SIR – If I had not been informed that you were at Paris, you should have had a letter from me by the earliest opportunity, announcing the birth of my Son, on the 9th instant; I have named him Alexander, after my father. I now write, as I suppose your fellow traveller, Mr Thrale, will return to London this week to attend his duty in parliament, and that you will not stay behind him.

I send another parcel of Lord Hailes's *Annals*. I have undertaken to solicit you for a favour to him, which he thus requests in a letter to me: 'I intend soon to give you the *Life of Robert Bruce*, which you will be pleased to transmit to Dr Johnson. I wish that you could assist me in a fancy which I have taken, of getting Dr Johnson to draw a character of Robert Bruce, from the account that I give of that prince. If he finds materials for it in my work, it will be a proof that I have been fortunate in selecting the most striking incidents.'

I suppose by the *Life of Robert Bruce*, his Lordship means that part of his *Annals* which relates the history of that prince, and not a separate work.

Shall we have *A Journey to Paris* from you in the winter? You will, I hope, at any rate be kind enough to give me some account of your French travels very soon, for I am very impatient. What a different scene have you

---

To the same.

Paris, Oct. 22, 1775.

DEAR SIR – We are still here, commonly very busy in looking about us. We have been today at Versailles. You have seen it, and I shall not describe it. We came yesterday from Fontainbleau, where the Court is now. We went to see the King and Queen at dinner, and the Queen was so impressed by Miss,[1] that she sent one of the Gentlemen to inquire who she was. I find all true that you have ever told me at Paris. Mr Thrale is very liberal, and keeps us two coaches, and a very fine table; but I think our cookery very bad. Mrs Thrale got into a convent of English nuns, and I talked with her through the grate, and I am very kindly used by the English Benedictine friars. But upon the whole I cannot make much acquaintance here; and though the churches, palaces, and some private houses are very magnificent, there is no very great pleasure after having seen many, in seeing more; at least the pleasure, whatever it be, must some time have an end, and we are beginning to think when we shall come home. Mr Thrale calculates that as we left Streatham on the fifteenth of September, we shall see it again about the fifteenth of November.

I think I had not been on this side of the sea five days before I found a sensible improvement in my health. I ran a race in the rain this day, and beat Baretti. Baretti is a fine fellow, and speaks French, I think, quite as well as English.

Make my compliments to Mrs Williams; and give my love to Francis; and tell my friends that I am not lost. I am, dear Sir,

Your affectionate humble, &c.

SAM. JOHNSON.

1   Miss Thrale.

viewed this autumn, from that which you viewed in autumn 1773! I ever am, my dear Sir,

Your much obliged, and affectionate humble servant,

JAMES BOSWELL.

To JAMES BOSWELL, Esq.

DEAR SIR – I am glad that the young Laird is born, and an end, as I hope, put to the only difference that you can ever have with Mrs Boswell.[1] I know that she does not love me, but I intend to persist in wishing her well till I get the better of her.

Paris is, indeed, a place very different from the Hebrides, but it is to a hasty traveller not so fertile of novelty, nor affords so many opportunities of remark. I cannot pretend to tell the public any thing of a place better known to many of my readers than to myself. We can talk of it when we meet.

I shall go next week to Streatham, from whence I purpose to send a parcel of the *History* every post. Concerning the character of Bruce, I can only say, that I do not see any great reason for writing it, but I shall not easily deny what Lord Hailes and you concur in desiring.

I have been remarkably healthy all the journey, and hope you and your family have known only that trouble and danger which has so happily terminated. Among all the congratulations that you may receive, I hope you believe none more warm and sincere, than those of, dear Sir,

Your most affectionate,

SAM. JOHNSON.

November 16, 1775.

To Mrs LUCY PORTER, in Lichfield.[2]

DEAR MADAM – This week I came home from Paris. I have brought you a little box, which I thought pretty; but I know not whether it is properly a snuff-box, or a box for some other use. I will send it, when I can find an opportunity. I have been through the whole journey remarkably well. My fellow-travellers were the same whom you saw at Lichfield, only we took Baretti with us. Paris is not so fine a place as you would expect. The palaces and churches, however, are very splendid and magnificent; and what would please you, there are many very fine pictures; but I do not think their way of life commodious or pleasant.

Let me know how your health has been all this while. I hope the fine summer has given you strength sufficient to encounter the winter.

Make my compliments to all my friends; and, if your fingers will let you,

---

1 This alludes to my old feudal principle of preferring male to female succession.

2 There can be no doubt that many years previous to 1775, he corresponded with this lady, who was his step-daughter, but none of his earlier letters to her have been preserved.

write to me, or let your maid write, if it be troublesome to you. I am, dear Madam,

     Your most affectionate humble servant,

SAM. JOHNSON.

    Nov. 16, 1775.

To the same.

DEAR MADAM – Some weeks ago I wrote to you, to tell you that I was just come home from a ramble, and hoped that I should have heard from you. I am afraid winter has laid hold on your fingers, and hinders you from writing. However, let somebody write, if you cannot, and tell me how you do, and a little of what has happened at Lichfield among our friends. I hope you are all well.

     When I was in France, I thought myself growing young, but am afraid that cold weather will take part of my new vigour from me. Let us, however, take care of ourselves, and lose no part of our health by negligence.

     I never knew whether you received the Commentary on the New Testament, and the Travels, and the glasses.

     Do, my dear love, write to me; and do not let us forget each other. This is the season of good wishes, and I wish you all good. I have not lately seen Mr Porter,[1] nor heard of him. Is he with you?

     Be pleased to make my compliments to Mrs Adey, and Mrs Cobb, and all my friends; and when I can do any good, let me know. I am, dear Madam,

     Yours most affectionately,

SAM. JOHNSON.

    December, 1775.

It is to be regretted, that he did not write an account of his travels in France; for as he is reported to have once said. that 'he could write the Life of a Broomstick', so, notwithstanding so many former travellers have exhausted almost every thing subject for remark in that great kingdom, his very accurate observation, and peculiar vigour of thought and illustration, would have produced a valuable work. During his visit to it, which lasted but about two months, he wrote notes or minutes of what he saw. He promised to show me them, but I neglected to put him in mind of it; and the greatest part of them have been lost, or, perhaps, destroyed in that precipitate burning of his papers a few days before his death, which must ever be lamented: One small paper-book, however, entitled 'FRANCE, II', has been preserved, and is in my possession. It is a diurnal register of his life and observations, from the 10th of October to the 4th of November, inclusive, being twenty-six days; and shows an extraordinary attention to various minute particulars. Being the only memorial of this tour that remains, my readers, I am confident, will peruse it with pleasure, though his notes are very short, and evidently written only to assist his own recollection.

---

1   Son of Mrs Johnson, by her first husband.

'Oct. 10. Tuesday. We saw the *Ecole Militaire*, in which one hundred and fifty young boys are educated for the army. They have arms of different sizes, according to the age – flints of wood. The building is very large, but nothing fine, except the council-room.. The French have large squares in the windows – they make good iron palisades. Their meals are gross.

'We visited the Observatory, a large building of a great height. The upper stones of the parapet very large, but not cramped with iron. The flat on the top is very extensive; but on the insulated part there is no parapet. Though it was broad enough, I did not care to go upon it. Maps were printing in one of the rooms.

'We walked to a small convent of the Fathers of the Oratory. In the reading-desk of the refectory lay the Lives of the Saints.

'Oct. 11. Wednesday. We went to see Hôtel de Chatlois, a house not very large, but very elegant. One of the rooms was gilt to a degree that I never saw before. The upper part for servants and their masters was pretty.

'Thence we went to Mr Monville's, a house divided into small apartments, furnished with effeminate and minute elegance. – Porphyry.

'Thence we went to St Roque's church, which is very large – the lower part of the pillars incrusted with marble. – Three chapels behind the high altar – the last a mass of low arches. – Altars, I believe, all round.

'We passed through *Place de Vendôme*, a fine square, about as big as Hanover-square – Inhabited by the high families. – Lewis XIV on horseback in the middle.

'Monville is the son of a farmer-general. In the house of Chatlois is a room furnished with japan, fitted up in Europe.

'We dined with Boccage, the Marquis Blanchetti, and his lady. – The sweetmeats taken by the Marchioness Blanchetti, after observing that they were dear. – Mr Le Roy, Count Manucci the Abbé, the Prior, and father Wilson, who staid with me, till I took him home in the coach.

'Bathiani is gone.

'The French have no laws for the maintenance of their poor. – Monk not necessarily a priest. – Benedictines rise at four – are at church an hour and half; at church again half an hour before, half an hour after dinner; and again from half an hour after seven to eight. They may sleep eight hours. – Bodily labour wanted in monasteries.

'The poor taken to hospitals, and miserably kept. – Monks in the convent fifteen – accounted poor.

'Oct. 12. Thursday. We went to the Gobelins. – Tapestry makes a good picture – imitates flesh exactly. – One piece with a gold ground – the birds not exactly coloured. – Thence we went to the King's cabinet – very neat, not, perhaps, perfect. – Gold ore. – Candles of the candle-tree. – Seeds. – Woods. – Thence to Gagnier's house, where I saw rooms nine, furnished with a profusion of wealth and elegance which I never have seen before – Vases – Pictures. – The dragon china. – The lustre said to be of crystal, and to have cost £3,500. – The whole furniture said to have cost £125,000. –

Damask hangings covered with pictures. – Porphyry. – This house struck me. – Then we waited on the ladies to Monville's. – Captain Irwin with us.[1] – Spain. County towns all beggars. – At Dijon he could not find the way to Orleans. – Cross roads of France very bad. – Five soldiers. – Woman. – Soldiers escaped. – The Colonel would not lose five men for the death of one woman – The magistrate cannot seize a soldier but by the Colonel's permission – Good inn at Nismes. – Moors of Barbary fond of Englishmen. – Gibraltar eminently healthy – it has beef from Barbary. – There is a large garden. – Soldiers sometimes fall from the rock.

'Oct. 13. Friday. I staid at home all day, only went to find the Prior, who was not at home. – I read something in Canus.[2] – *Nec admiror, nec multum laudo.*

'Oct. 14. Saturday. We went to the house of Mr Argenson, which was almost wainscotted with looking-glasses, and covered with gold. – The ladies' closet wainscotted with large squares of glass over painted paper. They always place mirrors to reflect their rooms.

'Then we went to Julien's, the Treasurer of the Clergy – £30,000 a year. – The house has no very large room, but is set with mirrors, and covered with gold. – Books of wood here, and in another library.

'At D—'s I looked into the books in the lady's closet, and, in contempt, showed them to Mr T. – *Prince Titi; Bibl. des Fées,* and other books. – She was offended, and shut up, as we heard afterwards, her apartment.

'Then we went to Julien Le Roy, the King's watch-maker, a man of character in his business, who showed a small clock made to find the longitude. – A decent man.

'Afterwards we saw the *Palais Marchand,* and the Courts of Justice, civil and criminal – Queries on the *Sellette.* – This building has the old Gothic passages, and a great appearance of antiquity. – Three hundred prisoners sometimes in the gaol.

'Much disturbed – hope no ill will be.[3]

'In the afternoon I visited Mr Freron the journalist. He spoke Latin very scantily, but seemed to understand me. – His house not splendid, but of commodious size. – His family, wife, son, and daughter, not elevated but decent. – I was pleased with my reception. – He is to translate my book, which I am to send him with notes.

'Oct. 15. Sunday. At Choisi, a royal palace on the banks of the Seine, about 7 m. from Paris. – The terrace noble along the river. – The rooms numerous and grand, but not discriminated from other palaces. – The chapel beautiful, but small. – China globes. – Inlaid table. – Labyrinth. – Sinking table. – Toilet tables.

---

1 The rest of this paragraph appears to be a minute of what was told by Captain Irwin.
2 Melchior Canus, a celebrated Spanish Dominican, who died at Toledo, in 1560. He wrote a treatise *De Locis Theologicis,* in twelve books.
3 This passage, which some may think superstitious, reminds me of Archbishop Laud's Diary.

'Oct. 16. Monday. The Palais Royal very grand, large, and lofty. – A very great collection of pictures. – Three of Raphael. – Two Holy Family. – One small piece of M. Angelo. – One room of Rubens. – I thought the pictures of Raphael fine.

'The Thuilleries. – Statues. – Venus. – Aen. and Anchises in his arms. – Nilus. – Many more. – The walks not open to mean persons. – Chairs at night hired for two sous a piece. – Pont tournant.

'Austin Nuns. – Grate. – Mrs Fermor, Abbess. – She knew Pope, and thought him disagreeable. – Mrs —— has many books – has seen life. – Their frontlet disagreeable. – Their hood. – Their life easy. – Rise about five; hour and half in chapel. – Dine at ten. – Another hour and half at chapel; half an hour about three, and half an hour more at seven – four hours in chapel. – A large garden. – Thirteen pensioners. – Teacher complained.

'At the Boulevards saw nothing, yet was glad to be there. – Rope-dancing and farce. – Egg dance.

'N. [Note.] Near Paris, whether on week-days or Sundays, the roads empty.

'Oct. 17. Tuesday. At the Palais Marchand. – I bought

A snuff-box	24 L.
———	6
Table book	15
Scissars 3 p [pair]	18
	63 = 2 12 6

'We heard the lawyers plead. – N. As many killed at Paris as there are days in the year. – *Chambre de question*. – Tournelle at the Palais Marchand. – An old venerable building.

'The Palais Bourbon, belonging to the Prince of Condé. Only one small wing shown – lofty – splendid – gold and glass. – The battles of the great Conde are painted in one of the rooms. The present Prince a grandsire at thirty-nine.

'The sight of palaces, and other great buildings, leaves no very distinct images, unless to those who talk of them, and impress them. As I entered, my wife was in my mind:[1] she would have been pleased. Having now nobody to please, I am little pleased.

'N. In France there is no middle rank.

'So many shops open, that Sunday is little distinguished at Paris. – The palaces of Louvre and Thuilleries granted out in lodgings.

'In the *Palais de Bourbon*, gilt globes of metal at the fireplace.

'The French beds commended. – Much of the marble only paste.

'The Colosseum a mere wooden building, at least much of it.

'Oct. 18. Wednesday. We went to Fontainebleau, which we found a large mean town, crowded with people. – The forest thick with woods, very extensive. – Manucci secured us lodgings. – The appearance of the country

---

1 His tender affection for his departed wife, of which there are many evidences in his *Prayers and Meditations*, appears very feelingly in this passage.

pleasant. – No hills, few streams, only one hedge. – I remember no chapels nor crosses on the road. – Pavement still, and rows of trees.

'N. Nobody but mean people walk in Paris.

'Oct. 19. Thursday. At court, we saw the apartments – the King's bed-chamber and council-chamber extremely splendid. – Persons of all ranks in the external rooms through which the family passes – servants and masters. – Brunet with us the second time.

'The introductor came to us – civil to me. – Presenting. – I had scruples. – Not necessary. – We went and saw the King and Queen at dinner. – We saw the other ladies at dinner. – Madame Elizabeth, with the Princess of Guimené. – At night we went to a comedy. I neither saw nor heard. – Drunken women. – Mrs Th. preferred one to the other.

'Oct. 20. Friday. We saw the Queen mount in the forest. – Brown habit; rode aside: one lady rode aside. – The Queen's horse light grey – martingale. – She galloped. – We then went to the apartments, and admired them. – Then wandered through the palace. – In the passages, stalls and shops. – Painting in fresco by a great master, worn out. – We saw the King's horses and dogs. – The dogs almost all English. – Degenerate.

'The horses not much commended. – The stables cool; the kennel filthy.

'At night the ladies went to the opera. I refused, but should have been welcome.

'The King fed himself with his left hand as we.

'Saturday, 21. In the night I got ground. – We came home to Paris. – I think we did not see the chapel. – Tree broken by the wind. – The French chairs made all of boards painted.

'N. Soldiers at the court of justice. – Soldiers not amenable to the magistrates. – Dijon woman.[1]

'Faggots in the palace. – Every thing slovenly, except in the chief rooms – Trees in the roads, some tall, none old, many very young and small.

'Women's saddles seem ill made. – Queen's bridle woven with silver. – Tags to strike the horse.

'Sunday, Oct. 22. To Versailles, a mean town. – Carriages of business passing. – Mean shops against the wall. – Our way lay through Sève, where the China manufacture. – Wooden bridge at Sève, in the way to Versailles. – The palace of great extent. – The front long; I saw it not perfectly. – The Menagerie. Cygnets dark; their black feet; on the ground; tame. – Halcyons, or gulls. – Stag and hind, young. – Aviary, very large; the net, wire. – Black flag of China, small. – Rhinoceros, the horn broken and pared away, which, I suppose, will grow; the basis, I think, four inches cross; the skin folds like loose cloth doubled over his body, and cross his hips; a vast animal though young; as big, perhaps, as four oxen. – The young elephant, with his tusks just appearing. – The brown bear put out his paws – all very tame. – The lion. – The tigers I did

2 See p. 457.

not well view. – The camel, or dromedary with two bunches, called the Huguin,[1] taller than any horse. – Two camels with one bunch. – Among the birds was a pelican, who being let out, went to a fountain, and swam about to catch fish. His feet well webbed: he dipped his head, and turned his long bill sidewise. He caught two or three fish, but did not eat them.

'Trianon is a kind of retreat appendant to Versailles. It has an open portico; the pavement, and, I think, the pillars, of marble. – There are many rooms which I do not distinctly remember. – A table of porphyry, about five feet long, and between two and three broad, given to Lewis XIV by the Venetian State. – In the council-room almost all that was not door or window, was, I think, looking-glass. – Little Trianon is a small palace like a gentleman's house. – The upper floor paved with brick. – Little Vienne. – The court is ill paved. – The rooms at the top are small, fit to sooth the imagination with privacy. In the front of Versailles are small basons of water on the terrace, and other basons, I think, below them. – There are little courts. – The great gallery is wainscotted with mirrors, not very large, but joined by frames. I suppose the large plates were not yet made. – The play-house was very large. – The chapel I do not remember if we saw. – We saw one chapel, but I am not certain whether there or at Trianon. – The foreign office paved with bricks. – The dinner half a Louis each, and, I think, a Louis over. – Money given at Menagerie, three livres; at palace, six livres.

'Oct. 23. Monday. Last night I wrote to Levet. – We went to see the looking-glasses wrought. They come from Normandy in cast plates, perhaps the third of an inch thick. At Paris they are ground upon a marble table, by rubbing one plate on another with grit between them. The various sands, of which there are said to be five, I could not learn. The handle, by which the upper glass is moved, has the form of a wheel, which may be moved in all directions. The plates are sent up with their surfaces ground, but not polished, and so continue till they are bespoken, lest time should spoil the surface, as we were told. Those that are to be polished, are laid on a table covered with several thick cloths, hard strained, that the resistance may be equal; they are then rubbed with a hand rubber, held down hard by a contrivance which I did not well understand. The powder which is used last seemed to me to be iron dissolved in aqua fortis: they called it, as Baretti said, *marc de l'eau forte*, which he thought was dregs. They mentioned vitriol and saltpetre. The cannon ball swam in the quicksilver. To silver them a leaf of beaten tin is laid, and rubbed with quicksilver, to which it unites. Then more quicksilver is poured upon it, which by its mutual [attraction] rises very high. Then a paper is laid at the nearest end of the plate, over which the glass is slided till it lies upon the plate, having driven much of the quicksilver before it. It is then, I think, pressed upon cloths, and then set sloping to drop the superfluous mercury; the slope is daily heightened towards a perpendicular.

1 This epithet should be applied to this animal with one bunch.

'In the way I saw the Grêve, the mayor's house, and the Bastile.

'We then went to Sans-terre, a brewer. He brews with about as much malt as Mr Thrale, and sells his beer at the same price, though he pays no duty for malt, and little more than half as much for beer. Beer is sold retail at 6d. a bottle. He brews 4,000 barrels a year. There are seventeen brewers in Paris, of whom none is supposed to brew more than he – reckoning them at 3,000 each, they make 51,000 a year. – They make their malt, for malting is here no trade.

'The moat of the Bastile is dry.

'Oct. 24. Tuesday. We visited the King's library – I saw the *Speculum humanae Salvationis*, rudely printed, with ink, sometimes pale, sometimes black; part supposed to be with wooden types, and part with pages cut on boards. – The Bible, supposed to be older than that of Mentz, in 62 [1462]: it has no date; it is supposed to have been printed with wooden types. – I am in doubt; the print is large and fair, in two folios. – Another book was shown me, supposed to have been printed with wooden types; I think, *Durandi Sanctuarium* in 58 [1458]. This is inferred from the difference of form, sometimes seen in the same letter, which might be struck with different puncheons. – The regular similitude of most letters proves better that they are metal. – I saw nothing but the *Speculum* which I had not seen, I think, before.

'Thence to the Sorbonne. – The library very large, not in lattices like the King's. *Marbone* and *Durandi*, q. collection 14 vol. *Scriptores de rebus Gallicis*, many folios. – *Histoire Généalogique* of France, 9 vol. – *Gallia Christiana*, the first edition, 4to. the last, f. 12 vol. – The Prior and Librarian dined [with us] – I waited on them home. – Their garden pretty, with covered walks, but small; yet may hold many students. – The Doctors of the Sorbonne are all equal – choose those who succeed to vacancies. – Profit little.

'Oct. 25. Wednesday. I went with the Prior to St Cloud, to see Dr Hooke. – We walked round the palace, and had some talk. – I dined with our whole company at the Monastery. – In the library, *Beroald – Cymon – Titus* – from Boccace *Oratio Proverbialis*; to the Virgin, from Petrarch; Falkland to Sandys – Dryden's Preface to the third vol. of Miscellanies.[1]

'Oct. 26. Thursday. We saw the china at Sève, cut, glazed, painted. Bellevue, a pleasing house, not great: fine prospect. – Meudon, an old palace. – Alexander in porphyry: hollow between eyes and nose, thin cheeks. – Plato and Aristotle. – Noble terrace overlooks the town. – St Cloud. – Gallery not very high, nor grand, but pleasing. – In the rooms, Michael Angelo, drawn by himself, Sir Thomas More, Des Cartes, Bochart, Naudaeus, Mazarine. – Gilded wainscot, so common that it is not minded. – Gough and Keene. – Hooke came to us at the inn. – A message from Drumgould.

---

1 He means, I suppose, that he *read* these different pieces, while he remained in the library.

'Oct. 27. Friday. I staid at home. – Gough and Keene, and Mrs S—'s friend dined with us. – This day we began to have a fire. – The weather is growing very cold, and I fear, has a bad effect upon my breath, which has grown much more free and easy in this country.

'Sat. Oct. 28. I visited the Grand Chartreux built by St Louis. – It is built for forty, but contains only twenty-four, and will not maintain more. – The friar that spoke to us had a pretty apartment. – Mr Baretti says, four rooms; I remember but three. – His books seemed to be French. – His garden was neat; he gave me grapes. – We saw the Place de Victoire, with the statues of the King, and the captive nations.

'We saw the palace and gardens of Luxembourg, but the gallery was shut. – We climbed to the top stairs. – I dined with Colbrooke, who had much company – Foote, Sir George Rodney, Motteux, Udson, Taaf. – Called on the Prior, and found him in bed.

'Hotel – a guinea a day. – Coach, three guineas a week. – Valet de place, three l. a day – *Avant-coureur*, a guinea a week – Ordinary dinner, six l. a head. – Our ordinary seems to be about five guineas a day – Our extra-ordinary expenses, as diversions, gratuities, clothes, I cannot reckon – Our travelling is ten guineas a day.

'White stockings, 18 l. Wig. – Hat.

'Sunday, Oct. 29. We saw the boarding-school. – The *Enfans trouvés*. – A room with about eighty-six children in cradles, as sweet as a parlour. – They lose a third; take in to perhaps more than seven [years old]; put them to trades; pin to them the papers sent with them. – Want nurses. – Saw their chapel.

'Went to St Eustatia; saw an innumerable company of girls catechised, in many bodies, perhaps 100 to a catechist. – Boys taught at one time, girls at another. – The sermon; the preacher wears a cap, which he takes off at the name – his action uniform, not very violent.

'Oct. 30. Monday. We saw the library of St Germain. – A very noble collection. – *Codex Divinorum Officiorum*, 1459 – a letter, square like that of the *Offices*, perhaps the same. – The *Codex*, by Fust and Gernsheym. – *Meursius*, 12 v. fol. – *Amadis*, in French, 3v. fol. – CATHOLICON *sine colophone*, but of 1460. – Two other editions,[1] one by . . . Augustin. *de Civitate Dei*, without name, date, or place, but of Fust's square letter as it seems.

'I dined with Col. Drumgould; had a pleasing afternoon.

'Some of the books of St Germain's stand in presses from the wall, like those at Oxford.

---

1 I have looked in vain into De Bure, Meerman, Mattaire, and other typographical books, for the two editions of the *Catholicon*, which Dr Johnson mentions here, with *names* which I cannot make out. I read 'one by *Latinius*, one by *Boedinus*'. I have deposited the original MS. in the British Museum, where the curious may see it. My grateful acknowledgements are due to Mr Planta for the trouble he was pleased to take in aiding my researches.

Oct. 31. Tuesday. I lived at the Benedictines; meagre day; soup meagre, herrings, eels, both with sauce; fryed fish; lentils, tasteless in themselves. In the library; where I found Masseus's *de Historia Indica: Promontorium flectere, to double the Cape.* I parted very tenderly from the Prior and Friar Wilkes.

'*Maitre es Arts*, 2 y. – *Bacc. Theol.* 3 y. – *Licentiate*, 2 y. – *Doctor Th.* 2 y. in all 9 years. – For the doctorate three disputations, *Major, Minor, Sorbonica.* – Several colleges suppressed, and transferred to that which was the Jesuits' College.

'Nov. 1. Wednesday. We left Paris. – St Denis a large town; the church not very large, but the middle isle is very lofty and awful. – On the left are chapels built beyond the line of the wall, which destroy the symmetry of the sides. – The organ is higher above the pavement than any I have ever seen. – The gates are of brass – On the middle gate is the history of our Lord. – The painted windows are historical, and said to be eminently beautiful. – We were at another church belonging to a convent, of which the portal is a dome; we could not enter further, and it was almost dark.

'Nov. 2. Thursday. We came this day to Chantilly, a seat belonging to the Prince of Condé – This place is eminently beautified by all varieties of waters starting up in fountains, falling in cascades, running in streams, and spread in lakes. – The water seems to be too near the house. – All this water is brought from a source or river three leagues off, by an artificial canal, which for one league is carried under ground. – The house is magnificent. – The cabinet seems well stocked: what I remember was, the jaws of a hippopotamus, and a young hippopotamus preserved, which, however, is so small that I doubt its reality. It seems too hairy for an abortion, and too small for a mature birth – Nothing was in spirits; all was dry. – The dog; the deer; the ant-bear with long snout. – The toucan, long broad beak. – The stables were of very great length. – The kennel had no scents. – There was a mockery of a village. – The Menagerie had few animals.[1] – Two faussans,[2] or Brasilian weasels, spotted, very wild. – There is a forest, and, I think, a park. – I walked till I was very weary, and next morning felt my feet battered, and with pains in the toes.

'Nov. 3. Friday. We came to Compiegne, a very large town, with a royal palace built round a pentagonal court. – The court is raised upon vaults, and has, I suppose, an entry on one side by a gentle rise. – Talk of painting. – The church is not very large, but very elegant and splendid. – I had at first great

---

1 The writing is so bad here, that the names of several of the animals could not be decyphered without much more acquaintance with natural history than I possess. Dr Blagden, with his usual politeness, most obligingly examined the MS. To that gentleman, and to Dr Gray, of the British Museum, who also very readily assisted me, I beg leave to express my best thanks.

2 It is thus written by Johnson, from the French pronunciation of *Fossane*. It should be observed, that the person who showed this Menagerie was mistaken in supposing the *fossane* and the Brasilian weasel to be the same, the *fossane* being a different animal, and a native of Madagascar. I find them, however, upon one plate in Pennant's *Synopsis of Quadrupeds*.

difficulty to walk, but motion grew continually easier. – At night we came to Noyon, an episcopal city. – The cathedral is very beautiful, the pillars alternately Gothic and Corinthian. – We entered a very noble parochial church – Noyon is walled, and is said to be three miles round.

'Nov. 4. Saturday. We rose very early, and came through St Quintin to Cambray, not long after three. – We went to an English nunnery, to give a letter to Father Welch, the confessor, who came to visit us in the evening.

'Nov. 5. Sunday. We saw the cathedral. – It is very beautiful, with chapels on each side. – The choir splendid. – The balustrade in one part brass. – The Neff very high and grand. – The Altar silver as far as it is seen. – The vestments very splendid – At the Benedictine's church —— '

Here his journal[1] ends abruptly. Whether he wrote any more after this time, I know not; but probably not much, as he arrived in England about the 12th of November. These short notes of his tour, though they may seem minute taken singly, make together a considerable mass of information, and exhibit such an ardour of enquiry and acuteness of examination, as, I believe, are found in but few travellers, especially at an advanced age. They completely refute the idle notion which has been propagated, *that he could not see*; and, if he had taken the trouble to revise and digest them, he undoubtedly could have expanded them into a very entertaining narrative.

When I met him in London the following year, the account which he gave me of his French tour, was, 'Sir, I have seen all the visibilities of Paris, and around it; but to have formed an acquaintance with the people there, would have required more time than I could stay. I was just beginning to creep into acquaintance by means of Colonel Drumgould, a very high man, Sir, head of *L'Ecole Militaire*, a most complete character, for he had first been a professor of rhetoric, and then became a soldier. And, Sir, I was very kindly treated by the English Benedictines, and have a cell appropriated to me in their convent.'

He observed, 'The great in France live very magnificently, but the rest very miserably. There is no happy middle state as in England. The shops of Paris are mean; the meat in the markets is such as would be sent to a gaol in England: and Mr Thrale justly observed, that the cookery of the French was forced upon them by necessity; for they could not eat their meat, unless they added some taste to it. The French are an indelicate people; they will spit upon any place. At Madame ——'s, a literary lady of rank, the footman took the sugar in his fingers, and threw it into my coffee. I was going to put it aside; but hearing it was made on purpose for me, I e'en tasted Tom's fingers. The same lady would needs make tea *à l'Angloise*. The spout of the tea-pot did not pour freely: she bade the footman blow into it. France is worse than Scotland in

1 My worthy and ingenious friend, Mr Andrew Lumisdane, by his accurate acquaintance with France, enabled me to make out many proper names, which Dr Johnson had written indistinctly, and sometimes spelt erroneously.

every thing but climate. Nature has done more for the French; but they have done less for themselves than the Scotch have done.'

It happened that Foote was at Paris at the same time with Dr Johnson, and his description of my friend while there was abundantly ludicrous. He told me, that the French were quite astonished at his figure and manner, and at his dress, which he obstinately continued exactly as in London – his brown clothes, black stockings, and plain shirt. He mentioned, that an Irish gentleman said to Johnson, 'Sir, you have not seen the best French players.' JOHNSON. 'Players, Sir! I look on them as no better than creatures set upon tables and joint-stools to make faces and produce laughter, like dancing dogs.' – 'But, Sir, you will allow that some players are better than others?' JOHNSON. 'Yes, Sir, as some dogs dance better than others.'

While Johnson was in France, he was generally very resolute in speaking Latin. It was a maxim with him that a man should not let himself down, by speaking a language which he speaks imperfectly. Indeed, we must have often observed how inferior, how much like a child a man appears, who speaks a broken tongue. When Sir Joshua Reynolds, at one of the dinners of the Royal Academy, presented him to a Frenchman of great distinction, he would not deign to speak French, but talked Latin, though his Excellency did not understand it, owing, perhaps, to Johnson's English pronunciation: yet upon another occasion he was observed to speak French to a Frenchman of high rank, who spoke English; and being asked the reason, with some expression of surprise, – he answered, 'Because I think my French is as good as his English.' Though Johnson understood French perfectly, he could not speak it readily, as I have observed at his first interview with General Paoli, in 1769; yet he wrote it, I imagine, very well, as appears from some of his letters in Mrs Piozzi's collection, of which I shall transcribe one.

A Madame La Comtesse de ——

July 16, 1771.

Oui, Madame, le moment est arrivé, et il faut que je parte. Mais pourquoi faut il partir? Est ce que je m'ennuye? Je m'ennuyerai ailleurs. Est ce que je cherche ou quelque plaisir, ou quelque soulagement? Je ne cherche rien, je n'espere rien. Aller voir ce que jai vû, etre un peu rejoué, un peu degouté, ne resouvenir que la vie se passe, et qu'elle se passe en vain, me plaindre de moi, m'endurcir aux dehors; voici le tout de ce qu'on compte pour les delices de l'année. Que Dieu vous donne, Madame, tous les agrémens de la vie, avec un esprit qui peut en jouir sans s'y livrer trop.

Here let me not forget a curious anecdote, as related to me by Mr Beauclerk, which I shall endeavour to exhibit as well as I can in that gentleman's lively manner; and in justice to him it is proper to add, that Dr Johnson told me, I might rely both on the correctness of his memory, and the fidelity of his narrative. 'When Madame de Boufflers was first in England (said Beauclerk), she was desirous to see Johnson. I accordingly went with her to his chambers in the Temple, where she was entertained with his conversation for some time. When our visit was over, she and I left him, and were got into Inner

Temple-lane, when all at once I heard a noise like thunder. This was occasioned by Johnson, who it seems upon a little recollection, had taken it into his head that he ought to have done the honours of his literary residence to a foreign lady of quality, and eager to show himself a man of gallantry, was hurrying down the staircase in violent agitation. He overtook us before we reached the Temple-gate, and brushing in between me and Madame de Boufflers, seized her hand, and conducted her to her coach. His dress was a rusty brown morning suit, a pair of old shoes by way of slippers, a little shrivelled wig sticking on the top of his head, and the sleeves of his shirt and the knees of his breeches hanging loose. A considerable crowd of people gathered round, and were not a little struck by this singular appearance.'

He spoke Latin with wonderful fluency and elegance. When Pere Boscovich was in England, Johnson dined in company with him at Sir Joshua Reynolds's, and at Dr Douglas's, now Bishop of Carlisle. Upon both occasions that celebrated foreigner expressed his astonishment at Johnson's Latin conversation.[a]

To Dr SAMUEL JOHNSON.

Edinburgh, Dec. 5, 1775.

MY DEAR SIR — Mr Alexander Maclean, the present young Laird of Col, being to set out tomorrow for London, I give him this letter to introduce him to your acquaintance. The kindness which you and I experienced from his brother, whose unfortunate death we sincerely lament, will make us always desirous to show attention to any branch of the family. Indeed, you have so much of the true Highland cordiality, that I am sure you would have thought me to blame if I had neglected to recommend to you this Hebridean prince, in whose island we were hospitably entertained. I ever am with respectful attachment, my dear Sir,

Your most obliged
And most humble Servant,

JAMES BOSWELL.

Mr Maclean returned with the most agreeable accounts of the polite attention with which he was received by Dr Johnson.

In the course of this year Dr Burney informs me, that 'he very frequently met Dr Johnson at Mr Thrale's, at Streatham, where they had many long conversations, often sitting up as long as the fire and candles lasted, and much longer than the patience of the servants subsisted.'

A few of Johnson's sayings, which that gentleman recollects, shall here be inserted.

'I never take a nap after dinner but when I have had a bad night, and then the nap takes me.'

---

[a] Add: When at Paris, Johnson thus characterised Voltaire to Freron the Journalist: 'Vir est acerrimi ingenii, et paucarum literarum.'

'The writer of an epitaph should not be considered as saying nothing but what is strictly true. Allowance must be made for some degree of exaggerated praise. In lapidary inscriptions a man is not upon oath.'

'There is now less flogging in our great schools than formerly, but then less is learned there; so that what the boys get at one end, they lose at the other.'

'More is learned in public than in private schools, from emulation; there is the collision of mind with mind, or the radiation of many minds pointing to one centre. Though few boys make their own exercises, yet if a good exercise is given up, out of a great number of boys, it is made by somebody.'

'I hate by-roads in education. Education is as well known, and has long been as well known, as ever it can be. Endeavouring to make children prematurely wise is useless labour. Suppose they have more knowledge at five or six years old than other children, what use can be made of it? It will be lost before it is wanted, and the waste of so much time and labour of the teacher can never be repaid. Too much is expected from precocity, and too little performed. Miss —— was an instance of early cultivation, but in what did it terminate? In marrying a little Presbyterian parson, who keeps an infant boarding-school, so that all her employment now is, "to suckle fools and chronicle small beer". She tells the children, "this is a cat, and that is a dog, with four legs and a tail; see there! You are much better than a cat or a dog, for you can speak." If I had bestowed such an education on a daughter, and had discovered that she thought of marrying such a fellow, I would have sent her to the *Congress*.'

After having talked slightingly of music, he was observed to listen very attentively while Miss Thrale played on the harpsichord, and with eagerness he called to her, 'Why don't you dash away like Burney?' Dr Burney upon this said to him, 'I believe, Sir, we shall make a musician of you at last.' Johnson with candid complacency replied, 'Sir, I shall be glad to have a new sense given to me.'

He had come down one morning to the breakfast-room, and been a considerable time by himself before any body appeared. When on a subsequent day, he was twitted by Mrs Thrale for being very late, which he generally was, he defended himself by alluding to the extraordinary morning, when he had been too early, 'Madam, I do not like to come down to *vacuity*.'

Dr Burney having remarked that Mr Garrick was beginning to look old, he said, 'Why, Sir, you are not to wonder at that; no man's face has had more wear and tear.'

Not having heard from him for a longer time than I supposed he would be silent, I wrote to him December 18, not in good spirits, 'Sometimes I have been afraid that the cold which has gone over Europe this year like a sort of pestilence, has seized you severely; sometimes my imagination, which is upon occasions prolific of evil, hath figured that you may have somehow taken offence at some part of my conduct.'

To James Boswell, Esq.

Dear Sir – Never dream of any offence, how should you offend me? I consider your friendship as a possession, which I intend to hold till you take it from me, and to lament if ever by my fault I should lose it. However, when such suspicions find their way into your mind, always give them vent; I shall make haste to disperse them; but hinder their first ingress if you can. Consider such thoughts as morbid.

Such illness as may excuse my omission to Lord Hailes I cannot honestly plead. I have been hindered I know not how, by a succession of petty obstructions. I hope to mend immediately, and to send next post to his Lordship. Mr Thrale would have written to you if I had omitted; he sends his compliments, and wishes to see you.

You and your lady will now have no more wrangling about feudal inheritance. How does the young Laird of Auchinleck? I suppose Miss Veronica is grown a reader and discourser.

I have just now got a cough, but it has never yet hindered me from sleeping: I have had quieter nights than are common with me.

I cannot but rejoice that Joseph[1] has had the wit to find the way back. He is a fine fellow, and one of the best travellers in the world.

Young Col brought me your letter. He is a very pleasing youth. I took him two days ago to the Mitre, and we dined together. I was as civil as I had the means of being.

I have had a letter from Rasay, acknowledging, with great appearance of satisfaction, the insertion in the Edinburgh paper. I am very glad that it was done.

My compliments to Mrs Boswell, who does not love me; and of all the rest, I need only send them to those that do; and I am afraid it will give you very little trouble to distribute them. I am, my dear, dear Sir,

Your affectionate humble servant,

Sam. Johnson.

December 23, 1775.

In 1776, Johnson wrote, so far as I can discover, nothing for the public: but that his mind was still ardent, and fraught with generous wishes to attain to still higher degrees of literary excellence, is proved by his private notes of this year, which I shall insert in their proper place.

To James Boswell, Esq.

Dear Sir – I have at last sent you all Lord Hailes's papers. While I was in France, I looked very often into Henault; but Lord Hailes, in my opinion,

---

1 Joseph Rieter, a Bohemian, who was in my service many years, and attended Dr Johnson and me in our Tour to the Hebrides. After having left me for some time, he had now returned to me.

leaves him far, and far, behind. Why I did not dispatch so short a perusal sooner, when I look back, I am utterly unable to discover: but human moments are stolen away by a thousand petty impediments which leave no trace behind them. I have been afflicted, through the whole Christmas, with the general disorder, of which the worst effect was a cough, which is now much mitigated, though the country, on which I look from a window at Streatham, is now covered with a deep snow. Mrs Williams is very ill: every body else is as usual.

Among the papers, I found a letter to you, which I think you had not opened; and a paper for *The Chronicle*, which I suppose it not necessary now to insert. I return them both.

I have, within these few days, had the honour of receiving Lord Hailes's first volume, for which I return my most respectful thanks.

I wish you, my dearest friend, and your haughty lady (for I know she does not love me), and the young ladies, and the young Laird, all happiness. Teach the young gentleman, in spite of his mamma, to think and speak well of, Sir,

Your affectionate humble servant,

SAM. JOHNSON.

Jan. 10, 1776.

At this time was in agitation a matter of great consequence to me and my family, which I should not obtrude upon the world, were it not that the part which Dr Johnson's friendship for me made him take in it was the occasion of an exertion of his abilities, which it would be injustice to conceal. That what he wrote upon the subject may be understood, it is necessary to give a state of the question, which I shall do as briefly as I can.

In the year 1504, the barony or manor of Auchinleck (pronounced *Affleck*), in Ayrshire, which belonged to a family of the same name with the lands, having fallen to the Crown by forfeiture, James the Fourth, King of Scotland, granted it to Thomas Boswell, a branch of an ancient family in the county of Fife, styling him in the charter, '*dilecto familiari nostro*'; and assigning, as the cause of the grant, '*pro bono et fideli servitio nobis praestito*'. Thomas Boswell was slain in battle, fighting along with his Sovereign, at the fatal field of Floddon, in 1513.

From this very honourable founder of our family, the estate was transmitted, in a direct series of heirs male, to David Boswell, my father's great grand uncle, who had no sons, but four daughters, who were all respectably married, the eldest to Lord Cathcart.

David Boswell, being resolute in the military feudal principle of continuing the male succession, passed by his daughters, and settled the estate on his nephew by his next brother, who approved of the deed, and renounced any pretensions which he might possibly have, in preference to his son. But the estate having been burthened with large portions to the daughters, and other debts, it was necessary for the nephew to sell a considerable part of it, and what remained was still much encumbered.

The frugality of the nephew preserved, and, in some degree, relieved the estate. His son, my grandfather, an eminent lawyer, not only repurchased a great part of what had been sold, but acquired other lands; and my father, who was one of the Judges of Scotland, and had added considerably to the estate, now signified his inclination to take the privilege allowed by our law,[1] to secure it to his family in perpetuity by an entail, which, on account of marriage articles, could not be done without my consent.

In the plan of entailing the estate, I heartily concurred with him, though I was the first to be restrained by it; but we unhappily differed as to the series of heirs which should be established, or in the language of our law, called to the succession. My father had declared a predilection for heirs general, that is, males and females indiscriminately. He was willing, however, that all males descending from his grandfather should be preferred to females; but would not extend that privilege to males deriving their descent from a higher source. I, on the other hand, had a zealous partiality for heirs male, however remote, which I maintained, by arguments which appeared to me to have considerable weight.[2] And in the particular case of our family, I apprehended that we were under an implied obligation, in honour and good faith, to transmit the estate by the same tenure which we held it, which was as heirs male, excluding nearer females. I therefore, as I thought conscientiously, objected to my father's scheme.

1 Acts of Parliament of Scotland, 1685, Cap. 22.

2 As first, the opinion of some distinguished naturalists, that our species is transmitted through males only, the female being all along no more than a *nidus*, or nurse, as Mother Earth is to plants of every sort; which notion seems to be confirmed by that text of scripture, 'He was *yet in the loins of his* FATHER when Melchisedeck met him' (Heb. vi. 10.): and consequently, that a man's grandson by a daughter, instead of being his *surest* descendant, as is vulgarly said, has, in reality, no connection whatever with his blood. – And secondly, independent of this theory (which, if true, should completely exclude heirs general), that if the preference of a male to a female, without regard to primogeniture (as a son, though much younger, nay, even a grandson by a son, to a daughter), be once admitted, as it universally is, it must be equally reasonable and proper in the most remote degree of descent from an original proprietor of an estate, as in the nearest; because – however distant from the representative at the time – that remote heir male, upon the failure of those nearer to the *original proprietor* than he is, becomes in fact the nearest male to *him*, and is, therefore, preferable as *his* representative, to a female descendant. – A little extension of mind will enable us easily to perceive that a son's son, in continuation to whatever length of time, is preferable to a son's daughter, in the succession to an ancient inheritance; in which regard should be had to the representation of the original proprietor, and not to that of one of his descendants.

I am aware of Blackstone's admirable demonstration of the reasonableness of the legal succession, upon the principle of there being the greatest probability that the nearest heir of the person who last dies proprietor of an estate, is of the blood of the first purchaser. But supposing a pedigree to be carefully authenticated through all its branches, instead of mere *probability* there will be a certainty that *the nearest heir male, at whatever period*, has the same right of blood with the first heir male, namely, *the original purchaser's eldest son.*

My opposition was very displeasing to my father, who was entitled to great respect and deference; and I had reason to apprehend disagreeable consequences from my non-compliance with his wishes. After much perplexity and uneasiness, I wrote to Dr Johnson, stating the case, with all its difficulties, at full length, and earnestly requesting that he would consider it at leisure, and favour me with his friendly opinion and advice.

To JAMES BOSWELL, Esq.

DEAR SIR — I was much impressed by your letter, and, if I can form upon your case any resolution satisfactory to myself, will very gladly impart it; but whether I am quite equal to it, I do not know. It is a case compounded of law and justice, and requires a mind versed in juridical disquisitions. Could you not tell your whole mind to Lord Hailes? He is, you know, both a Christian and a Lawyer. I suppose he is above partiality, and above loquacity; and, I believe, he will not think the time lost in which he may quiet a disturbed, or settle a wavering mind. Write to me, as any thing occurs to you; and if I find myself stopped by want of facts necessary to be known, I will make enquiries of you as my doubts arise.

If your former resolutions should be found only fanciful, you decide rightly in judging that your father's fancies may claim the preference; but whether they are fanciful or rational, is the question. I really think Lord Hailes could help us.

Make my compliments to dear Mrs Boswell; and tell her, that I hope to be wanting in nothing that I can contribute, to bring you all out of your troubles. I am, dear Sir, most affectionately,

Your humble servant,

SAM. JOHNSON.

London, Jan. 15, 1776.

To the same.

DEAR SIR — I am going to write upon a question which requires more knowledge of local law, and more acquaintance with the general rules of inheritance, than I can claim; but I write, because you request it.

Land is, like any other possession, by natural right wholly in the power of its present owner; and may be sold, given, or bequeathed, absolutely or conditionally, as judgement shall direct, or passion incite.

But natural right would avail little without the protection of law; and the primary notion of law is restraint in the exercise of natural right. A man is therefore, in society, not fully master of what he calls his own, but he still retains all the power which law does not take from him.

In the exercise of the right which law either leaves or gives, regard is to be paid to moral obligations.

Of the estate which we are now considering, your father still retains such possession, with such power over it, that he can sell it, and do with the money what he will, without any legal impediment. But when he extends his power beyond his own life, by settling the order of succession, the law makes your consent necessary.

Let us suppose that he sells the land to risk the money in some specious adventure, and in that adventure loses the whole: his posterity would be disappointed; but they could not think themselves injured or robbed. If he spent it upon vice or pleasure, his successors could only call him vicious and voluptuous; they could not say that he was injurious or unjust.

He that may do more, may do less. He that, by selling or squandering, may disinherit a whole family, may certainly disinherit part by a partial settlement.

Laws are formed by the manners and exigencies of particular times, and it is but accidental that they last longer than their causes: the limitation of feudal succession to the male arose from the obligation of the tenant to attend his chief in war.

As times and opinions are always changing, I know not whether it be not usurpation to prescribe rules to posterity, by presuming to judge of what we cannot know; and I know not whether I fully approve either your design or your father's, to limit that succession which descended to you unlimited. If we are to leave *sartum tectum* to posterity, what we have without any merit of our own received from our ancestors, should not choice and free-will be kept unviolated? Is land to be treated with more reverence than liberty? – If this consideration should restrain your father from disinheriting some of the males, does it leave you the power of disinheriting all the females?

Can the possessor of a feudal estate make any will? Can he appoint, out of the inheritance, any portions to his daughters? There seems to be a very shadowy difference between the power of leaving land, and of leaving money to be raised from land; between leaving an estate to females, and leaving the male heir, in effect, only their steward.

Suppose at one time a law that allowed only males to inherit, and during the continuance of this law many estates to have descended, passing by the females to remoter heirs. Suppose afterwards the law repealed in correspondence with a change of manners, and women made capable of inheritance; would not then the tenure of estates be changed? Could the women have no benefit from a law made in their favour? Must they be passed by upon moral principles for ever, because they were once excluded by a legal prohibition? Or may that which passed only to males by one law, pass likewise to females by another?

You mention your resolution to maintain the right of your brothers.[1] I do not see how any of their rights are invaded.

As your whole difficulty arises from the act of your ancestor, who diverted the succession from the females, you enquire, very properly, what were his motives, and what was his intention; for you certainly are not bound by his act more than he intended to bind you, nor hold your land on harder or stricter terms than those on which it was granted.

---

1 Which term I applied to all the heirs male.

Intentions must be gathered from acts. When he left the estate to his nephew, by excluding his daughters, was it, or was it not, in his power to have perpetuated the succession to the males? If he could have done it, he seems to have shown, by omitting it, that he did not desire it to be done; and, upon your own principles, you will not easily prove your right to destroy that capacity of succession which your ancestors have left.

If your ancestor had not the power of making a perpetual settlement; and if, therefore, we cannot judge distinctly of his intentions, yet his act can only be considered as an example; it makes not an obligation. And, as you observe, he set no example of rigorous adherence to the line of succession. He that overlooked a brother, would not wonder that little regard is shown to remote relations.

As the rules of succession are, in a great part, purely legal, no man can be supposed to bequeath any thing, but upon legal terms: he can grant no power which the law denies; and if he makes no special and definite limitation, he confers all the powers which the law allows.

Your ancestor, for some reason, disinherited his daughters; but it no more follows that he intended his[a] act as a rule for posterity, than the disinheriting of his brother.

If therefore, you ask by what right your father admits daughters to inheritance, ask yourself, first, by what right you require them to be excluded?

It appears, upon reflection, that your father excludes nobody; he only admits nearer females to inherit before males more remote; and the exclusion is purely consequential.

These, dear Sir, are my thoughts, immethodical and deliberative; but, perhaps, you may find in them some glimmering of evidence.

I cannot, however, but again recommend to you a conference with Lord Hailes, whom you know to be both a Lawyer and a Christian.

Make my compliments to Mrs Boswell, though she does not love me. I am, Sir,

Your affectionate servant,

SAM. JOHNSON.

Feb. 3, 1776.

I had followed his recommendation and consulted Lord Hailes, who upon this subject had a firm opinion contrary to mine. His Lordship obligingly took the trouble to write me a letter, in which he discussed with legal and historical learning, the points in which I saw much difficulty, maintaining that 'the succession of heirs general was the succession, by the law of Scotland, from the throne to the cottage, as far as we can learn it by record'; observing that the estate of our family had not been limited to heirs male, and that though an heir male had in one instance been chosen in preference to nearer females, that had been an arbitrary act, which had seemed to be best in the embarrassed state of affairs at that time; and the fact was, that upon a fair computation of the value

---

[a] Read: 'this'.

of land and money at the time, applied to the estate and the burthens upon it, there was nothing given to the heir male but the skeleton of an estate. 'The plea of conscience (said his Lordship) which you put, is a most respectable one, especially when *conscience* and *self* are on different sides. But I think that conscience is not well informed, and that *self* and *she* ought on this occasion to be of a side.'

This letter, which had considerable influence upon my mind, I sent to Dr Johnson, begging to hear from him again, upon this interesting question.

To JAMES BOSWELL, Esq.

DEAR SIR – Having not any acquaintance with the laws or customs of Scotland, I endeavoured to consider your question upon general princi-ples, and found nothing of much validity that I could oppose to this position. 'He who inherits a fief unlimited by his ancestor, inherits the power of limiting it according to his own judgement or opinion.' If this be true, you may join with your father.

Further consideration produced another conclusion, 'He who receives a fief unlimited by his ancestors, gives his heirs some reason to complain if he does not transmit it unlimited to posterity.' For why should he make the state of others worse than his own, without a reason? If this be true, though neither you nor your father are about to do what is quite right, but as your father violates (I think) the legal succession least, he seems to be nearer the right than yourself.

It cannot but occur that 'Women have natural and equitable claims as well as men, and these claims are not to be capriciously or lightly super-seded or infringed.' When fiefs implied military service, it is easily discerned why females could not inherit them; but that reason is now at an end. As manners make laws, manners likewise repeal them.

These are the general conclusions which I have attained. None of them are very favourable to your scheme of entail, nor perhaps to any scheme. My observation, that only he who acquires an estate may bequeath it capriciously,[1] if it contains any conviction includes this position likewise, that only he who acquires an estate may entail it capriciously. But I think it may be safely presumed, that 'he who inherits an estate inherits all the power legally concomitant.' And that 'He who gives or leaves unlimited an estate legally limitable, must be presumed to give that power of limitation which he omitted to take away, and to commit future contingencies to future prudence.' In these two positions I believe Lord Hailes will advise you to rest; every other notion of possession seems to me full of difficulties, and embarrassed with scruples.

If these axioms be allowed, you have arrived now at full liberty without the help of particular circumstances, which, however, have in your case great weight. You very rightly observe, that he who passing by his brother

1 I had reminded him of his observation mentioned on page 387.

gave the inheritance to his nephew, could limit no more than he gave, and by Lord Hailes's estimate of fourteen years' purchase, what he gave was no more than you may easily entail according to your own opinion, if that opinion should finally prevail.

Lord Hailes's suspicion that entails are encroachments on the dominion of Providence, may be extended to all hereditary privileges and all permanent institutions; I do not see why it may not be extended to any provision but for the present hour, since all care about futurity proceeds upon a supposition, that we know at least in some degree what will be future. Of the future we certainly know nothing; but we may form conjectures from the past; and the power of forming conjectures, includes, in my opinion, the duty of acting in conformity to that probability which we discover. Providence gives the power of which reason teaches the use. I am, dear Sir,

Your most faithful servant,

SAM. JOHNSON.

February 9, 1776.

I hope I shall get some ground now with Mrs Boswell; make my compliments to her, and to the little people.

Don't burn papers; they may be safe enough in your own box – you will wish to see them hereafter.

To the same.

DEAR SIR – To the letters which I have written about your great question I have nothing to add. If your conscience is satisfied, you have now only your prudence to consult. I long for a letter, that I may know how this troublesome and vexatious question is at last decided.[1] I hope that it will at last end well. Lord Hailes's letter was very friendly, and very seasonable, but I think his aversion from entails has something in it like superstition. Providence is not counteracted by any means which Providence puts into our power. The continuance and propagation of families makes a great part of the Jewish law, and is by no means prohibited in the Christian institution, though the necessity of it continues no longer. Hereditary tenures are established in all civilised countries, and are accompanied in most with hereditary authority. Sir William Temple considers our constitution as defective, that there is not an unalienable estate in land connected with a peerage: and Lord Bacon mentions as a proof that the Turks are Barbarians, their want of *Stirpes*, as he

---

1 The entail framed by my father with various judicious clauses, was executed by him and me, settling the estate upon the heirs male of his grandfather, which I found had been already done by my grandfather, imperfectly, but so as to be defeated only by selling the lands. I was freed by Dr Johnson from scruples of conscientious obligation, and could, therefore, gratify my father. But my opinion and partiality for male succession, in its full extent, remained unshaken. Yet let me not be thought harsh or unkind to daughters; for my notion is, that they should be treated with great affection and tenderness, and always participate of the prosperity of the family.

calls them, or hereditary rank. Do not let your mind, when it is freed from the supposed necessity of a rigorous entail, be entangled with contrary objections, and think all entails unlawful, till you have cogent arguments, which I believe you will never find; I am afraid of scruples.

I have now sent all Lord Hailes's papers; part I found hidden in a drawer in which I had laid them for security, and had forgotten them. Part of these are written twice, I have returned both the copies. Part I had read before.

Be so kind as to return Lord Hailes my most respectful thanks for his first volume; his accuracy strikes me with wonder; his narrative is far superior to that of Henault, as I have formerly mentioned.

I am afraid that the trouble, which my irregularity and delay has cost him, is greater, far greater, than any good that I can do him will ever recompense, but if I have any more copy, I will try to do better.

Pray let me know if Mrs Boswell is friends with me, and pay my respects to Veronica, and Euphemia, and Alexander. I am, Sir,

Your most humble servant,

SAM. JOHNSON.

Feb. 15, 1775.

Mr BOSWELL to Dr JOHNSON.

Edinburgh, Feb. 20, 1776.

. . . You have illuminated my mind and relieved me from imaginary shackles of conscientious obligation. Were it necessary, I could immediately join in an entail upon the series of heirs approved by my father; but it is better not to act too suddenly.

Dr JOHNSON to Mr BOSWELL.

DEAR SIR – I am glad that what I could think or say has at all contributed to quiet your thoughts. Your resolution not to act, till your opinion is confirmed by more deliberation, is very just. If you have been scrupulous, do not now be rash. I hope that as you think more, and take opportunities of talking with men intelligent in questions of property, you will be able to free yourself from every difficulty.

When I wrote last, I sent, I think, ten packets. Did you receive them all?

You must tell Mrs Boswell that I suspected her to have written without your knowledge,[1] and therefore did not return any answer, lest a clandestine correspondence should have been perniciously discovered. I will write to her soon . . . I am, dear Sir,

Most affectionately yours,

SAM. JOHNSON.

Feb. 24, 1776.

---

1 A letter to him on the interesting subject of the family settlement, which I had read.

Having communicated to Lord Hailes what Dr Johnson wrote concerning the question which perplexed me so much, his Lordship wrote to me, 'Your scruples have produced more fruit than I ever expected from them; an excellent dissertation on general principles of morals and law.'

I wrote to Dr Johnson on the 20th of February, complaining of melancholy, and expressing a strong desire to be with him; informing him that the ten packets came all safe; that Lord Hailes was much obliged to him, and said he had almost wholly removed his scruples against entails.

To JAMES BOSWELL, Esq.

DEAR SIR – I have not had your letter half an hour; as you lay so much weight upon my notions, I should think it not just to delay my answer.

I am very sorry that your melancholy should return, and should be sorry likewise if it could have no relief but from my company. My counsel you may have when you are pleased to require it; but of my company you cannot in the next month have much, for Mr Thrale will take me to Italy, he says, on the first of April.

Let me warn you very earnestly against scruples. I am glad that you are reconciled to your settlement, and think it a great honour to have shaken Lord Hailes's opinion of entails. Do not, however, hope wholly to reason away your troubles; do not feed them with attention, and they will die imperceptibly away. Fix your thoughts upon your business, fill your intervals with company, and sunshine will again break in upon your mind. If you will come to me, you must come very quickly, and even then I know not but we may scour the country together, for I have a mind to see Oxford and Lichfield before I set out on this long journey. To this I can only add, that I am, dear Sir,

Your most affectionate humble servant,

SAM. JOHNSON.

March 5, 1776.

To the same.

DEAR SIR – Very early in April we leave England, and in the beginning of the next week I shall leave London for a short time; of this I think it necessary to inform you, that you may not be disappointed in any of your enterprises. I had not fully resolved to go into the country before this day.

Please to make my compliments to Lord Hailes; and mention very particularly to Mrs Boswell my hope that she is reconciled to, Sir,

Your faithful servant,

SAM. JOHNSON.

March 12, 1776.

Above thirty years ago, the heirs of Lord Chancellor Clarendon presented the University of Oxford with the continuation of his History, and such other of his Lordship's manuscripts as had not been published, on condition that the profits arising from their publication should be applied to the establishment of a *Manege* in the University. The gift was accepted in full convocation. A person being now recommended to Dr Johnson, as fit to superintend this proposed riding-school, he exerted himself with that zeal for which he was remarkable upon every similar occasion. But, on enquiry into the matter, he found that the scheme was not likely to be soon carried into execution; the profits arising from the Clarendon press being, from some mismanagement, very scanty. This having been explained to him by a respectable dignitary of the church, who had good means of knowing it, he wrote a letter upon the subject, which at once exhibits his extraordinary precision and acuteness, and his warm attachment to his ALMA MATER.

To the Reverend Dr WETHERELL, Master of University-College, Oxford.

DEAR SIR – Few things are more unpleasant than the transaction of business with men who are above knowing or caring what they have to do; such as the trustees for Lord Cornbury's institution will, perhaps, appear, when you have read Dr ———'s letter.

The last part of the Doctor's letter is of great importance. The complaint[1] which he makes I have heard long ago, and did not know but it was redressed. It is unhappy that a practice so erroneous has not yet been altered; for altered it must be, or our press will be useless with all its privileges. The booksellers, who, like all other men, have strong prejudices in their own favour, are enough inclined to think the practice of printing and selling books by any but themselves, an encroachment on the rights of their fraternity, and have need of stronger inducements to circulate academical publications than those of one another; for, of that mutual co-operation by which the general trade is carried on, the University can bear no part. Of those whom he neither loves nor fears, and from whom he expects no reciprocation of good offices, why should any man promote the interest but for profit? I suppose, with all our scholastic ignorance of mankind, we are still too knowing to expect that the booksellers will erect themselves into patrons, and buy and sell under the influence of a disinterested zeal for the promotion of learning.

To the booksellers, if we look for either honour or profit from our press, not only their common profit, but something more must be allowed; and if books, printed at Oxford, are expected to be rated at a high price, that price must be levied on the public, and paid by the ultimate purchaser, not by the intermediate agents. What price shall be set upon the book, is, to the

---

1 I suppose the complaint was, that the trustees of the Oxford press did not allow the London booksellers a sufficient profit upon vending their publications.

booksellers, wholly indifferent, provided that they gain a proportionate profit by negotiating the sale.

Why books printed at Oxford should be particularly dear, I am, however, unable to find. We pay no rent; we inherit many of our instruments and materials; lodging and victuals are cheaper than at London; and, therefore, workmanship ought, at least, not to be dearer. Our expenses are naturally less than those of booksellers; and, in most cases, communities are content with less profit than individuals.

It is, perhaps, not considered through how many hands a book often passes, before it comes into those of the reader; or what part of the profit each hand must retain, as a motive for transmitting it to the next.

We will call our primary agent in London, Mr Cadell, who receives our books from us, gives them room in his warehouse, and issues them on demand; by him they are sold to Mr Dilly, a wholesale bookseller, who sends them into the country; and the last seller is the country bookseller. Here are three profits to be paid between the printer and the reader, or in the style of commerce, between the manufacturer and the consumer; and if any of these profits is too penuriously distributed, the process of commerce is interrupted.

We are now come to the practical question, what is to be done? You will tell me, with reason, that I have said nothing, till I declare how much, according to my opinion, of the ultimate price ought to be distributed through the whole succession of sale.

The deduction, I am afraid, will appear very great: but let it be considered before it is refused. We must allow, for profit, between thirty and thirty-five *per cent*, between six and seven shillings in the pound; that is, for every book which costs the last buyer twenty shillings, we must charge Mr Cadell with something less than fourteen. We must set the copies at fourteen shillings each, and superadd what is called the quarterly-book, or for every hundred books so charged we must deliver an hundred and four.

The profits will then stand thus:

Mr Cadell, who runs no hazard, and gives no credit, will be paid for warehouse room and attendance by a shilling profit on each book, and his chance of the quarterly-book.

Mr Dilly, who buys the book for fifteen shillings, and who will expect the quarterly-book if he takes five-and-twenty, will sell it to his country customer at sixteen and six-pence, by which, at the hazard of loss, and the certainty of long credit, he gains the regular profit of ten *per cent*, which is expected in the wholesale trade.

The country bookseller, buying at sixteen and six-pence, and commonly trusting a considerable time, gains but three and six-pence, and, if he trusts a year, not much more than two and six-pence; otherwise than as he may, perhaps, take as long credit as he gives.

With less profit than this, and more you see he cannot have, the country bookseller cannot live; for his receipts are small, and his debts sometimes bad.

Thus, dear Sir, I have been incited by Dr ——'s letter to give you a detail of the circulation of books, which, perhaps, every man has not had opportunity of knowing; and which those who know it, do not, perhaps, always distinctly consider.

I am, &c.

SAM. JOHNSON.[1]

March 12, 1776.

Having arrived in London late on Friday, the 15th of March, I hastened next morning to wait on Dr Johnson, at his house; but found he was removed from Johnson's-court, No. 7, to Bolt-court, No. 8, still keeping to his favourite Fleet-street. My reflection at the time upon this change as marked in my Journal, is as follows, 'I felt a foolish regret that he had left a court which bore his name;[a] but it was not foolish to be affected with some tenderness of regard for a place in which I had seen him a great deal, from whence I had often issued a better and a happier man than when I went in, and which had often appeared to my imagination while I trod its pavement, in the solemn darkness of the night, to be sacred to wisdom, and piety.' Being informed that he was at Mr Thrale's, in the Borough, I hastened thither, and found Mrs Thrale and him at breakfast. I was kindly welcomed. In a moment he was in a full glow of conversation, and I felt myself elevated as if brought into another state of being. Mrs Thrale and I looked to each other while he talked, and our looks expressed our congenial admiration and affection for him. I shall ever recollect this scene with great pleasure. I exclaimed to her, 'I am now, intellectually, *Hermippus redivivus*, I am quite restored by him, by transfusion of *mind*.' 'There are many (she replied) who admire and respect Mr Johnson, but you and I *love* him.'

He seemed very happy in the near prospect of going to Italy with Mr and Mrs Thrale. 'But (said he), before leaving England I am to take a jaunt to Oxford, Birmingham, my native city Lichfield, and my old friend, Dr Taylor's, at Ashbourne, in Derbyshire. I shall go in a few days, and you, Boswell, shall go with me.' I was ready to accompany him; being willing even to leave London to have the pleasure of his conversation.

I mentioned with much regret the extravagance of the representative of a great family of Scotland, by which there was danger of its being ruined; and as Johnson respected it for its antiquity, he joined with me in thinking it would be happy if this person should die. Mrs Thrale seemed shocked at this, as feudal barbarity; and said, 'I do not understand this preference of the estate to its owner; of the land to the man who walks upon that land.' JOHNSON. 'Nay, Madam, it is not a preference of the land to its owner, it is the preference of a

1 I am happy in giving this full and clear statement to the public, to vindicate, by the authority of the greatest author of his age, that respectable body of men, the Booksellers of London, from vulgar reflections, as if their profits were exorbitant, when, in truth, Dr Johnson has here allowed them more than they usually demand.

a Add the following note: He said, when he was in Scotland, that he was Johnson of *that ilk*.

family to an individual. Here is an establishment in a country, which is of importance for ages, not only to the chief but to his people; an establishment which extends upwards and downwards; that this should be destroyed by one idle fellow is a sad thing.'

He said, 'Entails are good, because it is good to preserve in a country, serieses of men, to whom the people are accustomed to look up as to their leaders But I am for leaving a quantity of land in commerce, to excite industry and keep money in the country; for if no land were to be bought in a country, there would be no encouragement to acquire wealth, because a family could not be founded there; or if it were acquired, it must be carried away to another country where land may be bought. And although the land in every country will remain the same, and be as fertile where there is no money, as where there is, yet all that portion of the happiness of civil life, which is produced by money circulating in a country, would be lost.' BOSWELL. 'Then, Sir, would it be for the advantage of a country that all its lands were sold at once?' JOHNSON. 'So far, Sir, as money produces good it would be an advantage; for, then that country would have as much money circulating in it as it is worth. But to be sure this would be counterbalanced by disadvantages attending a total change of proprietors.'

I expressed my opinion that the power of entailing should be limited thus: 'That there should be one third, or perhaps one half of the land of a country kept free for commerce; that the proportion allowed to be entailed, should be parcelled out so as that no family could entail above a certain quantity. Let a family according to the abilities of its representatives, be richer or poorer in different generations, or always rich if its representatives be always wise: but let its absolute permanency be moderate. In this way we should be certain of there being always a number of established roots; and as in the course of nature, there is in every age an extinction of some families, there would be continual openings for men ambitious of perpetuity, to plant a stock in the entail ground.'[1] JOHNSON. 'Why, Sir, mankind will be better able to regulate the system of entails, when the evil of too much land being locked up by them is felt, than we can do at present when it is not felt.'

I mentioned Dr Adam Smith's book on *The Wealth of Nations*, which was just published, and that Sir John Pringle had observed to me, that Dr Smith, who had never been in trade, could not be expected to write well on that subject any more than a lawyer upon physic. JOHNSON. 'He is mistaken, Sir; a man who has never been engaged in trade himself may undoubtedly write

---

1 The privilege of perpetuating in a family an estate and arms *indefeasibly* from generation to generation, is enjoyed by none of his Majesty's subjects except in Scotland, where the legal fiction of a *fine and recovery* is unknown. It is a privilege so proud, that I should think it would be proper to have the exercise of it dependent on the royal prerogative. It seems absurd to permit the power of perpetuating their representation, to men, who having had no eminent merit, have truly no name. The King, as the impartial father of his people, would never refuse to grant the privilege to those who deserved it.

well upon trade, and there is nothing which requires more to be illustrated by philosophy than trade does. As to mere wealth, that is to say, money, it is clear that one nation or one individual cannot increase its store but by making another poorer: but trade procures what is more valuable, the reciprocation of the peculiar advantages of different countries. A merchant seldom thinks but of his own particular trade. To write a good book upon it, a man must have extensive views. It is not necessary to have practised, to write well upon a subject.' I mentioned law as a subject on which no man could write well without practice. JOHNSON. 'Why, Sir, in England, where so much money is to be got by the practice of the law, most of our writers upon it have been in practice; though Blackstone had not been much in practice when he published his Commentaries. But upon the Continent, the great writers on law have not all been in practice: Grotius, indeed, was; but Puffendorf was not, Burlamaqui was not.'

When we had talked of the great consequence which a man acquired by being employed in his profession, I suggested a doubt of the justice of the general opinion, that it is improper in a lawyer to solicit employment; for why, I urged, should it not be equally allowable to solicit that as the means of consequence, as it is to solicit votes to be elected a member of parliament? Mr Strahan had told me, that a countryman of his and mine, who had risen to eminence in the law, had, when first making his way, solicited him to get him employed in city causes. JOHNSON. 'Sir, it is wrong to stir up law-suits; but when once it is certain that a law-suit is to go on, there is nothing wrong in a lawyer's endeavouring that he shall have the benefit, rather than another.' BOSWELL. 'You would not solicit employment, Sir, if you were a lawyer.' JOHNSON. 'No, Sir; but not because I should think it wrong, but because I should disdain it.' This was a good distinction, which will be felt by men of just pride. He proceeded: 'However, I would not have a lawyer to be wanting to himself in using fair means. I would have him to inject a little hint now and then, to prevent his being overlooked.'

Lord Mountstuart's bill for a Scotch militia, in supporting which his Lord-ship had made an able speech in the House of Commons, was now a pretty general topic of conversation. – JOHNSON. 'As Scotland contributes so little land-tax towards the general support of the nation, it ought not to have a militia paid out of the general fund, unless it should be thought for the general interest, that Scotland should be protected from an invasion, which no man can think will happen; for what enemy would invade Scotland, where there is nothing to be got? No, Sir; now that the Scotch have not the pay of English soldiers spent among them, as so many troops are sent abroad, they are trying to get money another way by having a militia paid. If they are afraid, and seriously desire to have an armed force to defend them, they should pay for it. Your scheme is to retain a part of your little land-tax, by making us pay and clothe your militia.' BOSWELL. 'You should not talk of we and you, Sir; there is now an *Union*.' JOHNSON. 'There must be a distinction of interest, while the proportions of land-tax are so unequal. If Yorkshire should say, "Instead of paying our land-tax, we will keep a greater number of militia", it would be unreasonable.' In this argument my friend was certainly in the wrong. The land-tax is as unequally proportioned between different parts of England, as between England and Scotland; nay, it is considerably unequal in Scotland itself. But the land-tax is but a small part of the numerous branches of public revenue, all of which Scotland pays precisely as England does. A French invasion made in Scotland would soon penetrate into England.

He thus discoursed upon supposed obligations in settling estates. – 'Where a man gets the unlimited property of an estate, there is no obligation upon him in *justice* to leave it to one person rather than to another. There is a motive of preference from *kindness*, and this kindness is generally entertained for the nearest relation. If I *owe* a particular man a sum of money, I am obliged to let that man have the next money I get, and cannot in justice let another have it: but if I owe money to no man, I may dispose of what I get as I please. There is not a *debitum justitiae* to a man's next heir; there is only a *debitum caritatis*. It is plain, then, that I have morally a choice, according to my liking. If I have a brother in want, he has a claim from affection to my assistance: but if I have also a brother in want, whom I like better, he has a preferable claim. The right of an heir at law is only this, that he is to have the succession to an estate, in case no other person is appointed to it by the owner. His right is merely preferable to that of the King.'

We got into a boat to cross over to Blackfriars; and as we moved along the Thames, I talked to him of a little volume, which, altogether unknown to him, was advertised to be published in a few days, under the title of '*Johnsoniana*, or *Bon Mots* of Dr Johnson'. JOHNSON. 'Sir, it is a mighty impudent thing.' BOSWELL. 'Pray, Sir, could you have no. redress if you were to prosecute a publisher for bringing out, under your name, what you never said, and ascribing to you dull stupid nonsense, or making you swear profanely, as many ignorant relaters of your *bon mots* do?' JOHNSON. 'No, Sir; there will always be some truth mixed with the falsehood, and how can it be ascertained how much is true and how much is false? Besides, Sir, what damages would a jury give me for having been represented as swearing?' BOSWELL. 'I think, Sir, you should at least disavow such a publication, because the world and posterity might with much plausible foundation say, "Here is a volume which was publicly advertised and came out in Dr Johnson's own time, and, by his silence, was admitted by him to be genuine." ' JOHNSON. 'I shall give myself no trouble about the matter.'

He was, perhaps, above suffering from such spurious publications; but I could not help thinking, that many men would be much injured in their reputation, by having absurd and vicious sayings imputed to them; and that redress ought in such cases to be given.

He said, 'The value of every story depends on its being true. A story is a picture either of an individual or of human nature in general: if it be false, it is a picture of nothing. For instance: suppose a man should tell that Johnson, before setting out for Italy, as he had to cross the Alps, sat down to make himself wings. This many people would believe; but it would be a picture of nothing. —— (naming a worthy friend of ours) used to think a story, a story, till I showed him that truth was essential to it.' I observed, that Foote entertained us with stories which were not true; but that, indeed, it was properly not as narratives that Foote's stories pleased us, but as collections of ludicrous images. JOHNSON. 'Foote is quite impartial, for he tells lies of every body.'

The importance of strict and scrupulous veracity cannot be too often inculcated. Johnson was known to be so rigidly attentive to it, that even in his common conversation the slightest circumstance was mentioned with exact precision. The knowledge of his having such a principle and habit made his friends have a perfect reliance on the truth of every thing that he told, however it might have been doubted if told by many others. As an instance of this, I may mention an odd incident which he related as having happened to him one night in Fleet-street. 'A gentlewoman (said he) begged I would give her my arm to assist her in crossing the street, which I accordingly did; upon which she offered me a shilling, supposing me to be the watchman. I perceived that she was somewhat in liquor.' This, if told by most people, would have been thought an invention: when told by Johnson, it was believed by his friends as much as if they had seen what passed.

We landed at the Temple-stairs, where we parted.

I found him in the evening in Mrs Williams's room. We talked of religious orders. He said, 'It is as unreasonable for a man to go into a Carthusian convent, for fear of being immoral, as for a man to cut off his hands for fear he should steal. There is, indeed, great resolution in the immediate act of dismembering himself; but when that is once done, he has no longer any merit: for though it is out of his power to steal, yet he may all his life be a thief in his heart. So when a man has once become a Carthusian, he is obliged to continue so, whether he chooses it or not. Their silence, too, is absurd. We read in the gospel of the apostles being sent to preach, but not to hold their tongues. All severity that does not tend to increase good, or prevent evil, is idle. I said to the Lady Abbess of a convent, "Madam, you are here, not for the love of virtue, but the fear of vice." She said, "she should remember this as long as she lived." ' I thought it hard to give her this view of her situation, when she could not help it; and, indeed, I wondered at the whole of what he now said; because, both in his *Rambler* and *Idler*, he treats religious austerities with much solemnity of respect.

Finding him still persevering in his abstinence from wine, I ventured to speak to him of it. – JOHNSON. 'Sir, I have no objection to a man's drinking wine, if he can do it in moderation. I found myself apt to go to excess in it, and therefore, after having been for some time without it, on account of illness, I thought it better not to return to it. Every man is to judge for himself, according to the effects which he experiences. One of the fathers tells us, he found fasting made him so peevish that he did not practise it.'

Though he often enlarged upon the evil of intoxication, he was by no means harsh and unforgiving to those who indulged in occasional excess in wine. One of his friends, I well remember, came to sup at a tavern with him and some other gentlemen, and too plainly discovered that he had drunk too much at dinner. When one who loved mischief, thinking to produce a severe censure, asked Johnson, some days afterwards, 'Well, Sir, what did your friend say to you, as an apology for being in such a situation?' Johnson answered, 'Sir, he said all that a man *should* say: he said he was sorry for it.'

I heard him once give a very judicious practical advice upon this subject: 'A man (said he), who has been drinking wine at all freely, should never go into a new company. With those who have partaken of wine with him, he may be pretty well in unison: but he will probably be offensive, or appear ridiculous, to other people.'

He allowed very great influence to education. 'I do not deny, Sir, but there is some original difference in minds; but it is nothing in comparison of what is formed by education. We may instance the science of *numbers*, which all minds are equally capable of attaining; yet we find a prodigious difference in the powers of different men, in that respect, after they are grown up, because their minds have been more or less exercised in it; and I think the same cause will explain the difference of excellence in other things, gradations admitting always some difference in the first principles.'

This is a difficult subject; but it is best to hope that diligence may do a great deal. We are *sure* of what it can do, in increasing our mechanical force and dexterity.

I again visited him on Monday. He took occasion to enlarge, as he often did, upon the wretchedness of a sea-life. 'A ship is worse than a gaol. There is, in a gaol, better air, better company, better conveniency of every kind; and a ship has the additional disadvantage of being in danger. When men come to like a sea-life, they are not fit to live on land.' – 'Then (said I), it would be cruel in a father to breed his son to the sea.' JOHNSON. 'It would be cruel in a father who thinks as I do. Men go to sea, before they know the unhappiness of that way of life; and when they have come to know it, they cannot escape from it, because it is then too late to choose another profession; as indeed is generally the case with men, when they have once engaged in any particular way of life.'

On Tuesday, March 19, which was fixed for our proposed jaunt, we met in the morning at the Somerset coffee-house in the Strand, where we were taken up by the Oxford coach. He was accompanied by Mr Gwyn, the architect; and a gentleman of Merton College, whom we did not know, had the fourth seat. We soon got into conversation; for it was very remarkable of Johnson, that the presence of a stranger was no restraint upon his talk. I observed that Garrick, who was about to quit the stage, would soon have an easier life. JOHNSON. 'I doubt that, Sir.' BOSWELL. 'Why, Sir, he will be Atlas with the burthen off his back.' JOHNSON. 'But I know not, Sir, if he will be so steady without his load. However, he should never play any more, but be entirely the gentleman, and not partly the player: he should no longer subject himself to be hissed by a mob, or to be insolently treated by performers, whom he used to rule with a high hand, and who would gladly retaliate.' BOSWELL. 'I think he should play once a year for the benefit of decayed actors, as it has been said he means to do.' JOHNSON. 'Alas, Sir! he will soon be a decayed actor himself.'

Johnson expressed his disapprobation of ornamental architecture, such as magnificent columns supporting a portico, or expensive pilasters supporting merely their own capitals, 'because it consumes labour disproportionate to its utility.' For the same reason he satyrised statuary. 'Painting (said he) consumes labour not disproportionate to its effect; but a fellow will hack half a year at a block of marble to make something in stone that hardly resembles a man. The value of statuary is owing to its difficulty. You would not value the finest head cut upon a carrot.' Here he seemed to me to be strangely deficient in taste; for surely statuary is a noble art of imitation, and preserves a wonderful expression of the varieties of the human frame; and although it must be allowed that the circumstances of difficulty enhance the value of a marble head, we should consider, that if it requires a long time in the performance, it has a proportionate value in durability.

Gwyn was a fine lively rattling fellow. Dr Johnson kept him in subjection, but with a kindly authority. The spirit of the artist, however, rose against what he thought a Gothic attack, and he made a brisk defence. 'What, Sir, will you allow no value to beauty in architecture or in statuary? Why should we allow it then in writing? Why do you take the trouble to give us so many fine allusions, and bright images, and elegant phrases? You might convey all your instruction without these ornaments.' Johnson smiled with complacency; but said, 'Why, Sir, all these ornaments are useful, because they obtain an easier reception for truth, but a building is not at all more convenient for being decorated with superfluous carved work.'

Gwyn at last was lucky enough to make one reply to Dr Johnson, which he allowed to be excellent. Johnson censured him for taking down a church which might have stood many years, and building a new one at a different place, for no other reason but that there might be a direct road to a new bridge; and his expression was, 'You are taking a church out of the way, that the people may go in a straight line to the bridge.' – 'No, Sir (said Gwyn), I am putting the church *in* the way, that the people may not *go out of the way.*' JOHNSON. (with a hearty loud laugh of approbation), 'Speak no more. Rest your colloquial fame upon this.'

Upon our arrival at Oxford, Dr Johnson and I went directly to University College, but were disappointed on finding that one of the fellows, his friend Mr Scott, who accompanied him from Newcastle to Edinburgh, was gone to the country. We put up at the Angel inn, and passed the evening by ourselves in easy and familiar conversation. Talking of constitutional melancholy, he observed, 'A man so afflicted, Sir, must divert distressing thoughts, and not combat with them.' BOSWELL. 'May not he think them down, Sir?' JOHNSON. 'No, Sir. To attempt to *think them down* is madness. He should have a lamp constantly burning in his bed-chamber during the night, and if wakefully disturbed, take a book, and read, and compose himself to rest. To have the management of the mind is a great art, and it may be attained in a considerable degree by experience and habitual exercise.' BOSWELL. 'Should not he provide amusements for himself? Would it not, for instance, be right for him to take a course of chemistry?' JOHNSON. 'Let him take a course of chemistry, or a course of rope-dancing, or a course of any thing to which he is inclined at the time. Let him contrive to have as many retreats for his mind as he can, as many things to which it can fly from itself. Burton's *Anatomy of Melancholy* is a valuable work. It is, perhaps, overloaded with quotation. But there is great spirit and great power in what Burton says, when he writes from his own mind.'

Next morning we visited Dr Wetherell, Master of University College, with whom Dr Johnson conferred on the most advantageous mode of disposing of the books printed at the Clarendon press, on which subject his letter has been inserted in a former page. I often had occasion to remark, Johnson loved business, loved to have his wisdom actually operate on real life. Dr Wetherell and I talked of him without reserve in his own presence. WETHERELL. 'I would have given him a hundred guineas if he would have written a preface to his *Political Tracts*, by way of a Discourse on the British Constitution.' BOSWELL. 'Dr Johnson, though in his writings, and upon all occasions a great friend to the constitution both in church and state, has never written expressly in support of either. There is really a claim upon him for both. I am sure he could give a volume of no great bulk upon each, which would comprise all the substance, and with his spirit would effectually maintain them. He should erect a fort on the confines of each.' I could perceive that he was displeased by this dialogue. He burst out, 'Why should *I* be always writing?' I hoped he was conscious that the debt was just, and meant to discharge it, though he disliked being dunned.

We then went to Pembroke College, and waited on his old friend Dr Adams, the master of it, whom I found to be a most polite, pleasing, communicative man. Before his advancement to the headship of his College, I had intended to go and visit him at Shrewsbury, where he was rector of St Chad's, in order to get from him what particulars he could recollect of Johnson's academical life. He now obligingly gave me part of that authentic information, which, with what I afterwards owed to his kindness, will be found incorporated in its proper place in this work.

Dr Adams had distinguished himself by an able answer to David Hume's 'Essay on Miracles'. He told me he had once dined in company with Hume in London; that Hume shook hands with him, and said, 'You have treated me much better than I deserve'; and that they exchanged visits. I took the liberty to object to treating an infidel writer with smooth civility. Where there is a controversy concerning a passage in a classic author, or concerning a question in antiquities, or any other subject in which human happiness is not deeply interested, a man may treat his antagonist with politeness and even respect. But where the controversy is concerning the truth of religion, it is of such vast importance to him who maintains it, to obtain the victory, that the person of an opponent ought not to be spared. If a man firmly believes that religion is an invaluable treasure, he will consider a writer who endeavours to deprive mankind of it as a *robber*; he will look upon him as *odious* though the Infidel may think himself in the right. A robber who reasons as the gang do in *The Beggar's Opera*, who call themselves *practical* philosophers, and may have as much sincerity as pernicious *speculative* philosophers, is not the less an object of just indignation. An abandoned profligate may think that it is not wrong to debauch my wife; but shall I, therefore, not detest him? And if I catch him making an attempt shall I treat him with politeness? No, I will kick him down stairs, or run him through the body: that is, if I really love my wife, or have a true rational notion of honour. An Infidel then should not be treated hand-somely by a Christian, merely because he endeavours to rob with ingenuity. I do declare, however, that I am exceedingly unwilling to be provoked to anger, and could I be persuaded that truth would not suffer from a cool moderation in its defenders, I should wish to preserve good humour, at least, in every controversy; nor, indeed, do I see why a man should lose his temper while he does all he can to refute an opponent. I think ridicule may be fairly used against an infidel; for instance, if he be an ugly fellow, and yet absurdly vain of his person, we may contrast his appearance with Cicero's beautiful image of Virtue, could she be seen. Johnson coincided with me and said, 'When a man voluntarily engages in an important controversy, he is to do all he can to lessen his antagonist, because authority from personal respect has much weight with most people, and often more than reasoning. If my antagonist writes bad language, though that may not be essential to the question, I will attack him for his bad language.' ADAMS. 'You would not jostle a chimney-sweeper.' JOHNSON. 'Yes, sir, if it were necessary to jostle him *down*.'

Dr Adams told us, that in some of the Colleges at Oxford, the fellows had excluded the students from social intercourse with them in the common room. JOHNSON. 'They are in the right, sir, for there can be no real convers-ation, no fair exertion of mind amongst them, if the young men are by; for a man who has a character does not choose to stake it in their presence.' BOSWELL. 'But, Sir, may there not be very good conversation without a contest for superiority?' JOHNSON. 'No animated conversation, sir, for it cannot be but one or other will come off superior. I do not mean that the victor must have the better of the argument, for he may take the weak side; but his superiority of parts and knowledge will necessarily appear: and he to whom he thus shews himself superior is lessened in the eyes of the young men. You know it was said, "*Mallem cum Scaligero errare quam cum Clavio recte sapere.*" In the same manner take Bentley's and Jason de Neres' Comments upon Horace, you will admire Bentley more when wrong, than Jason when right.'

We walked with Dr Adams into the master's garden, and into the common room. JOHNSON. (after a reverie of meditation), 'Aye! Here I used to play at drafts with Phil. Jones and Fludyer. Jones loved beer, and did not get very forward in the church. Fludyer turned out a scoundrel, a Whig, and said he was ashamed of having been bred at Oxford. He had a living at Putney, and got under the eye of some retainers to the court at that time, and so became a violent Whig: but he had been a scoundrel all along, to be sure.' BOSWELL. 'Was he a scoundrel, Sir, in any other way than being a political scoundrel? Did he cheat at drafts?' JOHNSON. 'Sir, we never played for *money*.'

He then carried me to visit Dr Bentham, Canon of Christ-Church, and Divinity Professor, with whose learned and lively conversation we were much pleased. He gave us an invitation to dinner, which Dr Johnson told me was a high honour. 'Sir, it is a great thing to dine with the Canons of Christ-

Church.' We could not accept his invitation, as we were engaged to dine at University College. We had an excellent dinner there, with the Master and Fellows, it being St Cuthbert's day, which is kept by them as a festival, as he was a saint of Durham, with which this College is much connected.

We drank tea with Dr Horne, President of Magdalen College, now Bishop of Norwich, of whose abilities, in different respects, the public has had eminent proofs, and the esteem annexed to whose character was increased by knowing him personally. He had talked of publishing an edition of Walton's Lives, but had laid aside that design, upon Dr Johnson's telling him, from mistake, that Lord Hailes intended to do it. I had wished to negotiate between Lord Hailes and him, that one or other should perform so good a work. JOHNSON. 'In order to do it well, it will be necessary to collect all the editions of Walton's Lives. By way of adapting the book to the taste of the present age, they have, in a later edition, left out a vision which he relates Dr Donne had, but it should be restored; and there should be a critical catalogue given of the works of the different persons whose lives were written by Walton, and therefore their works must be carefully read by the editor.'

We then went to Trinity College, where he introduced me to Mr Thomas Warton, with whom we passed a part of the evening. We talked of biography. – JOHNSON. 'It is rarely well executed. They only who live with a man can write his life with any genuine exactness and discrimination; and few people who have lived with a man know what to remark about him. The chaplain of a late Bishop, whom I was to assist in writing some memoirs of his Lordship, could tell me almost nothing.'[a]

I said, Mr Robert Dodsley's life should be written, as he had been so much connected with the wits of his time, and by his literary merit had raised himself from the station of a footman. Mr Warton said, he had published a little volume under the title of *The Muse in Livery*. JOHNSON. 'I doubt whether Dodsley's brother would thank a man who should write his life: yet Dodsley himself was not unwilling that his original low condition should be recollected. When Lord Lyttelton's *Dialogues of the Dead* came out, one of which is between Apicius, an ancient epicure, and Darteneuf, a modern epicure, Dodsley said to me, "I knew Darteneuf well, for I was once his footman." '

Biography led us to speak of Dr John Campbell, who had written a considerable part of the *Biographia Britannica*. Johnson, though he valued him highly, was of opinion that there was not so much in his great work, *A Political Survey of Great-Britain*, as the world had been taught to expect;[b] and had said to

---

[a] For 'almost nothing' read 'scarcely any thing'; and upon 'thing' put the following note:. It has been mentioned to me by an accurate English friend, that Dr Johnson could never have used the phrase *almost nothing*, as not being English; and therefore I have put another in its place. At the same time, I am not quite convinced it is not good English. For the best writers use this phrase '*little or nothing*'; i.e. almost so little as to be nothing.

[b] Add the following note: Yet surely it is a very useful work, and of wonderful research and labour for one man to have executed.

me, that he believed Campbell's disappointment, on account of the bad success of that work, had killed him. He this evening observed of it, 'That work was his death.' Mr Warton, not adverting to his meaning, answered, 'I believe so; from the great attention he bestowed on it.' JOHNSON. 'Nay, Sir, he died of *want* of attention, if he died at all by that book.'

We talked of a work much in vogue at that time, written in a very mellifluous style, but which, under pretext of another subject, contained much artful infidelity.[1] I said it was not fair to attack us thus unexpectedly; he should have warned us of our danger, before we entered his garden of flowery eloquence, by advertising, 'Spring-guns and mantraps set here.' The author had been an Oxonian, and was remembered there for having 'turned Papist'. I observed, that as he had changed several times – from the Church of England to the Church of Rome – from the Church of Rome to infidelity – I did not despair yet of seeing him a methodist preacher. JOHNSON. (laughing), 'It is said, that his range has been more extensive, and that he has once been Mahometan. However, now that he has published his infidelity, he will probably persist in it.' BOSWELL. 'I am not quite sure of that, Sir.'

I mentioned Sir Richard Steele having published his 'Christian Hero', with the avowed purpose of obliging himself to lead a religious life; yet, that his conduct was by no means strictly suitable. JOHNSON. 'Steele, I believe, practised the lighter vices.'

Mr Warton, being engaged, could not sup with us at our inn; we had therefore another evening by ourselves. I asked Johnson, whether a man's being forward in making himself known to eminent people, and seeing as much of life, and getting as much information as he could in every way, was not yet lessening himself by his forwardness. JOHNSON. 'No, Sir; a man always makes himself greater as he increases his knowledge.'

I censured some ludicrous fantastic dialogues between two coach-horses, and other such stuff, which Baretti had lately published. He joined with me, and said, 'Nothing odd will do long. *Tristram Shandy* did not last.' I expressed a desire to be acquainted with a lady who had been much talked of, and universally celebrated for extraordinary address and insinuation. JOHNSON. 'Never believe extraordinary characters which you hear of people. Depend upon it, Sir, they are exaggerated. You do not see one man shoot a great deal higher than another.' I mentioned Mr Burke. JOHNSON. 'Yes; Burke *is* an extraordinary man. His stream of mind is perpetual.' It is very pleasing to me to record, that Johnson's high estimation of the talents of this gentleman was uniform from their early acquaintance. Sir Joshua Reynolds informs me, that when Mr Burke was first elected a member of parliament, and Sir John Hawkins expressed a wonder at his attaining a seat, Johnson said, 'Now we who know Burke, know, that he will be one of the first men in this country.' And once, when Johnson was ill, and unable to exert himself as much as usual without fatigue, Mr Burke having been mentioned, he said, 'That fellow calls forth all my powers. Were I to see Burke now, it would kill me.' So much was

[a] [Gibbon, *The Decline and Fall of the Roman Empire*.]

he accustomed to consider conversation as a contest, and such was his notion of Burke as an opponent.

Next morning, Thursday, March 21, we set out in a post-chaise to pursue our ramble. It was a delightful day, and we drove through Blenheim Park. When I looked at the magnificent bridge built by John Duke of Marlborough, over a small rivulet, and recollected the Epigram made upon it –

> The lofty arch his high ambition shows,
> The stream, an emblem of his bounty flows.

and saw that now, by the genius of Brown, a magnificent body of water was collected, I said, 'They have *drowned* the Epigram.' I observed to him, while in the midst of the noble scene around us, 'You and I, Sir, have, I think, seen together the extremes of what can be seen in Britain; – the wild rough island of Mull, and Blenheim Park.'

We dined at an excellent inn at Chapel-house, where he expatiated on the felicity of England in its taverns and inns, and triumphed over the French for not having, in any perfection, the tavern life. 'There is no private house (said he) in which people can enjoy themselves so well, as at a capital tavern. Let there be ever so great plenty of good things, ever so much grandeur, ever so much elegance, ever so much desire that everybody should be easy; in the nature of things it cannot be: there must always be some degree of care and anxiety. The master of the house is anxious to entertain his guests; the guests are anxious to be agreeable to him: and no man, but a very impudent dog indeed, can as freely command what is in another man's house, as if it were his own. Whereas, at a tavern, there is a general freedom from anxiety. You are sure you are welcome: and the more noise you make, the more trouble you give, the more good things you call for, the welcomer you are. No servants will attend you with the alacrity which waiters do, who are incited by the prospect of an immediate reward, in proportion, as they please. No, Sir; there is nothing which has yet been contrived by man, by which so much happiness is produced as by a good tavern or inn.'[a] He then repeated, with great emotion, Shenstone's lines:

> Whoe'er has travell'd life's dull round,
> Where'er his stages may have been,
> May sigh to think he still has found
> The warmest welcome at an inn.[b]

---

[a] Add the following note: Sir John Hawkins has preserved very few *Memorabilia* of Johnson. There is, however, to be found in his bulky tome, a very excellent one upon this subject. 'In contradiction to those, who, having a wife and children, prefer domestic enjoyments to those which a tavern affords, I have heard him assert, *that a tavern chair was the throne of human felicity.* – "As soon (said he) as I enter the door of a tavern, I experience an oblivion of care, and a freedom from solicitude: when I am seated, I find the master courteous, and the servants obsequious to my call; anxious to know and ready to supply my wants: wine there exhilarates my spirits, and prompts me to free conversation and an interchange of discourse with those whom I most love: I dogmatise and am contradicted, and in this conflict of opinion and sentiments I find delight." '

[b] Add the following note: We happened to lie this night at the inn at Henley, where

In the afternoon, as we were driven rapidly along in the post-chaise, he said to me, 'Life has not many things better than this.'

We stopped at Stratford-upon-Avon, and drank tea and coffee; and it pleased me to be with him upon the classic ground of Shakspeare's native place.

He spoke slightingly of Dyer's 'Fleece'. – 'The subject, Sir, cannot be made poetical. How can a man write poetically of serges and druggets? Yet you will hear many people talk to you gravely of that *excellent* poem, 'The Fleece'. Having talked of Dr Grainger's 'Sugar-Cane', I mentioned to him Mr Langton's having told me, that this poem, when read in manuscript at Sir Joshua Reynolds's, had made all the assembled wits burst into a laugh, when, after much blank-verse pomp, the poet began a new paragraph thus:

> 'Now, Muse, let's sing of *rats*.'[a]

And what increased the ridicule was, that one of the company, who slily overlooked the reader, perceived that the word had been originally mice, and had been altered to *rats*, as more dignified.[1]

Johnson said, that Dr Grainger was an agreeable man; a man who would do any good that was in his power. His translation of Tibullus, he thought, was very well done; but 'The Sugar-Cane, a Poem', did not please him; for, he exclaimed, 'What could he make of a sugar-cane? One might as well write,

---

Shenstone wrote these lines, which I give as they are found in the corrected edition of his works, published after his death. In Dodsley's collection the stanza ran thus:

> Whoe'er has travelled life's dull round,
> Whate'er his *various tour has* been,
> May sigh to think *how oft* he found
> *His* warmest welcome at an inn.

Then read in the text as follows: My illustrious friend, I thought, did not sufficiently admire Shenstone. That ingenious and elegant gentleman's opinion of Johnson appears in one of his letters to Mr Greaves, dated Feb. 9, 1760. 'I have lately been reading one or two volumes of the *Rambler*; who, excepting against some few hardnesses in his manner, and the want of more examples to enliven, is one of the most nervous, most perspicuous, most concise, most harmonious prose writers I know. A learned diction improves by time.'

[a] Add: This passage does not appear in the printed work, Dr Grainger, or some of his friends, it should seem, having become sensible that introducing even *rats* in a grave poem might be liable to banter. He, however, could not bring himself to relinquish the idea; for they are thus, in a still more ludicrous manner, periphrastically exhibited in his poem as it now stands:

> Nor with less waste the whisker'd vermin race,
> A countless clan, despoil the lowland cane.

1 Such is this little laughable incident, which has been often related. Dr Percy, the Bishop of Dromore, who was an intimate friend of Dr Grainger, and has a particular regard for his memory, has communicated to me the following explanation:

'The passage in question was originally not liable to such a perversion; for the author having occasion in that part of his work to mention the havoc made by rats and

'The Parsley Bed: a Poem'; or, 'The Cabbage-Garden: a Poem'. BOSWELL. 'You must then *pickle* your cabbage with the *sal atticum*.' JOHNSON. 'You know there is already 'The Hop-Garden: a Poem': and, I think, one could say a great deal about cabbage. The poem might begin with the advantages of civilised society over a rude state, exemplified by the Scotch, who had no cabbages till Oliver Cromwell's soldiers introduced them; and one might thus show how arts are propagated by conquest, as they were by the Roman arms.' He seemed to be much diverted with the fertility of his own fancy.

I told him, that I heard Dr Percy was writing the history of the wolf in Great-Britain. JOHNSON. 'The wolf, Sir! Why the wolf? Why does he not write of the bear, which we had formerly? Nay, it is said we had the beaver. Or why does he not write of the grey rat, the Hanover rat, as it is called, because it is said to have come into this country about the time that the family of Hanover came? I should like to see '*The History of the Grey Rat. by Thomas Percy, D.D. Chaplain in Ordinary to his Majesty*', ' (laughing immoderately). BOSWELL. 'I am afraid a court chaplain could not decently write of the grey rat.' JOHNSON. 'Sir, he need not give it the name of the Hanover rat.' Thus could he indulge a luxuriant sportive imagination, when talking of a friend whom he loved and esteemed.

He mentioned to me the singular history of an ingenious acquaintance.[b] 'He settled as a physician in one of the Leeward Islands. A man was sent out to him merely to compound his medicines. This fellow set up as a rival to him in his practice of physic, and got so much the better of him in the opinion of the people of the island, that he carried away all the business; upon which he returned to England, and soon after died.'

---

mice, had introduced the subject in a kind of mock heroic, and a parody of Homer's battle of the frogs and mice, invoking the Muse of the old Grecian bard in an elegant and well-turned manner. In that state I had seen it; but afterwards, unknown to me and other friends, he had been persuaded, contrary to his own better judgement, to alter it, so as to produce the unlucky effect above mentioned.'[a]

The Bishop gives this character of Dr Grainger: 'He was not only a man of genius and learning, but had many excellent virtues; being one of the most generous, friendly, and benevolent men I ever knew.'

[a] Add to the note: The above was written by the bishop when he had not the Poem itself to recur to; and though the account given was true of it at one period, yet as Dr Grainger afterwards altered the passage in question, the remarks in the text do not now apply to the printed poem.

[b] Add: He had practised physic in various situations with no great emolument. A West-India gentleman, whom he delighted by his conversation, gave him a bond for a handsome annuity during his life, on the condition of his accompanying him to the West-Indies, and living with him there for two years. He accordingly embarked with the gentleman; but upon the voyage fell in love with a young woman who happened to be one of the passengers, and married the wench. From the imprudence of his disposition he quarrelled with the gentleman, and declared he would have no connection with him. So he forfeited the annuity.

On Friday, March 22, having set out early from Henley, where we had lain the preceding night, we arrived at Birmingham about nine o'clock, and, after breakfast, went to call on his old school-fellow Mr Hector. A very stupid maid, who opened the door, told us, that 'her master was gone out; he was gone to the country; she could not tell when he would return.' In short, she gave us a miserable reception; and Johnson observed, 'She would have behaved no better to people who wanted him in the way of his profession.' He said to her, 'My name is Johnson; tell him I called. Will you remember the name?' She answered with rustic simplicity, in the Warwickshire pronunciation, 'I don't understand you, Sir.' – 'Blockhead (said he), I'll write.' I never heard the word *blockhead* applied to a woman before, though I do not see why it should not, when there is evident occasion for it.[a] He, however, made another attempt to make her understand him, and roared loud in her ear, 'JOHNSON', and then she catched the sound.

We then called on Mr Lloyd, one of the people called Quakers. He too was not at home; but Mrs Lloyd was, and received us courteously, and asked us to dinner. Johnson said to me, 'After the uncertainty of all human things at Hector's, this invitation came very well.' We walked about the town, and he was pleased to see it increasing.

I talked of legitimation by subsequent marriage, which obtained in the Roman law, and still obtains in the law of Scotland. JOHNSON. 'I think it a bad thing; because the chastity of women being of the utmost importance, as all property depends upon it, they who forfeit it should not have any possibility of being restored to good character; nor should the children, by an illicit connection, attain the full rights of lawful children, by the posterior consent of the offending parties.' His opinion upon this subject deserves consideration. Upon his principle there may, at times, be a hardship, and seemingly a strange one, upon individuals; but the general good of society is better secured. And, after all, it is unreasonable in an individual to repine that he has not the advantage of a state which is made different from his own, by the social institution under which he is born. A woman does not complain that her brother, who is younger than her, gets their common father's estate. Why then should a natural son complain that a younger brother, by the same parents lawfully begotten, gets it? The operation of law is similar in both cases. Besides; an illegitimate son, who has a younger legitimate brother by the same father and mother, has no stronger claim to the father's estate, than if that legitimate brother had only the same father, from whom alone the estate descends.

Mr Lloyd joined us in the street; and in a little while we met *Friend Hector*, as

[a] Add the following note: My worthy friend Mr Langton, to whom I am under innumerable obligations in the course of my Johnsonian History, has furnished me with a droll illustration of this question. An honest carpenter, after giving some anecdote, in his presence, of the ill treatment which he had received from a clergyman's wife, who was a noted termagant, and whom he accused of unjust dealing in some transaction with him, added, 'I took care to let her know what I thought of her.' And being asked, 'What did you say?' answered, 'I told her she was a *scoundrel*.'

Mr Lloyd called him. It gave me pleasure to observe the joy which Johnson and he expressed on seeing each other again. Mr Lloyd and I left them together, while he obligingly showed me some of the manufactures of this very curious assemblage of artificers. We all met at dinner at Mr Lloyd's, where we were entertained with great hospitality. Mr and Mrs Lloyd had been married the same year with their Majesties, and, like them, had been blessed with a numerous family of fine children, their numbers being exactly the same. Johnson said, 'Marriage is the best state for man in general; and every man is a worse man, in proportion as he is unfit for the married state.'

I have always loved the simplicity of manners, and the spiritual-mindedness of the Quakers; and talking with Mr Lloyd, I observed that the essential part of religion was piety, a devout intercourse with the Divinity; and that many a man was a Quaker without knowing it.

As Dr Johnson had said to me in the morning, while we walked together, that he liked individuals among the Quakers, but not the sect; when we were at Mr Lloyd's I kept clear of introducing any question concerning the peculiarities of their faith. But I having asked to look at Baskerville's edition of *Barclay's Apology*, Johnson laid hold of it; and the chapter on baptism happening to open, Johnson remarked, 'He says there is neither precept nor practice for baptism, in the scriptures; that is false.' Here he was the aggressor, by no means in a gentle manner; and the good Quakers had the advantage of him; for he had read negligently, and had not observed that Barclay speaks of *infant* baptism, which they calmly made him perceive. Mr Lloyd, however, was in as great a mistake; for when insisting that the right of baptism with water was to cease, when the *spiritual* administration of CHRIST began, he maintained, that John the Baptist said, '*My baptism* shall decrease, but *his* shall increase.' Whereas the words are, '*He* must increase, but *I* must decrease.'[1]

One of them having objected to the 'observance of days, and months, and years,' Johnson answered, 'The Church does not superstitiously observe days, merely as days, but as memorials of important facts. Christmas might be kept as well upon one day of the year as another: but there should be a stated day for commemorating the birth of our Saviour, because there is danger that what may be done on any day, will be neglected.'[a]

Mr Hector was so good as to accompany me to see the great works of Mr Bolton, at a place which he has called Soho, about two miles from Birmingham,

---

[1] John iii. 30.

[a] Add: He said to me at another time, 'Sir, the holidays observed by our church are of great use in religion.' There can be no doubt of this in a limited sense, I mean if the number of such consecrated portions of time be not too extensive. The excellent Mr Nelson's *Festivals and Fasts*, which has, I understand, the greatest sale of any book ever printed in England, except the Bible, is a most valuable help to devotion; and in addition to it I would recommend two sermons on the same subject, by Mr Pott, Archdeacon of St Alban's, equally distinguished for piety and elegance. I am sorry to have it to say, that Scotland is the only Christian country, Catholic or Protestant, where the great events of our religion are not solemnly commemorated by its ecclesiastical establishment, on days set apart for the purpose.

which the very ingenious proprietor showed me himself to the best advantage. I wish that Johnson had been with us; for it was a scene which I should have been glad to contemplate by his light. The vastness and the contrivance of some of the machinery would have 'matched his mighty mind'. I shall never forget Mr Bolton's expression to me: 'I feel here, Sir, what all the world desires to have – Power.' He had about seven hundred people at work. I contemplated him as an *iron chieftan*, and he seemed to be a father to his tribe. One of them came to him, complaining grievously of his landlord for having distrained his goods. 'Your landlord is in the right, Smith (said Bolton). But I'll tell you what: find you a friend who will lay down one half of your rent, and I'll lay down the other half; and you shall have your goods again.'

From Mr Hector I now learnt many particulars of Dr Johnson's early life, which, with others that he gave me at different times since, have contributed to the formation of this work.

Dr Johnson said to me in the morning, 'You will see, Sir, at Mr Hector's, his sister, Mrs Careless, a clergyman's widow. She was the first woman with whom I was in love. It dropt out of my head imperceptibly; but she and I shall always have a kindness for each other.' He laughed at the notion that a man never can be really in love but once, and considered it as a mere romantic fancy.

On our return from Mr Bolton's, Mr Hector took me to his house, where we found Johnson sitting placidly at tea, with his *first love*; who, though now advanced in years, was a genteel woman, very agreeable, and well-bred.

Johnson lamented to Mr Hector the state of one of their school-fellows, Mr Charles Congreve, a clergyman, which he thus described: 'He obtained, I believe, considerable preferment in Ireland, but now lives in London, quite as a valetudinarian, afraid to go into any house but his own. He takes a short airing in his post-chaise every day. He has an elderly woman, whom he calls cousin, who lives with him, and jogs his elbow, when his glass has stood too long empty, and encourages him in drinking, in which he is very willing to be encouraged; not that he gets drunk, for he is a very pious man, but he is always muddy. He confesses to one bottle of port every day, and he probably drinks more. He is quite unsocial; his conversation is mono-syllabical: and when, at my last visit, I asked him what a clock it was, that signal of my departure had so pleasing an effect on him, that he sprung up to look at his watch like a greyhound bounding at a hare.' When Johnson took leave of Mr Hector, he said, 'Don't grow like Congreve; nor let me grow like him, when you are near me.'

When he again talked of Mrs Careless tonight, he seemed to have had his affection revived; for he said, 'If I had married her, it might have been as happy for me.' BOSWELL. 'Pray, sir, do you not suppose that there are fifty women in the world, with any one of whom a man may be as happy, as with any one woman in particular.' JOHNSON. 'Aye, fifty thousand.' BOSWELL. 'Then sir, you are not of opinion with some who imagine that certain men and certain women are made for each other; and that they cannot be happy if they miss their counterparts.' JOHNSON. 'To be sure not, sir. I believe marriages would in general be as happy, and often more so, if they were all made by the Lord

Chancellor upon a due consideration of characters and circumstances, without the parties having any choice in the matter.'

I wished to have staid at Birmingham to-night, to have talked more with Mr Hector; but my friend was impatient to reach his native city: so we drove on that[a] stage in the dark, and were long pensive and silent. When we came within the focus of the Lichfield lamps, 'Now (said he) we are getting out of a state of death.' We put up at the Three Crowns, not one of the great inns, but a good old fashioned one, which was kept by Mr Wilkins, and was the very next house to that in which Johnson was born and brought up, and which was still his own property.[1] We had a comfortable supper, and got into high spirits. I felt all my Toryism glow in this old capital of Staffordshire. I could have offered incense *genio loci*; and I indulged in libations of that ale, which Bonniface, in *The Beaux' Stratagem*, recommends with such an eloquent jollity.

Next morning he introduced me to Mrs Lucy Porter, his step-daughter. She was now an old maid, with much simplicity of manner. She had never been in London. Her brother, a Captain in the navy, had left her a fortune of ten thousand pounds; about a third of which she had laid out in building a stately house, and making a handsome garden, in an elevated situation in Lichfield. Johnson, when here by himself, used to live at her house. She reverenced him, and he had a parental tenderness for her.

We then visited Mr Peter Garrick, who had that morning received a letter from his brother David, announcing our coming to Lichfield. He was engaged to dinner, but asked us to tea, and to sleep at his house. Johnson, however, would not quit his old acquaintance Wilkins, of the Three Crowns. The family likeness of the Garricks was very striking; and Johnson thought that David's vivacity was not so peculiar to himself as was supposed. 'Sir (said he), I don't know but if Peter had cultivated all the arts of gaiety as much as David has done, he might have been as brisk and lively. Depend upon it, Sir, vivacity is much an art, and depends greatly on habit.' I believe there is a good deal of truth in this, notwithstanding a ludicrous story told me by a lady abroad, of a heavy German baron, who had lived much with the young English at Geneva, and was ambitious to be as lively as they; with which view, he, with assiduous exertion, was jumping over the tables and chairs in his lodgings; and when the people of the house ran in and asked with surprise, what was the matter, he answered, '*Sh' apprens t'etre fif.*'

We dined at our inn, and had with us a Mr Jackson, one of Johnson's schoolfellows, whom he treated with much kindness, though he seemed to be a low man, dull and untaught. He had a coarse grey coat, black waistcoat, greasy leather breeches, and a yellow uncurled wig; and his countenance had the ruddiness which betokens one who is in no haste to 'leave his can'. He drank only ale. He had tried to be a cutler at Birmingham, but had not

---

[a] For 'that' read 'another'.

1 I went through the house where my illustrious friend was born, with a reverence with which it doubtless will long be visited. An engraved view of it, with the adjacent buildings, is in the *Gentleman's Magazine* for February, 1785.

succeeded; and now he lived poorly at home, and had some scheme of dressing leather in a better manner than common; to his indistinct account of which, Dr Johnson listened with patient attention, that he might assist him with his advice. Here was an instance of genuine humanity and real kindness in this great man, who has been most unjustly represented as altogether harsh and destitute of tenderness. A thousand such instances might have been recorded in the course of his long life; though, that his temper was warm and hasty, and his manner often rough, cannot be denied.

I saw here, for the first time, *oat ale*; and oat cakes, not hard as in Scotland, but soft like a Yorkshire cake, were served at breakfast. It was pleasant to me to find, that '*Oats*', the '*food of horses*', were so much used as the *food of the people* in Dr Johnson's own town. He expatiated in praise of Lichfield and its inhabitants, who, he said, were 'the most sober, decent people in England, the genteelest in proportion to their wealth, and spoke the purest English.' I doubted as to the last article of this eulogy; for they had several provincial sounds; as, *there*, pronounced like *fear*, instead of like *fair*; *once*, pronounced *woonse*, instead of *wunse*, or *wonse*. Johnson himself never got entirely free of his provincial accent. Garrick sometimes used to take him off, squeezing a lemon into a punch-bowl, with uncouth gesticulations, looking round the company, and calling out, 'Who's for *poonsh*?'

Very little business appeared to be going forward in Lichfield. I found however two strange manufactures for so inland a place, sail-cloth and streamers for ships; and I observed them making saddle-cloths, and dressing sheepskins: but upon the whole, the busy hand of industry seemed to be quite slackened. 'Surely, Sir (said I), you are an idle set of people.' 'Sir (said Johnson), we are a city of philosophers: we work with our heads, and make the boobies of Birmingham work for us with their hands.'

There was at this time a company of players performing at Lichfield. The manager, Mr Stanton, sent his compliments, and requested leave to wait on Dr Johnson. Johnson received him very courteously, and he drank a glass of wine with us. He was a plain decent well-behaved man, and expressed his gratitude to Dr Johnson for having once got him permission from Dr Taylor at Ashbourne to play there upon moderate terms. Garrick's name was soon introduced. JOHNSON. 'Garrick's conversation is gay and grotesque. It is a dish of all sorts, but all good things. There is no solid meat in it: there is a want of sentiment in it. Not but that he has sentiment sometimes, and sentiment too very powerful and very pleasing: but it has not its full proportion in his conversation.'

When we were by ourselves he told me, 'Forty years ago, sir, I was in love with an actress here, Mrs Emmet, who acted Flora, in *Hob in the Well*.' What merit this lady had as an actress, or what was her figure, or her manner, I have not been informed: but if we may believe Mr Garrick, his old master's taste in theatrical merit was by no means refined; he was not an *elegans formarum spectator*. Garrick used to tell, that Johnson said of an actor, who played Sir Harry Wildair at Lichfield, 'There is a courtly vivacity about the fellow'; when in fact, according to Garrick's account, 'he was the most vulgar ruffian that ever went upon boards.'

We had promised Mr Stanton to be at his theatre on Monday. Dr Johnson jocularly proposed me to write a Prologue for the occasion: 'A Prologue, by James Boswell, Esq. from the Hebrides'. I was really inclined to take the hint. Methought, 'Prologue, spoken before Dr Samuel Johnson, at Lichfield, 1776'; would have sounded as well as, 'Prologue, spoken before the Duke of York, at Oxford', in Charles the Second's time. Much might have been said of what Lichfield had done for Shakspeare, by producing Johnson and Garrick. But I found he was averse to it.

We went and viewed the museum of Mr Richard Green, apothecary here, who told me he was proud of being a relation of Dr Johnson's. It was, truly, a wonderful collection, both of antiquities and natural curiosities, and ingenious works of art. He had all the articles accurately arranged, with their names upon labels, printed at his own little press; and on the staircase leading to it was a board, with the names of contributors marked in gold letters. A printed catalogue of the collection was to be had at a bookseller's. Johnson expressed his admiration of the activity and diligence and good fortune of Mr Green, in getting together, in his situation, so great a variety of things; and Mr Green told me, that Johnson once said to him, 'Sir, I should as soon have thought of building a man of war, as of collecting such a museum.' Mr Green's obliging alacrity in showing it was very pleasing. His engraved portrait, with which he has favoured me, has a motto truly characteristical of his disposition, '*Nemo sibi vivat.*'

A physician being mentioned who had lost his practice, because his whimsically changing his religion had made people distrustful of him, I maintained that this was unreasonable, as religion is unconnected with medical skill. JOHNSON. 'Sir, it is not unreasonable; for when people see a man absurd in what they understand, they may conclude the same of him in what they do not understand. If a physician were to take to eating of horse-flesh, nobody would employ him; though one may eat horse-flesh, and be a very skilful physician. If a man were educated in an absurd religion, his continuing to profess it would not hurt him, though his changing to it would.'

We drank tea and coffee at Mr Peter Garrick's, where was Mrs Aston, one of the maiden sisters of Mrs Walmsley, wife of Johnson's first friend, and sister also of the lady of whom Johnson used to speak with the warmest admiration, by the name of Molly Aston, who was afterwards married to Captain Brodie of the navy.

On Sunday, March 24, we breakfasted with Mrs Cobb, a widow lady, who lived in an agreeable sequestered place close by the town, called the Friary, it having been formerly a religious house. She and her niece, Miss Adey, were great admirers of Dr Johnson; and he behaved to them with a kindness and easy pleasantry, such as we see between old and intimate acquaintance. He accompanied Mrs Cobb to St Mary's church, and I went to the cathedral, where I was very much delighted with the music, finding it to be peculiarly solemn, and accordant with the words of the service.

We dined at Mr Peter Garrick's, who was in a very lively humour, and verified Johnson's saying, that if he had cultivated gaiety as much as his brother

David, he might have equally excelled in it. He was today quite a London narrator, telling us a variety of anecdotes with that earnestness and attempt at mimicry which we usually find in the wits of the metropolis. Dr Johnson went with me to the cathedral in the afternoon. It was grand and pleasing to contemplate this illustrious writer, now full of fame, worshipping in 'the solemn temple' of his native city.

I returned to tea and coffee at Mr Peter Garrick's, and then found Dr Johnson at the Reverend Mr Seward's, Canon Residentiary, who inhabited the Bishop's palace, in which Mr Walmsley lived, and which had been the scene of many happy hours in Johnson's early life. Mr Seward had, with ecclesiastical hospitality and politeness, asked me in the morning, merely as a stranger, to dine with him; and in the afternoon, when I was introduced to him, he asked Dr Johnson and me to spend the evening and sup with him. He was a genteel well-bred dignified clergyman, had travelled with Lord Charles Fitzroy, uncle of the present Duke of Grafton, who died when abroad, and he had lived much in the great world. He was an ingenious and literary man, had published an edition of Beaumont and Fletcher, and written verses in Dodsley's collection. His lady was the daughter of Mr Hunter, Johnson's first schoolmaster. And now, for the first time, I had the pleasure of seeing his celebrated daughter, Miss Anna Seward, to whom I have since been indebted for many civilities, as well as some obliging communications concerning Johnson.

Mr Seward mentioned to us the observations which he had made upon the strata of earth in volcanos, from which it appeared, that they were so very different in depth in different periods, that no calculation whatever could be made as to the time required for their formation. This fully refuted an anti-mosaical remark introduced into Captain Brydone's entertaining Tour, I hope heedlessly, from a kind of vanity which is too common in those who have not sufficiently studied the most important of all subjects. Dr Johnson, indeed, had said before, independent of this observation, 'Shall all the accumulated evidence of the history of the world; – shall the authority of what is unquestionably the most ancient writing, be overturned by an uncertain remark such as this?'

On Monday, March 25, we breakfasted at Mrs Lucy Porter's. He had sent an express to Dr Taylor's, acquainting him of our being at Lichfield, and Taylor had returned an answer that his post-chaise should come for us this day. While we sat at breakfast, Dr Johnson received a letter by the post, which seemed to agitate him very much. When he had read it, he exclaimed, 'One of the most dreadful things that has happened in my time.' The phrase *my time*, like the word *age*, is usually understood to refer to an event of a public or general nature. I imagined something like an assassination of the King – like a gun-powder plot carried into execution – or like another fire of London. When asked, 'What is it, Sir?' he answered, 'Mr Thrale has lost his only son!' This was, no doubt, a very great affliction to Mr and Mrs Thrale, which their friends would consider accordingly; but from the manner in which the intelligence of it was communicated by Johnson, it appeared for the moment to be comparatively small. I, however, soon felt a sincere concern, and was curious to observe how Dr

Johnson would be affected. He said, 'This is a total extinction to their family, as much as if they were sold into captivity.' Upon my mentioning that Mr Thrale had daughters, who might inherit his wealth; – 'Daughters (said Johnson, warmly), he'll no more value his daughters than —' I was going to speak. – 'Sir, (said he), don't you know how you yourself think? Sir, he wishes to propagate his name.' In short, I saw male succession strong in his mind, even where there was no name, no family of any long standing. I said, it was lucky he was not present when this misfortune happened. JOHNSON. 'It is lucky for *me*. People in distress never think that you feel enough.' BOSWELL. 'And, Sir, they will have the hope of seeing you, which will be a relief in the meantime; and when you get to them, the pain will be so far abated, that they will be capable of being consoled by you, which, in the first violence of it, I believe, would not be the case.' JOHNSON. 'No, Sir; violent pain of mind, as violent pain of body, must be severely felt.' BOSWELL. 'I own, Sir, I have not so much feeling for the distress of others as some people have, or pretend to have: but I know this, that I would do all in my power to relieve them.' JOHNSON. 'Sir, it is affectation to pretend to feel the distress of others, as much as they do themselves. It is equally so, as if one should pretend to feel as much pain while a friend's leg is cutting off, as he does. No, Sir; you have expressed the rational and just nature of sympathy. I would have gone to the extremity of the earth to have preserved this boy.'

He was soon quite calm. The letter was from Mr Thrale's clerk, and concluded, 'I need not say how much they wish to see you in London.' He said, 'We shall hasten back from Taylor's.'

Mrs Lucy Porter and some other ladies of the place talked a great deal of him when he was out of the room, not only with veneration but affection. It pleased me to find that he was so much *beloved* in his native city.

Mrs Aston, whom I had seen the preceding night, and her sister, Mrs Gastrel, a widow lady, had each a house and garden, and pleasure ground, prettily situated upon Stowhill, a gentle eminence adjoining to Lichfield. Johnson walked away to dinner there, leaving me by myself without any apology; I wondered at this want of that facility of manners, from which a man has no difficulty in carrying a friend to a house where he is intimate; I felt it very unpleasant to be thus left in solitude in a country town, where I was an entire stranger, and began to think myself unkindly deserted; but I was soon relieved, and convinced that my friend, instead of being deficient in delicacy, had conducted the matter with perfect propriety, for I received the following note in his handwriting: 'Mrs Gastrel, at the lower house on Stowhill, desires Mr Boswell's company to dinner at two.' I accepted of the invitation, and had here another proof how amiable his character was in the opinion of those who knew him best. I was not informed, till afterwards, that Mrs Gastrel's husband was the clergyman who, while he lived at Stratford upon Avon, where he was proprietor of Shakspeare's garden, with Gothic barbarity cut down his mulberry-tree,[a]

---

[a] Add the following note: See an accurate and animated statement of Mr Gastrel's barbarity, by Mr Malone, in a note on 'Some account of the Life of William Shakspeare', prefixed to his admirable edition of that Poet's works, Vol. I. p. 118.

and, as Dr Johnson told me, did it to vex his neighbours. His lady, I have reason to believe,[a] participated in the guilt of what the enthusiasts for our immortal bard deem almost a species of sacrilege.

After dinner Dr Johnson wrote a letter to Mrs Thrale, on the death of her son. I said it would be very distressing to Thrale, but she would soon forget it, as she had so many things to think of. JOHNSON. 'No, Sir, Thrale will forget it first. *She* has many things that she *may* think of. *He* has many things that he *must* think of.' This was a very just remark upon the different effect of those light pursuits which occupy a vacant and easy mind, and those serious engagements which arrest attention, and keep us from brooding over grief.

He observed of Lord Bute, 'It was said of Augustus, that it would have been better for Rome that he had never been born, or had never died. So it would have been better for this nation if Lord Bute had never been minister, or had never resigned.'

In the evening we went to the Town-hall, which was converted into a temporary theatre, and saw *Theodosius*, with *The Stratford Jubilee*. I was happy to see Dr Johnson sitting in a conspicuous part of the pit, and receiving affectionate homage from all his acquaintance. We were quite gay and merry. I afterwards mentioned to him that I condemned myself for being so, when poor Mr and Mrs Thrale were in such distress. JOHNSON. 'You are wrong, Sir; twenty years hence Mr and Mrs Thrale will not suffer much pain from the death of their son. Now, sir, you are to consider that distance of place, as well as distance of time, operates upon the human feelings. I would not have you be gay in the presence of the distressed, because it would shock them; but you may be gay at a distance. Pain for the loss of a friend, or of a relation whom we love, is occasioned by the want which we feel. In time the vacuity is filled with something else; or, sometimes the vacuity closes up of itself.'

Mr Seward and Mr Pearson, another clergyman here, supt with us at our inn, and after they left us, we sat up late as we used to do in London.

Here I shall record some fragments of my friend's conversation during this jaunt.

'Marriage, sir, is much more necessary to a man than to a woman; for he is much less able to supply himself with domestic comforts. You will recollect my saying to some ladies the other day, that I had often wondered why young women should marry, as they have so much more freedom, and so much more attention paid to them while unmarried, than when married. I indeed did not mention the *strong* reason for their marrying – the *mechanical* reason.' BOSWELL. 'Why that *is* a strong one. But does not imagination make it seem much more important than it is in reality? Is it not, to a certain degree, a delusion in us as well as in women?' JOHNSON. 'Why yes, sir; but it is a delusion that is always beginning again.' BOSWELL. 'I don't know but there is upon the whole more misery than happiness produced by that passion.' JOHNSON. 'I don't think so, Sir.'

---

[a] Add: 'on the same authority'.

'Never speak of a man in his own presence. It is always indelicate, and may be offensive.'

'Questioning is not the mode of conversation among gentlemen. It is assuming a superiority, and it is particularly wrong to question a man concerning himself. There may be parts of his former life which he may not wish to be made known to other persons, or even brought to his own recollection.'

'A man should be careful never to tell tales of himself to his own disadvantage. People may be amused and laugh at the time, but they will be remembered, and brought out against him upon some subsequent occasion.'

'Much may be done if a man puts his whole mind to a particular object. By doing so, Norton has made himself the great lawyer that he is allowed to be.'

I mentioned an acquaintance of mine, a sectary, who was a very religious man, who not only attended regularly on public worship with those of his communion, but made a particular study of the Scriptures, and even wrote a commentary on some parts of them, yet was known to be very licentious in indulging himself with women, maintaining that men are to be saved by faith alone, and that the Christian religion had not prescribed any fixed rule for the intercourse between the sexes. JOHNSON. 'Sir, there is no trusting to that crazy piety.'

I observed that it was strange how well Scotchmen were known to one another in their own country, though born in very distant counties; for we do not find that the gentlemen of neighbouring counties in England are mutually known to each other. Johnson, with his usual acuteness, at once saw and explained the reason of this; 'Why, Sir, you have Edinburgh, where the gentlemen from all your counties meet, and which is not so large but that they are all known. There is no such common place of collection in England, except London, where from its great size and diffusion, many of those who reside in contiguous counties of England may long remain unknown to each other.'

On Tuesday, March 26, there came for us an equipage properly suited to a wealthy well-beneficed clergyman – Dr Taylor's large, roomy post-chaise, drawn by four stout plump horses, and driven by two steady jolly postillions, which conveyed us to Ashbourne, where I found my friend's schoolfellow living upon an establishment perfectly corresponding with his substantial creditable equipage: his house, garden, pleasure-grounds, table, in short every thing good, and no scantiness appearing. Every man should form such a plan of living as he can execute completely. Let him not draw an outline wider than he can fill up. I have seen many skeletons of show and magnificence which excite at once ridicule and pity. Dr Taylor had a good estate of his own, and good preferment in the church, being a prebendary of Westminster, and rector of Bosworth. He was a diligent justice of the peace, and presided over the town of Ashbourne, to the inhabitants of which I was told he was very liberal; and as a proof of this it was mentioned to me, he had the preceding winter distributed two hundred pounds among such of them as stood in need of his assistance. He had consequently a considerable political interest in the county of Derby, which he employed to support the Devonshire family; for though the schoolfellow and friend of Johnson, he was a Whig. I could not perceive in his character much congeniality of any sort with that of Johnson, who, however, said to me, 'Sir, he has a very strong understanding.' His size and figure, and countenance, and manner, were that of a hearty English 'Squire, with the parson super-induced; and I took particular notice of his upper servant, Mr Peters, a decent grave man, in purple clothes, and a large white wig, like the butler or *major domo* of a Bishop.

Dr Johnson and Dr Taylor met with great cordiality; and Johnson soon gave him the same sad account of their schoolfellow, Congreve, that he had given to Mr Hector; adding a remark of such moment to the rational conduct of a man in the decline of life, that it deserves to be imprinted upon every mind: 'There is nothing against which an old man should be so much upon his guard as putting himself to nurse.' Innumerable have been the melancholy instances of men once distinguished for firmness, resolution, and spirit, who in their latter days have been governed like children, by interested female artifice.

Dr Taylor commended a physician who was known to him and Dr Johnson, and said, 'I fight many battles for him, as many people in the country dislike him.' JOHNSON. 'But you should consider, Sir, that by every one of your victories he is a loser; for, every man of whom you get the better, will be very angry, and will resolve not to employ him; whereas if people get the better of you in argument about him, they'll think, "We'll send for Dr —— nevertheless." ' This was an observation deep and sure in human nature.

Next day we talked of a book in which an eminent judge was arraigned before the bar of the public, as having pronounced an unjust decision in a great cause. Dr Johnson maintained that this publication would not give any uneasiness to the Judge. 'For (said he) either he acted honestly, or he meant to do injustice. If he acted honestly, his own consciousness will protect him; if he meant to do injustice, he will be glad to see the man who attacks him, so much vexed.'

Next day, as Dr Johnson had acquainted Dr Taylor of the reason for his returning speedily to London, it was resolved that we should set out after dinner. A few of Dr Taylor's neighbours were his guests that day.

Dr Johnson talked with approbation of one who had attained to the state of the philosophical wise man, that is, to have no want of anything. 'Then, Sir (said I), the savage is a wise man.' 'Sir (said he), I do not mean simply being without, – but not having a want.' I maintained, against this proposition, that it was better to have fine clothes, for instance, than not to feel the want of them. JOHNSON. 'No, Sir; fine clothes are good only as they supply the want of other means of procuring respect. Was Charles the Twelfth, think you, less respected for his coarse blue coat and black stock? And you find the King of Prussia dresses plain, because the dignity of his character is sufficient.' I here brought myself into a scrape, for I heedlessly said, 'Would not *you*, Sir, be the better for velvet and embroidery?' JOHNSON. 'Sir, you put an end to all argument when you introduce your opponent himself. Have you no better manners? There is *your want*.' I apologised by saying, I had mentioned him as an instance of one who wanted as little as any man in the world, and yet, perhaps, might receive some additional lustre from dress.

Having left Ashbourne in the evening, we stopped to change horses at Derby, and availed ourselves of a moment to enjoy the conversation of my countryman, Dr Butter, then physician there. He was in great indignation because Lord Mountstuart's bill for a Scotch militia had been lost. Dr Johnson was as violent against it. 'I am glad (said he), that Parliament has had the spirit to throw it out. You wanted to take advantage of the timidity of our scoundrels'[1] (meaning, I suppose, the ministry). It may be observed, that he used the epithet scoundrel very commonly, not quite in the sense in which it is generally understood, but as a strong term of disapprobation; as when he abruptly answered Mrs Thrale, who had asked him how he did, 'Ready to become a scoundrel, Madam; with a little more spoiling you will, I think, make me a complete rascal':[2] – he meant easy to become a capricious and self-indulgent valetudinarian; a character for which I have heard him express great disgust.

Johnson had with him upon this jaunt, *Il Palmerino d'Inghilterra*, a romance praised by Cervantes; but did not like it much. He said, he read it for the language, by way of preparation for his Italian expedition. – We lay this night at Loughborough.

On Thursday, March 28, we pursued our journey. I mentioned that old Mr Sheridan complained of the ingratitude of Mr Wedderburne and General Fraser, who had been much obliged to him when they were young Scotchmen entering upon life in England. JOHNSON. 'Why, Sir, a man is very apt to complain of the ingratitude of those who have risen far above him. A man when he gets into a higher sphere, into other habits of life, cannot keep up all his former connections. Then, Sir, those who knew him formerly upon a level with themselves, may think that they ought still to be treated as on a level, which cannot be; and an acquaintance in a former situation may bring out things which it would be very disagreeable to have mentioned before higher company, though, perhaps, every body knows of them.' He placed this subject in a new light to me, and showed that a man, who has risen in the world, must not be condemned too harshly, for being distant to former acquaintance, even though he may have been much obliged to them. It is, no doubt, to be wished that a proper degree of attention should be shown by great men to their early friends. But if either from obtuse insensibility to difference of situation, or presumptuous forwardness, which will not submit even to an exterior observance of it, the dignity of high place cannot be preserved, when they are admitted into the company of those raised above the state in which they once were, encroachment must be repelled, and the kinder feelings sacrificed. To one of the very fortunate persons whom I have mentioned, namely, Mr Wedderburne, now Lord Loughborough, I must do the justice to relate, that I have been assured by another early acquaintance of his, old Mr Macklin, who assisted him in improving his pronunciation, that he

1 See page 429.
2 *Anecdotes of Johnson*, p. 176.

had found him very grateful. Macklin, I suppose, had not pressed upon his elevation with so much eagerness as the gentleman who complained of him. Dr Johnson's remark as to the jealousy entertained of our friends who rise far above us, is certainly very just. By this was withered the early friendship between Charles Townshend and Akenside; and many similar instances might be adduced.

He said, 'It is commonly a weak man who marries for love.' We then talked of marrying women of fortune; and I mentioned a common remark, that a man may be, upon the whole, richer by marrying a woman with a very small portion, because a woman of fortune will be proportionally expensive; whereas a woman who brings none will be very moderate in expenses. JOHNSON. 'Depend upon it, Sir, this is not true. A woman of fortune being used to the handling of money spends it judiciously: but a woman who gets the command of money for the first time upon her marriage, has such a gust in spending it, that she throws it away with great profusion.'

He praised the ladies of the present age, insisting that they were more faithful to their husbands, and more virtuous in every respect, than in former times, because their understandings were better cultivated. It was an undoubted proof of his good sense and good disposition, that he was never querulous, never prone to inveigh against the present times, as is so common when superficial minds are on the fret. On the contrary, he was willing to speak favourably of his own age; and, indeed, maintained its superiority in every respect, except in its reverence for government; the relaxation of which he imputed, as its grand cause, to the shock which our monarchy received at the Revolution, though necessary; and secondly, to the timid concessions made to faction by successive administrations in the reign of his present Majesty. I am happy to think, that he lived to see the Crown at last recover its just influence.

At Leicester we read in the newspapers that Dr James was dead. I thought that the death of an old school-fellow, and one with whom he had lived a good deal in London, would have affected my fellow-traveller much: but he only said, 'Ah! poor Jamy.' Afterwards, however, when we were in the chaise, he said, with more tenderness, 'Since I set out on this jaunt, I have lost an old friend and a young one – Dr James, and poor Harry' (meaning Mr Thrale's son).

Having lain at St Alban's on Thursday, March 28, we breakfasted the next morning at Barnet. I expressed to him a weakness of mind which I could not help – an uneasy apprehension that my wife and children, who were at a great distance from me, might, perhaps, be ill. 'Sir (said he), consider how foolish you should think it in them to be apprehensive that you are ill.' This sudden turn relieved me for the moment; but I afterwards perceived it to be an ingenious fallacy. I might, to be sure, be satisfied that they had no reason to be apprehensive about me, because I knew that I myself was well: but we might have a mutual anxiety, without the charge of folly; because each was, in some degree, uncertain as to the condition of the other.

I enjoyed the luxury of our approach to London, that metropolis which we both loved so much, for the high and varied intellectual pleasure which it furnishes. I experienced immediate happiness while whirled along with such a companion, and said to him, 'Sir, you observed one day at General Oglethorpe's, that a man is never happy for the present, but when he is drunk. Will you not add – or when driving rapidly in a post-chaise?' JOHNSON. 'No, Sir, you are driving rapidly *from* something, or *to* something.'

Talking of melancholy, he said, 'Some men, and very thinking men too, have not those vexing thoughts.[a] Sir Joshua Reynolds is the same all the year round. Beauclerk, except when ill and in pain, is the same. But I believe most men have them in the degree in which they are capable of having them. If I were in the country, and were distressed by that malady, I would force myself to take a book; and every time I did it I should find it the easier. Melancholy, indeed, should be diverted by every means but drinking.'

We stopped at Messieurs Dillys, booksellers in the Poultry; from whence he hurried away, in a hackney coach, to Mr Thrale's in the Borough. I called at his house in the evening, having promised to acquaint Mrs Williams of his safe return; when, to my surprise, I found him sitting with her at tea, and, as I thought, not in a very good humour: for, it seems, when he got to Mr Thrale's, he found the coach was at the door waiting to carry Mrs and Miss Thrale, and Signor Baretti their Italian master, to Bath. This was not showing the attention which might have been expected to the 'Guide, Philosopher, and Friend', the *Imlack* who had hastened from the country to console a distressed mother, who he understood was very anxious for his return. They had, I found, without ceremony, proceeded on their intended journey. I was glad to understand from him that it was still resolved that his tour to Italy with Mr and Mrs Thrale should take place, of which he had entertained some doubt, on account of the loss which they had suffered; and his doubts afterwards proved to be well-founded. He observed, indeed very justly, that 'their loss was an additional reason for their going abroad; and if it had not been fixed that he should have been one of the party, he would force them out; but he would not advise them unless his advice was asked, lest they might suspect that he recommended what he wished on his own account.' I was not pleased that his intimacy with Mr Thrale's family, though it no doubt contributed much to his comfort and

---

[a] Add the following note: The phrase 'vexing thoughts' is, I think, very expressive. It has been familiar to me from my childhood; for it is to be found in the *Psalms in Metre*, used in the Churches (I believe I should say *kirks*) of Scotland, Psal. xliii. v. 5.

> Why art thou then cast down, my soul?
>   What should discourage thee?
> And why with *vexing thoughts* art thou
>   Disquieted in me?

Some allowance must no doubt be made for early prepossession. But at a maturer period of life, after looking at various metrical versions of the Psalms, I am well satisfied that the version used in Scotland, is, upon the whole, the best; and that it is vain to think of having a better. It has in general a simplicity and *unction* of sacred Poesy; and in many parts its transfusion is admirable.

enjoyment, was not without some degree of restraint. Not, as has been grossly suggested, that it was required of him as a task to talk for the entertainment of them and their company; but that he was not quite at his ease; which, however, might partly be owing to his own honest pride – that dignity of mind which is always jealous of appearing too compliant.

On Sunday, March 31, I called on him, and showed him as a curiosity which I had discovered, his 'Translation of Lobo's Account of Abyssinia', which Sir John Pringle had lent me, it being then little known as one of his works. He said, 'Take no notice of it, or don't talk of it.' He seemed to think it beneath him, though done at six-and-twenty. I said to him, 'Your style, Sir, is much improved since you translated this.' He answered with a sort of triumphant smile, 'Sir, I hope it is.'

On Wednesday, April 3, in the forenoon, I found him very busy putting his books in order, and as they were generally very old ones, clouds of dust were flying around him. He had on a pair of large gloves, such as hedgers use. His present appearance put me in mind of my uncle, Dr Boswell's description of him, 'A robust genius, born to grapple with whole libraries.'

I gave him an account of a conversation which had passed between me and Captain Cook, the day before at dinner at Sir John Pringle's, and he was much pleased with the conscientious accuracy of that celebrated circumnavigator, who set me right as to many of the exaggerated accounts given by Dr Hawkesworth of his Voyages. I told him that while I was with the Captain, I catched the enthusiasm of curiosity and adventure, and felt a strong inclination to go with him on his next voyage. JOHNSON. 'Why, Sir, a man does feel so, till he considers how very little he can learn from such voyages.' BOSWELL. 'But one is carried away with the general grand and indistinct notion of a voyage round the world.' JOHNSON. 'Yes, Sir, but a man is to guard himself against taking a thing in general.' I said I was certain that a great part of what we are told by the travellers to the South Sea must be conjecture, because they had not enough of the language of those countries to understand so much as they have related. Objects falling under the observation of the senses might be clearly known; but every thing intellectual, every thing abstract – politics, morals and religion, must be darkly guessed. Dr Johnson was of the same opinion. He upon another occasion, when a friend mentioned to him several extraordinary facts, as communicated to him by the circumnavigators, slily observed, 'Sir, I never before knew how much I was respected by these gentlemen; they told *me* none of these things.'

He had been in company with Omai, a native of one of the South Sea islands, after he had been some time in this country. He was struck with the elegance of his behaviour, and accounted for it thus: 'Sir, he had passed his time, while in England, only in the best company; so that all that he had acquired of our manners was genteel. As a proof of this, Sir, Lord Mulgrave and he dined one day at Streatham; they sat with their backs to the light fronting me, so that I could not see distinctly; and there was so little of the savage in Omai, that I was afraid to speak to either, lest I should mistake one for the other.'

We agreed to dine to-day at the Mitre-tavern, after the rising of the House of Lords, where a branch of the litigation concerning the Douglas estate, in which I was one of the counsel, was to come on. I brought with me Mr Murray, Solicitor-General of Scotland, now one of the Judges of the Court of Session, with the title of Lord Henderland. I mentioned Mr Solicitor's relation, Lord Charles Hay, with whom I knew Dr JOHNSON had been acquainted. JOHNSON. 'I wrote something for Lord Charles; and I thought he had nothing to fear from a court-martial. I suffered a great loss when he died; he was a mighty pleasing man in conversation, and a reading man. The character of a soldier is high. They who stand forth the foremost in danger, for the community, have the respect of mankind. An officer is much more respected than any other man who has as little money. In a commercial country money will always purchase respect. But you find, an officer, who has, properly speaking, no money, is every where well received and treated with attention. The character of a soldier always stands him in stead.' BOSWELL. 'Yet, Sir, I think that common soldiers are worse thought of than other men in the same rank of life; such as labourers.' JOHNSON. 'Why, Sir, a common soldier is usually a very gross man, and any quality which procures respect may be overwhelmed by grossness. A man of learning may be so vicious or so ridiculous that you cannot respect him. A common soldier too, generally eats more than he can pay for. But when a common soldier is civil in his quarters, his red coat procures him a degree of respect.' The peculiar respect paid to the military character in France was mentioned. BOSWELL. 'I should think that where military men are so numerous, they would be less valued as not being rare.' JOHNSON. 'Nay, Sir, wherever a particular character or profession is high in the estimation of a people, those who are of it will be valued above other men. We value an Englishman highly in this country, and yet Englishmen are not rare in it.'

Mr Murray praised the ancient philosophers for the candour and good humour with which those of different sects disputed with each other. JOHNSON. 'Sir, they disputed with good humour, because they were not in earnest as to religion. Had the ancients been serious in their belief, we should not have had their Gods exhibited in the manner we find them represented in the Poets. The people would not have suffered it. They disputed with good humour upon their fanciful theories, because they were not interested in the truth of them. When a man has nothing to lose, he may be in good humour with his opponent. Accordingly you see in Lucian, the Epicurean, who argues only negatively, keeps his temper; the Stoic, who has something positive to preserve, grows angry. Being angry with one who controverts an opinion which you value, is a necessary consequence of the uneasiness which you feel. Every man who attacks my belief, diminishes in some degree my confidence in it, and therefore makes me uneasy, and I am angry with him who makes me uneasy. Those only who believed in Revelation have been angry at having their faith called in question; because they only had something upon which they could rest as matter of fact.' MURRAY. 'It seems to me that we are not angry at a man for controverting an opinion which we believe and value; we rather pity him.' JOHNSON. 'Why, Sir; to be sure when you wish a man to have that belief which you think is of infinite advantage, you wish well to him; but your primary consideration is your own quiet. If a madman were to come into this room with a stick in his hand, no doubt we should pity the state of his mind; but our primary consideration would be to take care of ourselves. We should knock him down first, and pity him afterwards. No, Sir; every man will dispute with great good humour upon a subject in which he is not interested. I will dispute very calmly upon the probability of another man's son being hanged, but if a man zealously enforces the probability that my own son will be hanged, I shall certainly not be in very good humour with him.' I added this illustration, 'If a man endeavours to convince me that my wife, whom I love very much, and in whom I have great confidence, is a disagreeable woman, and is even unfaithful to me, I shall be very angry, – for he is putting me in fear of being unhappy.' MURRAY. 'But, Sir, truth will always bear an examination.' JOHNSON. 'Yes, Sir, but it is painful to be forced to defend it. Consider, Sir, how should you like, though conscious of your innocence, to be tried before a jury for a capital crime, once a week.'

We talked of education at great schools, the advantages and disadvantages of which Johnson displayed in a luminous manner; but his arguments preponderated so much in favour of the benefit which a boy of good parts might receive at one of them, that I have reason to believe Mr Murray was very much influenced by what he had heard today, in his determination to send his own son to Westminster school.[a]

I introduced the topic, which is often ignorantly urged, that the Universities of England are too rich,[b] so that learning does not flourish in them as it would do, if those who teach had smaller salaries, and depended on their assiduity for a great part of their income. JOHNSON. 'Sir, the very reverse of this is the truth; the English Universities are not rich enough. Our fellowships are only sufficient to support a man during his studies to fit him for the world, and accordingly in general they are held no longer than till an opportunity offers of getting away. Now and then, perhaps, there is a fellow who grows old in his college; but this is against his will, unless he be a man very indolent indeed. A hundred a year is reckoned a good fellowship, and that is no more than is necessary to keep a man decently as a scholar. We do not allow our fellows to marry, because we consider academical institutions as preparatory to a settlement in the world. It is only by being employed as a tutor, that a fellow can

[a] Add: I have acted in the same manner with regard to my own two sons; having placed the eldest at Eton, and the second at Westminster. I cannot say which is best. But in justice to both those noble seminaries, I with high satisfaction declare, that my boys have derived from them a great deal of good, and no evil: and I trust they will, like Horace, be grateful to their father for giving them so valuable an education.

[b] Add the following note: Dr Adam Smith, who was for some time a professor in the University of Glasgow, has uttered, in his *Wealth of Nations*, some reflections upon this subject which are certainly not well founded, and seem to be invidious.

obtain any thing more than a livelihood. To be sure a man, who has enough without teaching, will probably not teach; for we would all be idle if we could. In the same manner, a man who is to get nothing by teaching, will not exert himself. Gresham-College was intended as a place of instruction for London; able Professors were to read lectures gratis, they contrived to have no scholars; whereas, if they had been allowed to receive but six-pence a lecture from each scholar, they would have been emulous to have had many scholars. Every body will agree that it should be the interest of those who teach to have scholars; and this is the case in our Universities. That they are too rich is certainly not true; for they have nothing good enough to keep a man of eminent learning with them for his life. In the foreign Universities a professorship is a high thing. It is as much almost as a man can make by his learning; and therefore we find the most learned men abroad are in the Universities. It is not so with us. Our Universities are impoverished of learning, by the penury of their provisions. I wish there were many places of a thousand a-year at Oxford, to keep first-rate men of learning from quitting the University.' Undoubtedly, if this were the case, Literature would have a still greater dignity and splendour at Oxford, and there would be grander living sources of instruction.

I mentioned Mr Maclaurin's uneasiness on account of a degree of ridicule carelessly thrown on his deceased father, in Goldsmith's *History of Animated Nature*, in which that celebrated mathematician is represented as being subject to fits of yawning so violent as to render him incapable of proceeding in his lecture; a story altogether unfounded, but for the publication of which the law would give no reparation.[1] This led us to agitate the question, whether legal redress could be obtained, even when a man's deceased relation was calumniated in a publication. Mr Murray maintained there should be reparation, unless the author could justify himself by proving the fact. JOHNSON. 'Sir, it is of so much more consequence that truth should be told, than that individuals should not be made uneasy, that it is much better that the law does not restrain writing freely concerning the characters of the dead. Damages will be given to a man who is calumniated in his life-time, because he may be hurt in his worldly interest, or at least hurt in his mind: but the law does not regard that uneasiness which a man feels on having his ancestor calumniated. That is too nice. Let him deny what is said, and let the matter have a fair chance by discussion. But, if a man could say nothing against a character but what he can prove, history could not be written; for a great deal is known of men of which proof cannot be brought. A minister may be notoriously known to take bribes, and yet you may not be able to prove it.' Mr Murray suggested, that the author should be obliged to show some sort of evidence, though he would not require a strict

---

1 Dr Goldsmith was dead before Mr Maclaurin discovered the ludicrous error. But Mr Nourse, the bookseller, who was the proprietor of the work, upon being applied to by Sir John Pringle, agreed very handsomely to have the leaf on which it was contained cancelled, and re-printed without it, at his own expense.

legal proof: but Johnson firmly and resolutely opposed any restraint whatever, as adverse to a free investigation of the characters of mankind.[1]

1 What Dr Johnson has here said, is undoubtedly good sense; yet I am afraid that law, though defined by Lord Cole 'the perfection of reason', is not altogether with him; for it is held in the books, that an attack on the reputation even of a dead man, may be punished as a libel, because tending to a breach of the peace. There is however, I believe, no modern decided case to that effect. In the King's Bench, Trinity Term, 1790, the question occurred on occasion of an indictment, The King v. Topham, who, as a proprietor of a newspaper entitled The World, was found guilty of a libel against Earl Cowper, deceased, because certain injurious charges against his Lordship were published in that paper.[a] One of the counsel for Mr Topham, my friend Mr Const, who is very able to maintain the argument with learning and ingenuity, informs me that it is intended to move in arrest of judgement; so that we shall probably have a solemn determination, upon a point of universal importance. No man has a higher reverence for the law of England in general than I have; but, with all deference I cannot help thinking, that prosecution by indictment, if a defendant is never to be allowed to justify, must often be very oppressive, unless Juries, who I am more and more confirmed in holding to be judges of law as well as of fact, interpose.

[a] Delete the rest of this note after 'paper' and add: An arrest of judgement having been moved for, the case was afterwards solemnly argued. My friend Mr Const, whom I delight in having an opportunity to praise, not only for his abilities but his manners; a gentleman whose ancient German blood has been mellowed in England, and who may be truly said to unite the Baron and the Barrister, was one of the Counsel for Mr Topham. He displayed much learning and ingenuity upon the general question; which, however, was not decided, as the Court granted an arrest chiefly on the informality of the indictment. No man has a higher reverence for the law of England than I have; but, with all deference I cannot help thinking, that prosecution by indictment, if a defendant is never to be allowed to justify, must often be very oppressive, unless Juries, whom I am more and more confirmed in holding to be judges of law as well as of fact, resolutely interpose. Of late an act of Parliament has passed declaratory of their full right to one as well as the other, in matter of libel; and the bill having been brought in by a popular gentleman, many of his party have in most extravagant terms declaimed on the wonderful acquisition to the liberty of the press. For my own part, I ever was clearly of opinion that this right was inherent in the very constitution of a Jury, and indeed in sense and reason inseparable from their important function. To establish it, therefore, by statute, is, I think, narrowing its foundation, which is the broad and deep basis of Common Law. Would it not rather weaken the right of primo-geniture, or any other old and universally acknowledged right, should the legislature pass an act in favour of it? In my 'Letter to the People of Scotland, against diminishing the number of the Lords of Session', published in 1785, there is the following passage, which, as a concise, and I hope a fair and rational state of the matter, I presume to quote: 'The Juries of England are Judges of law as well as of fact in many civil and in all criminal trials. That my principles of resistance may not be misapprehended any more than my principles of submission, I protest that I should be the last man in the world to encourage Juries to contradict rashly, wantonly, or perversely, the opinion of the Judges. On the contrary, I would have them listen respectfully to the advice they receive from the Bench, by which they may often be well directed in forming their own opinion; which, 'and not another's', is the opinion they are to return upon their oaths. But where, after due attention to all that the Judge has said, they are decidedly of a different opinion from him, they have not only a power and a right, but they are bound in conscience to bring in a verdict accordingly.'

On Thursday, April 4, having called on Dr Johnson, I said, it was a pity that truth was not so firm as to bid defiance to all attacks, so that it might be shot at as much as people chose to attempt, and yet remain unhurt. JOHNSON. 'Then, Sir, it would not be shot at. Nobody attempts to dispute that two and two make four; but with contests concerning moral truth, human passions are generally mixed, and therefore it must ever be liable to assault and misrepresentation.'

On Friday, April 5, being Good-Friday, after having attended the morning service at St Clement's church, I walked home with Johnson. We talked of the Roman Catholic religion. JOHNSON. 'In the barbarous ages, Sir, priests and people were equally deceived; but afterwards there were gross corruptions introduced by the clergy, such as indulgences to priests to have concubines, and the worship of images, not, indeed, inculcated, but knowingly permitted.' He strongly censured the licensed stews at Rome. BOSWELL. 'So then, Sir, you would allow of no irregular intercourse whatever between the sexes?' JOHNSON. 'To be sure I would not, Sir. I would punish it much more than is done, and so restrain it. In all countries there has been fornication, as in all countries there has been theft; but there may be more or less of the one, as well as of the other, in proportion to the force of law. All men will naturally commit fornication, as all men will naturally steal. And, Sir, it is very absurd to argue, as has been often done, that prostitutes are necessary to prevent the violent effects of appetite from violating the decent order of life; nay, should be permitted, in order to preserve the chastity of our wives and daughters. Depend upon it, Sir, severe laws, steadily enforced, would be sufficient against those evils, and would promote marriage.'

I stated to him this case: 'Suppose a man has a daughter who he knows has been seduced, but her misfortune is concealed from the world: should he keep her in his house? Would he not, by doing so, be accessary to imposition? And, perhaps, a worthy unsuspecting man might come and marry this woman, unless the father inform him of the truth.' JOHNSON. 'Sir, he is accessary to no imposition. His daughter is in his house; and if a man courts her, he takes his chance. If a friend, or, indeed, if any man asks his opinion whether he should marry her, he ought to advise him against it, without telling why, because his real opinion is then required. Or, if he has other daughters who know of her frailty, he ought not to keep her in his house. You are to consider the state of life is this; we are to judge of one another's characters as well as we can; and a man is not bound, in honesty or honour, to tell us the faults of his daughter or of himself. A man who has debauched his friend's daughter is not obliged to say to every body – "Take care of me, don't let me into your houses without suspicion. I once debauched a friend's daughter: I may debauch yours." '

Mr Thrale called upon him, and appeared to bear the loss of his son with a manly composure. There was no affectation about him; and he talked, as usual, about indifferent subjects. He seemed to me to hesitate as to the intended Italian tour, on which, I flattered myself, he and Mrs Thrale and Dr Johnson were soon to set out; and, therefore, I pressed it as much as I could. I mentioned that Mr Beauclerk had said, that Baretti, whom they were to carry with them, would keep them so long in the little towns of his own district, that they would not have time to see Rome. I mentioned this, to put them on their guard. JOHNSON. 'Sir, we do not thank Mr Beauclerk for supposing that we are to be directed by Baretti. No, Sir; Mr Thrale is to go by my advice, to Mr Jackson (the all-knowing[a]), and get from him a plan for seeing the most that can be seen in the time that we have to travel. We must, to be sure, see Rome, Naples, Florence, and Venice, and as much more as we can' (speaking with a tone of animation).

When I expressed an earnest wish for his remarks on Italy, he said, 'I do not see that I could make a book upon Italy; yet I should be glad to get two hundred pounds, or five hundred pounds, by such a work.' This showed both that a journal of his Tour upon the Continent was not wholly out of his contemplation, and that he uniformly adhered to that strange opinion, which his indolent disposition made him utter: 'No man but a blockhead ever wrote, except for money.' Numerous instances to refute this will occur to all who are versed in the history of literature.

He gave us one of the many sketches of character which were treasured in his mind, and which he was wont to produce quite unexpectedly in a very entertaining manner. 'I lately (said he) received a letter from the East-Indies, from a gentleman whom I formerly knew very well; he had returned from that country with a handsome fortune, as it was reckoned, before means were found to acquire those immense sums which have been brought from thence of late; he was a scholar, and an agreeable man, and lived very prettily in London, till his wife died. After her death, he took to dissipation and gaming, and lost all he had. One evening he lost a thousand pounds to a gentleman whose name I am sorry I have forgotten. Next morning he sent the gentleman five hundred pounds, with an apology that it was all he had in the world. The gentleman sent the money back to him, declaring he would not accept it; and adding that if Mr —— had occasion for five hundred pounds more he would lend it to him. He resolved to go out again to the East-Indies, and make his fortune anew. He got a considerable appointment, and I had some intention of accompanying him. Had I thought then as I do now, I should have gone: but, at that time, I had objections to quitting England.'

It was a very remarkable circumstance about Johnson, whom shallow observers have supposed to have been ignorant of the world, that very few men had seen greater variety of characters; and none could observe them better, as was evident from the strong, yet nice portraits which he often drew. I have frequently thought that if he had made out what the French call *une catalogue raisonnée* of all the people who had passed under his observation, it would have afforded a very rich fund of instruction and entertainment. The suddenness with which his accounts of some of them started out in conversation, was not less pleasing than surprising. I remember he once observed to

---

[a] Add this note: A gentleman who, from his extraordinary stores of knowledge, has been styled *omniscient*. Johnson, I think very properly, altered it to all-knowing, as it is a *verbum solenne*, appropriated to the Supreme Being.

me, 'It is wonderful, Sir, what is to be found in London. The most literary conversation that I ever enjoyed, was at the table of Jack Ellis, a money-scrivener behind the Royal-Exchange, with whom I at one period used to dine generally once a week.'[1]

Volumes would be required to contain a list of his numerous and various acquaintance, none of whom he ever forgot; and could describe and discriminate them all with precision and vivacity. He associated with persons the most widely different in manners, abilities, rank, and accomplishments. He was at once the companion of the brilliant Colonel Forrester of the guards, who wrote *The Polite Philosopher*, and of the aukward and uncouth Robert Levett; of Lord Thurlow, and Mr Sastres, the Italian master; and has dined one day with the beautiful, gay, and fascinating Lady Craven,[2] and the next with good Mrs Gardiner the tallow-chandler, on Snow-hill.

On my expressing my wonder at his discovering so much of the knowledge peculiar to different professions, he told me, 'I learnt what I know of law, chiefly from Mr Ballow, a very able man. I learnt some too from Chambers; but was not so teachable then. One is not willing to be taught by a young man.' When I expressed a wish to know more about Mr Ballow,[a] Johnson said, 'Sir, I have seen him but once these twenty years. The tide of life has driven us different ways.' I was sorry at the time to hear this; but whoever quits the creeks of private connections, and fairly gets into the great ocean of London, will, by imperceptible degrees, unavoidably experience this.[b]

'My knowledge of physic (he added), I learnt from Dr James, whom I helped in writing the proposals for his Dictionary, and also a little in the

1 This Mr Ellis is, I believe, the last of that profession called Scriveners, which is one of the London companies, but of which the business is no longer carried on separately, but is transacted by attornies and others. He is a man of literature and talents. He is the author of a Hudibrastic version of Maphaeus's *Canto*, in addition to the *Aeneid*; of some poems in Dodsley's collection; and various other small pieces; but being a very modest man, has never put his name to anything. He has shown me a translation which he has made of Ovid's *Epistles*, very prettily done. There is a good engraved portrait of him by Peffer, from a picture by Fry, which hangs in the hall of the Scrivener's company. He is now a very old man. I have visited him this day (October 4, 1790), in his ninety-third year, and found his judgement distinct and clear, and his memory, though faded so as to fail him occasionally, yet, as he assured me, and I indeed perceived, able to serve him very well, after a little recollection. It was agreeable to observe, that he was free from the discontent and fretfulness which too often molest old age. He in the summer of this year walked to Rotherhithe, where he dined, and walked home in the evening.[c]

2 Lord Macartney, who with his other distinguished qualities, is remarkable also for an elegant pleasantry, told me, that he met Johnson at Lady Craven's, and that he seemed jealous of any interference; 'So (said his Lordship, smiling), I kept back.'

[a] Add the following note: There is an account of him in Sir John Hawkins's *Life of Johnson*.

[b] For 'this' read, 'such cessations of acquaintance'.

[c] Put the *past* instead of the *present* tense, and add: He died on the 31st December, 1791.

Dictionary itself.[a] I also learnt some from Dr Lawrence, but was then grown more stubborn.'

A curious incident happened today, while Mr Thrale and I sat with him. Francis announced that a large packet was brought to him from the post-office, said to have come from Lisbon, and it was charged *seven pounds ten shillings*. He would not receive it, supposing it to be some trick, nor did he even look at it. But upon enquiry afterwards he found that it was a real packet for him, from that very friend in the East-Indies of whom he had been speaking; and the ship which carried it having come to Portugal, this packet, with others, had been put into the post-office at Lisbon.

I mentioned a new gaming club, of which Mr Beauclerk had given me an account, where the members played to a desperate extent. JOHNSON. 'Depend upon it, Sir, this is mere talk. *Who* is ruined by gaming? You will not find six instances in an age. There is a strange rout made about deep play; whereas you have many more people ruined by adventurous trade, and yet we do not hear such an outcry against it.' THRALE. 'There may be few people absolutely ruined by deep play; but very many are much hurt in their circumstances by it.' JOHNSON. 'Yes, Sir; and so are very many by other kinds of expense.' I had heard him talk once before in the same manner; and at Oxford he said, 'he wished he had learnt to play at cards.' The truth, however, is, that he loved to display his ingenuity in argument; and therefore would sometimes in conversation maintain opinions which he was sensible were wrong, but in supporting which, his reasoning and wit would be most conspicuous. He would begin thus: 'Why, Sir, as to the good or evil of card-playing —' 'Now (said Garrick), he is thinking which side he shall take.' He appeared to have a pleasure in contradiction, especially when any opinion whatever was delivered with an air of confidence; so that there was hardly any topic, if not one of the great truths of Religion and Morality, that he might not have been incited to argue, either for or against it. Lord Elibank[1] had the highest admiration of his powers. He once observed to me, 'Whatever opinion Johnson maintains, I will not say that he convinces me; but he never fails to show me, that he has good reasons for it.' I have heard Johnson pay his Lordship this high compliment: 'I never was in Lord Elibank's company without learning something.'

We sat together till it was too late for the afternoon service. Thrale said, he had come with intention to go to church with us. We went at seven to evening prayers at St Clement's church, after having drank coffee; an indulgence, which I understood Johnson yielded to on this occasion, in compliment to Thrale.

On Sunday, April 7, Easter-day, after having been at St Paul's cathedral, I came to Dr Johnson, according to my usual custom. It seemed to me, that there was always something peculiarly mild and placid in his manner upon this holy festival, the commemoration of the most joyful event in the history of our

---

[a] Add this note: I have in vain endeavoured to find out what parts Johnson wrote for Dr James. Perhaps medical men may.

1 Patrick Lord Elibank, who died 1778.

world, the resurrection of our LORD and SAVIOUR, who, having triumphed over death and the grave, proclaimed immortality to mankind.

I repeated to him an argument of a lady of my acquaintance, who maintained, that her husband's having been guilty of numberless infidelities, released her from conjugal obligations, because they were reciprocal. JOHNSON. 'This is miserable stuff, Sir. To the contract of marriage, besides the man and wife, there is a third party — Society; and, if it be considered as a vow — GOD: and, therefore, it cannot be dissolved by their consent alone. Laws are not made for particular cases, but for mankind in general. A woman may be unhappy with her husband; but she cannot be freed from him without the approbation of the civil and ecclesiastical power. A man may be unhappy, because he is not so rich as another; but he is not to seize upon another's property with his own hand.' BOSWELL. 'But, Sir, this lady does not want that the contract should be dissolved; she only argues that she may indulge herself in gallantries with equal freedom as her husband does, provided she takes care not to introduce a spurious issue into his family. You know, Sir, what Macrobius has told us of Julia.[a] JOHNSON. 'This lady of yours, Sir, I think, is very fit for a brothel.'

Mr Macbean, author of the *Dictionary of ancient Geography*, came in. He mentioned, that he had been forty years absent from Scotland. 'Ah, Boswell! (said Johnson, smiling), what would you give to be forty years from Scotland?' I said, 'I should not like to be so long absent from the seat of my ancestors.' This gentleman, Mrs Williams, and Mr Levett, dined with us.

Dr Johnson made a remark, which both Mr Macbean and I thought new. It was this: that 'the law against usury is for the protection of creditors as well as of debtors; for if there were no such check, people would be apt, from the temptation of great interest, to lend to desperate persons, by whom they would lose their money. Accordingly there are instances of ladies being ruined, by having injudiciously sunk their fortunes for high annuities, which, after a few years, ceased to be paid, in consequence of the ruined circumstances of the borrower.'

Mrs Williams was very peevish; and I wondered at Johnson's patience with her now, as I had often done on similar occasions. The truth is, that his humane consideration of the forlorn and indigent state in which this lady was left by her father, induced him to treat her with the utmost tenderness, and even to be desirous of procuring her amusement, so as sometimes to incommode many of his friends, by carrying her with him to their houses, where, from her manner of eating, in consequence of her blindness, she could not but offend the delicacy of persons of nice sensations.

After coffee, we went to afternoon service in St Clement's church. Observing some beggars in the street as we walked along, I said to him I supposed there was no civilised country in the world, where the misery of want in the lowest classes of the people was prevented. JOHNSON. 'I believe, Sir, there is not; but it is better that some should be unhappy, than that none should be happy, which would be the case in a general state of equality.'

1 *Nunquam enim nisi navi plena tollo vectorem.* Lib. ii, ch. vi.

When the service was ended, I went home with him, and we sat quietly by ourselves. He recommended Dr Cheyne's books. I said, I thought Cheyne had been reckoned whimsical. – 'So he was (said he), in some things; but there is no end of objections. There are few books to which some objection or other may not be made.'[a]

Upon the question whether a man who had been guilty of vicious actions would do well to force himself into solitude and sadness; JOHNSON. 'No, Sir, unless it prevent him from being vicious again. With some people, gloomy penitence is only madness turned upside down. A man may be gloomy, till, in order to be relieved from gloom, he has recourse again to criminal indulgences.'

On Wednesday, April 10, I dined with him at Mr Thrale's, where were Mr Murphy and some other company. Before dinner, Dr Johnson and I passed some time by ourselves. I was sorry to find it was now resolved that the proposed journey to Italy should not take place this year. He said, 'I am disappointed, to be sure, but it is not a great disappointment.' I wondered to see him bear, with a philosophical calmness, what would have made most people peevish and fretful. I perceived, however, that he had so warmly cherished the hope of enjoying classical scenes, that he could not easily part with the scheme; for he said, 'I shall probably contrive to get to Italy some other way. But I won't mention it to Mr and Mrs Thrale, as it might vex them.' I suggested, that going to Italy might have done Mr and Mrs Thrale good. JOHNSON. 'I rather believe not, Sir. While grief is fresh, every attempt to divert only irritates. You must wait till grief be *digested*, and then amusement will dissipate the remains of it.'

At dinner, Mr Murphy entertained us with the history of Mr Joseph Simpson, a schoolfellow of Dr Johnson's, a barrister-at law, of good parts, but who fell into a dissipated course of life, incompatible with that success in his profession which he once had, and would otherwise have deservedly maintained; yet he still preserved a dignity in his deportment. He wrote a tragedy on the story of Leonidas, entitled *The Patriot*. He read it to a company of lawyers, who found so many faults, that he wrote it over again: so then there were two tragedies on the same subject, and with the same title. Dr Johnson told us, that one of them was still in his possession. This very piece was, after his death, published by some person who had been about him, and, for the sake of a little hasty profit, was positively averred[b] to have been written by Johnson himself.

I said, I disliked the custom which some people had of bringing their children into company, because it in a manner forced us to pay foolish compliments to please their parents. JOHNSON. 'You are right, Sir. We may be excused for not caring much about other people's children, for there are many who care very little about their own children. It may be observed, that men,

---

[a] After this passage, read: He added, 'I would not have you read any thing else of Cheyne, but his book on Health, and his *English Malady*.'

[b] For 'positively averred', read 'fallaciously advertised, so as to make it be believed'.

who from being engaged in business, or from their course of life in whatever way, seldom see their children, do not care much about them. I myself should not have had much fondness for a child of my own.' MRS THRALE. 'Nay, Sir, how can you talk so?' JOHNSON. 'At least, I never wished to have a child.'

Mr Murphy mentioned Dr Johnson's having a design to publish an edition of Cowley. Johnson said, he did not know but he should; and he expressed his disapprobation of Dr Hurd, for having published a mutilated edition under the title of 'Select Works of Abraham Cowley'. Mr Murphy thought it a bad precedent; observing, that any author might be used in the same manner; and that it was pleasing to see the variety of an author's compositions, at different periods.

We talked of Flatman's Poems; and Mrs Thrale observed, that Pope had partly borrowed from him, 'The dying Christian to his Soul'. Johnson repeated Rochester's verses upon Flatman, which I think by much too severe:

> Nor that slow drudge in swift Pindaric strains, ⎫
> Flatman, who Cowley imitates with pains, ⎬
> And rides a jaded Muse, whipt with loose reins. ⎭

I like to recollect all the passages that I heard Johnson repeat: it stamps a value on them.

He told us, that the book entitled 'The Lives of the Poets, by Mr Cibber', was entirely compiled by Mr Shiels, a Scotchman, one of his amanuenses. 'The booksellers (said he) gave Theophilus Cibber, who was then in prison, ten guineas, to allow Mr Cibber to be put upon the title-page, as the author; by this, a double imposition was intended: in the first place, that it was the work of a Cibber at all; and, in the second place, that it was the work of old Cibber.'[a]

---

[a] Add this note: In the *Monthly Review* for May, 1792, there is a circumstantial statement which seems to prove in a satisfactory manner that Johnson was mistaken. It is to be observed, however, that the story told by Johnson does not rest solely upon my record of his conversation, &c.' (*as in next note.*)[b]

[b] (*Second Edition*) In the *Monthly Review* for May, 1792, there is such a correction of the above passage, as I should think myself very culpable not to subjoin. 'This account is very inaccurate. The following statement of facts we know to be true, in every material circumstance: Shiels was the principal collector and digester of the materials for the work; but as he was very raw in authorship, an indifferent writer in prose, and his language full of Scotticisms, Cibber, who was a clever, lively fellow, and then soliciting employment among the booksellers, was engaged to correct the style and diction of the whole work, then intended to make only four volumes, with power to alter, expunge, or add, as he liked. He was also to supply *notes*, occasionally, especially concerning those dramatic poets with whom he had been chiefly conversant. He also engaged to write several of the Lives; which (as we are told), he, accordingly, performed. He was farther useful in striking out the Jacobitical and Tory sentiments, which Shiels had industriously interspersed wherever he could bring them in – and as the success of the work appeared, after all, very doubtful, he was content with twenty-one pounds for his labour besides a few sets of the books, to disperse among his

Mr Murphy said, that 'The Memoirs of Gray's Life set him much higher in his estimation than his poems did; for you there saw a man constantly at work in literature.' Johnson acquiesced in this, but depreciated the book, I thought, very unreasonably. For he said, 'I forced myself to read it, only because it was a common topic of conversation. I found it mighty dull; and, as to the style, it is fit for the second table.' Why he thought so, I was at a loss to conceive. He now gave it as his opinion, that 'Akenside was a superior poet both to Gray and Mason.'

---

friends. – Shiels had nearly seventy pounds, beside the advantage of many of the best Lives in the work being communicated by friends to the undertaking; and for which Mr Shiels had the same consideration as for the rest, being paid by the sheet for the whole. He was, however, so angry with his Whiggish supervisor (Theo., like his father, being a violent stickler for the political principles which prevailed in the reign of George the Second), for so unmercifully mutilating his copy, and scouting his politics, that he wrote Cibber a challenge: but was prevented from sending it, by the publisher, who fairly laughed him out of his fury. The proprietors, too, were discontented, in the end, on account of Mr Cibber's unexpected industry; for his corrections and alterations in the proof-sheets were so numerous and considerable, that the printer made for them a grievous addition to his bill; and, in fine, all parties were dissatisfied. On the whole, the work was productive of no profit to the undertakers, who had agreed, in case of success, to make Cibber a present of some addition to the twenty guineas which he had received, and for which his receipt is now in the booksellers' hands. We are farther assured, that he actually obtained an additional sum; when he, soon after (in the year 1758), unfortunately embarked for Dublin, on an engagement for one of the theatres there: but the ship was cast away, and every person on board perished. There were about sixty passengers, among whom was the Earl of Drogheda, with many other persons of consequence and property.

'As to the alleged design of making the compilement pass for the work of old Mr Cibber, the charges seem to have been founded on a somewhat uncharitable construction. We are assured that the thought was not harboured by some of the proprietors, who are still living: and we hope that it did not occur to the first designer of the work, who was also the printer of it, and who bore a respectable character.

'We have been induced to enter thus circumstantially into the foregoing detail of facts relating to the Lives of the Poets, compiled by Messrs Cibber and Shiels, from a sincere regard to that sacred principle of Truth, to which Dr Johnson so rigidly adhered, according to the best of his knowledge; and which, we believe, *no consideration* would have prevailed on him to violate. In regard to the matter, which we now dismiss, he had, no doubt, been misled by partial and wrong information: Shiels was the Doctor's amanuensis; he had quarrelled with Cibber; it is natural to suppose that he told his story in his own way; and it is certain that *he* was not "a very sturdy moralist".'

This explanation appears to me very satisfactory. It is, however, to be observed, that the story told by Johnson does not rest solely upon my record of his conversation; for be himself has published it in his life of Hammond, where he says, 'the manuscript of Shiels is now in my possession.' Very probably he had trusted to Shiels's word, and never looked at it so as to compare it with 'The Lives of the Poets', as published under Mr Cibber's name. What became of that manuscript I know not. I should have liked much to examine it. I suppose it was thrown into the fire in that impetuous combustion of papers, which Johnson I think rashly executed when *moribundus*.

Talking of the Reviews, Johnson said, 'I think them very impartial: I do not know an instance of partiality.' He mentioned what had passed upon the subject of the *Monthly* and *Critical* Reviews, in the conversation with which his Majesty had honoured him. He expatiated a little more on them this evening. 'The Monthly Reviewers (said he) are not Deists; but they are Christians with as little Christianity as may be; and are for pulling down all establishments. The Critical Reviewers are for supporting the constitution, both in church and state. The Critical Reviewers, I believe, often review without reading the books through; but lay hold of a topic, and write chiefly from their own minds. The Monthly Reviewers are duller men, and are glad to read the books through.'

He talked of Lord Lyttelton's extreme anxiety as an author; observing, that 'he was thirty years in preparing his History, and that he employed a man to point it for him, as if (laughing) another man could point his sense better than himself.' Mr Murphy said, he understood his History was kept back several years for fear of Smollet. JOHNSON. 'This seems strange to Murphy and me, who never felt that anxiety, but sent what we wrote to the press, and let it take its chance.' MRS THRALE. 'The time has been, Sir, when you felt it.' JOHNSON. 'Why really, Madam, I do not recollect a time when that was the case.'

Talking of *The Spectator*, he said, 'It is wonderful that there is such a proportion of bad papers, in the half of the work which was not written by Addison; for there was all the world to write that half, yet not a half of that half is good. One of the finest pieces in the English language is the paper on Novelty, yet we do not hear it talked of. It was written by Grove, a dissenting teacher.' He would not, I perceived, call him a *clergyman*, though he was candid enough to allow very great merit to his composition. Mr Murphy said, he remembered when there were several people alive in London, who enjoyed a considerable reputation merely from having written a paper in *The Spectator*. He mentioned particularly Mr Ince, who used to frequent Tom's coffee-house. 'But (said Johnson) you must consider how highly Steele speaks of Mr Ince.' He would not allow that the paper on carrying a boy to travel, signed *Philip Homebred*, which was written by the Lord Chancellor Hardwick, had merit. He said, 'it was quite vulgar, and had nothing luminous.'

Johnson mentioned Dr Barry's *System of Physic*. 'He was a man (said he) who had acquired a high reputation in Dublin, came over to England, and brought his reputation with him, but had not great success. His notion was, that pulsation occasions death by attrition; and that, therefore, the way to preserve life is to retard pulsation. But we know that pulsation is strongest in infants, and that we increase in growth while it operates in its regular course; so it cannot be the cause of destruction.' Soon after this, he said something very flattering to Mrs Thrale, which I do not recollect; but it concluded with wishing her long life. 'Sir (said I), if Dr Barry's system be true, you have now shortened Mrs Thrale's life, perhaps, some minutes, by accelerating her pulsation.'

On Thursday, April 11, I dined with him at General Paoli's, in whose house I now resided, and where I had ever afterwards the honour of being entertained with the kindest attention as his constant guest, while I was in London, till I had a house of my own there. I mentioned my having that morning introduced to Mr Garrick, Count Neni, a Flemish nobleman of great rank and fortune, to whom Garrick talked of Abel Drugger as *a small part*; and related, with pleasant vanity, that a Frenchman who had seen him in one of his low characters, exclaimed, '*Comment! je ne le crois pas. Ce n'est pas, Monsieur Garrick, ce Grand Homme!*' Garrick added, with an appearance of grave recollection, 'If I were to begin life again, I think I should not play those low characters.' Upon which I observed, 'Sir, you would be in the wrong; for your great excellence is your variety of playing, your representing so well, characters so very different.' JOHNSON. 'Garrick, Sir, was not in earnest in what he said; for, to be sure, his peculiar excellence is his variety; and, perhaps, there is not any one character which has not been as well acted by somebody else, as he could do it.' BOSWELL. 'Why then, Sir, did he talk so?' JOHNSON. 'Why, Sir, to make you answer as you did.' BOSWELL. 'I don't know, Sir; he seemed to dip deep into his mind for the reflection.' JOHNSON. 'He had not far to dip, Sir: he had said the same thing, probably, twenty times before.'

Of a nobleman raised at a very early period to high office, he said, 'His parts, Sir, are pretty well for a Lord, but would not be distinguished in a man who had nothing else but his parts.'

A journey to Italy was still in his thoughts. He said, 'A man who has not been in Italy, is always conscious of an inferiority, – from his not having seen what it is expected a man should see. The grand object of travelling is to see the shores of the Mediterranean. On those shores were the four great empires of the world; the Assyrian, the Persian, the Grecian, and the Roman. – All our religion, almost all our law, almost all our arts, almost all that sets us above savages, has come to us from the shores of the Mediterranean.' The General observed, that 'THE MEDITERRANEAN would be a noble subject for a poem.'

We talked of translation. I said, I could not define it, nor could I think of a similitude to illustrate it; but that it appeared to me the translation of poetry could be only imitation. JOHNSON. 'You may translate books of science exactly. You may also translate history, in so far as it is not embellished with oratory, which is poetical. Poetry, indeed, cannot be translated; and, therefore, it is the poets that preserve languages; for we would not be at the trouble to learn a language, if we could have all that is written in it just as well in a translation. But as the beauties of poetry cannot be preserved in any language except that in which it was originally written, we learn the language.'

A gentleman maintained that the art of printing had hurt real learning, by disseminating idle writings. – JOHNSON. 'Sir, if it had not been for the art of printing, we should now have no learning at all; for books would have perished faster than they could have been transcribed.' This observation seems not just, considering for how many ages books were preserved by writing alone.

The same gentleman maintained, that a general diffusion of knowledge among a people was a disadvantage; for it made the vulgar rise above their humble sphere. JOHNSON. 'Sir, while knowledge is a distinction, those who are possessed of it will naturally rise above those who are not. Merely to read and write was a distinction at first; but we see when reading and writing have become general, the common people keep their stations. And so, were higher attainments to become general, the effect would be the same.'

'Goldsmith (he said) referred every thing to vanity; his virtues, and his vices too, were from that motive. He was not a social man. He never exchanged mind with you.'

We spent the evening at Mr Hoole's. Mr Mickle, the excellent translator of *The Lusiad*, was there. I have preserved little of the conversation of this evening. Dr Johnson said, 'Thomson had a true poetical genius, the power of viewing every thing in a poetical light. His fault is such a cloud of words sometimes, that the sense can hardly peep through. Shiels, who compiled Cibber's *Lives of the Poets*, was one day sitting with me. I took down Thomson, and read aloud a large portion of him, and then asked – Is not this fine? Shiels having expressed the highest admiration: Well, Sir (said I), I have omitted every other line.'

I related a dispute between Goldsmith and Mr Robert Dodsley, one day when they and I were dining at Tom Davies's, in 1762. Goldsmith asserted, that there was no poetry produced in this age. Dodsley appealed to his own Collection, and maintained, that though you could not find a Palace like Dryden's 'Ode on St Cecilia's Day', you had villages composed of very pretty houses; and he mentioned particularly 'The Spleen'. JOHNSON. 'I think Dodsley gave up the question. He and Goldsmith said the same thing; only he said it in a softer manner than Goldsmith did: for he acknowledged that there was no poetry, nothing that towered above the common mark. You may find wit and humour in verse, and yet no poetry. *Hudibras* has a profusion of these; yet it is not to be reckoned a poem. 'The Spleen', in Dodsley's collection, on which you say he chiefly rested, is not poetry.' BOSWELL. 'Does not Gray's poetry, Sir, tower above the common mark?' JOHNSON. 'Yes, Sir; but we must attend to the difference between what men in general cannot do if they would, and what every man may do if he would. Sixteen-string Jack[a] towered above the common mark.' BOSWELL. 'Then, Sir, what is poetry?' JOHNSON. 'Why, Sir, it is much easier to say what it is not. We all *know* what light is; but it is not easy to *tell* what it is.'

On Friday, April 12, I dined with him at our friend Tom Davies's, where we met Mr Cradock,[b] a Leicestershire gentleman, author of *Zobeide*, a tragedy; and Dr Harwood, who has written and published various works.[c]

I introduced Aristotle's doctrine in his *Art of Poetry*, of 'the κάθαρσις τῶν

---

a Add this note: A noted highwayman, who after having been several times tried and acquitted, was at last hanged. He was remarkable for foppery in his dress, and particularly for wearing a bunch of sixteen strings at the knees of his breeches.

b After 'Mr Cradock', read: of Leicestershire, author of *Zobeide*, a tragedy; a very pleasing gentleman, to whom my friend Dr Farmer's very excellent 'Essay on the Learning of Shakspeare' is addressed.

c After 'works', add: particularly a fantastical translation of the New Testament, in modern phrase, and with a Socinian twist.

παθημάτων, the purging of the passions', as the purpose of tragedy.[a] 'But how are the passions to be purged by terror and pity?' (said I, with an assumed air of ignorance, to incite him to talk, for which it was often necessary to employ some address). JOHNSON. 'Why, Sir, you are to consider what is the meaning of purging in the original sense. It is to expel impurities from the human body. The mind is subject to the same imperfection. The passions are the great movers of human actions; but they are mixed with such impurities, that it is necessary they should be purged or refined by means of terror and pity. For instance, ambition is a noble passion; but by seeing upon the stage, that a man who is so excessively ambitious as to raise himself by injustice, is punished, we are terrified at the fatal consequences of such a passion. In the same manner a certain degree of resentment is necessary; but if we see that a man carries it too far, we pity the object of it, and are taught to moderate that passion.' My record upon this occasion does great injustice to Johnson's expression, which was so forcible and brilliant, that Mr Cradock whispered me, 'O that his words were written in a book!'

I observed the great defect of the tragedy of *Othello* was, that it had not a moral, for that no man could resist the circumstances of suspicion which were artfully suggested to Othello's mind. JOHNSON. 'In the first place, Sir, we learn from *Othello* this very useful moral, not to make an unequal match; in the second place, we learn not to yield too readily to suspicion. The handkerchief is merely a trick, though a very pretty trick; but there are no other circumstances of reasonable suspicion, except what is related by Iago of Cassio's warm expressions concerning Desdemona in his sleep; and that depended entirely upon the assertion of one man. No, Sir, I think *Othello* has more moral than almost any play.'

Talking of a penurious gentleman of our acquaintance, Johnson said, 'Sir, he is narrow, not so much from avarice, as from impotence to spend his money. He cannot find in his heart to pour out a bottle of wine; but he would not much care if it should sour.'

He said, he wished to see John Dennis's 'Critical Works' collected. Davies said they would not sell. Dr Johnson seemed to think otherwise.

Davies said of a well known dramatic author, that 'he lived upon potted stories, and that he made his way as Hannibal did, by vinegar; having begun by attacking people; particularly the players.'

He reminded Dr Johnson of Mr Murphy's having paid him the highest compliment that ever was paid to a layman, by asking his pardon for repeating some oaths in the course of telling a story.

Johnson and I supt this evening at the Crown and Anchor tavern, in company with Sir Joshua Reynolds, Mr Langton, Mr Nairne, now one of the Scotch Judges, with the title of Lord Dunsinan, and my very worthy friend, Sir William Forbes, of Pitsligo.

---

[a] Add this note: See an ingenious essay on this subject by the late Doctor Moor, Greek Professor at Glasgow.

We discussed the question whether drinking improved conversation and benevolence. Sir Joshua maintained it did. JOHNSON. 'No, Sir: before dinner men meet with great inequality of understanding; and those who are conscious of their inferiority, have the modesty not to talk. When they have drunk wine, every man feels himself happy, and loses that modesty, and grows impudent and vociferous; but he is not improved; he is only not sensible of his defects.' Sir Joshua said that the Doctor was talking of the effects of excess in wine; but that a moderate glass enlivened the mind, by giving a proper circulation to the blood. 'I am (said he) in very good spirits when I get up in the morning. By dinner-time I am exhausted; wine puts me in the same state as when I got up; and I am sure that moderate drinking makes people talk better.' JOHNSON. 'No, Sir; wine gives not light, gay, ideal hilarity, but tumultuous, noisy, clamorous merriment. I have heard none of those drunken – nay, drunken is a coarse word – none of those *vinous* flights.' SIR JOSHUA. 'Because you have sat by, quite sober, and felt an envy of the happiness of those who were drinking.' JOHNSON. 'Perhaps contempt. – And, Sir, it is not necessary to be drunk one's self, to relish the wit of drunkenness. Do we not judge of the drunken wit of the dialogue between Iago and Cassio, the most excellent in its kind, when we are quite sober? Wit is wit, by whatever means it is produced; and, if good, will appear so at all times. I admit that the spirits are raised by drinking, as by the common participation of any pleasure; cock-fighting, or bear-baiting, will raise the spirits of a company as drinking does, though surely they will not improve conversation. I also admit, that there are some sluggish men who are improved by drinking, as there are fruits which are not good till they are rotten. There are such men, but they are medlars. I indeed allow that there have been a very few men of talents who were improved by drinking, but I maintain that I am right as to the effects of drinking in general: and let it be considered, that there is no position, however false in its universality, which is not true of some particular man.' Sir William Forbes said, 'Might not a man warmed with wine be like a bottle of beer, which is made brisker by being set before the fire?' – 'Nay (said Johnson, laughing), I cannot answer that: that is too much for me.'

I observed, that wine did some people harm, by inflaming, confusing, and irritating their minds; but that the experience of mankind had declared in favour of moderate drinking. JOHNSON. 'Sir, I do not say it is wrong to produce self-complacency by drinking; I only deny that it improves the mind. When I drank wine, I scorned to drink it when in company. I have drunk many a bottle by myself: in the first place, because I had need of it to raise my spirits; in the second place, because I would have nobody to witness its effects upon me.'

He told us, 'almost all his *Ramblers* were written just as they were wanted for the press; that he sent a certain portion of the copy of an essay, and wrote the remainder, while the former part of it was printing. When it was wanted, and he had fairly sat down to it, he was sure it would be done.'

He said, that for general improvement, a man should read whatever his immediate inclination prompts him to; though, to be sure, if a man has a science to learn, he must regularly and resolutely advance. He added, 'what we read with inclination makes a much stronger impression. If we read without inclination, half the mind is employed in fixing the attention; so there is but one half to be employed on what we read.' He told us, he read Fielding's *Amelia* through without stopping.[1] He said, 'if a man begins to read in the middle of a book, and feels an inclination to go on, let him not quit it, to go to the beginning. He may, perhaps, not feel again the inclination.'

Sir Joshua mentioned Mr Cumberland's Odes, which were just published. JOHNSON. 'Why, Sir, they would have been thought as good as Odes commonly are, if Cumberland had not put his name to them; but a name immediately draws censure, unless it be a name that bears down every thing before it. Nay, Cumberland has made his Odes subsidiary to the fame of another man.[2] They might have run well enough by themselves; but he has not only loaded them with a name, but has made them carry double.'

We talked of the Reviews, and Dr Johnson spoke of them as he did at Thrale's.[3] Sir Joshua said, what I have often thought, that he wondered to find so much good writing employed in them, when the authors were to remain unknown, and so could not have the motive of fame. JOHNSON. 'Nay, Sir, those who write in them, write well, in order to be paid well.'

Soon after this day, he went to Bath with Mr and Mrs Thrale. I had never seen that beautiful city, and wished to take the opportunity of visiting it, while Johnson was there. Having written to him, I received the following answer:

To JAMES BOSWELL, Esq.

DEAR SIR – Why do you talk of neglect? When did I neglect you? If you will come to Bath, we shall all be glad to see you. Come, therefore, as soon as you can.

But I have a little business for you at London. Bid Francis look in the paper-drawer of the chest of drawers in my bed-chamber for two cases; one for the Attorney-General, and one for the Solicitor-General. They lie, I think, at the top of my papers; otherwise they are somewhere else, and will give me more trouble.

Please to write me immediately, if they can be found. Make my compliments to all our friends round the world, and to Mrs Williams at home.

I am, Sir, your, &c.

SAM. JOHNSON.

Search for the papers as soon as you can, that, if it is necessary, I may write to you again before you come down.

---

1 We have here an involuntary testimony to the excellence of this admirable writer, to whom we have seen that Dr Johnson *directly* allowed so little merit.
2 Mr Romney the painter, who has now deservedly established a high reputation.
3 Page 521.

On the 26th of April, I went to Bath; and on my arrival at the Pelican inn, found lying for me an obliging invitation from Mr and Mrs Thrale, by whom I was agreeably entertained almost constantly during my stay. They were gone to the rooms; but there was a kind note from Dr Johnson, that he should sit at home all the evening. I went to him directly, and before Mr and Mrs Thrale returned, we had by ourselves some hours of tea-drinking and talk.

I shall group together such of his sayings as I preserved during the few days that I was at Bath.

Of a person who differed from him in politics, he said, 'In private life he is a very honest gentleman; but I will not allow him to be so in public life. People *may* be honest, though they are doing wrong: that is between their Maker and them. But *we*, who are suffering by their pernicious conduct, are to destroy them. We are sure that —— acts from interest. We know what his genuine principles were. They who allow their passions to confound the distinctions between right and wrong, are criminal. They may be convinced; but they have not come honestly by their conviction.'

It having been mentioned, I know not with what truth, that a certain female political writer, whose doctrines he disliked, had of late become very fond of dress, sat hours together at her toilet, and even put on rouge; – JOHNSON. 'She is better employed at her toilet than using her pen. It is better she should be reddening her own cheeks, than blackening other people's characters.'

He told us that 'Addison wrote Budgell's papers in the *Spectator*, at least mended them so much, that he made them almost all his own; and that Draper, Tonson's partner, assured Mrs Johnson, that the much admired Epilogue to *The Distressed Mother*, which came out in Budgell's name, was in reality written by Addison.'

'The mode of government by one may be ill adapted to a small society, but is best for a great nation. The characteristic of our own government at present is imbecility. The magistrate dare not call the guards for fear of being hanged. The guards will not come, for fear of being given up to the blind rage of popular juries.'

Of the father of one of our friends. he observed, 'He never clarified his notions, by filtrating them through other minds. He had a canal upon his estate, where at one place the bank was too low. – I dug the canal deeper,' said he.

He told me that 'so long ago as 1748, he had read *The Grave: a Poem*,[1] but did not like it much.' I differed from him, for though it is not equal throughout, and is seldom elegantly correct, it abounds in solemn thought, and poetical imagery beyond the common reach. The world has differed from him, for the

---

1 I am sorry that there are no memoirs of the Reverend Robert Blair, the author of this poem. He was the representative of the ancient family of Blair, of Blair in Ayrshire, but the estate had descended to a female, and afterwards passed to the son of her husband by another marriage. He was minister of the parish of Athelstaneford, where Mr John Home was his successor; so that it may be truly called classic ground. His son, who is of the same name, and a man eminent for talents and learning, is now, with universal approbation, Solicitor-General of Scotland.

poem has passed through many editions, and is still much read by people of a serious cast of mind.

A literary lady of large fortune was mentioned, as one who did good to many, but by no means 'by stealth', and instead of 'blushing to find it fame', acted evidently from vanity. JOHNSON. 'I have seen no beings who do as much good from benevolence, as she does, from whatever motive. If there are such under the earth or in the clouds, I wish they would come up, or come down. What Soame Jennyns says upon this subject is not to be minded; he is a Wit. No, Sir, to act from pure benevolence is not possible for finite beings. Human benevolence is mingled with vanity, interest, or some other motive.'

He would not allow me to praise a lady then at Bath; observing, 'She does not gain upon me, Sir; I think her empty-headed.' He was, indeed, a stern critic upon characters and manners. Even Mrs Thrale did not escape his friendly animadversion at times. When he and I were one day endeavouring to ascertain article by article, how one of our friends could possibly spend as much money in his family as he told us he did, she interrupted us with a lively extravagant sally, on the expense of clothing his children, describing it in a very ludicrous and fanciful manner. Johnson looked a little angry, and said, 'Nay, Madam, when you are declaiming, declaim; and when you are calculating, calculate.' At another time, when she said, perhaps affectedly, 'I don't like to fly.' JOHNSON. 'With *your* wings, Madam, you *must* fly: but have a care, there are *clippers* abroad.' How very well was this said, and how fully has experience proved the truth of it! But have they not *clipped* rather *rudely*, and gone a great deal *closer* than was necessary?

A gentleman expressed a wish to go and live three years at Otaheite, or New-Zealand, in order to obtain a full acquaintance with people, so totally different from all that we have ever known, and be satisfied what pure nature can do for man. JOHNSON. 'What could you learn, Sir? What can savages tell, but what they themselves have seen? Of the past, or the invisible, they can tell nothing. The inhabitants of Otaheite and New-Zealand are not in a state of pure nature; for it is plain they broke off from some other people. Had they grown out of the ground, you might have judged of a state of pure nature. Fanciful people may talk of a mythology being amongst them; but it must be invention. They have once had religion, which has been gradually debased. And what account of their religion can you suppose to be learnt from savages? Only consider, Sir, our own state: Our religion is in a book; we have an order of men whose duty it is to teach it; we have one day in the week set apart for it, and this in general pretty well observed: yet ask the first ten gross men you meet, and hear what they can tell of their religion.'

On Monday, April 29, he and I made an excursion to Bristol, where I was entertained with seeing him inquire upon the spot, into the authenticity of 'Rowley's Poetry', as I had seen him inquire upon the spot into the authenticity of 'Ossian's Poetry'. George Catcot, the pewterer, who was as zealous for Rowley, as Dr Hugh Blair was for Ossian (I trust my Reverend friend will excuse the comparison), attended us at our inn, and with a triumphant air of lively simplicity called out, 'I'll make Dr Johnson a convert.' Dr Johnson, at his desire, read aloud some of Chatterton's fabricated verses, while Catcot stood at the back of his chair, moving himself like a pendulum, and beating time with his feet. and now and then looking into Dr Johnson's face, wondering that he was not yet convinced. We called on Mr Barret, the surgeon, and saw some of the *originals* as they were called, which were executed very artificially; but from a careful inspection of them, and a consideration of the circumstances with which they were attended, we were quite satisfied of the imposture, which, indeed, has been clearly demonstrated from internal evidence, by several able critics.[1]

Honest Catcot seemed to pay no attention whatever to any objections, but insisted, as an end of all controversy, that we should go with him to the tower of the church of St Mary, Redcliff, and *view with our own eyes* the ancient chest in which the manuscripts were found. To this, Dr Johnson good-naturedly agreed; and though troubled with a shortness of breathing, laboured up a long flight of steps, till we came to the place where the wondrous chest stood. 'There (said Catcot, with a bouncing confident credulity), *there* is the very chest itself.' After this *ocular demonstration*, there was no more to be said. He brought to my recollection a Scotch Highlander, a man of learning too, and who had seen the world, attesting, and at the same time giving his reasons for the authenticity of Fingal: 'I have heard all that poem when I was young.' – 'Have you, Sir? Pray what have you heard?' – 'I have heard Ossian, Oscar, and *every one of them.*'

Johnson said of Chatterton, 'This is the most extraordinary young man that has encountered my knowledge. It is wonderful how the whelp has written such things.'

We were by no means pleased with our inn at Bristol. 'Let us see now (said I), how we should describe it.' Johnson was ready with his raillery. 'Describe it, Sir? – Why, it was so bad that Boswell wished to be in Scotland!'

After Dr Johnson's return to London, I was several times with him at his house, where I occasionally slept, in the room that had been assigned to me. I dined with him at Dr Taylor's, at General Oglethorpe's, and at General Paoli's. To avoid a tedious minuteness, I shall group together what I have preserved of his conversation during this period also, without specifying each scene where it passed, except one, which will be found so remarkable as certainly to deserve a very particular relation. Where the place or the persons do not contribute to the zest of the conversation. it is unnecessary to encumber my page with mentioning them. To know of what vintage our wine is, enables us to judge of its value and to drink it with more relish: but to have the produce of each vine of one vineyard, in the same year, kept separate, would serve no purpose. To know that our wine (to use an advertising phrase) is 'of the stock of an Ambassador lately deceased', heightens its flavour: but it signifies nothing to know the bin where each bottle was once deposited.

'Garrick (he observed) does not play the part of Archer in *The Beaux' Stratagem* well. The gentleman should break out through the footman, which is not the case as he does it.'

1 Mr Tyrwhitt, Mr Warton, Mr Malone.

'Where there is no education, as in savage countries, men will have the upper hand of women. Bodily strength, no doubt, contributes to this: but it would be so, exclusive of that; for it is mind that always governs. When it comes to dry understanding, man has the better.'

'The little volumes entitled *Respublicae*, which are very well done, were a bookseller's work.'

'There is much talk of the misery which we cause to the brute creation, but they are recompensed by existence. If they were not useful to man, and therefore protected by him, they would not be nearly so numerous.' This argument is to be found in the able and benignant Hutchinson's *Moral Philosophy*. But the question is, whether the animals who endure such sufferings of various kinds, for the service and entertainment of man, would accept of existence upon the terms on which they have it. Madame Sevigne, who, though she had many enjoyments, felt with delicate sensibility the prevalence of misery, complains of the task of existence having been imposed upon her without her consent.

'That man is never happy for the present is so true, that all his relief from unhappiness is only forgetting himself for a little while. Life is a progress from want to want, not from enjoyment to enjoyment.'

'Though many men are nominally entrusted with the administration of hospitals and other public institutions, almost all the good is done by one man, by whom the rest are driven on; owing to confidence in him, and indolence in them.'

'Lord Chesterfield s Letters to his son, I think, might be made a very pretty book. Take out the immorality, and it should be put into the hands of every young gentleman. An elegant manner and easiness of behaviour are acquired gradually and imperceptibly. No man can say, 'I'll be genteel.' There are ten genteel women for one genteel man, because they are more restrained. A man without some degree of restraint is insufferable; but we are all less restrained than women. Were a woman sitting in company to put out her legs before her as most men do, we should be tempted to kick them in.'

No man was a more attentive and nice observer of behaviour in those in whose company he happened to be, than Johnson; or, however strange it may seem to many, had a higher estimation of its refinements. Lord Eliot informs me, that one day when Johnson and he were at dinner at a gentleman's house in London, upon Lord Chesterfield's Letters being mentioned, Johnson surprised the company by this sentence: 'Every man of any education would rather be called a rascal, than accused of deficiency in *the graces*.' Mr Gibbon, who was present, turned to a lady who knew Johnson well and lived much with him, and in his quaint manner, tapping his box, addressed her thus: 'Don`t you think, Madam (looking towards Johnson), that among *all* your acquaintance you could find *one* exception?' The lady smiled, and seemed to acquiesce.

'I read (said he) Sharpe's letters on Italy, over again when I was at Bath. There is a great deal of matter in them.'

'Mrs Williams was angry that Thrale's family did not send regularly to her every time they heard from me while I was in the Hebrides. Little people are apt to be jealous: but they should not be jealous; for they ought to consider, that superior attention will necessarily be paid to superior fortune or rank. Two persons may have equal merit and on that account may have an equal claim to attention; but one of them may have also fortune and rank, and so may have a double claim.'

Talking of his notes on Shakspeare, he said, 'I despise those who do not see that I am right in the passage where *as* is repeated, and "asses of great charge" introduced. That on "To be, or not to be", is disputable.'[1]

A gentleman, whom I found sitting with him one morning, said, that in his opinion the character of an infidel was more detestable than that of a man notoriously guilty of an atrocious crime. I differed from him, because we are surer of the odiousness of the one, than of the error of the other. JOHNSON. 'Sir, I agree with him; for the infidel would be guilty of any crime if he were inclined to it.'

'Many things which are false are transmitted from book to book and gain credit in the world. One of these is the cry against the evil of luxury. Now the truth is, that luxury produces much good. Take the luxury of building in London. Does it not produce real advantage in the conveniency and elegance of accommodation, and this all from the exertion of industry? People will tell you, with a melancholy face, how many builders are in gaol. It is plain they are in gaol, not for building; for rents are not fallen. − A man gives half a guinea for a dish of green peas. How much gardening does this occasion? How many labourers must the competition to have such things early in the market, keep in employment? You will hear it said, very gravely, "Why was not the half-guinea, thus spent in luxury, given to the poor? To how many might it have afforded a good meal?" Alas! Has it not gone to the *industrious* poor, whom it is better to support than the *idle* poor? You are much surer that you are doing good when you pay money to those who work, as the recompense of their labour, than when you give money merely in charity. Suppose the ancient luxury of a dish of peacock's brains were to be revived; how many carcases would be left to the poor at a cheap rate? And as to the rout that is made about people who are ruined by extravagance, it is no matter to the nation that some individuals suffer. When so much general productive exertion is the consequence of luxury, the nation does not care though there are debtors in gaol; nay, they would not care though their creditors were there too.'

The uncommon vivacity of General Oglethorpe's mind, and variety of knowledge, having sometimes made his conversation seem too desultory, Johnson observed, 'Oglethorpe, Sir, never *completes* what he has to say.'[a]

---

1 It may be observed, that Mr Malone, in his very valuable edition of Shakspeare, has fully vindicated Dr Johnson from the idle censures which the first of these notes has given rise to. The interpretation of the other passage, which Dr Johnson allows to be *disputable*, he has clearly shown to be erroneous.

a Add: He on the same account made a similar remark on Patrick Lord Elibank: 'Sir, there is nothing *conclusive* in his talk.'

When I complained of having dined at a splendid table without hearing one sentence of conversation worthy of being remembered, he said, 'Sir, there seldom is any such conversation.' BOSWELL. 'Why then meet at table?' JOHNSON. 'Why, to eat and drink together, and promote kindness; and, Sir, this is better done when there is no solid conversation; for when there is, people differ in opinion, and get into bad humour, or some of the company who are not capable of such conversation, are left out, and feel themselves uneasy. It was for this reason, Sir Robert Walpole said, he always talked bawdy at his table, because in that all could join.'

Being irritated by hearing a gentleman ask Mr Levett a variety of questions concerning him, when he was sitting by, he broke out, 'Sir, you have but two topics, yourself and me. I am sick of both.' – 'A man (said he) should not talk of himself, nor much of any particular person. He should take care not to be made a proverb; and, therefore, should avoid having any one topic of which people can say, "We shall hear him upon it." There was a Dr Oldfield, who was always talking of the Duke of Marlborough. He came into a coffee-house one day, and told that his Grace had spoken in the House of Lords for half an hour. "Did he indeed speak for half all hour?" (said Belchier, the surgeon.) – "Yes." – "And what did he say of Dr Oldfield?" – "Nothing." – "Why then, Sir, he was very ungrateful; for Dr Oldfield could not have spoken for a quarter of an hour without saying something of him." '

'Every man is to take existence on the terms on which it is given to him. To some men it is given on condition of not taking liberties, which other men may take without much harm. One man may drink wine and be nothing the worse for it, on another wine may have effects so inflammatory as to injure him both in body and mind, and perhaps make him commit something for which he may deserve to be hanged.'

'Lord Hailes's *Annals of Scotland* have not that pointed form which is the taste of this age; but it is a book which will always sell, it has such a stability of dates, such a certainty of facts, and such a punctuality of citation. I never before read Scotch history with certainty.'

I asked him whether he would advise me to read the Bible with a commentary, and what commentaries he would recommend. JOHNSON. 'To be sure, Sir, I would have you read the Bible with a commentary; and I would recommend Lowth and Patrick on the Old Testament, and Hammond on the New.'

During my stay in London this spring, I solicited his attention to another law case, in which I was engaged. In the course of a contested election for the borough of Dunfermline, which I attended, as one of my friend Colonel (now Sir Archibald) Campbell's counsel, a man, one of his political agents, who was charged with having been unfaithful to his employer, and having deserted to the opposite party for a pecuniary reward – attacked very rudely in a newspaper the Rev. Mr James Thomson, one of the ministers of that place, on account of a supposed allusion to him in one of his sermons. Upon this the minister, on a subsequent Sunday, arraigned him by name from the pulpit with some severity; and the agent, after the sermon was over, rose up and asked the minister aloud, 'What bribe he had received for telling so many lies from the chair of veracity.' I was present at this very extraordinary scene. The person arraigned, and his father and brother who had also had a share both of the reproof from the pulpit, and in the retaliation, brought an action against Mr Thomson, in the Court of Session, for defamation and damages, and I was one of the counsel for the reverend defendant. *The Liberty of the Pulpit* was our great ground of defence; but we argued also on the provocation of the previous attack, and on the instant retaliation. The Court of Session, however, the fifteen Judges, who are at the same time the jury, decided against the minister, contrary to my humble opinion; and several of them expressed themselves with indignation against him. He was an aged gentleman, formerly a military chaplain, and a man of high spirit and honour. Johnson was satisfied that the judgement was wrong, and dictated to me the following argument in confutation of it:

Of the censure pronounced from the pulpit, our determination must be formed, as in other cases, by a consideration of the action itself, and the particular circumstances with which it is invested.

The right of censure and rebuke seems necessarily appendant to the pastoral office. He, to whom the care of a congregation is entrusted, is considered as the shepherd of a flock, as the teacher of a school, as the father of a family. As a shepherd tending not his own sheep but those of his master, he is answerable for those that stray, and that lose themselves by straying. But no man can be answerable for losses which he has not power to prevent, or for vagrancy which he has not authority to restrain.

As a teacher giving instruction for wages, and liable to reproach if those whom he undertakes to inform make no proficiency, he must have the power of enforcing attendance, of awakening negligence, and repressing contradiction.

As a father, he possesses the paternal authority of admonition, rebuke, and punishment. He cannot, without reducing his office to an empty name, be hindered from the exercise of any practice necessary to stimulate the idle, to reform the vicious, to check the petulant, and correct the stubborn.

If we enquire into the practice of the primitive church, we shall, I believe, find the ministers of the Word exercising the whole authority of this complicated character. We shall find them not only encouraging the good by exhortation, but terrifying the wicked by reproof and denunciation. In the earliest ages of the Church, while religion was yet pure from secular advantages, the punishment of sinners was public censure, and open penance; penalties inflicted merely by ecclesiastical authority, at a time while the church had yet no help from the civil power, while the hand of the magistrate lifted only the rod of persecution; and when governors were ready to afford a refuge to all those who fled from clerical authority.

That the Church, therefore, had once a power of public censure is evident, because that power was frequently exercised. That it borrowed not its power from the civil authority, is likewise certain, because civil authority was at that time its enemy.

The hour came at length, when after three hundred years of struggle and distress, Truth took possession of imperial power, and the civil laws lent their aid to the ecclesiastical constitutions. The magistrate from that time co-operated with the priest, and clerical sentences were made efficacious by secular force. But the State, when it came to the assistance of the Church, had no intention to diminish its authority. Those rebukes and those censures which were lawful before, were lawful still. But they had hitherto operated only upon voluntary submission. The refractory and contemptuous were at first in no danger of temporal severities, except what they might suffer from the reproaches of conscience, or the detestation of their fellow Christians. When religion obtained the support of law, if admonitions and censures had no effect, they were seconded by the magistrates with coercion and punishment.

It therefore appears from ecclesiastical history, that the right of inflicting shame by public censure, has been always considered as inherent in the Church; and that this right was not conferred by the civil power; for, it was exercised when the civil power operated against it. By the civil power it was never taken away, for the Christian magistrate interposed his office not to rescue sinners from censure, but to supply more powerful means of reformation; to add pain where shame was insufficient; and when men were proclaimed unworthy of the society of the faithful, to restrain them by imprisonment, from spreading abroad the contagion of wickedness.

It is not improbable that from this acknowledged power of public censure, grew in time the practice of auricular confession. Those who dreaded the blast of public reprehension, were willing to submit themselves to the priest, by a private accusation of themselves; and to obtain a reconciliation with the Church by a kind of clandestine absolution and invisible penance; conditions with which the priest would in times of ignorance and corruption easily comply, as they increased his influence, by adding the knowledge of secret sins to that of notorious offences, and enlarged his authority, by making him the sole arbiter of the terms of reconcilement.

From this bondage the Reformation set us free. The minister has no longer power to press into the retirements of conscience, to torture us by interrogatories, or put himself in possession of our secrets and our lives. But though we have thus controlled his usurpations, his just and original power remains unimpaired. He may still see, though he may not pry: he may yet hear, though he may not question. And that knowledge which his eyes and ears force upon him it is still his duty to use for the benefit of his flock. A father who lives near a wicked neighbour, may forbid a son to frequent his company. A minister who has in his congregation a man of open and scandalous wickedness, may warn his parishioners to shun his conversation. To warn them is not only lawful, but not to warn them would be criminal. He may warn them one by one in friendly converse, or by a parochial visitation. But if he may warn each man singly, what shall forbid him to warn them all together? Of that which is to be made known to all, how is there any difference whether it be communicated to each singly, or to all together? What is known to all, must necessarily be public. Whether it shall be public at once, or public by degrees, is the only question. And of a sudden and solemn publication the impression is deeper, and the warning more effectual.

It may easily be urged, if a minister be thus left at liberty to delate sinners from the pulpit, and to publish at will the crimes of a parishioner, he may often blast the innocent, and distress the timorous. He may be suspicious, and condemn without evidence; he may be rash, and judge without examination; he may be severe, and treat slight offences with too much harshness; he may be malignant and partial, and gratify his private interest or resentment, under the shelter of his pastoral character.

Of all this there is possibility, and of all this there is danger. But if possibility of evil be to exclude good, no good ever can be done. If nothing is to be attempted in which there is danger, we must all sink into hopeless inactivity. The evils that may be feared from this practice arise not from any defect in the institution, but from the infirmities of human nature. Power, in whatever hands it is placed, will be sometimes improperly exerted; yet courts of law must judge, though they will sometimes judge amiss. A father must instruct his children, though he himself may often want instruction. A minister must censure sinners, though his censure may be sometimes erroneous by want of judgement, and sometimes unjust by want of honesty.

If we examine the circumstances of the present case, we shall find the sentence neither erroneous nor unjust; we shall find no breach of private confidence, no intrusion into secret transactions. The fact was notorious and indubitable; so easy to be proved, that no proof was desired. The act was base and treacherous, the perpetration insolent and open, and the example naturally mischievous. The minister, however, being retired and recluse, had not yet heard what was publicly known throughout the parish; and on occasion of a public election, warned his people, according to his duty, against the crimes which public elections frequently produce. His warning was felt by one of his parishioners, as pointed particularly at himself. But instead of producing as might be wished, private compunction and immediate reformation, it kindled only rage and resentment. He charged his minister, in a public paper, with scandal, defamation and falsehood. The minister, thus reproached, had his own character to vindicate, upon which his pastoral authority must necessarily depend. To be charged with a defamatory lie is an injury which no man patiently endures in common life. To be charged with polluting the pastoral office with scandal and falsehood was a violation of character still more atrocious, as it affected not only his personal but his clerical veracity. His indignation naturally rose in proportion to his honesty, and with all the fortitude of injured honesty, he dared this calumniator in the church, and at once exonerated himself from censure, and rescued his flock from deception and from danger. The man whom he accuses pretends not to be innocent, or at least only pretends, for he declines a trial. The crime of which he is accused has frequent opportunities and strong temptations. It has already spread far, with much depravation of private morals, and much injury to public happiness. To warn the people, therefore, against it was not wanton and officious, but necessary and pastoral.

What then is the fault with which this worthy minister is charged? He has usurped no dominion over conscience. He has exerted no authority in support of doubtful and controverted opinions. He has not dragged into light a bashful and corrigible sinner. His censure was directed against a breach of morality, against an act which no man justifies. The man who appropriated this censure to himself, is evidently and notoriously guilty. His consciousness of his own wickedness incited him to attack his faithful reprover with open insolence and printed accusations. Such an attack made defence necessary, and we hope it will be at last decided that the means of defence were just and lawful.

When I read this to Mr Burke, he was highly pleased, and exclaimed, 'Well, he does his work in a workman-like manner.'[1]

Mr Thomson wished to bring the cause by appeal before the House of Lords, but was dissuaded by the advice of the noble person who now presides so ably in that Most Honourable House, and who was then Attorney-General. As my readers will no doubt be glad also to read the opinion of this eminent man upon the same subject, I shall here insert it.

CASE

There is herewith laid before you,

1. Petition for the Reverend Mr James Thomson, minister of Dunfermline.
2. Answers thereto.
3. Copy of the judgement of the Court of Session upon both.
4. Notes of the opinions of the Judges, being the reasons upon which their decree is grounded.

These papers you will please to peruse, and give your opinion,

Whether there is a probability of the above decree of the Court of Session's being reversed, if Mr Thomson should appeal from the same?

I don't think the appeal advisable; not only because the value of the judgement is in no degree adequate to the expense, but because there are

---

1 As a proof of Dr Johnson's extraordinary powers of composition, it appears from the original manuscript of this excellent dissertation, of which he dictated the first eight paragraphs on the 10th of May, and the remainder on the 13th, that there are in the whole only seven corrections, or rather variations, and those not considerable. Such were at once the vigorous and accurate emanations of his mind.

many chances, that, upon the general complexion of the case, the impression will be taken to the disadvantage of the appellant.

It is impossible to approve the style of that sermon. But the *complaint* was not less ungracious from that man, – who had behaved so ill by his original libel, and, at the time, when he received the reproach he complains of. In the last article all the plaintiffs are equally concerned. It struck me also with some wonder, that the Judges should think so much fervour apposite to the occasion of reproving the defendant for a little excess.

Upon the matter, however, I agree with them in condemning the behaviour of the minister; and in thinking it a subject fit for ecclesiastical censure; and even for an action, if any individual could qualify[1] a wrong, and a damage arising from it. But this I doubt. The circumstance of publishing the reproach in a pulpit, though extremely indecent, and culpable in another view, does not constitute a different sort of wrong, or any other rule of law, than would have obtained, if the same words had been pronounced elsewhere. I don't know, whether there be any difference in the law of Scotland, in the definition of slander, before the Commissaries, or the Court of Session. The common law of England does not give way to actions for every reproachful word. An action cannot be brought for general damages, upon any words which import less than an offence cognisable by law; consequently no action could have been brought here for the words in question. Both laws admit the truth to be a justification in actions *for words*; and the law of England does the same in actions for libels. The judgement, therefore, seems to me to have been wrong, in that the Court repelled that defence.

E. Thurlow.

I am now to record a very curious incident in Dr Johnson's Life, which fell under my own observation; of which *pars magna fui*, and which I am persuaded will, with the liberal-minded, be much to his credit.

My desire of being acquainted with celebrated men of every description, had made me, much about the same time, obtain an introduction to Dr Samuel Johnson and to John Wilkes, Esq. Two men more different could perhaps not be selected out from all mankind. They had even attacked one another with some asperity in their writings; yet I lived in habits of friendship with both. I could fully relish the excellence of each; for I have ever delighted in that intellectual chemistry which can separate good qualities from evil in the same person.

Sir John Pringle, 'mine own friend and my Father's friend', between whom and Dr Johnson I in vain wished to establish an acquaintance, as I respected and lived in intimacy with both of them, observed to me once, very ingeniously, 'It

---

1 It is curious to observe that Lord Thurlow has here, perhaps in compliment to North-Britain, made use of a term of the Scotch law, which to an English reader may require explanation. To *qualify* a wrong, is to point out and establish it.

is not in friendship as in mathematics, where two things, each equal to a third, are equal between themselves. You agree with Johnson as a middle quality, and you agree with me as a middle quality; but Johnson and I should not agree.' Sir John was not sufficiently flexible; so I desisted; knowing, indeed, that the repulsion was equally strong on the part of Johnson; who, I know not from what cause, unless his being a Scotchman, had formed a very erroneous opinion of Sir John. But I conceived an irresistible wish, if possible, to bring Dr Johnson and Mr Wilkes together. How to manage it, was a nice and difficult matter.

My worthy booksellers and friends, Messieurs Dillys in the Poultry, at whose hospitable and well-covered table I have seen a greater number of literary men than at any other, except that of Sir Joshua Reynolds, had invited me to meet Mr Wilkes and some more gentlemen on Wednesday, May 15. 'Pray (said I), let us have Dr Johnson.' – 'What, with Mr Wilkes? Not for the world (said Mr Edward Dilly): Dr Johnson would never forgive me.' – 'Come (said I), if you'll let me negotiate for you, I will be answerable that all shall go well.' DILLY. 'Nay, if you will take it upon you, I am sure I shall be very happy to see them both here.'

Notwithstanding the high veneration which I entertained for Dr Johnson, I was sensible that he was sometimes a little actuated by the spirit of contradiction, and by means of that I hoped I should gain my point. I was persuaded that if I had come upon him with a direct proposal, 'Sir, will you dine in company with Jack Wilkes?' he would have flown into a passion, and would probably have answered, 'Dine with Jack Wilkes, Sir! I'd as soon dine with Jack Ketch?'[1] I therefore, while we were sitting quietly by ourselves at his house in an evening, took occasion to open my plan thus: 'Mr Dilly, Sir, sends his respectful compliments to you, and would be happy if you would do him the honour to dine with him on Wednesday next along with me, as I must soon go to Scotland.' JOHNSON. 'Sir, I am obliged to Mr Dilly. I will wait upon him — ' BOSWELL. 'Provided, Sir, I suppose, that the company which he is to have is agreeable to you.' JOHNSON. 'What do you mean, Sir? What do you take me for? Do you think I am so ignorant of the world, as to imagine that I am to prescribe to a gentleman what company he is to have at his table?' BOSWELL. 'I beg your pardon, Sir, for wishing to prevent you from meeting people whom you might not like. Perhaps he may have some of what he calls his patriotic friends with him.' JOHNSON. 'Well, Sir, and what then? What care *I* for his *patriotic friends*? Poh!' BOSWELL. 'I should not be surprised to find Jack Wilkes there.' JOHNSON. 'And if Jack Wilkes *should* be there, what is that to *me*, Sir? My dear friend, let us have no more of this. I am sorry to be angry with you; but really it is treating me strangely to talk to me as if I could not meet any company whatever, occasionally.' BOSWELL. 'Pray forgive me, Sir: I meant well. But you shall meet whoever comes, for me.' Thus I secured him, and told Dilly that he would find him very well pleased to be one of his guests on the day appointed.

1 This has been circulated as if actually said by Johnson, when the truth is it was only *supposed* by me.

Upon the much-expected Wednesday, I called on him about half an hour before dinner, as I often did when we were to dine out together, to see that he was ready in time, and to accompany him. I found him buffeting his books, as upon a former occasion,[1] covered with dust, and making no preparation for going abroad. 'How is this, Sir? (said I). Don't you recollect that you are to dine at Mr Dilly's?' JOHNSON. 'Sir, I did not think of going to Dilly's: it went out of my head. I have ordered dinner at home with Mrs Williams.' BOSWELL. 'But, my dear Sir, you know you were engaged to Mr Dilly, and I told him so. He will expect you, and will be much disappointed if you don't come.' JOHNSON. 'You must talk to Mrs Williams about this.'

Here was a sad dilemma. I feared that what I was so confident I had secured would yet be frustrated. He had accustomed himself to show Mrs Williams such a degree of humane attention, as frequently imposed some restraint upon him; and I knew that if she should be obstinate, he would not stir. I hastened down stairs to the blind lady's room, and told her I was in great uneasiness, for Dr Johnson had engaged to me to dine this day at Mr Dilly's, but that he had told me he had forgotten his engagement, and had ordered dinner at home. 'Yes, Sir (said she, pretty peevishly), Dr Johnson is to dine at home.' – 'Madam (said I), his respect for you is such, that I know he will not leave you unless you absolutely desire it. But as you have so much of his company, I hope you will be good enough to forego it for a day, as Mr Dilly is a very worthy man, has frequently had agreeable parties at his house for Dr Johnson, and will be vexed if the Doctor neglects him today. And then, Madam, be pleased to consider my situation; I carried the message, and I assured Mr Dilly that Dr Johnson was to come, and no doubt he has made a dinner, and invited a company, and boasted of the honour he expected to have. I shall be quite disgraced if the Doctor is not there.' She gradually softened to my solicitations, which were certainly as earnest as most entreaties to ladies upon any occasion, and was graciously pleased to empower me to tell Dr Johnson, 'That all things considered, she thought he should certainly go.' I flew back to him, still in dust, and careless of what should be the event, 'indifferent in his choice to go or stay'; but as soon as I had announced to him Mrs Williams's consent, he roared, 'Frank, a clean shirt', and was very soon drest. When I had him fairly seated in a hackney-coach with me, I exulted as much as a fortune-hunter who has got an heiress into a post-chaise with him to set out for Gretna-Green.

When we entered Mr Dilly's drawing-room, he found himself in the midst of a company he did not know. I kept myself snug and silent, watching how he would conduct himself. I observed him whispering to Mr Dilly, 'Who is that gentleman, Sir?' – 'Mr Arthur Lee.' – JOHNSON. 'Tut, tut, tut' (under his breath), which was one of his habitual mutterings. Mr Arthur Lee could not but be very obnoxious to Johnson, for he was not only a *patriot* but an *American*. He was afterwards minister from the United States at the court of Madrid. 'And who is the gentleman in lace?' – 'Mr Wilkes, Sir.' This

---

1 See page 508.

information confounded him still more; he had some difficulty to restrain himself, and taking up a book, sat down upon a windowseat and read, or at least kept his eye upon it intently for some time, till he composed himself. His feelings, I dare say, were awkward enough. But he no doubt recollected his having rated me for supposing that he could be at all disconcerted by any company, and he, therefore, resolutely set himself to behave quite as an easy man of the world, who could adapt himself at once to the disposition and manners of those whom he might chance to meet.

The cheering sound of 'Dinner is upon the table', dissolved his reverie, and we *all* sat down without any symptom of ill humour. There were present, besides Mr Wilkes, and Mr Arthur Lee, who was an old companion of mine when he studied physic at Edinburgh, Mr (now Sir John) Miller, Dr Lettsom, and Mr Slater the druggist. Mr Wilkes placed himself next to Dr Johnson, and behaved to him with so much attention and politeness, that he gained upon him insensibly. No man eat more heartily than Johnson, or loved better what was nice and delicate. Mr Wilkes was very assiduous in helping him to some fine veal. 'Pray give me leave, Sir – It is better here – A little of the brown – Some fat, Sir – A little of the stuffing – Some gravy – Let me have the pleasure of giving you some butter – Allow me to recommend a squeeze of this orange – or the lemon, perhaps, may have more zest.' – 'Sir, Sir, I am obliged to you, Sir,' cried Johnson, bowing and turning his head to him with a look for some time of 'surly virtue',[1] but, in a short while, of complacency.

Foote being mentioned, Johnson said, 'He is not a good mimic.' One of the company added, 'A merry Andrew, a buffoon.' JOHNSON. 'But he has wit too, and is not deficient in ideas, or in fertility and variety of imagery, and not empty of reading; he has knowledge enough to fill up his part. One species of wit he has in an eminent degree, that of escape. You drive him into a corner with both hands; but he's gone, Sir, when you think you have got him – like an animal that jumps over your head. Then he has a great range for his wit; he never lets truth stand between him and a jest, and he is sometimes mighty coarse. Garrick is under many restraints from which Foote is free.' WILKES. 'Garrick's wit is more like Lord Chesterfield's.' JOHNSON. 'The first time I was in company with Foote was at Fitzherbert's. Having no good opinion of the fellow, I was resolved not to be pleased, and it is very difficult to please a man against his will. I went on eating my dinner pretty sullenly, affecting not to mind him. But the dog was so very comical, that I was obliged to lay down my knife and fork, throw myself back upon my chair, and fairly laugh it out. No, Sir, he was irresistible.[2] He upon one occasion experienced, in an extraordinary degree, the efficacy of his powers of entertaining. Amongst the many and various modes which he tried of getting money, he became a partner with a small-beer brewer, and he was to have a share of the profits for procuring customers amongst his numerous acquaintance. Fitzherbert was one who took

1 Johnson's *London, a Poem*, v. 145.
2 Foote told me that Johnson said of him, 'For loud obstreperous broad-faced mirth, I know not his equal.'

his small-beer; but it was so bad that the servants resolved not to drink it. They were at some loss how to notify their resolution, being afraid of offending their master, who they knew liked Foote much as a companion. At last they fixed upon a little black boy, who was rather a favourite, to be their deputy, and deliver their remonstrance; and having invested him with the whole authority of the kitchen, he was to inform Mr Fitzherbert, in all their names, upon a certain day, that they would drink Foote's small-beer no longer. On that day Foote happened to dine at Fitzherbert's, and this boy served at table; he was so delighted with Foote's stories, and merriment, and grimace, that when he went down stairs, he told them, 'This is the finest man I have ever seen. I will not deliver your message. I will drink his small-beer.'

Somebody observed that Garrick could not have done this. WILKES. 'Garrick would have made the small-beer still smaller. He is now leaving the stage, but he will play *Scrub* all his life.' I knew that Johnson would let nobody attack Garrick but himself, as Garrick once said to me, and I had heard him praise his liberality; so to bring out his commendation of his celebrated pupil, I said, loudly, 'I have heard Garrick is liberal.' JOHNSON. 'Yes, Sir, I know that Garrick has given away more money than any man in England that I am acquainted with, and that not from ostentatious views. Garrick was very poor when he began life; so when he came to have money, he probably was very unskilful in giving away, and saved when he should not. But Garrick began to be liberal as soon as he could; and I am of opinion, the reputation of avarice which he has had, has been very lucky for him, and prevented his having many enemies. You despise a man for avarice, but do not hate him. Garrick might have been much better attacked for living with more splendour than is suitable to a player: if they had had the wit to have assaulted him in that quarter, they might have galled him more. But they have kept clamouring about his avarice, which has rescued him from much obloquy and envy.'

Talking of the great difficulty of obtaining authentic information for biography, Johnson told us, 'When I was a young fellow I wanted to write the Life of Dryden, and in order to get materials, I applied to the only two persons then alive who had seen him; these were old Swiney, and old Cibber. Swiney's information was no more than this, "That at Will's coffee-house Dryden had a particular chair for himself, which was set by the fire in winter, and was then called his winter-chair; and that it was carried out for him to the balcony in summer, and was then called his summer-chair." Cibber could tell no more but "That he remembered him a decent old man, arbiter of critical disputes at Will's." You are to consider that Cibber was then at a great distance from Dryden, had perhaps one leg only in the room, and durst not draw in the other.' BOSWELL. 'Yet Cibber was a man of observation?' JOHNSON. 'I think not.' BOSWELL. 'You will allow his *Apology* to be well done?' JOHNSON. 'Very well done, to be sure, Sir. That book is a striking proof of the justice of Pope's remark:

> Each might his several province well command,
> Would all but stoop to what they understand.'

BOSWELL. 'And his plays are good.' JOHNSON. 'Yes, but that was his trade; *l'esprit du corps*; he had been all his life among players and play-writers. I wondered that he had so little to say in conversation, for he had kept the best company, and learnt all that can be got by the ear. He abused Pindar to me, and then showed me an Ode of his own, with an absurd couplet, making a linnet soar on an eagle's wing.[1] I told him that when the ancients made a simile, they always made it like something real.'

Mr Wilkes remarked, that 'among all the bold flights of Shakspeare's imagination, the boldest was making Birnam-wood march to Dunsinane; creating a wood where there never was a shrub; a wood in Scotland! ha! ha! ha!' And he also observed, that 'the clannish slavery of the Highlands of Scotland was the single exception to Milton's remark of "The Mountain Nymph sweet Liberty", being worshipped in all hilly countries.' – 'When I was at Inverary (said he), on a visit to my old friend, Archibald, Duke of Argyle, his dependents congratulated me on being such a favourite of his Grace. I said, "It is then, gentlemen, truly lucky for me; for if I had displeased the Duke, and he had wished it, there is not a Campbell among you but would have been ready to bring John Wilkes's head to him in a charger. It would have been only

> Off with his head! So much for *Aylesbury*.

I was then member for Aylesbury.'

Dr Johnson and Mr Wilkes talked of the contested passage in Horace's *Art of Poetry*, '*Difficile est proprie communia dicere.*' Mr Wilkes, according to my note, gave the interpretation thus: 'It is difficult to speak with propriety of common things; as, if a poet had to speak of Queen Caroline drinking tea, he must endeavour to avoid the vulgarity of cups and saucers.' But upon reading my note, he tells me that he meant to say, that 'the word *communia*, being a Roman law term, signifies here things *communis juris*, that is to say, what have never yet been treated by any body; and this appears clearly from what followed,

> *Tuque*
> *Rectius Iliacum carmen deducis in actus*
> *Quam si proferres ignota indictaque primus.*

You will easier make a tragedy out of the *Iliad* than on any subject not handled before.'[2] JOHNSON. 'He means that it is difficult to appropriate to particular persons qualities which are common to all mankind, as Homer has done.'

---

1 See page 205.

2 My very pleasant friend himself, as well as others *who remember old stories*, will no doubt be surprised when I observe that John Wilkes here shows himself to be of the WARBURTONIAN SCHOOL. It is nevertheless true, as appears from Dr Hurd the Bishop of Worcester's very elegant commentary and notes on the *Epistola ad Pisones*.

It is necessary to a fair consideration of the question, that the whole passage in which the words occur should be kept in view:

> *Si quid inexpertum scenae committis, et audes*
> *Personam formare novam, servetur ad imum*

WILKES. 'We have no City-Poet now; that is an office which has gone into disuse. The last was Elkanah Settle. There something in *names* which one cannot help feeling. Now *Elkanah Settle* sounds so *queer*, who can expect much from that name? We should have no hesitation to give it for John Dryden, in preference to Elkanah Settle, from the names only, without known their different merits.' JOHNSON. 'I suppose, Sir, Settle did as well for Aldermen in his time, as John Home could do now. Where did Beckford and Trecothick learn English?'

Qualis ab incepto processerit, et sibi constet.
Difficile est proprie communia dicere: tuque
Rectius Iliacum carmen deducis in actus,
Quam si proferres ignota indictaque primus.
Publica materies privati juris erit, si
Non circa vilem patulumque moraberis orbem,
Nec verbum verbo curabis reddere fidus
Interpres; nec desilies imitator in artum
Unde pedem proferre pudor vetat aut operis lex.

The 'Commentary' thus illustrates it: 'But the formation of quite *new characters* is a work of great difficulty and hazard. For here there is no generally received and fixed *archetype* to work after, but every one *judges* of common right, according to the extent and comprehension of his own idea; therefore he advises to labour and refit *old characters and subjects*, particularly those made known and authorised by the practice of Homer and the Epic writers.'

The 'Note' is,

'*Difficile* EST PROPRIE COMMUNIA DICERE.' Lambin's Comment is '*Communia hoc loco appellat Horatius argumenta fabularum a nullo adhuc tractata: et ita, quae cuivis exposita sunt et in medio quodammodo posita, quasi vacua et a nemine occupata.*' And that this is the true meaning of *communia* is evidently fixed by the words *ignota indictaque*, which are explanatory of it; so that the sense given it in the commentary, is unquestionably the right one. Yet, notwithstanding the clearness of the case, a late critic hath this strange passage: '*Difficile quidem esse proprie communia dicere, hoc est, materiam vulgarem, notam et e medio petitam, ita immutare atque exornare, ut nova et scriptori propria videatur, ultro concedimus; et maximi procul dubio ponderis ista est observatio. Sed omnibus utrinque collatis, et tum difficilis, tum venusti, tam judicii quam ingenii ratione habita, major videtur esse gloria fabulam formare penitus novam, quam veterem, utcunque mutatam, de novo exhibere.* (Poet. Prael. v. ii. p. 164.) Where having first put a wrong construction on the word *communia*, he employs it to introduce an impertinent criticism. For where does the poet prefer the glory of refitting *old* subjects to that of inventing new ones? The contrary is implied in what he urges about the superior difficulty of the latter, from which he dissuades his countrymen, only in respect of their abilities and inexperience in these matters; and in order to cultivate in them, which is the main view of the Epistle, a spirit of correctness, by sending them to the old subjects, treated by the Greek writers.'

For my own part (with all deference for Dr Hurd, who thinks the *case clear*), I consider the passage, '*Difficile est proprie communia dicere*', to be a crux for the critics on Horace.

The explication which My Lord of Worcester treats with so much contempt, is nevertheless countenanced by authority which I find quoted by the learned Baxter, in his edition of Horace, '*Difficile est proprie communia dicere*, h. e. res vulgares disertis

Mr Arthur Lee mentioned some Scotch who had taken possession of a barren part of America, and wondered why they should choose it. JOHNSON. 'Why, Sir, all barrenness is comparative. The *Scotch* would not know it to be barren.' BOSWELL. 'Come, come, he is flattering the English. You have now been in Scotland, Sir, and say if you did not see meat and drink enough there.' JOHNSON. 'Why yes, Sir; meat and drink enough to give the inhabitants sufficient strength to run away from home.' All these quick and lively sallies were said sportively, quite in jest, and with a smile, which showed that he meant only wit. Upon this topic he and Mr Wilkes could perfectly assimilate; here was a bond of union between them, and I was conscious that as both of them had visited Caledonia, both were fully satisfied of the strange narrow ignorance of those who imagine that it is a land of famine. But they amused themselves with persevering in the old jokes. When I claimed a superiority for Scotland over England in one respect, that no man can be arrested there for a debt merely because another swears it against him; but there must first be the judgement of a court of law ascertaining its justice; and

---

verbis enarrare, vel humile thema cum dignitate tractare. *Difficile est communes res propriis explicare verbis.* Vet. Schol.'

I was much disappointed to find that the great critic, Dr Bentley, has no note upon this very difficult passage, as from his vigorous and illuminated mind I should have expected to receive more satisfaction than I have yet had.

Sanadon thus treats of it, '*Proprie communia dicere; c'est à dire qu'il n'est pas aisé de former à ces personnages d'imagination des caractères particuliers et cependant vraisemblables. Comme l'on a eté le maitre de les former tels qu'on a voulu, les fautes que l'on fait en cela sont moins pardonnables. C'est pourquoi Horace conseille de prendre toujours des sujets connus tels que sont par exemple ceux que l'on peut tirer des poèmes d'Homere.*'

And *Dacier* observes upon it, '*Apres avoir marqué les deux qualités qu'il faut donner aux personnages qu'on invente, il conseille aux Poètes tragiques, de n'user pas trop facilement de cette liberté qu'ils ont d'en inventer, car il est très difficile de réussir dans ces nouveaux caractères. Il est mal aisé, dit Horace,* de traiter proprement, *c'est à dire* convenablement, *des sujets communs; c'est à dire, des sujets inventés, et qui n'ont aucun fondement ni dans l'Histoire ni dans la Fable; et il les appelle* communs, *parce qu'ils sont en disposition à tout le monde, et que tout le monde a le droit de les inventer, et qu'ils sont, comme on dit, au premier occupant.*' See his observations at large on this expression and the following.

After all, I cannot help entertaining some doubt whether the words, '*Difficile est propria communia dicere*', may not have been thrown in by Horace to form a *separate* article in a 'choice of difficulties' which a poet has to encounter, who chooses a new subject; in which case it must be uncertain which of the various explanations is the true one, and every reader has a right to decide as it may strike his own fancy. And even should the words be understood as they generally are, to be connected both with what goes before, and what comes after, the exact sense cannot be absolutely ascertained; for instance, whether *proprie* is meant to signify *in an appropriated manner*, as Dr Johnson here understands it, or, as it is often used by Cicero, *with propriety*, or *elegantly*. In short, it is a rare instance of a defect in perspicuity in an admirable writer, who with almost every species of excellence, is peculiarly remarkable for that quality. The length of this note perhaps requires an apology. Many of my readers, I doubt not, will admit that a critical discussion of a passage in a favourite classic is very engaging.

that a seizure of the person before judgement is obtained can take place only, if his creditor should swear that he is about to fly from the country, or, as it is technically expressed, is *in meditatione fugae*. WILKES. 'That, I should think, may be safely sworn of all the Scotch nation.' JOHNSON. (to Mr Wilkes) 'You must know, Sir, I lately took my friend Boswell and showed him genuine civilised life in an English provincial town. I turned him loose at Lichfield, my native city, that he might see for once real civility: for you know he lives among savages in Scotland, and among rakes in London.' WILKES. 'Except when he is with grave, sober, decent people like you and me.' JOHNSON. (smiling) 'And we ashamed of him.'

They were quite frank and easy. Johnson told the story of his asking Mrs Macaulay to allow her footman to sit down with them; to prove the ridiculousness of the argument for the equality of mankind; and he said to me afterwards, with a nod of satisfaction, 'You saw Mr Wilkes acquiesced.' Wilkes talked with all imaginable freedom of the ludicrous title given to the Attorney-General, *Diabolus Regis*, adding, 'I have reason to know something about that officer, for I was prosecuted for a libel.' Johnson, who many people would have supposed must have been furiously angry at hearing this talked of so lightly, said not a word. He was now, *indeed*, 'a good-humoured fellow'.

After dinner we had an accession of Mrs Knowles, the Quaker lady, well known for her various talents, and of Mr Alderman Lee. Amidst some patriotic groans, somebody (I think the Alderman) said, 'Poor Old England is lost.' JOHNSON. 'Sir, it is not so much to be lamented that Old England is lost, as that the Scotch have found it.'[1] WILKES. 'Had Lord Bute governed Scotland only, I should not have taken the trouble to write his eulogy, and dedicate 'MORTIMER' to him.'

Mr Wilkes held a candle to show a fine print of a beautiful female figure which hung in the room, and pointed out the elegant contour of the bosom with the finger of an arch connoisseur. He afterwards waggishly insisted with me, that all the time Johnson showed visible signs of a fervent admiration of the corresponding charms of the fair Quaker.

This record, though by no means so perfect as I could wish, will serve to give a notion of a very curious interview, which was not only pleasing at the time, but had the agreeable and benignant effect of reconciling any animosity, and sweetening any acidity, which in the various bustle of political contest, had been produced in the minds of two men, who though widely different, had so many things in common – classical learning, modern literature, wit, and humour, and ready repartee – that it would have been much to be regretted if they had been for ever at a distance from each other.

Mr Burke gave me much credit for this successful *negotiation*; and pleasantly said, that 'there was nothing to equal it in the whole history of the *Corps Diplomatique*.'

I attended Dr Johnson home, and had the satisfaction to hear him tell Mrs

---

1 It would not become me to expatiate on this strong and pointed remark, in which a very great deal of meaning is condensed.

Williams how much he had been pleased with Mr Wilkes's company, and what an agreeable day he had passed.

I talked a good deal to him of the celebrated Margaret Caroline Rudd, whom I had visited, induced by the fame of her talents, address, and irresistible power of fascination. To a lady who disapproved of my visiting her, he said on a former occasion, 'Nay, Madam, Boswell is in the right; I should have visited her myself, were it not that they have now a trick of putting every thing into the newspapers.' This evening he exclaimed, 'I envy him his acquaintance with Mrs Rudd.'

I mentioned a scheme which I had of making a tour to the Isle of Man, and giving a full account of it; and that Mr Burke had playfully suggested as a motto,

'The proper study of mankind is MAN.'

JOHNSON. 'Sir, you will get more by the book than the jaunt will cost you; so you will have your diversion for nothing, and add to your reputation.'

On the evening of the next day I took leave of him, being to set out for Scotland. I thanked him with great warmth for all his kindness. 'Sir (said he), you are very welcome. Nobody repays it with more.'

How very false is the notion which has gone round the world of the rough, and passionate, and harsh manners of this great and good man. That he had occasional sallies of heat of temper, and that he was sometimes, perhaps, too 'easily provoked' by absurdity and folly, and sometimes too desirous of triumph in colloquial contest, must be allowed. The quickness both of his perception and sensibility disposed him to sudden explosions of satire; to which his extraordinary readiness of wit was a strong and almost irresistible incitement. To adopt one of the finest images in Mr Home's *Douglas*,

> On each glance of thought
> Decision followed, as the thunderbolt
> Pursues the flash!

I admit that the beadle within him was often so eager to apply the lash, that the Judge had not time to consider the case with sufficient deliberation.

That he was occasionally remarkable for violence of temper may be granted: but let us ascertain the degree, and not let it be supposed that he was in a perpetual rage, and never without a club in his hand, to knock down every one who approached him. On the contrary, the truth is, that by much the greatest part of his time he was civil, obliging, nay, polite in the true sense of the word; so much so, that many gentlemen, who were long acquainted with him, never received, or even heard a severe[a] expression from him.[b]

---

[a] *Second Edition*: 'severe' altered to 'strong'.

[b] After this passage, read: The following letters concerning an Epitaph which he wrote for the monument of Dr Goldsmith, in Westminster-Abbey, afford at once a proof of his unaffected modesty, his carelessness as to his own writings, and of the great respect which he entertained for the taste and judgement of the excellent and eminent person to whom they are addressed:

It was, I think, after I had left London this year, that an[a] Epitaph, which Dr Johnson had written for the monument of Dr Goldsmith in Westminster-Abbey, gave occasion to a *Remonstrance* to the MONARCH OF LITERATURE, for an account of which I am indebted to Sir William Forbes, of Pitsligo.

That my readers may have the subject more fully and clearly before them, I shall first insert the Epitaph.

OLIVARII GOLDSMITH,
Poetae, Physici, Historici,
Qui nullum fere scribendi genus
Non tetigit,
Nullum quod tetigit non ornavit:
Sive risus essent movendi,
Sive lacrymae,
Affectuum potens at lenis dominator,
Ingenio sublimis, vividus, versatilis,
Oratione grandis, nitidus, venustus:
Hoc monumento memoriam coluit
Sodalium amor,
Amicorum fides,
Lectorum veneratio.
Natus in Hibernia Forniae Longfordiensis
In loco cui nomen Pallas,
Nov. XXIX, M DCC XXXI;
Eblanae literis institutus;
Obiit Londini,
April IV. M DCC LXXIV.

To SIR JOSHUA REYNOLDS.

DEAR SIR – I have been kept away from you, I know not well how, and of these vexatious hindrances I know not when there will be an end. I therefore send you the poor dear Doctor's epitaph. Read it first yourself; and if you then think it right, show it to the Club. I am, you know, willing to be corrected. If you think any thing much amiss, keep it to yourself, till we come together. I have sent two copies, but prefer the card. The dates must be settled by Dr Percy. I am, Sir,

     Your most humble servant,   SAM. JOHNSON.
     May 16, 1776.

To the same.

SIR – Miss Reynolds has a mind to send the Epitaph to Dr Beattie; I am very willing, but having no copy, cannot immediately recollect it. She tells me you have lost it. Try to recollect, and put down as much as you retain; you perhaps may have kept what I have dropped. The lines for which I am at a loss are something of *rerum civilium sive naturalium*. It was a sorry trick to lose it; help me if you can. I am, Sir,

     Your most humble servant,   SAM. JOHNSON.
     June 22, 1776.

     The gout grows better but slowly.

[a] For 'an' read 'this', and delete the words between 'Epitaph' and 'gave'.

Sir William Forbes writes to me thus: 'I enclose the *Round Robin*. This *jeu d'esprit* took its rise one day at dinner at our friend Sir Joshua Reynolds's. All the company present, except myself, were friends and acquaintance of Dr Goldsmith. The Epitaph, written for him by Dr Johnson, became the subject of conversation, and various emendations were suggested, which it was agreed should be submitted to the Doctor's consideration. – But the question was, who should have the courage to propose them to him? At last it was hinted, that there could be no way so good as that of a *Round Robin*, as the sailors call it, which they make use of when they enter into a conspiracy, so as not to let it be known who puts his name first or last to the paper. This proposition was instantly assented to; and Dr Barnard, Dean of Derry, now Bishop of Killaloe, drew up an address to Dr Johnson on the occasion, replete with wit and humour, but which it was feared the Doctor might think treated the subject with too much levity. Mr Burke then proposed the address as it stands in the paper in writing, to which I had the honour to officiate as clerk.

'Sir Joshua agreed to carry it to Dr Johnson, who received it with much good humour,[1] and desired Sir Joshua to tell the gentlemen, that he would alter the Epitaph in any manner they pleased, as to the sense of it; but *he would never consent to disgrace the walls of Westminster-Abbey with an English inscription.*

'I consider this *Round Robin* as a species of literary curiosity worth preserving, as it marks, in a certain degree, Dr Johnson's character.'

---

1 He however, upon seeing Dr Warton's name to the suggestion that the Epitaph should be in English, observed to Sir Joshua, 'I wonder that Joe Warton, a scholar by profession, should be such a fool.'[a] Mr Langton, who was one of the company at Sir Joshua's, like a sturdy scholar, resolutely refused to sign the *Round Robin*. The epitaph is engraved upon Dr Goldsmith's monument without any alteration.[b]

[a] Add: He said, too, 'I should have thought Mund Burke would have had more sense.'

[b] Add to the note as follows: At another time, when somebody endeavoured to argue in favour of its being in English, Johnson said, 'The language of the country of which a learned man was a native, is not the language fit for his epitaph, which should be in ancient and permanent language. Consider, Sir, how you should feel, were you to find at Rotterdam an epitaph upon Erasmus *in Dutch!*' – For my own part, I think it would be best to have epitaphs written both in a learned language, and in the language of the country; so that they might have the advantage of being more universally understood, aud at the same time be secured of classical stability. I cannot, however, but be of opinion, that it is not sufficiently discriminative. Applying to Goldsmith equally the epithets of '*Poetae, Historici, Physici*', is surely not right; for as to his claim to the last of those epithets, I have heard Johnson himself say, 'Goldsmith, Sir, will give us a very fine book upon the subject; but if he can distinguish a cow from a horse, that, I believe, may be the extent of his knowledge of natural history.' His book is indeed an excellent performance, though in some instances he appears to have trusted too much to Buffon, who, with all his theoretical ingenuity and extraordinary eloquence, I suspect had little actual information in the science on which he wrote so admirably. For instance, he tells us that the *cow* sheds her horns every two years; a most palpable error, which Goldsmith has faithfully transferred into his book. It is wonderful that Buffon, who lived so much in the country, at his noble seat, should have fallen into such a blunder. I suppose he has confounded the *cow* with the *deer*.

ROUND ROBIN, *addressed to* SAMUEL JOHNSON, L.L.D. *with FAC SIMILES of the Signatures.*

We the Circumscribers, having read with great pleasure, an intended Epitaph for the Monument of Dr Goldsmith; which considered abstractedly, appears to be, for elegant Composition and Masterly Stile, in every respect worthy of the pen of its learned Author; are yet of opinion, that the Character of the Deceased as a Writer, particularly as a Poet, is, perhaps, not delineated with all the exactness which Dr Johnson is Capable of giving it. — We therefore, with deference to his Superior Judgement, humbly request, that he would at least take the trouble of revising it; & of making such additions and alterations as he shall think proper, upon a further perusal: — But if We might venture to express our Wishes, they would lead us to request, that he would write the Epitaph in English, rather than in Latin: As We think that the Memory of so eminent an English Writer ought to be perpetuated in the language, to which his Works are likely to be so lasting an Ornament, Which we also know to have been the opinion of The late Doctor himself.

My readers are presented with a faithful transcript of a paper which I doubt not of their being desirous to see.

Sir William Forbes's observation is very just. The anecdote now related proves, in the strongest manner, the reverence and awe with which Johnson was regarded, by some of the most eminent men of his time in various departments, and even by such of them as lived most with him; while it also confirms what I have again and again inculcated, that he was by no means of that ferocious and irascible character which has been ignorantly imagined.

This hasty composition is also to be remarked as one of a thousand instances which evince the extraordinary promptitude of Mr Burke; who while he is equal to the greatest things, can adorn the least; can, with equal facility, embrace the vast and complicated speculations of politics, or the ingenious topics of literary investigation.

Besides this Latin Epitaph, Johnson honoured the memory of his friend Goldsmith with a short one in Greek.[1]

Dr JOHNSON to Mrs BOSWELL.

Madam – You must not think me uncivil in omitting to answer the letter with which you favoured me some time ago. I imagined it to have been written without Mr Boswell's knowledge, and therefore supposed the answer to require, what I could not find, a private conveyance.

The difference with Lord Auchinleck is now over; and since young Alexander has appeared, I hope no more difficulties will arise among you; for I sincerely wish you all happy. Do not teach the young ones to dislike me, as you dislike me yourself; but let me at least have Veronica's kindness, because she is my acquaintance.

You will now have Mr Boswell home; it is well that you have him, he has led a wild life. I have taken him to Lichfield, and he has followed Mr Thrale to Bath. Pray take care of him, and tame him. The only thing in which I have the honour to agree with you is, in loving him; and while we are so much of a mind in a matter of so much importance, our other quarrels will, I hope, produce no great bitterness. I am, Madam,

Your most humble servant,

SAM. JOHNSON.

May 16, 1776.

Mr BOSWELL to Dr JOHNSON.

Edinburgh, June 25, 1776.

You have formerly complained that my letters were too long. There is no danger of that complaint being made at present; for I find it difficult for me to write to you at all. [Here an account of having been afflicted with a return of melancholy or bad spirits.]

The boxes of books[2] which you sent to me are arrived; but I have not yet examined the contents.

. . .

I send you Mr Maclaurin's paper for the negro, who claims his freedom in the Court of Session.

---

1 See page 399.

2 Upon a settlement of our account of expenses on our Tour to the Hebrides, there was a balance due to me, which Dr Johnson chose to discharge by sending books.

Dr JOHNSON to Mr BOSWELL.

DEAR SIR – These black fits, of which you complain, perhaps hurt your memory as well as your imagination. When did I complain that your letters were too long?[1] Your last letter, after a very long delay, brought very bad news. [Here a series of reflections upon melancholy, and – what I could not help thinking strangely unreasonable in him who had suffered so much from it himself – a good deal of severity and reproof, as if it were owing to my own fault, or that I was, perhaps, affecting it from a desire of distinction.]

Read Cheyne's *English Malady*; but do not let him teach you a foolish notion that melancholy is a proof of acuteness.

To hear that you have not opened your boxes of books is very offensive. The examination and arrangement of so many volumes might have afforded you an amusement very seasonable at present, and useful for the whole of life. I am, I confess, very angry that you manage yourself so ill.

. . .

I do not now say any more, than that I am, with great kindness and sincerity, dear Sir,

Your humble servant,

SAM. JOHNSON.

July 2, 1776.

It was last year determined by Lord Mansfield, in the Court of King's Bench, that a negro cannot be taken out of the kingdom without his own consent.

Dr JOHNSON to Mr BOSWELL.

DEAR SIR – I make haste to write again, lest my last letter should give you too much pain. If you are really oppressed with overpowering and involuntary melancholy, you are to be pitied rather than reproached . . .

Now, my dear Bozzy, let us have done with quarrels and with censure. Let me know whether I have not sent you a pretty library. There are, perhaps, many books among them which you need never read through; but there are none which it is not proper for you to know, and sometimes to consult. Of these books, of which the use is only occasional, it is often sufficient to know the contents, that, when any question arises, you may know where to look for information.

Since I wrote, I have looked over Mr Maclaurin's plea, and think it excellent. How is the suit carried on? If by subscription, I commission you to contribute, in my name, what is proper. Let nothing be wanting in such

---

1 Baretti told me that Johnson complained of my writing very long letters to him, when I was upon the continent; which was most certainly true; but it seems my friend did not remember it.

a case. Dr Drummond,[1] I see, is superseded. His father would have grieved; but he lived to obtain the pleasure of his son's election, and died before that pleasure was abated.

Langton's lady has brought him a girl, and both are well; I dined with him the other day. . . .

It vexes me to tell you, that on the evening of the 29th of May I was seized by the gout, and am not quite well. The pain has not been violent, but the weakness and tenderness were very troublesome, and what is said to be very uncommon, it has not alleviated my other disorders. Make use of youth and health while you have them; make my compliments to Mrs Boswell. I am, my dear Sir,

Your most affectionate,

SAM. JOHNSON.

July 6, 1776.

Mr BOSWELL to Dr JOHNSON.

Edinburgh, July 18, 1776.

MY DEAR SIR – Your letter of the second of this month was rather a harsh medicine; but I was delighted with that spontaneous tenderness, which, a few days afterwards, sent forth such balsam as your next brought me. I found myself for some time so ill that all I could do was to preserve a decent appearance, while all within was weakness and distress. Like a reduced garrison that has some spirit left, I hung out flags, and planted all the force I could muster, upon the walls. I am now much better, and I sincerely thank you for your kind attention and friendly counsel.

. . .

Count Manucci[2] came here last week from travelling in Ireland. I have shown him what civilities I could on his own account, your's, and on that of Mr and Mrs Thrale. He has had a fall from his horse, and been much hurt. I regret this unlucky accident, for he seems to be a very amiable man.

As the evidence of what I have mentioned at the beginning of this year, I select from his private register the following passage:

'July 25, 1776. O GOD, who hast ordained that whatever is to be desired should be sought by labour, and who, by thy blessing, bringest honest labour to good effect, look with mercy upon my studies and endeavours.

1 The son of Johnson's old friend, Mr William Drummond. (See pages 268–70.) He was a young man of such distinguished merit, that he was nominated to one of the medical professorships in the College of Edinburgh, without solicitation, while he was at Naples. Having other views, he did not accept of the honour, and soon afterwards died.

2 A Florentine nobleman, mentioned by Johnson, in his 'Notes of his Tour in France'. I had the pleasure of becoming acquainted with him in London, in the spring of this year.

Grant me, O LORD, to design only what is lawful and right; and afford me calmness of mind. and steadiness of purpose, that I may so do thy will in this short life, as to obtain happiness in the world to come, for the sake of JESUS CHRIST our Lord. Amen.[1]

It appears from a note subjoined, that this was composed when he 'purposed to apply vigorously to study, particularly of the Greek and Italian tongues.'

Such a purpose, so expressed, at the age of sixty-seven, is admirable and encouraging; and it must impress all the thinking part of my readers with a consolatory confidence in habitual devotion, when they see a man of such enlarged intellectual powers as Johnson, thus in the genuine earnestness of secrecy, imploring the aid of that Supreme Being, 'from whom cometh down every good and every perfect gift.'[a]

Mr BOSWELL to Dr JOHNSON.

Edinburgh, August 30, 1776.
[After giving him an account of my having examined the chests of books which he had sent to me, and which contained what may be truly called a numerous and miscellaneous *Stall Library*, thrown together at random:]

Lord Hailes was against the decree in the case of my client, the minister, not that he justified the minister, but because the parishioner both provoked and retorted. I sent his Lordship your able argument upon the case for his perusal. His observation upon it in a letter to me was, 'Dr Johnson's *Suasorium* is pleasantly[2] and artfully composed. I suspect, however, that he has not convinced himself; for, I believe that he is better read

---

[1] *Prayers and Meditations*, p. 151.

[a] After this passage, read:

To SIR JOSHUA REYNOLDS.

SIR – A young man, whose name is Paterson, offers himself this evening to the Academy. He is the son of a man for whom I have long had a kindness, and who is now abroad in distress. I shall be glad that you will be pleased to show him any little countenance, or pay him any small distinction. How much it is in your power to favour or to forward a young man I do not know; nor do I know how much this candidate deserves favour by his personal merit, or what hopes his proficiency may now give of future eminence. I recommend him as the son of my friend. Your character and station enable you to give a young man great encouragement by very easy means. You have heard of a man who asked no other favour of Sir Robert Walpole, than that he would bow to him at his levee. I am, Sir,
    Your most humble servant,
                                                        SAM. JOHNSON.
    August 3, 1776.

[2] Dr Johnson afterwards told me, that he was of opinion that a clergyman had this right.

in ecclesiastical history, than to imagine that a Bishop or a Presbyter has a right to begin censure or discipline *e cathedra*.[1]

. . .

For the honour of Count Manucci, as well as to observe that exactness of truth which you have taught me, I must correct what I said in a former letter. He did not fall from his horse, which might have been an imputation on his skill as an officer of cavalry; his horse fell with him.

I have, since I saw you, read every word of Granger's *Biographical History*. It has entertained me exceedingly, and I do not think him the Whig that you supposed. Horace Walpole's being his patron is, indeed, no good sign of his political principles. But he denied to Lord Mountstuart that he was a Whig, and said he had been accused by both parties of partiality. It seems he was like Pope,

> While Tories call me Whig, and Whigs a Tory.

I wish you would look more into his book; and as Lord Mountstuart wishes much to find a proper person to continue the work upon Granger's plan, and has desired I would mention it to you, if such a man occurs, please to let me know. His Lordship will give him generous encouragement.[a]

I again wrote to Dr Johnson on the 21st of October, informing him, that my father had, in the most liberal manner, paid a large debt for me, and that I had now the happiness of being upon very good terms with him; to which he returned the following answer:

1 Why his lordship uses the epithet *pleasantly*, when speaking of a grave piece of reasoning, I cannot conceive. But different men have different notions of pleasantry. I happened to sit by a gentleman one evening at the Opera-house in London, who, at the moment when Medea appeared to be in great agony at the thought of killing her children, turned to me with a smile, and said, '*funny* enough.'

a `After this passage, read:

To Mr ROBERT LEVETT.

DEAR SIR – Having spent about six weeks at this place, we have at length resolved upon returning. I expect to see you all in Fleet-street on the 30th of this month.

I did not go into the sea till last Friday, but think to go most of this week, though I know not that it does me any good. My nights are very restless and tiresome, but I am otherwise well.

I have written word of my coming to Mrs Williams. Remember me kindly to Francis and Betsy. I am, Sir,

> Your humble servant,

> > SAM. JOHNSON'[2]

Brighthelmston, Oct. 21, 1776.

2 For this and Dr Johnson's other letters to Mr Levett, I am indebted to my old acquaintance Mr Nathaniel Thomas, whose worth and ingenuity have been known to a respectable though not a wide circle; and whose collection of medals would do credit to persons of greater opulence.

To JAMES BOSWELL, Esq.

DEAR SIR – I had great pleasure in hearing that you are at last on good terms with your father. Cultivate his kindness by all honest and manly means. Life is but short; no time can be afforded but for the indulgence of real sorrow, or contests upon questions seriously momentous. Let us not throw any of our days away upon useless resentment, or contend who shall hold out longest in stubborn malignity. It is best not to be angry, and best, in the next place, to be quickly reconciled. May you and your father pass the remainder of your time in reciprocal benevolence!

. . .

Do you ever hear from Mr Langton? I visit him sometimes, but he does not talk. I do not like his scheme of life; but, as I am not permitted to understand it, I cannot set anything right that is wrong. His children are sweet babies.

I hope my irreconcileable enemy, Mrs Boswell, is well. Desire her not to transmit her malevolence to the young people. Let me have Alexander, and Veronica, and Euphemia, for my friends.

Mrs Williams, whom you may reckon as one of your well-wishers, is in a feeble and languishing state, with little hope of growing better. She went for some part of the autumn into the country, but is little benefited; and Dr Lawrence confesses that his art is at an end. Death is, however, at a distance; and what more than that can we say of ourselves? I am sorry for her pain, and more sorry for her decay. Mr Levett is sound, wind and limb.

I was some weeks this autumn at Brighthelmston. The place was very dull, and I was not well: the expedition to the Hebrides was the most pleasant journey that I ever made. Such an effort annually would give the world a little diversification.

Every year, however, we cannot wander, and must therefore endeavour to spend our time at home as well as we can. I believe it is best to throw life into a method, that every hour may bring its employment, and every employment have its hour. Xenophon observes, in his *Treatise of Economy*, that if every thing be kept in a certain place, when any thing is worn out or consumed, the vacuity which it leaves will show what is wanting; so, if every part of time has its duty, the hour will call into remembrance its proper engagement.

I have not practised all this prudence myself, but I have suffered much for want of it; and I would have you, by timely recollection and steady resolution, escape from those evils which have lain heavy upon me. I am, my dearest Boswell,

Your most humble servant,

SAM. JOHNSON.

Bolt-court, Nov. 16, 1776.

On the 16th of November I informed him that Mr Strahan had sent me *twelve* copies of the *Journey to the Western Islands*, handsomely bound, instead of the *twenty* copies which were stipulated, but which, I supposed, were to be only in sheets; requested to know how they should be distributed: and mentioned that I had another son born to me, who was named David, and was a sickly infant.

To James Boswell, Esq.

Dear Sir – I have been for some time ill of a cold, which, perhaps, I made an excuse to myself for not writing, when in reality I knew not what to say.

The books you must at last distribute as you think best, in my name, or your own, as you are inclined, or as you judge most proper. Every body cannot be obliged, but I wish that nobody may be offended. Do the best you can.

I congratulate you on the increase of your family, and hope that little David is by this time well, and his mamma perfectly recovered. I am much pleased to hear of the re-establishment of kindness between you and your father. Cultivate his paternal tenderness as much as you can. To live at variance at all is uncomfortable, and variance with a father is still more uncomfortable. Besides that, in the whole dispute you have the wrong side; at least you gave the first provocations, and some of them very offensive. Let it now be all over. As you have no reason to think that your new mother has shown you any foul play, treat her with respect, and with some degree of confidence; this will secure your father. When once a discordant family has felt the pleasure of peace, they will not willingly lose it. If Mrs Boswell would but be friends with me, we might now shut the temple of Janus.

What came of Dr Memis's cause? Is the question about the negro determined? Has Sir Allan any reasonable hopes? What is become of poor Macquarry? Let me know the event of all these litigations. I wish particularly well to the negro and Sir Allan.

Mrs Williams has been much out of order; and though she is something better, is likely, in her physician's opinion, to endure her malady for life, though she may, perhaps, die of some other. Mrs Thrale is big, and fancies that she carries a boy; if it were very reasonable to wish much about it, I should wish her not to be disappointed. The desire of male heirs is not appendant only to feudal tenures. A son is almost necessary to the continuance of Thrale's fortune; for what can misses do with a brewhouse? Lands are fitter for daughters than trades.

Baretti went away from Thrale's in some whimsical fit of disgust or ill-nature, without taking any leave. It is well if he finds in any other place as good an habitation, and as many conveniences. He has got five-and-twenty guineas by translating Sir Joshua's Discourses into Italian, and Mr Thrale gave him an hundred in the spring; so that he is yet in no difficulties.

Colman has bought Foote's patent, and is to allow Foote for life sixteen hundred pounds a year, as Reynolds told me, and to allow him to play so often on such terms that he may gain four hundred pounds more. What Colman can get by this bargain, but trouble and hazard, I do not see. I am, dear Sir,

Your humble servant,

SAM. JOHNSON.

Dec. 21, 1776.

The Reverend Dr Hugh Blair, who had long been admired as a preacher at Edinburgh, thought now of diffusing his excellent sermons more extensively, and increasing his reputation, by publishing a collection of them. He transmitted the manuscript to Mr Strahan, the printer, who after keeping it for some time, wrote a letter to him, discouraging the publication. Such at first was the unpropitious state of one of the most successful theological books that has ever appeared. Mr Strahan, however, had sent one of the sermons to Dr Johnson for his opinion; and after his unfavourable letter to Dr Blair had been sent off, he received from Johnson on Christmas-eve, a note in which was the following paragraph: 'I have read over Dr Blair's first sermon with more than approbation; to say it is good, is to say too little.'

I believe Mr Strahan had very soon after this time a conversation with Dr Johnson concerning them, and then he very candidly wrote again to Dr Blair, enclosing Johnson's note, and agreeing to purchase the volume, for which he and Mr Cadell gave one hundred pounds. The sale was so rapid and extensive, and the approbation of the public so high, that to their honour be it recorded, the proprietors made Dr Blair a present first of one sum, and afterwards of another, of fifty pounds, thus voluntarily doubling the stipulated price; and when he prepared another volume they gave him at once three hundred pounds, being in all five hundred pounds, by an agreement to which I am a subscribing witness; and now for a third octavo volume he has received no less than six hundred pounds.

In 1777, it appears from his *Prayers and Meditations*, that Johnson suffered much from a state of mind 'unsettled and perplexed', and from that constitutional gloom, which, together with his extreme humility and anxiety with regard to his religious state, made him contemplate himself through too dark and unfavourable a medium. It may be said of him, that he 'saw GOD in clouds'. Certain we may be of his injustice to himself in the following lamentable paragraph, which it is painful to think came from the contrite heart of this great man, to whose labours the world is so much indebted: 'When I survey my past life, I discover nothing but a barren waste of time, with some disorders of body, and disturbances of the mind very near to madness, which I hope He that made me will suffer to extenuate many faults, and excuse many deficiencies.'[1] But we find his devotions in this year eminently fervent, and we

1 *Prayers and Meditations*, p. 155.

are comforted by observing intervals of quiet, composure, and gladness.

On Easter-day we find the following emphatic prayer: 'Almighty and most merciful Father, who seest all our miseries, and knowest all our necessities, look down upon me, and pity me. Defend me from the violent incursion of evil thoughts, and enable me to form and keep such resolutions as may conduce to the discharge of the duties which thy providence shall appoint me; and so help me, by thy Holy Spirit, that my heart may surely there be fixed where true joys are to be found, and that I may serve Thee with pure affection and a cheerful mind. Have mercy upon me, O GOD, have mercy upon me; years and infirmities oppress me, terror and anxiety beset me. Have mercy upon me, my Creator and my Judge. In all perplexities relieve and free me; and so help me by thy Holy Spirit, that I may now so commemorate the death of thy Son our Saviour JESUS CHRIST, as that when this short and painful life shall have an end, I may, for his sake, be received to everlasting happiness. Amen.'[1]

While he was at church the agreeable impressions upon his mind are thus commemorated, 'I was for some time much distressed, but at last obtained, I hope from the GOD of Peace, more quiet than I have enjoyed for a long time. I had made no resolution, but as my heart grew lighter, my hopes revived, and my courage increased; and I wrote with my pencil in my Common Prayer Book,

> *Vita ordinanda.*
> *Biblia legenda.*
> *Theologiae opera danda.*
> *Serviendum et laetandum.*

Mr Steevens, whose generosity is well known, joined Dr Johnson in kind assistance to a female relation of Dr Goldsmith, and desired that on her return to Ireland she would procure authentic particulars of the life of her celebrated relation. Concerning her there is the following letter:

To GEORGE STEEVENS, Esq.

DEAR SIR – You will be glad to hear that from Mrs Goldsmith, whom we lamented as drowned, I have received a letter full of gratitude to us all, with promise to make the enquiries which we recommended to her.

I would have had the honour of conveying this intelligence to Miss Caulfield, but that her letter is not at hand, and I know not the direction. You will tell the good news. I am, Sir,

Your most, &c.

SAM. JOHNSON.

February 25, 1777.

---

1 *Prayers and Meditations*, p. 158.

Mr BOSWELL to Dr JOHNSON.

Edinburgh, Feb. 14, 1777.

MY DEAR SIR – My state of epistolary accounts with you at present is extraordinary. The balance, as to number, is on your side. I am indebted to you for two letters; one dated the 16th of November, upon which very day I wrote to you, so that our letters were exactly exchanged, and one dated the 21st of December last.

My heart was warmed with gratitude by the truly kind contents of both of them; and it is amazing and vexing that I have allowed so much time to elapse without writing to you. But delay is inherent in me, by nature or by bad habit. I waited till I should have an opportunity of paying you my compliments on a new year. I have procrastinated till the year is no longer new.

. . .

Dr Memis's cause was determined against him, with £40 costs. The Lord President, and two other of the Judges, dissented from the majority upon this ground: that although there may have been no intention to injure him by calling him *Doctor of Medicine*, instead of *Physician*, yet as he remonstrated against the designation before the charter was printed off, and represented that it was disagreeable and even hurtful to him, it was ill-natured to refuse to alter it, and let him have the designation to which he was certainly entitled. My own opinion is, that our court has judged wrong. The defendants were *in mala fide*, to persist in naming him in a way that he disliked. You remember poor Goldsmith, when he grew important and wished to appear *Doctor Major*, could not bear you calling him *Goldy*. Would it not have been wrong to have named him so in your 'Preface to Shakspeare', or in any serious permanent writing of any sort? The difficulty is, whether an action should be allowed on such petty wrongs. *De minimis non curat lex*.

The Negro cause is not yet decided. A memorial is preparing on the side of slavery. I shall send you a copy as soon as it is printed. Maclaurin is made happy by your approbation of his memorial for the black.

Macquarry was here in the winter, and we passed an evening together. The sale of his estate cannot be prevented.

Sir Allan Maclean's suit against the Duke of Argyle, for recovering the ancient inheritance of his family, is now fairly before all our Judges. I spoke for him yesterday, and Maclaurin today. Crosbie spoke to-day against him. Three more counsel are to be heard, and next week the cause will be determined. I send you the *Informations* or *Cases* on each side, which I hope you will read. You said to me when we were under Sir Allan's hospitable roof, 'I will help him with my pen.' You said it with a generous glow; and though his Grace of Argyle did afterwards mount you upon an excellent horse, upon which 'you looked like a Bishop', you must not swerve from your purpose at Inchkenneth. I wish you may understand the points at issue, amidst our Scotch law principles and phrases.

[Here followed a full state of the case, in which I endeavoured to make it as clear as I could to an Englishman, who had no knowledge of the formularies and technical language of the law of Scotland.]

I shall inform you how the cause is decided here. But as it may be brought under the review of our judges, and is certainly to be carried by appeal to the House of Lords, the assistance of such a mind as your's will be of consequence. Your paper on *Vicious Intromission* is a noble proof of what you can do even in Scotch law.

. . .

I have not yet distributed all your books. Lord Hailes and Lord Monboddo have each received one, and return you thanks. Monboddo dined with me lately, and having drank tea, we were a good while by ourselves, and as I knew that he had read the *Journey* superficially, as he did not talk of it as I wished, I brought it to him, and read aloud several passages, and then he talked so, that I told him he was to have a copy *from the author*. He begged *that* might be marked on it.

. . .

I ever am, my dear Sir,
Your most faithful
And affectionate humble servant,

JAMES BOSWELL.

Sir ALEXANDER DICK to Dr SAMUEL JOHNSON.

Prestonfield, Feb. 1777.

SIR – I had yesterday the honour of receiving your book of your *Journey to the Western Islands of Scotland*, which you was so good as to send me, by the hands of our mutual friend, Mr Boswell, of Auchinleck; for which I return you my most hearty thanks; and after carefully reading it over again, shall deposit it in my little collection of choice books, next our worthy friend's *Journey to Corsica*. As there are many things to admire in both performances, I have often wished that no Travels or Journeys should be published but those undertaken by persons of integrity and capacity, to judge well, and describe faithfully, and in good language, the situation, condition, and manners of the countries past through. Indeed our country of Scotland, in spite of the union of the crowns, is still in most places so devoid of cloathing, or cover from hedges and plantations, that it was well you gave your readers a sound *monitoire* with respect to that circumstance. The truths you have told, and the purity of the language in which they are expressed, as your *Journey* is universally read, may and already appear to have a very good effect. For a man of my acquaintance, who has the largest nursery for trees and hedges in this country, tells me, that of late the demand upon him for these articles is doubled, and sometimes tripled. I have, therefore, listed Dr Samuel Johnson in some of my memorandums of the principal planters and favourers of the enclosures, under a name which I took the liberty to invent from the Greek, *Papadendrion*. Lord Auchinleck and some few more are of the list. I am told that one gentleman in the shire of Aberdeen, *viz.* Sir Archibald Grant, has planted above fifty millions of trees on a piece of very wild ground at Monimusk: I must enquire if he has fenced them well, before he enters my list; for, that is the soul of enclosing. I began myself to plant a little, our ground being too valuable for much, and that is now fifty years ago; and the trees, now in my seventy-fourth year, I look up to with reverence, and show them to my eldest son, now in his fifteenth year, that they are full the height of my country-house here, where I had the pleasure of receiving you, and hope again to have that satisfaction with our mutual friend, Mr Boswell. I shall always continue with the truest esteem, dear Doctor,

Your much obliged, and obedient humble servant,

ALEXANDER DICK.[1]

To JAMES BOSWELL, Esq.

DEAR SIR — It is so long since I heard any thing from you,[2] that I am not easy about it; write something to me next post. When you sent your last letter every thing seemed to be mending, I hope nothing has lately grown worse. I suppose young Alexander continues to thrive, and Veronica is now very pretty company. I do not suppose the lady is yet reconciled to me, yet let her know that I love her very well, and value her very much.

Dr Blair is printing some sermons. If they are all like the first, which I have read, they are *sermones aurei, ac auro magis aurei*. It is excellently written both as to doctrine and language. Mr Watson's book[3] seems to be much esteemed.

. . .

Poor Beauclerk still continues very ill. Langton lives on as he is used to do. His children are very pretty, and, I think, his lady loses her Scotch. Paoli I never see.

I have been so distressed by difficulty of breathing, that I lost, as was computed, six-and-thirty ounces of blood in a few days. I am better, but not well.

I wish you would be vigilant and get me Graham's *Telemachus* that was printed at Glasgow, a very little book, and *Johnstoni Poemata*, another little book, printed at Middleburg.

Mrs Williams sends her compliments, and promises that when you come hither, she will accommodate you as well as ever she can in the old room. She wishes to know whether you sent her book to Sir Alexander Gordon.

1 For a character of this very amiable man, see *Journal of a Tour to the Hebrides*, 3d edit. p. 36.
2 By the then course of the post, my long letter of the 14th had not yet reached him.
3 *History of Philip the Second.*

My dear Boswell, do not neglect to write to me, for your kindness is one of the pleasures of my life, which I should be very sorry to lose. I am, Sir,

Your humble servant,

SAM. JOHNSON.

Feb. 18, 1777.

To Dr SAMUEL JOHNSON.

Edinburgh, Feb. 24, 1777.

MY DEAR SIR – Your letter dated the 18th instant, I had the pleasure to receive last post. Although my late long neglect, or rather delay was truly culpable, I am tempted not to regret it, since it has produced me so valuable a proof of your regard. I did indeed, during that inexcusable silence, sometimes divert the reproaches of my own mind, by fancying that I should hear again from you, inquiring with some anxiety about me, because, for aught you knew, I might have been ill.

You are pleased to show me, that my kindness is of some consequence to you. My heart is elated at the thought. Be assured, my dear Sir, that my affection and reverence for you are exalted and steady. I do not believe that a more perfect attachment ever existed in the history of mankind. And it is a noble attachment, for the attractions are Genius, Learning, and Piety.

Your difficulty of breathing alarms me, and brings into my imagination an event, which although in the natural course of things, I must expect at some period, I cannot view with composure . . .

My wife is much honoured by what you say of her. She begs you may accept of her best compliments. She is to send you some marmalade of oranges of her own making. . . .

I ever am, my dear Sir,

Your most obliged

And faithful humble servant,

JAMES BOSWELL.

To JAMES BOSWELL, Esq.

DEAR SIR – I have been much pleased with your late letter, and am glad that my old enemy, Mrs Boswell, begins to feel some remorse. As to Miss Veronica's Scotch, I think it cannot be helped. An English maid you might easily have; but she would still imitate the greater number, as they would be likewise those whom she must most respect. Her dialect will not be gross. Her Mamma has not much Scotch, and you have yourself very little. I hope she knows my name, and does not call me *Johnston*.[a]

---

[a] Add the following note: John*son* is the most common English formation of the surname from *John*; John*ston* the Scotch. My illustrious friend observed, that many North Britons pronounced his name in their own way.

The immediate cause of my writing is this: One Shaw, who seems a modest and a decent man, has written an Erse Grammar, which a very learned Highlander, Macbean, has, at my request, examined and approved.

The book is very little, but Mr Shaw has been persuaded by his friends to set it at half a guinea, though I had advised only a crown, and thought myself liberal. You, whom the author considers as a great encourager of ingenious men, will receive a parcel of his proposals and receipts. I have undertaken to give you notice of them, and to solicit your countenance. You must ask no poor man, because the price is really too high. Yet such a work deserves patronage.

It is proposed to augment our club from twenty to thirty, of which I am glad; for as we have several in it whom I do not much like to consort with,[1] I am for reducing it to a mere miscellaneous collection of conspicuous men, without any determinate character. . . . I am, dear Sir,

Most affectionately yours,

SAM. JOHNSON.

March 1, 1777.

My respects to Madam, to Veronica, to Alexander, to Euphemia, to David.

Mr BOSWELL to Dr JOHNSON.

Edinburgh, April 4, 1777.

[After informing him of the death of my little son David, and that I could not come to London this spring:]

I think it hard that I should be a whole year without seeing you. May I presume to petition for a meeting with you in the autumn? You have, I believe, seen all the cathedrals in England, except that of Carlisle. If you are to be with Dr Taylor, at Ashbourne, it would not be a great journey to come thither. We may pass a few most agreeable days there by ourselves, and I will accompany you a good part of the way to the southward again. Pray think of this.

You forget that Mr Shaw's Erse Grammar was put into your hands by myself last year. Lord Eglintoune put it into mine. I am glad that Mr Macbean approves of it. I have received Mr Shaw's Proposals for its publication, which I can perceive are written *by the hand of a* MASTER.

. . .

Pray get for me all the editions of Walton's *Lives*. I have a notion that the republication of them with Notes will fall upon me, between Dr Horne and Lord Hailes.

Mr Shaw's Proposals[†] for 'An Analysis of the Scotch Celtic Language', were thus illuminated by the pen of Johnson:

Though the Erse dialect of the Celtic language has, from the earliest times, been spoken in Britain, and still subsists in the northern parts and adjacent

---

[a] On account of their differing from him as to religion and politics.

islands, yet, by the negligence of a people rather warlike than lettered, it has hitherto been left to the caprice and judgement of every speaker, and has floated in the living voice, without the steadiness of analogy or direction of rules. An Erse Grammar is an addition to the stores of literature; and its author hopes for the indulgence always shown to those that attempt to do what was never done before. If his work shall be found defective, it is at least all his own: he is not like other grammarians, a compiler or transcriber; what he delivers, he has learned by attentive observation among his countrymen, who perhaps will be themselves surprised to see that speech reduced to principles, which they have used only by imitation.

The use of this book will, however, not be confined to the mountains and islands; it will afford a pleasing and important subject of speculation, to those whose studies lead them to trace the affinity of languages, and the migrations of the ancient races of mankind.

To Dr SAMUEL JOHNSON.

Glasgow, April 24, 1777.

MY DEAR SIR – Our worthy friend Thrale's death having appeared in the newspapers, and been afterwards contradicted, I have been placed in a state of very uneasy uncertainty, from which I hoped to be relieved by you: but my hopes have as yet been vain. How could you omit to write to me on such an occasion? I shall wait with anxiety.

I am going to Auchinleck to stay a fortnight with my father. It is better not to be there very long at one time. But frequent renewals of attention are agreeable to him.

Pray tell me about this edition of 'The English Poets, with a Preface, biographical and critical, to each Author, by Samuel Johnson, LL.D.' which I see advertised. I am delighted with the prospect of it. Indeed I am happy to feel that I am capable of being so much delighted with literature. But is not the charm of this publication chiefly owing to the *magnum nomen* in the front of it?

What do you say of Lord Chesterfield's Memoirs and last Letters?

My wife has made marmalade of oranges for you. I left her and my daughters and Alexander all well yesterday. I have taught Veronica to speak of you thus– Dr John*son*, not John*ston*. I remain, my dear Sir,

Your most affectionate

And obliged humble servant,

JAMES BOSWELL.

To JAMES BOSWELL, Esq.

DEAR SIR – The story of Mr Thrale's death, as he had neither been sick nor in any other danger, made so little impression upon me, that I never thought about obviating its effects on any body else. It is supposed to have been produced by the English custom of making April fools, that is, of sending one another on some foolish errand on the first of April.

Tell Mrs Boswell that I shall taste her marmalade cautiously at first, *Timeo Danaos et dona ferentes*. Beware, says the Italian proverb, of a reconciled enemy. But when I find it does me no harm, I shall then receive it and be thankful for it, as a pledge of firm, and I hope, of unalterable kindness. She is, after all, a dear, dear lady.

Please to return Dr Blair thanks for his sermons. The Scotch write English wonderfully well. . . .

Your frequent visits to Auchinleck, and your short stay there, are very laudable and very judicious. Your present concord with your father gives me great pleasure; it was all that you seemed to want.

My health is very bad, and my nights are very unquiet. What can I do to mend them? I have for this summer nothing better in prospect than a journey into Staffordshire and Derbyshire, perhaps with Oxford and Birmingham in my way.

Make my compliments to Miss Veronica; I must leave it to *her* philosophy to comfort you for the loss of little David. You must remember, that to keep three out of four is more than your share. Mrs Thrale has but four out of eleven.

I am engaged to write little Lives, and little Prefaces, to a little edition of the English Poets. I think I have persuaded the booksellers to insert something of Thomson, and if you could give me some information about him, for the life which we have is very scanty, I should be glad. I am, dear Sir,

Your most affectionate humble servant,

SAM. JOHNSON.

May 3, 1777.

To those who delight in tracing the progress of works of literature, it will be an entertainment to compare the limited design with the ample execution of that admirable performance, *The Lives of the English Poets*, which is the richest, most beautiful, and indeed most perfect production of his pen. His notion of it at this time appears in the preceding letter. He has a memorandum in this year, '29 May, Easter-Eve, I treated with booksellers on a bargain, but the time was not long.'[1] The bargain was concerning that undertaking, but his tender conscience seems alarmed lest it should have intruded too much on his devout preparation for the solemnity of the ensuing day. But, indeed, very little time was necessary for Johnson's concluding a treaty with the Booksellers; as he had, I believe, less attention to profit from his labours than any man to whom literature has been a profession. I shall here insert from a letter to me from a late worthy friend Mr Edward Dilly, though of a later date, an account of this plan so happily conceived; since it was the occasion of procuring for us an elegant collection of the best biography and criticism of which our language can boast.

1 *Prayers and Meditations*, p. 155.

To James Boswell, Esq.

Southill, Sept. 26, 1777.

Dear Sir — You will find by this letter, that I am still in the same calm retreat, from the noise and bustle of London, as when I wrote to you last. I am happy to find you had such an agreeable meeting with your old friend Dr Johnson; I have no doubt your stock is much increased by the interview; few men, nay I may say, scarcely any man has got that fund of knowledge and entertainment as Dr Johnson in conversation. When he opens freely, every one is attentive to what he says, and cannot fail of improvement as well as pleasure.

The edition of the Poets, now printing, will do honour to the English press, and a concise account of the life of each author, by Dr Johnson, will be a very valuable addition, and stamp the reputation of this edition superior to any thing that is gone before. The first cause that gave rise to this undertaking, I believe, was owing to the little trifling edition of the Poets, printing by the Martins at Edinburgh, and to be sold by Bell, in London. Upon examining the volumes which were printed, the type was found so extremely small, that many persons could not read them; not only this inconvenience attended it, but the inaccuracy of the press was very conspicuous. These reasons, as well as the idea of an invasion of what we call our Literary Property, induced the London Booksellers to print an elegant and accurate edition of all the English Poets of reputation, from Chaucer to the present time.

Accordingly a select number of the most respectable booksellers met on the occasion, and, on consulting together, agreed, that all the proprietors of copy-right in the various Poets should be summoned together; and when their opinions were given, to proceed immediately on the business. Accordingly a meeting was held, consisting of about forty of the most respectable booksellers of London, when it was agreed that an elegant and uniform edition of *The English Poets* should be immediately printed, with a concise account of the life of each author, by Dr Samuel Johnson; and that three persons should be deputed to wait upon Dr Johnson, to solicit him to undertake the Lives, *viz*. T. Davies, Strahan, and Cadell. The Doctor very politely undertook it, and seemed exceedingly pleased with the proposal. As to the terms, it was left entirely to the Doctor to name his own: he mentioned two hundred guineas: it was immediately agreed to; and a farther compliment, I believe, will be made him. A committee was likewise appointed to engage the best engravers, *viz*. Bartolozzi, Sherwin, Hall, &c. Likewise another committee for giving directions about the paper, printing, &c. so that the whole will be conducted with spirit, and in the best manner, with respect to authorship, editorship, engravings, &c. &c. My brother will give you a list of the Poets we mean to give, many of which are within the time of the Act of Queen Anne, which Martin and Bell cannot give, as they have no property in them; the proprietors are almost all the booksellers in London of consequence. I am, dear Sir,

Ever yours,

Edward Dilly.

I shall afterwards have occasion to consider the extensive and varied range which Johnson took, when he was once led upon ground which he trod with a peculiar delight, having long been intimately acquainted with all the circumstances of it that could interest and please.

Dr JOHNSON to CHARLES O'CONOR, Esq.[1]

SIR – Having had the pleasure of conversing with Dr Campbell about your character and your literary undertaking, I am resolved to gratify myself by renewing a correspondence which began and ended a great while ago, and ended, I am afraid, by my fault; a fault which, if you have not forgotten it, you must now forgive.

If I have ever disappointed you, give me leave to tell you, that you have likewise disappointed me. I expected great discoveries in Irish antiquity, and large publications in the Irish language; but the world still remains as it was, doubtful and ignorant. What the Irish language is in itself, and to what languages it has affinity, are very interesting questions; which every man wishes to see resolved, that has any philological or historical curiosity. Dr Leland begins his history too late: the ages which deserve an exact enquiry are those times (for such there were) when Ireland was the school of the west, the quiet habitation of·sanctity and literature. If you could give a history, though imperfect, of the Irish nation, from its conversion to Christianity to the invasion from England, you would amplify knowledge with new views and new objects. Set about it, therefore, if you can: do what you can easily do without anxious exactness. Lay the foundation, and leave the superstructure to posterity. I am, Sir,

Your most humble servant,

SAM. JOHNSON.

May 19, 1777.

Early in this year came out, in two volumes quarto, the posthumous works of the learned Dr Zachary Pearce, Bishop of Rochester; being 'A Commentary, with Notes, on the four Evangelists and the Acts of the Apostles', with other theological pieces. Johnson had now an opportunity of making a grateful return to that excellent prelate, who, we have seen, was the only person who gave him any assistance in the compilation of his Dictionary. The Bishop had left some account of his life and character, written by himself. To

1 Mr Walker, of the Treasury, Dublin, who obligingly communicated to me this and a former letter from Dr Johnson to the same gentleman (for which see page 164) writes to me as follows: 'Perhaps it would gratify you to have some account of Mr O'Conor. He is an amiable, learned, venerable old gentleman, of an independent fortune, who lives at Belanagar, in the county of Roscommon; he is an admired writer, and Member of the Irish Academy. – The above Letter is alluded to in the Preface to the 2d edit. of his Dissert. p.3.'[a]

[a] Add to this note: Mr O'Conor has since died at the age of eighty-two, July 1, 1791. See a well-drawn character of him in the *Gentleman's Magazine* for August, 1791.

this Johnson made some valuable additions,[†] and also furnished to the editor, the Reverend Mr Derby, a Dedication,[†] which I shall here insert, both because it will appear at this time with peculiar propriety; and because it will tend to propagate and increase that 'fervour of *Loyalty*', which in me, who boast of the name of TORY, is not only a principle but a passion.

To The King.

SIR – I presume to lay before your Majesty the last labours of a learned Bishop, who died in the toils and duties of his calling. He is now beyond the reach of all earthly honours and rewards; and only the hope of inciting others to imitate him, makes it now fit to be remembered, that he enjoyed in his life the favour of your Majesty.

The tumultuary life of Princes seldom permits them to survey the wide extent of national interest, without losing sight of private merit, to exhibit qualities which may be imitated by the highest and the humblest of mankind; and to be at once amiable and great.

Such characters, if now and then they appear in history, are contemplated with admiration. May it be the ambition of all your subjects to make haste with their tribute of reverence: and as posterity may learn from your Majesty how Kings should live, may they learn, likewise, from your people, how they should be honoured. I am,
May it please your Majesty,
With the most profound respect,
Your Majesty's
Most dutiful and devoted
Subject and servant.

In the summer he wrote a Prologue* which was spoken before *A Word to the Wise*, a comedy by Mr Hugh Kelly, which had been brought upon the stage in 1770; but its design being supposed favourable to the ministry,[a] it fell a sacrifice to popular fury, and, in the playhouse phrase, was *damned*. By the generosity of Mr Harris, the proprietor of Covent Garden theatre, it was now exhibited for one night, for the benefit of the author's widow and children. To conciliate the favour of the audience was the intention of Johnson's Prologue, which, as it is not long, I shall here insert, as a proof that his poetical talents were in no degree impaired.

> This night presents a play, which public rage,
> Or right or wrong, once hooted from the stage:
> From zeal, or malice, now no more we dread,
> For English vengeance *wars not with the dead*.
> A generous foe regards with pitying eye
> The man whom Fate has laid where all must lie.

---

[a] After 'its design being supposed favourable to the ministry,' read, 'he being a writer for ministry in one of the newspapers'.

> To wit, reviving from its author's dust,
> Be kind, ye judges, or at least be just:
> Let no renew'd hostilities invade
> Th' oblivious grave's inviolable shade.
> Let one great payment every claim appease,
> And him who cannot hurt, allow to please;
> To please by scenes, unconscious of offence,
> By harmless merriment or useful sense.
> Where aught of bright or fair the piece displays,
> Approve it only – 'tis too late to praise.
> If want of skill or want of care appear,
> Forbear to hiss; – the poet cannot hear.
> By all, like him, must praise and blame be found,
> At last a fleeting gleam, or empty sound.
> Yet then shall calm reflection bless the night,
> When liberal pity dignified delight;
> When pleasure fir'd her torch at virtue's flame,
> And mirth was bounty with an humbler name.

A circumstance which could not fail to be very pleasing to Johnson, occurred this year. The Tragedy of *Sir Thomas Overbury*, written by his early companion in London, Richard Savage, was brought out with alterations at Drury-lane theatre. The Prologue to it was written by Mr Richard Brinsley Sheridan; in which, after describing very pathetically the wretchedness of

> Ill-fated Savage, at whose birth was giv'n
> No parent but the Muse, no friend but Heav'n:

he concluded with[a] an elegant compliment to Johnson on his Dictionary, that wonderful performance which cannot be too often or too highly praised; of which Mr Harris, in his *Philological Inquiries*,[1] justly and liberally observes, 'Such is its merit, that our language does not possess a more copious, learned, and valuable work.' The concluding lines of this Prologue were these:

> So pleads the tale[2] that gives to future times
> The son's misfortunes and the parent's crimes;
> There shall his fame (if own'd to-night) survive,
> Fix'd by THE HAND THAT BIDS OUR LANGUAGE LIVE.

Mr Sheridan here at once did honour to his taste and to his liberality of sentiment, by showing that he was not prejudiced from the unlucky difference which had taken place between his worthy father and Dr Johnson. I have already mentioned, that Johnson was very desirous of reconciliation with old

---

[a] For 'concluded with', read 'introduced'.
1 Part First, Chap. 4.
2 *Life of Richard Savage*, by Dr Johnson.'

Mr Sheridan. It will, therefore, not seem at all surprising that he was zealous in acknowledging the brilliant merit of his son. While it had as yet been displayed only in the drama, Johnson proposed him as a member of THE LITERARY CLUB, observing that 'He who has written the two best comedies of his age, is surely a considerable man.' And he had, accordingly, the honour to be elected; for an honour it undoubtedly must be allowed to be, when it is considered of whom that society consists, and that a single black ball excludes a candidate.

Mr BOSWELL to Dr JOHNSON.

June 9, 1777.

MY DEAR SIR — For the health of my wife and children I have taken the little country-house at which you visited my uncle, Dr Boswell, who, having lost his wife, is gone to live with his son. We took possession of our villa about a week ago; we have a garden of three quarters of an acre, well stocked with fruit trees and flowers, and gooseberries and currants, and pease and beans, and cabbages, &c. &c. and my children are quite happy. I now write to you in a little study, from the window of which I see around me a verdant grove, and beyond it the lofty mountain, called Arthur's Seat.

Your last letter, in which you desire me to send you some additional information concerning Thomson, reached me very fortunately just as I was going to Lanark, to put my wife's two nephews, the young Campbells, to school there, under the care of Mr Thomson, the master of it, whose wife is sister to the author of the *Seasons*. She is an old woman; but her memory is very good; and she will with pleasure give me for you every particular that you wish to know, and she can tell. Pray then take the trouble to send me such questions as may lead to biographical materials. You say that the Life which we have of Thomson is scanty. Since I received your letter, I have read his Life, published under the name of Cibber, but as you told me, really written by a Mr Shiels;[1] that written by Dr Murdoch; one prefixed to an edition of the *Seasons*, published at Edinburgh, which is compounded of both, with the addition of an anecdote of Quin's relieving Thomson from prison; the abridgement of Murdoch's life of him, in the *Biographia Britannica*, and another abridgement of it in the *Biographical Dictionary*, enriched with Dr Joseph Warton's critical panegyric on the *Seasons* in his 'Essay on the Genius and Writings of Pope': from all these it appears to me that we have a pretty full account of this poet. However, you will, I doubt not, show me many blanks, and I shall do what can be done to have them filled up. As Thomson never returned to Scotland (which *you* will think very wise), his sister can speak from her own knowledge only as to the early part of his life. She has some letters from him, which may probably give light as to his more advanced progress, if she will let us see them, which I suppose she will. I believe George Lewis Scott and Dr Armstrong are now his only surviving com-

1 [See page 519.]

panions, while he lived in and about London; and they, I dare say, can tell more of him than is yet known. My own notion is, that Thomson was a much coarser man than his friends are willing to acknowledge. His *Seasons* are indeed full of elegant and pious sentiments: but a rank soil, nay a dunghill, will produce beautiful flowers.

Your edition of the *English Poets* will be very valuable, on account of the 'Prefaces and Lives'. But I have seen a specimen of an edition of the Poets at the Apollo press, at Edinburgh, which, for excellence in printing and engraving, highly deserves a liberal encouragement.

Most sincerely do I regret the bad health and bad rest with which you have been afflicted; and I hope you are better. I cannot believe that the prologue which you generously gave to Mr Kelly's widow and children the other day, is the effusion of one in sickness and in disquietude; but external circumstances are never sure indications of the state of man. I send you a letter which I wrote to you two years ago at Wilton; and did not send at the time, for fear of being reproved as indulging too much tenderness; and one written to you at the tomb of Melancthon, which I kept back, lest I should appear at once too superstitious and too enthusiastic. I now imagine that perhaps they may please you.

You do not take the least notice of my proposal for our meeting at Carlisle.[a] Though I have meritoriously refrained from visiting London this year, I ask you if it would not be wrong that I should be two years without having the benefit of your conversation, when, if you come down as far as Derbyshire, we may meet at the expense of a few days journeying, and not many pounds. I wish you to see Carlisle, which made me mention that place. But if you have not a desire to complete your tour of the English cathedrals, I will take a larger share of the road between this place and Ashbourne. So tell me *where* you will fix for our passing a few days by ourselves. Now don't cry 'foolish fellow', or 'idle dog'. Chain your humour, and let your kindness play.

You will rejoice to hear that Miss Macleod, of Rasay, is married to Colonel Mure Campbell, an excellent man, with a pretty good estate of his own, and the prospect of having the Earl of Loudoun's fortune and honours. Is not this a noble lot for our fair Hebridean? How happy am I that she is to be in Ayrshire. We shall have the Laird of Rasay, and old

[a] Add a note: Dr Johnson had himself talked of our seeing Carlisle together. *High* was a favourite word of his to denote a person of rank. He said to me, 'Sir, I believe we may meet at the house of a Roman Catholic lady in Cumberland; a high lady, Sir.' I afterwards discovered that he meant Mrs Strickland, sister of Charles Townley, Esq., whose very noble collection of statues and pictures is not more to be admired, than his extraordinary and polite readiness in showing it, which I and several of my friends have agreeably experienced. They who are possessed of valuable stores of gratification to persons of taste, should exercise their benevolence in imparting the pleasure. Grateful acknowledgements are due to Welbore Ellis Agar, Esq. for the liberal access which he is pleased to allow to his exquisite collection of pictures.

Malcolm, and I know not how many gallant Macleods, and bagpipes, &c. &c. at Auchinleck. Perhaps you may meet them all there.

Without doubt you have read what is called the *Life* of David Hume, written by himself, with the letter from Dr Adam Smith subjoined to it. Is not this an age of daring effrontery? My friend Mr Anderson, Professor of Natural Philosophy at Glasgow, at whose house you and I supped, and to whose care Mr Windham, of Norfolk, was entrusted at that University, paid me a visit lately; and after we had talked with indignation and contempt of the poisonous productions with which this age is infested, he said there was now an excellent opportunity for Dr Johnson to step forth. I agreed with him that you might knock Hume's and Smith's heads together, and make vain and ostentatious infidelity exceedingly ridiculous. Would it not be worth your while to crush such noxious weeds in the moral garden?

You have said nothing to me of Dr Dodd. I know not how you think on that subject; though the newspapers give us a saying of yours in favour of mercy to him. But I own I am very desirous that the royal prerogative of remission of punishment, should be employed to exhibit an illustrious instance of the regard which GOD'S VICEGERENT will ever show to piety and virtue. If for ten righteous men the ALMIGHTY would have spared Sodom, shall not a thousand acts of goodness done by Dr Dodd counter-balance one crime? Such an instance would do more to encourage goodness, than his execution would do to deter from vice. I am not afraid of any bad consequence to society; for who will persevere for a long course of years in a distinguished discharge of religious duties, with a view to commit a forgery with impunity?

Pray make my best compliments acceptable to Mr and Mrs Thrale, by assuring them of my hearty joy that the *Master* as you call him is alive. I hope I shall often taste his Champagne – soberly.

I have not heard from Langton for a long time. I suppose he is as usual,

'Studious the busy moments to deceive.'

. . .

I remain, my dear Sir,
Your most affectionate
And faithful humble servant,   JAMES BOSWELL.

On the 23d of June, I again wrote to Dr Johnson, enclosing a shipmaster's receipt for a jar of marmalade of oranges, and a large packet of Lord Hailes's *Annals of Scotland*.

To JAMES BOSWELL, Esq.

DEAR SIR – I have just received your packet from Mr Thrale's, but have not daylight enough to look much into it. I am glad that I have credit enough with Lord Hailes to be trusted with more copy. I hope to take more care of it than of the last. I return Mrs Boswell my affectionate thanks for her present, which I value as a token of reconciliation.

Poor Dodd was put to death yesterday, in opposition to the recommend-ation of the jury, the petition of the city of London, and a subsequent petition signed by three-and-twenty thousand hands. Surely the voice of the public, when it calls so loudly, and calls only for mercy, ought to be heard.

The saying that was given me in the papers I never spoke; but I wrote many of his petitions, and some of his letters. He applied to me very often. He was, I am afraid, long flattered with hopes of life; but I had no part in the dreadful delusion; for as soon as the King had signed his sentence, I obtained from Mr Chamier an account of the disposition of the court towards him, with a declaration that there was *no hope even of a respite*. This letter immediately was laid before Dodd; but he believed those whom he wished to be right, as it is thought, till within three days of his end. He died with pious composure and resolution. I have just seen the Ordinary that attended him. His Address to his fellow-convicts offended the Methodists; but he had a Moravian with him much of his time. His moral character is very bad: I hope all is not true that is charged upon him. Of his behaviour in prison an account will be published.

I give you joy of your country-house, and your pretty garden; and hope some time to see you in your felicity. I was much pleased with your two letters that had been kept so long in store;[1] and rejoice at Miss Rasay's advancement, and wish Sir Allan success.

I hope to meet you somewhere towards the north, but am loath to come quite to Carlisle. Can we not meet at Manchester? But we will settle it in some other letters.

---

[1] Since they have been so much honoured by Dr Johnson I shall here insert them:

To Mr SAMUEL JOHNSON.

MY EVER DEAR AND MUCH-RESPECTED SIR — You know my solemn enthusiasm of mind. You love me for it, and I respect myself for it, because in so far I resemble Mr Johnson. You will be agreeably surprised when you learn the reason of my writing this letter. I am at Wittemberg in Saxony. I am in the old church where the Reformation was first preached, and where some of the reformers lie interred. I cannot resist the serious pleasure of writing to Mr Johnson from the Tomb of Melancthon. My paper rests upon the grave-stone of that great and good man, who was undoubtedly the worthiest of all the reformers. He wished to reform abuses which had been introduced into the Church; but had no private resentment to gratify. So mild was he, that when his aged mother consulted him with anxiety on the perplexing disputes of the times, he advised her 'to keep to the old religion.' At this tomb, then, my ever dear and respected friend! I vow to thee an eternal attachment. It shall be my study to do what I can to render your life happy! And, if you die before me, I shall endeavour to do honour to your memory; and, elevated by the remembrance of you, persist in noble piety. May GOD, the Father of all beings, ever bless you! And may you continue to love

Your most affectionate friend, and devoted servant,

JAMES BOSWELL.

Sunday, Sept. 30, 1764.

Mr Seward,[1] a great favourite at Streatham, has been, I think, enkindled by our travels, with a curiosity to see the Highlands. I have given him letters to you and Beattie. He desires that a lodging may be taken for him at Edinburgh, against his arrival. He is just setting out.

Langton has been exercising the militia. Mrs Williams is, I fear, declining. Dr Lawrence says he can do no more. She is gone to summer in the country, with as many conveniences about her as she can expect; but I have no great hope. We must all die: may we all be prepared!

I suppose Miss Boswell reads her book, and young Alexander takes to his learning. Let me hear about them; for every thing that belongs to you, belongs in a more remote degree, and not, I hope, very remote, to, dear Sir,

Yours affectionately,

SAM. JOHNSON.

June 28, 1777.

To the same.

DEAR SIR — This gentleman is a great favourite at Streatham, and therefore you will easily believe that he has very valuable qualities. Our narrative has kindled him with a desire of visiting the Highlands, after having already seen a great part of Europe. You must receive him as a friend, and when you have directed him to the curiosities of Edinburgh, give him instructions and recommendations for the rest of his journey. I am, dear Sir,

Your most humble servant,

SAM. JOHNSON.

June 24, 1777.

To Dr SAMUEL JOHNSON.

Wilton House, April 22, 1775.

MY DEAR SIR — Every scene of my life confirms the truth of what you have told me — 'there is no certain happiness in this state of being.' — I am here, amidst all that you know is at Lord Pembroke's; and yet I am weary and gloomy. I am just setting out for the house of an old friend in Devonshire, and shall not get back to London for a week yet. You said to me last Good-Friday, with a cordiality that warmed my heart, that if I came to settle in London, we should have a day fixed every week, to meet by ourselves and talk freely. To be thought worthy of such a privilege cannot but exalt me. During my present absence from you, while, notwithstanding the gaiety which you allow me to possess, I am darkened by temporary clouds, I beg to have a few lines from you; a few lines merely of kindness, as a *viaticum* till I see you again. In your 'Vanity of human Wishes', and in Parnell's 'Contentment', I find the only sure means of enjoying happiness; or, at least, the hopes of happiness. I ever am, with reverence and affection,

Most faithfully yours,

JAMES BOSWELL.

1 William Seward, Esq., well known to a numerous and valuable acquaintance for his literature, love of the fine arts, and social virtues. I am indebted to him for several communications concerning Johnson.

Johnson's benevolence to the unfortunate was, I am confident, as steady and active as that of any of those who have been most eminently distinguished for that virtue. Innumerable proofs of it I have no doubt will be for ever concealed from mortal eyes. We may, however, form some judgement of it, from the many and very various instances which have been discovered. One which happened in the course of this summer is remarkable from the name and connection of the person who was the object of it. The circumstance to which I allude is ascertained by two letters, one to Mr Langton, and another to the Reverend Dr Vyse, rector of Lambeth, son of the respectable clergyman at Lichfield, who was contemporary with Johnson, and in whose father's family Johnson had the happiness of being kindly received in his early years.

Dr JOHNSON to BENNET LANGTON, Esq.

DEAR SIR — I have lately been much disordered by a difficulty of breathing, but am now better. I hope your house is well

You know we have been talking lately of St Cross, at Winchester; I have an old acquaintance whose distress makes him very desirous of an hospital, and I am afraid I have not strength enough to get him into the Chartreux. He is a painter, who never rose higher than to get his immediate living, and from that, at eighty-three, he is disabled by a slight stroke of the palsy, such as does not make him at all helpless on common occasions, though his hand is not steady enough for his art.

My request is, that you will try to obtain a promise of the next vacancy, from the Bishop of Chester. It is not a great thing to ask, and I hope we shall obtain it. Dr Warton has promised to favour him with his notice, and I hope he may end his days in peace. I am, Sir,

Your most humble servant,

SAM. JOHNSON.

June 29, 1777.

To The Reverend Dr VYSE, at Lambeth.

SIR — I doubt not but you will readily forgive me for taking the liberty of requesting your assistance in recommending an old friend to his Grace the Archbishop, as Governor of the Charter-house.

His name is De Groot; he was born at Gloucester; I have known him many years. He has all the common claims to charity, being old, poor, and infirm, in a great degree. He has likewise another claim, to which no scholar can refuse attention; he is by several descents the nephew of Hugo Grotius; of him, from whom perhaps every man of learning has learned something. Let it not be said that in any lettered country a nephew of Grotius asked a charity and was refused. I am, reverend Sir,

Your most humble servant,

SAM. JOHNSON.

July 19, 1777.

Rev. Dr Vyse to Mr Boswell.

Lambeth, June 9, 1787.

Sir – I have searched in vain for the letter which I spoke of, and which I wished, at your desire, to communicate to you. It was from Dr Johnson, to return me thanks for my application to Archbishop Cornwallis in favour of poor De Groot. He rejoices at the success it met with, and is lavish in the praise he bestows upon his favourite, Hugo Grotius. I am really sorry that I cannot find this letter, as it is worthy of the writer. That which I send you enclosed[1] is at your service. It is very short, and will not perhaps be thought of any consequence; unless you should judge proper to consider it as a proof of the very humane part which Dr Johnson took in behalf of a distressed and deserving person. I am, sir,

Your most obedient humble servant,

W. Vyse.

Dr Johnson to Mr Edward Dilly.

Sir – To the collection of English Poets, I have recommended the volume of Dr Watts to be added; his name has long been held by me in veneration, and I would not willingly be reduced to tell of him only that he was born and died. Yet of his life I know very little, and therefore must pass him in a manner very unworthy of his character, unless some of his friends will favour me with the necessary information; many of them must be known to you; and by your influence, perhaps I may obtain some instruction: My plan does not exact much; but I wish to distinguish Watts, a man who never wrote but for a good purpose. Be pleased to do for me what you can. I am, Sir,

Your humble servant,

Sam. Johnson.

Bolt-court, Fleet-street,
July 7, 1777.

To Dr Samuel Johnson.

Edinburgh, July 15, 1777.

My Dear Sir – The fate of Dr Dodd made a dismal impression upon my mind. . . .

I had sagacity enough to divine that you wrote his speech to the Recorder before sentence was pronounced. I am glad you have written so much for him; and I hope to be favoured with an exact list of the several pieces when we meet.

I received Mr Seward as the friend of Mr and Mrs Thrale, and as a gentleman recommended by Dr Johnson to my attention. I have introduced

1 The preceding letter.

him to Lord Kames, Lord Monboddo, and Mr Nairne. He is gone to the Highlands with Dr Gregory; when he returns I shall do more for him.

Sir Allan Maclean has carried that branch of his cause of which we had good hopes: the President and one other Judge only were against him. I wish the House of Lords may do as well as the Court of Session has done. But Sir Allan has not the lands of *Brolos* quite clear by this judgement, till a long account is made up of debts and interests on the one side, and rents on the other. I am, however, not much afraid of the balance.

Macquarry's estates, Staffa and all, were sold yesterday, and bought by a Campbell. I fear he will have little or nothing left out of the purchase money.

I send you the case against the negro, by Mr Cullen, son to Dr Cullen, in opposition to Maclaurin's for liberty, of which you have approved. Pray read this; and tell me what you think as a *Politician*, as well as a *Poet*, upon the subject.

Be so kind as to let me know how your time is to be distributed next autumn. I will meet you at Manchester, or where you please; but I wish you would complete your tour of the cathedrals, and come to Carlisle, and I will accompany you a part of the way homewards. I am ever

Most faithfully yours,

JAMES BOSWELL.

To JAMES BOSWELL, Esq.

DEAR SIR — Your notion of the necessity of an yearly interview is very pleasing to both my vanity and tenderness. I shall, perhaps, come to Carlisle another year; but my money has not held out so well as it used to do. I shall go to Ashbourne, and I purpose to make Dr Taylor invite you. If you live awhile with me at his house, we shall have much time to ourselves, and our stay will be no expense to us or him. I shall leave London the 28th; and after some stay at Oxford and Lichfield, shall probably come to Ashbourne about the end of your Session, but of all this you shall have notice. Be satisfied we will meet somewhere.

What passed between me and poor Dr Dodd you shall know more fully when we meet.

Of lawsuits there is no end; poor sir Allan must have another trial, for which, however, his antagonist cannot be much blamed, having two judges on his side. I am more afraid of the debts than of the House of Lords. It is scarcely to be imagined to what debts will swell, that are daily increasing by small additions, and how carelessly in a state of desperation debts are contracted. Poor Macquarry was far from thinking that when he sold his islands he should receive nothing. For what were they sold? And what was their yearly value? The admission of money into the Highland will soon put an end to the feudal modes of life, by making those men landlords who were not chiefs. I do not know that the people will suffer by the change, but there was in the patriarchal authority something venerable and pleasing. Every eye must look with pain on a *Campbell* turning the *Macquarries* at will out of their *sedes avitae*, their hereditary island.

Sir Alexander Dick is the only Scotsman liberal enough not to be angry that I could not find trees, where trees were not. I was much delighted by his kind letter.

I remember Rasay with too much pleasure not to partake of the happiness of any part of that amiable family. Our ramble in the islands hangs upon my imagination, I can hardly help imagining that we shall go again. Pennant seems to have seen a great deal which we did not see: When we travel again let us look better about us.

You have done right in taking your uncle's house. Some change in the form of life, gives from time to time a new epocha of existence. In a new place there is something new to be done, and a different system of thoughts rises in the mind. I wish I could gather currants in your garden. Now fit up a little study, and have your books ready at hand; do not spare a little money, to make your habitation pleasing to yourself.

I have dined lately with poor dear ——. I do not think he goes on well. His table is rather coarse, and he has his children too much about him.[1] But he is a very good man.

Mrs Williams is in the country to try if she can improve her health; she is very ill. Matters have come so about that she is in the country with very good accommodation; but, age and sickness, and pride, have made her so peevish that I was forced to bribe the maid to stay with her, by a secret stipulation of half a crown a week over her wages.

Our club ended its session about six weeks ago. We now only meet to dine once a fortnight. Mr Dunning, the great lawyer, is one of our members. The Thrales are well.

I long to know how the Negro's cause will be decided. What is the opinion of Lord Auchinleck, or Lord Hailes, or Lord Monboddo? I am, dear Sir,

Your most affectionate, &c.

SAM. JOHNSON.

July 22, 1777.

Dr JOHNSON to Mrs BOSWELL.

Madam – Though I am well enough pleased with the taste of sweetmeats, very little of the pleasure which I received at the arrival of your jar of marmalade arose from eating it. I received it as a token of friendship, as a proof of reconciliation, things much sweeter than sweetmeats, and upon

---

1 This very just remark I hope will be constantly held in remembrance by parents, who are in general too apt to indulge their own fond feelings for their children at expense of their friends. The common custom of introducing them after dinner is highly injudicious. It is agreeable enough that they should appear at any other time; but they should not be suffered to poison the moments of festivity by attracting the attention of the company, and in a manner compelling them from politeness to say what they do not think.

this consideration I return you, dear Madam, my sincerest thanks. By having your kindness I think I have a double security for the continuance of Mr Boswell's, which it is not to be expected that any man can long keep, when the influence of a lady so highly and so justly valued operates against him. Mr Boswell will tell you, that I was always faithful to your interest, and always endeavoured to exalt you in his estimation. You must now do the same for me. We must all help one another, and you must now consider me, as, dear Madam,

Your most obliged,

And most humble servant,

SAM. JOHNSON.

July 22, 1777.

Mr BOSWELL to Dr JOHNSON.

Edinburgh, July 22, 1777.

MY DEAR SIR – This is the day on which you were to leave London, and I have been amusing myself in the intervals of my law-drudgery, with figuring you in the Oxford post-coach. I doubt, however, if you have had so merry a journey as you and I had in that vehicle last year, when you made so much sport with Gwyn, the architect. Incidents upon a journey are recollected with peculiar pleasure; they are preserved in brisk spirits, and come up again in our minds, tinctured with that gaiety, or at least that animation with which we first perceived them.

. . .

[I added, that something had occurred, which I was afraid might prevent me from meeting him; and that my wife had been affected with complaints which threatened a consumption, but was now better.]

To JAMES BOSWELL, Esq.

DEAR SIR – Do not disturb yourself about our interviews; I hope we shall have many; nor think it any thing hard or unusual, that your design of meeting me is interrupted. We have both endured greater evils, and have greater evils to expect.

Mrs Boswell's illness makes a more serious distress. Does the blood rise from her lungs or from her stomach? From little vessels broken in the stomach there is no danger. Blood from the lungs is, I believe, always frothy, as mixed with wind. Your physicians know very well what is to be done. The loss of such a lady would, indeed, be very afflictive, and I hope she is in no danger. Take care to keep her mind as easy as is possible.

I have left Langton in London. He has been down with the militia, and is again quiet at home, talking to his little people, as, I suppose, you do sometimes. Make my compliments to Miss Veronica. The rest are too young for ceremony.

I cannot but hope that you have taken your country-house at a very seasonable time, and that it may conduce to restore, or establish Mrs

Boswell's health, as well as provide room and exercise for the young ones. That you and your lady may both be happy, and long enjoy your happiness, is the sincere and earnest wish of, dear Sir,

Your most, &c.

SAM. JOHNSON.

Oxford, Aug. 4, 1777.

Mr BOSWELL to Dr JOHNSON.

[Informing him that my wife had continued to grow better, so that my alarming apprehensions were relieved; and that I hoped to disengage myself from the other embarrassment which had occurred, and therefore requesting to know particularly when he intended to be at Ashbourne.]

To JAMES BOSWELL, Esq.

DEAR SIR – I am this day come to Ashbourne, and have only to tell you, that Dr Taylor says you shall be welcome to him, and you know how welcome you will be to me. Make haste to let me know when you may be expected.

Make my compliments to Mrs Boswell, and tell her, I hope we shall be at variance no more. I am, dear Sir,

Your most humble servant,

SAM. JOHNSON.

August 30, 1777.

To JAMES BOSWELL, Esq.

DEAR SIR – On Saturday I wrote a very short letter, immediately upon my arrival hither, to show you that I am not less desirous of the interview than yourself. Life admits not of delays; when pleasure can be had it is fit to catch it: Every hour takes away part of the things that please us, and perhaps part of our disposition to be pleased. When I came to Lichfield, I found my old friend Harry Jackson dead. It was a loss, and a loss not to be repaired, as he was one of the companions of my childhood. I hope we may long continue to gain friends, but the friends which merit or useful-ness can procure us, are not able to supply the place of old acquaintance, with whom the days of youth may be retraced, and those images revived which gave the earliest delight. If you and I live to be much older, we shall take great delight in talking over the Hebridean Journey.

In the mean time it may not be amiss to contrive some other little adventure, but what it can be I know not; leave it, as Sidney says,

To virtue, fortune, wine, and woman's breast;[1]

for I believe Mrs Boswell must have some part in the consultation.

---

1 [Note in later editions: By an odd mistake, in the first three editions we find a reading in this line to which Dr Johnson would by no means have subscribed, *wine*

One thing you will like. The Doctor, so far as I can judge, is likely to leave us enough to ourselves. He was out to-day before I came down, and, I fancy, will stay out till dinner. I have brought the papers about poor Dodd, to show you, but you will soon have dispatched them.

Before I came away I sent poor Mrs Williams into the country, very ill of a pituitous defluxion, which wastes her gradually away, and which her physician declares himself unable to stop. I supplied her as far as could be desired, with all conveniencies to make her excursion and abode pleasant and useful, but I am afraid she can only linger a short time in a morbid state of weakness and pain.

The Thrales, little and great, are all well, and purpose to go to Brighthelmston at Michaelmas. They will invite me to go with them, and perhaps I may go, but I hardly think I shall like to stay the whole time; but of futurity we know but little.

Mrs Porter is well; but Mrs Aston, one of the ladies at Stowhill, has been struck with a palsy, from which she is not likely ever to recover. How soon may such a stroke fall upon us!

Write to me, and let us know when we may expect you. I am, dear Sir, Your most humble servant,

SAM. JOHNSON.

Ashbourne, Sept. 1, 1777.

Mr BOSWELL to Dr JOHNSON.

Edinburgh, Sept. 9, 1777.

[After informing him that I was to set out next day, in order to meet him at Ashbourne –]

I have a present for you from Lord Hailes; the fifth book of Lactantius, which he has published with Latin notes. He is also to give you a few anecdotes for your 'Life of Thomson', who I find was private tutor to the present Earl of Hadington, Lord Hailes's cousin, a circumstance not mentioned by Dr Murdoch. I have keen expectations of delight from your edition of the English Poets.

I am sorry for poor Mrs Williams's situation. You will, however, have the comfort of reflecting on your kindness to her. Mr Jackson's death, and Mrs Aston's palsy, are gloomy circumstances, Yet surely we should be habituated to the uncertainty of life and health. When my mind is unclouded by melancholy, I consider the temporary distresses of this state of being, as light afflictions, by stretching my mental view into that glorious after existence, when they will appear to be as nothing. But present pleasures and present pains must be felt. I lately read *Rasselas* over again with great satisfaction.

---

having been substituted for *time*. That error probably was a mistake in the transcript of Johnson's original letter. The other deviation in the middle of the line (*virtue* instead of *nature*) must be attributed to his memory having deceived him.]

Since you are desirous to hear about Macquarry's sale I shall inform you particularly. The gentleman who purchased Ulva is Mr Campbell, of Auchnaba: our friend Macquarry was proprietor of two-thirds of it, of which the rent was £156 5s. 1⅛d. This parcel was set up at £4,069 15s. 1d., but it sold for no less than £5,540. The other third of Ulva, with the island of Staffa, belonged to Macquarry of Ormaig. Its rent, including that of Staffa, £83 12s. 2⅔d – set up at £2,178 16s. 4d. – sold for no less than £3,540. The Laird of Col wished to purchase Ulva, but he thought the price too high. There may, indeed, be great improvements made there, both in fishing and agriculture; but the interest of the purchase-money exceeds the rents so very much, that I doubt if the bargain will be profitable. There is an island called Little Colonsay, of £10 yearly rent, which I am informed has belonged to the Macquarrys of Ulva for many ages, but which was lately claimed by the Presbyterian Synod of Argyll, in consequence of a grant made to them by Queen Anne. It is believed that their claim will be dismissed, and that Little Colonsay will also be sold for the advantage of Macquarry's creditors. What think you of purchasing this island, and endowing a school or college there, the master to be a clergyman of the Church of England? How venerable would such an institution make the name of Dr Samuel Johnson in the Hebrides! I have, like yourself, a wonderful pleasure in recollecting our travels in those islands. The pleasure is, I think greater than it reasonably should be, considering that we had not much either of beauty and elegance to charm our imaginations, or of rude novelty to astonish. Let us, by all means, have another expedition. I shrink a little from our scheme of going up the Baltic.[1] I am sorry you have already been in Wales, for I wish to see it. Shall we go to Ireland, of which I have seen but little? We shall try to strike out a plan when we are at Ashbourne. I am ever

Your most faithful humble servant,

JAMES BOSWELL.

1 It appears that Johnson, now in his sixty-eighth year, was seriously inclined to realise the project of our going up the Baltic, which I had started when we were in the isle of Sky; for he thus writes to Mrs Thrale; *Letters*, Vol. I. page 366:

Ashbourne, Sept. 13, 1777.

Boswell, I believe, is coming. He talks of being here to-day: I shall be glad to see him; but he shrinks from the Baltic expedition, which, I think, is the best scheme in our power: what we shall substitute I know not. He wants to see Wales; but, except the woods of *Bachycraigh*, what is there in Wales that can fill the hunger of ignorance, or quench the thirst of curiosity? We may, perhaps, form some scheme or other; but, in the phrase of *Hockley in the Hole*, it is pity he has not a *better bottom*.

Such an ardour of mind, and vigour of enterprise, is admirable at any age; but more particularly so at the advanced period at which Johnson was then arrived. I am sorry now that I did not insist on our executing that scheme. Besides the other objects of curiosity and observation, to have seen my illustrious friend received, as he probably would have been, by a Prince so eminently distinguished for his variety of talents and

To JAMES BOSWELL, Esq.

DEAR SIR – I write to be left at Carlisle, as you direct me, but you cannot have it. Your letter, dated Sept. 6, was not at this place till this day, Thursday, Sept. 11; and I hope you will be here before this is at Carlisle.[1] However, what you have not going you may have returning; and as I believe I shall not love you less after our interview, it will then be as true as it is now, that I set a very high value upon your friendship, and count your kindness as one of the chief felicities of my life. Do not fancy that an intermission of writing is a decay of kindness. No man is always in a disposition to write; nor has any man at all times something to say.

That distrust which intrudes so often on your mind is a mode of melancholy, which, if it be the business of a wise man to be happy, it is foolish to indulge; and if it be a duty to preserve our faculties entire for their proper use, it is criminal. Suspicion is very often an useless pain. From that and all other pains, I wish you free and safe; for I am, dear Sir,

Most affectionately yours,

SAM. JOHNSON.

Ashbourne, Sept. 11, 1777.

On Sunday evening, September 14, I arrived at Ashbourne, and drove directly up to Dr Taylor's door. Dr Johnson and he appeared before I had got out of the post-chaise, and welcomed me cordially.

I told them that I had travelled all the preceding night, and gone to bed at Leek, in Staffordshire; and that when I rose to go to church in the afternoon, I was informed there had been an earthquake, of which, it seems, the shock had been felt, in some degree, at Ashbourne. JOHNSON. 'Sir, it will be much exaggerated in popular talk: for, in the first place, the common people do not accurately adapt their thoughts to the objects; nor, secondly, do they accurately adapt their words to their thoughts: they do not mean to lie; but, taking no pains to be exact, they give you very false accounts. A great part of their language is proverbial. If any thing rocks at all, they say *it rocks like a cradle*; and in this way they go on.'

The subject of grief for the loss of relations and friends being introduced, I observed that it was strange to consider how soon it in general wears away. Dr Taylor mentioned a gentleman of the neighbourhood as the only instance he had ever known of a person who had endeavoured to *retain* grief. He told Dr Taylor, that after his lady's death, which affected him deeply, he *resolved* that the grief, which he cherished with a kind of sacred fondness, should be lasting;

---

acquisitions as the King of Sweden; and by the Empress of Russia. whose extraordinary abilities, information, and magnanimity, astonish the world, would have afforded a noble subject for contemplation and record. This reflection may possibly be thought too visionary by the more sedate and cold-blooded part of my readers; yet I own, I frequently indulge it with an earnest, unavailing regret.

1 It so happened. The letter was forwarded to my house at Edinburgh.

but that he found he could not keep it long. JOHNSON. 'All grief for what cannot in the course of nature be helped, soon wears away; in some sooner, indeed, in some later; but it never continues very long, unless where there is madness, such as will make a man have pride so fixed in his mind, as to imagine himself a King; or any other passion in an unreasonable way: for all unnecessary grief is unwise, and therefore will not be long retained by a sound mind. If, indeed the cause of our grief is occasioned by our own misconduct, if grief is mingled with remorse of conscience, it should be lasting.' BOSWELL. 'But, Sir, we do not approve of a man who very soon forgets the loss of a wife or a friend.' JOHNSON. 'Sir we disapprove of him, not because he soon forgets his grief, for the sooner it is forgotten the better, but because we suppose, that if he forgets his wife or his friend soon, he has not had much affection for them.'

I was somewhat disappointed in finding that the edition of the English Poets, for which he was to write Prefaces and Lives, was not an undertaking directed by him; but that he was to furnish a Preface and Life to any poet the booksellers pleased. I asked him if he would do this to any dunce's works, if they should ask him. JOHNSON. 'Yes, Sir; and *say* he was a dunce.' My friend seemed now not much to relish talking of this edition.

On Monday, September 15, Dr Johnson observed, that every body commended such parts of his *Journey to the Western Islands*, as were in their own way. 'For instance (said he), Mr Jackson (the all-knowing) told me, there was more good sense upon trade in it, than he should hear in the House of Commons in a year, except from Burke. Jones commended the part which treats of language; Burke that which describes the inhabitants of mountainous countries.'

After breakfast, Johnson carried me to see the garden belonging to the school of Ashbourne, which is very prettily formed upon a bank, rising gradually behind the house. The Reverend Mr Langley, the head master, accompanied us.

While we sat basking in the sun upon a seat here, I introduced a common subject of complaint, the very small salaries which many curates have, and I maintained, 'that no man should be invested with the character of a clergyman, unless he has a security for such an income as will enable him to appear respectable; that, therefore, a clergyman should not be allowed to have a curate, unless he gives him a hundred pounds a year; if he cannot do that, let him perform the duty himself.' JOHNSON. 'To be sure, Sir, it is wrong that any clergyman should be without a reasonable income; but as the church revenues were sadly diminished at the Reformation, the clergy who have livings cannot afford, in many instances, to give good salaries to curates, without leaving themselves too little; and, if no curate were to be permitted, unless he had a hundred pounds a year, their number would be very small, which would be a disadvantage, as then there would not be such choice in the nursery for the church, curates being candidates for the higher ecclesiastical offices, according to their merit and good behaviour.' He explained the system of the English Hierarchy exceedingly well. 'It is not thought fit (said he) to trust a man with the care of a parish, till he has given proof as a curate that he shall deserve such a trust.' This is an excellent *theory*; and if the *practice* were according to it, the

Church of England would be admirable indeed. However, as I have heard Dr Johnson observe as to the Universities, bad practice does not infer that the *constitution* is bad.

We had with us at dinner several of Dr Taylor's neighbours, good civil gentlemen, who seemed to understand Dr Johnson very well, and not to consider him in the light that a certain person did, who being struck, or rather stunned by his voice and manner, when he was afterwards asked what he thought of him, answered, 'He's a tremendous companion.'

Johnson told me, that 'Taylor was a very sensible acute man, and had a strong mind; that he had great activity in some respects, and yet such a sort of indolence, that if you should put a pebble upon his chimney-piece, you would find it there, in the same state, a year afterwards.'

And here is the proper place to give an account of Johnson's humane and zealous interference in behalf of the Reverend Dr William Dodd, formerly Prebendary of Brecon, and chaplain in ordinary to his Majesty; celebrated as a very popular preacher, an encourager of charitable institutions, and author of a variety of works, chiefly theological. Having unhappily contracted expensive habits of living, partly occasioned by licentiousness of manners, he in an evil hour, when pressed by want of money, and dreading exposure of his circumstances, forged a bond of which he attempted to avail himself to support his credit, flattering himself with hopes that he might be able to repay its amount without being detected. The person, whose name he thus rashly and criminally presumed to falsify, was the Earl of Chesterfield, to whom he had been tutor, and who, he perhaps, in the warmth of his feelings, flattered himself would have[a] paid the money in case of an alarm being taken, rather than suffer him to fall a victim to the dreadful consequences of violating the law against forgery, the most dangerous crime in a commercial country; but the unfortunate divine had the mortification to find that he was mistaken. His noble pupil appeared against him, and he was capitally convicted.

Johnson told me that Dr Dodd was very little acquainted with him, having been but once in his company, many years previous to this period (which was precisely the state of my own acquaintance with Dodd); but in his distress he bethought himself of Johnson's persuasive power of writing, if haply it might avail to obtain for him the royal mercy. He did not apply to him directly, but, extraordinary as it may seem, through the late Countess of Harrington, who wrote a letter to Johnson, asking him to employ his pen in favour of Dodd. Mr Allen, the printer, who was Johnson's landlord and next neighbour in Bolt-court, and for whom he had much kindness, was one of Dodd's friends, of whom, to the credit of humanity be it recorded, that he had many who did not desert him, even after his infringement of the law had reduced him to the state of a man under sentence of death. Mr Allen told me that he carried Lady Harrington's letter to Johnson, that Johnson read it walking up and down his chamber, and seemed much agitated, after which he said, 'I will do what I can'; and certainly he did make extraordinary exertions.

[a] After 'have', read 'generously'.

He this evening, as he had obligingly promised in one of his letters, put into my hands the whole series of his writings upon this melancholy occasion, and I shall present my readers with the abstract which I made from the collection; in doing which I studied to avoid copying what had appeared in print, and now make part of the edition of *Johnson's Works*, published by the Booksellers of London, but taking care to mark Johnson's variations in some of the pieces there exhibited.

Dr Johnson wrote in the first place, Dr Dodd's 'Speech to the Recorder of London', at the Old-Bailey, when sentence of death was about to be pronounced upon him.

He wrote also 'The Convict's Address to his unhappy Brethren', a sermon delivered by Dr Dodd, in the chapel of Newgate. According to Johnson's manuscript it began thus after the text, *What shall I do to be saved?* – 'These were the words with which the keeper, to whose custody Paul and Silas were committed by their prosecutors, addressed his prisoners, when he saw them freed from their bonds by the perceptible agency of divine favour, and was, therefore, irresistibly convinced that they were not offenders against the laws, but martyrs to the truth.'

Dr Johnson was so good as to mark for me with his own hand, on a copy of this sermon which is now in my possession, such passages as were added by Dr Dodd. They are not many: Whoever will take the trouble to look at the printed copy and attend to what I mention, will be satisfied of this.

There is a short introduction by Dr Dodd, and he also inserted this sentence, 'You see with what confusion and dishonour I now stand before you; – no more in the pulpit of instruction, but on this humble seat with yourselves.' The *notes* are entirely Dodd's own, and Johnson's writing ends at the words, 'the thief whom he pardoned on the cross.' What follows was supplied by Dr Dodd himself.

The other pieces written by Johnson in the above mentioned collection, are two letters, one to the Lord Chancellor Bathurst (not Lord North, as is erroneously supposed) and one to Lord Mansfield; – A Petition from Dr Dodd to the King; – A Petition from Mrs Dodd to the Queen; – Observations of some length inserted in the newspapers, on occasion of Earl Percy's having presented to his Majesty a petition for mercy to Dodd, signed by twenty thousand people, but all in vain. He told me that he had also written a petition from the city of London; 'but (said he, with a significant smile) they *mended* it.'[a]

The last of these articles which Johnson wrote is 'Dr Dodd's last solemn Declaration', which he left with the sheriff at the place of execution. Here also my friend marked the variations on a copy of that piece now in my possession. Dodd inserted, 'I never knew or attended to the calls of frugality, or the needful minuteness of painful economy'; and in the next sentence he introduced the words which I distinguish by *Italics*, 'My life for some *few unhappy* years past has been *dreadfully erroneous*.' Johnson's expression was *hypocritical*; but his remark on the margin is 'With this he said he could not charge himself.'

[a] [See note on p. 919.]

Having thus authentically settled what part of the 'Occasional Papers', concerning Dr Dodd's miserable situation, came from the pen of Johnson, I shall proceed to present my readers with my record of the unpublished writings relating to that extraordinary and interesting matter.

I found a letter to Dr Johnson from Dr Dodd, May 23, 1777, in which 'The Convict's Address' seems clearly to be meant:

> I am so penetrated, my ever dear Sir, with a sense of your extreme benevolence towards me, that I cannot find words equal to the sentiments of my heart. . . .
>
> You are too conversant in the world to need the slightest hint from me, of what infinite utility the Speech[1] on the awful day has been to me. I experience, every hour, some good effect from it. I am sure that effects still more salutary and important, must follow from *your kind and intended favour*. I will labour – GOD being my helper – to do justice to it from the pulpit. I am sure, had I your sentiments constantly to deliver from thence, in all their mighty force and power, not a soul could he left unconvinced and unpersuaded. . . .

He added:

> May GOD ALMIGHTY bless and reward, with his choicest comforts, your philanthropic actions, and enable me at all times to express what I feel of the high and uncommon obligations which I owe to the *first man* in our times.

On Sunday, June 22, he writes, begging Dr Johnson's assistance in framing a supplicatory letter to his Majesty:

> If his Majesty could be moved of his royal clemency to spare me and my family the horrors and ignominy of a *public death*, which the *public* itself is solicitous to wave, and to grant me in some silent distant corner of the globe, to pass the remainder of my days in penitence and prayer, I would bless his clemency and be humbled.

This letter was brought to Dr Johnson when in church. He stooped down and read it, and wrote, when he went home, the following letter for Dr Dodd to the King:

> SIR – May it not offend your Majesty, that the most miserable of men applies himself to your clemency, as his last hope and his last refuge; that your mercy is most earnestly and humbly implored by a clergyman, whom your Laws and Judges have condemned to the horror and ignominy of a public execution.
>
> I confess the crime, and own the enormity of its consequences, and the danger of its example. Nor have I the confidence to petition for impunity; but humbly hope, that public security may be established, without the

1 His Speech at the Old-Bailey, when found guilty.

spectacle of a clergyman dragged through the streets, to a death of infamy, amidst the derision of the profligate and profane; and that justice may be satisfied with irrevocable exile, perpetual disgrace, and hopeless penury.

My life, Sir, has not been useless to mankind. I have benefited many. But my offences against GOD are numberless, and I have had little time for repentance. Preserve me, Sir, by your prerogative of mercy, from the necessity of appearing unprepared at that tribunal before which Kings and subjects must stand at last together. Permit me to hide my guilt in some obscure corner of a foreign country, where, if I can ever attain confidence to hope that my prayers will be heard, they shall be poured with all the fervour of gratitude for the life and happiness of your Majesty. I am, Sir,

Your Majesty's, &c.

Subjoined to it was written as follows:

To Dr DODD.

SIR — I most seriously enjoin you not to let it be at all known that I have written this letter, and to return the copy to Mr Allen in a cover to me. I hope I need not tell you, that I wish it success. — But do not indulge hope. — Tell nobody.

It happened luckily that Mr Allen was pitched on to assist in this melancholy office, for he was a great friend of Mr Akerman, the keeper of Newgate. Dr Johnson never went to see Dr Dodd. He said to me, it would have done *him* more harm, than good to Dodd, who once expressed a desire to see him, but not earnestly.

Dr Johnson, on the 20th of June, wrote the following letter:

To the Right Honourable CHARLES JENKINSON.

SIR — Since the conviction and condemnation of Dr Dodd, I have had, by the intervention of a friend, some intercourse with him, and I am sure I shall lose nothing in your opinion by tenderness and commiseration. Whatever be the crime, it is not easy to have any knowledge of the delinquent without a wish that his life may be spared, at least when no life has been taken away by him. I will, therefore, take the liberty of suggesting some reasons for which I wish this unhappy being to escape the utmost rigour of his sentence.

He is, so far as I can recollect, the first clergyman of our church who has suffered public execution for immorality; and I know not whether it would not be more for the interest of religion to bury such an offender in the obscurity of perpetual exile, than to expose him in a cart, and on the gallows, to all who for any reason are enemies to the clergy.

The supreme power has, in all ages, paid some attention to the voice of the people; and that voice does not least deserve to be heard, when it calls out for mercy. There is now a very general desire that Dodd's life should be spared. More is not wished; and, perhaps, this is not too much to be granted.

If you, Sir, have any opportunity of enforcing these reasons; you may, perhaps, think them worthy of consideration: but whatever you determine, I most respectfully intreat that you will be pleased to pardon for this intrusion, Sir,

Your most obedient

And most humble servant,

SAM. JOHNSON.

It has been confidently circulated, with invidious remarks, that to this letter no attention whatever was paid by Mr Jenkinson, now Lord Hawkesbury;[a] and that he did not even deign to show the common civility of owning the receipt of it. I could not but wonder at such conduct in the noble Lord, whose own character and just elevation in life, I thought, must have impressed him with all due regard for great abilities and attainments. As the story had been much talked of, and apparently from good authority, I could not but have animadverted upon it in this work, had it been as was alleged; but from my earnest love of truth, and having found reason to think that there might be a mistake, I presumed to write to his Lordship requesting an explanation; and it is with the sincerest pleasure that I am enabled to assure the world, that there is no foundation for it, the fact being, that owing to some neglect, or accident, Johnson's letter never came to Lord Hawkesbury's hands. I should have thought it strange indeed, if that noble Lord had undervalued my illustrious friend; but instead of this being the case, his Lordship, in the very polite answer with which he was pleased immediately to honour me, thus expresses himself: 'I have always respected the memory of Dr Johnson, and admire his writings; and I frequently read many parts of them with pleasure and great improvement.'

All applications for the Royal Mercy having failed, Dr Dodd prepared himself for death; and, with a warmth of gratitude, wrote to Dr Johnson as follows:

June 25. *Midnight.*

ACCEPT, thou *great* and *good* heart, my earnest and fervent thanks and prayers for all thy benevolent and kind efforts in my behalf. – Oh! Dr Johnson! as I sought your knowledge at an early hour in life, would to heaven I had cultivated the love and acquaintance of so excellent a man! – I pray GOD most sincerely to bless you with the highest transports – the infelt satisfaction of *humane* and benevolent exertions! – And admitted, as I trust I shall be, to the realms of bliss before you, I shall hail *your* arrival there with transport, and rejoice to acknowledge that you was my Comforter, my Advocate, and my *Friend*! GOD *be ever* with *you*!

Dr Johnson lastly wrote to Dr Dodd this solemn and soothing letter:

[a] *Third Edition.* Add: 'afterwards Earl of Liverpool'.

To the Reverend Dr DODD.

DEAR SIR – That which is appointed to all men is now coming upon you. Outward circumstances, the eyes and the thoughts of men, are below the notice of an immortal being about to stand the trial for eternity, before the Supreme Judge of heaven and earth. Be comforted: your crime, morally or religiously considered, has no very deep dye of turpitude. It corrupted no man's principles; it attacked no man's life. It involved only a temporary and reparable injury. Of this, and of all other sins, you are earnestly to repent; and may GOD, who knoweth our frailty and desireth not our death, accept your repentance, for the sake of his Son JESUS CHRIST our Lord.

In requital of those well-intended offices which you are pleased so emphatically to acknowledge, let me beg that you make in your devotions one petition for my eternal welfare. I am, dear Sir,

Your affectionate servant,

SAM. JOHNSON.

June 26, 1777.

Under the copy of this letter I found written, in Johnson's own hand, 'Next day, June 27, he was executed.'

To conclude this interesting episode with an useful application, let us now attend to the reflections of Johnson at the end of the 'Occasional Papers', concerning the unfortunate Dr Dodd. – 'Such were the last thoughts of a man whom we have seen exulting in popularity, and sunk in shame. For his reputation, which no man can give to himself, those who conferred it are to answer. Of his public ministry the means of judging were sufficiently attainable. He must be allowed to preach well, whose sermons strike his audience with forcible conviction. Of his life, those who thought it consistent with his doctrine did not originally form false notions. He was at first what he endeavoured to make others; but the world broke down his resolution, and he in time ceased to exemplify his own instructions.

'Let those who are tempted to his faults, tremble at his punishment; and those whom he impressed from the pulpit with religious sentiments, endeavour to confirm them by considering the regret and self-abhorrence with which he reviewed in prison his deviations from rectitude.'

Johnson gave us this evening, in his happy discriminating manner, a portrait of the late Mr Fitzherbert, of Derbyshire. 'There was (said he) no sparkle, no brilliancy in Fitzherbert; but I never knew a man who was so generally acceptable. He made every body quite easy, overpowered nobody by the superiority of his talents, made no man think worse of himself by being his rival, seemed always to listen, did not oblige you to hear much from him, and did not oppose what you said. Every body liked him; but he had no friend, as I understand the word, nobody with whom he exchanged intimate thoughts. People were willing to think well of every thing about him. A gentleman was making an affected rant, as many people do, of great feelings about "his dear son", who was at school near London, how anxious he was lest he might be ill, and what he would give to see him. "Can't you (said Fitzherbert), take a post-chaise and go to him?" This, to be sure, *finished* the affected man, but there was not much in it.[a] However, this was circulated as wit for a whole winter, and I believe part of a summer too; a proof that he was no very witty man. He was an instance of the truth of the observation, that a man will please more upon the whole by negative qualities than by positive; by never offending, than by giving a great deal of delight. In the first place, men hate more steadily than they love; and if I have said something to hurt a man once, I shall not get the better of this by saying many things to please him.'

Tuesday, September 16, Dr Johnson having mentioned to me the extraordinary size and price of some cattle reared by Dr Taylor, I rode out with our host, surveyed his farm, and was shown one cow which he had sold for a hundred and twenty guineas, and another for which he had been offered a hundred and thirty. Taylor thus described to me his old schoolfellow and friend, Johnson: 'He is a man of a very clear head, great power of words, and a very gay imagination; but there is no disputing with him. He will not hear you, and having a louder voice than you, must roar you down.'

In the afternoon I tried to get Dr Johnson to like the Poems of Mr Hamilton of Bangour, which I had brought with me: I had been much pleased with them at a very early age; the impression still remained on my mind: it was confirmed by the opinion of my friend the Honourable Andrew Erskine, himself both a good poet and a good critic, who thought Hamilton as true a poet as ever wrote, and that his not having fame was unaccountable. Johnson upon repeated occasions, while I was at Ashbourne, talked slightingly of Hamilton. He said there was no power of thinking in his verses, nothing that strikes one, nothing better than what you generally find in magazines; and that the highest praise they deserved was, that they were very well for a gentleman to hand about among his friends. He said the imitation of *Ne sit ancillae tibi amor &c.* was too solemn; he read part of it at the beginning. He read the beautiful pathetic song, 'Ah the poor shepherd's mournful fate', and did not seem to give attention to what I had been used to think tender elegant strains, but laughed at the rhyme, in Scotch pronunciation, *wishes* and *blushes*, reading *wushes* – and there he stopped. He owned that the epitaph on Lord Newhall was pretty well done. He read the 'Inscription in a Summer-house', and a little of the imitations of Horace's Epistles; but said, he found nothing to make him desire to read on. When I urged that there were some good poetical passages in the book,

---

[a] Add this note: Dr Gisborne, Physician to his Majesty's Household, has obligingly communicated to me a fuller account of this story than had reached Dr Johnson. The affected Gentleman was the late John Gilbert Cooper, Esq., author of a Life of Socrates, and of some poems in Dodsley's collection. Mr Fitzherbert found him one morning, apparently, in such violent agitation, on account of the indisposition of his son, as to seem beyond the power of comfort. At length, however, he exclaimed, 'I'll write an Elegy.' Mr Fitzherbert being satisfied, by this, of the sincerity of his emotions, slyly said, 'Had not you better take a post-chaise and go and see him?' It was the shrewdness of the insinuation which made the story be circulated.

'Where (said he) will you find so large a collection without some?' I thought the description of Winter might obtain his approbation:

> See Winter, from the frozen north,
> Drives his iron chariot forth!
> His grisly hand in icy chains
> Fair Tweeda's silver flood constrains, &c.

He asked why an '*iron* chariot'; and said 'icy chains' was an old image. I was struck with the uncertainty of taste, and somewhat sorry that a poet whom I had long read with fondness, was not approved by Dr Johnson. I comforted myself with thinking that the beauties were too delicate for his robust perceptions. Garrick maintained that he had not a taste for the finest product-ions of genius; but I was sensible, that when he took the trouble to analyse critically, he generally convinced us that he was right.

In the evening, the Reverend Mr Seward, of Lichfield, who was passing through Ashbourne in his way home, drank tea with us. Johnson described him thus: 'Sir, his ambition is to be a fine talker; so he goes to Buxton, and such places, where he may find companies to listen to him. And, Sir, he is a valetudinarian, one of those who are always mending themselves. I do not know a more disagreeable character than a valetudinarian, who thinks he may do any thing that is for his ease, and indulges himself in the grossest freedoms: Sir, he brings himself to the state of a hog in a stye.'

Dr Taylor's nose happening to bleed, he said, it was because he had omitted to have himself blooded four days after a quarter of a year's interval. Dr Johnson, who was a great dabbler in physic, disapproved much of periodical bleeding. 'For (said he) you accustom yourself to an evacuation which Nature cannot perform of herself, and therefore she cannot help you, should you, from forgetfulness or any other cause, omit it; so you may be suddenly suffocated. You may accustom yourself to other periodical evacuations, because should you omit them, Nature can supply the omission; but Nature cannot open a vein to blood you.' – 'I do not like to take an emetic (said Taylor), for fear of breaking some small vessels.' – 'Poh! (said Johnson) if you have so many things that will break, you had better break your neck at once, and there's an end on't. You will break no small vessels.' (blowing with high derision).

I mentioned to Dr Johnson, that David Hume's persisting in his infidelity, when he was dying, shocked me much. JOHNSON. 'Why should it shock you, Sir? Hume owned he had never read the New Testament with attention. Here then was a man who had been at no pains to inquire into the truth of religion, and had continually turned his mind the other way. It was not to be expected that the prospect of death would alter his way of thinking, unless GOD should send an angel to set him right.' I said, I had reason to believe that the thought of annihilation gave Hume no pain. JOHNSON. 'It was not so, Sir. He had a vanity in being thought easy. It is more probable that he should assume an appearance of ease, than that so very improbable a thing should be, as a man not afraid of going (as, in spite of his delusive theory, he cannot be sure but he may go), into an unknown state, and not being uneasy at leaving all he knew.

And you are to consider, that upon his own principle of annihilation he had no motive to speak the truth.' The horror of death which I had always observed in Dr Johnson, appeared strong to-night. I ventured to tell him, that I had been, for moments of my life, not afraid of death; therefore I could suppose another man in that state of mind for a considerable space of time. He said, 'he never had a moment in which death was not terrible to him.' He added, that it had been observed, that almost no man dies in public, but with apparent resolution; from that desire of praise which never quits us. I said, Dr Dodd seemed to be willing to die, and full of hopes of happiness. 'Sir (said he), Dr Dodd would have given both his hands and both his legs to have lived. The better a man is, the more afraid is he of death, having a clearer view of infinite purity.' He owned, that our being in an unhappy uncertainty as to our salvation, was mysterious; and said, 'Ah! we must wait till we are in another state of being, to have many things explained to us.' Even the powerful mind of Johnson seemed foiled by futurity. But I thought, that the gloom of uncertainty in solemn religious speculation, being mingled with hope, was yet more consolatory than the emptiness of infidelity. A man can live in thick air, but perishes in an exhausted receiver.

Dr Johnson was much pleased with a remark which I told him was made to me by General Paoli: 'That it is impossible not to be afraid of death; and that those who at the time of dying are not afraid, are not thinking of death, but of applause, or something else, which keeps death out of their sight: so that all men are equally afraid of death when they see it; only some have a power of turning their sight away from it better than others.'

On Wednesday, September 17, Dr Butter, physician at Derby, drank tea with us; and it was settled that Dr Johnson and I should go on Friday and dine with him. Johnson said, 'I'm glad of this.' He seemed weary of the uniformity of life at Dr Taylor's.

Talking of biography, I said, in writing a life a man's peculiarities should be mentioned, because they mark his character. JOHNSON. 'Sir, there is no doubt as to peculiarities: the question is, whether a man's vices should be mentioned; for instance, whether it should be mentioned that Addison and Parnel drank too freely; for people will probably more easily indulge in drinking from knowing this, so that more ill may be done by the example, than good by telling the whole truth.' Here was an instance of his varying from himself in talk; for when Lord Hailes and he sat one morning calmly conversing in my house at Edinburgh, I well remember that Dr Johnson maintained, that 'if a man is to write *A Panegyric*, he may keep vices out of sight; but if he professes to write *A Life*, he must represent it really as it was': and when I objected to the danger of telling that Parnel drank to excess, he said, that 'it would produce an instructive caution to avoid drinking, when it was seen, that even the learning and genius of Parnel could be debased by it.' And in the Hebrides he maintained, as appears from my *Journal*,[1] that a man's intimate friend should mention his faults, if he writes his life.

---

1 *Journal of a Tour to the Hebrides*, 3d edit. p. 240.

He had this evening, partly, I suppose, from the spirit of contradiction to his Whig friend, a violent argument with Dr Taylor, as to the inclinations of the people of England at this time towards the Royal Family of Stuart. He grew so outrageous as to say, 'that if England were fairly polled, the present King would be sent away to-night, and his adherents hanged to-morrow. Taylor, who was as violent a Whig as Johnson was a Tory, was roused by this to a pitch of bellowing. He denied, loudly, what Johnson said; and maintained, that there was an abhorrence against the Stuart family, though he admitted that the people were not much attached to the present King.[1] JOHNSON. 'Sir, the state of the country is this: the people knowing it to be agreed on all hands that this King has not the hereditary right to the crown, and there being no hope that he who has it can be restored, have grown cold and indifferent upon the subject of loyalty, and have no warm attachment to any King. They would not, therefore, risk any thing to restore the exiled family. They would not give twenty shillings a piece to bring it about. But, if a mere vote could do it, there would be twenty to one; at least, there would be a very great majority of voices for it. For, Sir, you are to consider, that all those who think a King has a right to his crown, as a man has to his estate, which is the just opinion, would be for restoring the King who certainly has the hereditary right, could he be trusted with it; in which there would be no danger now, when laws and every thing else are so much advanced; and every King will govern by the laws. And you must also consider, Sir, that there is nothing on the other side to oppose to this; for it is not alleged by any one that the present family has any inherent right: so that the Whigs could not have a contest between two rights.'

Dr Taylor admitted, that if the question as to hereditary right were to be tried by a poll of the people of England, to be sure the abstract doctrine would be given in favour of the family of Stuart; but he said, the conduct of that family, which occasioned their expulsion, was so fresh in the minds of the people, that they would not vote for a restoration. Dr Johnson, I think, was contented with the admission as to the hereditary right, leaving the original point in dispute, *viz.* what the people upon the whole would do, taking in right and affection; for he said, people were afraid of a change, even when they thought it right. Dr Taylor said something of the slight foundation of the hereditary right of the house of Stuart. 'Sir (said Johnson), the house of Stuart succeeded to the full right of both the houses of York and Lancaster, whose common source had the undisputed right. A right to a throne is like a right to any thing else. Possession is sufficient, where no better right can be shown. This was the case with the Royal Family of England, as it is now with the King of France: for as to the first beginning of the right, we are in the dark.'

Thursday, September 18. Last night Dr Johnson had proposed that the crystal lustre, or chandelier, in Dr Taylor's large room, should be lighted up

---

1 Dr Taylor was very ready to make this admission, because the party with which he was connected was not in power. There was then some truth in it, owing to the pertinacity of factious clamour. Had he lived till now, it would have been impossible for him to deny that his Majesty possesses the warmest affection of his people.

some time or other. Taylor said, it should be lighted up next night. 'That will do very well (said I), for it is Dr Johnson's birth-day.' When we were in the Isle of Sky, Johnson had desired me not to mention his birth-day. He did not seem pleased at this time that I mentioned it, and said (somewhat sternly) 'he would *not* have the lustre lighted the next night.'

Some ladies who had been present yesterday when I mentioned his birth-day, came to dinner to-day, and plagued him unintentionally, by wishing him joy. I know not why he disliked having his birth-day mentioned, unless it were that it reminded him of his approaching nearer to death, of which he had a constant dread.

I mentioned to him a friend of mine who was formerly gloomy from low spirits, and much distressed by the fear of death, but was now uniformly placid, and contemplated his dissolution without any perturbation. 'Sir (said Johnson), this is only a disordered imagination taking a different turn.'

We talked of a collection being made of all the English Poets who had published a volume of poems. Johnson told me, 'that a Mr Coxeter, whom he knew, had gone the greatest length towards this; having collected, I think, about five hundred volumes of poets whose works were little known, but that upon his death Tom Osborne bought them, and they were dispersed, which he thought a pity, as it was curious to see any series complete; and in every volume of poems something good may be found.'

He observed, that a gentleman of eminence in literature had got into a bad style of poetry of late. 'He puts (said he) a very common thing in a strange dress till he does not know it himself and thinks other people do not know it.' BOSWELL. 'That is owing to his being so much versant in old English Poetry.' JOHNSON. 'What is that to the purpose, Sir? If I say a man is drunk and you tell me it is owing to his taking much drink, the matter is not mended. No, Sir, —— has taken to an odd mode. For example; he'd write thus:

> Hermit hoar, in solemn cell,
>   Wearing out life's evening gray.

Gray evening is common enough; but *evening gray* he'd think fine. – Stay; – we'll make out the stanza:

> Hermit hoar, in solemn cell,
>   Wearing out life's evening gray;
> Smite thy bosom, sage, and tell,
>   What is bliss? and which the way?'

BOSWELL. 'But why smite his bosom, Sir?' JOHNSON. 'Why, to show he was in earnest' (smiling). – He at an after period added the following stanza:

> Thus I spoke; and speaking sigh'd;
>   – Scarce repress'd the starting tear; –
> When the smiling sage reply'd –
>   – Come, my lad, and drink some beer.'[1]

---

1 As some of my readers may be gratified by reading the precise progress of this little

I cannot help thinking the first stanza very good solemn poetry, as also the three first lines of the second. Its last line is an excellent burlesque surprise on gloomy sentimental enquirers. And, perhaps, the advice is as good as can be given to a low-spirited dissatisfied being. – 'Don't trouble your head with sickly thinking: take a cup, and be merry.'

Friday, September 19, after breakfast, Dr Johnson and I set out in Dr Taylor's chaise to go to Derby. The day was fine, and we resolved to go by Keddlestone, the seat of Lord Scarsdale, that I might see his Lordship's fine house. I was struck with the magnificence of the building; and the extensive park, with the finest verdure, covered with deer, and cattle, and sheep, delighted me. The number of old oaks, of an immense size, filled me with a sort of respectful admiration: for one of them sixty pounds was offered. The excellent smooth gravel roads; the large piece of water formed by his Lordship from some small brooks, with a handsome barge upon it; the venerable Gothic church, now the family chapel, just by the house; in short, the grand group of objects agitated and distended my mind in a most agreeable manner. 'One should think (said I) that the proprietor of all this *must* be happy.' – 'Nay, Sir (said Johnson), all this excludes but one evil – poverty.'[1]

Our names were sent up, and a well-drest elderly housekeeper, a most distinct articulator, showed us the house; which I need not describe, as it is published in Adam's *Works in Architecture*. Dr Johnson thought better of it to-day than when he saw it before; for the other night he attacked it violently, saying, 'It would do excellently for a town hall. The large room with the pillars (said he) would do for the Judges to sit in at the assizes; the circular room for a

---

composition, I shall insert it from my notes. 'When Dr Johnson and I were sitting *tête à tête* at the Mitre tavern, May 9, 1778, he said, '*Where* is bliss', would be better. He then added a ludicrous stanza, but would not repeat it, lest I should take it down. It was somewhat as follows; the last line I am sure I remember:

> While I thus . . . . cried,
> . . . . seer;
> The hoary . . . . reply'd,
>   Come, my lad, and drink some beer.

'In Spring, 1779, when in better humour, he made the second stanza, as in the text. There was only one variation afterwards made on my suggestion, which was changing *hoary* in the third line to *smiling*, both to avoid a sameness with the epithet in the first *lisse*, and to describe the hermit in his pleasantry. He was then very well pleased that I should preserve it.'

1 When I mentioned Dr Johnson's remark to a lady of admirable good sense and quickness of understanding, she observed, 'It is true, all this excludes only one evil; but how much good does it let in?'[a]

[a] To the note add: To this observation much praise has been justly given. Let me then now do myself the honour to mention that the lady who made it was the late Margaret Montgomerie, my very valuable wife, and the very affectionate mother of my children, who, if they inherit her good qualities, will have no reason to complain of their lot. *Dos magna parentum virtus.*

jury chamber; and the rooms above for prisoners.' Still he thought the large room ill lighted, and of no use but for dancing in; and the bed-chambers but indifferent rooms; and that the immense sum which it cost was injudiciously laid out. Dr Taylor had put him in mind of his *appearing* pleased with the house. 'But (said he) that was when Lord Scarsdale was present. Politeness obliges us to appear pleased with a man's works when he is present. No man will be so ill bred as to question you. You may therefore pay compliments without saying what is not true. I should say to Lord Scarsdale of his large room, "My Lord, this is the most *costly* room that I ever saw"; which is true.'

Dr Manningham, physician in London, who was visiting at Lord Scarsdale's, accompanied us through many of the rooms, and soon afterwards my Lord himself, to whom Dr Johnson was known, appeared, and did the honours of the house. We talked of Mr Langton. Johnson, with a warm vehemence of affectionate regard, exclaimed, 'The earth does not bear a worthier man than Bennet Langton.' We saw a good many fine pictures, which I think are described in one of *Young's Tours*. There is a printed catalogue of them which the housekeeper put into my hand; I should like to view them at leisure. I was much struck with Daniel interpreting Nebuchadnezzar's dream by Rembrandt. We were shown a pretty large library. In his Lordship's dressing-room lay Johnson's small Dictionary: he showed it to me, with some eagerness, saving, 'Look'ye! *Quae terra nostri non plena laboris.*' He observed, also, Goldsmith's *Animated Nature*; and said, 'Here's our friend! The poor Doctor would have been happy to hear of this.'

In our way, Johnson strongly expressed his love of driving fast in a post-chaise. 'If (said he) I had no duties, and no reference to futurity, I would spend my life in driving briskly in a post-chaise with a pretty woman, but she should be one who could understand me, and would add something to the conversation.' I observed, that we were this day to stop just where the Highland army did in 1745. JOHNSON. 'It was a noble attempt.' BOSWELL. 'I wish we could have an authentic history of it.' JOHNSON. 'If you were not an idle dog you might write it, by collecting from every body what they can tell, and putting down your authorities.' BOSWELL. 'But I could not have the advantage of it in my life-time.' JOHNSON. 'You might have the satisfaction of its fame, by printing it in Holland; and as to profit, consider how long it was before writing came to be considered in a pecuniary view. Baretti says, he is the first man that ever received copy-money in Italy.' I said, that I would endeavour to do what Dr Johnson suggested; and I thought that I might write so as to venture to publish my *History of the Civil War in Great-Britain in 1745 and 1746*, without being obliged to go to a foreign press.[1]

When we arrived at Derby, Dr Butter accompanied us to see the manufactory of china there. I admired the ingenuity and delicate art with

---

1 I am now happy to understand, that Mr John Home, who was himself gallantly in the field for the reigning family, in that interesting warfare, but is generous enough to do justice to the other side, is preparing an account of it for the press.

which a man fashioned clay into a cup, a saucer, or a tea-pot, while a boy turned round a wheel to give the mass rotundity. I thought this as excellent in its species of power, as making good verses in *its* species. Yet I had no respect for this potter. Neither, indeed, has a man of any extent of thinking for a mere verse-maker, in whose numbers, however perfect, there is no poetry, no mind. The china was beautiful; but Dr Johnson justly observed, it was too dear; for that he could have vessels of silver, of the same size, as cheap as what were here made of porcelain.

I felt a pleasure in walking about Derby, such as I always have in walking about any town to which I am not accustomed. There is an immediate sensation of novelty; and one speculates on the way in which life is passed in it, which, although there is a sameness every where upon the whole, is yet minutely diversified. The minute diversities in every thing are wonderful. Talking of shaving the other night at Dr Taylor's, Dr Johnson said, 'Sir, of a thousand shavers, two do not shave so much alike as not to be distinguished.' I thought this not possible, till he specified so many of the varieties in shaving; – holding the razor more or less perpendicular; – drawing long or short strokes; – beginning at the upper part of the face, or the under; – at the right side or the left side. Indeed, when one considers what variety of sounds can be uttered by the wind-pipe, in the compass of a very small aperture, we may be convinced how many degrees of difference there may be in the application of a razor.

We dined with Dr Butter, whose lady is daughter of my cousin Sir John Douglas, whose grandson is now presumptive heir of the noble family of Queensberry. Johnson and he had a good deal of medical conversation. Johnson said, he had somewhere or other given an account of Dr Nichols's discourse *De Anima Medica*. He told us, 'that whatever a man's distemper was, Dr Nichols would not attend him as a physician, if his mind was not at ease; for he believed that no medicines would have any influence. He once attended a man in trade, upon whom he found none of the medicines he prescribed had any effect; he asked the man's wife privately whether his affairs were not in a bad way? She said no. He continued his attendance some time, still without success. At length the man's wife told him, she had discovered that her husband's affairs *were* in a bad way. When Goldsmith was dying, Dr Turton said to him, "Your pulse is in greater disorder than it should be, from the degree of fever which you have: is your mind at ease?" Goldsmith answered it was not.'

After dinner, Mrs Butter went with me to see the silk-mill which Sir Thomas Lambe[a] had a patent for, having brought away the contrivance from Italy. I am not very conversant with mechanics; but the simplicity of this machine, and its multiplied operations, struck me with an agreeable surprise. I had learnt from Dr Johnson, during this interview, not to think with a dejected indifference of the works of art, and the pleasures of life, because life is uncertain and short; but to consider such indifference as a failure of reason, a morbidness of mind; for happiness should be cultivated as much as we can, and the objects which are instrumental to it should be steadily considered as of importance, with a reference not only to ourselves, but to multitudes in successive ages. Though it is proper to value small parts, as

> Sands make the mountain, moments make the year;[1]

yet we must contemplate, collectively, to have a just estimation of objects. One moment's being uneasy or not, seems of no consequence; yet this may be thought of the next, and the next, and so on, till there is a large portion of misery. In the same way one must think of happiness, of learning, of friendship. We cannot tell the precise moment when friendship is formed. As in filling a vessel drop by drop there is at last a drop which makes it run over; so in a series of kindnesses there is at last one which makes the heart run over. We must not divide objects of our attention into minute parts, and think separately of each part. It is by contemplating a large mass of human existence, that a man, while he sets a just value on his own life, does not think of his death as annihilating all that is great and pleasing in the world, as if actually *contained in his mind*, according to Berkeley's reverie. If his imagination be not sickly and feeble, it 'wings its distant way' far beyond himself, and views the world in unceasing activity of every sort. It must be acknowledged, however, that Pope's plaintive reflection, that all things would be as gay as ever on the day of his death, is natural and common. We are apt to transfer to all around us our own gloom, without considering that at any given point of time there is, perhaps, as much youth and gaiety in the world as at another. Before I came into this life, in which I have had so many pleasant scenes, have not thousands and ten thousands of deaths and funerals happened, and have not families been in grief for their nearest relations? But have those dismal circumstances at all affected *me*? Why then should the gloomy scenes which I experience, or which I know, affect others? Let us guard against imagining that there is an end of felicity upon earth, when we ourselves grow old, or are unhappy.

Dr Johnson told us at tea, that when some of Dr Dodd's pious friends were trying to console him by saying that he was going to leave 'a wretched world', he had honesty enough not to join in the cant; – 'No, no (said he), it has been a very agreeable world to me.' Johnson added, 'I respect Dodd for thus speaking the truth; for, to be sure, he had for several years enjoyed a life of great voluptuousness.'

He told us, that Dodd's city friends stood by him so, that a thousand pounds were ready to be given to the gaoler, if he would let him escape. He added, that he knew a friend of Dodd's, who walked about Newgate for some time on the evening before the day of his execution, with five hundred pounds in his pocket, ready to be paid to any of the turnkeys who could get him out: but

---

[1] Young.

[a] For 'Sir Thomas Lambe' read 'Mr John Lombe'; and on 'Lombe' add the following note: See Hutton's *History of Derby*, a book which is deservedly esteemed for its information, accuracy, and good narrative. Indeed the age in which we live is eminently distinguished by topographical excellence.

it was too late; for he was watched with much circumspection. He said, Dodd's friends had an image of him made of wax, which was to have been left in his place; and he believed it was carried into the prison.

Johnson disapproved of Dr Dodd's leaving the world persuaded that 'The Convict's Address to his unhappy Brethren', was of his own writing. 'But, Sir (said I), you contributed to the deception; for when Mr Seward expressed a doubt to you that it was not Dodd's own, because it had a great deal more force of mind in it than any thing known to be his, you answered, – "Why should you think so? Depend upon it, Sir, when a man knows he is to be hanged in a fortnight, it concentrates his mind wonderfully".' JOHNSON. 'Sir, as Dodd got it from me to pass as his own, while that could do him any good, there was an *implied promise* that I should not own it. To own it, therefore, would have been telling a lie, with the addition of breach of promise, which was worse than simply telling a lie to make it be believed it was Dodd's. Besides, Sir, I did not directly tell a lie: I left the matter uncertain. Perhaps I thought that Seward would not believe it the less to be mine for what I said; but I would not put it in his power to say I had owned it.'

He praised Blair's sermons: 'Yet,' said he (willing to let us see he was aware that fashionable fame, however deserved, is not always the most lasting), 'perhaps, they may not be reprinted after seven years; at least not after Blair's death.'

He said, 'Goldsmith was a plant that flowered late. There appeared nothing remarkable about him when he was young; though when he had got high in fame, one of his friends began to recollect something of his being distinguished at College. Goldsmith in the same manner recollected more of that friend's early years, as he grew a greater man.'

I mentioned that Lord Monboddo told me, he awaked every morning at four, and then for his health got up and walked in his room naked, with the window open, which he called taking *an air bath*; after which he went to bed again, and slept two hours more. Johnson, who was always ready to beat down any thing that seemed to be exhibited with disproportionate importance, thus observed: 'I suppose, Sir, there is no more in it than this, he awakes at four, and cannot sleep till he chills himself, and makes the warmth of the bed a grateful sensation.'

I talked of the difficulty of rising in the morning. Dr Johnson told me, 'that the learned Mrs Carter, at that period when she was eager in study, did not awake as early as she wished, and she therefore had a contrivance, that, at a certain hour, her chamber-light should burn a string to which a heavy weight was suspended, which then fell with a strong sudden noise: this roused her from sleep, and then she had no difficulty in getting up.' But I said that was my difficulty, and wished there could be some medicine invented which would make one rise without pain, which I never did, unless after lying in bed a very long time. Perhaps there may be something in the stores of Nature which can do this. I have thought of a pulley to raise me gradually; but that would give me pain, as it would counteract my internal inclination. I would have something that can dissipate the *vis inertiae*, and give elasticity to the muscles. As I imagine that the human body may be put, by the operation of other substances, into any state in which it has ever been; and as I have experienced a state in which rising from bed was not disagreeable but easy, nay, sometimes agreeable; I suppose that this state may be produced, if we knew by what. We can heat the body, we can cool it; we can give it tension or relaxation; and surely it is possible to bring it into a state in which rising from bed will not be a pain.

Johnson observed, 'that a man should take a sufficient quantity of sleep, which Dr Mead says is between seven and nine hours.' I told him, that Dr Cullen said to me, that a man should not take more sleep than he can take at once. JOHNSON. 'This rule, Sir, cannot hold in all cases; for many people have their sleep broken by sickness; and surely, Cullen would not have a man to get up, after having slept but an hour. Such a regimen would soon end in a *long sleep*.'[1] Dr Taylor remarked, I think very justly, 'that a man who does not feel an inclination to sleep at the ordinary time, instead of being stronger than other people, must not be well; for a man in health has all the natural inclinations to eat, drink, and sleep, in a strong degree.'

Johnson advised me to-night not to *refine* in the education of my children. 'Life (said he) will not bear refinement: you must do as other people do.'

As we drove back to Ashbourne, Dr Johnson recommended to me, as he had often done, to drink water only: 'For (said he) you are then sure not to get drunk; whereas if you drink wine you are never sure.' I said, drinking wine was a pleasure which I was unwilling to give up. 'Why, Sir (said he), there is no doubt that not to drink wine is a great deduction from life; but it may be necessary.' He however owned, that in his opinion, a free use of wine did not shorten life; and said, he would not give less for the life of a certain Scotch Lord (whom he named) celebrated for hard drinking, than for that of a sober man. 'But stay (said he, with his usual intelligence, and accuracy of enquiry), does it take much wine to make him drunk?' I answered, 'A great deal either of wine or strong punch.' – 'Then (said he) that is the worse.' I presume to illustrate my friend's observation thus: 'A fortress which soon surrenders has its walls less shattered, than when a long and obstinate resistance is made.'

I ventured to mention a person who was as violent a Scotchman as he was an Englishman; and literally had the same contempt for an Englishman compared with a Scotchman, that he had for a Scotchman compared with an Englishman;

---

1 This regimen was, however, practised by Bishop Ken, of whom Hawkins (not Sir John) in his Life of that venerable Prelate, page 4, tells us, 'And that neither his study might be the aggressor on his hours of instruction, or what he judged his duty prevent his improvements; or both, his closet addresses to his GOD; he strictly accustomed himself to but one sleep, which often obliged him to rise at one or two of the clock in the morning, and sometimes sooner; and grew so habitual, that it continued with him almost till his last illness. And so lively and cheerful was his temper, that he would be very facetious and entertaining to his friends in the evening, even when it was perceived that with difficulty he kept his eyes open; and then seemed to go to rest with no other purpose than the refreshing and enabling him with more vigour and cheerfulness to sing his morning hymn, as he then used to do to his lute, before he put on his cloaths.'

and that he would say of Dr Johnson, 'Damned rascal! to talk as he does of the Scotch.' This seemed, for a moment, 'to give him pause'. It, perhaps, presented his extreme prejudice against the Scotch in a point of view somewhat new to him, by the effect of *contrast*.

By the time when we returned to Ashbourne, Dr Taylor was gone to bed. Johnson and I sat up a long time by ourselves.

He was much diverted with an article which I showed him in the *Critical Review* of this year, giving an account of a curious publication, entitled, *A Spiritual Diary and Soliloquies*, by John Rutty, M.D. Dr Rutty was one of the people called Quakers, a physician of some eminence in Dublin, and author of several works. This *Diary*, which was kept from 1753 to 1775, the year in which he died, and was now published in two volumes, octavo, exhibited, in the simplicity of his heart, a minute and honest register of the state of his mind; which, though frequently laughable enough, was not more so than the history of many men would be, if recorded with equal fairness.

The following specimens were extracted by the Reviewers:

1753

Tenth month, 23rd	Indulgence in bed an hour too long.
Twelfth month, 17th	An hypochondriac obnubilation from wind and indigestion.
Ninth month, 28th	An over-dose of whisky.
29th	A dull, cross, choleric day.

1757

First month, 22nd	A little swinish at dinner and repast.
31st	Dogged on provocation.
Second month, 5th	Very dogged or snappish.
14th	Snappish on fasting.
26th	Cursed snappishness to those under me, on a bodily indisposition.
Third month, 11th	On a provocation, exercised a dumb resentment for two days, instead of scolding.
22nd	Scolded too vehemently.
23rd	Dogged again.
Fourth month, 29th	Mechanically and sinfully dogged.

Johnson laughed heartily at this good Quietist's self-condemning minutes; particularly at his mentioning, with such a serious regret, occasional instances of '*swinishness* in eating, and *doggedness of temper*'. He thought the observations of the *Critical Reviewers* upon the importance of a man to himself so ingenious and so well expressed, that I shall here introduce them.

After observing, that 'There are few writers who have gained any reputation by recording their own actions,' they say:

We may reduce the egotists to four classes. In the *first* we have Julius Caesar: he relates his own transactions; but he relates them with peculiar grace and dignity, and his narrative is supported by the greatness of his character and achievements. In the *second* class we have Marcus Antoninus: this writer has given us a series of reflections on his own life; but his sentiments are so noble, his morality so sublime, that his meditations are universally admired. In the *third* class we have some others of tolerable credit, who have given importance to their own private history by an intermixture of literary anecdotes, and the occurrences of their own times: the celebrated *Heutius* has published an entertaining volume upon this plan, *De rebus ad eum pertinentibus.* In the *fourth* class we have the journalists, temporal and spiritual: Elias Ashmole, William Lilly, George Whitefield, John Wesley, and a thousand other old women and fanatic writers of memoirs and meditations.

I mentioned to him that Dr Hugh Blair, in his lectures on Rhetoric and Belles Lettres, which I heard him deliver at Edinburgh, had animadverted on the Johnsonian style as too pompous; and attempted to imitate it, by giving a sentence of Addison in *The Spectator*, No. 411, in the manner of Johnson. When treating of the utility of the pleasures of imagination in preserving us from vice, it is observed of those 'who know not how to be idle and innocent', that their very first step out of business is into vice or folly; which Dr Blair supposed would have been expressed in *The Rambler*, thus: 'Their very first step out of the regions of business is into the perturbation of vice, or the vacuity of folly.'[1] JOHNSON. 'Sir, these are not the words I should have used. No, Sir; the imitators of my style have not hit it. Miss Aikin has done it the best; for she has imitated the sentiment as well as the diction.'

I intend, before this work is concluded, to exhibit specimens of imitation of my friend's style in various modes; some caricaturing or mimicking it, and some formed upon it, whether intentionally or with a degree of similarity to it, of which, perhaps, the writers were not conscious.

In Baretti's Review, which he published in Italy, under the title of *Frusta Letteraria*, it is observed, that Dr Robertson the historian had formed his style upon that of '*Il celebre Samuele Johnson*'. My friend himself was of that opinion; for he once said to me, in a pleasant humour, 'Sir, if Robertson's style be faulty, he owes it to me; that is, having too many words, and those too big ones.'

I read to him a letter which Lord Monboddo had written to me, containing some critical remarks upon the style of his *Journey to the Western Islands of Scotland.* His Lordship praised the very fine passage upon landing at Icolmkill;[2] but his own style being exceedingly dry and hard, he disapproved of the richness of Johnson's language, and of his frequent use of metaphorical

---

1 When Dr Blair published his Lectures, he was invidiously attacked for having omitted his censure on Johnson's style, and, on the contrary, praising it highly. But before that time Johnson's *Lives of the Poets* had appeared, in which his style was considerably easier than when he wrote *The Rambler.* It would, therefore, have been uncandid in Blair, even supposing his criticism to have been just, to have preserved it.

2 'WE were now treading that illustrious island, which was once the luminary of the Caledonian regions, whence savage clans and roving barbarians derived the benefits of knowledge, and the blessings of religion. To abstract the mind from all local emotion

expressions. JOHNSON. 'Why, Sir, this criticism would be just, if in my style, superfluous words, or words too big for the thoughts, could be pointed out; but this I do not believe can be done. For instance: in the passage which Lord Monboddo admires, "We were now treading that illustrious region", the word *illustrious*, contributes nothing to the mere narration; for the fact might be told without it: but it is not, therefore, superfluous; for it wakes the mind to peculiar attention, where something of more than usual importance is to be presented. "Illustrious!" – for what? and then the sentence proceeds to expand the circumstances connected with Iona. And, Sir, as to metaphorical expression, that is a great excellence in style, when it is used with propriety, for it gives you two ideas for one; – conveys the meaning more luminously, and generally with a perception of delight.'

He told me, that he had been asked to undertake the new edition of the *Biographia Britannica*, but had declined it; which he afterwards said to me he regretted. In this regret many will join, because it would have procured us more of Johnson's most delightful species of writing: and although my friend Dr Kippis has hitherto discharged the task judiciously, distinctly, and with more impartiality than might have been expected from a Separatist, it were to have been wished that the superintendance of this literary Temple of Fame, had been assigned to 'a friend to the constitution in Church and State'. We should not then have had it too much crowded with obscure dissenting teachers, doubtless men of merit and worth, but not quite to be numbered amongst 'the most eminent persons who have flourished in Great-Britain and Ireland'.[a]

On Saturday, September 20, after breakfast, when Taylor was gone out to his farm, Dr Johnson and I had a serious conversation by ourselves on melancholy and madness; which he was, I always thought, erroneously inclined to confound together. Melancholy, like 'great wit', may be 'near allied to madness'; but there is, in my opinion, a distinct separation between them. When he talked of madness, he was to be understood as speaking of

---

would be impossible, if it were endeavoured, and would be foolish if it were possible. Whatever withdraws us from the power of our senses, whatever makes the past, the distant, or the future, predominate over the present, advances us in the dignity of thinking beings. Far from me, and from my friends, be such frigid philosophy, as may conduct us, indifferent and unmoved, over any ground which has been dignified by wisdom, bravery, or virtue. That man is little to be envied, whose patriotism would not gain force upon the plain of Marathon, or whose piety would not grow warmer among the ruins of Iona.'

Had our Tour produced nothing else but this sublime passage, the world must have acknowledged that it was not made in vain. The present respectable President of the Royal Society was so much struck on reading it, that he clasped his hands together, and remained for some time in an attitude of silent admiration.

[a] Add this note: In this censure which has been carelessly uttered, I carelessly joined. But in justice to Dr Kippis, who with that manly candid good temper which marks his character, set me right, I now with pleasure retract it; and I desire it may be particularly observed, as pointed out by him to me, that, 'The new lives of dissenting Divines, in the first four volumes of the second edition of the *Biographia Britannica*, are

those who were in any great degree disturbed, or as it is commonly expressed, 'troubled in mind'. Some of the ancient philosophers held, that all deviations from right reason were madness; and whoever wishes to see the opinions both of ancients and moderns upon this subject, collected and illustrated with a variety of curious facts, may read Dr Arnold's very entertaining work.[1]

Johnson said, 'A madman loves to be with people whom he fears; not as a dog fears the lash; but of whom he stands in awe.' I was struck with the justice of this observation. To be with those of whom a person, whose mind is wavering and dejected, stands in awe, represses and composes an uneasy tumult of spirits, and consoles him with the contemplation of something steady, and at least comparatively great.

He added, 'Madmen are all sensual in the lower stages of the distemper. They are eager for gratifications to sooth their minds, and divert their attention from the misery which they suffer: but when they grow very ill, pleasure is too weak for them, and they seek for pain.[2] Employment, Sir, and hardships, prevent melancholy. I suppose in all our army in America there was not one man who went mad.'

---

those of John Abernethy, Thomas Amory, George Benson, Hugh Broughton the learned Puritan, Simon Browne, Joseph Boyse of Dublin, Thomas Cartwright the learned Puritan, and Samuel Chandler. The only doubt I have ever heard suggested is, whether there should have been an article of Dr Amory. But I was convinced, and am still convinced, that he was entitled to one, from the reality of his learning, and the excellent and candid nature of his practical writings.

'The new lives of clergymen of the church of England, in the same four volumes, are as follows: John Balguy, Edward Bentham, George Berkley Bishop of Cloyne, William Berriman, Thomas Birch, William Borlase, Thomas Bott, James Bradley, Thomas Broughton, John Brown, John Burton, Joseph Butler Bishop of Durham, Thomas Carte, Edmund Castell, Edmund Chishull, Charles Churchill, William Clarke, Robert Clayton Bishop of Clogher, John Conybeare Bishop of Bristol, George Costard, and Samuel Croxall. – I am not conscious (says Dr Kippis) of any partiality in conducting the work. I would not willingly insert a Dissenting Minister that does not justly deserve to be noticed, or omit an established clergyman that does. At the same time, I shall not be deterred from introducing Dissenters into the *Biographia* when I am satisfied that they are entitled to that distinction, from their writings, learning, and merit.'

Let me add that the expression 'A friend to the Constitution in Church and State', was not meant by me, as any reflection upon this Reverend Gentleman, as if he were an enemy to the political constitution of his country, as established at the revolution, but, from my steady and avowed predilection for a *Tory*, was quoted from Johnson's *Dictionary*, where that distinction is so defined.'

1 *Observations on Insanity*, by Thomas Arnold, M.D. London, 1782.

2 We read in the Gospels, that those unfortunate persons, who were possessed with evil spirits (which, after all, I think is the most probable cause of madness, as was first suggested to me by my respectable friend Sir John Pringle), had recourse to pain, tearing themselves, and jumping sometimes into the fire, sometimes into the water. Mr. Seward has furnished me with a remarkable anecdote in confirmation of Dr Johnson's observation. A tradesman, who had acquired a large fortune in London,

We entered seriously upon a question of much importance to me, which Johnson was pleased to consider with friendly attention. I had long complained to him that I felt myself discontented in Scotland, as too narrow a sphere, and that I wished to make my chief residence in London, the great scene of ambition, instruction, and amusement; a scene, which was to me, comparatively speaking, a heaven upon earth. JOHNSON. 'Why, Sir, I never knew any one who had such a *gust* for London as you have; and I cannot blame you for your wish to live there: yet, Sir, were I in your father's place, I should not consent to your settling there; for I have the old feudal notions, and I should be afraid that Auchinleck would be deserted, as you would soon find it more desirable to have a country-seat in a better climate. I own, however, that to consider it as a *duty* to reside on a family estate is a prejudice; for we must consider, that working-people get employment equally, and the produce of land is sold equally, whether a great family resides at home or not; and if the rents of an estate be carried to London, they return again in the circulation of commerce; nay, Sir, we must perhaps allow, that carrying the rents to a distance is a good, because it contributes to that circulation. We must, however, allow, that a well-regulated great family may improve a neighbourhood in civility and elegance, and give an example of good order, virtue, and piety; and so its residence at home may be of much advantage. But if a great family be disorderly and vicious, its residence at home is very pernicious to a neighbourhood. There is not now the same inducement to live in the country as formerly; the pleasures of social life are much better enjoyed in town; and there is no longer in the country that power and influence in proprietors of land which they had in old times, and which made the country so agreeable to them. The Laird of Auchinleck now is not near so great a man as the Laird of Auchinleck was a hundred years ago.'

I told him, that one of my ancestors never went from home without being attended by thirty men on horseback. Johnson's shrewdness and spirit of enquiry were exerted upon every occasion. 'Pray (said he), how did your ancestor support his thirty men and thirty horses, when he went at a distance from home, in an age when there was hardly any money in circulation?' I suggested the same difficulty to a friend, who mentioned Douglas's going to the Holy Land with a numerous train of followers. 'Douglas could, no doubt, maintain followers enough while living upon his own lands, the produce of which supplied them with food; but he could not carry that food to the Holy Land; and as there was no commerce by which he could be supplied with money, how could he maintain them in foreign countries?'

---

retired from business, and went to live at Worcester. His mind, being without its usual occupation, and having nothing else to supply its place, preyed upon itself, so that existence was a torment to him. At last he was seized with the stone; and a friend who found him in one of its severest fits, having expressed his concern, 'No, no, Sir (said he), don't pity me: what I now feel is ease, compared with that torture of mind from which it relieves me.'

I suggested a doubt, that if I were to reside in London, the exquisite zest with which I relished it in occasional visits might grow off, and I might grow tired of it. JOHNSON. 'Why, Sir, you find no man, at all intellectual, who is willing to leave London. No, Sir, when a man is tired of London, he is tired of life: for there is in London all that life can afford.'

To obviate his apprehension, that by settling in London I might desert the seat of my ancestors, I assured him, that I had old feudal principles to a degree of enthusiasm; and that I felt all the *dulcedo* of the *natale solum*. I reminded him, that the Laird of Auchinleck had an elegant house, in front of which he could ride ten miles forward upon his own territories, upon which he had upwards of six hundred people attached to him; that the family seat was rich in natural, romantic beauties of rock, wood, and water; and that in my 'morn of life' I had appropriated the finest descriptions in the ancient Classics to certain scenes there, which were thus associated in my mind. That when all this was considered, I should certainly pass a part of the year at home, and enjoy it the more from variety, and from bringing with me a share of the intellectual stores of the metropolis. He listened to all this, and kindly 'hoped it might be as I now supposed.'

He said, 'A country gentleman should bring his lady to visit London as soon as he can, that they may have agreeable topics for conversation when they are by themselves.'

As I meditated trying my fortune in Westminster Hall, our conversation turned upon the profession of the law in England. JOHNSON. 'You must not indulge too sanguine hopes, should you be called to our bar. I was told, by a very sensible lawyer, that there are a great many chances against any man s success in the profession of the law; the candidates are so numerous, and those who get large practice so few. He said, it was by no means true that a man of good parts and application is sure of having business, though he, indeed, allowed that if such a man could but appear in a few causes, his merit would be known, and he would get forward; but that the great risk was, that a man might pass half a life-time in the Courts, and never have an opportunity of showing his abilities.'[1]

We talked of employment being absolutely necessary to preserve the mind from wearying and growing fretful, especially in those who have a tendency to melancholy; and I mentioned to him a saying which somebody had related of an American savage, who, when an European was expatiating on all the advantages of money, put this question: 'Will it purchase *occupation*?' JOHNSON. 'Depend upon it, Sir, this saying is too refined for a savage. And, Sir, money

---

1 Now, at the distance of fifteen years since this conversation passed , the observation which I have had an opportunity of making in Westminster Hall has convinced me, that, however true the opinion of Dr Johnson's legal friend may have been some time ago, the same certainty or success cannot now be promised to the same display of merit. The reasons, however, of the rapid rise of some, and the disappointment of others equally respectable, are such as it might seem invidious to mention, and would require a longer detail than would be proper for this work.

will purchase occupation; it will purchase all the conveniences of life; it will purchase variety of company; it will purchase all sorts of entertainment.'

I talked to him of Forster's *Voyage to the South Seas*, which pleased me; but I found he did not like it. 'Sir (said he), there is a great affectation of fine writing in it.' BOSWELL. 'But he carries you along with him.' JOHNSON. 'No, Sir; he does not carry me along with him: he leaves me behind him: or rather, indeed, he sets me before him; for he makes me turn over many leaves at a time.'

On Sunday, September 21, we went to the church of Ashbourne, which is one of the largest and most luminous that I have seen in any town of the same size. I felt great satisfaction in considering that I was supported in my fondness for solemn public worship by the general concurrence and munificence of mankind.

Johnson and Taylor were so different from each other, that I wondered at their preserving such an intimacy. Their having been at school and college together, might, in some degree, account for this; but Sir Joshua Reynolds has furnished me with a stronger reason; for Johnson mentioned to him, that he had been told by Taylor he was to be his heir. I shall not take upon me to animadvert upon this; but certain it is, that Johnson paid great attention to Taylor. He now, however, said to me, 'Sir, I love him; but I do not love him more; my regard for him does not increase. As it is said in the Apocrypha, "his talk is of bullocks":[1] I do not suppose he is very fond of my company. His habits are by no means sufficiently clerical: this he knows that I see; and no man likes to live under the eye of perpetual disapprobation.'

I have no doubt that a good many sermons were composed for Taylor by Johnson. At this time I found, upon his table, a part of one which he had newly begun to write: and *Concio pro Tayloro* appears in one of his diaries. When to these circumstances we add the internal evidence from the power of thinking and style, in the collection which the Reverend Mr Hayes has published, with the *significant* title of 'Sermons *left for publication* by the Reverend John Taylor, LL.D.', our conviction will be complete.

I, however, would not have it thought, that Dr. Taylor, though he could not write like Johnson (as, indeed, who could?), did not sometimes compose sermons as good as those which we generally have from very respectable divines. He showed me one with notes on the margin in Johnson's hand-writing; and I was present when he read another to Johnson, that he might have his opinion of it, and Johnson said it was 'very well'. These, we may be sure, were not Johnson's; for he was above little arts, or tricks of deception.

Johnson was by no means of opinion, that every man of a learned profession should consider it as incumbent upon him, or as necessary to his credit, to appear as an author. When in the ardour of ambition for literary fame, I regretted to him one day that an eminent Judge had nothing of it, and therefore would leave no perpetual monument of himself to posterity. 'Alas, Sir (said

---

[1] *Ecclesiasticus*, ch. xxxviii. 25. The whole chapter may be read as an admirable illustration of the superiority of cultivated minds over the gross and illiterate.

Johnson), what a mass of confusion should we have, if every Bishop, and every Judge, every Lawyer, Physician, and Divine, were to write books.'

I mentioned to Johnson a respectable person of a very strong mind, who had little of that tenderness which is common to human nature; as an instance of which, when I suggested to him that he should invite his son, who had been settled ten years in foreign parts, to come home and pay him a visit, his answer was, 'No, no, let him mind his business.' JOHNSON. 'I do not agree with him, Sir, in this. Getting money is not all a man's business; to cultivate kindness is a valuable part of the business of life.'

In the evening, Johnson, being in very good spirits, entertained us with several characteristical portraits. I regret that any of them escaped my retention and diligence. I found, from experience, that to collect my friend's conversation so as to exhibit it with any degree of its original flavour, it was necessary to write it down without delay. To record his sayings, after some distance of time, was like preserving or pickling long-kept and faded fruits or other vegetables, which, when in that state, have little or nothing of their taste when fresh.

I shall present my readers with a series of what I gathered this evening from the Johnsonian garden.

'My friend, the late Earl of Corke, had a great desire to maintain the literary character of his family: he was a genteel man, but did not keep up the dignity of his rank. He was so generally civil, that nobody thanked him for it.'

'Did we not hear so much said of Jack Wilkes, we should think more highly of his conversation. Jack has great variety of talk, Jack is a scholar, and Jack has the manners of a gentleman. But after hearing his name sounded from pole to pole, as the phoenix of convivial felicity, we are disappointed in his company. He has always been *at me*: but I would do Jack a kindness, rather than not. The contest is now over.'

'Garrick's gaiety of conversation has delicacy and elegance: Foote makes you laugh more; but Foote has the air of a buffoon paid for entertaining the company. He, indeed, well deserves his hire.'

'Colley Cibber once consulted me as to one of his birthday Odes, a long time before it was wanted. I objected very freely to several passages. Cibber lost patience, and would not read his Ode to an end. When we had done with criticism, we walked over to Richardson's, the author of *Clarissa*, and I wondered to find Richardson displeased that I "did not treat Cibber with more *respect*". Now, Sir, to talk of *respect* for a *player*!' (smiling disdainfully). BOSWELL. 'There, Sir, you are always heretical: you never will allow merit to a player.' JOHNSON. 'Merit, Sir! What merit? Do you respect a rope-dancer, or a ballad-singer?' BOSWELL. 'No, Sir: but we respect a great player, as a man who can conceive lofty sentiments, and can express them gracefully.' JOHNSON. 'What, Sir, a fellow who claps a hump on his back, and a lump on his leg, and cries, "*I am Richard the Third*"? Nay, Sir, a ballad-singer is a higher man, for he does two things; he repeats and he sings: there is both recitation and music in his performance: the player only recites.' BOSWELL. 'My dear Sir! you may turn any thing into ridicule. I allow, that a player of farce is not entitled to respect; he does a little thing: but he who can represent exalted characters, and touch the noblest passions, has very respectable powers: and mankind have agreed in admiring great talents for the stage. We must consider, too, that a great player does what very few are capable to do: his art is a very rare faculty. *Who* can repeat Hamlet's Soliloquy, "To be, or not to be", as Garrick does it?' JOHNSON. 'Any body may. Jemmy, there (a boy about eight years old, who was in the room) will do it as well in a week.' BOSWELL. 'No, no, Sir: and as a proof of the merit of great acting, and of the value which mankind set upon it, Garrick has got a hundred thousand pounds.' JOHNSON. 'Is getting a hundred thousand pounds a proof of excellence? That has been done by a scoundrel commissary.'

This was most fallacious reasoning. I was *sure*, for once, that I had the best side of the argument. I boldly maintained the just distinction between a tragedian and a mere theatrical droll; between those who rouse our terror and pity, and those who only make us laugh. 'If (said I) Betterton and Foote were to walk into this room, you would respect Betterton much more than Foote.' JOHNSON. 'If Betterton were to walk into this room with Foote, Foote would soon drive him out of it. Foote, Sir, *quatenus* Foote, has powers superior to them all.'

On Monday, September 22, when at breakfast, I unguardedly said to Dr Johnson, 'I wish I saw you and Mrs Macaulay together.' He grew very angry; and, after a pause, while a cloud gathered on his brow, he burst out, 'No, Sir; you would not see us quarrel, to make you sport. Don't you know that it is very uncivil to *pit* two people against one another?' Then, checking himself, and wishing to be more gentle, he added, 'I do not say you should be hanged or drowned for this; but it *is* very uncivil.' Dr Taylor thought him in the wrong, and spoke to him privately of it; but I afterwards acknowledged to Johnson that I was to blame, for I candidly owned that I meant to express a desire to see a contest between Mrs Macaulay and him; but then I knew how the contest would end, so that I was to see him triumph. JOHNSON. 'Sir, you cannot be sure how a contest will end; and no man has a right to engage two people in a dispute by which their passions may be inflamed, and they may part with bitter resentment against each other. I would sooner keep company with a man from whom I must guard my pockets, than with a man who contrives to bring me into a dispute with somebody that he may hear it. This is the great fault of —— (naming one of our friends), endeavouring to introduce a subject upon which he knows two people in the company differ.' BOSWELL. 'But he told me, Sir, he does it for instruction.' JOHNSON. 'Whatever the motive be, Sir, the man who does so, does very wrong. He has no more right to instruct himself at such a risk, than he has to make two people fight a duel, that he may learn how to defend himself.'

He found great fault with a gentleman of our acquaintance for keeping a bad table. 'Sir (said he), when a man is invited to dinner, he is disappointed if he does not get something good. I advised Mrs Thrale, who has no card-parties at her house, to give sweet-meats, and such good things, in an evening, as are not commonly given, and she would find company enough come to her; for every body loves to have things which please the palate put in their way, without trouble or preparation.' Such was his attention to the minutiae of life and manners.

He thus characterised the Duke of Devonshire, grandfather of the present representative of that very respectable family: 'He was not a man of superior abilities, but he was a man strictly faithful to his word. If, for instance, he had promised you an acorn, and none had grown that year in his woods, he would not have contented himself with that excuse; he would have sent to Denmark for it. So unconditional was he in keeping his word; so high as to the point of honour.' This was a liberal testimony from the Tory Johnson to the virtue of a great Whig nobleman.

Mr Burke's 'Letter to the Sheriffs of Bristol, on the affairs of America', being mentioned, Johnson censured the composition much, and he ridiculed the definition of a free government, *viz.* 'For any practical purpose, it is what the people think so.'[1] – 'I will let the King of France govern me on those conditions (said he), for it is to be governed just as I please.' And when Dr Taylor talked of a girl being sent to a parish workhouse, and asked how much she could be obliged to work. 'Why (said Johnson), as much as is reasonable: and what is that? as much as *she thinks* reasonable.'

Dr Johnson obligingly proposed to carry me to see Islam, a romantic scene, now belonging to a family of the name of Port, but formerly the seat of the Congreves. I suppose it is well described in some of the Tours. Johnson described it distinctly and vividly, at which I could not but express to him my wonder, because, though my eyes, as he observed, were better than his, I could not by any means equal him in representing visible objects. I said, the difference between us in this respect was as that between a man who had a bad instrument, but plays well on it, and a man who has a good instrument, on which he can play very imperfectly.

I recollect a very fine amphitheatre, surrounded with hills covered with wood, and walks neatly formed along the side of a rocky steep, on the quarter next the house, with recesses under projections of rock, over-shadowed with trees; in one of which recesses, we were told, Congreve wrote his *Old Bachelor*. We viewed a remarkable natural curiosity at Islam; two rivers bursting near each other from the rock, not from immediate springs, but after having run for many miles under ground. Plott, in his *History of Staffordshire*,[2] gives an account of this curiosity; but Johnson would not believe it, though we had the attestation of the gardener, who said, he had put in corks, where the river *Manyfold* sinks into the ground, and had catched them in a net, placed before one of the openings where the water bursts out. Indeed, such subterraneous courses of water are found in various parts of our globe.[3]

1 Edit. 2, p. 53.
2 Page 89.
3 See Plott's *History of Staffordshire*, p. 88, and the authorities referred to by him.

Talking of Dr Johnson's unwillingness to believe extraordinary things, I ventured to say, 'Sir, you come near Hume's argument against miracles, "that it is more probable witnesses should lie, or be mistaken, than that they should happen." ' JOHNSON. 'Why Sir, Hume, taking the proposition simply, is right. But the Christian revelation is not proved by the miracles alone, but as connected with prophecies, and with the doctrines in confirmation of which the miracles were wrought.'

He repeated his observation, that the differences among Christians are really of no consequence. 'For instance (said he), if a Protestant objects to a Papist, "You worship images"; the Papist can answer, "I do not insist on *your* doing it; you may be a very good Papist without it: I do it only as a help to my devotion." ' I said the great article of Christianity is the revelation of immortality. Johnson admitted it was.

In the evening, a gentleman-farmer, who was on a visit at Dr Taylor's, attempted to dispute with Johnson in favour of Mungo Campbell, who shot Alexander, Earl of Eglintoune, upon his having fallen, when retreating from his Lordship, who he believed was about to seize his gun, as he had threatened to do. He said he should have done just as Campbell did. JOHNSON. 'Whoever would do as Campbell did, deserves to be hanged; not that I could, as a juryman, have found him legally guilty of murder; but I am glad they found means to convict him.' The gentleman-farmer said, 'A poor man has as much honour as a rich man; and Campbell had that to defend.' Johnson exclaimed, 'A poor man has no honour.' The English yeoman, not dismayed, proceeded: 'Lord Eglintoune was a damned fool to run on upon Campbell, after being warned that Campbell would shoot him if he did.' Johnson, who could not bear any thing like swearing, angrily replied, 'He was *not* a *damned* fool: he only thought too well of Campbell. He did not believe Campbell would be such a *damned* scoundrel, as to do so *damned* a thing.' His emphasis on *damned*, accompanied with frowning looks, reproved his opponent's want of decorum in his presence.

Talking of the danger of being mortified by rejection, when making approaches to the acquaintance of the great, I observed, 'I am, however, generally for trying, "Nothing venture, nothing have." ' JOHNSON. 'Very true, Sir; but I have always been more afraid of failing, than hopeful of success.' And, indeed, though he had all just respect for rank, no man ever less courted the favour of the great.

During this interview at Ashbourne, Johnson seemed to be more uniformly social, cheerful, and alert, than I had almost ever seen him. He was prompt on great occasions and on small. Taylor, who praised every thing of his own to excess, in short, 'whose geese were all swans', as the proverb says, expatiated on the excellence of his bull-dog, which he told us was 'perfectly well shaped'. Johnson, after examining the animal attentively, thus repressed the vain-glory of our host: 'No, Sir, he is *not* well shaped; for there is not the quick transition from the thickness of the fore-part to the *tenuity* – the thin part – behind, which a bull-dog ought to have.' This *tenuity*, was the only *hard word* that I heard him use during this interview, and it will be observed, he instantly put another expression in its place. Taylor said, a small bull-dog was as good as a large one. JOHNSON. 'No, Sir; for, in proportion to his size, he has strength: and your argument would prove, that a good bull-dog may be as small as a mouse.' It was amazing how he entered with perspicuity and keenness upon every thing that occurred in conversation. Most men, whom I know, would no more think of discussing a question about a bull-dog, than of attacking a bull.

I cannot allow any fragment whatever that floats in my memory concerning the great subject of this work to be lost. Though a small particular may appear trifling to some, it will be relished by others; while every little spark adds something to the general blaze: and to please the true, candid, warm admirers of Johnson, and in any degree increase the splendour of his reputation, I bid defiance to the shafts of ridicule, or even of malignity. Showers of them have been discharged at my *Journal of a Tour to the Hebrides*; yet it still sails unhurt along the stream of time, and, as an attendant upon Johnson,

> Pursues the triumph, and partakes the gale.

One morning after breakfast, when the sun shone bright, we walked out together, and 'pored' for some time with placid indolence upon an artificial waterfall, which Dr Taylor had made by building a strong dyke of stone across the river behind his garden. It was now somewhat obstructed by branches of trees and other rubbish, which had come down the river and settled close to it. Johnson, partly from a desire to see it play more freely, and partly from that inclination to activity which will animate, at times, the most inert and sluggish mortal, took a long pole which was lying on the bank, and pushed down several parcels of this wreck with painful assiduity, while I stood quietly by, wondering to behold the sage thus curiously employed, and smiling with an humorous satisfaction each time when he carried his point. He worked till he was quite out of breath; and having found a large dead cat so heavy that he could not move it after several efforts, 'Come (said he, throwing down the pole), *you* shall take it now'; which I accordingly did, and being a fresh man, soon made the cat tumble over the cascade. This may be laughed at as too trifling to record; but it is a small characteristic trait in the Flemish picture which I give of my friend, and in which, therefore, I mark the most minute particulars. And let it be remembered, that 'Aesop at play' is one of the instructive apologues of antiquity.

I mentioned an old gentleman of our acquaintance whose memory was beginning to fail. – JOHNSON. 'There must be a diseased mind, where there is a failure of memory at seventy. A man's head, Sir, must be morbid if he fails so soon.' My friend, being now himself sixty-eight, might think thus: but I imagine, that *threescore and ten*, the Psalmist's period of sound human life, in later ages may have a failure, though there be no disease in the constitution.

Talking of Rochester's Poems, he said, he had given them to Mr Steevens to castrate for the edition of the Poets, to which he was to write Prefaces. Dr

Taylor (the only time I ever heard him say any thing witty[1]) observed, that 'if Rochester had been castrated himself, his exceptional poems would not have been written.' I asked if Burnet had not given a good Life of Rochester. JOHNSON. 'We have a good *Death*: there is not much *Life*.' I asked whether Prior's Poems were to be printed entire: Johnson said they were. I mentioned Lord Hailes's censure of Prior, in his Preface to a collection of *Sacred Poems*, by various hands, published by him at Edinburgh a great many years ago, where he mentions, 'those impure tales which will be the eternal opprobrium of their ingenious author.' JOHNSON. 'Sir, Lord Hailes has forgot. There is nothing in Prior that will excite to lewdness. If Lord Hailes thinks there is, he must be more combustible than other people.' I instanced the tale of 'Paulo Purganti and his Wife'. JOHNSON. 'Sir, there is nothing there, but that his wife wanted to be kissed, when poor Paulo was out of pocket. No, Sir, Prior is a lady's book. No lady is ashamed to have it standing in her library.'

The hypochondriac disorder being mentioned, Dr Johnson did not think it so common as I supposed. – 'Dr Taylor (said he) is the same one day as another. Burke and Reynolds are the same. Beauclerk, except when in pain, is the same. I am not so myself; but this I do not mention commonly.'

I complained of a wretched changefulness, so that I could not preserve, for any long continuance, the same views of any thing. It was most comfortable to me to experience, in Dr Johnson's company, a relief from this uneasiness. His steady vigorous mind held firm before me those objects which my own feeble and tremulous imagination frequently presented, in such a wavering state, that my reason could not judge well of them.

Dr Johnson advised me to-day, to have as many books about me as I could; that I might read upon any subject upon which I had a desire for instruction at the time. 'What you read *then* (said he) you will remember; but if you have not a book immediately ready, and the subject moulds in your mind, it is a chance if you again have a desire to study it.' He added, 'If a man never has an eager desire for instruction, he should prescribe a task for himself. But it is better when a man reads from immediate inclination.'

He repeated a good many lines of Horace's Odes, while we were in the chaise. I remember particularly the Ode '*Eheu fugaces*'.

He said, the dispute as to the comparative excellence of Homer or Virgil[2] was inaccurate. 'We must consider (said he) whether Homer was not the greatest poet, though Virgil may have produced the finest poem. Virgil was indebted to Homer for the whole invention of the structure of an epic poem, and for many of his beauties.'

---

1 I am told, that the Honourable Horace Walpole has a collection of *Bon Mots* by persons who never said but one.

2 I am informed by Mr Langton, that a great many years ago he was present when this question was agitated between Dr Johnson and Mr Burke; and, to use Johnson's phrase, they 'talked their best'; Johnson for Homer, Burke for Virgil. It may well be supposed to have been one of the ablest and most brilliant contests that ever was exhibited. How much must we regret that it has not been preserved.

He told me, that Bacon was a favourite author with him, but he had never read his works till he was compiling the English Dictionary, in which, he said, I might see Bacon very often quoted. Mr Seward recollects his having mentioned, that a Dictionary of the English language might be compiled from Bacon's writings alone, and that he had once an intention of giving an edition of Bacon, at least of his English works, and writing the Life of that great man. Had he executed this intention, there can be no doubt that he would have done it in a most masterly manner. Mallet's Life of Bacon has no inconsiderable merit as an acute and elegant dissertation relative to its subject; but Mallet's mind was not comprehensive enough to embrace the vast extent of Lord Verulam's genius and research. Dr Warburton therefore observed, with witty justness, 'that Mallet in his Life of Bacon had forgotten that he was a philosopher; and if he should write the Life of the Duke of Marlborough, which he had undertaken to do, he would probably forget that he was a General.'

Wishing to be satisfied what degree of truth there was in a story which a friend of Johnson's and mine had told me to his disadvantage, I mentioned it to him in direct terms; and it was to this effect: that a gentleman who had lived in great intimacy with him, shown him much kindness, and even relieved him from a spunging-house, having afterwards fallen into bad circumstances, was one day, when Johnson was at dinner with him, seized for debt, and carried to prison; that Johnson sat still undisturbed, and went on eating and drinking; upon which the gentleman's sister, who was present, could not suppress her indignation: 'What, Sir (said she), are you so unfeeling, as not even to offer to go to my brother in his distress; you who have been so much obliged to him?' And that Johnson answered, 'Madam, I owe him no obligation; what he did for me he would have done for a dog.'

Johnson assured me, that the story was absolutely false; but like a man conscious of being in the right, and desirous of completely vindicating himself from such a charge, he did not arrogantly rest on a mere denial, and on his general character, but proceeded thus – 'Sir, I was very intimate with that gentleman, and was once relieved by him from an arrest; but I never was present when he was arrested, never knew that he was arrested, and I believe he never was in difficulties after the time when he relieved me. I loved him much; yet, in talking of his general character, I may have said, though I do not remember that I ever did[a] so, that as his generosity proceeded from no principle, but was part of his profusion, he would do for a dog what he would do for a friend: but I never applied this remark to any particular instance, and certainly not to his kindness to me. If a profuse man, who does not value his money, and gives a large sum to a whore, gives half as much, or an equally large sum to relieve a friend, it cannot be esteemed as virtue. This was all that I could say of that gentleman; and, if said at all, it must have been said after his death. Sir, I would have gone to the world's end to relieve him. The remark

a After 'did', read 'say'.

about the dog, if made by me, was such a sally as might escape one when painting a man highly.'

On Tuesday, September 23, Johnson was remarkably cordial to me. It being necessary for me to return to Scotland soon, I had fixed on the next day for my setting out, and I felt a tender concern at the thought of parting with him. He had, at this time, frankly communicated to me many particulars, which are inserted in this work in their proper places; and once, when I happened to mention that the expense of my jaunt would come to much more than I had computed, he said, 'Why, Sir, if the expense were to be an inconvenience, you would have reason to regret it: but, if you have had the money to spend, I know not that you could have purchased as much pleasure with it in any other way.'

During this interview at Ashbourne, Johnson and I frequently talked with wonderful pleasure of mere trifles which had occurred in our tour to the Hebrides; for it had left a most agreeable and lasting impression upon his mind.

He found fault with me for using the phrase to *make* money. 'Don't you see (said he) the impropriety of it? To *make* money is to *coin* it: you should say *get* money.' The phrase, however, is, I think, pretty current. But Johnson was at all times jealous of infractions upon the genuine English language, and prompt to repress colloquial barbarisms; such as, *pledging myself*, for *undertaking*; *line*, for *department* or *branch*, as, the *civil line*, the *banking* line. He was particularly indignant against the almost universal use of the word *idea* in the sense of notion or opinion when it is clear that *idea* can only signify something of which an image can be formed in the mind. We may have an *idea* or *image* of a mountain, a tree, a building; but we cannot surely have an *idea* or *image* of an *argument* or *proposition*. Yet we hear the sages of the law 'delivering their *ideas* upon the question under consideration'; and the first speakers in Parliament 'entirely coinciding in the *idea* which has been ably stated by an honourable member'; – or 'reprobating an *idea* unconstitutional, and fraught with the most dangerous consequences to a great and free country.' Johnson called this 'modern cant'.

I perceived that he pronounced the word *heard*, as if spelt with a double *e*, *heerd*, instead of sounding it *herd*, as is most usually done. He said, his reason was, that if it were pronounced *herd*, there would be a single exception from the English pronunciation of the syllable *ear*, and he thought it better not to have that exception.

He praised Granger's 'Ode on Solitude', in Dodsley's collection, and repeated, with great energy, the exordium:

> O Solitude, romantic maid,
> Whether by nodding towers you tread;
> Or haunt the desart's trackless gloom,
> Or hover o'er the yawning tomb;
> Or climb the Andes' clifted side,
> Or by the Nile's coy source abide;

> Or, starting from your half-year's sleep,
> From Hecla view the thawing deep;
> Or, at the purple dawn of day,
> Tadnor's marble wastes survey.

observing, 'This, Sir, is very noble.'

In the evening our gentleman-farmer, and two others, entertained themselves and the company with a great number of tunes on the fiddle. Johnson desired to have 'Let ambition fire thy mind', played over again, and appeared to give a patient attention to it; though he owned to me that he was very insensible to the power of music. I told him, that it affected me to such a degree, as often to agitate my nerves painfully, producing in my mind alternate sensations of pathetic dejection, so that I was ready to shed tears; and of daring resolution, so that I was inclined to rush into the thickest part of a battle. 'Sir (said he), I should never hear it, if it made me such a fool.'

Much of the effect of music, I am satisfied, is owing to association of ideas. That air, which instantly and irresistibly excites in the Swiss, when in a foreign land, the *maladie du pais*, has, I am told, no intrinsic power of sound. And I know from my own experience, that Scotch reels, though brisk, make me melancholy, because I used to hear them in my early years, at a time when Mr Pitt called for soldiers 'from the mountains of the north', and numbers of brave Highlanders were going abroad, never to return. Whereas the airs in *The Beggar's Opera*, many of which are very soft, never fail to render me gay, because they are associated with the warm sensations and high spirits of London. This evening, while some of the tunes of ordinary composition were played with no great skill, my frame was agitated, and I was conscious of a generous attachment to Dr Johnson, as my preceptor and friend, mixed with an affectionate regret that he was an old man, whom I should probably lose in a short time. I thought I could defend him at the point of my sword. My reverence and affection for him were in full glow. I said to him, 'My dear Sir, we must meet every year, if you don't quarrel with me.' JOHNSON. 'Nay, Sir, you are more likely to quarrel with me, than I with you. My regard for you is greater almost than I have words to express; but I do not choose to be always repeating it; write it down in the first leaf of your pocket-book, and never doubt of it again.'

I talked to him of misery being 'the doom of man', in this life, as displayed in his *Vanity of Human Wishes*. Yet I observed that things were done upon the supposition of happiness; grand houses were built, fine gardens were made, splendid places of public amusement were contrived, and crowded with company. JOHNSON. 'Alas, Sir, these are all only struggles for happiness. When I first entered Ranelagh, it gave an expansion and gay sensation to my mind, such as I never experienced any where else. But, as Xerxes wept when he viewed his immense army, and considered that not one of that great multitude would be alive a hundred years afterwards, so it went to my heart to consider that there was not one in all that brilliant circle, that was not afraid to go home and think; but that the thoughts of each individual there, would be distressing when alone.' This reflection was experimentally just. The feeling of languor,[1] which succeeds the animation of gaiety, is itself a very severe pain; and when the mind is then vacant, a thousand disappointments and vexations rush in and excruciate. Will not many even of my fairest readers allow this to be true?

I suggested, that being in love, and flattered with hopes of success; or having some favourite scheme in view for the next day, might prevent that wretchedness of which we had been talking. JOHNSON. 'Why, Sir, it may sometimes be so as you suppose; but my conclusion is in general but too true.'

While Johnson and I stood in calm conference by ourselves in Dr Taylor's garden, at a pretty late hour, in a serene autumn night, looking up to the heavens, I directed the discourse to the subject of a future state. My friend was in a placid and most benignant frame. 'Sir (said he), I do not imagine that all things will be made clear to us immediately after death, but that the ways of Providence will be explained to us very gradually.' I ventured to ask him whether although the words of some texts of Scripture seemed strong in support of the dreadful doctrine of an eternity of punishment, we might not hope that the denunciation was figurative, and would not literally be executed. JOHNSON. 'Sir, you are to consider the intention of punishment in a future state. We have no reason to be sure that we shall then be no longer liable to offend against GOD. We do not know that even the angels are quite in a state of security; nay we know that some of them have fallen. It may, therefore, perhaps be necessary, in order to preserve both men and angels in a state of rectitude, that they should have continually before them the punishment of those who have deviated from it; but we may hope that by some other means a fall from rectitude may be prevented. Some of the texts of Scripture upon this subject are, as you observe, indeed strong; but they may admit of a mitigated interpretation.' He talked to me upon this awful and delicate question in a gentle tone, and as if afraid to be decisive.

After supper I accompanied him to his apartment, and at my request he dictated to me an argument in favour of the negro who was then claiming his liberty, in an action in the Court of Session in Scotland.[2] He had always been very zealous against slavery in every form, in which I with all deference thought that he discovered 'a zeal without knowledge'. Upon one occasion, when in company with some very grave men at Oxford, his toast was, 'Here's

---

1 Pope mentions, 'Stretch'd on the rack of a too easy chair.' But I recollect a couplet quite apposite to my subject in *Virtue, an Ethic Epistle*, a beautiful and instructive poem, by an anonymous writer, in 1758; who, treating of pleasure in excess, says,

> Till languor, suffering on the rack of bliss,
> Confess that man was never made for this.

2 This being laid up somewhere amidst my multiplicity of papers at Auchinleck, has escaped my search for this work; but when found, I shall take care that my readers shall have it.

to the next insurrection of the negroes in the West-Indies.' His violent prejudice against our West-Indian and American settlers appeared whenever there was an opportunity. Towards the conclusion of his 'Taxation no Tyranny', he says, 'how is it that we hear the loudest *yelps* for liberty among the drivers of negroes?' and in his conversation with Mr Wilkes,[1] he asked, 'Where did Beckford and Trecothick learn English?' That Trecothick could both speak and write good English is well known. I myself was favoured with his correspondence concerning the brave Corsicans. And that Beckford could speak it with a spirit of honest resolution even to his Majesty, as his 'faithful Lord-Mayor of London', is commemorated by the noble monument erected to him in Guildhall.[a]

---

[1] See page 543 of this volume.

[a] *Third Edition* – The argument dictated by Dr Johnson was as follows:

'It must be agreed that in most ages many countries have had part or their inhabitants in a state of slavery; yet it may be doubted whether slavery can ever be supposed the natural condition of man. It is impossible not to conceive that men in their original state were equal; and very difficult to imagine how one would be subjected to another but by violent compulsion. An individual may, indeed, forfeit his liberty by a crime; but he cannot by that crime forfeit the liberty of his children. What is true of a criminal seems true likewise of a captive. A man may accept life from a conquering enemy on condition of perpetual servitude; but it is very doubtful whether he can entail that servitude on his descendants; for no man can stipulate without commission for another. The condition which he himself accepts, his son or grandson perhaps would have rejected. If we should admit, what perhaps may with more reason be denied, that there are certain relations between man and man which may make slavery necessary and just, yet it can never be proved that he who is now suing for his freedom ever stood in any of those relations. He is certainly subject by no law, but that of violence, to his present master; who pretends no claim to his obedience, but that he bought him from a merchant of slaves, whose right to sell him never was examined. It is said that according to the constitutions of Jamaica he was legally enslaved; these constitutions are merely positive; and apparently injurious to the rights of mankind, because whoever is exposed to sale is condemned to slavery without appeal; by whatever fraud or violence he might have been originally brought into the merchant's power. In our own time Princes have been sold, by wretches to whose care they were entrusted, that they might have an European education; but when once they were brought to a market in the plantations, little would avail either their dignity or their wrongs. The laws of Jamaica afford a Negro no redress. His colour is considered as a sufficient testimony against him. It is to be lamented that moral right should ever give way to political convenience. But if temptations of interest are sometimes too strong for human virtue, let us at least retain a virtue where there is no temptation to quit it. In the present case there is apparent right on one side, and no convenience on the other. Inhabitants of this island can neither gain riches nor power by taking away the liberty of any part of the human species. The sum of the argument is this: No man is by nature the property of another: The defendant is, therefore, by nature free: The rights of nature must be some way forfeited before they can be justly taken away: That the defendant has by any act forfeited the rights of nature we require to be proved; and if no proof of such forfeiture can be given, we doubt not but the justice of the court will declare him free.'

When I said now to Johnson, that I was afraid I kept him too late up. 'No, Sir (said he), I don't care though I sit all night with you.' This was an animated speech from a man in his sixty-ninth year.

Had I been as attentive not to displease him as I ought to have been, I know not but this vigil might have been fulfilled; but I unluckily entered upon the controversy concerning the right of Great-Britain to tax America, and attempted to argue in favour of our fellow-subjects on the other side of the Atlantic. I insisted that America might be very well governed, and made to yield a sufficient revenue by the means of *influence*, as exemplified in Ireland, while the people might be pleased with the imagination of their participating of the British constitution, by having a body of representatives without whose consent money could not be exacted from them. Johnson could not bear my thus opposing his avowed opinion, which he had exerted himself with an

---

I record Dr Johnson's argument fairly upon this particular case; where, perhaps, he was in the right. But I beg leave to enter my most solemn protest against his general doctrine with respect to the *Slave Trade*. For I will resolutely say – that his unfavourable notion of it was owing to prejudice, and imperfect or false information. The wild and dangerous attempt which has for some time been persisted in to obtain an act of our Legislature, to abolish so very important and necessary a branch of commercial interest, must have been crushed at once, had not the insignificance of the zealots who vainly took the lead in it, made the vast body of Planters, Merchants, and others, whose immense properties are involved in that trade, reasonably enough suppose that there could be no danger. The encouragement which the attempt has received excites my wonder and indignation; and though some men of superior abilities have supported it; whether from a love of temporary popularity, when prosperous; or a love of general mischief, when desperate, my opinion is unshaken. To abolish a *status*, which in all ages GOD has sanctioned, and man has continued, would not only be *robbery* to an innumerable class of our fellow-subjects; but it would be extreme cruelty to the African Savages, a portion of whom it saves from massacre, or intolerable bondage in their own country, and introduces into a much happier state of life; especially now when their passage to the West-Indies and their treatment there is humanely regulated. To abolish that trade would be to

. . . shut the gates of mercy on mankind.

Whatever may have passed elsewhere concerning it, The HOUSE OF LORDS is wise and independent:

> *Intaminatis fulget honoribus;*
> *Nec sumit aut ponit secures*
> *Arbitrio popularis aurae.*

I have read, conversed, and thought much upon the subject, and would recommend to all who are capable of conviction, an excellent Tract by my learned and ingenious friend John Ranby, Esq., entitled 'Doubts on the Abolition of the Slave Trade'. To Mr Ranby's 'Doubts', I will apply Lord Chancellor Hardwicke's expression in praise of a Scotch Law Book, called *Dirleton's Doubts*; 'HIS *Doubts* (said his Lordship), are better than most people's *Certainties*.

extreme degree of heat to enforce; and the violent agitation into which he was thrown while answering, or rather reprimanding me, alarmed me so that I heartily repented of my having unthinkingly introduced the subject. I myself however grew warm, and the change was great, from the calm state of philosophical discussion in which we had a little before been pleasingly employed.

I talked of the corruption of the British parliament, in which I alleged that any question, however unreasonable or unjust, might be carried by a venal majority; and I spoke with high admiration of the Roman Senate, as if composed of men sincerely desirous to resolve what they should think best for their country. My friend would allow no such character to the Roman Senate; and he maintained that the British parliament was not corrupt, and that there was no occasion to corrupt its members, asserting, that there was hardly ever any question of great importance before parliament, any question in which a man might not very well vote either upon one side or the other. He said there had been none in his time except that respecting America.

We were fatigued by the contest, which was produced by my want of caution; and he was not then in the humour to slide into easy and cheerful talk. It therefore so happened, that we were after an hour or two very willing to separate and go to bed.

On Wednesday, September 24, I went into Dr Johnson's room before he got up, and finding that the storm of the preceding night was quite laid, I sat down upon his bed-side, and he talked with as much readiness and good-humour as ever. He recommended to me to plant a considerable part of a large moorish farm which I had purchased, and he made several calculations of the expense and profit, for he delighted in exercising his mind on the science of numbers. He pressed upon me the importance of planting at the first in a very sufficient manner, quoting the saying, '*In bello non licet bis errare*'; and adding, 'this is equally true in planting.'

I spoke with gratitude of Dr Taylor's hospitality; and as evidence that it was not on account of his good table alone that Johnson visited him often, I mentioned a little anecdote which had escaped my friend's recollection, and at hearing which repeated, he smiled. One evening when I was sitting with him, Frank delivered this message, 'Sir, Dr Taylor sends his compliments to you, and begs you will dine with him to-morrow. He has got a hare.' – 'My compliments (said Johnson), and I'll dine with him, hare or rabbit.'

After breakfast I departed, and pursued my journey northwards. I took my post-chaise from the Green Man, a very good inn at Ashbourne, the mistress of which, a mighty civil gentlewoman, curtseying very low, presented me with an engraving of the sign of her house; to which she had subjoined, in her own hand-writing, an address in such singular simplicity of style, that I have preserved it pasted upon one of the boards of my original Journal at this time, and shall here insert it for the amusement of my readers:

M. Killingley's duty waits upon Mr Boswell, is exceedingly obliged to him for this favour; whenever he comes this way, hopes for a continuance of the same. Would Mr Boswell name the house to his extensive acquaintance, it would be a singular favour confer'd on one who has it not in her power to make any other return but her most grateful thanks, and sincerest prayers for his happiness in time, and in a blessed eternity.

Tuesday morn.

From this meeting at Ashbourne I derived a considerable accession to my Johnsonian store. I communicated my original Journal to Sir William Forbes, in whom I have always placed deserved confidence; and what he wrote to me concerning it is so much to my credit as the biographer of Johnson, that my readers will, I hope, grant me their indulgence for here inserting it, 'It is not once or twice going over it (says Sir William) that will satisfy me; for I find in it a high degree of instruction as well as entertainment; and I derive more benefit from Dr Johnson's admirable discussions than I should be able to draw from his personal conversation; for I suppose there is not a man in the world to whom he discloses his sentiments so freely as to yourself.'

I cannot omit a curious circumstance which occurred at Edensor-inn, close by Chatsworth, to survey the magnificence of which I had gone a considerable way out of my road to Scotland. The inn was then kept by a very jolly landlord, whose name I think was Malton. He happened to mention that 'the celebrated Dr Johnson had been in his house.' I inquired *who* this Dr Johnson was, that I might hear mine host's notion of him. 'Sir (said he), Johnson, the great writer; *Oddity*, as they call him. He's the greatest writer in England; he writes for the ministry; he has a correspondence abroad, and lets them know what's going on.'

My friend, who had a thorough dependance upon the authenticity of my relation without any *embellishment*, as *falsehood* or *fiction* is too gently called, laughed a good deal at this representation of himself.

Mr BOSWELL to Dr JOHNSON.

Edinburgh, Sept. 29, 1777.

MY DEAR SIR – By the first post I inform you of my safe arrival at my own house, and that I had the comfort of finding my wife and children all in good health.

When I look back upon our late interview, it appears to me to have answered expectation better than almost any scheme of happiness that I ever put in execution. My Journal is stored with wisdom and wit; and my memory is filled with the recollection of lively and affectionate feelings, which now, I think, yield me more satisfaction than at the time when they were first excited. I have experienced this upon other occasions. I will be obliged to you if you will explain it to me; for it seems wonderful that pleasure should be more vivid at a distance than when near. I wish you may find yourself in the humour to do me this favour; but I flatter myself with no strong hope of it; for I have observed, that unless upon very serious occasions, your letters to me are not answers to those which I write.

[I then expressed to him much uneasiness that I had mentioned to him the name of the gentleman who had told me the story so much to his disadvantage, the truth of which he had completely refuted; for that my having done so might be interpreted as a breach of confidence, and offend one whose society I valued: therefore earnestly requesting that no notice might be taken of it to any body, till I should be in London, and have an opportunity to talk it over with the gentleman.]

To JAMES BOSWELL, Esq.

DEAR SIR – You will wonder, or you have wondered, why no letter has come from me. What you wrote at your return, had in it such a strain of cowardly caution as gave me no pleasure. I could not well do what you wished; I had no need to vex you with a refusal. I have seen Mr ———, and as to him have set all right, without any inconvenience, so far as I know, to you. Mrs Thrale had forgot the story. You may now be at ease.

And at ease I certainly wish you, for the kindness that you showed in coming so long a journey to see me. It was pity to keep you so long in pain, but, upon reviewing the matter, I do not see what I could have done better than as I did.

I hope you found at your return my dear enemy and all her little people quite well, and had no reason to repent your journey. I think on it with great gratitude.

I was not well when you left me at the Doctor's, and I grew worse; yet I staid on, and at Lichfield was very ill. Travelling, however, did not make me worse; and when I came to London I complied with a summons to go to Brighthelmston, where I saw Beauclerk, and staid three days.

Our club has recommenced last Friday, but I was not there. Langton has another wench.[1] Mrs Thrale is in hopes of a young brewer. They got by their trade last year a very large sum, and their expenses are proportionate.

Mrs Williams's health is very bad. And I have had for some time a very difficult and laborious respiration, but I am better by purges, abstinence, and other methods. I am yet however much behind-hand in my health and rest.

Dr Blair's sermons are now universally commended, but let him think that I had the honour of first finding and first praising his excellencies. I did not stay to add my voice to that of the public.

My dear friend, let me thank you once more for your visit; you did me great honour, and I hope met with nothing that displeased you. I staid long at Ashbourne, not much pleased, yet awkward at departing. I then went to Lichfield, where I found my friend at Stowhill[2] very dangerously diseased. Such is life. Let us try to pass it well, whatever it be, for there is surely something beyond it.

1 A daughter born to him.
2 Mrs Aston.

Well, now I hope all is well, write as soon as you can to, dear Sir,
Your affectionate servant,

SAM. JOHNSON.

London, Nov. 25, 1777.

To Dr SAMUEL JOHNSON.

Edinburgh, Nov. 29, 1777.

MY DEAR SIR – This day's post has at length relieved me from much
uneasiness, by bringing me a letter from you. I was, indeed, doubly
uneasy; – on my own account and yours. I was very anxious to be secured
against any bad consequences from my imprudence in mentioning the
gentleman's name who had told me a story to your disadvantage; and as I
could hardly suppose it possible, that you would delay so long to make
me easy, unless you was ill, I was not a little apprehensive about you. You
must not be offended when I venture to tell you that you appear to me to
have been too rigid upon this occasion. The '*cowardly caution which gave
you no pleasure*', was suggested to me by a friend here, to whom I
mentioned the strange story and the detection of its falsity, as an instance
how one may be deceived by what is apparently very good authority.
But, as I am still persuaded, that as I might have obtained the truth,
without mentioning the gentleman's name, it was wrong in me to do it, I
cannot see that you are just in blaming my caution. But if you were ever
so just in your disapprobation, might you not have dealt more tenderly
with me?

I went to Auchinleck about the middle of October, and passed some
time with my father very comfortably. . . .

I am engaged in a criminal prosecution against a country schoolmaster,
for indecent behaviour to his female scholars. There is no statute against
such abominable conduct; but it is punishable at common law. I will be
obliged to you for your assistance in this extraordinary trial. I ever am, my
dear Sir,

Your faithful humble servant,

JAMES BOSWELL.

About this time I wrote to Johnson, giving him all account of the decision
of the *Negro cause*, by the Court of Session, which by those who hold even the
mildest and best regulated slavery in abomination (of which number I do not
hesitate to declare that I am none), should be remembered with high respect,
and to the credit of Scotland; for it went upon a much broader ground than
the case of *Somerset*, which was decided in England;[1] being truly the general
question, whether a perpetual obligation of service to one master in any mode
should be sanctioned by the law of a free country. A negro, then called *Joseph*

1 See State Trials, Vol. XI, p. 339, and Mr Hargrave's argument.

Knight, a native of Africa, who having been brought to Jamaica in the usual course of the slave trade, and purchased by a Scotch gentleman in that island, had attended his master to Scotland, where it was officiously suggested to him that he would be found entitled to his liberty without any limitation. He accordingly brought his action, in the course of which the advocates on both sides did themselves great honour. Mr Maclaurin has had the praise of Johnson, for his argument[1] in favour of the negro, and Mr Macconochie distinguished himself on the same side, by his ingenuity and extraordinary research. Mr Cullen, on the part of the master, discovered good information and sound reasoning; in which he was well supported by Mr James Fergusson, a man remarkable for a manly understanding, and a knowledge both of books and of the world. But I cannot too highly praise the speech which Mr Henry Dundas generously contributed to the cause of the sooty stranger. Mr Dundas's Scottish accent, which has been so often in vain obtruded as an objection to his powerful abilities in parliament, was no disadvantage to him in his own country. And I do declare, that upon this memorable question he impressed me, and I believe all his audience, with such feelings as were produced by some of the most eminent orations of antiquity. This testimony I liberally give to the excellence of an old friend, with whom it has been my lot to differ very widely upon many political topics; yet I persuade myself without malice. A great majority of the Lords of Session decided for the negro. But four of their number, the Lord President, Lord Elliock, Lord Monboddo, and Lord Covington, resolutely maintained the lawfulness of a *status*, which has been acknowledged in all ages and countries, and that when freedom flourished, as in old Greece and Rome.

To JAMES BOSWELL, Esq.

DEAR SIR – This is the time of the year in which all express their good wishes to their friends, and I send mine to you and your family. May your lives be long, happy, and good. I have been much out of order, but, I hope, do not grow worse.

The crime of the schoolmaster whom you are engaged to prosecute is very great, and may be suspected to be too common. In our law it would be a breach of the peace, and a misdemeanour; that is, a kind of indefinite crime, not capital, but punishable at the discretion of the court. You cannot want matter: all that needs to be said will easily occur.

---

1 The motto to it was happily chosen:

. . . *Nimium ne crede colori.*[a]

I cannot avoid mentioning a circumstance no less strange than true, that a brother Advocate in considerable practice, but of whom it certainly cannot be said, '*Ingenuas didicit fideliter artes*', asked Mr Maclaurin, with a face of flippant assurance, 'Are these words your own?'

a For '*Nimium ne crede colori*', read '*Quamvis ille niger, quamvis tu candidus esses.*'

Mr Shaw, the author of the Gaelic Grammar, desires me to make a request for him to Lord Eglintoune, that he may be appointed Chaplain to one of the new-raised regiments.

All our friends are as they were; little has happened to them of either good or bad. Mrs Thrale ran a great black hair-dressing pin into her eye; but by great evacuation she kept it from inflaming, and it is almost well. Miss Reynolds has been out of order, but is better. Mrs Williams is in a very poor state of health.

If I should write on, I should, perhaps, write only complaints, and therefore I will content myself with telling you, that I love to think on you, and to hear from you; and that I am, dear Sir,

Yours faithfully,

SAM. JOHNSON.

December 27, 1777.

In 1778, Johnson gave the world a luminous proof that the vigour of his mind in all its faculties, whether memory, judgement, or imagination, was not in the least abated; for this year came out the first four volumes of his *Prefaces, biographical and critical, to the most eminent of the English Poets,** published by the booksellers of London. The remaining volumes came out in the year 1780. The Poets were selected by the several booksellers who had the honorary copyright, which is still preserved among them by mutual compact, notwithstanding the decision of the House of Lords against the perpetuity of Literary Property. We have his own authority,[1] that by his recommendation the Poems of Blackmore, Watts, Pomfret, and Yalden, were added to the collection. Of this work I shall speak more particularly hereafter.[a]

To Dr SAMUEL JOHNSON.

Edinburgh, Jan. 8, 1778.

DEAR SIR – Your congratulations upon a new year are mixed with complaint: mine must be so too. My wife has for some time been very ill, having been confined to the house these three months by a severe cold, attended with alarming symptoms.

[Here I gave a particular account of the distress which the person, upon every account most dear to me, suffered; and of the dismal state of apprehension in which I now was. Adding, that I never stood more in need of his consoling philosophy.]

Did you ever look at a book written by Wilson, a Scotsman, under the Latin name of *Volusenus*, according to the custom of literary men at a certain period? It is entitled *De Animi Tranquillitate*. I earnestly desire

1 Life of Watts.

a *Second Edition.* – The paragraph beginning 'In 1778,' &c. shifted to the end of the year, and inserted after the paragraph following the letter to Hussey of December 29, 1778 on p. 708.

tranquillity. *Bona res quies*; but I fear I shall never attain it: for, when unoccupied, I grow gloomy, and occupation agitates me to feverishness.

. . .

I am, dear Sir,

Your most affectionate humble servant,

JAMES BOSWELL.

To JAMES BOSWELL, Esq.

DEAR SIR – To a letter so interesting as your last, it is proper to return some answer, however little I may be disposed to write.

Your alarm at your lady's illness was reasonable, and not disproportionate to the appearance of the disorder. I hope your physical friend's conjecture is now verified, and all fear of a consumption at an end: a little care and exercise will then restore her. London is a good air for ladies; and if you bring her hither, I will do for her what she did for me – I will retire from my apartments for her accommodation. Behave kindly to her, and keep her cheerful.

You always seem to call for tenderness. Know then, that in the first month of the present year I very highly esteem and very cordially love you. I hope to tell you this at the beginning of every year as long as we live; and why should we trouble ourselves to tell or hear it oftener?

Tell Veronica, Euphemia, and Alexander, that I wish them, as well as their parents, many happy years.

You have ended the negro's cause much to my mind. Lord Auchinleck and dear Lord Hailes were on the side of liberty. Lord Hailes's name reproaches me; but if he saw my languid neglect of my own affairs, he would rather pity than resent my neglect of his. I hope to mend, *ut et mihi vivam et amicis*. I am, dear Sir,

Your's affectionately,

SAM. JOHNSON.

January 24, 1778.

My service to my fellow-traveller, Joseph.[a]

[a] After this letter, read: Johnson maintained a long and intimate friendship with Mr Welch, who succeeded the celebrated Henry Fielding as one of his Majesty's Justices of the Peace for Westminster; kept a regular office for the police of that great district; and discharged his important trust, for many years, faithfully and ably. Johnson, who had an eager and unceasing curiosity to know human life in all its variety, told me, that he attended Mr Welch in his office for a whole winter, to hear the examinations of the culprits; but that he found an almost uniform tenor of misfortune, wretchedness, and profligacy. Mr Welch's health being impaired, he was advised to try the effect of a warm climate; and Johnson, by his interest with Mr Chamier, procured him leave of absence to go to Italy, and a promise that the pension or salary of two hundred pounds a year, which Government allowed him, should not be discontinued. Mr Welch accordingly went abroad, accompanied by his daughter Anne, a young lady of uncommon talents and literature.

To Dr SAMUEL JOHNSON.

Edinburgh, Feb. 26, 1778.

MY DEAR SIR – Why I have delayed, for near a month, to thank you for your last affectionate letter, I cannot say; for my mind has been in better health these three weeks than for some years past. I believe I have evaded till I could send you a copy of Lord Hailes's opinion on the negro's cause, which he wishes you to read, and correct any errors that there may be in the language; for, says he, 'we live in a critical, though not a learned age; and I seek to screen myself under the shield of Ajax.' I communicated to him your apology for keeping the sheets of his *Annals* so long. He says, 'I am sorry to see that Dr Johnson is in a state of languor. Why should a sober Christian, neither an enthusiast nor a fanatic, be very merry or very sad?' I envy his Lordship's comfortable constitution: but well do I know that

---

To SAUNDERS WELCH, Esq. at the English Coffee-house, Rome.

DEAR SIR – To have suffered one of my best and dearest friends to pass almost two years in foreign countries without a letter, has a very shameful appearance of inattention. But the truth is, that there was no particular time in which I had any thing particular to say; and general expressions of good will, I hope, our long friendship is grown too solid to want.

Of public affairs you have information from the news-papers wherever you go, for the English keep no secret; and of other things, Mrs Nollekens informs you. My intelligence could therefore be of no use; and Miss Nancy's letters made it unnecessary to write to you for information: I was likewise for some time out of humour, to find that motion, and nearer approaches to the sun, did not restore your health so fast as I expected. Of your health, the accounts have lately been more pleasing; and I have the gratification of imagining to myself a length of years which I hope you have gained, and of which the enjoyment will be improved by a vast accession of images and observations which your journies and various residence have enabled you to make and accumulate. You have travelled with this felicity, almost peculiar to yourself, that your companion is not to part from you at your journey's end; but you are to live on together, to help each other's recollection, and to supply each other's omissions. The world has few greater pleasures than that which two friends enjoy, in tracing back, at some distant time, those transactions and events through which they have passed together. One of the old man's miseries is, that he cannot easily find a companion able to partake with him of the past. You and your fellow-traveller have this comfort in store, that your conversation will be not easily exhausted; one will always be glad to say what the other will always be willing to hear.

That you may enjoy this pleasure long, your health must have your constant attention. I suppose you propose to return this year. There is no need of haste: do not come hither before the height of summer, that you may fall gradually into the inconveniences of your native clime. July seems to be the proper month. August and September will prepare you for the winter. After having travelled so far to find health, you must take care not to lose it at home; and I hope a little care will effectually preserve it.

Miss Nancy has doubtless kept a constant and copious journal. She must not expect to be welcome when she returns, without a great mass of information. Let

languor and dejection will afflict the best, however excellent their principles. I am in possession of Lord Hailes's opinion in his own hand-writing, and have had it for some time. My excuse then for procrastination must be, that I wanted to have it copied; and I have now put that off so long, that it will be better to bring it with me than send it, as I shall probably get you to look at it sooner when I solicit you in person.

My wife, who is, I thank GOD, a good deal better, is much obliged to you for your very polite and courteous offer of your apartment: but, if she goes to London, it will be best for her to have lodgings in the more airy vicinity of Hyde-Park. I, however, doubt much if I shall be able to prevail with her to accompany me to the metropolis, for she is so different from you and me, that she dislikes travelling; and she is so anxious about her children, that she thinks she should be unhappy if at a distance from them.

---

her review her journal often, and set down what she finds herself to have omitted, that she may trust to memory as little as possible, for memory is soon confused by a quick succession of things; and she will grow every day less confident of the truth of her own narratives, unless she can recur to some written memorials. If she has satisfied herself with hints, instead of full representations, let her supply the deficiencies now while her memory is yet fresh, and while her father's memory may help her. If she observes this direction, she will not have travelled in vain; for she will bring home a book with which she may entertain herself to the end of life. If it were not now too late, I would advise her to note the impression which the first sight of any thing new and wonderful made upon her mind. Let her now set her thoughts down as she can recollect them; for faint as they may already be, they will grow every day fainter.

Perhaps I do not flatter myself unreasonably when I imagine that you may wish to know something of me. I can gratify your benevolence with no account of health. The hand of time, or of disease, is very heavy upon me. I pass restless and uneasy nights, harassed with convulsions of my breast, and flatulencies at my stomach; and restless nights make heavy days. But nothing will be mended by complaints, and therefore I will make an end. When we meet, we will try to forget our cares and our maladies, and contribute, as we can, to the cheerfulness of each other. If I had gone with you, I believe I should have been better; but I do not know that it was in my power. I am, dear Sir,

Your most humble servant,

SAM. JOHNSON.

Feb. 3, 1778.

This letter, while it gives admirable advice how to travel to the best advantage, and will therefore be of very general use, is another eminent proof of Johnson's warm and affectionate heart.[1]

1 The friendship between Mr Welch and him was unbroken. Mr Welch died not many months before him, and bequeathed him five guineas for a ring, which Johnson received with tenderness, as a kind memorial, His regard was constant for his friend Mr Welch's daughters; of whom Jane is married to Mr Nollekens, the statuary, whose merit is too well known to require any praise from me.

She therefore wishes rather to go to some country place in Scotland, where she can have them with her.

I purpose being in London about the 20th of next month, as I think it creditable to appear in the House of Lords as one of Douglas's Counsel, in the great and last competition between Duke Hamilton and him.

. . .

I am sorry poor Mrs Williams is so ill: though her temper is unpleasant, she has always been polite and obliging to me. I wish many happy years to good Mr Levett, who I suppose holds his usual place at your breakfast-table.[1]

I ever am, my dear Sir,

Your affectionate humble servant,

JAMES BOSWELL.

To the same.

Edinburgh, Feb. 28, 1778.

MY DEAR SIR – You are at present busy amongst the English Poets, preparing, for the public instruction and entertainment, Prefaces, biographical and critical. It will not, therefore, be out of season to appeal to you for the decision of a controversy which has arisen between a lady and me concerning a passage in Parnell. That poet tells us, that his Hermit quitted his cell

> . . . to know the world by sight,
> To find if *books* or *swains* report it right;
> (For yet by *swains alone* the world he knew,
> Whose feet came wand'ring o'er the nightly dew).

I maintain that there is an inconsistency here; for as the Hermit's notions of the world were formed from the reports both of *books* and *swains*, he could not justly be said to know by *swains alone*. Be pleased to judge between us, and let us have your reasons.

What do you say to 'Taxation no Tyranny' now, after Lord North's declaration, or confession, or whatever else his conciliatory speech should be called? I never differed from you on politics but upon two points – the Middlesex Election, and the Taxation of the Americans by the British *Houses of Representatives*. There is a *charm* in the word *Parliament*, so I avoid it. As I am a steady and a warm Tory, I regret that the King does not see it to be better for him to receive constitutional supplies from his American subjects by the voice of their own assemblies, where his Royal Person is represented, than through the medium of his British subjects. I am persuaded that the power of the Crown, which I wish to increase, would

---

1 Dr Percy, the Bishop of Dromore, humorously observed, that Levett used to breakfast on the crust of a roll, which Johnson, after tearing out the crumb for himself, threw to his humble friend.

be greater when in contact with all its dominions, than if 'the rays of regal bounty'[1] were to 'shine' upon America, through that dense and troubled body – a modern British Parliament. But, enough of this subject; for your angry voice at Ashbourne upon it, still sounds awful 'in my mind's *ears*'. I ever am, my dear Sir,

Your most affectionate humble servant,

JAMES BOSWELL.

To the same.

Edinburgh, March 12, 1778.

MY DEAR SIR – The alarm of your late illness distressed me but for a few hours; for on the evening of the day that it reached me, I found it contradicted in the *London Chronicle*, which I could depend upon as authentic concerning you, Mr Strahan being the printer of it. I did not see the paper in which 'the approaching extinction of a bright luminary' was announced. Sir William Forbes told me of it; and he says, he saw me so uneasy, that he did not give me the report in such strong terms as he had read it. He afterwards sent me a letter from Mr Langton to him, which relieved me much. I am, however, not quite easy, as I have not heard from you; and now I shall not have that comfort before I see you, for I set out for London to-morrow before the post comes in. I hope to be with you on Wednesday morning; and I ever am, with the highest veneration, my dear Sir,

Your much obliged,

Faithful, and affectionate humble servant,

JAMES BOSWELL.

On Wednesday, March 18, I arrived in London, and was informed by good Mr Francis that his master was better, and was gone to Mr Thrale's at Streatham, to which place I wrote to him, begging to know when he would be in town. He was not expected for some time; but next day having called on Dr Taylor, in Dean's-yard, Westminster, I found him there, and was told he had come to town for a few hours. He met me with his usual kindness, but instantly returned to the writing of something on which he was employed when I came in, and on which he seemed much intent. Finding him thus engaged, I made my visit very short, and had no more of his conversation, except his expressing a serious regret that a friend of ours was living at too much expense, considering how poor an appearance he made: 'If (said he) a man has splendour from his expense, if he spends his money in pride or in pleasure, he has value; but if he lets others spend it for him, which is most commonly the case, he has no advantage from it.'

On Friday, March 20, I found him at his own house, sitting with Mrs

---

1 Alluding to a line in his *Vanity of Human Wishes*, when describing Cardinal Wolsey in his state of elevation:

Through him the rays of regal bounty shine.

Williams, and was informed that the room formerly allotted to me was now appropriated to a charitable purpose; Mrs Desmoulins,[1] and I think her daughter, and a Miss Carmichael, being all lodged in it. Such was his humanity, and such his generosity, that Mrs Desmoulins herself told me, he allowed her half-a-guinea a week. Let it be remembered, that this was above a twelfth part of his pension.

His liberality, indeed, was at all periods of his life very remarkable. Mr Howard, of Lichfield, at whose father's house Johnson had in his early years been kindly received, told me, that when he was a boy at the Charter-House, his father wrote to him to go and pay a visit to Mr Samuel Johnson, which he accordingly did, and found him in an upper room, of poor appearance. Johnson received him with much courteousness, and talked a great deal to him, as to a school-boy, of the course of his education, and other particulars. When he afterwards came to know and understand the high character of this great man, he recollected his condescension with wonder. He added, that when he was going away, Mr Johnson presented him with half-a-guinea; and this, said Mr Howard, was at a time when he probably had not another.

We retired from Mrs Williams to another room. Tom Davies soon after joined us. He had now unfortunately failed in his circumstances, and was much indebted to Dr Johnson's kindness for obtaining for him many alleviations of his distress. After he went away, Johnson blamed his folly in quitting the stage, by which he and his wife got five hundred pounds a year. I said, I believed it was owing to Churchill's attack upon him,

> He mouths a sentence as curs mouth a bone.

JOHNSON. 'I believe so too, Sir. But what a man is he who is to be driven from the stage by a line? Another line would have driven him from his shop.'

I told him, that I was engaged as Counsel at the bar of the House of Commons to oppose a road-bill in the county of Stirling, and asked him what mode he would advise me to follow in addressing such an audience. JOHNSON. 'Why, Sir, you must provide yourself with a good deal of extraneous matter, which you are to produce occasionally, so as to fill up the time; for you must consider, that they do not listen much. If you begin with the strength of your cause, it may be lost before they begin to listen. When you catch a moment of attention, press the merits of the question upon them.' He said, as to one point of the merits, that he thought 'it would be a wrong thing to deprive the small land-holders of the privilege of assessing themselves for making and repairing the high roads; it was destroying so much liberty, without a good reason, which was always a bad thing.' When I mentioned this observation next day to Mr Wilkes, he pleasantly said, 'What! does *he* talk of liberty? *Liberty* is as ridiculous in *his* mouth as *Religion* in *mine*.' Mr Wilkes's advice, as to the best mode of speaking at the bar of the House of Commons, was not more respectful towards the senate, than that of Dr Johnson. 'Be as impudent as you can, as merry as you can, and say whatever

1 Daughter of Dr Swinfen, Johnson's godfather, and widow of Mr Desmoulins, a writing-master.

comes uppermost. Jack Lee is the best heard there of any Counsel; and he is the most impudent dog, and always abusing us.'

In my interview with Dr Johnson this evening, I was quite easy, quite as his companion; upon which I find in my Journal the following reflection: 'So ready is my mind to suggest matter for dissatisfaction, that I felt a sort of regret that I was so easy. I missed that awful reverence with which I used to contemplate *Mr Samuel Johnson*, in the complex magnitude of his literary, moral, and religious character. I have a wonderful superstitious love of *mystery*; when, perhaps, the truth is, that it is owing to the cloudy darkness of my own mind. I should be glad that I am more advanced in my progress of being, so that I can view Dr Johnson with a steadier and clearer eye. My dissatisfaction tonight was foolish. Would it not be foolish to regret that we shall have less mystery in a future state? That we "now see in a glass darkly", but shall "then see face to face"?' – This reflection, which I thus freely communicate, will be valued by the thinking part of my readers, who may have themselves experienced similar states of mind.

He returned next day to Streatham, to Mr Thrale's; where, as Mr Strahan once complained to me, 'he was in a great measure absorbed from the society of his old friends.' I was kept in London by business, and wrote to him on the 27th, that 'a separation from him for a week, when we were so near, was equal to a separation for a year, when we were at four hundred miles distance.' I went to Streatham on Monday, March 30. Before he appeared, Mrs Thrale made a very characteristical remark: 'I do not know for certain what will please Dr Johnson: but I know for certain that it will displease him to praise any thing, even what he likes extravagantly.'

At dinner he laughed at querulous declamations against the age, on account of luxury – increase of London – scarcity of provisions – and other such topics. 'Houses (said he) will be built till rents fall; and corn is more plentiful now than ever it was.'

I had before dinner repeated a ridiculous story told me by an old man who had been a passenger with me in the stage-coach to-day. Mrs Thrale, having taken occasion to allude to it in talking to me, called it 'The story told you by the old *woman*.' – 'Now, Madam, (said I), give me leave to catch you in the fact: it was not an old *woman*, but an old *man*, whom I mentioned as having told me this.' I presumed to take an opportunity, in presence of Johnson, of shewing this lively lady how ready she was, unintentionally, to deviate from exact authenticity of narration.

'Thomas à Kempis (he observed) must be a good book, as the world has opened its arms to receive it. It is said to have been printed, in one language or other, as many times as there have been months since it first came out. I always was struck with this sentence in it: "Be not angry that you cannot make others as you wish them to be, since you cannot make yourself as you wish to be." '

He said, 'I was angry with Hurd about Cowley, for having published a selection of his works: but, upon better consideration, I think there is no impropriety in a man's publishing as much as he chooses of any author, if he does not put the rest out of the way. A man, for instance, may print the Odes of Horace alone.' He seemed to be in a more indulgent humour than when this subject was discussed between him and Mr Murphy.[1]

When we were at tea and coffee, there came in Lord Trimblestown, in whose family was an ancient Irish peerage, but it suffered by taking the generous side in the troubles of the last century. He was a man of pleasing conversation, and was accompanied by a young gentleman, his son.

I mentioned that I had in my possession the Life of Sir Robert Sibbald, the celebrated Scottish antiquary, and founder of the Royal College of Physicians at Edinburgh, in the original manuscript in his own hand-writing; and that it was I believed the most natural and candid account of himself that ever was given by any man. As an instance, he tells that the Duke of Perth, then Chancellor of Scotland, pressed him very much to come over to the Roman-Catholic Faith; that he resisted all his Grace's arguments for a considerable time, till one day he felt himself as it were instantaneously convinced, and with tears in his eyes ran into the Duke's arms, and embraced the ancient religion; that he continued very steady in it for some time, and accompanied his Grace to London one winter, and lived in his household; that there he found the rigid fasting prescribed by the church very severe upon him; that this disposed him to reconsider the controversy, and having then seen that he was in the wrong, he returned to Protestantism. I talked of some time or other publishing this curious life. MRS THRALE. 'I think you had as well let alone that publication. To discover such weakness exposes a man when he is gone.' JOHNSON. 'Nay, it is an honest picture of human nature. How often are the primary motives of our greatest actions as small as Sibbald's, for his re-conversion.' MRS THRALE. 'But may they not as well be forgotten?' JOHNSON. 'No, Madam, a man loves to review his own mind. That is the use of a diary, or journal.' LORD TRIMBLESTOWN. 'True, Sir. As the ladies love to see themselves in a glass; so a man likes to see himself in his journal.' BOSWELL. 'A very pretty allusion.' JOHNSON. 'Yes, indeed.' BOSWELL. 'And as a lady adjusts her dress before a mirror, a man adjusts his character by looking at his journal.' I next year found the very same thought in Atterbury's 'Sermon on Lady Cutts'. 'In this glass she every day dressed her mind.' This is a proof of coincidence, and not of plagiarism; for I had never read that sermon before.

Next morning, while we were at breakfast, Johnson gave a very earnest recommendation of what he himself practised with the utmost conscientious-ness: I mean a strict attention to truth, even in the most minute particulars. 'Accustom your children (said he) constantly to this; if a thing happened at one window, and they, when relating it, say that it happened at another, do not let it pass, but instantly check them; you do not know where deviation from truth will end.' BOSWELL. 'It may come to the door; and when once an account is at all varied in one circumstance, it may by degrees be varied so as to be totally different from what really happened.' Our lively hostess, whose fancy was impatient of the rein, fidgeted at this, and ventured to say, 'Nay, this is too much. If Mr Johnson should forbid me to drink tea I would comply, as I

[1] See page 519.

should feel the restraint only twice a day; but little variations in narrative must happen a thousand times a day, if one is not perpetually watching.' JOHNSON. 'Well, Madam, and you *ought* to be perpetually watching. It is more from carelessness about truth than from intentional lying, that there is so much falsehood in the world.'

In his review of Dr Warton's 'Essay on the Writings and Genius of Pope', Johnson has given the following salutary caution upon this subject: 'Nothing but experience could evince the frequency of false information, or enable any man to conceive that so many groundless reports should be propagated, as every man of eminence may hear of himself. Some men relate what they think, as what they know; some men of confused memories and habitual inaccuracy, ascribe to one man what belongs to another; and some talk on, without thought or care. A few men are sufficient to broach falsehoods, which are afterwards innocently diffused by successive relaters.'[1] Had he lived to read what Sir John Hawkins and Mrs Piozzi have related concerning himself, how much would he have found his observation illustrated. He was indeed so much impressed with the prevalence of falsehood, voluntary or unintentional, that I never knew any person who upon hearing an extraordinary circumstance told, discovered more of the *incredulus odi*. He would say with a significant look and decisive tone, 'It is not so. Do not tell this again.'[a] He inculcated upon all his friends the importance of perpetual vigilance against the slightest degrees of falsehood, the effect of which, as Sir Joshua Reynolds observed to me, has been, that all who were of his school are distinguished for a love of truth and accuracy, which they would not have possessed in the same degree, if they had not been known to Johnson.

Talking of ghosts, he said, 'It is wonderful that five thousand years have now elapsed since the creation of the world, and still it is undecided whether or not there has ever been an instance of the spirit of any person appearing after death. All argument is against it; but all belief is for it.'

He said, 'John Wesley's conversation is good, but he is never at leisure. He is always obliged to go at a certain hour. This is very disagreeable to a man who loves to fold his legs and have out his talk, as I do.'

On Friday, April 3, I dined with him in London, in a company where were present several eminent men, whom I shall not name, but distinguish their parts in the conversation by different letters.

F. 'I have been looking at this famous antique marble dog of Mr Jennings, valued at a thousand guineas, said to be Alcibiades's dog.' JOHNSON. 'His tail then must be docked. That was the mark of Alcibiades's dog.' E. 'A thousand

---

1 *Literary Magazine*, 1756, p. 37.

[a] Add this note: The following plausible, but over-prudent counsel on this subject is given by an Italian writer, quoted by '*Rhedi de generatione insectarum*', with the epithet of '*divini poetae*'.

> *Sempre a quel ver ch'ha faccia di menzogna*
> *De' l'uom chiuder le labbra fin ch'el pote,*
> *Però che senza colpa fa vergogna.*

guineas! The representation of no animal whatever is worth so much. At this rate a dead dog would indeed be better than a living lion.' JOHNSON. 'Sir, it is not the worth of the thing but the skill in forming it which is so highly estimated. Everything that enlarges the sphere of human powers, that shows man he can do what he thought he could not do, is valuable. The first man who balanced a straw on his nose; Johnston who rode three horses at a time; in short, all such men deserved the applause of mankind, not on account of the use of what they did, but of the dexterity which they exhibited.' BOSWELL. 'Yet a misapplication of time and assiduity is not to be encouraged. Addison, in one of his *Spectators*, commends the judgement of a King, who as a suitable reward to a man that by long perseverance had attained to the art of throwing a barleycorn through the eye of a needle, gave him a bushel of barley.' JOHNSON. 'He has been a King of Scotland, where barley is scarce.' F. 'One of the most remarkable antique figures of an animal is the boar at Florence.' JOHNSON. 'The first boar that is well made in marble should be preserved as a wonder. When men arrive at a facility of making boars well, then the workmanship is not of such value, but they should however be preserved as examples, and as a greater security for the restoration of the art, should it be lost.'

E. 'We hear prodigious complaints at present of emigration. I am convinced that emigration makes a country more populous.' J. 'That sounds very much like a paradox.' E. 'Exportation of men, like exportation of all other commodities, makes more be produced.' JOHNSON. 'But there would be more people were there not emigration, provided there were food for more.' E. 'No; leave a few breeders, and you'll have more people than if there were no emigration.' JOHNSON. 'Nay, Sir, it is plain there will be more people, if there are more breeders. Thirty cows in good pasture will produce more calves than ten cows, provided they have good bulls.' E. 'There are bulls enough in Ireland.' JOHNSON. (smiling), 'So, Sir, I should think from your argument.' BOSWELL. 'You said exportation of men, like exportation of other commodities, makes more be produced. But a bounty is given to encourage the exportation of corn, and no bounty is given for the exportation of men; though, indeed, those who go gain by it.' R. 'But the bounty on the exportation of corn is paid at home.' E. 'That's the same thing.' JOHNSON. 'No, Sir.' R. 'A man who stays at home gains nothing by his neighbour's emigrating.' BOSWELL. 'I can understand that emigration may be the cause that more people may be produced in a country; but the country will not therefore be from that the more populous, for the people issue from it. It can only be said that there is a flow of people. It is an encouragement to have children, to know that they can get a living by emigration.' R. 'Yes, if there were an emigration of children under six years of age. But they don't emigrate till they could earn their livelihood in some way at home.' C. 'It is remarkable that the most unhealthy countries, where there are the most destructive diseases, such as Egypt and Bengal, are the most populous.' JOHNSON. 'Countries which are the most populous have the most destructive diseases. *That* is the true state of the proposition.' C. 'Holland is very unhealthy, yet it is exceedingly populous.' JOHNSON. 'I know not that Holland is unhealthy. But its populousness is owing to an influx of people from all other countries. Disease cannot be the cause of populousness, for it not only carries off a great proportion of the people; but those who are left are weakened, and unfit for the purposes of increase.'

R. 'Mr E., I don't mean to flatter, but when posterity reads one of your speeches in parliament, it will be difficult to believe that you took so much pains, knowing with certainty that it could produce no effect, that not one vote would be gained by it.' E. 'Waving your compliment to me, I shall say in general, that it is very well worth while for a man to take pains to speak well in parliament. A man, who has vanity, speaks to display his talents and if a man speaks well, he gradually establishes a certain reputation and consequence in the general opinion, which sooner or later will have its political reward. Besides, though not one vote is gained, a good speech has its effect. Though an act which has been ably opposed passes into a law, yet in its progress it is modelled, it is softened in such a manner, that we see plainly the minister has been told, that the members attached to him are so sensible of its injustice or absurdity from what they have heard, that it must be altered.' JOHNSON. 'And, Sir, there is a gratification of pride. Though we cannot out-vote them we will out-argue them. They shall not do wrong without its being shown both to themselves and to the world.' E. 'The House of Commons is a mixed body. (I except the minority, which I hold to be pure [smiling], but I take the whole House.) It is a mass by no means pure; but neither is it wholly corrupt, though there is a large proportion of corruption in it. There are many members who generally go with the minister, who will not go all lengths. There are many honest well-meaning country gentlemen who are in parliament only to keep up the consequence of their families. Upon most of these a good speech will have influence.' JOHNSON. 'We are all more or less governed by interest. But interest will not make us do every thing. In a case which admits of doubt, we try to think on the side which is for our interest, and generally bring ourselves to act accordingly. But the subject must admit of diversity of colouring; it must receive a colour on that side. In the House of Commons there are members enough who will not vote what is grossly unjust or absurd. No, Sir, there must always be right enough, or appearance of right, to keep wrong in countenance.' BOSWELL. 'There is surely always a majority in parliament who have places, or who want to have them, and who therefore will be generally ready to support government without requiring any pretext.' E. 'True, Sir; that majority will always follow

> *Quo clamor vocat et turba faventium.'*

BOSWELL. 'Well now, let us take the common phrase, Place-hunters. I thought they had hunted without regard to any thing, just as their huntsman, the minister, leads, looking only to the prey.'[1] J. 'But taking your metaphor,

---

1 Lord Bolingbroke, who, however detestable as a metaphysician, must be allowed to have had admirable talents as a political writer, thus describes the House of Commons, in his 'Letter to Sir William Windham': 'You know the nature of that assembly; they grow, like hounds, fond of the man who shows them game, and by whose halloo they are used to be encouraged.'

you know that in hunting there are few so desperately keen as to follow without reserve. Some do not choose to leap ditches and hedges and risk their necks, or gallop over steeps, or even to dirty themselves in bogs and mire.' Boswell. 'I am glad there are some good, quiet, moderate political hunters.' E. 'I believe in any body of men in England I should have been in the minority; I have always been in the minority.' P. 'The House of Commons resembles a private company. How seldom is any man convinced by another's argument; passion and pride rise against it.' R. 'What would be the consequence, if a minister, sure of a majority in the House of Commons, should resolve that there should be no speaking at all upon his side.' E. 'He must soon go out. That has been tried; but it was found it would not do.'

E. 'The Irish language is not primitive; it is Teutonic, a mixture of the northern tongues: it has much English in it.' Johnson. 'It may have been radically Teutonic; but English and High Dutch have no similarity to the eye, though radically the same. Once when looking into Low Dutch, I found, in a whole page, only one word similar to English; *stroem*, like *stream*, and it signified *tide*.' E. 'I remember having seen a Dutch Sonnet, in which I found this word, *roesnopies*. Nobody would, at first, think that this could be English; but, when we enquire, we find *roes*, rose, and *nopie*, knob; so we have *rose-buds*.'

Johnson. 'I have been reading Thickness's travels which I think are entertaining.' Boswell. 'What, Sir, a good book?' Johnson. 'Yes, Sir, to read once; I do not say you are to make a study of it, and digest it; and I believe it to be a true book in his intention. All travellers generally mean to tell truth; though Thickness observes, upon Smollet's account of his alarming a whole town in France by firing a blunderbuss, and frightening a French nobleman till he made him tie on his portmanteau, that he would be loth to say Smollet had told two lies in one page; but he had found the only town in France where these things could have happened. Travellers must often be mistaken. In every thing, except where mensuration can be applied, they may honestly differ. There has been, of late, a strange turn in travellers to be displeased.'

E. 'From the experience which I have had – and I have had a great deal – I have learnt to think better of mankind.' Johnson. 'From my experience I have found them worse in commercial dealings, more disposed to cheat, than I had any notion of, but more disposed to do one another good than I had conceived.' J. 'Less just and more beneficent.' Johnson. 'And really it is wonderful, considering how much attention is necessary for men to take care of themselves, and ward off immediate evils which press upon them, it is wonderful how much they do for others. As it is said of the greatest liar, that he tells more truth than falsehood; so it may be said of the worst man, that he does more good than evil.' Boswell. 'Perhaps from experience men may be found happier than we suppose.' Johnson. 'No, Sir; the more we enquire we shall find men the less happy.' P. 'As to thinking better or worse of mankind from experience, some cunning people will not be satisfied unless they have put men to the test, as they think. There is a very good story told of Sir Godfrey Kneller, in his character of a Justice of the peace. A gentleman brought his servant before him, upon an accusation of having stolen some money from him; but it having come out that he had laid it purposely in the servant's way, in order to try his honesty, Sir Godfrey sent the master to prison.'ª JOHNSON. 'To resist temptation once, is not a sufficient proof of honesty. If a servant, indeed, were to resist the continued temptation of silver lying in a window, as some people let it lie, when he is sure his master does not know how much there is of it, he would give a strong proof of honesty. But this is a proof to which you have no right to put a man. You know, humanly speaking, there is a certain degree of temptation which will overcome any virtue. Now, in so far as you approach temptation to a man, you do him an injury; and, if he is overcome, you share his guilt.' P. 'And, when once overcome, it is easier for him to be got the better of again.' BOSWELL. 'Yes, you are his seducer; you have debauched him. I have known a man resolve to put friendship to the test, by asking a friend to lend him money, merely with that view, when he did not want it.' JOHNSON. 'That is very wrong, Sir. Your friend may be a narrow man, and yet have many good qualities: narrowness may be his only fault. Now you are trying his general character as a friend, by one particular singly, in which he happens to be defective, when, in truth, his character is composed of many particulars.'

E. 'I understand the hogshead of claret, which this society was favoured with by our friend the Dean, is nearly out; I think he should be written to, to send another of the same kind. Let the request be made with a happy ambiguity of expression, so that we may have the chance of his sending it also a present.' JOHNSON. 'I am willing to offer my services as secretary on this occasion.' P. 'As many as are for Dr Johnson being secretary hold up your hands. – Carried unanimously.' BOSWELL. 'He will be our Dictator.' JOHNSON. 'No, the company is to dictate to me. I am only to write for wine; and I am quite disinterested, as I drink none; I shall not be suspected of having forged the application. I am no more than humble *scribe*. E. 'Then you shall *pre*scribe.' BOSWELL. 'Very well. The first play of words to-day.' J. 'No, no; the *bulls* in Ireland.' JOHNSON. 'Were I your Dictator you should have no wine. It would be my business *cavere ne quid detrimenti Respublica caperet*, and wine is dangerous. Rome was ruined by luxury' (smiling). E. 'If you allow no wine as Dictator, you shall not have me for your master of horse.'

On Saturday, April 4, I drank tea with Johnson at Dr Taylor's, where he had dined. He entertained us with an account of a tragedy written by a Dr Kennedy (not the Lisbon physician). 'The catastrophe of it (said he) was, that a King, who was jealous of his Queen with his prime-minister, castrated

---

ª Add the following note: Pope thus introduces this story:

> Faith in such case if you should prosecute,
> I think Sir Godfrey should decide the suit,
> Who sent the thief who stole the cash away,
> And punish'd him that put it in his way.

Imitations of Horace, Book II. Epist. ii.

himself.[a] This tragedy was actually shown about in manuscript to several
people, and, amongst others, to Mr Fitzherbert, who repeated to me two lines
of the Prologue:

> Our hero's fate we have but gently touch'd;
> The fair might blame us if it were less couch'd.

It is hardly to be believed what absurd and indecent images men will introduce
into their writings, without being sensible of the absurdity and indecency. I
remember Lord Orrery told me, that there was a pamphlet written against Sir
Robert Walpole, the whole of which was an allegory on the *phallic obscenity*.
The Duchess of Buckingham asked Lord Orrery *who* this person was? He
answered, he did not know. She said, she would send to Mr Pulteney, who,
she supposed, could inform her. So then, to prevent her from making herself
ridiculous, Lord Orrery sent her Grace a note, in which he gave her to
understand what was meant.'

He was very silent this evening; and read in a variety of books; suddenly
throwing down one, and taking up another.

He talked of going to Streatham that night. TAYLOR. 'You'll be robbed if
you do; or you must shoot a highwayman. Now I would rather be robbed
than do that: I would not shoot a highwayman.' JOHNSON. 'But I would
rather shoot him in the instant when he is attempting to rob me, than
afterwards swear against him at the Old-Bailey to take away his life, after he
has robbed me. I am surer I am right in the one case than in the other. I may
be mistaken as to the man when I swear: I cannot be mistaken if I shoot him
in the act. Besides, we feel less reluctance to take away a man's life when we
are heated by the injury, than to do it at a distance of time by an oath, after we
have cooled.' BOSWELL. 'So, Sir, you would rather act from the motive of
private passion, than that of public advantage.' JOHNSON. 'Nay, Sir, when I
shoot the highwayman I act from both.' BOSWELL. 'Very well, very well. –
There is no catching him.' JOHNSON. 'At the same time one does not know
what to say. For perhaps one may, a year after, hang himself from uneasiness
for having shot a man.[1] Few minds are fit to be trusted with so great a thing.'

---

[a] Add the following note: The reverse of the story of *Combabus*, on which Mr David
Hume told Lord Macartney, that a friend of his had written a tragedy. It is, however,
possible, that I may have been inaccurate in my perception of what Dr Johnson
related, and that he may have been talking of the same ludicrous tragical subject that
Mr Hume has mentioned.

1 The late Duke of Montrose was generally said to have been uneasy on that account;
but I can contradict the report from his Grace's own authority. As he used to admit me
to very easy conversation with him, I took the liberty to introduce the subject. His
Grace told me, that when riding one night near London, he was attacked by two
highwaymen on horseback, and that he instantly shot one of them, upon which the
other galloped off; that his servant, who was very well mounted, proposed to pursue
him and take him, but that his Grace said, 'No, we have had blood enough: I hope the
man may live to repent.' His Grace, upon my presuming to put the question, assured
me, that his mind was not at all clouded by what he had thus done in self-defence.

BOSWELL. 'Then, Sir, you would not shoot him?' JOHNSON. 'But I might be vexed afterwards for that too.'

Thrale's carriage not having come for him, as he expected, I accompanied him some part of the way home to his own house. I told him, that I had talked of him to Mr Dunning a few days before, and had said, that in his company we did not so much interchange conversation, as listen to him; and that Dunning observed, upon this, 'One is always willing to listen to Dr Johnson': to which I answered, 'That is a great deal from you, Sir.' – 'Yes, Sir (said Johnson), a great deal indeed. Here is a man willing to listen, to whom the world is listening all the rest of the year.' BOSWELL. 'I think, Sir, it is right to tell one man of such a handsome thing, which has been said of him by another. It tends to increase benevolence.' JOHNSON. 'Undoubtedly it is right, Sir.'

On Tuesday, April 7, I breakfasted with him at his house. He said, 'nobody was content.' I mentioned to him a respectable person in Scotland whom he knew; and I asserted, that I really believed he was always content. JOHNSON. 'No, Sir, he is not content with the present; he has always some new scheme, some new plantation, something which is future. You know he was not content as a widower; for he married again.' BOSWELL. 'But he is not restless.' JOHNSON. 'Sir, he is only locally at rest. A chemist is locally at rest; but his mind is hard at work. This gentleman has done with external exertions. It is too late for him to engage in distant projects.' BOSWELL. 'He seems to amuse himself quite well, to have his attention fixed, and his tranquillity preserved by very small matters. I have tried this, but it would not do with me.' JOHNSON. (laughing) 'No, Sir; it must be born with a man to be contented to take up with little things. Women have a great advantage that they may take up with little things, without disgracing themselves: a man cannot, except with fiddling. Had I learnt to fiddle, I should have done nothing else.' BOSWELL. 'Pray, Sir, did you ever play on any musical instrument?' JOHNSON. 'No, Sir. I once bought me a flagelet; but I never made out a tune.' BOSWELL. 'A flagelet, Sir! – so small an instrument?[1] I should have liked to hear you play on the violincello. *That* should have been *your* instrument.' JOHNSON. 'Sir, I might as well have played on the violincello as another; but I should have done nothing else. No, Sir; a man would never undertake great things could he be amused with small. I once tried knotting. Dempster's sister undertook to teach me; but I could not learn it.' BOSWELL. 'So, Sir, it will be related in pompous narrative, "Once for his amusement he tried knotting; nor did this Hercules disdain the distaff. Once for his amusement he tried knotting."' JOHNSON. 'Knitting of stockings is a good amusement. As a freeman of Aberdeen I should be a knitter of stockings.'

He asked me to go down with him and dine at Mr Thrale's at Streatham, to which I agreed. I had lent him *An Account of Scotland, in 1702*, written by a man of various enquiry, an English chaplain to a regiment stationed there.

1 When I told this to Miss Seward, she smiled, and repeated, with admirable readiness, from *Acis and Galatea*,

> Bring me a hundred reeds of ample growth,
> To make a pipe for my CAPACIOUS MOUTH.

JOHNSON. 'It is sad stuff, Sir, miserably written, as books in general then were. There is now an elegance of style universally diffused. No man now writes so ill as Martin's Account of the Hebrides is written. A man could not write so ill, if he should try. Set a merchant's clerk now to write, and he'll do better.'

He talked to me with serious concern of a certain female friend's 'laxity of narration, and inattention to truth'. – 'I am as much vexed (said he) at the ease with which she hears it mentioned to her, as at the thing itself. I told her, "Madam, you are contented to hear every day said to you, what the highest of mankind have died for, rather than bear." – You know, Sir, the highest of mankind have died rather than bear to be told they had uttered a falsehood. Do talk to her of it: I am weary.'

BOSWELL. 'Was not Dr John Campbell a very inaccurate man in his narrative, Sir? He once told me that he drank thirteen bottles of port at a sitting.'[a] JOHNSON. 'Why, Sir, I do not know that Campbell ever lied with pen and ink; but you could not entirely depend on any thing he told you in conversation, if there was fact mixed with it. However, I loved Campbell: he was a solid orthodox man; he had a reverence for religion. Though defective in practice, he was religious in principle; and he did nothing grossly wrong that I have heard.'

I told him, that I had been present the day before when Mrs Montagu, the literary lady, sat to Miss Reynolds for her picture; and that she said, 'she had bound up Mr Gibbon's History without the last two offensive chapters; for that she thought the book so far good, as it gave, in an elegant manner, the substance of the bad writers *medii aevi*, which the late Lord Lyttelton advised her to read.' JOHNSON. 'Sir, she has not read them: she shows none of this impetuosity to me: she does not know Greek, and, I fancy, knows little Latin. She is willing you should think she knows them; but she does not say she does.' BOSWELL. 'Mr Harris, who was present, agreed with her.' JOHNSON. 'Harris was laughing at her, Sir. Harris is a sound sullen scholar; he does not like interlopers. Harris, however, is a prig, and a bad prig;[1] I looked into his

---

[a] Add the following note: Lord Macartney observes upon this passage, 'I have heard him tell many things, which, though embellished by their mode of narrative, had their foundation in truth; but I never remember any thing approaching to this. If he had written it, I should have supposed some wag had put the figure of one before the three.' – I am, however, absolutely certain that Dr Campbell told me it, and I gave particular attention to it, being myself a lover of wine, and therefore curious to hear whatever is remarkable concerning drinking. There can be no doubt that some men can drink, without suffering any injury, such a quantity as to others appears incredible. It is but fair to add, that Dr Campbell told me, he took a very long time to this great potation; and I have heard Dr Johnson say, 'Sir, if a man drinks very slowly, and lets one glass evaporate before he takes another, I know not how long he may drink.' Dr Campbell mentioned a Colonel of Militia who sat with him all the time, and drank equally.

1 What my friend meant by these words concerning the amiable philosopher of Salisbury, I am at a loss to understand.[a]

[a] *Third Edition.* – Add to note: A friend suggests that Johnson thought his *manner* as a writer affected, while at the same time, the *matter* did not compensate for the fault. In short, that he meant to make a remark quite different from that which a celebrated gentleman made on a very eminent physician: 'He is a coxcomb, but a *satisfactory coxcomb*.'

book, and thought he did not understand his own system.' BOSWELL. 'He says plain things in a formal and abstract way, to be sure; but his method is good: for to have clear notions upon any subject we must have recourse to analytic arrangement.' JOHNSON. 'Sir, it is what every body does, whether they will or no. But sometimes things may be made darker by definition. I see a *cow*. I define her, *Animal quadrupes ruminans cornutum*. But a goat ruminates, and a cow may have no horns. *Cow* is plainer.' BOSWELL. 'I think Dr Franklin's definition of *Man* is a good one — "A tool-making animal".' JOHNSON. 'But many a man never made a tool: and suppose a man without arms, he could not make a tool.'

Talking of drinking wine, he said, 'I did not leave off wine because I could not bear it: I have drunk three bottles of port without being the worse for it. University College has witnessed this.' BOSWELL. 'Why, then, Sir, did you leave it off?' JOHNSON. 'Why, Sir, because it is so much better for a man to be sure that he is never to be intoxicated, never to lose the power over himself. I shall not begin to drink wine again till I grow old, and want it.' BOSWELL. 'I think, Sir, you once said to me, that not to drink wine was a great deduction from life.'[1] JOHNSON. 'It is a diminution of pleasure, to be sure; but I do not say a diminution of happiness. There is more happiness in being rational.' BOSWELL. 'But if we could have pleasure always, should not we be happy? The greatest part of men would compound for pleasure.' JOHNSON. 'Supposing we could have pleasure always, an intellectual man would not compound for it. The greatest part of men would compound, because the greatest part of men are gross.' BOSWELL. 'I allow there may be greater pleasure than from wine. I have had more pleasure from your conversation. I have indeed; I assure you I have.' JOHNSON. 'When we talk of pleasure, we mean sensual pleasure. When a man says he had pleasure with a woman, he does not mean conversation, but something of a very different nature. Philosophers tell you, that pleasure is *contrary* to happiness. Gross men prefer animal pleasure. So there are men who have preferred living among savages. Now what a wretch must he be, who is content with such conversation as can be had among savages! You may remember an officer at Fort Augustus, who had served in America, told us of a woman whom they were obliged to *bind*, in order to get her back from savage life.' BOSWELL. 'She must have been an animal, a beast.' JOHNSON. 'Sir, she was a speaking cat.'

I mentioned to him that I had become very weary in a company where I heard not a single intellectual sentence, except that 'a man who had been settled ten years in Minorca was become a much inferior man to what he was in London, because a man's mind grows narrow in a narrow place.' JOHNSON. 'A man's mind grows narrow in a narrow place, whose mind is enlarged only because he has lived in a large place: but what is got by books and thinking is preserved in a narrow place as well as in a large place. A man cannot know modes of life as well in Minorca as in London; but he may study mathematics

1 See page 601.

as well in Minorca.' BOSWELL. 'I don't know, Sir: if you had remained ten years in the Isle of Col, you would not have been the man that you now are.' JOHNSON. 'Yes, Sir, if I had been there from fifteen to twenty-five; but not if from twenty-five to thirty-five.' BOSWELL. 'I own, Sir, the spirits which I have in London make me do every thing with more readiness and vigour. I can talk twice as much in London as any where else.'

Of Goldsmith he said, 'He was not an agreeable companion, for he talked always for fame. A man who does so never can be pleasing. The man who talks to unburthen his mind is the man to delight you. An eminent friend of ours is not so agreeable as the variety of his knowledge would otherwise make him, because he talks partly from ostentation.'

Soon after our arrival at Thrale's, I heard one of the maids calling eagerly on another, to go to Dr Johnson. I wondered what this could mean. I afterwards learnt, that it was to give her a Bible which he had brought from London as a present to her.

He was for a considerable time occupied in reading *Mémoires de Fontenelle*; leaning and swinging upon the low gate into the court, without his hat.

I looked into Lord Kames's *Sketches of the History of Man*; and mentioned to Dr Johnson his censure of Charles the Fifth, for celebrating his funeral obsequies in his life-time, which, I told him, I had been used to think a solemn and affecting act. JOHNSON. 'Why, Sir, a man may dispose his mind to think so of that act of Charles; but it is so liable to ridicule, that if one man out of ten thousand laughs at it, he'll make the other nine thousand nine hundred and ninety-nine laugh too.' I could not agree with him in this.

Sir John Pringle had expressed a wish that I would ask Dr Johnson's opinion what were the best English sermons for style. I took an opportunity today of mentioning several to him. *Atterbury*? JOHNSON. 'Yes, Sir, one of the best.' BOSWELL. '*Tillotson?*' JOHNSON. 'Why not now. I should not advise a preacher at this day to imitate Tillotson's style: though I don't know; I should be cautious of objecting to what has been applauded by so many suffrages. – *South* is one of the best, if you except his peculiarities, and his violence, and sometimes coarseness of language. – *Seed* has a very fine style; but he is not very theological. – *Jortin's* sermons are very elegant. – *Sherlock's* style too is very elegant, though he has not made it his principal study. – And you may add *Smallridge*. All the latter preachers have a good style. Indeed, nobody now talks much of style: Every body composes pretty well. There are no such unharmonious periods as there were a hundred years ago. I should recommend Dr *Clarke's* sermons, were he orthodox. However, it is very well known *where* he was not orthodox, which was upon the doctrine of the Trinity, as to which he is a condemned heretic; so one is aware of it.' BOSWELL. 'I like Ogden's sermons on prayer very much, both for neatness of style and subtilty of reasoning.' JOHNSON. 'I should like to read all that Ogden has written.' BOSWELL. 'What I wish to know is, what sermons afford the best specimen of English pulpit eloquence.' JOHNSON. 'We have no sermons addressed to the passions that are good for any thing; if you mean that kind of eloquence.' A CLERGYMAN. (whose name I do not recollect) 'Were not

Dodd's sermons addressed to the passions?' JOHNSON. 'They were nothing, Sir, be they addressed to what they may.'

At dinner, Mrs Thrale expressed a wish to go and see Scotland. JOHNSON. 'Seeing Scotland, Madam, is only seeing a worse England. It is seeing the flower gradually fade away to the naked stalk. Seeing the Hebrides, indeed, is seeing quite a different scene.'

Our poor friend, Mr Thomas Davies, was soon to have a benefit at Drury-lane theatre, as some relief to his unfortunate circumstances. We were all warmly interested for his success, and had contributed to it. However, we thought there was no harm in having our joke when he could not be hurt by it. I proposed that he should be brought on to speak a Prologue upon the occasion; and I began to mutter fragments of what it might be: as, that when now grown *old*, he was obliged to cry, 'Poor Tom's *a-cold*'; – that he owned he had been driven from the stage by a Churchill, but that this was no disgrace, for a Churchill had beat the French; – that he had been satyrised as 'mouthing a sentence as curs mouth a bone', but he was now glad of a bone to pick. – 'Nay (said Johnson), I would have him to say,

> Mad Tom is come to see the world again.'

He and I returned to town in the evening. Upon the road I endeavoured to maintain, in argument, that a landed gentleman is not under any obligation to reside upon his estate; and that by living in London he does no injury to his country. JOHNSON. 'Why, Sir, he does no injury to his country in general, because the money which he draws from it gets back again in circulation; but to his particular district, his particular parish, he does an injury. All that he has to give away is not given to those who have the first claim to it. And though I have said that the money circulates back, it is a long time before that happens. Then, Sir, a man of family and estate ought to consider himself as having the charge of a district, over which he is to diffuse civility and happiness.'

Next day I found him at home in the forenoon. He praised Delaney's *Observations on Swift*; said that his book and Lord Orrery's might both be true, though one viewed Swift more, and the other less favourably; and that, between both, we might have a complete notion of Swift.

Talking of a man's resolving to deny himself the use of wine, from moral and religious considerations, he said, 'He must not doubt about it. When one doubts as to pleasure, we know what will be the conclusion. I now no more think of drinking wine, than a horse does. The wine upon the table is no more for me, than for the dog that is under the table.'

On Thursday, April 9, I dined with him at Sir Joshua Reynolds's, with the Bishop of St Asaph (Dr Shipley), Mr Allan Ramsay, Mr Gibbon, Mr Cambridge, and Mr Langton. Mr Ramsay had lately returned from Italy, and entertained us with his observations upon Horace's villa, which he had examined with great care. I relished this much, as it brought fresh into my mind what I had viewed with great pleasure thirteen years before. The Bishop, Dr Johnson, and Mr Cambridge, joined with Mr Ramsay, in recollecting the various lines in Horace relating to the subject.

Horace's journey to Brundusium being mentioned, Johnson observed that the brook which he describes is to be seen now, exactly as at that time; and that he had often wondered how it happened, that small brooks, such as this, kept the same situation for ages, notwithstanding earthquakes, by which even mountains have been changed, and agriculture, which produces such a variation upon the surface of the earth. CAMBRIDGE. 'A Spanish writer has this thought in a poetical conceit. After observing that most of the solid structures of Rome are totally perished, while the Tiber remains the same, he adds,

> *Lo que era Firme huio solamente,*
> *Lo Fugitivo permanece y dura.'*

JOHNSON. 'Sir, that is taken from *Janus Vitalis:*

> *. . . immota labescunt;*
> *Et quae perpetuo sunt agitata manent.'*

The Bishop said, it appeared from Horace's writings that he was a cheerful contented man. JOHNSON. 'We have no reason to believe that, my Lord. Are we to think Pope was happy, because he says so in his writings? We see in his writings what he wished the state of his mind to appear. Dr Young, who pined for preferment, talks with contempt of it in his writings, and affects to despise every thing that he did not despise.' BISHOP OF ST ASAPH. 'He was like other chaplains, looking for vacancies: but that is not peculiar to the clergy. I remember when I was with the army, after the battle of Lafeldt, the officers seriously grumbled that no General was killed.' CAMBRIDGE. 'We may believe Horace when he says,

> *Romae Tibur amem ventosus Tibure Romam.'*[a]

BOSWELL. 'How hard is it that man can never be at rest.' RAMSAY. 'It is not in his nature to be at rest. When he is at rest he is in the worst state that he can be in, for he has nothing to agitate him. He is then like the man in the Irish song,

> There was an old fellow at Ballanacrazy,[b]
> Who wanted a wife for to make him un*a*isy.'

Goldsmith being mentioned, Johnson observed that it was long before his merit came to be acknowledged. That he once complained to him, in ludicrous terms of distress, 'Whenever I write anything the public make a point to know nothing about it': but that his *Traveller* brought him into high reputation. LANGTON. 'There is not one bad line in that poem; not one of Dryden's careless verses.' SIR JOSHUA. 'I was glad to hear Charles Fox say it

---

[a] Add: more than when he boasts of his consistency:

> *Me constare mihi scis, et decedere tristem,*
> *Quandocunque trahunt invisa negotia Romam.*

[b] For 'was an old fellow at Ballanacrazy', read 'lived a young man in Ballinacrazy'.

was one of the finest poems in the English language.' LANGTON. 'Why was you glad? You surely had no doubt of this before.' JOHNSON. 'No; the merit of *The Traveller* is so well established, that Mr Fox's praise cannot augment it, nor his censure diminish it.' SIR JOSHUA. 'But his friends may suspect they had a too great partiality for him.' JOHNSON. 'Nay, Sir, the partiality of his friends was all against him. It was with difficulty we could give him a hearing. Goldsmith had no settled notions upon any subject; so he talked always at random. It seemed to be his intention to blurt out whatever was in his mind, and see what would become of it. He was angry too when catched in an absurdity; but it did not prevent him from falling into another the next minute. I remember Chamier, after talking with him for some time, said, 'Well, I do believe he wrote this poem himself: and, let me tell you, that is believing a great deal.' Chamier once asked him what he meant by slow, the last word in the first line of *The Traveller*,

> Remote, unfriended, melancholy, slow.

Did he mean tardiness of locomotion? Goldsmith, who would say something without consideration, answered, "Yes". I was sitting by, and said, "No, Sir; you do not mean tardiness of locomotion; you mean, that sluggishness of mind which comes upon a man in solitude.' Chamier believed then that I had written the line, as much as if he had seen me write it. Goldsmith, however, was a man, who, whatever he wrote, did it better than any other man could do. He deserved a place in Westminster-Abbey, and every year he lived, would have deserved it better. He had, indeed, been at no pains to fill his mind with knowledge. He transplanted it from one place to another; and it did not settle in his mind; so he could not tell what was in his own books.'

We talked of living in the country. JOHNSON. 'No wise man will go to live in the country, unless he has something to do which can be better done in the country. For instance: if he is to shut himself up for a year to study a science, it is better to look out to the fields, than to an opposite wall. Then, if a man walks out in the country, there is nobody to keep him from walking in again: but if a man walks out in London, he is not sure when he shall walk in again. A great city is, to be sure, the school for studying life; and "the proper study of mankind is man", as Pope observes.' BOSWELL. 'I fancy London is the best place in the world for society; though I have heard that the very first society of Paris is still beyond any thing that we have here.' JOHNSON. 'Sir, I question if in Paris such a company as is sitting round this table could be got together in less than half a year. They talk in France of the felicity of men and women living together: the truth is, that there the men are not higher than the women, they know no more than women do, and they are not held down in their conversation by the presence of women.' RAMSAY. 'Literature is upon the growth, it is in its spring in France. Here it is rather *passée*.' JOHNSON. 'Literature was in France long before we had it. Paris was the second city for the revival of letters: Italy had it first, to be sure. What have we done for literature, equal to what was done by the Stephani and others in France? Our literature came to us through France. Caxton printed only two books,

Chaucer and Gower, that were not translations from the French; and Chaucer, we know, took much from the Italians. No Sir, if literature be in its spring in France, it is a second spring; it is after a winter. We are now before the French in literature; but we had it long after them. In England, any man who wears a sword and a powdered wig is ashamed to be illiterate. I believe it is not so in France. Yet there is, probably, a great deal of learning in France, because they have such a number of religious establishments; so many men who have nothing else to do but to study. I do not know this; but I take it upon the common principles of chance. Where there are many shooters, some will hit.'

We talked of old age. Johnson (now in his seventieth year) said, 'It is a man's own fault, it is from want of use, if his mind grows torpid in old age.' The Bishop asked, if an old man does not lose faster than he gets. JOHNSON. 'I think not, my Lord, if he exerts himself.' One of the company rashly observed, that he thought it was happy for an old man that insensibility comes upon him. JOHNSON. (with a noble elevation and disdain) 'No, Sir, I should never be happy by being less rational.' BISHOP OF ST ASAPH. 'Your wish then, Sir, is γεράσκειν διδασκόμενος.' JOHNSON. 'Yes; my Lord.'

His Lordship mentioned a charitable establishment in Wales where people were maintained, and supplied with every thing, upon the condition of their contributing the weekly produce of their labour; and he said, they grew quite torpid for want of property. JOHNSON. 'They have no object for hope. Their condition cannot be better. It is rowing without a port.'

One of the company asked him the meaning of the expression in Juvenal, *unius lacertae.* JOHNSON. 'I think it clear enough; as much ground as one may have a chance to find a lizard upon.'

Commentators have differed as to the exact meaning of the expression by which the Poet intended to enforce the sentiment contained in the passage where these words occur. It is enough that they mean to denote even a very small possession, provided it be a man's own.

> *Est aliquid quocunque loco quocunque recessu*
> *Unius sese dominum fecisse lacertae.*

This season there was a whimsical fashion in the newspapers of applying Shakspeare's words to describe living people well known in the world; which was done under the title of *Modern Characters from Shakspeare*; many of which were admirably adapted. The fancy took so much, that they were afterwards collected into a pamphlet. Somebody said to Johnson, across the table, that he had not been in those characters. 'Yes (said he) I have. I should have been sorry to be left out.' He then repeated what had been applied to him,

> I must borrow GARAGANTUA's mouth.

Miss Reynolds not perceiving at once the meaning of this, he was obliged to explain it to her, which had something of an awkward and ludicrous effect. 'Why, Madam, it has a reference to me as using big words, which require the mouth of a giant to pronounce them. Garagantua is the name of a giant in

Rabelais.' BOSWELL. 'But, Sir, there is another amongst them for you:

> He would not flatter Neptune for his trident,
> Or Jove for his power to thunder.'

JOHNSON. 'There is nothing marked in that. No, Sir, Garagantua is the best.' Notwithstanding this ease and good humour, when I, a little while afterwards, repeated his sarcasm on Kenrick,[1] which was received with applause, he asked, '*Who* said that?' and on my suddenly answering, *Garagantua*, he looked serious, which was a sufficient indication that he did not wish it to be kept up.

When we went to the drawing-room there was a rich assemblage. Besides the company who had been at dinner, there were Mr Garrick, Mr Harris of Salisbury, Dr Percy, Dr Burney, Honourable Mrs Cholmondeley, Miss Hannah More, &c. &c.

After wandering about in a kind of pleasing distraction for some time, I got into a corner, with Johnson, Garrick, and Harris. GARRICK. (to Harris) 'Pray, Sir, have you read Potter's Aeschylus?' HARRIS. 'Yes; and think it pretty.' GARRICK. (to Johnson) 'And what think you, Sir, of it?' JOHNSON. 'I thought what I read of it *verbiage*: but upon Mr Harris's recommendation I will read a play. (to Mr Harris) Don't prescribe two.' Mr Harris suggested one, I do not remember which. JOHNSON. 'We must try its effect as an English poem; that is the way to judge of the merit of a translation. Translations are, in general, for people who cannot read the original.' I mentioned the vulgar saying, that Pope's Homer was not a good representation of the original. JOHNSON. 'Sir, it is the greatest work of the kind that has ever been produced.' BOSWELL. 'The truth is, it is impossible perfectly to translate poetry. In a different language it may be the same tune, but it has not the same tone. Homer plays it on a bassoon; Pope on a flagelet.' HARRIS. 'I think heroic poetry is best in blank verse; yet it appears that rhyme is essential to English poetry, from our deficiency in metrical quantities. In my opinion the chief excellence of our language is numerous prose.' JOHNSON. 'Sir William Temple was the first writer who gave cadence to English prose. Before his time they were careless of arrangement and did not mind whether a sentence ended with an important word or an insignificant word, or with what part of speech it was concluded.' Mr Langton, who now had joined us, commended Clarendon. JOHNSON. 'He is objected to for his parentheses, his involved clauses, and his want of harmony. But he is supported by his matter. It is, indeed, owing to a plethora of matter that his style is so faulty. Every *substance* (smiling to Mr Harris) has so many *accidents*. – To be distinct, we must talk *analytically*. If we analyse language, we must speak of it grammatically: if we analyse argument, we must speak of it logically.' GARRICK. 'Of all the translations that ever were attempted, I think Elphinston's Martial the most extraordinary. He consulted me upon it, who am a little of an epigrammatist myself, you know. I told him freely, "You don't seem to have that turn." I asked him if he was serious; and finding he was, I advised him against publishing. Why, his translation is more

1 See p. 250.

difficult to understand than the original. I thought him a man of some talents; but he seems crazy in this.' JOHNSON. 'Sir, you have done what I had not courage to do. But he did not ask my advice, and I did not force it upon him to make him angry with me.' GARRICK. 'But as a friend, Sir – .' JOHNSON. 'Why, such a friend as I am with him – no.' GARRICK. 'But if you see a friend going to tumble over a precipice?' JOHNSON. 'That is an extravagant case, Sir. You are sure a friend will thank you for hindering him from tumbling over a precipice: but, in the other case, I should hurt his vanity, and do him no good. He would not take my advice. His brother-in-law, Strahan, sent him a subscription of fifty pounds, and said he would send him fifty more, if he would not publish.' GARRICK. 'What! eh! is Strahan a good judge of an Epigram? Is not he rather an *obtuse* man, eh?' JOHNSON. 'Why, Sir, he may not be a judge of an Epigram: but you see he is a judge of what is *not* an Epigram.' BOSWELL. 'It is easy for you, Mr Garrick, to talk to an author as you talked to Elphinston: you, who have been so long the manager of a theatre, rejecting the plays of poor authors. You are an old Judge, who have often pronounced sentence of death. You are a practised surgeon, who have often amputated limbs; and though this may have been for the good of your patients, they cannot like you. Those who have undergone a dreadful operation are not very fond of seeing the operator again.' GARRICK. 'Yes, I know enough of that. There was a reverend gentleman (Mr Hawkins) who wrote a tragedy, the siege of something,[a] which I refused.' HARRIS. 'So the siege was raised.' JOHNSON. 'Aye, he came to me and complained; and told me, that Garrick said his play was wrong in the *concoction*. Now, what is the concoction of a play?' (Here Garrick started, and twisted himself, and seemed sorely vexed, for Johnson told me he believed the story was true.) GARRICK. 'I – I – I – said *first* concoction.' JOHNSON. (smiling) 'Well, he left out *first*. And Rich, he said, refused him *in false English*: he could show it under his hand.' GARRICK. 'He wrote to me in violent wrath for having refused his play: "Sir, this is growing a very serious and terrible affair. I am resolved to publish my play. I will appeal to the world; and how will your judgement appear?" I answered, "Sir, notwithstanding all the seriousness, and all the terrors, I have no objection to your publishing your play; and as you live at a great distance (Devonshire, I believe), if you will send me it, I will convey it to the press." I never heard more of it, ha! ha! ha!'

On Friday, April 10, I found Johnson at home in the forenoon. We resumed the conversation of yesterday. He put me in mind of some of it which had escaped my memory, and enabled me to record it more perfectly than I otherwise could have done. He was much pleased with my paying so great attention to his recommendation in 1763, the beginning of our acquaintance, to keep a journal; and I could perceive he was secretly pleased to find so much of the fruit of his mind preserved; and as he had been used to imagine and say

---

[a] Add the following note: It was called *The Siege of Aleppo*. Mr Hawkins, the author of it, was formerly Professor of Poetry at Oxford. It is printed in his *Miscellanies*, 3 Vols. 8vo.

that he always laboured when he said a good thing – it delighted him, on a review, to find that his conversation teemed with point and imagery.

I said to him, 'You were yesterday, Sir, in remarkably good humour: but there was nothing to offend you, nothing to produce irritation or violence. There was no bold offender. There was not one capital conviction. It was a maiden assize. You had on your white gloves.'

He found fault with our friend Langton for having been too silent. 'Sir (said I), you will recollect, that he very properly took up Sir Joshua for being glad that Charles Fox had praised Goldsmith's *Traveller*, and you joined him.' JOHNSON. 'Yes, Sir, I knocked Fox on the head, without ceremony. Reynolds is too much under Fox and Burke at present. He is under the *Fox star* and the *Irish constellation*. He is always under some planet.' BOSWELL. 'There is no Fox star.' JOHNSON. 'But there is a dog star. BOSWELL. 'They say, indeed, a fox and a dog are the same animal.'

I reminded him of a gentleman who, Mrs Cholmondeley said, was first talkative from affectation, and then silent from the same cause; that he first thought, 'I shall be celebrated as the liveliest man in every company'; and then, all at once, 'O! it is much more respectable to be grave and look wise.' 'He has reversed the Pythagorean discipline, by being first talkative, and then silent. He reverses the course of Nature too: he was first the gay butterfly, and then the creeping worm.' Johnson laughed loud and long at this expansion and illustration of what he himself had told me.

We dined together with Mr Scott (now Sir William Scott, his Majesty's Advocate) at his chambers in the Temple, nobody else there. The company being small, Johnson was not in such spirits as he had been yesterday, and for a considerable time little was said. At last he burst forth, 'Subordination is sadly broken down in this age. No man, now, has the same authority which his father had – except a gaoler. No master has it over his servants: it is diminished in our colleges; nay, in our grammar-schools.' BOSWELL. 'What is the cause of this, Sir? JOHNSON. 'Why, the coming in of the Scotch.' (laughing sarcastically). BOSWELL. 'That is to say, things have been turned topsy turvey. – But your serious cause.' JOHNSON. 'Why, Sir, there are many causes, the chief of which is, I think, the great increase of money. No man now depends upon the Lord of a Manor, when he can send to another country, and fetch provisions. The shoe-black at the entry of my court does not depend on me. I can deprive him but of a penny a day, which he hopes somebody else will bring him; and that penny I must carry to another shoe-black, so the trade suffers nothing. I have explained in my *Journey to the Hebrides*, how gold and silver destroy feudal subordination. But, besides, there is a general relaxation of reverence. No son now depends upon his father as in former times. Paternity used to be considered as of itself a great thing, which had a right to many claims. That is, in general, reduced to very small bounds. My hope is, that as anarchy produces tyranny, this extreme relaxation will produce *freni strictio*.'

Talking of fame, for which there is so great a desire, I observed how little there is of it in reality, compared with the other objects of human attention. 'Let every man recollect, and he will be sensible how small a part of his time is employed in talking or thinking of Shakspeare, Voltaire, or any of the most celebrated men that have ever lived, or are now supposed to occupy the attention and admiration of the world. Let this be extracted and compressed; into what a narrow space will it go!' I then slily introduced Mr Garrick's fame, and his assuming the airs of a great man. JOHNSON. 'Sir, it is wonderful how little Garrick assumes. No, Sir, Garrick *fortunam reverenter habet*. Consider, Sir: celebrated men, such as you have mentioned, have had their applause at a distance; but Garrick had it dashed in his face, sounded in his ears, and went home every night with the · plaudits of a thousand in his cranium. Then, Sir, Garrick did not *find*, but *made* his way to the tables, the levees, and almost the bed-chambers, of the great. Then, Sir, Garrick had under him a numerous body of people; who, from fear of his power, and hopes of his favour, and admiration of his talents, were constantly submissive to him. And here is a man who has advanced the dignity of his profession. Garrick has made a player a higher character.' SCOTT. 'And he is a very sprightly writer too.' JOHNSON. 'Yes, Sir; and all this supported by great wealth of his own acquisition. If all this had happened to me, I should have had a couple of fellows with long poles walking before me, to knock down every body that stood in the way. Consider, if all this had happened to Cibber or Quin, they'd have jumped over the moon. – Yet Garrick speaks to *us*' (smiling). BOSWELL. 'And Garrick is a very good man, a charitable man.' JOHNSON. 'Sir, a liberal man. He has given away more money than any man in England. There may be a little vanity mixed: but he has shown, that money is not his first object.' BOSWELL. 'Yet Foote used to say of him, that he walked out with an intention to do a generous action; but, turning the corner of a street, he met with the ghost of a half-penny, which frightened him.' JOHNSON. 'Why, Sir, that is very true, too; for I never knew a man of whom it could be said with less certainty today, what he will do tomorrow, than Garrick; it depends so much on his humour at the time.' SCOTT. 'I am glad to hear of his liberality. He has been represented as very saving.' JOHNSON. 'With his domestic saving we have nothing to do. I remember drinking tea with him long ago, when Peg Woffington made it, and he grumbled at her for making it too strong.[1] He had then begun to feel money in his purse, and did not know when he should have enough of it.'

On the subject of wealth, the proper use of it, and the effects of that art which is called economy, he observed, 'It is wonderful to think how men of very large estates not only spend their yearly income, but are often actually in want of money. It is clear they have not value for what they spend. Lord Shelburne told me, that a man of high rank, who looks into his own affairs, may have all that he ought to have, all that can be of any use, or appear with any advantage, for five thousand pounds a year. Therefore, a great proportion must go in waste; and, indeed, this is the case with most people, whatever their fortune is.' BOSWELL. 'I have no doubt, Sir, of this. But how is it? What is

---

[1] When Johnson told this little anecdote to Sir Joshua Reynolds, he mentioned a circumstance which he omitted to-day: 'Why (said Garrick), it is as red as blood.'

waste?' JOHNSON. 'Why, Sir, breaking bottles, and a thousand other things. Waste cannot be accurately told, though we are sensible how destructive it is. Economy on the one hand, by which a certain income is made to maintain a man genteelly, and waste on the other, by which, on the same income, another man lives shabbily, cannot be defined. It is a very nice thing: as one man wears his coat out much sooner than another, we cannot tell how.'

We talked of war. JOHNSON. 'Every man thinks meanly of himself for not having been a soldier, or not having been at sea.' BOSWELL. 'Lord Mansfield does not.' JOHNSON. 'Sir, if Lord Mansfield were in a company of General Officers and Admirals who have been in service, he would shrink; he'd wish to creep under the table.' BOSWELL. 'No; he'd think he could *try* them all.' JOHNSON. 'Yes, if he could catch them: but they'd try him much sooner. No, Sir; were Socrates and Charles the Twelfth of Sweden both present in any company, and Socrates to say, "Follow me, and hear a lecture in philosophy", and Charles, laying his hand on his sword, to say, "Follow me, and dethrone the Czar"; a man would be ashamed to follow Socrates. Sir, the impression is universal: yet it is strange. As to the sailor, when you look down from the quarterdeck to the space below, you see the utmost extremity of human misery: such crowding, such filth, such stench!' BOSWELL. 'Yet sailors are happy.' JOHNSON. 'They are happy as brutes are happy, with a piece of fresh meat, with the grossest sensuality. But, Sir, the profession of soldiers and sailors has the dignity of danger. Mankind reverence those who have got over fear, which is so general a weakness.' SCOTT. 'But is not courage mechanical, and to be acquired?' JOHNSON. 'Why yes, Sir, in a collective sense. Soldiers consider themselves only as parts of a great machine.' SCOTT. 'We find people fond of being sailors.' JOHNSON. 'I cannot account for that, any more than I can account for other strange perversions of imagination.'

His abhorrence of the profession of a sailor was uniformly violent; but in conversation he always exalted the profession of a soldier. And yet I have, in my large and various collection of his writings, a letter to an eminent friend, in which he expresses himself thus: 'My god-son called on me lately. He is weary, and rationally weary, of a military life. If you can place him in some other state, I think you may increase his happiness, and secure his virtue. A soldier's time is passed in distress and danger, or in idleness and corruption.' Such was his cool reflection in his study; but whenever he was warmed and animated by the presence of company, he, like other philosophers, whose minds are impregnated with poetical fancy, caught the common enthusiasm for splendid renown.

He talked of Mr Charles Fox, of whose abilities he thought highly, but observed, that he did not talk much at our club. I have heard Mr Gibbon remark, 'that Mr Fox could not be afraid of Dr Johnson; yet he certainly was very shy of saying any thing in Dr Johnson's presence.' Mr Scott now quoted what was said of Alcibiades by a Greek poet, to which Johnson assented.

He told us, that he had given Mrs Montagu a catalogue of all Daniel Defoe's works of imagination; most, if not all of which, as well as of his other works, he now enumerated, allowing a considerable share of merit to a man, who, bred a silversmith, had written so variously and so well. Indeed, his *Robinson Crusoe* is enough of itself to establish his reputation.

He expressed great indignation at the imposture of the Cock-lane Ghost, and related, with much satisfaction, how he had assisted in detecting the cheat, and had published an account of it in the newspapers. Upon this subject I incautiously offended him, by pressing him with too many questions, and he showed his displeasure. I apologised, saying that 'I asked questions in order to be instructed and entertained; I repaired eagerly to the fountain; but that the moment he gave me a hint, the moment he put a lock upon the well, I desisted.' – 'But, Sir (said he), that is forcing one to do a disagreeable thing'; and he continued to rate me. 'Nay, Sir (said I), when you have put a lock upon the well, so that I can no longer drink, do not make the fountain of your wit play upon me and wet me.'

He sometimes could not bear being teased with questions. I was once present when a gentleman asked so many, as, 'What did you do, Sir?' 'What did you say, Sir?' that he at last grew enraged, and said, 'I will not be put to the *question*. Don't you consider, Sir, that these are not the manners of a gentleman? I will not be baited with *what*, and *why*; what is this? what is that? why is a cow's tail long? why is a fox's tail bushy?' The gentleman, who was a good deal out of countenance, said, 'Why, Sir, you are so good, that I venture to trouble you.' JOHNSON. 'Sir, my being so *good* is no reason why you should be so *ill*.'

Talking of the *Justitia* hulk at Woolwich, in which criminals were punished, by being confined to labour, he said, 'I do not see that they are punished by this: they must have worked equally had they never been guilty of stealing. They now only work; so, after all, they have gained; what they stole is clear gain to them; the confinement is nothing. Every man who works is confined: the smith to his shop, the tailor to his garret.' BOSWELL. 'And Lord Mansfield to his Court.' JOHNSON. 'Yes, Sir. You know the notion of confinement may be extended, as in the song, 'Every island is a prison'. There is, in Dodsley's collection, a copy of verses to the author of that song.'

Smith's Latin verses on Pococke, the great traveller, were mentioned. He repeated some of them, and said they were Smith's best verses.

He talked with an uncommon animation of travelling into distant countries; that the mind was enlarged by it, and that an acquisition of dignity of character was derived from it. He expressed a particular enthusiasm with respect to visiting the wall of China. I catched it for the moment, and said I really believed I should go and see the wall of China had I not children, of whom it was my duty to take care. 'Sir (said he), by doing so, you would do what would be of importance in raising your children to eminence. There would be a lustre reflected upon them from your spirit and curiosity. They would be at all times regarded as the children of a man who had gone to view the wall of China. I am serious, Sir.'

When we had left Mr Scott's, he said, 'Will you go home with me?' 'Sir (said I), it is late; but I'll go with you for three minutes.' JOHNSON. 'Or *four*.' We went to Mrs Williams's room, where we found Mr Allen, the printer, who was the landlord of his house in Bolt-court, a worthy obliging man, and his very old acquaintance; and what was exceedingly amusing, though he was of a very diminutive size, he used, even in Johnson's presence, to imitate the stately periods and slow and solemn utterance of the great man. I this evening boasted, that although I did not write what is called stenography, or short-hand, in appropriated characters devised for the purpose, I had a method of my own of writing half words, and leaving out some altogether, so as yet to keep the substance and language of any discourse which I heard so much in view, that I could give it very completely soon after taking it down. He defied me, as he had once defied an actual short-hand writer; and he made the experiment by reading slowly and distinctly a part of Robertson's *History of America*, while I endeavoured to write it in my way of taking notes. It was found that I had it very imperfectly; the conclusion from which was, that its excellence was principally owing to a studied arrangement of words, which could not be varied or abridged without an essential injury.

On Sunday, April 12, I found him at home before dinner; Dr Dodd's poem entitled 'Thoughts in Prison', was lying upon his table. This appearing to me an extraordinary effort by a man who was in Newgate for a capital crime, I was desirous to hear Johnson's opinion of it: to my surprise, he told me he had not read a line of it. I took up the book and read a passage to him. JOHNSON. 'Pretty well, if you are previously disposed to like them.' I read another passage, with which he was better pleased. He then took the book into his own hands, and having looked at the prayer at the end of it, he said, 'What *evidence* is there that this was composed the night before he suffered. *I* do not believe it.' He then read aloud where he prays for the King, &c. and observed, 'Sir, do you think that a man the night before he is to be hanged cares for the succession of a royal family? Though he *may* have composed this prayer then. A man who has been canting all his life may cant to the last. And yet a man who has been refused a pardon after so much petitioning, would hardly be praying thus fervently for the King.'

He and I, and Mrs Williams, went to dine with the Reverend Dr Percy. Talking of Goldsmith, Johnson said, he was very envious. I defended him, by observing that he owned it frankly upon all occasions. JOHNSON. 'Sir, you are enforcing the charge. He had so much envy that he could not conceal it. He was so full of it that he overflowed. He talked of it to be sure often enough. Now, Sir, what a man avows, he is not ashamed to think; though many a man thinks, what he is ashamed to avow. We are all envious naturally; but by checking envy we get the better of it. So we are all thieves naturally; a child always tries to get at what it wants, the nearest way; by good instruction and good habits this is cured, till a man has not even an inclination to seize what is another's; has no struggle with himself about it.'

And here I shall record a scene of too much heat between Dr Johnson and Dr Percy, which I should have suppressed, were it not that it gave occasion to display the truly tender and benevolent heart of Johnson, who as soon as he found a friend was at all hurt by any thing which he had 'said in his wrath', was not only prompt and desirous to be reconciled, but exerted himself to make ample reparation.

Books of Travels having been mentioned, Johnson praised Pennant very highly, as he did at Dunvegan, in the Isle of Sky.[1] Dr Percy still holding himself as the heir male of the ancient Percies,[a] and having the warmest and most dutiful attachment to the noble house of Northumberland, could not sit quietly and hear a man praised, who had spoken disrespectfully of Alnwick-Castle and the Duke's pleasure-grounds, especially as he thought meanly of his travels. He therefore opposed Johnson eagerly. JOHNSON. 'Pennant in what he has said of Alnwick, has done what he intended; he has made you very angry.' PERCY. 'He has said the garden is *trim*, which is representing it like a citizen's parterre, when the truth is, there is a very large extent of fine turf and gravel walks.' JOHNSON. 'According to your own account, Sir, Pennant is right. It *is* trim. Here is grass cut close, and gravel rolled smooth. Is not that trim? The extent is nothing against that; a mile may be as trim as a square yard. Your extent puts me in mind of the citizens' enlarged dinner, two pieces of roast beef, and two puddings. There is no variety, no mind exerted in laying out the ground, no trees.' PERCY. 'He pretends to give the natural history of Northumberland, and yet takes no notice of the immense number of trees planted there of late.' JOHNSON. 'That, Sir, has nothing to do with the *natural* history; that is *civil* history. A man who gives the natural history of the oak, is not to tell how many oaks have been planted in this place or that. A man who gives the natural history of the cow, is not to tell how many cows are milked at Islington. The animal is the same, whether milked in the Park or at Islington.' PERCY. 'Pennant does not describe well; a carrier who goes along the side of Loch-lomond would describe it better.' JOHNSON. 'I think he describes very well.' PERCY. 'I travelled after him.' JOHNSON. 'And *I* travelled after him.' PERCY. 'But, my good friend, you are short-sighted, and do not see so well as I do.' I wondered at Dr Percy's venturing thus. Dr Johnson said nothing at the time; but inflammable particles were collecting for a cloud to burst. In a little while Dr Percy said something more in disparagement of Pennant. JOHNSON. (pointedly) 'This is the resentment of a narrow mind, because he did not find every thing in Northumberland.' PERCY. (feeling the stroke) 'Sir, you may be

---

[1] *Journal of a Tour to the Hebrides*, edit. 3, p. 221.

[a] Add the following note: See this accurately stated, and the descent of his family from the Earls of Northumberland clearly deduced in the Reverend Dr Nash's excellent *History of Worcestershire*, vol. ii, p. 318. The Doctor has subjoined a note, in which he says, 'The Editor hath seen, and carefully examined the proofs of all the particulars above-mentioned, now in the possession of the Reverend Thomas Percy.'

The same proofs I have also myself carefully examined, and have seen some additional proofs which have occurred since the Doctor's book was published; and both as a Lawyer accustomed to the consideration of evidence, and as a Genealogist versed in the study of pedigrees, I am fully satisfied. I cannot help observing, as a circumstance of no small moment, that in tracing the Bishop of Dromore's genealogy, essential aid was given by the late Elizabeth Duchess of Northumberland, heiress of that illustrious House; a lady not only of high dignity of spirit, such as became her noble blood, but of excellent understanding and lively talents. With a fair pride I can boast of the honour of her Grace's correspondence, specimens of which adorn my archives.

as rude as you please.' JOHNSON. 'Hold, Sir! Don't talk of rudeness; remember, Sir, you told me (puffing hard with passion struggling for a vent) I was short-sighted. We have done with civility. We are to be as rude as we please.' PERCY. 'Upon my honour, Sir, I did not mean to be uncivil.' JOHNSON. 'I cannot say so, Sir; for I *did* mean to be uncivil, thinking you had been uncivil.' Dr Percy rose, ran up to him, and taking him by the hand, assured him affectionately that his meaning had been misunderstood; upon which a reconciliation instantly took place. JOHNSON. 'My dear Sir, I am willing you shall *hang* Pennant.' PERCY. (resuming the former subject) 'Pennant complains that the helmet is not hung out to invite to the hall of hospitality. Now I never heard that it was a custom to hang out a *helmet*.' JOHNSON. 'Hang him up, hang him up.' BOSWELL. (humouring the joke) 'Hang out his skull instead of a helmet, and you may drink ale out of it in your hall of Odin, as he is your enemy; that will be truly ancient. *There* will be *Northern Antiquities*.'[a] JOHNSON. 'He's a *Whig*, Sir; a *sad dog* (smiling at his own violent expressions, merely for *political* difference of opinion). But he's the best traveller I ever read; he observes more things than any one else does.'

I could not help thinking that this was too high praise of a writer who traversed a wide extent of country in such haste, that he could put together only curt frittered fragments of his own, and afterwards procured supplemental intelligence from parochial ministers, and others not the best qualified or most impartial narrators, whose ungenerous prejudice against the house of Stuart glares in misrepresentation; a writer, who at best treats merely of superficial objects, and shows no philosophical investigation of character and manners, such as Johnson has exhibited in his masterly *Journey*, over part of the same ground; and who it should seem from a desire of ingratiating himself with the Scotch, has flattered the people of North-Britain so inordinately and with so little discrimination, that the judicious and candid amongst them must be disgusted, while they value more the plain, just, yet kindly report of Johnson.[b]

We had a calm after the storm, staid the evening and supt, and were pleasant and gay. But Dr Percy told me he was very uneasy at what had passed; for there was a gentleman there who had recently been admitted into the confidence of the Northumberland family, to whom he hoped to appear more

---

[a] Add a note: The title of a book translated by Dr Percy.

[b] After this passage, read as follows: Having impartially censured Mr Pennant, as a Traveller in Scotland, let me allow him from authorities much better than mine, his deserved praise as an able Zoologist; and let me also from my own understanding and feelings, acknowledge the merit of his *London*, which, though said to be not quite accurate in some particulars, is one of the most pleasing topographical performances that ever appeared in any language. Mr Pennant, like his countrymen in general, has the true spirit of a *Gentleman*. As a proof of it, I shall quote from his *London* the passage, in which he speaks of my illustrious friend. 'I must by no means omit *Bolt-court*, the long residence of DOCTOR SAMUEL JOHNSON, a man of the strongest natural abilities, great learning, a most retentive memory, of the deepest and most unaffected piety and morality, mingled with those numerous weaknesses and prejudices which his friends

respectable, by showing him how intimate he was with the great Dr Johnson; and now the gentleman would go away with an impression much to his disadvantage, as if Johnson treated him with disregard, which might do him an essential injury. He begged I would mention this to Dr Johnson, which I afterwards did. His observation upon it was, 'This comes of *stratagem*; had he told me that he wished to appear to advantage before that gentleman, he should have been at the top of the house all the time.' He spoke of Dr Percy in the handsomest terms. 'Then, Sir (said I), may I be allowed to suggest a mode by which you may effectually counteract any unfavourable report of what passed. I will write a letter to you upon the subject of the unlucky contest of that day, and you will be kind enough to put in writing as an answer to that letter, what you have now said, and in short all that you can say to Dr Percy's advantage; and as Lord Percy is to dine with us at General Paoli's soon, I will take an opportunity to read the correspondence in his Lordship's presence.' This friendly scheme was accordingly carried into execution without Dr Percy's knowledge. Johnson's letter was studiously framed to place Dr Percy's unquestionable merit in the fairest point of view; and I contrived that Lord Percy should hear the correspondence, by introducing it at General Paoli's, as an instance of Dr Johnson's kind disposition towards one in whom his Lordship was interested. Thus our friend Percy was raised higher in the estimation of those by whom he wished most to be regarded. I breakfasted the day after with him, and informed him of my scheme, and its happy completion, for which he thanked me in the warmest terms, and was highly delighted with Dr Johnson's letter in his praise, of which I gave him a copy. He said, 'I would rather have this than degrees from all the Universities in Europe. It will be for me, and my children and grandchildren.' Dr Johnson having afterwards asked me if I had given him a copy of it, and being told I had, was offended, and insisted that I should get it back, which I did. As, however, he did not desire me to destroy either the original or the copy, or forbid me to let it be seen, I think myself at liberty to apply to it his general declaration to me concerning his other letters, 'That he did not choose they should be published

---

have kindly taken care to draw from their dread abode.[1] I brought on myself his transient anger, by observing that in his tour in Scotland, he once had 'long and woeful experience of oats being the food of men in *Scotland* as they were of horses in *England*." It was a national reflection unworthy of him, and I shot my bolt. In return he gave me a tender hug. *Con amore* he also said of me "*The dog is a Whig*": I admired the virtues of Lord *Russel*, and pitied his fall. I should have been a Whig at the Revolution. There have been periods since, in which I should have been, what I now am, a moderate Tory, a supporter, as far as my little influence extends, of a well-poised balance between the crown and people: but should the scale preponderate against the *Salus populi*, that moment may it be said "The dog's a *Whig*!" '

1 This is the common cant against faithful Biography. Does the worthy gentleman mean that I, who was taught discrimination of character by Johnson, should have omitted his frailties, and, in short, have *bedaubed* him as the worthy gentleman was bedaubed Scotland?

in his life-time; but had no objection to their appearing after his death.' I shall therefore insert this kindly correspondence, having faithfully narrated the circumstances accompanying it.

To Dr SAMUEL JOHNSON.

MY DEAR SIR – I beg leave to address you in behalf of our friend Dr Percy, who was much hurt by what you said to him that day we dined at his house;[1] when in the course of the dispute as to Pennant's merit as a traveller, you told Percy that "he had the resentment of a narrow mind against Pennant, because he did not find every thing in Northumberland." Percy is sensible that you did not mean to injure him; but he is vexed to think that your behaviour to him upon that occasion may be interpreted as a proof that he is despised by you, which I know is not the case. I have told him, that the charge of being narrow-minded was only as to the particular point in question; and that he had the merit of being a martyr to his noble family.

Earl Percy is to dine with General Paoli next Friday; and I should be sincerely glad to have it in my power to satisfy his Lordship how well you think of Dr Percy, who, I find, apprehends that your good opinion of him may be of very essential consequence; and who assures me, that he has the highest respect and the warmest affection for you.

I have only to add, that my suggesting this occasion for the exercise of your candour and generosity, is altogether unknown to Dr Percy, and proceeds from my good-will towards him, and my persuasion that you will be happy to do him an essential kindness. I am, more and more, my dear Sir,
    Your most faithful and affectionate humble servant,
                                                    JAMES BOSWELL.
    Sunday, April 12, 1778.

To JAMES BOSWELL, Esq.

SIR – The debate between Dr Percy and me is one of those foolish controversies, which begin upon a question of which neither party cares how it is decided, and which is, nevertheless, continued to acrimony, by the vanity with which every man resists confutation. Dr Percy's warmth proceeded from a cause which, perhaps, does him more honour than he could have derived from juster criticism. His abhorrence of Pennant proceeded from his opinion that Pennant had wantonly and indecently censured his patron. His anger made him resolve that for having been once wrong, he never should be right. Pennant has much in his notions that I do not like; but still I think him a very intelligent traveller. If Percy is really offended, I am sorry; for he is a man whom I never knew to offend any one. He is a man very willing to learn, and very able to teach; a man, out of

1 Sunday, April 12, 1778.

whose company I never go without having learned something. It is sure that he vexes me sometimes, but I am afraid it is by making me feel my own ignorance. So much extension of mind, and so much minute accuracy of enquiry, if you survey your whole circle of acquaintance, you will find so scarce, if you find it at all, that you will value Percy by comparison. Lord Hailes is somewhat like him: but Lord Hailes does not, perhaps, go beyond him in research; and I do not know that he equals him in elegance. Percy's attention to poetry has given grace and splendour to his studies of antiquity. A mere antiquarian is a rugged being.

Upon the whole, you see that what I might say in sport or petulance to him, is very consistent with full conviction of his merit. I am, dear Sir,

Your most, &c.

SAM. JOHNSON.

April 23, 1778.

To the Reverend Dr PERCY, Northumberland-house.

DEAR SIR – I wrote to Dr Johnson on the subject of the *Pennantian* controversy; and have received from him an answer which will delight you. I read it yesterday to Dr Robertson, at the Exhibition; and at dinner to Lord Percy, General Oglethorpe, &c. who dined with us at General Paoli's; who was also a witness to the high *testimony* to your honour.

General Paoli desires the favour of your company next Tuesday to dinner, to meet Dr Johnson. If I can, I will call on you today. I am, with sincere regard,

Your most obedient humble servant,

JAMES BOSWELL.[a]

South Audley-street, April 25.

On Monday, April 13, I dined with Johnson at Mr Langton's, where were Dr Porteus, then Bishop of Chester, now of London, and Dr Stinton. He was at first in a very silent frame. Before dinner he said nothing but 'Pretty baby', to one of the children. Langton said very well to me afterwards, that he could repeat Johnson's conversation before dinner, as Johnson had said that he could repeat a complete chapter of *The Natural History of Iceland*, from the Danish of *Horrebow*, the whole of which was exactly thus:

'CHAP. LXXII. *Concerning snakes*.

'There are no snakes to be met with throughout the whole island.'

---

[a] Add the following note: Though the Bishop of Dromore kindly answered the letters which I wrote to him, relative to Dr Johnson's early history; yet, in justice to him, I think it proper to add, that the account of the foregoing conversation, and the subsequent transaction, as well as of some other conversations in which he is mentioned, has been given to the public without previous communication with his Lordship.

At dinner we talked of another mode in the news-papers of giving modern characters in sentences from the classics, and of the passage

> Parcus Deorum cultor, et infrequens,
> Insanientis dum sapientiae
> Consultus erro, nunc retrorsum
> Vela dare, atque iterare cursus
> Cogor relictos:

being well applied to Soame Jennyns; who, after having wandered in the wilds of infidelity, had returned to the Christian faith. Mr Langton asked Johnson as to the propriety of *sapientiae consultus.* JOHNSON. 'Though *consultus* was primarily an adjective, like *amicus* it came to be used as a substantive. So we have *Jurisconsultus,* a consult in law.'

We talked of the styles of different painters, and how certainly a connoisseur could distinguish them. I asked if there was as clear a difference of styles in language as in painting, or even as in hand-writing, so that the composition of every individual may be distinguished? JOHNSON. 'Yes. Those who have a style of eminent excellence, such as Dryden and Milton, can always be distinguished.' I had no doubt of this; but what I wanted to know was, whether there was really a peculiar style to every man whatever, as there is certainly a peculiar hand-writing, a peculiar countenance, not widely different in many, yet always enough to be distinctive:

> . . . facies non omnibus una
> Nec diversa tamen.

The Bishop thought not; and said, he supposed that many pieces in Dodsley's collection of poems, though all very pretty, had nothing appropriated in their style, and in that particular could not be at all distinguished. JOHNSON. 'Why, Sir, I think every man whatever has a peculiar style, which may be discovered by nice examination and comparison with others: but a man must write a great deal to make his style obviously discernible. As logicians say, this appropriation of style is infinite *in potestate,* limited *in actu.*'

Mr Topham Beauclerk came in the evening, and he and Dr Johnson and I staid to supper. It was mentioned that Dr Dodd had once wished to be a member of THE LITERARY CLUB. JOHNSON. 'I should be sorry if any of our club were hanged. I will not say but some of them deserve it.'[1] BEAUCLERK. (supposing this to be aimed at persons for whom he had at that time a wonderful fancy, which, however, did not last long), was irritated, and eagerly said, 'You, Sir, have a friend (naming him) who deserves to be hanged; for he speaks behind their backs against those with whom he lives on the best terms, and attacks them in the news-papers. *He* certainly ought to be *kicked.*' JOHNSON. 'Sir, we all do this in some degree, "*Veniam petimus damusque vicissim.*" To be sure it may be done so much that a man may deserve to be

1 See note, p. 563.

kicked.' BEAUCLERK. 'He is very malignant.' JOHNSON. 'No, Sir; he is not malignant. He is mischievous, if you will. He would do no man an essential injury; he may, indeed, love to make sport of people by vexing their vanity. I, however, once knew an old gentleman who was absolutely malignant. He really wished evil to others, and rejoiced at it.' BOSWELL. 'The gentleman, Mr Beauclerk, against whom you are so violent, is I know, a man of good principles.' BEAUCLERK. 'Then he does not wear them out in practice.'

Dr Johnson, who as I have observed before, delighted in discrimination of character, and having a masterly knowledge of human nature, was willing to take men as they are, imperfect and with a mixture of good and bad qualities, I suppose thought he had said enough in defence of his friend; of whose merits, notwithstanding his exceptionable points, he had a just value, and added no more on the subject.

On Tuesday, April 14, I dined with him at General Oglethorpe's, with General Paoli and Mr Langton. General Oglethorpe declaimed against luxury. JOHNSON. 'Depend upon it, Sir, every state of society is as luxurious as it can be. Men always take the best they can get.' OGLETHORPE. 'But the best depends much upon ourselves; and if we can be as well satisfied with plain things, we are in the wrong to accustom our palates to what is high-seasoned and expensive. What says Addison in his *Cato*, speaking of the Numidian:

> Coarse are his meals, the fortune of the chace,
> Amid the running stream he slakes his thirst,
> Toils all the day, and at the approach of night,
> On the first friendly bank he throws him down,
> Or rests his head upon a rock till morn;
> And if the following day he chance to find
> A new repast, or an untasted spring,
> Blesses his stars! and thinks it luxury!

Let us have *that* kind of luxury, Sir, if you will.' JOHNSON. 'But hold, Sir; to be merely satisfied is not enough. It is in refinement and elegance that the civilized man differs from the savage. A great part of our industry, and all our ingenuity is exercised in procuring pleasure; and, Sir, a hungry man has not the same pleasure in eating a plain dinner, that a hungry man has in eating a luxurious dinner. You see I put the case fairly. A hungry man may have as much, nay, more pleasure in eating a plain dinner, than a man grown fastidious has in eating a luxurious dinner. But I suppose the man who decides between the two dinners, to be equally a hungry man.'

Talking of different governments, – JOHNSON. 'The more contracted that power is, the more easily it is destroyed. A country governed by a despot is an inverted cone. Government there cannot be so firm as when it rests upon a broad basis gradually contracted, as the government of Great-Britain, which is founded on the parliament, then is in the privy-council, then in the King.' BOSWELL. 'Power when contracted into the person of a despot may be easily destroyed, as the prince may be cut off. So Caligula wished that the people of Rome had but one neck, that he might cut them off at a blow.' OGLETHORPE.

'It was of the Senate he wished that. The Senate by its usurpation controlled both the Emperor and the people. And don't you think that we see too much of that in our own parliament?'

Dr Johnson endeavoured to trace the etymology of Maccaronic verses, which he thought were of Italian invention from Maccaroni: but on being informed that this would infer that they were the most common and easy verses, maccaroni being the most ordinary and simple food, he was at a loss; for he said, 'He rather should have supposed it to import in its primitive signification, a composition of several things; for Maccaronic verses are verses made out of a mixture of different languages, that is, of one language with the termination of another.' I suppose there is almost no language in any country where there is any learning, in which that motley ludicrous species of composition may not be found. It is particularly droll in Low Dutch. The *Polemomiddinia* of Drummond of Hawthornden, in which there is a jumble of many languages moulded, as if it were, all in Latin, is well known. Mr Langton made us laugh heartily at one in the Grecian mould, by Joshua Barnes, in which are to be found such comical *Anglo-Ellenisms* as Κλυββοισιν ἐβανχθεν: they were banged with clubs.

On Wednesday, April 15, I dined with Dr Johnson at Mr Dilly's, and was in high spirits, for I had been a good part of the morning with Mr Orme, the able and eloquent historian of Hindostan, who expressed a high admiration of Johnson. 'I do not care (said he) on what subject Johnson talks; but I love better to hear him talk than any body. He either gives you new thoughts, or a new colouring. It is a shame to the nation that he has not been more liberally rewarded. Had I been George the Third, and thought as he did about America, I would have given Johnson three hundred a year for his 'Taxation no Tyranny' alone.' I repeated this, and Johnson was much pleased with such praise from such a man as Orme.

At Mr Dilly's today were Mrs Knowles, the ingenious Quaker lady,[1] Miss Seward, the poetess of Lichfield, the Rev. Dr Mayo, and the Rev. Mr Beresford, Tutor to the Duke of Bedford. Before dinner Dr Johnson seized upon Mr Charles Sheridan's *Account of the late Revolution in Sweden*, and seemed to read it ravenously as if he devoured it, which was to all appearance his method of studying. 'He knows how to read better than any one (said Mrs Knowles); he gets at the substance of a book directly; he tears out the heart of it.' He kept it wrapt up in the tablecloth in his lap during the time of dinner, from an avidity to have one entertainment in readiness when he should have finished another, resembling (if I may use so coarse a simile) a dog who holds a bone in his paws in reserve, while he eats something else which has been thrown to him.

The subject of cookery having been very naturally introduced at a table where Johnson, who boasted of the niceness of his palate, owned that 'he

---

1 Dr Johnson, describing her needle-work in one of his letters to Mrs Thrale, Vol. I. p. 326, uses the learned word *sutile*; which Mrs Thrale has mistaken, and made the phrase injurious by writing '*futile* pictures'.

always found a good dinner', he said, 'I could write a better book of cookery than has ever yet been written; it should be a book upon philosophical principles. Pharmacy is now made much more simple. Cookery may be made so too. A prescription which is now compounded of five ingredients, had formerly fifty in it. So in cookery, if the nature of the ingredients be well known, much fewer will do. Then as you cannot make bad meat good, I would tell what is the best butcher's meat, the best beef, the best pieces; how to choose young fowls; the proper season of different vegetables; and then how to roast and boil, and compound.' DILLY. 'Mrs Glasse's *Cookery*,which is the best, was written by Dr Hill. Half the *trade*[a] know this.' JOHNSON. 'Well, Sir. This shows how much better the subject of Cookery may be treated by a philosopher. I doubt if the book be written by Dr Hill; for, in Mrs Glasse's *Cookery*, which I have looked into, salt-petre and sal-prunella are spoken of as different substances, whereas sal-prunella is only salt-petre burnt on charcoal, and Hill could not be ignorant of this. However, as the greatest part of such a book is made by transcription, this mistake may have been carelessly adopted. But you shall see what a Book of Cookery I shall make! I shall agree with Mr Dilly for the copy-right.' MISS SEWARD. 'That would be Hercules with the distaff indeed.' JOHNSON. 'No, Madam. Women can spin very well; but they cannot make a good book of cookery.'

JOHNSON. 'O! Mr Dilly – you must know that an English Benedictine Monk at Paris has translated the Duke of Berwick's *Memoirs*, from the original French, and has sent them to me to sell. I offered them to Strahan, who sent them back with this answer: "That the first book he had published was the Duke of Berwick's Life, by which he had lost; and he hated the name." – Now I honestly tell you, that Strahan has refused them; but I also honestly tell you, that he did it upon no principle, for he never looked into them.' DILLY. 'Are they well translated, Sir?' JOHNSON. 'Why, Sir, very well – in a style very current and very clear. I have written to the Benedictine to give me an answer upon two points – What evidence is there that the letters are authentic? For if they are not authentic they are nothing. – And how long will it be before the original French is published? For if the French edition is not to appear for a considerable time, the translation will be almost as valuable as an original book. They will make two volumes in octavo; and I have undertaken to correct every sheet as it comes from the press.' Mr Dilly desired to see them, and said he would send for them. He asked Dr Johnson if he would write a Preface to them. JOHNSON. 'No, Sir. The Benedictines were very kind to me, and I'll do what I undertook to do; but I will not mingle my name with them. I am to gain nothing by them. I'll turn them loose upon the world, and let them take their chance.' DR MAYO. 'Pray, Sir, are Ganganelli's letters authentic?' JOHNSON. 'No, Sir. Voltaire put the same question to the editor of them, that I did to Macpherson – Where are the originals?'

[a] Add the following note: As Physicians are called *the Faculty*, and Counsellors at Law *the Profession*, the Booksellers of London are denominated *the Trade*. Johnson disapproved of these denominations.

Mrs Knowles affected to complain that men had much more liberty allowed them than women. JOHNSON. 'Why, Madam, women have all the liberty they should wish to have. We have all the labour and the danger, and the women all the advantage. We go to sea, we build houses, we do every thing, in short, to pay our court to the women.' MRS KNOWLES. 'The Doctor reasons very wittily, but not convincingly. Now, take the instance of building; the mason's wife, if she is ever seen in liquor, is ruined. The mason may get himself drunk as often as he pleases, with little loss of character, nay, may let his wife and children starve.' JOHNSON. 'Madam, you must consider, if the mason does get himself drunk, and let his wife and children starve, the parish will oblige him to find security for their maintenance. We have different modes of restraining evil. Stocks for the men, a ducking-stool for women, and a pound for beasts. If we require more perfection from women than from ourselves, it is doing them honour. And women have not the same temptations that we have: they may always live in virtuous company; men must mix in the world indiscriminately. If a woman has no inclination to do what is wrong, being secured from it is no restraint to her. I am at liberty to walk into the Thames; but if I were to try it, my friends would restrain me in Bedlam, and I should be obliged to them.' MRS KNOWLES. 'Still, Doctor, I cannot help thinking it a hardship that more indulgence is allowed to men than to women. It gives a superiority to men, to which I do not see how they are entitled.' JOHNSON. 'It is plain, Madam, one or other must have the superiority. As Shakspeare says, "If two men ride on horseback, one must ride behind." ' DILLY. 'I suppose, Sir, Mrs Knowles would have them to ride in panniers, one on each side.' JOHNSON. 'Then, Sir, the horse would throw them both.' MRS KNOWLES. 'Well, I hope that in another world the sexes will be equal.' BOSWELL. 'That is being too ambitious, Madam. *We* might as well desire to be equal with the angels. We shall all, I hope, be happy in a future state, but we must not expect to be all happy in the same degree. It is enough if we be happy according to our several capacities. A worthy carman will get to heaven as well as Sir Isaac Newton. Yet, though equally good, they will not have the same degrees of happiness.' JOHNSON. 'Probably not.'

Upon this subject I had once before sounded him, by mentioning the late Reverend Mr Brown, of Utrecht's image; that a great and small glass, though equally full, did not hold an equal quantity; which he threw out to refute David Hume's saying, that a little miss, going to dance at a ball, in a fine new dress, was as happy as a great orator, after having made an eloquent and applauded speech. After some thought, Johnson said, 'I come over to the parson.' As an instance of coincidence of thinking, Mr Dilly told me, that Dr King, a late dissenting minister in London, said to him, upon the happiness in a future state of good men of different capacities, 'A pail does not hold so much as a tub; but, if it be equally full, it has no reason to complain. Every saint in heaven will have as much happiness as he can hold.' Mr Dilly thought this a clear, though a familiar illustration of the phrase, 'One star differeth from another in brightness.'

Dr Mayo having asked Johnson's opinion of Soame Jennyns's 'View of the internal Evidence of the Christian Religion'; – JOHNSON. 'I think it a pretty book; not very theological indeed; and there seems to be an affectation of ease and carelessness, as if it were not suitable to his character to be very serious about the matter.' BOSWELL. 'He may have intended this to introduce his book the better among genteel people, who might be unwilling to read too grave a treatise. There is a general levity in the age. We have physicians now with bag-wigs; may we not have airy divines, at least somewhat less solemn in their appearance than they used to be?' JOHNSON. 'Jennyns might mean as you say.' BOSWELL. '*You* should like his book, Mrs Knowles, as it maintains, as you *friends* do, that courage is not a Christian virtue.' MRS KNOWLES. 'Yes, indeed, I like him there; but I cannot agree with him, that friendship is not a Christian virtue.' JOHNSON. 'Why, Madam, strictly speaking, he is right. All friendship is preferring the interest of a friend, to the neglect, or, perhaps, against the interest of others; so that an old Greek said, "He that has *friends* has *no friend*." Now Christianity recommends universal benevolence, to consider all men as our brethren, which is contrary to the virtue of friendship, as described by the ancient philosophers. Surely, Madam, your sect must approve of this; for you call all men *friends*.' MRS KNOWLES. 'We are commanded to do good to all men, "but especially to them who are of the household of Faith".' JOHNSON. 'Well, Madam. The household of Faith is wide enough.' MRS KNOWLES. 'But, Doctor, our Saviour had twelve Apostles, yet there was one whom he *loved*. John was called "the disciple whom JESUS loved".' JOHNSON. (with eyes sparkling benignantly) 'Very well indeed, Madam. You have said very well.' BOSWELL. 'A fine application. Pray, Sir, had you ever thought of it?' JOHNSON. 'I had not, Sir.'

From this amiable and pleasing subject, he, I know not how or why, made a sudden transition to one upon which he was a violent aggressor; for he said, 'I am willing to love all mankind, *except an American*': and his inflammable corruption bursting into horrid fire, he 'breathed out threatenings and slaughter'; calling them 'Rascals – Robbers – Pirates'; and exclaiming, he'd 'burn and destroy them'. Miss Seward, looking to him with mild but steady astonishment, said, 'Sir, this is an instance that we are always most violent against those whom we have injured.' – He was irritated still more by this delicate and keen reproach; and roared out another tremendous volley, which one might fancy could be heard across the Atlantic. During this tempest I sat in great uneasiness, lamenting his heat of temper; till, by degrees, I diverted his attention to other topics.

DR MAYO. (to Dr Johnson) 'Pray, Sir, have you read Edwards, of New England, on Grace?' JOHNSON. 'No, Sir.' BOSWELL. 'It puzzled me so much as to the freedom of the human will, by stating, with wonderful acute ingenuity, our being actuated by a series of motives which we cannot resist, that the only relief *I* had was to forget it.' MAYO. 'But he makes the proper distinction between moral and physical necessity.' BOSWELL. 'Alas, Sir, they come both to the same thing. You may be bound as hard by chains when covered by leather, as when the iron appears. The argument for the moral necessity of human actions is always, I observe, fortified by supposing universal prescience to be one of the attributes of the Deity.' JOHNSON. 'You are surer that you are free, than you are of prescience; you are surer that you can lift up your finger or not as you please, than you are of any conclusion from a deduction of reasoning. But let us consider a little the objection from prescience. It is certain I am either to go home tonight or not; that does not prevent my freedom.' BOSWELL. 'That it is certain you are *either* to go home or not, does not prevent your freedom; because the liberty of choice between the two is compatible with that certainty. But if *one* of these events be certain *now*, you have no *future* power of volition. If it be certain you are to go home tonight, you *must* go home.' JOHNSON. 'If I am well acquainted with a man, I can judge with great probability how he will act in any case, without his being restrained by my judging. GOD may have this probability increased to certainty.' BOSWELL. 'When it is increased to *certainty* freedom ceases, because that cannot be certainly foreknown which is not certain at the time; but if it be certain at the time, it is a contradiction in terms to maintain that there can be afterwards any *contingency* dependent upon the exercise of will or any thing else.' JOHNSON. 'All theory is against the freedom of the will; all experience for it.' – I did not push the subject any farther. I was glad to find him so mild in discussing a question of the most abstract nature, which is involved with theological tenets, which he generally would not suffer to be in any degree opposed.[1]

He as usual defended luxury; 'You cannot spend money in luxury without doing good to the poor. Nay, you do more good to them by spending it in luxury than by giving it; for by spending it in luxury you make them exert industry, whereas by giving it you keep them idle. I own, indeed, there may be more virtue in giving it immediately in charity than in spending it in luxury; though there may be a pride in that too.' Miss Seward asked if this was not Mandeville's doctrine of 'private vices public benefits'. JOHNSON. 'The fallacy of that book is, that Mandeville defines neither vices nor benefits. He reckons among vices every thing that gives pleasure. He takes the narrowest system of morality, monastic morality, which holds pleasure itself to be a vice, such as eating salt with our fish, because it makes it taste better; and he reckons wealth as a public benefit, which is by no means always true. Pleasure of itself is not a vice. Having a garden, which we all know to be perfectly innocent, is a great pleasure. At the same time, in this state of being there are many pleasures vices, which however are so immediately agreeable that we can hardly abstain from them. The happiness of heaven will be, that pleasure and virtue will be perfectly consistent. Mandeville puts the case of a man who gets drunk at an alehouse; and says it is a public benefit, because so much money is got by it to the public. But it must be considered, that all the good gained by this, through the gradation of alehouse-keeper, brewer, maltster, and farmer, is overbalanced by the evil caused to the man and his family by his getting

1 If any of my readers are disturbed by this thorny question, I beg leave to recommend to them Letter 69 of Montesquieu's *Lettres Persanes*; and the late Mr John Palmer of Islington's Answer to Dr Priestley's mechanical arguments for what he calls 'Philosophical Necessity'.

drunk. This is the way to try what is vicious, by ascertaining whether more evil than good is produced by it upon the whole, which is the case in all vice. It may happen that good is produced by vice; but not as vice; for instance, a robber may take money from its owner, and give it to one who will make a better use of it. Here is good produced; but not by the robbery as robbery, but as translation of property. I read Mandeville forty, or I believe fifty years ago. He did not puzzle me; he opened my views into real life very much. No, it is clear that the happiness of society depends on virtue. In Sparta theft was allowed by general consent; theft, therefore, was *there* not a crime, but then there was no security; and what a life must they have had when there was no security. Without truth there must be a dissolution of society. As its is, there is so little truth that we are almost afraid to trust our ears; but how should we be, if falsehood were multiplied ten times? Society is held together by communication and information; and I remember this remark of Sir Thomas Brown's 'Do the devils lie? No; for then Hell could not subsist.'

Talking of Miss ——, a literary lady, he said, 'I was obliged to speak to Miss Reynolds, to let her know that I desired she would not flatter me so much.' Somebody now observed, 'She flatters Garrick.' JOHNSON. 'She is in the right to flatter Garrick. She is in the right for two reasons; first, because she has the world with her, who have been praising Garrick these thirty years; and secondly, because she is rewarded for it by Garrick. Why should she flatter *me*? I can do nothing for her. Let her carry her praise to a better market. (Then turning to Mrs Knowles) You, Madam, have been flattering me all the evening; I wish you would give Boswell a little now. If you knew his merit as well as I do, you would say a great deal; he is the best travelling companion in the world .'

Somebody mentioned the Reverend Mr Mason's prosecution of Mr Murray, the bookseller, for having inserted in a collection of Gray's Poems, only fifty lines, of which Mr Mason had still the exclusive property, under the statute of Queen Anne; and that Mr Mason had persevered, notwithstanding his being requested to name his own terms of compensation.[1] Johnson signified his displeasure at Mr Mason's conduct very strongly; but added by way of showing that he was not surprised at it, 'Mason's a Whig.' MRS KNOWLES. (not hearing distinctly) 'What! a Prig, Sir?' JOHNSON. 'Worse, Madam; a Whig! But he is both.'

I expressed a horror at the thought of death. MRS KNOWLES. 'Nay, thou should'st not have a horror for what is the gate of life.' JOHNSON. (standing upon the hearth rolling about, with a serious, solemn, and somewhat gloomy air) 'No rational man can die without uneasy apprehension.' MRS KNOWLES. 'The Scriptures tell us, "the righteous shall have *hope* in his death." ' JOHNSON. 'Yes, Madam; that is, he shall not have despair. But, consider, his hope of salvation must be founded on the terms on which it is promised, that the mediation of our SAVIOUR shall be applied to us, namely, obedience; and where obedience has failed, then as suppletory to it, repentance. But what man can say that his obedience has been such, as he would approve of in another, or even in

---

1 See *A letter to W. Mason*, A.M. *from J. Murray, Bookseller in London*; 2d edition, p. 29.

himself upon close examination, or that his repentance has not been such as to require being repented of? No man can be sure that his obedience and repentance will obtain salvation.' MRS KNOWLES. 'But divine intimation of acceptance may be made to the soul.' JOHNSON. 'Madam, it may; but I should not think the better of a man who should tell me on his death-bed he was sure of salvation. A man cannot be sure himself that he has divine intimation of acceptance; much less can he make others sure that he has it.' BOSWELL. 'Then, Sir, we must be contented to acknowledge that death is a terrible thing.' JOHNSON. 'Yes, Sir, I have made no approaches to a state which can look on it as not terrible.' MRS KNOWLES. (seeming to enjoy a pleasing serenity in the persuasion of benignant divine light) 'Does not St Paul say, "I have fought the good fight of faith, I have finished my course; henceforth is laid up for me a crown of life"?' JOHNSON. 'Yes, Madam; but here was a man inspired, a man who had been converted by supernatural interposition.' BOSWELL. 'In prospect death is dreadful; but in fact we find that people die easy.' JOHNSON. 'Why, Sir, most people have not *thought* much of the matter, so cannot *say* much, and it is supposed they die easy. Few believe it certain they are then to die; and those who do, set themselves to behave with resolution, as a man does who is going to be hanged. He is not the less unwilling to be hanged.' MISS SEWARD. 'There is one mode of the fear of death, which is certainly absurd; and that is the dread of annihilation, which is only a pleasing sleep without a dream.' JOHNSON. 'It is neither pleasing nor sleep; it is nothing. Now mere existence is so much better than nothing, that one would rather exist even in pain, than not exist.' BOSWELL. 'If annihilation be nothing, then existing in pain is not a comparative state, but is a positive evil, which I cannot think we should choose. I must be allowed to differ here; and it would lessen the hope of a future state founded on the argument, that the Supreme Being, who is good as he is great, will hereafter compensate for our present sufferings in this life. For if existence, such as we have it here, be comparatively a good, we have no reason to complain, though no more of it should be given to us. But if our only state of existence were in this world, then we might with some reason complain that we are so dissatisfied with our enjoyments compared with our desires.' JOHNSON. 'The lady confounds annihilation, which is nothing, with the apprehension of it, which is dreadful. It is in the apprehension of it that the horror of annihilation consists.'

Of John Wesley he said, 'He can talk well on any subject.' BOSWELL. 'Pray, Sir, what has he made of his story of a ghost?' JOHNSON. 'Why, Sir, he believes it; but not on sufficient authority. He did not take time enough to examine the girl. It was at Newcastle, where the ghost was said to have appeared to a young woman several times, mentioning something about the right to an old house, advising application to be made to an attorney, which was done; and, at the same time, saying the attorney would do nothing, which proved to be the fact. "This (says John) is a proof that a ghost knows our thoughts." Now (laughing) it is not necessary to know our thoughts to tell that an attorney will sometimes do nothing. Charles Wesley, who is a more stationary man, does not believe the story. I am sorry that John did not take more pains to inquire into the evidence for it.' MISS SEWARD. (with an incredulous smile) 'What, Sir! about a ghost?' JOHNSON. (with solemn vehemence) 'Yes, Madam: this is a question which, after five thousand years, is yet undecided; a question, whether in theology or philosophy, one of the most important that can come before the human understanding.'

Mrs Knowles mentioned, as a proselyte to Quakerism, Miss ——, a young lady well known to Dr Johnson, for whom he had shown much affection; while she ever had, and still retained, a great respect for him. Mrs Knowles at the same time took an opportunity of letting him know 'that the amiable young creature was sorry at finding that he was offended at her leaving the Church of England and embracing a simpler faith'; and, in the gentlest and most persuasive manner, solicited his kind indulgence for what was sincerely a matter of conscience. JOHNSON. (frowning very angrily) 'Madam, she is an odious wench. She could not have any proper conviction that it was her duty to change her religion, which is the most important of all subjects, and should be studied with all care, and with all the helps we can get. She knew no more of the Church which she left, and that which she embraced, than she did of the difference between the Copernican and Ptolemaic systems.' MRS KNOWLES. 'She had the New Testament before her.' JOHNSON. 'Madam, she could not understand the New Testament, the most difficult book in the world, for which the study of a life is required.' MRS KNOWLES. 'It is clear as to essentials.' JOHNSON. 'But not as to controversial points. The heathens were easily converted, because they had nothing to give up; but we ought not, without very strong conviction indeed, to desert the religion in which we have been educated. That is the religion given you, the religion in which it may be said Providence has placed you. If you live conscientiously in that religion, you may be safe. But error is dangerous indeed, if you err when you choose a religion for yourself.' MRS KNOWLES. 'Must we then go by implicit faith?' JOHNSON. 'Why, Madam, the greatest part of our knowledge is implicit faith; and as to religion, have we heard all that a disciple of Confucius, all that a Mahometan can say for himself?' He then rose again into passion, and attacked the young proselyte in the severest terms of reproach, so that both the ladies seemed to be much shocked.[a]

[a] Add the following note: Mrs Knowles, not satisfied with the fame of her needlework, the 'sutile pictures' mentioned by Johnson, in which she has indeed displayed much dexterity, nay, with the fame of reasoning better than women generally do, as I have fairly shown her to have done, communicated to me a Dialogue of considerable length, which after many years had elapsed, she wrote down as having passed between Dr Johnson and her at this interview. As I had not the least recollection of it, and did not find the smallest trace of it in my Record taken at the time, I could not in consistency with my firm regard to authenticity, insert it in my work. It has however, been published in the *Gentleman's Magazine* for June 1791. It chiefly relates to the principles of the sect called *Quakers*; and no doubt the lady appears to have greatly the advantage of Dr Johnson in argument as well as expression. From what I have now stated, and from the internal evidence of the paper itself, any one who may have the curiosity to peruse it, will judge whether it was wrong in me to reject it, however willing to gratify Mrs Knowles.

We remained together till it was pretty late. Notwithstanding occasional explosions of violence, we were all delighted upon the whole with Johnson. I compared him at this time to a warm West-Indian climate, where you have a bright sun, quick vegetation, luxuriant foliage, luscious fruits; but where the same heat sometimes produces thunder, lightning, and earthquakes in a terrible degree.

April 17, being Good-Friday, I waited on Johnson as usual. I observed at breakfast that although it was a part of his abstemious discipline on this most solemn fast, to take no milk in his tea, yet when Mrs Desmoulins inadvertently poured it in, he did not reject it. I talked of the strange indecision of mind, and imbecility in the common occurrences of life, which we may observe in some people. JOHNSON. 'Why, Sir, I am in the habit of getting others to do things for me.' BOSWELL. 'What, Sir! have you that weakness?' JOHNSON. 'Yes, Sir. But I always think afterwards I should have done better for myself.'

I told him that at a gentleman's house where there was thought to be such extravagance or bad management, that he was living much beyond his income, his lady had objected to the cutting of a pickled mango, and that I had taken an opportunity to ask the price of it, and found it was only two shillings; so here was a very poor saving. JOHNSON. 'Sir, that is the blundering economy of a narrow understanding. It is stopping one hole in a sieve.'

I expressed some inclination to publish an account of my Travels upon the continent of Europe, for which I had a variety of materials collected. JOHNSON. 'I do not say, Sir, you may not publish your travels; but I give you my opinion, that you would lessen yourself by it. What can you tell of countries so well known as those upon the continent of Europe, which you have visited?' BOSWELL. 'But I can give an entertaining narrative, with many incidents, anecdotes, *jeux d'esprit*, and remarks, so as to make very pleasant reading.' JOHNSON. 'Why, Sir, most modern travellers in Europe who have published their travels, have been laughed at: I would not have you added to the number.[1] The world is now not contented to be merely entertained by a traveller's narrative; they want to learn something. Now some of my friends asked me why I did not give some account of my travels in France. The reason is plain; intelligent readers had seen more of France than I had. *You* might have liked my *Travels in France*, and THE CLUB might have liked them; but upon the whole there would have been more ridicule than good produced by them.' BOSWELL. 'I cannot agree with you, Sir. People would like to read what you say of any thing. Suppose a face has been painted by fifty painters before; still we love to see it done by Sir Joshua.' JOHNSON. 'True, Sir, but Sir Joshua cannot paint a face when he has not time to look on it.' BOSWELL. 'Sir, a sketch of any sort by him is valuable. And, Sir, to talk to you in your own style (raising my voice, and shaking my head), you *should* have given us your Travels in France. I am sure I am right, *and there's an end on't.*'

---

1 I believe, however, I shall follow my own opinion; for the world has shown a very flattering partiality to my writings, on many occasions.

I said to him that it was certainly true, as my friend Dempster had observed in his letter to me upon the subject, that a great part of what was in his *Journey to the Western Islands of Scotland*, had been in his mind before he left London. JOHNSON. 'Why, yes, Sir, the topics were; and books of travels will be good in proportion to what a man has previously in his mind; his knowing what to observe; his power of contrasting one mode of life with another. As the Spanish proverb says, "He, who would bring home the wealth of the Indies, must carry the wealth of the Indies with him." So it is in travelling; a man must carry knowledge with him if he would bring home knowledge.' BOSWELL. 'The proverb, I suppose, Sir, means, he must carry a large stock with him to trade with.' JOHNSON. 'Yes, Sir.'

It was a delightful day: as we walked to St Clement's church, I again remarked that Fleet-street was the most cheerful scene in the world. 'Fleet-street (said I) is in my mind more delightful than Tempé.' JOHNSON. 'Aye, Sir; but let it be compared with Mull.'

There was a very numerous congregation today at St Clement's church, which Dr Johnson said he observed with pleasure.

And now I am to give a pretty full account of one of the most curious incidents in Johnson's life, of which he himself has made the following minute on this day: 'In my return from church, I was accosted by Edwards, an old fellow-collegian, who had not seen me since 1729. He knew me, and asked if I remembered one Edwards; I did not at first recollect the name, but gradually as we walked along, recovered it, and told him a conversation that had passed at an alehouse between us. My purpose is to continue our acquaintance.'[1]

It was in Butcher-row that this meeting happened. Mr Edwards, who was a decent-looking elderly man in grey clothes, and a wig of many curls, accosted Johnson with familiar confidence, knowing who he was, while Johnson returned his salutation with a courteous formality, as to a stranger. But as soon as Edwards had brought to his recollection their having been at Pembroke-College together nine-and-thirty years ago, he seemed much pleased, asked where he lived, and said he should be glad to see him in Bolt-Court. EDWARDS. 'Ah, Sir! we are old men now.' JOHNSON. (who never liked to think of being old) 'Don't let us discourage one another.' EDWARDS. 'Why, Doctor, you look stout and hearty, I am happy to see you so; for the newspapers told us you were very ill.' JOHNSON. 'Aye, Sir, they are always telling lies of *us old fellows*.'

Wishing to be present at more of so singular a conversation as that between two fellow collegians, who had lived near forty years in London without ever having chanced to meet, I whispered to Mr Edwards that Dr Johnson was going home, and that he had better accompany him now. So Edwards walked along with us, I eagerly assisting to keep up the conversation. Mr Edwards informed Dr Johnson that he had practised long as a solicitor in Chancery, but that he now lived in the country upon a little farm about sixty acres, just by

---

1 *Prayers and Meditations*, p. 164.

Stevenage in Hertfordshire, and that he came to London (to Barnard's Inn, No. 6), generally twice a week. Johnson appearing to be in a reverie, Mr Edwards addressed himself to me, and expatiated on the pleasure of living in the country. BOSWELL. 'I have no notion of this, Sir. What you have to entertain you, is, I think, exhausted in half an hour.' EDWARDS. 'What! don't you love to have hope realised? I see my grass, and my corn, and my trees growing. Now, for instance, I am curious to see if this frost has not nipped my fruit trees.' JOHNSON. (who we did not imagine was attending) 'You find, Sir, you have fears as well as hopes.' – So well did he see the whole, when another saw but the half of a subject.

When we got to Dr Johnson's house, and were seated in his library, the dialogue went on admirably. EDWARDS. 'Sir, I remember you would not let us say *prodigious* at College. For even then, Sir (turning to me), he was delicate in language, and we all feared him.'[1] JOHNSON. (to Edwards) 'From your having practised the law long, Sir, I presume you must be rich.' EDWARDS. 'No, Sir, I got a good deal of money; but I had a number of poor relations to whom I gave a great part of it.' JOHNSON. 'Sir, you have been rich in the most valuable sense of the word.' EDWARDS. 'But I shall not die rich.' JOHNSON. 'Nay, sure, Sir, it is better to *live* rich than to *die* rich.' EDWARDS. 'I wish I had continued at College.' JOHNSON. 'Why do you wish that, Sir?' EDWARDS. 'Because I think I should have had a much easier life than mine has been. I should have been a parson, and had a good living, like Bloxam and several others, and lived comfortably.' JOHNSON. 'Sir, the life of a parson, of a conscientious clergyman, is not easy. I have always considered a clergyman as the father of a larger family than he is able to maintain. I would rather have Chancery suits upon my hands than the cure of souls. No, Sir, I do not envy a clergyman's life as an easy life, nor do I envy the clergyman who makes it an easy life.' – Here taking himself up all of a sudden, he exclaimed, 'O! Mr Edwards! I'll convince you that I recollect you. Do you remember our drinking together at an alehouse near Pembroke gate. At that time you told me of the Eton boy, who, when verses on our SAVIOUR's turning water into wine were prescribed as an exercise, brought up a single line, which was highly admired:

> *Vidit et erubuit lympha pudica* DEUM.

and I told you of another fine line in Camden's *Remains*, an eulogy upon one of our Kings, who was succeeded by his son, a prince of equal merit:

> *Mira cano, Sol occubuit, nox nulla secuta est.'*

EDWARDS. 'You are a philosopher, Dr Johnson. I have tried too in my time to be a philosopher; but, I don't know how, cheerfulness was always breaking in.' – Mr Burke, Sir Joshua Reynolds, Mr Courtenay, Mr Malone, and,

---

1 Johnson said to me afterwards, 'Sir, they respected me for my literature; and yet it was not great but by comparison. Sir, it is amazing how little literature there is in the world.'

indeed, all the eminent men to whom I have mentioned this, have thought it an exquisite trait of character. The truth is, that philosophy, like religion, is too generally supposed to be hard and severe, at least so grave as to exclude all gaiety.

EDWARDS. 'I have been twice married, Doctor. You, I suppose, have never known what it was to have a wife.' JOHNSON. 'Sir, I have known what it was to have a wife, and (in a solemn tender faltering tone) I have known what it was to *lose a wife*. - It had almost broke my heart.'

EDWARDS. 'How do you live, Sir? For my part, I must have my regular meals, and a glass of good wine. I find I require it.' JOHNSON. 'I now drink no wine, Sir. Early in life I drank wine: for many years I drank none. I then for some years drank a great deal.' EDWARDS. 'Some hogsheads, I warrant you.' JOHNSON. 'I then had a severe illness, and left it off, and I have never begun it again. I never felt any difference upon myself from eating one thing rather than another, nor from one kind of weather rather than another. There are people, I believe, who feel a difference; but I am not one of them. And as to regular meals, I have fasted from the Sunday's dinner to the Tuesday's dinner, without any inconvenience. I believe it is best to eat just as one is hungry; but a man who is in business, or a man who has a family, must have stated meals. I am a straggler. I may leave this town and go to Grand Cairo, without being missed here or observed there.' EDWARDS. 'Don't you eat supper, Sir?' JOHNSON. 'No, Sir.' EDWARDS. 'For my part now, I consider supper as a turnpike through which one must pass, in order to get to bed.'[1]

JOHNSON. 'You are a lawyer, Mr Edwards. Lawyers know life practically. A bookish man should always have them to converse with. They have what he wants.' EDWARDS. 'I am grown old: I am sixty-five.' JOHNSON. 'I shall be sixty-eight next birthday. Come, Sir, drink water, and put in for a hundred.'

Mr Edwards mentioned a gentleman who had left his whole fortune to Pembroke College. JOHNSON. 'Whether to leave one's whole fortune to a College be right, must depend upon circumstances. I would leave the interest of the fortune I bequeathed to a College to my relations or my friends, for their lives. It is the same thing to a College, which is a permanent society, whether it gets the money now or twenty years hence; and I would wish to make my relations or friends feel the benefit of it.'

This interview confirmed my opinion of Johnson's most humane and benevolent heart. His cordial and placid behaviour to an old fellow-collegian, a man so different from himself; and his telling him that he would go down to his farm and visit him, showed a kindliness of disposition very rare at an advanced age. He observed, 'how wonderful it was that they had both been in London almost forty years, without having ever once met, and both walkers in the street too!' Mr Edwards, when going away, again recurred to his consciousness of senility, and looking full in Johnson's face, said to him,

---

1 I am not absolutely sure but this was my own suggestion, though it is truly in the character of Edwards.

'You'll find in Dr Young,

> O my coevals! remnants of yourselves.'

Johnson did not relish this at all; but shook his head with impatience. Edwards walked off, seemingly highly pleased with the honour of having been thus noticed by Dr Johnson. When he was gone, I said to Johnson, that I thought him but a weak man. JOHNSON. 'Why, yes, Sir. Here is a man who has passed through life without experience: yet I would rather have him with me than a more sensible man who will not talk readily. This man is always willing to say what he has to say.' Yet Dr Johnson had himself by no means that willingness which he praised so much, and I think so justly; for who has not felt the painful effect of the dreary void, when there is a total silence in a company for any length of time; or, which is as bad, or perhaps worse, when the conversation is with difficulty kept up by a perpetual effort?

Johnson once observed to me, 'Tom Tyers described me the best: "Sir (said he), you are like a ghost: you never speak till you are spoken to." '

The gentleman whom he thus familiarly mentioned was Mr Thomas Tyers, son of Mr Jonathan Tyers, the founder of that excellent place of public amusement, Vauxhall Gardens, which must ever be an estate to its proprietor, as it is peculiarly adapted to the taste of the English nation; there being a mixture of curious show – gay exhibition – music, vocal and instrumental, not too refined for the general ear – for all which only a shilling is paid[a] – and, though last not least, good eating and drinking for those who choose to purchase that regale. Mr Thomas Tyers was bred to the law; but having a handsome fortune, vivacity of temper, and eccentricity of mind, he could not confine himself to the regularity of practice. He therefore ran about the world with a pleasant carelessness, amusing every body by his desultory conversation. He abounded in anecdote, but was not sufficiently attentive to accuracy. I therefore cannot venture to avail myself much of a biographical sketch of Johnson which he published, being one among the various persons ambitious of appending their names to that of my illustrious friend. That sketch is, however, an entertaining little collection of fragments. Those which he published of Pope and Addison are of higher merit; but his fame must chiefly rest upon his 'Political Conferences', in which he introduces several eminent persons delivering their sentiments in the way of dialogue, and discovers a considerable share of learning, various knowledge, and discernment of character. This much may I be allowed to say of a man who was exceedingly obliging to me, and who lived with Dr Johnson in as easy a manner as almost any of his very numerous acquaintance.

---

[a] Add this note: In summer, 1792, additional and more expensive decorations having been introduced, the price of admission was raised to two shillings. I cannot approve of this. The company may be more select; but a number of the honest commonalty are, I fear, excluded from sharing in elegant and innocent entertainment. An attempt to abolish the one-shilling gallery at the playhouse has been very properly counteracted.

Mr Edwards had said to me aside, that Dr Johnson should have been of a profession. I repeated the remark to Johnson that I might have his own thoughts on the subject. JOHNSON. 'Sir, it *would* have been better that I had been of a profession. I ought to have been a lawyer.' BOSWELL. 'I do not think, Sir, it would have been better, for we should not have had the English Dictionary.' JOHNSON. 'But you would have had Reports.' BOSWELL. 'Aye; but there would not have been another who could have written the Dictionary. There have been many very good Judges. Suppose you had been Lord Chancellor; you would have delivered opinions with more extent of mind, and in a more ornamented manner, than perhaps any Chancellor ever did, or ever will do. But, I believe, causes have been as judiciously decided as you could have done.' JOHNSON. 'Yes, Sir. Property has been as well settled.'

Johnson, however, had a noble ambition floating in his mind, and had, undoubtedly, often speculated on the possibility of his super-eminent powers being rewarded in this great and liberal country by the highest honours of the state. Sir William Scott informs me that upon the death of the late Lord Lichfield, who was Chancellor of the University of Oxford, he said to Johnson, 'What a pity it is, Sir, that you did not follow the profession of the law. You might have been Lord Chancellor of Great-Britain, and attained to the dignity of the peerage; and now that the title of Lichfield, your native city, is extinct, you might have had it.' Johnson, upon this, seemed much agitated; and, in an angry tone, exclaimed, 'Why will you vex me by suggesting this, when it is too late?'

But he did not repine at the prosperity of others. The late Dr Thomas Leland told Mr Courtenay, that when Mr Edmund Burke showed Johnson his fine house and lands near Beaconsfield, Johnson coolly said, '*Non equidem invideo; miror magis.*'[a]

---

[a] Add the following note: I am not entirely without suspicion that Johnson may have felt a little momentary envy; for no man loved the good things of this life better than he did; and he could not but be conscious that he deserved a much larger share of them, than he ever had. I attempted in a news-paper to comment on the above passage in the manner of Warburton, who must be allowed to have shown uncommon ingenuity, in giving to any author's text whatever meaning he chose it should carry. As this imitation may amuse my readers, I shall here introduce it:

No saying of Dr JOHNSON's has been more misunderstood than his applying to Mr BURKE when he first saw him at his fine place at Beaconsfield, *Non equidem invideo; miror magis.* These two celebrated men had been friends for many years before Mr Burke entered on his parliamentary career. They were both writers, both members of THE LITERARY CLUB; when, therefore, Dr Johnson saw Mr Burke in a situation so much more splendid than that to which he himself had attained, he did not mean to express that he thought it a disproportionate prosperity; but while he, as a philosopher, asserted an exemption from envy, *non equidem invideo*, he went on in the words of the poet, *miror magis*; thereby signifying, either that he was occupied in admiring what he was glad to see; or, perhaps, that considering the general lot of men of superior abilities, he wondered, that Fortune, who is represented as blind, should, in this instance, have been so just.

Yet no man had a higher notion of the dignity of literature than Johnson, or was more determined in maintaining the respect which he justly considered as due to it. Of this, besides the general tenor of his conduct in society, some characteristical instances may be mentioned.

He told Sir Joshua Reynolds, that once when he dined in a numerous company of booksellers, where the room being small, the head of the table, at which he sat, was almost close to the fire, he persevered in suffering a great deal of inconvenience from the heat, rather than quit his place, and let one of them sit above him.

Goldsmith, in his diverting simplicity, complained one day, in a mixed company, of Lord Camden. I met him (said he) at Lord Clare's house in the country, and he took no more notice of me than if I had been an ordinary man. The company having laughed heartily, Johnson stood forth in defence of his friend. Nay, gentlemen (said he), Dr Goldsmith is in the right. A nobleman ought to have made up to such a man as Goldsmith; and I think it is much against Lord Camden that he neglected him.

Nor could he patiently endure to hear that such respect as he thought due only to higher intellectual qualities, should be bestowed on men of slighter, though perhaps more amusing talents. I told him, that one morning, when I went to breakfast with Garrick, who was very vain of his intimacy with Lord Camden, he accosted me thus – 'Pray now, did you? – did you meet a little lawyer turning the corner, eh?' – 'No, Sir (said I). Pray what do you mean by the question?' – 'Why (replied Garrick, with an affected indifference, yet as if standing on tip-toe), Lord Camden has this moment left me. We have had a long walk together.' JOHNSON. 'Well, Sir, Garrick talked very properly. Lord Camden *was* a little lawyer to be associated so familiarly with a player.'

Sir Joshua Reynolds has observed, with great truth, that Johnson considered Garrick to be as it were his *property*. He would allow no man either to blame or to praise Garrick in his presence, without contradicting him.

Having fallen into a very serious frame, in which mutual expressions of kindness passed between us, such as would be thought too vain in me to repeat, I talked with regret of the sad inevitable certainty that one of us must survive the other. JOHNSON. 'Yes, Sir, that is an affecting consideration. I remember Swift, in one of his letters to Pope, says, "I intend to come over, that we may meet once more; and when we must part, it is what happens to all human beings." ' BOSWELL. 'The hope that we shall see our departed friends again must support the mind.' JOHNSON. 'Why yes, Sir.' BOSWELL. 'There is a strange unwillingness to part with life, independent of serious fears as to futurity. A reverend friend of ours (naming him) tells me, that he feels an uneasiness at the thoughts of leaving his house, his study, his books.' JOHNSON. 'This is foolish in ——. A man need not be uneasy on these grounds; for, as he will retain his consciousness, he may say with the philosopher, *Omnia mea mecum porto*.' BOSWELL. 'True, Sir: we may carry our books in our head; but still there is something painful in the thought of leaving for ever what has given us pleasure. I remember many years ago, when my imagination was warm, and I happened to be in a melancholy mood, it distressed me to think of going into a state of being in which Shakspeare's poetry did not exist. A lady whom I then much admired, a very amiable woman, humoured my fancy, and relieved me by saying, "the first thing you will meet in the other world, will be an elegant copy of Shakspeare's works presented to you." ' Dr Johnson smiled benignantly at this, and did not appear to disapprove of the notion.

We went to St Clement's church again in the afternoon, and then returned and drank tea and coffee in Mrs Williams's room; Mrs Desmoulins doing the honours of the tea-table. I observed that he would not even look at a proof sheet of his 'Life of Waller' on Good-Friday.

Mr Allen, the printer, brought a book on agriculture, which was printed, and was soon to be published. It was a very strange performance, the author having mixed in it his own thoughts upon various topics, along with his remarks on ploughing, sowing, and other farming operations. He seemed to be an absurd profane fellow, and had introduced in his book many sneers at religion, with equal ignorance and conceit. Dr Johnson permitted me to read some passages aloud. One was, that he resolved to work on Sunday, and did work, but he owned he felt *some* weak compunction; and he had this very curious reflection: 'I was born in the wilds of Christianity, and the briars and thorns still hang about me.' Dr Johnson could not help laughing at this ridiculous image, yet was very angry at the fellow's impiety. 'However (said he), the Reviewers will make him hang himself.' He however observed, 'that formerly there might have been a dispensation obtained for working on Sunday in the time of harvest.' Indeed in ritual observances, were all the ministers of religion what they should be, and what many of them are, such a power might be wisely and safely lodged with the Church.

On Saturday, April 14, I drank tea with him. He praised the late Mr Duncombe, of Canterbury, as a pleasing man. 'He used to come to me: I did not seek much after *him*. Indeed I never sought much after any body.' BOSWELL. 'Lord Orrery, I suppose.' JOHNSON. 'No, Sir, I never went to him but when he sent for me.' BOSWELL. 'Richardson?' JOHNSON. 'Yes, Sir. But I sought after George Psalmanazar the most. I used to go and sit with him at an alehouse in the city.'

I am happy to mention another instance which I discovered of his seeking after a man of merit. Soon after the Honourable Daines Barrington had published his excellent *Observations on the Statutes*, Johnson waited on that worthy and learned gentleman; and, having told him his name, courteously said, 'I have read your book, Sir, with great pleasure, and wish to be better known to you.' Thus began an acquaintance, which was continued with mutual regard as long as Johnson lived.

Talking of a recent seditious delinquent, he said, 'They should set him in the pillory, that he may be punished in a way that would disgrace him.' I observed, that the pillory does not always disgrace. And I mentioned an instance of a gentleman who I thought was not dishonoured by it. JOHNSON. 'Aye, but he was, Sir. He could not mouth and strut as he used to do, after having been there. People are not very willing to ask a man to their tables who has stood in the pillory.'

The gentleman who had dined with us at Dr Percy's[1] came in. Johnson attacked the Americans with intemperate vehemence of abuse. I said something in their favour; and added, that I was always sorry when he talked on that subject. This, it seems, exasperated him; though he said nothing at the time. The cloud was charged with sulphureous vapour, which was afterwards to burst in thunder. – We talked of a gentleman who was running out his fortune in London; and I said, 'We must get him out of it. All his friends must quarrel with him, and that will soon drive him away.' JOHNSON. 'Nay, Sir, we'll send *you* to him. If your company does not drive a man out of his house, nothing will.' This was a horrible shock, for which there was no visible cause. I afterwards asked him why he had said so harsh a thing. JOHNSON. 'Because, Sir, you had made me angry about the Americans.' BOSWELL. 'But why did not you take your revenge directly?' JOHNSON. (smiling) 'Because, Sir, I had nothing ready. A man cannot strike till he has his weapons.' This was a candid and pleasant confession.

He showed me tonight his drawing-room, very genteelly fitted up; and said, 'Mrs Thrale sneered when I talked of my having asked you and your lady to live at my house. I was obliged to tell her, that you would be in as respectable a situation in my house as in hers. Sir, the insolence of wealth will creep out.' BOSWELL. 'She has a little both of the insolence of wealth, and the conceit of parts.' JOHNSON. 'The insolence of wealth is a wretched thing; but the conceit of parts has some foundation. To be sure it should not be. But who is without it?' BOSWELL. 'Yourself, Sir.' JOHNSON. 'Why, I play no tricks: I lay no traps.' BOSWELL. 'No, Sir. You are six feet high, and you only do not stoop.'

We talked of the numbers of people that sometimes have composed the household of great families. I mentioned that there were a hundred in the family of the present Earl of Eglintoune's father. Dr Johnson seeming to doubt it, I began to enumerate. 'Let us see: my Lord and my lady two.' JOHNSON. 'Nay, Sir, if you are to count by twos, you may be long enough.' BOSWELL. 'Well, but now I add two sons and seven daughters, and a servant for each, that will make twenty; so we have the fifth part already.' JOHNSON. 'Very true. You get at twenty pretty readily; but you will not so easily get further on. We grow to five feet pretty readily; but it is not so easy to grow to seven.'

On Sunday, April 19, being Easter-day, after the solemnities of the festival in St Paul's church, I visited him, but could not stay to dinner. I expressed a wish to have the arguments for Christianity always in readiness, that my religious faith might be as firm and clear as any proposition whatever, so that I need not be under the least uneasiness when it should be attacked. JOHNSON. 'Sir, you cannot answer all objections. You have demonstration for a First Cause: you see he must be good as well as powerful, because there is nothing to make him otherwise, and goodness of itself is preferable. Yet you have against this, what is very certain, the unhappiness of human life. This, however, gives us reason to hope for a future state of compensation, that

1 See p. 658.

there may be a perfect system. But of that we were not sure till we had a positive revelation.' I told him, that his *Rasselas* had often made me unhappy; for it represented the misery of human life so well, and so convincingly to a thinking mind, that if at any time the impression wore off, and I felt myself easy, I began to suspect some delusion.

On Monday, April 20, I found him at home in the morning. We talked of a gentleman who we apprehended was gradually involving his circumstances by bad management. JOHNSON. 'Wasting a fortune is evaporation by a thousand imperceptible means. If it were a stream, they'd stop it. You must speak to him. It is really miserable. Were he a gamester, it could be said he had hopes of winning. Were he a bankrupt in trade, he might have grown rich; but he has neither spirit to spend, nor resolution to spare. He does not spend fast enough to have pleasure from it. He has the crime of prodigality, and the wretchedness of parsimony. If a man is killed in a duel, he is killed as many a one has been killed; but it is a sad thing for a man to lie down and die; to bleed to death, because he has not fortitude enough to sear the wound, or even to stitch it up.' I cannot but pause a moment to admire the fecundity of fancy, and choice of language, which in this instance, and, indeed, on almost all occasions, he displayed. It was well observed by Dr Percy, now Bishop of Dromore, 'The conversation of Johnson is strong and clear, and may be compared to an antique statue, where every vein and muscle is distinct and bold. Ordinary conversation resembles an inferior cast.'

On Saturday, April 25, I dined with him at Sir Joshua Reynolds's, with the learned Dr Musgrave, Counsellor Leland of Ireland, son to the historian, Mrs Cholmondeley, and some more ladies. 'The Project', a new poem, was read to the company by Dr Musgrave. JOHNSON. 'Sir, it has no power. Were it not for the well-known names with which it is filled, it would be nothing: the names carry the poet, not the poet the names.' MUSGRAVE. 'A temporary poem always entertains us.' JOHNSON. 'So does an account of the criminals hanged yesterday entertain us.'

He proceeded: 'Demosthenes Taylor, as he was called (that is, the translator[a] of Demosthenes), was the most silent man, the merest statue of a man that I have ever seen. I once dined in company with him, and all he said during the whole time was no more than *Richard*. How a man should say only Richard, it is not easy to imagine. But it was thus: Dr Douglas was talking of Dr Zachary Grey, and ascribing to him something that was written by Dr Richard Grey. So to correct him, Taylor said (imitating his affected sententious emphasis and nod), "Richard".'

Mrs Cholmondeley, in a high flow of spirits, exhibited some lively sallies of hyperbolical compliment to Johnson, with whom she had been long acquainted, and was very easy. He was quick in catching the manner of the moment, and answered her somewhat in the style of the hero of a romance, 'Madam, you crown me with unfading laurels.'

---

[a] *Second Edition.* Alter 'translator' to 'editor'.

I happened, I know not how, to say that a pamphlet meant a prose piece. JOHNSON. 'No, Sir. A few sheets of poetry unbound are a pamphlet, as much as a few sheets of prose.' MUSGRAVE. 'A pamphlet may be understood to mean a poetical piece, in Westminster-Hall, that is in formal language; but in common language it is understood to mean prose.' JOHNSON. (and here was one of the many instances of his knowing clearly and telling exactly how a thing is) 'A pamphlet is understood in common language to mean prose, only from this, that there is so much more prose written than poetry; as when we say a *book*, prose is understood for the same reason, though a book may as well be in poetry as in prose. We understand what is most general, and we name what is less frequent.'

We talked of a certain lady's verses on Ireland. MISS REYNOLDS. 'Have you seen them, Sir?' JOHNSON. 'No, Madam. I have seen a translation from Horace, by one of her daughters. She showed it me.' MISS REYNOLDS. 'And how was it, Sir?' JOHNSON. 'Why, very well for a young Miss's verses; – that is to say, compared with excellence, nothing; but, very well, for the person who wrote them. I am vexed at being shown verses in that manner.' MISS REYNOLDS. 'But if they should be good, why not give them hearty praise?' JOHNSON. 'Why, Madam, because I have not then got the better of my bad humour from having been shown them. You must consider, Madam; beforehand they may be bad as well as good. Nobody has a right to put another under such a difficulty, that he must either hurt the person by telling the truth, or hurt himself by telling what is not true.' BOSWELL. 'A man often shows his writings to people of eminence, to obtain from them, either from their good-nature, or from their not being able to tell the truth firmly, a commendation, of which he may afterwards avail himself.' JOHNSON. 'Very true, Sir. Therefore a man, who is asked by an author what he thinks of his work, is put to the torture, and is not obliged to speak the truth; so that what he says is not to be considered as his opinion; yet he has said it, and cannot retract it; and this author, when mankind are hunting him with a cannister at his tail, can say, "I would not have published, had not Johnson, or Reynolds, or Musgrave, or some other good judge commended the work." Yet I consider it as a very difficult question in conscience, whether one should advise a man not to publish a work, if profit be his object; for the man may say, "Had it not been for you, I should have had the money." Now you cannot be sure; for you have only your own opinion, and the public may think very differently.' SIR JOSHUA REYNOLDS. 'You must upon such an occasion have two judgements; one as to the real value of the work, the other as to what may please the general taste at the time.' JOHNSON. 'But you can be *sure* of neither; and therefore I should scruple much to give a suppressive vote. Both Goldsmith's comedies were once refused; his first by Garrick, his second by Colman, who was prevailed on at last by much solicitation, nay, a kind of force, to bring it on. His *Vicar of Wakefield* I myself did not think would have had much success. It was written and sold to a bookseller before his *Traveller*, but published after; so little expectation had the bookseller from it. Had it been sold after the *Traveller*, he might have had twice as much money for it, though sixty guineas was no mean price. The bookseller had the advantage of Goldsmith's reputation from *The Traveller* in the sale, though he had it not in selling the copy.' SIR JOSHUA REYNOLDS. '*The Beggar's Opera* affords a proof how strangely people will differ in opinion about a literary performance. Burke thinks it has no merit.' JOHNSON. 'It was refused by one of the houses; but I should have thought it would succeed, not from any great excellence in the writing, but from the novelty, and the general spirit and gaiety of the piece, which keeps the audience always attentive, and dismisses them in good humour.'

We went to the drawing-room, where was a considerable increase of company. Several of us got round Dr Johnson, and complained that he would not give us an exact catalogue of his works, that there might be a complete edition. He smiled, and evaded our intreaties. That he intended to do it I have no doubt, because I have heard him say so; and I have in my possession an imperfect list, fairly written out, which he entitles *Historia Studiorum*. I once got from one of his friends a list, which there was pretty good reason to suppose was accurate, for it was written down in his presence by this friend, who enumerated each article aloud, and had some of them mentioned to him by Mr Levett, in concert with whom it was made out; and Johnson, who heard all this, did not contradict it. But when I showed a copy of this list to him, and mentioned the evidence for its exactness, he laughed, and said, 'I was willing to let them go on as they pleased, and never interfered.' Upon which I read it to him, article by article, and got him positively to own or refuse; and then having obtained certainty so far, I got some other articles confirmed by him directly, and afterwards, from time to time, made additions under his sanction.

His friend Edward Cave having been mentioned, he told us, 'Cave used to sell ten thousand of *The Gentleman's Magazine*: yet such was then his minute attention and anxiety that the sale should not feel the smallest diminution, that he would name a particular person who he heard had talked of leaving off the magazine, and would say, "Let us have something good next month." '

It was observed, that avarice was inherent in some dispositions. JOHNSON. 'No man was born a miser, because no man was born to possession. Every man is born *cupidus* – desirous of getting; but not *avarus* – desirous of keeping.' BOSWELL. 'I have heard old Mr Sheridan maintain, with much ingenuity, that a complete miser is a happy man; a miser who gives himself wholly to the one passion of saving.' JOHNSON. 'That is flying in the face of all the world, who have called an avaricious man a miser, because he is miserable. No, Sir; a man who both spends and saves money is the happiest man, because he has both enjoyments.'

The conversation having turned on *Bon Mots*, he quoted from one of the *Ana* an exquisite instance of flattery in a maid of honour in France, who being asked by the Queen what o'clock it was, answered, 'What your Majesty pleases.' He admitted that Mr Burke s classical pun upon Mr Wilkes's being carried on the shoulders of the mob,

> . . . *Numerisque fertur*
> *Lege solutus, . . .*

was admirable; and though he was strangely unwilling to allow to that extraordinary man the talent of wit,[1] he also laughed with approbation at another of his playful conceits; which was, that 'Horace has in one line given a description of a good desirable manor:

> Est modus in rebus, sunt certi denique fines.

that is to say, a *modus* as to the tithes and certain *fines*.'

He observed, 'A man cannot with propriety speak of himself, except he relates simple facts; as, "I was at Richmond": or what depends on mensuration; as, "I am six feet high." He is sure he has been at Richmond; he is sure he is six feet high: but he cannot be sure he is wise, or that he has any other excellence. Then, all censure of a man's self is oblique praise. It is in order to show how much he can spare. It has all the invidiousness of self-praise, and all the reproach of falsehood.' BOSWELL. 'Sometimes it may proceed from a man's strong consciousness of his faults being observed. He knows that others would throw him down, and therefore he had better lie down softly of his own accord.'

On Tuesday, April 28, he was engaged to dine at General Paoli's, where, as I have already observed, I was still entertained in elegant hospitality, and with all the ease and comfort of a home. I called on him, and accompanied him in a hackney-coach. We stopped first at the bottom of Hedge-lane, into which he went to leave a letter, 'with good news for a poor man in distress', as he told me. I did not question him particularly as to this. He himself often resembled Lady Bolingbroke's lively description of Pope: that 'he was *un politique aux choux et aux raves.*' He would say, 'I dine to-day in Grosvenor-square'; this might be with a Duke: or, perhaps, 'I dine to-day at the other end of the town': or, 'A gentleman of great eminence called on me yesterday.' – He loved thus to keep things floating in conjecture: *Omne ignotum pro magnifico est.* I believe I ventured to dissipate the cloud, to unveil the mystery, more freely and frequently than any of his friends. We stopped again at Wirgman's, the corner of St James's-street, a *toy-shop* to which he had been directed, but not clearly, for he searched about some time, and could not find it at first; and said, 'To direct one only to a corner shop is *toying* with one.' I suppose he meant this as a play upon the word *toy*: it was the first time that I knew him stoop to such sport. After he had been some time in the shop, he sent for me to come out of the coach, and help him to choose a pair of silver buckles, as those he had were too small. Probably this alteration in dress had been suggested by Mrs Thrale,

---

1 See this question fully investigated in the Notes upon my *Journal of a Tour to the Hebrides*, edit. 3, p. 21, *et seq*. And here, as a lawyer mindful of the maxim *Suum cuique tribuito*, I cannot forbear to mention, that the Note beginning with 'I find since the former edition', is not mine, but was originally furnished by Mr Malone, who was so kind as to superintend the press while I was in Scotland, and the first part of the second edition was printing. He would not allow me to ascribe it to its proper author; but as it is exquisitely acute and elegant, I take this opportunity, without his knowledge, to do him justice.

by associating with whom, his external appearance was much improved. He got better clothes; and the dark colour, from which he never deviated, was enlivened by metal buttons. His wigs, too, were much better; and during their travels in France, he was furnished with a Paris-made wig, of handsome construction. This choosing of silver buckles was a negotiation: 'Sir (said he), I will not have the ridiculous large ones now in fashion; and I will give no more than a guinea for a pair.' Such were the *principles* of the business; and, after some examination, he was fitted. As we drove along, I found him in a talking humour, of which I availed myself. BOSWELL. 'I was this morning in Ridley's shop, Sir; and was told, that the collection called *Johnsoniana* has sold very much.' JOHNSON. 'Yet the *Journey to the Hebrides* has not had a great sale.'[1] BOSWELL. 'That is strange.' JOHNSON, 'Yes, Sir; for in that book I have told the world a great deal that they did not know before.'

BOSWELL. 'I drank chocolate, Sir, this forenoon with Mr Eld; and, to my no small surprise, found him to be a Staffordshire Whig, a being which I did not believe had existed.' JOHNSON. 'Sir, there are rascals in all countries.' BOSWELL. 'Eld said, a Tory was a creature generated between a non-juring parson and one's grandmother.' JOHNSON. 'And I have always said, the first Whig was the Devil.' BOSWELL. 'He certainly was, Sir. The Devil was impatient of subordination; he was the first who resisted power:

Better to reign in Hell than serve in Heaven.'

At General Paoli's were Sir Joshua Reynolds, Mr Langton, Marchese Gherardi of Lombardy, and Mr John Spottiswoode, of Spottiswoode,[2] the solicitor. At this time fears of an invasion were circulated; to obviate which, Mr Spottiswoode observed, that Mr Fraser the engineer, who had lately come from Dunkirk, said, that the French had the same fears of us. JOHNSON. 'It is thus that mutual cowardice keeps us in peace. Were one half of mankind brave, and one half cowards, the brave would be always beating the cowards. Were all brave, they would lead a very uneasy life; all would be continually fighting: but being all cowards, we go on very well.'

We talked of drinking wine. JOHNSON. 'I require wine only when I am alone. I have then often wished for it, and often taken it.' SPOTTISWOODE. 'What, by way of a companion, Sir?' JOHNSON. 'To get rid of myself, to send myself away. Wine gives great pleasure; and every pleasure is of itself a good. It is a good, unless counterbalanced by evil. A man may have a strong reason not to drink wine; and that may be greater than the pleasure. Wine makes a man better

---

1 Here he either was mistaken, or had a different notion of an extensive sale from what is generally entertained: for the fact is, that four thousand copies of that excellent work were sold very quickly. A new edition has been printed since his death, besides that in the collection of his works.

2 In the phraseology of Scotland, I should have said, 'Mr Spottiswoode, *of that ilk*'. Johnson knew that sense of the word very well, and has thus explained it in his Dictionary, *voce* ILK – 'It also signifies "the same"; as, *Mackintosh of that ilk*, denotes a gentleman whose surname and the title of his estate are the same.'

pleased with himself. I do not say that it makes him more pleasing to others. Sometimes it does. But the danger is, that while a man grows better pleased with himself, he may be growing less pleasing to others.[1] Wine gives a man nothing. It neither gives him knowledge nor wit; it only animates a man, and enables him to bring out what a dread of the company has repressed. It only puts in motion what has been locked up in frost. But this may be good, or it may be bad.' SPOTTISWOODE. 'So, Sir, wine is a key which opens a box: but this box may be either full or empty.' JOHNSON. 'Nay, Sir, conversation is the key: wine is a pick-lock which forces open the box and injures it. A man should cultivate his mind so as to have that confidence and readiness without wine, which wine gives.' BOSWELL. 'The great difficulty of resisting wine is from benevolence. For instance, a good worthy man asks you to taste his wine which he has had twenty years in his cellar.' JOHNSON. 'Sir, all this notion about benevolence arises from a man imagining himself to be of more importance to others, than he really is. They don't care a farthing whether he drinks wine or not.' SIR JOSHUA REYNOLDS. 'Yes, they do for the time.' JOHNSON. 'For the time! – If they care this minute, they forget it the next. And as for the good worthy man; how do we know he is good and worthy? No good and worthy man will insist upon another man's drinking wine. As to the wine twenty years in the cellar – of ten men, three say this, merely because they must say something; – three are telling a lie, when they say they have had the wine twenty years; – three would rather save the wine; – one, perhaps, cares. I allow it is something to please one's company, and people are always pleased with those who partake pleasure with them. But after a man has brought himself to relinquish the great personal pleasure which arises from drinking wine, any other consideration is a trifle. To please others by drinking wine, is something, only if there be nothing against it. I should, however, be sorry to offend worthy men:

> Curst be the verse, how well soe'er it flow,
> That tends to make one worthy man my foe.'

BOSWELL. 'Curst be the spring, the water.' JOHNSON. 'But let us consider what a sad thing it would be, if we were obliged to drink or do any thing else that may happen to be agreeable to the company where we are.' LANGTON. 'By the same rule you must join with a gang of cut-purses.' JOHNSON. 'Yes, Sir: but yet we must do justice to wine; we must allow it the power it possesses. To make a man pleased with himself, let me tell you, is doing a very great thing;

> *Si patriae volumus, si Nobis vivere cari.*'

I was at this time myself a water-drinker upon trial by Johnson's recommendation. JOHNSON. 'Boswell is a bolder combatant than Sir Joshua: he

---

1 It is observed in Waller's Life, in the *Biographia Britannica*, that he drank only water; and that while he sat in a company who were drinking wine, 'he had the dexterity to accommodate his discourse to the pitch of theirs as it *sunk*.' If excess in drinking be meant, the remark is acutely just. But surely, a moderate use of wine gives a gaiety of spirits which water-drinkers know not.

argues for wine without the help of wine; but Sir Joshua with it.' SIR JOSHUA REYNOLDS. 'But to please one's company is a strong motive.' JOHNSON. (who, from drinking only water, supposed every body who drank wine to be elevated), 'I won't argue any more with you, Sir. You are too far gone.' SIR JOSHUA. 'I should have thought so indeed, Sir, had I made such a speech as you have now done.' JOHNSON. (drawing himself in, and, I really thought, blushing), 'Nay, don't be angry. I did not mean to offend you.' SIR JOSHUA. 'At first the taste of wine was disagreeable to me; but I brought myself to drink it, that I might be like other people. The pleasure of drinking wine is so connected with pleasing your company, that altogether there is something of social goodness in it.' JOHNSON. 'Sir, this is only saying the same thing over again.' SIR JOSHUA. 'No, this is new.' JOHNSON. 'You put it in new words, but it is an old thought. This is one of the disadvantages of wine. It makes a man mistake words for thoughts.' BOSWELL. 'I think it is a new thought; at least, it is in a new *attitude*.' JOHNSON. 'Nay, Sir, it is only in a new coat or an old coat with a new facing. (Then laughing heartily) It is the old dog in a new doublet. – An extraordinary instance however may occur where a man's patron will do nothing for him, unless he will drink: there may be a good reason for drinking.'

I mentioned a nobleman who I believed was really uneasy if his company would not drink hard. JOHNSON. 'That is from having had people about him whom he has been accustomed to command.' BOSWELL. 'Supposing I should be *tête à tête* with *him* at table.' JOHNSON. 'Sir, there is no more reason for your drinking with him, than his being sober with *you*.' BOSWELL. 'Why that is true; for it would do him less hurt to be sober, than it would do me to get drunk.' JOHNSON. 'Yes, Sir; and from what I have heard of him, one would not wish to sacrifice himself to such a man. If he must always have somebody to drink with him, he should buy a slave, and then he would be sure to have it. They who submit to drink as another pleases, make themselves his slaves.' BOSWELL. 'But, Sir, you will surely make allowance for the duty of hospitality. A gentleman who loves drinking comes to visit me.' JOHNSON. 'Sir, a man knows whom he visits; he comes to the table of a sober man.' BOSWELL. 'But, Sir, you and I should not have been so well received in the Highlands and Hebrides, if I had not drank with our worthy friends. Had I drunk water only as you did, they would not have been so cordial.' JOHNSON. 'Sir William Temple mentions that in his travels through the Netherlands he had two or three gentlemen with him, and when a bumper was necessary he put it on *them*. Were I to travel again through the Highlands, I would have Sir Joshua with me to take the bumpers.' BOSWELL. 'But, Sir, let me put a case. Suppose Sir Joshua should take a jaunt into Scotland; he does me the honour to pay me a visit at my house in the country; I am overjoyed at seeing him, we are quite by ourselves; shall I unsociably and churlishly let him sit drinking by himself? No, no, my dear Sir Joshua, you shall not be treated so, I *will* take a bottle with you.'

The celebrated Mrs Rudd being mentioned, JOHNSON. 'Fifteen years ago I should have gone to see her.' SPOTTISWOODE. 'Because she was fifteen years younger?' JOHNSON. 'No, Sir; but now they have a trick of putting every thing into the newspapers.'

He begged of General Paoli to repeat one of the introductory stanzas of the first book of Tasso's *Jerusalem*, which he did, and then Johnson found fault with the simile of sweetening the edges of a cup for a child, being transferred from Lucretius into an epic poem. The General said he did not imagine Homer's poetry was so ancient as is supposed, because he ascribes to a Greek colony circumstances of refinement not found in Greece itself at a later period, when Thucydides wrote. JOHNSON. 'I recollect but one passage quoted by Thucydides from Homer, which is not to be found in our copies of Homer's works; I am for the antiquity of Homer, and think that a Grecian colony by being nearer Persia might be more refined than the mother country.'

On Wednesday, April 29, I dined with him at Mr Allan Ramsay's, where were Lord Binning, Dr Robertson the historian, Sir Joshua Reynolds, and the Honourable Mrs Boscawen, widow of the Admiral, and mother of the present Viscount Falmouth, of whom, if it be not presumptuous in me to praise her, I would say, that her manners are the most agreeable, and her conversation the best of any lady with whom I ever had the happiness to be acquainted. Before Johnson came we talked a good deal of him; Ramsay said he had always found him a very polite man, and that he treated him with great respect, which he did very sincerely. I said I worshipped him. ROBERTSON. 'But some of you spoil him; you should not worship him; you should worship no man.' BOSWELL. 'I cannot help worshipping him, he is so much superior to other men.' ROBERTSON. 'In criticism, and in wit in conversation he is no doubt very excellent; but in other respects he is not above other men; he will believe any thing, and will strenuously defend the most minute circumstance connected with the Church of England.' BOSWELL. 'Believe me, Doctor, you are much mistaken as to this; for when you talk with him calmly in private, he is very liberal in his way of thinking.' ROBERTSON. 'He and I have been always very gracious; the first time I met him was one evening at Strahan's, when he had just had an unlucky altercation with Adam Smith, to whom he had been so rough, that Strahan, after Smith was gone, had remonstrated with him, and told him that I was coming soon, and that he was uneasy to think that he might behave in the same manner to me. "No, no, Sir (said Johnson), I warrant you Robertson and I shall do very well." Accordingly he was gentle and good-humoured, and courteous with me the whole evening; and he has been so upon every occasion that we have met since. I have often said (laughing) that I have been in a great measure indebted to Smith for my good reception.' BOSWELL. 'His power of reasoning is very strong, and he has a peculiar art of drawing characters, which is as rare as good portrait painting.' SIR JOSHUA REYNOLDS. 'He is undoubtedly admirable in this; but, in order to mark the characters which he draws, he overcharges them, and gives people more than they really have, whether of good or bad.'

No sooner did he, of whom we had been thus talking so easily, arrive, than we were all as quiet as a school upon the entrance of the headmaster; and were very soon set down to a table covered with such variety of good things as contributed not a little to dispose him to be pleased.

RAMSAY. 'I am old enough to have been a contemporary of Pope. His poetry was highly admired in his life-time, more a great deal than after his death.' JOHNSON. 'Sir, it has not been less admired after his death; no authors ever had so much fame in their own life-time as Pope and Voltaire; and Pope's poetry has been as much admired after his death as during his life; it has only not been as much talked of, but that is owing to its being now more distant, and people having other writings to talk of. Virgil is less talked of than Pope, and Homer is less talked of than Virgil, but they are not less admired. We must read what the world reads at the moment. It has been maintained that this superfoetation, this teeming of the press in modern times, is prejudicial to good literature, because it obliges us to read so much of what is of inferior value, in order to be in the fashion; so that better works are neglected for want of time, because a man will have more gratification of his vanity in conversation, from having read modern books than from having read the best works of antiquity. But it must be considered, that we have now more knowledge generally diffused; all our ladies read now, which is a great extension. Modern writers are the moons of literature, they shine with reflected light, with light borrowed from the ancients. Greece appears to me to be the fountain of knowledge; Rome of elegance.' RAMSAY. 'I suppose Homer's *Iliad* to be a collection of pieces which had been written before his time. I should like to see a translation of it in poetical prose like the book of Ruth or Job.' ROBERTSON. 'Would you, Dr Johnson, who are master of the English language, but try your hand upon a part of it.' JOHNSON. 'Sir, you could not read it without the pleasure of verse.'[1]

We talked of antiquarian researches. JOHNSON. 'All that is really *known* of the ancient state of Britain is contained in a few pages. We *can* know no more than what the old writers have told us; yet what large books have we upon it, the whole of which excepting such parts as are taken from those old writers is all a dream, such as Whitaker's *Manchester*. I have heard Henry's *History of Britain* well spoken of: I am told it is carried on in separate divisions, as the civil, the military, the religious history; I wish much to have one branch well done, and that is the history of manners, of common life.' ROBERTSON. 'Henry should have applied his attention to that alone, which is enough for any man; and he might have found a great deal scattered in various books, had he read solely with that view. Henry erred in not selling his first volume at a moderate price to the booksellers, that they might have pushed him on till he had got reputation. I sold my *History of Scotland* at a moderate price, as a work by which the booksellers might either gain or not; and Cadell has told me that Millar and he have got six thousand pounds by it. I afterwards received a

1 This experiment which Madame Dacier made in vain, has since been tried in our own language, by the editor of Ossian, and we must either think very meanly of his abilities, or allow that Dr Johnson was in the right.[a]

a Add to the note as follows: And Mr Cowper, a man of real genius, has miserably failed in his blank verse translation.

much higher price for my writings. An author should sell his first work for what the booksellers will give, till it shall appear whether he is an author of merit, or, which is the same thing as to purchase-money, an author who pleases the public.'

Dr Robertson expatiated on the character of a certain nobleman; that he was one of the strongest-minded men that ever lived; that he would sit in company quite sluggish, while there was nothing to call forth his intellectual vigour; but the moment that any important subject was started, for instance, how this country is to be defended against a French invasion, he would rouse himself, and show his extraordinary talents with the most powerful ability and animation.' JOHNSON. 'Yet this man cut his own throat. The true strong and sound mind is the mind that can embrace equally great things and small. Now I am told the King of Prussia will say to a servant, "Bring me a bottle of such a wine, which came in such a year; it lies in such a corner of the cellars." I would have a man to be great in great things, and elegant in little things.' He said to me afterwards, when we were by ourselves, 'Robertson was in a mighty romantic humour, he talked of one whom he did not know; but I *downed* him with the King of Prussia.' – 'Yes, Sir (said I), you threw a *bottle* at his head.'

An ingenious gentleman was mentioned, concerning whom both Robertson and Ramsay agreed that he had a constant firmness of mind; for after a laborious day, and amidst a multiplicity of cares a and anxieties, he would sit down with his sisters and be quite cheerful and good-humoured. Such a disposition, it was observed, was a happy gift of nature. JOHNSON. 'I do not think so; a man has from nature a certain portion of mind; the use he makes of it depends upon his own free will. That a man has always the same firmness of mind I do not say; because every man feels his mind less firm at one time than at another; but I think a man's being in a good or bad humour depends upon his will.' I, however, could not help thinking that a man's humour is often uncontrollable by his will.

Johnson harangued against drinking wine. 'A man (said he) may choose whether he will have abstemiousness and knowledge, or claret and ignorance.' Dr Robertson (who is very companionable) was beginning to dissent as to the proscription of claret. JOHNSON. (with a placid smile) 'Nay, Sir, you shall not differ with me; as I have said that the man is most perfect who takes in the most things, I am for knowledge and claret.' ROBERTSON. (holding a glass of generous claret in his hand) 'Sir, I can only drink your health.' JOHNSON. 'Sir, I should be sorry if you should be ever in such a state as to be able to do nothing more.' ROBERTSON. 'Dr Johnson, allow me to say, that in one respect I have the advantage of you; when you were in Scotland you would not come to hear any of our preachers, whereas when I am here I attend your public worship without scruple, and indeed, with great satisfaction.' JOHNSON. 'Why, Sir, that is not so extraordinary: the King of Siam sent ambassadors to Louis the Fourteenth, but Louis the Fourteenth sent none to the King of Siam.'[1]

1 Mrs Piozzi confidently mentions this as having passed in Scotland, *Anecdotes*, p. 62.

Here my friend for once discovered a want of knowledge or forgetfulness; for Louis the Fourteenth did send an embassy to the King of Siam, and the Abbé Choisis, who was employed in it, published an account of it in two volumes.

Next day, Thursday, April 30, I found him at home by himself. JOHNSON. 'Well, Sir, Ramsay gave us a splendid dinner. I love Ramsay. You will not find a man in whose conversation there is more instruction, more information, and more elegance, than in Ramsay's.' BOSWELL. 'What I admire in Ramsay, is his continuing to be so young.' JOHNSON. 'Why yes, Sir, it is to be admired. I value myself upon this, that there is nothing of the old man in my conversation. I am now sixty-eight, and I have no more of it than at twenty-eight.' BOSWELL. 'But, Sir, would not you wish to know old age? He who is never an old man does not know the whole of human life; for old age is one of the divisions of it.' JOHNSON. 'Nay, Sir, what talk is this?' BOSWELL 'I mean, Sir, the Sphinx's description of it – morning, noon, and night. I would know night, as well as morning and noon.' JOHNSON. 'What, Sir, would you know what it is to feel the evils of old age? Would you have the gout? Would you have decrepitude?' – Seeing him heated, I would not argue any farther; but I was confident that I was in the right. I would, in due time, be a Nestor, an elder of the people; and there *should* be some difference between the conversation of twenty-eight and sixty-eight. A grave picture should not be gay. There is a serene, solemn, placid old age. JOHNSON. 'Mrs Thrale's mother said of me what flattered me much. A clergyman was complaining of want of society in the country where he lived; and said, "they talk of *runts*" (that is, young cows). "Sir (said Mrs Salusbury), Mr Johnson would learn to talk of runts": meaning that I was a man who would make the most of my situation, whatever it was.' He added, 'I think myself a very polite man.'

On Saturday, May 2, I dined with him at Sir Joshua Reynolds's, where there was a very large company, and a great deal of conversation; but owing to some circumstance which I cannot now recollect, I have no record of any part of it, except that there were several people there by no means of the Johnsonian school; so that less attention was paid to him than usual, which put him out of humour; and upon some imaginary offence from me, he attacked me with such rudeness, that I was vexed and angry because it gave those persons an opportunity of enlarging upon his supposed ferocity, and ill treatment of his best friends. I was so much hurt, and had my pride so much roused, that I kept away from him for a week; and, perhaps, might have kept away much longer, nay, gone to Scotland without seeing him again, had not we fortunately met and been reconciled. To such unhappy chances are human friendships liable.

On Friday, May 8, I dined with him at Mr Langton's. I was reserved and silent, which I suppose he perceived, and might recollect the cause. After dinner, when Mr Langton was called out of the room, and we were by ourselves, he drew his chair near to mine, and said, in a tone of conciliating courtesy, 'Well, how have you done?' BOSWELL. 'Sir, you have made me very uneasy by your behaviour to me when we were last at Sir Joshua Reynolds's. You know, my dear Sir, no man has a greater respect and affection for you, or would sooner go to the end of the world to serve you. Now to treat me so — .' He insisted that I had interrupted him, which I assured him was not the case; and proceeded, 'But why treat me so before people who neither love you nor me?' JOHNSON. 'Well, I am sorry for it. I'll make it up to you twenty different ways, as you please.' BOSWELL. 'I said to-day to Sir Joshua, when he observed that you tossed me sometimes, I don't care how often, or how high he tosses me, when only friends are present, for then I fall upon soft ground: but I do not like falling on stones, which is the case when enemies are present. – I think this a pretty good image, Sir.' JOHNSON. 'Sir, it is one of the happiest I have ever heard.'

The truth is, there was no venom in the wounds which he inflicted at any time, unless they were irritated by some malignant infusion by other hands. We were instantly as cordial again as ever, and joined in hearty laugh at some ludicrous but innocent peculiarities of one of our friends. BOSWELL. 'Do you think, Sir, it is always culpable to laugh at a man to his face?' JOHNSON. 'Why, Sir, that depends upon the man and the thing. If it is a slight man, and a slight thing, you may; for you take nothing valuable from him.'

He said, 'I read yesterday Dr Blair's sermon on Devotion, from the text "Cornelius, a devout man". His doctrine is the best limited, the best expressed: there is the most warmth without fanaticism, the most rational transport. There is one part of it which I disapprove, and I'd have him correct it; which is, that "he who does not feel joy in religion is far from the kingdom of heaven." There are many good men whose fear of GOD predominates over their love. It may discourage. It was rashly said. A noble sermon it is indeed. I wish Blair would come over to the Church of England.'

When Mr Langton returned to us, the 'flow of talk' went on. An eminent author being mentioned; – JOHNSON. 'He is not a pleasant man. His conversation is neither instructive nor brilliant. He does not talk as if impelled by any fullness of knowledge or vivacity of imagination. His conversation is like that of any other sensible man. He talks with no wish either to inform or to hear, but only because he thinks it does not become —— to sit in a company and say nothing.'

Mr Langton having repeated the anecdote of Addison having distinguished between his powers in conversation and in writing, by saying 'I have only nine-pence in my pocket; but I can draw for a thousand pounds'; – JOHNSON. 'He had not that retort ready, Sir; he had prepared it before-hand.' LANGTON. (turning to me) 'A fine surmise. Set a thief to catch a thief.'

Johnson called the East-Indians barbarians. BOSWELL. 'You will except the Chinese, Sir? JOHNSON. 'No, Sir.' BOSWELL. 'Have they not arts?' JOHNSON. 'They have pottery.' BOSWELL.'What do you say to the written characters of their language?' JOHNSON. 'Sir, they have not an alphabet. They have not been able to form what all other nations have formed.' BOSWELL. 'There is more learning in their language than in any other, from the immense number of their characters.' JOHNSON. 'It is only more difficult from its rudeness; as there is more labour in hewing down a tree with a stone than with an axe.'

He said, 'I have been reading Lord Kames's *Sketches of the History of Man*. In treating of severity of punishment, he mentions that of Madame Lapouchin, in

Russia, but he does not give it fairly; for I have looked at *Chappe D'Auteroche*, from whom he has taken it. He stops where it is said that the spectators thought her innocent, and leaves out what follows; that she nevertheless was guilty. Now this is being as culpable as one can conceive, to misrepresent fact in a book, and for what motive? It is like one of those lies which people tell, one cannot see why. The woman's life was spared; and no punishment is too great for the favourite of an Empress who had conspired to dethrone her mistress.' BOSWELL. 'He was only giving a picture of the lady in her sufferings.' JOHNSON. 'Nay, don't endeavour to palliate this. Guilt is a principal feature in the picture. Kames is puzzled with a question that puzzled me when I was a very young man. Why is it that the interest of money is lower, when money is plentiful; for five pounds has the same proportion of value to a hundred pounds when money is plentiful, as when it is scarce? A lady explained it to me. "It is (said she) because when money is plentiful there are so many more who have money to lend, that they bid down one another. Many have then a hundred pounds; and one says, Take mine rather than another's, and you shall have it at four *per cent*." ' BOSWELL. 'Does Lord Kames decide the question?' JOHNSON. 'I think he leaves it as he found it.' BOSWELL. 'This must have been an extraordinary lady who instructed you, Sir. May I ask who she was?' JOHNSON. 'Molly Aston,[1] Sir, the sister of those ladies with whom you dined at Lichfield. – I shall be at home to-morrow.' BOSWELL. 'Then let us dine by ourselves at the Mitre, to keep up the old custom, "the custom of the Manor", the custom of the mitre.' JOHNSON. 'Sir, so it shall be.'

On Saturday, May 9, we fulfilled our purpose of dining by ourselves at the Mitre, according to old custom. There was, on these occasions, a little circumstance of kind attention to Mrs Williams, which must not be omitted.

1

Johnson had an extraordinary admiration of this lady, notwithstanding she was a violent Whig. In answer to her high-flown speeches for *Liberty*, he addressed to her the following Epigram, of which I presume to offer a translation:

> *Liber ut esse velim suasisti pulchra Maria,*
> *Ut maneam liber pulchra Maria vale.*

Adieu, Maria! since you'd have me free;
For, who beholds thy charms a slave must be.[a]

[a] Add to the note as follow: A correspondent of *The Gentleman's Magazine*, who subscribes himself SCIOLUS, to whom I am indebted for several excellent remarks, observes, 'The turn of Dr Johnson's lines to Miss Aston, whose Whig principles he had been combating, appears to me to be taken from an ingenious epigram in the *Menagiana* (Vol. III. p. 376, edit. 1716), on a young lady who appeared at a masquerade, *habillé en Jesuite*, during the fierce contentions of the followers of Molinos and Jansenius concerning free-will:

> *On s'étonne ici que Caliste*
> *Ait pris l'habit de Moliniste.*
> *Puisque cette jeune beauté*
> *Ote à chacun sa liberté;*
> *N'est-ce pas une Janseniste?'*

Before coming out, and leaving her to dine alone, he gave her her choice of a chicken, a sweetbread, or any other little nice thing, which was carefully sent to her from the tavern, ready drest.

Our conversation to-day, I know not how, turned (I think for the only time at any length, during our long acquaintance), upon the sensual intercourse between the sexes, the delight of which he ascribed chiefly to imagination. 'Were it not for imagination, Sir (said he), a man would be as happy in the arms of a chamber-maid as of a Duchess. But such is the adventitious charm of fancy, that we find men who have violated the best principles of society, and ruined their fame and their fortune, that they might possess a woman of rank.' It would not be proper to record the particulars of such a conversation in moments of unreserved frankness, when nobody was present on whom it could have any hurtful effect. That subject, when philosophically treated, may surely employ the mind in as curious discussion, and as innocently as anatomy; provided that those who do treat it keep clear of inflammatory incentives.

'From grave to gay, from lively to severe', – we were soon engaged in very different speculation; humbly and reverently considering and wondering at the universal mystery of all things, as our imperfect faculties can now judge of them. 'There are (said he) innumerable questions to which the inquisitive mind can in this state receive no answer: Why do you and I exist? Why was this world created? Since it was to be created, why was it not created sooner?'

On Sunday, May 10, I supped with him at Mr Hoole's, with Sir Joshua Reynolds. I have neglected the memorial of this evening, so as to remember no more of it than two particulars; one, that he strenuously opposed an argument by Sir Joshua, that virtue was preferable to vice, considering this life only; and that a man would be virtuous were it only to preserve his character: and, that he expressed much wonder at the curious formation of the bat, a mouse with wings; saying that 'it was almost as strange a thing in physiology, as if the fabulous dragon could be seen.'

On Tuesday, May 12, I waited on the Earl of Marchmont, to know if his Lordship would favour Dr Johnson with information concerning Pope, whose Life he was about to write. Johnson had not flattered himself with the hopes of receiving any civility from this nobleman; for he said to me, when I mentioned Lord Marchmont as one who could tell him a great deal about Pope, 'Sir, he will tell me nothing.' I had the honour of being known to his Lordship, and applied to him of myself, without being commissioned by Johnson. His Lordship behaved in the most polite and obliging manner, promised to tell all he recollected about Pope, and was so very courteous as to say, 'Tell Dr Johnson I have a great respect for him, and am ready to show it in any way I can. I am to be in the city tomorrow, and will call at his house as I return.' His Lordship however asked, 'Will he write the Lives of the Poets impartially? He was the first that brought Whig and Tory into a Dictionary. And what do you think of his definition of Excise? Do you know the history of his aversion to the word *transpire*?' Then taking down the folio Dictionary, he showed it with this censure on its secondary sense: ' "To escape from secresy to notice; a sense lately innovated from France, without necessity." '

The truth was, Lord Bolingbroke, who left the Jacobites, first used it; therefore, it was to be condemned. He should have shown what word would do for it, if it was unnecessary.' I afterwards put the question to Johnson: 'Why, Sir (said he), *get abroad.*' BOSWELL. 'That, Sir, is using two words. JOHNSON. 'Sir, there's no end of this. You may as well insist to have a word for old age.' BOSWELL. 'Well, Sir, *Senectus.*' JOHNSON. 'Nay, Sir, to insist always that there should be one word to express a thing in English, because there is one in another language, is to change the language.'

I availed myself of this opportunity to hear from his Lordship many particulars both of Pope and Lord Bolingbroke, which I have in writing.

I proposed to Lord Marchmont that he should revise Johnson's Life of Pope: 'So (said his Lordship) you would put me in a dangerous situation. You know he knocked down Osborne the bookseller.'

Elated with the success of my spontaneous exertion to procure material and respectable aid to Johnson for his very favourite work, *The Lives of the Poets*, I hastened down to Mr Thrale's at Streatham, where he now was, that I might insure his being at home next day; and after dinner, when I thought he would receive the good news in the best humour, I announced it eagerly: 'I have been at work for you to-day, Sir. I have been with Lord Marchmont. He bid me tell you he has a great respect for you, and will call on you to-morrow at one o'clock, and communicate all he knows about Pope.' – Here I paused, in full expectation that he would be pleased with this intelligence, would praise my active merit, and would be alert to embrace such an offer from a nobleman. But whether I had shown an over exultation, which provoked his spleen; or whether he was seized with a suspicion that I had obtruded him on Lord Marchmont, and had humbled him too much; or whether there was any thing more than an unlucky fit of ill humour, I know not; but, to my surprise, the result was, – JOHNSON. 'I shall not be in town tomorrow. I don't care to know about Pope.' MRS THRALE. (surprised as I was, and a little angry) 'I suppose, Sir, Mr Boswell thought, that as you are to write Pope's Life, you would wish to know about him.' JOHNSON. 'Wish! why yes. If it rained knowledge I'd hold out my hand; but I would not give myself the trouble to go in quest of it.' There was no arguing with him at the moment. Some time afterwards he said, 'Lord Marchmont will call on me, and then I shall call on Lord Marchmont.' Mr Thrale was uneasy at his unaccountable caprice; and told me, that if I did not take care to bring about a meeting between Lord Marchmont and him, it would never take place, which would be a great pity. I sent a card to his Lordship, to be left at Johnson's house, acquainting him, that Dr Johnson could not be in town next day, but would do himself the honour of waiting on him at another time. – I give this account fairly, as a specimen of that unhappy temper with which this great and good man had occasionally to struggle, from something morbid in his constitution. Let the most censorious of my readers suppose himself to have a violent fit of the tooth-ache, or to have received a severe stroke on the shin-bone, and when in such a state to be asked a question; and if he has any candour, he will not be surprised at the answers which Johnson sometimes gave in moments of irritation, which, let me assure them, is exquisitely painful. But it must not be erroneously supposed that he was, in the smallest degree, careless concerning any work which he undertook, or that he was generally thus peevish. It will be seen, that in the following year he had a very agreeable interview with Lord Marchmont, at his Lordship's house; and this very afternoon he soon forgot any fretfulness, and fell into conversation as usual.

I mentioned a reflection having been thrown out against four Peers for having presumed to rise in opposition to the opinion of the twelve Judges, in a cause in the House of Lords, as if that were indecent. JOHNSON. 'Sir, there is no ground for censure. The Peers are Judges themselves: and supposing them really to be of a different opinion, they might from duty be in opposition to the Judges, who were there only to be consulted.'

In this observation I fully concurred with him; for, unquestionably, all the Peers are vested with the highest judicial powers; and, when they are confident that they understand a cause, are not obliged, nay ought not to acquiesce in the opinion of the ordinary law Judges, or even in that of those who from their studies and experience are called the Law Lords. I consider the Peers in general as I do a Jury, who ought to listen with respectful attention to the sages of the law; but, if after hearing them, they have a firm opinion of their own, are bound, as honest men, to decide accordingly. Nor is it so difficult for them to understand even law questions, as is generally thought; provided they will bestow sufficient attention upon them. This observation was made by my honoured relation the late Lord Cathcart, who had spent his life in camps and courts; yet assured me, that he could form a clear opinion upon most of the causes that came before the House of Lords, 'as they were so well enucleated in the Cases.'

Mrs Thrale told us, that a curious clergyman of our acquaintance had discovered a licentious stanza, which Pope had originally in his *Universal Prayer*, before the stanza

> What conscience dictates to be done,
>   Or warns us not to do, &c.

It was this:

> Can sins of moment claim the rod
>   Of everlasting fires?
> And that offend great Nature's GOD,
>   Which Nature's self inspires?

and that Dr Johnson observed, 'it had been borrowed from *Guarini*.' There are, indeed, in *Pastor Fido*, many such flimsy superficial reasonings, as that in the two last lines of this stanza.

BOSWELL. 'In that stanza of Pope's, "*rod* of *fires*", is certainly a bad metaphor.' MRS THRALE. 'And "sins of *moment*" is a faulty expression; for its true import is *momentous*, which cannot be intended.' JOHNSON. 'It must have been written "of *moments*". Of *moment*, is *momentous*; of *moments*, *momentary*. I warrant you, however, Pope wrote this stanza, and some friend struck it out.

Boileau wrote some such thing, and Arnaud struck it out, saying, "*Vous gagnerez deux ou trois impies, et perdrez je ne sais combien des honnettes gens.*" These fellows want to say a daring thing, and don't know how to go about it. Mere poets know no more of fundamental principles than – ' Here he was inter-rupted somehow. Mrs Thrale mentioned Dryden. JOHNSON. 'He puzzled himself about predestination. – How foolish was it in Pope to give all his friendship to Lords, who thought they honoured him by being with him; and to choose such Lords as Burlington, and Cobham, and Bolingbroke? Bathurst was negative, a pleasing man; and I have heard no ill of Marchmont: and then always saying, "I do not value you for being a Lord"; which was a sure proof that he did. I never say, I do not value Boswell more for being born to an estate, because I do not care.' BOSWELL. 'Nor for being a Scotchman?' JOHNSON. 'Nay, Sir, I do value you more for being a Scotchman. You are a Scotchman without the faults of Scotchmen. You would not have been so valuable as you are, had you not been a Scotchman.'

Talking of divorces, I asked if Othello's doctrine was not plausible:

> He who is robb'd, not wanting what is stolen,
> Let him not know't, and he's not robb'd at all.

Dr Johnson and Mrs Thrale joined against this. JOHNSON. 'Ask any man if he'd wish not to know of such an injury.' BOSWELL. 'Would you tell your friend to make him unhappy?' JOHNSON. 'Perhaps, Sir, I should not; but that would be from prudence on my own account. A man would tell his father.' BOSWELL. 'Yes; because he would not have spurious children to get any share of the family inheritance.' MRS THRALE. 'Or he would tell his brother.' BOSWELL. 'Certainly his elder brother.' JOHNSON. 'You would tell your friend of a woman's infamy, to prevent his marrying a whore: there is the same reason to tell him of his wife's infidelity, when he is married, to prevent the conse-quences of imposition. It is a breach of confidence not to tell a friend.' BOSWELL. 'Would you tell Mr ——?' (naming a gentleman who assuredly was not in the least danger of such a miserable disgrace, though married to a fine woman.) JOHNSON 'No, Sir; because it would do no good: he is so sluggish, he'd never go to parliament and get through a divorce.'

He said of one of our friends, 'He is ruining himself without pleasure. A man who loses at play, or who runs out his fortune at court, makes his estate less, in hopes of making it bigger (I am sure of this word, which was often used by him): but it is a sad thing to pass through the quagmire of parsimony, to the gulph of ruin. To pass over the flowery path of extravagance is very well.'

Amongst the numerous prints pasted on the walls of the dining-room at Streatham, was Hogarth's 'Modern Midnight Conversation'. I asked him what he knew of Parson Ford, who makes a conspicuous figure in the riotous group. JOHNSON. 'Sir, he was my acquaintance and relation, my mother's nephew. He had purchased a living in the country, but not simoniacally. I never saw him but in the country. I have been told he was a man of great parts; very profligate, but I never heard he was impious.' BOSWELL. 'Was there not a story of his ghost having appeared?' JOHNSON. 'Sir, it was believed. A waiter at the Hummums, in which house Ford died, had been absent for some time, and returned, not knowing that Ford was dead. Going down to the cellar, according to the story, he met him; going down again he met him a second time. When he came up, he asked some of the people of the house what Ford could be doing there. They told him Ford was dead. The waiter took a fever, in which he lay for some time. When he recovered, he said he had a message to deliver to some women from Ford; but he was not to tell what, or to whom. He walked out; he was followed; but somewhere about St Paul's they lost him. He came back, and said he had delivered the message, and the women exclaimed, "Then we are all undone!" Dr Pellet, who was not a credulous man, inquired into the truth of this story, and he said, the evidence was irresistible. My wife went to the Hummums; (it is a place where people get themselves cupped.) I believe she went with intention to hear about this story of Ford. At first they made difficulty to tell her; but, after they had talked to her, she came away satisfied that it was true. To be sure, the man had a fever; and this vision may have been the beginning of it. But if the message to the women, and their behaviour upon it were true as related, there was something super-natural. That rests upon his word; and there it remains.'

After Mrs Thrale was gone to bed, Johnson and I sat up late. We resumed Sir Joshua Reynolds's argument on Sunday last, that a man would be virtuous though he had no other motive than to preserve his character. JOHNSON. 'Sir, it is not true: for as to this world vice does not hurt a man's character.' BOSWELL. 'Yes, Sir; debauching a friend's wife will.' JOHNSON. 'No, Sir. Who thinks the worse of —— for it?' BOSWELL. 'Lord —— was not his friend.' JOHNSON. 'That is only a circumstance, Sir; a slight distinction. He could not get into the house but by Lord ——. A man is chosen Knight of the shire, not the less for having debauched ladies.' BOSWELL. 'What, Sir, if he debauched the ladies of gentle-men in the county, will not there be a general resentment against him?' JOHNSON. 'No, Sir. He will lose those particular gentlemen; but the rest will not trouble their heads about it' (warmly). BOSWELL. 'Well, Sir, I cannot think so.' JOHNSON. 'Nay, Sir, there is no talking with a man who will dispute what everybody knows (angrily). Don't you know this?' BOSWELL, 'No, Sir; and I wish to think better of your country than you represent it. I knew in Scotland a gentleman obliged to leave it for debauching a lady; and in one of our counties an Earl's brother lost his election, because he had debauched the lady of another Earl in that county, and broken the peace of a noble family.'

Still he would not yield. He proceeded: 'Will you not allow, Sir, that vice does not hurt a man's character so as to obstruct his prosperity in life, when you know that ——, was loaded with wealth and honours; a man who had acquired his fortune by such crimes, that his consciousness of them impelled him to cut his own throat.' BOSWELL. 'You will recollect, Sir, that Dr Robert-son said, he cut his throat because he was weary of still life; little things not being sufficient to move his great mind.' JOHNSON. (very angry) 'Nay, Sir, what stuff is this? You had no more this opinion after Robertson said it, than before. I know nothing more offensive than repeating what one knows to be foolish things, by way of continuing a dispute, to see what a man will answer, to make him your butt!' (angrier still). BOSWELL. 'My dear Sir, I had no such intention as you seem to suspect; I had not indeed. Might not this nobleman have felt every thing "weary, stale, flat, and unprofitable", as Hamlet says?' JOHNSON. 'Nay, if you are to bring in gabble, I'll talk no more. I will not, upon my honour.' My readers will decide upon this dispute.

Next morning I stated to Mrs Thrale at breakfast, before he came down, the dispute of last night as to the influence of character upon success in life. She said he was certainly wrong; and told me, that a Baronet lost an election in Wales, because he had debauched the sister of a gentleman in the county, whom he made one of his daughters invite as her companion at his seat in the country, when his lady and his other children were in London. But she would not encounter Johnson upon the subject.

I stayed all this day with him at Streatham. He talked a great deal, in very good humour.

Looking at Messrs. Dilly's splendid edition of Lord Chesterfield's miscellaneous works, he laughed, and said, 'Here now are two speeches ascribed to him, both of which were written by me: and the best of it is, they have found out that one is like Demosthenes, and the other like Cicero.'

He censured Lord Kames's *Sketches of the History of Man*, for misrepresenting Clarendon's account of the appearance of Sir George Villiers's ghost, as if Clarendon were weakly credulous; when the truth is, that Clarendon only says, that the story was upon a better foundation of credit, than usually such discourses are founded upon; nay, speaks thus of the person who was reported to have seen the vision, 'the poor man, *if he had been at all waking*'; which Lord Kames has omitted. He added, 'in this book it is maintained that virtue is natural to man, and that if we would but consult our own hearts we should be virtuous. Now after consulting our own hearts all we can, and with all the helps we have, we find how few of us are virtuous. This is saying a thing which all mankind know not to be true.' BOSWELL. 'Is not modesty natural?' JOHNSON. 'I cannot say, Sir, as we find no people quite in a state of nature; but I think the more they are taught, the more modest they are. The French are a gross, ill-bred, untaught people; a lady there will spit on the floor and rub it with her foot. What I gained by being in France was, learning to be better satisfied with my own country. Time may be employed to more advantage from nineteen to twenty-four almost in any way than in travelling; when you set travelling against mere negation, against doing nothing, it is better to be sure; but how much more would a young man improve were he to study during those years. Indeed, if a young man is wild, and must run after women and bad company, it is better this should be done abroad, as, on his return, he can break off such connections, and begin at home a new man, with a character to form, and acquaintances to make. How little does travelling supply to the conversation of any man who has travelled? How little to Beauclerk?' BOSWELL. 'What say you to Lord ——?' JOHNSON. 'I never but once heard him talk of what he had seen, and that was of a large serpent in one of the Pyramids of Egypt.' BOSWELL. 'Well, I happened to hear him tell the same thing, which made me mention him.'

I talked of a country life. – JOHNSON. 'Were I to live in the country I would not devote myself to the acquisition of popularity; I would live in a much better way, much more happily; I would have my time at my own command.' BOSWELL. 'But, Sir, is it not a sad thing to be at a distance from all our literary friends?' JOHNSON. 'Sir, you will by and by have enough of this conversation, which now delights you so much.'

As he was a zealous friend of subordination, he was at all times watchful to repress the vulgar cant against the manners of the great; 'High people, Sir (said he), are the best; take a hundred ladies of quality, you'll find them better wives, better mothers, more willing to sacrifice their own pleasure to their children, than a hundred other women. Tradeswomen (I mean the wives of tradesmen) in the city, who are worth from ten to fifteen thousand pounds, are the worst creatures upon the earth, grossly ignorant, and thinking viciousness fashionable. Farmers, I think, are often worthless fellows. Few lords will cheat; and, if they do, they'll be ashamed of it: farmers cheat and are not ashamed of it: they have all the sensual vices too of the nobility, with cheating into the bargain. There is as much fornication and adultery amongst farmers as amongst noblemen.' BOSWELL. 'The notion of the world, Sir, however is, that the morals of women of quality are worse than those in lower stations.' JOHNSON. 'Yes, Sir, the licentiousness of one woman of quality makes more noise than that of a number of women in lower stations; then, Sir, you are to consider the malignity of women in the city against women of quality, which will make them believe any thing of them, such as that they call their coachmen to bed. No, Sir, so far as I have observed, the higher in rank, the richer ladies are, they are the better instructed and the more virtuous.'

This year the Reverend Mr Horne published his 'Letter to Mr Dunning, on the English Particle'; Johnson read it, and though not treated in it with sufficient respect, he had candour enough to say to Mr Seward, 'Were I to make a new edition of my Dictionary, I would adopt several[1] Of Mr Horne's etymologies; I hope they did not put the dog in the pillory for his libel; he has too much literature for that.'

On Saturday, May 16, I dined with him at Mr Beauclerk's, with Mr Langton, Mr Steevens, Dr Higgins, and some others. I regret very feelingly every instance of my remissness in recording his *memorabilia*; I am afraid it is the condition of humanity (as Mr Windham, of Norfolk, once observed to me, after having made an admirable speech in the House of Commons, which was highly applauded, but which he afterwards perceived might have been better): 'that we are more uneasy from thinking of our wants, than happy in thinking of our acquisitions.' This is an unreasonable mode of disturbing our tranquillity, and should be corrected; let me then comfort myself with the

---

1 In Mr Horne Tooke's enlargement of that 'Letter', which he has since published with the title of 'Επεα πτεροεντα; or, the Diversions of Purley'; he mentions this compliment, as if Dr Johnson instead of *several* of his etymologies had said *all*. His recollection having thus magnified it, shows how ambitious he was of the approbation of so great a man.

large treasure of Johnson's conversation which I have preserved for my own enjoyment and that of the world, and let me exhibit what I have upon each occasion, whether more or less, whether a bulse, or only a few sparks of diamond.

He said, 'Dr Mead lived more in the broad sunshine of life than almost any man.'

The disaster of General Burgoyne's army was then the common topic of conversation. It was asked why piling their arms was insisted upon as a matter of such consequence, when it seemed to be a circumstance so inconsiderable in itself. JOHNSON. 'Why, Sir, a French author says, "*Il y a beaucoup de puerilités dans la guerre.*" All distinctions are trifles, because great things can seldom occur, and those distinctions are settled by custom. A savage would as willingly have his meat sent to him in the kitchen, as eat it at the table here; as men become civilised, various modes of denoting honourable preference are invented.'

He this day made the observations upon the similarity between *Rasselas* and *Candide*, which I have inserted in its proper place, when considering his admirable philosophical Romance. He said *Candide* he thought had more power in it than any thing that Voltaire had written.

He said, 'The lyrical part of Horace never can be perfectly translated; so much of the excellence is in the numbers and the expression. Francis has done it the best; I'll take his, five out of six, against them all.'

On Sunday, May 17, I presented to him Mr Fullarton, of Fullarton, who has since distinguished himself so much in India, to whom he naturally talked of travels, as Mr Brydone accompanied him in his tour to Sicily and Malta. He said, 'The information which we have from modern travellers is much more authentic than what we had from ancient travellers; ancient travellers guessed; modern travellers measure. The Swiss admit that there is but one error in Stanyan. If Brydone were more attentive to his Bible, he would be a good traveller.'

He said, 'Lord Chatham was a Dictator; he possessed the power of putting the State in motion; now there is no power, all order is relaxed.' BOSWELL. 'Is there no hope of a change to the better?' JOHNSON. 'Why, yes, Sir, when we are weary of this relaxation. So the City of London will appoint its Mayors again by seniority.' BOSWELL. 'But is not that taking a mere chance for having a good or a bad Mayor?' JOHNSON. 'Yes, Sir; but the evil of competition is greater than that of the worst Mayor that can come; besides, there is no more reason to suppose that the choice of a rabble will be right, than that chance will be right.'

On Tuesday, May 19, I was to set out for Scotland in the evening. He was engaged to dine with me at Mr Dilly's, I waited upon him to remind him of his appointment and attend him thither; he gave me some salutary counsel, and recommended vigorous resolution against any deviation from moral duty. BOSWELL. 'But you would not have me to bind myself by a solemn obligation?' JOHNSON. (much agitated) 'What! a vow – O, no, Sir, a vow is a horrible thing, it is a snare for sin. The man who cannot go to Heaven without a vow – may go – ' Here, standing erect, in the middle of his library, and rolling grand, his pause was truly a curious compound of the solemn and the ludicrous; he half-whistled in his usual way, when pleasant, and he paused, as if checked by religious awe. – Methought he would have added – to Hell – but was restrained. I humoured the dilemma. 'What! Sir (said I), "*In caelum jusseris ibit,*" ' alluding to his imitation of it,

> And bid him go to Hell, to Hell he goes.

I had mentioned to him a slight fault in his noble *Imitation of the Tenth Satire of Juvenal*, a too near recurrence of the verb *spread*, in his description of the young Enthusiast at College:

> Through all his veins the fever of renown,
> *Spreads* from the strong contagion of the gown;
> O'er Bodley's dome his future labours *spread*,
> And Bacon's mansion trembles o'er his head.

He had desired me to change *spreads* to *burns*, but for perfect authenticity, I now had it done with his own hand.[1] I thought this alteration not only cured the fault, but was more poetical, as it might carry an illusion to the shirt by which Hercules was inflamed.

We had a quiet comfortable meeting at Mr Dilly's; nobody there but ourselves, Mr Dilly mentioned somebody having wished that Milton's 'Tractate on Education' should be printed along with his Poems in the edition of the English Poets then going on. JOHNSON. 'It would be breaking in upon the plan; but would be of no great consequence. So far as it would be any thing it would be wrong. Education in England has been in danger of being hurt by two of its greatest men, Milton and Locke. Milton's plan is impractic-able, and I suppose has never been tried. Locke's, I fancy has been tried often enough, but is very imperfect; it gives too much to one side, and too little to the other; it gives too little to literature. I shall do what I can for Dr Watts; but my materials are very scanty. His poems are by no means his best works; I cannot praise his poetry itself highly; but I can praise its design.'

My illustrious friend and I parted with assurances of affectionate regard.

I wrote to him on the 25th of May, from Thorpe, in Yorkshire, one of the seats of Mr Bosville, and gave him an account of my having passed a day at Lincoln, unexpectedly, and therefore without having any letters of introduc-tion, but that I had been honoured with civilities from the Reverend Mr Simpson, an acquaintance of his, and Captain Broadley, of the Lincolnshire Militia; but more particularly from the Reverend Dr Gordon, the Chancellor, who first received me with great politeness as a stranger, and when I had informed him who I was, entertained me at his house with the most flattering

---

1 The slip of paper on which he made the correction, is deposited by me in the noble library to which it relates, and to which I have presented other specimens of his hand-writing.

attention; I also expressed the pleasure with which I had found that our worthy friend Langton was highly esteemed in his own county town.

To Dr SAMUEL JOHNSON.

Edinburgh, June 18, 1778.

MY DEAR SIR — . . .
Since my return to Scotland, I have been again at Lanark, and have had more conversation with Thomson's sister. It is strange that Murdoch, who was his intimate friend, should have mistaken his mother's maiden name, which he says was Hume, whereas Hume was the name of his grand-mother by the mother's side. His mother's name was Beatrix Trotter,[1] a daughter of Mr Trotter, of Fogo, a small proprietor of land. Thomson had one brother, whom he had with him in England as his amanuensis; but he was seized with a consumption, and having returned to Scotland, to try what his native air would do for him, died young. He had three sisters, one married to Mr Bell, minister of the parish of Strathaven; one to Mr Craig, father of the ingenious architect, who gave the plan of the New Town of Edinburgh; and one to Mr Thomson, master of the grammar-school at Lanark. He was of a humane and benevolent disposition; not only sent valuable presents to his sisters, but an yearly allowance in money, and was always wishing to have it in his power to do them more good. Lord Lyttelton's observation, that 'he lothed much to write', was very true. His letters to his sister, Mrs Thomson, were not frequent, and in one of them he says, 'All my friends who know me, know how backward I am to write letters; and never impute the negligence of my hand to the coldness of my heart.' I send you a copy of the last letter which she had from him; she never heard that he had any intention of going into holy orders. From this late interview with his sister, I think much more favourably of him, as I hope you will. I am eager to see more of your Prefaces to the Poets; I solace myself with the few proof-sheets which I have.

I send another parcel of Lord Hailes's *Annals*, which you will please to return to me as soon as you conveniently can. He says, 'he wishes you would cut a little deeper'; but he may be proud that there is so little occasion to use the critical knife. I ever am, my dear Sir,
    Your faithful and affectionate humble servant,

JAMES BOSWELL.

Mr Langton has been pleased, at my request, to favour me with some particulars of Dr Johnson's visit to Warley-Camp, where this gentleman was at the time stationed, as a Captain in the Lincolnshire militia. I shall give them in his own words in a letter to me.

---

1 Dr Johnson was by no means attentive to minute accuracy in his *Lives of the Poets*; for notwithstanding my having detected this mistake, he has continued it.

It was in the summer of the year 1778, that he complied with my invitation to come down to the Camp at Warley, and he staid with me about a week; the scene appeared, notwithstanding a great degree of ill health that he seemed to labour under, to interest and amuse him, as agreeing with the disposition that I believe you know he constantly manifested towards enquiring into subjects of the military kind. He sat, with a patient degree of attention, to observe the proceedings of a regimental court-martial, that happened to be called in the time of his stay with us; and one night, as late as at eleven o'clock, he accompanied the Major of the regiment in going what are styled the *Rounds*, where he might observe the forms of visiting the guards, for the seeing that they and their sentries are ready in their duty on their several posts. He took occasion to converse at times on military topics, one in particular, that I see the mention of, in your *Journal of a Tour to the Hebrides*, which lies open before me,[1] as to gun-powder; which he spoke of to the same effect, in part, that you relate.

On one occasion, when the regiment were going through their exercise, he went quite close to the men at one of the extremities of it, and watched all their practices attentively; and, when he came away, his remark was, "the men indeed do load their musquets and fire with wonderful celerity." He was likewise particular in requiring to know what was the weight of the musquet-balls in use, and within what distance they might be expected to take effect when fired off.

In walking among the tents, and observing the difference between those of the officers and private men, he said that the superiority of accommodation of the better conditions of life, to that of the inferior ones, was never exhibited to him in so distinct a view. The civilities paid to him in the camp were, from the gentlemen of the Lincolnshire regiment, one of the officers of which accommodated him with a tent in which he slept; and from General Hall, who very courteously invited him to dine with him, where he appeared to be very well pleased with his entertainment, and the civilities he received on the part of the General;[2] the attention likewise of the General's aide-de-camp, Captain Smith, seemed to be very welcome to him, as appeared by their engaging in a great deal of discourse together. The gentlemen of the East York regiment likewise on being informed of his coming, solicited his company at dinner, but by that time he had fixed his departure, so that he could not comply with the invitation.

1 Third Edition, p. 111.
2 When I one day at Court expressed to General Hall my sense of the honour he had done my friend, he politely answered, 'Sir, I did *myself* honour.'

To James Boswell, Esq.

Dear Sir — I have received two letters from you, of which the second complains of the neglect shown to the first. You must not tie your friends to such punctual correspondence. You have all possible assurances of my affection and esteem; and there ought to be no need of reiterated professions. When it may happen that I can give you either counsel or comfort, I hope it will never happen to me that I should neglect you; but you must not think me criminal or cold if I say nothing, when I have nothing to say.

You are now happy enough. Mrs Boswell is recovered; and I congratulate you upon the probability of her long life. If general approbation will add any thing to your enjoyment, I can tell you that I have heard you mentioned as *a man whom every body likes*. I think life has little more to give.

—— has gone to his regiment. He has laid down his coach, and talks of making more contractions of his expense: how he will succeed I know not. It is difficult to reform a household gradually; it may be better done by a system totally new. I am afraid he has always something to hide. When we pressed him to go to ——, he objected the necessity of attending his navigation; yet he could talk of going to Aberdeen, a place not much nearer his navigation. I believe he cannot bear the thought of living at —— in a state of diminution; and of appearing among the gentlemen of the neighbourhood *shorn of his beams*. This is natural, but it is cowardly. What I told him of the encreasing expense of a growing family seems to have struck him. He certainly had gone on with very confused views, and we have, I think, shown him that he is wrong; though, with the common deficience of advisers, we have not shown him how to do right.

I wish you would a little correct or restrain your imagination, and imagine that happiness, such as life admits, may be had at other places as well as London. Without asserting Stoicism, it may be said, that it is our business to exempt ourselves as much as we can from the power of external things. There is but one solid basis of happiness; and that is, the reasonable hope of a happy futurity. This may be had every where.

I do not blame your preference of London to other places, for it is really to be preferred, if the choice is free; but few have the choice of their place, or their manner of life; and mere pleasure ought not to be the prime motive of action.

Mrs Thrale, poor thing, has a daughter. Mr Thrale dislikes the times, like the rest of us. Mrs Williams is sick; Mrs Desmoulins is poor. I have miserable nights. Nobody is well but Mr Levett. I am, dear Sir,

Your most, &c.

SAM. JOHNSON.

London, July 3, 1778.

In the course of this year there was a difference between him and his friend Mr Strahan; the particulars of which it is unnecessary to relate. Their reconciliation was communicated to me in a letter from Mr Strahan, in the following words:

The notes I showed you that past between him and me were dated in March last. The matter lay dormant till July 27, when he wrote to me as follows:

To WILLIAM STRAHAN, Esq.

SIR – It would be very foolish for us to continue strangers any longer. You can never by persistency make wrong right. If I resented too acrimoniously, I resented only to yourself. Nobody ever saw or heard what I wrote. You saw that my anger was over, for in a day or two I came to your house. I have given you longer time; and I hope you have made so good use of it, as to be no longer on evil terms with, Sir,
  Your, &c.

SAM. JOHNSON.

On this I called upon him; and he has since dined with me.

After this time, the same friendship as formerly continued between Mr Johnson and Mr Strahan. My friend mentioned to me a little circumstance of his attention, which, though we may smile at it, must be allowed to have its foundation in a nice and true knowledge of human life. 'When I write to Scotland (said he), I employ Strahan to frank my letters, that he may have the consequence of appearing a Parliament-man among his countrymen.'

To CAPTAIN LANGTON,[1] at Warley Camp.

DEAR SIR – When I recollect how long ago I was received with so much kindness at Warley Common, I am ashamed that I have not made some enquiries after my friends.

Pray how many sheep-stealers did you convict? and how did you punish them? When are you to be cantoned in better habitations? The air grows cold, and the ground damp. Longer stay in the camp cannot be without much danger to the health of the common men, if even the officers can escape.

You see that Dr Percy is now Dean of Carlisle; about five hundred a year, with a power of presenting himself to some good living. He is provided for.

The session of the club is to commence with that of the parliament. Mr Banks desires to be admitted; he will be a very honourable accession.

Did the King please you? The Coxheath men, I think, have some reason to complain: Reynolds says your camp is better than theirs.

---

1 Dr Johnson here addresses his worthy friend, Bennet Langton, Esq. by his title, as a Captain of the Lincolnshire militia.

I hope you find yourself able to encounter this weather. Take care of your own health; and, as you can, of your men. Be pleased to make my compliments to all the gentlemen whose notice I have had, and whose kindness I have experienced. I am, dear Sir,

Your most humble servant,

SAM. JOHNSON.

Oct. 31, 1778.

I wrote to him on the 18th of August, the 18th of September, and the 6th of November; informing him of my having had another son born, whom I had called James; that I had passed some time at Auchinleck; that the Countess of Loudoun, now in her ninety-ninth year, was as fresh as when he saw her, and remembered him with respect; and that his mother by adoption, the Countess of Eglintoune, had said to me, 'Tell Mr Johnson I love him exceedingly'; that I had again suffered much from bad spirits; and that as it was very long since I heard from him, I was not a little uneasy.

The continuance of his regard for his friend Dr Burney, appears from the following letters:

To the Reverend Dr WHEELER, Oxford.

DEAR SIR – Dr Burney, who brings this paper, is engaged in a History of Music; and having been told by Dr Markham of some MSS. relating to his subject, which are in the library of your College, is desirous to examine them. He is my friend; and therefore I take the liberty of intreating your favour and assistance in his enquiry: and can assure you, with great confidence, that if you knew him he would not want any intervenient solicitation to obtain the kindness of one who loves learning and virtue as you love them.

I have been flattering myself all the summer with the hope of paying my annual visit to my friends, but something has obstructed me; I still hope not to be long without seeing you. I should be glad of a little literary talk; and glad to show you, by the frequency of my visits, how eagerly I love it, when you talk it. I am, dear Sir,

Your most humble servant,

SAM. JOHNSON.

London, Nov. 2, 1778.

To the Reverend Dr EDWARDS, Oxford.

SIR – The bearer, Dr Burney, has had some account of a Welsh Manuscript in the Bodleian library, from which he hopes to gain some materials for his History of Music; but, being ignorant of the language, is at a loss where to find assistance. I make no doubt but you, Sir, can help him through his difficulties, and therefore take the liberty of recommending him to your favour, as I am sure you will find him a man worthy of every civility that can be shown, and every benefit that can be conferred.

But we must not let Welsh drive us from Greek. What comes of Xenophon? If you do not like the trouble of publishing the book, do not let your commentaries be lost; contrive that they may be published somewhere. I am, Sir,

Your humble servant,

SAM. JOHNSON.

London, Nov. 2, 1778.

These letters procured Dr Burney great kindness and friendly offices from both of these gentlemen, not only on that occasion, but in future visits to the university. The same year Dr Johnson not only wrote to Dr Joseph Warton in favour of Dr Burney's youngest son, who was to be placed in the college there, but accompanied him to Winchester, when he went thither.

We surely cannot but admire the benevolent exertions of this great and good man, especially when we consider how grievously he was afflicted with bad health, and how uncomfortable his home was made by the perpetual jarring of those whom he charitably accommodated under his roof. He has sometimes suffered me to talk jocularly of his group of females, and call them his *Seraglio*. He thus mentions them, together with honest Levett, in one of his letters to Mrs Thrale:[1] 'Williams hates every body; Levett hates Desmoulins, and does not love Williams; Desmoulins hates them both; Poll[2] loves none of them.'

To James Boswell, Esq.

DEAR SIR — It is indeed a long time since I wrote, and I think you have some reason to complain; however, you must not let small things disturb you, when you have such a fine addition to your happiness as a new boy, and I hope your lady's health restored by bringing him. It seems very probable that a little care will now restore her, if any remains of her complaints are left.

You seem, if I understand your letter, to be gaining ground at Auchinleck, an incident that would give me great delight. . . .

When any fit of anxiety, or gloominess, or perversion of mind, lays hold upon you, make it a rule not to publish it by complaints, but exert your whole care to hide it; by endeavouring to hide it, you will drive it away. Be always busy.

The Club is to meet with the parliament; we talk of electing Banks, the traveller; he will be a reputable member.

Langton has been encamped with his company of militia on Warley-common; I spent five days amongst them; he signalized himself as a diligent officer, and has very high respect in the regiment. He presided when I was

1 Vol. ii, page 38.
2 Miss Carmichael.

there at a court-martial; he is now quartered in Hertfordshire; his lady and little ones are in Scotland. Paoli came to the camp and commended the soldiers.

Of myself I have no great matter to say, my health is not restored, my nights are restless and tedious. The best night that I have had these twenty years was at Fort-Augustus.

I hope soon to send you a few lives to read. I am, dear Sir,
Your most affectionate,

SAM. JOHNSON.

Nov. 21, 1778.

About this time Mr John Hussey,[a] who had been some time in trade, and is now[b] a clergyman of the Church of England, being about to undertake a journey to Aleppo, and other parts of the East, which he accomplished, Dr Johnson[c] honoured him with the following letter:

To Mr JOHN HUSSEY.

DEAR SIR – I have sent you the *Grammar*, and have left you two books more, by which I hope to be remembered; write my name in them; we may perhaps see each other no more, you part with my good wishes, nor do I despair of seeing you return. Let no opportunities of vice corrupt you; let no bad example seduce you; let the blindness of Mahometans confirm you in Christianity. GOD bless you. I am, dear Sir,
Your affectionate humble servant,

SAM. JOHNSON.

Dec. 29, 1778.

Johnson this year expressed great satisfaction at the publication of the first volume of *Discourses to the Royal Academy*, by Sir Joshua Reynolds, whom he always considered as one of his literary school. Much praise indeed is due to those excellent Discourses, which are so universally admired, and for which the author lately received from the Empress of Russia a gold snuff-box, adorned with her profile in *bas relief*, set in diamonds; and containing what is infinitely more valuable, a slip of paper, on which are written with her Imperial Majesty's own hand, the following words: '*Pour le Chevalier Reynolds en temoignage du contentement que j'ai ressentie à la lecture de ses excellens discours sur la peinture.*'[d]

In 1779, Johnson proceeded, at intervals, in writing his *Lives of the Poets.*[d]

---

[a] Read 'the Reverend Mr John Hussey'.

[b] For 'is now' read 'was then'.

[c] Add: 'with whom he had long been in habits of intimacy'.

[d] This paragraph is removed, and the following substituted [see p. 626 and note]: This year, Johnson gave the world a luminous proof that the vigour of his mind in all its faculties, whether memory, judgement, or imagination, was not in the least abated; for this year came out the first four volumes of his *Prefaces, biographical and critical, to the*

On the 22nd of January, I wrote to him on several topics, and mentioned that as he had been so good as to permit me to have the proof sheets of his *Lives of the Poets*, I had written to his servant, Francis, to take care of them for me.

Mr BOSWELL to Dr JOHNSON.

Edinburgh, Feb. 2, 1779.

MY DEAR SIR – Garrick's death is a striking event; not that we should be surprised with the death of any man, who has lived sixty-two years. But because there was a *vivacity* in our late celebrated friend, which drove away the thoughts of *death* from any association with *him*; I am sure you will be tenderly affected with his departure; and I would wish to hear from you upon the subject. I was obliged to him in my days of effervescence in London, when poor Derrick was my governor; and since that time I received many civilities from him. Do you remember how pleasing it was, when I received a letter from him at Inverary, upon our first return to civilized living after our Hebridean journey. I shall always remember him with affection as well as admiration.

On Saturday last, being the 30th of January, I drank coffee and old port, and had solemn conversation with the Reverend Mr Falconer, a non-juring bishop, a very learned and worthy man. He gave two toasts, which you will believe I drank with cordiality, Dr Samuel Johnson and Flora Macdonald. I sat about four hours with him, and it was really as if I had been living in the last century. The Episcopal Church of Scotland, though faithful to the royal house of Stuart, has never accepted of any *congé d'élire*, since the Revolution; it is the only true Episcopal Church in Scotland, as it has its own succession of bishops. For as to the episcopal clergy who take the oaths to the present government, they indeed follow the rites of the Church of England, but, as Bishop Falconer observed, they are not *Episcopals*; for they are under no bishop, as a bishop cannot have authority beyond his diocese.

This venerable gentleman did me the honour to dine with me yesterday, and he laid his hands upon the heads of my little ones. We had a good deal of curious literary conversation, particularly about Mr Thomas Ruddiman, with whom he lived in great friendship.

Any fresh instance of the uncertainty of life makes one embrace more

---

most eminent of the English Poets,* published by the booksellers of London. The remaining volumes came out in the year 1780. The Poets were selected by the several booksellers who had the honorary copy-right, which is still preserved among them by mutual compact, notwithstanding the decision of the House of Lords against the perpetuity of Literary Property. We have his own authority, that by his recommendation the poems of Blackmore, Watts, Pomfret, and Yalden, were added to the collection. Of this work I shall speak more particularly hereafter.

closely a valuable friend. My dear and much respected Sir, may GOD preserve you long in this world while I am in it. I am ever,

Your much obliged,

And affectionate humble servant,

JAMES BOSWELL.

On the 23rd of February I wrote to him again, complaining of his silence, as I had heard he was ill, and had written to Mr Thrale for information concerning him; and I announced my intention of soon being again in London.

To JAMES BOSWELL, Esq.

DEAR SIR – Why should you take such delight to make a bustle, to write to Mr Thrale that I am negligent, and to Francis to do what is so very unnecessary. Thrale, you may be sure, cared not about it; and I shall spare Francis the trouble, by ordering a set both of the *Lives* and *Poets* to dear Mrs Boswell,[1] in acknowledgement of her marmalade. Persuade her to accept them, and accept them kindly. If I thought she would receive them scornfully, I would send them to Miss Boswell, who, I hope, has yet none of her mamma's ill-will to me.

I would send sets of *Lives*, four volumes, to some other friends, to Lord Hailes first. His second volume lies by my bed-side; a book surely of great labour, and to every just thinker of great delight. Write me word to whom I shall send besides; would it please Lord Auchinleck? Mrs Thrale waits in the coach.

I am, dear Sir, &c.

SAM. JOHNSON.

March 13, 1779.

This letter crossed me on the road to London, where I arrived on Monday, March 15, and next morning at a late hour, found Dr Johnson sitting over his tea, attended by Mrs Desmoulins, Mr Levett, and a clergyman, who had come to submit some poetical pieces to his revision. It is wonderful what a number and variety of writers, some of them even unknown to him, prevailed on his good-nature to look over their works, and suggest corrections and improvements. My arrival interrupted for a little while, the important business of this true representative of Bayes; upon its being resumed, I found that the subject under immediate consideration was a translation, yet in manuscript, of the *Carmen Seculare* of Horace, which had this year been set to music, and performed as a public entertainment in London, for the joint benefit of Monsieur Philidor and Signor Baretti. When

---

[1] He sent a set elegantly bound and gilt, which was received as a very handsome present.

Johnson had done reading, the author asked him bluntly, 'If upon the whole it was a good translation?' Johnson, whose regard for truth was uncommonly strict, seemed to be puzzled for a moment, what answer to make, as he certainly could not honestly commend the performance: with exquisite address he evaded the question thus, 'Sir, I do not say that it may not be made a very good translation.' Here nothing whatever in favour of the performance was affirmed, and yet the writer was not shocked. A printed 'Ode to the Warlike Genius of Britain', came next in review; the bard was a lank bony figure, with short black hair; he was writhing himself in agitation, while Johnson read, and showing his teeth in a grin of earnestness, exclaimed in broken sentences, and in a keen sharp tone, 'Is that poetry, Sir? – Is it Pindar?' JOHNSON. 'Why, Sir, there is here a great deal of what is called poetry.' Then turning to me, the poet cried, 'My muse has not been long upon the town, and (pointing to the Ode) it trembles under the hand of the great critic.' Johnson in a tone of displeasure asked him, 'Why do you praise Anson?' I did not trouble him by asking his reason for this question. He proceeded, 'Here is an error, Sir; you have made Genius feminine.' – 'Palpable, Sir (cried the enthusiast); I know it. But (in a lower tone) it was to pay a compliment to the Duchess of Devonshire, with which her Grace was pleased. She is walking across Coxheath, in the military uniform, and I suppose her to be the Genius of Britain.' JOHNSON. 'Sir, you are giving a reason for it, but that will not make it right. You may have a reason why two and two should make five; but they will still make but four.'

Although I was several times with him in the course of the following days, such it seems were my occupations, or such my negligence, that I have preserved no memorial of his conversation till Friday, March 26, when I visited him. He said he expected to be attacked on account of his *Lives of the Poets*. 'However (said he), I would rather be attacked than unnoticed. For the worst thing you can do to an author is to be silent as to his works. An assault upon a town is a bad thing; but starving it is still worse; an assault may be unsuccessful; you may have more men killed than you kill; but if you starve the town you are sure of a victory.'

Talking of a friend of our's associating with persons of very discordant principles and characters; I said he was a very universal man, quite a man of the world. JOHNSON. 'Yes, Sir; but one may be so much a man of the world as to be nothing in the world. I remember a passage in Goldsmith's *Vicar of Wakefield*, which he was afterwards fool enough to expunge: "I do not love a man who is zealous for nothing." ' BOSWELL. 'That was a fine passage.' JOHNSON. 'Yes, Sir: there was another fine passage too, which he struck out: "When I was a young man, being anxious to distinguish myself, I was perpetually starting new propositions. But I soon gave this over; for, I found that generally what was new was false." ' I said I did not like to sit with people of whom I had not a good opinion. JOHNSON. 'But you must not indulge your delicacy too much; or you will be a *tête à tête* man all your life.'

During my stay in London, this spring, I find I was unaccountably negligent in preserving Johnson's sayings, more so than at any time when I was happy enough to have an opportunity of hearing his wisdom and wit. There is no help for it now. I must content myself with presenting such scraps as I have. But I am nevertheless ashamed and vexed to think how much has been lost. It is not that there was a bad crop this year; but that I was not sufficiently careful in gathering it in. I, therefore, in some instances can only exhibit a few detached fragments.

Talking of the wonderful concealment of the author of the celebrated letters signed *Junius*; he said, 'I should have believed Burke to be Junius, because I know no man but Burke who is capable of writing these letters; but Burke spontaneously denied it to me. The case would have been different had I asked him if he was the author; a man so questioned, as to an anonymous publication, may think he has a right to deny it.'

He observed that his old friend, Mr Sheridan, had been honoured with extraordinary attention in his own country, by having had an exception made in his favour in an Irish Act of Parliament concerning insolvent debtors. 'To be thus singled out (said he) by a legislature, as an object of public consideration and kindness, is a proof of no common merit.'

At Streatham, on Monday, March 29, at breakfast he maintained that a father had no right to control the inclinations of his daughters in marriage.

On Wednesday, March 31, when I visited him, and confessed an excess of which I had very seldom been guilty; that I had spent a whole night in playing at cards, and that I could not look back on it with satisfaction. Instead of a harsh animadversion, he mildly said, 'Alas, Sir, on how few things can we look back with satisfaction.'

On Thursday, April 1, he commended one of the Dukes of Devonshire for 'a dogged veracity'.[1] He said too, 'London is nothing to some people; but to a man whose pleasure is intellectual, London is the place. And there is no place where economy can be so well practised as in London. More can be had here for the money, even by ladies, than any where else. You cannot play tricks with your fortune in a small place; you must make an uniform appearance. Here a lady may have well-furnished apartments, and elegant dress, without any meat in her kitchen.'

I was amused by considering with how much ease and coolness he could write or talk to a friend, exhorting him not to suppose that happiness was not to be found as well in other places as in London; when he himself was at all times sensible of its being, comparatively speaking, a heaven upon earth. The truth is, that by those who from sagacity, attention, and experience, have learnt the full advantage of London, its pre-eminence over every other place, not only for variety of enjoyment, but for comfort, will be felt with a philosophical exultation. The freedom from remark and petty censure, with which life may be passed there, is a circumstance which a man who knows the teasing restraint of a narrow circle must relish highly. Mr Burke, whose orderly and amiable domestic habits might make the eye of observation less

1 See p. 609.

irksome to him than to most men, said once very pleasantly, in my hearing, 'Though I have the honour to represent Bristol, I should not like to live there; I should be obliged to be so much *upon my good behaviour.*' In London, a man may live in splendid society at one time, and in frugal retirement another, without animadversion,

There, and there alone, a man's own house is truly his *castle*, in which he can be in perfect safety from intrusion whenever he pleases. I never shall forget how well this was expressed to me one day by Mr Meynell: 'The chief advantage of London (said he) is, that a man is always *so near his burrow.*'

He said of one of his old acquaintances, 'He is very fit for a travelling governor. He knows French very well. He is a man of good principles; and there would be no danger that a young gentleman should catch his manner; for it is so very bad, that it must be avoided. In that respect he would be like the drunken Helot.'[a]

On Friday, April 2, being Good-Friday, I visited him in the morning as usual; and finding that we insensibly fell into a train of ridicule upon the foibles of one of our friends, a very worthy man, I, by way of a check, quoted some good admonition from *The Government of the Tongue*, that very pious book. It happened also remarkably enough, that the subject of the sermon preached to us to-day by Dr Burrows, the rector of St Clement Danes, was the certainty that at the last day we must give an account of 'the deeds done in the body'; and, amongst various acts of culpability he mentioned evil-speaking. As we were moving slowly along in the crowd from church, Johnson jogged my elbow, and said, 'Did you attend to the sermon?' – 'Yes, Sir (said I), it was very applicable to *us.*' He, however, stood upon the defensive. 'Why, Sir, the sense of ridicule is given us, and may be lawfully used. The author of *The Government of the Tongue* would have us to treat all men alike.'

In the interval between morning and evening service, he endeavoured to employ himself earnestly in devotional exercises; and, as he has mentioned in his *Prayers and Meditations*,[1] gave me *Les Pensées de Pascal*, that I might not interrupt him. I preserve the book with reverence. His presenting it to me is marked upon it with his own hand, and I have found in it a truly divine unction. We went to church again in the afternoon.

On Saturday, April 3, I visited him at night, and found him sitting in Mrs Williams's room, with her, and one who he afterwards told me was a natural son of the second Lord Southwell.

The table had a singular appearance, being covered with a heterogeneous assemblage of oysters and porter for his company, and tea for himself. I mentioned my having heard an eminent physician, who was himself a Christian, argue in favour of universal toleration, and maintain, that no man could be hurt by another man's differing from him in opinion. JOHNSON. 'Sir,

---

[a] Add: A gentleman has informed me, that Johnson said of the same person, 'Sir, he has the most inverted understanding of any man whom I have ever known.'

1 Page 173.

you are to a certain degree hurt by knowing that even one man does not believe.'

On Easter-day, after solemn service at St Paul's, I dined with him: Mr Allen the printer was also his guest. He was uncommonly silent; and I have not written down any thing, except a single curious fact, which, having the sanction of his inflexible veracity, may be received as a striking instance of human insensibility and inconsideration. As he was passing by a fishmonger who was skinning an eel alive, he heard him 'curse it, because it would not lie still.'

On Wednesday, April 7, I dined with him at Sir Joshua Reynolds's. I have not marked what company was there. Johnson harangued upon the qualities of different liquors, and spoke with great contempt of claret, as so weak, that 'a man would be drowned by it before it made him drunk.' He was persuaded to drink one glass of it, that he might judge, not from recollection, which might be dim, but from immediate sensation. He shook his head, and said, 'Poor stuff. No, Sir, claret is the liquor for boys; port, for men: but he who aspires to be a hero (smiling) must drink brandy. In the first place, the flavour of brandy is most grateful to the palate; and then brandy will do soonest for a man what drinking *can* do for him. There are, indeed, few who are able to drink brandy. That is a power rather to be wished for than attained. And yet (proceeded he) as in all pleasure hope is a considerable part, I know not but fruition comes too quick by brandy. Florence wine I think the worst; it is wine only to the eye; it is wine neither while you are drinking it, nor after you have drunk it; it neither pleases the taste, nor exhilarates the spirits.' I reminded him how heartily he and I used to drink wine together when we were first acquainted; and how I used to have a head-ache after sitting up with him. He did not like to have this recalled, or, perhaps, thinking that I boasted improperly, resolved to have a witty stroke at me: 'Nay, Sir, it was not the *wine* that made your head ache, but the *sense* that I put into it.' BOSWELL. 'What, Sir! will sense make the head ache?' JOHNSON. 'Yes, Sir, (with a smile) when it is not used to it.' No man who has a true relish of pleasantry could be offended at this; especially if Johnson in a long intimacy had given him repeated proofs of his regard and good estimation. I used to say, that as he had given me a thousand pounds in praise, he had a good right now and then to take a guinea from me.

On Thursday, April 8, I dined with him at Mr Allan Ramsay's, with Lord Graham and some other company. We talked of Shakspeare's witches. JOHNSON. 'They are beings of his own creation; they are a compound of malignity and meanness, without any abilities; and are quite different from the Italian magician. King James says, in his *Daemonology*, "Magicians command the devils; witches are their servants." The Italian magicians are elegant beings.' RAMSAY. 'Opera witches, not Drury-lane witches.' Johnson observed, that abilities might be employed in a narrow sphere, as in getting money, which he said he believed no man could do, without vigorous parts, though concentrated to a point. RAMSAY. 'Yes, like a strong horse in a mill: he pulls better.'

Lord Graham, while he praised the beauty of Lochlomond, on the banks of which is his family seat, complained of the climate, and said he could not bear it. JOHNSON. 'Nay, my Lord, don't talk so: you may bear it well enough. Your ancestors have borne it more years than I can tell.' This was a handsome compliment to the antiquity of the house of Montrose. His Lordship told me afterwards, that he had only affected to complain of the climate; lest, if he had spoken as favourably of his country as he really thought, Dr Johnson might have attacked it. Johnson was very courteous to Lady Margaret Macdonald. 'Madam (said he), when I was in the Isle of Sky, I heard of the people running to take the stones off the road, lest Lady Margaret's horse should stumble.'

Lord Graham commended Dr Drummond at Naples, as a man of extraordinary talents; and added, that he had a great love of liberty. JOHNSON. 'He is *young*, my Lord; (looking to his Lordship with an arch smile) all *boys* love liberty, till experience convinces them they are not fit so to govern themselves as they imagined. We are all agreed as to our own liberty: we would have as much of it as we can get; but we are not agreed as to the liberty of others: for in proportion as we take, others must lose. I believe we hardly wish that the mob should have liberty to govern us. When that was the case some time ago, no man was at liberty not to have candles in his windows.' RAMSAY. 'The result is, that order is better than confusion.' JOHNSON. 'The result is, that order cannot be had but by subordination.'

On Friday, April 16, I had been present at the trial of the unfortunate Mr Hackman, who, in a fit of frantic jealous love, had shot Miss Ray, the favourite of a nobleman. Johnson, in whose company I dined today, with some other friends, was much interested by my account of what passed, and particularly with his prayer for the mercy of heaven. He said, in a solemn fervid tone, 'I hope he *shall* find mercy.'

This day a violent altercation arose between Johnson and Beauclerk, which having made much noise at the time, I think it proper, in order to prevent any future misrepresentation, to give a minute account of it.

In talking of Hackman, Johnson argued, as Judge Blackstone had done, that his being furnished with two pistols was a proof that he meant to shoot two persons. Mr Beauclerk said, 'No; for that every wise man who intended to shoot himself, took two pistols, that he might be sure of doing it at once. Lord ——'s cook shot himself with one pistol, and lived ten days in great agony. Mr ——, who loved buttered muffins, but durst not eat them because they disagreed with his stomach, resolved to shoot himself; and then he eat three buttered muffins for breakfast, before shooting himself, knowing that he should not be troubled with indigestion: *he* had two charged pistols; one was found lying charged upon the table by him, after he had shot himself with the other.' – 'Well (said Johnson, with an air of triumph), you see here one pistol was sufficient.' Beauclerk replied smartly, 'Because it happened to kill him.' And either then, or a very little afterwards, being piqued at Johnson's triumphant remark, added, 'This is what you don't know, and I do.' There was then a cessation of the dispute; and some minutes intervened, during which, dinner and the glass went on cheerfully; when Johnson suddenly and abruptly exclaimed, 'Mr Beauclerk, how came you to talk so petulantly to me, as "This is what you don't know, but what I know?" One thing *I* know which *you* don't seem to know, that you are very uncivil.' BEAUCLERK. 'Because *you* began by being uncivil (which you always are).' The words in parenthesis were, I believe, not heard by Dr Johnson. Here again there was a cessation of arms. Johnson told me, that the reason why he waited some time at first without taking any notice of what Mr Beauclerk said, was because he was thinking whether he should resent it. But when he considered that there were present a young Lord and an eminent traveller, two men of the world with whom he had never dined before, he was apprehensive that they might think they had a right to take such liberties with him as Beauclerk did, and therefore resolved he would not let it pass; adding, that 'he would not appear a coward.' A little while after this, the conversation turned on the violence of Hackman's temper. Johnson then said, 'It was his business to *command* his temper, as my friend Mr Beauclerk should have done some time ago.' BEAUCLERK. 'I should learn of *you*, Sir.' JOHNSON. 'Sir, you have given *me* opportunities enough of learning, when I have been in *your* company. No man loves to be treated with contempt.' BEAUCLERK. (with a polite inclination towards Johnson) 'Sir, you have known me twenty years, and however I may have treated others, you may be sure I could never treat you with contempt.' JOHNSON. 'Sir, you have said more than was necessary.' Thus it ended; and Beauclerk's coach not having come for him till very late, Dr Johnson and another gentleman sat with him a long time after the rest of the company were gone; and he and I dined at Beauclerk's on the Saturday se'nnight following.

After this tempest had subsided, I recollect the following particulars of his conversation:

'I am always for getting a boy forward in his learning; for that is a sure good. I would let him at first read a*ny* English book which happens to engage his attention; because you have done a great deal when you have brought him to have entertainment from a book. He'll get better books afterwards.'

'Mallet, I believe, never wrote a single line of his projected Life of the Duke of Marlborough. He groped for materials; and thought of it, till he had exhausted his mind. Thus it sometimes happens that men entangle themselves in their own schemes.'

'To be contradicted, in order to force you to talk, is mighty unpleasing. You *shine*, indeed; but it is by being *ground*.'

Of a gentleman who made some figure among the *Literati* of his time, he said, 'What eminence he had was by a felicity of manner: he had no more learning than what he could not help.'

On Saturday, April 24, I dined with him at Mr Beauclerk's, with Sir Joshua Reynolds, Mr Jones (now Sir William), Mr Langton, Mr Steevens, Mr Paradise, and Dr Higgins. I mentioned that Mr Wilkes had attacked Garrick to me, as a man who had no friend. JOHNSON. 'I believe he is right, Sir. Οἱ φίλοι οὐ φίλος. He had friends, but no friend. Garrick was so diffused, he had no man to whom he wished to unbosom himself. He found people always ready to applaud him, and that always for the same thing: so he saw life with great uniformity.' I took upon me, for once, to fight with Goliath's weapons, and play the sophist. – 'Garrick did not need a friend, as he got from every body all he wanted. What is a friend? One who supports you and comforts you, while others do not. Friendship, you know, Sir, is the cordial drop, "to make the nauseous draught of life go down": but if the draught be not nauseous, if it be all sweet, there is no occasion for that drop.' JOHNSON. 'Many men would not be content to live so. I hope I should not. They would wish to have an intimate friend, with whom they might compare minds, and cherish private virtues.' One of the company mentioned Lord Chesterfield, as a man who had no friend. JOHNSON. 'There were more materials to make friendship in Garrick, had he not been so diffused.' BOSWELL. 'Garrick was pure gold, but beat out to thin leaf. Lord Chesterfield was tinsel.' JOHNSON. 'Garrick was a very good man, the cheerfullest man of his age; a decent liver in a profession which is supposed to give indulgence to licentiousness; and a man who gave away, freely, money acquired by himself. He began the world with a great hunger for money; the son of a half-pay officer, bred in a family whose study was to make four-pence do as much as others made four-pence halfpenny do. But, when he had got money, he was very liberal.' – I presumed to animadvert on his eulogy on Garrick, in his *Lives of the Poets*. 'You say, Sir, his death eclipsed the gaiety of nations.' JOHNSON. 'I could not have said more nor less. It is the truth; *eclipsed*, not *extinguished*; and his death *did* eclipse; it was like a storm.' BOSWELL. 'But why nations? Did his gaiety extend farther than his own nation?' JOHNSON. 'Why, Sir, some exaggeration must be allowed. Besides, nations may be said if we allow the Scotch to be a nation, and to have gaiety, which they have not. *You* are an exception though. Come, gentlemen, let us candidly admit that there is one Scotchman who is cheerful.' BEAUCLERK. 'But he is a very unnatural Scotchman.' I, however, continued to think the compliment to Garrick hyperbolically untrue. His acting had ceased some time before his death; at any rate he had acted in Ireland but a short time, at an early period of his life, and never in Scotland. I objected also to what appears an anticlimax of praise, when contrasted with the preceding panegyric – 'and diminished the public stock of harmless pleasure!' – 'Is not *harmless pleasure* very tame?' JOHNSON. 'Nay, Sir, harmless pleasure is the highest praise. Pleasure is a word of dubious import; pleasure is in general dangerous, and pernicious to virtue; to be able therefore to furnish pleasure that is harmless, pleasure pure and unalloyed, is as great a power as man can possess.' This was, perhaps, as ingenious a defence as could be made; still, however, I was not satisfied.

A celebrated wit being mentioned, he said, 'One may say of him as was said of a French wit, *Il n'a de l'esprit que contre Dieu*. I have been several times in company with him, but never perceived any strong power of wit. He produces a general effect by various means; he has a cheerful countenance and a gay voice; besides his trade is wit. It would be as wild in him to come into company without merriment, as for a highwayman to take the road without his pistols.'

Talking of the effects of drinking, he said, 'Drinking may be practised with great prudence; a man who exposes himself when he is intoxicated, has not the art of getting drunk; a sober man who happens occasionally to get drunk, readily enough goes into a new company, which a man who has been drinking should never do. Such a man will undertake any thing; he is without skill in inebriation. I used to slink home when I had drunk too much. A man accustomed to self-examination will be conscious when he is drunk, though an habitual drunkard will not be conscious of it. I knew a physician who for twenty years was not sober; yet in a pamphlet, which he wrote upon fevers, he appealed to Garrick and me for his vindication from a charge of drunkenness. A bookseller (naming him) who got a large fortune by trade, was so habitually and equably drunk, that his most intimate friends never perceived that he was more sober at one time than another.'

Talking of celebrated and successful irregular practisers in physic; he said, 'Taylor was the most ignorant man I ever knew; but sprightly. Ward the dullest. Taylor challenged me once to talk Latin with him; (laughing). I quoted some of Horace, which he took to be a part of my own speech. He said a few words well enough.' BEAUCLERK. 'I remember, Sir, you said that Taylor was an instance how far impudence could carry ignorance.' Mr Beauclerk was very entertaining this day, and told us a number of short stories in a lively elegant manner, and with that air of *the world* which has I know not what impressive effect, as if there were something more than is expressed, or than perhaps we could perfectly understand. As Johnson and I accompanied Sir Joshua Reynolds in his coach, Johnson said, 'There is in Beauclerk a predominance over his company, that one does not like. But he is a man who has lived so much in the world, that he has a short story on every occasion; he is always ready to talk and is never exhausted.'

Johnson and I passed the evening at Miss Reynolds's, Sir Joshua's sister. I mentioned that an eminent friend of our's talking of the common remark, that affection descends, said that 'this was wisely contrived for the preservation of mankind; for which it was not so necessary that there should be affection from children to parents, as from parents to children; nay there would be no harm in that view though children should at a certain age eat their parents.' JOHNSON. 'But, Sir, if this were known generally to be the case, parents would not have affection for children.' BOSWELL. 'True, Sir; for it is in expectation of a return that parents are so attentive to their children; and I know a very pretty instance of a little girl of whom her father was very fond, who once when he was in a melancholy fit, and had gone to bed, persuaded him to rise in good-humour, by saying, "My dear papa, please to get up, and let me help you on with your clothes, that I may learn to do it when you are an old man." '

Soon after this time a little incident occurred, which I will not suppress, because I am desirous that my work should be, as much as is consistent with the strictest truth, an antidote to the false and injurious notions of his character, which have been given by others, and therefore I infuse every drop of genuine sweetness into my biographical cup.

To Dr JOHNSON.

MY DEAR SIR – I am in great pain with an inflamed foot, and obliged to keep my bed, so am prevented from having the pleasure to dine at Mr Ramsay's today, which is very hard; and my spirits are sadly sunk. Will you be so friendly as to come and sit an hour with me in the evening. I am ever
Your most faithful,
And affectionate humble servant,   JAMES BOSWELL.
South Audley-street,
Monday, April 26.

To Mr BOSWELL.

Mr JOHNSON laments the absence of Mr Boswell, and will come to him.
Harley-street.

He came to me in the evening, and brought Sir Joshua Reynolds. I need scarcely say, that their conversation, while they sat by my bedside, was the most pleasing opiate to pain that could have been administered.

Johnson being now better disposed to obtain information concerning Pope than he was last year,[1] sent by me to my Lord Marchmont, a present of those volumes of his *Lives of the Poets*, which were at this time published, with a request to have permission to wait on him, and his Lordship, who had called on him twice, obligingly appointed Saturday, the first of May, for receiving us.

On that morning Johnson came to me from Streatham, and after drinking chocolate, at General Paoli's, in South-Audley-street, we proceeded to Lord Marchmont's, in Curzon-street. His Lordship met us at the door of his library, and with great politeness said to Johnson, 'I am not going to make an encomium upon myself, by telling you the high respect I have for you, Sir.' Johnson was exceedingly courteous, and the interview, which lasted about two hours, during which the Earl communicated his anecdotes of Pope, was as agreeable as I could have wished. When we came out, I said to Johnson, that considering his Lordship's civility, I should have been vexed if he had again failed to come. 'Sir (said he), I would rather have given twenty pounds than not have come.' I accompanied him to Streatham, where we dined, and returned to town in the evening.

On Monday, May 3, I dined with him at Mr Dilly's; I pressed him this day for his opinion on the passage in Parnell, concerning which I had in vain questioned him in several letters, and at length obtained it in *due form of law*;

CASE for Dr JOHNSON's Opinion; 3d of May, 1779.

'PARNELL, in his *Hermit*, has the following passage:

> To clear this doubt, to know the world by sight,
> To find if *books* and *swains* report it right:
> (For yet by *swains alone* the world he knew,
> Whose feet came wandering o'er the nightly dew).

1 See p. 694.

Is there not a contradiction in its being *first* supposed that the Hermit knew *both* what books and swains reported of the world; yet *afterwards* said, that he knew it by swains *alone*?'

'*I think it an inaccuracy. – He mentions two instructors in the first line, and says he had only one in the next.*'[a]

This evening I set out for Scotland.

To Mrs LUCY PORTER, in Lichfield.

DEAR MADAM – Mr Green has informed me that you are much better; I hope I need not tell you that I am glad of it. I cannot boast of being much better; my old nocturnal complaint still pursues me, and my respiration is difficult, though much easier than when I left you the summer before last. Mr and Mrs Thrale are well; Miss has been a little indisposed; but she is got well again. They have since the loss of their boy had two daughters; but they seem likely to want a son.

I hope you had some books which I sent you. I was sorry for poor Mrs Adey's death, and am afraid you will be sometimes solitary; but endeavour, whether alone or in company, to keep yourself cheerful. My friends likewise die very fast; but such is the state of man. I am, dear love,

Your most humble servant,

SAM. JOHNSON.

May 4, 1779.

He had, before I left London, resumed the conversation concerning the appearance of a ghost at Newcastle upon Tyne, which Mr John Wesley believed, but to which Johnson did not give credit. I was, however, desirous to examine the question closely, and at the same time wished to be made acquainted with Mr John Wesley; for though I differed from him in some points, I admired his various talents, and loved his pious zeal. At my request, therefore, Dr Johnson gave me a letter of introduction to him.

To the Reverend Mr JOHN WESLEY.

SIR – Mr Boswell, a gentleman who has been long known to me, is desirous of being known to you, and has asked this recommendation, which I give him with great willingness, because I think it very much to be wished that worthy and religious men should be acquainted with each other. I am, Sir,

Your most humble servant,   SAM. JOHNSON.

May 3, 1779.

---

[a] Add this note: Mr Malone, it must be owned, has shown much critical ingenuity in his explanation of this passage. His interpretation, however, seems to me much too recondite. The *meaning* of the passage may be certain enough; but surely the expression is confused, and one part of it contradictory to the other.

Mr Wesley being in the course of his ministry at Edinburgh, I presented this letter to him, and was very politely received. I begged to have it returned to me, which was accordingly done. His state of the evidence as to the ghost, did not satisfy me.

I did not write to Johnson, as usual, upon my return to my family; but tried how he would be affected by my silence. Mr Dilly sent me a copy of a note which he received from him on the 3rd of July, in these words:

To Mr DILLY.

SIR – Since Mr Boswell's departure I have never heard from him; please to send word what you know of him, and whether you have sent my books to his lady. I am, &c.

SAM. JOHNSON.

My readers will not doubt that his solicitude about me was very flattering.

To JAMES BOSWELL, Esq.

DEAR SIR – What can possibly have happened, that keeps us two such strangers to each other? I expected to have heard from you when you came home; I expected afterwards. I went into the country, and returned; and yet there is no letter from Mr Boswell. No ill I hope has happened; and if ill should happen, why should it be concealed from him who loves you? Is it a fit of humour, that has disposed you to try who can hold out longest without writing? If it be, you have the victory. But I am afraid of something bad; set me free from my suspicions.

My thoughts are at present employed in guessing the reason of your silence: you must not expect that I should tell you any thing, if I had any thing to tell. Write, pray write to me, and let me know what is, or what has been the cause of this long interruption. I am, dear Sir,

Your most affectionate humble servant,

SAM. JOHNSON.

July 13, 1779.

To Dr SAMUEL JOHNSON.

Edinburgh, July 17, 1779.

MY DEAR SIR – What may be justly denominated a supine indolence of mind has been my state of existence since I last returned to Scotland. In a livelier state I had often suffered severely from long intervals of silence on your part; and I had even been chid by you for expressing my uneasiness. I was willing to take advantage of my insensibility, and while I could bear the experiment, to try whether your affection for me, would, after an unusual silence on my part, make you write first. This afternoon I have had very high satisfaction by receiving your kind letter of inquiry, for which I most gratefully thank you. I am doubtful if it was right to make the experiment; though I have gained by it. I was beginning to grow tender, and to upbraid myself, especially after having dreamt two nights ago that I was with you. I and my wife, and my four children, are all well. I would not delay one post to answer your letter; but as it is late, I have not time to do more. You shall soon hear from me, upon many and various particulars; and I shall never again put you to any test. I ever am, with veneration, my dear Sir,

Your much obliged

And faithful humble servant,

JAMES BOSWELL.

On the 22nd of July, I wrote to him again; and gave him an account of my last interview with my worthy friend, Mr Edward Dilly, at his brother's house at Southill, in Bedfordshire, where he died soon after I parted from him, leaving me a very kind remembrance of his regard.

I informed him that Lord Hailes, who had promised to furnish him with some anecdotes for his *Lives of the Poets*, had sent me three instances of Prior's borrowing from *Gombauld*, in *Recueil des Poetes*, tome 3. Epigram 'To John I owed great obligation', p. 25. 'To the Duke of Noailles', p. 32. 'Sauntering Jack and idle Joan', p. 25.

My letter was a pretty long one, and contained a variety of particulars; but he, it would seem, had not attended to it; for his next to me was as follows:

To JAMES BOSWELL, Esq.

MY DEAR SIR —Are you playing the same trick again, and trying who can keep silence longest? Remember that all tricks are either knavish or childish; and that it is as foolish to make experiments upon the constancy of a friend, as upon the chastity of a wife.

What can be the cause of this second fit of silence, I cannot conjecture; but after one trick, I will not be cheated by another, nor will harass my thoughts with conjectures about the motives of a man who, probably, acts only by caprice. I therefore suppose you are well, and that Mrs Boswell is well too; and that the fine summer has restored Lord Auchinleck. I am much better than you left me; I think I am better than when I was in Scotland.

I forgot whether I informed you that poor Thrale has been in great danger. Mrs Thrale likewise has miscarried, and been much indisposed. Every body else is well; Langton is in camp. I intend to put Lord Hailes's description of Dryden[1] into another edition, and as I know his accuracy, wish he would consider the dates, which I could not always settle to my own mind.

Mr Thrale goes to Brighthelmston, about Michaelmas, to be jolly and

1 Which I communicated to him from his Lordship, but it has not yet been published. I have a copy of it.

ride a hunting. I shall go to town, or perhaps to Oxford. Exercise and gaiety, or rather carelessness, will, I hope, dissipate all remains of his malady; and I likewise hope by the change of place, to find some opportunities of growing yet better myself. I am, dear Sir,

Your humble servant,

SAM. JOHNSON.

Streatham, Sept. 9, 1779.

My readers will not be displeased at being told every slight circumstance of the manner in which Dr Johnson contrived to amuse his solitary hours. He sometimes employed himself in chemistry, sometimes in watering and pruning a vine, and sometimes in small experiments, at which those who may smile, should recollect that there are moments which admit of being soothed only by trifles.[1]

On the 20th of September I defended myself against his suspicion of me, which I did not deserve; and I added, 'Pray let us write frequently. A whim strikes me, that we should each send off a sheet once a week, like a stage-coach, whether it be full or not; nay, though it should be empty. The very sight of your handwriting would comfort me; and were a sheet to be thus sent regularly, we should much oftener convey something, were it only a few kind words.'

My friend Colonel James Stuart, second son of the Earl of Bute, who had distinguished himself as a good officer of the Bedfordshire militia, had taken a public-spirited resolution to serve his country in its difficulties, by raising a regular regiment, and taking the command of it himself. This, in the heir of the immense property of Wortley, was highly honourable. Having been in Scotland recruiting, he obligingly asked me to accompany him to Leeds, then the head-quarters of his corps; from thence to London for a short time, and afterwards to other places to which the regiment might be ordered. Such an offer, at a time of the year when I had full leisure, was very pleasing; especially as I was to accompany a man of sterling good sense, information, discernment, and conviviality; and was to have a second crop, in one year, of London and Johnson. Of this I informed my illustrious friend, in characteristic warm terms, in a letter dated the 30th of September, from Leeds.

---

1 In one of his manuscript Diaries, there is the following entry, which marks his curious minute attention: 'Aug. 7, 1779. *Partem brachii dextri carpo proximam et cutem pectoris circa maxillam[a] dextram rasi, ut notum fieret quanto temporis pili renovarentur.*'

Another of the same kind appears, 'July 26, 1768. I shaved my nail by accident in whetting the knife, about an eighth of an inch from the bottom, and about a fourth from the top. This I measure that I may know the growth of nails; the whole is about five eighths of an inch.'

And, 'Aug. 15, 1783. I cut from the vine 41 leaves, which weighed five oz. and a half, and eight scruples: I lay them upon my book-case to see what weight they will lose by drying.'

[a] For 'maxillam' read 'mamillam'.

On Monday, October 4, I called at his house before he was up. He sent for me to his bedside, and expressed his satisfaction at this incidental meeting, with as much vivacity as if he had been in the gaiety of youth. He called briskly, 'Frank, go and get coffee, and let us breakfast in splendour.'

During this visit to London I had several interviews with him, which it is unnecessary to distinguish particularly. I consulted him as to the appointment of guardians to my children, in case of my death. 'Sir (said he), do not appoint a number of guardians. When they are many, they trust one to another, and the business is neglected. I would advise you to choose only one; let him be a man of respectable character, who, for his own credit, will do what is right; let him be a rich man, so that he may be under no temptation to take advantage; and let him be a man of business, who is used to conduct affairs with ability and expertness, to whom, therefore, the execution of the trust will not be burthensome.'

On Sunday, October 10, we dined together at Mr Strahan's. The conversation having turned on the prevailing practice of going to the East-Indies in quest of wealth; – JOHNSON. 'A man had better have ten thousand pounds at the end of ten years passed in England, than twenty thousand pounds at the end of ten years passed in India, because you must compute what you *give* for money; and a man who has lived ten years in India, has given up ten years of social comfort and all those advantages which arise from living in England. The ingenious Mr Brown, distinguished by the name of *Capability Brown*, told me, that he was once at the seat of Lord Clive, who had returned from India with great wealth; and that he showed him at the door of his bed-chamber a large chest, which he said he had once had full of gold; upon which Brown observed, "I am glad you can bear it so near your bed-chamber." '

We talked of the state of the poor in London. – JOHNSON. 'Saunders Welch, the Justice, who was once High-Constable of Holborn, and had the best opportunities of knowing the state of the poor, told me, that I underrated the number, when I computed that twenty a week, that is, above a thousand a year, died of hunger; not absolutely of immediate hunger, but of the wasting and other diseases which are the consequences of hunger. This happens only in so large a place as London, where people are not known. What we are told about the great sums got by begging is not true: the trade is overstocked. And, you may depend upon it, there are many who cannot get work. A particular kind of manufacture fails. Those who have been used to work at it can, for some time, work at nothing else. You meet a man begging; you charge him with idleness: he says, 'I am willing to labour. Will you give me work?' – 'I cannot.' – 'Why then you have no right to charge me with idleness.'

We left Mr Strahan's at seven, as Johnson had said he intended to go to evening prayers. As we walked along, he complained of a little gout in his toe, and said, 'I shan't go to prayers to-night; I shall go to-morrow. Whenever I miss church on a Sunday, I resolve to go another day. But I do not always do it.' This was a fair exhibition of that vibration between pious resolutions and indolence, which many of us have too often experienced.

I went home with him, and we had a long quiet conversation.

I read him a letter from Dr Hugh Blair, concerning Pope, (in writing whose life he was now employed), which I shall insert as a literary curiosity.[1]

To JAMES BOSWELL, Esq.

DEAR SIR – In the year 1763, being at London, I was carried by Dr John Blair, Prebendary of Westminster, to dine at old Lord Bathurst's; where we found the late Mr Mallet, Sir James Porter, who had been Ambassador at Constantinople, the late Dr Macaulay, and two or three more. The conversation turning on Mr Pope, Lord Bathurst told us, that the *Essay on Man* was originally composed by Lord Bolingbroke in prose, and that Mr Pope did no more than put it into verse: that he had read Lord Bolingbroke's manuscript in his own hand-writing; and remembered well, that he was at a loss whether most to admire the elegance of Lord Bolingbroke's prose, or the beauty of Mr Pope's verse. When Lord Bathurst told this, Mr Mallet bade me attend, and remember this remarkable piece of information; as, by the course of Nature, I might survive his Lordship, and be a witness of his having said so. The conversation was indeed too remarkable to be forgotten. A few days after, meeting with you, who were then also at London, you will remember that I mentioned to you what had passed on this subject, as I was much struck with this anecdote. But what ascertains my recollection of it beyond doubt, is, that being accustomed to keep a journal of what passed when I was at London, which I wrote out every evening, I find the particulars of the above information, just as I have now given them, distinctly marked; and am thence enabled to fix this conversation to have passed on Friday, the 22nd of April, 1763.

I remember also distinctly (though I have not for this the authority of my journal), that the conversation going on concerning Mr Pope, I took notice of a report which had been sometimes propagated that he did not understand Greek. Lord Bathurst said to me, that he knew that to be false; for that part of the *Iliad* was translated by Mr Pope in his house in the country; and that in the mornings, when they assembled at breakfast, Mr Pope used frequently to repeat, with great rapture, the Greek lines

---

1 The Reverend Dr Law, Bishop of Carlisle, in the Preface to his valuable edition of Archbishop King's *Essay on the Origin of Evil*, mentions that the principles maintained in it had been adopted by Pope in his *Essay on Man*; and adds, 'The fact, notwithstanding such denial (Bishop Warburton's), might have been strictly verified by an unexceptionable testimony, *viz.* that of the late Lord Bathurst, who saw the very same system of the τὸ βέλτιον (taken from the Archbishop) in Lord Bolingbroke's own hand, lying before Mr Pope while he was composing his *Essay*.' This is respectable evidence; but that of Dr Blair is more direct from the fountain-head, as well as more full.[a]

a Add to this note: Let me add to it that of Dr Joseph Warton; 'The late Lord Bathurst repeatedly assured me that he had read the whole scheme of the *Essay on Man*, in the hand-writing of Bolingbroke, and drawn up in a series of propositions, which Pope was to versify and illustrate.' *Essay on the Genius and Writings of Pope*, vol. ii. p.62.

which he had been translating, and then to give them his version of them, and to compare them together.

If these circumstances can be of any use to Dr Johnson, you have my full liberty to give them to him. I beg you will, at the same time, present to him my most respectful compliments, with best wishes for his success and fame in all his literary undertakings. I am, with great respect, my dearest Sir,

Your most affectionate

And obliged humble servant,

HUGH BLAIR.

Broughton-Park,
Sept. 21, 1779.

JOHNSON. 'Depend upon it, Sir, this is too strongly stated. Pope may have had from Bolingbroke the philosophic stamina of his Essay: and admitting this to be true, Lord Bathurst did not intentionally falsify. But the thing is not true in the latitude that Blair seems to imagine; we are sure that the poetical imagery, which makes a great part of the poem, was Pope's own. It is amazing, Sir, what deviations there are from precise truth, in the account which is given of almost every thing. I told Mrs Thrale, "You have so little anxiety about truth, that you never tax your memory with the exact thing." Now what is the use of the memory to truth, if one is careless of exactness? Lord Hailes's *Annals of Scotland* are very exact: but they contain mere dry particulars. They are to be considered as a Dictionary. You know such things are there; and may be looked at when you please. Robertson paints; but the misfortune is, you are sure he does not know the people whom he paints: so you cannot suppose a likeness. Characters should never be given by an historian unless he knew the people whom he describes, or copies from those who knew them.'

BOSWELL. 'Why, Sir, do people play this trick which I observe now, when I look at your grate, putting the shovel against it to make the fire burn?' JOHNSON. 'They play the trick, but it does not make the fire burn. *There* is a better (setting the poker perpendicularly up at right angles with the grate). In days of superstition they thought, as it made a cross with the bars, it would drive away the witch.'

BOSWELL. 'By associating with you, Sir, I am always getting an accession of wisdom. But perhaps a man, after knowing his own character – the limited strength of his own mind, should not be desirous of having too much wisdom, considering, *quid valeant humeri*, how little he can carry.' JOHNSON. 'Sir, be as wise as you can; let a man be *aliis laetus, sapiens sibi*:

> Though pleas'd to see the dolphins play,
> I mind my compass and my way.

You may be wise in your study in the morning, and gay in company at a tavern in the evening. Every man is to take care of his own wisdom and his own virtue, without minding too much what others think.'

He said, 'Dodsley first mentioned to me the scheme of an English Dictionary; but I had long thought of it.' BOSWELL. 'You did not know what you was undertaking.' JOHNSON. 'Yes, Sir, I knew very well what I was undertaking – and very well how to do it – and have done it very well.' BOSWELL. 'An excellent climax! and it *has* availed you. In your Preface you say, "What would it avail me in this gloom of solitude?" You have been agreeably mistaken.'

In his Life of Milton he observes, 'I cannot but remark a kind of respect, perhaps unconsciously, paid to this great man by his biographers: every house in which he resided is historically mentioned, as if it were an injury to neglect naming any place that he honoured by his presence.' I had, before I read this observation, been desirous of showing that respect to Johnson, by various inquiries. Finding him this evening in a very good humour, I prevailed on him to give me an exact list of his places of residence, since he entered the metropolis as an author, which I subjoin in a note.[1]

I mentioned to him a dispute between a friend of mine and his lady, concerning conjugal infidelity, which my friend had maintained was by no means so bad in the husband, as in the wife. JOHNSON. 'Your friend was in the right, Sir. Between a man and his Maker it is a different question; but between a man and his wife, a husband's infidelity is nothing. They are connected by children, by fortune, by serious considerations of community. Wise married women don't trouble themselves about infidelity in their husbands.' BOSWELL. 'To be sure there is a great difference between the offence of infidelity in a man and that of his wife.' JOHNSON. 'The difference is boundless. The man imposes no bastards upon his wife.'

Here it may be questioned whether Johnson was entirely in the right. I suppose it will not be controverted that the difference in the degree of criminality is very great, on account of consequences: but still it may be maintained, that, independent of moral obligation, infidelity is by no means a light offence in a husband; because it must hurt a delicate attachment, in which a mutual constancy is implied, with such refined sentiments as Massinger has exhibited in his play of *The Picture*. Johnson probably at another time would have admitted this opinion. And let it be kept in remembrance, that he was very careful not to give any encouragement to irregular conduct. A gentleman, not adverting to the distinction made by him upon this subject, supposed a case of singular perverseness in a wife, and heedlessly said, 'That then he thought a husband might do as he pleased with a safe conscience.' JOHNSON. 'Nay, sir, this is wild indeed (smiling); you must consider that

---

1   1 Exeter-street, off
         Catherine-street, Strand.
      2 Greenwich.
      3 Woodstock-street, near
         Hanover-square.
      4 Castle-street, Cavendish
         square.
      5 Strand.
      6 Boswell-court.
      7 Strand, again.
      8 Bow-street.
      9 Holborn.
     10 Fetter-lane.
     11 Holborn, again.
     12 Gough-square.
     13 Staple Inn.
     14 Gray's Inn.
     15 Inner Temple-lane, No. 1.
     16 Johnson's-court, No. 7.
     17 Bolt-court, No. 8.

fornication is a crime in a single man; and you cannot have more liberty by being married.'

He this evening expressed himself strongly against the Roman Catholics; observing, 'In every thing in which they differ from us they are wrong.' He was even against the invocation of Saints; in short, he was in the humour of opposition.

Having regretted to him that I had learnt little Greek, as is too generally the case in Scotland, that I had for a long time hardly applied at all to the study of that noble language, and that I was desirous of being told by him what method to follow; he recommended to me as easy helps, Sylvanus's First Book of the *Iliad*, Dawson's *Lexicon to the Greek New Testament*; and Hesiod, with *Pasoris Lexicon* at the end of it.

On Tuesday, October 12, I dined with him at Mr Ramsay's, with Lord Newhaven, and some other company, none of whom I recollect, but a beautiful Miss Graham,[a] a relation of his Lordship's, who asked Dr Johnson to hob or nob with her. He was flattered by such pleasing attention, and politely told her, he never drank wine; but if she would drink a glass of water, he was much at her service. She accepted. 'Oho, Sir! (said Lord Newhaven) you are caught.' JOHNSON. 'Nay, I do not see *how* I am *caught*; but if I am caught I don't want to get free again. If I am caught, I hope to be kept.' Then when the two glasses of water were brought, smiling placidly to the young lady, 'Madam, let us *reciprocate*.'

Lord Newhaven and Johnson carried on an argument for some time, concerning the Middlesex election. Johnson said, 'Parliament may be considered as bound by law, as a man is bound where there is nobody to tie the knot. As it is clear that the House of Commons may expel, and expel again and again, why not allow of the power to incapacitate for that parliament, rather than have a perpetual contest kept up between parliament and the people.' Lord Newhaven took the opposite side, but respectfully said, 'I speak with great deference to you, Dr Johnson; I speak to be instructed.' This had its full effect upon my friend. He bowed his head almost as low as the table, to a complimenting nobleman; and called out, 'My Lord, my Lord, I do not desire all this ceremony; let us tell our minds to one another quietly.' After the debate was over, he said, 'I have got lights on the subject to-day, which I had not before.' This was a great deal from him, especially as he had written a pamphlet upon it.

He observed, 'The House of Commons was originally not a privilege of the people, but a check for the Crown on the House of Lords. I remember Henry the Eighth wanted them to do something; they hesitated in the morning, but did it in the afternoon. He told them, "It is well you did, or half your heads should have been upon Temple-bar." But the House of Commons is now no longer under the power of the crown, and therefore must be bribed.' He added, 'I have no delight in talking of public affairs.'

---

[a] Add this note: Now the lady of Sir Henry Dashwood, Baronet.

Of his fellow-collegian, the celebrated Mr George Whitefield, he said, 'Whitefield never drew as much attention as a mountebank does; he did not draw attention by doing better than others, but by doing what was strange. Were Astley to preach a sermon standing upon his head on a horse's back, he would collect a multitude to hear him; but no wise man would say he had made a better sermon for that. I never treated Whitefield's ministry with contempt; I believe he did good. He had devoted himself to the lower classes of mankind, and among them he was of use. But when familiarity and noise claim the praise due to knowledge, art, and elegance, we must beat down such pretensions.'

What I have preserved of his conversation during the remainder of my stay in London at this time, is only what follows: I told him that when I objected to keeping company with a notorious infidel, a celebrated friend of our's said to me, 'I do not think that men who live laxly in the world, as you and I do, can with propriety assume such an authority. Dr Johnson may, who is uniformly exemplary in his conduct. But it is not very consistent to shun an infidel today, and get drunk tomorrow.' JOHNSON. 'Nay, Sir, this is sad reasoning. Because a man cannot be right in all things, is he to be right in nothing? Because a man sometimes gets drunk, is he therefore to steal? This doctrine would very soon bring a man to the gallows.

'After all, however, it is a difficult question how far sincere Christians should associate with the avowed enemies of religion; for in the first place, almost every man's mind may be more or less corrupted by evil communications; secondly, the world may very naturally suppose that they are not really in earnest in religion, who can easily bear its opponents; and thirdly, if the profane find themselves quite well received by the pious, one of the checks upon an open declaration of their infidelity, and one of the probable chances of obliging them seriously to reflect, which their being shunned would do, is removed.'

He, I know not why, showed upon all occasions an aversion to go to Ireland, where I proposed to him that we should make a tour. JOHNSON. 'It is the last place where I should wish to travel.' BOSWELL. 'Should you not like to see Dublin, Sir?' JOHNSON. 'No, Sir, Dublin is only a worse capital.' BOSWELL. 'Is not the Giant's-Causeway worth seeing?' JOHNSON. 'Worth seeing, yes; but not worth going to see.'[a]

Of an acquaintance of ours, whose manners and every thing about him, though expensive, were coarse, he said, 'Sir, you see in him vulgar prosperity.'

A foreign minister of no very high talents, who had been in his company for a considerable time quite overlooked, happened luckily to mention that he had read some of his *Rambler* in Italian, and admired it much. This pleased him

---

[a] After this passage, read: Yet he had a kindness for the Irish nation, and thus generously expressed himself to a gentleman from that country, on the subject of an UNION which artful Politicians have often had in view – 'Do not make an union with us, Sir. We should unite with you, only to rob you. We should have robbed the Scotch, if they had had anything of which we could have robbed them.'

greatly; he observed, that the title had been translated, *Il Genio errante*, though I have been told it was rendered more ludicrously, *Il Vagabondo*; and finding that this minister gave such a proof of his taste, he was all attention to him, and on the first remark which he made, however simple, exclaimed, 'The Ambassador says well – His Excellency observes —— ' And then he expanded and enriched the little that had been said in so strong a manner, that it appeared something of consequence. This was exceedingly entertaining to the company who were present, and many a time afterwards it furnished a pleasant topic of merriment: '*The Ambassador says well*,' became a laughable term of applause, when no mighty matter had been expressed.

I left London on Monday, October 18, and accompanied Colonel Stuart to Chester, where his regiment was to lie for some time.

Mr BOSWELL to Dr JOHNSON.

Chester, 22 October, 1779.
MY DEAR SIR – It was not till one o'clock on Monday morning, that Colonel Stuart and I left London; for we chose to bid a cordial adieu to Lord Mountstuart, who was to set out on that day on his embassy to Turin. We drove on excellently, and reached Lichfield in good time enough that night. The Colonel had heard so preferable a character of the George, that he would not put up at the Three Crowns, so that I did not see our host Wilkins. We found at the George as good accommodation as we could wish to have, and I fully enjoyed the comfortable thought that *I was in Lichfield again.* Next morning it rained very hard; and as I had much to do in a little time, I ordered a post-chaise, and between eight and nine sallied forth to make a round of visits. I first went to Mr Green, hoping to have had him to accompany me to all my other friends, but he was engaged to attend the Bishop of Sodor and Man, who was then lying at Lichfield very ill of the gout. Having taken a hasty glance at the additions to Green's museum, from which it was not easy to break away, I next went to the Friery, where I at first occasioned some tumult in the ladies, who were not prepared to receive *company* so early, but my *name,* which has by wonderful felicity come to be so closely associated with yours, soon made all easy; and Mrs Cobb and Miss Adye re-assumed their seats at the breakfast-table, which they had quitted with some precipitation. They received me with the kindness of old acquaintance; and after we had joined in a cordial chorus to *your* praise, Mrs Cobb gave *me* the high satisfaction of hearing that you said, 'Boswell is a man who I believe never left a house without leaving a wish for his return.' And she afterwards added, that she bid you tell me, that if ever I came to Lichfield, she hoped I would take a bed at the Friery. From thence I drove to Peter Garrick's, where I also found a very flattering welcome. He appeared to me to enjoy his usual cheerfulness; and he very kindly asked me to come when I could, and pass a week with him. From Mr Garrick's I went to the Palace to wait on Mr Seward. I was first entertained by his lady and daughter, he himself being in bed with a cold,

according to his valetudinary custom. But he desired to see me; and I found him drest in his black gown, with a white flannel night-gown above it; so that he looked like a Dominican friar. He was good humoured and polite; and under his roof too my reception was very pleasing. I then proceeded to Stowhill, and first paid my respects to Mrs Gastrell, whose conversation I was not willing to quit. But my sand-glass was now beginning to run low, as I could not trespass too long on the Colonel's kindness, who obligingly waited for me; so I hastened to Mrs Aston's, whom I found much better than I feared I should; and there I met a brother-in-law of these ladies, who talked much of you, and very well too, as it appeared to me. It then only remained to visit Mrs Lucy Porter, which I did, I really believe, with sincere satisfaction on both sides. I am sure I was glad to see her again; and, as I take her to be very honest, I trust she was glad to see me again; for she expressed herself so, that I could not doubt of her being in earnest. What a great key-stone of kindness, my dear Sir, was you that morning! for we were all held together by our common attachment to you. I cannot say that I ever passed two hours with more self-complacency than I did those two at Lichfield. Let me not entertain any suspicion that this is idle vanity. Will not you confirm me in my persuasion, that he who finds himself so regarded has just reason to be happy?

We got to Chester about midnight on Tuesday; and here again I am in a state of much enjoyment. Colonel Stuart and his officers treat me with all the civility I could wish; and I play my part admirably. *Laetus aliis, sapiens sibi*, the classical sentence which you, I imagine, invented the other day, is exemplified in my present existence. The Bishop, to whom I had the honour to be known several years ago, shows me much attention; and I am edified by his conversation. I must not omit to tell you, that his Lordship admires, very highly, your Prefaces to the Poets. I am daily obtaining an extension of agreeable acquaintance, so that I am kept in animated variety; and the study of the place itself, by the assistance of books, and of the Bishop, is sufficient occupation. Chester pleases my fancy more than any town I ever saw. But I will not enter upon it at all in this letter.

How long I shall stay here, I cannot yet say. I told a very pleasing young lady,[a] niece to one of the Prebendaries, at whose house I saw her, 'I have come to Chester, Madam, I cannot tell how; and far less can I tell how I am to get away from it.' Do not think me too juvenile. I beg it of you, my dear Sir, to favour me with a letter while I am here, and add to the happiness of a happy friend, who is ever, with affectionate veneration,

Most sincerely yours,

JAMES BOSWELL.

If you do not write directly, so as to catch me here, I shall be disappointed. Two lines from you will keep my lamp burning bright.

---

[a] Add this note: Miss Letitia Barnston.

To JAMES BOSWELL, Esq.

DEAR SIR – Why should you importune me so earnestly to write? Of what importance can it be to hear of distant friends, to a man who finds himself welcome wherever he goes, and makes new friends faster than he can want them? If, to the delight of such universal kindness of reception, any thing can be added by knowing that you retain my good-will, you may indulge yourself in the full enjoyment of that small addition.

I am glad that you made the round of Lichfield with so much success: the oftener you are seen, the more you will be liked. It was pleasing to me to read that Mrs Aston was so well; and that Lucy Porter was so glad to see you.

In the place where you now are, there is much to be observed; and you will easily procure yourself skilful directors. But what will you do to keep away the *black dog* that worries you at home? If you would, in compliance with your father's advice, enquire into the old tenures, and old charters of Scotland, you would certainly open to yourself many striking scenes of the manners of the middle ages. The feudal system, in a country half barbarous, is naturally productive of great anomalies in civil life. The knowledge of past times is naturally growing less in all cases not of public record; and the past time of Scotland is so unlike the present, that it is already difficult for a Scotchman to imagine the economy of his grandfather. Do not be tardy, nor negligent; but gather up eagerly what can yet be found.[1]

We have, I think, once talked of another project, a History of the late insurrection in Scotland, with all its incidents. Many falsehoods are passing into uncontradicted history. Voltaire, who loved a striking story, has told what we could not find to be true.

You may make collections for either of these projects, or for both, as opportunities occur, and digest your materials at leisure. The great direction which Burton has left to men disordered like you,[a] *Be not solitary; be not idle*: which I would thus modify; – If you are idle, be not solitary; if you are solitary, be not idle.

There is a letter for you, from

Your humble servant,

SAM. JOHNSON.

London, Oct. 27, 1779.

---

1 I have a valuable collection made by my Father, which, with some additions and illustrations of my own, I intend to publish. I have some hereditary claim to be an Antiquary; not only from my Father, but as being descended, by the mother's side, of the able and learned Sir John Skene, whose merit bids defiance to all the attempts which have been made to lessen his fame.

a After 'you' read 'is this'.

To Dr SAMUEL JOHNSON.

Carlisle, Nov. 7, 1779.

MY DEAR SIR – That I should importune you to write to me at Chester, is not wonderful, when you consider what an avidity I have for delight; and that the *amor* of pleasure, like the *amor nummi*, increases in proportion with the quantity which we possess of it Your letter, so full of polite kindness and masterly counsel, came like a large treasure upon me, while already glittering with riches. I was quite enchanted at Chester, so that I could with difficulty quit it. But the enchantment was the reverse of that of Circe; for so far was there from being any thing sensual in it, that I was *all mind*. I do not mean all reason only; for my fancy was kept finely in play. And why not? – If you please I will send you a copy, or an abridgement of my Chester Journal, which is truly a log-book of felicity.

The Bishop treated me with a kindness which was very flattering. I told him, that you regretted you had seen so little of Chester. His Lordship bid me tell you, that he should be glad to show you more of it. I am proud to find the friendship with which you honour me is known in so many places.

I arrived here late last night. Our friend the Dean has been gone from hence some months; but I am told at my inn, that he is very *populous* (popular). However, I found Mr Law, the Archdeacon, son to the Bishop, and with him I have breakfasted and dined very agreeably. I got acquainted with him at the assizes here, about a year and a half ago; he is a man of great variety of knowledge, uncommon genius, and I believe, sincere religion. I received the holy sacrament in the cathedral in the morning, this being the first Sunday of the month; and was at prayers there in the evening. It is divinely cheering to me to think that there is a Cathedral so near Auchinleck; and I now leave Old England in such a state of mind as I am thankful to God for granting me.

The *black dog* that worries me at home I cannot but dread; yet as I have been for some time past in a military train, I trust I shall *repulse* him. To hear from you will animate me like the sound of a trumpet, I therefore hope that soon after my return to the Northern field, I shall receive a few lines from you.

Colonel Stuart did me the honour to escort me in his carriage to show me Liverpool, and from thence back again to Warrington, where we parted.[1] In justice to my valuable wife, I must inform you, that as I was so happy, she would not be so selfish as to wish me to return sooner than business absolutely required my presence. She made my clerk write to me a post or two after to the same purpose, by commission from her, and this

---

1 His regiment was afterwards ordered to Jamaica, where he accompanied it, and almost lost his life by the climate. This impartial order I should think a sufficient refutation of the idle rumour that 'there was something behind the throne greater than the throne itself.'

day a kind letter from her met me at the Post-Office here, acquainting me that she and the little ones were well, and expressing all their wishes for my return home. I am, more and more, my dear Sir,

Your affectionate,

And obliged humble servant,

JAMES BOSWELL.

To JAMES BOSWELL, Esq.

Dear Sir — Your last letter was not only kind but fond. But I wish you to get rid of all intellectual excesses, and neither to exalt your pleasures, nor aggravate your vexations, beyond their real and natural state. Why should you not be as happy at Edinburgh as at Chester, *In culpa est animus, qui se non effugit usquam.* Please yourself with your wife and children, and studies and practice.

I have sent a petition[1] from Lucy Porter, with which I leave it to your discretion whether it is proper to comply. Return me her letter, which I have sent that you may know the whole case, and not be seduced to any thing that you may afterwards repent. Miss Doxy perhaps you know to be Mr Garrick's's niece.

If Dean Percy can be popular at Carlisle, he may be very happy. He has in his disposal two livings, each equal, or almost equal in value to the deanery; he may take one himself, and give the other to his son.

How near is the Cathedral to Auchinleck, that you are so much delighted with it? It is, I suppose, at least an hundred and fifty miles off. However, if you are pleased, it is so far well.

Let me know what reception you have from your father, and the state of his health. Please him as much as you can, and add no pain to his last years.

Of our friends here I can recollect nothing to tell you. I have neither seen nor heard of Langton. Beauclerk is just returned from Brighthelmston, I am told, much better. Mr Thrale and his family are still here; and his health is said to be visibly improved he has not bathed, but hunted.

At Bolt-court there is much malignity but of late little open hostility. I have had a cold, but it is gone.

Make my compliments to Mrs Boswell, &c. I am, Sir,

Your humble servant,

SAM. JOHNSON.

London, November 13, 1779.

---

1 Requesting me to inquire concerning the family of a gentleman who was then paying his addresses to Miss Doxy.

On November 22, and December 21, I wrote to him from Edinburgh, giving a very favourable report of the family of Miss Doxy's lover; – that after a good deal of inquiry I had discovered the sister of Mr Francis Stewart, one of his amanuenses when writing his Dictionary; – that I had, as desired by him, paid her a guinea or an old pocket-book of her brother's which he had retained; and that the good woman, who was in very moderate circumstances, but contented and placid, wondered at his scrupulous and liberal honesty, and received the guinea as if sent her by Providence. – That I had repeatedly begged of him to keep his promise to send me his letter to Lord Chesterfield, and that this *memento*, like *Delenda est Carthago*, must be in every letter that I should write to him, till I had obtained my object.

In 1780 the world was kept in impatience for the completion of his *Lives of the Poets*, upon which he was employed so far as his indolence allowed him to labour.

I wrote to him on January 1, and March 13, sending him my notes of Lord Marchmont's information concerning Pope; – complaining that I had not heard from him for almost four months, though he was two letters in my debt; – that I had suffered again from melancholy; – hoping that he had been in so much better company (the Poets), that he had not time to think of his distant friends; for if that were the case, I should have some recompense for my uneasiness; – that the state of my affairs did not admit of my coming to London this year; – and, begging he would return me Goldsmith's two poems, with his lines marked.

His friend Dr Lawrence having now suffered the greatest affliction to which a man is liable, and which Johnson himself had felt in the most severe manner; Johnson wrote to him in an admirable strain of sympathy and pious consolation.

To Dr LAWRENCE.

DEAR SIR – At a time when all your friends ought to show their kindness, and with a character which ought to make all that know you your friends, you may wonder that you have yet heard nothing from me.

I have been hindered by a vexatious and incessant cough, for which within these ten days I have been bled once, fasted four or five times, taken physic five times, and opiates, I think, six. This day seems to remit.

The loss, dear Sir, which you have lately suffered, I felt many years ago, and know therefore how much has been taken from you, and how little help can be had from consolation. He that outlives a wife whom he has long loved, sees himself disjoined from the only mind that has the same hopes, and fears, and interest; from the only companion with whom he has shared much good or evil; and with whom he could set his mind at liberty, to retrace the past, or anticipate the future. The continuity of being is lacerated; the settled course of sentiment and action is stopped; and life stands suspended and motionless, till it is driven by external causes into a new channel. But the time of suspense is dreadful.

Our first recourse in this distressful solitude, is, perhaps, for want of habitual piety, to a gloomy acquiescence in necessity. Of two mortal beings, one must lose the other; but surely there is a higher and a better comfort to be drawn from the consideration of that Providence which watches over all, and a belief that the living and the dead are equally in the hands of GOD, who will reunite those whom he has separated, or who sees that it is best not to reunite them. I am, dear Sir,

Your most affectionate,

And most humble servant,

SAM. JOHNSON.

Jan. 20, 1780.

To JAMES BOSWELL, Esq.

DEAR SIR – Well, I had resolved to send you the Chesterfield letter; but I will write once again without it. Never impose tasks upon mortals. To require two things is the way to have them both undone.

For the difficulties which you mention in your affairs I am sorry; but difficulty is now very general: it is not therefore less grievous, for there is less hope of help. I pretend not to give you advice, not knowing the state of your affairs; and general counsels about prudence and frugality would do you little good. You are, however, in the right not to increase your own perplexity by a journey hither; and I hope that by staying at home you will please your father.

Poor dear Beauclerk – *nec, ut soles, dabis joca*. His wit and his folly, his acuteness and maliciousness, his merriment and his reasoning, are now over. Such another will not often be found among mankind. He directed himself to be buried by the side of his mother, an instance of tenderness which I hardly expected. He has left his children to the care of Lady Di. and if she dies, of Mr Langton, and of Mr Leicester, his relation, and a man of good character. His library has been offered to sale to the Russian ambassador.

Dr Percy, notwithstanding all the noise of the newspapers, has had no literary loss.[1] Clothes and moveables were burnt to the value of about one hundred pounds; but his papers, and I think his books, were all preserved.

Poor Mr Thrale has been in extreme danger from an apoplectical disorder, and recovered, beyond the expectation of his physicians; he is now at Bath, that his mind may be quiet, and Mrs Thrale and Miss are with him.

Having told you what has happened to your friends, let me say something to you of yourself. You are always complaining of melancholy, and I conclude from those complaints that you are fond of it. No man talks of that which he is desirous to conceal, and every man desires to conceal that of which he is ashamed. Do not pretend to deny it; *manifestum habemus furem*; make it an invariable and obligatory law to yourself, never to

---

1 By a fire in Northumberland-house, where he had an apartment, in which I have passed many an agreeable hour.

mention your own mental diseases; If you are never to speak of them you will think on them but little, and if you think little of them, they will molest you rarely. When you talk of them, it is plain that you want either praise or pity; for praise there is no room, and pity will do you no good; therefore, from this hour speak no more, think no more about them.

Your transaction with Mrs Stuart gave me great satisfaction; I am much obliged to you for your attention. Do not lose sight of her, your countenance may be of great credit, and of consequence of great advantage to her. The memory of her brother is yet fresh ill my mind; he was an ingenious and worthy man.

Please to make my compliments to your lady, and to the young ladies. I should like to see them, pretty loves. I am dear Sir,

Yours, affectionately,

SAM. JOHNSON.

April 8, 1780.

Mrs Thrale being now at Bath with her husband, the correspondence between Johnson and her was carried on briskly. I shall present my readers with one of her original letters to him at this time, which will amuse them probably more than those well-written but studied epistles which she has inserted in her collection, because it exhibits the easy vivacity of their literary intercourse. It is also of value as a key to Johnson's answer, which she has printed by itself, and of which I shall subjoin extracts.

Mrs THRALE to Dr JOHNSON.

I had a very kind letter from you yesterday, dear Sir, with a most circumstantial date. You took trouble with my circulating letter, Mr Evans writes me word, and I thank you sincerely for so doing: one might do mischief else, not being on the spot.

Yesterday's evening was passed at Mrs Montagu's: there was Mr Melmoth; I do not like him though, nor he me; it was expected we should have pleased each other; he is, however, just Tory enough to hate the Bishop of Peterborough for Whiggism, and Whig enough to abhor you for Toryism.

Mrs Montagu flattered him finely; so he had a good afternoon on't. This evening we spend at a concert. Poor Queeney's[1] sore eyes have just released her; she had a long confinement, and could neither read nor write, so my master[2] treated her very good-naturedly with the visits of a young woman in this town, a taylor's daughter, who professes music, and teaches so as to give six lessons a day to ladies, at five and three-pence a lesson. Miss Burney says she is a great performer; and I respect the wench for getting

---

1 A kind of nick-name given to Mrs Thrale's eldest daughter, whose name being Esther, she might be assimilated to a *Queen*.
2 Mr Thrale.

her living so prettily; she is very modest and pretty mannered, and not seventeen years old.

You live in a fine whirl indeed, if I did not write regularly you would half forget me, and that would be very wrong, for I *felt* my regard for you in my *face* last night, when the criticisms were going on.

This morning it was all connoisseurship; we went to see some pictures painted by a gentleman artist, Mr Taylor, of this place; my master makes one every where, and he has got a dawling[a] companion to ride with him now. . . . He looks well enough, but I have no notion of health for a man whose mouth cannot be sewed up. Burney and I and Queeney teize him every meal he eats, and Mr Montagu is quite serious with him, but what *can* one do? He will eat, I think, and if he does eat I know he will not live; it makes me very unhappy, but I must bear it. Let me always have your friendship. I am, most sincerely, dear Sir,

Your faithful servant,

H. L. T.

Bath, Friday, April 28.

Dr JOHNSON to Mrs THRALE.

DEAREST MADAM – Mr Thrale never will live abstinently, till he can persuade himself to live by rule.[1] . . . Encourage, as you can, the musical girl.

Nothing is more common than mutual dislike where mutual approbation is particularly expected. There is often on both sides a vigilance not over benevolent, and as attention is strongly excited, so that nothing drops unheeded, any difference in taste or opinion, and some difference where there is no restraint will commonly appear, immediately generates dislike.

Never let criticism operate upon your face or your mind, it is very rarely that an author is hurt by his critics. The blaze of reputation cannot be blown out, but it often dies in the socket; a very few names may be considered as perpetual lamps that shine unconsumed. From the author of *Fitzosborne's Letters* I cannot think myself in much danger. I met him only once about thirty years ago, and in some small dispute reduced him to whistle; having not seen him since, that is the last impression. Poor Moore, the fabulist, was one of the company.

Mrs Montagu's long stay, against her own inclination, is very convenient. You would, by your own confession, want a companion; and she is *par pluribus*; conversing with her you may *find variety in one*.

London, May 1, 1780.

---

a *Second Edition* – A *good* dawling companion.
1 I have taken the liberty to leave out a few lines.

On the 2nd of May I wrote to him, and requested that we might have another meeting somewhere in the North of England, in the autumn of this year.

From Mr Langton I received soon after this time a letter, of which I extract a passage, relative at once to Mr Beauclerk and Dr Johnson.

The melancholy information you have received concerning Mr Beauclerk's death is true. Had his talents been directed in any sufficient degree as they ought, I have always been strongly of opinion that they were calculated to make an illustrious figure; and that opinion, as it had been in part formed upon Dr Johnson's judgement, receives more and more confirmation by hearing, what since his death, Dr Johnson has said concerning them; a few evenings ago, he was at Mr Vesey's, where Lord Althorpe, who was one of a numerous company there, addressed Dr Johnson on the subject of Mr Beauclerk's death, saying, 'Our CLUB has had a great loss since we met last.' He replied, 'A loss that perhaps the whole nation could not repair!' The Doctor then went on to speak of his endowments, and particularly extolled the wonderful ease with which he uttered what was highly excellent. He said, that no man ever was so free when he was going to say a good thing, from a *look* that expressed that it was coming; or, when he had said it, from a look that expressed that it *had* come. At Mr Thrale's, some days before, when we were talking on the same subject, he said, referring to the same idea of his wonderful facility, 'That Beauclerk's talents were those which he had felt himself more disposed to envy, than those of any whom he had known.'

At the evening I have spoken of above, at Mr Vesey's, you would have been much gratified, as it exhibited an instance of the high importance in which Dr Johnson's character is held, I think even beyond any I ever before was witness to. The company consisted chiefly of ladies, among whom were the Duchess Dowager of Portland, the Duchess of Beaufort, whom I suppose from her rank I must name before her mother Mrs Boscawen, and her elder sister Mrs Lewson, who was likewise there; Lady Lucan, Lady Clermont, and others of note both for their station and understandings. Among the gentlemen were, Lord Althorpe, whom I have before named, Lord Macartney, Sir Joshua Reynolds, Lord Lucan, Mr Wraxal, whose book you have probably seen, *The Tour to the Northern Parts of Europe*; a very agreeable ingenious man, Dr Warren, Mr Pepys, the Master in Chancery, whom I believe you know, and Dr Barnard, the Provost of Eton. As soon as Dr Johnson was come in and had taken a chair, the company began to collect round him till they became not less than four if not five deep; those behind standing, and listening over the heads of those that were sitting near him. The conversation for some time was chiefly between Dr Johnson and the Provost of Eton, while the others contributed occasionally their re-marks. Without attempting to detail the particulars of the conversation, which perhaps if I did, I should spin my account out to a tedious length, I thought, my dear Sir, this general account of the respect with which our valued friend was attended to, might be acceptable.

To the Reverend Dr FARMER.

May 23, 1780.

SIR – I know your disposition to second any literary attempt, and therefore venture upon the liberty of entreating you to procure from College or University registers, all the dates, or other informations which they can supply relating to Ambrose Philips, Broom, and Gray, who were all of Cambridge, and of whose lives I am to give such accounts as I can gather. Be pleased to forgive this trouble, from, Sir,

    Your most humble servant,

SAM. JOHNSON.

While Johnson was thus engaged in preparing a delightful literary entertainment for the world, the tranquillity of the metropolis of Great Britain was unexpectedly disturbed, by the most horrid series of outrage that ever disgraced a civilized country. A relaxation of some of the severe penal provisions against our fellow subjects of the Catholic communion had been granted by the legislature, with an opposition so inconsiderable, that the genuine mildness of Christianity, united with liberal policy, seemed to have become general in this island. But a dark and malignant spirit of persecution soon showed itself, in an unworthy petition for the repeal of the wise and humane statute. That petition was brought forward by a mob, with the evident purpose of intimidation, and was justly rejected. But the attempt was accompanied and followed by such daring violence as is unexampled in history. Of this extraordinary tumult, Dr Johnson has given the following concise, lively, and just account in his *Letters to Mrs Thrale*:[1]

'On Friday, the good Protestants met in St George's-Fields, at the summons of Lord George Gordon, and marching to Westminster, insulted the Lords and Commons, who all bore it with great tameness. At night the outrages began by the demolition of the mass-house by Lincoln's-Inn.'

'An exact journal of a week's defiance of government I cannot give you. On Monday, Mr Strahan, who had been insulted, spoke to Lord Mansfield, who had I think been insulted too, of the licentiousness of the populace; and his Lordship treated it as a very slight irregularity. On Tuesday night they pulled down Fielding's house, and burnt his goods in the street. They had gutted on Monday Sir George Savile's house, but the building was saved. On Tuesday evening, leaving Fielding's ruins, they went to Newgate to demand their companions who had been seized demolishing the chapel. The keeper could not release them but by the Mayor's permission, which he went to ask; at his return he found all the prisoners released, and Newgate in a blaze. They then went to Bloomsbury, and fastened upon Lord Mansfield's house, which they pulled down; and as for his goods, they totally burnt them. They have since

1 Vol. ii. p. 143, *et seq.* I have selected passages from several letters, without mentioning dates.

gone to Caen-wood, but a guard was there before them. They plundered some Papists, I think, and burnt a mass-house in Moorfields the same night.'

'On Wednesday I walked with Dr Scot to look at Newgate, and found it in ruins, with the fire yet glowing. As I went by, the Protestants were plundering the Sessions house at the Old Bailey. There were not, I believe, a hundred; but they did their work at leisure, in full security, without sentinels, without trepidation, as men lawfully employed, in full day. Such is the cowardice of a commercial place. On Wednesday they broke open the Fleet, and the King's-bench, and the Marshalsea, and Wood-street Compter, and Clerkenwell Bridewell, and released all the prisoners.'

'At night they set fire to the Fleet, and to the King's-bench, and I know not how many other places; and one might see the glare of conflagration fill the sky from many parts. The light was dreadful. Some people were threatened: Mr Strahan advised me to take care of myself. Such a time of terror you have been happy in not seeing.'

'The King said in council, "that the magistrates had not done their duty, but that he would do his own", and a proclamation was published, directing us to keep our servants within doors, as the peace was now to be preserved by force. The soldiers were sent out to different parts, and the town is now at quiet.'

'The soldiers are stationed so as to be every where within call: there is no longer any body of rioters, and the individuals are haunted to their holes, and led to prison; Lord George was last night sent to the Tower. Mr John Wilkes was this day in my neighbourhood, to seize the publishers of a seditious paper.'

'Several chapels have been destroyed, and several inoffensive Papists have been plundered: but the high sport was to burn the gaols. This was a good rabble trick. The debtors and criminals were all set at liberty; but of the criminals, as has always happened, many are already retaken; and two pirates have surrendered themselves, and it is expected that they will be pardoned.'

'Government now acts again with its proper force; and we are all again under the protection of the King and the law. I thought that it would be agreeable to you and my master to have my testimony to the public security; and that you would sleep more quietly when I told you that you are safe.'

'There has, indeed, been an universal panic, from which the King was the first that recovered. Without the concurrence of his ministers, or the assistance of the civil magistrate, he put the soldiers in motion, and saved the town from calamities, such as a rabble's government must naturally produce.'

'The public has escaped a very heavy calamity. The rioters attempted the Bank on Wednesday night, but in no great number; and like other thieves, with no great resolution. Jack Wilkes headed the party that drove them away. It is agreed, that if they had seized the Bank on Tuesday, at the height of the panic, when no resistance had been prepared, they might have carried irrecoverably away whatever they had found. Jack, who was always zealous for order and decency, declares, that if he be trusted with power, he will not leave a rioter alive. There is, however, now no longer any need of heroism or bloodshed; no blue ribband is any longer worn.'

Such was the end of this miserable sedition, from which London was delivered by the magnanimity of the Sovereign himself. Whatever some may maintain, I am satisfied that there was no combination or plan, either domestic or foreign; but that the mischief spread by a gradual contagion of frenzy, augmented by the quantities of fermented liquors, of which the deluded populace possessed themselves in the course of their depredations.

I should think myself very much to blame, did I here neglect to do justice to my esteemed friend Mr Akerman, the keeper of Newgate, who has long discharged a very important trust with an uniform intrepid firmness, and at the same time a tenderness and a liberal charity, which entitle him to be recorded with distinguished honour.

Upon this occasion, from the timidity and negligence of magistracy on the one hand, and the almost incredible exertions of the mob on the other, the first prison of this great country was laid open, and the prisoners set free; but that Mr Akerman, whose house was burnt, would have prevented all this, had proper aid been sent to him in due time, there can be no doubt.

Many years ago, a fire broke out in the brick part which was built as an addition to the old gaol of Newgate. The prisoners were in consternation and tumult, calling out, 'We shall be burnt – we shall be burnt! Down with the gate – down with the gate!' Mr Akerman hastened to them, showed himself at the gate, and having, after some confused vociferation of 'Hear him – hear him!' obtained a silent attention, he then calmly told them, that the gate must not go down; that they were under his care, and that they should not be permitted to escape; but that he could assure them, they need not be afraid of being burnt, for that the fire was not in the prison, properly so called, which was strongly built with stone; and that if they would engage to be quiet, he himself would come in to them, and conduct them to the further end of the building, and would not go out till they gave him leave. To this proposal they agreed; upon which Mr Akerman, having first made them fall back from the gate, went in, and with a determined resolution ordered the outer turnkey upon no account to open the gate, even though the prisoners (though he trusted they would not) should break their word, and by force bring himself to order it. 'Never mind me (said he), should that happen.' The prisoners peaceably followed him, while he conducted them through passages, of which he had the keys, to the extremity of the gaol, which was most distant from the fire. Having, by this very judicious conduct, fully satisfied them that there was no immediate risk, if any at all, he then addressed them thus: 'Gentlemen, you are now convinced that I told you true. I have no doubt that the engines will soon extinguish this fire: if they should not, a sufficient guard will come, and you shall all be taken out and be lodged in the Compters. I assure you, upon my word and honour, that I have not a farthing insured. I have left my house that I might take care of you. I will keep my promise, and stay with you, if you insist upon it: but if you will allow me to go out and look after my family and property, I will be obliged to you.' Struck with his behaviour, they called out, 'Master Akerman, you have done bravely; it was very kind in you: by all means go and take care of your own concerns.' He did so accordingly, while they remained and were all preserved.

Johnson has been heard to relate the substance of this story with high praise, in which he was joined by Mr Burke. My illustrious friend, speaking of Mr Akerman's kindness to his prisoners, pronounced this eulogy upon his character: 'He who has long had constantly in his view the worst of mankind, and is yet eminent for the humanity of his disposition, must have had it originally in a great degree, and continued to cultivate it very carefully.'

In the course of this month my brother David waited upon Dr Johnson, with the following letter of introduction, which I had taken care should be lying ready on his arrival in London.

To Dr SAMUEL JOHNSON.

Edinburgh, April 29, 1780.

MY DEAR SIR – This will be delivered to you by my brother David, on his return from Spain. You will be glad to see the man who vowed to 'stand by the old castle of Auchinleck, with heart, purse, and sword'; that romantic family solemnity devised by me, of which you and I talked with complacency upon the spot. I trust that twelve years of absence have not lessened his feudal attachment; and that you will find him worthy of being introduced to your acquaintance.

I have the honour to be, with affectionate veneration, my dear Sir,
Your most faithful humble servant,

JAMES BOSWELL.

Johnson received him very politely, and has thus mentioned him in a letter to Mrs Thrale:[1] 'I have had with me a brother of Boswell's, a Spanish merchant,[2] whom the war has driven from his residence at Valencia; he is gone to see his friends, and will find Scotland but a sorry place after twelve years' residence in a happier climate. He is a very agreeable man, and speaks no Scotch.'

To Dr BEATTIE at Aberdeen.

SIR – More years[3] than I have any delight to reckon, have past since you and I saw one another; of this, however, there is no reason for making any reprehensory complaint, *Sic fata ferunt*. But methinks there might pass some small interchange of regard between us. If you say, that I ought to have written, I now write, and I write to tell you, that I have much kindness for you and Mrs Beattie; and that I wish your health better, and your life long. Try change of air, and come a few degrees Southwards; a softer climate may do you good; winter is coming on; and London will be warmer, and gayer, and busier, and more fertile of amusement than Aberdeen.

My health is better; but that will be little in the balance, when I tell you that Mrs Montagu has been very ill, and is I doubt now but weakly. Mr

1 Vol ii, p. 163. Mrs Piozzi has omitted the name, she best knows why.
2 Now settled in London.
3 I had been five years absent from London. BEATTIE.

Thrale has been very dangerously disordered; but is much better, and I hope will totally recover. He has withdrawn himself from business the whole summer. Sir Joshua and his sister are well; and Mr Davies has had great success as an author,[1] generated by the corruption of a bookseller. More news I have not to tell you, and therefore you must be contented with hearing, what I know not whether you much wish to hear,[2] that I am, Sir,

Your most humble servant,

SAM. JOHNSON.

Bolt-court, Fleet-street,
August 21, 1780.

To JAMES BOSWELL, Esq.

DEAR SIR – I find you have taken one of your fits of taciturnity, and have resolved not to write till you are written to; it is but a peevish humour, but you shall have your way.

I have sat at home in Bolt-court, all the summer, thinking to write the Lives, and a great part of the time only thinking. Several of them, however, are done, and I still think to do the rest

Mr Thrale and his family have, since his illness, passed their time first at Bath, and then at Brighthelmston; but I have been at neither place. I would have gone to Lichfield, if I could have had time, and I might have had time, if I had been active, but I have missed much, and done little.

In the late disturbances, Mr Thrale's house and stock were in great danger; the mob was pacified at their first invasion, with about fifty pounds in drink and meat, and at their second, were driven away by the soldiers. Mr Strahan got a garrison into his house, and maintained them a fortnight; he was so frighted that he removed part of his goods. Mrs Williams took shelter in the country.

I know not whether I shall get a ramble this autumn, it is now about the time when we were travelling. I have, however, better health than I had then, and hope you and I may yet show ourselves on some parts of Europe, Asia, or Africa.[3] In the mean time let us play no trick, but keep each other's kindness by all means in our power.

1 Meaning his entertaining *Memoirs of David Garrick, Esq.*, of which Johnson (as Davies informed me) wrote the first sentence; thus giving, as it were, the key-note to the performance. It is, indeed, very characteristical of its author, beginning with a maxim, and proceeding to illustrate. – 'All excellence has a right to be recorded. I shall, therefore, think it superfluous to apologise for writing the life of a man, who by an uncommon assemblage of private virtues, adorned the highest eminence in a public profession.'

2 I wish he had omitted the suspicion expressed here, though I believe he meant nothing but jocularity; for though he and I differed sometimes in opinion, he well knew how much I loved and revered him. BEATTIE.

3 It will, no doubt, be remarked how he avoids the *rebellious* land of America. This puts me in mind of an anecdote, for which I am obliged to my worthy friend, Governor Penn: 'At one of Miss E. Hervey's assemblies, Dr Johnson was following

The bearer of this is Dr Dunbar, of Aberdeen, who has written and published a very ingenious book,[1] and who I think has a kindness for me, and will when he knows you have a kindness for you.

I suppose your little ladies are grown tall; and your son is become a learned young man. I love them all, and I love your naughty lady, whom I never shall persuade to love me. When the Lives are done, I shall send them to complete her collection, but must send them in paper, as for want of a pattern, I cannot bind them to fit the rest. I am, Sir,

Yours most affectionately,

SAM. JOHNSON.

London, Aug. 21, 1780.

This year he wrote to a young clergyman in the country, the following very excellent letter, which contains valuable advice to Divines in general:

DEAR SIR – Not many days ago Dr Lawrence showed me a letter, in which you make mention of me: I hope, therefore, you will not be displeased that I endeavour to preserve your good-will by some observations which your letter suggested to me.

You are afraid of falling into some improprieties in the daily service, by reading to an audience that requires no exactness. Your fear, I hope, secures you from danger. They who contract absurd habits are such as have no fear. It is impossible to do the same thing very often, without some peculiarity of manner: but that manner may be good or bad, and a little care will at least preserve it from being bad: to make it very good, there must, I think, be something of natural or casual felicity, which cannot be taught.

Your present method of making your sermons seems very judicious. Few frequent preachers can be supposed to have sermons more their own than yours will be. Take care to register, somewhere or other, the authors from whom your several discourses are borrowed; and do not imagine that you shall always remember, even what perhaps you now think it impossible to forget.

My advice, however, is, that you attempt, from time to time, an original sermon; and in the labour of composition, do not burden your mind with too much at once; do not exact from yourself, at one effort of excogitation, propriety of thought and elegance of expression. Invent first, and then embellish. The production of something, where nothing was before, is an act of greater energy than the expansion or decoration of the thing produced. Set down diligently your thoughts as they rise, in the first words

---

her up and down the room; upon which Lord Abingdon observed to her, "Your great friend is very fond of you, you can go no where without him." – "Aye (said she), he would follow me to any part of the world." – Then (said the Earl) ask him to go with you to *America*." '

1 *Essays on the History of Mankind.*

that occur; and, when you have matter, you will easily give it form: nor, perhaps, will this method be always necessary; for, by habit, your thoughts and diction will flow together.

The composition of sermons is not very difficult: the divisions not only help the memory of the hearer, but direct the judgement of the writer; they supply sources of invention, and keep every part in its proper place.

What I like least in your letter is your account of the manners of your parish; from which I gather, that it has been long neglected by the parson. The Dean of Carlisle,[1] who was then a little rector in Northamptonshire, told me, that it might be discerned whether or no there was a clergyman resident in a parish, by the civil or savage manner of the people. Such a congregation as yours stands in much need of reformation; and I would not have you think it impossible to reform them. A very savage parish was civilised by a decayed gentlewoman, who came among them to teach a petty school. My learned friend Dr Wheeler of Oxford, when he was a young man, had the care of a neighbouring parish for fifteen pounds a year, which he was never paid; but he counted it a convenience that it compelled him to make a sermon weekly. One woman he could not bring to the communion; and when he reproved or exhorted her, she only answered, that she was no scholar. He was advised to set some good woman or man of the parish, a little wiser than herself, to talk to her in language level to her mind. Such honest, I may call them holy artifices, must be practised by every clergyman; for all means must be tried by which souls may be saved. Talk to your people, however, as much as you can, and you will find, that the more frequently you converse with them upon religious subjects, the more willingly they will attend, and the more submissively they will learn. A clergyman's diligence always makes him venerable. I think I have now only to say, that in the momentous work you have undertaken, I pray GOD to bless you. I am, Sir,

Your most humble servant,

SAM. JOHNSON.

Bolt-court, Aug. 30, 1780.

My next letters to him were of dates August 24, September 6, and October 1, and from them I extract the following passages:

My brother David and I find the long indulged fancy of our comfortable meeting again at Auchinleck, so well realised, that it in some degree confirms the pleasing hope of O! praeclarum diem! in a future state.

I beg that you may never again harbour a suspicion of my indulging a peevish humour, or playing tricks; you will recollect, that when I confessed to you, that when I had once been intentionally silent to try your regard, I gave you my word and honour that I should not do so again.

1 Dr Percy, now Bishop of Dromore.

'I rejoice to hear of your good state of health; I pray GOD to continue it long. I have often said, that I would willingly have ten years added to my life, to have ten taken from yours; I mean, that I would be ten years older, to have you ten years younger. But let me be thankful for the years during which I have enjoyed your friendship, and please myself with the hopes of enjoying it many years to come in this state of being, trusting always, that in another state, we shall meet never to be separated. Of this we can form no notion; but the thought, though indistinct, is delightful, when the mind is calm and clear.

The riots in London were certainly horrible; but you give me no account of your own situation, during the barbarous anarchy. A description of it by DR JOHNSON would be a great painting;[1] you might write another *London, a Poem.*

I am charmed with your condescending affectionate expression, 'let us keep each other's kindness by all the means in our power'; my revered Friend! how elevating is it to my mind, that I am found worthy to be a companion to Dr Samuel Johnson! All that you have said in grateful praise of Mr Walmsley, I have long thought of you, but we are both Tories, which has a very general influence upon our sentiments. I hope that you will agree to meet me at York, about the end of this month; or if you will come to Carlisle, that would be better still, in case the Dean be there. Please to consider, that to keep each other's kindness, we should every year have that free and intimate communication of mind which can be had only when we are together. We should have both our solemn and our pleasant talk.

I write now for the third time, to tell you that my desire for our meeting this autumn, is much increased. I wrote to 'Squire Godfrey Bosville, my Yorkshire Chief, that I should, perhaps, pay him a visit, as I was to hold a conference with Dr Johnson, at York. I give you my word and honour that I said not a word of his inviting you; but he wrote to me as follows:

'I need not tell you I shall be happy to see you here the latter end of this month, as you propose; and I shall likewise be in hopes that you will persuade Dr Johnson to finish the conference here. It will add to the favour of your own company, if you prevail upon such an associate, to assist your observations. I have often been entertained with his writings, and I once belonged to a club of which he was a member, and I never spent an evening there, but I heard something from him well worth remembering.'

We have thus, my dear Sir, good comfortable quarters in the neighbour-hood of York, where you may be assured we shall be heartily welcome. I pray you then resolve to set out; and let not the year 1780 be a blank in our social calendar, and in that record of wisdom and wit, which I keep with so much diligence, to your honour, and the instruction and delight of others.

---

1 I had not then seen his letters to Mrs Thrale.

Mr Thrale had now another contest for the representation in parliament of the borough of Southwark, and Johnson kindly lent him his assistance, by writing advertisements and letters for him. I shall insert one as a specimen:*

To the worthy ELECTORS of the Borough of SOUTHWARK.

GENTLEMEN – A new Parliament being now called, I again solicit the honour of being elected for one of your representatives, and solicit it with the greater confidence, as I am not conscious of having neglected my duty, or of having acted otherwise than as becomes the independent representative of independent constituents, superior to fear, hope, and expectation, who has no private purposes to promote, and whose prosperity is involved in the prosperity of his country. As my recovery from a very severe distemper is not yet perfect, I have declined to attend the Hall, and hope an omission so necessary will not be harshly censured.

I can only send my respectful wishes, that all your deliberations may tend to the happiness of the kingdom, and the peace of the borough. I am, Gentlemen,

Your most faithful and obedient servant,

HENRY THRALE.

Southwark, Sept. 5, 1780.

On his birth-day, Johnson has this note, 'I am now beginning the seventy-second year of my life, with more strength of body, and greater vigour of mind, than I think is common at that age.' But still he complains of sleepless nights and idle days, and forgetfulness, or neglect of resolutions. He thus pathetically expresses himself, 'Surely I shall not spend my whole life with my own total disapprobation.'[1]

Mr Macbean, whom I have mentioned more than once, as one of Johnson's humble friends, a deserving but unfortunate man, being now oppressed by age and poverty, Johnson solicited the Lord Chancellor Thurlow, to have him admitted into the Charter-house. I take the liberty to insert his Lordship's answer, as I am eager to embrace every occasion of augmenting the respectable notion which should ever be entertained of my illustrious friend:

To Dr SAMUEL JOHNSON.

London, Oct. 24, 1780.

SIR – I have this moment received your letter, dated the 19th, and returned from Bath.

In the beginning of the summer I placed one in the Chartreux, without the sanction of a recommendation so distinct, and so authoritative as yours of Macbean; and I am afraid, that according to the establishment of the House, the opportunity of making the charity so good amends will not

---

1 *Prayers and Meditations*, p. 185.

soon recur. But whenever a vacancy shall happen, if you'll favour me with notice of it, I will try to recommend him to the place, even though It should not be my turn to nominate. I am, Sir, with great regard,

Your most faithful

And obedient servant,

THURLOW.

To JAMES BOSWELL, Esq.

DEAR SIR – I am sorry to write you a letter that will not please you, and yet it is at last what I resolve to do. This year must pass without an interview; the summer has been foolishly lost, like many other of my summers and winters. I hardly saw a green field, but staid in town to work, without working much.

Mr Thrale's loss of health has lost him the election; he is now going to Brighthelmston, and expects me to go with him, and how long I shall stay I cannot tell. I do not much like the place, but yet I shall go, and stay while my stay is desired. We must, therefore, content ourselves with knowing what we know as well as man can know the mind of man, that we love one another, and that we wish each other's happiness, and that the lapse of a year cannot lessen our mutual kindness.

I was pleased to be told that I accused Mrs Boswell unjustly, in supposing that she bears me ill-will. I love you so much, that I would be glad to love all that love you, and that you love; and I have love very ready for Mrs Boswell, if she thinks it worthy of acceptance. I hope all the young ladies and gentlemen are well.

I take a great liking to your brother. He tells me that his father received him kindly, but not fondly; however, you seem to have lived well enough at Auchinleck, while you staid. Make your father as happy as you can.

You lately told me of your health: I can tell you in return, that my health has been for more than a year past, better than it has been for many years before. Perhaps it may please GOD to give us some time together before we are parted. I am, dear Sir,

Yours, most affectionately,

SAM. JOHNSON.

Oct. 17, 1780.

Being disappointed in my hopes of meeting Johnson this year, so that I could hear none of his admirable sayings, I shall compensate for this want by inserting a collection of them, for which I am indebted to my worthy friend Mr Langton, whose kind communications have been separately interwoven in many parts of this work. A very few articles of this collection were committed to writing by himself, he not having that habit; which he regrets, and which those who know the numerous opportunities he had of gathering the rich fruits of *Johnsonian* wit and wisdom must ever regret. I however found, in conversations with him, that a good store of *Johnsoniana* was treasured in his mind; and I compared it to Herculaneum, or some old Roman field, which, when dug, fully rewards the labour employed. The authenticity of every article is unquestionable. For the expression, I, who wrote them down in his presence, am partly answerable.

'Theocritus is not deserving of very high respect as a writer; as to the pastoral part, Virgil is very evidently superior. He wrote when there had been a larger influx of knowledge into the world than when Theocritus lived. Theocritus does not abound in description, though living in a beautiful country: the manners painted are coarse and gross. Virgil has much more description, more sentiment, more of Nature, and more of art. Some of the most excellent parts of Theocritus are, where Castor and Pollux, going with the other Argonauts, land on the Bebrycian coast, and there fall into a dispute with Amycus, the King of that country; which is as well conducted as Euripides could have done it; and the battle is well related. Afterwards they carry off a woman, whose two brothers come to recover her, and expostulate with Castor and Pollux on their injustice; but they pay no regard to the brothers, and a battle ensues, where Castor and his brother are triumphant. Theocritus seems not to have seen that the brothers have the advantage in their argument over his Argonaut heroes. – *The Sicilian Gossips* is a piece of merit.'

'Callimachus is a writer of little excellence. The chief thing to be learned from him is his account of Rites and Mythology; which, though desirable to be known for the sake of understanding other parts of ancient authors, is the least pleasing or valuable part of their writings.'

'Mattaire's account of the Stephani is a heavy book. He seems to have been a puzzle-headed man, with a large share of scholarship, but with little geometry or logic in his head, without method, and possessed of little genius. He wrote Latin verses from time to time, and published a set in his old age, which he called *Senilia*; in which he shows so little learning or taste in writing, as to make *Carteret* a dactyl. – In matters of genealogy it is necessary to give the bare names as they are; but in poetry, and in prose of any elegance in the writing, they require to have inflection given to them. – His book of the Dialects is a sad heap of confusion; the only way to write on them is to tabulate them with Notes, added at the bottom of the page, and references.'

'It may be questioned, whether there is not some mistake as to the methods of employing the poor, seemingly on the supposition that there is a certain portion of work left undone for want of persons to do it; but if that is otherwise, and all the materials we have are actually worked up, or all the manufactures we can use or dispose of are already executed, then what is given to the poor, who are to be set at work, must be taken from some who now have it, as time must be taken for learning, according to Sir William Petty's observation; a certain part of those very materials that, as it is, are properly worked up, must be spoiled by the unskilfulness of novices. We may apply to well-meaning, but misjudging persons in particular of this nature, what Giannone said to a monk, who wanted what he called to *convert* him: "*Tu sei santo, ma tu non sei filosofo.*" – It is an unhappy circumstance that one might give away five hundred pounds in a year to those that importune in the streets, and not do any good.'

'There is nothing more likely to betray a man into absurdity than *condescension*; when he seems to suppose his understanding too powerful for his company.'

'Having asked Mr Langton if his father and mother had sat for their pictures, which he thought it right for each generation of a family to do, and being told they had opposed it, he said, "Sir, among the anfractuosities of the human mind, I know not if it may not be one, that there is a superstitious reluctance to sit for a picture." '

'John Gilbert Cooper related, that soon after the publication of his Dictionary, Garrick being asked by Johnson what people said of it, told him, that among other animadversions, it was objected that he cited authorities which were beneath the dignity of such a work, and mentioned Richardson. "Nay, (said Johnson), I have done worse than that: I have cited thee, David." '

'Talking of expense, he observed, with what munificence a great merchant will spend his money, both from his having it at command, and from his enlarged views by calculation of a good effect upon the whole. "Whereas (said he) you will hardly ever find a country gentleman who is not a good deal disconcerted at an unexpected occasion for his being obliged to lay out ten pounds." '

'When in good humour he would talk of his own writings, with a wonderful frankness and candour, and would even criticise them with the closest severity. One day, having read over one of his Ramblers, Mr Langton asked him how he liked that paper; he shook his head, and answered, "too wordy". And at another time, when one was reading his tragedy of *Irene*, to a company at a house in the country, he left the room; and somebody having asked him the reason of this, he replied, "Sir, I thought it had been better." '

'Talking of a point of delicate scrupulosity of moral conduct, he said to Mr Langton, "Men of harder minds than ours will do many things from which you and I would shrink; yet, Sir, they will, perhaps, do more good in life than we. But let us try to help one another. If there be a wrong twist, it may be set right. It is not probable that two people can be wrong the same way." '

'Of the Preface to Capel's Shakspeare, he said, "If the man would have come to me, I would have endeavoured to 'endow his purposes with words;' for, as it is, 'he doth gabble monstrously'." '

'He related, that he had once in a dream a contest of wit with some other person, and that he was very much mortified by imagining that his opponent had the better of him. "Now (said he) one may mark here the effect of sleep in weakening the power of reflection; for had not my judgement failed me, I should have seen, that the wit of this supposed antagonist, by whose superiority I felt myself depressed, was as much furnished by me, as that which I thought I had been uttering in my own character." '

'One evening in company, an ingenious and learned gentleman read a letter of compliment to him from one of the Professors of a foreign University. Johnson, in an irritable fit, thinking there was too much ostentation, said, "I never receive any of these tributes of applause from abroad. One instance I recollect of a foreign publication, in which mention is made of *l'illustre Lockman*." 'ᵃ

'Of Sir Joshua Reynolds he said, "Sir, I know no man who has passed through life with more observation than Reynolds." '

'He repeated to Mr Langton, with great energy, in the Greek, our SAVIOUR'S gracious expression concerning the forgiveness of Mary Magdalen, Ἡ πίστις σου σέσωκέ σε· πορεύου εἰς εἰρήνην. "Thy faith hath saved thee; go in peace."[1] He said, "the manner of this dismission is exceedingly affecting." '

'He thus defined the difference between physical and moral truth; "Physical truth, is, when you tell a thing as it actually is. Moral truth, is, when you tell a thing sincerely and precisely as it appears to you. I say such a one walked across the street; if he really did so I told a physical truth. If I thought so, though I should have been mistaken, I told a moral truth." '

'Huggins, the translator of Ariosto, and Mr Thomas Warton, in the early part of his literary life, had a dispute concerning that poet, of whom Mr Warton, in his 'Observations on Spencer's Fairy Queen', gave some account, which Huggins attempted to answer with violence, and said, "I will *militate* no longer against his nescience." Huggins was master of the subject, but wanted expression. Mr Warton's knowledge of it was then imperfect, but his manner lively and elegant. Johnson said, "It appears to me, that Huggins has ball without powder, and Warton powder without ball." '

'Talking of the Farce of *High Life below Stairs*, he said, "Here is a Farce, which is really very diverting when you see it acted; and yet one may read it, and not know that one has been reading any thing at all." '

'He used at one time to go occasionally to the green-room of Drury-lane Theatre, where he was much regarded by the players, and was very easy and facetious with them. He had a very high opinion of Mrs Clive's comic powers, and conversed more with her than with any of them. He said, "Clive, Sir, is a good thing to sit by, she always understands what you say." And she said of him, "I love to sit by Dr Johnson, he always entertains me." One night, when *The Recruiting Officer* was acted, he said to Mr Holland, who had been expressing an apprehension that Dr Johnson would disdain the works of Farquhar; "No, Sir, I think Farquhar a man whose writings have considerable merit." '

'His friend Garrick was so busy in conducting the drama, that they could not have so much intercourse as Mr Garrick used to profess an anxious wish that there should be. There might indeed be something in the contemptuous severity as to the merit of acting which his old preceptor nourished in himself, that would mortify Garrick after the great applause which he received from the audience. For though Johnson said of him, "Sir, a man who has a nation to admire him every night, may well be expected to be somewhat elated"; yet he would treat theatrical matters with a ludicrous slight. He mentioned one

---

ᵃ Add the following note: Secretary to the British Herring Fishery, remarkable for an extraordinary number of occasional verses, not of eminent merit.

1 Luke vii. 50.

evening, "I met David coming off the stage, drest in a woman's riding-hood, when he acted in *The Wonder*; I came full upon him, and I believe he was not pleased." '

'Once he asked Tom Davies, whom he saw drest in a fine suit of clothes, "And what art thou to-night?" Tom answered, "The Thane of Ross" (which it will be recollected is a very inconsiderable character). "O brave!" said Johnson.'

'Of Mr Longley, at Rochester, a gentleman of very considerable learning, whom Dr Johnson met there, he said, "My heart warms towards him. I was surprised to find in him such a nice acquaintance with the metre in the learned languages; though I was somewhat mortified that I had it not so much to myself, as I should have thought." '

'Talking of the minuteness with which people will record the sayings of eminent persons, a story was told, that when Pope was on a visit to Spence at Oxford, as they looked from the window they saw a Gentleman Commoner, who was just come in from riding, amusing himself with whipping at a post. Pope took occasion to say, "That young gentleman seems to have little to do." Mr Beauclerk observed, "Then, to be sure, Spence turned round and wrote that down"; and went on to say to Dr Johnson, "Pope, Sir, would have said the same of you, if he had seen you distilling." JOHNSON. "Sir, if Pope had told me of my distilling, I would have told him of his grotto." '

'He would allow no settled indulgence of idleness upon principle, and always repelled every attempt to urge excuses for it. A friend one day suggested, that it was not wholesome to study soon after dinner. JOHNSON. "Ah, Sir, don't give way to such a fancy. At one time of my life I had taken it into my head that it was not wholesome to study between breakfast and dinner." '

'Mr Beauclerk one day repeated to Dr Johnson, Pope's lines,

> Let modest Foster, if he will, excel
> Ten metropolitans in preaching well:

Then asked the Doctor, "Why did Pope say this?" JOHNSON. "Sir, he hoped it would vex somebody." '

'Dr Goldsmith, upon occasion of Mrs Lennox's bringing out a play, said to Dr Johnson at the CLUB, that a person had advised him to go and hiss it, because she had attacked Shakspeare in her book called *Shakspeare Illustrated*. JOHNSON. "And did not you tell him that he was a rascal?" GOLDSMITH. "No, Sir, I did not. Perhaps he might not mean what he said." JOHNSON. "Nay, Sir, if he lied it is a different thing." Colman slily said (but it is believed Dr Johnson did not hear him), "Then the proper expression should have been – Sir, if you don't lie, you're a rascal." '

'His affection for Topham Beauclerk was so great, that when Beauclerk was labouring under that severe illness which at last occasioned his death, Johnson said (with a voice faltering with emotion), "Sir, I would walk to the extent of the diameter of the earth to save Beauclerk." '

'One night at the CLUB he produced a translation of an Epitaph which Lord Elibank had written in English, for his Lady, and requested of Johnson to turn into Latin for him. Having read *Domina de North et Gray*, he said to Dyer, "You see, Sir, what barbarisms we are compelled to make use of, when modern titles are to be specifically mentioned in Latin inscriptions." When he had read it once aloud, and there had been a general approbation expressed by the company, he addressed himself to Mr Dyer in particular, and said, "Sir, I beg to have your judgement, for I know your nicety." Dyer then very properly desired to read it over again; which, having done, he pointed out an incongruity in one of the sentences. Johnson immediately assented to the observation, and said, "Sir, this is owing to an alteration of a part of the sentence, from the form in which I had first written it, and I believe, Sir, you may have remarked, that it is a very frequent cause of error in composition, when one has made a partial change, without a due regard to the general structure of the sentence." '

'Johnson was well acquainted with Mr Dossie, author of a treatise on Agriculture; and said of him, "Sir, of the objects which the Society of Arts have chiefly in view, the chemical effects of bodies operating upon other bodies, he knows more than almost any man." Johnson, in order to give Mr Dossie his vote to be a member of this Society, paid up an arrear which had run on for two years. On this occasion he mentioned a circumstance, as characteristic of the Scotch. "One of that nation (said he), who had been a candidate, against whom I had voted, came up to me with a civil salutation. Now, Sir, this is their way. An Englishman would have stomached it, and been sulky, and never have taken further notice of you: but a Scotchman, Sir, though you vote nineteen times against him, will accost you with equal complaisance after each time, and the twentieth time, Sir, he will get your vote." '

'Talking on the subject of toleration, one day when some friends were with him in his study, he made his usual remark, that the State has a right to regulate the religion of the people, who are the children of the State. A clergyman having readily acquiesced in this, Johnson, who loved discussion, observed, "But, Sir, you must go round to other States than our own. You do not know what a Bramin has to say for himself.[a] In short, Sir, I have got no farther than this. Every man has a right to utter what he thinks truth, and every other man has a right to knock him down for it. Martyrdom is the test." '

'A man, he observed, should begin to write soon; for, if he waits till his judgement is matured, his inability, through want of practice to express his conceptions, will make the disproportion so great between what he sees, and what he can attain, that he will probably be discouraged from writing at all. As a proof of the justness of this remark, we may instance what is related of the great Lord Granville; that after he had written his letter, giving an account of the battle of Dettingen, he said, "Here is a letter, expressed in terms not good enough for a tallow-chandler to have used." '

[a] Add the following note: Here Lord Macartney remarks, 'A Bramin or any cast of the Hindoos will neither admit you to be of their religion, nor be converted to yours: a thing which struck the Portuguese with the greatest astonishment, when they first discovered the East Indies.

'Talking of a Court-martial that was sitting upon a very momentous public occasion, he expressed much doubt of an enlightened decision; and said, that perhaps there was not a member of it, who in the whole course of his life, had ever spent an hour by himself in balancing probabilities.'

'Goldsmith one day brought to the CLUB a printed Ode, which he, with others, had been hearing read by its author in a public room, at the rate of five shillings each for admission. One of the company having read it aloud, Dr Johnson said, "Bolder words, and more timorous meaning, I think never were brought together." '

'Talking of Gray's Odes, he said, "They are forced plants, raised in a hot-bed; and they are poor plants; they are but cucumbers after all." A gentleman present, who had been running down Ode-writing in general, as a bad species of poetry, unluckily said, "Had they been literally cucumbers, they had been better things than Odes." - "Yes, Sir (said Johnson), for a *hog*." '

'His distinction of the different degrees of attainment of learning was thus marked upon two occasions. Of Queen Elizabeth he said, "She had learning enough to have given dignity to a Bishop": and of Mr Thomas Davies he said, "Sir, Davies has learning enough to give credit to a clergyman." '

'He used to quote, with great warmth, the saying of Aristotle recorded by Diogenes Laertius; that there was the same difference between one learned and unlearned, as between the living and the dead.'

'It is very remarkable, that he retained in his memory very slight and trivial, as well as important things. As an instance of this, it seems that an inferior domestic of the Duke of Leeds had attempted to celebrate his Grace's marriage in such homely rhymes as he could make; and this curious composition having been sung to Dr Johnson he got it by heart, and used to repeat it in a very pleasant manner. Two of the stanzas were these:

> When the Duke of Leeds shall married be
> To a fine young lady of high quality,
> How happy will that gentlewoman be
> In his Grace of Leeds's good company.
>
> She shall have all that's fine and fair,
> And the best of silk and sattin shall wear;
> And ride in a coach to take the air,
> And have a house in St James's-square.[a]

To hear a man, of the weight and dignity of Johnson, repeating such humble attempts at poetry, had a very amusing effect. He, however, seriously observed of the last stanza, that it nearly comprized all the advantages that wealth can give.'

[a] Add the following note: The correspondent of the *Gentleman's Magazine* who subscribes himself SCIOLUS, furnishes the following supplement:

'An eminent foreigner, when he was shown the British Museum, was very troublesome with many absurd inquiries. "Now, there, Sir (said he), is the difference between an Englishman and a Frenchman. A Frenchman must be always talking, whether he knows any thing of the matter or not: an Englishman is content to say nothing, when he has nothing to say." '

'His unjust contempt for foreigners was, indeed, extreme. One evening, at Old Slaughter's coffee-house, when a number of them were talking loud about little matters, he said, "Does not this confirm old Meynell's observation – For any thing I see, foreigners are fools." '

'He said, that once, when he had a violent tooth-ache, a Frenchman accosted him thus: *Ah, Monsieur, vous etudiez trop.*'

'Having spent an evening at Mr Langton's, with the Reverend Dr Parr, he was much pleased with the conversation of that learned gentleman; and, after he was gone, said to Mr Langton, "Sir, I am obliged to you for having asked me this evening. Parr is a fair man. I do not know when I have had an occasion of such free controversy. It is remarkable how much of a man's life may pass without meeting with any instance of this kind of open discussion." '

'We may fairly institute a criticism between Shakspeare and Corneille, as they both had, though in a different degree, the lights of a latter age. It is not so just between the Greek dramatic writers and Shakspeare. It may be replied to what is said by one of the remarkers on Shakspeare, that though Darius's shade had *prescience*, it does not necessarily follow that he had all *past* particulars revealed to him.'

'Spanish plays, being wildly and improbably farcical, would please children here, as children are entertained with stories full of prodigies; their experience not being sufficient to cause them to be so readily startled at deviations from the natural course of life. The machinery of the Pagans is uninteresting to us: when a Goddess appears in Homer or Virgil, we grow weary; still more so in

---

'A lady of my acquaintance remembers to have heard her uncle sing those homely stanzas more than forty-five years ago. He repeated the second thus:

> She shall breed young lords and ladies fair,
> And ride abroad in a coach and three pair,
> And the best, &c.
> And have a house, &c.

And remembered a third which seems to have been the introductory one, and is believed to have been the only remaining one:

> When the Duke of Leeds shall have made his choice
> Of a charming young lady that's beautiful and wise,
> She'll be the happiest young gentlewoman under the skies,
> As long as the sun and moon shall rise,
> And how happy shall, &c.'

It is with pleasure I add that this stanza could never be more truly applied than at this present time.

the Grecian tragedies, as in that kind of composition a nearer approach to Nature is intended. Yet there are good reasons for reading romances; as the fertility of invention, the beauty of style, and expression, the curiosity of seeing with what kind of performances the age and country in which they were written was delighted: for it is to be apprehended, that at the time when very wild improbable tales were well received, the people were in a barbarous state, and so on the footing of children, as has been explained.'

'It is evident enough that no one who writes now can use the Pagan deities and mythology; the only machinery, therefore, seems that of ministering spirits, the ghosts of the departed, witches, and fairies, though these latter, as the vulgar superstition concerning them (which, while in its force, infected at least the imagination of those that had more advantage in education, and only their reason set them free from it) is every day wearing out, seem likely to be of little further assistance in the machinery of poetry. As I recollect, Hammond introduces a hag or witch into one of his love elegies, where the effect is unmeaning and disgusting.'

'The man who uses his talent of ridicule in creating or grossly exaggerating the instances he gives, who imputes absurdities that did not happen, or when a man was a little ridiculous, describes him as having been very much so, abuses his talents greatly. The great use of delineating absurdities is, that we may know how far human folly can go; the account, therefore, ought to be of absolute necessity to be faithful. A certain character (naming the person) as to the general cast of it, is well described by Garrick, but a great deal of the phraseology he uses in it, is quite his own, particularly in the proverbial comparisons, "obstinate as a pig", &c., but I don't know whether it might not be true of him, that from a too great eagerness for praise and popularity, and a politeness carried to a ridiculous excess, he was likely, after asserting a thing in general, to give it up again in parts. For instance, if he had said Reynolds was the first of painters, he was capable enough of giving up, as objections might happen to be severally made; first, his outline – then the grace in form – then the colouring – and lastly, to have owned that he was such a mannerist, that the disposition of his pictures was all alike.'

'For hospitality, as formerly practised, there is no longer the same reason; heretofore the poorer people were more numerous, and from want of commerce, their means of getting a livelihood more difficult; therefore the supporting them was an act of great benevolence; now that the poor can find maintenance for themselves and their labour is wanted, a general undiscerning hospitality tends to ill, by withdrawing them from their work to idleness and drunkenness. Then formerly rents were received in kind, so that there was a great abundance of provisions in possession of the owners of the lands, which since the plenty of money afforded by commerce is no longer the case.'

'Hospitality to strangers and foreigners in our country is now almost at an end, since from the increase of them that come to us, there have been a sufficient number of people that have found an interest in providing inns and proper accommodations, which is in general a more expedient method for the entertainment of travellers. Where the travellers and strangers are few, more of that hospitality subsists, as it has not been worth while to provide places of accommodation. In Ireland there is still hospitality to strangers, in some degree; in Hungary and Poland probably more.'

'Colman, in a note on his translation of Terence, talking of Shakspeare's learning, asks, "What says Farmer to this? – What says Johnson?" Upon this he observed, "Sir, let Farmer answer for himself: *I* never engaged in this controversy. I always said, Shakspeare had Latin enough to grammaticise his English." '

'A clergyman, whom he characterised as one who loved to say little oddities, was affecting one day, at a Bishop's table, a sort of slyness and freedom not in character, and repeated, as if part of *The Old Man's Wish*, a song by Dr Walter Pope, a verse bordering on licentiousness. Johnson rebuked him in the finest manner by first showing him that he did not know the passage he was aiming at, and thus humbling him: "Sir, that is not the song: it is thus." And he gave it right. Then looking steadfastly on him, "Sir, there is a part of that song which I should wish to exemplify in my own life:

May I govern my passions with absolute sway." '

'Being asked if Barnes knew a good deal of Greek, he answered, "I doubt, Sir, he was *unoculus inter caecos*." '

'He used frequently to observe, that men might be very eminent in a profession, without our perceiving any particular power of mind in them in conversation. "It seems strange (said he), that a man should see so far to the right, who sees so short a way to the left. Burke is the only man whose common conversation corresponds with the general fame which he had in the world. Take up whatever topic you please, he is ready to meet you." '

'A gentleman, by no means deficient in literature, having discovered less acquaintance with one of the Classics than Johnson expected, when the gentleman left the room he observed, "You see, now, how little any body reads." Mr Langton happening to mention his having read a good deal in Clenardus's Greek Grammar, "Why, Sir (said he), who is there in this town who knows any thing of Clenardus but you and I?" And upon Mr Langton's mentioning that he had taken the pains to learn by heart the Epistle of St Basil, which is given in that Grammar as a praxis, "Sir (said he), I never made such an effort to attain Greek." '

'Of Dodsley's *Public Virtue: a Poem*, he said, "It was fine *blank* (meaning to express his usual contempt for blank verse): however, this miserable poem did not sell, and my poor friend Doddy said, Public Virtue was not a subject to interest the age." '

'Mr Langton, when a very young man, read Dodsley's *Cleone: a Tragedy* to him, not aware of his extreme impatience to be read to. As it went on he turned his face to the back of his chair, and put himself into various attitudes, which marked his uneasiness. At the end of an act, however, he said, "Come let's have some more, let's go into the slaughter-house again, Lanky. But I am afraid there is more blood than brains." Yet he afterwards said, "When I heard you read it, I thought higher of its power of language. When I read it myself, I was more sensible of its pathetic effect," and then paid it a compliment which many will think very extravagant. "Sir (said he), if Otway had written this play, no other of his pieces would have been remembered." Dodsley himself, upon this being repeated to him, said, "It was too much": it must be remembered, that Johnson always appeared not to be sufficiently sensible of the merit of Otway.'

'Snatches of reading (said he) will not make a Bentley or a Clarke. They are, however, in a certain degree advantageous. I would put a child into a library (where no unfit books are) and let him read at his choice. A child should not be discouraged from reading any thing that he takes a liking to, from a notion that it is above his reach. If that be the case, the child will soon find it out and desist; if not, he of course gains the instruction; which is so much the more likely to come, from the inclination with which he takes up the study.'

'Though he used to censure carelessness with great vehemence, he owned, that he once, to avoid the trouble of locking up five guineas, hid them, he forgot where, so that he could not find them.'

'A gentleman who introduced his brother to Dr Johnson, was earnest to recommend him to the Doctor's notice, which he did by saying, "When we have sat together some time, you'll find my brother grow very entertaining." – "Sir (said Johnson), I can wait." '

'When the rumour was strong that we should have a war, because the French would assist the Americans; he rebuked a friend with some asperity for supposing it, saying, "No, Sir, national faith is not yet sunk so low." '.

'In the latter part of his life, in order to satisfy himself whether his mental faculties were impaired, he resolved that he would try to learn a new language, and fixed upon the Low Dutch, for that purpose, and this he continued till he had read about one half of Thomas à Kempis; and finding that there appeared no abatement of his power of acquisition, he then desisted, as thinking the experiment had been duly tried. Mr Burke justly observed, that this was not the most vigorous trial, Low Dutch being a language so near to our own; had it been one of the languages entirely different, he might have been very soon satisfied.'

'Mr Langton and he having gone to see a Freemason's funeral procession, when they were at Rochester, and some solemn music being played on French-horns, he said, "This is the first time that I have ever been affected by musical sounds": adding, "that the impression made upon him was of a melancholy kind." Mr Langton saying, that this effect was a fine one, – JOHNSON. "Yes, if it softens the mind so as to prepare it for the reception of salutary feelings, it may be good. But inasmuch as it is melancholy *per se*, it is bad." '

'Goldsmith had long a visionary project, that some time or other when his circumstances should be easier, he would go to Aleppo, in order to acquire a knowledge as far as might be, of any arts peculiar to the East, and introduce them into Britain. When this was talked of in Dr Johnson's company, he said, "Of all men Goldsmith is the most unfit to go out upon such an inquiry, for he is utterly ignorant of such arts as we already possess, and consequently could not know what would be accessions to our present stock of mechanical knowledge. Sir, he would bring home a grinding-barrow, which you see in every street in London, and think that he had furnished a wonderful improvement." '

'Greek, Sir (said he), is like lace; every man gets as much of it as he can.'

'When Lord Charles Hay, after his return from America, was preparing his defence to be offered to the Court-Martial which he had demanded, having heard Mr Langton as high in expressions of admiration of Johnson, as he usually was, he requested that Dr Johnson might be introduced to him; and Mr Langton having mentioned it to Johnson, he very kindly and readily agreed; and being presented to his Lordship, while under arrest, by Mr Langton, he saw him several times; upon one of which occasions Lord Charles read to him what he had prepared, which Johnson signified his approbation of, saying, "It is a very good soldierly defence." Johnson said, that he had advised his Lordship, that as it was in vain to contend with those who were in possession of power, if they would offer him the rank of Lieutenant-General, and a government, it would be better judged to desist from urging his complaints. It is well known that his Lordship died before the trial came on.'[a]

'Johnson one day gave high praise to Dr Bentley's verses[1] in Dodsley's Collection, which he recited with his usual energy. Dr Adam Smith, who was present, observed in his decisive professorial manner, "Very well – very well."

[a] For 'trial came on' read 'sentence was made known'.

[1] Dr Johnson, in his Life of Cowley, says, that these are 'the only English verses which Bentley is known to have written'. I shall here insert them, and hope my readers will apply them.

Who strives to mount Parnassus' hill,
　And thence poetick laurels bring,
Must first acquire due force and skill,
　Must fly with swan's or eagle's wing.

Who Nature's treasures would explore,
　Her mysteries and arcana know;
Must high as lofty Newton soar,
　Must stoop as delving Woodward low.

'Who studies ancient laws and rites,
　Tongues, arts, and arms, and history;
Must drudge, like Seldon, days
　　　　　　　　　and nights,
And in the endless labour die.

Who travels in religious jars,
　(Truth mixt with errour, shades
　　　　　　　　　with rays);
Like Whiston, wanting pyx or stars,
　In ocean wide, or sinks or strays.

But grant our hero's hope, long toil
　And comprehensive genius crown,
All sciences, all arts his spoil,
　Yet what reward, or what renown?

Envy, innate in vulgar souls,
　Envy steps in and stops his rise,
Envy with poison'd tarnish fouls
　His lustre and his worth decries.

He lives inglorious or in want,
　To College and old books confin'd;
Instead of learn'd he's call'd pedant,
　Dunces advanc'd, he's left behind:
Yet left content a genuine Stoick he,
Great without patron, rich without
　　　　　　　　　　South Sea.

Johnson however added, "Yes, they are very well, Sir, but you may observe in what manner they are well. They are the forcible verses of a man of a strong mind, but not accustomed to write verse; for there is some uncouthness in the expression." 'ª

'Drinking tea one day at Garrick's with Mr Langton, he was questioned if he was not somewhat of a heretic as to Shakspeare; said Garrick, "I doubt he is a little of an infidel." – "Sir (said Johnson), I will stand by the lines I have written on Shakspeare, in my Prologue at the opening of your Theatre." Mr Langton suggested, that in the line

And panting Time toil'd after him in vain;

Johnson might have had in his eye the passage in *The Tempest*, where Prospero says of Miranda,

. . . She will outstrip all praise,
And make it halt behind her.

Johnson said nothing. Garrick then ventured to observe, "I do not think that the happiest line in the praise of Shakspeare." Johnson exclaimed (smiling) "Prosaical rogues; next time I write, I'll make both time and space pant." '¹

'It is well known that there was formerly a rude custom for those who were sailing upon the Thames, to accost each other as they passed in the most abusive language they could invent, generally, however, with as much satirical humour as they were capable of producing. Addison gives a specimen of this

---

ª Add this note: The difference between Johnson and Smith is apparent even in this slight instance. Smith was a man of extraordinary application, and had his mind crowded with all manner of subjects; but the force, acuteness, and vivacity of Johnson were not to be found there. He had book-making so much in his thoughts, and was so chary of what might be turned to account in that way, that he once said to Sir Joshua Reynolds, that he made it a rule when in company, never to talk of what he understood. Beauclerk had for a short time a pretty high opinion of Smith's conversation. Garrick, after listening to him for a while, as to one of whom his expectations had been raised, turned slyly to a friend, and whispered him, 'What say you to this? – eh? *flabby*, I think.'

1 I am sorry to see in the *Transactions of the Royal Society of Edinburgh*, Vol. II, 'An Essay on the Character of Hamlet', written, I should suppose, by a very young man, though called 'Reverend'; who speaks with presumptuous petulance of the first literary character of his age. Amidst a cloudy confusion of words (which hath of late too often passed in Scotland for *Metaphysics*), he thus ventures to criticise one of the noblest lines in our language: 'Dr Johnson has remarked, that "time toil'd after him in vain." But I should apprehend, that this is *entirely to mistake the character*. Time toils after *every great man*, as well as after Shakspeare. The *workings* of an ordinary mind *keep pace*, indeed, with time; they move no faster; *they have their beginning, their middle, and their end*; but superior natures can *reduce these into a point*. They do not, indeed, *suppress* them; but they *suspend*, or they *lock them up in the breast*.' The learned Society, under whose sanction such gabble is ushered into the world, would do well to offer a premium to any one who will discover its meaning.

ribaldry, in Number 383 of *The Spectator*, when Sir Roger de Coverley and he are going to Spring-garden. Johnson was once eminently successful in this species of contest; a fellow having attacked him with some coarse raillery, Johnson answered thus: "Sir, your wife, *under pretence of keeping a bawdy-house*, is a receiver of stolen-goods." One evening when he and Mr Burke and Mr Langton were in company together, and the admirable scolding of Timon of Athens was mentioned, this instance of Johnson's was quoted, and thought to have at least equal excellence.'

'As Johnson always allowed the extraordinary talents of Mr Burke, so Mr Burke was fully sensible of the wonderful powers of Johnson. Mr Langton recollects having passed an evening with both of them, when Mr Burke repeatedly entered upon topics which it was evident he would have illustrated with extensive knowledge and richness of expression; but Johnson always seized upon the conversation, in which, however, he acquitted himself in a most masterly manner. As Mr Burke and Mr Langton were walking home, Mr Burke observed that Johnson had been very great that night; Mr Langton joined in this, but added, he could have wished to hear more from another person (plainly intimating that he meant Mr Burke). "O, no (said Mr Burke), it is enough for me to have rung the bell to him."[a]

---

[a] *Second Edition.* – Read:

THE FOLLOWING ADDITIONAL COMMUNICATIONS BY MR LANGTON

'Beauclerk having observed to him of one of their friends, that he was awkward at counting money, "Why, Sir, said Johnson, I am likewise awkward at counting money. But then, Sir, the reason is plain; I have had very little money to count." '

'He had an abhorrence of affectation. Talking of old Mr Langton, of whom he said, "Sir, you will seldom see such a gentleman, such are his stores of literature, such his knowledge in divinity, and such his exemplary life"; he added, "and, Sir, he has no grimace, no gesticulation, no bursts of admiration on trivial occasion; he never embraces you with an overacted cordiality." '

'Being in company with a gentleman who thought fit to maintain Dr Berkeley's ingenious philosophy, that nothing exists but as perceived by some mind; when the gentleman was going away, Johnson said to him, "Pray, Sir, don't leave us; for we may perhaps forget to think of you, and then you will cease to exist." '

'Goldsmith, upon being visited by Johnson one day in the Temple, said to him with a little jealousy of the appearance of his accommodation, "I shall soon be in better chambers than these." Johnson at the same time checked him and paid him a handsome compliment, implying that a man of his talent should be above attention to such distinctions. – "Nay, Sir, never mind that: *nil te quaesiveris extra.*" '

'At the time when his pension was granted to him, he said with a noble literary ambition, "Had this happened twenty years ago, I should have gone to Constantinople to learn Arabic, as Pococke did." '

'As an instance of the niceness of his taste, though he praised West's translation of Pindar, he pointed out the following passages as faulty, by expressing a circumstance so minute as to detract from the general dignity which should prevail:

Down then from thy glittering *nail*,
Take, O muse, thy Dorian lyre.'

This year the Reverend Dr Franklin having published a translation of Lucian, inscribed to him the *Demonax* thus:

> To Dr SAMUEL JOHNSON, the Demonax of the present age, this piece is inscribed by a sincere admirer of his respectable talents,
>
> THE TRANSLATOR.

'When Mr Vesey was proposed as a member of the LITERARY CLUB, Mr Burke began by saying, that he was a man of gentle manners. "Sir," said Johnson, "you need say no more. When you have said a man of gentle manners, you have said enough." '

'The late Mr Fitzherbert told Mr Langton, that Johnson said to him, "Sir, a man has no more right to *say* an uncivil thing, than to *act* one; no more right to say a rude thing to another than to knock him down." '

'My dear friend Dr Bathurst (said he with a warmth of approbation) declared, he was glad that his father, who was a West-Indian planter, had left his affairs in total ruin, because, having no estate, he was not under the temptation of having slaves.'

'Richardson had little conversation, except about his own works, of which Sir Joshua Reynolds said he was always willing to talk, and glad to have them introduced. Johnson, when he carried Mr Langton to see him, professed that he could bring him out into conversation, and used this allusive expression, "Sir, I can make him *rear*." But he failed; for in that interview Richardson said little else than that there lay in the room a translation of his *Clarissa* into German.'[a]

'Once when somebody produced a newspaper in which there was a letter of stupid abuse of Sir Joshua Reynolds, of which Johnson himself came in for a share, – "Pray, said he, let us have it read aloud from beginning to end"; which being done, he with a ludicrous earnestness, and not directing his look to any particular person, called out, "Are we alive after all this satire!" '

'He had a strong prejudice against the political character of Secker, one instance of which appeared at Oxford, where he expressed great dissatisfaction, at his varying the old established toast, Church and King. "The Archbishop of Canterbury, said he (with an affected smooth smiling grimace), drinks, Constitution in Church and State." Being asked what difference there was between the two toasts, he said, "Why, Sir, you may be sure he meant something." Yet when the life of that prelate, prefixed to his sermons by Dr Porteus and Dr Stinton, his chaplains, first came out, he read it with the utmost avidity, and said, "It is a life well written, and that well deserves to be recorded." '

note continues overleaf

---

[a] A literary lady has favoured me with a characteristic anecdote of Richardson. One day at his country house at Northend, where a large company was assembled at dinner, a gentleman who was just returned from Paris, willing to please Mr Richardson, mentioned to him a very flattering circumstance – that he had seen his *Clarissa* lying on the King's brother's table. Richardson observing that part of the company were engaged in talking to each other, affected then not to attend to it; but by and by, when there was a general silence, and he thought that the flattery might be fully heard, he addressed himself to the gentleman, 'I think, Sir, you were saying something about,' – pausing in a high flutter of expectation. The gentleman provoked at his inordinate vanity, resolved not to indulge it, and with an exquisitely sly air of indifference answered, 'A mere trifle, Sir, not worth repeating.' The mortification of Richardson was visible, and he did not speak ten words more the whole day. Dr Johnson was present, and appeared to enjoy it much.

Though upon a particular comparison of Demonax and Johnson there does not seem to be a great deal of similarity between them; this Dedication is a just compliment from the general character given by Lucian of the ancient Sage, 'ἄριστον ὧν οἶδα ἐγὼ φιλοσόφων γενόμενον, the best philosopher whom I have ever seen or known.'

'Of a certain noble Lord, he said, "Respect him, you could not; for he had no mind of his own. Love him you could not; for that which you could do with him, every one else could." '

'Of Dr Goldsmith he said, "No man was more foolish when he had not a pen in his hand, or more wise when he had." '

'He told in his lively manner the following literary anecdote: "Green and Guthrie, an Irishman and a Scotchman, undertook a translation of Duhalde's history of China. Green said of Guthrie, that he knew no English, and Guthrie of Green, that he knew no French; and these two undertook to translate Duhalde's history of China. In this translation there was found – "the twenty-sixth day of the new moon". Now, as the whole age of the moon is but twenty-eight days, the moon, instead of being new, was nearly as old as it could be. The blunder arose from their mistaking the word *neuvieme*, ninth, for *nouvelle*, or *neuve*, new." '

'Talking of Dr Blagden's copiousness and precision of communication, Dr Johnson said, "Blagden, Sir, is a delightful fellow." '

'On occasion of Dr Johnson's publishing his pamphlet of 'The False Alarm', there came out a very angry answer (by many supposed to be by Mr Wilkes). Dr Johnson determined on not answering it; but, in conversation with Mr Langton, mentioned a particular or two, which if he *had* replied to it, he might perhaps have inserted. – In the answerer's pamphlet, it had been said with solemnity, "Do you consider, Sir, that a House of Commons is to the people as a creature is to its Creator?" To this question, said Dr Johnson, I could have replied, that – in the first place – the idea of a CREATOR must be such as that he has a power to unmake or annihilate his creature.

'Then it cannot be conceived that a creature can make laws for its CREATOR.'[a]

'Depend upon it, said he, that if a man *talks* of his misfortunes, there is something in them that is not disagreeable to him; for where there is nothing but pure misery, there never is any recourse to the mention of it.'

'A man must be a poor beast, that should read no more in quantity than he could *utter* aloud.'

'Imlac in *Rasselas*, I spelt with a *c* at the end, because it is less like English, which should always have the Saxon *k* added to the *c*.'[b]   *note continues overleaf*

[a] His profound adoration of the GREAT FIRST CAUSE was such as to set him above that 'Philosophy and vain deceit', with which men of narrow conceptions have been infected. I have heard him strongly maintain that 'what is right is not so from any natural fitness, but because GOD wills it to be right'; and it is certainly so, because he has predisposed the relations of things so, as that which he wills must be right. – BOSWELL.

[b] I hope the authority of the great Master of our language will stop that curtailing innovation, by which we see *critic*, *public*, &c., frequently written instead of *critick*, *publick*, &c. [With the passage of more than two hundred years since Boswell wrote this note, it is hoped that readers will pardon the adoption of the 'curtailing innovation' which Johnson disliked.]

In 1781 Johnson at last completed his *Lives of the Poets*, of which he gives this account: 'Sometime in March I finished the *Lives of the Poets*, which I wrote in my usual way, dilatorily and hastily, unwilling to work, and working with

---

'Many a man is mad in certain instances, and goes through life without having it perceived; – for example, a madness has seized a person, of supposing himself obliged literally to pray continually; had the madness turned the opposite way, and the person thought it a crime ever to pray, it might not improbably have continued unobserved.'

'He apprehended that the delineation of *characters* in the end of the first Book of the *Retreat of the Ten Thousand* was the first instance of the kind that was known.'

'Supposing (said he) a wife to be of a studious or argumentative turn, it would be very troublesome: for instance – if a woman should continually dwell upon the subject of the Arian heresy.'

'No man speaks concerning another, even suppose it be in his praise, if he thinks he does not hear him, exactly as he would, if he thought he was within hearing.'

' "The applause of a single human being is of great consequence." This he said to me with great earnestness of manner, very near the time of his decease, on occasion of having desired me to read a letter addressed to him from some person in the North of England; which when I had done, and he asked me what the contents were, as I thought being particular upon it might fatigue him, it being of great length, I only told him in general that it was highly in his praise; – and then he expressed himself as above.

'He mentioned with an air of satisfaction what Baretti had told him; that, meeting, in the course of his studying English, with an excellent paper in the *Spectator*, one of four that were written by the respectable Dissenting Minister Mr Grove of Taunton, and observing the genius and energy of mind that it exhibits, it greatly quickened his curiosity to visit our country; as he thought, if such were the lighter periodical essays of our authors, their productions on more weighty occasions must be wonderful indeed!'

'He observed once, at Sir Joshua Reynolds's, that a beggar in the street will more readily ask alms from a *man*, though there should be no marks of wealth in his appearance, than from even a well-dressed *woman*;[a] which he accounted for from the great degree of carefulness as to money, that is to be found in women; saying farther upon it, that, the opportunities in general that they possess of improving their condition are much fewer than men have; and adding, as he looked round the company, which consisted of men only, – there is not one of us who does not think he might be richer, if he would use his endeavour.'

'He thus characterised an ingenious writer of his acquaintance: "Sir, he is an enthusiast by rule." '

'*He may hold up that* SHIELD *against all his enemies*' – was an observation on Homer, in reference to his description of the shield of Achilles, made by Mrs Fitzherbert, wife to his friend Mr Fitzherbert of Derbyshire, and respected by Dr Johnson as a very fine one. He had in general a very high opinion of that lady's understanding.'

'An observation of Bathurst's may be mentioned, which Johnson repeated, appearing to acknowledge it to be well founded; namely, it was somewhat remarkable how seldom, on occasion of coming into the company of any new person, one felt any wish or inclination to see him again.'

---

[a] Sterne is of a direct contrary opinion. See his *Sentimental Journey*, Article, 'The Mystery'. – BOSWELL.

1 *Prayers and Meditations*, p. 190.

vigour and haste.'[1] In a memorandum previous to this, he says of them: 'Written I hope, in such a manner as may tend to the promotion of piety.'[2]

This is the work which of all Dr Johnson's writings will perhaps be read most generally, and with most pleasure. Philology and biography were his favourite pursuits, and those who lived most in intimacy with him, heard him upon all occasions, when there was a proper opportunity, take delight in expatiating upon the various merits of the English Poets; upon the niceties of their characters, and the events of their progress through the world which they contributed to illuminate. His mind was so full of that kind of information, and it was so well arranged in his memory, that in performing what he had undertaken in this way, he had little more to do than to put his thoughts upon paper, exhibiting first each Poet's life, and then subjoining a critical examination of his genius and works. But when he began to write, the subject swelled in such a manner, that instead of prefaces to each poet of no more than a few pages as he had originally intended,[3] he produced an ample, rich, and most entertaining view of them in every respect. In this he resembled Quintilian, who tells us, that in the composition of his Institutions of Oratory, '*Latius se tamen aperiente materia plus quam imponebatur oneris sponte suscepi.*' The booksellers, justly sensible of the great additional value of the copy-right, presented him with another hundred pounds, over and above two hundred, for which his agreement was to furnish such prefaces as he thought fit.

This was, however, but a small recompense for such a collection of biography, and such principles and illustrations of criticisms as, if digested and arranged in one system by some modern Aristotle or Longinus, might form a code upon that subject such as no other nation can show. As he was so good as to make me a present of the greatest part of the original, and indeed only manuscript of this admirable work, I have an opportunity of observing with wonder the correctness with which he rapidly struck off such glowing composition. He may be assimilated to the Lady in Waller, who could impress with 'Love at first sight':

> Some other nymphs with colours faint,
> And pencil slow may Cupid paint,
> And a weak heart in time destroy;
> She has a stamp and prints the boy.

---

2 Ibid. 174.

3 His design is thus announced in his *Advertisement*: 'The Booksellers having determined to publish a body of English Poetry, I was persuaded to promise them a Preface to the works of each author; an undertaking, as it was then presented to my mind, not very tedious or difficult.

'My purpose was only to have allotted to every poet an Advertisement, like that which we find in the French Miscellanies, containing a few dates, and a general character; but I have been led beyond my intention, I hope by the honest desire of giving useful pleasure.'

1 Thus: 'In the Life of Waller, Mr Nichols will find a reference to the *Parliamentary*

That he, however, had a good deal of trouble and some anxiety in carrying on the work, we see from a series of his notes to Mr Nichols, the printer,[1] whose variety of literary inquiry and obliging disposition, rendered him very useful to Johnson. Mr Steevens appears, from the papers in my possession, to have supplied him with some anecdotes and quotations; and I observe the fair hand of Mrs Thrale as one of his copyists of select passages.[a]

It is not my intention to dwell upon each of Johnson's *Lives of the Poets*, or attempt an analysis of their merits, which were I able to do it, would take up too much room in this work; yet I shall make a few observations upon some of them, and insert a few various readings.

The Life of COWLEY he himself considered as the best of the whole, on account of the dissertation which it contains on the *Metaphysical Poets*. Dryden,

History, from which a long quotation is to be inserted. If Mr Nichols cannot easily find the book, Mr Johnson will send it from Streatham.'

'Clarendon is here returned.'

'By some accident, I laid *your* note upon Duke up so safely, that I cannot find it. Your informations have been of great use to me. I must beg it again; with another list of our authors, for I have laid that with the other. I have sent Stepney's Epitaph. Let me have the revises as soon as can be. Dec. 1778.'

'I have sent Philips, with his Epitaphs, to be inserted. The fragment of a Preface is hardly worth the impression, but that we may seem to do something. It may be added to the Life of Philips. The Latin page is to be added to the Life of Smith. I shall be at home, to revise the two sheets of Milton. March 1, 1779.'

'Please to get me the last edition of Hughes's Letters; and try to get Dennis upon Blackmore, and upon Cato, and anything of the same writer against Pope. Our materials are defective.'

'As Waller professed to have imitated Fairfax, do you think a few pages of Fairfax would enrich our edition? Few readers have seen it, and it may please them. But it is not necessary.'

' "An account of the Lives and Works of some of the most eminent English Poets. By, &c." – "The English Poets, biographically and critically considered, by SAM. JOHNSON." – Let Mr Nichols take his choice, or make another to his mind. May, 1781.'

'You somehow forgot the advertisement for the new edition. It was not inclosed. Of Gay's letters I see not that any use can be made, for they give no information of any thing. That he was a member of the Philosophical Society is something; but surely he could be but a corresponding member. However, not having his Life here, I know not how to put it in, and it is of little importance.'

See several more in the *Gentleman's Magazine*, 1785. The Editor of that *Miscellany*, in which Johnson wrote for several years, seems justly to think that every fragment of so great a man is worthy of being preserved.

[a] Add: But he was principally indebted to my steady friend Mr Isaac Reed, of Staple-inn, whose extensive and accurate knowledge of English literary History I do not express with exaggeration, when I say it is wonderful; indeed his labours have proved it to the world; and all who have the pleasure of his acquaintance can bear testimony to the frankness of his communications in private society.

whose critical abilities were equal to his poetical, had mentioned them in one of his excellent prefatory discourses to his Plays,[a] but had barely mentioned them. Johnson has exhibited them at large, with such happy illustration from their writings, and in so luminous a manner, that indeed he may be allowed the full merit of novelty,[b] to have discovered to us as it were, a new planet in the poetical hemisphere.

It is remarked by Johnson, in considering the works of a poet,[1] that 'amendments are seldom made without some token of a rent'; but I do not find that this is applicable to prose. We shall see that though his amendments in this work are for the better, there is nothing of the *pannus assutus*; the texture is uniform, and indeed what has been there at first, is very seldom unfit to have remained.

Various readings[2] *in the Life of* COWLEY.

All [future votaries of] *that may hereafter pant for* solitude.

To conceive and execute the [agitation or perception] *pains and the pleasures* of other minds.

The wide effulgence of [the blazing] *a summer* noon.

In the Life of WALLER, Johnson gives a distinct and animated narrative of public affairs in that variegated period, with strong yet nice touches of character, and having a fair opportunity to display his political principles, does it with an unqualified manly confidence, and satisfies his readers how nobly he might have executed a *Tory History* of his country.

So easy is his style in these Lives, that I do not recollect more than three uncommon or learned words; one, when giving an account of the approach of Waller's mortal disease, he says, 'he found his legs grow *tumid*'; by using the expression his legs *swelled*, he would have avoided this; and there would have been no impropriety in its being followed by the interesting question to his physician, 'What that *swelling* meant?' Another, when he mentions that Pope had *emitted* proposals; when *published* or *issued*, would have been more readily understood; and a third, when he calls Orrery and Dr Delany, writers both undoubtedly *veracious*; when *true*, *honest*, or *faithful*, might have been used. Yet, it must be owned, that none of these are *hard* or *too big* words; that custom would make them seem as easy as any others; and that a language is richer and capable of more beauty of expression, by having a greater variety of synonimes.

His dissertation upon the unfitness of poetry for the awful subjects of our holy religion, though I do not entirely agree with him, has all the merit of originality, with uncommon force of reasoning.

---

[a] Delete 'one of'; and for 'prefatory discourses to his plays' read 'dedication of his Juvenal'.

[b] After 'novelty', insert 'and'.

1 Life of Sheffield.

2 The original reading is inclosed in brackets, and the present one is printed in italics.

Various readings in the Life of WALLER.

Consented to [the insertion of their names] *their own nomination.*

[After] *paying* a fine of ten thousand pounds.

Congratulating Charles the Second on his [coronation] *recovered right.*

He that has flattery ready for all whom the vicissitudes of the world happen to exalt, must be [confessed to degrade his powers] *scorned as a prostituted mind.*

The characters by which Waller intended to distinguish his writings are [elegance] *sprightliness* and dignity.

Blossoms to be valued only as they [fetch] *foretell* fruits.

Images such as the superficies of nature [easily] *readily* supplies.

[His] *Some* applications [are sometimes] *may be thought* too remote and unconsequential.

His images are [sometimes confused] *not always distinct.*

Against his Life of MILTON, the hounds of Whiggism have opened in full cry. But of Milton's great excellence as a poet, where shall we find such a blazon as by the hand of Johnson? I shall select only the following passage concerning *Paradise Lost*:

> Fancy can hardly forbear to conjecture with what temper Milton surveyed the silent progress of his work, and marked his reputation stealing its way in a kind of subterraneous current, through fear and silence. I cannot but conceive him calm and confident, little disappointed, not at all dejected, relying on his own merit with steady consciousness, and waiting without impatience, the vicissitudes of opinion, and the impartiality of a future generation.

Indeed, even Dr Towers, who may be considered as one of the warmest zealots of *The Revolution Society* itself, allows, that 'Johnson has spoken in the highest terms of the abilities of that great poet, and has bestowed on his principal poetical compositions, the most honourable encomiums.'[1]

---

1 See *An Essay on the Life, Character, and Writings of Dr Samuel Johnson*, London, 1787; which is very well written, making a proper allowance for the democratical bigotry of its author; whom I cannot however but admire for his liberality in speaking thus of my illustrious friend:

> He possessed extraordinary powers of understanding, which were much cultivated by study, and still more by meditation and reflection. His memory was remarkably retentive, his imagination uncommonly vigorous, and his judgement keen and penetrating. He had a strong sense of the importance of religion; his piety was sincere, and sometimes ardent; and his zeal for the interests of virtue was often manifested in his conversation and in his writings. The same energy which was displayed in his literary productions was exhibited also in his conversation, which was various, striking, and instructive; and perhaps no man ever equalled him for nervous and pointed repartees.
>
> His Dictionary, his moral Essays, and his productions in polite literature, will convey useful instruction, and elegant entertainment, as long as the language in which they are written shall be understood.

That a man, who venerated the Church and Monarchy as Johnson did, should speak with a just abhorrence of Milton as a politician, or rather as a daring foe to good polity, was surely to be expected; and to those who censure him, I would recommend his commentary on Milton's celebrated complaint of his situation, when by the lenity of Charles the Second, 'a lenity of which (as Johnson well observes) the world has had perhaps no other example; he, who had written in justification of the murder of his Sovereign, was safe under an *Act of Oblivion*.' No sooner is he safe than he finds himself in danger, *fallen on evil days and evil tongues, and with darkness and with danger compass'd round.* This darkness, had his eyes been better employed, had undoubtedly deserved compassion; but to add the mention of danger was ungrateful and unjust. He was fallen, indeed, on evil days; the time was come in which regicides could no longer boast their wickedness. But of *evil tongues*[a] to complain, required impudence at least equal to his other powers: Milton, whose warmest advocates must allow, 'that he never spared any asperity of reproach, or brutality of insolence.'

I have, indeed, often wondered how Milton, 'an acrimonious and surly Republican',[b] a man 'who in his domestic relations was so severe and arbitrary', and whose head was filled with the hardest and most dismal tenets of Calvinism, should have been such a poet; should not only have written with sublimity, but with beauty, and even gaiety; should have exquisitely painted the sweetest sensations of which our nature is capable; imaged the delicate raptures of connubial love; nay, seemed to be animated with all the spirit of revelry. It is a proof that in the human mind the departments of judgement and imagination, perception and temper, may sometimes be divided by strong partitions; and that the light and shade in the same character may be kept so distinct as never to be blended.[c]

In the Life of Milton, Johnson took occasion to maintain his own and the general opinion of the excellence of rhyme over blank verse, in English poetry, and quotes this apposite illustration of it by 'an ingenious critic', *that it seems to be verse only to the eye*.[1] The gentleman whom he thus characterises is (as he told Mr Seward) Mr Lock, of Norbury Park, in Surrey, whose knowledge and taste in the fine arts is universally celebrated; with whose elegance of manners the writer of the present work has felt himself much impressed, and to whose virtues a common friend, who has known him long, and is not much addicted to flattery, gives the highest testimony.

[a] After '*tongues*', read 'for Milton'.

[b] Johnson's Life of Milton.

[c] Add the following note: Mr Malone thinks it is rather a proof that he felt nothing of these cheerful sensations which he has described: that on these topics it is the *poet*, and not the *man*, that writes.

1 One of the most natural instances of the effect of blank verse happened to the late Earl of Hopeton. His Lordship observed one of his shepherds poring in the fields upon Milton's *Paradise Lost*; and, having asked him what book it was, the man answered, 'An't please your Lordship, this is a very odd sort of an author: he would fain rhyme, but cannot get at it.'

Various readings in the Life of MILTON.

I cannot find any meaning but this which [his most bigoted advocates] *even kindness and reverence* can give.

[Perhaps no] *scarcely any* man ever wrote so much, and praised so few.

A certain [rescue] *preservative* from oblivion.

Let me not be censured for this digression, as [contracted] *pedantic* or paradoxical.

Socrates rather was of opinion, that what we had to learn was how to [obtain and communicate happiness] *do good and avoid evil*.

Its elegance [who can exhibit?] *is less attainable*.

I could, with pleasure, expatiate upon the masterly execution of the Life of DRYDEN, which we have seen[1] was one of Johnson's literary projects at an early period, and which it is remarkable, that after desisting from it, from a supposed scantiness of materials, he should, at an advanced age, have performed so amply.

His defence of that great poet against the illiberal attacks upon him, as if his embracing the Roman Catholic communion had been a time-serving measure, is a piece of reasoning at once able and candid. Indeed, Dryden himself, in his 'Hind and Panther', hath given such a picture of his mind, that they who know the anxiety for repose as to the awful subject of our state beyond the grave, though they may think his opinion ill-founded, must think charitably of his sentiment,

> But, gracious GOD, how well dost thou provide
> For erring judgements an unerring guide!
> Thy throne is darkness in th' abyss of light,
> A blaze of glory that forbids the sight.
> O! teach me to believe thee thus conceal'd,
> And search no farther than thyself reveal'd;
> But Her alone for my director take,
> Whom thou hast promis'd never to forsake.
> My thoughtless youth was wing'd with vain desires;
> My manhood, long misled by wand'ring fires,
> Follow'd false lights; and when their glimpse was gone,
> My pride struck out new sparkles of her own.
> Such was I, such by Nature still I am;
> Be thine the glory, and be mine the shame.
> Good life be now my task: my doubts are done;
> What more could shock my faith than Three in One?

In drawing Dryden's character, Johnson has given, though I suppose unintentionally, some touches of his own. Thus, 'The power that predominated in his intellectual operations was rather strong reason than quick sensibility. Upon all occasions that were presented, he studied rather than felt;

1 See page 541.

and produced sentiments not such as Nature enforces, but meditation sup-plies. With the simple and elemental passions as they spring separate in the mind, he seems not much acquainted. He is, therefore, with all his variety of excellence, not often pathetic; and had so little sensibility of the power of effusions purely natural, that he did not esteem them in others.' – It may indeed be observed, that in all the numerous writings of Johnson, whether in prose or verse, and even in his tragedy, of which the subject is the distress of an unfortunate Princess, there is not a single passage that ever drew a tear.

Various readings in the Life of DRYDEN.

The reason of this general perusal, Addison has attempted to [find in] *derive from* the delight which the mind feels in the investigation of secrets.

His best actions are but [convenient] *inability of* wickedness.

When once he had engaged himself in disputation, [matter] *thoughts* flowed in on either side.

The abyss of un-ideal [emptiness] *vacancy*.

These, like [many other harlots] *the harlots of other men*, had his love though not his approbation.

He [sometimes displays] *descends to display* his knowledge with pedantic ostentation.

French words which [were then used in] *had then crept into* conversation.

The Life of POPE was written by Johnson *con amore*, both from the early possession which that writer had taken of his mind, and from the pleasure which he must have felt, in for ever silencing all attempts to lessen his poetical fame, by demonstrating his excellence, and pronouncing a triumphant apotheosis.[a] – 'After all this, it is surely superfluous to answer the question that has once been asked, Whether Pope was a poet? otherwise than by asking in return, If Pope be not a poet, where is poetry to be found? To circumscribe poetry by a definition, will only show the narrowness of the definer; though a definition which shall exclude Pope will not easily be made. Let us look round upon the present time, and back upon the past; let [us] enquire to whom the voice of mankind has decreed the wreath of poetry; let their productions be examined, and their claims stated, and the pretensions of Pope will be no more disputed.'

I remember once to have heard Johnson say, 'Sir, a thousand years may elapse before there shall appear another man with a power of versification equal to that of Pope.' That power must undoubtedly be allowed its due share in enhancing the value of his captivating composition.

Johnson, who had done liberal justice to Warburton in his edition of Shakspeare, which was published during the life of that powerful writer, with still greater liberality took an opportunity of paying the tribute due to him when he was no longer in 'high place,' but numbered with the dead.[1]

---

[a] For 'apotheosis' read 'eulogium'.

[1] Of Johnson's conduct towards Warburton, a very honourable notice is taken by the editor of *Tracts by Warburton, and a Warburtonian, not admitted into the Collection of their*

It seems strange, that two such men as Johnson and Warburton, who lived in the same age and country, should not only not have been in any degree of intimacy, but been almost personally unacquainted. But such instances, though we must wonder at them, are not rare. If I am rightly informed, after a careful inquiry, they never met but once, which was at the house of Mrs French, in London, well known for her elegant assemblies, and bringing eminent characters together. The interview proved to be mutually agreeable.

I am well informed, that Warburton said of Johnson, 'I admire him, but I cannot bear his style': and that Johnson being told of this, said, 'That is exactly my case as to him.' The manner in which he expressed his admiration of the

---

respective Works. After an able and 'fond, though not undistinguishing', consideration of Warburton's character, he says, 'In two immortal works, Johnson has stood forth in the foremost rank of his admirers. By the testimony of such a man, impertinence must be abashed, and malignity itself must be softened. Of literary merit, Johnson, as we all know, was a sagacious but a most severe judge. Such was his discernment, that he pierced into the most secret Springs of human actions; and such was his integrity, that he always weighed the moral characters of his fellow-creatures in the "balance of the sanctuary". He was too courageous to propitiate a rival, and too proud to truckle to a superior. Warburton he knew, as I know him, and as every man of sense and virtue would wish to be known – I mean, both from his own writings, and from the writings of those who dissented from his principles, or who envied his reputation. But, as to favours, he had never received or asked any from the Bishop of Gloucester; and, if my memory fails me not, he had seen him only once, when they met almost without design, conversed without much effort, and parted without any lasting impressions of hatred or affection. Yet, with all the ardour of sympathetic genius, Johnson has done that, spontaneously and ably, which, by some writers, had been before attempted injudiciously, and which, by others, from whom more successful attempts might have been expected, has not *hitherto* been done at all. He spoke well of Warburton, without insulting those whom Warburton despised. He suppressed not the imperfections of this extraordinary man, while he endeavoured to do justice to his numerous and transcendental excellencies. He defended him when living, amidst the clamours of his enemies; and praised him when dead, amidst the *silence of his friends.'*

Having availed myself of this editor's eulogy on my departed friend, for which I warmly thank him, let me not suffer the lustre of his reputation, honestly acquired by profound learning and vigorous eloquence, to be tarnished by a charge of illiberality. He has been accused of invidiously dragging again into light certain writings of a person respectable by his talents, his learning, his station, and his age, which were published a great many years ago, and have since, it is said, been silently given up by their author. But when it is considered that these writings were not *sins of youth*, but deliberate works of one well advanced in life, overflowing at once with flattery to a great man of great interest in the Church, and with unjust and acrimonious abuse of two men of eminent merit; and that, though it would have been unreasonable to expect an humiliating recantation, no apology whatever has been made in the cool of the evening, for the oppressive fervour of the heat of the day; no slight relenting indication has appeared in any note, or any corner of later publications; is it not fair to understand him as superciliously persevering? When he allows the shafts to remain in the wounds, and will not stretch forth a lenient hand, is it wrong, is it not generous to become an indignant avenger?

fertility of Warburton's genius and of the variety of his materials, was, 'The table is always full, Sir. He brings things from the north, and the south, and from every quarter. In his *Divine Legation*, you are always entertained. He carries you round and round, without carrying you forward to the point; but then you have no wish to be carried forward.' He said to the Reverend Mr Strahan, 'Warburton is perhaps the last man who has written with a mind full of reading and reflection.'

It is remarkable, that in the Life of Broome, Johnson takes notice of Dr Warburton's using a mode of expression which he himself used, and that not seldom, to the great offence of those who did not know him. Having occasion to mention a note, stating the different parts which were executed by the associated translators of the *Odyssey*, he says, 'Dr Warburton told me, in his warm language, that he thought the relation given in the not*e a lie*.' The language is *warm* indeed; and, I must own, cannot be justified in consistency with a decent regard to the established forms of speech. Johnson had accustomed himself to use the word *lie*, to express a mistake or an error in relation; in short, when the thing *was not so as told*, though the relator did not *mean* to deceive. When he thought there was intentional falsehood in the relator, his expression was, 'He *lies*, and he *knows* he *lies*.'

Speaking of Pope's not having been known to excel in conversation, Johnson observes, that 'traditional memory retains no sallies of raillery, or sentences of observation; nothing either pointed or solid, wise or merry; and that one apophthegm only is recorded.' In this respect, Pope differed widely from Johnson, whose conversation was, perhaps, more admirable than even his writings, however excellent. Mr Wilkes has, however, favoured me with one repartee of Pope, of which Johnson was not informed. Johnson, after justly censuring him for having 'nursed in his mind a foolish dis-esteem of Kings', tells us, 'yet a little regard shown him by the Prince of Wales melted his obduracy; and he had not much to say when he was asked by his Royal Highness, *how he could love a Prince, while he disliked Kings?*' The answer which Pope made, was, 'The young lion is harmless, and even playful; but when his claws are full grown he becomes cruel, dreadful, and mischievous.'

But although we have no collection of Pope's sayings, it is not therefore to be concluded, that he was not agreeable in social intercourse; for Johnson himself has been heard to say, that 'the happiest conversation is that of which nothing is distinctly remembered but a general effect of pleasing impression.' The late Lord Somerville,[1] who saw much both of great and brilliant life, told

---

1 Let me here express my grateful remembrance of Lord Somerville's kindness to me, at a very early period. He was the first person of high rank that took particular notice of me in the way most flattering to a young man, fondly ambitious of being distinguished for his literary talents; and by the honour of his encouragement made me think well of myself, and aspire to deserve it better. He had a happy art of communicating his varied knowledge of the world, in short remarks and anecdotes, with a quiet pleasant gravity, that was exceedingly engaging. Never shall I forget the hours which I enjoyed with him at his apartments in the Royal Palace of Holy-Rood House, and at his seat near Edinburgh, which he himself had formed with an elegant taste.

me, that he had dined in company with Pope, and that after dinner the *little man*, as he called him, drank his bottle of Burgundy, and was exceedingly gay and entertaining.

I cannot with-hold from my great friend a censure of at least culpable inattention, to a nobleman, who, it has been shown, behaved to him with uncommon politeness. He says, 'Except Lord Bathurst, none of Pope's noble friends were such as that a good man would wish to have his intimacy with them known to posterity.' This will not apply to Lord Mansfield, who was not ennobled in Pope's life-time; but Johnson should have recollected, that Lord Marchmont was one of those noble friends. He includes his Lordship along with Lord Bolingbroke, in a charge of neglect of the papers which Pope left by his will; when, in truth, as I myself pointed out to him, before he wrote that poet's life, the papers were 'committed to *the sole care and judgement* of Lord Bolingbroke, unless he (Lord Bolingbroke) shall not survive me'; so that Lord Marchmont had no concern whatever with them. After the first edition of the Lives, Mr Malone, whose love of justice is equal to his accuracy, made, in my hearing, the same remark to Johnson; yet he omitted to correct the erroneous statement. These particulars I mention, in the belief that there was only forgetfulness in my friend; but I owe this much to the Earl of Marchmont's reputation, who, were there no other memorials, will be immortalised by that line of Pope, in the verses on his Grotto:

> And the bright flame was shot through Marchmont's soul.

Various readings in the Life of POPE.

[Somewhat free] *sufficiently bold* in his criticisms.

All the gay [niceties] *varieties* of diction.

Strikes the imagination with far [more] *greater* force.

It is [probably] *certainly* the noblest version of poetry which the world has ever seen.

Every sheet enabled him to write the next with [less trouble] *more facility*.

'No man sympathizes with [vanity depressed] *the sorrows of vanity*.

It had been [criminal] *less easily excused*.

When he [threatened to lay down] *talked of laying down* his pen.

Society [is so named emphatically in opposition to] *politically regulated, is a state contra-distinguished from* a state of nature.

A fictitious life of an [absurd] *infatuated* scholar.

A foolish [contempt, disregard] *disesteem* of Kings.

His hopes and fears, his joys and sorrows [were like those of other mortals] *acted strongly upon his mind*.

Eager to pursue knowledge and attentive to [accumulate] *retain it*.

A mind [excursive] *active*, ambitious, and adventurous.

In its [noblest] *widest* searches still longing to go forward.

He wrote in such a manner as might expose him to few [neglects] *hazards*.

The [reasonableness] *justice* of my determination.

A [favourite] *delicious* employment of the poets.

More terrific and more powerful [beings] *phantoms* perform on the stormy ocean.

The inventor of [those] *this* petty [beings] *nation*.

The [mind] *heart* naturally loves truth.

In the Life of ADDISON we find an unpleasing account of his having lent Steele a hundred pounds, and 'reclaimed his loan by an execution'. In the new edition of the *Biographia Britannica*, the authenticity of this anecdote is denied. But Mr Malone has obliged me with the following note concerning it:

> Many persons having doubts concerning this fact, I applied to Dr Johnson to learn on what authority he asserted it. He told me, he had it from Savage, who lived in intimacy with Steele, and who informed him, that Steele told him the story with tears in his eyes. – Ben Victor, Dr Johnson said, likewise informed him of this remarkable transaction, from the relation of Mr Wilkes the comedian, who was also an intimate of Steele's. – Some, in defence of Addison, have said, that 'the act was done with the good-natured view of rousing Steele, and correcting that profusion which always made him necessitous.' – 'If that were the case (said Johnson), and that he only wanted to alarm Steele, he would afterwards have *returned* the money to his friend, which it is not pretended he did.' – 'This, too (he added), might be retorted by an advocate for Steele, who might allege, that he did not repay the loan *intentionally*, merely to see whether Addison would be mean and ungenerous enough to make use of legal process to recover it. But of such speculations there is no end: we cannot dive into the hearts of men; but their actions are open to observation.'
>
> I then mentioned to him that some people thought that Mr Addison's character was so pure, that the fact, *though true*, ought to have been suppressed. He saw no reason for this. 'If nothing but the bright side of characters should be shown, we should sit down in despondency, and think it utterly impossible to imitate them in *any thing*. The sacred writers (he observed) related the vicious as well as the virtuous actions of men; which had this moral effect, that it kept mankind from *despair*, into which otherwise they would naturally fall, were they not supported by the recollection that others had offended like themselves, and by penitence and amendment of life had been restored to the favour of Heaven.
>
> E. M.

March 15, 1782.

The last paragraph of this note is of great importance; and I request that my readers may consider it with particular attention. It will be afterwards referred to in this work.

Various readings in the Life of ADDISON.

[But he was our first great example] *He was, however, one of our earliest examples* of correctness.

And [overlook] *despise* their masters.

His instructions were such as the [state] *character* of his [own time] *readers* made [necessary] *proper.*

His purpose was to [diffuse] *infuse* literary curiosity by gentle and unsuspected conveyance [among] *into* the gay, the idle, and the wealthy.

Framed rather for those that [wish] *are learning* to write.

Domestic [manners] *scenes.*

In his Life of PARNELL, I wonder that Johnson omitted to insert an Epitaph which he had long before composed for that amiable man, without ever writing it down, but which he was so good as, at my request, to dictate me, by which means it has been preserved.

> *Hic requiescit* THOMAS PARNELL, *S. T. P.*
> *Qui sacerdos pariter et Poeta,*
> *Utrasque partes ita implevit,*
> *Ut neque sacerdoti suavitas poetae,*
> *Nec poetae sacerdotis sanctitas deesset.*

Various readings in the Life of PARNELL.

About three years [after] *afterwards.*

[Did not much want] *was in no great need of* improvement.

But his prosperity *did not last long* [was clouded by that which took away all his powers of enjoying either profit or pleasure, the death of his wife, whom he is said to have lamented with such sorrow, as hastened his end.][1]

His end, whatever was the cause, was now approaching.

In the Hermit, the [composition] *narrative,* as it is less airy, is less pleasing.

In the Life of BLACKMORE, we find that writer's reputation generously cleared by Johnson, from the cloud of prejudice which the malignity of contemporary wits had raised around it. In this spirited exertion of justice, he has been imitated by Sir Joshua Reynolds, in his praise of the architecture of Vanburgh.

We trace Johnson's own character in his observation on Blackmore's 'magnanimity as an author'. – 'The incessant attacks of his enemies, whether serious or merry, are never discovered to have disturbed his quiet, or to have lessened his confidence in himself.' Johnson, I recollect, once told me, laughing heartily, that he understood it had been said of him, 'He *appears* not to feel; but, when he is *alone*, depend upon it, he *suffers sadly.*' I am as certain as I can be of any man's real sentiments, that he *enjoyed* the perpetual shower of little hostile arrows, as evidences of his fame.

---

1 I should have thought that Johnson, who had felt the severe affliction from which Parnell never recovered, would have preserved this passage.

Various readings in the Life of BLACKMORE.

To [set] *engage* poetry [on the side] *in the cause* of virtue.

He likewise [established] *enforced* the truth of Revelation.

[Kindness] *benevolence* was ashamed to favour.

His practice, which was once [very extensive] *invidiously great.*

There is scarcely any distemper of dreadful name [of] which he has not [shown] *taught his reader* how [it is to be opposed] *to oppose.*

Of this [contemptuous] *indecent* arrogance.

[He wrote] *but produced* likewise a work of a different kind.

At least [written] *compiled* with integrity.

Faults which many tongues [were desirous] *would have made haste* to publish.

But though he [had not] *could not boast of* much critical knowledge.

He [used] *waited for* no felicities of fancy.

Or had ever elevated his [mind] *views* to that ideal perfection which every [mind] *genius* born to excel is condemned always to pursue and never overtake.

The [first great] *fundamental* principle of wisdom and of virtue.

Various readings in the Life of PHILIPS.

His dreaded [rival] *antagonist* Pope.

They [have not often much] *are not loaded with* thought.

In his translations from Pindar, he [will not be denied to have reached] *found the art of reaching* all the obscurity of the Theban bard.

Various readings in the Life of CONGREVE.

Congreve's conversation must surely have been *at least* equally pleasing with his writings.

It apparently [requires] *pre-supposes* a familiar knowledge of male characters.

Reciprocation of [similes] *conceits.*

The dialogue is quick and [various] *sparkling.*

Love for Love; a comedy [more drawn from life] *of nearer alliance to life.*

The general character of his miscellanies is, that they show little wit and [no] *little* virtue.

[Perhaps] *certainly* he had not the fire requisite for the higher species of lyric poetry.

Various readings in the Life of TICKELL.

[Longed] *long wished* to peruse it.

At the [accession] *arrival* of King George.

Fiction [unnaturally] *unskilfully* compounded of Grecian deities and Gothic fairies.

Various readings in the Life of AKENSIDE.

For [another] *a different* purpose.

[A furious] *an unnecessary* and outrageous zeal.

[Something which] *what* he called and thought liberty.

A [favourer of innovation] *lover of contradiction.*

Warburton's [censure] *objections.*

His rage [for liberty] *of patriotism.*

Mr Dyson with [a zeal] *an ardour* of friendship.

In the Life of LYTTELTON, Johnson seems to have been not favourably disposed towards that nobleman. Mrs Thrale suggests that he was offended by *Molly Aston's* preference of his Lordship to him.[1] I can by no means join the censure bestowed by Johnson on his Lordship, whom he calls 'poor Lyttelton', for returning thanks to the Critical Reviewers, for having 'kindly commended' his *Dialogues of the Dead.* Such 'acknowledgements (says my friend) never can be proper, since they must be paid either for flattery or for justice.' In my opinion, the most upright man, who has been tried on a false accusation, may, when he is acquitted, make a bow to his jury. And when those who, no matter by what right, are so much the arbiters of literary merit, as in a considerable degree to influence the public opinion, review an author's work, *placido lumine*, when I am afraid mankind in general are better pleased with severity, he may surely express a grateful sense of their civility.

Various readings in the Life of LYTTELTON.

He solaced [himself] *his grief* by writing a long poem to her memory.

The production rather [of a mind that means well than thinks vigorously] *as it seems of leisure than of study, rather effusions than compositions.*

His last literary [work] *production.*

[Found the way] *undertook* to persuade.

---

1 Let not my readers smile to think of Johnson's being a candidate for female favour; Mr Peter Garrick assured me, that he was told by a lady, that in her opinion Johnson was 'a very seducing man'. Disadvantages of person and manner may be forgotten, where intellectual pleasure is communicated to a susceptible mind; and that Johnson was capable of feeling the most delicate and disinterested attachment, appears from the following letter, which is published by Mrs Thrale, with some others to the same person, of which the excellence is not so apparent:

To Miss BOOTHBY.

January, 1755.

DEAREST MADAM – Though I am afraid your illness leaves you little leisure for the reception of airy civilities, yet I cannot forbear to pay you my congratulations on the new year; and to declare my wishes that your years to come may be many and happy. In this wish, indeed, I include myself, who have none but you on whom my heart reposes; yet surely I wish your good, even though your situation were such as should permit you to communicate no gratifications to, dearest, dearest Madam,

Your, &c.

SAM. JOHNSON.

As the introduction to his critical examination of the genius and writings of
YOUNG, he did Mr Herbert Croft, then a Barrister of Lincoln's-inn, now a
clergyman, the honour to adopt a Life of Young written by that gentleman,
who was the friend of Dr Young's son, and wished to vindicate him from
some very mistaken remarks to his prejudice. Mr Croft's performance was
subjected to the revision of Dr Johnson, as appears from the following note to
Mr John Nichols:

> This Life of Dr Young was written by a friend of his son. What is crossed
> with black is expunged by the author, what is crossed with red is expunged
> by me. If you find any thing more that can be well omitted, I shall not be
> sorry to see it yet shorter.

It has always appeared to me to have a considerable share of merit, and to
display a pretty successful imitation of Johnson's style. When I mentioned this to
a very eminent literary character, he opposed me vehemently, exclaiming, 'No,
no, it is *not* a good imitation of Johnson; it has all his pomp without his force; it
has all the nodosities of the oak without its strength.' This was an image so
happy, that one might have thought he would have been satisfied with it; but he
was not. And setting his mind again to work, he added, with exquisite felicity,
'It has all the contortions of the Sybil, without the inspiration.'

Mrs Croft very properly guards us against supposing that Young was a
gloomy man; and mentions, that 'his parish was indebted to the good-humour
of the author of the *Night Thoughts* for an Assembly and a Bowling-Green.' A
letter from a noble foreigner is quoted, in which he is said to have been 'very
pleasant in conversation'.

Mr Langton, who frequently visited him, informs me, that there was an air
of benevolence in his manner, but that he could obtain from him less
information than he had hoped to receive from one who had lived so much in
intercourse with the brightest men of what has been called the Augustan age of
England; and that he showed a degree of eager curiosity concerning the
common occurrences that were then passing, which appeared somewhat
remarkable in a man of such intellectual stores, of such an advanced age, and
who had retired from life with declared disappointment in his expectations.

An instance at once of his pensive turn of mind, and his cheerfulness of
temper, appeared in a little story which he himself told to Mr Langton, when
they were walking in his garden: 'Here (said he) I had put a handsome sun-
dial, with this inscription, *Eheu fugaces!* which (speaking with a smile) was sadly
verified, for by the next morning my dial had been carried off.'[a]

---

[a] Add this note: The Late Mr James Ralph told Lord Macartney, that he passed an
evening with Dr Young at Lord Melcombe's (then Mr Doddington) at Hammersmith.
The Doctor happening to go out into the garden, Mr Doddington observed to him,
on his return, that it was a dreadful night, as in truth it was, there being a violent storm
of rain and wind. 'No, Sir (replied the Doctor), it is a very fine night. THE LORD is
abroad.'

It gives me much pleasure to observe, that however Johnson may have casually talked, yet when he sits, as 'an ardent judge zealous to his trust, giving sentence', upon the excellent works of Young, he allows them the high praise to which they are justly entitled. The *Universal Passion* (says he) is indeed a very great performance – his distichs have the weight of solid sentiment, and his points the sharpness of resistless truth.'

But I was most anxious concerning Johnson's decision upon *Night Thoughts*, which I esteem as a mass of the grandest and richest poetry that human genius has ever produced; and was delighted to find this character of that work: 'In his *Night Thoughts* he has exhibited a very wide display of original poetry, variegated with deep reflections and striking allusions; a wilderness of thought, in which the fertility of fancy scatters flowers of every hue and of every odour. This is one of the few poems in which blank verse could not be changed for rhyme but with disadvantage.' And afterwards, 'Particular lines are not to be regarded, the power is in the whole, and in the whole there is a magnificence like that ascribed to Chinese plantation, the magnificence of vast extent and endless diversity.'

But there is in this Poem not only all that Johnson so well brings in view, but a power of the *Pathetic* beyond almost any example that I have seen. He who does not feel his nerves shaken, and his heart pierced by many passages in this extraordinary work, particularly by that most affecting one, which describes the gradual torment suffered by the contemplation of an object of affectionate attachment, visibly and certainly decaying into dissolution, must be of a hard and obstinate frame.

To all the other excellencies of *Night Thoughts* let me add the great and peculiar one, that they contain not only the noblest sentiments of virtue, and the immortality of the soul, but the *Christian Sacrifice*, the *Divine Propitiation*, with all its interesting circumstances, and consolations to 'a wounded spirit', solemnly and poetically displayed in such imagery and language, as cannot fail to exalt, animate, and soothe the truly pious. No book whatever can be recommended to young persons, with better hopes of seasoning their minds with *vital religion* than YOUNG's *Night Thoughts*.

In the Life of SWIFT, it appears to me that Johnson had a certain degree of prejudice against that extraordinary man, of which I have elsewhere had occasion to speak. Mr Thomas Sheridan imputed it to a supposed apprehension in Johnson, that Swift had not been sufficiently active in obtaining for him an Irish degree when it was solicited,[1] but of this there was not sufficient evidence; and let me not presume to charge Johnson with injustice, because he did not think so highly of the writings of this author, as I have done from my youth upwards. Yet that he had an unfavourable bias is evident, were it only from that passage in which he speaks of Swift's practice of saving, as, 'first ridiculous and at last detestable'; and yet after some examination of circumstances, finds himself obliged to own, that 'it will perhaps appear that he only liked one mode of expense better than another, and saved merely that he might have something to give.'

1 See pp. 68–69.

One observation which Johnson makes in Swift's life should be often inculcated: 'It may be justly supposed, that there was in his conversation what appears so frequently in his letters, an affectation of familiarity with the great, an ambition of momentary equality, sought and enjoyed by the neglect of those ceremonies which custom has established as the barriers between one order of society and another. This transgression of regularity was by himself and his admirers termed greatness of soul; but a great mind disdains to hold any thing by courtesy, and therefore never usurps what a lawful claimant may take away. He that encroaches on another's dignity puts himself in his power; he is either repelled with helpless indignity, or endured by clemency and condescension.'

Various readings in the Life of SWIFT.

Charity may be persuaded to think that it might be written by a man of *a* peculiar [opinions] *character*, without ill intention.

He did not [disown] *deny* it.

[To] *by* whose kindness it is not unlikely that he was [indebted for] *advanced to* his benefices.

[With] *for* this purpose he had recourse to Mr Harley.

Sharpe, whom he [represents] *describes* as 'the harmless tool of others' hate.'

Harley was slow because he was [irresolute] *doubtful*.

When [readers were not many] *we were not yet a nation of readers*.

[Every man who] *he that could say he* knew him.

Every man of known influence has so many [more] petitions [than] *which* he [can] *cannot* grant, that he must necessarily offend more than he [can gratify] *gratifies*.

Ecclesiastical [preferments] *benefices*.

Swift [procured] *contrived* an interview.

[As a writer] *In his works* he has given very different specimens.

On all common occasions he habitually [assumes] *affects* a style of [superiority] *arrogance*.

By the [omission] *neglect* of those ceremonies.

That their merits filled the world [and] *or that* there was no [room for] *hope of* more.

I have not confined myself to the order of the *Lives*, in making my few remarks. Indeed a different order is observed in the original publication, and in the collection of Johnson's Works. And should it be objected, that many of my various readings are inconsiderable, those who make the objection will be pleased to consider, that such small particulars are intended for those who are nicely critical in composition, to whom they will be an acceptable selection.

Spence's *Anecdotes*, which are frequently quoted and referred to in Johnson's *Lives of the Poets*, are in a manuscript collection, made by the Reverend Dr Joseph Spence, containing a number of particulars concerning eminent men. To each anecdote is marked the name of the person on whose authority it is mentioned. This valuable collection is the property of the Duke of Newcastle, who upon the application of Sir Lucas Pepys, was pleased to permit it to be put into the hands of Dr Johnson, who I am sorry to think made but an awkward

return. 'Great assistance (says he) has been given me by Mr Spence's Collection, of which I consider the communication as a favour worthy of public
acknowledgement'; but he has not owned to whom he was obliged; so that
the acknowledgement is unappropriated to his Grace.

While the world in general was filled with admiration of Johnson's *Lives of
the Poets*, there were narrow circles in which prejudice and resentment were
fostered, and from whence attacks of different sorts issued against him.[a] By
some violent Whigs he was arraigned of injustice to Milton; by some
Cambridge men of depreciating Gray; and his expressing with a dignified
freedom what he really thought of George, Lord Lyttelton, gave offence to
some of the friends of that nobleman, and particularly produced a declaration
of war against him from Mrs Montague, the ingenious Essayist on Shakspeare,
between whom and his Lordship a commerce of reciprocal compliments had
long been carried on. In this war the smaller powers in alliance with him were
of course led to engage, at least on the defensive, and thus I for one, was
excluded from the enjoyment of 'A Feast of Reason', such as Mr Cumberland
has described, with a keen, yet just and delicate pen, in his *Observer*. These
minute inconveniencies gave not the least disturbance to Johnson. He nobly
said, when I talked to him of the feeble, though shrill outcry which had been
raised, 'Sir, I considered myself as entrusted with a certain portion of truth. I
have given my opinion sincerely; let them show where they think me
wrong.'

While my friend is thus contemplated in the splendour derived from his last
and perhaps most admirable work, I introduce him with peculiar propriety as
the correspondent of WARREN HASTINGS, a man whose regard reflects dignity
even upon JOHNSON; a man, the extent of whose abilities was equal to that of
his power; and who, by those who are fortunate enough to know him in
private life, is admired for his literature and taste, and beloved for the candour,
moderation, and mildness of his character. Were I capable of paying a suitable
tribute of admiration to him, I should certainly not withhold it at a moment[1]
when it is not possible that I should be suspected of being an interested
flatterer. But how weak would be my voice after that of the millions whom he
governed. His condescending and obliging compliance with my solicitation, I
with humble gratitude acknowledge; and while by publishing his letter to me,
accompanying the valuable communication, I do eminent honour to my great
friend, I shall entirely disregard any invidious suggestions, that as I in some
degree participate in the honour, I have, at the same time, the gratification of
my own vanity in view.

[a] Add the following note: From this disreputable class, I except an ingenious, though
not satisfactory defence of HAMMOND, which I did not see till lately, by the favour of
its author, my amiable friend, the Reverend Mr Bevil, who published it without his
name. It is a juvenile performance, but elegantly written, with classical enthusiasm of
sentiment, and yet with a becoming modesty, and great respect for Dr Johnson.

1 January, 1791.

To James Boswell, Esq.

Park-lane, Dec. 2, 1790.

Sir – I have been fortunately spared the troublesome suspense of a long search, to which, in performance of my promise, I had devoted this morning, by lighting upon the objects of it among the first papers that I laid my hands on: my veneration for your great and good friend, Dr Johnson, and the pride, or I hope something of a better sentiment, which I indulged in possessing such memorials of his goodwill towards me, having induced me to bind them in a parcel containing other select papers, and labelled with the titles appertaining to them. They consist but of three letters, which I believe were all that I ever received from Dr Johnson. Of these, one, which was written in quadruplicate, under the different dates of its respective dispatches, has already been made public, but not from any communication of mine. This, however, I have joined to the rest; and have now the pleasure of sending them to you for the use to which you informed me it was your desire to destine them.

My promise was pledged with the condition, that if the letters were found to contain any thing which should render them improper for the public eye, you would dispense with the performance of it. You will have the goodness, I am sure, to pardon my recalling this stipulation to your recollection, as I should be loth to appear negligent of that obligation which is always implied in an epistolary confidence. In the reservation of that right I have read them over with the most scrupulous attention, but have not seen in them the slightest cause on that ground to with-hold them from you. But, though not on that, yet on another ground I own I feel a little, yet but a little, reluctance to part with them: I mean on that of my own credit, which I fear will suffer by the information conveyed by them, that I was early in the possession of such valuable instructions for the beneficial employment of the influence of my late station, and (as it may seem) have so little availed myself of them. Whether I could, if it were necessary, defend myself against such an imputation, it little concerns the world to know. I look only to the effect which these relics may produce, considered as evidences of the virtues of their author: and believing that they will be found to display an uncommon warmth of private friendship, and a mind ever attentive to the improvement and extension of useful knowledge, and solicitous for the interests of mankind, I can cheerfully submit to the little sacrifice of my own fame to contribute to the illustration of so great and venerable a character. They cannot be better applied, for that end, than by being entrusted to your hands. Allow me, with this offering, to infer from it a proof of the very great esteem with which I have the honour to profess, myself, Sir,

Your most obedient

And most humble servant,

Warren Hastings.

P.S. At some future time, and when you have no further occasion for these papers, I shall be obliged to you if you would return them.

The last of the three letters thus graciously put into my hands, and which has already appeared in public, belongs to this year; but I shall previously insert the two first in the order of their dates. They altogether form a grand group in my biographical picture.

To the Honourable WARREN HASTINGS, Esq.

SIR – Though I have had but little personal knowledge of you, I have had enough to make me wish for more; and though it be now a long time since I was honoured by your visit, I had too much pleasure from it to forget it. By those whom we delight to remember, we are unwilling to be forgotten; and therefore I cannot omit this opportunity of reviving myself in your memory by a letter which you will receive from the hands of my friend Mr Chambers;[1] a man, whose purity of manners and vigour of mind are sufficient to make every thing welcome that he brings.

That this is my only reason for writing, will be too apparent by the uselessness of my letter to any other purpose. I have no questions to ask; not that I want curiosity after either the ancient or present state of regions, in which have been seen all the power and splendour of wide-extended empire; and which, as by some grant of natural superiority, supply the rest of the world with almost all that pride desires, and luxury enjoys. But my knowledge of them is too scanty to furnish me with proper topics of enquiry; I can only wish for information, and hope that a mind comprehensive like yours will find leisure, amidst the cares of your important station, to enquire into many subjects of which the European world either thinks not at all, or thinks with deficient intelligence and uncertain conjecture. I shall hope, that he who once intended to increase the learning of the Persian language, will examine nicely the traditions and histories of the East; that he will survey the wonders of its ancient edifices, and trace the vestiges of its ruined cities; and that, at his return, we shall know the arts and opinions of a race of men, from whom very little has been hitherto derived.

You, Sir, have no need of being told by me, how much may be added by your attention and patronage to experimental knowledge and natural history. There are arts of manufacture practised in the countries in which you preside, which are yet very imperfectly known here, either to artificers or philosophers. Of the natural productions, animate and inanimate, we yet have so little intelligence, that our books are filled, I fear, with conjectures about things which an Indian peasant knows by his senses.

Many of those things my first wish is to see, my second to know by such accounts as a man like you will be able to give.

As I have not skill to ask proper questions, I have likewise no such access to great men as can enable me to send you any political information. Of the

---

1 Now Sir Robert Chambers, one of his Majesty's Judges in India.

agitations of an unsettled government, and the struggles of a feeble minis-try, care is doubtless taken to give you more exact accounts than I can obtain. If you are inclined to interest yourself much in public transactions, it is no misfortune to you to be so distant from them.

That literature is not totally forsaking us, and that your favourite lan-guage is not neglected, will appear from the book,[1] which I should have pleased myself more with sending, if I could have presented it bound; but time was wanting. I beg, however, Sir, that you will accept it from a man very desirous of your regard; and that if you think me able to gratify you by any thing more important, you will employ me.

I am now going to take leave, perhaps a very long leave, of my dear Mr Chambers. That he is going to live where you govern, may justly alleviate the regret of parting; and the hope of seeing both him and you again, which I am not willing to mingle with doubt, must at present, comfort as it can, Sir,

Your most humble servant,

SAM. JOHNSON.

March 30, 1774.

To the same.

SIR — Being informed that by the departure of a ship, there is now an opportunity of writing to Bengal, I am unwilling to slip out of your memory by my own negligence, and therefore take the liberty of remind-ing you of my existence, by sending you a book which is not yet made public.

I have lately visited a region less remote, and less illustrious than India, which afforded some occasions for speculation; what occurred to me, I have put into the volume,[2] of which I beg your acceptance.

Men in your station seldom have presents totally disinterested; my book is received, let me now make my request.

There is, Sir, somewhere within your government, a young adventurer, one Chauncy Lawrence, whose father is one of my oldest friends. Be pleased to show the young man what countenance is fit, whether he wants to be restrained by your authority, or encouraged by your favour. His father is now President of the College of Physicians, a man venerable for his knowledge, and more venerable for his virtue.

I wish you a prosperous government, a safe return, and a long enjoyment of plenty and tranquillity. I am, Sir,

Your most obedient

And most humble servant,

SAM. JOHNSON.

London, Dec. 20, 1774.

1 Jones's *Persian Grammar.*
2 *Journey to the Western Islands of Scotland.*

To the same.

Jan. 9, 1781.

SIR – Amidst the importance and multiplicity of affairs in which your great office engages you, I take the liberty of recalling your attention for a moment to literature, and will not prolong the interruption by an apology, which your character makes needless.

Mr Hoole, a gentleman long known, and long esteemed in the India-House, after having translated Tasso, has undertaken Ariosto. How well he is qualified for his undertaking he had already shown. He is desirous, Sir, of your favour in promoting his proposals, and flatters me by supposing that my testimony may advance his interest.

It is a new thing for a clerk of the India-House to translate poets – it is new for a Governor of Bengal to patronize learning. That he may find his ingenuity rewarded, and that learning may flourish under your protection, is the wish of, Sir,

Your most humble servant,

SAM. JOHNSON.

I wrote to him in February, complaining of having been troubled by a recurrence of the perplexing question of Liberty and Necessity – and mentioning that I hoped soon to meet him again in London.

To JAMES BOSWELL, Esq.

DEAR SIR – I hoped you had got rid of all this hypocrisy of misery. What have you to do with Liberty and Necessity? Or what more than to hold your tongue about it? Do not doubt but I shall be most heartily glad to see you here again, for I love every part about you but your affectation of distress.

I have at last finished my Lives, and have laid up for you a load of copy, all out of order, so that it will amuse you a long time to set it right. Come to me, my dear Bozzy, and let us be as happy as we can. We will go again to the Mitre, and talk old times over. I am, dear Sir,

Yours, affectionately,

SAM. JOHNSON.

March 14, 1781.

On Monday, March 19, I arrived in London, and on Tuesday, the 20th, met him in Fleet-street, walking, or rather indeed moving along; for his march is thus described in a very just and picturesque manner, in a short Life[1] of him

---

1 With this well-chosen motto:

> . . . From his cradle
> He was a SCHOLAR, and a ripe and good one:
> And to add greater honours to his age
> Than man could give him, he died fearing Heaven. SHAKSPEARE

published by Kearsley,[a] very soon after his death: 'When he walked the streets, what with the constant roll of his head, and the concomitant motion of his body, he appeared to make his way by that motion, independent of his feet.' That he was often much stared at while he advanced in this manner, may easily be believed; but it was not safe to make sport of one so robust as he was. Mr Langton saw him one day, in a fit of absence, by a sudden start, drive the load off a porter's back, and walk forward briskly, without being conscious of what he had done. The porter was very angry, but stood still, and eyed the huge figure with much earnestness, till he was satisfied that his wisest course was to be quiet, and take up his burthen again.

Our accidental meeting in the street after a long separation was a pleasing surprise to us both. He stepped aside with me into Falcon-court, and made kind inquiries about my family, and as we were in a hurry going different ways, I promised to call on him next day; he said he was engaged to go out in the morning. 'Early, Sir?' said I. JOHNSON. 'Why, Sir, a London morning does not go with the sun.'

I waited on him next evening, and he gave me a quantity of his original manuscript of his *Lives of the Poets*, which he had preserved for me.

I found that his friend, Mr Thrale, was now very ill, and had removed, I suppose by the solicitation of Mrs Thrale, to a house in Grosvenor-square. I was sorry to find him sadly changed in his appearance.

He told me I might now have the pleasure to see Dr Johnson drink wine again, for he had lately returned to it. When I mentioned this to Johnson, he said, 'I drink it now sometimes, but not socially.' The first evening that I was with him at Thrale's, I observed he poured a quantity of it into a large glass, and swallowed it greedily. Every thing about his character and manners was forcible and violent; there never was any moderation; many a day did he fast, many a year did he refrain from wine; but when he did eat, it was voraciously; when he did drink wine, it was copiously. He could practise abstinence, but not temperance.

Mrs Thrale and I had a dispute, whether Shakspeare or Milton had drawn the most admirable picture of a man.[1] I was for Shakspeare; Mrs Thrale for Milton; and upon a fair hearing, Johnson decided for my opinion.

---

[a] Omit 'published by Kearsley' from the text, and transfer to note before the words 'With this well-chosen motto (previous page).'

1 Shakspeare makes Hamlet thus describe his father:

> See what a grace was seated on this brow,
> Hyperion's curls, the front of Jove himself,
> An eye like Mars, to threaten and command,
> A station like the herald, Mercury,
> New lighted on a Heaven-kissing hill:
> A combination and a form indeed,
> Where every god did seem to set his seal,
> To give the world assurance of a man.

I told him of one of Mr Burke's playful sallies upon Dean Marlay. 'I don't like the Deanery of *Ferns*, it sounds so like a *barren* title.' – 'Dr *Heath* should have it'; said I. Johnson laughed, and condescending to trifle in the same mode of conceit, suggested Dr *Moss*.

He said, 'Mrs Montagu has dropt me. Now, Sir, there are people whom one should like very well to drop, but would not wish to be dropped by.' He certainly was vain of the society of ladies, and could make himself very agreeable to them when he chose it; Sir Joshua Reynolds agreed with me that he could. Mr Gibbon, with his usual sneer, controverted it, perhaps in resentment of Johnson's having talked with some disgust of his ugliness, which one should think a *philosopher* would not mind. Dean Marlay wittily observed, 'A lady may be vain when she can turn a wolfdog into a lap-dog.'

The Election for Ayrshire, my own county, was this spring tried upon a petition, before a Committee of the House of Commons. I was one of the Counsel for the sitting member, and took the liberty of previously stating different points to Johnson, who never failed to see them clearly, and to supply me with some good hints. He dictated to me the following note upon the registration of deeds:

All laws are made for the convenience of the community; what is legally done, should be legally recorded, that the state of things may be known, and that wherever evidence is requisite, a evidence may be had. For this reason, the obligation to frame and establish a legal register is enforced by a legal penalty, which penalty is the want of that perfection and plenitude of right which a register would give. Thence it follows, that this is not an objection merely legal; for the reason on which the law stands being equitable, makes it an equitable objection.

This (said he) you must enlarge on, when speaking to the Committee. You must not argue there, as if you were arguing in the schools; close reasoning will not fix their attention; you must say the same thing over and over again, in different words. If you say it but once, they miss it in a moment of inattention. It is unjust, Sir, to censure lawyers for multiplying words when they argue; it is *necessary* for them to multiply words.

His notion of the duty of a member of Parliament, sitting upon an election committee, was very high; and when he was told of a gentleman upon one of those committees, who read the newspapers part of the time, and slept the rest, while the merits of a vote were examined by the counsel, and as an excuse,

---

Milton thus portrays our first parent, Adam:

His fair large front and eye sublime declar'd
Absolute rule; and hyacinthin locks
Round from his parted forelock manly hung
Clust'ring, but not beneath his shoulders broad.

when challenged by the chairman for such behaviour, bluntly answered, 'I had made up my mind upon that case'; – Johnson, with an indignant contempt, said, 'If he was such a rogue as to make up his mind upon a case without hearing it, he should not have been such a fool as to tell it.' – 'I think (said Mr Dudley Long) the Doctor has pretty plainly made him out to be both rogue and fool.'

Johnson's profound reverence for the Hierarchy made him expect from Bishops the highest degree of decorum; he was offended even at their going to taverns; 'A bishop (said he) has nothing to do at a tippling-house. It is not indeed immoral in him to go to a tavern; neither would it be immoral in him to whip a top in Grosvenor-square. But, if he did, I hope the boys would fall upon him and apply the whip to *him*. There are gradations in conduct, there is morality – decency – propriety. None of these should be violated by a bishop. A bishop should not go to a house where he may meet a young fellow leading out a wench.' BOSWELL. 'But, Sir, every tavern does not admit women.' JOHNSON. 'Depend upon it, Sir, any tavern will admit a well-drest man and a well-drest woman; they will not perhaps admit a woman whom they see every night walking by their door, in the street. But a well-drest man may lead in a well-drest woman to any tavern in London. Taverns sell meat and drink, and will sell them to any body who can eat and can drink. You may as well say that a mercer will not sell silks to a woman of the town.'

He also disapproved of bishops going to routs, at least of their staying at them longer than their presence commanded respect. He mentioned a particular bishop. 'Poh (said Mrs Thrale), the Bishop of —— is never minded at a rout.' BOSWELL. 'When a Bishop places himself in a situation where he has no distinct character, and is of no consequence, he degrades the dignity of his order.' JOHNSON. 'Mr Boswell, Madam, has said it as correctly as could be.'

Nor was it only in the dignitaries of the Church that Johnson required a particular decorum and delicacy of behaviour; he justly considered that the clergy, as men set apart for the sacred office of serving at the altar, and impressing the minds of men with the awful concerns of a future state, should be somewhat more serious than the generality of mankind, and have a suitable composure of manners. A due sense of the dignity of their profession, independent of higher motives, will ever prevent them from losing their distinction in an indiscriminate sociality; and did such as affect this, know how much it lessens them in the eyes of those whom they think to please by it, they would feel themselves much mortified.

Johnson, and his friend, Beauclerk, were once together in company with several clergymen, who thought they should appear to advantage, by assuming the lax jollity of *men of the world*; which, as it may be observed in similar cases, they carried to noisy excess. Johnson, who they expected would be *entertained*, sat grave and silent for some time; at last, turning to Beauclerk, he said, by no means in a whisper, 'This merriment of parsons is mighty offensive.'

Even the dress of a clergyman should be in character, and nothing can be more despicable than conceited attempts at avoiding the appearance of the clerical order; attempts, which are as ineffectual as they are pitiful. Dr Porteus, now Bishop of London, in his excellent charge when presiding over the diocese of Chester, justly animadverts upon this subject; and observes of a reverend fop, that he 'can be but *half a beau.*'

Addison, in *The Spectator*, has given us a fine portrait of a clergyman, who is supposed to be a member of his *Club*; and Johnson has exhibited a model, in the character of Mr Mudge,[1] which has escaped the collectors of his works, but which he owned to me, and which indeed he showed to Sir Joshua Reynolds at the time when it was written. It bears the genuine marks of Johnson's best manner, and is as follows:

> The Reverend Mr *Zachariah Mudge*, Prebendary of Exeter, and Vicar of St Andrews in Plymouth; a man equally eminent for his virtues and abilities, and at once beloved as a companion and reverenced as a pastor. He had that general curiosity to which no kind of knowledge is indifferent or superfluous; and that general benevolence by which no order of men is hated or despised.
>
> His principles both of thought and action were great and comprehensive. By a solicitous examination of objections, and judicious comparison of opposite arguments, he attained what enquiry never gives but to industry and perspicuity, a firm and unshaken settlement of conviction. But his firmness was without asperity, for knowing with how much difficulty truth was sometimes found, he did not wonder that many missed it.
>
> The general course of his life was determined by his profession; he studied the sacred volumes in the original languages; with what diligence and success, his *Notes upon the Psalms* give sufficient evidence. He once endeavoured to add the knowledge of Arabic to that of Hebrew; but finding his thoughts too much diverted from other studies, after some time, desisted from his purpose.
>
> His discharge of parochial duties was exemplary. How his *Sermons* were composed, may be learned from the excellent volume which he has given to the public; but how they were delivered can be known only to those that heard them, for as he appeared in the pulpit, words will not easily describe him. His delivery, though unconstrained was not negligent, and though forcible was not turbulent; disdaining anxious nicety of emphasis, and laboured artifice of action, it captivated the hearer by its natural dignity, it roused the sluggish, and fixed the volatile, and detained the mind upon the subject, without directing it to the speaker.
>
> The grandeur and solemnity of the preacher did not intrude upon his general behaviour; at the table of his friends he was a companion communicative and attentive, of unaffected manners, of manly cheerfulness, willing to please, and easy to be pleased. His acquaintance was universally solicited, and his presence obstructed no enjoyment which religion did

1 See p. 194.

not forbid. Though studious he was popular; though argumentative he was modest; though inflexible he was candid; and though metaphysical yet orthodox.[1]

On Friday, March 30, I dined with him at Sir Joshua Reynolds's with the Earl of Charlemont, Sir Annesley Stewart, Mr Eliot, of Port-Eliot, Mr Burke, Dean Marlay, now Bishop of Clonfert, Mr Langton; a most agreeable day, of which I regret that every circumstance is not preserved; but it is unreasonable to require such a multiplication of felicity.

Mr Eliot, with whom Dr Walter Harte had travelled, talked to us of his *History of Gustavus Adolphus*, which he said was a very good book in the German translation. JOHNSON. 'Harte was excessively vain. He put copies of his book in manuscript into the hands of Lord Chesterfield and Lord Granville, that they might revise it. Now, how absurd was it to suppose that two such noblemen would revise so big a manuscript. Poor man! He left London the day of the publication of his book, that he might be out of the way of the great praise he was to receive; and he was ashamed to return, when he found how ill his book had succeeded. It was unlucky in coming out on the same day with Robertson's *History of Scotland*. His husbandry, however, is good.' BOSWELL. 'So he was fitter for that than for heroic history. He did well when he turned his sword into a ploughshare.'

Mr Eliot mentioned a curious liquor peculiar to his country, which the Cornish fishermen drink. They call it *Mahogany*; and it is made of two parts gin, and one part treacle, well beat together. I begged to have some of it made, which was done with proper skill by Mr Eliot. I thought it very good liquor; and said it was a counterpart of what is called *Athol Porridge* in the Highlands of Scotland, which is a mixture of whisky and honey. Johnson said, 'that must be a better liquor than the Cornish, for both its component parts are better.' He also observed, '*Mahogany* must be a modern name; for it was not long since the wood called mahogany was known in this country.' I mentioned his scale of liquors; – claret for boys – port for men – brandy for heroes. 'Then (said Mr Burke) let me have claret: I love to be a boy; to have the careless gaiety of boyish days.' JOHNSON. 'I should drink claret too, if it would give me that; but it does not: it neither makes boys men, nor men boys. You'll be drowned by it before it has any effect upon you.'

I ventured to mention a ludicrous paragraph in the newspapers, that Dr Johnson was learning to dance of Vestris. Lord Charlemont, wishing to excite him to talk, proposed, in a whisper, that he should be asked, whether it was true. 'Shall I ask him?' said his Lordship. We were, by a great majority, clear for the experiment. Upon which his Lordship very gravely and with a courteous air said 'Pray, Sir, is it true that you are taking lessons of Vestris?' This was risking a good deal, and required the boldness of a General of Irish

---

1 *London Chronicle*, May 2, 1769. This respectable man is there mentioned to have died on the 3d of April, that year, at Cofflect, the seat of Thomas Veale, Esq. in his way to London.

Volunteers to make the attempt. Johnson was at first startled, and in some heat answered, 'How can your Lordship ask so simple a question?' But immediately recovering himself, whether from unwillingness to be deceived, or to appear deceived, or whether from real good humour, he kept up the joke: 'Nay, but if any body were to answer the paragraph, and contradict it, I'd have a reply, and would say, that he who contradicted it was no friend either to Vestris or me. For why should not Dr Johnson add to his other powers a little corporeal agility? Socrates learnt to dance at an advanced age, and Cato learnt Greek at an advanced age. Then it might proceed to say, that this Johnson, not content with dancing on the ground, might dance on the rope; and they might introduce the elephant dancing on the rope. A nobleman[a] wrote a play, called *Love in a hollow Tree*. He found out that it was a bad one, and therefore wished to buy up all the copies, and burn them. The Duchess of Marlborough had kept one; and when he was against her at an election, she had a new edition of it printed, and prefixed to it, as a frontispiece, an elephant dancing on a rope; to show, that his Lordship's writing comedy was as awkward as an elephant dancing on a rope.'

On Sunday, April 1, I dined with him at Mr Thrale's, with Sir Philip Jennings Clerk and Mr Perkins, who had the superintendence of Mr Thrale's brewery, with a salary of five hundred pounds a year. Sir Philip had the appearance of a gentleman of ancient family, well advanced in life. He wore his own white hair in a bag of goodly size, a black velvet coat, with an embroidered waistcoat and very rich laced ruffles; which Mrs Thrale said were old fashioned, but which, for that reason, I thought the more respectable, more like a Tory; yet Sir Philip was then in opposition in parliament. 'Ah, Sir (said Johnson), ancient ruffles and modern principles do not agree.' Sir Philip defended the opposition to the American war ably and with temper, and I joined him. He said, the majority of the nation was against the ministry. Johnson. '*I*, Sir, am against the ministry; but it is for having too little of that of which opposition thinks they have too much. Were I minister, if any man wagged his finger against me, he should be turned out; for that which it is in the power of Government to give at pleasure to one or to another, should be given to the supporters of Government. If you will not oppose at the expense of losing your place, your opposition will not be honest, you will feel no serious grievance; and the present opposition is only a contest to get what others have. Sir Robert Walpole acted as I would do. As to the American war, the *sense* of the nation is *with* the ministry. The majority of those who can *understand* is with it; the majority of those who can only *hear* is against it; and as those who can only hear are more numerous than those who can understand, and opposition is always loudest, a majority of the rabble will be for opposition.'

This boisterous vivacity entertained us; but the fact really was, that those who could understand the best were against the American war, as almost every man now is, when the question has been coolly considered.

[a] Add: William, the first Viscount Grimston.

Mrs Thrale gave high praise to a gentleman of our acquaintance.[a] JOHNSON. 'Nay, my dear lady, don't talk so. Mr ——'s[b] character is very *short*. It is nothing. He fills a chair. He is a man of a genteel appearance, and that is all.[c] I know nobody who blasts by praise as you do: for whenever there is exaggerated praise, every body is set against a character. They are provoked to attack it. Now there is ——:[d] you praised that man with such disproportion, that I was incited to lessen him, perhaps more than he deserves. His blood is upon your head. By the same principle, your malice defeats itself; for your censure is too violent. And yet (looking to her with a leering smile) she is the first woman in the world could she but restrain that wicked tongue of hers – she would be the only woman could she but command that little whirligig.'

Upon the subject of exaggerated praise I took the liberty to say, that I thought there might be very high praise given to a known character which deserved it, and therefore it would not be exaggerated. Thus, one might say of Mr Edmund Burke, He is a very wonderful man. JOHNSON. 'No, Sir, you would not be safe if another man had a mind perversely to contradict. He might answer, Where is all the wonder? Burke is, to be sure, a man of uncommon abilities, with a great quantity of matter in his mind and a great fluency of language in his mouth. But we are not to be stunned and astonished by him. So you see, Sir, even Burke would suffer, not from any fault of his own, but from your folly.'

Mrs Thrale mentioned a gentleman who had acquired a fortune of four thousand a year in trade, but was absolutely miserable, because he could not talk in company; so miserable, that he was impelled to lament his situation in the street to ——, whom he hates, and who he knows despises him. 'I am a most unhappy man (said he). I am invited to conversations. I go to conversations; but, alas! I have no conversation.' JOHNSON. 'Man commonly cannot be successful in different ways. This gentleman has spent, in getting four thousand pounds a year, the time in which he might have learnt to talk; and now he cannot talk.' Mr Perkins made a shrewd and droll remark: 'If he had got his four thousand a year as a mountebank, he might have learnt to talk at the same time that he was getting his fortune.'

a For 'gentleman of our acquaintance' read 'Mr Dudley Long (now North)'.

b For 'Mr ——'s' read 'Mr Long's'.

c Here Johnson condescended to play upon the words *Long* and *short*. But little did he know that, owing to Mr Long's reserve in his presence, he was talking thus of a gentleman distinguished amongst his acquaintance, for acuteness of wit; one to whom I think the French expression, '*Il petille d'esprit*,' is particularly suited. He has gratified me by mentioning that he heard Dr Johnson say, 'Sir, if I were to lose Boswell, it would be a limb amputated.'

d For '——' read 'Pepys'; William Weller Pepys, Esq. one of the Masters in the High Court of Chancery, and well known in polite circles. My acquaintance with him is not sufficient to enable me to speak of him from my own judgement. But I know that both at Eton and Oxford he was the intimate friend of the late Sir James Macdonald, the *Marcellus* of Scotland, whose extraordinary talents, learning, and virtues, will ever be remembered with admiration and regret.

Some other gentlemen came in. The conversation concerning the person whose character Dr Johnson had treated so slightingly, as he did not know his merit, was resumed. Mrs Thrale said, 'You think so of him, Sir, because he is quiet, and does not exert himself with force. You'll be saying the same thing of Mr —— there, who sits as quiet – .' This was not well bred; and Johnson did not let it pass without correction. 'Nay, Madam, what right have you to talk thus? Both Mr —— and I have reason to take it ill. *You* may talk so of Mr ——: but why do you make *me* do it? Have I said any thing against Mr ——? You have *set* him, that I might shoot him: but I have not shot him.'

One of the gentlemen said, he had seen three folio volumes of Dr Johnson's sayings collected by me. 'I must put you right, Sir (said I); for I am very exact in authenticity. You could not see folio volumes, for I have none: you might have seen some in quarto and octavo. This is inattention which one should guard against.' JOHNSON. 'Sir, it is a want of concern about veracity. He does not know that he saw *any* volumes. If he had seen them he could have remembered their size.'

Mr Thrale appeared very lethargic to-day. I saw him again on Monday evening, at which time he was not thought to be in immediate danger; but early in the morning of Wednesday the 4th, he expired. Johnson was in the house, and thus mentions the event: 'I felt almost the last flutter of his pulse, and looked for the last time upon the face that for fifteen years had never been turned upon me but with respect and benignity.'[1] Upon that day there was a *Call* of the LITERARY CLUB; but Johnson apologised for his absence by the following note:

> MR JOHNSON knows that Sir Joshua Reynolds and the other Gentlemen will excuse his incompliance with the Call, when they are told that Mr Thrale died this morning.
> Wednesday.

Mr Thrale's death was a very essential loss to Johnson, who, although he did not foresee all that afterwards happened, was sufficiently convinced that the comforts which Mr Thrale's family afforded him would now in a great measure cease. He, however, continued to show a kind attention to his widow and children as long as it was acceptable; and he took upon him, with a very earnest concern, the office of one of his executors, the importance of which seemed greater than usual to him, from his circumstances having been always such that he had scarcely any share in the real business of life. His friends of the CLUB were in hopes that Mr Thrale might have made a liberal provision for him for his life, which, as Mr Thrale left no son, and a very large fortune, it would have been highly to his honour to have done; and, considering Dr Johnson's age, could not have been of long duration: but he bequeathed him only two hundred pounds, which was the legacy given to each of his executors. I could not but be somewhat diverted by hearing Johnson talk in a pompous manner of his new office, and particularly of the

---

1 *Prayers and Meditations*, p. 191.

concerns of the brewery, which it was at last resolved should be sold. Lord Lucan tells a very good story, which, if not precisely exact, is certainly characteristical: that when the sale of Thrale's brewery was going forward, Johnson appeared bustling about, with an ink-horn and pen in his button-hole, like an exciseman; and on being asked what he really considered to be the value of the property which was to be disposed of, answered, 'We are not here to sell a parcel of boilers and vats, but the potentiality of growing rich, beyond the dreams of avarice.'

On Friday, April 6, he carried me to dine at a club, which, at his desire, had been lately formed at the Queen's Arms, in St Paul's Church-yard. He told Mr Hoole, that he wished to have a *City Club*, and asked him to collect one; but, said he, 'Don't let them be *patriots*.' The company today were very sensible well-behaved men. I have preserved only two particulars of his conversation. He said, he was glad Lord George Gordon had escaped, rather than that a precedent should be established for hanging a man for *constructive treason*; which, in consistency with his true, manly, constitutional Toryism, he considered would be a dangerous engine of arbitrary power. And upon its being mentioned that an opulent and very indolent Scotch nobleman, who totally resigned the management of his affairs to a man of knowledge and abilities, had claimed some merit by saying, 'The next best thing to managing a man's own affairs well, is being sensible of incapacity, and not attempting it, but having full confidence in one who can do it'; JOHNSON. 'Nay, Sir, this is paltry. There is a middle course. Let a man give application, and depend upon it he will soon get above a despicable state of helplessness, and attain the power of acting for himself.'

On Saturday, April 7, I dined with him at Mr Hoole's, with Governor Bourchier and Captain Orme, both of whom had been long in the East-Indies; and being men of good sense and observation, were very entertaining. Johnson defended the oriental regulation of different *casts* of men, which was objected to as totally destructive of the hopes of rising in society by personal merit. He showed that there was a *principle* in it sufficiently plausible by analogy. 'We see (said he) in metals that there are different species, and so likewise in animals, though one species may not differ very widely from another, as in the species of dogs – the cur, the spaniel, the mastiff. The Bramins are the mastiffs of mankind.'

On Thursday, April 12, I dined with him at a Bishop's, where were Sir Joshua Reynolds, Mr Berrenger, and some more company. He had dined the day before at another Bishop's. I have unfortunately recorded none of his conversation at the Bishop's where we dined together: but I have preserved his ingenious defence of his dining twice abroad in Passion-week; a laxity, in which I am convinced he would not have indulged himself at the time when he wrote his solemn paper in *The Rambler*, upon that awful season. It appeared to me, that by being much more in company, and enjoying more luxurious living, he had contracted a keener relish of pleasure, and was consequently less rigorous in his religious rites. This he would not acknowledge; but he reasoned, with admirable sophistry, as follows: 'Why, Sir, a Bishop's calling company together in this week, is, to use the vulgar phrase, not *the thing*. But you must consider laxity is a bad thing; but preciseness is also a bad thing; and your general character may be more hurt by preciseness than by dining with a Bishop in Passion-week. There might be a handle for reflection. It might be said, "He refused to dine with a Bishop in Passion-week, but was three Sundays absent from church." ' BOSWELL. 'Very true, Sir. But suppose a man to be uniformly of good conduct, would it not be better that he should refuse to dine with a Bishop in this week, and so not encourage a bad practice by his example?' JOHNSON. 'Why, Sir, you are to consider whether you might not do more harm by lessening the influence of a Bishop's character by your disapprobation in refusing him, than by going to him.'

To Mrs LUCY PORTER, in Lichfield.

Dear Madam – Life is full of troubles. I have just lost my dear friend Thrale. I hope he is happy; but I have had a great loss. I am otherwise pretty well. I require some care[a] myself, but that care is not ineffectual; and when I am out of order I think it often my own fault.

The spring is now making quick advances. As it is the season in which the whole world is enlivened and invigorated, I hope that both you and I shall partake of its benefits. My desire is to see Lichfield; but being left executor to my friend, I know not whether I can be spared; but I will try, for it is now long since we saw one another, and how little we can promise ourselves many more interviews, we are taught by hourly examples of mortality. Let us try to live so as that mortality may not be an evil. Write to me soon, my dearest; your letters will give me great pleasure.

I am sorry that Mr Porter has not had his box; but by sending it to Mr Mathias, who very readily undertook its conveyance, I did the best I could, and perhaps before now he has it.

Be so kind as to make my compliments to my friends; I have a great value for their kindness, and hope to enjoy it before summer is past. Do write to me. I am, dearest love,

Your most humble servant,

SAM. JOHNSON.

London, April 12, 1781.

On Friday, April 13, being Good-Friday, I went to St Clement's church with him, as usual. There I saw again his old fellow-collegian, Edwards, to whom I said, 'I think, Sir, Dr Johnson and you meet only at church.' – 'Sir (said he), it is the best place we can meet in except Heaven, and I hope we shall meet there too.' Dr Johnson told me that there was very little communication between Edwards and him, after their unexpected renewal of acquaintance. 'But (said he, smiling) he met me once, and said, "I am told you

---

a

´ After 'care' read 'of'.

have written a very pretty book called *The Rambler*." I was unwilling that he should leave the world in total darkness, and sent him a set.'

Mr Berrenger visited him to-day, and was very pleasing. We talked of an evening society for conversation at a house in town, of which we were all members, but of which Johnson said, 'It will never do, Sir. There is nothing served about there, neither tea, nor coffee, nor lemonade, nor any thing whatever; and depend upon it, Sir, a man does not love to go to a place from whence he comes out exactly as he went in.' I endeavoured for argument's sake, to maintain that men of learning and talents might have very good intellectual society, without the aid of any little gratifications of the senses. Berrenger joined with Johnson, and said that without these any meeting would be dull and insipid. He would therefore have all the slight refreshments; nay, it would not be amiss to have some cold meat, and a bottle of wine upon a sideboard. 'Sir (said Johnson to me, with an air of triumph), Mr Berrenger knows the world. Every body loves to have good things furnished to them without any trouble. I told Mrs Thrale once, that as she did not choose to have card-tables, she should have a profusion of the best sweet-meats, and she would be sure to have company enough come to her.' The event[a] proved the justice of Johnson's opinion, as to the impracticability of getting people to meet, when they know there is absolutely nothing to touch the palate; for this Society, though held at the house of a person deservedly much esteemed, and composed of very eminent men, could not be preserved from gradual decay.

On Sunday, April 15, being Easter-day, after solemn worship in St Paul's church, I found him alone; Dr Scott, of the Commons, came. He talked of its having been said, that Addison wrote some of his best papers in *The Spectator*, when warm with wine. Dr Johnson did not seem willing to admit this. Dr Scott, as a confirmation of it related, that Blackstone[b] composed his *Commentaries* with a bottle of port before him.[c]

I told him, that in a company where I had lately been, a desire was expressed to know his authority for the shocking story of Addison's sending an execution into Steele's house. Sir (said he), it is generally known, it is known to all who are acquainted with the literary history of that period. It is as well known, as that he wrote *Cato*.' Mr Thomas Sheridan once defended Addison to me, by alleging that he did it in order to cover Steele's goods from other creditors, who were going to seize them.[d]

---

[a] Delete 'The event,' and all the remainder of that paragraph, and read as follows: 'I agreed with my illustrious friend upon this subject; for it has pleased GOD to make man a composite animal, and where there is nothing to refresh the body, the mind will languish.'

[b] After 'Blackstone,' read 'a sober man.'

[c] After 'him,' read 'and found his mind invigorated and supported in the fatigue of his great work by a temperate use of it.'

[d] Add this note: See this explained, p. 776.

We talked of the difference between the mode of education at Oxford, and that in the Colleges, where instruction is chiefly conveyed by lectures. JOHNSON. 'Lectures were once useful but now, when all can read, and books are so numerous, lectures are unnecessary. If your attention fails, and you miss a part of a lecture, it is lost, you cannot go back as you do upon a book.' Dr Scott agreed with him. 'But yet (said I), Dr Scott, you yourself gave lectures at Oxford.' He smiled. 'You laughed (then said I) at those who came to you.'

Dr Scott left us, and soon afterwards we went to dinner. Our company consisted of Mrs Williams, Mrs Desmoulins, Mr Levett, Mr Allen, the printer, and Mrs Hall, sister of the Reverend Mr John Wesley, and resembling him, as I thought, both in figure and manner. Johnson produced now, for the first time, some handsome silver salvers, which he told me he had bought fourteen years ago; so it was a great day. I was not a little amused by observing Allen perpetually struggling to talk in the manner of Johnson, like the little frog in the fable, blowing himself up to resemble the stately ox.

I mentioned a kind of religious Robinhood Society, which met every Sunday evening, at Coachmaker's-hall, for free debate; and that the subject for this night was, the text which relates, with other miracles, which happened at our SAVIOUR's death, 'And the graves were opened, and many bodies of the saints which slept arose, and came out of the graves after his resurrection, and went into the holy city, and appeared unto many.' Mrs Hall said it was a very curious subject, and she should like to hear it discussed. JOHNSON. (somewhat warmly) 'One would not go to such a place to hear it – one would not be seen in such a place – to give countenance to such a meeting.' I, however, resolved that I would go. 'But, Sir (said she to Johnson), I should like to hear you discuss it.' He seemed reluctant to engage in it. She talked of the resurrection of the human race in general, and maintained that we shall be raised with the same bodies. JOHNSON. 'Nay, Madam, we see that it is not to be the same body; for the Scripture uses the illustration of grain sown, and we know that the grain which grows is not the same with what is sown. You cannot suppose that we shall rise with a diseased body; it is enough if there be such a sameness as to distinguish identity of person.' She seemed desirous of knowing more, but he left the question in obscurity.

Of apparitions, he observed, 'A total disbelief of them is adverse to the opinion of the existence of the soul between death and the last day; the question simply is, whether departed spirits ever have the power of making themselves perceptible to us; a man who thinks he has seen an apparition, can only be convinced himself; his authority will not convince another, and his conviction, if rational, must be founded on being told something which cannot be known but by supernatural means.'

He mentioned a thing as not unfrequent, of which I had never heard before – being *called*, that is, hearing one's name pronounced by the voice of a known person at a great distance, far beyond the possibility of being reached by any sound, uttered by human organs. 'An acquaintance, on whose veracity I can depend, told me, that walking home one evening to Kilmarnock, he heard himself called from a wood, by the voice of a brother who had gone to America;

and the next packet brought accounts of that brother's death.' Macbean asserted that this inexplicable calling was a thing very well known. Dr Johnson said, that one day at Oxford, as he was turning the key of his chamber, he heard his mother distinctly call *Sam*. She was then at Lichfield; but nothing ensued. This phenomenon is, I think, as wonderful as any other mysterious fact, which many people are very slow to believe, or rather, indeed, reject with an obstinate contempt.

Some time after this, upon his making a remark which escaped my attention, Mrs Williams and Mrs Hall were both together striving to answer him. He grew angry, and called out loudly, 'Nay, when you both speak at once it is intolerable.' But checking himself, and softening, he said, 'This one may say, though you *are* ladies.' Then he brightened into gay humour, and addressed them in the words of one of the songs in *The Beggar's Opera*,

> But two at a time there's no mortal can bear.

'What, Sir (said I), are you going to turn Captain Macheath?' There was something as pleasantly ludicrous in this scene as can be imagined. The contrast between Macheath, Polly, and Lucy – and Dr Samuel Johnson, blind, peevish Mrs Williams, and lean, lank, preaching Mrs Hall, was exquisite.

I stole away to Coachmaker's-hall, and heard the difficult text of which we had talked, discussed with great decency, and some intelligence, by several speakers. There was a difference of opinion as to the appearance of ghosts in modern times, though the arguments for it, supported by Mr Addison's authority, preponderated. The immediate subject of debate was embarrassed by the *bodies* of the saints having been said to rise, and by the question what became of them afterwards; did they return again to their graves? Or were they translated to Heaven? Only one evangelist mentions the fact,[1] and the commentators whom I have looked at, do not make the passage clear. There is, however, no occasion for our understanding it farther, than to know that it was one of the extraordinary manifestations of divine power, which accompanied the most important event that ever happened.

On Friday, April 20, I spent with him one of the happiest days that I remember to have enjoyed in the whole course of my life. Mrs Garrick, whose grief for the loss of her husband was, I believe, as sincere as wounded affection and admiration could produce, had this day, for the first time since his death, a select party of his friends to dine with her. The company was Miss Hannah More. who lived with her, and whom she called her Chaplain; Mrs Boscawen,[a] Mrs Elizabeth Carter, Sir Joshua Reynolds, Dr Burney, Dr Johnson, and myself. We found ourselves very elegantly entertained at her house in the Adelphi, where I have passed many a pleasing hour with him 'who gladdened life'. She looked very well, talked of her husband with complacency, and while she cast her eyes on his portrait, which hung over

---

1 St Matthew, ch. xxvii, 52, 53.
a Add a note: See page 687.

the chimney-piece, said, that 'death was now the most agreeable object to her.' The very semblance of David Garrick was cheering. Mr Beauclerk, with happy propriety, inscribed under that fine portrait of him, which by Lady Diana's kindness is now the property of my friend Mr Langton, the following passage from his beloved Shakspeare:

> A merrier man,
> Within the limit of becoming mirth,
> I never spent an hour's talk withal.
> His eye begets occasion for his wit;
> For ev'ry object that the one doth catch,
> The other turns to a mirth-moving jest;
> Which his fair tongue (Conceit's expositor)
> Delivers in such apt and gracious words,
> That aged ears play truant at his tales,
> And younger hearings are quite ravished;
> So sweet and voluble is his discourse.

We were all in fine spirits; and I whispered to Mrs Boscawen, 'I believe this is as much as can be made of life.' In addition to a splendid entertainment, we were regaled with Lichfield ale, which had a peculiar appropriated value. Sir Joshua, and Dr Burney, and I, drank cordially of it to Dr Johnson's health; and though he would not join us, he as cordially answered, 'Gentlemen, I wish you all as well as you do me.'

The general effect of this day dwells upon my mind in fond remembrance; but I do not find much conversation recorded. What I have preserved shall be faithfully given.

Somebody mentioned Mr Thomas Hollis, the strenuous Whig, who used to send over Europe presents of democratical books, with their boards stamped with daggers and caps of liberty. Mrs Carter said, 'He was a bad man. He used to talk uncharitably.' JOHNSON. 'Poh! poh! Madam; who is the worse for being talked of uncharitably? Besides, he was a dull poor creature as ever lived. And I believe he would not have done harm to a man whom he knew to be of very opposite principles to his own. I remember once at the Society of Arts, when an advertisement was to be drawn up, he pointed me out as the man who could do it best. This, you will observe, was kindness to me. I however slipt away and escaped it.'

Mrs Carter having said of a certain[a] person, 'I doubt he was an Atheist.' JOHNSON. 'I don't know that. He might perhaps have become one, if he had had time to ripen (smiling). He might have *exuberated* into an Atheist.'

Sir Joshua Reynolds praised Mudge's Sermons. JOHNSON. 'Mudge's Sermons are good, but not practical. He grasps more sense than he can hold; he takes more corn than he can make into meal; he opens a wide prospect, but it is so distant, it is indistinct. I love Blair's Sermons. Though the dog is a Scotchman,

---

[a] For 'a certain' read 'the same'.

and a Presbyterian, and every thing he should not be, I was the first to praise them. Such was my candour' (smiling). MRS BOSCAWEN. 'Such his great merit to get the better of all your prejudices.' JOHNSON. 'Why, Madam, let us compound the matter; let us ascribe it to my candour, and his merit.'

In the evening we had a large company in the drawing-room, several ladies, the Bishop of Killaloe, Dr Percy, Mr Chamberlayne of the Treasury, &c. &c. Somebody said the life of a mere literary man could not be very entertaining. JOHNSON. 'But it certainly may. This is a remark which has been made, and repeated, without justice; why should the life of a literary man be less entertaining than the life of any other man? Are there not as interesting varieties in such a life? As *a literary life* it may be very entertaining.' BOSWELL. 'But it must be better surely, when it is diversified with a little active variety – such as his having gone to Jamaica; – or – his having gone to the Hebrides.' Johnson was not displeased at this.

Talking of a very respectable author, he told us a curious circumstance in his life, which was, that he had married a printer's devil. REYNOLDS. 'A printer's devil, Sir! Why, I thought a printer's devil was a creature with a black face and in rags.' JOHNSON. 'Yes, Sir. But I suppose, he had her face washed, and put clean clothes on her. (Then looking very serious, and very earnest) And she did not disgrace him – the woman had a bottom of good sense.' The word *bottom* thus introduced, was so ludicrous, when contrasted with his gravity, that most of us could not forbear tittering and laughing, though I recollect that the Bishop of Killaloe kept his countenance with perfect steadiness, while Miss Hannah More slyly hid her face behind a lady's back who sat on the same settee with her. His pride could not bear that any expression of his should excite ridicule, when he did not intend it; he therefore resolved to assume and exercise despotic power, glanced sternly around, and called out in a strong tone, 'Where's the merriment?' Then collecting himself, and looking awful, to make us feel how he could impose restraint, and as it were searching his mind for a still more ludicrous word, he slowly pronounced, 'I say the *woman* was *fundamentally* sensible'; as if he had said, hear this now, and laugh if you dare. We all sat composed as at a funeral.

He and I walked away together; we stopped a little while by the rails of the Adelphi, looking on the Thames, and I said to him with tenderness, that I thought of two friends we had lost, who once lived in the buildings behind us, Beauclerk and Garrick. 'Aye, Sir (said he, tenderly), and two such friends as cannot be supplied.'

For some time after this day I did not see him very often, and of the conversation which I did enjoy, I am sorry to find I have preserved but little. I was at this time engaged in a variety of other matters, which required exertion and assiduity, and necessarily occupied almost all my time.

One day having spoken very freely of those who were then in power, he said to me, 'Between ourselves, Sir, I do not like to give opposition the satisfaction of knowing how much I disapprove of the ministry.' And when I mentioned that Mr Burke had boasted how quiet the nation was in George the Second's reign, when Whigs were in power, compared with the present reign, when

Tories governed. 'Why, Sir (said he), you are to consider that Tories having more reverence for government, will not oppose with the same violence as Whigs, who being unrestrained by that principle, will oppose by any means.'

This month he lost not only Mr Thrale, but another friend, Mr William Strahan, Junior, printer, the eldest son of his old and constant friend, Printer to his Majesty.

To Mrs STRAHAN.

Dear Madam – The grief which I feel for the loss of a very kind friend is sufficient to make me know how much you must suffer by the death of an amiable son; a man, of whom I think it may truly be said, that no one knew him who does not lament him. I look upon myself as having a friend, another friend taken from me.

Comfort, dear Madam, I would give you if I could, but I know how little the forms of consolation can avail. Let me, however, counsel you not to waste your health in unprofitable sorrow, but go to Bath, and endeavour to prolong your own life; but when we have all done all that we can, one friend must in time lose the other. I am, dear Madam,

Your most humble servant,

SAM. JOHNSON.

April 23, 1781.

On Tuesday, May 8, I had the pleasure of again dining with him and Mr Wilkes, at Mr Dilly's. No *negotiation* was now required to bring them together; for Johnson was so well satisfied with the former interview, that he was very glad to meet Wilkes again, who was this day seated between Dr Beattie and Dr Johnson (between Truth and Reason, as General Paoli said, when I told him of it). WILKES. 'I have been thinking, Dr Johnson, that there should be a bill brought into parliament that the controverted elections for Scotland should be tried in that country, at their own Abbey of Holy-Rood House, and not here; for the consequence of trying them here is, that we have an inundation of Scotchmen who come up and never go back again. Now here is Boswell, who has come up upon the election for his own county, which will not last a fortnight.' JOHNSON. 'Nay, Sir, I see no reason why they should be tried at all; for, you know, one Scotchman is as good as another.' WILKES. 'Pray, Boswell, how much may be got in a year by an Advocate at the Scotch bar?' BOSWELL. 'I believe two thousand pounds.' WILKES. 'How can it be possible to spend that money in Scotland?' JOHNSON. 'Why, Sir, the money may be spent in England: but there is a harder question. If one man in Scotland gets possession of two thousand pounds, what remains for all the rest of the nation?' WILKES. 'You know, in the last war, the immense booty which Thurot carried off from the complete plunder of seven Scotch isles. He re-embarked with *three and six-pence*.' Here again Johnson and Wilkes joined in extravagant sportive raillery upon the supposed poverty of Scotland, which Dr Beattie and I did not think it worth our while to dispute.

The subject of quotation being introduced, Mr Wilkes censured it as pedantry. JOHNSON. 'No, Sir, it is a good thing; there is a community of mind in it. Classical quotation is the *parole* of literary men all over the world.' WILKES. 'Upon the continent they all quote the vulgate Bible. Shakspeare is chiefly quoted here; and we quote also Pope, Prior, Butler, Waller, and sometimes Cowley.'

We talked of Letter-writing. JOHNSON. 'It is now become so much the fashion to publish letters, that in order to avoid it, I put as little into mine as I can.' BOSWELL. 'Do what you will, Sir, you cannot avoid it. Should you even write as ill as you can, your letters would be published as curiosities.

> Behold a miracle! instead of wit
> See two dull lines with Stanhope's pencil writ.'

He gave us an entertaining account of *Bet Flint*, a woman of the town, who, with some eccentric talents and much effrontery, forced herself upon his acquaintance. 'Bet (said he) wrote her own Life in verse,[1] which she brought to me, wishing that I would furnish her with a Preface to it (laughing). I used to say of her, that she was generally slut and drunkard – occasionally, whore and thief. She had, however, genteel lodgings, a spinet on which she played, and a boy that walked before her chair. Poor Bet was taken up on a charge of stealing a counterpane, and tried at the Old-Bailey. Chief Justice ——, who loved a wench, summed up favourably, and she was acquitted. After which, Bet said, with a gay and satisfied air, "Now that the counterpane is my own, I shall make a petticoat of it." '

Talking of oratory, Mr Wilkes described it as accompanied with all the charms of poetical expression. JOHNSON. 'No, Sir; oratory is the power of beating down your adversary's arguments, and putting better in their place.' WILKES. 'But this does not move the passions.' JOHNSON. 'He must be a weak man who is to be so moved.' WILKES. (naming a celebrated orator) 'Amidst all the brilliancy of ——'s imagination, and the exuberance of his wit, there is a strange want of *taste*. It was observed of Apelles's Venus, that her flesh seemed as if she had been nourished by roses: his oratory would sometimes make one suspect that he eats potatoes and drinks whisky.'

Mr Wilkes observed, how tenacious we are of forms in this country, and gave us an instance, the vote of the House of Commons for remitting money to pay the army in America *in Portugal pieces*, when, in reality, the remittance is made not in Portugal money but in our own specie. JOHNSON. 'Is there not a law, Sir, against exporting the current coin of the realm?' WILKES. 'Yes, Sir:

---

1 Johnson, whose memory was wonderfully retentive, remembered the first four lines of this curious production, which have been communicated to me by a young lady of his acquaintance:

> 'When first I drew my vital breath,
> A little minikin I came upon earth;
> And then I came from a dark abode,
> Into this gay and gaudy world.'

but might not the House of Commons, in case of real evident necessity, order our own current coin to be sent into our own colonies?' – Here Johnson, with that quickness of recollection which distinguished him so eminently, gave the *Middlesex Patriot* an admirable retort upon his own ground. 'Sure, Sir, *you* don't think a *resolution of the House of Commons* equal to *the law of the land*.' WILKES. (at once perceiving the application) 'GOD forbid, Sir.' – To hear what had been treated with such violence in 'The False Alarm', now turned into pleasant repartee, was extremely agreeable. Johnson went on – 'Locke observes well, that a prohibition to export the current coin is impolitic; for when the balance of trade happens to be against a state, the current coin *must* be exported.'

Mr Beauclerk's great library was this season sold in London by auction. Mr Wilkes said, he wondered to find in it such a numerous collection of sermons, seeming to think it strange that a gentleman of Mr Beauclerk's character in the gay world, should have chosen to have many compositions of that kind. JOHNSON. 'Why, Sir, you are to consider, that sermons make a considerable branch of English literature; so that a library must be very imperfect if it has not a numerous collection of sermons:[1] and in all collections,

---

1 Mr Wilkes probably did not know that there is in an English sermon the most comprehensive and lively account of that entertaining faculty, for which he himself is so much admired. It is in Dr Barrow's first volume, and fourteenth sermon, '*Against foolish Talking and Jesting*'. My old acquaintance, the late Corbyn Morris, in his ingenious 'Essay on Wit, Humour, and Ridicule', calls it 'a *profuse* description of Wit': but I do not see how it could be curtailed, without leaving out some good circumstance of discrimination. As it is not generally known, and may perhaps dispose some to read sermons, from which they may receive real advantage, while looking only for entertainment, I shall here quote it.

'But first (says the learned preacher) it may be demanded, what the thing we speak of is? Or what this facetiousness (or *wit*, as he calls it before) doth import? To which questions I might reply, as Democritus did to him that asked the definition of a man, ' 'Tis that which we all see and know.' Any one better apprehends what it is by acquaintance, than I can inform him by description. It is, indeed, a thing so versatile and multiform, appearing in so many shapes, so many postures, so many garbs, so variously apprehended by several eyes and judgements, that it seemeth no less hard to settle a clear and certain notion thereof, than to make a portrait of Proteus, or to define the figure of the fleeting air. Sometimes it lieth in pat allusion to a known story, or in seasonable application of a trivial saying, or in forging an apposite tale: sometimes it playeth in words and phrases, taking advantage from the ambiguity of their sense, or the affinity of their sound: sometimes it is wrapped in a dress of humorous expression: sometimes it lurketh under an odd similitude: sometimes it is lodged in a sly question, in a smart answer, in a quirkish reason, in a shrewd intimation, in cunningly diverting or cleverly retorting an objection: sometimes it is couched in a bold scheme of speech, in a tart irony, in a lusty hyperbole, in a startling metaphor, in a plausible reconciling of contradictions, or in acute nonsense: sometimes a scenical representation of persons or things, a counterfeit speech, a mimical look or gesture, passeth for it: sometimes an affected simplicity, sometimes a presumptuous bluntness giveth it being: sometimes it riseth only from a lucky hitting upon what is strange, sometimes from a crafty wresting obvious matter to the purpose. Often it consisteth in one knows not what, and

Sir, the desire of augmenting it grows stronger in proportion to the advance in acquisition; as motion is accelerated by the continuance of the impetus. Besides, Sir (looking at Mr Wilkes with a placid but significant smile), a man may collect sermons with intention of making himself better by them. I hope Mr Beauclerk intended, that some time or other that should be the case with him.'

Mr Wilkes said to me, loud enough for Dr Johnson to hear, 'Dr Johnson should make me a present of his *Lives of the Poets*, as I am a poor patriot who cannot afford to buy them.' Johnson seemed to take no notice of this hint; but in a little while, he called to Mr Dilly, 'Pray, Sir, be so good as to send a set of my Lives to Mr Wilkes, with my compliments.' This was accordingly done; and Mr Wilkes paid Dr Johnson a visit, was courteously received, and sat with him a long time.

The company gradually dropped away. Mr Dilly himself was called down stairs upon business; I left the room for some time; when I returned, I was struck with observing Dr Samuel Johnson and John Wilkes, Esq. literally *tête à tête*; for they were reclined upon their chairs, with their heads leaning almost close to each other, and talking earnestly, in a kind of confidential whisper, of the personal quarrel between George the Second and the King of Prussia. Such a scene of perfectly easy sociality between two such opponents in the war of political controversy, as that which I now beheld, would have been an excellent subject for a picture. It presented to my mind the happy days which are foretold in Scripture, when the lion shall lie down with the kid.[1]

---

springeth up one can hardly tell how. Its ways are unaccountable, and inexplicable; being answerable to the numberless rovings of fancy, and windings of language. It is, in short, a manner of speaking out of the simple and plain way (such as reason teacheth and proveth things by), which by a pretty surprising uncouthness in conceit or expression, doth affect and amuse the fancy, stirring in it some wonder, and breeding some delight thereto. It raiseth admiration, as signifying a nimble sagacity of apprehension, a special felicity of invention, a vivacity of spirit, and reach of wit more than vulgar; it seeming to argue a rare quickness of parts, that one can fetch in remote conceits applicable; a notable skill, that he can dexterously accommodate them to the purpose before him; together with a lively briskness of humour, not apt to damp those sportful flashes of imagination. (Whence in Aristotle such persons are termed ἐπιδέξιοι, dexterous men, and εὔστροφοι, men of facile or versatile manners, who can easily turn themselves to all things, or turn all things to themselves.) It also procureth delight, by gratifying curiosity with its rareness, as semblance of difficulty (as monsters, not for their beauty, but their rarity; as juggling tricks, not for their use, but their abstruseness, are beheld with pleasure): by diverting the mind from its road of serious thoughts; by instilling gaiety and airiness of spirit; by provoking to such dispositions of spirit in way of emulation or complaisance; and by seasoning matters, otherwise distasteful or insipid, with an unusual and thence grateful tang.'

1 When I mentioned this to the Bishop of Killaloe, 'With the *goat*', said his Lordship. Such, however, is the engaging politeness and pleasantry of Mr Wilkes, and such the social good humour of the Bishop, that when they dined together at Mr Dilly's, where I also was, they were mutually agreeable.

After this day there was another pretty long interval, during which Dr Johnson and I did not meet. When I mentioned it to him with regret, he was pleased to say, 'Then, Sir, let us live double.'

About this time it was much the fashion for several ladies to have evening assemblies, where the fair sex might participate in conversation with literary and ingenious men, animated by a desire to please. These societies were denominated *Blue-stocking Clubs*, the origin of which title being little known, it may be worth while to relate it. One of the most eminent members of those societies when they first commenced, was Mr Stillingfleet, whose dress was remarkably grave, and in particular it was observed, that he wore blue-stockings. Such was the excellence of his conversation, that his absence was felt as so great a loss, that it used to be said, 'We can do nothing without the *blue-stockings*'; and thus by degrees the title was established. Miss Hannah More has admirably described a *Blue-stocking Club*, in her '*Bas Bleu*', poem in which many of the persons who were most conspicuous there are mentioned.

Johnson was prevailed with to come sometimes into these circles, and did not think himself too grave even for the lively Miss Monckton (now Countess of Corke) who used to have the finest *bit of blue* at the house of her mother, Lady Galway. Her vivacity enchanted the Sage, and they used to talk together with all imaginable ease. A singular instance happened one evening, when she insisted that some of Sterne's writings were very pathetic. Johnson bluntly denied it. 'I am sure (said she) they have affected *me*.' – 'Why (said Johnson, smiling, and rolling himself about), that is, because, dearest, you're a dunce.' When she some time afterwards mentioned this to him, he said with equal truth and politeness; 'Madam, if I had thought so, I certainly should not have said it.'

Another evening Johnson's kind indulgence towards me had a pretty difficult trial. I had dined at the Duke of Montrose's, with a very agreeable party, and his Grace, according to his usual custom, had circulated the bottle very freely. Lord Graham and I went together to Miss Monckton's, where I certainly was in extraordinary spirits, and above all fear or awe. In the midst of a great number of persons of the first rank, amongst whom I recollect with confusion, a noble lady of the most stately decorum, I placed myself next to Johnson, and thinking myself now fully his match, talked to him in a loud and boisterous manner, desirous to let the company know how I could contend with Ajax. I particularly remember pressing him upon the value of the pleasures of the imagination, and as an illustration of my argument, asking him, 'What, Sir, supposing I were to fancy that the[a] (naming the most charming Duchess in his Majesty's dominions) were in love with me, should I not be very happy?' My friend with much address evaded my interrogatories, and kept me as quiet as possible; but it may easily be conceived how he must have felt.[1] When a few days afterwards I waited upon him and made an apology, he behaved with the most friendly gentleness.

---

[a] Alter 'that the' to 'that the —— '.

1 Next day I endeavoured to give what had happened the most ingenious turn I could, by the following verses:

While I remained in London this year, Johnson and I dined together at several places. I recollect a placid day at Dr Butters's, who was now removed from Derby to Lower Grosvenor-street, London; but of his conversation on that and other occasions during this period, I neglected to keep any regular record, and shall therefore insert here some miscellaneous articles which I find in my Johnsonian notes.

His disorderly habits, when 'making provision for the day that was passing over him', appear from the following anecdote, communicated to me by Mr John Nichols: 'In the year 1763, a young bookseller, who was an apprentice to Mr Whiston, waited on him with a subscription to his *Shakspeare*; and observing that the Doctor made no entry in any book of the subscriber's name, ventured diffidently to ask, whether he would please to have the gentleman's address, that it might be properly inserted in the printed list of subscribers. – "*I shall print no List of Subscribers*," said Johnson, with great abruptness: but almost immediately recollecting himself, added, very complacently, "Sir, I have two very cogent reasons for not printing any list of subscribers – one, that I have lost all the names – the other, that I have spent all the money." '

Johnson could not brook appearing to be worsted in argument, even when he had taken the wrong side, to show the force and dexterity of his talents. When, therefore, he perceived that his opponent gained ground, he had recourse to some sudden mode of robust sophistry. Once when I was pressing

---

To the Honourable Miss MONCKTON.

NOT that with th' excellent Montrose
    I had the happiness to dine;
Not that I late from table rose,
    From Graham's wit, from generous wine.

It was not these alone which led
    On sacred manners to encroach;
And made me feel what most I dread,
    JOHNSON's just frown, and self-reproach.

But when I enter'd, not abash'd,
    From your bright eyes were shot such rays,
At once intoxication flash'd,
    And all my frame was in a blaze!

But not a brilliant blaze I own,
    Of the dull smoak I'm yet asham'd;
I was a dreary ruin grown,
    And not enlighten'd though inflam'd.

Victim at once to wine and love,
    I hope, MARIA, you'll forgive;
While I invoke the powers above,
    That henceforth I may wiser live.

The lady was generously forgiving, returned me an obliging answer, and I thus obtained an *Act of Oblivion*, and took care never to offend again.

upon him with visible advantage, he stopped me thus: 'My dear Boswell, let's have no more of this; you'll make nothing of it. I'd rather have you whistle a Scotch tune.'

Care, however, must be taken to distinguish between Johnson when he 'talked for victory', and Johnson when he had no desire but to inform and illustrate. – 'One of Johnson's principal talents (says an eminent friend) was shown in maintaining the wrong side of an argument, and in a splendid perversion of the truth. – If you could contrive to have his fair opinion on a subject, and without any bias from personal prejudice, or from a wish to be victorious in argument, it was wisdom itself, not only convincing, but overpowering.'

He had, however, all his life habituated himself to consider conversation as a trial of intellectual vigour and skill; and to this, I think, we may venture to ascribe that unexampled richness and brilliancy which appeared in his own. As a proof at once of his eagerness for colloquial distinction, and his high notion of this eminent friend, he once addressed him thus: '——, we now have been several hours together; and you have said but one thing for which I envied you.'

He disliked much all speculative desponding considerations, which tended to discourage men from diligence and exertion. He was in this like Dr Shaw, the great traveller, who, Mr Daines Barrington told me, used to say, 'I hate a *cui bono* man.' Upon being asked by a friend what he should think of one who was apt to say, *non est tanti*; – 'That he's a stupid fellow, Sir (answered Johnson). What would these *tanti* men be doing the while?' When I, in a low-spirited fit, was talking to him with indifference of the pursuits which generally engage us in a course of action, and inquiring a *reason* for taking so much trouble; 'Sir, (said he, in an animated tone), it is driving on the system of life.'

He told me, that he was glad that I had, by General Oglethorpe's means, become acquainted with Dr Shebbeare. Indeed that gentleman, whatever objections were made to him, had knowledge and abilities much above the class of ordinary writers, and deserves to be remembered as a respectable name in literature, were it only for his admirable *Letters on the English Nation*, under the name of 'Battista Angeloni, a Jesuit'.

Johnson and Shebbeare[1] were frequently named together, as having in former reigns had no predilection for the family of Hanover. The author of the celebrated 'Heroic Epistle to Sir William Chambers', introduces them in one line, in a list of those who 'tasted the sweets of his present Majesty's reign'. Such was Johnson's fair taste of the merit of that satire, that he allowed Dr Goldsmith, as he told me, to read it to him from beginning to end, and did not refuse his praise to its execution.

Goldsmith could sometimes take adventurous liberties with him, and escape unpunished. Beauclerk told me that when Goldsmith talked of a project for having a third Theatre in London, solely for the exhibition of new plays, in

---

1 I recollect a ludicrous paragraph in the newspapers, that the King had pensioned both a *He*-bear and a *She*-bear.

order to deliver authors from the supposed tyranny of managers, Johnson treated it slightingly; upon which Goldsmith said, 'Aye, aye, this may be nothing to you, who can now shelter yourself behind the corner of a pension'; and that Johnson bore this with good-humour.

Johnson praised the Earl of Carlisle's Poems, which his Lordship had published with his name, as not disdaining to be a candidate for literary fame. My friend was of opinion, that when a man of rank appeared in that character, he deserved to have his merit handsomely allowed.[1] In this I think he was more liberal than Mr William Whitehead, in his 'Elegy to Lord Villiers', in which under the pretext of 'superior toils, demanding all their care', he discovers a jealousy of the great paying their court to the Muses.

> To the chosen few
> Who dare excel, thy fost'ring aid afford,
> Their arts, their magic powers, with honours due
> Exalt; – but be thyself what they record.

Johnson had called twice on the Bishop of Killaloe before his Lordship set out for Ireland, having missed him the first time. He said, 'It would have hung heavy on my heart if I had not seen him. No man ever paid more attention to another than he has done to me;[1] and I have neglected him, not wilfully, but

---

1 Men of rank and fortune however should be pretty well assured of having a real claim to the approbation of the public as writers, before they venture to stand forth. Dryden in his Preface to *All for Love*, thus expresses himself:

Men of pleasant conversation (at least esteemed so) and endued with a trifling kind of fancy, perhaps helped out by a smattering of Latin, are ambitious to distinguish themselves from the herd of gentlemen, by their poetry:

> *Rarus enim ferme sensus communis in illa*
> *Fortuna.*

And is not this a wretched affectation, not to be contented with what fortune has done for them, and sit down quietly with their estates, but they must call their wits in question, and needlessly expose their nakedness to public view? Not considering that they are not to expect the same approbation from sober men which they have found from their flatterers after the third bottle. If a little glittering discourse has passed them on us for witty men, where was the necessity of undeceiving the world? Would a man who has an ill title to an estate, but yet is in possession of it, would he bring it of his own accord to be tried at Westminster? We who write, if we want the talents, yet have the excuse that we do it for a poor subsistence; but what can be urged in their defence, who not having the vocation of poverty to scribble, out of mere wantonness take pains to make themselves ridiculous? Horace was certainly in the right where he said, 'that no man is satisfied with his own condition.' A Poet is not pleased, because he is not rich; and the rich are discontented because the poets will not admit them of their number.

1 This gave me a very great pleasure, for there had been once a pretty smart alter-cation between Dr Barnard and him, upon a question, whether a man could improve himself after the age of forty-five; when Johnson in a hasty humour, expressed himself in a manner not quite civil. Dr Barnard made it the subject of a copy of pleasant verses,

from being otherwise occupied. Always, Sir, set a high value on spontaneous kindness. He, whose inclination prompts him to cultivate your friendship of his own accord, will love you more than one whom you have been at pains to attach to you.'

Johnson told me, that he was once much pleased to find that a carpenter, who lived near him, was very ready to show him some things in his business which he wished to see. 'It was paying (said he) respect to literature.'

I asked him if he was not dissatisfied with having so small a share of wealth, and none of those distinctions in the state which are the objects of ambition. He had only a pension of three hundred a year. Why was he not in such circumstances as to keep his coach? Why had he not some considerable office? JOHNSON. 'Sir, I have never complained of the world; nor do I think that I have reason to complain. It is rather to be wondered at that I have so much. My pension is more out of the usual course of things than any instance that I have known. Here, Sir, was a man avowedly no friend to the Government at the time, gets[a] a pension without asking for it. I never courted the great; they sent for me: but I think they now give me up. They are satisfied. They have seen enough of me.' Upon my observing that I could not believe this, for they must certainly be highly pleased by his conversation; conscious of his own superiority, he answered, 'No, Sir; great Lords and great Ladies don't love to have their mouths stopped.' This was very expressive of the effect which the force of his understanding and brilliancy of his fancy could not but produce; and, to be sure, they must have found themselves strangely diminished in his company. When I warmly declared how happy I was at all times to hear him; – 'Yes, Sir (said he). But if you were Lord Chancellor, it would not be so: you would then consider your own dignity.'

There was much truth and knowledge of human nature in this remark. But certainly one should think, that in whatever elevated state of life a man who *knew* the value of the conversation of Johnson might be placed, though he might prudently avoid a situation in which he might appear lessened by comparison; yet he would frequently gratify himself in private with the participation of the rich intellectual entertainment which Johnson could furnish. Strange, however, it is, to consider how few of the great sought his

---

in which he supposed himself to learn different perfections from different men. They concluded with delicate irony:

> Johnson shall teach me how to place
> In fairest light each borrow'd grace;
>   From him I'll learn to write:
> Copy his clear familiar style,
> And by the roughness of his file,
>   Grow – like *himself* – polite.

I know not whether Johnson ever saw the Poem, but I had occasion to find that as Dr Barnard and he knew each other better, their mutual regard increased.

[b] For 'gets' read 'who got'.

society; so that if one were disposed to take occasion for satire on that account, very conspicuous objects present themselves. His noble friend, Lord Elibank, well observed, that if a great man procured an interview with Johnson, and did not wish to see him more, it showed a mere idle curiosity, and a wretched want of relish for extraordinary powers of mind. Mrs Thrale justly and wittily accounted for such conduct by saying, that Johnson's conversation was by much too strong for a person accustomed to obsequiousness and flattery; it was *mustard in a young child's mouth!*

One day, when I told him that I was a zealous Tory, but not enough 'according to knowledge', and should be obliged to him for 'a reason', he was so candid, and expressed himself so well, that I begged of him to repeat what he had said, and I wrote down as follows:

Of Tory and Whig.

A wise Tory and a wise Whig, I believe, will agree. Their principles are the same, though their modes of thinking are different. A high Tory makes Government unintelligible: it is lost in the clouds. A violent Whig makes it impracticable: he is for allowing so much liberty to every man, that there is not power enough to govern any man. The prejudice of the Tory is for establishment: the prejudice of the Whig is for innovation. A Tory does not wish to give more real power to Government; but that Government should have more reverence. Then they differ as to the Church. The Tory is not for giving more legal power to the Clergy, but wishes they should have a considerable influence, founded on the opinion of mankind: the Whig is for limiting and watching them with a narrow jealousy.[a]

On Saturday, June 2, I set out for Scotland, and had engaged, as I sometimes did, to pay a visit, in my way, at Southill, in Bedfordshire, at the hospitable mansion of 'Squire Dilly, the elder brother of my worthy friends the booksellers in the Poultry. Dr Johnson agreed to be of the party this year, with Mr Charles Dilly and me, and to go and see Lord Bute's seat at Luton Hoe. He talked little to us in the carriage, being chiefly occupied in reading

---

[a] After this passage, read:

To Mr Perkins.

Sir – However often I have seen you, I have hitherto forgotten the note, but I have now sent it: with my good wishes for the prosperity of you and your partner,[1] of whom, from our short conversation, I could not judge otherwise than favourably. I am, Sir,

Your most humble servant,

                                             Sam. Johnson.

June 2, 1781.

1 Mr Barclay, a descendant of Robert Barclay, of Ury, the celebrated apologist of the people called Quakers, and remarkable for maintaining the principles of his venerable progenitor, with as much of the elegance of modern manners as is consistent with primitive simplicity.

Dr Watson's[a] second volume of *Chemical Essays*, which he liked very well, and his own *Prince of Abyssinia*, on which he seemed to be intensely fixed; having told us, that he had not looked at it since it was first published. I happened to take it out of my pocket to-day, and he seized upon it with avidity. He pointed out to me the following remarkable passage: 'By what means (said the Prince) are the Europeans thus powerful; or why, since they can so easily visit Asia and Africa for trade or conquest, cannot the Asiatics and Africans invade their coasts, plant colonies in their ports, and give laws to their natural princes? The same wind that carries them back would bring us thither.' – 'They are more powerful, Sir, than we (answered Imlac), because they are wiser. Knowledge will always predominate over ignorance, as man governs the other animals. But why their knowledge is more than ours, I know not what reason can be given, but the unsearchable will of the Supreme Being.' He said, 'This, Sir, no man can explain otherwise.'

We stopped at Welwyn, where I wished much to see, in company with Dr Johnson, the residence of the author of *Night Thoughts*, which was then possessed by his son, Mr Young. Here some address was requisite, for I was not acquainted with Mr Young, and had I proposed to Dr Johnson that we should send to him, he would have checked my wish, and perhaps been offended. I therefore concerted with Mr Dilly, that I should steal away from Dr Johnson and him, and try what reception I could procure from Mr Young; if unfavourable nothing was to be said; but if agreeable I should return and notify it to them. I hastened to Mr Young's, found he was at home, sent in word that a gentleman desired to wait upon him, and was shown into a parlour, where he and a young lady, his daughter, were sitting. He appeared to be a plain, civil, country gentleman; and when I begged pardon for presuming to trouble him, but said I wished much to see his place, if he would give me leave; he behaved very courteously, and answered, 'By all means, Sir; we are just going to drink tea; will you sit down?' I thanked him, but said, that Dr Johnson had come with me from London, and I must return to the inn and drink tea with him; that my name was Boswell, I had travelled with him in the Hebrides. 'Sir (said he), I should think it a great honour to see Dr Johnson here. Will you allow me to send for him?' Availing myself of this opening, I said that 'I would go myself and bring him, when he had drunk tea; he knew nothing of my calling here.' Having been thus successful, I hastened back to the inn, and informed Dr Johnson that 'Mr Young, son of Dr Young, the author of *Night Thoughts*, whom I had just left, desired to have the honour of seeing him at the house where his father lived.' Dr Johnson luckily made no inquiry how this invitation had arisen, but

---

[a] Add the following note: Now Bishop of Llandaff, one of the *poorest* Bishoprics in this Kingdom. His Lordship has written with much zeal to show the propriety of *equalizing* the revenues of Bishops. He has informed us that he has burnt all his Chemical papers. The friends of our excellent constitution, now assailed on every side by innovators and levellers, would have less regretted the suppression of some of his Lordship's other writings.

agreed to go, and when we entered Mr Young's parlour, he addressed him with a very polite bow, 'Sir, I had a curiosity to come and see this place. I had the honour to know that great man, your father.' We went into the garden, where we found a gravel walk, on each side of which was a row of trees, planted by Dr Young, which formed a handsome Gothic arch; Dr Johnson called it a fine grove. I beheld it with reverence.

We sat some time in the summer-house, on the outside wall of which was inscribed, *'Ambulantes in horto audiebant vocem Dei.'* And in reference to a brook by which it is situated, *'Vivendi recte qui prorogat horam, &c.'* I said to Mr Young, that I had been told his father was cheerful. 'Sir (said he), he was too well-bred a man not to be cheerful in company; but he was gloomy when alone. He never was cheerful after my mother's death, and he had met with many disappointments.' Dr Johnson observed to me afterwards, 'That this was no favourable account of Dr Young; for it is not becoming in a man to have so little acquiescence in the ways of Providence, as to be gloomy because he has not obtained as much preferment as he expected; nor to continue gloomy for the loss of his wife. Grief has its time.' The last part of this censure was theoretically made. Practically, we know that grief for the loss of a wife may be continued very long, in proportion as affection has been sincere. No man knew this better than Dr Johnson.

We went into the church, and looked at the monument erected by Mr Young, to his father. Mr Young mentioned an anecdote, that his father had received several thousand pounds of subscription money for his *Universal Passion*, but had lost it in the South-Sea. Dr Johnson thought this must be a mistake; for he had never seen a subscription-book.

Upon the road we talked of the uncertainty of profit with which authors and booksellers engage in the publication of literary works. JOHNSON. 'My judgement I have found is no certain rule as to the sale of a book.' BOSWELL. 'Pray, Sir, have you been much plagued with authors sending you their works to revise?' JOHNSON. 'No, Sir; I have been thought a sour surly fellow.' BOSWELL. 'Very lucky for you, Sir – in that respect.' I must however observe, that notwithstanding what he now said, which he no doubt imagined at the time to be the fact, there was, perhaps, no man who more frequently yielded to the solicitations even of very obscure authors, to read their manuscripts, or more liberally assisted them with advice and correction.

He found himself very happy at Mr Dilly's, where there is always abundance of excellent fare and hearty welcome.

On Sunday, June 3, we all went to Southill church, which is very near to Mr Dilly's house. It being the first Sunday of the month, the holy sacrament was administered, and I staid to partake of it. When I came afterwards into Dr Johnson's room, he said, 'You did right to stay and receive the communion; I had not thought of it.' This seemed to imply that he did not choose to approach the altar without a previous preparation, as to which good men entertain different opinions, some holding that it is irreverent to partake of that ordinance without considerable premeditation; others, that whoever is a sincere Christian, and in a proper frame to discharge any other ritual duty of our religion, may, without scruple, discharge this most solemn one. A middle notion I believe to be the just one, which is, that communicants need not think a long train of preparatory forms indispensibly necessary; but neither should they rashly and lightly venture upon so awful and mysterious an institution. Christians must judge each for himself, what degree of retirement and self-examination is necessary upon each occasion.

Being in a frame, which, I hope for the felicity of human nature, many experience – in fine weather – at the country-house of a friend – consoled and elevated by pious exercises – I expressed myself with an unrestrained fervour to my 'Guide, Philosopher, and Friend'; 'My dear Sir, I would fain be a good man; and I am very good now. I fear GOD, and honour the King, I wish to do no ill, and to be benevolent to all mankind.' He looked at me with a benignant indulgence; but took occasion to give me able and salutary caution. 'Do not, Sir, accustom yourself to trust to *impressions*. There is a middle state of mind between conviction and hypocrisy, of which many are conscious. By trusting to impressions, a man may gradually come to yield to them, and at length be subject to them, so as not to be a free agent, or what is the same thing in effect, to *suppose* that he is not a free agent. A man who is in that state, should not be suffered to live; if he declares he cannot help acting in a particular way, but is irresistibly impelled, there can be no confidence in him, no more than in a tiger. But, Sir, no man believes himself to be impelled irresistibly; we know that he who says he believes it, lies. Favourable impressions at particular moments, as to the state of our souls, may be deceitful and dangerous. In general no man can be sure of his acceptance with GOD; some, indeed, may have had it revealed to them. St Paul, who wrought miracles, may have had a miracle wrought on himself, and may have obtained supernatural assurance of pardon, and mercy, and beatitude; yet St Paul, though he expresses strong hope, also expresses fear, lest having preached to others, he himself should be a cast-away.'

The opinion of a learned Bishop of our acquaintance, as to there being merit in religious faith, being mentioned; – JOHNSON. 'Why, yes, Sir, the most licentious man, were hell open before him, would not take the most beautiful strumpet to his arms. We must, as the Apostle says, live by faith, not by sight.'

I talked to him of original sin,[1] in consequence of the fall of man, and of the atonement made by our SAVIOUR. After some conversation, which he desired me to remember, he at my request dictated to me as follows:

---

1 Dr Ogden, in his second sermon 'On the Articles of the Christian Faith', with admirable acuteness thus addresses the opposers of that doctrine, which accounts for the confusion, sin, and misery, which we find in this life: 'It would be severe in GOD, you think, to *degrade* us to such a sad state as this, for the offence of our first parents; but you can allow him to *place* us in it, without any inducement. Are our calamities lessened for not being ascribed to Adam? If your condition be unhappy, is it not still unhappy, whatever was the occasion? With the aggravation of this reflection, that if it was as good as it was at first designed, there seems to be somewhat the less reason to look for its amendment.'

With respect to original sin, the inquiry is not necessary; for whatever is the cause of human corruption, men are evidently and confessedly corrupt, that all the laws of heaven and earth are insufficient to restrain them from crimes.

Whatever difficulty there may be in the conception of vicarious punishments, it is an opinion which has had possession of mankind in all ages. There is no nation that has not used the practice of sacrifices. Whoever, therefore, denies the propriety of vicarious punishments, holds an opinion which the sentiments and practice of mankind have contradicted, from the beginning of the world. The great sacrifice for the sins of mankind was offered at the death of the MESSIAH, who is called in scripture, 'the Lamb of GOD, that taketh away the sins of the world'. To judge of the reasonableness of the scheme of redemption, it must be considered as necessary to the government of the universe, that GOD should make known his perpetual and irreconcileable detestation of moral evil. He might indeed punish, and punish only the offenders: but as the end of punishment is not revenge of crimes, but propagation of virtue, it was more becoming the divine clemency to find another manner of proceeding, less destructive to man, and at least equally powerful to promote goodness. The end of punishment is to reclaim and warn. *That* punishment will both reclaim and warn, which shows evidently such abhorrence of sin in GOD, as may deter us from it, or strike us with dread of vengeance when we have committed it. This is effected by vicarious punishment. Nothing could more testify the opposition between the nature of GOD and moral evil, or more amply display his justice, to men and angels, to all orders and successions of beings, than that it was necessary for the highest and purest nature, even for DIVINITY itself, to pacify the demands of vengeance, by a painful death; of which the natural effect would be, that when justice is appeased, there is a proper place for the exercise of mercy; and that such propitiation shall supply, in some degree, the imperfections of our obedience, and the inefficacy of our repentance. For, obedience and repentance, such as we can perform, are still necessary. Our SAVIOUR has told us, that he did not come to destroy the law, but to fulfil: to fulfil the typical law, by the performance of what those types had foreshown; and the moral law, by precepts of greater purity and higher exaltation.

[Here he said, 'God bless you with it.' I acknowledged myself much obliged to him; but I begged that he would go on as to the propitiation being the chief object of our most holy faith. He then dictated this one other paragraph.]

The peculiar doctrine of Christianity is, that of an universal sacrifice, and perpetual propitiation. Other prophets only proclaimed the will and the threatenings of GOD. CHRIST satisfied his justice.

The Reverend Mr Palmer,[a] Fellow of Queen's-College, Cambridge, dined

---

[a] Add the following note: This unfortunate person, whose full name was Thomas Fysche Palmer, afterwards went to Dundee, in Scotland, where he officiated as

with us. He expressed a wish that a better provision were made for parish-clerks. JOHNSON. 'Yes, Sir; a parish-clerk should be a man who is able to make a will, or write a letter for any body in the parish.'

I mentioned Lord Monboddo's notion that the ancient Egyptians, with all their learning, and all their arts, were not only black, but woolly-haired. Mr Palmer asked how did it appear upon examining the mummies? Dr Johnson approved of this test.

Although upon most occasions I never heard a more strenuous advocate for the advantages of wealth, than Dr Johnson; he this day, I know not from what caprice, took the other side. 'I have not observed (said he) that men of very large fortunes enjoy any thing extraordinary that makes happiness. What has the Duke of Bedford? What has the Duke of Devonshire? The only great instance that I have ever known of the enjoyment of wealth was, that of Jamaica Dawkins, who going to visit Palmyra, and hearing that the way was infested by robbers, hired a troop of Turkish horse to guard him.'

Dr Gibbons, the Dissenting minister, being mentioned, he said, 'I took to Dr Gibbons.' And addressing himself to Mr Charles Dilly, added, 'I shall be glad to see him. Tell him, if he'll call on me, and dawdle over a dish of tea in an afternoon, I shall take it kind.'

The Reverend Mr Smith, Vicar of Southill, a very respectable man, with a very agreeable family, sent an invitation to us to drink tea. I remarked Dr Johnson's very formal politeness. Though always fond of changing the scene, he said, 'We must have Mr Dilly's leave. We cannot go from your house, Sir, without your permission.' We all went, and were well satisfied with our visit. I however remember nothing particular, except a nice distinction which Dr Johnson made with respect to the power of memory, maintaining that forgetfulness was a man's own fault. 'To remember and to recollect (said he) are different things. A man has not the power to recollect what is not in his mind; but when a thing is in his mind he may remember it.' The remark was occasioned by my leaning back on a chair, which a little before I had perceived to be broken, and pleading forgetfulness as an excuse. 'Sir (said he), its being broken was certainly in your mind.'

---

minister to a congregation of the sect who call themselves *Unitarians*, from a notion that they distinctively worship ONE GOD, because they *deny* the mysterious doctrine of the TRINITY. They do not advert that the great body of the Christian Church in maintaining that mystery, maintain also the *Unity* of the GODHEAD: the 'TRINITY in UNITY! – three persons and ONE GOD'. The Church humbly adores the DIVINITY as exhibited in the holy Scriptures. The Unitarian sect vainly presumes to comprehend and define the ALMIGHTY. Mr Palmer having heated his mind with political speculations, became so much dissatisfied with our excellent Constitution, as to compose, publish, and circulate writings, which were found to be so seditious and dangerous, that upon being found guilty by a Jury, the Court of Justiciary in Scotland sentenced him to transportation for fourteen years. A loud clamour against this sentence was made by some Members of both Houses of Parliament; but both Houses approved of it by a great majority; and he was conveyed to the settlement for convicts in New South Wales. – (*Boswell or Malone.*)

When I observed that a housebreaker was in general very timorous; JOHNSON. 'No wonder, Sir; he is afraid of being shot getting *into* a house, or hanged when he has got *out* of it.'

He told us, that he had in one day written six sheets of a translation from the French; adding, 'I should be glad to see it now. I wish that I had copies of all the pamphlets written against me, as it is said Pope had. Had I known that I should make so much noise in the world, I should have been at pains to collect them. I believe there is hardly a day in which there is not something about me in the newspapers.'

On Monday, June 4, we all went to Luton-Hoe, to see Lord Bute's magnificent seat, for which I had obtained a ticket. As we entered the park, I talked in a high style of my old friendship with Lord Mountstuart, and said, 'I shall probably be much at this place.' The Sage, aware of human vicissitudes, gently checked me: 'Don't you be too sure of that.' He made two or three peculiar observations, as when shown the botanical garden, 'Is not every garden a botanical garden?' When told that there was a shrubbery to the extent of several miles; 'That is making a very foolish use of the ground; a little of it is very well.' When it was proposed that we should walk on the pleasure-ground; 'Don't let us fatigue ourselves. Why should we walk there? Here's a fine tree, let's get to the top of it.' But upon the whole, he was very much pleased. He said, 'This is one of the places I do not regret having come to see. It is a very stately place, indeed; in the house magnificence is not sacrificed to convenience, nor convenience to magnificence. The library is very splendid; the dignity of the rooms is very great; and the quantity of pictures is beyond expectation, beyond hope.'

It happened without any previous concert, that we visited the seat of Lord Bute upon the King's birthday; we dined and drank his Majesty's health at an inn, in the village of Luton.

In the evening I put him in mind of his promise to favour me with a copy of his celebrated Letter to the Earl of Chesterfield,[1] and he was at last pleased to comply with this earnest request, by dictating it to me from his memory; for he believed that he himself had no copy. There was an animated glow in his countenance while he thus recalled his high-minded indignation.

He laughed heartily at a ludicrous action in the Court of Session, in which I was Counsel. The Society of *Procurators*, or Attornies, entitled to practise in the inferior Courts at Edinburgh, had obtained a royal charter, in which they had taken care to have their ancient designation of *Procurators*, changed into that of *Solicitors*, from a notion, as they supposed, that it was more *genteel*; and this new title they displayed by a public advertisement for a *General Meeting* at their HALL.

It has been said, that the Scottish nation is not distinguished for humour; and, indeed, what happened on this occasion may in some degree justify the remark: for although this society had contrived to make themselves a very

1 See page 132.

prominent object for the ridicule of such as might stoop to it, the only joke that appeared was the following paragraph, sent as a card to the news-paper called the *Caledonian Mercury*:

> A correspondent informs us, that the Worshipful Society of *Chaldeans*, *Cadies*, or *Running Stationers* of this city, are resolved, in imitation, and encouraged by the singular success of their brethren, of an *equally respectable* Society, to apply for a Charter of their Privileges, particularly of the sole privilege of PROCURING, in the most extensive sense of the word, exclusive of chairmen, porters, penny-post men, and other *inferior* ranks; their brethren the R–Y– S–LL–RS, alias P–C–RS, *before the* INFERIOR Courts of this City, always excepted.
>
> Should the Worshipful Society be successful, they are farther resolved not to be *puffed up* thereby, but to demean themselves with more equanimity and decency than their *R–y–l*, *learned*, and *very modest* brethren above mentioned have done, upon their late dignification and exaltation.

A majority of the members of the Society prosecuted Mr Robertson, the publisher of the paper, for damages; and the first judgement of the whole Court very wisely dismissed the action, *Solventur risu tabulae, tu missus abibis*. But a new trial or review was granted upon a petition, according to the forms in Scotland. This petition I was engaged to answer, and Dr Johnson with great alacrity furnished to-night what follows:

> All injury is either of the person, the fortune, or the fame. Now, it is a certain thing, it is proverbially known, that *a jest breaks no bones*. They never have gained half-a-crown less in the whole profession since this mischievous paragraph has appeared: and, as to their reputation, What is their reputation but an instrument of getting money? If, therefore, they have lost no money, the question upon reputation may be answered by a very old position, *De minimis non curat Praetor*.
>
> Whether there was, or was not, an *animus injuriandi*, is not worth inquiring, if no *injuria* can be proved. But the truth is, there was no *animus injuriandi*. It was only an *animus irritandi*,[1] which, happening to be exercised upon a *genus irritabile*, produced unexpected violence of resentment. Their irritability arose only from an opinion of their own importance, and their delight in their new exaltation. What might have been borne by a *Procurator* could not be borne by a *Solicitor*. Your Lordships well know, that *honores mutant mores*. Titles and dignities play strongly upon the fancy. As a mad-man is apt to think himself grown suddenly great; so he that grows suddenly great is apt to borrow a little from the mad-man. To co-operate with their resentment would be to promote their phrenzy; nor is it possible to guess to what they might proceed, if to the new title of Solicitor, should be added the elation of victory and triumph.

---

[1] Mr Robertson altered this word to *jocandi*, he having found in Blackstone that to *irritate* is actionable.

We consider your Lordships as the protectors of our rights, and the guardians of our virtues; but believe it not included in your high office, that you should flatter our vices, or solace our vanity: and, as vanity only dictates this prosecution, it is humbly hoped your Lordships will dismiss it.

If every attempt, however light or ludicrous, to lessen another's reputation, is to be punished by a judicial sentence, what punishment can be sufficiently severe for him who attempts to diminish the reputation of the Supreme Court of Justice, by reclaiming upon a cause already determined, without any change in the state of the question? Does it not imply hopes that the Judges will change their opinion? Is not uncertainty and inconstancy in the highest degree disreputable to a Court? Does it not suppose, that the former judgement was temerarious or negligent? Does it not lessen the confidence of the public? Will it not be said, that *jus est aut incognitum, aut vagum*? and will not the consequence be drawn, *misera est servitus*? Will not the rules of action be obscure? Will not he who knows himself wrong today, hope that the Courts of Justice will think him right tomorrow? Surely, my Lords, these are attempts of dangerous tendency, which the Solicitors, as men versed in the law, should have foreseen and avoided. It was natural for an ignorant printer to appeal from the Lord Ordinary; but from lawyers, the descendents of lawyers, who have practised for three hundred years, and have now raised themselves to a higher denomination, it might be expected, that they should know the reverence due to a judicial determination; and, having been once dismissed, should sit down in silence.

I am ashamed to mention, that the Court, by a plurality of voices, without having a single additional circumstance before them, reversed their own judgement, made a serious matter of this dull and foolish joke, and adjudged Mr Robertson to pay to the Society five pounds (sterling money) and costs of suit. The decision will seem strange to English lawyers.

On Tuesday, June 5, Johnson was to return to London. He was very pleasant at breakfast; I mentioned a friend of mine having resolved never to marry a pretty woman. JOHNSON. 'Sir, it is a very foolish resolution to resolve not to marry a pretty woman. Beauty is of itself very estimable. No, Sir, I would prefer a pretty woman, unless there are objections to her. A pretty woman may be foolish; a pretty woman may be wicked; a pretty woman may not like me. But there is no such danger in marrying a pretty woman as is apprehended; she will not be persecuted if she does not invite persecution. A pretty woman, if she has a mind to be wicked, can find a readier way than another; and that is all.'

I accompanied him in Mr Dilly's chaise to Shefford, where talking of Lord Bute's never going to Scotland, he said, 'As an Englishman, I should wish all the Scotch gentlemen to be educated in England; Scotland would become a province; they would spend all their rents in England.' This is a subject of much consequence and much delicacy. The advantage of an English education is unquestionably very great to Scotch gentlemen of talents and ambition; and regular visits, and I should think other means,[a] might be effectually used to prevent them from being totally estranged from their native country, any more than a Cumberland or Northumberland gentleman, who has been educated in the South of England. I own, indeed, that it is no small misfortune for Scotch gentlemen who have neither talents nor ambition, to be educated in England, where they may be perhaps distinguished only by a nick-name, lavish their fortune in giving expensive entertainments to those who laugh at them, and saunter about as mere idle insignificant hangers on even upon the foolish great; when if they had been judiciously brought up at home, they might have been comfortable and creditable members of society.

At Shefford, I had another affectionate parting from my revered friend, who was taken up by the Bedford coach, and carried to the metropolis. I went with Messieurs Dilly, to see some friends at Bedford; dined with the officers of the militia of the county, and next day proceeded on my journey.

To BENNET LANGTON, Esq.

DEAR SIR – How welcome your account of yourself and your invitation to your new house was to me, I need not tell you, who consider our friendship not only as formed by choice, but as matured by time. We have been now long enough acquainted to have many images in common; and, therefore, to have a source of conversation which neither the learning nor the wit of a new companion can supply.

My Lives are now published; and if you will tell me whither I shall send them that they may come to you, I will take care that you shall not be without them.

You will, perhaps, be glad to hear, that Mrs Thrale is disincumbered of her brewhouse; and that it seemed to the purchaser so far from an evil, that he was content to give for it an hundred and thirty-five thousand pounds. Is the nation ruined?

Please to make my respectful compliments to Lady Rothes, and keep me in the memory of all the little dear family, particularly pretty Mrs Jane. I am, Sir,

Your affectionate humble servant,

SAM. JOHNSON.

Bolt-court, June 16, 1781.[b]

---

[a] After 'visits' read 'to Scotland'. Delete 'I should think', and read 'perhaps'.
[b] After the letter to Mr Langton read: Johnson's charity to the poor was uniform and extensive, both from inclination and principle. He not only bestowed liberally out of his own purse, but what is more difficult as well as rare, would beg from others, when he had proper objects in view. This he did judiciously as well as humanely. Mr Philip Metcalfe tells me, that when he has asked him for some money for persons in distress, and Mr Metcalfe has offered what Johnson thought too much, he insisted on taking less, saying, 'No, no, Sir; we must not *pamper* them.'

To Thomas Astle, Esq.

Sir – I am ashamed that you have been forced to call so often for your books, but it has been by no fault on either side. They have never been out of my hands, nor have I ever been at home without seeing you; for to see a man so skilful in the antiquities of my country, is an opportunity of improvement not willingly to be missed.

Your notes on Alfred[1] appear to me very judicious and accurate, but they are too few. Many things familiar to you are unknown to me, and to most others; and you must not think too favourably of your readers: by supposing them knowing, you will leave them ignorant. Measure of land, and value of money, it is of great importance to state with care. Had the Saxons any gold coin?

I have much curiosity after the manners and transactions of the middle ages, but have wanted either diligence or opportunity in both.[a] You, Sir, have great opportunities, and I wish you both diligence and success.

I am, Sir, &c.

SAM. JOHNSON.

July 17, 1781.

The following curious anecdote I insert in Dr Burney's own words. 'Dr Burney related to Dr Johnson the partiality which his writings had excited in a friend of Dr Burney's, the late Mr Bewley, well known in Norfolk by the name of the *Philosopher of Massingham*; who, from the *Ramblers* and plan of his Dictionary, and long before the author's fame was established by the Dictionary itself, or any other work, had conceived such a reverence for him, that he urgently begged Dr Burney to give him the cover of the first letter he had received from him, as a relic of so estimable a writer. This was in 1755. In 1760, when Dr Burney visited Dr Johnson at the Temple in London, where he had

---

I am indebted to Mr Malone, one of Sir Joshua Reynolds's executors, for the following note, which was found among his papers after his death, and which, we may presume, his unaffected modesty prevented him from communicating to me with the other letters from Dr Johnson with which he was pleased to furnish me. However slight in itself, as it does honour to that illustrious painter, and most amiable man, I am happy to introduce it:

To Sir Joshua Reynolds.

Dear Sir – It was not before yesterday that I received your splendid benefaction. To a hand so liberal in distributing, I hope nobody will envy the power of acquiring. I am, dear Sir,

Your obliged and most humble servant,

SAM. JOHNSON.

June 23, 1781.

1 The Will of King Alfred, alluded to in this letter, is now printing from the original Saxon, in the library of Mr Astle, at the expense of the University of Oxford. It is not to be sold, but is to be distributed in presents.

a For 'in' read 'or'.

then Chambers, he happened to arrive there before he was up, and being shown into the room where he was to breakfast, finding himself alone, he examined the contents of the apartment, to try whether he could undiscovered steal any thing to send to his friend Bewley, as another relic of the admirable Dr Johnson. But finding nothing better to his purpose, he cut some bristles off his hearth-broom, and inclosed them in a letter to his country enthusiast, who received them with due reverence. The Doctor was so sensible of the honour done him by a man of genius and science, to whom he was an utter stranger, that he said to Dr Burney, "Sir there is no man possessed of the smallest portion of modesty, but must be flattered with the admiration of such a man. I'll give him a set of my Lives if he will do me the honour to accept of them." In this he kept his word; and Dr Burney had not only the pleasure of gratifying his friend with a present more worthy of his acceptance than the segment from the hearth-broom, but soon after of introducing him to Dr Johnson himself in Bolt-court, with whom he had the satisfaction of conversing a considerable time, not a fortnight before his death; which happened in St Martin's-street, during his visit to Dr Burney, in the house where the great Sir Isaac Newton had lived and died before.

In one of his little memorandum-books is the following minute:

> August 9, 3 p.m. aetat. 72, in the summer-house at Streatham.
>
> After innumerable resolutions formed and neglected, I have retired hither, to plant a life of greater diligence, in hope that I may yet be useful, and be daily better prepared to appear before my Creator and my Judge, from whose infinite mercy I humbly call for assistance and support.
>
> My purpose is,
>
> To pass eight hours every day in some serious employment.
>
> Having prayed, I purpose to employ the next six weeks upon the Italian language, for my settled study.

How venerably pious does he appear in these moments of solitude, and how spirited are his resolutions for the improvement of his mind, even in elegant literature, at a very advanced period of life, and when afflicted with many complaints.

In autumn he went to Oxford, Birmingham, Lichfield, and Ashbourne, for which very good reasons might be given, in the conjectural yet positive manner of writers, who are proud to account for every event which they relate. He himself however says, 'The motives of my journey I hardly know; I omitted it last year, and am not willing to miss it again.'[1] But some good considerations arise, amongst which is the kindly recollection of Mr Hector, surgeon, at Birmingham. 'Hector is likewise an old friend, the only companion of my childhood that passed through the school with me. We have always loved one another; perhaps we may be made better by some serious conversation, of which however I have no distinct hope.'

He says too, 'At Lichfield, my native place, I hope to show a good example by frequent attendance on public worship.'

---

1 *Prayers and Meditations*, p. 201.

My correspondence with him during the rest of this year was I know not why very scanty, and all on my side. I wrote him one letter to introduce Mr Sinclair (now Sir John), the member for Caithness, to his acquaintance; and informed him in another, that my wife had again been affected with alarming symptoms of illness.

In 1782, his complaints increased, and the history of his life for this year, is little more than a mournful recital of the variations of his illness, in the midst of which, however, it will appear from his letters, that the powers of his mind were in no degree impaired.

To JAMES BOSWELL, Esq.

DEAR SIR – I sit down to answer your letter on the same day in which I received it, and am pleased that my first letter of the year is to you. No man ought to be at ease while he knows himself in the wrong; and I have not satisfied myself with my long silence. The letter relating to Mr Sinclair, however, was, I believe, never brought.

My health has been tottering this last year; and I can give no very laudable account of my time. I am always hoping to do better than I have ever hitherto done.

My journey to Ashbourne and Staffordshire was not pleasant; for what enjoyment has a sick man visiting the sick? Shall we ever have another frolic like our journey to the Hebrides?

I hope that dear Mrs Boswell will surmount her complaints; in losing her you would lose your anchor, and be tost, without stability, by the waves of life.[1] I wish both her and you very many years, and very happy.

For some months past I have been so withdrawn from the world, that I can send you nothing particular. All your friends, however, are well, and will be glad of your return to London. I am, dear Sir,

Yours most affectionately,

SAM. JOHNSON.

January 5, 1782.

At a time when he was less able than he had once been to sustain a shock, he was suddenly deprived of Mr Levett, which he thus communicated to Dr Lawrence:

Sir – Our old friend, Mr Levett, who was last night eminently cheerful, died this morning. The man who lay in the same room, hearing an uncommon noise, got up and tried to make him speak, but without effect. He then called Mr Holder, the apothecary, who though when he came he thought him dead, opened a vein, but could draw no blood. So has ended the long life of a very useful and very blameless man. I am, Sir,

Your most humble servant,

SAM. JOHNSON.

Jan. 17, 1782.

1 The truth of this has been proved by sad experience.

In one of his memorandum-books in my possession, is the following entry: 'January 20. Sunday. Robert Levett was buried in the church-yard of Bridewell, between one and two in the afternoon. He died on Thursday 17, about seven in the morning, by an instantaneous death. He was an old and faithful friend; I have known him from about 46. *Commendari*. May GOD have mercy on him. May he have mercy on me.'

Such was Johnson's affectionate regard for Levett,[1] that he honoured his memory with the following verses:

> CONDEMN'D to Hope's delusive mine,
>   As on we toil from day to day,
> By sudden blast or slow decline,
>   Our social comforts drop away.
>
> Well try'd through many a varying year,
>   See LEVETT to the grave descend;
> Officious, innocent, sincere,
>   Of ev'ry friendless name the friend.
>
> Yet still he fills Affection's eye,
>   Obscurely wise and coarsely kind;
> Nor, letter'd arrogance,[2] deny
>   The praise to merit unrefin'd.
>
> When fainting Nature call'd for aid,
>   And hov'ring Death prepar'd the blow,
> His vigorous remedy display'd
>   The pow'r of art without the show.
>
> In Misery's darkest caverns known,
>   His ready help was ever nigh,
> Where hopeless Anguish pours his groan,
>   And lonely Want retir'd to die.[3]
>
> No summons mock'd by chill delay,
>   No petty gains disdain'd by pride;
> The modest wants of ev'ry day
>   The toil of ev'ry day supply'd.
>
> His virtues walk'd their narrow round,
>   Nor made a pause nor left a void;
> And sure th' Eternal Master found
>   His single talent well employ'd.

---

1 See an account of him in *Gentleman's Magazine*, Feb. 1785.

2 In both editions of Sir John Hawkins's *Life of Dr Johnson*, 'letter'd *ignorance*' is printed.

3 Johnson repeated this line to me thus: 'And Labour steals an hour to die.' But he afterwards altered it to the present reading.

The busy day, the peaceful night,
  Unfelt, uncounted, glided by;
His frame was firm, his powers were bright,
  Though now his eightieth year was nigh.

Then, with no throbs of fiery pain,
  No cold gradations of decay,
Death broke at once the vital chain,
  And freed his soul the nearest way.

In one of his registers of this year, there occurs the following curious passage: 'Jan. 20. The ministry is dissolved. I prayed with Francis, and gave thanks.'[1] It has been the subject of discussion, whether there are two distinct particulars mentioned here, or that we are to understand the giving of thanks to be in consequence of the dissolution of the ministry. In support of the last of these conjectures, may be urged his mean opinion of that ministry, which has frequently appeared in the course of this work; and it is strongly confirmed by what he said on the subject to Mr Seward: 'I am glad the ministry is removed. Such a bunch of imbecility never disgraced a country. If they sent a messenger into the City to take up a printer, the messenger was taken up instead of the printer, and committed by the sitting Alderman. If they sent one army to the relief of another, the first army was defeated and taken before the second arrived. I will not say that what they did was always wrong; but it was always done at a wrong time.'

To Mrs STRAHAN.

DEAR MADAM – Mrs Williams showed me your kind letter. This little habitation is now but a melancholy place, clouded with the gloom of disease and death. Of the four inmates, one has been suddenly snatched away; two are oppressed by very afflictive and dangerous illness; and I tried yesterday to gain some relief by a third bleeding, from a disorder which has for some time distressed me, and I think myself to-day much better.

I am glad, dear Madam, to hear that you are so far recovered as to go to Bath. Let me once more entreat you to stay till your health is not only obtained but confirmed. Your fortune is such as that no moderate expense deserves your care; and you have a husband who, I believe, does not regard it. Stay, therefore, till you are quite well. I am, for my part, very much deserted; but complaint is useless. I hope GOD will bless you, and I desire you to form the same wish for me. I am, dear Madam,

  Your most humble servant,

                                    SAM. JOHNSON.

Feb. 4, 1782.

1 *Prayers and Meditations*, p. 209.

To EDMOND MALONE, Esq.

SIR – I have for many weeks been so much out of order, that I have gone out only in a coach to Mrs Thrale's, where I can use all the freedom that sickness requires. Do not, therefore, take it amiss, that I am not with you and Dr Farmer. I hope hereafter to see you often. I am, Sir,

Your most humble servant,

SAM. JOHNSON.

Feb. 27, 1782.

To the same.

DEAR SIR – I hope I grow better, and shall soon be able to enjoy the kindness of my friends. I think this wild adherence to Chatterton more unaccountable than the obstinate defence of Ossian. In Ossian there is a national pride, which may be forgiven, though it cannot be applauded. In Chatterton there is nothing but the resolution to say again what has once been said. I am, Sir,

Your humble servant,

SAM. JOHNSON.

March 2, 1782.

These short letters show the regard which Dr Johnson entertained for Mr Malone, who the more he is known is the more highly valued. It is much to be regretted that Johnson was prevented from sharing the elegant hospitality of that gentleman's table, at which he would in every respect have been fully gratified. Mr Malone, who has so ably succeeded him as an Editor of Shakspeare, has, in his Preface, done great and just honour to Johnson's memory.

To Mrs LUCY PORTER, in Lichfield.

DEAR MADAM – I went away from Lichfield ill, and have had a trouble-some time with my breath; for some weeks I have been disordered by a cold, of which I could not get the violence abated, till I had been let blood three times. I have not, however, been so bad but that I could have written, and I am sorry that I neglected it.

My dwelling is but melancholy; both Williams, and Desmoulins, and myself are very sickly; Frank is not well; and poor Levett died in his bed the other day, by a sudden stroke; I suppose not one minute passed between health and death; so uncertain are human things.

Such is the appearance of the world about me; I hope your scenes are more cheerful. But whatever befals us, though it is wise to be serious, it is useless and foolish, and perhaps sinful to be gloomy. Let us, therefore, keep ourselves as easy as we can; though the loss of friends will be felt, and poor Levett had been a faithful adherent for thirty years.

Forgive me, my dear love, the omission of writing; I hope to mend that and my other faults. Let me have your prayers.

Make my compliments to Mr Cobb, and Miss Adey, and Mr Pearson, and the whole company of my friends. I am, my dear,

Your most humble servant,

SAM. JOHNSON.

London, March 2, 1782.

To the same.

DEAR MADAM – My last was but a dull letter, and I know not that this will be much more cheerful; I am however willing to write, because you are desirous to hear from me.

My disorder has now begun its ninth week, for it is not yet over. I was last Thursday blooded for the fourth time, and have since found myself much relieved, but I am very tender and easily hurt; so that since we parted I have had little comfort, but I hope that the spring will recover me; and that in the summer I shall see Lichfield again, for I will not delay my visit another year to the end of autumn.

I have, by advertising, found poor Mr Levett's brothers in Yorkshire, who will take the little that he has left; it is but little, yet it will be welcome, for I believe they are of very low condition.

To be sick, and to see nothing but sickness and death, is but a gloomy state, but I hope better times, even in this world will come, and whatever this world may with-hold or give, we shall be happy in a better state. Pray for me, my dear Lucy.

Make my compliments to Mrs Cobb, and Miss Adey, and my old friend, Hetty Bailey, and to all the Lichfield ladies. I am, dear Madam,

Yours, affectionately,

SAM. JOHNSON.

Bolt-court, Fleet-street,
March 19, 1782.

On the day on which this letter was written, he thus feelingly mentions his respected friend and physician, Dr Lawrence: 'Poor Lawrence has almost lost the sense of hearing; and I have lost the conversation of a learned, intelligent, and communicative companion, and a friend whom long familiarity has much endeared. Lawrence is one of the best men whom I have known. – *Nostrum omnium miserere Deus.*'[1]

It was Dr Johnson's custom when he wrote to Dr Lawrence concerning his own health, to use the Latin language. I have been favoured by Miss Lawrence with one of these letters as a specimen:

1 *Prayers and Meditations*, p. 207.

T. Lawrentio, *Medico S.*

Novum frigus, nova tussis, nova spirandi difficultas, novam sanguinis missionem suadent, quam tamen te inconsulto nolim fieri. Ad te venire vix possum, nec est cur ad me venias. Licere vel non licere uno verbo dicendum est; cetera mihi et Holdero[1] reliqueris. Si per te licet, imperatur nuncio Holderum ad me deducere.

   Maiis Calendis, 1782.

   Postquam tu discesseris quo me vertam?[2]

To Captain Langton,[3] in Rochester.

Dear Sir – It is now long since we saw one another, and whatever has been the reason neither you have written to me, nor I to you. To let friendship die away by negligence and silence, is certainly not wise. It is voluntarily to throw away one of the greatest comforts of this weary pilgrimage, of which when it is, as it must be, taken finally away, he that travels on alone, will wonder how his esteem could be so little. Do not forget me; you see that I do not forget you. It is pleasing in the silence of solitude to think, that there is one at least, however distant, of whose benevolence there is little doubt, and whom there is yet hope of seeing again.

1   Mr Holder, Dr Johnson's apothecary.[a]

2   Soon after the above letter, Dr Lawrence left London, but not before the palsy had made so great a progress as to render him unable to write for himself. – The following are extracts from letters addressed to one of his daughters:

   'You will easily believe with what gladness I read that you had heard once again that voice to which we have all so often delighted to attend. May you often hear it. If we had his mind, and his tongue, we could spare the rest.

   'I am not vigorous, but much better than when dear Dr Lawrence held my pulse the last time. Be so kind as to let me know, from one little interval to another, the state of his body. I am pleased that he remembers me, and hope that it never can be possible for me to forget him. July 22, 1782.'

   'I am much delighted even with the small advances which dear Dr Lawrence makes towards recovery. If we could have again but his mind, and his tongue in his mind, and his right hand, we should not much lament the rest. I should not despair of helping the swelled hand by electricity, if it were frequently and diligently supplied.

   'Let me know from time to time whatever happens; and I hope I need not tell you, how much I am interested in every change. Aug. 26, 1782.'

   'Though the accounts with which you favoured me in your last letter could not give me the pleasure that I wished, yet I was glad to receive it; for my affection to my dear friend makes me desirous of knowing his state, whatever it be. I beg, therefore, that you continue to let me know, from time to time, all that you observe.

   'Many fits of severe illness have, for about three months past, forced my kind physician often upon my mind. I am now better, and hope gratitude, as well as distress, can be a motive to remembrance. Bolt-court, Fleet-street, Feb. 4, 1783.'

3   Mr Langton being at this time on duty at Rochester, he is addressed by his military title.

a   Add: 'in the Strand'.

Of my life, from the time we parted, the history is mournful. The spring of last year deprived me of Thrale, a man whose eye for fifteen years had scarcely been turned upon me but with respect or tenderness; for such another friend, the general course of human things will not suffer man to hope. I passed the summer at Streatham, but there was no Thrale; and having idled away the summer with a weakly body and neglected mind, I made a journey to Staffordshire on the edge of winter. The season was dreary, I was sickly, and found the friends sickly whom I went to see. After a sorrowful sojourn, I returned to a habitation possessed for the present by two sick women, where my dear old friend, Mr Levett, to whom as he used to tell me, I owe your acquaintance, died a few weeks ago, suddenly in his bed; there passed not, I believe, a minute between health and death. At night, as at Mrs Thrale's I was musing in my chamber, I thought with uncommon earnestness, that however I might alter my mode of life, or whithersoever I might remove, I would endeavour to retain Levett about me; in the morning my servant brought me word that Levett was called to another state, a state for which, I think, he was not unprepared, for he was very useful to the poor. How much soever I valued him, I now wish that I had valued him more.

I have myself been ill more than eight weeks of a disorder, from which at the expense of about fifty ounces of blood, I hope I am now recovering.

You, dear Sir, have, I hope, a more cheerful scene; you see George fond of his book, and the pretty misses airy and lively, with my own little Jenny equal to the best; and in whatever can contribute to your quiet or pleasure, you have Lady Rothes ready to concur. May whatever you enjoy of good be increased, and whatever you suffer of evil be diminished.

I am, dear Sir, your humble servant,

SAM JOHNSON.

Bolt-court, Fleet-street,
March 20, 1782.

To Mr HECTOR, in Birmingham.[1]

DEAR SIR – I hope I do not very grossly flatter myself to imagine that you and dear Mrs Careless will be glad to hear some account of me. I performed the journey to London with very little inconvenience, and came safe to my habitation, where I found nothing but ill-health, and, of consequence, very little cheerfulness. I then went to visit a little way into the country, where I got a complaint by a cold which has hung eight weeks upon me, and from which I am, at the expense of fifty ounces of blood, not yet free. I am afraid I must once more owe my recovery to warm weather, which seems to make no advances towards us.

---

1 A part of this letter having been torn off, I have, from the evident meaning, supplied a few words and half words at the ends and beginnings of lines.

Such is my health, which will, I hope, soon grow better. In other respects I have no reason to complain. I know not that I have written any thing more generally commended than the Lives of the Poets; and have found the world willing enough to caress me, if my health had invited me to be in much company: but this season I have been almost wholly employed in nursing myself.

When summer comes I hope to see you again, and will not put off my visit to the end of the year. I have lived so long in London, that I did not remember the difference of seasons.

Your health, when I saw you, was much improved. You will be prudent enough not to put it in danger. I hope, when we meet again, we shall all congratulate each other upon fair prospects of longer life; though what are the pleasures of the longest life, when placed in comparison with a happy death? I am, dear Sir, yours most affectionately,

SAM. JOHNSON.

London, March 21, 1782.

To the same.

[*Without a date, but supposed to be about this time.*]
DEAR SIR – That you and dear Mrs Careless should have care or curiosity about my health, gives me that pleasure which every man feels from finding himself not forgotten. In age we feel again that love of our native place and our early friends, which, in the bustle or amusements of middle life, were overborn and suspended. You and I should now naturally cling to one another: we have outlived most of those who could pretend to rival us in each other's kindness. In our walk through life we have dropped our companions, and are now to pick up such as chance may offer us, or to travel on alone. You, indeed, have a sister, with whom you can divide the day: I have no natural friend left; but Providence has been pleased to preserve me from neglect; I have not wanted such alleviations of life as friendship could supply. My health has been, from my twentieth year, such as has seldom afforded me a single day of ease; but it is at least not worse: and I sometimes make myself believe that it is better. My disorders are, however, still sufficiently oppressive.

I think of seeing Staffordshire again this autumn, and intend to find my way through Birmingham, where I hope to see you and dear Mrs Careless well. I am, Sir, your affectionate friend,

SAM. JOHNSON.

I wrote to him at different dates; regretted that I could not come to London this spring, but hoped we should meet somewhere in the summer; mentioned the state of my affairs, and suggested hopes of some preferment; informed him, that as *The Beauties of Johnson* had been published in London, some obscure scribbler had published at Edinburgh, what he called *Deformities of Johnson*.

To James Boswell, Esq.

Dear Sir – The pleasure which we used to receive from each other on Good-Friday and Easter-day, we must be this year content to miss. Let us, however, pray for each other, and hope to see one another yet from time to time with mutual delight. My disorder has been a cold, which impeded the organs of respiration, and kept me many weeks in a state of great uneasiness, but by repeated phlebotomy it is now relieved; and next to the recovery of Mrs Boswell, I flatter myself, that you will rejoice at mine.

What we shall do in the summer it is yet too early to consider. You want to know what you shall do now; I do not think this time of bustle and confusion likely to produce any advantage to you. Every man has those to reward and gratify who have contributed to his advancement. To come hither with such expectations at the expense of borrowed money, which, I find, you know not where to borrow, can hardly be considered as prudent. I am sorry to find, what your solicitation seems to imply, that you have already gone the whole length of your credit. This is to set the quiet of your whole life at hazard. If you anticipate your inheritance, you can at last inherit nothing; all that you receive must pay for the past. You must get a place, or pine in penury, with the empty name of a great estate. Poverty, my dear friend, is so great an evil, and pregnant with so much temptation, and so much misery, that I cannot but earnestly enjoin you to avoid it. Live on what you have, live if you can on less; do not borrow either for vanity or pleasure; the vanity will end in shame, and the pleasure in regret; stay therefore at home, till you have saved money for your journey hither.

The Beauties of Johnson are said to have got money to the collector; if the *Deformities* have the same success, I shall be still a more extensive benefactor.

Make my compliments to Mrs Boswell, who is, I hope, reconciled to me; and to the young people, whom I never have offended.

You never told me the success of your plea against the Solicitors.

I am, dear Sir, your most affectionate,

Sam. Johnson.

London, March 28, 1782.

Notwithstanding his afflicted state of body and mind this year, the following correspondence affords a proof not only of his benevolence and conscientious readiness to relieve a good man from error, but by his clothing one of the sentiments in his *Rambler* in different language, not inferior to that of the original, shows his extraordinary command of clear and forcible expression.

A clergyman at Bath wrote to him, that in the *Morning Chronicle*, a passage in *The Beauties of Johnson*, article Death, had been pointed out as supposed by some readers to recommend suicide, the words being, 'To die is the fate of man; but to die with lingering anguish is generally his folly'; and respectfully suggesting to him, that such an erroneous notion of any sentence in the writings of an acknowledged friend of religion and virtue, should not pass uncontradicted.

Johnson thus answered the clergyman's letter:

To the Reverend Mr ——, at Bath.

SIR – Being now in the country in a state of recovery, as I hope, from a very oppressive disorder, I cannot neglect the acknowledgement of your Christian letter. The book called *The Beauties of Johnson*, is the production of I know not whom: I never saw it but by casual inspection, and considered myself as utterly disengaged from its consequences. Of the passage you mention, I remember some notice in some paper; but, knowing that it must be misrepresented, I thought of it no more, nor do I know where to find it in my own books. I am accustomed to think little of news-papers, but an opinion so weighty and serious as yours has determined me to do, what I should, without your seasonable admonition, have omitted; and I will direct my thought to be shown in its true state.[1] If I could find the passage, I would direct you to it. I suppose the tenor is this: – 'Acute diseases are the immediate and inevitable strokes of Heaven, but of them the pain is short, and the conclusion speedy: chronical disorders, by which we are suspended in tedious torture between life and death, are commonly the effect of our own misconduct and intemperance. To die, &c.' – This, Sir, you see, is all true, and all blameless. I hope, some time in the next week, to have all rectified. My health has been lately much shaken; if you favour this with any answer, it will be a comfort to me to know that I have your prayers.

I am, &c.

SAM. JOHNSON.

May 15, 1782.

This letter, as might be expected, had its full effect, and the clergyman acknowledged it in grateful and pious terms.[2]

The following letters require no extracts from mine to introduce them.

---

1 What follows appeared in the *Morning Chronicle* of May 29, 1782. – 'A correspondent having mentioned, in the *Morning Chronicle* of December 12, the last clause of the following paragraph, as seeming to favour suicide; we are requested to print the whole passage, that its true meaning may appear, which is not to recommend suicide, but exercise.

Exercise cannot secure us from that dissolution to which we are decreed; but while the soul and body continue united, it can make the association pleasing, and give probable hopes that they shall be disjoined by an easy separation. It was a principle among the ancients, that acute diseases are from Heaven, and chronical from ourselves; the dart of death, indeed, falls from Heaven, but we poison it by our own misconduct: to die is the fate of man; but to die with lingering anguish is generally his folly.

2 The Correspondence may be seen at length in the *Gentleman's Magazine*, Feb. 1786.

To James Boswell, Esq.

Dear Sir – The earnestness and tenderness of your letter is such, that I cannot think myself showing it more respect than it claims by sitting down to answer it the day on which I received it.

This year has afflicted me with a very irksome and severe disorder. My respiration has been much impeded, and much blood has been taken away. I am now harrassed by a catarrhous cough from which my purpose is to seek relief by change of air; and I am, therefore, preparing to go to Oxford.

Whether I did right in dissuading you from coming to London this spring, I will not determine. You have not lost much by missing my company; I have scarcely been well for a single week. I might have received comfort from your kindness, but you would have seen me afflicted, and, perhaps, found me peevish. Whatever might have been your pleasure or mine, I know not how I could have honestly advised you to come hither with borrowed money. Do not accustom yourself to consider debt only as an inconvenience: you will find it a calamity. Poverty takes away so many means of doing good, and produces so much inability to resist evil, both natural and moral, that it is by all virtuous means to be avoided. Consider a man whose fortune is very narrow; whatever be his rank by birth, or whatever his reputation by intellectual excellence, what good can he do? or what evil can he prevent? That he cannot help the needy is evident, he has nothing to spare. But, perhaps, his advice or admonition may be useful. His poverty will destroy his influence: many more can find that he is poor, than that he is wise; and few will reverence the understanding that is of so little advantage to its owner. I say nothing of the personal wretchedness of a debtor, which, however, has passed into a proverb. Of riches, it is not necessary to write the praise. Let it, however, be remembered, that he who has money to spare, has it always tn his power to benefit others; and of such power a good man must always be desirous.

I am pleased with your account of Easter.[1] We shall meet, I hope, in autumn, both well and both cheerful; and part each the better for the other's company.

Make my compliments to Mrs Boswell, and to the young charmers.

I am, &c.

SAM. JOHNSON.

London, June 3, 1782.[a]

[1] Which I celebrated in the Church-of-England chapel at Edinburgh, founded by Lord Chief Baron Smith, of respectable and pious memory.

[a] Between the two letters to Mr Boswell, read:

To Mr Perkins.

Dear Sir – I am much pleased that you are going a very long journey, which may by proper conduct restore your health and prolong your life.

Observe these rules:

1. Turn all care out of your head as soon as you mount the chaise.

To JAMES BOSWELL, Esq.

DEAR SIR – Being uncertain whether I should have any call this autumn into the country, I did not immediately answer your kind letter. I have no call, but if you desire to meet me at Ashbourne, I believe I can come thither; if you had rather come to London, I can stay at Streatham; take your choice.

This year has been very heavy. From the middle of January to the middle of June I was battered by one disorder after another; I am now very much recovered, and hope still to be better. What happiness it is that Mrs Boswell has escaped.

My *Lives* are reprinting, and I have forgotten the author of Gray's character;[1] write immediately, and it may be perhaps yet inserted.

Of London or Ashbourne you have your free choice; at any place I shall be glad to see you. I am, dear Sir, your, &c.

SAM. JOHNSON.

Aug. 24, 1782.

On the 30th of August, I informed him that my honoured father had died that morning; a complaint under which he had long laboured, having suddenly come to a crisis, while I was upon a visit at the seat of Sir Charles Preston, from whence I had hastened the day before, upon receiving a letter by express.

To JAMES BOSWELL, Esq.

DEAR SIR – I have struggled through this year with so much infirmity of body, and such strong impressions of the fragility of life, that death, wherever it appears, fills me with melancholy; and I cannot hear without emotion, of the removal of any one, whom I have known, into another state.

Your father's death had every circumstance that could enable you to bear it; it was at a mature age, and it was expected; and as his general life had been pious, his thoughts had doubtless for many years past been turned upon eternity. That you did not find him sensible must doubtless grieve

---

2. Do not think about frugality; your health is worth more than it can cost.
3. Do not continue any day's journey to fatigue.
4. Take now and then a day's rest.
5. Get a smart sea sickness, if you can.
6. Cast away all anxiety, and keep your mind easy.

This last direction is the principal; with an unquiet mind, neither exercise, nor diet, nor physic, can be of much use.

I wish you, dear Sir, a prosperous journey, and a happy recovery. I am, dear Sir, Your most affectionate, humble servant,

SAM. JOHNSON.

July 28, 1782.

1 The Reverend Mr Temple, Vicar of St Gluvias, Cornwall.

you; his disposition towards you was undoubtedly that of a kind, though not of a fond father. Kindness, at least actual, is in our power, but fondness is not; and if by negligence or imprudence you had extinguished his fondness, he could not at will rekindle it. Nothing then remained between you but mutual forgiveness of each other's faults, and mutual desire of each other's happiness.

I shall long to know his final disposition of his fortune.

You, dear Sir, have now a new station, and have therefore new cares, and new employments. Life, as Cowley seems to say, ought to resemble a well ordered poem; of which one rule generally received is, that the exordium should be simple, and should promise little. Begin your new course of life with the least show, and the least expense possible; you may at pleasure increase both, but you cannot easily diminish them. Do not think your estate your own, while any man can call upon you for money which you cannot pay; therefore, begin with timorous parsimony. Let it be your first care not to be in any man's debt.

When the thoughts are extended to a future state, the present life seems hardly worthy of all those principles of conduct, and maxims of prudence, which one generation of men has transmitted to another; but upon a closer view, when it is perceived how much evil is produced, and how much good is impeded by embarrassment and distress, and how little room the expedients of poverty leave for the exercise of virtue; it grows manifest that the boundless importance of the next life, enforces some attention to the interests of this.

Be kind to the old servants, and secure the kindness of the agents and factors; do not disgust them by asperity, or unwelcome gaiety, or apparent suspicion. From them you must learn the real state of your affairs, the characters of your tenants, and the value of your lands.

Make my compliments to Mrs Boswell; I think her expectations from air and exercise are the best that she can form. I hope she will live long and happily.

I forget whether I told you that Rasay has been here; we dined cheerfully together. I entertained lately a young gentleman from Coriatachat.

I received your letters only this morning. I am, dear Sir, yours, &c.

SAM. JOHNSON.

London, Sept. 7, 1782.

In answer to my next letter, I received one from him, dissuading me from hastening to him as I had proposed; what is proper for publication is the following paragraph, equally just and tender:

One expense, however, I would not have you to spare: let nothing be omitted that can preserve Mrs Boswell, though it should be necessary to transplant her for a time into a softer climate. She is the prop and stay of your life. How much must your children suffer by losing her.

My wife was now so much convinced of his sincere friendship for me, and regard for her, that she without any suggestion on my part, wrote him a very polite and grateful letter.

Dr JOHNSON to Mrs BOSWELL.

DEAR LADY — I have not often received so much pleasure as from your invitation to Auchinleck. The journey thither and back is, indeed, too great for the latter part of the year; but if my health were fully recovered, I would suffer no little heat and cold, nor a wet or a rough road to keep me from you. I am, indeed, not without hope of seeing Auchinleck again, but to make it a pleasant place I must see its lady well, and brisk, and airy. For my sake, therefore, among many greater reasons, take care, dear Madam, of your health, spare no expense, and want no attendance that can procure ease, or preserve it. Be very careful to keep your mind quiet; and do not think it too much to give an account of your recovery to, Madam, your, &c.

SAM. JOHNSON.

London, Sept. 7, 1782.

To JAMES BOSWELL, Esq.

DEAR SIR — Having passed almost this whole year in a succession of disorders, I went in October to Brighthelmston, whither I came in a state of so much weakness, that I rested four times in walking between the inn and the lodging. By physic and abstinence I grew better, and am now reasonably easy, though at a great distance from health. I am afraid, however, that health begins, after seventy, and often long before, to have a meaning different from that which it had at thirty. But it is culpable to murmur at the established order of the creation, as it is vain to oppose it. He that lives, must grow old; and he that would rather grow old than die, has GOD to thank for the infirmities of old age.

At your long silence I am rather angry. You do not, since now you are the head of your house, think it worth your while to try whether you or your friend can live longer without writing, nor suspect after so many years of friendship, that when I do not write to you, I forget you. Put all such useless jealousies out of your head, and disdain to regulate your own practice by the practice of another, or by any other principle than the desire of doing right.

Your economy, I suppose, begins now to be settled; your expenses are adjusted to your revenue, and all your people in their proper places. Resolve not to be poor: whatever you have, spend less. Poverty is a great enemy to human happiness; it certainly destroys liberty, and it makes some virtues impracticable, and others extremely difficult.

Let me know the history of your life, since your accession to your estate. How many houses, how many cows, how much land in your own hand, and what bargains you make with your tenants. . . .

Of my *Lives of the Poets*, they have printed a new edition in octavo, I hear, of three thousand. Did I give a set to Lord Hailes? If I did not, I will do it out of these. What did you make of all your copy?

Mrs Thrale and the three Misses are now for the winter, in Argyll-street. Sir Joshua Reynolds has been out of order, but is well again; and I am, dear Sir, your affectionate humble servant,

SAM. JOHNSON.

London, Dec. 7, 1782.

To Dr SAMUEL JOHNSON.

Edinburgh, Dec. 20, 1782.

DEAR SIR – I was made happy by your kind letter, which gave us the agreeable hopes of seeing you in Scotland again.

I am much flattered by the concern you are pleased to take in my recovery. I am better, and hope to have it in my power to convince you by my attention, of how much consequence I esteem your health to the world and to myself. I remain, Sir, with grateful respect,

Your obliged and obedient servant,

MARGARET BOSWELL.

The death of Mr Thrale had made a very material alteration upon Johnson, with respect to his reception in that family. The manly authority of the husband no longer curbed the lively exuberance of the lady; and as her vanity had been fully gratified, by having the Colossus of Literature attached to her for many years, she gradually became less assiduous to please him. Whether her attachment to him was already divided by another object, I am unable to ascertain; but it is plain that Johnson's penetration was alive to her neglect or forced attention; for on the 6th of October this year, we find him making a 'parting use of the library' at Streatham, and pronouncing a prayer, which he composed 'On leaving Mr Thrale's family'.[1]

Almighty GOD, Father of all mercy, help me by thy grace, that I may, with humble and sincere thankfulness, remember the comforts and conveniencies which I have enjoyed at this place; and that I may resign them with holy submission, equally trusting in thy protection when Thou givest, and when Thou takest away. Have mercy upon me, O LORD, have mercy upon me.

To thy fatherly protection, O LORD, I commend this family. Bless, guide, and defend them, that they may so pass through this world, as finally to enjoy in thy presence everlasting happiness, for JESUS CHRIST's sake. Amen.

One cannot read this prayer, without some emotions not very favourable to the lady whose conduct occasioned it.

In one of his memorandum-books I find, 'Sunday, went to church at Streatham. *Templo valedixi cum osculo.*'

---

1 *Prayers and Meditations*, p. 214.

He met Mr Philip Metcalfe often at Sir Joshua Reynolds's, and other places, and was a good deal with him at Brighthelmston this autumn, being pleased at once with his excellent table and animated conversation. Mr Metcalfe showed him great respect, and sent him a note that he might have the use of his carriage whenever he pleased. Johnson (3d October, 1782) returned this polite answer: 'Mr Johnson is very much obliged by the kind offer of the carriage; but he has no desire of using Mr Metcalfe's carriage, except when he can have the pleasure of Mr Metcalfe's company.' Mr Metcalfe could not but be highly pleased that his company was thus valued by Johnson, and he frequently attended him in airings. They also went together to Cirencester, and they visited Petworth and Cowdery, the venerable seat of the Lords Montacute. 'Sir (said Johnson), I should like to stay here four-and-twenty hours. We see here how our ancestors lived.'

That his curiosity, however, was unabated, appears from two letters to Mr John Nichols, of the 10th and 20th of October this year. In one he says, 'I have looked into your *Anecdotes*, and you will hardly thank a lover of literary history for telling you, that he has been much informed and gratified. I wish you would add your own discoveries and intelligence to those of Dr Rawlinson, and undertake the Supplement to Wood. Think of it.' In the other, 'I wish, Sir, you could obtain some fuller information of Jortin, Markland, and Thirlby. They were three contemporaries of great eminence.'

To Sir JOSHUA REYNOLDS.

DEAR SIR – I heard yesterday of your late disorder, and should think ill of myself if I had heard of it without alarm. I heard likewise of your recovery, which I sincerely wish to be complete and permanent. Your country has been in danger of losing one of its brightest ornaments, and I of losing one of my oldest and kindest friends: but I hope you will still live long, for the honour of the nation; and that more enjoyment of your elegance, your intelligence, and your benevolence, is still reserved for, dear Sir,

Your most affectionate, &c.

SAM. JOHNSON.

Brighthelmston, Nov. 14, 1782.

The Reverend Mr Wilson having dedicated to him his *Archæological Dictionary*, that mark of respect was thus acknowledged.

To the Reverend Mr WILSON, Clitheroe, Lancashire.

REVEREND SIR – That I have long omitted to return you thanks for the honour conferred upon me by your Dedication, I intreat you with great earnestness not to consider as more faulty than it is. A very importunate and oppressive disorder has for some time debarred me from the pleasures, and obstructed me in the duties of life. The esteem and kindness of wise and good men is one of the last pleasures which I can be content to lose; and gratitude to those from whom this pleasure is received, is a duty of which I hope never to be reproached with the final neglect. I therefore now return you thanks for the notice which I have received from you; and which I consider as giving to my name not only more bulk, but more weight; not only as extending its superficies, but as increasing its value. Your book was evidently wanted, and will, I hope, find its way into the school, to which, however, I do not mean to confine it; for no man has so much skill in ancient rites and practices as not to want it. As I suppose myself to owe part of your kindness to my excellent friend Dr Patten, he has likewise a just claim to my acknowledgements, which I hope you, Sir, will transmit. There will soon appear a new edition of my Poetical Biography; if you will accept of a copy to keep me in your mind, be pleased to let me know how it may be conveniently conveyed to you. The present is small, but it is given with good will by, Reverend Sir, your most, &c.

SAM. JOHNSON.

Dec. 31, 1782.

In 1783 he was more severely afflicted than ever, as will appear in the course of his correspondence; but still the same ardour for literature, the same constant piety, the same kindness for his friends, and the same vivacity, both in conversation and writing, distinguished him.

Having given Dr Johnson a full account of what I was doing at Auchinleck, and particularly mentioned what I knew would please him – my having brought an old man of eighty-eight from a lonely cottage to a comfortable habitation within my enclosures, where he had good neighbours near to him, I received an answer in February, of which I extract what follows:

I am delighted with your account of your activity at Auchinleck, and wish the old gentleman, whom you have so kindly removed, may live long to promote your prosperity by his prayers. You have now a new character and new duties; think on them, and practise them.

Make an impartial estimate of your revenue, and whatever it is, live upon less. Resolve never to be poor. Frugality is not only the basis of quiet, but of beneficence. No man can help others that wants help himself; we must have enough before we have to spare.

I am glad to find that Mrs Boswell grows well; and hope that to keep her well, no care nor caution will be omitted. May you long live happily together.

When you come hither, pray bring with you Baxter's Anacreon. I cannot get that edition in London.

On Friday, March 21, having arrived in London the night before, I was glad to find him at Mrs Thrale's house, in Argyll-street, appearances of friendship between them being still kept up. I was shown into his room, and after the first salutation he said, 'I am glad you are come. I am very ill.' He looked pale, and was distressed with a difficulty of breathing. But he soon assumed his usual strong animated style of conversation. Seeing me now for the first time as a *Laird*, or proprietor of land, he began, 'Sir, the superiority of a country-gentleman over the people upon his estate is very agreeable; and he who says he does not feel it to be agreeable, lies: for it must be agreeable to have a casual superiority over those who are by nature equal with us.' BOSWELL. 'Yet, Sir, we see great proprietors of land who prefer living in London.' JOHNSON. 'Why, Sir, the pleasure of living in London, the intellectual superiority that is enjoyed there, may counterbalance the other. Besides, Sir, a man may prefer the state of the country gentleman upon the whole, and yet there may never be a moment when he is willing to make the change to quit London for it.' He said, 'It is better to have five *per cent.* out of land than out of money, because it is more secure; but the readiness of transference, and promptness of interest, make many people rather choose the funds. Nay, there is another disadvantage belonging to land, compared with money. A man is not so much afraid of being a hard creditor as of being a hard landlord.' BOSWELL. 'Because there is a sort of kindly connection between a landlord and his tenants.' JOHNSON. 'No, Sir; many landlords with us never see their tenants. It is because if a landlord drives away his tenants, he may not get others; whereas the demand for money is so great, it may always be lent.'

He talked with regret and indignation of the factious opposition to Government at this time, and imputed it, in a great measure, to the Revolution. 'Sir, (said he, in a low voice, having come nearer to me, while his old prejudices seemed to be fermenting in his mind), this Hanoverian family is *isolée* here. They have no friends. Now the Stuarts had friends who stuck by them so late as 1745. When the right of the King is not reverenced, there will not be reverence for those appointed by the King.'

His observation that the present royal family has no friends, has been too much justified by the very ungrateful behaviour of many who were under great obligations to his Majesty; at the same time there are honourable exceptions; and the very next year after this conversation, and ever since, the King has had as extensive and generous support as ever was given to any monarch, and has had the satisfaction of knowing that he was more and more endeared to his people.

He repeated to me his verses on Mr Levett, with an emotion which gave them full effect; and then he was pleased to say, 'You must be as much with me as you can. You have done me good. You cannot think how much better I am since you came in.'

He sent a message to acquaint Mrs Thrale that I was arrived. I had not seen her since her husband's death. She soon appeared, and favoured me with an invitation to stay to dinner, which I accepted. There was no other company but herself and three of her daughters, Dr Johnson, and I. She too, said she was very glad I was come, for she was going to Bath, and should have been sorry to leave Dr Johnson before I came. This seemed to be attentive and kind, and I who had not been informed of any change, imagined all to be as well as formerly. He was little inclined to talk at dinner, and went to sleep after it; but when he joined us in the drawing-room, he seemed revived, and was again himself.

Talking of conversation, he said, 'There must, in the first place, be knowledge, there must be materials; — in the second place, there must be a command of words; — in the third place, there must be imagination, to place things in such views as they are not commonly seen in; – and in the fourth place, there must be presence of mind, and a resolution that is not to be overcome by failures; this last is an essential requisite; for want of it many people do not excel in conversation. Now *I* want it, I throw up the game upon losing a trick.' I wondered to hear him talk thus of himself, and said, 'I don't know, Sir, how this may be, but I am sure you beat other people's cards out of their hands.' I doubt whether he heard this remark. While he went on talking triumphantly, I was fixed in admiration, and said to Mrs Thrale, 'O, for short-hand to take this down.' – 'You'll carry it all in your head (said he); a long head is as good as short-hand.'

It has been observed and wondered at, that Mr Charles Fox never talked with any freedom in the presence of Dr Johnson, though it is well known, and I myself can witness, that his conversation is various, fluent, and exceedingly agreeable. Johnson's experience, however, founded him in going on thus: 'Fox never talks in private company, not from any determination not to talk, but because he has not the first motion. A man who is used to the applause of the House of Commons, has no wish for that of a private company. A man accustomed to throw for a thousand pounds, if set down to throw for sixpence, would not be at the pains to count his dice. Burke's talk is the ebullition of his mind; he does not talk from a desire of distinction, but because his mind is full.'

He thus curiously characterised one of our old acquaintance: '—— is a good man, Sir; but he is a vain man, and a liar. He, however, only tells lies of vanity; of victories, for instance, in conversation which never happened.' This alluded to a story which I had repeated from that gentleman, to entertain Johnson with its wild bravado: 'This Johnson, Sir (said he), whom you are all afraid of, will shrink if you come close to him in argument, and roar as loud as he. He once maintained the paradox, that there is no beauty but in utility. "Sir (said I), what say you to the peacock's tail, which is one of the most beautiful objects in nature, but would have as much utility if its feathers were all of one colour." He *felt* what I thus produced, and had recourse to his usual expedient, ridicule; exclaiming, "A peacock has a tail, and a fox has a tail"; and then he burst out into a laugh. "Well, Sir (said I, with a strong voice, looking him full in the face), you have unkennelled your fox; pursue him if you dare." He had not a word to say, Sir.' Johnson told me that this was a fiction from beginning to end.[1]

---

1 Were I to insert all the stories which have been told of contests boldly maintained with him, imaginary victories obtained over him, of reducing him to silence, and of making him own that his antagonists had the better of him in argument, my volumes would swell to an immoderate size. One instance, I find, has circulated both in conversation and in print; that when he would not allow the Scotch writers to have merit, the late Dr Rose, of Chiswick, asserted, that he could name one Scotch writer, who Dr Johnson himself would allow to have written better than any man of the age; and upon Johnson's asking who it was, answered, 'Lord Bute, when he signed the warrant for your pension.' Upon which Johnson, struck with the repartee, acknowledged that this *was* true. When I mentioned it to Johnson, 'Sir (said he), if Rose said this, I never heard it.'

After musing for some time, he said, 'I wonder how I should have any enemies; for I do harm to nobody.'[1] BOSWELL. 'In the first place, Sir, you will be pleased to recollect, that you set out with attacking the Scotch; so you got a whole nation for your enemies.' JOHNSON. 'Why I own, that by my definition of *oats* I meant to vex them.' BOSWELL. 'Pray, Sir, can you trace the cause of your antipathy to the Scotch?' JOHNSON. 'I cannot, Sir.' BOSWELL. 'Old Mr Sheridan says, it was because they sold Charles the First.' JOHNSON. 'Then, Sir, old Mr Sheridan has found out a very good reason.'

Surely the most obstinate and sulky nationality, the most determined aversion to this great and good man, must be cured, when he is seen thus playing with one of his prejudices, of which he candidly admitted that he could not tell the reason. It was, however, probably owing to his having had in his view the worst part of the Scottish nation, the needy adventurers, many of whom he thought were advanced beyond their merits, by means which he did not approve. Had he in his early life been in Scotland, and seen the worthy, sensible, independent gentlemen, who live rationally and hospitably at home, he never could have entertained such unfavourable and unjust notions of his fellow-subjects. And accordingly we find, that when he did visit Scotland, in the latter period of his life, he was fully sensible of all that it deserved, as I have already pointed out, when speaking of his *Journey to the Western Islands*.

Next day, Saturday, March 22, I found him still at Mrs Thrale's, but he told me that he was to go to his own house in the afternoon. He was better, but I perceived he was but an unruly patient, for Dr Pepys,[a] who visited him, while I was with him said, 'If you were *tractable*, Sir, I should prescribe for you.'

I related to him a remark which a respectable friend had made to me, upon the then state of Government, when those who had been long in opposition had attained to power, it was supposed against the inclination of the Sovereign. 'You need not be uneasy (said this gentleman) about the King. He laughs at them all; he plays them one against another.' JOHNSON. 'Don't think so, Sir. The King is as much oppressed as a man can be. If he plays them one against another he *wins* nothing.'

I had paid a visit to General Oglethorpe in the morning, and was told by him that Dr Johnson saw company on Saturday evenings, and he would meet me at Johnson's, that night. When I mentioned this to Johnson, not doubting that it would please him, as he had a great value for Oglethorpe, the fretfulness of his disease unexpectedly showed itself; his anger suddenly kindled, and he said with vehemence, 'Did not you tell him not to come? Am I to be *hunted* in this manner?' I satisfied him that I could not divine that the visit would not be convenient, and that I certainly could not take it upon me of my own accord, to forbid the General.

---

1 This reflection was very natural in a man of a good heart, who was not conscious of any ill-will to mankind, though the sharp sayings which were sometimes produced by his discrimination and vivacity, and which he perhaps did not recollect, were, I am afraid, too often remembered with resentment.

a Alter 'Dr Pepys' to 'Sir Lucas Pepys'.

I found Dr Johnson in the evening in Mrs Williams's room, at tea and coffee with her and Mrs Desmoulins, who were also both ill; it was a sad scene, and he was not in a very good humour. He said of a performance that had lately come out, 'Sir, if you should search all the mad-houses in England, you would not find ten men who would write so, and think it sense.'

I was glad when General Oglethorpe's arrival was announced; and we left the ladies. Dr Johnson attended him in the parlour and was as courteous as ever. The General said he was busy reading the writers of the middle age. Johnson said they were very curious. OGLETHORPE. 'The House of Commons has usurped the power of the nation's money, and used it tyrannically. Government is now carried on by corrupt influence, instead of the inherent right in the King.' JOHNSON. 'Sir, the want of inherent right in the King occasions all this disturbance. What we did at the Revolution was necessary: but it broke our constitution.'[1] OGLETHORPE. 'My father did not think it necessary.'

On Sunday, March 23, I breakfasted with Dr Johnson, who seemed much relieved, having taken opium the night before. He however protested against it, as a remedy that should be given with the utmost reluctance, and only in extreme necessity. I mentioned how commonly it was used in Turkey, and therefore it could not be so pernicious as he apprehended. He grew warm, and said, 'Turks take opium, and Christians take opium; but Russel, in his account of Aleppo, tells us, that it is as disgraceful in Turkey to take too much opium, as it is with us to get drunk. Sir, it is amazing how things are exaggerated. A gentleman was lately telling in a company where I was present, that in France, as soon as a man of fashion marries, he takes an opera girl into keeping; and this he mentioned as a general custom. Pray, Sir (said I), how many opera girls may there be? He answered, "About fourscore." Well then, Sir (said I), you see there can be no more than fourscore men of fashion who can do this.'

Mrs Desmoulins made tea; and she and I talked before him upon a topic which he had once borne patiently from me, when we were by ourselves – his not complaining of the world, because he was not called to some great office, nor had attained to great wealth. He flew into a violent passion, I confess with some justice, and commanded us to have done. 'Nobody (said he) has a right to talk in this manner, to bring before a man his own character, and the events of his life, when he does not choose it should be done. I never have sought the world; the world was not to seek me. It is rather wonderful that so much has been done for me. All the complaints which are made of the world are unjust. I never knew a man of merit neglected. It was generally by his own fault that he failed of success. A man may hide his head in a hole. He

---

1 I have, in my *Journal of a Tour to the Hebrides*, fully expressed my sentiments upon this subject. The Revolution was *necessary*, but not a subject for *glory*; because it for a long time blasted the generous feelings of *Loyalty*. And now, when by the benignant effect of time the present Royal Family are established in our *affections*, how unwise is it to revive by celebrations the memory of a shock, which it would surely have been better that our constitution had not required.

may go into the country, and publish a book now and then, which nobody reads, and then complain he is neglected. There is no reason why any person should exert himself for a man who has written a good book. He has not written it for any individual. I may as well make a present to the post-man who brings me a letter. When patronage was limited, an author expected to find a Maecenas and complained if he did not find one. Why should he complain? This Maecenas has others as good as he, or others who have got the start of him.' Boswell. 'But surely, Sir, you will allow that there are many men of merit at the bar who never get practice.' Johnson. 'Sir, you are sure that practice is got from an opinion that the person employed deserves it best; so that if a man of merit at the bar does not get practice, it is from error, not from injustice. He is not neglected. A horse that is brought to market may not be bought, though he is a very good horse: but that is from ignorance, not from intention.'

There was in this discourse much novelty, ingenuity, and discrimination, such as is seldom to be found. Yet I cannot help thinking that men of merit, who have no success in life, may be forgiven for *lamenting*, if they are not allowed to *complain*. They may consider it as *hard* that their merit should not have its suitable distinction. If there is no intentional[a] injustice towards them on the part of the world, because their merit has not been perceived, they may repine against *fortune*, or *fate*, or by whatever name they choose to call the supposed mythological power of *Destiny*. It has, however, occurred to me, as a consolatory thought, that men of merit should consider thus: How much harder would it be if the same men had both all the merit and all the prosperity? Would not this be a miserable distribution for the poor dunces? Would men of merit exchange their intellectual superiority, and the enjoyments arising from it, for external distinction, and the pleasures of wealth? If they would not, let them not envy others, who are poor where they are rich, a compensation which is made to them. Let them look inwards and be satisfied; recollecting with conscious pride what Virgil finely says of the *Corycius Senex*, and which I have, in another place,[1] with truth and sincerity applied to Mr Burke:

Regum aequabat opes animis.

On the subject of the right employment of wealth, Johnson observed, 'A man cannot make a bad use of his money, so far as regards Society, if he does not hoard it. For if he either spends it or lends it out, Society has the benefit. It is in general better to spend money than to give it away; for industry is more promoted by spending money, than by giving it away. A man who spends his money is sure he is doing good with it: he is not so sure when he gives it away. A man who spends ten thousand a year will do more good than a man who spends two thousand and gives away eight.'

1 Letter to the People of Scotland against the Attempt to diminish the Number of the Lords of Session. 1785.

In the evening I came to him again. He was rather fretful[a] from his illness. A gentleman asked him, whether he had been abroad to-day. 'Don't talk so childishly, (said he). You may as well ask if I hanged myself to-day.' I mentioned politics. JOHNSON. 'Sir, I'd as soon have a man to break my bones as talk to me of public affairs, internal or external. I have lived to see things all as bad as they can be.'

Having mentioned his friend the second Lord Southwell, he said, 'Lord Southwell was the highest bred man without insolence that I ever was in company with; the most *qualitied* I ever saw. Lord Orrery was not dignified: Lord Chesterfield was, but he was insolent. Lord —— is a man of coarse manners, but a man of abilities and information. I don't say he is a man I would set at the head of a nation, though perhaps he may be as good as the next Prime Minister that comes. But he is a man to be at the head of a Club; – I don't say *our* CLUB; – for there's no such Club.' BOSWELL. 'But, Sir, was not he once a factious man?' JOHNSON. 'O yes, Sir; as factious a fellow as could be found: one who was for sinking us all into the mob.' BOSWELL. 'How then, Sir, did he get into favour with the King?' JOHNSON. 'Because, Sir, I suppose he promised the King to do whatever the King pleased.'

He said, 'Goldsmith's blundering speech to Lord Shelburne, which has been so often mentioned, and which he really did make to him, was only a blunder in emphasis: – "I wonder they should call your Lordship *Malagrida*, for Malagrida was a very good man"; – meant, I wonder they should use *Malagrida* as a term of reproach.'

Soon after this time I had an opportunity of seeing, by means of one of his friends, a proof that his talents, as well as his obliging service to authors, were ready as ever. He had revised *The Village*, an admirable poem, by the Reverend Mr Crabbe. Its sentiments as to the false notions of rustic happiness and rustic virtue, were quite congenial with his own; and he had taken the trouble not only to suggest slight corrections and variations, but to furnish some lines, when he thought he could give the writer's meaning better than in the words of the manuscript.[1]

[a] For 'rather' read 'somewhat'.

[1] I shall give an instance, marking the original by Roman, and Johnson's substitution in Italic characters:

> In fairer scenes, where peaceful pleasures spring,
> Tityrus, the pride of Mantuan swains, might sing:
> But charm'd by him, or smitten with his views,
> Shall modern poets court the Mantuan muse?
> From Truth and Nature shall we widely stray,
> Where Fancy leads, or Virgil leads the way?

> *On Mincio's banks, in Caesar's bounteous reign,*
> *If Tityrus found the golden age again,*
> *Must sleepy bards the flattering dream prolong,*
> *Mechanick echos of the Mantuan song?*
> From Truth and Nature shall we widely stray,
> *Where Virgil, not where Fancy, leads the way?*

On Sunday, March 30, I found him at home in the evening, and had the pleasure to meet with Dr Brocklesby, whose reading, and knowledge of life, and good spirits, supply him with a never-failing source of conversation. He mentioned a respectable gentleman, who became extremely penurious near the close of his life. Johnson said there must have been a degree of madness about him. 'Not at all Sir (said Dr Brocklesby), his judgement was entire.' Unluckily, however, he mentioned that although he had a fortune of twenty-seven thousand pounds, he denied himself many comforts, from an apprehension that he could not afford them. 'Nay, Sir (cried Johnson), when the judgement is so disturbed that a man cannot count, that is pretty well.'

I shall here insert a few of Johnson's sayings, without the formality of dates, as they have no reference to any particular time or place.

'The more a man extends and varies his acquaintance the better.' This, however, was meant with a just restriction; for, he on another occasion said to me, 'Sir, a man may be so much of every thing, that he is nothing of any thing.'

'Raising the wages of day-labourers is wrong; for it does not make them live better, but only makes them idler, and idleness is a very bad thing for human nature.'

'It is a very good custom to keep a journal for a man's own use; he may write upon a card a day all that is necessary to be written, after he has had experience of life. At first there is a great deal to be written, because there is a great deal of novelty. But when once a man has settled his opinions, there is seldom much to be set down.'

'There is nothing wonderful in the journal which we see Swift kept in London, for it contains slight topics, and it might soon be written.'

I praised the accuracy of an account book of a private person[a] whom I mentioned. JOHNSON. "Keeping accounts, Sir, is of no use when a man is spending his own money, and has nobody to whom he is to account. You won't eat less beef to-day, because you have written down what it cost yesterday." I mentioned a[b] lady who thought as he did, so that her husband could not get her to keep an account of the expence of the family, as she thought it enough that she never exceeded the sum allowed her. JOHNSON. "Sir, it is fit she should keep an account, because her husband wishes it; but I do not see its use." I maintained that keeping an account has this advantage, that it satisfies a man that his money has not been lost or stolen, which he might sometimes be apt to imagine, were there no written state of his expense; and besides, a calculation of economy so as not to exceed one's income, cannot be made without a view of the different articles in figures, that one may see how to retrench in some particulars less necessary than others. This he did not attempt to answer.

Here we find Johnson's poetical and critical powers undiminished. I must, however, observe, that the aids he gave to this poem, as to The Traveller and Deserted Village of Goldsmith, were so small as by no means to impair the distinguished merit of the author.

[a] For 'private person' read 'lady'.

[b] For 'a' read 'another'.

Talking of an acquaintance of ours, whose narratives, which abounded in curious and interesting topics, were unhappily found to be very fabulous; I mentioned Lord Mansfield having said to me, 'Suppose we believe one *half* of what he tells.' JOHNSON. 'Aye; but we don't know *which* half to believe. By his lying we lose not only our reverence for him, but all comfort in his conversation.' BOSWELL. 'May we not take it as amusing fiction?' JOHNSON. 'Sir, the misfortune is, that you will insensibly believe as much of it as you incline.'

It is remarkable, that notwithstanding their congeniality in politics, he never was acquainted with a late eminent noble judge, whom I have heard speak of him as a writer, with great respect. Johnson, I know not upon what degree of investigation, entertained no exalted opinion of his Lordship's intellectual character. Talking of him to me one day, he said, 'It is wonderful, Sir, with how little real superiority of mind men can make an eminent figure in public life.' He expressed himself to the same purpose concerning another law Lord, who, it seems, once took a fancy to associate with the wits of London; but with so little success, that Foote said, 'What can he mean by coming among us? He is not only dull himself, but the cause of dullness in others.' Trying him by the test of his colloquial powers, Johnson had found him very defective. He once said to Sir Joshua Reynolds, 'This man now has been ten years about town, and has made nothing of it'; meaning as a companion.[1] He said to me, 'I never heard any thing from him in company that was at all striking; and depend upon it, Sir, it is when you come close to a man in conversation, that you discover what his real abilities are; to make a speech in a public assembly is a knack. Now I honour Thurlow, Sir; Thurlow is a fine fellow; he fairly puts his mind to yours.'

After repeating to him some of his pointed lively sayings, I said, 'It is a pity, Sir, you don't always remember your own good things, that you may have a laugh when you will.' JOHNSON. 'Nay, Sir, it is better that I forget them, that I may be reminded of them and have a laugh[a] brought to my recollection.'

When I recalled his having said as we sailed upon Lochlomond, 'That if he wore any thing fine, it should be *very* fine'; I observed that all his thoughts were upon a great scale. JOHNSON. 'Depend upon it, Sir, every man will have as fine a thing as he can get; as a large diamond for his ring.' BOSWELL. 'Pardon me, Sir; a man of a narrow mind will not think of it, a slight trinket will satisfy him.

Nec sufferre queat majoris pondera gemmae.

I told him I should send him some 'Essays' which I had written, which I hoped he would be so good as to read, and pick out the good ones. JOHNSON. 'Nay, Sir, send me only the good ones; don't make me pick them.'[b]

---

1 Knowing as well as I do, what precision and elegance of oratory his Lordship can display, I cannot but suspect that his unfavourable appearance in a social circle, which drew such animadversions upon him, must be owing to a cold affectation of consequence, from being reserved and stiff. If it be so, and he might be an agreeable man if he would, we cannot be sorry that he misses his aim.

a After 'laugh' read 'on their being'.

b Add: I heard him once say, 'Though the proverb *Nullum numen abest, si sit prudentia,*

On Thursday, April 10, I introduced to him, at his house in Bolt-court, the Honourable and Reverend William Stuart, son of the Earl of Bute; a gentleman truly worthy of being known to Johnson, being, with all the advantages of high birth, learning, travel, and elegant manners, an exemplary parish priest in every respect.

---

does not always prove true, we may be certain of the converse of it, *Nullum numen adest, si sit imprudentia.*

Once, when Mr Seward was going to Bath, and asked his commands, he said, 'Tell Dr Harrington that I wish he would publish another volume of the *Nugae antiquae;* it is a very pretty book.'[1] Mr Seward seconded this wish, and recommended to Dr Harrington to dedicate it to Johnson, and take for his motto, what Catullus says to Cornelius Nepos:

> *namque tu solebas*
> *Meas esse aliquid putare* NUGAS.

As a small proof of his kindliness and delicacy of feeling, the following circumstance may be mentioned: One evening when we were in the street together, and I told him I was going to sup at Mr Beauclerk's, he said, 'I'll go with you.' After having walked part of the way, seeming to recollect something, he suddenly stopped and said, 'I cannot go, – but *I do not love Beauclerk the less.*'

On the frame of his portrait, Mr Beauclerk had inscribed,

> *Ingenium ingens*
> *Inculto latet hoc sub corpore.*

After Mr Beauclerk's death, when it became Mr Langton's property, he made the inscription be defaced. Johnson said complacently, 'It was kind in you to take it off'; and then after a short pause, added, 'and not unkind in him to put it on.'

He said, 'How few of his friends' houses would a man choose to be at, when he is sick!' He mentioned one or two. I recollect only Thrale's.

He observed, 'There is a wicked inclination in most people to suppose an old man decayed in his intellects. If a young or middle-aged man, when leaving a company, does not recollect where he laid his hat, it is nothing; but if the same inattention is discovered in an old man, people will shrug up their shoulders, and say, "His memory is going." '

When I once talked to him of some of the sayings which every body repeats, but nobody knows where to find, such as, *Quos* DEUS *vult perdere, prius dementat*; he told me that he was once offered ten guineas to point out from whence *Semel insanivimus omnes* was taken. He could not do it; but many years afterwards met with it by chance in *Johannes Baptista Mantuanus.*

I am very sorry that I did not take a note of an eloquent argument in which he maintained that the situation of Prince of Wales was the happiest of any person's in the kingdom, even beyond that of the Sovereign. I recollect only – the enjoyment of hope, – the high superiority of rank, without the anxious cares of government, – and a great degree of power, both from natural influence wisely used and from the sanguine expectations of those who look forward to the chance of future favour.

Sir Joshua Reynolds communicated to me the following particulars:

Johnson thought the poems published as translations from Ossian, had so little merit, that he said, 'Sir, a man might write such stuff for ever, if he would *abandon* his mind to it.' *note continued overleaf*

---

1 It has since appeared.

After some compliments on both sides, the tour which Johnson and I had made to the Hebrides was mentioned. – JOHNSON. 'I got an acquisition of more ideas by it than by any thing that I remember. I saw quite a different system of life.' BOSWELL. 'You would not like to make the same journey again.' JOHNSON. 'Why no, Sir; not the same: it is a tale told. *Gravina*, an Italian critic, observes, that every man desires to see that of which he has read; but no

---

He said, 'A man should pass a part of his time with *the laughers*, by which means any thing ridiculous or particular about him might be presented to his view, and corrected.' I observed, he must have been a bold laugher who would have ventured to tell Dr Johnson of any of his particularities.[1]

Having observed the vain ostentatious importance of many people in quoting the authority of Dukes and Lords, as having been in their company, he said, he went to the other extreme, and did not mention his authority when he should have done it, had it not been that of a Duke or a Lord.

Dr Goldsmith said once to Dr Johnson, that he wished for some additional members to the LITERARY CLUB, to give it an agreeable variety; for (said he) there can now be nothing new among us: we have travelled over one another's minds. Johnson seemed a little angry, and said, 'Sir, you have not travelled over *my* mind, I promise you.' Sir Joshua, however, thought Goldsmith right; observing, that 'when people have lived a great deal together, they know what each of them will say on every subject. A new understanding, therefore, is desirable; because though it may only furnish the same sense upon a question which would have been furnished by those with whom we are accustomed to live, yet this sense will have a different colouring; and colouring is of much effect in every thing else as well as in painting.'

Johnson used to say that he made it a constant rule to talk as well as he could, both as to sentiment and expression; by which means, what had been originally effort became familiar and easy. The consequence of this, Sir Joshua observed, was, that his common conversation in all companies was such as to secure him universal attention, as something above the usual colloquial style was expected.

Yet, though Johnson had this habit in company, when another mode was necessary, in order to investigate truth, he could descend to a language intelligible to the meanest capacity. An instance of this was witnessed by Sir Joshua Reynolds, when they were present at an examination of a little blackguard boy, by Mr Saunders Welch, the late Westminster Justice. Welch, who imagined that he was exalting himself in Dr Johnson's eyes by using big words, spoke in a manner that was utterly unintelligible to the boy; Dr Johnson perceiving it, addressed himself to the boy, and changed the pompous phraseology into colloquial language. Sir Joshua Reynolds, who was much amused by this procedure, which seemed a kind of reversing of what might have been expected from the two men, took notice of it to Dr Johnson, as they walked away by themselves. Johnson said, that it was continually the case; and that he was always obliged to *translate* the Justice's swelling diction (smiling), so as that his meaning might be understood by the vulgar, from whom information was to be obtained.

note continued overleaf

1 I am happy, however, to mention a pleasing instance of his enduring with great gentleness to hear one of his most striking particularities pointed out: Miss Hunter, a niece of his friend Christopher Smart, when a very young girl, struck by his extraordinary motions, said to him, 'Pray, Dr Johnson, why do you make such strange gestures?' – 'From bad habit (he replied). Do you, my dear, take care to guard against bad habits.' This I was told by the young lady's brother at Margate.

man desires to read an account of what he has seen. So much does description fall short of reality. Description only excites curiosity: seeing satisfies it. Other people may go and see the Hebrides.' BOSWELL. 'I should wish to go and see

---

Sir Joshua once observed to him, that he had talked above the capacity of some people with whom they had been in company together. 'No matter, Sir (said Johnson); they consider it as a compliment to be talked to, as if they were wiser than they are. So true is this, Sir, that Baxter made it a rule in every sermon that he preached, to say something that was above the capacity of his audience.'[1]

Johnson's dexterity in retort, when he seemed to be driven to an extremity by his adversary, was very remarkable. Of his power in this respect, our common friend, Mr Windham, of Norfolk, has been pleased to furnish me with an eminent instance. However unfavourable to Scotland, he uniformly gave liberal praise to George Buchanan, as a writer. In a conversation concerning the literary merits of the two countries, in which Buchanan was introduced, a Scotchman, imagining that on this ground he should have an undoubted triumph over him, exclaimed, 'Ah, Dr Johnson, what would you have said of Buchanan, had he been an Englishman?' – 'Why, Sir (said Johnson, after a little pause), I should *not* have said of Buchanan, had he been an *Englishman*, what I will now say of him as a *Scotchman*, – that he was the only man of genius his country ever produced.'

And this brings to my recollection another instance of the same nature. I once reminded him that when Dr Adam Smith was expatiating on the beauty of Glasgow, he had cut him short by saying, 'Pray, Sir, have you ever seen Brentford?' and I took the liberty to add, 'My dear Sir, surely that was *shocking*.' – 'Why, then, Sir (he replied), you have never seen Brentford.'

Though his usual phrase for conversation was *talk*, yet he made a distinction; for when he once told me that he dined the day before at a friend's house, with 'a very pretty company'; and I asked him if there was good conversation, he answered, 'No, Sir; we had *talk* enough, but no *conversation*; there was nothing *discussed*.'

Talking of the success of the Scotch in London, he imputed it in a considerable degree to their spirit of nationality. 'You know, Sir (said he), that no Scotchman publishes a book, or has a play brought upon the stage, but there are five hundred people ready to applaud him.'

He gave much praise to his friend Dr Burney's elegant and entertaining travels, and told Mr Seward that he had them in his eye, when writing his *Journey to the Western Islands of Scotland*.

Such was his sensibility, aud so much was he affected by pathetic poetry, that, when he was reading Dr Beattie's *Hermit*, in my presence, it brought tears into his eyes.

He disapproved much of mingling real facts with fiction. On this account he censured a book entitled *Love and Madness*.

Mr Hoole told him, he was born in Moorfields, and had received part of his early instruction in Grub-street. 'Sir, (said Johnson, smiling) you have been *regularly* educated.' Having asked who was his instructor, and Mr Hoole having answered, 'My uncle, Sir, who was a tailor'; Johnson, recollecting himself, said, 'Sir, I knew him; we called him the *metaphysical tailor*. He was of a club in Old-street, with me and George Psalmanazar, and some others: but pray, Sir, was he a good tailor?' Mr Hoole having

note continued overleaf

---

1 The justice of this remark is confirmed by the following story, for which I am indebted to Lord Eliot: A country Parson, who was remarkable for quoting scraps of Latin in his sermons, having died, one of his parishioners was asked how he liked his successor; 'He is a very good preacher (was his answer), but no *latiner*.'

some country totally different from what I have been used to; such as Turkey, where religion and every thing else are different.' JOHNSON. 'Yes, Sir; there are

---

answered that he believed he was too mathematical, aud used to draw squares and triangles on his shop-board, so that he did not excel in the cut of a coat; – 'I am sorry for it (said Johnson), for I would have every man to be master of his own business.'

In pleasant reference to himself and Mr Hoole, as brother authors, he often said, 'Let you and I, Sir, go together, and eat a beaf-steak in Grub-street.'

Sir William Chambers, that great Architect,[1] whose works show a sublimity of genius, and who is esteemed by all who knew him, for his social, hospitable, and generous qualities, submitted the manuscript of his *Chinese Architecture*, to Dr Johnson's perusal. Johnson was much pleased with it, and said, 'It wants no addition nor correction, but a few lines of introduction'; which he furnished, and Sir William adopted.[2]

He said to Sir William Scott, 'The age is running mad after innovation; and all the business of the world is to be done in a new way; men are to be hanged in a new way; Tyburn itself is not safe from the fury of innovation.' It having been argued that this was an improvement. – 'No, Sir (said be, eagerly), it is *not* an improvement; they object, that the old method drew together a number of spectators. Sir, executions are intended to draw spectators. If they do not draw spectators, they don't answer their purpose. The old method was most satisfactory to all parties; the public was gratified by a procession; the criminal was supported by it. Why is all this to be swept away?' I perfectly agree with Dr Johnson upon this head, and am persuaded that executions now, the solemn procession being discontinued, have not nearly the effect which they formerly had. Magistrates both in London, and elsewhere, have, I am afraid, in this, had too much regard to their own ease.

Of Dr Hurd, Bishop of Worcester, Johnson said to a friend, – 'Hurd, Sir, is one of a set of men who account for every thing systematically; for instance, it has been a fashion to wear scarlet breeches; these men would tell you, that according to causes and effects, no other wear could at that time have been chosen.' He, however, said of him at another time to the same gentleman, 'Hurd, Sir, is a man whose acquaintance is a valuable acquisition.'

That learned and ingenious Prelate it is well known published at one period of his life *Moral and Political Dialogues*, with a woefully whiggish cast. Afterwards, his Lordship having thought better, came to see his error, and republished the work with a more constitutional spirit. Johnson, however, was unwilling to allow him full

note continued overleaf

1 The Honourable Horace Walpole, now Earl of Orford, thus bears testimony to this gentleman's merit as a writer: Mr Chambers's *Treatise on Civil Architecture*, is the most sensible book, and the most exempt from prejudices, that ever was written on that science. – Preface to *Anecdotes of Painting in England*.

2 The introductory lines are these: 'It is difficult to avoid praising too little or too much. The boundless panegyrics which have been lavished upon the Chinese learning, policy, and arts, show with what power novelty attracts regard, and how naturally esteem swells into admiration.

'I am far from desiring to be numbered among the exaggerators of Chinese excellence. I consider them as great, or wise, only in comparison with the nations that surround them; and have no intention to place them in competition either with the antients or with the moderns of this part of the world; yet they must be allowed to claim our notice as a distinct and very singular race of men: as the inhabitants of a region divided by its situation from all civilized countries, who have formed their own manners, and invented their own arts, without the assistance of example.'

two objects of curiosity – the Christian world and the Mahometan world. All
the rest may be considered as barbarous.' BOSWELL. 'Pray, Sir, is the *Turkish*

---

credit for his political conversion. I remember when his Lordship declined the honour
of being Archbishop of Canterbury, Johnson said, 'I am glad he did not go to
Lambeth; for, after all, I fear he is a Whig in his heart.'

Johnson's attention to precision and clearness in expression was very remarkable. He
disapproved of a parenthesis; and I believe in all his voluminous writings, not half a
dozen of them will be found. He never used the phrases *the former and the latter*, having
observed, that they often occasioned obscurity; he therefore contrived to construct his
sentences so as not to have occasion for them, and would even rather repeat the same
words, in order to avoid them. Nothing is more common than to mistake surnames,
when we hear them carelessly uttered for the first time. To prevent this, he used not
only to pronounce them slowly and distinctly, but to take the trouble of spelling them;
a practice which I have often followed, and which I wish were general.

Such was the heat and irritability of his blood, that not only did he pare his nails to
the quick, but scraped the joints of his fingers with a pen-knife, till they seemed quite
red and raw.

The heterogeneous composition of human nature was remarkably exemplified in
Johnson. His liberality in giving his money to persons in distress was extraordinary.
Yet there lurked about him a propensity to paltry saving. One day I owned to hint,
that 'I was occasionally troubled with a fit of *narrowness*.' 'Why, Sir (said he), so am I.
But I do not tell it.' He has now and then borrowed a shilling of me; and when I asked
him for it again, seemed to be rather out of humour. A droll little circumstance once
occurred: As if he meant to reprimand my minute exactness as a creditor, he thus
addressed me; – 'Boswell, *lend* me sixpence – *not to be repaid.*'

This great man's attention to small things was very remarkable. As an instance of it,
he one day said to me, 'Sir, when you get silver in change for a guinea, look carefully
at it; you may find some curious piece of coin.'

Though a stern *true-born Englishman*, and fully prejudiced against all other nations,
he had discernment enough to see, and candour enough to censure, the cold reserve
too common among Englishmen towards strangers: 'Sir (said he), two men of any
other nation who are shown into a room together, at a house where they are both
visitors, will immediately find some conversation. But two Englishmen will probably
go each to a different window, and remain in obstinate silence. Sir, we as yet do not
enough understand the common rights of humanity.'

Johnson was at a certain period of his life a good deal with the Earl of Shelburne,
now Marquis of Lansdown, as he doubtless could not but have a due value for that
nobleman's activity of mind, and uncommon acquisitions of important knowledge,
however much he might disapprove of other parts of his Lordship's character, which
were widely different from his own.

Maurice Morgann, Esq., author of the very ingenious 'Essay on the character of
Falstaff',[1] being a particular friend of his Lordship, had once an opportunity of
entertaining Johnson for a day or two at Wycombe, when its Lord was absent, and by
him I have been favoured with two anecdotes.

One is not a little to the credit of Johnson's candour. Mr Morgann and he had a
dispute pretty late at night, in which Johnson would not give up, though he had the

note continued overleaf

1 Johnson being asked his opinion of this Essay, answered, 'Why, Sir, we shall have
the man come forth again; and as he has proved Falstaff to be no coward, he may
prove Iago to be a very good character.'

Spy a genuine book?' JOHNSON. 'No, Sir. Mrs Manley, in her Life, says, that her father wrote the two first volumes. And in another book, Dunton's *Life and Errors*, we find that the rest was written by one *Sault*, at two guineas a sheet, under the direction of Dr Midgeley.'

---

wrong side; and in short, both kept the field. Next morning, when they met in the breakfasting-room, Dr Johnson accosted Mr Morgann thus: 'Sir, I have been thinking on our dispute last night; – *You were in the right.*'

The other was as follows: Johnson, for sport perhaps, or from the spirit of contradiction, eagerly maintained that Derrick had merit as a writer. Mr Morgann argued with him directly, in vain. At length he had recourse to this device. 'Pray, Sir (said he), whether do you reckon Derrick or Smart the best poet?' Johnson at once felt himself roused; and answered, 'Sir, there is no settling the point of precedency between a louse and a flea.'

Once, when checking my boasting too frequently of myself in company, he said to me, 'Boswell, you often vaunt so much as to provoke ridicule. You put me in mind of a man who was standing in the kitchen of an inn with his back to the fire, and thus accosted the person next him, "Do you know, Sir, who I am?" "No, Sir (said the other), I have not that advantage." "Sir (said he), I am the great TWALMLEY, who invented the New Floodgate."[1] The Bishop of Killaloe, on my repeating the story to him, defended TWALMLEY, by observing that he was entitled to the epithet of *great*; for Virgil in his group of worthies in the Elysian fields –

> *Hic manus ob patriam pugnando vulnera passi*; &c.

mentions

> *Inventas aut qui vitam excoluere per artes.*

He was pleased to say to me one morning when we were left alone in his study, 'Boswell, I think, I am easier with you than with almost any body.'

He would not allow Mr David Hume any credit for his political principles, though similar to his own; saying of him, 'Sir, he was a Tory by chance.'

His acute observation of human life made him remark, 'Sir, there is nothing by which a man exasperates most people more, than by displaying a superior ability of brilliancy in conversation. They seem pleased at the time; but their envy makes them curse him at their hearts.'

My readers will probably be surprised to hear that the great Dr Johnson could amuse himself with so slight and playful a species of composition as a *Charade*. I have recovered one which he made on Dr Barnard, now Lord Bishop of Killaloe; who has been pleased for many years to treat me with so much intimacy and social ease, that I may presume to call him not only my Right Reverend, but my very dear, Friend. I therefore with peculiar pleasure give to the world a just and elegant compliment thus paid to his Lordship by Johnson.

CHARADE

My *first* shuts out thieves from your house or your room,[2]
My *second* expresses a Syrian perfume.[3]
My *whole* is a man in whose converse is shar'd[4]
The strength of a Bar and the sweetness of Nard.'

note continued overleaf

---

1 What the *great* TWALMLEY was so proud of having invented, was neither more or less than a kind of box-iron for smoothing linen.

2 Bar.   3 Nard.   4 Barnard.

BOSWELL. 'This has been a very factious reign, owing to the too great indulgence of Government. JOHNSON. '*I* think so, Sir. What at first was lenity, grew timidity. Yet this is reasoning *a posteriori*, and may not be just. Supposing

---

Johnson asked Richard Owen Cambridge, Esq. if he had read the Spanish translation of Sallust, said to be written by a Prince of Spain, with the assistance of his tutor, who is professedly the author of a treatise annexed, on the Phoenician language.

Mr Cambridge commended the work, particularly as he thought the Translator understood his author better than is commonly the case with Translators; but said, he was disappointed in the purpose for which he borrowed the book; to see whether a Spaniard could be better furnished with inscriptions from monuments, coins, or other antiquities, which he might more probably find on a coast, so immediately opposite to Carthage, than the Antiquaries of any other countries. JOHNSON. 'I am very sorry you were not gratified in your expectations.' CAMBRIDGE. 'The language would have been of little use, as there is no history existing in that tongue to balance the partial accounts which the Roman writers have left us.' JOHNSON. 'No, Sir. They have not been *partial*, they have told their own story, without shame or regard to equitable treatment of their injured enemy; they had no compunction, no feeling for a Carthaginian. Why, Sir, they would never have borne Virgil's description of Aeneas's treatment of Dido, if she had not been a Carthaginian.'

I gratefully acknowledge this and other communications from Mr Cambridge, whom, if a beautiful villa on the banks of the Thames, a few miles distant from London, a numerous and excellent library, which he accurately knows and reads, a choice collection of pictures, which he understands and relishes, an easy fortune, an amiable family, an extensive circle of friends and acquaintance, distinguished by rank, fashion, and genius, a literary fame, various, elegant and still increasing, colloquial talents rarely to be found, and with all these means of happiness, enjoying, when well advanced in years, health and vigour of body, serenity and animation of mind, do not entitle to be addressed *fortunate senex!* I know not to whom, in, any age, that expression could with propriety have been used. Long may he live to hear and to feel it!

Johnson's love of little children, which he discovered upon all occasions, calling them, 'pretty dears', and giving them sweetmeats, was an undoubted proof of the real humanity and gentleness of his disposition.

His uncommon kindness to his servants, and serious concern, not only for their comfort in this world, but their happiness in the next, was another unquestionable evidence of what all, who were intimately acquainted with him, knew to be true.

Nor would it be just under this head, to omit the fondness which he showed for animals which he had taken under his protection. I never shall forget the indulgence with which he treated Hodge, his cat; for whom he himself used to go out and buy oysters, lest the servants, having that trouble, should take a dislike to the poor creature. I am, unluckily, one of those who have an antipathy to a cat, so that I am uneasy when in the room with one; and I own, I frequently suffered a good deal from the presence of this same Hodge. I recollect him one day scrambling up Dr Johnson's breast, apparently with much satisfaction, while my friend smiling and half-whistling, rubbed down his back, and pulled him by the tail; and when I observed he was a fine cat, saying, 'why, yes, Sir, but I have had cats whom I liked better than this'; and then as if perceiving Hodge to be out of countenance, adding, 'but he is a very fine cat, a very fine cat indeed.'

This reminds me of the ludicrous account which he gave Mr Langton, of the despicable state of a young gentleman of good family. 'Sir, when I heard of him last, he was running about town shooting cats.' And then in a sort of kindly reverie, he

a few had at first been punished, I believe faction would have been crushed; but it might have been said, that it was a sanguinary reign. A man cannot tell *a priori* what will be best for Government to do. This reign has been very unfortunate. We have had an unsuccessful war; but that does not prove that we have been ill governed. One side or other must prevail in war, as one or other must win at play. When we beat Louis, we were not better governed; nor were the French better governed when Louis beat us.'

On Saturday, April 12, I visited him, in company with Mr Windham, of Norfolk, whom, though a Whig, he highly valued. One of the best things he ever said was to this gentleman; who before he set out for Ireland as Secretary to Lord Northington, when Lord Lieutenant, expressed to the Sage some modest and virtuous doubts, whether he could bring himself to practise those arts which it is supposed a person in that situation has occasion to employ. Don't be afraid, Sir (said Johnson, with a pleasant smile), you will soon make a very pretty rascal.'

He talked to-day a good deal of the wonderful extent and variety of London, and observed, that men of curious enquiry might see in it such modes of life as very few could even imagine. He in particular recommended to us to *explore Wapping*, which we resolved to do, and certainly shall.[a]

Mr Lowe the painter, who was with him, was very much distressed that a large picture which he had painted was refused to be received into the

---

bethought himself of his own favourite cat, and said, 'But Hodge shan't be shot: no, no, Hodge shall not be shot.'

He thought Mr Beauclerk made a shrewd and judicious remark to Mr Langton, who, after having been for the first time in company with a well-known wit about town, was warmly admiring and praising him, – 'See him again,' said Beauclerk.

His respect for the Hierarchy, and particularly the Dignitaries of the Church, has been more than once exhibited in the course of this work. Mr Seward saw him presented to the Archbishop of York, and described his *Bow to an* ARCH-BISHOP as such a studied elaboration of homage, such an extension of limb, such a flexion of body, as have seldom or ever been equalled.

I cannot help mentioning with much regret, that by my own negligence I lost an opportunity of having the history of my family from its founder Thomas Boswell, in 1504, recorded and illustrated by Johnson's pen. Such was his goodness to me that when I presumed to solicit him for so great a favour, he was pleased to say, 'Let me have all the materials you can collect, and I will do it both in Latin and English; then let it be printed, and copies of it be deposited in various places for security and preservation.' I can now only do the best I can to make up for this loss, keeping my great Master steadily in view. Family histories, like the *imagines majorum* of the ancients, excite to virtue; and I wish that they who really have blood, would be more careful to trace and ascertain its course. Some have affected to laugh at the history of the house of Yvery: it would be well if many others would transmit their pedigrees to posterity, with the same accuracy and generous zeal, with which the Noble Lord who compiled that work has honoured and perpetuated his ancestry.

a Delete 'and certainly shall', and add the following note: We accordingly carried our scheme into execution, in October, 1792; but whether from that uniformity which has in modern times, in a great degree, spread through every part of the metropolis, or from our want of sufficient exertion, we were disappointed.

exhibition of the Royal Academy. Mrs Thrale knew Johnson's character so superficially, as to represent him as unwilling to do small acts of benevolence; and mentions, in particular, that he would hardly take the trouble to write a letter in favour of his friends. The truth, however, is, that he was remarkable, in an extraordinary degree, for what she denies to him; and, above all, for this very sort of kindness, writing letters for those to whom his solicitations might be of service. He now gave Mr Lowe the following, of which I was diligent enough, with his permission, to take copies at the next coffee-house, while Mr Windham was so good as to stay by me.

To Sir Joshua Reynolds.

Sir – Mr Lowe considers himself as cut off from all credit and all hope, by the rejection of his picture from the Exhibition. Upon this work he has exhausted all his powers, and suspended all his expectations: and certainly, to be refused an opportunity of taking the opinion of the public, is in itself a very great hardship. It is to be condemned without a trial.

If you could procure the revocation of this incapacitating edict, you would deliver an unhappy man from great affliction. The Council has sometimes reversed its own determination; and I hope, that by your interposition this luckless picture may be got admitted. I am, &c.

SAM. JOHNSON.

April 12, 1783.

To Mr Barry.

Sir – Mr Lowe's exclusion from the Exhibition gives him more trouble than you and the other gentlemen of the Council could imagine or intend. He considers disgrace and ruin as the inevitable consequence of your determination.

He says, that some pictures have been received after rejection; and if there be any such precedent, I earnestly entreat that you will use your interest in his favour. Of his work, I can say nothing: I pretend not to judge of painting; and this picture I never saw: but I conceive it extremely hard to shut out any man from the possibility of success; and therefore I repeat my request that you will propose the reconsideration of Mr Lowe's case; and if there be any among the Council with whom my name can have any weight, be pleased to communicate to them the desire of, Sir,

Your most humble servant,

SAM. JOHNSON.

April 12, 1783.

Such intercession was too powerful to be resisted, and Mr Lowe's perform-ance was admitted at Somerset-house. The subject, as I recollect, was the Deluge, at that point of time when the water was verging to the top of the last uncovered mountain. Near to the spot was seen the last of the antediluvian race, exclusive of those who were saved in the ark of Noah. This was one of those giants, then the inhabitants of the earth, who had still strength to swim, and with one of his hands held aloft his infant child. Upon the small remaining dry spot appeared a famished lion, ready to spring at the child and devour it. Mr Lowe told me that Johnson said to him, 'Sir, your picture is noble and probable.' – 'A compliment, indeed (said Mr Lowe), from a man who cannot lie, and cannot be mistaken.'

About this time he wrote to Mrs Lucy Porter, mentioning his bad health, and that he intended a visit to Lichfield. 'It is (says he) with no great expectation of amendment that I make every year a journey into the country; but it is pleasant to visit those whose kindness has been often experienced.'

On April 18 (being Good-Friday), I found him at breakfast, in his usual manner upon that day, drinking tea without milk, and eating a cross-bun to prevent faintness; we went to St Clement's church, as formerly. When we came home from church he placed himself on one of the stone seats at his garden-door, and I took the other, and thus in the open air and in a placid frame, he talked away very easily. JOHNSON. 'Were I a country gentleman, I should not be very hospitable, I should not have crowds in my house.' BOSWELL. 'Sir Alexander Dick tells me, that he remembers having a thousand people in a year to dine at his house; that is reckoning each person one each time that he dined there.' JOHNSON. 'That, Sir, is about three a day.' BOSWELL. 'How your statement lessens the idea.' JOHNSON. 'That, Sir, is the good of counting. It brings every thing to a certainty which before floated in the mind indefinitely.' BOSWELL. 'But *Omne ignotum pro magnifico est*. One is sorry to have this diminished.' JOHNSON. 'Sir, you should not allow yourself to be delighted with error.' BOSWELL. 'Three a day seem but few.' JOHNSON. 'Nay, Sir, he who entertains three a day does very liberally. And if there is a large family the poor entertain those three, for they eat what the poor would get; there must be superfluous meat; it must be given to the poor, or thrown out.' BOSWELL. 'I observe in London, that the poor go about and gather bones, which I understand are manufactured.' JOHNSON. 'Yes, Sir; they boil them, and extract a grease from them for greasing wheels and other purposes. Of the best pieces they make a mock ivory, which is used for hafts to knives, and various other things. The coarser pieces they burn and pound them, and sell the ashes.' BOSWELL. 'For what purpose, Sir?' JOHNSON. 'Why, Sir, for making a furnace for the chemists for melting iron. A paste made of burnt bones will stand a stronger heat than any thing else. Consider, Sir, if you are to melt iron, you cannot line your pot with brass, because it is softer than iron and would melt sooner; nor with iron, for though malleable iron is harder than cast iron, yet it would not do; but a paste of burnt bones will not melt.' BOSWELL. 'Do you know, Sir, I have discovered a manufacture to a great extent, of what you only piddle at – scraping and drying the peel of oranges.[a] At a place in Newgate-street, there is a prodigious quantity

---

[a] Add this note: It is suggested to me by an anonymous Annotator on my Work, that the reason why Dr Johnson collected the peels of squeezed oranges, may be found in the 358th Letter in Mrs Piozzi's Collection, where it appears that he recommended 'dried orange-peel, finely powdered', as a medicine.

done, which they sell to the distillers.' JOHNSON. 'Sir, I believe they make a higher thing out of them than a spirit; they make what is called orange-butter, the oil of the orange inspissated, which they mix perhaps with common pomatum, and make it fragrant. The oil does not fly off in the drying.'

BOSWELL. 'I wish to have a good walled garden.' JOHNSON. 'I don't think it would be worth the expense to you. We compute in England, a park-wall at a thousand pounds a mile; now a garden wall must cost at least as much. You intend your trees should grow higher than a deer will leap. Now let us see – for a hundred pounds you could only have forty-four square yards, which is very little; for two hundred pounds, you may have eighty-four square yards, which is very well. But when will you get the value of two hundred pounds of walls in your climate? No, Sir, such contention with nature is not worth while. I would plant an orchard, and have plenty of such fruit as ripen well in your country. My friend, Dr Madden, of Ireland, said, that in an orchard there should be enough to eat, enough to lay up, enough to be stolen, and enough to rot upon the ground. Cherries are an early fruit, you may have them and you may have the early apples and pears.' BOSWELL. 'We cannot have nonpareils.' JOHNSON. 'Sir, you can no more have nonpareils than you can have grapes.' BOSWELL. 'We have them, Sir; but they are very bad.' JOHNSON. 'Nay, Sir, never try to have a thing merely to show that you *cannot* have it. For ground that would let for forty shillings you may have a large orchard; and you see it costs you only forty shillings. Nay, you may graze the ground when the trees are grown up, you cannot while they are young.' BOSWELL. 'Is not a good garden a very common thing in England, Sir?' JOHNSON. 'Not so common, Sir, as you imagine. In Lincolnshire there is hardly an orchard; in Staffordshire very little fruit.' BOSWELL. 'Has Langton no orchard?' JOHNSON. 'No, Sir.' BOSWELL. 'How so, Sir?' JOHNSON. 'Why, Sir, from the general negligence of the county. He has it not, because nobody else has it.' BOSWELL. 'A hot-house is a certain thing; I may have that.' JOHNSON. 'A hot-house is pretty certain; but you must first build it, then you must keep fires in it, and you must have a gardener to take care of it.' BOSWELL. 'But if I have a gardener at any rate.' JOHNSON. 'Why, yes.' BOSWELL. 'I'd have it near my house; there is no need to have it in the orchard.' JOHNSON. 'Yes, I'd have it near my house – I would plant a great many currants; the fruit is good, and they make a pretty sweetmeat.'

I record this minute detail, which some may think trifling, in order to show clearly how this great man, whose mind could grasp such large and extensive subjects as he has shown in his literary labours, was yet well-informed in the common affairs of life, and loved to illustrate them.

Mr Walker, the celebrated master of elocution came, and then we went up stairs into the study. I asked him if he had taught many clergymen. JOHNSON. 'I hope not.' WALKER. 'I have taught only one, and he is the best reader I ever heard, not by my teaching, but by his own natural talents.' JOHNSON. 'Were he the best reader in the world, I would not have it told that be was taught.' Here was one of his peculiar prejudices. Could it he any disadvantage to the clergyman, to have it known that he was taught an easy and graceful delivery? BOSWELL. 'Will you not allow, Sir, that a man may be taught to read well?'

JOHNSON. 'Why, Sir, so far as to read better than he might do without being taught, yes. Formerly it was supposed that there was no difference in reading, but that one read as well as another.' BOSWELL. 'It is wonderful to see old Sheridan as enthusiastic about oratory as ever.' WALKER. 'His enthusiasm as to what oratory will do may be too great. But he reads well.' JOHNSON. 'He reads well, but he reads low; and you know it is much easier to read low than to read high; for when you read high you are much more limited, your loudest note can be but one, and so in proportion to loudness. Now some people have occasion to speak to an extensive audience, and must speak loud to be heard.' WALKER. 'The art is to read strong, though low.'

Talking of the origin of language – JOHNSON. 'It must have come by inspiration. A thousand, nay a million of children could not invent a language. While the organs are pliable, there is not understanding enough to form a language: by the time that there is understanding enough, the organs are become stiff. We know that after a certain age we cannot learn to pronounce a new language. No foreigner, who comes to England when advanced in life, ever pronounces English tolerably well; at least such instances are very rare. When I maintain that language must have come by inspiration, I do not mean that inspiration is required for rhetoric, and all the beauties of language; for when once man has language, we can conceive that he may gradually form modifications of it. I mean only, that inspiration seems to me to be necessary to give man the faculty of speech; to inform him that he may have speech; which I think he could no more find out without inspiration, than cows or hogs would think of such a faculty.' WALKER. 'Do you think, Sir, that there are any perfect synonyms in any language?' JOHNSON. 'Originally there were not; but by using words negligently, or in poetry, one word comes to be confounded with another.'

He talked of Dr Dodd. 'A friend of mine (said he) came to me and told me, that a lady wished to have Dodd's picture in a bracelet, and asked me for a motto. I said, I could think of no better than *Currat Lex*. I was very willing to have him pardoned, that is, to have the sentence changed to transportation: but, when he was once hanged, I did not wish he should be made a saint.'

Mrs Burney, wife of his friend Dr Burney, came in, and he seemed to be entertained with her conversation.

Garrick's funeral was talked of as extravagantly expensive. Johnson, from his dislike to exaggeration, would not allow that it was distinguished by any extraordinary pomp. 'Were there not six horses in each coach?' said Mrs Burney. JOHNSON. 'Madam, there were no more six horses than six phoenixes.'

Mrs Burney wondered that some very beautiful new buildings should be erected in Moorfields, in so shocking a situation as between Bedlam and St Luke's Hospital; and said, she could not live there. JOHNSON. 'Nay, Madam, you see nothing there to hurt you. You no more think of madness by having windows that look to Bedlam, than you think of death by having windows that look to a church-yard.' MRS BURNEY. 'We may look to a church-yard, Sir; for it is right that we should be kept in mind of death.' JOHNSON. 'Nay, Madam, if you go to that it is right that we should be kept in mind of madness, which is occasioned by too much indulgence of imagination. I think a very moral use may be made of these new buildings. I would have those who have heated imaginations live there, and take warning.' MRS BURNEY. 'But, Sir, many of the poor people that are mad have become so from disease, or from distressing events. It is, therefore, not their faults, but their misfortune; and, therefore, to think of them, is a melancholy consideration.'

Time passed on in conversation till it was too late for the service of the church at three o'clock. I took a walk, and left him alone for some time; then returned, and we had coffee and conversation again by ourselves.

I stated the character of a noble friend of mine, as a curious case for his opinion: 'He is the most inexplicable man to me that I ever knew. Can you explain him, Sir? He is, I really believe, noble-minded, generous, and princely. But his most intimate friends may be separated from him for years, without his ever asking a question concerning them. He will meet them with a formality, a coldness, a stately indifference; but when they come close to him, and fairly engage him in conversation, they find him as easy, pleasant, and kind as they could wish. One then supposes that what is so agreeable will soon be renewed; but stay away from him for half a year, and he will neither call on you, nor send to inquire about you.' JOHNSON. 'Why, Sir, I cannot ascertain his character exactly, as I do not know him; but I should not like to have such a man for my friend. He may love study, and wish not to be interrupted by his friends; *Amici fures temporis*. He may be a frivolous man, and be so much occupied with petty pursuits, that he may not want friends. Or he may have a notion that there is a dignity in appearing indifferent, while he in fact may not be more indifferent at his heart than another.'

We went to evening prayers at St Clement's, at seven, and then parted.

On Sunday, April 20, being Easter-day, after attending solemn service at St Paul's, I came to Dr Johnson, and found Mr Lowe, the painter, sitting with him. Mr Lowe mentioned the great number of new buildings of late in London, yet that Dr Johnson had observed, that the number of inhabitants was not increased. JOHNSON. 'Why, Sir, the bills of mortality prove that no more people die now than formerly; so it is plain no more live. Births are[a] nothing, for not one tenth of the people of London are born there.' BOSWELL. 'I believe, Sir, a great many of the children born in London die early.' JOHNSON. 'Why yes, Sir.' BOSWELL. 'But those who do live are as stout and strong people as any. Dr Price says, they must be naturally stronger to get through.' JOHNSON. 'That is system, Sir. A great traveller observes, that it is said there are no weak or deformed people among the Indians; but he with much sagacity assigns the reason of this, which is, that the hardship of their life as hunters and fishers, does not allow weak or diseased children to grow up. Now had I been an Indian I must have died early, my eyes would not have served me to get food. I indeed now could fish, give me English tackle; but had I been an Indian I must have starved, or they would have knocked me on the head when they saw I could do nothing.' BOSWELL. 'Perhaps they would have taken care of you; we

[a] For 'births are' read 'the register of births proves'.

are told they are fond of oratory, you would have talked to them.' JOHNSON. 'Nay, Sir, I should not have lived long enough to be fit to talk; I should have been dead before I was ten years old. Depend upon it, Sir, a savage when he is hungry will not carry about with him a looby of nine years old, who cannot help himself. They have no affection, Sir.' BOSWELL. 'I believe natural affection, of which we hear so much, is very small.' JOHNSON. 'Sir, natural affection is nothing. But affection from principle and established duty is sometimes wonderfully strong.' LOWE. 'A hen, Sir, will feed her chickens in preference to herself.' JOHNSON. 'But we don't know that the hen is hungry; let the hen be fairly hungry, and I'll warrant she'll peck the corn herself. A cock, I believe, will feed hens instead of himself; but we don't know that the cock is hungry.' BOSWELL. 'And that, Sir, is not from affection but gallantry. But some of the Indians have affection.' JOHNSON. 'Sir, that they help some of their children is plain; for some of them live which could not do without being helped.'

I dined with him; the company were, Mrs Williams, Mrs Desmoulins, and Mr Lowe. He seemed not to be well, talked little, grew drowsy soon after dinner and retired, upon which I went away.

Having next day gone to Mr Burke's seat in the country, from whence I was recalled by an express, that a near relation of mine had killed his antagonist in a duel, and was himself dangerously wounded, I saw little of Dr Johnson till Monday, April 28, when I spent a considerable part of the day with him, and introduced the subject, which chiefly occupied my mind. JOHNSON. 'I do not see, Sir, that fighting is absolutely forbidden in Scripture; I see revenge forbidden, but not self-defence.' BOSWELL. 'The Quakers say it is; "Unto him that smiteth thee on one cheek, offer also the other." ' JOHNSON. 'But stay, Sir, the text is meant only to have the effect of moderating passion; it is plain that we are not to take it in a literal sense. We see this from the context, where there are other recommendations, which I warrant you the Quaker will not take literally, as for instance, "From him that would borrow of thee, turn thou not away." Let a man whose credit is bad come to a Quaker, and say, "Well, Sir, lend me a hundred pounds"; he'll find him as unwilling as any other man. No, Sir, a man may shoot the man who invades his character, as he may shoot him who attempts to break into his house.[a] So in 1745, my friend, Tom Cumming,

---

[a] Add the following note: I think it necessary to caution my readers against concluding that in this or any other conversation of Dr Johnson, they have his serious and deliberate opinion on the subject of duelling. In my *Journal of a Tour to the Hebrides*, 3rd edit. p. 386, it appears that he made this frank confession: 'Nobody at times, talks more laxly than I do'; and, ibid. p. 231, 'He fairly owned he could not explain the rationality of duelling.' We may, therefore, infer, that he could not think that justifiable, which seems so inconsistent with the spirit of the Gospel. At the same time it must be confessed, that from the prevalent notions of honour, a gentleman who receives a challenge is reduced to a dreadful alternative. A remarkable instance of this is furnished by a clause in the will of the late Colonel Thomas, of the Guards, written the night before he fell in a duel, September 3, 1783: 'In the first place, I commit my soul to Almighty GOD, in hopes of his mercy and pardon for the irreligious step I now (in compliance with the unwarrantable customs of this wicked world) put myself under the necessity of taking.'

the Quaker, said, he would not fight, but he would drive an ammunition-cart; and we know that the Quakers have sent flannel waistcoats to our soldiers, to enable them to fight better.' BOSWELL. 'When a man is the aggressor, and by ill-usage forces on a duel in which he is killed, have we not little ground to hope that he is gone into a state of happiness?' JOHNSON. 'Sir, we are not to judge determinately of the state in which a man leaves this life. He may in a moment have repented effectually, and it is possible may have been accepted by GOD. There is in Camden's *Remains*, an epitaph upon a very wicked man, who was killed by a fall from his horse, in which he is supposed to say,

> Between the stirrup and the ground,
> I mercy asked, I mercy found.'

BOSWELL. 'Is not the expression in the Burial-service, "In the *sure* and *certain* hope of a blessed resurrection", too strong to be used indiscriminately, and, indeed, sometimes when those over whose bodies it is said, have been notoriously profane?' JOHNSON. 'It is sure and certain *hope*, Sir; not *belief.*' I did not insist further; but cannot help thinking that less positive words would be more proper.[a]

Talking of a man who was grown very fat, so as to be incommoded with corpulency; he said, 'He eats too much, Sir.' BOSWELL. 'I don't know, Sir, you will see one man fat who eats moderately, and another lean who eats a great deal.' JOHNSON. 'Nay, Sir, whatever may be the quantity that a man eats, it is plain that if he is too fat, he has eaten more than he should have done. One man may have a digestion that consumes food better than common; but it is certain that solidity is increased by putting something to it.' BOSWELL. 'But may not solids swell and be distended?' JOHNSON. 'Yes, Sir, they may swell and be distended; but that is not fat.'

We talked of the accusation against a gentleman for supposed delinquencies in India. JOHNSON. 'What foundation there is for accusation I know not, but they will not get at him. Where bad actions are committed at so great a distance, a delinquent can obscure the evidence till the scent becomes cold; there is a cloud between, which cannot be penetrated, therefore all distant power is bad. I am clear that the best plan for the government of India is a despotic governor; for if he be a good man it is evidently the best government; and supposing him to be

---

[a] Add this note: Upon this objection the Reverend Mr Ralph Churton, Fellow of Brazenose College, Oxford, has favoured me with the following satisfactory observation. 'The passage in the Burial-service does not mean the resurrection of the person interred, but the general resurrection; it is in sure and certain hope of *the* resurrection; not *his* resurrection. Where the deceased is really spoken of, the expression is very different – "as our hope is this our brother doth" [rest in Christ]; a mode of speech consistent with every thing but absolute certainty that the person departed doth *not* rest in Christ, which no one can be assured of, without immediate revelation from Heaven. In the first of these places also, "eternal life" does not necessarily mean eternity of bliss, but merely the eternity of the state, whether in happiness or in misery, to ensue upon the resurrection; which is probably the sense of "the life everlasting", in the Apostles Creed. See Wheatly and Bennet on the Common Prayer.'

a bad man, it is better to have one plunderer than many. A governor whose power is checked, lets others plunder that he himself may be allowed to plunder. But if despotic, he sees that the more he lets others plunder the less there will be for himself, so he restrains them; and though he himself plunders, the country is a gainer, compared with being plundered by numbers.'

I mentioned the very liberal payment which had been received for reviewing; and, as evidence of this, that it had been proved in a trial that Dr Shebbeare had received six guineas a sheet for that kind of literary labour. JOHNSON. 'Sir, he might get six guineas for a particular sheet, but not *communibus sheetibus*.' BOSWELL. 'Pray, Sir, by a sheet of review is it meant that it shall be all of the writer's own composition; or are extracts, made from the book reviewed, deducted?' JOHNSON. 'No, Sir: it is a sheet, no matter of what.' BOSWELL. 'I think that it is not reasonable.' JOHNSON. 'Yes, Sir, it is. A man will more easily write a sheet all his own than read an octavo volume to get extracts.' To one of Johnson's wonderful fertility of mind, I believe writing was really easier than reading and extracting; but with ordinary men the case is very different. A great deal, indeed, will depend upon the care and judgement with which the extracts are made. I can suppose the operation to be tedious and difficult: but in many instances we must observe crude morsels cut out of books as if at random; and when a large extract is made from one place, it surely may be done with very little trouble. One, however, I must acknowledge, might be led, from the practice of Reviewers, to suppose that they take a pleasure in original writing; for we often find that, instead of giving an accurate account of what has been done by the author whose work they are reviewing, which is surely the proper business of a literary journal, they produce some plausible and ingenious conceits of their own, upon the topics which have been discussed.

Upon being told that old Mr Sheridan, indignant at the neglect of his oratorical plans, bad threatened to go to America; – JOHNSON. 'I hope he will go to America.' BOSWELL. 'The Americans don't want oratory.' JOHNSON. 'But we can want Sheridan.'

On Monday, April 29,[a] I found him at home in the forenoon, and Mr Seward with him. Horace having been mentioned; – BOSWELL. 'There is a great deal of thinking in his works. One finds there almost every thing but religion.' SEWARD. 'He speaks of his returning to it in his Ode *Parcus Deorum cultor et infrequens*.' JOHNSON. 'Sir, he was not in earnest. This was merely poetical.' BOSWELL. 'There are, I am afraid, many people who have no religion at all.' SEWARD. 'And sensible people too.' JOHNSON. Why, Sir, not sensible in that respect. There must be either a natural or a moral stupidity, if one lives in a total neglect of so very important a concern.' SEWARD. 'I wonder that there should be people without religion.' JOHNSON. 'Sir, you need not wonder at this, when you consider how large a proportion of almost every man's life is passed without thinking of it. I myself was for some years totally

---

[a] Alter to 'April 28'. [But this should read 'Wednesday, April 30'.]

regardless of religion. It had dropped out of my mind. It was at an early part of my life. Sickness brought it back, and I hope I have never lost it since.' BOSWELL. 'My dear Sir, what a man must you have been without religion! Why, you must have gone on drinking, and swearing, and —' JOHNSON. (with a smile) 'I drank enough and swore enough, to be sure.' SEWARD. 'One should think that sickness, and the view of death, would make more men religious.' JOHNSON. 'Sir, they do not know how to go about it. They have not the first notion. A man who has never had religion before, no more grows religious when he is sick, than a man who has never learnt figures can count when he has need of calculation.'

I mentioned a worthy friend of ours whom we valued much, but observed that he was too ready to introduce religious discourse upon all occasions. JOHNSON. 'Why yes, Sir; he will introduce religious discourse without seeing whether it will end in instruction and improvement, or produce some profane jest. He would introduce it in the company of Wilkes, and twenty more such.'

I mentioned Dr Johnson's excellent distinction between liberty of conscience and liberty of teaching. JOHNSON. 'Consider, Sir; if you have children whom you wish to educate in the principles of the Church of England, and there comes a Quaker who tries to pervert them to his principles; you would drive away the Quaker. You would not trust to the predomination of right, which you believe is in your opinions; you would keep wrong out of their heads. Now the vulgar are the children of the State. If any one attempts to teach them doctrines contrary to what the State approves, the magistrate may and ought to restrain him.' SEWARD. Would you restrain private conversation, Sir?' JOHNSON. 'Why, Sir, it is difficult to say where private conversation begins, and where it ends. If we three should discuss even the great question concerning the existence of a Supreme Being by ourselves, we should not be restrained; for that would be to put an end to all improvement. But if we should discuss it in the presence of ten boarding-school girls, and as many boys, I think the magistrate would do well to put us in the stocks, to finish the debate there.'

Lord Hailes had sent him a present of a curious little printed poem, on repairing the University of Aberdeen, by David *Malloch*, which he thought would please Johnson, as affording clear evidence that Mallet had appeared even as a literary character by the name of Malloch; his changing which to one of softer sound, had given Johnson occasion to introduce him into his Dictionary, under the article *Alias*. This piece was, I suppose, one of Mallet's first essays. It is preserved in his works, with several variations. Johnson now read aloud, from the beginning of it, where there were some common-place assertions as to the superiority of ancient times. 'How false is all this to say that in ancient times learning was not a disgrace to a Peer as it is now. In ancient times a Peer was as ignorant as any one else. He would have been angry to have it thought he could write his name. Men in ancient times dared to stand forth with a degree of ignorance with which nobody would dare now to stand forth. I am always angry when I hear ancient times praised at the expense of modern times. There is now a great deal more learning in the world than there was formerly; for it is universally diffused. You have, perhaps, no man who knows as much Greek and Latin as Bentley; or no man who knows as much mathematics as Newton: but you have many more men who know Greek and Latin, and who know mathematics.'

On Thursday, May 1, I visited him in the evening along with young Mr Burke. He said, 'It is strange that there should be so little reading in the world, and so much writing. People in general do not willingly read, if they can have any thing else to amuse them. There must be an external impulse; emulation, or vanity, or avarice. The progress which the understanding makes through a book, has more pain than pleasure in it. Language is scanty, and inadequate to express the nice gradations and mixtures of our feelings. No man reads a book of science from pure inclination. The books that we do read with pleasure are light compositions, which contain a quick succession of events. However, I have this year read all Virgil through. I read a book of the *Aeneid* every night, so it was done in twelve nights, and I had great delight in it. The *Georgics* did not give me so much pleasure, except the fourth book. The *Eclogues* I have almost all by heart. I do not think the story of the *Aeneid* interesting. I like the story of the *Odyssey* much better; and this not on account of the wonderful things which it contains; for there are wonderful things enough in the *Aeneid*; – the ships of the Trojans turned to sea-nymphs – the tree at Polydorus's tomb dropping blood. The story of the *Odyssey* is interesting, as a great part of it is domestic. It has been said, there is pleasure in writing, particularly in writing verses. I allow you may have pleasure from writing after it is over, if you have written well; but you don't go willingly to it again. I know when I have been writing verses, I have run my finger down the margin to see how many I had made, and how few I had to make.'

He seemed to be in a very placid humour, and although I have no note of the particulars of young Mr Burke's conversation, it is but justice to mention in general, that it was such that Dr Johnson said to me afterwards, 'He did very well indeed; I have a mind to tell his father.'[a]

I have no minute of any interview with Johnson till Thursday, May 15, when I find what follows: BOSWELL. 'I wish much to be in Parliament, Sir.' JOHNSON. 'Why, Sir, unless you come resolved to support any administration, you would be the worse for being in Parliament, because you would be obliged to live more expensively.' BOSWELL. 'Perhaps, Sir, I should be the less

---

[a]   After this passage, read:

To Sir JOSHUA REYNOLDS.

DEAR SIR – The gentleman who waits on you with this, is Mr Cruikshanks, who wishes to succeed his friend Dr Hunter, as Professor of Anatomy in the Royal Academy. His qualifications are very generally known, and it adds dignity to the institution that such men are candidates. I am, Sir,
  Your most humble servant,

                                                            SAM. JOHNSON.
May 2, 1783.

happy for being in Parliament. I never would sell my vote, and I should be vexed if things went wrong.' JOHNSON. 'That's cant, Sir. It would not vex you more in the house, than in the gallery. Public affairs vex no man.' BOSWELL. 'Have not they vexed yourself a little, Sir? Have not you been vexed by all the turbulence of this reign, and by that absurd vote of the House of Commons, "That the influence of the Crown has increased, is increasing, and ought to be diminished?" ' JOHNSON. 'Sir, I have never slept an hour less, nor eat an ounce less meat. I would have knocked the factious dogs on the head, to be sure; but I was not *vexed*.' BOSWELL. 'I declare, Sir, upon my honour, I did imagine I was vexed, and took a pride in it. But it *was*, perhaps, cant; for I own I neither eat less nor slept less.' JOHNSON. 'My dear friend, clear your *mind* of cant. You may *talk* as other people do. You may say to a man, "Sir, I am your most humble servant." You are *not* his most humble servant. You may say, "These are sad times; it is a melancholy thing to be reserved to such times." You don't mind the times. You tell a man, "I am sorry you had such bad weather the last day of your journey, and were so much wet." You don't care six-pence whether he was wet or dry. You may *talk* in this manner; it is a mode of talking in Society: but don't *think* foolishly.'

I talked of living in the country. JOHNSON. 'Don't set up for what is called hospitality; it is a waste of time, and a waste of money; you are eat up, and not the more respected for your liberality. If your house be like an inn, nobody cares for you. A man who stays a week with another, makes him a slave for a week.' BOSWELL. 'But there are people, Sir, who make their houses a home to their guests, and are themselves quite easy.' JOHNSON. 'Then, Sir, home must be the same to the guests, and they need not come.'

Here he discovered a notion common enough in persons not much accustomed to entertain company; that there must be a degree of elaborate attention, otherwise company will think themselves neglected; and such attention is no doubt very fatiguing. He proceeded, 'I would not, however, be a stranger in my own county; I would visit my neighbours, and receive their visits; but I would not be in haste to return visits. If a gentleman comes to see me, I tell him he does me a great deal of honour. I do not go to see him perhaps for ten weeks, then we are very complaisant to each other. No, Sir, you will have much more influence by giving or lending money where it is wanted, than by hospitality.'

On Saturday, May 17, I saw him for a short time. Having mentioned that I had that morning been with old Mr Sheridan, he remembered their former intimacy with a cordial warmth, and said to me, 'Tell Mr Sheridan, I shall be glad to see him and shake hands with him.' BOSWELL. 'It is to me very wonderful that resentment should be kept up so long.' JOHNSON. 'Why, Sir, it is not altogether resentment that he does not visit me; it is partly falling out of the habit – partly disgust, as one has at a drug that has made him sick. Besides, he knows that I laugh at his oratory.'

Another day I spoke of one of our friends, of whom he, as well as I, had a very high opinion. He expatiated in his praise; but added, 'Sir, he is a cursed Whig, a *bottomless* Whig, as they all are now.'

I mentioned my expectations from the interest of an eminent person then in power; adding, 'but I have no claim but the claim of friendship. However, some people will go a great way from that motive.' JOHNSON. 'Sir, they will go all the way from that motive.' A gentleman talked of retiring. 'Never think of that,' said Johnson. The gentleman urged, 'I should then do no ill.' JOHNSON. 'Nor no good either. Sir, it would be a civil suicide.'

On Monday, May 26, I found him at tea, and the celebrated Miss Burney, the author of *Evelina and Cecilia*, with him. I asked if there would be any speakers in parliament, if there were no places to be obtained? JOHNSON. 'Yes, Sir. Why do you speak here? Either to instruct and entertain, which is a benevolent motive; or for distinction, which is a selfish motive.' I mentioned *Cecilia*. JOHNSON. (with an air of animated satisfaction) 'Sir, if you talk of *Cecilia*, talk on.'

We talked of Mr Barry's exhibition of his pictures. JOHNSON. 'Whatever the hand may have done, the mind has done its part. There is a grasp of mind there which you find no where else.'[1]

I asked whether a man naturally virtuous, or one who has overcome wicked inclinations, is the best. JOHNSON. 'Sir, to *you*, the man who has overcome wicked inclinations is not the best. He has more merit to *himself*. I would rather trust my money to a man who has no hands, and so a physical impossibility to steal, than to a man of the most honest principles. There is a witty satirical story of Foote. He had a small bust of Garrick placed upon his bureau. "You may be surprised (said he) that I allow him to be so near my gold; but you will observe he has no hands."'

On Friday, May 29, being to set out for Scotland next morning, I passed a part of the day with him in more than usual earnestness; as his health was in a more precarious state than at any time when I had parted from him. He however was quick and lively, and critical as usual. I mentioned one who was a very learned man. JOHNSON. 'Yes, Sir, he has a great deal of learning; but it never lies straight. There is never one idea by the side of another; 'tis all entangled: and then he drives it so awkwardly upon conversation.'

I stated to him an anxious thought, by which a sincere Christian might be disturbed, even when conscious of having lived a good life, so far as is consistent with human infirmity; he might fear that he should afterwards fall away, and be guilty of such crimes as would render all his former religion vain. 'Could there be, upon this awful subject, such a thing as balancing of accounts? Suppose a man who has led a good life for seven years, commits an act of wickedness, and instantly dies; will his former good life have any effect in his favour?' JOHNSON. 'Sir, if a man has led a good life for seven years, and then is hurried by passion to do what is wrong, and is suddenly carried off, depend upon it he will have the reward of his seven years' good life; GOD will not take a catch of him. Upon this principle Richard Baxter believes, that a

---

1 In Mr Barry's printed analysis, or description of these pictures, he speaks of Johnson's character in the highest terms.

Suicide may be saved. "If (says he) it should be objected that what I maintain may encourage suicide, I answer, I am not to tell a lie to prevent it." ' BOSWELL. 'But does not the text say, "As the tree falls, so it must lie?" ' JOHNSON. 'Yes, Sir; as the tree falls. But – (after a little pause) – that is meant as to the general state of the tree, not what is the effect of a sudden blast.' In short, he interpreted the expression as referring to condition, not to position. The common notion, therefore, seems to be erroneous; and Shenstone's witty remark on Divines trying to give the tree a jerk upon a death-bed, to make it lie favourably, is not well founded.

I asked him what works of Richard Baxter's I should read. He said, 'Read any of them; they are all good.'

He said, 'Get as much force of mind as you can. Live within your income. Always have something saved at the end of the year. Let your imports be more than your exports, and you'll never go far wrong.'

I assured him, that in the extensive and various range of his acquaintance there never had been any one who had a more sincere respect and affection for him than I had. He said, 'I believe it, Sir. Were I in distress, there is no man to whom I should sooner come than to you. I should like to come and have a cottage in your park, toddle about, live mostly on milk, and be taken care of by Mrs Boswell. She and I are good friends now; are we not?'

Talking of devotion, he said, 'Though it be true that "GOD dwelleth not in temples made with hands", yet in this state of being our minds are more piously affected in places appropriated to divine worship, than in others. Some people have a particular room in their house where they say their prayers, of which I do not disapprove, as it may animate their devotion.'

He embraced me, and gave me his blessing, as usual when I was leaving him for any length of time. I walked from his door to-day with a fearful apprehension of what might happen before I returned.

To the Right Honourable WILLIAM WINDHAM.

SIR – The bringer of this letter is the father of Miss Philips,[a] a singer, who comes to try her voice on the stage at Dublin.

Mr Philips is one of my old friends; and as I am of opinion that neither he nor his daughter will do any thing that can disgrace their benefactors, I take the liberty of entreating you to countenance and protect them so far as may be suitable to your station[b] and character; and shall consider myself as obliged by any favourable notice which they shall have the honour of receiving from you. I am, Sir, your most humble servant,

SAM. JOHNSON.

London, May 31, 1783.

---

[a] Add this note: Now the celebrated Mrs Crouch.
[b] Add this note: Mr Windham was at this time in Dublin, Secretary to the Earl of Northington, then Lord Lieutenant of Ireland.

The following is another instance of his active benevolence:

To Sir JOSHUA REYNOLDS.

DEAR SIR - I have sent you some of my god-son's[a] performances, of which I do not pretend to form any opinion. When I took the liberty of mentioning him to you, I did not know what I have since been told, that Mr Moser had admitted him among the Students of the Academy. What more can be done for him I earnestly entreat you to consider; for I am very desirous that he should derive some advantage from my connection with him. If you are inclined to see him, I will bring him to wait on you at any time that you shall be pleased to appoint. I am, Sir, your most humble servant,

SAM. JOHNSON.

June 2, 1783.

My anxious apprehensions at parting with him this year proved to be but too well founded; for not long afterwards he had a dreadful stroke of the palsy, of which there are very full and accurate accounts in letters written by himself, which show with what composure[b] his steady piety enabled him to behave.[c]

To the Reverend Dr JOHN TAYLOR.

DEAR SIR - It has pleased GOD, by a paralytic stroke in the night, to deprive me of speech.

I am very desirous of Dr Heberden's assistance, as I think my case is not past remedy. Let me see you as soon as it is possible. Bring Dr Heberden with you, if you can; but come yourself at all events. I am glad you are so well, when I am so dreadfully attacked.

I think that by a speedy application of stimulants much may be done. I question if a vomit, vigorous and rough, would not rouse the organs of speech to action. As it is too early to send, I will try to recollect what I can, that can be suspected to have brought on this dreadful distress.

---

[a] Add the following note: Young Paterson, the son of Mr Samuel Paterson.
[b] After 'composure' read, 'of mind and resignation to the Divine Will'.
[c] Before the letter to the Reverend Dr Taylor, insert:

To MR EDMUND ALLEN.

DEAR SIR – It has pleased GOD, this morning, to deprive me of the powers of speech; and as I do not know but that it may be his further good pleasure to deprive me soon of my senses, I request you will on the receipt of this note, come to me, and act for me, as the exigencies of my case may require.
I am,
Sincerely your's,

SAM. JOHNSON.

June 17, 1783.

I have been accustomed to bleed frequently for an asthmatic complaint, but have forborne for some time by Dr Pepys's persuasion, who perceived my legs beginning to swell. I sometimes alleviate a painful, or more properly an oppressive constriction of my chest, by opiates; and have lately taken opium frequently, but the last, or two last times, in smaller quantities. My largest dose is three grains, and last night I took but two. You will suggest these things (and they are all that I can call to mind) to Dr Heberden. I am, &c.

SAM. JOHNSON.

June 17, 1783.

Two days after he wrote thus to Mrs Thrale:[1]

On Monday the 16th I sat for my picture, and walked a considerable way with little inconvenience. In the afternoon and evening I felt myself light and easy, and began to plan schemes of life. Thus I went to bed, and in a short time waked and sat up, as has been long my custom, when I felt a confusion and indistinctness in my head, which lasted, I suppose, about half a minute. I was alarmed, and prayed GOD, that however he might afflict my body, he would spare my understanding. This prayer, that I might try the integrity of my faculties, I made in Latin verse. The lines were not very good, but I knew them not to be very good: I made them easily, and concluded myself to be unimpaired in my faculties.

Soon after I perceived that I had suffered a paralytic stroke, and that my speech was taken from me. I had no pain, and so little dejection in this dreadful state, that I wondered at my own apathy, and considered that perhaps death itself, when it should come, would excite less horror than seems now to attend it.

In order to rouse the vocal organs, I took two drachms. Wine has been celebrated for the production of eloquence. I put myself into violent motion, and I think repeated it; but all was vain. I then went to bed, and, strange as it may seem, I think, slept. When I saw light, it was time to contrive what I should do. Though GOD stopped my speech, he left me my hand; I enjoyed a mercy which was not granted to my dear friend Lawrence, who now perhaps overlooks me as I am writing, and rejoices that I have what he wanted. My first note was necessarily to my servant, who came in talking, and could not immediately comprehend why he should read what I put into his hands.

I then wrote a card to Mr Allen, that I might have a discreet friend at hand, to act as occasion should require. In penning this note, I had some difficulty; my hand, I knew not how nor why, made wrong letters. I then wrote to Dr Taylor to come to me, and bring Dr Heberden; and I sent to Dr Brocklesby, who is my neighbour. My physicians are very friendly and

1 Vol. ii. p. 268, of Mrs Thrale's Collection.

give me great hopes; but you may imagine my situation. I have so far recovered my vocal powers, as to repeat the Lord's Prayer with no very imperfect articulation. My memory, I hope, yet remains as it was; but such an attack produces solicitude for the safety of every faculty.

To Mr THOMAS DAVIES.

DEAR SIR — I have had, indeed, a very heavy blow; but GOD, who yet spares my life, I humbly hope will spare my understanding, and restore my speech. As I am not at all helpless, I want no particular assistance, but am strongly affected by Mrs Davies's tenderness; and when I think she can do me good, shall be very glad to call upon her. I had ordered friends to be shut out, but one or two have found the way in; and if you come you shall be admitted: for I know not whom I can see that will bring more amusement on his tongue, or more kindness in his heart. I am, &c.

SAM. JOHNSON.

June 18, 1783.

It gives me great pleasure to preserve such a memorial of Johnson's regard for Mr Davies, to whom I was indebted for my introduction to him.[1] He indeed loved Davies cordially, of which I shall give the following little evidence. One day, when he had treated him with too much asperity, Tom, who was not without pride and spirit, went off in a passion; but he had hardly reached home, when Frank, who had been sent after him, delivered this note: 'Come, come, dear Davies, I am always sorry when we quarrel; send me word that we are friends.'

To JAMES BOSWELL, Esq.

DEAR SIR — Your anxiety about my health is very friendly, and very agreeable with your general kindness. I have, indeed, had a very frightful blow. On the 17th of last month, about three in the morning, as near as I can guess, I perceived myself almost totally deprived of speech. I had no pain. My organs were so obstructed, that I could say no, but could scarcely say yes. I wrote the necessary directions, for it pleased GOD to spare my hand, and sent for Dr Heberden and Dr Brocklesby. Between the time in which I discovered my own disorder, and that in which I sent for the doctors, I had, I believe, in spite of my surprise and solicitude, a little sleep, and Nature began to renew its operations. They came, and gave the directions which the disease required, and from that time I have been continually improving in articulation. I can now speak, but the nerves are weak, and I cannot continue discourse long; but strength, I hope, will return. The physicians consider me as cured. I was last Sunday at church. On Tuesday I took an

---

1 Poor Derrick, however, though he did not himself introduce me to Dr Johnson as he promised, had the merit of introducing me to Davies, the immediate introductor.

airing to Hampstead, and dined with the Club, where Lord Palmerston was proposed, and, against my opinion, was rejected.[1] I design to go next week with Mr Langton to Rochester, where I purpose to stay about ten days, and then try some other air. I have many kind invitations. Your brother has very frequently enquired after me. Most of my friends have, indeed, been very attentive. Thank dear Lord Hailes for his present.

I hope you found at your return every thing gay and prosperous, and your lady, in particular, quite recovered and confirmed. Pay her my respects.

I am, dear Sir, your most humble servant,

SAM. JOHNSON.

London, July 3, 1783.

To Mrs LUCY PORTER, in Lichfield.

DEAR MADAM — The account which you give of your health is but melancholy. May it please GOD to restore you. My disease affected my speech, and still continues, in some degree, to obstruct my utterance; my voice is distinct enough for awhile, but the organs being still weak are quickly weary: but in other respects I am, I think, rather better than I have lately been; and can let you know my state without the help of any other hand.

In the opinion of my friends, and in my own, I am gradually mending. The physicians consider me as cured; and I had leave, four days ago, to wash the cantharides from my head. Last Tuesday I dined at the Club.

I am going next week into Kent, and purpose to change the air frequently this summer; whether I shall wander so far as Staffordshire I cannot tell. I should be glad to come. Return my thanks to Mrs Cobb, and Mr Pearson, and all that have shown attention to me.

Let us, my dear, pray for one another, and consider our sufferings as notices mercifully given us to prepare ourselves for another state.

I live now but in a melancholy way. My old friend Mr Levett is dead, who lived with me in the house, and was useful and companionable; Mrs Desmoulins is gone away; and Mrs Williams is so much decayed, that she can add little to another's gratifications. The world passes away, and we are passing with it; but there is, doubtless, another world, which will endure for ever. Let us all fit ourselves for it. I am, &c.

SAM. JOHNSON.

London, July 5, 1783.

Such was the general vigour of his constitution, that he recovered from this alarming and severe attack with wonderful quickness; so that in July he was able to make a visit to Mr Langton at Rochester, where he passed about a fortnight, and made little excursions as easily as at any time of his life. In August he went as far as the neighbourhood of Salisbury, to Heale, the seat of

1 His Lordship was soon after chosen, and is now a member of the Club.

William Bowles, Esq., a gentleman whom I have heard him praise for exemplary religious order in his family. In his diary I find a short but honourable mention of this visit: 'August 28, I came to Heale without fatigue. 30. I am entertained quite to my mind.'

To Dr Brocklesby.

Heale, near Salisbury, Aug. 29, 1783.
Dear Sir - Without appearing to want a just sense of your kind attention, I cannot omit to give an account of the day which seemed to appear in some sort perilous. I rose at five, and went out at six, and having reached Salisbury about nine, went forward a few miles in my friend's chariot. I was no more wearied with the journey, though it was a high hung rough coach, than I should have been forty years ago. We shall now see what air will do. The country is all a plain; and the house in which I am, so far as I can judge from my window, for I write before I have left my chamber, is sufficiently pleasant.

'Be so kind as to continue your attention to Mrs Williams; it is great consolation to the well, and still greater to the sick, that they find themselves not neglected; and I know that you will be desirous of giving comfort even where you have no great hope of giving help.

Since I wrote the former part of the letter, I find that by the course of the post I cannot send it before the thirty-first. I am, &c.

Sam. Johnson.

While he was here he had a letter from Dr Brocklesby, acquainting him of the death of Mrs Williams, which affected him a good deal. Though for several years her temper had not been complacent, she had valuable qualities, and her departure left a blank in his house. Upon this occasion he, according to his habitual course of piety, composed a prayer.[1]

I shall here insert a few particulars concerning him, with which I have been favoured by one of his friends.

He had once conceived the design of writing the Life of Oliver Cromwell, saying, that he thought it must be highly curious to trace his extraordinary rise to the supreme power, from so obscure a beginning. He at length laid aside his scheme, on discovering that all that can be told of him is already in print; and that it is impracticable to procure any authentic information in addition to what the world is already possessed of.[a]

---

1 *Prayers and Meditations*, p. 226.
[a] Add this note: Mr Malone observes, 'This, however, was entirely a mistake, as appears from the Memoirs published by Mr Noble. Had Johnson been furnished with the materials which the industry of that gentleman has procured, and with others which, it is believed, are yet preserved in manuscript, he would, without doubt, have produced a most valuable and curious history of Cromwell's life.'

He had likewise projected, but at what part of his life is not known, a work to show how small a quantity of REAL FICTION there is in the world; and how the same images, with very little variation, have served all the authors who have ever written.

His thoughts in the latter part of his life were frequently employed on his deceased friends. He often muttered these, or such like sentences, 'Poor man! and then he died.'

Speaking of a certain literary friend, 'He is a very pompous puzzling fellow (says the Doctor); he lent me a letter once that somebody had written to him, no matter what it was about; but he wanted to have the letter back, and expressed a mighty value for it, he hoped it was to be met with again, he would not lose it for a thousand pounds. I layed my hand upon it soon afterwards, and gave it him. I believe I said, I was very glad to have met with it. O then he did not know that it signified any thing. So you see, when the letter was lost it was worth a thousand pounds, and when it was found it was not worth a farthing.'

The style and character of his conversation is pretty generally known; it was certainly conducted in conformity with a precept of Lord Bacon, but it is not clear, I apprehend, that this conformity was either perceived or intended by Johnson. The precept alluded to is as follows: 'In all kinds of speech, either pleasant, grave, severe, or ordinary, it is convenient to speak leisurely, and rather drawingly than hastily: because hasty speech confounds the memory, and oftentimes, besides the unseemliness, drives a man either to stammering, a non-plus, or harping on that which should follow; whereas a slow speech confirmeth the memory, addeth a conceit of wisdom to the hearers, besides a seemliness of speech and countenance.' Dr Johnson's method of conversation was certainly calculated to excite attention, and to amuse or instruct (as it happened), without wearying or confusing his company. He was always most perfectly clear and conspicuous;[a] and his language was so accurate, and his sentences so neatly constructed, that his conversation might have been all printed without any correction. At the same time, it was easy and natural; the accuracy of it had no appearance of labour, constraint, or stiffness; he seemed more correct than others by the force of habit and the customary exercises of his powerful mind.

He spoke often in praise of French literature. 'The French are excellent in this (he would say), they have a book on every subject.' From what he had seen of them he denied them the praise of superior politeness, and mentioned, with very visible disgust, the custom they have of spitting on the floors of their apartment. 'This (says[b] the Doctor) is as gross a thing as can well be done; and one wonders how any man, or set of men, can persist in so offensive a practice for a whole day together; one should expect that the first effort toward civilization would remove it even amongst savages.'

[a] For 'conspicuous' read 'perspicuous'.
[b] For 'says' read 'said'.

Baxter's *Reasons of the Christian Religion*, he thought contained the best collection of the evidences of the divinity of the Christian system.

Chemistry was always an interesting pursuit with Dr Johnson. Whilst he was in Wiltshire, he attended some experiments that were made by a physician at Salisbury, on the new kinds of air. In the course of the experiments frequent mention being made of Dr Priestley, Dr Johnson knit his brows, and in a stern manner enquired, 'Why do we hear so much of Dr Priestley?'[1] He was very properly answered, 'Sir, because we are indebted to him for these important discoveries.' On this, Dr Johnson appeared well content; and replied, 'Well, well, I believe we are; and let every man have the honour he has merited.'

A friend was one day, about two years before his death, struck with some instance of Dr Johnson's great candour. 'Well, Sir (said he), I will always say that you are a very candid man.' – 'Will you (replied the Doctor), I doubt then you will be very singular. But, indeed, Sir (continued he), I

1 I do not wonder at Johnson's displeasure when the name of Dr Priestley was mentioned; for I know no writer who has been suffered to publish more pernicious doctrines. I shall instance only three. First, *Materialism*; by which *mind* is denied to human nature, which, if believed, must deprive us of every elevated principle. Secondly, *Necessity*; or the doctrine that every action, whether good or bad, is included in an unchangeable and unavoidable system; a notion utterly subversive of moral government. Thirdly, that we have no reason to think that the *future* world (which, as he is pleased to *inform* us, will be adapted to our merely improved nature) will be materially different from *this*; which, if believed, would sink wretched mortals into despair, as they could no longer hope for the 'rest that remaineth for the people of GOD', or for that happiness which is revealed to us as something beyond our present conceptions; but would feel themselves doomed to a continuation of the uneasy state under which they now groan. I say nothing of the petulant intemperance with which he dares to insult the venerable establishments of his country.

As a specimen of his writings, I shall quote the following passage, which appears to me equally absurd and impious, and which might have been retorted upon him by the men who were prosecuted for burning his house. 'I cannot (says he) as a *necessarian* [meaning *necessitarian*], hate *any man*; because I consider him as *being*, in all respects, just what GOD has *made him to be*; and also as *doing with respect to me*, nothing but what he was *expressly designed* and *appointed* to do: GOD being the *only cause*, and men nothing more than the *instruments* in his hands to *execute all his pleasure*.' – *Illustrations of Philosophical Necessity*, p. 111.

The Reverend Dr Parr, in a late tract, appears to suppose that *Dr Johnson not only endured, but almost solicited, an interview with Dr Priestley*. In justice to Dr Johnson, I declare my firm belief that he never did. My illustrious friend was particularly resolute in not giving countenance to men whose writings he considered as pernicious to society. I was present at Oxford when Dr Price, even before he had rendered himself so generally obnoxious by his zeal for the French revolution, came into a company where Johnson was, who instantly left the room. Much more would he have reprobated Dr Priestley.

Whoever wishes to see a perfect delineation of this *Literary Jack of all Trades*, may find it in an ingenious tract, entitled, 'A SMALL WHOLE-LENGTH OF DR PRIESTLEY', printed for Rivingtons in St Paul's Church Yard.

look upon myself to be a man very much misunderstood. I am not an uncandid, nor am I a severe man. I sometimes say more than I mean in jest, and people are apt to believe me serious: however, I am more candid than I was when I was younger. As I know more of mankind I expect less of them, and am ready now to call a man *a good man*, upon easier terms than I was formerly.'

On his return from Heale he wrote to Dr Burney. 'I came home on the 18th at noon to a very disconsolate house. You and I have lost our friends, but you have more friends at home. My domestic companion is taken from me. She is much missed, for her acquisitions were many, and her curiosity universal; so that she partook of every conversation. I am not well enough to go much out; and to sit, and eat, or fast alone, is very wearisome. I always mean to send my compliments to all the ladies.'

His fortitude and patience met with severe trials during this year. The stroke of the palsy has been related circumstantially; but he was also afflicted with the gout, and was besides troubled with a complaint which not only was attended with immediate inconvenience, but threatened him with a painful chirurgical operation, from which most men would shrink. The complaint was a *sarcocele*, which Johnson bore with uncommon firmness, and was not at all frightened while he looked forward to amputation. He was attended by Mr Pott and also Mr Cruikshank. I have before me a letter of the 30th of July this year, to Mr Cruikshank, in which he says, 'I am going to put myself into your hands'; and another, accompanying a set of his *Lives of the Poets*, in which he says, 'I beg your acceptance of these volumes, as an acknowledgement of the great favours which you have bestowed on, Sir, your most obliged and most humble servant.' I have in my possession several more letters from him to Mr Cruikshank, and also to Dr Mudge at Plymouth, which it would be improper to insert, as they are filled with unpleasing technical details. I shall, however, extract from his letters to Dr Mudge such passages as show either a felicity of expression, or the undaunted state of his mind.

'My conviction of your skill, and my belief of your friendship, determine me to intreat your opinion and advice.' – 'In this state I with great earnestness desire you to tell me what is to be done. Excision is doubtless necessary to the cure, and I know not any means of palliation. The operation is doubtless painful; but is it dangerous? The pain I hope to endure with decency; but I am loth to put life into much hazard.' – 'By representing the gout as an antagonist to the palsy, you have said enough to make it welcome. This is not strictly the first fit, but I hope it is as good as the first; for it is the second that ever confined me; and the first was ten years ago, much less fierce and fiery than this.' – 'Write, dear Sir, what you can, to inform or encourage me. The operation is not delayed by any fears or objections of mine.'

Happily the complaint abated without his being put to the torture of amputation. But we must surely admire the manly resolution which he discovered while it hung over him.

To Bennet Langton, Esq.

Dear Sir - You may very reasonably charge me with insensibility of your kindness, and that of Lady Rothes, since I have suffered so much time to pass without paying any acknowledgement. I now, at last, return my thanks; and why I did it not sooner I ought to tell you. I went into Wiltshire as soon as I well could, and was there much employed in palliating my own malady. Disease produces much selfishness. A man in pain is looking after ease; and lets most other things go as chance shall dispose of them. In the mean time I have lost a companion, to whom I have had recourse for domestic amusement for thirty years, and whose variety of knowledge never was exhausted; and now return to a habitation vacant and desolate. I carry about a very troublesome and dangerous complaint, which admits no cure but by the chirurgical knife. Let me have your prayers. I am, &c.

SAM. JOHNSON.

London, Sept. 29, 1783.

In his next letter to the same gentleman he writes, 'The gout has within these four days come upon me with a violence which I never experienced before. It made me helpless as an infant.' - And in the following, having mentioned Mrs Williams, says, 'Whose death following that of Levett, has now made my house a solitude. She left her little substance to a charity-school. She is, I hope, where there is neither darkness, nor want, nor sorrow.'

I wrote to him, begging to know the state of his health, and mentioned that 'Baxter's Anacreon, which is in the library at Auchinleck, was, I find, collated by my father in 1727, with the MS. belonging to the University of Leyden, and he has made a number of Notes upon it. Would you advise me to publish a new edition of it?'

His answer was dated September 30. - 'You should not make your letters such rarities, when you know) or might know, the uniform state of my health. It is very long since I heard from you; and that I have not answered is a very insufficient reason for the silence of a friend. - Your Anacreon is a very uncommon book; neither London nor Cambridge can supply a copy of that edition. Whether it should be reprinted, you cannot do better than consult Lord Hailes. - Besides my constant and radical disease, I have been for these ten days much harrassed with the gout, but that has now remitted. I hope GOD will yet grant me a little longer life, and make me less unfit to appear before him.'

He this autumn received a visit from the celebrated Mrs Siddons. He gives this account of it in one of his letters to Mrs Thrale: 'Mrs Siddons, in her visit to me, behaved with great modesty and propriety, and left nothing behind her to be censured or despised. Neither praise nor money, the two powerful corrupters of mankind, seem to have depraved her. I shall be glad to see her again. Her brother Kemble calls on me, and pleases me very well. Mrs Siddons and I talked of plays; and she told me her intention of exhibiting this winter the characters of Constance, Catherine, and Isabella, in Shakspeare.'

Mr Kemble has favoured me with the following minute of what passed at this visit.

> When Mrs Siddons came into the room, there happened to be no chair ready for her, which he observing, said with a smile, 'Madam, you who so often occasion a want of seats to other people, will the more easily excuse the want of one yourself.' Having placed himself by her, he with great good humour entered upon a consideration of the English drama; and, among other enquiries, particularly asked her which of Shakspeare's characters she was most pleased with. Upon her answering that she thought the character of Queen Catherine in Henry the Eighth the most natural: 'I think so too, Madam (said he); and whenever you perform it I will once more hobble out to the theatre myself.' Mrs Siddons promised she would do herself the honour of acting his favourite part for him; but many circumstances happened to prevent the representation of King Henry the Eighth during the Doctor's life.

> In the course of the evening he thus gave his opinion upon the merits of some of the principal performers whom he remembered to have seen upon the stage. 'Mrs Porter, in the vehemence of rage, and Mrs Clive in the sprightliness of humour, I have never seen equalled. What Clive did best, she did better than Garrick; but could not do half so many things well; she was a better romp than any I ever saw in nature. Pritchard, in common life, was a vulgar idiot; she would talk of her *gownd*: but, when she appeared upon the stage, seemed to be inspired by gentility and understanding. I once talked with Colley Cibber, and thought him ignorant of the principles of his art. Garrick, Madam, was no declaimer; there was not one of his own scene-shifters who could not have spoken *To be, or not to be*, better than he did; yet he was the only actor I ever saw whom I could call a master both in tragedy and comedy; though I liked him best in comedy. A true conception of character, and natural expression of it were his distinguishing excellencies.' Having expatiated, with his usual force and eloquence, on Mr Garrick's extraordinary eminence as an actor, he concluded with this compliment to his social talents: 'And after all, Madam, I thought him less to be envied on the stage than at the head of a table.'

Johnson, indeed, had thought more upon the subject of acting than might be generally supposed. Talking of it one day to Mr Kemble, he said, 'Are you, Sir, one of those enthusiasts who believe yourself transformed into the very character you represent?' Upon Mr Kemble's answering that he had never felt so strong a persuasion himself; 'To be sure not, Sir (said Johnson). The thing is impossible. And if Garrick really believed himself to be that monster Richard the Third, he deserved to be hanged every time he performed it.'[a]

---

[a] Add the following note: My worthy friend, Mr John Nichols, was present when Mr Henderson, the actor, paid a visit to Dr Johnson; and was received in a very courteous manner. See *Gentleman's Magazine*, June 1791. *note continued overleaf*

A pleasing instance of the generous attention of one of his friends has been discovered by the publication of Mrs Thrale's collection of Letters. In a letter to one of the Miss Thrales,[1] he writes, 'A friend, whose name I will tell when your mamma has tried to guess it, sent to my physician to enquire whether this long train of illness had brought me into difficulties for want of money, with an invitation to send to him for what occasion required. I shall write this night to thank him, having no need to borrow.' And afterwards, in a letter to Mrs Thrale, 'Since you cannot guess, I will tell you, that the generous man was Gerard Hamilton. I returned him a very thankful and respectful letter.'[2]

I applied to Mr Hamilton, by a common friend, and he has been so obliging as to let me have Johnson's letter to him upon this occasion, to adorn my collection.

To the Right Honourable WILLIAM GERARD HAMILTON.

DEAR SIR – Your kind enquiries after my affairs, and your generous offers have been communicated to me by Dr Brocklesby. I return thanks with great sincerity, having lived long enough to know what gratitude is due to such friendship; and entreat that my refusal may not be imputed to sullenness or pride. I am, indeed, in no want. Sickness is, by the generosity of my physicians, of little expense to me. But if any unexpected exigence should press me, you shall see, dear Sir, how cheerfully I can be obliged to so much liberality. I am, Sir, your most obedient and most humble servant,

SAM. JOHNSON.

Nov. 19, 1783.

I found among Dr Johnson's papers, the following letter to him, from the celebrated Mrs Bellamy:

To Dr JOHNSON.

SIR – The flattering remembrance of the partiality you honoured me with, some years ago, as well as the humanity you are known to possess, has encouraged me to solicit your patronage at my Benefit.

By a long Chancery suit, and a complicated train of unfortunate events, I am reduced to the greatest distress; which obliges me, once more, to request the indulgence of the public.

Give me leave to solicit the honour of your company, and to assure you, if you grant my request, the gratification I shall feel, from being patronized by Dr Johnson, will be infinitely superior to any advantage that may arise from the Benefit; as I am, with the profoundest respect, Sir,

Your most obedient, humble servant,

G. A. BELLAMY.

No. 10, Duke-street, St James's,
May 11, 1783.

I am happy in recording these particulars, which prove that my illustrious friend lived to think much more favourably of Players than he appears to have done in the early part of his life.

1 Vol. ii, p. 328.
2 Ibid. p. 342.

I find in this, as in former years, notices of his kind attention to Mrs Gardiner, who, though in the humble station of a tallow-chandler upon Snow-hill, was a woman of excellent good sense, pious, and charitable. She told me, she had been introduced to him by Mrs Masters the poetess, whose volumes he revised, and, it is said, illuminated here and there with a ray of his own genius. Mrs Gardiner was very zealous for the support of a Welch charity-school; and Johnson this year, I find, obtained for it a sermon from the late Bishop of St Asaph, Dr Shipley, whom he, in one of his letters to Mrs Thrale, characterises as 'knowing and conversible'; and whom all who knew his Lordship, even those who differed from him in politics, remember with much respect.

The Earl of Carlisle having written a tragedy entitled *The Father's Revenge*, some of his Lordship's friends applied to Mrs Chapone, to prevail on Dr Johnson to read and give his opinion of it, which he accordingly did, in a letter to that lady. Sir Joshua Reynolds having informed me that this letter was in Lord Carlisle's possession, though not fortunate enough to have the honour of being known to his Lordship, trusting to the general courtesy of literature, I wrote to him, requesting the favour of a copy of it, and to be permitted to insert it in my life of Dr Johnson. His Lordship was so good as to comply with my request, and has thus enabled me to enrich my work with a very fine piece of writing, which displays at once the critical skill and politeness of my illustrious friend; and perhaps the curiosity which it will excite, may induce the noble and elegant author to gratify the world by the publication[1] of a performance, of which Dr Johnson has spoken in such terms.

To Mrs CHAPONE.

MADAM – By sending the tragedy to me a second time,[2] I think that a very honourable distinction has been shown me, and I did not delay the perusal, of which I am now to tell the effect.

The construction of the play is not completely regular; the stage is too often vacant, and the scenes are not sufficiently connected. This, however, would be called by Dryden only a mechanical defect; which takes away little from the power of the poem, and which is seen rather than felt.

A rigid examiner of the diction might, perhaps, wish some words changed, and some lines more vigorously terminated. But from such petty imperfections what writer was ever free?

The general form and force of the dialogue is of more importance. It seems to want that quickness of reciprocation which characterises the English drama, and is not always sufficiently fervid or animated.

Of the sentiments, I remember not one that I wished omitted. In the imagery I cannot forbear to distinguish the comparison of joy succeeding

---

1 A few copies only of this tragedy have been printed, and given to the author's friends.

2 Dr Johnson, having been very ill when the tragedy was first sent to him, had declined the consideration of it.

grief to light rushing on the eye accustomed to darkness. It seems to have all that can be desired to make it please. It is new, just, and delightful.[1]

With the characters, either as conceived or preserved, I have no fault to find; but was much inclined to congratulate a writer who, in defiance of prejudice and fashion, made the Archbishop a good man, and scorned all thoughtless applause, which a vicious churchman would have brought him.

The catastrophe is affecting. The Father and Daughter both culpable, both wretched, and both penitent, divide between them our pity and our sorrow.

Thus, Madam, I have performed what I did not willingly undertake, and could not decently refuse. The noble writer will be pleased to remember, that sincere criticism ought to raise no resentment, because judgement is not under the control of will; but involuntary criticism, as it has still less of choice, ought to be more remote from possibility of offence. I am, &c.

SAM. JOHNSON.

Nov. 28, 1783.

I consulted him on two questions, of a very different nature: one, whether the unconstitutional influence exercised by the Peers of Scotland in the election of the representatives of the Commons, by means of fictitious qualifications, ought not to be resisted? – the other, What, in propriety and humanity, should be done with old horses unable to labour? I gave him some account of my life at Auchinleck; and expressed my satisfaction that the gentlemen of the county had, at two public meetings, elected me their *Praeses*, or Chairman.

To JAMES BOSWELL, Esq.

DEAR SIR – Like all other men who have great friends, you begin to feel the pangs of neglected merit, and all the comfort that I can give you is, by telling you that you have probably more pangs to feel, and more neglect to suffer. You have, indeed, begun to complain too soon; and I hope I am the only confidant of your discontent. Your friends have not yet had leisure to gratify personal kindness; they have hitherto been busy in strengthening their ministerial interest. If a vacancy happens in Scotland, give them early intelligence; and as you can serve Government as powerfully as any of your probable competitors, you may make in some sort a warrantable claim.

Of the exaltations and depressions of your mind you delight to talk, and I hate to hear. Drive all such fancies from you.

On the day when I received your letter, I think, the foregoing page was written; to which, one disease or another has hindered me from making any additions. I am now a little better. But sickness and solitude press me very heavily. I could bear sickness better, if I were relieved from solitude.

---

1   I could have borne my woes; that stranger Joy
           Wounds while it smiles: The long imprison'd wretch,
           Emerging from the night of his damp cell,
           Shrinks from the sun's bright beams; and that which flings
           Gladness o'er all, to him is agony.

The present dreadful confusion of the public ought to make you wrap yourself up in your hereditary possessions, which, though less than you may wish, are more than you can want; and in an hour of religious retirement return thanks to GOD, who has exempted you from any strong temptation to faction, treachery, plunder, and disloyalty.

As your neighbours distinguish you by such honours as they can bestow, content yourself with your station, without neglecting your profession. Your estate and the Courts will find you full employment; and your mind well occupied will be quiet.

The usurpation of the nobility, for they apparently usurp all the influence they gain by fraud, and misrepresentation, I think it certainly lawful, perhaps your duty to resist. What is not their own they have only by robbery.

Your question about the horses gives me more perplexity. I know not well what advice to give you. I can only recommend a rule which you do not want – give as little pain as you can. I suppose that we have a right to their service while their strength lasts; what we can do with them afterwards I cannot so easily determine. But let us consider. Nobody denies that man has a right first to milk the cow, and to sheer the sheep, and then to kill them for his table. May he not, by parity of reason, first work a horse, and then kill him the easiest way, that he may have the means of another horse, or food for cows and sheep? Man is influenced in both cases by different motives of self-interest. He that rejects the one must reject the other.

I am, &c.

SAM. JOHNSON.

London, Dec. 24, 1783.

A happy and pious Christmas; and many happy years to you, your lady, and children.

The late ingenious Mr Mickle, some time before his death, wrote me a letter concerning Dr Johnson, in which he mentions, 'I was upwards of twelve years acquainted with him, was frequently in his company, always talked with ease to him, and can truly say, that I never received from him one rough word.'

In this letter he relates his having, while engaged in translating the *Lusiad*, had a dispute of considerable length with Johnson, who, as usual, declaimed upon the misery and corruption of a sea life, and used this expression: 'It had been happy for the world, Sir, if your hero Gama, Prince Henry of Portugal, and Columbus, had never been born, or that their schemes had never gone farther than their own imaginations.' – 'This sentiment (says Mr Mickle), which is to be found in his 'Introduction to the World displayed', I, in my Dissertation prefixed to the *Lusiad*, have controverted; and though authors are said to be bad judges of their own works, I am not ashamed to own to a friend, that that dissertation is my favourite above all that I ever attempted in prose. Next year, when the *Lusiad* was published, I waited on Dr Johnson, who addressed me with one of his good-humoured smiles: 'Well, you have remembered our dispute about Prince Henry, and have cited me too. You have done your part very well indeed; you have made the best of your argument: but I am not convinced yet.'

'Before publishing the *Lusiad*, I sent Mr Hoole a proof of that part of the introduction, in which I make mention of Dr Johnson, yourself, and other well-wishers to the work, begging it might be shown to Dr Johnson. This was accordingly done; and in place of the simple mention of him which I had made, he dictated to Mr Hoole the sentence as it now stands.

'Dr Johnson told me in 1772, that about twenty years before that time, he himself had a design to translate the *Lusiad*, of the merit of which he spoke highly, but had been prevented by a number of other engagements.'

Mr Mickle reminds me in this letter of a conversation, when dining one day at Mr Hoole's with Dr Johnson, when Mr Nicol, the King's bookseller, and I attempted to controvert the maxim, 'Better that ten guilty should escape, than one innocent person suffer'; and were answered by Dr Johnson with great power of reasoning and eloquence. I am very sorry that I have no record of that day; but I well recollect my illustrious friend's having ably shown, that unless civil institutions insure protection to the innocent, all the confidence which mankind should have in them would be lost.

I shall here mention what should properly have appeared in my account of last year, though the controversy was not closed till this. The Reverend Mr Shaw, a native of one of the Hebrides, having entertained doubts of the authenticity of the poems ascribed to Ossian, divested himself of national bigotry; and having travelled in the Highlands and Islands of Scotland, and also in Ireland, in order to furnish himself with materials for a Gaelic Dictionary, which he afterwards compiled, was so fully satisfied that Dr Johnson was in the right upon the question, that he fairly published a pamphlet, stating his conviction, and the proofs and reasons on which it was founded. A person at Edinburgh of the name of Clark, answered this pamphlet with much zeal, and much abuse of its author. Johnson took Mr Shaw under his protection, and gave him his assistance in writing a reply, which has been admired by the best judges, and, by many been considered as conclusive. A few paragraphs, which sufficiently mark their great author, shall be selected.

My assertions are, for the most part, purely negative: I deny the existence of Fingal, because in a long and curious peregrination through the Gaelic regions I have never been able to find it. What I could not see myself I suspect to be equally invisible to others; and I suspect with the more reason, as among all those who have seen it no man can show it.

Mr Clark compares the obstinacy of those who disbelieve the genuineness of Ossian to a blind man, who should dispute the reality of colours, and deny that the British troops are clothed in red. The blind man's doubt would be rational, if he did not know by experience that others have a power which he himself wants: but what perspicacity has Mr Clark which Nature has with-held from me or the rest of mankind?

The true state of the parallel must be this. Suppose a man, with eyes like his neighbours, was told by a boasting corporal, that the troops, indeed, wore red clothes for their ordinary dress, but that every soldier had likewise a suit of black velvet, which he put on when the King reviews them. This he thinks strange, and desires to see the fine clothes, but finds nobody in forty thousand men that can produce either coat or waistcoat. One, indeed, has left them in his chest at Port Mahon; another has always heard that he ought to have velvet clothes somewhere; and a third has heard somebody say, that soldiers ought to wear velvet. Can the enquirer be blamed if he goes away believing that a soldier's red coat is all that he has?

But the most obdurate incredulity may be shamed or silenced by facts. To overpower contradictions, let the soldier show his velvet coat, and the Fingalist the original of Ossian.

The difference between us and the blind man is this: the blind man is unconvinced, because he cannot see; and we, because though we can see, we find that nothing can be shown.

Notwithstanding the complication of disorders under which Johnson now laboured, he did not resign himself to despondency and discontent, but with wisdom and spirit endeavoured to console and amuse his mind with as many innocent enjoyments as he could procure. Sir John Hawkins has mentioned the cordiality with which he insisted that such of the members of the old club in Ivy-lane as survived should meet again and dine together, which they did, twice at a tavern, and once at his house: and in order to insure himself society in the evening for three days in the week, he instituted a Club at the Essex Head, in Essex-street, then kept by Samuel Greaves, an old servant of Mr Thrale's.

To Sir JOSHUA REYNOLDS.

DEAR SIR – It is inconvenient to me to come out, I should else have waited on you with an account of a little evening Club which we are establishing in Essex-street, in the Strand, and of which you are desired to be one. It will be held at the Essex Head, now kept by an old servant of Thrale's. The company is numerous, and, as you will see by the list, miscellaneous. The terms are lax, and the expenses light. Mr Barry was adopted by Dr Brocklesby, who joined with me in forming the plan. We meet thrice a week, and he who misses forfeits two-pence.

If you are willing to become a member, draw a line under your name. Return the list. We meet for the first time on Monday at eight. I am, &c.
                                                            SAM. JOHNSON.
    Dec. 4, 1783.

It did not suit Sir Joshua to be one of this club. But when I mention only Mr Daines Barrington, Dr Brocklesby, Mr Murphy,[a] Mr Cooke, Mr Joddrel,

---

[a] After 'Mr Murphy', add 'Mr John Nichols'.

Mr Paradise, Dr Horsley, Mr Windham,[1] I shall sufficiently obviate the misrepresentation of it by Sir John Hawkins, as if it had been a low ale-house association, by which Johnson was degraded. Johnson himself, like his name-sake Old Ben, composed the Rules of his Club.[2]

In the end of this year he was seized with a spasmodic asthma of such violence, that he was confined to the house in great pain, being sometimes obliged to sit all night in his chair, a recumbent posture being so hurtful to his respiration, that he could not endure lying in bed; and there came upon him at

---

1 I was in Scotland when this Club was founded, and during all the winter. Johnson, however, declared I should be a member, and invented a word upon the occasion: 'Boswell (said he) is a very *clubable* man.' When I came to town I was proposed by Mr Barrington, and chosen. I believe there are few societies where there is better conversation or more decorum. Several of us resolved to continue it after our great founder was removed by death. Other members were added; and now, above six years since that loss, we go on happily.

2   RULES.

'Today deep thoughts with me resolve to drench
In mirth, which after no repenting draws.'   MILTON.

The Club shall consist of four-and-twenty.

The meetings shall be on the Monday, Thursday, and Saturday of every week; but in the week before Easter there shall be no meeting.

Every member is at liberty to introduce a friend once a week; but not oftener.

Two members shall oblige themselves to attend in their turn every night from eight to ten, or to procure two to attend in their room.

Every member present at the Club shall spend at least six-pence; and every member who stays away shall forfeit three-pence.

The master of the house shall keep an account of the absent members; and deliver to the President of the night a list of the forfeits incurred.

When any member returns after absence, he shall immediately lay down his forfeits; which if he omits to do, the President shall require.

There shall be no general reckoning, but every man shall adjust his own expences.

The night of indispensable attendance will come to every member once a month. Whoever shall for three months together omit to attend himself, or by substitution, nor shall make any apology in the fourth month, shall be considered as having abdicated the Club.

When a vacancy is to be filled, the name of the candidate, and of the member recommending him, shall stand in the Club-room three nights. On the fourth he may be chosen by ballot; six members, at least, being present, and two-thirds of the ballot being in his favour; or the majority, should the numbers not be divisible by three.

The master of the house shall give notice, six days before, to each of those members whose turn of necessary attendance is come.

The notice may be in these words : 'Sir, On ——— the ——— of ———, will be your turn of presiding at the Essex Head. Your company is therefore earnestly requested.'

One penny shall be left by each member for the waiter.

Johnson's definition of a Club in this sense in his Dictionary is, 'An assembly of good fellows, meeting under certain conditions'.

the same time that oppressive and fatal disease, a dropsy. It was a very severe winter, which probably aggravated his complaints; and the solitude in which Mr Levett and Mrs Williams had left him, rendered his life very gloomy. Mrs Desmoulins, who still lived, was herself so very ill that she could contribute very little to his relief. He, however, had none of that unsocial shyness which we commonly see in people afflicted with sickness. He did not hide his head in abstraction; he did not deny himself to the visits of his friends and acquaintances; but at all times, when he was not overcome by sleep, was ready for conversation as in his best days.

To Mrs LUCY PORTER, in Lichfield.

DEAR MADAM – You may perhaps think me negligent that I have not written to you again upon the loss of your brother; but condolences and consolations are such common and such useless things, that the omission of them is no great crime; and my own diseases occupy my mind, and engage my care. My nights are miserably restless, and my days, therefore, are heavy. I try, however, to hold up my head as high as I can.

I am sorry that your health is impaired; perhaps the spring and the summer may, in some degree, restore it; but if not, we must submit to the inconveniencies of time, as to the other dispensations of Eternal Goodness. Pray for me, and write to me, or let Mr Pearson write for you. I am, &c.

SAM. JOHNSON.

London, Nov. 29, 1783.

And now I am arrived at the last year of the life of SAMUEL JOHNSON, an year in which, although passed in severe indisposition, he nevertheless gave many evidences of the continuance of those wondrous powers of mind, which raised him so high in the intellectual world. His conversation and his letters of this year were in no respect inferior to those of former years.

The following is a remarkable proof of his being alive to the most minute curiosities of literature.

To Mr DILLY, Bookseller in the Poultry.

SIR – There is in the world a set of books, which used to be sold by the booksellers on the bridge, and which I must entreat you to procure me. They are called, *Burton's Books*; the title of one is, *Admirable Curiosities, Rarities, and Wonders in England*. I believe there are about five or six of them; they seem very proper to allure backward readers; be so kind as to get them for me, and send me them with the best printed edition of Baxter's *Call to the Unconverted*. I am, &c.

SAM. JOHNSON.

Jan. 6, 1784.[a]

---

[a] After the letter to Mr Dilly, add the following:

His attention to the Essex Head Club appears from the following letter to Mr Alderman Clark, a gentleman for whom he deservedly entertained a great regard.

To Richard Clark, Esq.

Dear Sir – You will receive a requisition, according to the rules of the Club, to be at the house as President of the night. This turn comes once a month, and the member is obliged to attend, or send another in his place. You were enrolled in the Club by my invitation, and I ought to introduce you; but as I am hindered by sickness, Mr Hoole will very properly supply my place as introductor, or yours as President. I hope in milder weather to be a very constant attendant. I am, Sir, &c.

SAM. JOHNSON.

Jan. 27, 1784.

You ought to be informed, that the forfeits began with the year, and that every night of non-attendance incurs the mulct of three-pence, that is, nine-pence a week.

On the 8th of January I wrote to him, anxiously enquiring as to his health, and enclosing my 'Letter to the People of Scotland, on the present State of the Nation'. – 'I trust (said I) that you will be liberal enough to make allowance for my differing from you on two points [the Middlesex Election and the American War], when my general principles of government are according to your own heart, and when, at a crisis of doubtful event I stand forth with honest zeal as an ancient and faithful Baron. My reason for introducing those two points was, that as my opinions with regard to them had been declared at the periods when they were least favourable, I might have the credit of a man who is not a worshipper of ministerial power.'

To James Boswell, Esq.

Dear Sir – I hear of many inquiries which your kindness has disposed you to make after me. I have long intended you a long letter, which perhaps the imagination of its length hindered me from beginning. I will, therefore, content myself with a shorter.

To Mr Perkins.

Dear Sir – I was very sorry not to see you, when you were so kind as to call on me; but to disappoint friends, and if they are not very good-natured, to disoblige them, is one of the evils of sickness. If you will please to let me know which of the afternoons in this week I shall be favoured with another visit by you and Mrs Perkins, and the young people, I will take all the measures that I can to be pretty well at that time. I am, dear Sir,

Your most humble servant,

SAM. JOHNSON.

Jan. 21, 1784.

Having promoted the institution of a new Club in the neighbourhood, at the house of an old servant of Thrale's, I went thither to meet the company, and was seized with a spasmodic asthma so violent, that with difficulty I got to my own house, in which I have been confined eight or nine weeks, and from which I know not when I shall be able to go even to church. The asthma, however, is not the worst. A dropsy gains ground upon me; my legs and thighs are very much swollen with water, which I should be content if I could keep there, but I am afraid that it will soon be higher. My nights are very sleepless and very tedious. And yet I am extremely afraid of dying.

My physicians try to make me hope, that much of my malady is the effect of cold, and that some degree at least of recovery is to be expected from vernal breezes and summer suns. If my life is prolonged to autumn, I should be glad to try a warmer climate; though how to travel with a diseased body, without a companion to conduct me, and with very little money, I do not well see. Ramsay has recovered his limbs in Italy; and Fielding was sent to Lisbon, where, indeed, he died; but he was, I believe, past hope when he went. Think for me what I can do.

I received your pamphlet, and when I write again may perhaps tell you some opinion about it; but you will forgive a man struggling with disease his neglect of disputes, politics, and pamphlets. Let me have your prayers. My compliments to your lady, and young ones. Ask your physicians about my case; and desire Sir Alexander Dick to write me his opinion.

I am, dear Sir, &c.

SAM. JOHNSON.

Feb. 1, 1784.

To Mrs LUCY PORTER, in Lichfield.

MY DEAREST LOVE — I have been extremely ill of an asthma and dropsy, but received, by the mercy of GOD, sudden and unexpected relief last Thursday, by the discharge of twenty pints of water. Whether I shall continue free, or shall fill again, cannot be told. Pray for me.

Death, my dear, is very dreadful; let us think nothing worth our care but how to prepare for it: what we know amiss in ourselves let us make haste to amend, and put our trust in the mercy of GOD, and the intercession of our SAVIOUR. I am, dear Madam,

Your most humble servant,

SAM. JOHNSON.

Feb. 23, 1784.

To JAMES BOSWELL, Esq.

DEAR SIR — I have just advanced so far towards recovery as to read a pamphlet; and you may reasonably suppose that the first pamphlet which I read was yours. I am very much of your opinion, and, like you, feel great indignation at the indecency with which the King is every day treated. Your paper contains very considerable knowledge of history and of the constitution, very properly produced and applied. It will certainly raise your character,[1] though perhaps it may not make you a Minister of State.

. . .

I desire you to see Mrs Stewart once again, and tell her, that in the letter-case was a letter relating to me, for which I will give her, if she is willing to give it me, another guinea. The letter is of consequence only to me. I am, dear Sir, &c.

SAM. JOHNSON.

London, Feb. 27, 1784.

In consequence of Johnson's request that I should ask our physicians about his case, and desire Sir Alexander Dick to send his opinion, I transmitted him a letter from that very amiable Baronet, then in his eighty-first year, with his faculties as entire as ever; and mentioned his expressions to me in the note accompanying it: 'With my most affectionate wishes for Dr Johnson's recovery, in which his friends, his country, and all mankind have so deep a stake': and at the same time a full opinion upon his case by Dr Gillespie, who, like Dr Cullen, had the advantage of having passed through the gradations of surgery and pharmacy, and by study and practice had attained to such skill, that my father settled on him two hundred pounds a year for five years, and fifty pounds a year during his life, as an *honorarium* to secure his particular attendance. The opinion was conveyed in a letter to me beginning, 'I am sincerely sorry for the bad state of health your very learned and illustrious friend, Dr Johnson, labours under at present.'

To JAMES BOSWELL, Esq.

DEAR SIR – Presently after I had sent away my last letter, I received your kind medical packet. I am very much obliged both to you and your physicians for your kind attention to my disease. Dr Gillespie has sent an excellent *consilium medicum*, all solid practical experimental knowledge. I am at present, in the opinion of my physicians (Dr Heberden and Dr Brocklesby) as well as my own, going on very hopefully. I have just begun to take vinegar of squills. The powder hurt my stomach so much, that it could not be continued.

---

1 I sent it to Mr Pitt, with a letter, in which I thus expressed myself: 'My principles may appear to you too monarchical; but I know and am persuaded, they are not inconsistent with the true principles of liberty. Be this as it may, you, Sir, are now the Prime Minister, called by the Sovereign to maintain the rights of the Crown, as well as those of the people, against a violent faction. As such, you are entitled to the warmest support of every good subject in every department.' He answered, 'I am extremely obliged to you for the sentiments you do me the honour to express, and have observed with great pleasure the *zealous and able support* given to the CAUSE OF THE PUBLIC in the work you were so good to transmit to me.'

Return Sir Alexander Dick my sincere thanks for his kind letter; and bring with you the rhubarb[1] which he so tenderly offers me.

I hope dear Mrs Boswell is now quite well, and that no evil, either real or imaginary, now disturbs you. I am, &c.

SAM. JOHNSON.

London, March 2, 1784.

I also applied to three of the eminent physicians who had chairs in our celebrated school of medicine at Edinburgh, Doctors Cullen, Hope, and Monro, to each of whom I sent the following letter:

DEAR SIR – Dr Johnson has been very ill for some time; and in a letter of anxious apprehension he writes to me, 'Ask your physicians about my case.'

This, you see, is not authority for a regular consultation: but I have no doubt of your readiness to give your advice to a man so eminent, and who, in his Life of Garth, has paid your profession a just and elegant compliment: 'I believe every man has found in physicians great liberality and dignity of sentiment, very prompt effusions of beneficence, and willingness to exert a lucrative art, where there is no hope of lucre.'

Dr Johnson is aged seventy-four. Last summer he had a stroke of the palsy, from which he recovered almost entirely. He had, before that, been troubled with a catarrhous cough. This winter he was seized with a spasmodic asthma, by which he has been confined to his house for about three months. Dr Brocklesby writes to me, that upon the least admission of cold, there is such a constriction upon his breast, that he cannot lie down in his bed, but is obliged to sit up all night, and gets rest, and sometimes sleep, only by means of laudanum and syrup of poppies; and that there are oedematous tumours on his legs and thighs. Dr Brocklesby trusts a good deal to the return of mild weather. Dr Johnson says, that a dropsy gains ground upon him; and he seems to think that a warmer climate would do him good. I understand he is now rather better, and is using vinegar of squills. I am, with great esteem, dear Sir,

Your most obedient humble servant,

JAMES BOSWELL.

March 7, 1784.

All of them paid the most polite attention to my letter, and its venerable object. Dr Cullen's words concerning him were, 'It would give me the greatest pleasure to be of any service to a man whom the public properly esteem, and whom I esteem and respect as much as I do Dr Johnson.' Dr Hope's, 'Few people have a better claim on me than your friend, as hardly a day passes that I

1 From his garden at Prestonfield, where he cultivated that plant with such success, that he was presented with a gold medal by the Society of London for the Encouragement of Arts and Sciences.[a]

a For 'and Sciences' read 'Manufactures and Commerce'.

do not ask his opinion about this or that word.' Dr Monro's, 'I most sincerely join you in sympathizing with that very worthy and ingenious character, from whom his country has derived much instruction and entertainment.'

Dr Hope corresponded with his friend Dr Brocklesby. Doctors Cullen and Monro wrote their opinions and prescriptions to me, which I afterwards carried with me to London, and, so far as they were encouraging, communicated to Johnson. The liberality on one hand, and grateful sense of it on the other, I have great satisfaction in recording.

To James Boswell, Esq.

Dear Sir – I am too much pleased with the attention which you and your dear lady[1] show to my welfare, not to be diligent in letting you know the progress which I make towards health. The dropsy, by God's blessing, has now run almost totally away by natural evacuation; and the asthma, if not irritated by cold, gives me little trouble. While I am writing this, I have not any sensation of debility or disease. But I do not yet venture out, having been confined to the house from the thirteenth of December, now a quarter of a year.

When it will be fit for me to travel as far as Auchinleck, I am not able to guess; but such a letter as Mrs Boswell's might draw any man, not wholly motionless, a great way. Pray tell the dear lady how much her civility and kindness have touched and gratified me.

Our parliamentary tumults have now begun to subside, and the King's authority is in some measure re-established. Mr Pitt will have great power; but you must remember, that what he has to give must, at least for some time, be given to those who gave, and those who preserve his power. A new minister can sacrifice little to esteem or friendship; he must, till he is settled, think only of extending his interest.

. . .

If you come hither through Edinburgh, send for Mrs Stewart, and give from me another guinea for the letter in the old case, to which I shall not be satisfied with my claim, till she gives it me.

Please to bring with you Baxter's Anacreon; and if you procure heads of Hector Boece, the historian, and Arthur Johnston, the poet, I will put them in my room, or any other of the fathers of Scottish literature.

I wish you an easy and happy journey, and hope I need not tell you that you will be welcome to, dear Sir, your most affectionate humble servant,

Sam. Johnson.

London, March 18, 1784.

I wrote to him, March 28, from York, informing him that I had a high gratification in the triumph of monarchical principles over aristocratical influence, in that great county, in an address to the King; that I was thus far on my way to him, but that news of the dissolution of Parliament having arrived,

1 Who had written him a very kind letter.

I was to hasten back to my own county, where I had carried an address to his Majesty by a great majority, and had some intention of being a candidate to represent the county in Parliament.

To JAMES BOSWELL, Esq.

DEAR SIR – You could do nothing so proper as to haste back when you found the Parliament dissolved. With the influence which your address must have gained you, it may reasonably be expected that your presence will be of importance, and your activity of effect.

Your solicitude for me gives me that pleasure which every man feels from the kindness of such a friend; and it is with delight I relieve it by telling, that Dr Brocklesby's account is true, and that I am, by the blessing of GOD, wonderfully relieved.

You are entering upon a transaction which requires much prudence. You must endeavour to oppose without exasperating; to practise temporary hostility, without producing enemies for life. This is, perhaps, hard to be done; yet it has been done by many, and seems most likely to be effected by opposing merely upon general principles, without descending to personal or particular censures or objections. One thing I must enjoin you, which is seldom observed in the conduct of elections; – I must entreat you to be scrupulous in the use of strong liquors. One night's drunkenness may defeat the labours of forty days well employed. Be firm, but not clamorous; be active, but not malicious; and you may form such an interest, as may not only exalt yourself, but dignify your family.

We are, as you may suppose, all busy here. Mr Fox resolutely stands for Westminster, and his friends say will carry the election. However that be, he will certainly have a seat. Mr Hoole has just told me, that the city leans towards the King.

Let me hear, from time to time, how you are employed, and what progress you make.

Make dear Mrs Boswell, and all the young Boswells, the sincere compliments of, Sir, your affectionate humble servant,

SAM. JOHNSON.

London, March 30, 1784.

To Mr Langton he wrote with that cordiality which was suitable to the long friendship which had subsisted between him and that gentleman.

March 27 – Since you left me, I have continued in my own opinion, and in Dr Brocklesby's, to grow better with respect to all my formidable and dangerous distempers; though to a body battered and shaken as mine has lately been, it is to be feared that weak attacks may be sometimes mischievous. I have, indeed, by standing carelessly at an open window, got a very troublesome cough, which it has been necessary to appease by opium, in larger quantities than I like to take, and I have not found it give way so readily as I expected; its obstinacy, however, seems at last disposed to submit to the remedy, and I know not whether I should then have a right to complain of any morbid sensation. My asthma is, I am afraid, constitutional and incurable; but it is only occasional, and unless it be excited by labour or by cold, gives me no molestation, nor does it lay very close siege to life; for Sir John Floyer, whom the physical race consider as author of one of the best books upon it, panted on to ninety, as was supposed; and why were we content with supposing a fact so interesting, of a man so conspicuous, because he corrupted, at perhaps seventy or eighty, the register, that he might pass for younger than he was? He was not much less than eighty, when to a man of rank who modestly asked him his age, he answered, 'Go look'; though he was in general a man of civility and elegance.

The ladies, I find, are at your house all well, except Miss Langton, who will probably soon recover her health by light suppers. Let her eat at dinner as she will, but not take a full stomach to bed. Pay my sincere respects to the two principal ladies in your house; and when you write to dear Miss Langton in Lincolnshire, let her know that I mean not to break our league of friendship, and that I have a set of *Lives* for her, when I have the means of sending it.

April 8 – I am still disturbed by my cough; but what thanks have I not to pay, when my cough is the most painful sensation that I feel? And from that I expect hardly to be released, while winter continues to gripe us with so much pertinacity. The year has now advanced eighteen days beyond the equinox, and still there is very little remission of the cold. When warm weather comes, which surely must come at last, I hope it will help both me and your young lady.

The man so busy about addresses is neither more nor less than our own Boswell, who had come as far as York towards London, but turned back on the dissolution, and is said now to stand for some place. Whether to wish him success, his best friends hesitate.

Let me have your prayers for the completion of my recovery: I am now better than I ever expected to have been. May GOD add to his mercies the grace that may enable me to use them according to his will. My compliments to all.

April 13 – I had this evening a note from Lord Portmore,[1] desiring that I would give you an account of my health. You might have had it with less circumduction. I am, by GOD's blessing, I believe, free from all morbid sensations, except a cough, which is only troublesome. But I am still weak, and can have no great hope of strength till the weather shall be softer. The

---

1 To which Johnson returned this answer:

To the Right Honourable Earl of PORTMORE.

Dr JOHNSON acknowledges with great respect the honour of Lord Portmore's notice. He is better than he was; and will, as his Lordship directs, write to Mr Langton. Bolt-court, Fleet-street, Apr. 13, 1784.

summer, if it be kindly, will, I hope, enable me to support the winter. GOD, who has so wonderfully restored me, can preserve me in all seasons.

Let me enquire in my turn after the state of your family, great and little. I hope Lady Rothes and Miss Langton are both well. That is a good basis of content. Then how goes George on with his studies? How does Miss Mary? And how does my own Jenny? I think I owe Jenny a letter, which I will take care to pay. In the mean time tell her that I acknowledge the debt.

Be pleased to make my compliments to the ladies. If Mrs Langton comes to London, she will favour me with a visit, for I am not well enough to go out.

To OZIAS HUMPHREY,[1] Esq.

SIR – Mr Hoole has told me with what benevolence you listened to a request which I was almost afraid to make, of leave to a young painter,[2] to attend you from time to time in your painting-room, to see your operations, and receive your instructions.

The young man has perhaps good parts, but has been without a regular education. He is my god-son, and therefore I interest myself in his progress and success, and shall think myself much favoured if I receive from you a permission to send him.

My health is, by GOD's blessing, much restored, but I am not yet allowed by my physicians to go abroad; nor, indeed, do I think myself yet able to endure the weather. I am, Sir, your most humble servant,

SAM. JOHNSON.

April 5, 1784.

To the same.

SIR – The bearer is my god-son, whom I take the liberty of recommending to your kindness; which I hope he will deserve by his respect to your excellence, and his gratitude for your favours. I am, Sir,

Your most humble servant,

SAM. JOHNSON.

April 10, 1784.

---

1 The eminent painter, representative of the ancient family of Homfrey (now spelt Humphrey) in the west of England; who, as appears from their arms which they have invariably used, have been (as I have seen authenticated by the best authority) one of those among the Knights and Esquires of honour who are represented by Holingshead as having issued from the Tower of London on coursers apparelled for the justes, accompanied by ladies of honour, leading every one a Knight, with a chain of gold, passing through the streets of London into Smithfield, on Sunday at three o'clock in the afternoon, being the first Sunday after Michaelmas, in the fourteenth year of King Richard the Second. This family once enjoyed large possessions, but, like others, have lost them in the progress of ages. Their blood, however, remains to them well ascertained; and they may hope, in the revolution of events, to recover that rank in society for which, in modern times, fortune seems to be an indispensable requisite.

2 Son of Mr Samuel Paterson, eminent for his knowledge of books.

To the same.

SIR – I am very much obliged by your civilities to my god-son, but must beg of you to add to them the favour of permitting him to see you paint, that he may know how a picture is begun, advanced, and completed.

If he may attend you in a few of your operations, I hope he will show that the benefit has been properly conferred, both by his proficiency and his gratitude. At least I shall consider you as enlarging your kindness to, Sir,
    Your humble servant,

SAM. JOHNSON.

    May 31, 1784.

To the Reverend Dr TAYLOR, Ashbourne, Derbyshire.

DEAR SIR – What can be the reason that I hear nothing from you? I hope nothing disables you from writing. What I have seen, and what I have felt, gives me reason to fear every thing. Do not omit giving me the comfort of knowing, that after all my losses I have yet a friend left.

I want every comfort. My life is very solitary and very cheerless. Though it has pleased GOD wonderfully to deliver me from the dropsy, I am yet very weak, and have not passed the door since the 13th of December. I hope for some help from warm weather, which will surely come in time.

I could not have the consent of the physicians to go to church yesterday; I therefore received the holy Sacrament at home, in the room where I communicated with dear Mrs Williams, a little before her death. O! my friend, the approach of death is very dreadful. I am afraid to think on that which I know I cannot avoid. It is vain to look round and round for that help which cannot be had. Yet we hope and hope, and fancy that he who has lived to-day may live to-morrow. But let us learn to derive our hope only from GOD.

In the mean time, let us be kind to one another. I have no friend now living, but you and Mr Hector, that was the friend of my youth. Do not neglect, dear Sir, yours affectionately,

SAM. JOHNSON.

    London. Easter-Monday,
    April 12, 1784.

What follows is a beautiful specimen of his gentleness and complacency to a young lady his god-child, one of the daughters of his friend Mr Langton, then I think in her seventh year. He took the trouble to write it in a large round hand, nearly resembling printed characters, that she might have the satisfaction of reading it herself. The original lies before me, but shall be faithfully restored to her; and I dare say will be preserved by her as a jewel as long as she lives.

To Miss JANE LANGTON, in Rochester, Kent.

MY DEAREST MISS JENNY – I am sorry that your pretty letter has been so long without being answered; but, when I am not pretty well, I do not always write plain enough for young ladies. I am glad, my dear, to see that you write so well, and hope that you mind your pen, your book, and your needle, for they are all necessary. Your books will give you knowledge, and make you respected; and your needle will find you useful employment when you do not care to read. When you are a little older, I hope you will be very diligent in learning arithmetic; and, above all, that through your whole life you will carefully say your prayers, and read your bible. I am, my dear,

Your most humble servant,

SAM. JOHNSON.

May 10, 1784.

On Wednesday, May 5, I arrived in London, and next morning had the pleasure to find Dr Johnson greatly recovered. I but just saw him; for a coach was waiting to carry him to Islington, to the house of his friend the Reverend Mr Strahan, where he went sometimes for the benefit of good air, which, notwithstanding his having formerly laughed at the general opinion upon the subject, he now acknowledged was conducive to health.

One morning afterwards, when I found him alone, he communicated to me, with solemn earnestness, a very remarkable circumstance which had happened in the course of his illness, when he was much distressed by the dropsy. He had shut himself up, and employed a day in particular exercises of religion, - fasting, humiliation, and prayer. On a sudden he obtained extra-ordinary relief, for which he looked up to heaven with grateful devotion. He made no direct inference from this fact; but from his manner of telling it, I could perceive that it appeared to him as something more than an incident in the common course of events. For my own part, I have no difficulty to avow that cast of thinking, which by many modern pretenders to wisdom, is called *superstitious*. But here I think even men of pretty dry rationality may believe, that there was an intermediate interposition of divine Providence, and that 'the fervent prayer of this righteous man' availed.[1]

On Sunday, May 9, I found Colonel Vallancy, the celebrated antiquarian and engineer of Ireland, with him. On Monday the 10th I dined with him at

---

1 Upon this subject there is a very fair and judicious remark in the Life of Dr Abernethy, in the first edition of the *Biographia Britannica*, which I should have been glad to see in his Life which has been written for the second edition of that valuable work. 'To deny the exercise of a particular providence in the Deity's government of the world is certainly impious: yet nothing serves the cause of the scorner more than an incautious forward zeal in determining the particular instances of it.'

In confirmation of my sentiments, I am also happy to quote that sensible and elegant writer Mr *Melmoth*, in Letter VIII of his collection, published under the name of *Fitzosborne*. 'We may safely assert, that the belief of a particular Providence is founded upon such probable reasons as may well justify our assent. It would scarce, therefore, be wise to renounce an opinion which affords so firm a support to the soul, in those seasons wherein she stands in most need of assistance, merely because it is not possible, in questions of this kind, to solve every difficulty which attends them.'

Mr Paradise's, where was a large company; Mr Bryant, Mr Joddrel, Mr Hawkins Browne, &c. On Thursday the 13th I dined with him at Mr Joddrel's, with another large company; the Bishop of Exeter, Lord Monboddo,[1] Mr Murphy, &c.

On Saturday, May 15, I dined with him at Dr Brocklesby's, where were Colonel Vallancy, Mr Murphy, and that ever-cheerful companion Mr Devaynes, apothecary to his Majesty. Of these days, and others on which I saw him, I have no memorials, except the general recollection of his being able and animated in conversation, and appearing to relish society as much as the youngest man. I find only these three small particulars. One, when a person was mentioned who said, 'I have lived fifty-one years to this world without having had ten minutes of uneasiness'; he exclaimed, 'The man who says so lies. He attempts to impose on human credulity.' The Bishop of Exeter in vain observed, that men were very different. His Lordship's manner was not impressive, and I learnt afterwards that Johnson did not find out that the person who talked to him was a Prelate; if he had, I doubt not that he would have treated him with more respect; for once talking of George Psalmanazar, whom he reverenced for his piety, he said, 'I should as soon think of contradicting a bishop.' One of the company provoked him greatly by doing what he could least of all bear, which was quoting something of his own writing, against what he then maintained. 'What, Sir (cried the gentleman), do you say to

> The busy day, the peaceful night,
> Unfelt, uncounted, glided by?'

Johnson having thus had himself presented as giving an instance of a man who had lived without uneasiness was much offended, for he looked upon such quotation as unfair. His anger burst out in an unjustifiable retort, insinuating that the gentleman's remark was a sally of ebriety; 'Sir, there is one passion I would advise you to command. When you have drunk out that glass, don't drink another.' Here was exemplified what Goldsmith said of him, with the aid of a very witty image from one of Cibber's Comedies, 'There is no arguing with Johnson; for if his pistol misses fire, he knocks you down with the butt end of it.' – Another, when a gentleman of eminence in the literary world was violently censured for attacking people by anonymous paragraphs in newspapers; he, from the spirit of contradiction as I thought, took up his defence,

---

1 I was sorry to observe Lord Monboddo avoid any communication with Dr Johnson. I flattered myself that I had made them very good friends (see *Journal of a Tour to the Hebrides*, third edition, page 67), but unhappily his Lordship had resumed and cherished a violent prejudice against my illustrious friend, to whom I must do the justice to say, there was on his part not the least anger, but a good-humoured sportiveness. Nay, though he knew of his Lordship's disposition[a] towards him, he was even kindly; as appeared from his inquiring of me after him, by an abbreviation of his name, 'Well, how does *Monny*?'

a For 'disposition' read 'indisposition'.

and said, 'Come, come, this is not so terrible a crime; he means only to vex them a little. I do not say that I should do it; but there is a great difference between him and me; what is fit for Hephaestion is not fit for Alexander.' – Another, when I told him that a young and handsome Countess had said to me, 'I should think that to be praised by Dr Johnson would make one a fool all one's life'; and that I answered, 'Madam, I shall make him a fool to-day, by repeating this to him,' he said, 'I am too old to be made a fool; but if you say I am, I shall not deny it. I am much pleased with a compliment, especially from a pretty woman.'

On the evening of Saturday, May 15, he was in fine spirits, at our Essex-Head-Club. He told us, 'I dined yesterday at Mrs Garrick's, with Mrs Carter, Miss Hannah More, and Miss Fanny Burney. Three such women are not to be found. I know not where I could find a fourth, except Mrs Lennox, who is superior to them all.' BOSWELL. 'What! had you them all to yourself, Sir?' JOHNSON. 'I had them all as much as they were had; but it might have been better had there been more company there.' BOSWELL. 'Might not Mrs Montagu have been a fourth?' JOHNSON. 'Sir, Mrs Montagu does not make a trade of her wit. But Mrs Montagu is a very extraordinary woman; she has a constant stream of conversation, and it is always impregnated; it has always meaning.' BOSWELL. 'Mr Burke has a constant stream of conversation.' JOHNSON. 'Yes, Sir; if a man were to go by chance at the same time with Burke under a shed, to shun a shower, he would say this is an extraordinary man. If Burke should go into a stable to see his horse drest, the ostler would say we have had an extraordinary man here.' BOSWELL. 'Foote was a man who never failed in conversation. If he had gone into a stable – ' JOHNSON. 'Sir, if he had gone into a stable, the ostler would have said here has been a comical fellow; but he would not have respected him.' BOSWELL. 'And, Sir, the ostler would have answered him, would have given him as good as he brought, as the common saying is.' JOHNSON. 'Yes, Sir; and Foote would have answered the ostler. – When Burke does not descend to be merry, his conversation is very superior indeed. There is no proportion between the powers which he shows in serious talk and in jocularity. When he lets himself down to that, he is in the kennel.' I have in another place[1] opposed, and I hope with success, Dr Johnson's very singular and erroneous notion as to Mr Burke's pleasantry. Mr Windham now said low to me, that he differed from our great friend in this observation; for that Mr Burke was often very happy in his merriment. It would not have been right for either of us to have contradicted Johnson at this time, in a Society all of whom did not know and value Mr Burke as much as we did. It might have occasioned something more rough, and at any rate would probably have checked the flow of Johnson's good-humour. He called to us with a sudden air of exultation, as the thought started into his mind, 'O! Gentlemen, I must tell you a very great thing. The Empress of Russia has ordered the *Rambler* to be translated into the

---

1 *Journal of a Tour to the Hebrides*, edit. 3, p. 20.

Russian language.[1] So I shall be read on the banks of the Wolga. Horace boasts that his fame would extend as far as the banks of the Rhone; now the Wolga is farther from me than the Rhone was from Horace.' BOSWELL. 'You must certainly be pleased with this, Sir.' JOHNSON. 'I am pleased, Sir, to be sure. A man is pleased to find he has succeeded in that which he has endeavoured to do.'

One of the company mentioned his having seen a noble person driving in his carriage, and looking exceedingly well, notwithstanding his great age. JOHNSON. 'Ah, Sir, that is nothing. Bacon observes, that a stout healthy old man is like a tower undermined.'

On Sunday, May 16, I found him alone; he talked of Mrs Thrale with much concern, saying, 'Sir, she has done every thing wrong, since Thrale's bridle was off her neck'; and was proceeding to mention some circumstances which have since been the subject of public discussion, when he was interrupted by the arrival of Dr Douglas, now Bishop of Carlisle.

Dr Douglas, upon this occasion, refuted a mistaken notion which is very common in Scotland, that the ecclesiastical discipline of the Church of England, though duly enforced, is insufficient to preserve the morals of the clergy, inasmuch as all delinquents may be screened by appealing to the Convocation, which being never authorized by the King to sit for the dispatch of business, the appeal never can be heard. Dr Douglas observed, that this was founded upon ignorance; for that the Bishops have sufficient power to maintain discipline, and that the sitting of the Convocation was wholly immaterial in this respect, it being not a Court of judicature, but like a parliament, to make Canons and regulations as times may require.

Johnson, talking of the fear of death, said, 'Some people are not afraid, because they look upon salvation as the effect of an absolute decree, and think they feel in themselves the marks of sanctification. Others, and those the most rational in my opinion, look upon salvation as conditional; and as they never can be sure that they have complied with the conditions, they are afraid.'

In one of his little manuscript diaries, about this time, I find a short notice, which marks his amiable disposition more certainly than a thousand studied declarations. − 'Afternoon spent cheerfully and elegantly, I hope without offence to GOD or man; though in no holy duty, yet in the general exercise and cultivation of benevolence.'

On Monday, May 17, I dined with him at Mr Dilly's, where were Colonel Vallancy, Reverend Dr Gibbons, and Mr Capel Lofft, who, though a most zealous Whig, has a mind so full of learning and knowledge, and so much in exercise in various exertions,[a] and withal so much liberality, that the stupendous powers of the literary Goliath, though they did not frighten this little David of popular spirit, could not but excite his admiration. There was also

---

1 I have since heard that the report was not well-founded; but the elation discovered by Johnson in the belief that it was true, showed a noble ardour for literary fame.

a For 'exertions' read 'departments'.

Mr Braithwaite of the Post-office, that amiable and friendly man, who, with modest and unassuming manners, has associated with many of the wits of the age. Johnson was very quiescent today. Perhaps too I was indolent. I find nothing more of him in my notes, but that when I mentioned that I had seen in the King's library sixty-three editions of my favourite Thomas à Kempis, amongst which it was in eight languages, Latin, German, French, Italian, Spanish, English, Arabic, and Armenian, he said, he thought it unnecessary to collect many editions of a book, which were all the same, except as to the paper and print; he would have the original, and all the translations, and all the editions which had any variations in the text. He approved of the famous collection of editions of Horace by Douglas, mentioned by Pope, who is said to have had a closet filled with them; and he said, every man should try to collect one book in that manner, and present it to a public library.

On Tuesday, May 17, I saw him for a short time in the morning. I told him that the mob had called out, as the King passed, 'No Fox – No Fox,' which I did not like. He said, 'They were right, Sir.' I said, I thought not, for it seemed to be making Mr Fox the King's competitor. There being no audience, so that there could be no triumph in a victory, he fairly agreed with me. I said it might do very well, if explained thus: 'Let us have no Fox'; understanding it as a prayer to his Majesty not to appoint that gentleman minister.

On Wednesday, May 19, I sat a part of the evening with him, by ourselves. I observed, that the death of our friends might be a consolation against the fear of our own dissolution, because we might have more friends in the other world than in this. He perhaps felt this as a reflection upon his apprehension as to death; and said, with heat, 'How can a man know *where* his departed friends are, or whether they will be his friends in the other world? How many friendships have you known formed upon principles of virtue? Most friendships are formed by caprice or by chance, mere confederacies in vice or leagues in folly.'

We talked of our worthy friend Mr Langton. He said, 'I know not who will go to Heaven if Langton does not. Sir, I could almost say, *Sit anima mea cum Langtono.*' I mentioned a very eminent friend as a virtuous man. JOHNSON. 'Yes, Sir; but —— has not the evangelical virtue of Langton. ——, I am afraid, would not scruple to pick up a wench.'

He however charged Mr Langton with what he thought want of judgement upon an interesting occasion. 'When I was ill (said he) I desired he would tell me sincerely in what he thought my life was faulty. Sir, he brought me a sheet of paper, on which he had written down several texts of Scripture, recommending christian charity. And when I questioned him what occasion I had given for such an animadversion, all that he could say amounted to this – that I sometimes contradicted people in conversation. Now what harm does it do to any man to be contradicted?' BOSWELL. 'I suppose he meant the *manner* of doing it; roughly – and harshly.' JOHNSON. 'And who is the worse for that?' BOSWELL. 'It hurts people of weak nerves.' JOHNSON. 'I know no such weak-nerved people.' Mr Burke, to whom I related this conference, said, 'It is well, if when a man comes to die, he has nothing heavier upon his conscience than having been a little rough in conversation.'

Johnson, at the time when the paper was presented to him, though at first pleased with the attention of his friend, whom he thanked in an earnest manner, soon exclaimed, in a loud and angry tone, 'What is your drift, Sir?' Sir Joshua Reynolds pleasantly observed, that it was a scene for a comedy, to see a penitent get into a violent passion and belabour his confessor.[1]

I have preserved no more of his conversation at the times when I saw him during the rest of this month, till Sunday, the 30th of May, when I met him in the evening at Mr Hoole's, where there was a large company both of ladies and gentlemen; Sir James Johnston happened to say, that he paid no regard to the arguments of counsel at the bar of the House of Commons, because they were paid for speaking. JOHNSON. 'Nay, Sir, argument is argument. You cannot help paying regard to their arguments if they are good. If it were testimony you might disregard it, if you knew that it were purchased. There is a beautiful image in Bacon upon this subject; testimony is like an arrow shot from a long bow; the force of it depends on the strength of the hand that draws it. Argument is like an arrow from a cross-bow, which has equal force though shot by a child.'

He had dined that day at Mr Hoole's, and Miss Helen Maria Williams being expected in the evening, Mr Hoole put into his hands her beautiful 'Ode on the Peace';[2] Johnson read it over, and when this amiable, elegant, and accomplished young lady[a] was presented to him, he took her by the hand in the most courteous manner, and repeated the finest stanza of her poem; this was the most delicate and pleasing compliment he could pay. Her respectable

1 After all, I cannot but be of opinion, that as Mr Langton was seriously requested by Dr Johnson to mention what appeared to him erroneous in the character of his friend, he was bound, as an honest man, to intimate what he really thought, which he certainly did in the most delicate manner; so that Johnson himself, when in a quiet frame, was pleased with it. The texts suggested are now before me, and I shall quote a few of them. 'Blessed are the meek, for they shall inherit the earth.' Matt. v. 5. – 'I therefore, the prisoner of the LORD, beseech you, that ye walk worthy of the vocation wherewith ye are called. With all lowliness and meekness, with long-suffering, forbearing one another in love.' Ephes. v. 1, 2. – 'And above all these things put on charity, which is the bond of perfectness.' Col. iii. 14. – 'Charity suffereth long, and is kind; charity envieth not, charity vaunteth not itself, is not puffed up: doth not behave itself unseemly, is not easily provoked.' 1 Cor. xiii. 4.

2 The Peace made by that very able statesman, the Earl of Shelburne, now Marquis of Lansdowne, which may fairly be considered as the foundation of all the prosperity of Great Britain since that time.

a Delete 'amiable'. In the first edition of my Work, the epithet *amiable* was given. I was sorry to be obliged to strike it out; but I could not in justice suffer it to remain, after this young lady had not only written in favour of the savage Anarchy with which France has been visited, but had (as I have been informed by good authority) walked, without horror, over the ground at the Thuilleries when it was strewed with the naked bodies of the faithful Swiss Guards, who were barbarously massacred for having bravely defended, against a crew of ruffians, the Monarch whom they had taken an oath to defend. From Dr Johnson she could now expect not endearment but repulsion.

1784 THE LIFE OF SAMUEL JOHNSON 903

friend, Dr Kippis, from whom I had this anecdote, was standing by, and was not a little gratified.

Miss Williams told me, that the only other time she was fortunate enough to be in Dr Johnson's company, he asked her to sit down by him, which she did, and upon her enquiring how he was, he answered, 'I am very ill indeed, Madam. I am very ill even when you are near me; what should I be were you at a distance.'

He had now a great desire to go to Oxford, as his first jaunt after his illness; we talked of it for some days, and I had promised to accompany him. He was impatient and fretful to-night, because I did not at once agree to go with him on Thursday. When I considered how ill he had been, and what allowance should be made for the influence of sickness upon his temper, I resolved to indulge him, though with some inconvenience to myself, as I wished to attend the musical meeting in honour of Handel, in Westminster-Abbey, on the following Saturday.

In the midst of his own diseases and pains, he was ever compassionate to the distresses of others, and actively earnest in procuring them aid, as appears from a note to Sir Joshua Reynolds, of June 1, in these words: 'I am ashamed to ask for some relief for a poor man, to whom, I hope, I have given what I can be expected to spare. The man importunes me, and the blow goes round. I am going to try another air on Thursday.'

On Thursday, June 3, the Oxford post-coach took us up in the morning at Bolt-court. The other two passengers were Mrs Beresford and her daughter, two very agreeable ladies from America; they were going to Worcestershire, where they then resided. Frank had been sent by his master the day before to take places for us; and I found from the way-bill, that Dr Johnson had made our names be put down. Mrs Beresford, who had read it, whispered me, 'Is this the great Dr Johnson?' I told her it was; so she was then prepared to listen. As she soon happened to mention in a voice so low that Johnson did not hear it, that her husband had been a member of the American Congress, I cautioned her to beware of introducing that subject, as she must know how very violent Johnson was against the people of that country. He talked a great deal, but I am sorry I have preserved little of the conversation. Miss Beresford was so much charmed, that she said to me aside, 'How he does talk! Every sentence is an essay.' She amused herself in the coach with knotting; he would scarcely allow this species of employment any merit. 'Next to mere idleness (said he) I think knotting is to be reckoned in the scale of insignificance; though I once attempted to learn knotting. Dempster's sister (looking to me) endeavoured to teach me it; but I made no progress.'

I was surprised at his talking without reserve in the public post-coach of the state of his affairs; 'I have (said he) about the world I think above a thousand pounds, which I intend shall afford Frank an annuity of seventy pounds a year.'[a]

---

[a] After 'year', read: He said once to Mr Langton, 'I think I am like Squire Richard in 'The Journey to London', *I'm never strange in a strange place.*' He was truly *social*. He strongly censured what is much too common in England among persons of condition – maintaining an absolute silence, when unknown to each other; as for instance, when

At the inn where we stopped he was exceedingly dissatisfied with some roast mutton which we had for dinner. The ladies I saw wondered to see the great philosopher, whose wisdom and wit they had been admiring all the way, get into ill-humour from such a cause. He scolded the waiter, saying, 'It is as bad as bad can be. It is ill-fed, ill-killed, ill-kept, and ill-drest.'

He bore the journey very well, and seemed to feel himself elevated as he approached Oxford, that magnificent and venerable seat of Learning, Orthodoxy, and Toryism. Frank came in the heavy coach, in readiness to attend him; and we were received with the most polite hospitality at the house of his old friend Dr Adams, Master of Pembroke College, who had given us a kind invitation. Before we were set down, I communicated to Johnson my having engaged to return to London directly, for the reason I have mentioned, but that I would hasten down to him again. He was pleased that I had made this journey merely to keep him company. He was easy and placid, with Dr Adams, Mrs and Miss Adams, and Mrs Kennicot, widow of the learned Hebraean, who was here on a visit. He soon dispatched the inquiries which were made about his illness and recovery, by a short and distinct narrative; and then assuming a gay air, repeated from Swift,

> 'Nor think on our approaching ills,
> And talk of spectacles and pills.'

Dr Newton, the Bishop of Bristol, having been mentioned, Johnson, recollecting the manner in which he had been mentioned by that Prelate,[1]

---

occasionally brought together in a room before the master or mistress of the house has appeared. 'Sir, that is being so uncivilized as not to understand the common rights of humanity.'

1 Dr Newton in his Account of his own Life, after animadverting upon Mr Gibbon's History, says, 'Dr Johnson's *Lives of the Poets* afforded more amusement; but candour was much hurt and offended at the malevolence that predominates in every part. Some passages, it must be allowed, are judicious and well written, but make not sufficient compensation for so much spleen and ill humour. Never was any biographer more sparing of his praise, or more abundant in his censures. He seemingly delights more in exposing blemishes, than in recommending beauties; slightly passes over excellencies, enlarges upon imperfections, and not content with his own severe reflections, revives old scandal, and produces large quotations from the forgotten works of former critics. His reputation was so high in the republic of letters, that it wanted not to be raised upon the ruins of others. But these Essays, instead of raising a higher idea than was before entertained of his understanding, have certainly given the world a worse opinion of his temper.' The Bishop was therefore the more surprised and concerned for his townsman, for he '*respected him not only for his genius and learning, but valued him much more for the more amiable part of his character, his humanity and charity, his morality and religion.*' The last sentence we may consider as the general and permanent opinion of Bishop Newton; the remains which precede it must, by all who have read Johnson's admirable work, be imputed to the disgust and peevishness of old age. I wish it had not appeared, and that Dr Johnson had not been provoked by it to express himself, not in respectful terms, of a Prelate, whose labours were certainly of considerable advantage both to literature and religion.

thus retaliated: 'Tom knew he should be dead before what he has said of me would appear. He durst not have printed it while he was alive.' DR ADAMS. 'I believe his *Dissertations on the Prophecies* is his great work.' JOHNSON. 'Why, Sir, it is Tom's great work; but how far it is great, or how much of it is Tom's, are other questions. I fancy a considerable part of it was borrowed.' DR ADAMS. 'He was a very successful man.' JOHNSON. 'I don't think so, Sir. – He did not get very high. He was late in getting what he did get; and he did not get it by the best means. I believe he was a gross flatterer.'

I fulfilled my intention by going to London, and returned to Oxford on Wednesday the 9th of June, when I was happy to find myself again in the same agreeable circle at Pembroke College, with the comfortable prospect of making some stay. Johnson welcomed my return with more than ordinary glee.

He talked with great regard of the Honourable Archibald Campbell, whose character he had given at the Duke of Argyll's table, when we were at Inveraray;[1] and at this time wrote out for me, in his own hand, a fuller account of that learned and venerable writer, which I have published in its proper place. Johnson made a remark this evening which struck me a good deal. 'I never (said he) knew a nonjuror who could reason.'[a] Surely he did not mean to deny that faculty to many of their writers; to Hickes, Brett, and other eminent divines of that persuasion; and did not recollect that the seven Bishops, so justly celebrated for their magnanimous resistance of arbitrary power, were yet Nonjurors to the new Government. The nonjuring clergy of Scotland, indeed, who, excepting a few, have lately, by a sudden stroke, cut off all ties of allegiance to the house of Stuart, and resolved to pray for our present lawful Sovereign by name, may be thought to have confirmed this remark; as it may be said, that the divine indefeasible hereditary right which they professed to believe, if ever true, must be equally true still. Many of my readers will be surprised when I mention, that Johnson assured me he had never in his life been in a nonjuring meeting-house.

Next morning at breakfast, he pointed out a passage in Savage's 'Wanderer', saying, 'These are fine verses.' – 'If (said he) I had written with hostility of Warburton in my Shakspeare, I should have quoted this couplet:

> Here Learning, blinded first, and then beguil'd,
> Looks dark as Ignorance, as Fancy wild.

---

1 *Journal of a Tour to the Hebrides*, 3d edit. p. 371.

a Add the following note: The Rev. Mr Agutter has favoured me with a note of a dialogue between Mr John Henderson and Dr Johnson on this topic, as related by Mr Henderson, and it is evidently so authentic that I shall here insert it – HENDERSON. 'What do you think, Sir, of William Law?' JOHNSON. 'William Law, Sir, wrote the best piece of Parenetic Divinity; but William Law was no reasoner.' HENDERSON. 'Jeremy Collier, Sir?' JOHNSON. 'Jeremy Collier fought without a rival, and therefore could not claim the victory.' Mr Henderson mentioned Kenn and Kettlewell; but some objections were made; at last he said, 'But, Sir, what do you think of Lesley?' JOHNSON. 'Charles Lesley I had forgotten. Lesley *was* a reasoner, and *a reasoner who was not to be reasoned against.*'

You see they'd have fitted him to a *T*' (smiling). Dr Adams. But you did not write against Warburton.' Johnson. 'No, Sir, I treated him with great respect both in my Preface and in my Notes.'

Mrs Kennicot spoke of her brother, the Reverend Mr Chamberlayne, who had given up good preferments[a] in the Church of England on his conversion to the Roman Catholic faith. Johnson, who warmly admired every man who acted from a conscientious regard to principle, erroneous or not, exclaimed fervently, 'GOD bless him.'

Mrs Kennicot, in confirmation of Dr Johnson's opinion, that the present was not worse than former ages, mentioned that her brother assured her, there was now less infidelity on the Continent than there had been; Voltaire and Rousseau were less read. I asserted, from good authority, that Hume's infidelity was certainly less read. Johnson. 'All infidel writers drop into oblivion, when personal connections and the floridness of novelty are gone; though now and then a foolish fellow, who thinks he can be witty upon them, may bring them again into notice. There will sometimes start up a College joker, who does not consider that what is a joke in a College will not do in the world. To such defenders of Religion I would apply a stanza of a poem which I remember to have seen in some old collection:

> Henceforth be quiet and agree,
>   Each kiss his empty brother;
> Religion scorns a foe like thee,
>   But dreads a friend like t'other.

The point is well, though the expression is not correct; *one*, and not *thee*, should be opposed to *t'other*.'[1]

On the Roman Catholic religion he said, 'If you join the Papists externally, they will not interrogate you strictly as to your belief in their tenets. No reasoning Papist believes every article of their faith. There is one side on which a good man might be persuaded to embrace it. A good man, of a timorous disposition, in great doubt of his acceptance with GOD, and pretty

---

[a] For 'good preferments' read 'great prospects'.

[1] I have inserted the stanza as Johnson repeated it from memory; but I have since found the poem itself, in *The Foundling Hospital for Wit*, printed at London, 1749. It is as follows:

> Epigram, *occasioned by a religious Dispute at Bath.*
>
> On Reason, Faith, and Mystery high,
>   Two wits harangue the table;
> B——y believes he knows not why,
>   N—— swears 'tis all a fable.
>
> Peace, coxcombs, peace, and both agree,
>   N——, kiss thy empty brother;
> Religion laughs at foes like thee,
>   And dreads a friend like t'other.

credulous, might be glad to be of a church where there are so many helps to get to Heaven. I would be a Papist if I could. I have fear enough; but an obstinate rationality prevents me. I shall never be a Papist, unless on the near approach of death, of which I have a very great terror. I wonder that women are not all Papists.' BOSWELL. 'They are not more afraid of death than men are.' JOHNSON. 'Because they are less wicked.' DR ADAMS. 'They are more pious.' JOHNSON. 'No, hang 'em, they are not more pious. A wicked fellow is the most pious when he takes to it. He'll beat you all at piety.'

He argued in defence of some of the peculiar tenets of the Church of Rome. As to the giving the bread only to the laity, he said, 'They may think, that in what is merely ritual, deviations from the primitive mode may be admitted on the ground of convenience, and I think they are as well warranted to make this alteration, as we are to substitute sprinkling in the room of the ancient baptism.' As to the invocation of saints, he said, 'Though I do not think it authorised, it appears to me, that "the communion of saints" in the Creed means the communion with the saints in Heaven, as connected with "the holy catholic church".'[1] He admitted the influence of evil spirits upon our minds, and said, 'Nobody who believes the New Testament can deny it.'

I brought a volume of Dr Hurd, the Bishop of Worcester's Sermons, and read to the company some passages from one of them, upon this text, '*Resist the Devil and he will fly from you.*' James iv. 7. I was happy to produce so judicious and elegant a supporter[2] of a doctrine, which, I know not why, should in this world of imperfect knowledge, and therefore of wonder and mystery in a thousand instances, be contested by some with an unthinking assurance and flippancy.

---

1 Waller, in his *Divine Poesie*, Canto first, has the same thought finely expressed:

> The Church triumphant, and the Church below,
> In songs of praise their present union show:
> Their joys are full; our expectation long,
> In life we differ, but we join in song;
> Angels and we assisted by this art,
> May sing together, though we dwell apart.

2 The Sermon thus opens: 'That there are angels and spirits good and bad; that at the head of these last there is ONE more considerable and malignant than the rest, who in the form, or under the name of a *serpent*, was deeply concerned in the fall of man, and whose *head*, as the prophetic language is, the son of man was one day to *bruise*; that this evil spirit, though that prophecy be in part completed, has not yet received his death's wound, but is still permitted, for ends unsearchable to us, and in ways which we cannot particularly explain, to have a certain degree of power in this world hostile to its virtue and happiness, and sometimes exerted with too much success; all this is so clear from Scripture, that no believer, unless he be first of all *spoiled by philosophy and vain deceit*, can possibly entertain a doubt of it.'

Having treated of *possessions*, his Lordship says, 'As I have no authority to affirm that there *are* now any such, so neither may I presume to say with confidence, that there are *not* any.'

'But then with regard to the influence of evil spirits at this day upon the SOULS of

After dinner, when one of us talked of there being a great enmity between Whig and Tory; JOHNSON. 'Why, not so much, I think, unless when they come into competition with each other. There is none when they are only common acquaintance, none when they are of different sexes. A Tory will marry into a Whig family, and a Whig into a Tory family, without any reluctance. But indeed in a matter of much more concern than political tenets, and that is religion, men and women do not concern themselves much about difference of opinion. And ladies set no value on the moral character of men who pay their addresses to them; the greatest profligate will be as well received as the man of the greatest virtue, and this by a very good woman, by a woman who says her prayers three times a day.' Our ladies endeavoured to defend their sex from this charge; but he roared them down! 'No, no; a lady will take Jonathan Wild as readily as St Austin, if he has three-pence more; and, what is worse, her parents will give her to him. Women have a perpetual envy of our vices; they are less vicious than we, not from choice, but because we restrict them; they are the slaves of order and fashion; their virtue is of more consequence to us than our own, so far as concerns this world.'

Miss Adams mentioned a gentleman of licentious character, and said, 'Suppose I had a mind to marry that gentleman, would my parents consent?' JOHNSON. 'Yes, they'd consent, and you'd go. You'd go though they did not consent.' MISS ADAMS. 'Perhaps their opposing might make me go.' JOHNSON. 'O, very well; you'd take one whom you think a bad man, to have the pleasure of vexing your parents. You put me in mind of Dr Barrowby the physician, who was very fond of swine's flesh. One day when he was eating it, he said, "I wish I was a Jew." – "Why so? (said somebody); the Jews are not allowed to eat your favourite meat." – "Because (said he) I should then have the gust of eating it, with the pleasure of sinning." ' He then proceeded in his declamation.

Miss Adams soon afterwards made an observation that I do not recollect, which pleased him much; he said with a good-humoured smile, 'That there should be so much excellence united with so much depravity is strange.'

Indeed, this lady's good qualities, merit, and accomplishments, and her

---

men, I shall take leave to be a great deal more peremptory. – [Then, having stated the various proofs] All this I say is so manifest to every one who reads the Scriptures, that if we respect their authority, the question concerning the reality of the demonic influence upon the minds of men is clearly determined.'

Let it be remembered, that these are not the words of an antiquated or obscure enthusiast, but of a learned and polite Prelate now alive; and were spoken, not to a vulgar congregation, but to the Honourable Society of Lincoln-Inn. His Lordship in this Sermon explains the words, 'deliver us from evil', in the Lord's Prayer, as signifying a request to be protected from 'the evil one', that is, the Devil. This is well illustrated in a short but excellent Commentary by my late worthy friend, the Reverend Dr Lort, of whom it may truly be said, *Multis ille bonis flebilis occidit.* It is remarkable that Waller in his 'Reflections on the several Petitions', in that sacred form of devotion, has understood this in the same sense,

'Guard us from all temptations of the FOE.'

constant attention to Dr Johnson, were not lost upon him. She happened to tell him that a little coffee-pot, in which she had made his coffee, was the only thing she could call her own. He turned to her with a complacent gallantry, 'Don't say so, my dear; I hope you don't reckon my heart as nothing.'

I asked him if it was true as reported, that he had said lately, 'I am for the King against Fox; but I am for Fox against Pitt.' JOHNSON. 'Yes, Sir; the King is my master; but I do not know Pitt; and Fox is my friend.'

'Fox (added he) is a most extraordinary man; here is a man (describing him in strong terms of objection in some respects according as he apprehended, but which exalted his abilities the more) who has divided the kingdom with Caesar; so that it was a doubt whether the nation should be ruled by the sceptre of George the Third, or the tongue of Fox.'

Dr Wall, physician at Oxford, drank tea with us. Johnson had in general a peculiar pleasure in the company of physicians, which was certainly not abated by the conversation of this learned, ingenious, and pleasing gentleman. Johnson said, 'It is wonderful how little good Radcliffe's travelling fellowships have done. I know nothing that has been imported by them; yet many additions to our medical knowledge might be got in foreign countries. Inoculation, for instance, has saved more lives than war destroys. And the cures performed by the Peruvian-bark are innumerable. But it is in vain to send our travelling physicians to France, and Italy, and Germany, for all that is known there is known here; I'd send them out of Christendom; I'd send them among barbarous nations.'

On Friday, June 11, we talked at breakfast, of forms of prayer. JOHNSON. 'I know of no good prayers but those in the Book of Common Prayer.' DR ADAMS. (in a very earnest manner) 'I wish, Sir, you would compose some family prayers.' JOHNSON. 'I will not compose prayers for you, Sir, because you can do it for yourself. But I have thought of getting together all the books of prayers which I could, selecting those which should appear to me the best, putting out some, inserting others, adding some prayers of my own, and prefixing a discourse on prayer.' We all now gathered about him, and two or three of us at a time joined in pressing him to execute this plan. He seemed to be a little displeased at the manner of our importunity, and in great agitation called out, 'Do not talk thus of what is so awful. I know not what time GOD will allow me in this world. There are many things which I wish to do.' Some of us persisted, and Dr Adams said, 'I never was more serious about any thing in my life.' JOHNSON. 'Let me alone, let me alone; I am overpowered.' And then he put his hands before his face, and reclined for some time upon the table.

I mentioned Jeremy Taylor's using, in his forms of prayer, 'I am the chief of sinners', and other such self-condemning expressions. 'Now (said I) this cannot be said with truth by every man, and therefore is improper for a general printed form. I myself cannot say that I am the worst of men. I *will* not say so.' JOHNSON. 'A man may know, that physically, that is, in the real state of things, he is not the worst man; but that morally he may be so. Law observes, that "Every man knows something worse of himself, than he is sure of in others." You may not have committed such crimes as some men have done; but you do not know against what degree of light they have sinned. Besides, Sir, the "chief of sinners" is a mode of expression for "I am a great sinner." So St Paul, speaking of our SAVIOUR'S having died to save sinners, says, "of whom I am the chief": yet he certainly did not think himself so bad as Judas Iscariot.' BOSWELL. 'But, Sir, Taylor means it literally, for he founds a conceit upon it. When praying for the conversion of sinners, and of himself in particular, he says, "Lord, thou wilt not leave thy *chief* work undone." ' JOHNSON. 'I do not approve of figurative expressions in addressing the Supreme Being; and I never use them. Taylor gives a very good advice: "Never lie in your prayers; never confess more than you really believe; never promise more than you mean to perform." I recollected this precept in his *Golden Grove*. But his *example* for prayer contradicts his *precept*.'

Dr Johnson and I went in Dr Adams' coach to dine with Dr Nowell, Principal of St Mary Hall, at his beautiful villa at Iffley, on the banks of the Isis, about two miles from Oxford. While we were upon the road, I had the resolution to ask Johnson whether he thought that the roughness of his manner had been an advantage or not, and if he would not have done more good if he had been more gentle? I proceeded to answer myself thus: 'Perhaps it has been of advantage, as it has given weight to what you said. You could not, perhaps, have talked with such authority without it.' JOHNSON. 'No, Sir; I have done more good as I am. Obscenity and Impiety have always been repressed in my company.' BOSWELL. 'True, Sir; and that is more than can be said of every Bishop. Greater liberties have been taken in the presence of a Bishop, though a very good man, from his being milder, and therefore not commanding such awe. Yet, Sir, many people who might have been benefited by your conversation, have been frightened away. A worthy friend of ours has told me, that he has often been afraid to talk to you.' JOHNSON. 'Sir, he need not have been afraid, if he had any thing rational to say. If he had not, it was better he did not talk.'

Dr Nowell is celebrated for having preached a sermon before the House of Commons, on the 30th of January, 1772, full of high Tory sentiments, for which he was thanked as usual, and printed it at their request; but, in the midst of that turbulence and faction which disgraced a part of the present reign, the thanks were afterwards ordered to be expunged. This strange conduct sufficiently exposes itself; and Dr Nowell will ever have the honour which is due to a lofty friend of our monarchical constitution. Dr Johnson said to me, 'Sir, the Court will be very much to blame if he is not promoted.' I told this to Dr Nowell, and asserting my humbler, though not less zealous exertions in the same cause, I suggested that whatever return we might receive, we should still have the consolation of being like Butler's steady and generous Royalist,

> True as the dial to the sun,
> Although it be not shone upon.

We were well entertained and very happy at Dr Nowell's, where was a very agreeable company, and we drank 'Church and King' after dinner, with true Tory cordiality.

We talked of a certain clergyman of extraordinary character, who by exerting his talents in writing on temporary topics, and displaying uncommon intrepidity, had raised himself to affluence. I maintained that we ought not to be indignant at his success; for merit of every sort was entitled to reward. JOHNSON. 'Sir, I will not allow this man to have merit. No, Sir; what he has is rather the contrary; I will, indeed, allow him courage, and on this account we so far give him credit. We have more respect for a man who robs boldly on the highway, than for a fellow who jumps out of a ditch, and knocks you down behind your back. Courage is a quality so necessary for maintaining virtue, that it is always respected, even when it is associated with vice.'

I censured the coarse invective which was become fashionable in the House of Commons, and said that if members of parliament must attack each other personally in the heat of debate, it should be done more genteelly. JOHNSON. 'No, Sir; that would be much worse. Abuse is not so dangerous when there is no vehicle of wit or delicacy, no subtle conveyance. The difference between coarse and refined abuse is as the difference between being bruised by a club, and wounded by a poisoned arrow.' I have since observed his position elegantly expressed by Dr Young:

> As the soft plume gives swiftness to the dart,
> Good breeding sends the satire to the heart.

On Saturday, June 12, there drank tea with us at Dr Adams's, Mr John Henderson, student of Pembroke-College, celebrated for his wonderful acquirements in Alchemy, Judicial Astrology, and other abstruse and curious learning;[a] and the Reverend Herbert Croft, who I am afraid was somewhat mortified by Dr Johnson's not being highly pleased with some *Family Discourses*, which he had printed; they were in too familiar a style to be approved of by so manly a mind. I have no note of this evening's conversation, except a single fragment. When I mentioned Thomas Lord Lyttelton's vision, the prediction of the time of his death, and its exact fulfilment; JOHNSON. 'It is the most extraordinary thing that has happened in my day. I heard it with my own ears, from his uncle, Lord Westcote. I am so glad to have every evidence of the spiritual world, that I am willing to believe it.' DR ADAMS. 'You have evidence enough; good evidence, which needs not such support.' JOHNSON. 'I like to have more.'

Mr Henderson, with whom I had sauntered in the venerable walks of Merton-College, and found him a very learned and pious man, supt with us. Dr Johnson surprised him not a little, by acknowledging with a look of horror, that he was much oppressed by the fear of death. The amiable Dr Adams suggested that GOD was infinitely good. JOHNSON. 'That he is infinitely good, as far as the perfection of his nature will allow, I certainly believe; but it is necessary for good upon the whole, that individuals should be punished. As to an *individual* therefore, he is not infinitely good; and as I cannot be *sure* that I

---

[a] Add this note: See an account of him in a sermon by the Reverend Mr Agutter.

have fulfilled the conditions on which salvation is granted, I am afraid I may be one of those who shall be damned.' (looking dismally). DR ADAMS. 'What do you mean by damned?' JOHNSON. (passionately and loudly) 'Sent to Hell, Sir, and punished everlastingly.' DR ADAMS. 'I don't believe that doctrine.' JOHNSON. 'Hold, Sir; do you believe that some will be punished at all?' DR ADAMS. 'Being excluded from Heaven will be a punishment; yet there may be no great positive suffering.' JOHNSON. 'Well, Sir; but, if you admit any degree of punishment, there is an end of your argument for infinite goodness simply considered; for, infinite goodness would inflict no punishment whatever. There is not infinite goodness physically considered; morally there is.' BOSWELL. 'But may not a man attain to such a degree of hope as not to be uneasy from the fear of death?' JOHNSON. 'A man may have such a degree of hope as to keep him quiet. You see I am not quiet, from the vehemence with which I talk; but I do not despair.' MRS ADAMS. 'You seem, Sir, to forget the merits of our Redeemer.' JOHNSON. 'Madam, I do not forget the merits of my Redeemer; but my Redeemer has said that he will set some on his right-hand, and some on his left.' – He was in gloomy agitation, and said, 'I'll have no more on't.' If what has now been stated should be urged by the enemies of Christianity, as if its influence on the mind were not benignant, let it be remembered, that Johnson's temperament was melancholy, of which such direful apprehensions of futurity are often a common effect. We shall presently see that when he approached nearer to his awful change, his mind became tranquil, and he exhibited as much fortitude as becomes a thinking man in that situation.

From the subject of death we passed to discourse of life, whether it was upon the whole more happy or miserable. Johnson was decidedly for the balance of misery:[a] in confirmation of which I maintained, that no man would choose to

---

[a] Add this note: The Reverend Mr Ralph Churton, Fellow of Brazen-Nose College, Oxford, has favoured me with the following remarks on my Work, which he is pleased to say, 'I have hitherto extolled, and cordially approve.'

'The chief part of what I have to observe is contained in the following transcript from a letter to a friend, which, with his concurrence, I copied for this purpose; and, whatever may be the merit or justness of the remarks, you may be sure that being written to a most intimate friend, without any intention that they ever should go further, they are the genuine and undisguised sentiments of the writer.'

Jan. 6, 1792.

Last week, I was reading the second volume of Boswell's Johnson, with increasing esteem for the worthy author, and increasing veneration of the wonderful and excellent man who is the subject of it. The writer throws in, now and then very properly, some serious religious reflections; but there is one remark, in my mind an obvious and just one, which I think he has not made, that Johnson's 'morbid melancholy', and constitutional infirmities, were intended by Providence, like St Paul's thorn in the flesh, to check intellectual conceit and arrogance; which the consciousness of his extraordinary talents, awake as he was to the voice of praise, might otherwise have generated in a very culpable degree. Another observation strikes me, that in consequence of the same natural indisposition, and habitual

lead over again the life which he had experienced. Johnson acceded to that opinion in the strongest terms. This is an inquiry often made; and its being a subject of disquisition is a proof that much misery presses upon human

---

sickliness (for he says he scarcely passed one day without pain after his twentieth year), he considered and represented human life, as a scene of much greater misery than is generally experienced. There may be persons bowed down with affliction all their days; and there are those, no doubt, whose iniquities rob them of rest; but neither calamities nor crimes, I hope and believe, do so much and so generally abound, as to justify the dark picture of life which Johnson's imagination designed, and his strong pencil delineated. This I am sure, the colouring is far too gloomy for what I have experienced, though as far as I can remember, I have had more sickness (I do not say more severe, but only more in quantity), than falls to the lot of most people. But then daily debility and occasional sickness were far overbalanced by intervenient days, and, perhaps, weeks void of pain, and overflowing with comfort. So that in short, to return to the subject, human life, as far as I can perceive from experience or observation, is not that state of constant wretchedness which Johnson always insisted it was: which misrepresentation (for such it surely is), his Biographer has not corrected, I suppose, because, unhappily, he has himself a large portion of melancholy in his constitution, and fancied the portrait a faithful copy of life.

The learned writer then proceeds thus in his letter to me:

I have conversed with some sensible men on this subject, who all seem to entertain the same sentiments respecting life with those which are expressed or implied in the foregoing paragraph. It might be added, that as the representation here spoken of, appears not consistent with fact and experience, so neither does it seem to be countenanced by Scripture. There is, perhaps, no part of the sacred volume which at first sight promises so much to lend its sanction to these dark and desponding notions as the book of Ecclesiastes, which so often, and so emphatically, proclaims the vanity of things sublunary. But the design of this whole book (as it has been justly observed), is not to put us out of conceit with life, but to cure our vain expectation of a complete and perfect happiness in this world; to convince us, that there is no such thing to be found in mere external enjoyments; – and to teach us – to seek for happiness in the practice of virtue, in the knowledge and love of God, and in the hopes of a better life. For this is the application of all: *Let us hear*, &c. xii. 13. Not only his duty, but his happiness too: *For* GOD, &c. ver. 14. – See Sherlock on *Providence*, p. 299.

The New Testament tells us, indeed, and most truly, that 'sufficient unto the day is the evil thereof'; and, therefore, wisely forbids us to increase our burden by forebodings of sorrows; but I think it nowhere says that even our ordinary afflictions are not consistent with a very considerable degree of positive comfort and satisfaction. And, accordingly, one whose sufferings as well as merits were conspicuous, assures us, that in proportion 'as the sufferings of Christ abounded in them, so their consolation also abounded by Christ.' 2 Cor. i. 5. It is needless to cite, as indeed it would be endless even to refer to, the multitude of passages in both Testaments holding out, in the strongest language, promises of blessings, even in this world, to the faithful servants of GOD. I will only refer to St Luke xviii. 29, 30, and 1 Tim. iv. 8.

Upon the whole, setting aside instances of great and lasting bodily pain, of

feelings; for those who are conscious of a felicity of existence, would never hesitate to accept of a repetition of it. I have met with very few who would. I have heard Mr Burke make use of a very ingenious and plausible argument on this subject; 'Every man (said he) would lead his life over again; for, every man is willing to go on and take an addition to his life, which as he grows older, he has no reason to think will be better, or even so good as what has preceded.' I imagine, however, the truth is, that there is a deceitful hope that the next part

---

minds peculiarly oppressed by melancholy, and of severe temporal calamities, from which extraordinary cases we surely should not form our estimate of the general tenor and complexion of life; excluding these from the account, I am convinced that as well the gracious constitution of things which Providence has ordained, as the declarations of Scripture and the actual experience of individuals, authorize the sincere Christian to hope that his humble and constant endeavours to perform his duty, chequered as the best life is with many failings, will be crowned with a greater degree of present peace, serenity, and comfort, than he could reasonably permit himself to expect if he measured his views and judged of life from the opinion of Dr Johnson, often and energetically expressed in the Memoirs of him, without any animadversion or censure by his ingenious Biographer. If He himself, upon reviewing the subject, shall see the matter in this light, he will, in an octavo edition, which is eagerly expected, make such additional remarks or corrections as he shall judge fit; less the impressions which these discouraging passages may leave on the reader's mind, should in any degree hinder what otherwise the whole spirit and energy of the work tends, and, I hope, successfully, to promote – pure morality and true religion.

Though I have, in some degree, obviated any reflections against my illustrious friend's dark views of life when considering, in the course of this Work, his *Rambler* and his *Rasselas*, I am obliged to Mr Churton for complying with my request of his permission to insert his remarks, being conscious of the weight of what he judiciously suggests as to the melancholy in my own constitution. His more pleasing views of life, I hope, are just. *Valeant, quantum valere possunt.*

Mr Churton concludes his letter to me in these words: 'Once, and only once, I had the satisfaction of seeing your illustrious friend; and as I feel a particular regard for all whom he distinguished with his esteem and friendship, so I derive much pleasure from reflecting that I once beheld, though but transiently near our College-gate, one whose works will for ever delight and improve the world, who was a sincere and zealous son of the Church of England, an honour to his country, and an ornament to human nature.'

His letter was accompanied with a present from himself of his *Sermons at the Bampton Lecture*, and from his friend, Dr Townson, the venerable Rector of Malpas in Cheshire, of his *Discourses on the Gospels*, together with the following extract of a letter from that excellent person, who is now gone to receive the reward of his labours: 'Mr Boswell is not only very entertaining in his works, but they are so replete with moral and religious sentiments, without an instance, as far as I know, of contrary tendency, that I cannot help having a great esteem for him; and if you think such a trifle as a copy of the Discourses, *ex dono authoris*, would be acceptable to him, I should be happy to give him this small testimony of my regard.'

Such spontaneous testimonies of approbation from such men, without any personal acquaintance with me, are truly valuable and encouraging.

of life will be free from the pains, and anxieties, and sorrows which we have already felt. We are for wise purposes 'Condemn'd to Hope's delusive mine'; as Johnson finely says; and I may also quote the celebrated lines of Dryden, equally philosophical and poetical:

> When I consider life, 'tis all a cheat,
> Yet fool'd with hope, men favour the deceit;
> Trust on and think to-morrow will repay;
> To-morrow's falser than the former day;
> Lies worse; and while it says we shall be blest
> With some new joys, cuts off what we possest.
> Strange cozenage! none would live past years again;
> Yet all hope pleasure in what yet remain;
> And from the dregs of life think to receive,
> What the first sprightly running could not give.[1]

It was observed to Dr Johnson, that it seemed strange that he, who has so often delighted his company by his lively and brilliant conversation, should say he was miserable. JOHNSON. 'Alas! it is all outside; I may be cracking my joke and cursing the sun. *Sun, how I hate thy beams!*' I knew not well what to think of this declaration; whether to hold it as a genuine picture of his mind,[2] or as the effect of his persuading himself contrary to fact, that the position which he had assumed as to human unhappiness, was true. We may apply to him a sentence in Mr Greville's *Maxims, Characters, and Reflections*;[3] a book which is entitled to much more praise than it has received: 'ARISTARCHUS is charming: how full of knowledge, of sense, of sentiment. You get him with difficulty to your supper; and after having delighted every body and himself for a few hours, he is obliged to return home; – he is finishing his treatise, to prove that unhappiness is the portion of man.'

On Sunday, June 13, our philosopher was calm at breakfast. There was something exceedingly pleasing in our leading a College life, without restraint, and with superior elegance, in consequence of our living in the Master's house, and having the company of ladies. Mrs Kennicot related, in his presence, a lively saying of Dr Johnson to Miss Hannah More, who had expressed a wonder that the poet who had written *Paradise Lost*, should write such poor Sonnets: 'Milton, Madam, was a genius that could cut a Colossus from a rock; but could not carve heads upon cherry-stones.'

We talked of the casuistical question, Whether it was allowable at any time to depart from *Truth*? JOHNSON. 'The general rule is, that Truth should never be violated, because it is of the utmost importance to the comfort of life, that we should have a full security by mutual faith; and occasional inconveniencies

1 *Aurungzebe.*
2 Yet there is no doubt that a man may appear very gay in company who is sad at heart. His merriment is like the sound of drums aud trumpets in a battle, to drown the groans of the wounded and dying.
3 Page 139.

should be willingly suffered that we may preserve it. There must, however, be some exceptions. If, for instance, a murderer should ask you which way a man is gone, you may tell him what is not true, because you are under a previous obligation not to betray a man to a murderer.' BOSWELL. 'Supposing the person who wrote *Junius* were asked whether he was the author, might he deny it?' JOHNSON. 'I don't know what to say to this. If you were *sure* that he wrote Junius, would you, if he denied it, think as well of him afterwards? Yet it may be urged, that what a man has no right to ask, you may refuse to communicate; and there is no other effectual mode of preserving a secret, and an important secret, the discovery of which may be very hurtful to you, but a flat denial; for if you are silent, or hesitate, or evade, it will be held equivalent to a confession. But stay, Sir; here is another case. Supposing the author had told me confidentially that he had written *Junius*, and I were asked if he had, I should hold myself at liberty to deny it, as being under a previous promise, express or implied, to conceal it. Now what I ought to do for the author, may I not do for myself? But I deny the lawfulness of telling a lie to a sick man for fear of alarming him. You have no business with consequences: you are to tell the truth. Besides, you are not sure what effect your telling him that he is in danger may have. It may bring his distemper to a crisis, and that may cure him. Of all lying I have the greatest abhorrence at[a] this, because I believe it has been frequently practised on myself.'

I cannot help thinking, that there is much weight in the opinion of those who have held, that Truth, as an eternal and immutable principle, ought, upon no account whatever, to be violated, from supposed previous or superior obligations, of which every man being the judge for himself, there is great danger that we may too often, from partial motives, persuade ourselves that they exist; and probably whatever extraordinary instances may sometimes occur, where some evil may be prevented by violating this noble principle, it would be found that human happiness would, upon the whole, be more perfect were Truth universally preserved.

In the Notes to the *Dunciad* we find the following elegant and pathetic verses, addressed to Pope:[1]

> While malice, Pope, denies thy page
>   Its own celestial fire;
> While critics, and while bards in rage
>   Admiring, won't admire:
>
> While wayward pens thy worth assail,
>   And envious tongues decry;
> These times, though many a friend bewail,
>   These times bewail not I.

---

[a] For 'at' read 'of'.

[1] The annotator calls them 'amiable verses'.

> But when the world's loud praise is thine,
>   And spleen no more shall blame;
> When with thy Homer thou shalt shine
>   In one establish'd fame;
>
> When none shall rail, and every lay
>   Devote a wreath to thee:
> That day (for come it will) that day
>   Shall I lament to see.

It is surely not a little remarkable, that they should appear without a name. Miss Seward, knowing Dr Johnson's almost universal and minute literary information, signified a desire that I should ask him who was the author. He was prompt with his answer: 'Why, Sir, they were written by one Lewis, an under-master or usher of Westminster school, who published a miscellany, in which 'Grongar Hill' first came out.' Johnson praised them highly, and repeated them with a noble animation. In the twelfth line, instead of 'one established fame', he repeated 'one unclouded flame', which he thought was the reading in former editions; but I believe was a flash of his own genius. It is much more poetical than the other.

On Monday 14, and Tuesday, June 15, Dr Johnson and I dined on one of them, I forget which, with Mr Mickle, translator of the *Lusiad*, at Wheatley, a very pretty country place a few miles from Oxford; and on the other with Dr Wetherell, Master of University-College. From Dr Wetherell's he went to visit Mr Sackville Parker the bookseller; and when he returned to us, gave the following account of his visit, saying, 'I have been to see my old friend, Sack. Parker; I find he has married his maid; he has done right. She had lived with him many years in great confidence, and they had mingled minds; I do not think he could have found any wife that would have made him so happy. The woman was very attentive and civil to me; she pressed me to fix a day for dining with them, and to say what I liked, and she would be sure to get it for me. Poor Sack! He is very ill, indeed. We parted as never to meet again. It has quite broke me down.' This pathetic narrative was strangely diversified with the grave and earnest defence of a man's having married his maid. I could not but feel it as in some degree ludicrous.

In the morning of Tuesday, June 15, while we sat at Dr Adams's, we talked of a printed letter from the Reverend Herbert Croft, to a young gentleman who had been his pupil, in which he advised him to read to the end of whatever books he should begin to read. JOHNSON. 'This is surely a strange advice; you may as well resolve that whatever men you happen to get acquainted with, you are to keep to them for life. A book may be good for nothing; or there may be only one thing in it worth knowing; are we to read it all through? These Voyages (pointing to the three large volumes of *Voyages to the South Sea*, which were just come out), *who* will read them through? A man had better work his way before the mast, than read them through; they will be eaten by rats and mice, before they are read through. There can be little entertainment in such books; one set of Savages is like another.' BOSWELL. 'I do not think the people of Otaheite can be reckoned Savages.' JOHNSON. 'Don't cant in defence of Savages.' BOSWELL. 'They have the art of navigation.' JOHNSON. 'A dog or a cat can swim.' BOSWELL. 'They carve very ingeniously.' JOHNSON. 'A cat can scratch, and a child with a nail can scratch.' I perceived this was none of the *mollia tempora fandi*, so desisted.

Upon his mentioning that when he came to College he wrote his first exercise twice over, but never did so afterwards, MISS ADAMS. 'I suppose, Sir, you could not make them better.' JOHNSON. 'Yes, Madam, to be sure, I could make them better. Thought is better than no thought.' MISS ADAMS. 'Do you think, Sir, you could make your Ramblers better?' JOHNSON. 'Certainly I could.' BOSWELL. 'I'll lay a bet, Sir, you cannot.' JOHNSON. 'But I will, Sir, if I choose. I shall make the best of them you shall pick out, better.' BOSWELL. 'But you may add to them. I will not allow of that.' JOHNSON. 'Nay, Sir, there are three ways of making them better; – putting out – adding – or correcting.'

During our visit at Oxford, the following conversation passed between him and me on the subject of my trying my fortune at the English bar: Having asked whether a very extensive acquaintance in London, which was very valuable, and of great advantage to a man at large, might not be prejudicial to a lawyer, by preventing him from giving sufficient attention to business. JOHNSON. 'Sir, you will attend to business as business lays hold of you. When not actually employed, you may see your friends as much as you do now. You may dine at a Club every day, and sup with one of the members every night; and you may be as much at public places as one who has seen them all would wish to be. But you must take care to attend constantly in Westminster-Hall; both to mind your business, as it is almost all learnt there (for nobody reads now); and to show that you want to have business. And you must not be too often seen at public places, that competitors may not have it to say, "He is always at the Playhouse or at Ranelagh, and never to be found at his chambers." And, Sir, there must be a kind of solemnity in the manner of a professional man. I have nothing particular to say to you on the subject. All this I should say to any one; I should have said it to Lord Thurlow twenty years ago.'

THE PROFESSION may probably think this representation of what is required in a Barrister who would hope for success, to be by much too indulgent; but certain it is, that as

> The wits of Charles found easier ways to fame,

some of the lawyers of this age who have risen high, have by no means thought it absolutely necessary to submit to that long and painful course of study which a Plowden, a Coke, a Hale considered as requisite. My respected friend, Mr Langton, has shown me in the hand-writing of his grandfather, a curious account of a conversation which he had with Lord Chief Justice Hale, in which that great man tells him, 'That for two years after he came to the inn of court, he studied sixteen hours a day; however (his Lordship added) that by this intense application he almost brought himself to his grave, though he were of a very strong constitution, and after reduced himself to eight hours; but that he would not advise any body to so much; that he thought six hours a day, with attention and constancy was sufficient; that a man must use his body as he would his horse, and his stomach; not tire him at once, but rise with an appetite.'

On Wednesday, June 19, Dr Johnson and I returned to London; he was not well today, and said very little, employing himself chiefly in reading Euripides. He expressed some displeasure at me, for not observing sufficiently the various objects upon the road. 'If I had your eyes, Sir (said he), I should count the passengers.' It was wonderful how accurate his observations of visual objects was, notwithstanding his imperfect eyesight, owing to a habit of attention. That he was much satisfied with the respect paid to him at Dr Adams's, is thus attested by himself: 'I returned last night from Oxford, after a fortnight's abode with Dr Adams, who treated me as well as I could expect or wish; and he that contents a sick man, a man whom it is impossible to please, has surely done his part well.'[1]

After his return to London from this excursion, I saw him frequently, but have few memorandums; I shall therefore here insert some particulars which I collected at various times.[2]

The Reverend Mr Astle, of Ashbourne in Derbyshire, brother to the learned and ingenious Thomas Astle, Esq. was from his early years known to Dr Johnson, who obligingly advised him as to his studies, and recommended to him the following books, of which a list which he has been pleased to communicate, lies before me in Johnson's own hand-writing. – *Universal History* (*ancient*) – Rollin's *Ancient History* – Puffendorf's *Introduction to History* – Vertot's *History of Knights of Malta* – Vertot's *Revolution of Portugal* – Vertot's *Revolutions*

---

1 *Letters to Mrs Thrale*, Vol. ii, page 372.

2 Having unexpectedly by the favour of Mr Stone, of London-Field, Hackney, seen the original in Johnson's handwriting, of 'The Petition of the City of London to his Majesty, in favour of Dr Dodd', I now present it to my readers, with such passages as were omitted, inclosed in crotchets, and the additions or variations marked in Italics.

That William Dodd, Doctor of Laws, now lying under sentence of death *in your Majesty's gaol of Newgate*, for the crime of forgery, has for a great part of his life set an useful and laudable example of diligence in his calling, [and as we have reason to believe, has exercised his ministry with great fidelity and efficacy,] *which in many instances has produced the most happy effect.*

That he has been the first institutor, [or] *and* a very earnest and active promoter of several modes of useful charity, and [that] therefore [he] may be considered as having been on many occasions a benefactor to the public.

[That when they consider his past life, they are willing to suppose his late crime to have been not the consequence of habitual depravity, but the suggestion of some sudden and violent temptation.]

[That] *Your Petitioners*, therefore considering his case as in some of its circumstances unprecedented and peculiar, *and encouraged by your Majesty's known clemency* [they] most humbly recommend the said William Dodd to [his] *your* Majesty's most gracious consideration, in hope that he will be found not altogether [unfit] *unworthy* to stand an example of royal mercy.'[a]

a *Second Edition.* – Above note shifted back to page 586, on the words 'they *mended* it.'

of Sweden – Carte's H*istory of England* – *Present State of England* – *Geographical Grammar* – Prideaux's *Connection* – Nelson's *Feasts and Fasts* – *Duty of Man* – *Gentleman's Religion* – Clarendon's *History* – Watts's *Improvement of the Mind* – Watts's *Logic* – *Nature Displayed* – Lowth's *English Grammar* – *Blackwall on the Classics* – Sherlock's *Sermons* – Burnet's *Life of Hale* – Dupin's *History of the Church* – Shuckford's *Connections* – Law's *Serious Call* – Walton's *Complete Angler* – Sandys's *Travels* – Sprat's *History of the Royal Society* – England's *Gazetteer* – Goldsmith's *Roman History* – Some Commentaries on the Bible.

It having been mentioned to Dr Johnson that a gentleman who had a son whom he imagined to have an extreme degree of timidity, resolved to send him to a public school, that he might acquire confidence. 'Sir (said Johnson), this is a preposterous expedient for removing his infirmity; such a disposition should be cultivated in the shade. Placing him at a public school is forcing an owl upon day.'

Speaking of a gentleman whose house was much frequented by low company; 'Rags, Sir (said he), will always make their appearance where they have a right to do it.'

Of the same gentleman's mode of living, he said, 'Sir, the servants, instead of doing what they are bid, stand round the table in idle clusters, gaping upon the guests; and seem as unfit to attend a company, as to steer a man of war.'

A dull country magistrate gave Johnson a long tedious account of his exercising his criminal jurisdiction, the result of which was his having sentenced four convicts to transportation. Johnson, in an agony of impatience to get rid of such a companion, exclaimed, I heartily wish, Sir, that I were a fifth.'

Johnson was present when a tragedy was read, in which there occurred this line:

> Who rules o'er freemen should himself be free.

The company having admired it much, 'I cannot agree with you (said Johnson): It might as well be said,

> Who drives fat oxen should himself be fat.'

He was pleased with the kindness of Mr Cator, who was joined with him in Mr Thrale's important trust, and thus describes him:[1] 'There is much good in his character, and much usefulness in his knowledge.' He found a cordial solace at that gentleman's seat of Beckenham, in Kent, which is indeed one of the finest places at which I ever was a guest.

Johnson seldom encouraged general censure of any profession; but he was willing to allow a due share of merit to the various departments necessary in civilised life. In a splenetic, sarcastical, or jocular frame, however, he would sometimes utter a pointed saying of that nature. One instance has been mentioned,[2] where he gave a sudden satirical stroke to the character of an

---

1 *Letters to Mrs Thrale*, Vol. ii, p. 284.
2 See p. 316.

attorney. The too indiscriminate admission to that employment, which requires both abilities and integrity, has given rise to injurious reflections, which are totally inapplicable to many very respectable men who exercise it with reputation and honour.

Johnson having argued for some time with a pertinacious gentleman; his opponent, who had talked in a very puzzling manner, happened to say, 'I don't understand you, Sir': upon which Johnson observed, 'Sir, I have found you an argument; but I am not obliged to find you an understanding.'

Talking to me of Horry Walpole (as the Honourable Horace Walpole is often called), Johnson allowed that he got together a great many curious little things, and told them in an elegant manner. Mr Walpole thought Johnson a more amiable character after reading his Letters to Mrs Thrale; but never was one of the true admirers of that great man. We may suppose a prejudice conceived, if he ever heard Johnson's account to Sir George Staunton, that when he made the speeches in parliament for the *Gentleman's Magazine,* 'he always took care to put Sir Robert Walpole in the wrong, and to say everything he could against the electorate of Hanover.' The celebrated Heroic Epistle, in which Johnson is satirically introduced, has been ascribed both to Mr Walpole and Mr Mason. One day at Mr Courtenay's, when a gentleman expressed his opinion that there was more energy in that poem than could be expected from Mr Walpole; Mr Warton, the late Laureat, observed, 'It may have been written by Walpole, and *buckram'd* by Mason.'

He disapproved of Lord Hailes for having modernised the language of the ever-memorable John Hailes of Eton, in an edition which his Lordship published of that writer's works. 'An author's language, Sir (said he), is a characteristical part of his composition, and is also characteristical of the age in which he writes. Besides, Sir, when the language is changed we are not sure that the sense is the same. No, Sir; I am sorry Lord Hailes has done this.'

Here it may be observed, that his frequent use of the expression, *No, Sir,* was not always to intimate contradiction; for he would say so, when he was about to enforce an affirmative proposition which had not been denied, as in the instance last mentioned. I used to consider it as a kind of flag of defiance; as if he had said, 'Any argument you may offer against this is not just. No, Sir, it is not.' It was like Falstaff's 'I deny your Major.'

Sir Joshua Reynolds having said that he took the altitude of a man's taste by his stories and his wit, and of his understanding by the remarks which he repeated; being always sure that he must be a weak man who quotes common things with an emphasis as if they were oracles. Johnson agreed with him; and Sir Joshua having also observed that the real character of a man was found out by his amusements – JOHNSON. 'Yes, Sir; no man is a hypocrite in his pleasures.[a]'

---

[a] After this passage, read: I have mentioned Johnson's general aversion to a pun. He once, however, endured one of mine. When we were talking of a numerous company in which he had distinguished himself highly, I said, 'Sir, you were a COD surrounded by smelts. Is not this enough for you? at a time too when you were not *fishing* for a compliment?' He laughed at this with a complacent approbation. Old Mr Sheridan

Had Johnson treated at large *De Claris Oratoribus*, he might have given us an admirable work. When the Duke of Bedford attacked the ministry as vehemently as he could, for having taken upon them to extend the time for the importation of corn, Lord Chatham, in his first speech in the House of Lords, boldly avowed himself to be an adviser of that measure. 'My colleagues (said he), as I was confined by indisposition, did me the signal honour of coming to the bed-side of a sick man, to ask his opinion. But, had they not thus condescended, I should have *taken up my bed and walked*, in order to have delivered that opinion at the Council Board.' Mr Langton, who was present, mentioned this to Johnson, who observed, 'Now, Sir, we see that he took these words as he found them; without considering, that though the expression in Scripture, *take up thy bed and walk*, strictly suited the instance of the sick man restored to health and strength, who would of course be supposed to carry his bed with him, it could not be proper in the case of a man who was lying in a state of feebleness, and who certainly would not add to the difficulty of moving at all, that of carrying his bed.'

When I pointed out to him in the news-paper one of Mr Grattan's animated and glowing speeches, in favour of the freedom of Ireland, in which this expression occurred (I know not if accurately taken): 'We will persevere, till there is not one link of the English chain left to clank upon the rags of the meanest beggar in Ireland.' – 'Nay, Sir (said Johnson), don't you perceive that one link cannot clank.'

Mrs Thrale has published,[1] as Johnson's, a kind of parody or counterpart of a fine poetical passage in one of Mr Burke's speeches on American Taxation. It is vigorously but somewhat coarsely executed; and I am inclined to suppose, is not quite correctly exhibited. I hope he did not use the words '*vile agents* for the Americans in the House of Parliament'; and if he did so, in an extempore effusion, I wish the lady had not committed it to writing.

Mr Burke uniformly showed Johnson the greatest respect; and when Mr Townshend, now Lord Sydney, at a period when he was conspicuous in opposition, threw out some reflection in parliament upon the grant of a pension to a man of such political principles as Johnson; Mr Burke, though then of the same party with Mr Townshend, stood warmly forth in defence of his friend, to whom, he justly observed, the pension was granted solely on account of his eminent literary merit. I am well assured, that Mr Townshend's attack upon Johnson was the occasion of his 'hitching in a rhyme'; for, that in the original copy of Goldsmith's character of Mr Burke, in his *Retaliation*, another person's name stood in the couplet where Mr Townshend is now introduced:

---

observed, upon my mentioning it to him, 'He liked your compliment so well, he was willing to take it with *pun sauce*.' For my own part I think no innocent species of wit or pleasantry should be suppressed: and that a good pun may be admitted among the smaller excellencies of lively conversation.

1 *Anecdotes*, p. 43.

> Though fraught with all learning, kept straining his throat,
> To persuade *Tommy Townshend* to lend him a vote.

It may be worth remarking, among the *minutiae* of my collection, that Johnson was once drawn for the militia, the Trained Bands of the City of London, and that Mr·Rackstrow, of the Museum in Fleet-street, was his Colonel. It may be believed he did not serve in person; but the idea, with all its circumstances, is certainly laughable. He upon that occasion provided himself with a musket, and with a sword and belt, which I have seen hanging in his closet.

He was very constant to those whom he once employed, if they gave him no reason to be displeased. When somebody talked of being imposed on in the purchase of tea and sugar, and such articles; 'That will not be the case (said he), if you go to a *stately shop*, as I always do. In such a shop it is not worth their while to take a petty advantage.'

An author of most anxious and restless vanity being mentioned, 'Sir (said he), there is not a young sapling upon Parnassus more severely blown about by every wind of criticism than that poor fellow.'

The difference, he observed, between a well-bred and an ill-bred man is this: 'One immediately attracts your liking, the other your aversion. You love the one till you find reason to hate him; you hate the other till you find reason to love him.'

The wife of one of his acquaintance had fraudulently made a purse to herself out of her husband's fortune. Feeling a proper compunction in her last moments, she confessed how much she had secreted; but before she could tell where it was placed, she was seized with a convulsive fit and expired. Her husband said, he was more hurt by her want of confidence in him, than by the loss of his money. 'I told him (said Johnson) that he should console himself; for *perhaps* the money might be *found*, and he was *sure* that his wife was *gone*.'

A foppish physician imagined that Johnson had animadverted on his wearing a fine coat, and mentioned it to him. 'I did not notice you'; was his answer. The physician still insisted. 'Sir (said Johnson), had you been dipt in Pactolus, I should not have noticed you.'[a]

He seemed to take a pleasure in speaking in his own style; for when he had carelessly missed, he would repeat the thought translated into it. Talking of the Comedy of *The Rehearsal*, he said, 'It has not wit enough to keep it sweet.' This was easy; – he therefore caught himself, and pronounced a more rounded sentence, 'It has not vitality enough to preserve it from putrefaction.'

He censured a writer of entertaining Travels for assuming a feigned character, saying (in his sense of the word), 'He carries out one lie; we know not how many he brings back.'

---

[a] Instead of the last paragraph read: A foppish physician once reminded Johnson of his having been in company with him on a former occasion, 'I do not remember it, Sir.' The physician still insisted; adding that he that day wore so fine a coat that it must have attracted his notice. 'Sir (said Johnson), had you been dipt in Pactolus, I should not have noticed you.'

Though he had no taste for painting, he admired much the manner in which Sir Joshua Reynolds treated of his art, in his *Discourses to the Royal Academy*. He observed of a passage one day, 'I think I might as well have said this myself.' And once when Mr Langton was sitting by him, he read one of them very eagerly, and expressed himself thus: 'Very well, Master Reynolds; very well, indeed. But it will not be understood.'[a]

No man was more ready to make an apology when he had censured unjustly than Johnson. When a proof-sheet of one of his works was brought to him, he found fault with the mode in which a part of it was arranged, refused to read it, and in a passion desired that the compositor[1] might be sent to him. The compositor was Mr Manning, a decent sensible man, who had composed about one half of his *Dictionary*, when in Mr Strahan's printing-house; and a great part of his *Lives of the Poets*, when in Mr Nichols's printing-house; and now (in his seventy-seventh year) when in Mr Baldwin's printing-house, has composed a part of this work concerning him. By producing the manuscript, he at once satisfied Dr Johnson that he was not to blame. Upon which Johnson candidly and earnestly said to him, 'Mr Compositor, I ask your pardon. Mr Compositor, I ask your pardon, again and again.'

His generous humanity to the miserable was almost beyond example. The following instance is well attested: Coming home late one night, he found a poor woman lying in the street, so much exhausted that she could not walk; he took her upon his back, and carried her to his house, where he discovered that she was one of those wretched females who had fallen into the lowest state of vice, poverty, and disease. Instead of harshly upbraiding her, he had her taken care of with all tenderness for a long time, at a considerable expense, till she was restored to health, and endeavoured to put her into a virtuous way of living.[2]

He thought Mr Caleb Whitefoord singularly happy in hitting on the signature of *Papyrius Cursor*, to his ingenious and diverting cross-readings of the news-papers; it being a real name of an ancient Roman, and clearly expressive of the thing done in this lively conceit.

He once in his life was known to have uttered what is called a *bull*; Sir Joshua Reynolds, when they were riding together in Devonshire, complained that he had a very bad horse, for that even when going down hill he moved slowly step by step. 'Ay (said Johnson), and when he *goes* up hill, he *stands still*.'

[a] Add: When I observed to him that Painting was so far inferior to Poetry, that the story or even emblem which it communicates must be previously known, and mentioned as a natural and laughable instance of this, that a little miss, on seeing a picture of Justice with the scales, had exclaimed to me, 'See, there's a woman selling sweetmeats'; he said, 'Painting, Sir, can illustrate, but cannot inform.'

1 Compositor, in the art of printing, means, the person who adjusts the types in the order in which they are to stand for printing; one who arranges what is called the form, from which an impression is taken.

2 This circumstance therefore alluded to in Mr Courtenay's 'Poetical Character' of him is strictly true.[b]

[b] Add: My informer was Mrs Desmoulins, who lived many years in Dr Johnson's house.

He had a great aversion to gesticulating in company. He called once to a gentleman who offended him in that point, 'Don't attitudenise.' And when another gentleman thought he was giving additional force to what he uttered, by expressive movements of his hands, Johnson fairly seized them, and held them down.

An author of considerable eminence having engrossed a good share of the conversation in the company of Johnson, and having said nothing but what was very trifling and insignificant; Johnson when he was gone, observed to us, 'It is wonderful what a difference there sometimes is between a man's powers of writing and of talking. —— writes with great spirit, but is a poor talker; had he held his tongue we might have supposed him to have been restrain'd by modesty; but he has spoken a great deal to-day; and you have heard what stuff it was.'

A gentleman having said that a *congé d'elire*, has not perhaps the force of a command, but may be considered only as a strong recommendation. 'Sir (replied Johnson, who overheard him), it is such a recommendation, as if I should throw you out of a two-pair-of-stairs window, and recommend to you to fall soft.'[1]

Mr Steevens, who passed many a social hour with him during their long acquaintance, which commenced when they both lived in the Temple, has preserved a good number of particulars concerning him, most of which are to be found in the department of Apothegms, &c. in the Collection of Johnson's Works. But he has been pleased to favour me with the following, which are original:

> One evening, previous to the trial of Baretti, a consultation of his friends was held at the house of Mr Cox, the Solicitor, in Southampton-buildings, Chancery-lane. Among others present were, Mr Burke and Dr Johnson, who differed in sentiments concerning the tendency of some part of the defence the prisoner was to make. When the meeting was over, Mr Steevens observed, that the question between him and his friend had been agitated with rather too much warmth. 'It may be so, Sir (replied the Doctor), for Burke and I should have been of one opinion, if we had had no audience.'
>
>   Dr Johnson once assumed a character in which perhaps even Mr Boswell never saw him. His curiosity having been excited by the praises bestowed on the celebrated Torre's fireworks at Marybone-Gardens, he desired Mr Steevens to accompany him thither. The evening had proved showery; and soon after the few people present were assembled, public notice was given, that the conductors to the wheels, suns, stars, &c. were so thoroughly water-soaked, that it was impossible any part of the exhibition should be made. 'This is a mere excuse (says the Doctor) to save their

---

1 This has been printed in other publications, 'fall *to the ground*', But Johnson himself gave me the true expression which he had used, as above; meaning that the recommendation left as little choice in the one case as the other.

crackers for a more profitable company. Let us but hold up our sticks, and threaten to break those coloured lamps that surround the Orchestra, and we shall soon have our wishes gratified. The core of the fire-works cannot be injured; let the different pieces be touched in their respective centers, and they will do their offices as well as ever.' – Some young men who overheard him, immediately began the violence he had recommended, and an attempt was speedily made to fire some of the wheels which appeared to have received the smallest damage; but to little purpose were they lighted, for most of them completely failed. – The author of *The Rambler*, however, may be considered on this occasion, as the ringleader of a successful riot, though not as a skilful pyrotechnist.

It has been supposed that Dr Johnson, so far as fashion was concerned, was careless of his appearance in public. But this is not altogether true, as the following slight instance may show. – Goldsmith's last Comedy was to be represented during some court-mourning; and Mr Steevens appointed to call on Dr Johnson, and carry him to the tavern where he was to dine with others of the Poet's friends. The Doctor was ready dressed, but in coloured cloaths; yet being told that he would find every one else in black, received the intelligence with a profusion of thanks, hastened to change his attire, all the while repeating his gratitude for the information that had saved him from an appearance so improper in the front row of a front box. 'I would not (added he) for ten pounds, have seemed so retrograde to any general observance.'

He would sometimes found his dislikes on very slender circumstances. Happening one day to mention Mr Flexman, a Dissenting minister, with some compliment to his exact memory in chronological matters; the Doctor replied, 'Let me hear no more of him, Sir. That is the fellow who made the Index to my *Ramblers*, and set down the name of Milton thus: "Milton, *Mr* John".'

Mr Steevens adds this testimony, 'It is unfortunate however for Johnson, that his particularities and frailties can be more distinctly traced than his good and amiable exertions. Could the many bounties he studiously concealed, the many acts of humanity he performed in private, be displayed with equal circumstantiality, his defects would be so far lost in the blaze of his virtues, that the latter only would be regarded.'

Though from my very great[a] admiration of Johnson, I have wondered that he was not courted by all the great and all the eminent persons of his time, it ought fairly to be considered, that no man of humble birth, who lived entirely by literature, in short no author by profession, ever rose in this country, into that personal notice which he did. In the course of this work a numerous variety of names have been mentioned, to which many might be added. I cannot omit Lord and Lady Lucan, at whose house he often enjoyed all that an

[a] For 'great' read 'high'.

elegant table, and the best company can contribute to happiness; he found hospitality united with extraordinary accomplishments, and embellished with charms of which no man could be insensible.

On Tuesday, June 22, I dined with him at THE LITERARY CLUB, the last time of his being in that respectable society. The other members present were the Bishop of St Asaph, Lord Eliot, Lord Palmerston, Dr Fordyce, and Mr Malone. He looked ill; but had such a manly fortitude, that he did not trouble the company with melancholy complaints. They all showed evident marks of concern about him, with which he was much pleased, and he exerted himself to be as entertaining as his indisposition allowed him.

The anxiety of his friends to preserve so estimable a life, as long as human means might be supposed to have influence, made them plan for him a retreat from the severity of a British winter, to the mild climate of Italy. This scheme was at last brought to a serious resolution at General Paoli's, where I had often talked of it. One essential matter, however, I understood was necessary to be previously settled, which was obtaining such an addition to his income, as would be sufficient to enable him to defray the expense in a manner becoming the first literary character of a great nation, and, independent of all his other merits, the Author of THE DICTIONARY OF THE ENGLISH LANGUAGE. The person to whom I above all others thought I should apply to negotiate this business, was the Lord Chancellor,[1] because I knew that he highly valued Johnson, and that Johnson highly valued his Lordship; so that it was no degradation of my illustrious friend to solicit for him the favour of such a man, I have mentioned what Johnson said of him to me when he was at the bar;[2] and after his Lordship was advanced to the seals, he said of him, 'I would prepare myself for no man in England but Lord Thurlow. When I am to meet with him I should wish to know a day before.' How he would have prepared himself I cannot conjecture. Would he have selected certain topics, and considered them in every view so as to be in readiness to argue them at all points? And what may we suppose those topics to have been? I once started the curious enquiry to the great man who was the subject of this compliment: he smiled, but did not pursue it.

I first consulted with Sir Joshua Reynolds, who perfectly coincided in opinion with me; and I therefore, though personally very little known to his Lordship, wrote to him,[3] stating the case, and requesting his good offices for Dr Johnson. I mentioned that I was obliged to set out for Scotland early in the week after, so that if his Lordship should have any commands for me as to this pious negotiation, he would be pleased to send them before that time; otherwise Sir Joshua Reynolds would give all attention to it.

---

1 Edward Lord Thurlow.

2 Page 848.

3 It is strange that Sir John Hawkins should have related that the application was made by Sir Joshua Reynolds, when he could so easily have been informed of the truth by inquiring of Sir Joshua. Sir John's carelessness to ascertain facts is very remarkable.

This application was made not only without any suggestion on the part of Johnson himself, but was utterly unknown to him, nor had he the smallest suspicion of it. Any insinuations, therefore, which since his death have been thrown out, as if he had stooped to ask what was superfluous, are without any foundation. But, had he asked it, it would not have been superfluous; for though the money he had saved proved to be more than his friends imagined, or than I believe he himself, in his carelessness concerning worldly matters, knew it to be, had he travelled upon the Continent, an augmentation of his income would by no means have been unnecessary.

On Wednesday, June 23, I visited him in the forenoon, after having been present at the shocking sight of fifteen men executed before Newgate. I said to him, I was sure that human life was not machinery, that is to say, a chain of fatality planned and directed by the Supreme Being, as it had in it so much wickedness and misery, so many instances of both, as that by which my mind was now clouded. Were it machinery it would be better than it is in these respects, though less noble, as not being a system of moral government. He agreed with me now, as he always did, upon the great question of the liberty of the human will, which has been in all ages perplexed with so much sophistry. 'But, Sir, as to the doctrine of Necessity, no man believes it. If a man should give me arguments that I do not see, though I could not answer them, should I believe that I do not see?' It will be observed, that Johnson at all times made the just distinction between doctrines *contrary* to reason, and doctrines *above* reason.

Talking of the religious discipline proper for unhappy convicts, he said, 'Sir, one of our regular clergy will probably not impress their minds sufficiently: they should be attended by a Methodist preacher,[a] or a Popish priest.' Let me however observe, in justice to the Reverend Mr Vilette, who has been Ordinary of Newgate for no less than seventeen years, in the course of which he has attended many hundreds of wretched criminals, that his earnest and humane exhortations have been very effectual. His extraordinary diligence is highly praise-worthy, and merits a distinguished reward.[b]

On Thursday, June 24, I dined with him at Mr Dilly's, where were the Reverend Mr Knox, master of Tunbridge-school, Mr Smith, Vicar of Southill, Dr Beattie, Mr Pinkerton, author of various literary performances, and the Reverend Dr Mayo. At my desire old Mr Sheridan was invited, as I was earnest to have Johnson and him brought together again by chance, that a reconciliation might be effected. Mr Sheridan happened to come early, and having learnt that Dr Johnson was to be there, went away; so I found, with sincere regret, that my friendly intentions were hopeless. I recollect nothing that

---

[a] Add this note: A friend of mine happened to be passing by a *field congregation* in the environs of London, when a Methodist preacher quoted this passage with triumph.

[b] Add this note: I trust that THE CITY OF LONDON, now happily in unison with THE COURT, will have the justice and generosity to obtain preferment for this Reverend Gentleman, now a worthy old servant of that magnificent Corporation.

passed this day, except Johnson's quickness, who, when Dr Beattie observed, as something remarkable which bad happened to him, that he had chanced to see both No.1, and No. 1,000, of the hackney-coaches, the first and the last; 'Why, Sir (said he), there is an equal chance for one's seeing those two numbers as any other two.' He was clearly right; yet the seeing of the two extremes, each of which is in some degree more conspicuous than the rest, could not but strike one in a stronger manner than the sight of any other two numbers. – Though I have neglected to preserve his conversation, it was perhaps at this interview that Mr Knox formed the notion of it which he has exhibited in his *Winter Evenings*.

On Friday, June 25, I dined with him at General Paoli's, where he says, in one of his letters to Mrs Thrale, 'I love to dine.' There were a variety of dishes much to his taste, of all which he seemed to me to eat so much, that I was afraid he might be hurt by it; and I whispered to the General my fear, and begged he might not press him. 'Alas! (said the General) see how very ill he looks; he can live but a very short time. Would you refuse any slight gratifications to a man under sentence of death? There is a humane custom in Italy, by which persons in that melancholy situation are indulged with having whatever they like best to eat and drink, even with expensive delicacies.'

I showed him some verses on Lichfield by Miss Seward, which I had that day received from her, and had the pleasure to hear him approve of them. He confirmed to me the truth of a high compliment which I had been told he had paid to that lady, when she mentioned to him *The Colombiade*, an epic poem, by Madame du Boccage: 'Madam, there is not in it any thing equal to your description of the sea round the North Pole, in your Ode on the death of Captain Cook.'

On Sunday, June 27, I found him rather better. I mentioned to him a young man who was going to Jamaica with his wife and children, in expectation of being provided for by two of her brothers settled in that island, one a clergyman and the other a physician. JOHNSON. 'It is a wild scheme, Sir, unless he has a positive and deliberate invitation. There was a poor girl, who used to come about me, who had a cousin in Barbadoes, that, in a letter to her, expressed a wish she would come out to that island, and expatiated on the comforts and happiness of her situation. The poor girl went out: her cousin was much surprised, and asked her how she could think of coming. "Because (said she) you invited me." – "Not I" (answered the cousin). The letter then was produced. "I see it is true (said she), that I did invite you; but I did not think you would come." They lodged her in an out-house, where she passed her time miserably; and as soon as she had an opportunity she returned to England. Always tell this, when you hear of people going abroad to relations, upon a notion of being well received. In the case which you mention, it is probable the clergyman spends all he gets, and the physician does not know how much he is to get.'

We this day dined at Sir Joshua Reynolds's, with General Paoli, Lord Eliot (formerly Mr Eliot, of Port Eliot), Dr Beattie, and some more company. Talking of Lord Chesterfield; – JOHNSON. 'His manner was exquisitely elegant, and he had more knowledge than I expected.' BOSWELL. 'Did you find, Sir, his conversation to be of a superior style?' JOHNSON. 'Sir, in the conversation which I had with him I had the best right to superiority, for it was upon philology and literature.' Lord Eliot, who had travelled at the same time with Mr Stanhope, Lord Chesterfield's natural son, justly observed, that it was strange that a man who showed he had so much affection for his son as Lord Chesterfield did, by writing so many long and anxious letters to him, almost all of them when he was Secretary of State, which certainly was a proof of great goodness of disposition, should endeavour to make his son a rascal. His Lordship told us, that Foote had intended to bring on the stage a father who had thus tutored his son, and to show the son an honest man to every thing else, but practising his father's maxims upon him, and cheating him. JOHNSON. 'I am much pleased with this design; but I think there was no occasion to make the son honest at all. No; he should be a consummate rogue: the contrast between honesty and knavery would be the stronger. It should be contrived so that the father should be the only sufferer by the son's villainy, and thus there would be poetical justice.'

He put Lord Eliot in mind of Dr Walter Harte. 'I know (said he) Harte was your Lordship's tutor, and he was also tutor to the Peterborough family. Pray, my Lord, do you recollect any particulars that he told you of Lord Peterborough? He is a favourite of mine, and is not enough known: his character has been only ventilated in party pamphlets.' Lord Eliot said, if Dr Johnson would be so good as to ask him any questions, he would tell what he could recollect. Accordingly some things were mentioned. 'But (said his Lordship) the best account of Lord Peterborough that I have happened to meet with, is, Captain Carleton's *Memoirs*. Carleton was descended of an ancestor who had distinguished himself at the siege of Derry. He was an officer; and, what was rare at that time, had some knowledge of engineering.' Johnson said, he had never heard of the book. Lord Eliot had it at Port Eliot; but, after a good deal of enquiry, procured a copy in London, and sent it to Johnson, who told Sir Joshua Reynolds that he was going to bed when it came, but was so much pleased with it, that he sat up till he had read it through, and found in it such an air of truth, that he could not doubt of its authenticity; adding, with a smile (in allusion to Lord Eliot's having recently been raised to the peerage), 'I did not think a *young Lord* could have mentioned to me a book in the English history that was not known to me.'

An addition to our company came after we went up to the drawing-room; Dr Johnson seemed to rise in spirits as his audience increased. He said, 'He wished that Lord Orford's pictures, and Sir Ashton Lever's Museum, might be purchased by the public, because both the money, and the pictures, and the curiosities, would remain in the country. Whereas, if they were sold into another kingdom, the nation would indeed get some money, but would lose the pictures and curiosities, which it would be desirable we should have for improvement in taste and natural history. The only question was, that as the nation was much in want of money, whether it would not be better to take a large price from a foreign state.'

He entered upon a curious discussion of the difference between intuition and sagacity, one being immediate in its effect, the other requiring a circuitous process; one he observed, was the *eye* of the mind, the other the *nose* of the mind.

A gentleman[a] present took up the argument against him, and maintained that no man ever thinks of the *nose of the mind*, not adverting that though that figurative phrase seems strange to us, as very unusual, it is truly not more forced than Hamlet's 'In my *mind's eye*, Horatio'. He persisted much too long, and appeared to Johnson as putting himself forward as his antagonist with too much presumption; upon which he called to him in a loud tone, 'What is it you are contending for, if you *be* contending?' And afterwards imagining that the gentleman retorted upon him with a kind of smart drollery, he said, 'Mr ——, it does not become you to talk so to me. Besides, ridicule is not your talent; you have *there* neither intuition nor sagacity.' – The gentleman protested that he had intended no improper freedom, but had the greatest respect for Dr Johnson. After a short pause, during which we were somewhat uneasy – JOHNSON. 'Give me your hand, Sir. You were too tedious, and I was too short.' MR ——. 'Sir, I am honoured by your attention in any way.' JOHNSON. 'Come, Sir, let's have no more of it. We offended one another by our contention; let us not offend the company by our compliments.'

He now said, 'He wished much to go to Italy, and that he dreaded passing the winter in England.' I said nothing; but enjoyed a secret satisfaction in thinking that I had taken the most effectual measures to make such a scheme practicable.

On Monday, June 28, I had the honour to receive from the Lord Chancellor the following letter:

To JAMES BOSWELL, Esq.

SIR – I should have answered your letter immediately; if (being much engaged when I received it) I had not put it in my pocket, and forgot to open it till this morning.

I am much obliged to you for the suggestion; and I will adopt and press it as far as I can. The best argument, I am sure, and I hope it is not likely to fail, is Dr Johnson's merit. – But it will be necessary, if I should be so unfortunate as to miss seeing you, to converse with Sir Joshua on the sum it will be proper to ask – in short, upon the means of setting him out. It would be a reflection on us all, if such a man should perish for want of the means to take care of his health. Yours, &c.

THURLOW.

This letter gave me a very high satisfaction; I next day went and showed it to Sir Joshua Reynolds, who was exceedingly pleased with it. He thought that I should now communicate the negotiation to Dr Johnson, who might

[a] *Third Edition*: 'A young gentleman'.

afterwards complain if the attention with which it had been honoured, should be too long concealed from him. I intended to set out for Scotland next morning, but Sir Joshua cordially insisted that I should stay another day, that Johnson and I might dine with him, that we three might talk of his Italian Tour, and as Sir Joshua expressed himself, 'have it all out'. I hastened to Johnson, and was told by him that he was rather better to-day. BOSWELL. 'I am very anxious about you, Sir, and particularly that you should go to Italy for the winter, which I believe is your own wish.' JOHNSON. 'It is, Sir.' BOSWELL. 'You have no objection, I presume, but the money it would require.' JOHNSON. 'Why no, Sir.' Upon which I gave him a particular account of what had been done, and read to him the Lord Chancellor's letter. – He listened with much attention; then warmly said, 'This is taking prodigious pains about a man.' – 'O! Sir (said I, with most sincere affection), your friends would do every thing for you.' He paused – grew more and more agitated – till tears started into his eyes, and he exclaimed with fervent emotion, 'GOD bless you all.' I was so affected that I also shed tears. – After a short silence, he renewed and extended his grateful benediction, 'GOD bless you all, for JESUS CHRIST's sake.' We both remained for some time unable to speak. – He rose suddenly and quitted the room quite melted in tenderness. He staid but a short time, till he had recovered his firmness; soon after he returned I left him, having first engaged him to dine at Sir Joshua Reynolds's, next day – I never was again under that roof which I had so long reverenced.

On Wednesday, June 30, the friendly confidential dinner with Sir Joshua Reynolds took place, no other company being present. Had I known that this was the last time that I should enjoy in this world, the conversation of a friend whom I so much respected, and from whom I derived so much instruction and entertainment, I should have been deeply affected. When I now look back to it, I am vexed that a single word should have been forgotten.

Both Sir Joshua and I were so sanguine in our expectations, that we expatiated with confidence on the large provision which we were sure would be made for him, conjecturing whether munificence would be displayed in one large donation, or in an ample increase of his pension. He himself catched so much of our enthusiasm, as to allow himself to suppose it not impossible that our hopes might in one way or other be realised. He said that he would rather have his pension doubled than a grant of a thousand pounds; 'For (said he) though probably I may not live to receive as much as a thousand pounds, a man would have the consciousness that he should pass the remainder of his life in splendour, how long soever it might be.' Considering what a moderate proportion an income of six hundred pounds a year bears to innumerable fortunes in this country, it is worthy of remark, that a man so truly great should think it splendour.

As an instance of extraordinary liberality of friendship, he told us, that Dr Brocklesby had upon this occasion, offered him a hundred a year for his life. A grateful tear started into his eye, as he spoke this in a faltering tone.

Sir Joshua and I endeavoured to flatter his imagination with agreeable prospects of happiness in Italy. 'Nay (said he), I must not expect much of that;

when a man goes to Italy merely to feel how he breathes the air, he can enjoy very little.'

Our conversation turned upon living in the country, which Johnson, whose melancholy mind required the dissipation of quick successive variety, had habituated himself to consider as a kind of mental imprisonment. 'Yet, Sir (said I), there are many people who are content to live in the country.' JOHNSON. 'Sir, it is in the intellectual world as in the physical world; we are told by natural philosophers, that a body is at rest in the place that is fit for it; they who are content to live in the country are *fit* for the country.'

Talking of various enjoyments, I argued that a refinement of taste was a disadvantage, as they who have attained to it must be seldomer pleased than those who have no nice discrimination, and are therefore satisfied with every thing that comes in their way. JOHNSON. 'Nay, Sir; that is a paltry notion. Endeavour to be as perfect as you can in every respect.'

I accompanied him in Sir Joshua Reynolds's coach, to the entry of Bolt-court. He asked me whether I would not go with him to his house; I declined it, from an apprehension that my spirits would sink. We bade adieu to each other affectionately in the carriage. When he had got down upon the foot-pavement, he called out, 'Fare you well'; and without looking back, sprung away with a kind of pathetic briskness, if I may use that expression, which seemed to indicate a struggle to conceal uneasiness, and impressed me with a foreboding of our long, long separation.

I remained one day more in town, to have the chance of talking over my negotiation with the Lord Chancellor; but the multiplicity of his Lordship's important engagements did not allow of it; so I left the management of the business in the hands of Sir Joshua Reynolds.

Soon after this time Dr Johnson had the mortification of being informed by Mrs Thrale, that 'what she supposed he never believed',[1] was true, namely, that she was actually going to marry Signor Piozzi, an Italian music-master. He endeavoured to prevent it, but in vain. If she would publish the whole of the correspondence that passed between Dr Johnson and her on the subject, we should have a full view of his real sentiments. As it is, our judgement must be biassed by that characteristic specimen, which Sir John Hawkins has given us: 'Poor Thrale! I thought that either her virtue or her vice would have restrained her from such a marriage. She is now become a subject for her enemies to exult over, and for her friends, if she has any left, to forget, or pity.'[2]

It must be admitted that Johnson derived a considerable portion of happiness from the comforts and elegancies which he enjoyed in Mr Thrale's family; but Mrs Thrale assures us he was indebted for these to her husband alone, who certainly respected him sincerely.[3] Her words are, '*Veneration for his virtue,*

1 *Letters to Mrs Thrale*, Vol. ii, p. 375.
2 Dr Johnson's Letter to Sir John Hawkins, *Life*, p. 570.
3 *Anecdotes*, p. 293.

reverence for his talents, delight *in his conversation, and* habitual endurance of a yoke my husband first put upon me, *and of which he contentedly bore his share for sixteen or seventeen years, made me go on so long with Mr Johnson; but the perpetual confinement I will own to have been* terrifying, *in the first years of our friendship, and* irksome *in the last; nor could I pretend to* support *it without help when my coadjutor was no more.*' Alas! how different is this from the declarations which I have heard Mrs Thrale make in his life-time, without a single murmur against any peculiarities, or against any one circumstance which attended their intimacy.

As a sincere friend of the great man whose Life I am writing, I think it necessary to guard my readers against the mistaken notion of Dr Johnson's character, which this lady's *Anecdotes* of him suggest; for from the very nature and form of her book, it 'lends deception lighter wings to fly.'

Let it be remembered (says an eminent critic[1]), that she has comprised in a small volume all that she could recollect of Dr Johnson in *twenty years,* during which period, doubtless, some severe things were said by him; and they who read the book in *two hours,* naturally enough suppose that his whole conversation was of this complexion. But the fact is, I have been often in his company, and never *once* heard him say a severe thing to any one; and many others can attest the same. When he did say a severe thing it was generally extorted by ignorance pretending to knowledge, or by extreme vanity or affectation.

Two instances of inaccuracy (adds he) are peculiarly worthy of notice:

It is said,[2] '*That natural roughness of his manner so often mentioned, would, notwithstanding the regularity of his notions, burst through them all from time to time; and he once bade a very celebrated lady, who praised him with too much zeal perhaps, or perhaps too strong an emphasis (which always offended him), consider what her flattery was worth before she choked him with it.*'

Now let the genuine anecdote be contrasted with this. – The person thus represented as being harshly treated, though a very celebrated lady, was *then* just come to London from an obscure situation in the country. At Sir Joshua Reynolds's one evening she met Dr Johnson. She very soon began to pay her court to him in the most fulsome strain. 'Spare me, I beseech you, dear Madam,' was his reply. She still *laid it on.* 'Pray, Madam, let us have no more of this,' he rejoined. Not paying any attention to these warnings, she continued still her eulogy. At length, provoked by this indelicate and *vain* obtrusion of compliment, he exclaimed, 'Dearest lady, consider with your-self what your flattery is worth before you bestow it so freely.'

How different does this story appear, when accompanied with all these circumstances which really belong to it, but which Mrs Thrale either did not know, or has suppressed.

She says,[3] '*One gentleman, however, who dined at a nobleman's house in his*

1 Who has been pleased to furnish me with his remarks.
2 *Anecdotes,* p. 183.
3 Ibid. p. 202.

company, and that of Mr Thrale, to whom I was obliged for the anecdote, was willing to enter the lists in defence of King William's character; and having opposed and contradicted Johnson two or three times, petulantly enough, the master of the house began to feel uneasy, and expect disagreeable consequences; to avoid which, he said, loud enough for the Doctor to hear – Our friend here has no meaning now in all this, except just to relate at club to-morrow how he teased Johnson at dinner to-day; this is all to do himself honour. *– No, upon my word, (replied the other), I see no honour in it, whatever you may do. – Well, Sir (returned Mr Johnson, sternly), if you do not see the honour, I am sure I feel the disgrace.'*

This is all sophisticated. Mr Thrale was not in the company, though he might have related the story to Mrs Thrale. A friend, from whom I had the story, was present; and it was not at the house of a nobleman. On the observation being made by the master of the house on a gentleman's contradicting Johnson, that he had talked for the honour, &c. the gentleman muttered, in a low voice, 'I see no honour in it'; and Dr Johnson said nothing: so all the rest (though *bien trouvée*) is mere garnish.

I have had occasion several times, in the course of this work, to point out the incorrectness of Mrs Thrale, as to particulars which consisted with my own knowledge. But indeed she has, in flippant terms enough, expressed her disapprobation of that anxious desire of authenticity which prompts a person who is to record conversations, to write them down *at the moment.*[1] Unquestionably, if they are to be recorded at all, the sooner it is done the better. This lady herself says,[2] '*To recollect, however, and to repeat the sayings of Dr Johnson, is almost all that can be done by the writers of his Life; as his life, at least since my acquaintance with him, consisted in little else than talking, when he was not employed in some serious piece of work.*' She boasts of her having kept a common-place book; and, we find she noted, at one time or other, in a very lively manner, specimens of the conversation of Dr Johnson, and of those who talked with him; but had she done it recently, they probably would have been less erroneous; and we should have been relieved from those disagreeable doubts of their authenticity, with which we must now peruse them.

She says of him,[3] '*He was the most charitable of mortals, without being what we call an* active *friend. Admirable at giving counsel; no man saw his way so clearly; but he* would not stir a finger *for the assistance of those to whom he was willing enough to give advice.*' And again on the same page, '*If you wanted* a slight favour, *you must apply to people of other dispositions; for* not a step would Johnson move *to obtain a man a vote in a society, to repay a compliment which might be useful or pleasing, to write a letter of request, &c. or to obtain a hundred pounds a year more for a friend who perhaps had already two or three. No force could urge him to diligence, no importunity could conquer his resolution to stand still.*'

It is amazing that one who had such opportunities of knowing Dr Johnson,

---

1 *Anecdotes*, p. 44.
2 Ibid. p. 23.
3 Ibid. p. 51.

should appear so little acquainted with his real character. I am sorry this lady does not advert, that she herself contradicts the assertion of his being obstinately defective in the *petite morale*, in the little endearing charities of social life in conferring smaller favours; for she says,[1] '*Dr Johnson was liberal enough in granting literary assistance to others, I think; and innumerable are the Prefaces, Sermons, Lectures, and Dedications which he used to make for people who begged of him.*' I am certain that a *more active friend* has rarely been found in any age. This work, which I fondly hope will rescue his memory from obloquy, contains a thousand instances of his benevolent exertions in almost every way that can be conceived; and particularly in employing his pen with a generous readiness for those to whom its aid could be useful. Indeed his obliging activity in doing little offices of kindness, both by letters and personal application, was one of the most remarkable features in his character; and for the truth of this I can appeal to a number of his respectable friends: Sir Joshua Reynolds, Mr Langton, Mr Hamilton, Mr Burke, Mr Windham, Mr Malone, the Bishop of Dromore, Sir William Scott, Sir Robert Chambers. – And can Mrs Thrale forget the advertisements which he wrote for her husband at the time of his election contest; the epitaphs on him and her mother; the playful and even trifling verses, for the amusement of her and her daughters; his corresponding with her children, and entering into their minute concerns, which shows him in the most amiable light?

She relates,[2] that Mr Ch—lm—ley unexpectedly rode up to Mr Thrale's carriage, in which Mr Thrale and she, and Dr Johnson were travelling; that he paid them all his proper compliments, but observing that Dr Johnson, who was reading, did not see him, '*tapt him gently on the shoulder. " 'Tis Mr Ch—lm—ley"; says my husband. "Well, Sir – and what if it is Mr Ch—lm—ley"; says the other, sternly, just lifting his eyes a moment from his book, and returning to it again, with renewed avidity.*' This surely conveys a notion of Johnson, as if he had been grossly rude to Mr Cholmondeley,[a] a gentleman whom he always loved and esteemed. If, therefore, there was an absolute necessity for mentioning the story at all, it might have been thought that her tenderness for Dr Johnson's character would have disposed her to state any thing that could soften it. Why then is there a total silence as to what Mr Cholmondeley told her? – That Johnson, who had known him from his earliest years, having been made sensible of what had doubtless a strange appearance, took occasion, when he afterwards met him, to make a very courteous and kind apology. There is another little circumstance which I cannot but remark. Her book was published in 1785, she had then in her possession a letter from Dr Johnson, dated in 1777,[3] which begins thus:

1 *Anecdotes*, p. 193.
2 Ibid. p. 258.
a Add this note: George James Cholmondeley, Esq. grandson of George, third Earl of Cholmondeley, and one of the Commissioners of Excise; a gentleman respected for his abilities and elegance of manners.
3 *Letters to Mrs Thrale*, Vol. ii, p. 12.

'Cholmondeley's story shocks me, if it be true, which I can hardly think, for I am utterly unconscious of it: I am very sorry, and very much ashamed.' Why then publish the anecdote? Or if she did, why not add the circumstances, with which she was well acquainted?

In his social intercourse she thus describes him:[1] '*Ever musing till he was called out to converse, and conversing till the fatigue of his friends, or the promptitude of his own temper to take offence, consigned him back again to silent meditation.*' Yet in the same book[2] she tells, '*He was, however, seldom inclined to be silent, when any moral or literary question was started; and it was on such occasions that, like the Sage in 'Rasselas', he spoke, and attention watched his lips; he reasoned, and conviction closed his periods.*' His conversation, indeed, was so far from ever fatiguing his friends, that they regretted when it was interrupted or ceased, and could exclaim in Milton's language,

> With thee conversing, I forget all time.

I certainly, then, do not claim too much in behalf of my illustrious friend in saying, that however smart and entertaining Mrs Thrale's *Anecdotes* are, they must not be held as good evidence against him; for wherever an instance of harshness and severity is told, I beg leave to doubt its perfect authenticity; for though there may have been *some* foundation for it, yet, like that of his reproof to the 'very celebrated lady', it may be so exhibited in the narration as to be very unlike the real fact.

The evident tendency of the following anecdote[3] is to represent Dr Johnson very deficient in affection, tenderness, or even common civility. '*When I one day lamented the loss of a first cousin killed in America – "Pr'ythee, my dear (said he), have done with canting; how would the world be the worse for it, I may ask, if all your relations were at once spitted like larks, and roasted for Presto's supper?" – Presto was the dog that lay under the table while we talked.*' – I suspect this too of exaggeration and distortion. I allow that he made her an angry speech; but let the circumstances fairly appear as told by Mr Baretti who was present:

> Mrs Thrale, while supping very heartily upon larks, laid down her knife and fork, and abruptly exclaimed, 'O, my dear Mr Johnson, do you know what has happened? The last letters from abroad have brought us an account that our poor cousin's head was taken off by a cannon-ball.' Johnson, who was shocked both at the fact, and her light unfeeling manner of mentioning it, replied, 'Madam, it would give *you* very little concern if all your relations were spitted like those larks, and drest for Presto's supper.'[a]

1 *Anecdotes*, p. 23.
2 Ibid. p. 302.
3 Ibid. p. 63.
[a] Upon mentioning this to my friend Mr Wilkes, he, with his usual readiness, pleasantly matched it with the following *sentimental anecdote*. He was invited by a young man of fashion at Paris, to sup with him and a lady, who had been for some time his mistress, but with whom he was going to part. He said to Mr Wilkes that he

It is with concern that I find myself obliged to animadvert on the inaccuracies of Mrs Piozzi's *Anecdotes*, and perhaps I may be thought to have dwelt too long upon her little collection. But as from Johnson's long residence under Mr Thrale's roof, and his intimacy with her, the account which she has given of him may have made an unfavourable and unjust impression, my duty, as a faithful biographer, has obliged me reluctantly to perform this unpleasing task.

Having left the *pious negotiation*, as I called it, in the best hands, I shall here insert what relates to it. Johnson wrote to Sir Joshua Reynolds on July 6, as follows: 'I am going, I hope, in a few days, to try the air of Derbyshire, but hope to see you before I go. Let me, however, mention to you what I have much at heart. – If the Chancellor should continue his attention to Mr Boswell's request, and confer with you on the means of relieving my languid state, I am very desirous to avoid the appearance of asking money upon false pretences. I desire you to represent to his Lordship, what, as soon as it is suggested, he will perceive to be reasonable. – That, if I grow much worse, I shall be afraid to leave my physicians, to suffer the inconveniences of travel, and pine in the solitude of a foreign country. – That, if I grow much better, of which indeed there is now little appearance, I shall not wish to leave my friends and my domestic comforts; for I do not travel for pleasure or curiosity; yet if I should recover, curiosity would revive. – In my present state, I am desirous to make a struggle for a little longer life, and hope to obtain some help from a softer climate. Do for me what you can.' He wrote to me July 26: 'I wish your affairs could have permitted a longer and continued exertion of your zeal and kindness. They that have your kindness may want your ardour. In the mean time I am very feeble, and very dejected.'

By a letter from Sir Joshua Reynolds I was informed, that the Lord Chancellor had called on him, and acquainted him that the application had not been successful; but that his Lordship, after speaking highly in praise of Johnson, as a man who was an honour to his country, desired Sir Joshua to let him know, that on granting a mortgage of his pension, he should draw on his Lordship to the amount of five or six hundred pounds; and that his Lordship explained the meaning of the mortgage to be, that he wished the business to be conducted in such a manner, as that Dr Johnson should appear to be under the least possible obligation. Sir Joshua mentioned, that he had by the same post communicated all this to Dr Johnson.

How Johnson was affected upon the occasion will appear from what he wrote to Sir Joshua Reynolds:

---

really felt very much for her, she was in such distress, and that he meant to make her a present of two hundred louis-d'ors. Mr Wilkes observed the behaviour of Mademoiselle, who sighed indeed very piteously, and assumed every pathetic air of grief; but eat no less than three French pigeons, which are as large as English partridges, besides other things. Mr Wilkes whispered the gentleman, 'We often say in England, *Excessive sorrow is exceeding dry*, but I never heard *Excessive sorrow is exceeding hungry*. Perhaps *one* hundred will do.' The gentleman took the hint.

Ashbourne, Sept. 9.

Many words I hope are not necessary between you and me, to convince you what gratitude is excited in my heart by the Chancellor's liberality, and your kind offices. . . .

I have enclosed a letter to the Chancellor, which, when you have read it, you will be pleased to seal with a head, or any other general seal, and convey it to him: had I sent it directly to him, I should have seemed to overlook the favour of your intervention.

To the LORD HIGH CHANCELLOR.[1]

MY LORD – After a long and not inattentive observation of mankind, the generosity of your Lordship's offer raises in me not less wonder than gratitude. Bounty, so liberally bestowed, I should gladly receive, if my condition made it necessary; for, to such a mind, who would not be proud to own his obligations? But it has pleased GOD to restore me to so great a measure of health, that if I should now appropriate so much of a fortune destined to do good, I could not escape from myself the charge of advancing a false claim. My journey to the continent, though I once thought it necessary, was never much encouraged by my physicians; and I was very desirous that your Lordship should be told of it by Sir Joshua Reynolds, as an event very uncertain; for if I grew much better, I should not be willing, if much worse, not able, to migrate. – Your Lordship was first solicited without my knowledge; but, when I was told, that you were pleased to honour me with your patronage, I did not expect to hear of a refusal; yet, as I have had no long time to brood hope, and have not rioted in imaginary opulence, this cold reception has been scarce a disappointment; and, from your Lordship's kindness, I have received a benefit, which only men like you are able to bestow. I shall now live *mihi carior*, with a higher opinion of my own merit. I am, my Lord,

Your Lordship's most obliged,

Most grateful, and most humble servant,

SAM. JOHNSON.

Sept. 1784.

Upon this unexpected failure I abstain from presuming to make any remarks, or offer any conjectures.

Having after repeated reasonings, brought Dr Johnson to agree to my removing to London, and even to furnish me with arguments in favour of what he had opposed; I wrote to him requesting he would write them for me; he was

---

1 Sir Joshua Reynolds, on account of the excellence both of the sentiment and expression of this letter, took a copy of it, which he showed to some of his friends; one of whom, who admired it, being allowed to peruse it leisurely at home, a copy was made, and found its way into the news-papers and magazines. It was transcribed with some inaccuracies. I print it from the original draft in Johnson's own hand-writing.

so good as to comply, and I shall extract that part of his letter to me of June 11, as a proof how well he could exhibit a cautious yet encouraging view of it:

> I remember, and intreat you to remember, that *virtus est vitium fugere*; the first approach to riches is security from poverty. The condition upon which you have my consent to settle in London is, that your expense never exceeds your annual income. Fixing this basis of security, you cannot be hurt, and you may be very much advanced. The loss of your Scottish business, which is all that you can lose, is not to be reckoned as any equivalent to the hopes and possibilities that open here upon you. If you succeed, the question of prudence is at an end: every body will think that done right which ends happily; and though your expectations, of which I would not advise you to talk too much, should not be totally answered, you can hardly fail to get friends who will do for you all that your present situation allows you to hope: and if, after a few years, you should return to Scotland, you will return with a mind supplied by various conversation, and many opportunities of enquiry, with much knowledge and materials for reflection and instruction.

Let us now contemplate Johnson thirty years after the death of his wife, still retaining for her all the tenderness of affection.

To the Reverend Mr BAGSHAW, at Bromley.[a]

SIR – Perhaps you may remember, that in the year 1753, you committed to the ground my dear wife. I now entreat your permission to lay a stone upon her; and have sent the inscription, that, if you find it proper, you may signify your allowance.

You will do me a great favour by showing the place where she lies, that the stone may protect her remains.

Mr Ryland will wait on you for the inscription,[1] and procure it to be engraved. You will easily believe that I shrink from this mournful office. When it is done, if I have strength remaining, I will visit Bromley once again, and pay you part of the respect to which you have a right from, Reverend Sir,

Your most humble servant,

SAM. JOHNSON.

July 12, 1784.

On the same day he wrote to Mr Langton: 'I cannot but think that in my languid and anxious state, I have some reason to complain that I receive from

---

[a] Add this note: I am obliged for this, and a former letter, to John Loveday, of the Commons, a son of the late learned and pious John Loveday, Esq., of Caversham, in Berkshire. This worthy gentleman having retired from business, now lives in Warwickshire.

[1] Printed in his Works.

you neither enquiry nor consolation. You know how much I value your friendship, and with what confidence I expect your kindness, if I wanted any act of tenderness that you could perform; at least, if you do not know it, I think your ignorance is your own fault. Yet how long is it that I have lived almost in your neighbourhood without the least notice. – I do not, however, consider this neglect as particularly shown to me; I hear two of your most valuable friends make the same complaint. But why are all thus overlooked? You are not oppressed by sickness, you are not distracted by business; if you are sick, you are sick of leisure. – And allow yourself to be told, that no disease is more to be dreaded or avoided. Rather to do nothing than to do good, is the lowest state of a degraded mind. Boileau says to his pupil,

> *Que les vers ne soient pas votre eternel emploi,*
> *Cultivez vos amis.*

That voluntary debility, which modern language is content to term indolence, will, if it is not counteracted by resolution, render in time the strongest faculties lifeless, and turn the flame to the smoke of virtue. – I do not expect nor desire to see you, because I am much pleased to find that your mother stays so long with you, and I should think you neither elegant nor grateful, if you did not study her gratification. You will pay my respects to both the ladies, and to all the young people. – I am going Northward for a while, to try what help the country can give me; but, if you will write, the letter will come after me.'

Next day he set out on a jaunt to Staffordshire and Derbyshire, flattering himself that he might be in some degree relieved.

During his absence from London he kept up a correspondence with several of his friends, from which I shall select what appears to me proper for publication, without attending nicely to chronological order.

To Dr BROCKLESBY, he writes:

Ashbourne, July 20 – The kind attention which you have so long shown to my health and happiness, makes it as much a debt of gratitude as a call of interest, to give you an account of what befals me, when accident recovers me from your immediate care. – The journey of the first day was performed with very little sense of fatigue; the second day brought me to Lichfield, without much lassitude, but I am afraid that I could not have borne such violent agitation for many days together. Tell Dr Heberden, that in the coach I read *Ciceronianus*, which I concluded as I entered Lichfield. My affection and understanding went along with Erasmus, except that once or twice he somewhat unskilfully entangles Cicero's civil or moral, with his rhetorical character. – I staid five days at Lichfield, but, being unable to walk, had no great pleasure, and yesterday (19th) I came hither, where I am to try what air and attention can perform. – Of any improvement in my health I cannot yet please myself with the perception. . . . – The asthma has no abatement. Opiates stop the fit, so as that I can sit and sometimes lie easy, but they do not now procure me the power of motion; and I am afraid that my general strength of body does not increase. The weather indeed is not benign; but how low is he sunk whose strength depends upon the weather! – I am now looking into Floyer, who lived with his asthma to almost his ninetieth year. His book by want of order is obscure, and his asthma, I think, not of the same kind with mine. Something however I may perhaps learn. – My appetite still continues keen enough; and what I consider as a symptom of radical health, I have a voracious delight in raw summer fruit, of which I was less eager a few years ago. – You will be pleased to communicate this account to Dr Heberden, and if anything is to be done, let me have your joint opinion. – Now – *abite curae* – let me enquire after the Club.[1]

July 31 – Not recollecting that Dr Heberden might be at Windsor, I thought your letter long in coming. But, you know, *nocitura petuntur*, the letter which I so much desired, tells me that I have lost one of my best and tenderest friends.[2] My comfort is, that he appeared to live like a man that had always before his eyes the fragility of our present existence, and was therefore, I hope, not unprepared to meet his judge. – Your attention, dear Sir, and that of Dr Heberden, to my health is extremely kind. I am loth to think that I grow worse; and cannot fairly prove even to my own partiality, that I grow much better.

August 5 – I return you thanks, dear Sir, for your unwearied attention, both medicinal and friendly, and hope to prove the effect of your care by living to acknowledge it.

August 12 – Pray be so kind as to have me in your thoughts, and mention my case to others as you have opportunity. I seem to myself neither to gain nor lose strength. I have lately tried milk, but have yet found no advantage, and am afraid of it merely as a liquid. My appetite is still good, which I know is dear Dr Heberden's criterion of the *vis vitae*. – As we cannot now see each other, do not omit to write, for you cannot think with what warmth of expectation I reckon the hours of a post-day.

August 14. – I have hitherto sent you only melancholy letters, you will be glad to hear some better account. Yesterday the asthma remitted, perceptibly remitted, and I moved with more ease than I have enjoyed for many weeks. May GOD continue his mercy. – This account I would not delay, because I am not a lover of complaints, or complainers, and yet I have since we parted, uttered nothing till now but terror and sorrow. Write to me, dear Sir.

August 16 – Better I hope, and better. My respiration gets more and more ease and liberty. I went to church yesterday, after a very liberal dinner, without any inconvenience; it is indeed no long walk, but I never walked it without difficulty, since I came, before. . . . the intention was only to

1 At the Essex Head, Essex-street.
2 Mr Allen, the printer.

overpower the seeming *vis inertiae* of the pectoral and pulmonary muscles. – I am favoured with a degree of ease that very much delights me, and do not despair of another race upon the stairs of the Academy. – If I were, however, of a humour to see, or to show the state of my body, on the dark side, I might say,

Quid te exempta juvat spinis de pluribus una?

The nights are still sleepless, and the water rises, though it does not rise very fast. Let us, however, rejoice in all the good that we have. The remission of one disease will enable nature to combat the rest. – The squills I have not neglected; for I have taken more than a hundred drops a day, and one day took two hundred and fifty, which, according to the popular equivalence of a drop to a grain, is more than half an ounce. – I thank you, dear Sir, for your attention in ordering the medicines; your attention to me has never failed. If the virtue of medicines could be enforced by the benevolence of the prescriber, how soon should I be well.

August 19 – The relaxation of the asthma still continues, yet I do not trust it wholly to itself, but soothe it now and then with an opiate. I not only perform the perpetual act of respiration with less labour, but I can walk with fewer intervals of rest, and with greater freedom of motion. – I never thought well of Dr James's compounded medicines; his ingredients appeared to me sometimes inefficacious and trifling, and sometimes heterogeneous and destructive of each other. This prescription exhibits a composition of about three hundred and thirty grains, in which there are four grains of emetic tartar, and six drops thebaic tincture. He that writes thus, surely writes for show. The basis of his medicine is the gum ammoniacum, which dear Dr Lawrence used to give, but of which I never saw any effect. We will, if you please, let this medicine alone. The squills have every suffrage, and in the squills we will rest for the present.

August 21 – The kindness which you show by having me in your thoughts upon all occasions, will, I hope, always fill my heart with gratitude. Be pleased to return my thanks to Sir George Baker, for the consideration which he has bestowed upon me. – Is this the balloon that has been so long expected, this balloon to which I subscribed, but without payment? It is pity that philosophers have been disappointed, and shame that they have been cheated; but I know not well how to prevent either. Of this experiment I have read nothing; where was it exhibited? And who was the man that ran away with so much money? – Continue, dear Sir, to write often and more at a time; for none of your prescriptions operate to their proper uses more certainly than your letters operate as cordials.

August 26 – I suffered you to escape last post without a letter, but you are not to expect such indulgence very often, for I write not so much because I have any thing to say, as because I hope for an answer; and the vacancy of my life here makes a letter of great value. – I have here little company and

little amusement, and thus abandoned to the contemplation of my own miseries, I am sometimes gloomy and depressed; this too I resist as I can, and find opium, I think, useful, but I seldom take more than one grain. – Is not this strange weather? Winter absorbed the spring, and now autumn is come before we have had summer. But let not our kindness for each other imitate the inconstancy of the seasons.

Sept. 2 – Mr Windham has been here to see me; he came, I think, forty miles out of his way, and staid about a day and a half, perhaps I make the time shorter than it was. Such conversation I shall not have again till I come back to the regions of literature, and there Windham is, *inter stellas*[1] *Luna minores*. [He then mentions the effects of certain medicines, as taken, that] Nature is recovering its original powers, and the functions returning to their proper state. God continue his mercies, and grant me to use them rightly.

Sept. 9 – Do you know the Duke and Duchess of Devonshire? And have you ever seen Chatsworth? I was at Chatsworth on Monday: I had indeed seen it before, but never when its owners were at home; I was very kindly received, and honestly pressed to stay, but I told them that a sick man is not a fit inmate of a great house. But I hope to go again some time.

Sept. 11 – I think nothing grows worse, but all rather better, except sleep, and that of late has been at its old pranks. Last evening, I felt what I had not known for a long time, an inclination to walk for amusement; I took a short walk, and came back again neither breathless nor fatigued. – This has been a gloomy, frigid, ungenial summer, but of late it seems to mend; I hear the heat sometimes mentioned, but I do not feel it,

> *Praeterea minimus gelido jam in corpore sanguis*
> *Febre calet sola.*

I hope, however, with good help, to find means of supporting a winter at home, and to hear and tell at the Club what is doing, and what ought to be doing in the world. I have no company here, and shall naturally come home hungry for conversation. – To wish you, dear Sir, more leisure would not be kind; but what leisure you have, you must bestow upon me.

Sept. 16 – I have now let you alone for a long time, having indeed little to say. You charge me somewhat unjustly with luxury. At Chatsworth, you should remember, that I have eaten but once; and the Doctor, with whom I live, follows a milk diet. I grow no fatter, though my stomach, if it be not disturbed by physic, never fails me. – I now grow weary of solitude, and think of removing next week to Lichfield, a place of more society, but otherwise of less convenience. When I am settled, I shall write again. – Of

---

1 It is remarkable that so good a Latin scholar as Johnson, should have been so inattentive to the metre, as by mistake to have written *stellas* instead of *ignes*.

the hot weather that you mention, we have had in Derbyshire very much, and for myself I seldom feel heat, and suppose that my frigidity is the effect of my distemper, a supposition which naturally leads me to hope that a hotter climate may be useful. But I hope to stand another English winter.

Lichfield, Sept. 29 – On one day I had three letters about the air-balloon: yours was far the best, and has enabled me to impart to my friends in the country an idea of this species of amusement. In amusement, mere amusement, I am afraid it must end, for I do not find that its course can be directed so as that it should serve any purposes of communication; and it can give no new intelligence of the state of the air at different heights, till they have ascended above the height of mountains, which they seem never likely to do. – I came hither on the 27th. How long I shall stay, I have not determined. My dropsy is gone, and my asthma much remitted, but I have felt myself a little declining these two days, or at least to-day; but such vicissitudes must be expected. One day may be worse than another; but this last month is far better than the former; if the next should be as much better than this, I shall run about the town on my own legs.

October 6 – The fate of the balloon I do not much lament: to make new balloons is to repeat the jest again. We now know a method of mounting into the air, and, I think, are not likely to know more. The vehicles can serve no use till we can guide them; and they can gratify no curiosity till we mount with them to greater heights than we can reach without, till we rise above the tops of the highest mountains, which we have yet not done. We know the state of the air in all its regions, to the top of Teneriffe, and therefore learn nothing from those who navigate a balloon below the clouds. The first experiment, however, was bold, and deserved applause and reward. But since it has been performed, and its event is known, I had rather now find a medicine that can ease an asthma.

October 25 – You write to me with a zeal that animates, and a tenderness that melts me. I am not afraid either of a journey to London, or a residence in it. I came down with little fatigue, and am now not weaker. In the smoky atmosphere I was delivered from the dropsy, which I consider as the original and radical disease. The town is my element;[1] there are my friends, there are my books, to which I have not yet bidden farewell, and there are my

---

1 His love of London continually appears.[a] Once upon reading that line in the curious epitaph quoted in *The Spectator*,

Born in New-England, did in London die;

he laughed and said, 'I do not wonder at this. It would have been strange, if born in London, he had died in New-England.'

[a] After 'appears', read: In a letter from him to Mrs Smart, wife of his friend the poet, which is published in a well-written life of him, prefixed to an edition of his poems, in 1791, there is the following sentence: 'To one that has passed so many years in the pleasures and opulence of London, there are few places that can give much delight.'

amusements. Sir Joshua told me long ago, that my vocation was to public life, and I hope still to keep my station, till GOD shall bid me *Go in peace*.

To Mr HOOLE:

Ashbourne, Aug. 7 – Since I was here, I have two little letters from you, and have not had the gratitude to write. But every man is most free with his best friends, because he does not suppose that they can suspect him of intentional incivility. – One reason for my omission is, that being in a place to which you are wholly a stranger, I have no topics of correspondence. If you had any knowledge of Ashbourne, I could tell you of two Ashbourne men, who, being last week condemned at Derby to be hanged for a robbery, went and hanged themselves in their cell. But this, however it may supply us with talk, is nothing to you. – Your kindness, I know, would make you glad to hear some good of me, but I have not much good to tell; if I grow not worse, it is all that I can say. – I hope Mrs Hoole receives more help from her migration. Make her my compliments, and write again to, dear Sir, your affectionate servant.

Aug. 13 – I thank you for your affectionate letter. I hope we shall both be the better for each other's friendship, and I hope we shall not very quickly be parted. – Tell Mr Nichols, that I shall be glad of his correspondence, when his business allows him a little remission; though to wish him less business, that I may have more pleasure, would be too selfish. – To pay for seats at the balloon is not very necessary, because, in less than a minute, they who gaze at a mile's distance will see all that can be seen. About the wings, I am of your mind; they cannot at all assist it, nor I think regulate its motion. – I am now grown somewhat easier in my body, but my mind is sometimes depressed. – About the Club, I am in no great pain. The forfeitures go on, and the house, I hear, is improved for our future meetings. I hope we shall meet often, and sit long.

Sept. 4 – Your letter was, indeed, long in coming, but it was very welcome. Our acquaintance has now subsisted long, and our recollection of each other involves a great space, and many little occurrences, which melt the thoughts to tenderness. Write to me, therefore, as frequently as you can. – I hear from Dr Brocklesby and Mr Ryland, that the Club is not crowded. I hope we shall enliven it when winter brings us together.

To Dr BURNEY:

August 2 – The weather, you know, has not been balmy; I am now reduced to think, and am at last content to talk of the weather. Pride must have a fall.[1] – I have lost dear Mr Allen, and wherever I turn, the dead or

---

1 There was no information for which Dr Johnson was less grateful than for that which concerned the weather. It was in allusion to his impatience with those who were reduced to keep conversation alive by observations on the weather, that he

the dying meet my notice, and force my attention upon misery and mortality. Mrs Burney's escape from so much danger, and her ease after so much pain, throws, however, some radiance of hope upon the gloomy prospect. May her recovery be perfect, and her continuance long. – I struggle hard for life. I take physic, and take air; my friend's chariot is always ready. We have run this morning twenty-four miles, and could run forty-eight more. *But who can run the race with death?*

Sept. 4 – [Concerning a private transaction, in which his opinion was asked, and after giving it he makes the following reflections, which are applicable on other occasions.] Nothing deserves more compassion than wrong conduct with good meaning; than loss or obloquy suffered by one who, as he is conscious only of good intentions, wonders why he loses that kindness which he wishes to preserve; and not knowing his own fault, if, as may sometimes happen, nobody will tell him, goes on to offend by his endeavours to please. – I am delighted by finding that our opinions are the same. – You will do me a real kindness by continuing to write. A post-day has now been long a day of recreation.

Nov. 1 – Our correspondence paused for want of topics. I had said what I had to say on the matter proposed to my consideration; and nothing remained but to tell you, that I waked or slept; that I was more or less sick. I drew my thoughts in upon myself, and supposed yours employed upon your book. – That your book has been delayed I am glad, since you have gained an opportunity of being more exact. – Of the caution necessary in adjusting narratives there is no end. Some tell what they do not know, that they may not seem ignorant, and others from mere indifference about truth. All truth is not, indeed, of equal importance; but, if little violations are allowed, every violation will in time be thought little; and a writer should keep himself vigilantly on his guard against the first temptations to negligence or supineness. – I had ceased to write, because respecting you I had no more to say, and respecting myself could say little good. I cannot boast of advancement, and in cases of convalescence it may be said, with few exceptions, *non progredi, est regredi.* I hope I may be excepted. – My great difficultly was with my sweet Fanny,[a] who, by her artifice of inserting her letter in yours, had given me a precept of frugality which I was not at liberty to neglect; and I know not who were in town under whose cover I could send my letter. I rejoice to hear that you are all so well, and have a delight particularly sympathetic in the recovery of Mrs Burney.

applied the old proverb to himself. If any one of his intimate acquaintance told him it was hot or cold, wet or dry, windy or calm, he would stop them, by saying, 'Poh! poh! you are telling us that of which none but men in a mine or a dungeon can be ignorant. Let us bear in patience, or enjoy in quiet, elementary changes, whether for the better or the worse, as they are never secrets.'   BURNEY.

[a] Add this note: The celebrated Miss Fanny Burney.

To Mr LANGTON:

Aug. 25 – The kindness of your last letter, and my omission to answer it, begins to give you, even in my opinion, a right to recriminate, and to charge me with forgetfulness of the absent. I will therefore delay no longer to give an account of myself, and wish I could relate what would please either myself or my friend. – On July 13, I left London, partly in hope of help from new air and change of place, and partly excited by the sick man's impatience of the present. I got to Lichfield in a stage vehicle, with very little fatigue, in two days, and had the consolation to find, that since my last visit my three old acquaintance are all dead. – July 20, I went to Ashbourne, where I have been till now; the house in which we live is repairing. I live in too much solitude, and am often deeply dejected: I wish we were nearer, and rejoice in your removal to London. A friend, at once cheerful and serious, is a great acquisition. Let us not neglect one another for the little time which Providence allows us to hope. – Of my health I cannot tell you, what my wishes persuaded me to expect, that it is much improved by the season or by remedies. I am sleepless; my legs grow weary with a very few steps, and the water breaks its boundaries in some degree. The asthma, however, has remitted; my breath is still much obstructed, but is more free than it was. Nights of watchfulness produce torpid days; I read very little, though I am alone; for I am tempted to supply in the day what I lost in bed. – This is my history, like all other histories, a narrative of misery. Yet am I so much better than in the beginning of the year, that I ought to be ashamed of complaining. I now sit and write with very little sensibility of pain or weakness; but when I rise, I shall find my legs betraying me. – Of the money which you mentioned I have no immediate need; keep it, however for me, unless some exigence requires it. Your papers I will show you certainly when you would see them, but I am a little angry at you for not keeping minutes of your own *acceptum et expensum*, and think a little time might be spared from Aristophanes, for the *res familiares*. Forgive me, for I mean well. – I hope, dear Sir, that you and Lady Rothes, and all the young people, too many to enumerate, are well and happy. GOD bless you all.

To Mr WINDHAM:

August – The tenderness with which you have been pleased to treat me, through my long illness, neither health or sickness can I hope make me forget; and you are not to suppose, that after we parted you were no longer in my mind. But what can a sick man say, but that he is sick? His thoughts are necessarily concentred in himself; he neither receives nor can give delight; his enquiries are after alleviations of pain, and his efforts are to catch some momentary comfort – Though I am now in the neighbour- hood of the Peak, you must expect no account of its wonders, of its hills, its waters, its caverns, or its mines; but I will tell you, dear Sir, what I hope you will not hear with less satisfaction, that for about a week past my asthma has been less afflictive.

October 2 – I believe you have been long enough acquainted with the *phaenomena* of sickness, not to be surprised that a sick man wishes to be where he is not, and where it appears to every body but himself that he might easily be, without having the resolution to remove. I thought Ashbourne a solitary place, but did not come hither till last Monday. – I have here more company, but my health has for this last week not advanced; and in the languor of disease how little can be done? Whither or when I shall make my next remove, I cannot tell; but I entreat you, dear Sir, to let me know, from time to time, where you may be found, for your residence is a very powerful attractive to, Sir, your most humble servant.'[a]

To the Right Honourable WILLIAM GERARD HAMILTON.

DEAR SIR – Considering what reason you gave me in the spring to conclude that you took part in whatever good or evil might befal me, I ought not to have omitted so long the account which I am now about to give you. – My diseases are an asthma and a dropsy, and, what is less curable, seventy-five. Of the dropsy, in the beginning of the summer, or in the spring, I recovered to a degree which struck with wonder both me and my physicians: the asthma now is likewise, for a time, very much relieved. I went to Oxford, where the asthma was very tyrannical, and the dropsy began again to threaten me, but seasonable physic stopped the inundation: I then returned to London, and in July took a resolution to visit Staffordshire and Derby-shire, where I am yet struggling with my diseases. The dropsy made another attack, and was not easily ejected, but at last gave way. The asthma suddenly remitted in bed, on the 13th of August, and, though now very oppressive, is, I think, still something gentler than it was before the remission. My limbs are miserably debilitated, and my nights are sleepless and tedious. – When you read this, dear Sir, you are not sorry that I wrote no sooner. I will not prolong my complaints. I hope still to see you *in a happier hour*, to talk over

---

[a] After this letter, read:

To Mr PERKINS.

DEAR SIR – I cannot but flatter myself that your kindness for me will make you glad to know where I am, and in what state.

I have been struggling very hard with my diseases. My breath has been very much obstructed, and the water has attempted to encroach upon me again. I past the first part of the summer at Oxford, afterwards I went to Lichfield, thence to Ashbourne, in Derbyshire, and a week ago I returned to Lichfield.

My breath is now much easier, and the water is in a great measure run away, so that I hope to see you again before winter.

Please make my compliments to Mrs Perkins, and to Mr and Mrs Barclay. I am, dear Sir,

Your most humble servant,

SAM. JOHNSON.

Lichfield, Oct. 4, 1784.

what we have often talked, and perhaps to find new topics of merriment, or new incitements to curiosity. I am, dear Sir, &c.

SAM. JOHNSON.

Lichfield, Oct. 20, 1784.

To JOHN PARADISE, Esq.[a]

DEAR SIR – Though in all my Summer's excursion I have given you no account of myself, I hope you think better of me than to imagine it possible for me to forget you, whose kindness to me has been too great and too constant not to have made its impression on a harder breast than mine. – Silence is not very culpable when nothing pleasing is suppressed. It would have alleviated none of your complaints to have read my vicissitudes of evil. I have struggled hard with very formidable and obstinate maladies; and though I cannot talk of health, think all praise due to my Creator and Preserver for the continuance of my life. The dropsy has made two attacks, and has given way to medicine; the asthma is very oppressive, but that has likewise once remitted. I am very weak, and very sleepless; but it is time to conclude the tale of misery. – I hope, dear Sir, that you grow better, for you have likewise your share of human evil, and that your lady and the young charmers are well. I am, dear Sir, &c.

SAM. JOHNSON.

Lichfield, Oct. 20, 1784.

To Mr GEORGE NICOLL.[1]

DEAR SIR – Since we parted I have been much oppressed by my asthma, but it has lately been less laborious. When I sit I am almost at ease, and I can walk, though yet very little, with less difficulty for this week past than before. I hope I shall again enjoy my friends, and that you and I shall have a little more literary conversation. – Where I now am, every thing is very liberally provided for me but conversation. My friend is sick himself, and the reciprocation of complaints and groans affords not much of either pleasure or instruction. What we have not at home this town does not supply, and I shall be glad of a little imported intelligence, and hope that you will bestow now and then a little time on the relief and entertainment of, Sir, yours, &c.

SAM. JOHNSON.

Ashbourne, August 19, 1784.

---

[a] Add the following note: Son of the late Peter Paradise, Esq., his Britannic Majesty's Consul at Salonica, in Macedon, and his lady, a native of that country. He studied at Oxford, and has been honoured by that University with the degree of LL.D. He is distinguished not only by his learning and talents, but by an amiable disposition, gentleness of manners, and a very general acquaintance with well-informed and accomplished persons of almost all nations.

1 Bookseller to his Majesty.

To Mr CRUIKSHANK.

DEAR SIR – Do not suppose that I forget you; I hope I shall never be accused of forgetting my benefactors. I had, till lately, nothing to write but complaints upon complaints, of miseries upon miseries, but within this fortnight I have received great relief. – Have your Lectures any vacation? If you are released from the necessity of daily study, you may find time for a letter to me. [In this letter he states the particulars of his case.] – In return for this account of my health, let me have a good account of yours, and of your prosperity in all your undertakings. I am, dear Sir, your, &c.

SAM. JOHNSON.

Ashbourne, Sept. 4, 1784.

To Mr THOMAS DAVIES:

August 14 – The tenderness with which you always treat me, makes me culpable in my own eyes for having omitted to write in so long a separation; I had, indeed, nothing to say that you could wish to hear. All has been hitherto misery accumulated upon misery, disease corroborating disease, till yesterday my asthma was perceptibly and unexpectedly mitigated. I am much comforted with this short relief, and am willing to flatter myself that it may continue and improve. I have at present, such a degree of ease, as not only may admit the comforts, but the duties of life. Make my compliments to Mrs Davies. – Poor dear Allen, he was a good man.[a]

To Sir JOSHUA REYNOLDS:

August 19 – Having had since our separation, little to say that could please you or myself by saying, I have not been lavish of useless letters; but I flatter myself that you will partake of the pleasure with which I can now tell you, that about a week ago, I felt suddenly a sensible remission of my asthma, and consequently a greater lightness of action and motion. – Of this grateful alleviation I know not the cause, nor dare depend upon its continuance, but while it lasts I endeavour to enjoy it, and am desirous of communicating, while it lasts, my pleasure to my friends. – Hitherto, dear

[a] After this letter, read:

To Sir JOSHUA REYNOLDS.

Ashbourne, July 21.

The tenderness with which I am treated by my friends, makes it reasonable to suppose that they are desirous to know the state of my health, and a desire so benevolent ought to be gratified. – I came to Lichfield in two days without any painful fatigue, and on Monday came hither, where I purpose to stay and try what air and regularity will effect. I cannot yet persuade myself that I have made much progress in recovery. My sleep is little, my breath is very much encumbered, and my legs are very weak. The water has increased a little, but has again run off. The most distressing symptom is want of sleep.

Sir, I had written before the post, which stays in this town but a little while, brought me your letter. Mr Davies seems to have represented my little tendency to recovery in terms too splendid. I am still restless, still weak, still watry, but the asthma is less oppressive. – Poor Ramsay![1] On which side soever I turn, mortality presents its formidable frown. I left three old friends at Lichfield, when I was last there, and now found them all dead. I no sooner lose sight of dear Allen, than I am told that I shall see him no more. That we must all die, we always knew; I wish I had sooner remembered it. Do not think me intrusive or importunate, if I now call, dear Sir, on you to remember it.

Sept. 2[b] – I still continue, by GOD's mercy, to mend. My breath is easier, my nights are quieter, and my legs are less in bulk, and stronger in use. I have, however, yet a great deal to overcome, before I can yet attain even an old man's health. – Write, do write to me now and then; we are now old acquaintance, and perhaps few people have lived so much and so long together, with less cause of complaint on either side. The retrospection of this is very pleasant, and I hope we shall never think on each other with less kindness.[c]

---

1 Allan Ramsay, Esq. painter to his Majesty, who died about this time,[a] much regretted by his friends.

[a] For 'about this time' read 'Aug. 10, 1784, in the 71st year of his age'.

[b] Add:

I am glad that a little favour from the court has intercepted your furious purposes. I could not in any case have approved such public violence of resentment, and should have considered any who encouraged it, as rather seeking sport for themselves, than honour for you. Resentment gratifies him who intended an injury, and pains him unjustly who did not intend it. But all this is now superfluous.

[c] Add:

Sept. 9 – I could not answer your letter before this day, because I went on the sixth to Chatsworth, and did not come back till the post was gone. – Many words, I hope, are not necessary between you and me to convince you what gratitude is excited in my heart by the Chancellor's liberality and your kind offices. I did not indeed expect that what was asked by the Chancellor would have been refused, but since it has, we will not tell that any thing has been asked. – I have enclosed a letter to the Chancellor, which when you have read it, you will be pleased to seal with a head, or other general seal, and convey it to him; had I sent it directly to him, I should have seemed to overlook the favour of your intervention. – My last letter told you of my advance in health, which, I think, in the whole still continues. Of the hydropic tumour there is now very little appearance; the asthma is much less troublesome, and seems to remit something day after day. I do not despair of supporting an English winter. – At Chatsworth, I met young Mr Burke, who led me very commodiously into conversation with the Duke and Duchess. We had a very good morning. The dinner was public.

Sept. 18 – I flattered myself that this week would have given me a letter from you, but none has come. Write to me now and then, but direct your next to Lichfield. – I think, and I hope, am sure, that I still grow better; I have sometimes good nights; but am still in my legs weak, but so much mended, that I go to Lichfield in hope of being able to pay my visits on foot, for there are no coaches. – I have three letters this day, all about the balloon, I could have been content with one. Do not write about the balloon, whatever else you may think proper to say.[a]

To Mr JOHN NICHOLS:

Lichfield, Oct. 20 – When you were here, you were pleased, as I am told, to think my absence an inconvenience. I should certainly have been very glad to give so skilful a lover of antiquities any information about my native place, of which, however, I know not much, and have reason to believe that not much is known. – Though I have not given you any amusement, I have received amusement from you. At Ashbourne, where I had very little company, I had the luck to borrow Mr Bowyer's Life; a book so full of contemporary history, that a literary man must find some of his old friends. I thought that I could now and then have told you some hints worth your notice; and perhaps we may talk a life over. I hope we shall be much together; you must now be to me what you were before, and what dear Mr Allen was, besides. He was taken unexpectedly away, but I think he was a very good man. – I have made little progress in recovery. I am very weak, and very sleepless; but I live on and hope.

This various mass of correspondence, which I have thus brought together, is valuable both as an addition to the store which the public already has of Johnson's writings, and as exhibiting a genuine and noble specimen of vigour and vivacity of mind, which neither age nor sickness could impair or diminish.

It may be observed, that his writing in every way, whether for the public, or privately to his friends, was by fits and starts; for we see frequently, that a number of letters are written on the same day. When he had once overcome his aversion to begin, he was, I suppose, desirous to go on in order to relieve his mind from the uneasy reflection of delaying what he ought to do.

[a] Add:

October 2 – I am always proud of your approbation, and therefore was much pleased that you liked my letter. When you copied it, you invaded the Chancellor's right rather than mine. – The refusal I did not expect, but I had never thought much about it, for I doubted whether the Chancellor had so much tenderness for me as to ask. He, being keeper of the King's conscience, ought not to be supposed capable of an improper petition. – All is not gold that glitters, as we have often been told; and the adage is verified in your place and my favour; but if what happens does not make us richer, we must bid it welcome, if it makes us wiser. – I do not at present grow better, nor much worse; my hopes, however, are somewhat abated, and a very great loss is the loss of hope, but I struggle on as I can.

While in the country, notwithstanding the accumulation of illness which he endured, his mind did not lose its powers. He translated an Ode of Horace, which is printed in his Works, and composed several prayers. I shall insert one of them, which is so wise and energetic, so philosophical and so pious, that I doubt not of its affording consolation to many a sincere Christian, when in a state of mind to which I believe the best are sometimes liable.[1]

And here I am enabled fully to refute a very unjust reflection both against Dr Johnson, and his faithful servant, Mr Francis Barber, by Sir John Hawkins, as if both of them had been guilty of culpable neglect towards a person of the name of Heely, whom Sir John chooses to call a *relation* of Dr Johnson's. The fact is, that Mr Heely was not his relation; he had indeed been married to one of his cousins, but she had died without having children, and he had married another woman, so that even the slight connection which there once had been by *alliance* was dissolved. Dr Johnson, who had shown very great liberality to this man while his first wife was alive, as has appeared in a former part of this work,[2] was humane and charitable enough to continue his bounty to him occasionally; but surely there was no strong call of duty upon him or upon his legatee, to do more. The following letter, obligingly communicated to me by Mr Andrew Strahan, will confirm what I have stated

To Mr HEELY, No. 5, in Pye-street, Westminster.

SIR – As necessity obliges you to call so soon again upon me, you should at least have told the smallest sum that will supply your present wants; you cannot suppose that I have much to spare. Two guineas is as much as you ought to be behind with your creditor. – If you wait on Mr Strahan, in New-street, Fetter-lane, or in his absence, on Mr Andrew Strahan, show this, by which they are entreated to advance you two guineas, and to keep this as a voucher. I am, Sir, your humble servant,

SAM. JOHNSON.

Ashbourne, August 12, 1784.

---

1 *Against inquisitive and perplexing thoughts.* 'O LORD, my Maker and Protector, who hast graciously sent me into this world to work out my salvation, enable me to drive from me all such unquiet and perplexing thoughts as may mislead or hinder me in the practice of those duties which Thou hast required. When I behold the works of thy hands, and consider the course of thy providence, give me grace always to remember that thy thoughts are not my thoughts, nor thy ways my ways. And while it shall please Thee to continue me in this world, where much is to be done, and little to be known, teach me, by thy Holy Spirit, to withdraw my mind from unprofitable and dangerous enquiries, from difficulties vainly curious, and doubts impossible to be solved. Let me rejoice in the light which Thou hast imparted, let me serve Thee with active zeal and humble confidence, and wait with patient expectation for the time in which the soul which Thou receivest shall be satisfied with knowledge. Grant this, O LORD, for JESUS CHRIST's sake. Amen.'

2 Page 261.

Indeed it is very necessary to keep in mind that Sir John Hawkins has unaccountably viewed Johnson's character and conduct in almost every particular with an unhappy prejudice.[1]

We now behold Johnson for the last time, in his native city, for which he ever retained a warm affection, and which by a sudden apostrophe under the word *Lich*, he introduces with reverence, into his immortal work THE ENGLISH DICTIONARY – *Salve magna parens!*[2] While here, he felt a revival of all the tenderness of filial affection, an instance of which appeared in his ordering the gravestone and inscription, over Elizabeth Blaney,[3] to be substantially and carefully renewed.

1 I shall add one instance only to those on which I have thought it incumbent on me to observe. Talking of Mr Garrick's having signified his willingness to let Johnson have the loan of any of his books to assist him in his edition of Shakspeare; Sir John says (page 444), 'Mr Garrick knew not what risque he ran by this offer. Johnson had so strange a forgetfulness of obligations of this sort, that few who lent him books ever saw them again.' This surely conveys a most unfavourable insinuation, and has been so understood. Sir John mentions the single case of a curious edition of Politian, which he tells us, 'appeared to belong to Pembroke-College, and which, probably, had been considered by Johnson as his own, for upwards of fifty years.' Would it not be fairer to consider this as an inadvertence, and draw no general inference? The truth is, that Johnson was so attentive, that in one of his manuscripts in my possession, he has marked in two columns books borrowed, and books lent.

In Sir John Hawkins's compilation, there are, however, some passages concerning Johnson which have unquestionable merit. One of them I shall transcribe, in justice to a writer whom I have had too much occasion to censure, and to show my fairness as the biographer of my illustrious Friend: 'There was wanting in his conduct and behaviour, that dignity which results from a regular and orderly course of action, and by an irresistible power commands esteem. He could not be said to be a stayed man, nor so to have adjusted in his mind the balance of reason and passion, as to give occasion to say what may be observed of some men, that all they do is just, fit, and right.'[a]

[a] Add: Yet a judicious friend well suggests, 'It might, however, have been added, that such men are often merely just, and rigidly correct, while their hearts are cold and unfeeling; and that Johnson's virtues were of a much higher tone than those of the *stayed, orderly man*, here described.'

2 The following circumstance, mutually to the honour of Johnson and the corporation of his native city, has been communicated to me by the Reverend Dr Vyse, from the Town-Clerk: 'Mr Simpson has now before him a record of the respect and veneration which the Corporation of Lichfield, in the year 1767, had for the merits and learning of Dr Johnson. His father built the corner house in the Market-place, the two fronts of which, towards Market and Broad-market-street, stood upon waste land of the Corporation, under a forty years' lease, which was then expired. On the 15th of August, 1767, at a common-hall of the bailiffs and citizens, it was ordered (and that without any solicitation) that a lease should be granted to Samuel Johnson, Doctor of Laws, of the encroachments at his house, for the term of ninety-nine years, at the old rent, which was five shillings. Of which, as Town-Clerk, Mr Simpson had the honour and pleasure of informing him, and that he was desired to accept it, without paying any fine on the occasion, which lease was afterwards granted, and the Doctor died possessed of this property.'

3 See p. 17.

To Mr Henry White, a young clergyman, with whom he now formed an intimacy, so as to talk to him with great freedom, he mentioned that he could not in general accuse himself of having been an undutiful son. 'Once, indeed (said he), I was disobedient; I refused to attend my father to Uttoxeter-market. Pride was the source of that refusal, and the remembrance of it was painful. A few years ago, I desired to atone for this fault; I went to Uttoxeter in very bad weather, and stood for a considerable time bare-headed in the rain, on the spot where my father's stall used to stand. In contrition I stood, and I hope the penance was expiatory.'

'I told him (says Miss Seward) in one of my latest visits to him, of a wonderful learned pig, which I had seen at Nottingham; and which did all that we have observed exhibited by dogs and horses. The subject amused him. "Then (said he) the pigs are a race unjustly calumniated. *Pig* has, it seems, *not* been wanting to *man*, but *man* to *pig*. We do not allow *time* for his education, we kill him at a year old." Mr Henry White, who was present, observed that if this instance had happened in or before Pope's time, he would not have been justified in instancing the swine as the lowest degree of groveling instinct. Doctor Johnson seemed pleased with the observation, while the person who made it proceeded to remark, that great torture must have been employed, ere the indocility of the animal could have been subdued. – "Certainly (said the Doctor), but (turning to me) how old is your pig?" I told him three years old. "Then (said he) the pig has no cause to complain; he would have been killed the first year if he had not been *educated*, and protracted existence is a good recompense for very considerable degrees of torture." '

As Johnson had now very faint hopes of recovery, and as Mrs Thrale was no longer devoted to him, it might have been supposed that he would naturally have chosen to remain in the comfortable house of his beloved wife's daughter, and end his life where he began it. But there was in him an animated and lofty spirit,[1] and however complicated diseases might depress ordinary mortals, all who saw him, beheld and acknowledged the *invictum animum Catonis*. Such was his intellectual ardour even at this time, that he said to one friend, 'Sir, I look upon every day to be lost in which I do not make a new acquaintance.' And to another, when talking of his illness, 'I will be conquered; I will not capitulate.' And such was his love of London, so high a relish had he of its magnificent extent, and variety of intellectual entertainment, that he languished when absent from it, his mind having become quite luxurious from the long habit of enjoying the metropolis; and therefore although at Lichfield, surrounded with friends, who loved and revered him, and for whom he had a very sincere affection, he still found that such conversation as London affords, could be found no where else. These feelings,

---

1 Mr Burke suggested to me as applicable to Johnson, what Cicero, in his *Cato Major*, says of Appius, '*Intentum enim animum tanquam arcum habebat, nec languescens succumbebat senectuti*'; repeating at the same time, the following noble words in the same passage: '*Ita enim senectus honesta est si se ipsa defendit, si jus suum retinet, si nemini emancipata est, si usque ad extremum vitae spiritum vindicet jus suum.*'

joined probably to some flattering hopes of aid, from the eminent physicians and surgeons in London, who kindly and generously attended him without accepting of fees, made him resolve to return to the capital.

From Lichfield he came to Birmingham, where he passed a few days with his worthy old schoolfellow, Mr Hector, who thus writes to me: 'He was very solicitous with me to recollect some of our most early transactions, and transmit them to him, for I perceived nothing gave him greater pleasure than calling to mind those days of our innocence. I complied with his request, and he only received them a few days before his death. I have transcribed for your inspection, exactly the minutes I wrote to him.' This paper having been found in his repositories after his death, Sir John Hawkins has inserted it entire, and I have made occasional use of it, and other communications from Mr Hector,[a] in the course of this work. I have both visited and corresponded with him since Dr Johnson's death, and by asking a great variety of particulars have obtained additional information. I followed the same mode with the Reverend Dr Taylor, in whose presence I wrote down a good deal of what he could tell: and he, at my request, signed his name, to give it authenticity. It is very rare to find any person who is able to give a distinct account of the life even of one whom he has known intimately, without questions being put to them. My friend, Dr Kippis, has told me, that on this account it is a practice with him to draw out a biographical catechism.

Johnson then proceeded to Oxford, where he was again kindly received by Dr Adams, who was pleased to give me the following account in one of his letters (17th Feb. 1785): 'His last visit was, I believe, to my house, which he left after a stay of four or five days. We had much serious talk together, for which I ought to be the better as long as I live. You will remember some discourse which we had in the summer upon the subject of prayer, and the difficulty of this sort of composition. He reminded me of this, and of my having wished him to try his hand, and to give us a specimen of the style and manner that he approved. He added, that he was now in a right frame of mind, and as he could not possibly employ his time better, he would in earnest set about it. But I find upon enquiry, that no papers of this sort were left behind him, except a few short ejaculatory forms suitable to his present situation.'

Dr Adams had not then received accurate information on this subject; for it has since appeared that various prayers had been composed by him at different periods, which intermingled with pious resolutions, and some short notes of his life, were entitled by him *Prayers and Meditations*, and have in pursuance of

---

[a] Add this note: It is a most agreeable circumstance attending the publication of this Work, that Mr Hector has survived his illustrious school-fellow so many years; that he still retains his health and spirits; and has gratified me with the following acknowledgement: 'I thank you, most sincerely thank you, for the great and long continued entertainment your Life of Dr Johnson has afforded me, and others, of my particular friends.' Mr Hector, besides setting me right as to the verses on a sprig of Myrtle (see note on page 46), has favoured me with two English odes, written by Dr Johnson, at an early period of his life, which will appear in my edition of his Poems.

his earnest requisition in the hopes of doing good, been published, with a judicious well-written Preface, by the Reverend Mr Strahan, to whom he delivered them. This admirable collection, to which I have frequently referred in the course of this work, evinces, beyond all his compositions for the public, and all the eulogies of his friends and admirers, the sincere virtue and piety of Johnson. It proves with unquestionable authenticity, that amidst all his constitutional infirmities, his earnestness to conform his practice to the precepts of Christianity was unceasing, and that he habitually endeavoured to refer every transaction of his life to the will of the Supreme Being.

He arrived in London on the 16th of November, and next day sent to Dr Burney, the following note, which I insert as the last token of his remembrance of this ingenious and amiable man, and as another of the many proofs of the tenderness and benignity of his heart.

'Mr JOHNSON, who came home last night, sends his respects to dear Dr Burney, and all the dear Burneys, little and great.'

To Mr HECTOR, in Birmingham.

DEAR SIR - I did not reach Oxford until Friday morning, and then I sent Francis to see the balloon fly, but could not go myself. I staid at Oxford 'till Tuesday, and then came in the common vehicle easily to London. I am as I was, and having seen Dr Brocklesby, am to ply the squills; but whatever be their efficacy, this world must soon pass away. Let us think seriously on our duty. – I send my kindest respects to dear Mrs Careless; let me have the prayers of both. We have all lived long, and must soon part. GOD have mercy on us, for the sake of our Lord JESUS CHRIST. Amen. I am, &c.

SAM. JOHNSON.

London, Nov. 17, 1784.

His correspondence with me after his letter on the subject of my settling in London, shall now so far as is proper, be produced in one series.

July 26, he wrote to me from Ashbourne – On the 14th I came to Lichfield, and found every body glad enough to see me. On the 20th, I came hither, and found a house half built, of very uncomfortable appearance, but my own room has not been altered. That a man worn with diseases, in his seventy-second or third year, should condemn part of his remaining life to pass among ruins and rubbish, and that no inconsiderable part, appears to me very strange. – I know that your kindness makes you impatient to know the state of my health, in which I cannot boast of much improvement. I came through the journey without much inconvenience, but when I attempt self-motion I find my legs weak, and my breath very short; this day I have been much disordered. I have no company; the Doctor is busy in his fields, and goes to bed at nine, and his whole system is so different from mine, that we seem formed for different elements; I have, therefore, all my amusement to seek within myself.

Having written to him in bad spirits, a letter filled with dejection and fretfulness, and at the same time expressing anxious apprehensions concerning him, on account of a dream which had disturbed me; his answer was chiefly in terms of reproach, for a supposed charge of 'affecting discontent, and indulging the vanity of complaint.' It however proceeded, 'Write to me often, and write like a man. I consider your fidelity and tenderness as a great part of the comforts which are yet left me, and sincerely wish we could be nearer to each other. . . . – My dear friend, life is very short and very uncertain; let us spend it as well as we can. – My worthy neighbour, Allen, is dead. Love me as well as you can. Pay my respects to dear Mrs Boswell. – Nothing ailed me at that time; let your superstition at last have an end.'

Feeling very soon, that the manner in which he had written might hurt me, he in two days after, July 28, wrote to me again, giving me an account of his suffering, after which follows: 'Before this letter you will have had one which I hope you will not take amiss; for it contains only truth, and that truth kindly intended. . . . *Spartam quam nactus es orna*; make the most and best of your lot, and compare yourself not with the few that are above you, but with the multitudes which are below you. . . . Go steadily forward with lawful business or honest diversions. "*Be* (as Temple says of the Dutchmen) *well when you are not ill, and pleased when you are not angry*," . . . This may seem but an ill return for your tenderness; but I mean it well, for I love you with great ardour and sincerity. Pay my respects to dear Mrs Boswell, and teach the young ones to love me.'

I unfortunately was so much indisposed during a considerable part of the year, that it was not, or at least I thought it was not, in my power to write to my illustrious friend as formerly, or without expressing such complaints as offended him. Having conjured him not to do me the injustice of charging me with affectation, I was with much regret long silent. His last letter to me then came, and affected me very tenderly:

To JAMES BOSWELL, Esq.

DEAR SIR – I have this summer sometimes amended and sometimes relapsed, but upon the whole, have lost ground very much. My legs are extremely weak, and my breath very short, and the water is now increasing upon me. In this uncomfortable state your letters used to relieve; what is the reason that I have them no longer? Are you sick, or are you sullen? Whatever be the reason, if it be less than necessity, drive it away, and of the short life that we have, make the best use for yourself and for your friends. . . . I am sometimes afraid that your omission to write has some real cause, and shall be glad to know that you are not sick, and that nothing ill has befallen dear Mrs Boswell, or any of your family. I am, Sir, your, &c.

SAM. JOHNSON.

Lichfield, Nov. 3, 1784.

Yet it was not a little painful to me to find, that in a paragraph of this letter, which I have omitted, he still persevered in arraigning me as before, which was strange in him who had so much experience of what I suffered. I however wrote to him two as kind letters as I could; the last of which came too late to be read by him, for his illness increased more rapidly upon him than I had apprehended; but I had the consolation of being informed that he spoke of me on his death-bed, with affection, and I look forward with humble hope of renewing our friendship in a better world.

I now relieve the readers of this work from any farther personal notice of its author, who if he should be thought to have obtruded himself too much upon their attention, requests them to consider the peculiar plan of his biographical undertaking.

Soon after Johnson's return to the metropolis, both the asthma and dropsy became more violent and distressful. He had for some time kept a journal in Latin, of the state of his illness, and the remedies which he used, under the title of *Aegri Ephemeris*, which he began on the 6th of July, but continued it no longer than the 8th of November; finding, I suppose, that it was a mournful and unavailing register. It is in my possession; and is written with great care and accuracy.

Still his love of literature[1] did not fail. He drew out and gave to his friend Mr John Nichols, what perhaps he alone could have done, a list of the authors of the *Universal History*, mentioning their several shares in that work. It has, according to his direction, been deposited in the British Museum, and is printed in the *Gentleman's Magazine* for December, 1784.

---

1 It is truly wonderful to consider the extent and constancy of Johnson's literary ardor, notwithstanding the melancholy which clouded and embittered his existence. Besides the numerous and various works which he executed, he had at different times formed schemes of a great many more, of which the following catalogue was given by him to Mr Langton, and by that gentleman presented to his Majesty.

DIVINITY.

A small book of precepts and directions for piety: the hint taken from the directions in Morton's exercise.

PHILOSOPHY, HISTORY, and LITERATURE in general.

History of Criticism, as it relates to judging of authors, from Aristotle to the present age. An account of the rise and improvements of that art; of the different opinions of authors, ancient and modern.

Translation of the History of Herodian.

New edition of Fairfax's Translation of Tasso, with notes, glossary, &c.

Chaucer, a new edition of him, from manuscripts and old editions, with various readings, conjectures, remarks on his language, and the changes it had undergone from the earliest times to his age, and from his to the present: with notes explanatory of customs, &c. and references to Boccace, and other authors from whom he has borrowed, with an account of the liberties he has taken in telling the stories; his life, and an exact etymological glossary.

Aristotle's *Rhetoric*, a translation of it into English.

During his sleepless nights he amused himself by translating into Latin verse, from the Greek, many of the epigrams in the *Anthologia*. These translations, with some other poems by him in Latin, he gave to his friend Mr Langton,

---

A Collection of Letters, translated from the modern writers, with some account of the several authors.

Oldham's Poems, with notes historical and critical.

Roscommon's Poems, with notes.

Lives of the Philosophers, written with a polite air, in such a manner as may divert as well as instruct.

History of the Heathen Mythology, with an explication of the fables, both allegorical and historical; with references to the poets.

History of the State of Venice, in a compendious manner.

Aristotle's *Ethics*, an English translation of them with notes.

Geographical Dictionary from the French.

Hierocles upon Pythagoras, translated into English, perhaps with notes. This is done by Norris.

A book of Letters upon all kinds of subjects.

Claudian, a new edition of his works, *cum notis variorum*, in the manner of Burman.

Tully's *Tusculan Questions*, a translation of them.

Tully's *De Natura Deorum*, a translation of those books.

Benzo's *New History of the New World*, to be translated.

Machiavel's *History of Florence*, to be translated.

History of the Revival of Learning in Europe, containing an account of whatever contributed to the restoration of literature; such as controversies, printing, the destruction of the Greek empire, the encouragement of great men, with the lives of the most eminent patrons and most eminent early professors of all kinds of learning in different countries.

A body of chronology, in verse, with historical notes.

A table of the *Spectators*, *Tatlers*, and *Guardians*, distinguished by figures into six degrees of value, with notes giving the reasons of preference or degradation.

A Collection of Letters from English authors, with a preface giving some account of the writers; with reasons for selection, and criticism upon styles; remarks on each letter, if needful.

A collection of Proverbs from various languages. Jan. 6, 1753.

A Dictionary to the Common Prayer, in imitation of Calmet's *Dictionary of the Bible*. March, 1752.

A Collection of Stories and Examples, like those of Valerius Maximus. Jan. 10, 1753.

From Aelian, a volume of select Stories, perhaps from others. Jan. 28, 1753.

Collection of Travels, Voyages, Adventures, and Descriptions of Countries.

Dictionary of Ancient History and Mythology.

Treatise on the Study of Polite Literature, containing the history of learning, directions for editions, commentaries, &c.

Maxims, Characters, and Sentiments, after the manner of Bruyère, collected out of ancient authors, particularly the Greek, with Apophthegms.

Classical Miscellanies, Select Translations from ancient Greek and Latin authors.

Lives of illustrious persons, as well of the active as the learned, in imitation of Plutarch.

Judgement of the learned upon English authors.

Poetical Dictionary of the English tongue.

Considerations upon the present state of London.

who, having added a few notes, sold them to the booksellers for a small sum, to be given to some of Johnson's relations, which was accordingly done; and they are printed in the collection of his works.

Collection of Epigrams, with notes and observations.
Observations on the English language, relating to words, phrases, and modes of Speech.
Minutiae Literariae, Miscellaneous reflections, criticisms, emendations, notes.
History of the Constitution.
Comparison of Philosophical and Christian Morality, by sentences collected from the moralists and fathers.
Plutarch's *Lives* in English, with notes.

POETRY and works of IMAGINATION.

Hymn to Ignorance.
The Palace of Sloth – a vision.
Coluthus, to be translated.
Prejudice – a poetical essay.
The Palace of Nonsense – a vision.

Johnson's extraordinary facility of composition, when he shook off his constitutional indolence, and resolutely sat down to write, is admirably described by Mr Courtenay, in his *Poetical Review*, which I have several times quoted:

> While through life's maze he sent a piercing view,
> His mind expansive to the object grew.
> With various stores of erudition fraught,
> The lively image, the deep-searching thought,
> Slept in repose; – but when the moment press'd,
> The bright ideas stood at once confess'd;
> Instant his genius sped its vigorous rays,
> And o'er the letter'd world diffus'd a blaze:
> As womb'd with fire the cloud electric flies,
> And calmly o'er th' horizon seems to rise;
> Touch'd by the pointed steel, the lightning flows,
> And all th' expanse with rich effulgence glows.

We shall in vain endeavour to know with exact precision every production of Johnson's pen. He owned to me, that he had written about forty sermons; but as I understood that he had given or sold them to different persons, who were to preach them as their own, he did not consider himself at liberty to acknowledge them. Would those who were thus aided by him, who are still alive, and the friends of those who are dead, fairly inform the world, it would be obligingly gratifying a reasonable curiosity, to which there should, I think, now be no objection. – I have lying before me, in his hand-writing, a fragment of twenty quarto leaves, of a translation into English of Sallust, *De Bello Catilinario*. When it was done I have no notion; but it seems to have no very superior merit to mark it as his. Besides those publications, which with all my chronological care I have ascertained in the course of this work, I am satisfied, from internal evidence, to admit also as genuine the following:

Considerations on the Case of Dr Trapp's Sermons,[†] published in 1739, in the *Gentleman's Magazine*. It is a very ingenious defence of the right of abridging an author's work, without being held as infringing his property. This is one of the nicest questions in the *Law of Literature*; and I cannot help thinking, that the

A very erroneous notion has circulated as to Johnson's deficiency in the knowledge of the Greek language, partly owing to the modesty with which, from knowing how much there was to be learnt, he used to mention his own comparative acquisitions. When Mr Cumberland[1] talked to him of the Greek fragments which are so well illustrated in *The Observer*, and of the Greek dramatists in general, he candidly acknowledged his insufficiency in that particular branch of Greek literature. Yet it may be said, that though not a great, he was a good Greek scholar. Mr Burney,[a] who is universally acknowledged by the best judges, to be one of the few men of this age who are very eminent for their

---

   indulgence of abridging is often exceedingly injurious to authors and booksellers, and should in very few cases be permitted.[b]

Dedication for Mrs Lennox to the Earl of Middlesex, of her *Female Quixote*, in 1762.[†]

Preface to the Catalogue of the Artists' Exhibition in 1762.[†]

Preface to Baretti's 'Easy Lessons in Italian and English', in 1775.[†]

But, though it has been confidently ascribed to him, I cannot allow that he wrote a Dedication to both Houses of Parliament of a book entitled *The Evangelical History Harmonized*. He was no *croaker*; no declaimer against *the times*. He would not have written, 'That we are fallen upon an age in which corruption is not barely universal, is universally confessed.' Nor, 'Rapine preys on the public without opposition, and perjury betrays it without inquiry.' Nor would he, to excite a speedy reformation, have conjured up such phantoms of terror as these: 'A few years longer, and perhaps all endeavours will be in vain. We may be swallowed by an earthquake; we may be delivered to our enemies.' This is not Johnsonian.

There are indeed, in this Dedication, several sentences constructed upon the model of those of Johnson. But the imitation of the form, without the spirit of his style, has been so general, that this of itself is not sufficient evidence. Even our news-paper writers aspire to it. In an account of the funeral of Edwin the comedian, in *The Diary* of Nov. 9, 1790, that son of drollery is thus described: 'A man who had so often cheered the sullenness of vacancy, and suspended the approaches of sorrow.' And in the *Dublin Evening Post*, August 16, 1791, there is the following paragraph: 'It is a singular circumstance, that in a city like this, containing 200,000 people, there are three months in the year during which no place of public amusement is open. Long vacation is here a vacation from pleasure, as well as business; nor is there any mode of passing the listless evenings of declining summer, but in the riots of a tavern, or the stupidity of a coffee-house.'

I have not thought it necessary to specify every copy of verses written by Johnson, it being my intention to publish an authentic edition of all his Poetry, with Notes.

1 Mr Cumberland assures me, that he was always treated with great courtesy by Dr Johnson, who, in his *Letters to Mrs Thrale*, Vol. ii, p. 68, thus speaks of that learned, ingenious, and accomplished gentleman: 'The want of company is an inconvenience: but Mr Cumberland is a million.'

[a] For 'Mr Burney', read 'Dr Charles Burney the younger'.

---

[b] Add : At any rate, to prevent difficult and uncertain discussion, and give an absolute security to authors in the property of their labours, no abridgement whatever should be permitted, till after the expiration of such a number of years as the Legislature may be pleased to fix.

skill in that noble language, has assured me, that Johnson could give a Greek word for almost every English one; and that although not sufficiently conversant in the niceties of the language, he upon some occasions discovered, even in these, a considerable degree of critical acumen. Mr Dalzell, Professor of Greek at Edinburgh, whose skill in it is unquestionable, mentioned to me, in very liberal terms, the impression which was made upon him by Johnson, in a conversation which they had in London concerning that language. As Johnson, therefore, was undoubtedly one of the first Latin scholars in modern times, let us not deny to his fame some additional splendour from Greek.

I shall now fulfil my promise of exhibiting specimens of various sorts of imitations of Johnson's style.

In the *Transactions of the Royal Irish Academy*, 1787, there is an 'Essay on the Style of Dr Samuel Johnson', by the Rev. Robert Burrowes, whose respect for the great object of his criticism[1] is thus evinced in the concluding paragraph: 'I have singled him out from the whole body of English writers, because his universally acknowledged beauties would be most apt to induce imitation; and I have treated rather on his faults than his perfections, because an essay might comprize all the observations I could make upon his faults, while volumes would not be sufficient for a treatise on his perfections.'

Mr Burrowes has analysed the composition of Johnson, and pointed out its peculiarities with much acuteness; and I would recommend a careful perusal of his Essay to those, who being captivated by the union of perspicuity and splendour which the writings of Johnson contain, without having a sufficient portion of his vigour of mind, may be in danger of becoming bad copyists of his manner. I however cannot but observe, and I observe it to his credit, that this learned gentleman has himself caught no mean degree of the expansion and harmony which, independent of all other circumstances, characterise the sentences of Johnson. Thus, in the Preface to the volume in which his Essay appears, we find, 'If it be said that in societies of this sort, too much attention is frequently bestowed on subjects barren and speculative, it may be answered, that no one science is so little connected with the rest, as not to afford many principles whose use may extend considerably beyond the science to which they primarily belong; and that no proposition is so purely theoretical as to be totally incapable of being applied to practical purposes. There is no apparent connection between duration and the cycloidal arch, the properties of which duly attended to, have furnished us with our best regulated methods of measuring time: and he who has made himself master of the nature and affections of the logarithmic curve, is not aware that he has advanced considerably towards ascertaining the proportionable density of the air at its various distances from the surface of the earth.'

---

1 We must smile at a little inaccuracy of metaphor in the Preface to the *Transactions*, which is written by Mr Burrowes. The *critic of the style of Johnson* having, with a just zeal for literature, observed, that the whole nation are called on to exert themselves, afterwards says: 'They are *called on* by every *tye* which can have a laudable influence on the heart of man.'

The ludicrous imitators of Johnson's style are innumerable. Their general method is to accumulate hard words, without considering, that although he was fond of introducing them occasionally, there is not a single sentence in all his writings where they are crowded together, as in the first verse of the following imaginary Ode by him to Mrs Thrale,[1] which appeared in the newspapers:

> *Cervisial coctor's viduate* dame,
> *Opin'st* thou this gigantic frame,
>   *Procumbing* at thy shrine:
> Shall, *catenated* by thy charms,
> A captive in thy *ambient* arms,
>   *Perennially* be thine?

This, and a thousand other such attempts, are totally unlike the original, which the writers imagined they were turning into ridicule. There is not similarity enough for burlesque, or even for caricature.

Mr COLMAN, in his 'Prose on several Occasions', has 'A Letter from LEXIPHANES; containing Proposals for a *Glossary* or *Vocabulary* of the *Vulgar Tongue*: intended as a supplement to a larger DICTIONARY.' It is evidently meant as a sportive sally of ridicule on Johnson, whose style is thus imitated, without being grossly overcharged. 'It is easy to foresee, that the idle and illiterate will complain that I have increased their labours by endeavouring to diminish them; and that I have explained what is more easy by what is more difficult – *ignotum per ignotius*. I expect, on the other hand, the liberal acknowledgements of the learned. He who is buried in scholastic retirement, secluded from the assemblies of the gay, and remote from the circles of the polite, will at once comprehend the definitions, and be grateful for such a

---

1 Johnson's wishing to unite himself with this rich widow was much talked of; but I believe without foundation. The report, however, gave occasion for a poem, not without characteristical merit, entitled, 'Ode to Mrs Thrale, by Samuel Johnson, LL.D. on their supposed approaching Nuptials': printed for Mr Faulder, in Bond-street.[a]

[a] Add the following to this note: I shall quote as a specimen, the first three stanzas:

> If e'er my fingers touch'd the lyre,
>   In satire fierce, in pleasure gay;
> Shall not my THRALIA's smiles inspire?
>   Shall SAM refuse the sportive lay?
>
> My dearest Lady! view your slave,
>   Behold him as your very *Scrub*;
> Eager to write as author grave,
>   Or govern well, the brewing-tub.
>
> To rich felicity thus raised,
>   My bosom glows with amorous fire,
> Porter no longer shall be praised,
>   'Tis I MYSELF am *Thrale's Entire*.

seasonable and necessary elucidation of his mother tongue.' Annexed to this letter is a short specimen of the work, thrown together in a vague and desultory manner, not even adhering to alphabetical concatenation.[1]

The serious imitators of Johnson's style, whether intentionally or by the imperceptible effect of its strength and animation, are, as I have had already occasion to observe, so many, that I might introduce quotations from a great proportion of the writers in our language since he appeared. I shall point out only the following.

WILLIAM ROBERTSON, D.D.

'In other parts of the globe, man, in his rudest state, appears as lord of the creation, giving law to various tribes of animals which he has tamed and reduced to subjection. The Tartar follows his prey on the horse which he has reared, or tends his numerous herds, which furnish him both with food and clothing; the Arab has rendered the camel docile, and avails himself of its persevering strength; the Laplander has formed the reindeer to be subservient to his will; and even the people of Kamschatka have trained their dogs to labour. This command over the inferior creatures is one of the noblest prerogatives of man, and among the greatest efforts of his wisdom and power. Without this, his dominion is incomplete. He is a monarch who has no subjects; a master without servants; and must perform every operation by the strength of his own arm.'[2]

EDWARD GIBBON, Esq.

'Of all our passions and appetites, the love of power is of the most imperious and unsociable nature, since the pride of one man requires the submission of the multitude. In the tumult of civil discord the laws of society lose their force, and their place is seldom supplied by those of humanity. The ardour of contention, the pride of victory, the despair of success, the memory of past injuries, and the fear of future dangers, all contribute to inflame the mind, and to silence the voice of pity.'[3]

---

1 *Higgledy-piggledy* – Conglomeration and confusion.
   Hodge-podge – A culinary mixture of heterogeneous ingredients; applied
      metaphorically to all discordant combinations.
   Tit-for-Tat – Adequate retaliation.
   Shilly Shally – Hesitation and irresolution.
   Fee! fa! fum! – Gigantic intonations.
   Rigmarole – Discourse, incoherent and rhapsodical.
   Crincum-crancum – Lines of irregularity and involution.
   Ding-dong – Tintinabulary chimes, used metaphorically to signify dispatch and
      vehemence.
2 *History of America*, Vol. I, quarto, p. 332.
3 *Decline and Fall of the Roman Empire*, Vol. I, Chap. IV.

Miss BURNEY.

'My family mistaking ambition for honour, and rank for dignity, have long planned a splendid connection for me, to which, though my invariable repugnance has stopped any advances, their wishes and their views immoveably adhere. I am but too certain they will now listen to no other. I dread therefore to make a trial where I despair of success; I know not how to risk a prayer with those who may silence me by a command.'[1]

Reverend Mr NARES.[2]

'In an enlightened and improving age, much perhaps is not to be apprehended from the inroads of mere caprice; at such a period it will generally be perceived, that needless irregularity is the worst of all deformities, and that nothing is so truly elegant in language as the simplicity of unviolated analogy. – Rules will therefore be observed, so far as they are known and acknowledged: but, at the same time, the desire of improvement having been once excited will not remain inactive; and its efforts, unless assisted by knowledge, as much as they are prompted by zeal, will not unfrequently be found pernicious; so that the very persons whose intention it is to perfect the instrument of reason, will deprave and disorder it unknowingly. At such a time, then, it becomes peculiarly necessary that the analogy of language should be fully examined and understood; that its rules should be carefully laid down; and that it should be clearly known how much it contains, which being already right should be defended from change and violation: how much it has that demands amendment; and how much that, for fear of greater inconveniences, must perhaps be left unaltered, though irregular.'

A distinguished author in *The Mirror,*[3] a periodical paper published at Edinburgh, has imitated Johnson very closely. Thus, in No. 16 – 'The effects of the return of spring have been frequently remarked as well in relation to the human mind as to the animal and vegetable world. The reviving power of this season has been traced from the fields to the herds that inhabit them, and from the lower classes of beings up to man. Gladness and joy are described as prevailing through universal Nature, animating the low of the cattle, the carol of the birds, and the pipe of the shepherd.'

---

1 *Cecilia*, Book VII, Chap. I.

2 The passage which I quote is taken from that gentleman's 'ELEMENTS OF ORTHOEPY; containing a distinct View of the whole Analogy of the ENGLISH LANGUAGE, so far as it relates to *Pronunciation, Accent, and Quantity*', London, 1784. I beg leave to offer my particular acknowledgements to the author of a work of uncommon merit and great utility. I know no book which contains, in the same compass, more learning, polite literature, sound sense, accuracy of arrangement, and perspicuity of expression.

3 That collection was presented to Dr Johnson I believe by its authors; and I heard him speak very well of it.

The Reverend Dr KNOX, master of Tunbridge school, appears to have the *imitari aveo* of Johnson's style perpetually in his mind; and to his assiduous study of it we may partly ascribe the extensive popularity of his writings.[1]

In his *Essays, Moral and Literary*, No. 3, we find the following passage: 'The polish of external grace may indeed be deferred till the approach of manhood. When solidity is obtained by pursuing the modes prescribed by our fore-fathers, then may the file be used. The firm substance will bear attrition, and the lustre then acquired will be durable.'

There is, however, one in No. 11, which is blown up into such tumidity as to be truly ludicrous. The writer means to tell us, that Members of Parliament, who have run in debt by extravagance, will sell their votes to avoid an arrest,[2] which he thus expresses: 'They who build houses and collect costly pictures and furniture, with the money of an honest artisan or mechanic, will be very glad of emancipation from the hands of a bailiff, by a sale of their senatorial suffrage.'

But I think the most perfect imitation of Johnson is a professed one, entitled 'A Criticism on Gray's Elegy in a Country Churchyard', said to be written by Mr YOUNG, Professor of Greek at Glasgow, and of which let him have the credit, unless a better title can be shown. It has not only the peculiarities of Johnson's style, but that very species of literary discussion and illustration for which he was eminent. Having already quoted so much from others, I shall refer the curious to this performance, with an assurance of much entertainment.

Yet whatever merit there may be in any imitations of Johnson's style, every good judge must see that they are obviously different from the original; for all of them are either deficient in its force, or overloaded with its peculiarities; and the powerful sentiment to which it is suited is not to be found.

Johnson's affection for his departed relations seemed to grow warmer as he approached nearer to the time when he might hope to see them again. It

---

1 It were to be wished, that he had imitated that great man in every respect, and had not followed the example of Dr Adam Smith, in ungraciously attacking his venerable Alma Mater, Oxford.[a]

[a] Add: It must, however, be observed, that he is much less to blame than Smith: he only objects to certain particulars; Smith to the whole institution; though indebted for much of his learning to an exhibition which he enjoyed for many years at Baliol College. Neither of them, however, will do any hurt to the noblest university in the world. While I animadvert on what appears to me exceptionable in some of the works of Dr Knox, I cannot refuse due praise to others of his productions; particularly his sermons, and to the spirit with which he maintains, against presumptuous heretics, the consolatory doctrines peculiar to the Christian Revelation. This he has done in a manner equally strenuous and conciliating. Neither ought I to omit mentioning a remarkable instance of his candour. Notwithstanding the wide difference of our opinions, upon the important subject of University education, in a letter to me concerning this Work, he thus expresses himself: 'I thank you for the very great entertainment your Life of Johnson gives me. It is a most valuable work. Yours is a new species of biography. Happy for Johnson, that he had so able a recorder of his wit and wisdom.'

2 Dr Knox, in his *Moral and Literary Abstraction*, may be excused for not knowing the political regulations of his country. No senator can be in the hands of a bailiff.

probably appeared to him that he should upbraid himself with unkind inattention, were he to leave the world, without having paid a tribute of respect to their memory.

To Mr GREEN, Apothecary at Lichfield.

DEAR SIR — I have enclosed the Epitaph[a] for my Father, Mother, and Brother, to be all engraved on the large size, and laid in the middle aisle in St Michael's church, which I request the clergyman and church-wardens to permit.

The first care must be to find the exact place of interment, that the stone may protect the bodies. Then let the stone be deep, massy, and hard; and do not let the difference of ten pounds, or more, defeat our purpose.

I have enclosed ten pounds, and Mrs Porter will pay you ten more, which I gave her for the same purpose. What more is wanted shall be sent; and I beg that all possible haste may be made, for I wish to have it done while I am yet alive. Let me know, dear Sir, that you receive this. I am, Sir, your most humble servant,

SAM. JOHNSON.

Dec. 2, 1784.

To Mrs LUCY PORTER, in Lichfield.

DEAR MADAM — I am very ill, and desire your prayers. I have sent Mr Green the Epitaph, and a power to call on you for ten pounds.

I laid this summer a stone over Tetty, in the chapel of Bromley in Kent. The inscription is in Latin, of which this is the English. [Here a translation.]

That this is done, I thought it fit that you should know. What care will be taken of us, who can tell? May GOD pardon and bless us, for JESUS CHRIST's sake. I am, &c.

SAM. JOHNSON.

Dec. 2, 1784.

My readers are now at last to behold SAMUEL JOHNSON preparing himself for that doom from which the most exalted powers afford no exemption to man. Death had always been to him an object of terror; so that though by no means happy, he still clung to life with an eagerness at which many have wondered. At any time when he was ill, he was very much pleased to be told that he

---

[a] No man understood that species of composition better than Johnson. I should have mentioned in 1773, his Epitaph on Mrs Bell, wife of his friend JOHN BELL, Esq. It is printed in his Works, as well as the above.

Second Edition. This note omitted in this place, and put on the word 'Preface', page 357 thus: He, however, wrote, or partly wrote, an Epitaph on Mrs Bell, wife of his friend John Bell, Esq., brother of the Rev. Dr Bell, Prebendary of Westminster, which is printed in his works. It is in English prose, and has so little of his manner, that I did not believe he had any hand in it, till I was satisfied of the fact by the authority of Mr Bell.

looked better. An ingenious member of the *Eumelian Club*[1] informs me, that upon one occasion when he said to him that he saw health returning to his cheek, Johnson seized him by the hand and exclaimed, 'Sir, you are one of the kindest friends I ever had.'

His own state of his views of futurity will appear truly rational, and may perhaps impress the unthinking with seriousness.

You know (says he)[2] I never thought confidence with respect to futurity any part of the character of a brave, a wise, or a good man. Bravery has no place where it can avail nothing; wisdom impresses strongly the conscious-ness of those faults, of which it is perhaps itself an aggravation; and goodness, always wishing to be better, and imputing every deficience to criminal negligence, and every fault to voluntary corruption, never dares to suppose the condition of forgiveness fulfilled, nor what is wanting in the crime supplied by penitence.

This is the state of the best; but what must be the condition of him whose heart will not suffer him to rank himself among the best, or among the good? Such must be his dread of the approaching trial, as will leave him little attention to the opinion of those whom he is leaving for ever; and the serenity that is not felt, it can be no virtue to feign.

His great fear of death, and the strange dark manner in which Sir John Hawkins imparts the uneasiness which he expressed on account of offences with which he charged himself, may give occasion to injurious suspicions, as if there had been something of more than ordinary criminality weighing upon his conscience. On that account, therefore, as well as from the regard to truth which he inculcated,[3] I am to mention (with all possible respect and delicacy however), that his conduct after he came to London, and had associated with Savage and others, was not so strictly virtuous, in one respect, as when he was a younger man It was well known, that his amorous inclinations were uncommonly strong and impetuous. He owned to many of his friends, that he used to take women of the town to taverns, and hear them relate their history. – In short, it must not be concealed, that like many other good and pious men, amongst whom we may place the Apostle Paul, upon his own authority, Johnson was not free from propensities which were ever 'warring against the law of his mind.' – and that in his combats with them, he was sometimes overcome.

Here let the profane and licentious pause; – let them not thoughtlessly say that Johnson was an *hypocrite*, or that his *principles* were not firm, because his *practice* was not uniformly conformable to what he professed.

---

1 A Club in London, founded by the learned and ingenious physician, Dr Ash, in honour of whose name it was called Eumelian, from the Greek Εὐμέλιας; though it was warmly contended, and even put to a vote, that it should have the more obvious appellation of *Fraxinean*, from the Latin.

2 *Letters to Mrs Thrale*, Vol. ii, p. 350.

3 See what he said to Mr Malone, p. 776.

Let the question be considered independent of moral and religious association; and no man will deny that thousands, in many instances, act against conviction. Is a prodigal, for example, an hypocrite, when he owns he is satisfied that his extravagance will bring him to ruin and misery? We are *sure* he *believes* it; but immediate inclination, strengthened by indulgence, prevails over that belief in influencing his conduct. Why then shall credit be refused to the *sincerity* of those who acknowledge their persuasion of moral and religious duty, yet sometimes fail of living as it requires? I heard Dr Johnson once observe, 'There is something noble in publishing truth, though it condemns one's self.'[1] And one who said in his presence, 'he had no notion of people being in earnest in their good professions, whose practice was not suitable to them,' was thus reprimanded by him: 'Sir, are you so grossly ignorant of human nature as not to know that a man may be very sincere in good principles, without having good practice?'[2]

But let no man encourage or soothe himself in 'presumptuous sin', from knowing that Johnson was sometimes hurried into indulgences which he thought criminal. I have exhibited this circumstance as a shade in so great a character, both from my sacred love of truth, and to show that he was not so weakly scrupulous as he has been represented by those who imagine that the sins of which a deep sense was upon his mind, were merely such little venial trifles as pouring milk into his tea on Good-Friday. His understanding will be defended by my statement, if his consistency of conduct be in some degree impaired. But what wise man would, for momentary gratifications, deliberately subject himself to suffer such uneasiness as we find was experienced by Johnson in reviewing his conduct as compared with his notion of the ethics of the gospel? Let the following passages be kept in remembrance: 'O GOD, giver and preserver of all life, by whose power I was created, and by whose providence I am sustained, look down upon me with tenderness and mercy; grant that I may not have been created to be finally destroyed; that I may not be preserved to add wickedness to wickedness.'[3] – 'O LORD, let me not sink into total depravity; look down upon me, and rescue me at last from the captivity of sin.'[4] – 'Almighty and most merciful Father, who hast continued my life from year to year, grant that by longer life I may become less desirous of sinful pleasures, and more careful of eternal happiness.'[5] – 'Let not my years be multiplied to increase my guilt; but as

---

1 *Journal of a Tour to the Hebrides*, 3d edit. p. 209.[a]

a

To this note add: On the same subject, in his Letter to Mrs Thrale, dated Nov. 29, 1783, he makes the following just observation: 'Life, to be worthy of a rational being, must be always in progression; we must always purpose to do more or better than in time past. The mind is enlarged and elevated by mere purposes, though they end as they began, by airy contemplation. We compare and judge, though we do not practise.'

2 *Journal of a Tour to the Hebrides*, 3d edit. p. 374.

3 *Prayers and Meditations*, p. 47.

4 Ibid. p. 68.

5 Ibid. p. 84.

my age advances, let me become more pure in my thoughts, more regular in my desires, and more obedient to thy laws.'[1] – 'Forgive, O merciful LORD, whatever I have done contrary to thy laws. Give me such a sense of my wickedness as may produce true contrition and effectual repentance; so that when I shall be called into another state, I may be received among the sinners to whom sorrow and reformation have obtained pardon, for JESUS CHRIST's sake. Amen.'[2]

Such was the distress of mind, such the penitence of Johnson in his hours of privacy, and in his devout approaches to his Maker. His *sincerity* therefore must appear to every candid mind unquestionable.

It is of essential consequence to keep in view, that there was in this excellent man's conduct no false principle of *commutation*, no *deliberate* indulgence in sin, in consideration of a counterbalance of duty. His offending, and his repenting, were distinct and separate:[3] and when we consider his almost unexampled attention to truth, his inflexible integrity, his constant piety, who will dare to 'cast a stone' at him? Besides, let it never be forgotten, that he cannot be charged with any offence indicating badness of *heart*, any thing dishonest, base, or malignant; but that, on the contrary, he was charitable in an extraordinary degree: so that even in one of his own rigid judgements of himself (Easter-eve, 1781), while he says, 'I have corrected no external habits'; he is obliged to own, 'I hope that since my last communion I have advanced by pious reflections in my submission to GOD, and my benevolence to man.'[4]

I am conscious that this is the most difficult and dangerous part of my biographical work, and I cannot but be very anxious concerning it. I trust that I have got through it, preserving at once my regard to truth – to my friend – and to the interests of virtue and religion. Nor can I apprehend that more harm can ensue from the knowledge of the irregularity of Johnson, guarded as I have stated it, than from knowing that Addison and Parnell were intemperate in the use of wine; which Johnson himself, in his Lives of those celebrated writers, and pious men, has not forborne to record.

It is not my intention to give a very minute detail of the particulars of Johnson's remaining days, of whom it was now evident, that the crisis was fast approaching, when he must '*die like men, and fall like one of the Princes*'. Yet it will be instructive, as well as gratifying to the curiosity of my readers, to record a few circumstances, on the authenticity of which they may perfectly rely, as I have been at the utmost pains to obtain them from the best authority.

Dr Heberden, Dr Brocklesby, Dr Warren, and Dr Butter, physicians, generously attended him, without accepting of any fees, as did Mr Cruikshank, surgeon; and all that could be done from professional skill and ability

---

1 *Prayers and Meditations.* p. 120.

2 Ibid. p. 130.

3 Dr Johnson related, with an earnestness of approbation, a story of a gentleman, who, in an impulse of passion, overcame the virtue of a young woman. When she said to him, 'I am afraid we have done wrong!' he answered, 'Yes, we have done wrong; – for I would not *debauch her mind.*'

4 *Prayers and Meditations*, p. 192.

was tried, to prolong a life so truly valuable. He himself, indeed, having on account of his very bad constitution been perpetually applying himself to medical inquiries, united his own efforts with those of the gentlemen who attended him; and imagining that the dropsical collection of water which oppressed him, might be drawn off, by making incisions in his body, he, with his usual resolute defiance of pain, cut deep, when he thought that his surgeon had done it too tenderly.[1]

About eight or ten days before his death, when Dr Brocklesby paid him his morning visit, he seemed very low and desponding, and said, 'I have been as a dying man all night.' He then emphatically broke out, in the words of Shakspeare,

> Can'st thou not minister to a mind diseas'd?
> Pluck from the memory a rooted sorrow?
> Raze out the written troubles of the brain?
> And with some sweet oblivious antidote,
> Cleanse the full bosom of that perilous stuff,
> Which weighs upon the heart.

To which Dr Brocklesby readily answered from the same great poet

> therein the patient
> Must minister unto himself.

Johnson expressed himself much satisfied with the application.

On another day after this, when talking on the subject of prayer, Dr Brocklesby repeated from Juvenal,

> *Orandum est ut sit mens sana in corpore sano,*

and so on to the end of the tenth satire; but in running it quickly over he happened in the line

> *Qui spatium vitae extremum inter munera ponat,*

to pronounce *supremum* for *extremum*; at which Johnson's critical ear instantly took offence, and discoursing vehemently on the unmetrical effect of such a lapse, he showed himself as full as ever of the spirit of the grammarian.

Having no near relations, it had been for some time Johnson's intention to make a liberal provision for his faithful servant, Mr Francis Barber, whom he looked upon as particularly under his protection, and whom he had all along treated truly as an humble friend. Having asked Dr Brocklesby what would be a proper annuity to bequeath to a favourite servant, and being answered that it

---

1 This bold experiment, Sir John Hawkins has related in such a manner as to suggest a charge against Johnson of intentionally hastening his end; a charge so very inconsistent with his character in every respect, that it is injurious even to refute it, as Sir John has thought it necessary to do. It is evident, that what Johnson did in hopes of relief indicated an extraordinary eagerness to retard his dissolution.

must depend on the circumstances of the master; and that in the case of a nobleman fifty pounds a year was considered as an adequate reward for many years faithful service; 'Then (said Johnson) shall I be *nobilissimus*, for I mean to leave Frank seventy pounds a year, and I desire you to tell him so.' It is strange, however, to think, that Johnson was not free from that general weakness of being averse to execute a will, so that he delayed it from time to time; and had it not been for Sir John Hawkins's repeatedly urging it, I think it is probable that his kind resolution would not have been fulfilled. After making one which, as Sir John Hawkins informs us, extended no further than the promised annuity, Johnson's final disposition of his property was established by a Will and Codicil, of which copies are subjoined.[1]

1 'IN THE NAME OF GOD. AMEN. I SAMUEL JOHNSON, being in full possession of my faculties, but fearing this night may put an end to my life, do ordain this my last Will and Testament. I bequeath to GOD a soul polluted with many sins, but I hope purified by JESUS CHRIST. – I leave seven hundred and fifty pounds in the hands of Bennet Langton, Esq.; three hundred pounds in the hands of Mr Barclay and Mr Perkins, brewers; one hundred and fifty pounds in the hands of Dr Percy, Bishop of Dromore; one thousand pounds, three *per cent.* annuities, in the public funds; and one hundred pounds now lying by me in ready money: all these before-mentioned sums and property I leave, I say, to Sir Joshua Reynolds, Sir John Hawkins, and Dr William Scott, of Doctors Commons, in trust, for the following uses: That is to say, to pay to the representatives of the late William Innys, bookseller, in St Paul's Church-yard, the sum of two hundred pounds; to Mrs White, my female servant, one hundred pounds stock in the three *per cent.* annuities aforesaid. The rest of the aforesaid sums of money and property, together with my books, plate, and house-hold furniture, I leave to the before-mentioned Sir Joshua Reynolds, Sir John Hawkins, and Dr William Scott, also in trust, to be applied, after paying my debts, to the use of Francis Barber, my man-servant, a negro, in such a manner as they shall judge most fit and available to his benefit. And I appoint the aforesaid Sir Joshua Reynolds, Sir John Hawkins, and Dr William Scott, sole executors of this my last will and testament, hereby revoking all former wills and testaments whatever. In witness whereof I hereunto subscribe my name, and affix my seal, this eighth day of December, 1784.

SAM. JOHNSON, (L. S.)

'Signed, sealed, published, declared, and delivered by the said testator, as his last will and testament, in the presence of us, the word *two* being first inserted in the opposite page.'

GEORGE STRAHAN.
JOHN DESMOULINS.

'By way of Codicil to my last Will and Testament, I SAMUEL JOHNSON, give, devise, and bequeath, my messuage or tenement, situate at Lichfield, in the county of Stafford, with the appurtenances, in the tenure or occupation of Mrs Bond, of Lichfield aforesaid, or of Mr Hinchman, her under-tenant, to my executors in trust, to sell and dispose of the same; and the money arising from such sale I give and bequeath as follows, viz. to Thomas and Benjamin the sons of Fisher Johnson, late of Leicester, and — Whiting, daughter of Thomas Johnson, late of Coventry, and the grand-daughter of the said Thomas Johnson, one full and equal fourth part each; but in case there shall be more grand-daughters than one of the said Thomas Johnson, living at the time of my decease, I give and bequeath the part or share of that one to,

The consideration of the numerous papers of which he was possessed, seems to have struck Johnson's mind with a sudden anxiety, and as they were in great

---

and equally between such grand-daughters. I give and bequeath to the Reverend Mr Rogers, of Berkley, near Froome, in the county of Somerset, the sum of one hundred pounds, requesting him to apply the same towards the maintenance of Elizabeth Herne, a lunatic. I also give and bequeath to my god-children, the son and daughter of Mauritius Lowe, painter, each of them, one hundred pounds of my stock in the three *per cent*. consolidated annuities, to be applied and disposed of by and at the discretion of my Executors, in the education or settlement in the world of them my said legatees. Also I give and bequeath to Sir John Hawkins, one of my Executors, the Annales Ecclesiastici of Baronius, and Holingshed's and Stowe's Chronicles, and also an octavo Common Prayer Book. To Bennet Langton, Esq. I give and bequeath my Polyglot Bible. To Sir Joshua Reynolds, my great French Dictionary, by Martiniere, and my own copy of my folio English Dictionary, of the last revision. To Dr William Scott, one of my Executors, the Dictionnaire de Commerce, and Lectius's edition of the Greek Poets. To Mr Windham, Poetae Graeci Heroici per Henricum Stephanum. To the Reverend Mr Strahan, Vicar of Islington, in Middlesex, Mills's Greek Testament, Beza's Greek Testament by Stephens, all my Latin Bibles, and my Greek Bible by Wechelius. To Dr Heberden, Dr Brocklesby, Dr Butter, and Mr Cruikshank the surgeon who attended me, Mr Holder my apothecary, Gerard Hamilton, Esq., Mrs Gardiner, of Snow-hill, Mrs Frances Reynolds, Mr Hoole, and the Reverend Mr Hoole, his son, each a book at their election, to keep as a token of remembrance. I also give and bequeath to Mr John Desmoulins, two hundred pounds consolidated three *per cent*. annuities; and to Mr Sastres, the Italian master, the sum of five pounds, to be laid out in books of piety for his own use. And whereas the said Bennet Langton hath agreed, in consideration of the sum of seven hundred and fifty pounds, mentioned in my Will to be in his hands, to grant and secure an annuity of seventy pounds, payable during the life of me and my servant Francis Barber, and the life of the survivor of us, to Mr George Stubbs in trust for us; my mind and will is, that in case of my decease before the said agreement shall be perfected, the said sum of seven hundred and fifty pounds, and the bond for securing the said sum, shall go to the said Francis Barber; and I hereby give and bequeath to him the same, in lieu of the bequest in his favour, contained in my said Will. And I hereby empower my Executors to deduct and retain all expences that shall or may be incurred in the execution of my said Will, or of this Codicil thereto, out of such estates and effects as I shall die possessed of. All the rest, residue, and remainder of my estate and effects, I give and bequeath to my said Executors, in trust for the said Francis Barber, his Executors, and Administrators. Witness my hand and seal this ninth day of December, 1784.

SAM. JOHNSON, (L. S.)

'Signed, sealed, published, declared, and delivered by the said Samuel Johnson, as, and for a Codicil to his last Will and Testament, in the presence of us, who, in his presence, and at his request, and also in the presence of each other, have hereto subscribed our names as witnesses.'

JOHN COPLEY.
WILLIAM GIBSON.
HENRY COLE.

Upon these testamentary deeds it is proper to make a few observations.
His express declaration with his dying breath of his faith as a Christian, as it had

confusion, it is much to be lamented that he had not entrusted some faithful and discreet person with the care and selection of them; instead of which, he, in a precipitate manner, burnt large masses of them, as I should apprehend,

---

been often practised in such solemn writings, was of real consequence from this great man, as the conviction of a mind equally acute and strong might well overbalance the doubts of others who were his contemporaries. The expression *polluted* may to some convey an impression of more than ordinary contamination; but that is not warranted by its genuine meaning. as appears from *The Rambler*, No. 42. The same word is used in the will of Dr Sanderson, Bishop of Lincoln, who was piety itself.

His legacy of two hundred pounds to the representatives of Mr Innys, bookseller in St Paul's Church-yard, was the effect of a very worthy motive. He told Sir John Hawkins, that his father having become bankrupt, Mr Innys had assisted him with money or credit to continue his business. 'This (said he) I consider as an obligation on me to be grateful to his descendants.'

The amount of his property proved to be considerably more than he had supposed it to be. Sir John Hawkins estimates the bequest to Francis Barber at a sum little short of fifteen hundred pounds, including an annuity of seventy pounds to be paid to him by Mr Langton, in consideration of seven hundred and fifty pounds, which Johnson had lent to that gentleman. Sir John seems not a little angry at this bequest, and mutters 'a caveat against ostentatious bounty and favour to negroes'. But surely when a man has money entirely of his own acquisition, especially when he has no near relations, he may, without blame, dispose of it as he pleases, and with great propriety to a faithful servant. Mr Barber, by the recommendation of his master, retired to Lichfield, where he might pass the rest of his days in comfort.

It has been objected that Johnson has omitted many of his best friends when leaving books to several as tokens of his last remembrance. The names of Dr Adams, Dr Taylor, Dr Burney, Mr Hector, Mr Murphy, the Author of this Work, and others who were intimate with him, are not to be found in his Will. This may be accounted for by considering, that as he was very near his dissolution at the time, he probably mentioned such as happened to occur to him; and that he may have recollected, that he had formerly shown others such proofs of his regard, that it was not necessary to crowd his Will with their names. Mrs Lucy Porter was much displeased that nothing was left to her; but besides what I have now stated, she should have considered, that she had left nothing to Johnson by her Will, which was made during his life-time, as appeared at her decease.

His enumerating several persons in one group, and leaving them 'each a book at their election', might possibly have given occasion to a curious question as to the order of choice, had they not luckily fixed on different books. His library, though by no means handsome in its appearance, was sold by Mr Christie for two hundred and forty-seven pounds, nine shillings, many people being desirous to have a book which had belonged to Dr Johnson. In many of them he had written little notes, sometimes tender memorials of his departed wife; as, 'This was dear Tetty's book': sometimes occasional remarks of different sorts. Mr Lysons, of Clifford's Inn, has favoured me with the two following:

In *Holy Rules and Helps to Devotion*, by Bryan Duppa, Lord Bishop of Winton, '*Preces quidam videtur diligenter tractasse; spero non inauditus.*'

In *The Rosicrucian infallible Axiomata*, by John Heydon, Gent., prefixed to which are some verses addressed to the author, signed Ambr. Waters, A.M. coll. Ex. Oxon. '*These Latin verses were written to Hobbes by Bathurst, upon his Treatise on Human Nature, and have no relation to the book. – An odd fraud.*'

with little regard to discrimination. Not that I suppose we have thus been deprived of any compositions which he had ever intended for the public eye; but, from what escaped the flames, I judge that many curious circumstances relating both to himself and other literary characters have perished.

Two very valuable articles, I am sure, we have lost, which were two quarto volumes, containing a full, fair, and most particular account of his own life, from his earliest recollection. I owned to him, that having accidentally seen them, I had read a great deal in them; and apologising for the liberty I had taken, asked him if I could help it. He placidly answered, 'Why, Sir, I do not think you could have helped it.' I said that I had for once in my life felt half an inclination to commit theft. It had come into my mind to carry off those two volumes, and never see him more. Upon my inquiring how this would have affected him, 'Sir (said he), I believe I should have gone mad.'[1]

During his last illness, Johnson experienced the steady and kind attachment of his numerous friends. Mr Hoole has drawn up a narrative of what passed in the visits which he paid to him during that time, from the 10th of November to the 13th of December, the day of his death inclusive, and has favoured me with a perusal of it.[a] Nobody was more attentive to him than Mr Langton, to whom he tenderly said, *Te teneam moriens deficiente manu.* And I think it highly to the honour of Mr Windham, that his important occupations as an active statesman did not prevent him from paying assiduous respect to the dying Sage, whom he revered. Mr Langton informs me, that 'one day he found Mr Burke and four or five more friends sitting with Johnson. Mr Burke said to him, "I am afraid, Sir, such a number of us may be oppressive to you." – "No, Sir (said Johnson), it is not so; and I must be in a wretched state indeed, when your company would not be a delight to me." Mr Burke, in a tremulous voice, expressive of being very tenderly affected, replied, "My dear Sir, you have always been too good to me." Immediately afterwards he went away. This was the last circumstance in the acquaintance of these two eminent men.'[b]

1 One of these volumes, Sir John Hawkins informs us he put into his pocket; for which the excuse he states is, that he meant to preserve it from falling into the hands of a person whom he describes so as to make it sufficiently clear who is meant; 'having strong reasons (says he) to suspect that this man might find and make an ill use of the book.' Why Sir John should suppose that the gentleman alluded to would act in this manner, he has not thought fit to explain. But what he did was not approved of by Johnson; who, upon being acquainted of it without delay by a friend, expressed great indignation, and warmly insisted on the book being delivered up; and, in the supposition of his afterwards missing it, without knowing by whom it had been taken, he said, 'Sir, I should have gone out of the world distrusting half mankind.' Sir John next day wrote a letter to Johnson, assigning the reasons for his conduct; upon which Johnson observed to Mr Langton. 'Bishop Sanderson could not have dictated a better letter. I could almost say, *Melius est sic penituisse quam non errasse.*' The agitation into which Johnson was thrown by this incident, probably made him hastily burn those precious records which must ever be regretted.

a After 'it,' read 'with permission to make extracts, which I have done.'

b Add here: The following particulars of his conversation within a few days of his death, I give on the authority of Mr John Nichols:

'He said, that the Parliamentary Debates were the only part of his writings which

It is to the mutual credit of Johnson and divines of different communions, that although he was a steady Church-of-England man, there was nevertheless much agreeable intercourse between him and them. Let me particularly name the late Mr La Trobe, and Mr Hutton of the Moravian profession. His intimacy with the English Benedictines at Paris has been mentioned; and as an

---

then gave him any compunction: but that at the time he wrote them, he had no conception he was imposing upon the world, though they were frequently written from very slender materials, and often, from none at all – the mere coinage of his own imagination. He never wrote any part of his works with equal velocity. Three columns of the *Magazine*, in an hour, was no uncommon effort, which was faster than most persons could have transcribed that quantity.

'Of his friend Cave, he always spoke with great affection. "Yet (said he), Cave (who never looked out of his window, but with a view to the *Gentleman's Magazine*), was a penurious pay-master; he would contract for lines by the hundred, and expect the long hundred; but he was a good man, and always delighted to have his friends at his table."

'When talking of a regular edition of his own works, he said, that he had power]from the booksellers] to print such an edition, if his health admitted it; but had no power to assign over any edition, unless he could add notes, and so alter them as to make them new works; which his state of health forbade him to think of. "I may possibly live (said he), or rather breathe, three days, or perhaps three weeks; but find myself daily and gradually weaker."

'He said at another time, three or four days only before his death, speaking of the little fear he had of undergoing a chirurgical operation, "I would give one of these legs for a year more of life, I mean of comfortable life, not such as that which I now suffer'; – and lamented much his inability to read during his hours of restlessness. "I used formerly (he added), when sleepless in bed, *to read like a Turk*."

'Whilst confined by his last illness, it was his regular practice to have the church service read to him, by some attentive and friendly divine. The Rev. Mr Hoole performed this kind office in my presence for the last time, when, by his own desire, no more than the litany was read; in which his responses were in the deep and sonorous voice which Mr Boswell has occasionally noticed, and with the most profound devotion that can be imagined. His hearing not being quite perfect, he more than once interrupted Mr Hoole, with, "Louder, my dear Sir, louder, I entreat you, or you pray in vain!" – and, when the service was ended, he, with great earnestness, turned round to an excellent lady who was present, saying, "I thank you, Madam, very heartily, for your kindness in joining me in this solemn exercise. Live well, I conjure you; and you will not feel the compunction at the last, which I now feel." So truly humble were the thoughts which this great and good man entertained of his own approaches to religious perfection.

'He was earnestly invited to publish a volume of *Devotional Exercises*; but this (though he listened to the proposal with much complacency, and a large sum of money was offered for it), he declined, from motives of the sincerest modesty.

'He seriously entertained the thought of translating *Thuanus*. He often talked to me on the subject; and once, in particular, when I was rather wishing that he would favour the world, and gratify his Sovereign, by a Life of Spenser (which he said that he would readily have done, had he been able to obtain any new materials for the purpose), he added, "I have been thinking again, Sir, of

additional proof of the charity in which he lived with good men of the Romish Church, I am happy in this opportunity of recording his friendship

---

> *Thuanus*: it would not be the laborious task which you have supposed it. I should have no trouble but that of dictation, which would be performed as speedily as an amanuensis could write." '

On the same undoubted authority, I give a few articles, which should have been inserted in chronological order; but which, now that they are before me, I should be sorry to omit:

'In 1736, Dr Johnson had a particular inclination to have been engaged as an assistant to the Reverend Mr Budworth, then head master of the Grammar-school, at Brewood, in Staffordshire, "an excellent person, who possessed every talent of a perfect instructor of youth, in a degree which (to use the words of one of the brightest ornaments of literature, the Reverend Dr Hurd, Bishop of Worcester), has been rarely found in any of that profession since the days of Quintilian." Mr Budworth, "who was less known in his life-time, from that obscure situation to which the caprice of fortune oft condemns the most accomplished characters, than his highest merit deserved", had been bred under Mr Blackwell, at Market Bosworth, where Johnson was some time an usher; which might naturally lead to the application. Mr Budworth was certainly no stranger to the learning or abilities of Johnson, as he more than once lamented his having been under the necessity of declining the engagement, from an apprehension that the paralytic affection, under which our great Philologist laboured through life, might become the object of imitation or of ridicule, among his pupils.' – Captain Budworth, his grandson, has confirmed to me this anecdote.

'Among the early associates of Johnson, at St John's Gate, was Samuel Boyse, well known by his ingenious productions; and not less noted for his imprudence. It was not unusual for Boyse to be a customer to the pawnbroker. On one of these occasions, Dr Johnson collected a sum of money to redeem his friend's clothes, which in two days after were pawned again. "The sum (said Johnson), was collected by sixpences, at a time when to me sixpence was a serious consideration."

'Speaking one day of a person for whom he had a real friendship, but in whom vanity was somewhat too predominant, he observed, that "Kelly was so fond of displaying on his side-board the plate which he possessed, that he added to it his spurs. For my part (said he), I never was master of a pair of spurs, but once; and they are now at the bottom of the ocean. By the carelessness of Boswell's servant, they were dropped from the end of the boat, on our return from the Isle of Sky."

'The late Reverend Mr Samuel Badcock, having been introduced to Dr Johnson, by Mr Nichols, some years before his death, thus expressed himself in a letter to that gentleman:

> How much I am obliged to you for the favour you did me in introducing me to Dr Johnson! *Tantum vidi Virgilium*. But to have seen him, and to have received a testimony of respect from him, was enough. I recollect all the conversation, and shall never forget one of his expressions. – Speaking of Dr P—— (whose writings, I saw, he estimated at a low rate), he said, 'You have proved him as deficient in probity as he is in learning.' – I called him an '*Index-scholar*'; but he was not willing to allow him a claim even to that merit. He said, 'that he borrowed from those who had been borrowers themselves, and did not know that the mistakes he adopted had been answered by others.' – I often think of our short, but precious, visit to this great man. I shall consider it as a kind of *era* in my life.

with the Reverend Thomas Hussey, D.D., His Catholic Majesty's Chaplain of Embassy at the Court of London, that very respectable man, eminent not only for his powerful eloquence as a preacher, but for his various abilities and acquisitions. – Nay, though Johnson loved a Presbyterian the least, this did not prevent his having a long and uninterrupted social connection with the Reverend Dr James Fordyce, who, since his death, hath gratefully celebrated him in a warm strain of devotional composition.

Amidst the melancholy clouds which hung over the dying Johnson, his characteristical manner showed itself on different occasions.

When Dr Warren, in the usual style, hoped that he was better; his answer was, 'No, Sir. You cannot conceive with what acceleration I advance towards death.'

A man whom he had never seen before was employed one night to sit up with him. Being asked next morning how he liked his attendant, his answer was, 'Not at all, Sir. The fellow's an idiot; he is as awkward as a turn-spit when first put into the wheel, and as sleepy as a dormouse.'

Mr Windham having placed a pillow conveniently to support him, he thanked him for his kindness, and said, 'That will do – all that a pillow can do.'[a]

---

[a] Omit next paragraph, and read: He repeated with great spirit a poem, consisting of several stanzas, in four lines, in alternate rhyme, which he said he had composed some years before, on occasion of a rich, extravagant young gentleman's coming of age; saying he had never repeated it but once since he composed it, and had given but one copy of it. That copy was given to Mrs Thrale, now Piozzi, who has published it in a book which she entitles *British Synonimy*, but which is truly a collection of entertaining remarks and stories, no matter whether accurate or not. Being a piece of exquisite satire, conveyed in a strain of pointed vivacity and humour, and in a manner of which no other instance is to be found in Johnson's writings, I shall here insert it:

> Long-expected one-and-twenty,
>   Ling'ring year, at length is flown;
> Pride and pleasure, pomp and plenty,
>   Great — —, are now your own.
>
> Loosen'd from the Minor's tether,
>   Free to mortgage or to sell,
> Wild as wind, and light as feather,
>   Bid the sons of thrift farewell.
>
> Call the Betseys, Kates, and Jennies,
>   All the names that banish care;
> Lavish of your grandsire's guineas,
>   Show the spirit of an heir.
>
> All that prey on vice and folly
>   Joy to see their quarry fly;
> There the gamester, light and jolly,
>   There the lender, grave and sly.
>
> Wealth, my lad, was made to wander,
>   Let it wander as it will;
> Call the jockey, call the pander,
>   Bid them come and take their fill.

He repeated with great spirit a poem, consisting of about fifteen stanzas in four lines, in alternate rhymes, which he said he had composed some years before, on occasion of a young gentleman's coming of age; saying he had never repeated it but once since he composed it, and had given but one copy of it. From the specimen of it which Mrs Piozzi has given of it in her *Anecdotes*, p. 196, it is much to be wished that we could see the whole.

As he opened a note which his servant brought to him, he said, 'An odd thought strikes me. – We shall receive no letters in the grave.'

He requested three things of Sir Joshua Reynolds: To forgive him thirty pounds which he had borrowed of him – to read the Bible – and never to use his pencil on a Sunday. Sir Joshua readily acquiesced.

Indeed he showed the greatest anxiety for the religious improvement of his friends, to whom he discoursed on its infinite consequence. He begged of Mr Hoole to think of what he had said, and to commit it to writing; and upon being afterwards assured that this was done, pressed his hands, and in an earnest tone, thanked him. Dr Brocklesby having attended him with the utmost assiduity and kindness as his physician and friend, he was peculiarly desirous that this gentleman should not entertain any loose speculative notions, but be confirmed in the truths of Christianity, and insisted on his writing down in his presence, as nearly as he could collect it, the import of what passed on the subject; and Dr Brocklesby having complied with the request, he made him sign the paper, and urged him to keep it in his own custody as long as he lived.

Johnson, with that native fortitude which amidst all his bodily distress and mental sufferings never forsook him, asked Dr Brocklesby, as a man in whom he had confidence, to tell him plainly whether he could recover. 'Give me (said he) a direct answer.' The Doctor having first asked him if he could bear the whole truth, which way soever it might lead, and being answered that he could, declared that in his opinion he could not recover without a miracle. 'Then (said Johnson) I will take no more physic, not even my opiates; for I have prayed that I may render up my soul to GOD unclouded.' In this resolution he persevered, and at the same time used only the weakest kinds of sustenance.[a]

The Reverend Mr Strahan, who was the son of his friend, and had been always one of his great favourites, had, during Johnson's last illness, the

---

When the bonny blade carouses,
  Pockets full, and spirits high –
What are acres? what are houses?
  Only dirt, or wet or dry.

Should the guardian friend or mother
  Tell the woes of wilful waste:
Scorn their counsel, scorn their pother, –
  You can hang or drown at last.

[a] Add: Being pressed by Mr Windham to take somewhat more generous nourishment, lest too low a diet should have the very effect he dreaded by debilitating his mind, he said 'I will take anything but inebriating substance.'

satisfaction of contributing to soothe and comfort him. That gentleman's house at Islington, of which he is Vicar, afforded occasionally and easily an agreeable change of place and fresh air; and he attended also upon Johnson in town in the discharge of the sacred offices of his profession.

Mr Strahan has given me the agreeable assurance, that after being in much agitation, Johnson became quite composed, and continued so till his death.

Dr Brocklesby, who will not be suspected of fanaticism, obliged me with the following accounts:

> For some time before his death all his fears were calmed and absorbed by the prevalence of his faith, and his trust in the merits and propitiation of JESUS CHRIST.
>
> He talked often to me about the necessity of faith in the *sacrifice* of JESUS, as necessary beyond all good works whatever for the salvation of mankind.
>
> He pressed me to study Dr Clarke, and to read his Sermons. I asked him why he pressed Dr Clarke, an Arian.[1] 'Because (said he) he is fullest on the *propitiatory sacrifice*.'

Johnson having thus in his mind the true Christian scheme, at once rational and consolatory, uniting justice and mercy in the Divinity, with the improvement of human nature, previous to his receiving the Holy Sacrament in his apartment, composed and fervently uttered this prayer:[2]

> Almighty and most merciful Father, I am now, as to human eyes it seems, about to commemorate, for the last time, the death of thy Son JESUS CHRIST our Saviour and Redeemer. Grant, O LORD, that my whole hope and confidence may be in his merits, and thy mercy; enforce and accept my imperfect repentance; make this commemoration available to the confirmation of my faith, the establishment of my hope, and the enlargement of my charity; and make the death of thy Son JESUS CHRIST effectual to my redemption. Have mercy upon me, and pardon the multitude of my offences. Bless my friends; have mercy upon all men. Support me, by thy Holy Spirit, in the days of weakness, and at the hour of death; and receive me, at my death, to everlasting happiness, for the sake of JESUS CHRIST. Amen.

---

1 The change of his sentiments with regard to Dr Clarke, is thus mentioned to me in a letter from the late Dr Adams, Master of Pembroke College, Oxford. – 'The Doctor's prejudices were the strongest, and certainly in another sense the weakest, that ever possessed a sensible man. You know his extreme zeal for orthodoxy. But did you ever hear what he told me himself? That he had made it a rule not to admit Dr Clarke's name in his Dictionary. This, however, wore off. At some distance of time he advised with me what books he should read in defence of the Christian Religion. I recommended Clarke's *Evidences of Natural and Revealed Religion*, as the best of the kind; and I find in what is called his *Prayers and Meditations*, that he was frequently employed in the latter part of his time in reading Clarke's Sermons.'

2 The Reverend Mr Strahan took care to have it preserved, and has inserted it in *Prayers and Meditations*, p. 222.

From my brother Thomas David I have these particulars:[a]

The Doctor, from the time that he was certain his death was near, appeared to be perfectly resigned, was seldom or never fretful or out of temper, and often said to his faithful servant, who gave me this account, 'Attend, Francis, to the salvation of your soul, which is the object of greatest importance': he also explained to him passages in the scripture, and seemed to have pleasure in talking upon religious subjects.

On Monday the 13th of December, the day on which he died, a Miss Morris, daughter to a particular friend of his, called, and said to Francis, that she begged to be permitted to see the Doctor, that she might earnestly request him to give her his blessing. Francis went into the room, followed by the young lady, and delivered the message. The Doctor turned himself in the bed, and said 'GOD bless you, my dear!' These were the last words he spoke. – His difficulty of breathing increased till about seven o'clock in the evening, when Mr Barber and Mrs Desmoulins, who were sitting in the room, observing that the noise he made in breathing had ceased, went to the bed, and found he was dead.

About two days after his death, the following very agreeable account was communicated to Mr Malone, in a letter by the Honourable John Byng, to whom I am much obliged for granting me permission to introduce it in my work.

DEAR SIR – Since I saw you, I have had a long conversation with Cawston,[1] who sat up with Dr Johnson from nine o'clock on Sunday evening till ten o'clock on Monday morning. And from what I can gather from him, it should seem, that Dr Johnson was perfectly composed, steady in hope, and resigned to death. At the interval of each hour, they assisted him to sit up in his bed, and move his legs, which were in much pain; when he regularly addressed himself to fervent prayer; and though sometimes his voice failed him, his senses never did during that time. The only sustenance he received was cyder and water. He said his mind was prepared, and the time to his dissolution seemed long. At six in the morning he enquired the hour, and on being informed, said that all went on regularly, and he felt he had but a few hours to live.

At ten o'clock in the morning he parted from Cawston, saying, 'You should not detain Mr Windham's servant. – I thank you; – bear my remembrance to your master.' Cawston says, that no man could appear

---

[a] Delete this line, and add instead: Having, as has been already mentioned, made his will on the 8th and 9th of December, and settled all his worldly affairs, he languished till Monday, the 13th of that month, when he expired, about seven o'clock in the evening, with so little apparent pain that his attendants hardly perceived when his dissolution took place. Of his last moments, my brother Thomas David has furnished me with the following particulars.

1 Servant to the Right Honourable William Windham.

more collected, more devout, or less terrified at the thoughts of the approaching minute.

This account, which is so much more agreeable than, and somewhat different from yours, has given us the satisfaction of thinking that that great man died as he lived, full of resignation, strengthened in faith, and joyful in hope.

A few days before his death he had asked Sir John Hawkins, as one of his executors, where he should be buried; and on being answered, 'Doubtless in Westminster Abbey', seemed to feel a satisfaction very natural to a poet, and indeed, in my opinion, very natural to every man of any imagination, who has no family sepulchre in which he can be laid with his fathers. Accordingly, upon Monday, December 20, his remains were deposited in that noble and renowned edifice; and over his grave was placed a large blue flagstone, with this inscription:

> SAMUEL JOHNSON, LL.D.
> *Obiit* XIII *die Decembris,*
> *Anno Domini*
> M.DCC.LXXXIV.
> *Aetatis suae* LXXV.

His funeral was attended by a respectable number of his friends, particularly by many of the members of THE LITERARY CLUB, who were then in town; and was also honoured by the presence of several of the Reverend Chapter of Westminster.[a] His school-fellow, Dr Taylor, performed the mournful office of reading the service.[b]

I trust I shall not be accused of affectation when I declare, that I find myself unable to express all that I felt upon the loss of such a 'Guide, Philosopher, and Friend'. I shall therefore not say one word of my own, but adopt those of an eminent friend,[c] which he uttered with an abrupt excellence, superior to all

---

[a] After 'Westminster', read: Mr Burke, Sir Joseph Banks, Mr Windham, Mr Langton, Sir Charles Bunbury, and Mr Colman, bore his pall.

[b] Before 'service', read 'burial'.

[c] Add this note: On the subject of Johnson I may adopt the words of Sir John Harrington, concerning his venerable Tutor and Diocesan, Dr John Still, Bishop of Bath and Wells; 'who hath given me some helps, more hopes, all encouragements in my best studies: to whom I never came but I grew more religious; from whom I never went, but I parted better instructed. Of him therefore, my acquaintance, my friend, my instructor, if I speak much, it were not to be marvelled; if I speak frankly, it is not to be blamed; and though I speak partially, it were to be pardoned.' – *Nugae Antiquae*, Vol. I, p. 136. There is one circumstance in Sir John's character of Bishop Still, which is peculiarly applicable to Johnson: 'He became so famous a disputer, that the learnedest were even afraid to dispute with him: and he finding his own strength, could not stick to warn them in their arguments to take heed to their answers, like a perfect fencer that will tell aforehand in which button he will give the venew, or like a cunning chess-player that will appoint aforehand with which pawn, and in which place he will give the mate.'

studied composition: 'He has made a chasm, which not only nothing can fill up, but which nothing has a tendency to fill up. – Johnson is dead. – Let us go to the next best. – There is nobody. – No man can be said to put you in mind of Johnson.'

As Johnson had abundant homage paid to him during his life,[1] so no writer

---

[1] Besides the Dedications to him by Dr Goldsmith, the Reverend Dr Franklin, and the Reverend Mr Wilson, which I have mentioned according to their dates, there was one by a lady, of a versification of *Aningait and Ajut*, and one by the ingenious Mr Walker, of his *Rhetorical Grammar*. I have introduced into this work several compliments paid to him in the writings of his contemporaries; but the number of them is so great, that we may fairly say that there was almost a general tribute.

Let me not be forgetful of the honour done to him by Colonel Myddelton, of Gwaynynog, near Denbigh; who, on the banks of a rivulet in his Park, where Johnson delighted to stand and repeat verses, erected an urn with the following inscription:

> This spot was often dignified by the presence of
> SAMUEL JOHNSON, LL.D.
> Whose moral writings, exactly conformable to the precepts of Christianity,
> Give ardour to Virtue and confidence to Truth.

As no inconsiderable circumstance of his fame, we must reckon the extraordinary zeal of the artists to extend and perpetuate his image. I can enumerate a bust by Mr Nollekens, and the many casts which are made from it; several pictures by Sir Joshua Reynolds;[a] one by Mr Zoffani; and one by Mr Opie; and the following engravings of his portrait: 1. One by Cooke, from Sir Joshua, for the Proprietors' edition of his folio Dictionary – 2. One from ditto by ditto, for their quarto edition – 3. One from Opie, by Heath, for Harrison's edition of his Dictionary – 4. One from Nollekens's bust of him, by Bartolozzi, for Fielding's quarto edition of his Dictionary – 5. One small from Harding, by Trotter, for his *Beauties* – 6. One small from Sir Joshua, by Trotter, for his *Lives of the Poets* – 7. One small one from Sir Joshua, by Hall, for *The Rambler* – 8. One small from an original drawing in the possession of Mr John Simco, etched by Trotter, for another edition of his *Lives of the Poets* – 9. One small, no painter's name, etched by Taylor, for his *Johnsoniana* – 10. One folio whole length, with his oak stick, as described in Boswell's *Tour*, drawn and etched by Trotter – 11. One large mezzotinto rom Sir Joshua, by Doughty – 12. One large Roman head from Sir Joshua, by Marchi – 13. One octavo, holding a book to his eye, from Sir Joshua, by Hall, for his works – 14. One small from a drawing from the life, and engraved by Trotter, for his Life published by Kearsley – 15. One large from Opie, by Mr Townley,[b] an ingenious engraver now at Berlin. This is one of the finest mezzotintos that ever was executed; and what renders it of extraordinary value, the plate was destroyed after four or five impressions only were taken off. One of them is in the possession of Sir William Scott[b] – 16. One

[a] Add: From one of which, in the possession of the Duke of Dorset, Mr Humphry executed a beautiful miniature in enamel; one by Mrs Frances Reynolds, Sir Joshua's sister.

[b] Add: (brother of Mr Townley, of the Commons), an ingenious artist, who resided some time at Berlin, and has the honour of being engraver to his Majesty the King of Prussia.

[c] Add: Mr Townley has lately been prevailed with to execute and publish another of the same, that it may be more generally circulated among the admirers of Dr Johnson.

in this nation ever had such an accumulation of literary honours after his death. A sermon upon that event was preached in St Mary's church, Oxford, before the University, by the Reverend Mr Agutter, of Magdalen College.[a] The Lives, the Memoirs, the Essays, both in prose and verse, which have been published concerning him, would make many volumes. The numerous attacks too upon him, I consider as making part of his consequence, upon the principle which he himself so well knew and asserted. Many who trembled at his presence were forward in assault when they no longer apprehended danger. When one of his little pragmatical foes was invidiously snarling at his fame,[b] the Reverend Dr Parr exclaimed, with his usual bold animation, 'Aye, now that the old lion is dead, every ass thinks he may kick at him.'

A monument for him in Westminster-Abbey was resolved upon soon after his death, and has been supported by a most respectable contribution;[c] and in the cathedral of his native city of Lichfield a smaller one is to be erected. To compose his epitaph has excited[d] the warmest competition of genius.[e] If *laudari*

---

large from Sir Joshua's first picture of him, by Heath, for this work – 17. And one for Lavater's Essay on Physiognomy, in which Johnson's countenance is analysed upon the principles of that fanciful writer.[f]

[a] Add: It is not yet published – In a letter to me, Mr Agutter says, 'My sermon before the University was more engaged with Dr Johnson's moral than his intellectual character. It particularly examined his fear of death, and suggested several reasons for the apprehensions of the good, and the indifference of the infidel in their last hours; this was illustrated by contrasting the death of Dr Johnson and Mr Hume; the text was Job xxi, 22–26.

[b] Add: at Sir Joshua Reynolds's table.

[c] Correction: But the Dean and Chapter of St Paul's having come to a resolution of admitting monuments there, upon a liberal and magnificent plan, that cathedral was afterwards fixed on as the place.

[d] For 'has excited' read 'could not but excite.'

[e] Add the following note: The Reverend Dr Parr, on being requested to undertake it, thus expressed himself in a letter to William Seward, Esq.

> I leave this mighty task to some hardier and some abler writer. The variety and splendour of Johnson's attainments, the peculiarities of his character, his private virtues, and his literary publications, fill me with confusion and dismay, when I reflect upon the confined and difficult species of composition, in which alone they can be expressed, with propriety, upon his monument.

But I understand that this great scholar, and warm admirer of Johnson, has yielded to repeated solicitations, and executed the very difficult undertaking.

---

[f] Add: There are also several seals with his head cut on them, particularly a very fine one by that eminent artist, Edward Birch, Esq. R.A., in the possession of the younger Dr Charles Burney.

Let me add, as a proof of the popularity of his character, that there are copper pieces struck at Birmingham with his head impressed on them, which pass current as halfpence there, and in the neighbouring parts of the country.

a laudato viro be praise which is highly estimable, I should not forgive myself were I to omit the following sepulchral verses on the author of THE ENGLISH DICTIONARY, written by the Right Honourable Henry Flood:[a]

> No need of Latin or of Greek to grace
> Our JOHNSON's mem'ry, or inscribe his grave;
> His native language claims this mournful space,
> To pay the Immortality he gave.

The character of SAMUEL JOHNSON has, I trust, been so developed in the course of this work, that they who have honoured it with a perusal, may be considered as well acquainted with him. As, however, it may be expected that I should collect into one view the capital and distinguishing features of this extraordinary man, I shall endeavour to acquit myself of that part of my biographical undertaking,[1] however difficult it may be to do that which many of my readers will do better for themselves.

His figure was large and well formed, and his countenance of the cast of an ancient statue; yet his appearance was rendered strange and somewhat uncouth, by convulsive cramps, by the scars of that distemper which it was once imagined the royal touch could cure, and by a slovenly mode of dress. He had the use only of one eye; yet so much does mind govern and even supply the deficiency of organs, that his visual perceptions, as far as they extended, were uncommonly quick and accurate. So morbid was his temperament, that he never knew the natural joy of a free and vigorous use of his limbs: when he walked, it was like the struggling gait of one in fetters; when he rode, he had no command or direction of his horse, but was carried as if in a balloon. That with his constitution and habits of life he should have lived seventy-five years, is a proof that an inherent *vivida vis* is a powerful preservative of the human frame.

---

[a] Add this note: To prevent any misconception on this subject, Mr Malone, by whom these lines were obligingly communicated, requests me to add the following remark:

> In justice to the late Mr Flood, now himself wanting, and highly meriting, an epitaph from his country, to which his transcendent talents did the highest honour, as well as the most important service; it should be observed, that these lines were by no means intended as a regular monumental inscription for Dr Johnson. Had he undertaken to write an appropriate and discriminative epitaph for that excellent and extraordinary man, those who knew Mr Flood's vigour of mind, will have no doubt that he would have produced one worthy of his illustrious subject. But the fact was merely this: In Dec. 1789, after a large subscription had been made for Dr Johnson's monument, to which Mr Flood liberally contributed, Mr Malone happened to call on him at his house, in Berners-street, and the conversation turning on the proposed monument, Mr Malone maintained that the epitaph, by whomsoever it should be written, ought to be in Latin. Mr Flood thought differently. The next morning, in the postscript to a note on another subject. he mentioned that he continued of the same opinion as on the preceding day, and subjoined the lines above given.

1 As I do not see any reason to give a different character of my illustrious friend now, from what I formerly gave, the greatest part of the sketch of him in my *Journal of a Tour to the Hebrides*, is here adopted.

Man is in general made up of contradictory qualities, and these will ever show themselves in strange succession, where a consistency in appearance at least, if not in reality, has not been attained by long habits of philosophical discipline. In proportion to the native vigour of the mind, the contradictory qualities will be the more prominent, and more difficult to be adjusted; and therefore we are not to wonder, that Johnson exhibited an eminent example of this remark which I have made upon human nature. At different times he seemed a different man, in some respects; not, however, in any great or essential article, upon which he had fully employed his mind and settled certain principles of duty, but only in his manners, and in displays of argument and fancy in his talk. He was prone to superstition, but not to credulity. Though his imagination might incline him to a belief of the marvellous and the mysterious, his vigorous reason examined the evidence with jealousy. He was a sincere and zealous Christian, of high Church-of-England and monarchical principles, which he would not tamely suffer to be questioned; and had perhaps, at an early period, narrowed his mind somewhat too much, both as to religion and politics. His being impressed with the danger of extreme latitude in either, though he was of a very independent spirit, occasioned his appearing somewhat unfavourable to the prevalence of that noble freedom of sentiment which is the best possession of man. Nor can it be denied, that he had many prejudices; which, however, frequently suggested many of his pointed sayings, that rather show a playfulness of fancy than any settled malignity. He was steady and inflexible in maintaining the obligations of religion and morality, both from a regard for the order of society, and from a veneration for the Great Source of all order; correct, nay stern in his taste; hard to please, and easily offended; impetuous and irritable in his temper, but of a most humane and benevolent heart,[1] which showed itself not only in a most liberal charity, as far as his circumstances would allow, but in a thousand instances of active benevolence. He was afflicted with a bodily disease which made him often restless and fretful, and with a constitutional melancholy, the clouds of which darkened the brightness of his fancy, and gave a gloomy cast to his whole course of thinking: we therefore ought not to wonder at his sallies of impatience and passion at any time, especially when provoked by obtrusive ignorance or presuming petulance; and allowance must be made for his uttering hasty and satirical sallies, even against his best friends. And surely, when it is considered that 'amidst sickness and sorrow' he exerted his faculties in so many works for the benefit of mankind, and particularly that he achieved the great and admirable Dictionary of our language, we must be astonished at his resolution. The solemn text of 'him to

---

1 In the *Olla Podrida*, a collection of Essays published at Oxford, there is an excellent paper upon the character of Johnson, said to be written by the Reverend Dr Horne, now Bishop of Norwich. The following passage is eminently happy: 'To reject wisdom, because the person of him who communicates it is uncouth, and his manners are inelegant; – what is it, but to throw away a pineapple, and assign for a reason the roughness of its coat?'

whom much is given, much will be required', seems to have been ever present to his mind in a rigorous sense, and to have made him dissatisfied with his labours and acts of goodness, however comparatively great; so that the unavoidable consciousness of his superiority was in that respect a cause of disquiet. He suffered so much from this, and from the gloom which perpetually haunted him, and made solitude frightful, that it may be said of him, 'If in this life only he had hope, he was of all men most miserable.' He loved praise when it was brought to him; but was too proud to seek for it. He was somewhat susceptible of flattery. As he was general and unconfined in his studies, he cannot be considered as master of any one particular science; but he had accumulated a vast and various collection of learning and knowledge, which was so arranged in his mind, as to be ever in readiness to be brought forth. But his superiority over other learned men consisted chiefly in what may be called the art of thinking, the art of using his mind; a certain continual power of seizing the useful substance of all that he knew, and exhibiting it in a clear and forcible manner; so that knowledge which we often see to be no better than lumber in men of dull understanding, was in him true, evident, and actual wisdom. His moral precepts are practical; for they are drawn from an intimate acquaintance with human nature. His maxims carry conviction; for they are founded on the basis of common sense. His mind was so full of imagery, that he might have been perpetually a poet; yet it is remarkable, that however rich his prose is in that respect, the poetical pieces which he wrote in general have not much of that splendour, but are rather distinguished by strong sentiment, and acute observation, conveyed in harmonious and energetic verse, particularly in heroic couplets. Though usually grave and even awful in his deportment, he possessed uncommon and peculiar powers of wit and humour; he frequently indulged himself in colloquial pleasantry; and the heartiest merriment was often enjoyed in his company; with this great advantage, that as it was entirely free from any poisonous tincture of vice or impiety, it was salutary to those who shared in it. He had accustomed himself to such accuracy in his common conversation,[1] that he at all times delivered

---

1 Though a perfect resemblance of Johnson is not to be found in any age, parts of his character are admirably expressed by Clarendon, in drawing that of Lord Falkland, whom the noble and masterly historian describes at his seat near Oxford: 'Such an immenseness of wit, such a solidity of judgement, so infinite a fancy, bound in by a most logical ratiocination. – His acquaintance was cultivated by the most polite and accurate men, so that his house was a University in less volume, whither they came not so much for repose as study, and to examine and refine those grosser propositions, which laziness and consent made current in conversation.'

Bayle's account of Menage may also be quoted as exceedingly applicable to the great subject of this work: 'His illustrious friends erected a very glorious monument to him in the collection entitled *Menagiana*. Those who judge of things aright, will confess that this collection is very proper to show the extent of genius and learning which was the character of Menage. And I may be bold to say, that *the excellent works he published will not distinguish him from other learned men so advantageously as this*. To publish books of great learning, to make Greek and Latin verses exceedingly well turned, is not a common talent, I own; neither is it extremely rare. It is incomparably

himself with a force, and elegant choice of expression, the effect of which was aided by his having a loud voice, and a slow deliberate utterance. He united a most logical head with a most fertile imagination, which gave him an extra-ordinary advantage in arguing; for he could reason close or wide, as he saw best for the moment. Exulting in his intellectual strength and dexterity, he could, when he pleased, be the greatest sophist that ever contended in the lists of declamation; and from a spirit of contradiction, and a delight in showing his powers, he would often maintain the wrong side with equal warmth and ingenuity: so that, when there was an audience, his real opinions could seldom be gathered from his talk; though when he was in company with a single friend, he would discuss a subject with genuine fairness. But he was too conscientious to make error permanent and pernicious, by deliberately writ-ing it; and in all his numerous works he earnestly inculcated what appeared to him to be the truth. His piety was constant, and was the ruling principle of all his conduct; and the more we consider his character, we shall be the more disposed to regard him with admiration and reverence.[a]

---

more difficult to find men who can furnish discourse about an infinite number of things, and who can diversify them an hundred ways. How many authors are there, who are admired for their works, on account of the vast learning that is displayed in them, who are not able to sustain a conversation. Those who know Menage only by his books, might think he resembled those learned men: but if you show the *Menagiana*, you distinguish him from them, and make him known by a talent which is given to very few learned men. There it appears that he was a man who spoke off hand a thousand good things. His memory extended to what was ancient and modern; to the court and to the city; to the dead and to the living languages; to things serious and things jocose; in a word, to a thousand sorts of subjects. That which appeared a trifle to some readers of the *Menagiana*, who did not consider circumstances, caused admiration in other readers, who minded the difference between what a man speaks without preparation, and that which he prepares for the press. And therefore we cannot sufficiently commend the care which his illustrious friends took to erect to him a monument so capable of giving him immortal glory. They were not obliged to rectify what they had heard him say; for in so doing they had not been faithful historians of his conversations.'

[a] Read: 'his piety being constant, and the ruling principle of all his conduct.' After 'conduct', read: 'Such was SAMUEL JOHNSON, a man whose talents, acquirements, and virtues, were so extraordinary, that the more his character is considered, the more he will be regarded by the present age, and by posterity, with admiration and reverence.'

A CHRONOLOGICAL CATALOGUE
OF THE PROSE WORKS¹ OF SAMUEL JOHNSON, LL.D.

[Works cited below and marked with an asterisk were acknowledged by Dr Johnson as his own. Those marked with a dagger are fully believed to be his work from internal evidence.]

1735 Abridgement and translation of Lobo's Voyage to Abyssinia.*

1738 Part of a translation of Father Paul Sarpi's History of the Council of Trent.* As this work after some sheets were printed, suddenly stopped, I know not whether any part of it is now to be found.

For the *Gentleman's Magazine*
Preface.†
Life of Father Paul.*

1739 A complete vindication of the Licenser of the Stage from the malicious and scandalous aspersions of Mr Brooke, author of *Gustavus Vasa*.*

Marmor Norfolciense: or, an Essay on an ancient prophetical inscription in monkish rhyme, lately discovered near Lynne in Norfolk; by PROBUS BRITANNICUS.*

For the *Gentleman's Magazine*
Life of Boerhave.*
Address to the Reader.†
Appeal to the Public in behalf of the Editor.†
Considerations on the case of Dr Trapp's Sermons; a plausible attempt to prove that an author's work may be abridged without injuring his property.*

1740 **For the** *Gentleman's Magazine*
Preface.†
Life of Admiral Drake.*
Life of Admiral Blake.*
Life of Philip Barretier.*
Essay on Epitaphs.*

1741 **For the** *Gentleman's Magazine*
Preface.†

1 I do not here include his Poetical Works; for, excepting his Latin Translation of Pope's *Messiah*, his *London*, and his *Vanity of Human Wishes*, imitated from Juvenal; his Prologue on the opening of Drury-Lane Theatre by Mr Garrick, and his *Irene*, a Tragedy, they are very numerous, and in general short; and I have promised a complete edition of them, in which I shall with the utmost care ascertain their authenticity, and illustrate them with notes and various readings.

A free translation of the Jests of Hierocles, with an introduction.†
Debate on the Humble Petition and Advice of the Rump Parliament
     to Cromwell in 1657, to assume the title of King; abridged,
     methodized and digested.†
Translation of Abbe Guyon's Dissertation on the Amazons.†
Translation of Fontenelle's Panegyric on Dr Morin.†

1742   **For the** *Gentleman's Magazine*
     Preface.†
     Essay on the Account of the Conduct of the Duchess of Marlborough.*
     An Account of the Life of Peter Burman.*
     The Life of Sydenham, afterwards prefixed to Dr Swan's Editions of
          his Works.*
     Proposals for Printing *Bibliotheca Harleiana*, or a Catalogue of the
          Library of the Earl of Oxford, afterwards prefixed to the first
          Volume of that Catalogue, in which the Latin Accounts of the
          Books were written by him.*
     Abridgement intitled, Foreign History.†
     Essay on the Description of China, from the French of Du Halde.†

1743   **Dedication to Dr Mead of Dr James's** *Medicinal Dictionary.*†

     For the *Gentleman's Magazine*
     Preface.†
     Parliamentary Debates, under the Name of Debates in the Senate of
          Lilliput, from Nov. 19, 1740, to Feb. 23, 1742–3, inclusive.*
     Considerations on the Dispute between Crousaz and Warburton on
          Pope's Essay on Man.†
     A Letter announcing that the Life of Mr Savage was speedily to be
          published by a Person who was favoured with his Confidence.†
     Advertisement for Osborne concerning the Harleian Catalogue.

1744   Life of Richard Savage.*
     Preface to the Harleian Miscellany.*

     For the *Gentleman's Magazine*
     Preface.†.

1745   Miscellaneous Observations on the *Tragedy of Macbeth*, with remarks
          on Sir T. H.'s (Sir Thomas Hanmer's) Edition of Shakspeare, and
          Proposals for a new Edition of that Poet.*

1747   Plan for a Dictionary of the ENGLISH LANGUAGE, addressed to Philip
          Dormer Earl of Chesterfield.*

1748   Life of Roscommon in the *Gentleman's Magazine.*

     For Dodsley's *Preceptor*
     Preface.*
     Vision of Theodore the Hermit.*

1750   *The Rambler*, the first Paper of which was published 20th of March
         this Year, and the last 17th of March, 1752, the Day on which
         Mrs Johnson died.*
       Letter in the General Advertiser to excite the attention of the Public
         to the Performance of *Comus*, which was next Day to be acted at
         Drury-Lane Playhouse for the Benefit of Milton's Grand-daughter.*
       Preface and Postscript to Lauder's Pamphlet, intitled, 'An Essay on
         Milton's Use and Imitation of the Moderns in his *Paradise Lost*'.*

1751   Life of Cheynel in the Miscellany called 'The Student'.*
       Letter for Lauder, addressed to the Reverend Dr John Douglas,
         acknowledging his Fraud concerning Milton in Terms of suitable
         Contrition.*
       Dedication to the Earl of Middlesex of Mrs Charlotte Lennox's
         Female Quixote.†

1753   Dedication to John Earl of Orrery, of Shakspeare Illustrated, by Mrs
         Charlotte Lennox.*
       During this and the following year he wrote and gave to his much
         loved friend Dr Bathurst the Papers in the *Adventurer*, signed T.*

1754   Life of Edw. Cave in the *Gentleman's Magazine*.*

1755   A DICTIONARY, with a Grammar and History, of the ENGLISH
         LANGUAGE.*
       An Account of an Attempt to ascertain the Longitude at Sea, by an
         exact Theory of the Variations of the Magnetical Needle, with a
         Table of the Variations at the most remarkable Cities in Europe
         from the Year 1660 to 1680.* This he wrote for Mr Zachariah
         Williams, an ingenious ancient Welch Gentleman, Father of Mrs
         Anna Williams whom he for many Years kindly lodged in his
         House. It was published with a Translation into Italian by Signor
         Baretti. In a Copy of it which he presented to the Bodleian Library
         at Oxford, is pasted a Character of the late Mr Zachariah Williams,
         plainly written by Johnson.†

1756   An Abridgement of his Dictionary.*
       Several Essays in the *Universal Visitor*, which there is some difficulty in
         ascertaining. All that are marked with two Asterisks, have been
         ascribed to him, although I am confident from internal Evidence,
         that we should except from these 'The Life of Chaucer',
         'Reflections on the State of Portugal', and 'An Essay on
         Architecture': And from the same Evidence I am confident that he
         wrote 'Further Thoughts on Agriculture', and 'A Dissertation on
         the State of Literature and Authors'. The Dissertation on the
         Epitaphs written by Pope he afterwards acknowledged, and added
         to his *Idler*.
       Life of Sir Thomas Browne prefixed to a new Edition of his *Christian
         Morals*.*

In the *Literary Magazine; or, Universal Review*, which began in
January 1756, his Original Essays are:
Preliminary Address.[†]
An Introduction to the Political State of Great-Britain.[†]
Remarks on the Militia Bill.[†]
Observations on his Britannic Majesty's Treaties with the Empress of
Russia and the Landgrave of Hesse Cassel.[†]
Observations on the Present State of Affairs.[†]
Memoirs of Frederick III, King of Prussia.[†]

In the same Magazine his Reviews are of the following Books:
Birch's *History of the Royal Society* – Browne's *Christian Morals* –
Warton's *Essay on the Writings and Genius of Pope*, Vol. I –
Hampton's Translation of Polybius – Sir Isaac Newton's *Arguments
in Proof of a Deity* – Borlase's *History of the Isles of Scilly* – Home's
Experiments on Bleaching – Browne's *History of Jamaica* – Hales on
*Distilling Sea Waters, Ventilators in Ships, and curing an ill Taste in
Milk* – Lucas's *Essay on Waters* – Keith's *Catalogue of the Scottish
Bishops* – *Philosophical Transactions*, Vol. XLIX – *Miscellanies* by
Elizabeth Harrison – Evans's *Map and Account of the Middle Colonies
in America* – *The Cadet, a Military Treatise* – 'The Conduct of the
Ministry relating to the present War impartially examined'.[†]
Mrs Lennox's Translation of Sully's *Memoirs* – 'Letter on the Case of
Admiral Byng' – 'Appeal to the People concerning Admiral Byng' –
Hanway's *Eight Days Journey*, and *Essay on Tea* – 'Some further
Particulars in Relation to the Case of Admiral Byng', by a
Gentleman of Oxford.
Mr Jonas Hanway having written an angry Answer to the Review of
his *Essay on Tea*, Johnson in the same Collection made a Reply to
it.[*] This is the only Instance, it is believed, when he condescended
to take Notice of any Thing that had been written against him; and
here his chief Intention seems to have been to make Sport.
Dedication to the Earl of Rochford of, and Preface to, Mr Payne's
Introduction to the Game of Draughts.[*]
Introduction to the *London Chronicle*, an Evening Paper which still
subsists with deserved credit.[*]

1757 Speech on the Subject of an Address to the Throne after the Expedition
to Rochefort; delivered by one of his Friends in some public
Meeting: it is printed in the *Gentleman's Magazine* for October 1785.[†]
The two first Paragraphs of the Preface to Sir William Chambers's
Designs of Chinese Buildings, &c.[*]

1758 *The Idler*, which began April 5, in this year, and was continued till
April 5, 1760.[*]
An Essay on the Bravery of the English Common Soldiers was added
to it when published in Volumes.[*]

1759 Rasselas Prince of Abyssinia, a Tale.*

Advertisement for the Proprietors of the *Idler* against certain Persons
who pirated those Papers as they came out singly in a Newspaper
called the *Universal Chronicle or Weekly Gazette*.†

For Mrs Charlotte Lennox's English Version of Brumoy –
A Dissertation on the Greek Comedy, and the General Conclusion of
the Book.†

Introduction to *The World Displayed*, a Collection of Voyages and
Travels.*

Three Letters in the *Gazetteer*, concerning the best Plan for
Blackfriars Bridge.*

1760 Address of the Painters to George III on his Accession to the
Throne.†

Dedication of Baretti's Italian and English Dictionary to the Marquis
of Abreu, then Envoy-Extraordinary from Spain at the Court of
Great Britain.†

Review in the *Gentleman's Magazine* of Mr Tytler's acute and able
Vindication of Mary Queen of Scots.*

Introduction to the Proceedings of the Committee for Cloathing
the French Prisoners.*

1761 Preface to Rolt's Dictionary of Trade and Commerce.*

Corrections and Improvements for Mr Gwyn the Architect's
Pamphlet, intitled 'Thoughts on the Coronation of George III'.*

1762 Dedication to the King of the Reverend Dr Kennedy's *Complete
System of Astronomical Chronology*, unfolding the Scriptures, Quarto
Edition.*

Concluding Paragraph of that Work.†

Preface to the Catalogue of the Artists' Exhibition.†

1763 Character of Collins in the Poetical Calendar, published by Fawkes
and Woty.*

Dedication to the Earl of Shaftesbury of the Edition of Roger
Ascham's English Works, published by the Reverend Mr Bennet.*

The Life of Ascham, also prefixed to that Edition,*

Review of *Telemachus*, a Masque, by the Reverend George Graham of
Eton College, in the *Critical Review*.*

Dedication to the Queen of Mr Hoole's Translation of Tasso.*

Account of the Detection of the Imposture of the Cock-Lane Ghost,
published in the Newspapers and *Gentleman's Magazine*.*

1764 Part of a Review of Grainger's 'Sugar Cane, a Poem', in the *London
Chronicle*.*

Review of Goldsmith's *Traveller*, a Poem, in the *Critical Review*.*

1765 The Plays of William Shakspeare, with Notes.*

1766 *The Fountains*, a Fairy Tale, in Mrs Williams's Miscellanies.*

1767   Dedication to the King of Mr Adams's *Treatise on the Globes.**

1769   Character of the Reverend Mr Zachariah Mudge, in the *London Chronicle.**

1770   *The False Alarm.**

1771   Thoughts on the late Transactions respecting Falkland's Islands.*

1772   Defence of a Schoolmaster; dictated to me for the House of Lords.*
       Argument in Support of the Law of Vicious Intromission; dictated to me for the Court of Session in Scotland.*

1773   Preface to Macbean's *Dictionary of Ancient Geography.**
       Argument in favour of the Rights of Lay Patrons; dictated to me for the General Assembly of the Church of Scotland.*

1774   *The Patriot.**

1775   *A Journey to the Western Islands of Scotland.**
       Proposals for publishing the Works of Mrs Charlotte Lennox, in Three Volumes Quarto.*
       Preface to Baretti's *Easy Lessons in Italian and English.*†
       Taxation no Tyranny; an Answer to the Resolutions and Address of the American Congress.*
       Argument on the case of Dr Memis; dictated to me for the Court of Session in Scotland.*
       Argument to prove that the Corporation of Stirling was corrupt; dictated to me for the House of Lords.*

1776   Argument in Support of the Right of immediate, and personal reprehension from the Pulpit; dictated to me.*
       Proposals for publishing an Analysis of the Scotch Celtic Language, by the Reverend William Shaw.*

1777   Dedication to the King of the Posthumous Works of Dr Pearce, Bishop of Rochester.*
       Additions to the Life and Character of that Prelate; prefixed to those Works.*
       Various Papers and Letters in Favour of the Reverend Dr Dodd.*

1780   Advertisement for his Friend Mr Thrale to the Worthy Electors of the Borough of Southwark.*
       The first Paragraph of Mr Thomas Davies's Life of Garrick.*

1781   Prefaces Biographical and Critical to the Works of the most eminent English Poets; afterwards published with the Title of *Lives of the English Poets.**
       Argument on the Importance of the Registration of Deeds; dictated to me for an Election Committee of the House of Commons.*
       On the Distinction between Tory and Whig; dictated to me.*

On Vicarious Punishments, and the great Propitiation for the Sins of the World, by JESUS CHRIST; dictated to me.*

Argument in favour of Joseph Knight an African Negro, who claimed his Liberty in the Court of Session in Scotland, and obtained it; dictated to me.*

Defence of Mr Robertson, Printer of the *Caledonian Mercury*, against the Society of Procurators in Edinburgh, for having inserted in his Paper a ludicrous Paragraph against them; demonstrating that it was not an injurious Libel; dictated to me.*

1782 The greatest Part, if not the whole, of a Reply, by the Reverend Mr Shaw, to a Person at Edinburgh of the Name of Clark, refuting his arguments for the authenticity of the Poems published by Mr James Macpherson as Translations from Ossian.†

1784 List of the Authors of the *Universal History*, deposited in the British Museum, and printed in the *Gentleman's Magazine* for December this Year.*

Various years.

Letters to Mrs Thrale.*

Prayers and Meditations, which he delivered to the Rev. Mr Strahan, enjoining him to publish them.*

Sermons left for Publication by John Taylor, LL.D., Prebendary of Westminster, and given to the World by the Reverend Samuel Hayes, A.M.†

Such was the number and variety of the Prose Works of this extraordinary man, which I have been able to discover and am at liberty to mention; but we ought to keep in mind, that there must undoubtedly have been many more which are yet concealed; and we may add to the account, the numerous Letters which he wrote, of which a considerable part are yet unpublished. It is hoped that those persons in whose possession they are, will favour the world with them.

JAMES BOSWELL.